MARYLAND
A Middle Temperament

1634–1980

Maryland Paperback Bookshelf
Also available in the Series:

CONTENTS

Contents

To Robert G. Merrick,
Banker, Civic Leader, Philanthropist
and
David Herbert Donald,
Whose Students Thank Him

PREFACE AND
ACKNOWLEDGMENTS

A few years ago, when Virginia first adopted the tourism slogan Virginia Is for Lovers, Marylanders printed tee shirts that read Maryland Is for Crabs. Following time-honored tradition by twitting an older sister, the pranksters also knew what they were talking about. As both quarry and entrée the hard-shell crab helps to illustrate what makes Maryland Maryland. Ugly yet grace-ful, its pincers sharp, its quickest move sideways, the blue crab seeks a mix of salty and fresh water. Marylanders steam their catch with just the right amount of spicy seasoning and serve this meal—fit for royalty though one has to pick for it—on tables covered with ordinary newsprint.

So small, so varied, clinging tenaciously to its independence, Maryland from the beginning served itself as a rich subject. An early planter jokingly named himself "poet laureate" and then set about putting the rankness of Maryland life to verse. With deeper sympathy the late-nineteenth-century romancer George Alfred Townsend described Maryland as "only a rim of shore, a shell of mountain, but all gold!" and H. L. Mencken, while making piquant comments about his home state, always made a point of his choice to live by the Chesapeake rather than on the Hudson. Historians recently have been drawn to the state for their own reasons. The Maryland State Archives in Annapolis preserves some of the most inviting sources available for early America. They, along with shifts in scholarly interests and meth-ods, have led to an outpouring of important late work on the social, eco-nomic, and political life of colonial Maryland. In the past few years historians also have produced valuable new studies of revolutionary conflict in the state, the early growth and development of Baltimore, the nature of mid-nineteenth-century politics, slavery, emancipation, and changes in the state since 1940.

Owing a heavier debt than is usual to writers who have gone before, this book aims to combine a zestful story with the study of historical issues—to weave a narrative out of Maryland's colorful materials while giving the whole a meaningful pattern. On one level I have tried to let Maryland speak for itself; one need only step aside for topics like the Maryland love of food and sport or Maryland's blend of land and water, black and white, English and German, Christian and Jew, native and immigrant, town and country, rich and poor. These pages introduce some, not all, of the interesting personali-ties in the Maryland record and sketch the things Marylanders have done (and still do): growing tobacco, sailing for foreign ports, building ships and railroads, banking, milling wheat and weaving cotton, canning food, mining coal, laying roads, crafting airplanes, and—by means of tonging, dredging, crabbing, and fishing—bringing up the bounty of the Chesapeake Bay. The work and fragrances of Maryland carry their own appeal.

On another plane Maryland escapes the convention that state histories foster only local interest—it supplies an instructive study in American history. Here the tensions and ironies of the American experience have taken concrete form and become vividly, at times painfully, a part of everyday life. Marylanders both championed liberty and relied on slavery. They welcomed opportunity yet clung to tradition. In weighing the benefits of individual freedom and local liberty against those of moral experiment and the power of central government, citizens of this oldest border state have divided more than once. Maryland illustrates the local effect of broad trends in American life—growing transportation and communications links, the rise of industry, the growing influence of organizations, corporate offices, and government bureaus. Maryland history highlights the truth that we have built up and grown wealthy as a nation while acquiring debts to nature; it tells of economic development, but also of diminishing and polluted natural resources. The Maryland past demonstrates how easily democratic politics can give rise to political scandal; it recalls the Founding Fathers' warning that the garden of self-rule needs constant weeding.

Maryland finally deserves our attention for the particular results American issues brought to this place combining North and South, Cavalier and Yankee, business and pleasure. Over three and one-half centuries, Marylanders in a sense developed a culture all their own. As they came to grips with (or sidestepped) the choices facing them, they cultivated a middle-state ethos— a sensibility founded on compromise given conflict, on toleration given differences among people and their failings, on the pursuit of happiness given the brevity of life and the allurements of Maryland scenery and the Chesapeake Bay. Marylanders at their best have stood for moderation, skepticism, ironic humor, love of place, and a sense of proportion that reminds one of the sailor's heed to both sail and ballast. My title hints at this unifying theme: the elusive character of Maryland may lie in its search for what we can abbreviate as a middle way, between extremes, where the human spirit thrives.

Maryland, A Middle Temperament could not have appeared without the generous support of the late Robert G. Merrick, whose long life gave renewed meaning to the phrase "amiable Baltimorean." In early 1983, as Marylanders prepared to mark their 350th anniversary, he and leaders of the Maryland Historical Society, including then-director Romaine Stec Somerville, agreed to a plan by which Mr. Merrick personally, the Jacob and Annita France Foundation, and the Robert G. and Anne M. Merrick Foundation made grants to the society for the purpose of sponsoring a new state history. This volume,

I hope a fitting tribute to Maryland and to Mr. Merrick's devotion to the state, thus plays a small, late part in the 1984 celebration. Mr. Merrick died in November 1986. He gave me his personal encouragement from the beginning, and it saddens all of us that he did not live to see the project to completion.

Warm thanks go to Ms. Somerville, J. Jefferson Miller II, present director of the society, and to the committee that chose an author and saw the book to completion. Committee members Jean H. Baker, D. Randall Beirne, Gary L. Browne, Leonard C. Crewe, Jr., the late William L. Marbury, Roland C. McConnell, and J. Fife Symington, Jr.—have proven helpful, warmhearted, and lighthanded. Thomas M. Caplan, chairman and humanist of rare dimension, has been full of cheer and keen in judgment. Members of the society's staff—especially Sherri Sweep, Jeff D. Goldman, and Karen A. Stuart—gave unstintingly of their time to carry the work forward.

Cynthia, Mary Ellen, Ric, and I also acknowledge the many professional people who went out of their way to aid us. The staff of the Alderman Library, University of Virginia—including the circulation librarians and William H. Runge and Mildred K. Abraham of the Rare Books Department—left no request unfilled; thanks to H. C. Erik Midelfort, Sada Crismond, and former colleagues on the *Papers of James Madison* staff—Bob Rutland, Jeanne Sisson, Tom Mason, and Robert R. Crout—I was there able to work in a study offering enough (though not too much) peace and quiet. Both Gary L. Browne, earlier editor of the *Maryland Historical Magazine*, and Bonnie Joe Ayers, editor of *Maryland Magazine*, gladly loaned me files of those journals. We enjoyed equally warm cooperation from Susan Cummings, Phebe R. Jacobsen, Ben Primer, and Mame Warren of the Maryland State Archives, Annapolis; Wesley Wilson, Eva Slezak, and all others in the Maryland Room, Enoch Pratt Free Library; Nancy Brennan, Richard Flint, and Dean Krimmel of the Baltimore City Life Museums; Frederick N. Rasmussen and Carolyn J. Hardnett, Baltimore Sunpapers; Dennis M. Zembala (director), Ann Steele, and Peter Liebhold of Baltimore's splendid Museum of Industry; Peter H. Curtis, curator, Marylandia Department, McKeldin Library, University of Maryland at College Park; Paula Johnson, Calvert Marine Museum; and librarians at the Johns Hopkins University, the Maryland State Law Library, and the public libraries of Montgomery and Prince George's counties. Barbara Graebner of the Johns Hopkins University Center for Metropolitan Planning and Research lent me a large number of center publications. The University of Baltimore made available the files of the Baltimore Neighborhood Heritage Project. Gerry Watkins Yeager, University of Baltimore, opened the massive WMAR television newsfilm collection to us. Orlando Ridout V, Maryland Historical Trust, supplied answers to architectural history questions with admirable care and sharp wit; Mark Edwards of the same office sent us a draft report on state historic-preservation planning. I am grateful to Juanita Jackson Mitchell, Judge Robert Watts, William Boucher III,

Garrett Power, and Joseph L. Arnold for sharing their knowledge of post–World War II Baltimore; to James H. Bready for umpiring passages on baseball; and to Drs. A. McGehee Harvey and Gert H. Brieger (director), Institute for Medical History, Johns Hopkins University School of Medicine, for kindly answering medical history queries. Friends on the *Papers of Dwight D. Eisenhower* staff at Johns Hopkins, allowing me afterhours use of their word-processing system, spared much time and trouble in the last stages of copyediting; Daun van Ee and Elizabeth S. Hughes also made valuable substantive and editorial suggestions.

Additional thanks to Susan Alderman and Richard F. Noll of the Maryland Planning Department; Robert Snyder, L. G. Hermes, and Richard L. Daff, Sr., Department of Transportation; Karen Trent, Office of Licenses and Consumer Services; Kathie Hiatt, Department of Education; Tony Abato, Bureau of Mines; Arlene Jenkins, Baltimore City Police Department; and Charla Dicus, Maryland Port Administration. For searches, permissions, delightful guided tours, or particular expertise we express appreciation to Edward G. Uhl, formerly of Martin-Marietta; Theron K. Rinehart, retired from Fairchild Aircraft; Nancy McReynolds, Fairchild Industries; Elwood L. Loh, Prince George's County Public Schools; Martha Hahn of the Allegany County Historical Society; Jane C. Sween, Montgomery County Historical Society; Mary C. Ternes, Washingtoniana Division and the Washington Star Collection, District of Columbia Public Library; Emily Greenberg, University of Baltimore School of Law; Philip W. Tawes, Jr.; G. Raquel Mitchell, Lillie Carroll Jackson Museum; Elizabeth Schaaf, Peabody Institute; Garry Wheeler Stone, St. Mary's City Commission; John P. Hankey, consultant to the B&O Museum; Brigadier General Bernard Feingold (Ret.) and Major Howard S. Freedlander, Twenty-ninth Division museum and public affairs office, respectively; William L. Brown III, National Park Service historian and former officer in the re-created First Maryland; John Kish of the H. L. Mencken House; Susan Ulrich, Cornell University Press; Mark N. Schatz and the Ann Arrundell County Historical Society; Barbara Kellner, Columbia (Maryland) Archives; Nicholas M. Prevas; Aimee Fine, Mayor's Advisory Committee on Art and Culture, Baltimore; Bernard Fishman and Steven Shapiro, Jewish Historical Society of Maryland; Helen Campbell, Babe Ruth Birthplace/Baltimore Orioles Museum; John Beck, Albin O. Kuhn Library and Gallery, University of Maryland, Baltimore County; Linda Vlasac, Maryland State Arts Council; Yvonne Hardy, Eubie Blake Cultural Center; Ira Swadow, Baltimore Gas and Electric Company; David W. Harp; Susan Yardley Wheltle; Middleton Evans; Betsey R. and Philip Kahn, Jr.; and Bonnie S. Thompson of the Yeshiva School, Silver Spring. Jacques Kelly overcame every obstacle in the quest for post–World War II illustrations.

For reading the book or parts of it in manuscript form (when, rough and wrinkled, it needs the pressing of further thought and more work), I extend special thanks to everyone on the Caplan Committee, particularly to Mr.

Marbury for his detailed and thoughtful remarks; to Lois Green Carr, director of research, St. Mary's City Commission; Edward C. Papenfuse, Maryland State Archivist; Gregory A. Stiverson, director, Maryland Office for the Bicentennial of the U.S. Constitution and Assistant Maryland State Archivist; Ronald Hoffman, University of Maryland at College Park; Garrett Power, University of Maryland School of Law; W. Theodore Dürr, University of Baltimore; and most of all to George H. Callcott, University of Maryland at College Park, whose close reading and constructive suggestions reminded me of how much I profited from once being his seminar student. James F. DiLisio, Department of Geography, Towson State University, and Kay DiLisio rendered complete cooperation and many a helpful hint in putting together graphics. Jackie Wehmueller bravely took on the task of copyediting the manuscript, which benefited immensely from her work, as it did from the attention of Barbara Lamb, Henry Y. K. Tom, Joyce Kachergis, and Jess Bell. All errors and awkward passages in these pages are mine alone; I am deeply grateful to all these persons for helping me try to avoid them.

Cynthia and Ric—rummaging for illustrative material, running down obscure bits of evidence, debating which print or photo to use—shared the experience every step of the way (along with Barbara Grace Cottom) and have my affection for all their support and simply for keeping me company. Mary Ellen Hayward, maritime curator, Maryland Historical Society, on her own time and with patience far exceeding the normal person's, saw to the work of completing illustrations and writing captions for them, reconciling the various parts of the book, and helping with the index. I cannot adequately thank my father or the rest of our family for their help during the last few years, or say enough for the kindly Thomsens of Mechums River, Virginia. Nor could I properly acknowledge the devotion of two wonderful daughters, Laura and Rebecca.

MARYLAND
A Middle Temperament

1634–1980

Robert J. Brugger

with the assistance of
Cynthia Horsburgh Requardt, Robert I. Cottom, Jr.,
and Mary Ellen Hayward

Published by
THE JOHNS HOPKINS UNIVERSITY PRESS
in association with the
MARYLAND HISTORICAL SOCIETY

A Robert G. Merrick Edition

This book was originally brought to publication with the generous
assistance of the Jacob and Anita France Foundation, Inc., and the
Robert G. and Anne M. Merrick Foundation, Inc.

Maryland Paperback Bookshelf edition
05 04 03 02 01 00 99 98 97 96   5 4 3 2 1

The Johns Hopkins University Press, 2715 North Charles Street, Baltimore,
Maryland 21218-4319
The Johns Hopkins Press Ltd., London

LIBRARY OF CONGRESS CATALOGING-IN-PUBLICATION DATA

Brugger, Robert J.
Maryland, a middle temperament, 1634–1980
Bibliography: p.
Includes index.
1. Maryland—History.   I. Maryland Historical Society.
II. Title.
F181.B85   1988   975.2   88-7238
ISBN 0-8018-3399-x (alk. paper)
ISBN 0-8018-5465-2 (pbk.: alk. paper)

MARYLAND
A Middle Temperament

1634–1980

CHAPTER 1

From Province to Colony

In 1634 a successful voyage across the Atlantic left one grateful to see land of any kind. Father Andrew White's first observations were of the water he found and of the unsurpassed beauty of the earth—*Terra Maria* in the Latin charter—that he and other members of the group had set out to cultivate. They offered thanks not only for a safe ocean crossing; they seemed to have arrived in Paradise itself. "This baye is the most delightfull water I ever saw," White wrote in one version of his account. Its wide channel teemed with fish. Broad rivers, including one the natives called Patawomeck, emptied into it. Up the bay swampy and sickly shores gave way to "two sweet landes" firm and fertile—beckoning rather than forbidding. The woods were abundant and yet the trees so widely spaced and free of underbrush, he reported, that one could easily drive a four-horse coach among them. He took evident pleasure in describing the walnuts, oaks, and cedars, the "sallad-herbes and such like," the strawberries, raspberries, and "fallen mulberry vines" that were so thick one could scarcely walk without stepping on them. The soil was rich, black on top, reddish underneath, and the settlers had discovered "delicate springs" that provided good drink. The Indians daily caught partridge, deer, turkeys, and squirrels; there were also eagles, swans, herons, geese, and ducks whose bright feathers made them look as if dressed for a party, he thought, "by which will appeare, the place abounds not alone with profit, but also with pleasure." Father White noted that this promising land lay between the extremes of New England and Virginia. Maryland preserves, he wrote, "a middle temperature between the two, and enjoys the advantages, and escapes the evils, of each."[1]

The Maryland expedition had roots in the tangled bed of seventeenth-century English life and politics and in the venturesome energy of George Calvert. Calvert, son of a Yorkshire landholder, graduated from Oxford University in 1597, traveled on the Continent, and then began a long career in government service. Though first serving in minor posts, Calvert soon received the help of influential patrons, among them Sir Robert Cecil, who recognized his keen political sense and skills of expression. In 1613 King James himself took notice of Calvert by appointing him clerk of the Privy Council; after 1619 he was one of two principal secretaries of state, among the king's closest advisors. James had rewarded Calvert's loyal service by knighting him, then by making him a commissioner of the treasury with an annual pension of £1,000 and a lucrative subsidy on imported raw silk. In the Parliament of 1621 Calvert represented Yorkshire, trying to reconcile militant Protestants in Commons to the royal hope of an alliance with Spain. Two years later James granted Calvert twenty-three hundred acres in County Longford, Ireland, where his home was known as the Manor of Baltimore.

Meantime Calvert, like so many leading Europeans of his day, found the allurement of riches in the New World and the Orient irresistible. Since early in the century he had been a shareholder in the East India Company. In 1609 he purchased shares in the Virginia Company, which then faced serious difficulties with the Jamestown settlement, and later sat on its board of governors. Taking note of the problems plaguing Virginia during these years, Calvert in the 1620s made his own plans to settle Englishmen in America—on the shores of Newfoundland, where he expected farming and fishing to support a profitable colony. He acquired a royal grant or patent to the southeast coast of the island and called the place Avalon after the mythical point where Christianity entered Britain.

Possibly Calvert busied himself with Avalon because he was growing tired of Stuart statecraft. He had little taste for intrigue—a French minister to England half-correctly believed him so honorable, sensible, and courteous as to be "entirely without consideration or importance"[2]—and by 1624 the tide had turned against Spain in the court. His own rivals had grown in political influence. In 1625 Calvert resigned his secretaryship and next, after soul-searching both temporal and spiritual, declared to his Protestant king that he had converted to Catholicism. Unable any longer to take the Oath of Supremacy (to recognize the ultimate authority of the king in English ecclesiastical affairs), he withdrew entirely from political strife. James nonetheless remained grateful to Calvert, who in leaving service received the title Baron of Baltimore.

Calvert redoubled his efforts to found a settlement in America. Twice he traveled to Newfoundland, taking new settlers with him, yet late in the summer of 1629, shivering in Avalon, he had decided that its cold climate and rocky soil would never support a thriving colony. He wrote James's successor, Charles I, and asked for another grant, this one in the northern Chesapeake within the now-royal colony of Virginia. He and Lady Baltimore then sailed southward and visited Jamestown, whose leaders greeted him with guarded politeness; besides being "Romish" in religion, Calvert threatened to reduce the original compass of Virginia. When the impatient Virginians

Calvert family coat of arms. Detail from "Confirmation of Arms to Sir George Calvert," granted
by Richard St. George Norroy, King at Arms,
3 December 1622. *MHS*

asked him to take the Oath of Supremacy the Lord of Avalon left and re
turned home to work levers in the office of the privy seal. As he struggled
against poor health he managed to win a deadly backstairs and official game
with agents of Virginia. In June 1632, two months after Calvert died, King
Charles signed the final charter and established a new English colony in
honor of Queen Henrietta Maria. The grant went to Calvert's eldest son and
heir, Cecil, namesake of Sir Robert Cecil.

The second Lord Baltimore, who never entered public life, set about planning the Maryland settlement in a climate of stern political and religious
orthodoxy. Having dismissed Parliament, Charles ruled according to the
largest claims of royal prerogative. Puritans and Catholics suffered for failing
to conform to the Church of England. Old shareholders in the Virginia Company cloaked their opposition to the Catholic's venture by circulating what
Calvert called "monstrous charges" and spreading "scandalous reports to
discourage men from it." In mid-September 1633 he had organized about
seventeen gentlemen, most if not all of them the younger sons of Catholic
gentry, to make the voyage and help finance it. More than a hundred ordinary folk, mostly Protestants who had some experience at farming, joined

Left, Queen Henrietta Maria (1609–69), by Sir Anthony Van Dyck, c. 1632. *Collection of Her Majesty Queen Elizabeth II. Right*, Cecil Calvert (1606–75), second Lord Baltimore, ex-

tends the first "authorized" map of Maryland to his grandson, Cecil Calvert II (1667–81). By Gerard Soest, c. 1670. *Enoch Pratt Free Library*

the expedition. Perhaps a few men brought their wives; probably no couple brought children too young to work. With assistance from backers and members of his family, Calvert outfitted two vessels for the ocean journey. The *Ark*, of 350 tons, carried four small guns and measured between 90 and 110 feet in length; the *Dove*, an armed pinnace, was about one-seventh the size. Once loaded at Gravesend, the ships in October sailed down the Thames estuary. Suspicious authorities recalled the settlers for investigation and oath administering. Released, they set off again and then stopped at Cowes on the Isle of Wight, where they furtively took on two Jesuit priests, Andrew White and John Altham, along with their servants and possibly a few Catholic settlers, increasing the size of the party to 130 or 140. Cecil Calvert had intended to accompany the group, but fears of further attacks at home kept him there. As leaders of the small band he sent his brother Leonard to act as governor and Jerome Hawley and Thomas Cornwallis, Catholic gentlemen, to serve as commissioners or assistants.[3]

Baltimore's handwritten instructions reached the expedition before it left Cowes. They revealed his highest hopes and darkest forebodings. He ordered the colonists while on board ship to examine all "the private plotts" against them; he specified that after the party landed within the Maryland grant, one of its Anglican members was to visit the Virginians and pledge them "good correspondency." In practical terms Calvert, scarcely an experienced adventurer, drew heavily from Captain John Smith's published account of early Virginia. Baltimore warned the settlers against dangerous dispersal in the hostile wilderness (eleven years before, the natives had risen up and killed more than three hundred Virginians). He advised them to seat themselves in a town, frame their houses "in as decent and uniforme a manner as their abilities and the place" would afford, and build homes adjoining one another with land enough behind them for gardens. Drawing on Smith's laments about needless starvation, he told his own party to plant "a sufficient quantity of corne and other provision of victuall." His Lordship hoped not to fight Indians but to convert them. He expected the colonists all the same to take necessary precautions: to train able-bodied men in military skills and place the settlement where there was land enough for a fort. Calvert went on record as a loyal subject, listing as one of his aims the spread of King Charles's dominion. He also enlisted the colonists' self-interest; he wanted them to "reape the fruites of their charges and labors . . . with as much freedome comfort and incouragement" as they could want.[4]

His most admirable purpose, mixed in with the others, was religious toleration. Calvert counseled Leonard, Hawley, and Cornwallis above all to be "very carefull to preserve unity and peace" between Protestants and Catholics, both on the voyage and afterward. Protestants received guarantees of "mildness and favor" as justice permitted; Catholics on board ship he adjured to practice their faith as privately as possible.[5] Lord Baltimore's colony was indeed to locate a middle ground. Maryland settlers, like the Virginians, listed the pursuit of earthly gain high among their aims; like New England, though more discreetly, Maryland would provide religious asylum.

Turning design into reality tested the strength and courage of every settler. Sailing with fair winds on 22 November 1633, the ships followed the usual winter route to the Americas by first plying to the southwest and the Canary Islands. Sailors kept a sharp lookout for predators—murderous North African and Turkish pirates and the ships of England's seafaring enemies. Everyone watched the weather, which turned foul only a few nights out. At the height of the storm the *Dove* put up two distress lanterns and then disappeared from view, leaving passengers on the larger craft to fear the worst. The *Ark* later met a squall so severe it ripped the mainsail completely in two before it could be taken in. Even the stoutest hearts were amazed, wrote Father White. Catholics confessed their sins and fell to prayer, and the ship, "left without saile or government to the windes and waves, floated at hull like a dish till god were pleased to take pittie upon her."[6] Thus spared, the

Ark in December caught the trade winds that blew across three thousand miles of ocean to the West Indies. All the while the colonists, most of them probably on their maiden voyage, endured the daily privations of seventeenth-century seafaring. They fought boredom, lived in cramped quarters below deck, and slept on thin, straw-filled mats. The women had scant privacy. Men took turns at the bilge pumps. One could bathe only in saltwater, and certainly personal discomfort and dirty linen weighed less in the balance than the danger of being washed overboard. Meals of salted meat, hard biscuits, and dried peas made one wish for more fresh water. On Christmas Day men and women on the *Ark* let themselves go by drinking some Canary Island wine with supper. Thirty people fell sick and twelve of them died. In early January the voyagers at last reached landfall at Barbados, where they found the island's servants in rebellion and supplies costing five times what they usually did.

Later events enabled White to make happier entries in his journal. The main party cheered on 17 January when the little *Dove*, not sunk after all, sailed into port in the company of a British merchantman. Later in the month the Calvert vessels struck off for St. Christopher, where they took on more provisions. In early February they cleared the Leeward Islands and made for the Virginia Capes. Lord Baltimore had instructed his brother to avoid Jamestown; presuming the Virginia councillors hostile (and expecting them to offer no material help), he wished not to provoke them. Now on the scene, Governor Calvert chose a different form of politeness and sailed up the James anyway, hoping to pay a friendly call. A tense moment passed when the ships glided under the guns protecting the river mouth. Once anchored, the Maryland party found Governor John Harvey, George Calvert's old friend, hospitable and full of promises of future aid. Other Virginians stood aloof. A few of them hoped to put off the newcomers with word that the northern-Chesapeake Indians had armed after hearing rumors of an upcoming Spanish raid. Father White, noting that some Virginians wanted "noething more then our ruine," never doubted the source of those rumors. Virginia merchant-traders had developed a lush commerce with Indians within the Maryland grant. Among them, Henry Fleet bowed to the new order by agreeing to help the Calvert party locate a landing site. After a week of largely warm hospitality, the expedition set sail on 3 March for the upper bay.[7]

The colonists reached the mouth of the Potomac and slowly sailed upriver—naming landmarks as they proceeded—until the water narrowed at an island they called St. Clement's. There they felt safe enough to drop anchor and venture ashore. The exciting work of building an English settlement began with the banality of doing laundry, much of it lost when a boat overturned, but after a few days at St. Clement's the settlers had erected a wooden cross on the island and taken "solemne possession of the Country." Father White said a mass of thanksgiving on the Feast of the Annunciation,

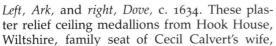

Left, Ark, and *right, Dove,* c. 1634. These plaster relief ceiling medallions from Hook House, Wiltshire, family seat of Cecil Calvert's wife, supply the only known contemporary images of any of the vessels that brought the original settlers to British North America. *MHS*

25 March, which by the calendar then in use was the first day of the new year, and Governor Calvert formally read Lord Baltimore's charter. With similar solemnity Calvert sought peace with the natives. A small force in the *Dove* sailed up the river far enough to treat with the Piscataway Indians and put away any fears they had of "Spanish invaders." Employing Fleet, a Protestant, as interpreter, the new settlers could only speak vaguely of their wish to convert the Indians, but a chieftain on the Virginia side had a striking reply to Father Altham's pledge of peaceful intentions. "We will use one table," he said. "My people shall hunt for my brother, and all things shall be in common." Farther up, on the northern bank, a Piscataway child-emperor and his advisors offered the hand of friendship; in the minds of the Indians, tribal land belonged to everyone. Calvert made the most of this pristine sense of property and satisfied his own. Next dealing with the Yaocomacoes below St. Clement's, he traded English-made axes, hoes, hatchets, and cloth for about thirty miles of land below what the English called the Wicomico River.[8]

The settlers could hardly have hoped for such a welcome. Father White described the natives as painted in ghastly colors—red and blue lines on their faces—dressed in deerskin, and decorated with shells, teeth, beads, and feathers. They could throw a stick in the air and strike it with an arrow before it fell. The Indians looked warlike; miraculously, they seemed to be "of a very loveing and kinde nature." He may have portrayed a people who knew the futility of resistance. Some of them visited the *Ark,* marveling at the tree it had been dug out of. "They trembled," White wrote, "to heare our ordinance thinking them fearefuller than any thunder they had ever heard." Most of these Indians already had begun trading with Englishmen and knew of their cruelty at war.[9]

Even so, Marylanders benefited from a lucky draw and the results of long-standing Indian struggles in the region. The tribes living within Baltimore's grant, for the most part members of the Algonquin family, were truly peaceful, loosely governed, and fairly weak in comparison to the powerful Virginia Algonquins under Chief Powhatan. They farmed, fished, hunted, and lived settled lives in hamlets. Fewer than fifteen hundred of them dwelled on the eastern side of the Chesapeake, where they formed Choptank, Nanticoke, Pocomoke, and Assateague tribes. On the western shore there were many villages on what the settlers named the Patuxent River—Patuxent and Mattapanient sites—and, on the Potomac, clusters of Conoy subtribes. Besides the Yaocomaco and Piscataway, the Conoy included Chopticos, Potapacos, Pamunkeys, Mattowomans, and Anacostanks. In all, these native peoples of the western shore numbered about another fifteen hundred. Much of the upper Chesapeake had cleared of heavy Algonquin population because the warlike Susquehannocks, a tribe numbering perhaps two thousand and living in a cluster of villages forty miles up the river that the colonists named after them, had conducted raiding parties to the south. For twenty years after the Maryland settlers landed they successfully befriended the closest Indian tribes by promising them protection from the Susquehannocks, who for their part acted as a buffer against their aggressive Iroquois enemies farther north. Both whites and Indians had later examples of the other's treachery. Even so, good fortune promised to fulfill Baltimore's hope for peace with the Maryland Indians.

The first months of the settlement were auspicious indeed. Around the spot the settlers soon called St. Mary's, they built a palisade with seven small cannon, began felling trees for their homes, and put in first crops. The Yaocomaco Indians made these pioneering efforts far easier by sharing their cleared land and village with the settlers and bringing them food like small game and boiled or roasted oysters. The new settlers purchased Virginia cattle, hogs, and slips for fruit trees. Marylanders thus escaped the hard times of early Jamestown. Having arrived prepared to work, Calvert's group planned their arrival for the planting time. Marylanders had brought seasoned timbers for a barge that they quickly assembled and put into the water. Concern for food crops and the early appearance of women (if none came on the *Ark*) gave the Maryland settlement a domestic character Virginia at the onset had lacked. Later visitors found a few wooden houses and outbuildings on lots that averaged a hundred acres or more and a water-powered grist mill. Learning of the successful landing at St. Mary's, Lord Baltimore hoped that one day it would resemble the English town he had envisioned.

"Their manner of fishynge." Engraving by Theodore de Bry from an original drawing by John White, who accompanied Sir Walter Raleigh's expedition to the Chesapeake in 1585. From Thomas Hariot, *A Briefe and True Report of the New Found Land of Virginia* (Frankfurt, 1590). *John Work Garrett Collections of the Milton S. Eisenhower Library, The Johns Hopkins University*

In fact, Calvert's original intent was to duplicate old England as accurately as possible. By charter Maryland was his fiefdom, a royal gift that resembled the land grants medieval English kings made in return for the military knight service of their loyal retainers—though in this case the substitute for such fealty was Baltimore's symbolic annual tribute of two Indian arrows. King Charles placed Maryland on the same footing as the old county palatine of Durham. From the time of William the Conquerer until the sixteenth century the bishop of that northern border city had held wide-ranging political and military authority. As Lord Proprietor, Baltimore answered only to the king for his government of Maryland; while the settlers were to enjoy the rights of Englishmen, Calvert owned all the territory within the boundaries of his grant, expected to receive traditional rents, taxes, and fees, appointed all officials necessary to enforce the law, and exercised final political and judicial authority in his domain. He received full power to build fortifications and wage defensive war, to confer honors and titles, incorporate boroughs and towns, and license trade. As head of the church, he had authority to erect and consecrate chapels and churches. Like a baron of old, Baltimore also enjoyed the right of subinfeudation, the power to grant lands within his realm just as the king had bestowed Maryland on him. All these "ample rights, liberties, immunities, and temporal franchises" belonged as an inheritance to the lords Baltimore for all time.[10]

No one knew how these prerogatives would weather the climate of the New World. Baltimore's first challenge came from William Claiborne, a Kent County Englishman who had arrived in Virginia as a young man in 1621 and risen from surveyor to Indian fighter, trader, and member of the council. Like John Smith, he had sailed up the bay and marveled at its potential riches. Along with Virginia investors and English merchants, he managed to organize the northern Chesapeake fur trade and also profited by supplying corn to English settlements farther north. On Kent Island, largest piece of land in the bay, well drained, and located ideally for dealings with upper-Chesapeake Indians, Claiborne in 1631 had built a stockade, church, and store. He persuaded a number of Virginians to settle the island, and after pledging him military support they moved there to plant crops and orchards. Claiborne named a smaller, thousand-acre island to the south after his friend Richard Popely and sent men first to graze hogs and then to clear fields there. In about 1634 Richard Thompson, a Claiborne lieutenant, took his family to live on Popely's Island. Having made such investments, Claiborne had angrily resisted Baltimore's request for a Chesapeake land grant; probably he was the one who in 1634 told Indians that the approaching Marylanders were hostile Spanish. Now he brushed aside messages noting the bounds of Lord Baltimore's domain and inviting Claiborne to cast his lot with Maryland. The Maryland grant, he declared, excluded places already settled—a view that carried legal substance. But Claiborne was no lawyer.

He typified the swashbucklers that English ambition of the day sprouted in foreign parts. Proud, impulsive, and untamed, he sought out adventure and loved a good fight.

Calvert prepared for trouble, and in the spring of 1635 two Maryland vessels under Cornwallis's command clashed with one of Claiborne's armed trading wherries, *Cockatrice*, at a river mouth on the lower eastern shore of the bay. She surrendered only after suffering several casualties. Soon afterward the Virginian got revenge when another small naval battle ended in his favor. Fortunately for the Lord Proprietor and for peace in the Chesapeake, Claiborne's resistance led to a drop in his fur exports, and his London sponsors replaced him with another agent, more tractable, George Evelin. The Kent Islanders eventually came to terms with Calvert, though not before a Maryland expeditionary party landed on the island in December 1637 and subdued rebel leaders. Claiborne, first in England and then in Virginia, nursed his wounded pride and sat on plots he hoped would hatch in the future.

Questions of governance posed serious problems of a different sort. The benevolent intentions of Lord Baltimore—still in England—and the interests of settlers on the Potomac frontier almost certainly had to clash, and even during the Claiborne controversy differences arose over the fundamental issue of lawmaking. In the beginning Baltimore's view was that he would make all needful statutes for the settlement, submitting them to the advice and consent of freemen (males not bound in service) assembled as the charter contemplated. Before long, many constituents, probably most of the Protestants, concluded that fairness would be better served by reversing the order. They wished to frame laws that the proprietor then would seal with his approval. Records of the first assembly session in January 1635 do not survive, but during that meeting members apparently tried to take the first step in legislating. Governor Leonard Calvert, who sat as head of the one-house body, objected to the "acts"; their content aside, he said, they represented an unjustified assumption of authority. Baltimore's own reply arrived in April 1637, when he directed his brother to call another assembly for the following January "and then and there to signify to them, that we do dissent to all their laws, by them heretofore . . . made within our said province, and do hereby declare them to be void." He enclosed his own statutes and ordered the governor to have them confirmed. When the assembly met it formally rejected Baltimore's statutes and formed a committee to write its own. The committee drafted twenty-six bills covering "enormous" criminal offenses and protecting property rights; it also adopted seventeen of the proposals Baltimore had made—which included procedures for obtaining land and the enforcement of military discipline. Among the homegrown measures was one that members knew would tempt Baltimore; it declared Claiborne an outlaw and all his property forfeited to the proprietor. With the gauntlet thrown down, Baltimore might have taken the course of King Charles and asserted absolute authority over this fledgling legislature. In August he decided to yield. Thereafter legislative initiative lay with the assembly.[11]

At the same time, establishing proprietary offices, Baltimore claimed every privilege of the Maryland charter. In his 1637 letter of commission to Leonard Calvert, Baltimore named his brother chancellor and chief judge as well as governor, entrusting him with all judicial powers, civil and criminal— although the governor was to share with the council jurisdiction over offenses involving penalty of life or limb. Calvert was empowered to issue grants, writs, and pardons, and was to establish public ports and markets. Baltimore made Hawley and Cornwallis councillors; as the proprietor's trusted advisors, they received a personal writ of summons to the assembly sessions. A third councillor, John Lewger, conveyed the commission itself. Lewger, Baltimore's old Oxford friend and a recent convert to Catholicism, was also to act as provincial secretary—the source of many more proprietary officials later in the century—and head of the land office.

⚬⚬⚬

In places Maryland soil was every bit as rich as Father White had described it—centuries of mulch on top of water-deposited sandy loam made for earth far more fecund than the Englishmen had known. The more of it Baltimore could see settled, the better for himself and his province. In a booklet entitled *A Relation of Maryland*, Jerome Hawley and John Lewger, surely with Baltimore's blessing, tried in 1635 to entice Englishmen to take up land on the Potomac and Patuxent rivers. The pamphlet relied heavily on White's description of the land and Indians; it included a crude map of the province, an English translation of Baltimore's charter, and his "conditions" to those "as shall goe, or adventure to Maryland."[12]

Even before the original settlers left England, Lord Baltimore had made known his plan for making land grants, which generally rewarded a colonist's contribution to the enterprise. They also established a peculiar pattern in Maryland, for Baltimore made these grants to colonists and their heirs in perpetuity—their holdings were secure—yet he required an annual quitrent or fee as lord of the province, and if a landholder died intestate (without a will or known heirs) the land reverted or escheated to the proprietor. To "adventurers" who provided for their own transport and the passage of five "able men" between the ages of sixteen and fifty, Baltimore first promised two thousand, after 1635 one thousand, acres. Obtaining such a grant entitled a subscriber to erect and name as he wished a manor of the kind the English gentry enjoyed at home—complete with the power to hold court to settle minor affairs among tenants. Settlers accompanied by fewer than five servants received one hundred acres for themselves and another hundred for each additional servant. Married settlers received two hundred acres plus one hundred per servant. For each child under sixteen the reward was fifty

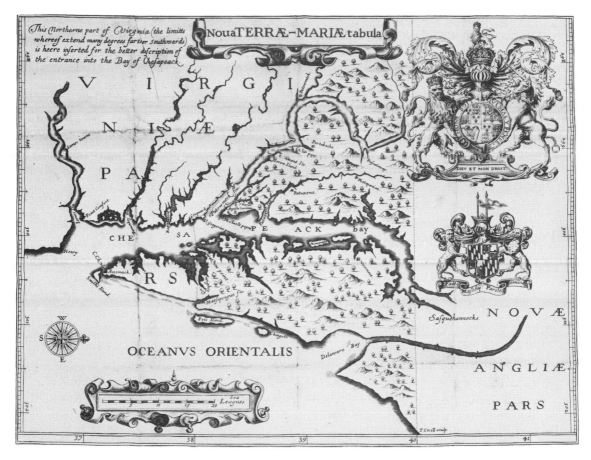

"Nova Terrae-Mariae Tabula." The first "authorized" map of Maryland, bound into copies of *A Relation of Maryland* (London, 1635), depicted Virginia as a wasteland and used the Indian name to identify Kent Island, William Claiborne's territorial claim. *MHS*

acres. Though grants to couples listed the husband as landholder—reflecting the lowly status of women in English law at the time—widows with children received the same grants as men; unmarried women with servants were entitled to fifty acres for each. The Lord Proprietor's annual quitrent in 1635 ranged from twenty shillings—"in the commodity of the country"—for a manor to twelve pence per fifty acres for a family of settlers. Though these rates underwent changes, the principle of exchanging land for settling oneself and perhaps others remained in place for nearly fifty years. A settler who met the conditions of plantation approached the secretary of the province, recorded his right, and requested a grant. The governor or secretary presented a warrant of survey to the surveyor general, who located and surveyed an appropriate tract of land. His report eventually led to the secretary's issuing a patent that described the reasons for the grant, the boundaries of the land, and the conditions of tenure. Settlers paid rent on surveyed land

and did not hold secure title until they received their patent, signed by the governor on Lord Baltimore's behalf.[13]

The Lewger and Hawley booklet offered a sample indenture, a form for binding a servant. This device enabled men who could not afford the cost of a voyage to make the trip in exchange for time in service. The servant might accompany his master to Maryland, as the authors suggested, or, as in later practice, he might sign papers with a sea captain who then sold his obligation on landing. This model indenture bound the master to furnish transportation, "Meat, Drinke, Apparell and Lodging, with other necessaries" during the servant's term and then, on its completion, to supply him with clothes, a year's provision of corn, and the right to fifty acres of land. Though the usual length of service in Maryland was four or five years, Lewger and Hawley noted that one did well to shorten that term in the cases of skilled workers, who were especially valuable in the province.[14]

The land yielded so much grain in the first year that the *Dove* carried a full load to Massachusetts in trade. But tobacco was the crop that the Virginia enterprise recommended and for which a marketing system already extended from the Chesapeake to London. Indians had smoked it and then John Rolfe of Virginia had discovered the weed as a cash crop. While King James had denounced its use, he finally seized upon its popularity as a revenue source. Without doubt the exportation of tobacco after 1619 had saved the Virginia colony from ruin. Just as clearly, the economy that linked itself to changing tobacco prices in England laid itself open to merciless market fluctuations. Virginia planters, after reacting to towering prices in the early 1620s by planting as much acreage as possible, suffered hard times during the ensuing tobacco glut. By 1635 the market had returned to a more profitable level, four to six pence a pound, and Maryland settlers wasted no time getting into it. They eagerly sought patents on lands that faced onto the rivers and creeks of the western shore, thus accommodating the annual visits of tobacco vessels. They and their servants set to work attacking the hardwoods and pines that loomed over settlers from the water's edge to wherever they obtained a grant. Killing trees by girdling (cutting a ring around their base), the newcomers allowed light into their "fields" and planted mostly tobacco. Tobacco was so valuable that it became common currency. As early as 1639 the province produced 100,000 pounds of the "sotte weed," and within a generation tobacco growing had become a way of life. A transplanted Englishman later called Maryland tobacco "our meat, drinke, cloathing and monies."[15]

It was tedious business, requiring "a great deal of trouble in the right management of it." The first step was to seed specially prepared beds in late winter to early spring, then, after warmer weather and a good rainstorm, to transplant the seedlings into hills spaced three feet apart in rows that wound around tree stumps. Later, to ensure fullest possible leaf growth, the grower or his servants had to top the plants. In performing this task they used their thumbnails, giving rise to the seventeenth-century saying that one could always tell a tobacco planter by his calloused and green-stained thumb. During the summer, besides constant weeding that left the light, loose soil liable to runoff during thunderstorms, the planter had to pull suckers from the base of the leaves and check them for worms and grubs.[16]

Once the tobacco ripened it was cut with a special knife and left in the field to wilt, then tied to sticks that were placed in an airy barn for the thorough drying necessary to prevent rotting in shipment to England. When "in proper case" the plants were piled in the barns until there was time for stemming (which then meant pulling the leaves from the stalks) and stripping (taking the largest fibers out of the leaves). Finally, using their feet, workers forced the cured tobacco leaves, bundled in "hands," into homemade barrels or hogsheads, each containing as much as the planter could press into it—usually between two and three hundred pounds (packing became increasingly efficient; in the middle of the next century large hand-operated presses packed thousand-pound casks). By the time Marylanders began planting tobacco, two varieties had displaced the indigenous plant the Indians grew. One, known as "sweet scented," always brought a high price but flourished only in several Virginia counties. The other, Orinoco, came from South America and yielded a bulkier and stronger-scented leaf. Less valuable, it grew well in Maryland soils. Bound to plant no more than he could care for, a single grower at the time of Maryland settlement could expect to produce perhaps 800 or 1,000 pounds of tobacco each season (in the early eighteenth century that figure rose to between 1,500 and 1,700 pounds). With each successive season, yield tended to drop as erosion and soil exhaustion took their toll. Planters worked their fields as long as possible, then moved on, further scattering the population.

By 1642 Lord Baltimore's settlement on the lower Potomac had grown into St. Mary's County. In it lived nearly four hundred persons, spread over several smaller jurisdictions or hundreds. Near St. Mary's, where a dozen households occupied five square miles, there were hundreds named St. George's and St. Michael's. More distant were St. Clement's, up the Potomac at the mouth of the Wicomico, and Mattapanient, five miles north of St. Mary's on the Patuxent. On Kent Island settlers remained on the southern side, fearful of the Susquehannocks. Throughout the province there were sixteen manors, belonging to the men who had done the most to finance Lord Baltimore's colony. While just four of the seventeen original gentlemen-immigrants remained in Maryland, large landholders like Leonard Calvert, Cornwallis, Thomas Weston, and Thomas Gerard (Gerard's own lands amounted to more than six thousand acres) offered proof that some of Baltimore's subscribers had realized his vision of a replicated English gentry. More than 80 percent of the land surveyed at the time fell within a manor. Four-fifths of the freemen had not claimed land. In St. Mary's, 136 out of 173 of them worked as tenant farmers or as wage-earning laborers who lived in dwellings the landholders supplied for them. Smaller tracts or "plantations" commonly adjoined the manor properties, a pattern suggesting that mano-rial gentlemen chose rich locations in the early province and also that manors might have provided security in the wilderness. But surveys of such inde-pendent holdings also demonstrated that as long as land was abundant few freemen in the palatinate would choose to live as subjects on another's manor.[17]

⌒⋙⋘⌒

Stretched along the rivers and creeks of Baltimore's province, this string of settlement was fragile enough without trouble from home. For nearly twenty years in the middle of the century, a period the settlers later referred to as a "time of troubles," Maryland suffered the full consequences of English po-litical and religious warring and its own weak political structure. Lord Balti-more found the time personally difficult. His wife, Lady Anne Arundel, daughter of a leading Catholic member of Lords, died in 1639. In the next few years Calvert must have wished he himself were free to seek refuge in Maryland. Parliament convened in 1640, challenged royal absolutism, and charged some of King Charles's advisors with counseling tyranny and trea-son against the English people. The House of Commons executed a longtime Yorkshire friend of the Calverts, Thomas Wentworth, Earl of Strafford, in 1641. In August 1642 the king defied Parliament and took his cause to the battlefield. During the ensuing civil war Charles and his royalist or Cavalier friends enlisted the help of Scots Presbyterians and Irish Catholics in the struggle against Cromwell's forces, while the Puritan or "Roundhead" Parlia-ment showed a willingness to deal with its enemies as it did with Charles, who was beheaded in early 1649. Politics and conscience had so combined as to leave Calvert's every move suspect; in the Puritan order his tolerant province was more anomalous than ever.

Little wonder that the ambitions of some members of the Jesuit community in Maryland embarrassed and angered him. The original Jesuit priests had brought with them men sufficient to claim six thousand acres of land under the first conditions of plantation. White, uninterested in secular things, had devoted attention not to the grant but to preaching and teaching among the Indian tribes, even baptizing a Piscataway chief, Kittamaquund, in 1640. By the late 1630s other priests had arrived in the province and the Jesuits' worldly business had grown considerably. In 1637 Father Philip Fisher as-sumed charge of secular details. Using the name Thomas Copley (and ignor-ing the papal order to keep God's affairs outside of civil interference), he laid claim to more lands, began dealing with the Indians for grants indepen-dently of provincial authority, and wrote Baltimore seeking further privi-leges and exemptions that the proprietor found "very extravagant." Not only did Fisher challenge established authority, he acted as if he exercised palatine powers within the palatinate—as if Maryland were harboring a papal enclave. Baltimore responded by separating church and state for reasons both pragmatic and principled. He set aside Fisher's agreements with the Indians and revised the conditions of land grants to exclude any "corporation, society, fraternity, municipality, political body (whether ecclesiastical or temporal)."[18] To discuss this and other issues too serious to develop in writing, Baltimore asked his brother Leonard to return to England.

Lord Baltimore hoped to hold Maryland above the religious strife that beset Britain, but at this point the English civil war reached the Chesapeake in the person of Richard Ingle. A Roundhead shipmaster and merchant, Ingle voiced sympathy for Cromwell from the quarterdeck of his aptly named vessel, *Reformation*. On a 1641 visit to Maryland he had done business with the Brent family, which had arrived with servants in 1638, taken up large holdings of land, and as relatives of the Calverts apparently grown close to the governor. The Brents believed Ingle had treated them badly. When Ingle reappeared at St. Mary's in early 1644 Leonard Calvert was in London to consult with his brother, and Giles Brent was acting provincial governor. By later accounts Ingle arrived with the usual bluster, waving parliamentary papers allowing him to take royalist ships as prizes and scornfully declaring that "the king was no king." Brent had him arrested for treason. There followed some division among Maryland political leaders as to the wisdom of Ingle's arrest and then either confusion or conspiracy involving Thomas Cornwallis, who along with the sheriff returned Ingle to his ship. Ingle sailed to England, Cornwallis with him.[19]

Ingle's next visit to Maryland early in 1645 was a marauding expedition, justified in his view because Baltimore's province had proven itself to be a royalist camp as well as a nest of papists. Governor Calvert had returned to America, but when Ingle's force landed at St. Mary's he again was absent, this time on a working visit to Virginia. Well armed and expecting booty in payment, Ingle's men quickly subdued the settlers in and around the provincial capital. Ingle demanded that Marylanders take an oath of submission to the Puritan Parliament. Those who refused—Protestants and Catholics alike—found their estates eagerly set upon and pillaged. Ingle even plundered the home of his earlier benefactor, Cornwallis, whose eventual suit in English court outlined the terror Ingle and his men visited on their enemies: they burned fences, killed or scattered livestock, and carried off everything of value in the house, including ironwork, door fixtures, and window glass. Ingle destroyed government records and Lord Baltimore's great seal. He and a council calling itself the assembly of Protestants broke up the missionary work of Jesuit priests among the Indians. Meantime, taking full advantage of the chaos, William Claiborne returned to Kent Island and attempted to reestablish control over his former trading post. Not until late 1646 was Governor Calvert able to organize an expedition to challenge the rebels' rule. By that time Ingle himself had set sail for England and Claiborne once again had retreated to Virginia. In the December assembly Baltimore's friends complained to him of their sufferings during the "heinous rebellion" of Ingle, "his accomplices and confederates."[20]

Ingle was gone, but peace and order remained elusive. Governor Calvert issued a general pardon to the Kent Islanders who renewed their oath of allegiance to Lord Baltimore. He began making arrangements for paying the armed band that had helped him regain control of the province. With the government treasury low, he worried about mutiny. Suddenly taken ill in these straits, Leonard Calvert died, only hours after naming as his successor a Catholic planter, Thomas Greene, and appointing Margaret Brent—Giles Brent's sister and herself a highly respected landholder—to manage his private affairs. One could scarcely distinguish the late governor's personal and political lives; he had pledged his own money or proprietary property in payment to his troops. Strong enough to carry that plan into execution (and to request a seat in the assembly for the purpose), Margaret Brent played a key role in satisfying those men before their impatience turned to violence. Lord Baltimore both protested Brent's seizure of his property and bowed to expediency. In August 1648 he removed Greene and named as governor a Virginian and Protestant, William Stone.

One of Stone's first public acts, offering refuge to a band of persecuted Virginia Puritans, both confirmed Baltimore's ideal of tolerance and helped to safeguard his province as long as Puritans ruled in England. It also complicated the already difficult social situation in Maryland. Richard Bennett, the Puritan leader, settled his flock of three hundred at the mouth of the Severn River, calling the settlement Providence. At the 1649 assembly session legislators in An Act Concerning Religion fulfilled the promise of toleration Stone had made to the Puritans before they removed to the Severn. The law recognized the informal free exercise of religion that had marked the province since Cecil Calvert's instructions to the first settlers. It imposed heavy fines for making references to the religious practice of others—for using the pointed and derogatory phrases of the day that included "heretick, Scismatick, Idolater, puritan, Independant, Prespitarian, popish priest, Jesuite, Jesuited papist," along with "Roundhead" and "Sepratist." The act had two edges. Designed to curb sectarian animosity, it also established penalties for denying Christ as the Savior and doubting the Holy Trinity or God's existence; Jacob Lumbrozo, a Jewish physician, later learned its limits when authorities bound him over for trial for explaining Christ's miracles and Resurrection as so much magicianship and shrewd body-stealing. Still, the measure marked a notable departure from Old World oppression. Henceforward no Christian in the province would "bee any wais troubled, molested or discountenanced for or in respect of his or her religion nor in the free exercise thereof"; no man or woman could be "any way compelled to the beleife or exercise of any other Religion against his or her consent."[21] The work of Protestant and Catholic lawmakers alike, the act gave assurances to Puritan newcomers while also protecting Catholic families, who more than ever stood in the minority.

The Toleration Act, as it came to be known, represented a high achievement in provincial government, the result of a balance of forces that worked for the general good. It was a precarious balance, as became evident a short time later. Congregationalists on the Severn began to doubt that they could submit in conscience to the oath of allegiance to Lord Baltimore—it seemed to contain royalist implications and required sworn commitment to officials whose spiritual head was the "Antichrist," the pope himself.[22] While the Puritans entertained these scruples, word reached the Chesapeake of Charles's execution and of a Parliament act declaring it treasonous to speak of an heir to the throne, to support the claims of Charles's exiled son. Like Virginia under William Berkeley, Maryland in November 1649—while Stone visited his Virginia lands and Thomas Greene acted as governor—pronounced Prince Charles rightful king of England. Though Stone quickly retracted the endorsement, Baltimore's enemies in England plotted to lump Virginia and Maryland together as mainland governments in need of chastisement. Parliament named commissioners to obtain the submission of Berkeley and Virginia, and in 1652 two of them, Richard Bennett and William Claiborne, sailed to St. Mary's to accept the deference of Maryland. After two confusing years, during which a council appointed by Bennett and Claiborne vied with the proprietary governor for authority, the Puritans finally succeeded in portraying Stone as rebellious to Cromwell and persuading Bennett and Claiborne—who were serving as governor and secretary of Virginia—to place Maryland government in the hands of a ten-man Puritan council.

The Toleration Act became one of the first victims of Puritan rule—a new law passed in October 1654 forbade Catholics openly to practice their faith. No longer were Marylanders required to take an oath of loyalty to the Lord Proprietor upon receiving land grants. Other statutes outlawed sin, vice, and sabbath breaking. William Fuller, now leading the three hundred or more Providence Puritans, scoffed at Stone's word that Cromwell himself had agreed to a restoration of Lord Baltimore's Maryland rights. Governor Stone bravely mounted a counterattack. He retrieved the provincial records from a private dwelling at Patuxent, where the Puritans had met, and then in the spring of 1655 assembled a small force that embarked in boats and proceeded toward the Severn River. On 25 March the proprietary troops landed and met a murderous fire both from the large number of infantrymen under Fuller's command and from an armed vessel, *Golden Lion*, whose guns supported the Puritans. Stone's heavy losses and surrender only produced an uneasy quiet in Maryland. In England a pamphlet war between Lord Baltimore and his enemies generated much heat and titles like *Babylon's Fall in Maryland* and *Lord Baltimore's printed Case, uncased and answered*. An exception was John Hammond's booklet, *Leah and Rachel, or, The Two Fruitfull Sisters Virginia and Mary-land*. Hammond, who had lived on both sides of the Potomac, saw the roots of religious strife in the nagging Calvert-Claiborne controversy. He counseled the siblings of the Chesapeake to take their example from the Old Testament sisters who learned to live in peace and prosperity.

Hammond's advice may or may not have moved his immediate audience, but finally, in 1657, Bennett and Claiborne signed a peace agreement with Lord Baltimore. In exchange for Calvert's amnesty, Puritans in the province recognized His Lordship's proprietorship and restored religious toleration. Baltimore dismissed the case against Lumbrozo and granted him full citizenship. Claiborne at last bowed to the Maryland patent. The proprietor and most of his tenants hoped that the violence and divisiveness had ended.

In the mid-seventeenth century, uncertainty colored more than government in Maryland, for life could be as unpredictable as politics. The number of settlers in the province ebbed and flowed—dropping in the decade of Ingle's rebellion, then, after 1650, climbing sharply as troubles like the civil war, high food prices, and an oversupply of labor drove young people away from the British Isles. Nearly half of all these migrants landed in the Chesapeake region, many of them in Maryland. There in 1660 the population reached about twenty-five hundred—still only ten times the size of the original expedition. Twenty years later some twenty thousand persons lived in Lord Baltimore's province. But numbers masked the uncertainty and bleakness of human experience. New planters established homes in forested isolation, the trees they had girdled standing starkly about them. Kent Island farmers and traders, along with settlers on what John Smith had named the Eastern Shore, relied on boats to conduct business and visit any close neighbors on the creeks and rivers; on the bay their small craft were vulnerable to sudden changes in weather. Traveling by land between St. Mary's and outlying plantations, one might follow a path running from Point Lookout to the Patuxent settlements. Marked by thrice-notched trees, it wound through somber forest and the gullies and brambles that took over abandoned tobacco fields.

The greatest doubt surrounded life itself. Despite Father White's expectant praise for the Maryland climate, Lord Baltimore's settlers, like the Virginians, underwent a "seasoning" ordeal as their bodies struggled to adjust to new habitat, diet, and maladies. The Maryland marshes bred "muskeetoes" that pestered the immigrants, many of whom, complaining of "agues and fevers" or "great sickness and much weakness," caught malaria. Its deadly combination of fevers and chills left them miserable for the better part of a year if they did not die sooner. "A fiery Pulse beat in my Veins / From Cold I felt resembling Pains," wrote a poetic victim of the "intermitting fever." "This cursed seasoning I remember, / Lasted from *March* to cold *December*." Malarial fever not only took a heavy toll of lives, it left survivors weak, suscep-

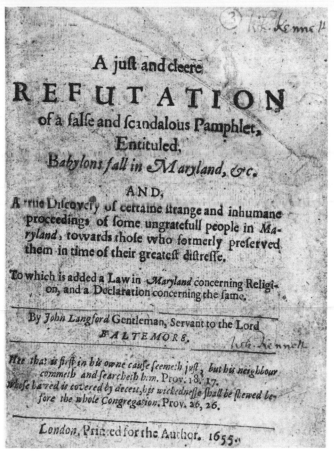

Title page from John Langford's entry in the pamphlet war surrounding the good care Lord Baltimore gave the Church of England in Maryland. *John Work Garrett Collections of the Milton S. Eisenhower Library, The Johns Hopkins University*

tible to later attacks, and vulnerable to other common diseases like smallpox, diphtheria, and yellow fever. Epidemics of influenza between 1675 and 1677 and smallpox in 1685 and 1686 accounted for periods of unusually high mortality in the province. At any time settlers might fall to the bloody flux or "Grypes of the Gutts"—which likely referred to amoebic dysentery.[23]

Thus the Chesapeake region both enticed newcomers with its richness and killed them with its illness. In seventeenth-century New England, males who reached the age of twenty generally lived for another forty-five years. By contrast, youthful immigrants to Maryland (most men made the voyage in their late teens) died on average only twenty-three years later. Almost one in five male settlers who reached age twenty-two succumbed to disease before his thirtieth birthday. Seven of ten died before reaching age fifty. From another perspective, two-thirds of married or widowed men who died in these years left all minor children. Only a few fathers, about 6 percent, lived to see any offspring grow to maturity. Immigrant women, of whom the records spoke less clearly, apparently did not live long lives, either. Roughly half the children born in seventeenth-century Maryland died before reaching age twenty.

Frequent loss of spouses, parents, and youngsters left these settlers anxious and guarded. Husbands and fathers expected their widows to face the burden of young children. Because English common law sharply curtailed a married woman's powers, widows, before remarrying, often deeded portions of their estate to children as a way of protecting family property. Every locality offered examples of eldest orphans caring for younger siblings, of private and public accommodations for children. Orphans might go to relatives, godparents, or guardians; authorities frequently bound them as servants until they reached adulthood. When native-born children married they generally took that step with comparative freedom, parents either being dead or reluctant to impose their will. Aware of death's frequent visits, parents and children alike may have prepared themselves for loss by watching their affections. At the least, parental death—leading to remarriages, minor stepchildren, and legal wards—made for complex households that tended to differ from those in old or New England.

No less than death and disease, the labor system shaped early Maryland society. Between the 1640s and late 1670s most newcomers arrived as indentured servants, largely single men, who paid fully for their passage. By Elizabethan custom they worked twelve or fourteen hours a day, every day but Saturday (when by usage they had afternoons free) and Sunday. They were liable to sale and subject to their master's discipline, which included what the statutes described as reasonable corporal punishment. Running away carried formal penalties of lengthened service. Though allowed a hearing in court if they felt abused, mistreated servants presumably did not visit the courthouse as part of their monthly regimen. Neither men nor women could marry until they had completed or purchased their service contract. Women (whom men outnumbered by a ratio of two or three to one) generally arrived in their early twenties. Four or five years later, by the time they were freed, they were likely to bear few children and were subject to the poor health that lowered fertility. The indenture system played its own part in undermining English custom. Strapped between length of service and healthy sexuality, youthful newcomers bent and broke moral codes. References to illegitimate children appeared often in local records. Bridal pregnancy in seventeenth-century Maryland reached levels more than twice the ratio in England. Though occasionally joining another male, a "mate," to keep house and put a crop in the ground, young men leaving servitude much preferred the contract of marriage. If they were fortunate enough to find a partner, they took the step far from home—escaping parental controls and losing family assistance. Wedding celebrations often fell to the necessity of saving money or getting back to work.

Nothing spoke truer of the coarseness of life than housing. Married or not, the typical Maryland planter lived in a one- or two-room, timber-frame house that combined English skills with the rule of simplicity—and the abundance of wood. Working with hand tools, one turned logs into posts, beams, rafters, and clapboards. Wooden roofing—usually shingles, sometimes boards—contrasted with the familiar English thatch, tile, or slate. Unlike New Englanders, who built homes drawing most domestic functions under one roof, settlers in the Chesapeake region put up houses surrounded with various outbuildings like storage sheds and summer kitchens. Hammond, in *Leah and Rachel*, commended the huts as "contrived so delightfull, that your ordinary houses in England are not so handsome." He noted their large rooms, white-limed walls, and "very pritty" shutters in the absence of glazed windows. Visitors to the province later offered another assessment. "The dwellings are so wretchedly constructed," read one account, "that if you are not so close to the fire as almost to burn yourself, you cannot keep warm, for the wind blows through them everywhere."[24] Built of green boards that shrank as they dried, walls required constant daubing with clay. Furnishings usually consisted of rough woolen and cotton bedclothes, hand-hewn furniture, and homemade utensils. A loft overhead made room for any children to sleep in. Clay spread over sticks and poles sufficed to make a chimney that stood outside the house at one gable end. Bricks, like hardware and window glass, awaited good tobacco crops and high prices; most planters in these years got along without them.

In short supply and highly sought after, women also worked very hard. Married partners relied heavily on each another. Typically former servants with experience growing tobacco, both of them—unless they could afford their own servants—spent long hours hoeing, topping, and suckering the plants. On small plantations the wife milked the cow, made uncured cheese and perhaps butter, fed the chickens, and gathered eggs; she planted and tended the kitchen garden, where she grew English peas and native vegetables like beans, squash, and pumpkins. Wives left butchering to the men but handled or supervised the curing, which usually meant smoking pork— the most common meat, in the form of bacon and ham—and salting or pickling beef. At the time doing without grist mills, settlers had to grind corn, the principal cereal food, using a mortar and pestle or a hand-cranked mill. Squaws' work among the Indians (whom some Englishmen scorned for mistreating their women), pounding corn left one so exhausted that the job went to servants where possible or to young men in the family; often, however, the planter's wife shared the chore. If skilled enough, she might also make clothes—though the spinning wheel seems to have been a rarity in early Maryland homes. She did laundry using homemade soap, hauling either water to clothes or clothes to water. Perhaps the rough work women did inclined their husbands to accept them more as partners than as inferiors.

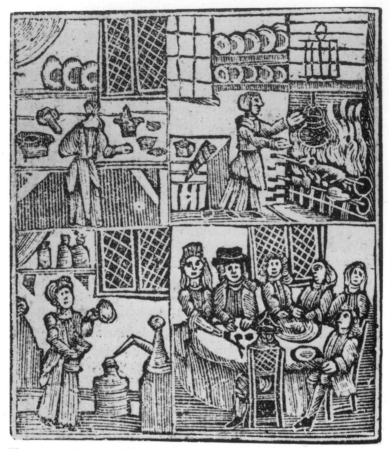

The many chores of the seventeenth-century British housewife.
Unidentified contemporary woodcut.

Doubtless the woman's large role in a planter's success explained why so
many men, besides making their wives executors of their wills (common English practice), also left them more than a dower.[25]

Restless young people considering a move to America heard both the
claims of promotional literature and rumors of death, cruelty, and failure. In
1666, as Maryland competed with other colonies for settlers, Lord Baltimore
aided a former indentured servant, George Alsop, in publishing a homely
pamphlet that painted a bright picture of the common man's fate in Maryland. Alsop mentioned nothing of the seasoning experience save an aside
explaining that he had written his booklet, titled *A Character of the Province of
Maryland*, "in the intermitting time" of his sickness. He downplayed sectarian differences and held back nothing in describing the game animals,
wild fowl, fish, and unfenced hogs in Maryland. Stories of enslavement
there—of English subjects drawing carts like horses—he called damnable

lies. In summer, he wrote, servants received three hours' "repose" at midday and in winter had nothing much to do except chop firewood and hunt. Alsop made "freedom dues" (a former master's gift of clothing and corn) and rights to fifty acres sound like an ample stake. Actually the costs of surveying and patenting a tract were too high for the average former servant, who, if he stayed in Maryland, continued as earlier in the century to spend seven or eight years as a sharecropper, tenant, or wage earner while trying to save enough cash or tobacco to start a plantation. More accurately, Alsop said that masters esteemed skilled workers, who remained in high demand, and that women servants scarcely landed on shore when men began pursuing them with "Copulative Matrimony the object."[26]

Alsop wrote that former servants lived "passingly well." To give him and his sponsor their due, some freemen in these years did survive to realize their wildest dreams. The largest proportion of them became small planters with fifty to several hundred acres; a few rose to the highest levels of wealth and power in the province. Fourteen persons in the mid-seventeenth century managed to climb from servitude to ownership of a thousand or more acres of land—among them Zachary Wade, who in the 1670s held about five thousand acres. Robert Vaughan and John Hatch began as servants and finally reached the governor's council. After 1642 Vaughan, an assemblyman in 1638 and later a militia sergeant, served as Governor Calvert's chief representative on Kent Island; Hatch, appointed sheriff of St. Mary's County in 1647, first sat on the council in 1654. With death rates high, and the impulse to remarry strong among widows, ex-servants could hope to wed well and thus hasten their upward rise. Henry Adams married Mary Cockshutt, daughter and stepdaughter of large landholders, whose dowry included twelve hundred acres of land her mother had set aside for her in 1649. Though usually illiterate, former servants sat on juries, attended sessions of the assembly, and served as militia leaders, justices of the peace, and sheriffs.

Obviously opportunity owed much to the pace of growth in the province. Lord Baltimore appointed Josias Fendall governor following Stone's defeat at the Battle of the Severn and finally, in February 1658, Fendall issued writs for an assembly session to meet in Patuxent (later Calvert) County—about midway between St. Mary's City and the Puritan settlements in what had become Anne Arundel County in 1650. By 1660 orders in council had created two new counties: Baltimore, on the northwestern edge of settlement, and Charles. Former servants found themselves filling many Charles County offices. Of six original justices of the peace there, four had arrived in Maryland as laborers—besides John Hatch and Henry Adams, James Lindsey and James Walker. Nicholas Gwyther, a former indentured servant, served as Charles County sheriff, and four of the five men who succeeded him also had entered the province under indenture. The income that went with officeholding proved of material benefit to more than one ex-servant. William Empson toiled as a tenant until 1659, when Gwyther appointed him a deputy sheriff;

next year Empson bought a plantation from his former landlord. With mortality rates leaving gaps to be filled, tobacco (despite price fluctuations) bringing profits, wages holding at fifteen to twenty pounds of tobacco per day, and land abundant, luck and industry could pay high dividends in mid-seventeenth-century Maryland. The province developed a reputation, partially deserved, as "a fine poor man's country."[27]

〜ᘉᘉ〜

Living with so much uncertainty, settlers in Maryland understandably felt an emptiness that only religious experience could fill, a yearning for order and legitimacy. Many of them missed the regular weekly services of the established Church of England, its familiar baptisms, marriage ceremonies, and burial rites. Of course Lord Baltimore left Anglicans free to found parishes and appoint ministers at will. Yet only a few churches so organized. Several of them relied on lay readers; at various times ordained ministers served five: one in St. Mary's, another in Charles, the others on the Eastern Shore. In 1665, when a small planter named Giles Tomkinson appeared in Charles County Court to answer charges that he was keeping a pregnant concubine in his house, he admitted that the woman who lived with him was pregnant and that he was the unborn child's father. But she was his "lawful wiffe." Without a minister, he explained, the "marriage was as good as possibly it Coold bee maed by the Protestants," and for the world's satisfaction, Tomkinson went on defiantly, "they hear publish themselves man and wife till death them doe part."[28]

The patchwork quilt of Maryland religious life had been growing colorful for years, and it soon became more so. Presbyterians, attacked in England and Scotland under the Puritans, had begun to make their mark on Maryland at mid-century, when refugees and captives (whom the English sent to be sold as servants) first arrived in the Chesapeake. In about 1657 Francis Doughty, an unordained Presbyterian who earlier had run afoul of authorities in Massachusetts Bay and New Netherland, sought refuge in Charles County; there another English dissenter, Matthew Hill, also preached until his death in 1679. On occasion both of them may have journeyed to the Eastern Shore, where, in Somerset County (created in 1666) and Accomack, Virginia, Scottish Presbyterians grew in number. In that sparsely settled region loneliness brought a deep thirst for religious community. Late in 1680 William Stevens—a Rehoboth landowner, militia colonel, and Anglican member of Baltimore's council—wrote on behalf of local Presbyterians requesting the Laggan Presbytery in Ireland to send a minister.

Soon afterward the Reverend Francis Makemie settled near Onancock, on the Virginia side, and began preaching to all on the lower Eastern Shore. Makemie labored in a vineyard composed of "poor, desolate people" whose ignorance, remoteness, and spiritual carelessness he called a "melancholy consideration." His appearance answered many prayers; his powerful sermons helped to strengthen or form churches at Rehoboth and Snow Hill on the Pocomoke River and others on the Manokin and Wicomico. Involved in Caribbean trade and married to the daughter of a large landowner, Makemie knew the world. But he dedicated his life to building Presbyterianism and identifying its enemies. He traveled in the colonies to inspect possible sites for more congregations and wrote theological tracts. Makemie condemned Anglicans for subordinating the spiritual life to outward forms and official trifles. Like a sentry he fixed his eye on the "deep projects" of the "Jesuitical Party" in Maryland.[29]

Makemie had no higher regard for the Society of Friends, which in his view neglected sacred Scripture in favor of the mysterious Inner Light. While seeking to withdraw from profane strife, the Quakers (as they called themselves) suffered in old and New England alike during much of the seventeenth century. Under Puritan rule in Maryland, especially in 1658–59, they were also fined, whipped, jailed, and banished in Baltimore's province; the Indians, they said, treated them with more love and mercy than "the mad, rash rulers of Mariland." Afterward Calvert's tolerance—and his steady hope of thwarting Protestant opposition by settling non-Catholics—beckoned once again to dissenters. Fleeing the hostility of Virginia Anglicans, Quakers after 1661 moved into the Patapsco River region, into Talbot County (created in about 1660), and the lower Eastern Shore. Wenlocke Christison, a notorious Quaker in Massachusetts Bay, had been whipped for heresy and driven out of New England. Establishing himself in Talbot, on Fausley Creek, he gratefully named his patent "The Ending of Controversie." Meantime Quaker missionaries visited the spiritually needy in the province. In 1656, when Boston authorities disrobed Quaker women searching for the marks of witchcraft, Elizabeth Harris had preached to unchurched Protestants along the Severn and Patuxent rivers and on Kent Island. Within a decade the Quakers had four meeting houses in Talbot County. In 1672 the founder of Quakerism himself, George Fox, left England to preach in Maryland. His meetings, by his own admission, attracted not only the converted but "many of the World, both Protestants of divers sorts, and some Papists"; in all, it was "wonderful glorious." By the late 1670s the number of Quaker meetings in the province had grown to about fifteen, most of them in Anne Arundel (where the Friends gained converts among Puritans), Talbot, and Somerset counties.[30]

Though Maryland tolerance left the Quakers free to practice their faith after 1660, their role in public life remained irregular. Aloof from military service, Quakers frequently though at first not always refused to swear oaths, declined to serve on juries (to become embroiled in hostilities), and refused to doff their hats before civil magistrates (to show obeisance to worldly authority). In 1674 members of the society, Christison among them, petitioned the assembly to permit Friends to affirm—to say yea or nay twice, with double assurance—rather than swear in courtroom proceedings. Lord

Baltimore's council refused then and again in 1681. All the same, after Baltimore's restoration Maryland law exempted Friends from militia service and the hats-off rule. A measure of 1658 accepted a promise of loyalty to the proprietor in place of the customary English oath of fidelity or allegiance— an accommodation that permitted Quakers to hold offices. Only in Maryland and Rhode Island could they participate in politics, and for a time they did. Because Quakers generally were known for their sobriety, literacy, and reliability, the proprietor appointed some of them to local posts like sheriff and justice of the peace. Between 1661 and 1675 thirteen Quakers won election as burgesses.

After Fox's visit the Quakers developed doubts about any participation in civil affairs. Fox exhorted them to weed out heresy, conform to the practices of English Quakers, and become *"well established* in the Truth." In obedience they began to draw boundaries between themselves and the rest of the world. By the 1680s they frowned on marriages between Friends and outsiders and avoided burying Friends in plots with nonbelievers. They used their own resources to care for the Quaker poor and enforced with greater strictness the Quaker teaching against oath taking. Largely disappearing from the rolls of burgesses, justices, and sheriffs, Quakers in the late seventeenth century refused every oath. In giving up entirely the protections of a court system based on sworn testimony, they left themselves vulnerable to enemies who could sue them for property and never doubt the result. Their newly troublesome scruples angered the Lord Proprietor, who in 1681 published an attack on the Quakers. Many settlers worried that the Friends would refuse to fight were the province invaded; the Quakers, in common belief, would extend the invaders aid out of mistaken brotherly love.[31]

Besides religious minorities like Catholics and Puritans and growing congregations of Presbyterians and Friends, odder nonconformists found a home in Maryland. In 1680 a small group of Labadists, a Dutch independent sect, sent Jaspar Danckaerts and Peter Sluyter to America in search of a refuge from religious persecution. The two agents landed at Manhattan, where apparently by happenstance they met and converted the eldest son of a large Maryland landholder, Augustine Herrman.

Herrman, a German-born merchant, first had entered the province twenty years earlier. He arrived as a diplomatic representative of Governor Peter Stuyvesant of New Netherland, whose government and the Calvert family alike claimed the Atlantic coast below Delaware Bay and the defeated settlement of New Sweden. By then Herrman had sensed the decline of Dutch power in America and also grown tired of the turmoil in New Amsterdam. Educated, ambitious, and a man of means, he found the Calvert plan of manors and nobility highly attractive. He offered to draw a map of Maryland that would help Lord Baltimore establish the proper boundaries of his grant, an offer (Herrman made a complementary one to Stuyvesant) that Cecil Calvert quickly accepted. In 1660 Herrman moved to Maryland and took up lands in the northeastern part of the province, naming his seat Bohemia Manor. Between 1660 and 1670 he drew and redrew the map—a work of cartographic art whose accuracy made it essential in Calvert's boundary struggles. In 1663 the assembly naturalized Herrman. Baltimore gave him the title of lord and a special seal with baronial powers. By 1674, when the governor created Cecil County, Herrman's twenty thousand acres or more made him the largest private landholder in America. Bohemia Manor, its lands sloping down to the Bohemia River and Chesapeake Bay, became well known for its size, Dutch grooming, and beautiful location. In finding Ephraim Herrman, Danckaerts and Sluyter must have felt guided by the hand of Providence.

Ephraim brought the two Dutchmen home to Bohemia Manor, where the elder Herrman greeted them sympathetically. Much to their delight—they noted in their journal that "Maryland is considered the most fertile portion of America"—Herrman invited them to take up land on his manor. In 1683 a hundred or so Labadists settled there, growing corn, tobacco, flax, and hemp and manufacturing linen. The order adhered to the communal Christian teachings of Jean de Labadie, a Jesuit-turned-Calvinist reformer who pointed his followers down a straight and narrow road to salvation. Avoiding all luxury, the Labadists spurned sinful trappings like winter fires. They kept to themselves, owned property in common, and ate meals in silence. They slept in monastic simplicity—men and women separate. Though like the Quakers they dressed plainly, they had no kind words for the Friends, whom the Indians, according to Danckaerts and Sluyter, hated "very much on account of their deceit and covetousness." Local Quakers suspected the same of Sluyter, who became the Labadist bishop and ruled like an Old Testament patriarch. He also alienated many members of his flock, whose lean asceticism won few converts. Eventually the community dispersed.[32]

Swiftly growing, religiously diverse, the province faced serious economic, military, and legal problems in these years. Further developments in the structure of government served to sharpen political differences. Before the troubles between the proprietary regime and Puritans, assembly members successfully had petitioned the governor and his councillors to meet in separate session. During Fendall's governorship that division into upper and lower houses survived, as did the claim of the lower house that proprietary measures like new duties and taxes required its consent before becoming law. An informal system of representation—by which freemen attended personally, gave their assembly votes to others by proxy, or selected burgesses—gave way after 1658 to elections for four delegates per county. Though as a rule only heads of households sat on juries and held minor offices, all freemen were entitled to vote. The "people" and the proprietor each had a house adhering to its interests. So earnest were delegates in

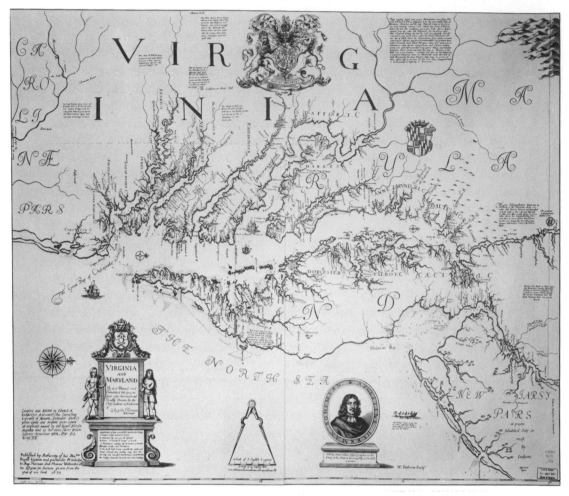

Augustine Herrman's map of Maryland, 1673. *MHS*

pressing against the limits of their political power that in 1660, with the collusion of Fendall, who evidently agreed to exchange Baltimore's commission
for one from the delegates, they briefly challenged the council and the Lord
Proprietor for supreme control in the province.

At the local level the growing responsibilities of county courts drew an
ever-larger number of men, mostly Protestants, into places of public trust in
the last decades of the seventeenth century. Justices of the peace by 1660
heard and decided all civil actions involving three thousand pounds of tobacco or less and all criminal cases except those for which penalties extended
to loss of life or limb. In 1679, probably because of the distance from many
counties to the provincial court—made up of governor and council—at
St. Mary's, the governor granted counties jurisdiction of civil suits to any
amount. Given the primacy of credit, of contractual agreements, in the to-

bacco economy, this authority over private dealings considerably enhanced the power of the county justices. They also handled an increasing administrative load: laying out and maintaining public roads, licensing taverns, policing weights and measures, hearing disputes between masters and servants, overseeing the placement and welfare of orphans, and supervising elections of delegates to the assembly. After 1671 they exercised powers of taxation for local projects like courthouses, jails, poor relief, ferries, and bridges. Though commissioned by the governor, justices stood in a position to represent the grass roots of the province against him.[33]

The Calvert family and its councillors aroused opposition among assemblymen, justices of the peace, and struggling Protestant planters. Protection against Indians became a critical issue in mid-century, when provincial leaders responded to tribal unrest. The peaceful natives of the Maryland tidewater posed no threat; they had proven resourceful in adapting to proprietary rule, even manipulating the Englishman's scruples to win small concessions. By 1650 disease had reduced their villages to mere shells. More troublesome were the Susquehannocks, whom Alsop described as seven feet tall, deep voiced, and "for the most part great Warriours." With firearms supplied by Dutch and Swedish traders, they had aimed strikes at the Patuxent and Piscataway Indians, threatening Kent Island in the attempt. Between 1639 and 1649 the province mounted several expeditions against the Susquehannocks. In 1652 Maryland leaders persuaded them to sign a treaty ceding the greater part of their lands. Soon they, too, lay ravaged by disease, and when in 1673 their Seneca enemies soundly defeated them, they requested a refuge on the Potomac. Alarm soon spread in Maryland as the Senecas, truly a dangerous tribe, pursued their quarry into the province, wreaking havoc on outlying households as they did. Reports of Indian attacks in frontier Virginia did nothing to allay fear.[34]

While responsibility for building forts and organizing a militia lay with Lord Baltimore, the charter did not specify who would shoulder the costs. Able-bodied men in the province over the age of sixteen served in the militia, which mustered four times a year in each county. To pay the salary of the militia supervisor, the mustermaster general, taxable persons paid four pounds of tobacco annually. To house provincial arms and ammunition, the assembly in 1664 appropriated funds for a public magazine. In 1670 Cecil Calvert's son Charles, then in his early thirties and provincial governor since 1661, submitted a proposal for port duties. Approving a tax of two shillings on each hogshead exported, delegates in the lower house stipulated that half the revenue go toward maintenance of the militia and related government expenses. Delegates demanded that taxes for the mustermaster general's support and the public magazine cease at once. They demanded further that the governor accept proprietary fees like quitrents and alienation fees in tobacco at the rate of two pence per pound—at the time a rate double tobacco's "farm price" or real market value. During the fearful Seneca raids of the

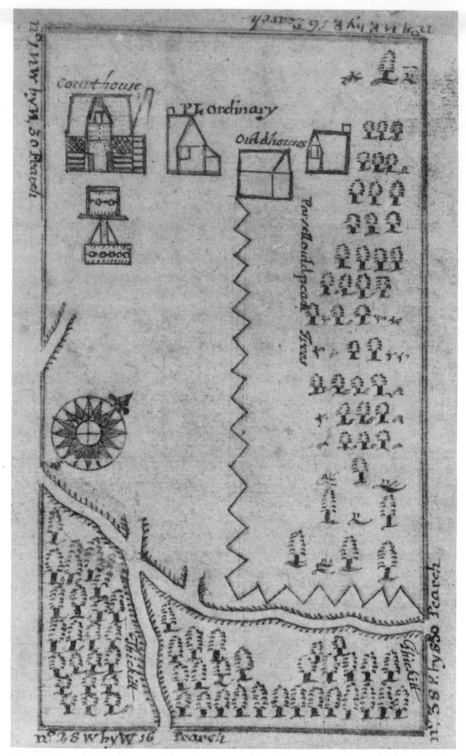

Plat of the Charles County Courthouse and Ordinary, 1697. Maryland's wealthiest seventeenth-century families lived in houses similar to the riven-clapboard courthouse with casement windows, two-story porch, and brick chimney. Most people lived in one-room, single-story structures like the "Ouldhouses" here depicted. *MSA*

years following, the burgesses doubted Calvert's word that one shilling per exported hogshead did in fact support defense. Members of the lower house also complained that the governor kept military stores in St. Mary's rather than in the counties, where in emergencies they were needed.

Other problems in these years, though legalistic in appearance, raised fundamental political issues. The Calverts and their settlers quarreled over the place of English law and over who should decide. Delegates argued that as representatives of freeholders they should establish its extent in Maryland, and they worked to implant its "full force & Power" (it included provisions unkind to Catholics and Quakers) as one means of limiting proprietary discretion. On the other side, Charles Calvert struggled to maintain his prerogative. English common and statute law might apply, he said, where "the necessity and exigencyes of the Provynce" had not produced Maryland laws, but only his appointed justices of the peace and ultimately he and his councillors could decide whether and where it did apply.[35] Calvert had fully employed discretionary power in 1670 when he tightened suffrage qualifications, restricting the vote in the growing province to men with a fifty-acre freehold or forty pounds worth of property. Then, in his orders for elections in 1676, he directed voters in each county to return two instead of four delegates to the assembly. Calvert's reasons—the principle of government by persons with a stake in society; the need to keep the number of burgesses manageable—may have had merit, but these decisions provoked much protest.

Worsening economic conditions produced more tension. After 1660 overproduction in Maryland and Virginia had led to a drop in tobacco prices and talk of public measures to cut the supply. Governor Berkeley of Virginia approached Maryland leaders about a "stint"—a one-year moratorium on tobacco growing. The leading planters who sat in his assembly supported the plan. While Governor Calvert and large growers in Maryland leaned toward it, Virginians complained that Maryland delegates refused to step into line. Indeed many of them, having humble origins, noted that such a measure would fall hardest on small planters. Lord Baltimore opposed the plan for his own reasons. While he preferred a diversity of crops, the proposed stint encouraged long-range tobacco growing. Schooled in human nature, he also predicted disobedience; if adopted, the measure would force servants to spy on masters, divide families, promote corruption, and "wholly ruin the poor, who are the generality of the Provinces." With Governor Calvert's prodding the assembly in 1666 nonetheless passed a bill "to encourage trade" by outlawing tobacco culture for the year following February 1667. Virginia provided for its own stint. Then, to Berkeley's sputtering disbelief, Baltimore vetoed the Maryland law. Virginia leaders considered the episode proof of Calvert perversity. As it turned out, nature imposed an unexpected stint: during the summer of 1667 a devastating hurricane swept through the region and leveled almost every tobacco field in its path.[36]

Cecil Calvert's death in 1675 sent Charles to London to assume baronial rank, and both his English and Maryland adversaries used the occasion to smite him. In 1676, when a disgruntled Virginian, Nathaniel Bacon, challenged Governor Berkeley, a group of disaffected Maryland planters met in Calvert County to protest against the Calverts. The insurgents published a furious, partially literate petition to royal authorities entitled a *Complaint from Heaven with a Huy and Crye . . . out of Virginia and Maryland*. It listed many grievances, and especially indicted the province for lacking an established church. "The province of Maryland is in a deplorable condition," declared the Anglican minister John Yeo that year in a letter to the archbishop of Canterbury. Yeo's message marked his disgust at the mix of Maryland faiths; from his perspective variety meant laxity and license. "The Lord's day is profaned," he reported. "Religion is despised, and all notorious vices are committed; so that it is become a Sodom of uncleanliness and a pest-house of iniquity." Calvert's council hanged two of the would-be rebels, but the planters' hue and cry, together with Yeo's unhappy letter, raised questions that members of the king's Privy Council asked the third Lord Baltimore to answer. His reply only confirmed Maryland's heterodoxy. Most settlers, wrote Calvert, were "Presbiterians, Independents, Anabaptists, and Quakers, those of the Church of England as well as those of the Romish being the fewest." The promise of free religious practice, Calvert pointed out, had brought these sundry Christians to the Chesapeake; it would be "a most difficult task," he continued, referring to suggestions of an established church, "to draw such persons to consent unto a Law which shall compel them to maintaine Ministers of a contrary perswasion to themselves."[37]

Threats from both within and without weakened Charles Lord Baltimore's hold on his province. In 1681 open rebellion nearly flared up again under Josias Fendall—the former governor whom Calvert had barred from office for his part in the legislative assumption of power in 1660—and a member of the lower house, John Coode. Both men, but especially Coode, illustrated the meanness of conflict in early Maryland. Born in Cornwall in 1648, Coode briefly had attended Oxford and served as an Anglican priest before mysteriously being "turned out" of his parish. In 1672 he migrated (or was shipped off) to Maryland, where he took sick, recovered, and then landed in jail for refusing to pay a physician's bill of ten thousand pounds of tobacco. Coode's troubles seem often to have grown out of his personality, which must have owed something to physical deformity and appearance. Clubfooted, with a face that a sheriff's warrant once described as "resembling that of a baboon or monkey," he was quick tempered, boastful, and resentful of all authority. He also was resourceful. Coode soon married a wealthy St. Mary's County widow, a daughter of Thomas Gerard, whose landholdings—after Coode won them in legal struggles—made him a leading figure there. At first Charles Calvert directed patronage toward him; eventually Coode's naked ambition or perhaps his Protestantism forestalled higher rise and Coode, who liked to tear up official documents in front of Catholic burgesses, became an outspoken—some said blasphemous—critic of proprietary rule. Calvert dismissed him and Fendall as "rank Baconists." In 1681 the provincial court found Fendall guilty of plotting to seize and imprison the third Lord Baltimore. It fined him forty thousand pounds of tobacco and banished him from Maryland (Secretary William Calvert observed that the court could have bored his tongue or cropped his ears). While Coode escaped conviction as a co-conspirator, a struggle ensued between the council and lower house over seating him in the next assembly.[38]

"Maryland is now in torment," reported the new governor of Virginia, "and not only troubled with our disease, poverty, but in very great danger of falling in pieces; whether it be that old Lord Baltimore's politic maxims are not pursued or that they are unsuited to this age."[39] In fact nothing but rancor governed relations between the Calverts and the lower house. By the 1680s tobacco prices had dropped 50 percent from levels thirty years earlier to a mere .9 or .7 pence sterling a pound. Several acts of the assembly in the 1680s established places where visiting ships were to take on tobacco and sell their cargoes; by stopping only at these "towns," vessels might save time and money and therefore pay more for the planters' product. Fines were to be levied on those who loaded elsewhere. The failure of these measures to create towns—where some delegates owned land they counted on to appreciate in value—soon became evident, and later, when Baltimore abolished penalties for loading at private wharves, the assembly objected to his high-handedness. Delegates alleged that certain large planters, Calvert's Catholic friends, had evaded the "town" loading law, apparently with the governor's approval.

In 1688 the governor's council offered several bills that the lower house regarded with understandable distaste. The measures would have helped to increase the supply of coin in the province by ending the use of tobacco as money and making all proprietary fees payable in hard currency. Calvert's failure to appoint proprietary naval officers as fee collectors on the Eastern Shore, burgesses complained, stunted prosperity in the counties of Talbot, Somerset, and Dorchester. Members of the lower house accused Baltimore of being in league with the Lords of Trade, who in the late 1680s requested the Maryland assembly to cooperate in outlawing tobacco shipments in bulk. Besides being an aid to smugglers, the practice promoted the shipment of poor-grade, "trashy" tobacco to England. But shipmasters who brought the manufactured tools and other commodities that Marylanders imported from western England preferred carrying in bulk. More important, many Maryland planters, growing Orinoco tobacco on inferior soils, loudly protested efforts to impose standards of quality, especially in hard times.

Two irreducible elements made conflict especially bitter. The third Lord Baltimore did hold medieval charter powers; a Catholic, he gathered around him advisors and friends who shared his faith. In yet another exercise of his palatine authority, Calvert in 1683 abolished the headright system of acquiring land and substituted payment of "caution money": 100 pounds (later 120) of tobacco for each fifty acres. His purpose, he explained, was to end the unseemly market in headrights, by which speculators on the docks bought them cheaply from ship captains who had paid servants' passage and then sold them for what the market would bear. Although the purchase price may have been well within the reach of most hopeful landowners, this change in longstanding policy fired resentment against proprietary authority. A policy that Calvert did not change had the same effect. Between 1666 and 1689 twenty-seven men sat on the governor's council. Only eight of them were Protestants. Fifteen, mostly Catholics, were related to Calvert's immediate family by blood or marriage. One of them, former governor Philip Calvert, Charles Lord Baltimore's uncle and the provincial chancellor, aspired to live in regal splendor at St. Peter's, south of the St. Mary's town lands. In 1676 the province had begun work on a new state house, the first one of brick in Maryland. Calvert began building his large brick mansion, surrounded by a stout wall, shortly afterward. Along with the Jesuits' brick chapel and the new state house, St. Peter's symbolized Calvert-Catholic property and prerogative; after Philip's death without children in 1682 it fell to Charles. Meantime Baltimore's Catholic friends, besides making up a majority on the highest bench in the province, served as militia officers, managed the land office, and filled the abundant patronage posts that the provincial secretary's office had spawned. Not surprisingly, common tenants and large Protestant landholders alike suspected Romish plots and feared for their English liberties.

Already preoccupied with problems in Maryland, Baltimore now became embroiled in serious boundary disputes. King Charles II in 1681 had granted William Penn a vague proprietorship north of Maryland. Penn's commissioners then began laying out a capital city below the fortieth parallel, in Maryland territory. Adding to the confusion, Charles's brother, the Duke of York (since 1664 in possession of formerly Dutch possessions in mainland America), gave Penn the Dutch claim to New Sweden. Yet Delaware Bay and the seacoast below it—the territory that had helped bring Augustine Herrman to the Chesapeake—arguably belonged to Maryland by the terms of the original Calvert grant. Baltimore and Penn met twice without settling their differences while, in London, Baltimore's enemies threatened quo warranto proceedings against his charter. In 1684 Lord Charles had to choose between serious problems in Maryland and urgent business at court. He cut short a controversy with the lower house by disallowing all laws it had passed in 1678 except those he formally approved. He then set off for England to pursue his boundary claims.

The third Lord Baltimore never returned. Protestant fears subsided neither in Maryland nor in England—where, after 1685, York, as James II, attempted to rule as both a Catholic and an autocrat of his father's stripe. Like so many of their predecessors, the men whom Baltimore deputized to govern the province suffered lapses in judgment. The error of George Talbot—Calvert's nephew, president of the governor's council, and acting governor—was to stab to death a royal customs collector on board his vessel in the Patuxent River. Baltimore had objected to such collections as an infringement on his proprietary rights; Talbot's crime put Calvert on the defensive almost as soon as he arrived in London. To succeed Talbot he sent a Catholic, William Joseph, whose address to the assembly in November 1688 astounded listeners by trumpeting divine right authority and impugning their morality. All power is derived from God, Joseph declared, from whom it flowed "to the King, and from the King to his Excellency the Lord Proprietor, and from his said Lordship to Us." Joseph chastised the provincials for their sins, which in addition to drunkenness and breaking the sabbath included "that most horrid and damnable sin of adultery" (earlier a Captain William Mitchell had been forced to resign after such a scandal); in these days, Joseph declared, sexual license "is grown to that height that with the prophet we may justly say the land is full of Adulterers."[40] He finished by reminding the delegates not to be violators of the laws before being lawmakers. Heaped on the grievances of many years, such insult promised to keep Joseph's term of office uncomfortable if not brief.

That month events took a decisive turn. William of Orange landed in England and deposed the widely despised James. Sketchy reports of what became the "Glorious Revolution" reached Maryland in December. Though Lord Baltimore sent orders to proclaim William's rule, the carrier of the message died before leaving England, and if Baltimore did send a duplicate, as he later claimed, the orders never arrived. Protestant suspicions of Catholic plots climbed higher the next year as Governor Joseph refused to convene the assembly and then recalled, ostensibly for repair, the weapons that had been sent to county depositories by an act of 1678. Once again Lord Baltimore's Protestant settlers revolted. In July 1689 Coode along with other non-Catholic leaders—among them Kenylm Cheseldyne and Nehemiah Blakiston of St. Mary's, Henry Jowles and Ninian Beale of Calvert, and John Addison and John Courts of Charles County—met in Charles to organize a Protestant Association. Almost all of them had arrived in Maryland as young immigrants, succeeded in tobacco planting, and then served in the county courts. Coode styled himself commander and chief of the Protestant Associators, whose spokesmen issued a high-sounding "Declaration of the reason and motive for the present appearing in arms of His Majesties Protestant Subjects in the Province of Maryland." The manifesto listed the grievances that long had divided the proprietor and so many of his people, declared allegiance to the new monarchs, William and Mary, and prayed them to take Maryland under their protection. Armed and resolute, members of the Association marched toward St. Mary's City, gathering strength on the way. At the capital councillors loyal to Lord Baltimore, overwhelmed in numbers, chose not to resist. Proprietary government fell virtually without a shot.

The province of Maryland, a Calvert family venture, next became a royal colony subject directly to the Crown. The change represented failure. Settlers in Maryland had made their homes between New England (and now Pennsylvania and New York) and Virginia (and the Carolinas). Avoiding geographic extremes, they had groped less successfully for "middleness" of a different kind: a political center in a society made up of diverse elements.

CHAPTER 2

Tobacco Coast

F
ew visitors to the new seat of government at Proctor's Landing or Anne Arundell Town (renamed Annapolis in 1695) saw the sleepy village as the work of art it was. Governor Francis Nicholson had been in London when John Evelyn and Christopher Wren laid plans for rebuilding that city after the great fire of 1666. Apparently from their example this talented soldier and administrator, who later designed the Virginia capital at Williamsburg, learned how a city of connected circles and squares made the most of natural features, fixed a viewer's eyes on major buildings, and provided imposing homes with focus and privacy. There were two hills at the Annapolis site. On the more dominating elevation Nicholson planned a building for assembly and court, laying out a circle 520 feet in diameter to encompass them. On the nearby knoll he placed an Anglican church surrounded by a smaller circle. Nicholson made provision for a large square, named after the Bloomsbury section of London, to the northwest of the circles, where the houses were to face inward upon a green. A smaller market square south of the state house circle lent some balance to the design, which borrowed from Europe principles of urban planning no one before had applied in America.

Not for many years did Nicholson's town fill out the form he had drawn. Someone called the state house of 1704 "a very neat little brick building." Together with the small academy on the state house grounds and St. Anne's—the Anglican church at Church Circle—the capitol did offer visible proof of colonial development. Yet early tobacco growers preferred the country to city life, and even residents of young Annapolis had misgivings about the costs of urban diversity. A town ordinance directed bakers, brewers, tanners, and other tradesmen to ply their crafts outside the village so as not to "anoy or disquiett the neighbours or Inhabitants." Annapolis long had unpaved streets; St. Anne's, when finished, stood on an ungraded hill. A condescending clergyman described the Maryland capital as a state house and school making "a great shew among a parscell of wooden houses." There were sharper critics. In 1708 Ebenezer Cook, an English immigrant and for-

41

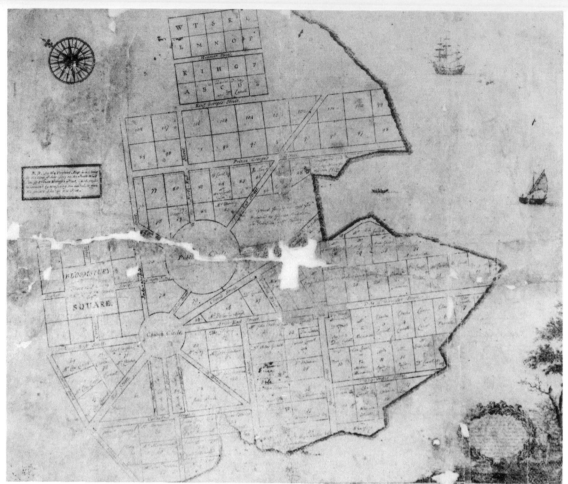

Plat of Annapolis. Drawn by James Stoddert in 1743 after his original survey of 1718. *MSA*

mer tobacco agent who eventually claimed the title "laureate of Maryland," published *The Sot-Weed Factor*, a poetic commentary on the sickness, rascality, and rawness of early Maryland. Noticing a gap between design and reality (also satirizing the disillusioned European visitor to America), Cook wrote that Annapolis was "A City Situate on a Plain / Where scarce a house will keep out Rain."[1]

❧

Along the Tobacco Coast—the name eighteenth-century English merchants and seafarers might well have given the Chesapeake region—African slavery supplied a prime reason for the stability Annapolis built upon. As a long-term answer to the labor problem, slavery had emerged slowly. Until the late 1680s Maryland growers who could afford slaves or servants were far more likely to rely on Englishmen with indentures. Only 15 of 151 estates probated on the lower Western Shore between 1658 and 1670 included slaves as assets; in Maryland as a whole between 1674 and 1679 inventories enumerated more servants than slaves by a ratio of four to one.

To be sure, there had been blacks in Maryland from the beginning. Virginians had employed Negro labor before the *Ark* and *Dove* landed, so Marylanders scarcely found the idea novel. In both colonies, however, the status of blacks for much of the seventeenth century left room for ambiguity and depended on particular circumstances. Not all Africans were "heathens." Not all blacks were "slaves"—meaning that their service extended their entire lives and that their children inherited lifetime bondage. Father White, who in 1634 had been accompanied by a mulatto servant named Mathias de Sousa, later imported another named Francisco. These unfree men, likely Christians, may have served for only a fixed term. In 1653 a black servant named John Babtiste successfully petitioned the provincial court for his freedom. He stated that he had agreed to work for his former master a limited time and later had been sold as a slave. Thomas Hagleton, an African and a Catholic, testified in 1676 that he had been brought from England by a master who indentured him to serve four years with Major Thomas Truman, who then attempted to keep Hagleton in bondage past his term. The court ordered his release. In 1678 and 1693, in similar cases, black men proved that their servitude had been contractual and won their freedom, one winning a suit of clothes and supply of corn from his former master.[2] A few blacks in early Maryland followed the path of white indentured servants.

Other evidence, gleaned from statute books and probate records, leaves a drearier impression: as the seventeenth century wore on, blacks in Maryland were treated less like men, more and more like a labor commodity. The 1638 act claiming the protection of English law as a challenge to Baltimore's authority, for example, had clearly excepted slaves—presumably meaning blacks—and thus begun to establish legal distinctions between white persons (including servants with limited terms) and black chattels (slaves who as property had no claim to civic rights). Inventories of estates probated at the owner's death demonstrated that most Maryland blacks in the seventeenth century, serving without term and therefore more valuable than indentured servants, already wore the collar of slavery. In the same records African women carried especially high value; they could be used for field work, and their children reaped reward for their owners. A law of 1663 recognized that black service usually was perpetual. It scheduled punishments for English servants who ran away with "Negroes & other Slaves, who are incapeable of makeing S[a]tisfaction by Addition of Tyme." An act of the next year, clearly decreeing that all blacks in Maryland and all who arrived afterward were servants "durante vita" (during their lives), evidently sanctioned what had become familiar practice.[3] Unless a black could prove that he had contracted his labor for a matter of years, the law presumed him to be a slave.

THE

Negro's & Indians ADVOCATE,

Suing for their Admiſſion into the

CHURCH:

OR

A PERSUASIVE to the Inſtructing
and Baptizing of the *Negro's* and
Indians in our Plantations.

SHEWING,

That as the Compliance therewith can prejudice
no Mans juſt Intereſt; So the wilful Neglecting
and Oppoſing of it, is no leſs than a manifeſt
Apoſtacy from the Chriſtian Faith.

To which is added, A brief Account of Religion in *Virginia.*

By MORGAN GODWYN,

Sometime St. of Ch. Ch. Oxon.

Judges 19. 30. And it was ſo, that all that ſaw it ſaid, There was
no ſuch deed done nor ſeen from the day that the Children of Iſrael
came up out of the Land of Egypt, unto this Day.
Acts 4. 20. We cannot but ſpeak the things which we have ſeen and heard.

If we muſt anſwer for our idle Words, how much more for our idle
ſilence? St. Auguſtin.

LONDON, Printed for the Author, by J. D. and are
to be Sold by moſt Bookſellers. 1680.

Title page, Morgan Godwyn, *The Negro's & Indians Advocate, Suing for their Admission into the Church* (London, 1680). When Godwyn's volume appeared, many Maryland colonists may have shared his view that non-English people deserved an opportunity to win salvation. *John Work Garrett Collections of the Milton S. Eisenhower Library, The Johns Hopkins University*

Even before white Maryland settlers associated blacks with lifetime bondage, they placed them in a category far beneath their own. In the sixteenth century, when Englishmen penetrated sub-Saharan Africa, they lacked the Portuguese and Spanish traders' familiarity with black culture. Thereafter in English lore the Negro assumed brutish qualities. So strikingly different in color, so strange in native customs, clothing, and religion, Negroes appeared to be violent and libidinous creatures. In seventeenth-century Maryland such perceptions surfaced in laws covering sexual misconduct. Fornication and adultery had been subjects of early legislation and many court cases. Miscegenation whites regarded as far more sinister, and in the 1660s both Maryland and Virginia passed laws directed against it. The 1664 "durante vita" statute evidently sought, among its other objects, to discourage interracial marriages. Addressing the same point, an act of 1681 described unions between white women and blacks as being "always to the Satisfaction of theire Lascivious and Lustfull desires, and to the disgrace not only of the English butt allso of many other Christian Nations."[4] Thus slavery, providing a labor supply, had another function in placing controls on a disturbing social element. Negroes, English colonists decided, belonged in slavery; better for everyone that they remain under white control. Converting to Christianity did not change skin color, and two acts of this period ensured that baptism did not bring freedom to slaves.

Large-scale slavery in Maryland, though it depended on racial prejudice, emerged as planters made incremental decisions based on the urge for profit under conditions that limited their choices. For most of the seventeenth century planters found that steadily dropping tobacco prices (with occasional upward bursts) provided them a margin of profit because production costs remained low. Another price drop in the late 1660s forced them as never before to seek expanded production and to be mindful of every expense, especially labor costs. The price of an indentured servant, with few exceptions, stood at about £10 or £12 in constant money throughout the period 1660 to 1720. Though slaves cost more—about £23 for a healthy, young male in 1674, £36 by 1720—they carried benefits of lifetime labor and possible offspring. At least some planters, making these calculations, were prepared to shift to slave labor by the 1660s; "I find wee are nott men of estates good enough to undertake such a business," Charles Calvert wrote his father in 1663, "but could wish wee were for wee are naturally inclin'd to love neigros."[5] Besides the objection of higher cost, there were problems of supply, especially after England and France went to war in 1689. West Indian shipments were infrequent and unreliable. Parliamentary navigation acts, passed after the Restoration, forbade the Dutch slave trade in the colonies and consigned that enterprise to the Royal African Company. Its directors found it more profitable to supply slaves to sugar planters in Barbados than to tobacco growers in the Chesapeake.

The Maryland planter who preferred a white servant faced his own difficulties. In the spring of 1689 King William joined with the Dutch in a war against the French, a conflict that made Atlantic crossings hazardous, depressed tobacco prices further, and stemmed the flow of indentures. Fewer young men from the middling classes of English society found service in America appealing in any case, for opportunities at home improved in the late seventeenth century, and those Englishmen willing to journey to the colonies might well choose to settle not in Maryland but in Pennsylvania or the Carolinas. Maryland planters complained that arriving servants did not appear as attractive as they had earlier—they came from lower classes or from impoverished Ireland. Meantime former indentured servants, struggling to establish their own tobacco farms in Maryland, kept prices high for the fewer indentures.

Then in the 1690s a series of changes helped the uncertain planter make up his mind on the labor question. King William's War ended in 1697. Sugar prices fell—giving the advantage to tobacco investment and making the Chesapeake a more profitable destination for slave traders. Parliament in 1698 abolished the Royal African Company monopoly, opening up the trade in slaves. A slight upturn in the farm price of Maryland tobacco between 1697 and 1702 enabled larger planters to purchase slaves. Though the servant-to-slave price ratio held at about the same level from 1698 to 1708, demonstrating persistent demand for white indentures, Maryland tobacco growers who could afford the investment took an important step and chose blacks.[6] The Tobacco Coast had met the Slave Coast.

Port records proved how quickly Maryland planters seized upon Negro labor. In October 1695 a "parcel" of 160 blacks landed. The next year the ship *Society* sailed into Annapolis with 175. Governor Nicholson in 1698 reported that 470 had been imported during the summer alone. Between May and August 1699 three ships landed a total of 352 slaves. In July 1700 a single vessel, the *John Hopewell* of London, brought 320 blacks to Maryland. About 4,000 slaves arrived in the colony between 1695 and 1708, an average of 300 per year. Major demographic changes took place in the counties of Prince George's (established in 1695), Calvert, Charles, and St. Mary's—where more than half of all Maryland slaves lived. While in 1658, 100 blacks in those counties made up only 3 percent of the population, by 1710, when the colonial government conducted an early head count, the number had grown to 3,500 and accounted for almost 25 percent of the total. Slaves in Anne Arundel County made up a considerable share of the population, in Baltimore County a somewhat smaller share—between 10 and 20 percent. On the Eastern Shore, where in 1680 blacks had numbered about 300, that figure rose to 1,390 in 1704 and six years later to 1,640—10 to 15 percent of all inhabitants. Among the American colonies only Virginia imported more slaves than Maryland.

While few sources shed light on the experience of the first Maryland blacks, they clearly knew cruelty, sickness, and bewilderment. Ships from the West Indies typically carried 30 or more Negroes, or, with other Caribbean products aboard, 10 or 12. Planters looked upon them suspiciously, believing sugar growers likely to cast off only those "Rogues" who had resisted bondage. After the 1680s highest prices went for blacks who had been brought directly from Africa, especially from the west coast in cargoes of about 170 persons. During the six weeks or more at sea they remained chained below deck with minimal food and water, poor ventilation, and abounding filth. Shipping records show that slavers from Angola, sailing a longer distance, hedged against loss during passage by crowding well over 300 blacks into the hold. Wherever they had embarked, blacks often arrived in the Chesapeake ill and weakened.

Blacks next found themselves subjected to sale and confined to a life in

"The Tobacco House and its Variety." From William Tatham, *Historical and Practical Essay on the Culture and Commerce of Tobacco* (London, 1800). *McGregor Library, University of Virginia*

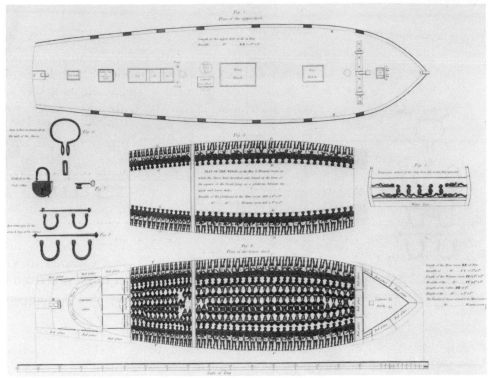

Detail, "The Representation of the brig *Vigilante* from Nantes, a vessel employed in the Slave Trade," 1822. *National Maritime Museum, Greenwich, England*

which there was little to hope for. Branded by color as chattels, savages, and inferiors, they could expect no release after a term of service. Few slaves at first could understand what their owners said; indeed, the Negroes often had to overcome language differences among themselves. Black in a white society, unfamiliar with their surroundings, they stood small chance of successful escape and after recapture could count on severe whippings. Although many of them had been born in agricultural villages, they now were forced to learn the peculiar, painstaking care tobacco plants required. Though not as vulnerable as immigrant whites to malaria, Africans frequently fell prey to respiratory disease in the winter and early spring. In the late seventeenth century and early years of the next, slaves mostly lived dispersed in small groups, men exceeding women by about one and a half to one. Black slaves—in the only way they resembled white servants earlier—commonly lived and worked without the meager comforts a family might have afforded them.[7]

Slave masters preferred order to chaos, and in this respect the rebellion of 1689 was at first disappointing. For several years afterward the only courts in the province to sit were the county courts and the only executive authority was a committee of Protestant Associators. Rumors of Baltimore's wrathful return and of various Indian conspiracies kept confusion at high levels. In May 1690, when Francis Nicholson arrived in the Chesapeake as newly appointed lieutenant governor of Virginia, he carried with him a letter from King William authorizing John Coode and the Associators to "continue in our name your care in the administration of the Government and preservation of the peace and properties of our Subjects." The new monarch, for whom the outbreak of war with France caused more alarm than Maryland politics, reserved time to examine the case against Lord Baltimore's proprietary rule. Meanwhile Coode and his interim government felt strong enough to pursue their most vocal critics, among them Richard Hill of Anne Arundel, who admitted having "somewhat opposed their illegal and arbitrary proceedings." Luckier than other Coode opponents, Hill escaped to Virginia. In April 1692 the king's appointed governor, Lionel Copley, arrived to take Maryland under the "immediate Care and Protection" that William and Mary had promised the Associators.[8]

As during the earlier, proprietary period, the lower house of assembly did not easily submit to the care and protection of anyone. First meeting under royal rule in the spring of 1692, delegates—taking full advantage of Copley's newness and the unsettled situation—assumed the power to name their own clerk, John Lewellin, ignoring the man the governor sent for that purpose. For the most part made up of men who had supported the revolt against proprietary government, the house also moved to establish within itself several standing committees that gave the legislature structure and continuity. A committee on elections and privileges represented the members' belief that they alone should decide who would sit in the house. Another committee on "aggrievances" assumed the busy work of handling petitions from the citizenry. Two more permanent committees, those on laws and accounts, provided stations in the house for legal talent and financial experience, promising formal or textual improvement in Maryland statutes and the likelihood that economic legislation could pass only with the approval of men aware of—and of course interested in—the shipping and credit arrangements of the colony. These committees enabled members to handle recurrent issues with dispatch, promoted a few leaders to positions of parliamentary influence, and further strengthened the house against the claims of governor and council. These claims often touched on rights and liberties.

The struggle among delegates, councillors, and governors also had a seedy side. Feeling a bit obliged by the terms of the 1632 charter, King William promised Lord Baltimore that the royal government would collect the quitrents landholders owed him and the export and other fees due him by palatine privilege. But William stripped Calvert of his political authority, thus leaving to royal prerogative appointments that carried heavy financial reward. Next to the governorship, chief among them was the office of provincial secretary, which brought with it fees both statutory and traditional. The now-royal secretary kept official records, served as a notary public, appointed county clerks, licensed taverns, and sat on the governor's council. In the early eighteenth century this post returned an annual profit approaching one thousand pounds. To fill it King William chose a professional bureaucrat or placeman, Sir Thomas Lawrence, son of a minor baronet of Middlesex County and a man determined to make the most of a good thing.

Before leaving England Lawrence began his tenure by squabbling with Governor Copley over the spoils they would divide. Then, having refused to ship to Maryland on the same vessel as Copley, Lawrence arrived in September 1692 to find two clerks exercising the authority of the secretary's office and collecting his revenue. They refused to pay him for the period between the date of his commission and his appearance in the colony. Lawrence also discovered that the governor had used his earlier arrival to reach an accommodation with leading Marylanders, some of whom unsuccessfully had applied to the Crown for the secretary's office. For many members of the assembly the perquisites of the secretary had been one of the grievances justifying revolt against the Calverts, whose concern for remunerative offices and rewarding friends did not disappear easily. In 1692 delegates asserted themselves by specifying the amount each government official would receive and entitling the act one for the limitation of officers' fees.

Perhaps nowhere but in Maryland would the next series of alliances have developed. Copley approved the statute, and the assembly returned the favor by taking fees for licensing ordinaries from the secretary and placing them in the governor's hands. The delegates took other fees from the secretary as well, and some of them the governor distributed to Nehemiah Blakiston. Along with several other leaders of the revolution of 1689, Blakiston now sat on the council and was in a position to benefit from official profits. Secretary Lawrence protested in vain before the council, whose members unblushingly cited him for an "avaritious and greedy appetite."[9] Lawrence then turned his attention to the county court clerkships. Violating the terms of his commission, which empowered him to fill vacant clerkships, he replaced some incumbents with men who shared their fees but whose qualifications were nil, and drove hard bargains with others already in place. The Byzantine struggle over lucrative offices served as a primitive form of checks and balances. When Blakiston had Lawrence arrested for his brazen dismissal of incumbent clerks, the secretary found himself supported by Marylanders who opposed Copley and the council and saw Lawrence as a means of dividing and weakening their rule. In the same way the assembly supported Copley against the surveyor general of the customs, Edward Randolph, during an inspection tour that revealed irregularities both on the docks and in the governor's office.

When not distracted by issues surrounding Lawrence, members of the first assembly under royal government responded to a Crown order that they revise the laws, write them clearly, and repeal those statutes no longer necessary. Some revised statutes noted the shortcomings of an old law. Almost all of them reinstated earlier measures, often covering earthy subjects like the proper height of fences in animal trespass cases, hog stealing, controlling wild horses that bred in the Maryland woods and trampled corn crops, and bounties for wolf heads. The assembly required planters to build a "good tight house," with a lock and key, where for as long as a year they might store tobacco sold but not called for. Lawmakers limited the damages a foreign creditor could collect when a Maryland planter's bill of exchange (a form of check) exceeded his promised tobacco shipment. Among other economic acts, the assembly established a system of weights and measures, standardized the size of hogsheads, and promoted the building of roads and water-powered mills. The new militia act retained a force of rangers to guard the forests of Charles, Anne Arundel, and Baltimore counties against northern Indians. Clad in green, the rangers drew strength from two volumes the assembly provided each of them—the Bible and *A Brief Discourse on the Whole Duty of Man*. Legislators made new efforts to record and publish the laws, in order to deter the "evilly disposed" in the province from pleading ignorance.

A few important measures addressed grievances that had prompted revolt. The assembly repealed an Act for Deserted Plantations, thus forcing Baltimore to sue for back rents. An Act for Proceedings at Law hastened trials, regulated appeals on writs of error, discouraged "vexatious & unnecessary" debt suits, improved procedures for probating wills, and stiffened the punishment for perjury. The assembly for a time had the last word in one of its bitterest proprietary disputes; it declared that English law would stand in Maryland courts when, in civil proceedings, no Maryland measure supplied a rule. A new law limited county sheriffs to two-year terms. By an Act for Elections the burgesses ensured that they would meet every year and that four delegates would represent each county.[10]

Legislators in the royal colony strengthened the labor system that planters increasingly depended upon. A 1692 statute repeated that baptism did nothing to alter the status of black slaves; another revised and strengthened provisions covering runaways. Complaints of blacks "wandering about on Sundays" and leaving their owners' land without a ticket or certificate led in 1695 to an act restraining the "frequent Assembly" of blacks. So confident were lawmakers of the demand for slaves that in the same session they installed a duty on each slave imported into the colony. When in 1704 the General Assembly undertook another comprehensive listing of Maryland law, it restated the penalites for harboring fugitive blacks and for miscegenation, and prohibited a slave from carrying a firearm or other "Offensive Weapon" without his master's written permission. Hoping to encourage Marylanders to trade more adventurously in rum, sugar, "Negroes and other Commoditys," the assembly in 1704 waived all duties on those imports when they arrived in Maryland-built and -owned vessels.[11] These acts clarified the rule of government and aimed to achieve a stable economic order.

⚬⚬⚬

The law that struck most deeply at Lord Baltimore's old system touched not on bills of exchange but on religious practice. In 1692, after recognizing William and Mary as sovereigns, the assembly in an Act for the Service of Almighty God and the Establishment of the Protestant Religion within this Province made the Church of England the official faith in Maryland. The colony adopted the union of church and state that Englishmen knew from home experience. No longer would "wicked Lewd and disorderly people" profane the sabbath. Besides renewing the proviso against Sunday work, delegates outlawed "drunkenness, Swearing, Gaming, fowling, fishing, hunting, or any other Sports Pastimes or Recreations whatsoever" on the Lord's Day—when sheriffs were no longer to serve warrants or make arrests that would discourage persons from attending services. To remedy a standing complaint, the assembly assured Maryland Anglicans of solemn marriages; requiring published banns and the presence of five witnesses, the new law provided that the wedding conclude "in manner and forme as set down & expressed in the Liturgy of the Church of England." Justices of the peace were to divide counties into parishes and then hold parish elections for six vestrymen. These laymen would oversee construction of churches or chapels where necessary. Sheriffs collected an annual poll of forty pounds of tobacco per taxable person in the parish. Turned over to vestrymen, that tax went toward building churches and paying the salaries of Anglican ministers.[12]

A driving force behind church establishment appeared after Copley's death in September 1693 and a series of short-time successors. The new royal governor, Francis Nicholson, arrived in the summer of 1694 and immediately made his presence felt. Skilled in governing, he knew the value of symbolic action. When he convened the assembly that fall he obtained a bill permanently moving the colonial capital away from St. Mary's City—the seat of Calvert and Catholic power. Petitioners from the lower counties pleaded humbly for reconsideration, citing the harbor at St. Mary's, noting how much had been spent on its public buildings—even offering to erect a new home for the governor. Under Nicholson's influence the delegates answered curtly that these stated benefits hardly deserved any reply at all. Not long afterward seventeen barrels of gunpowder stored in the cellar of the Philip Calvert house mysteriously exploded, leaving the fine brick mansion (where Nicholson himself lived briefly) a pile of rubble.

Nicholson campaigned for the Anglican church with the same firmness he took to relocating the colonial capital. In July 1694, soon after his arrival, he offered five pounds sterling to every congregation that built a parsonage and surveyed glebe lands for the support of a minister (Secretary Lawrence for his part offered an incentive of a thousand pounds of tobacco). At the end of the year twenty-two of the thirty-nine Anglican parishes in the colony had churches and nine had ministers. Some congregations employed makeshift churches. Services were held in the Dorchester County courthouse. At St. Mary's City, Anglicans overrode Catholic objections and used the old provincial court for the same purpose. In 1696, after learning that King William's council found legal fault with the 1692 establishment act, Nicholson urged the assembly to pass another one. He petitioned the bishop of London, Henry Compton, to aid in filling clerical vacancies in Maryland and himself put up seventy-five pounds toward King William's School, chartered the year of the second establishment measure. Eventually located on the state house grounds, the academy promised to promote "Good Letters and manners"— the stuff of improved colonial clerks.[13] It also would prepare young men for the Anglican ministry.

Once Bishop Compton appointed the Reverend Thomas Bray his commissary for the Maryland Church, Anglican prospects brightened further. Bray, in his forties, took to the Maryland episcopacy all the energy and ability that he later applied in founding the Society for the Propagation of the Gospel. Before leaving London he spent about three years searching for ministers willing to move to the Chesapeake and collecting books that he sent ahead for the libraries of Maryland parsonages. The Anglican majority in the assembly, having assigned him St. Anne's parish, Annapolis, nearly despaired of ever seeing Bray in Maryland. He arrived in the spring of 1700 and immediately called a visitation of the fifteen Anglican clergy then serving in the colony. His agenda addressed the shaky condition of the nominally established church. Lacking a bishop to administer confirmation, Anglicans in all the colonies faced the problem of raising parishioners to full membership. Bray stressed well-prepared sermons on the catechism; he and his ministers resolved to admit to the faith all persons "desirous and ready." They set aside twenty-five pounds for a mission to the Pennsylvania Quakers. More practically, they voted a sum for Bray's return to England, where he could encourage other clergy to settle in Maryland parishes. In London Bray sent a circular letter to Maryland ministers reminding them of the "Fundamental Work of Catechising," wrote a pamphlet describing the plight of the Maryland church, and finally in 1702 used his influence to press passage in Annapolis of an establishment act that Crown lawyers had approved in advance.[14]

Royal government—its oaths, militia duties, and crusade to organize and sanction the Anglican church in Maryland—cast the religious diversity of the colony into bold relief. Prominent Friends elected to the first royal assembly—John Edmondson of Talbot, John Goddin and Thomas Everden of Somerset, and George Warner of Cecil—departed when Governor Copley required them to swear the fidelity oath. The provincial court afterward

banned the testimony of unsworn Quakers, who resisted the demand of
royal officials that they support and join the militia. Early on Presbyterians
like the Scots immigrant and burgess Ninian Beale supported church establishment; the Reverend Francis Makemie at first had praised the Protestant
victory of 1689. Finally Puritans and Presbyterians (under the church act,
county courts recognized but also registered all dissenters) joined Quakers
in resenting the forty-pound poll, which they took pains to pay in the lowest-
grade tobacco. Nonconformists scoffed at Anglican frets over glebes and
parish boundaries. Disdaining Anglican forms and laboring to send more
itinerant preachers into Maryland, Makemie preferred to focus solely on
spiritual needs. His church continued to flourish in poorer regions where
established ministers complained of their "very naked & poor Condition."
Heavily Presbyterian counties "produce very mean tobacco," wrote a chronicler of the Chesapeake early in the eighteenth century, "and for that reason
can't get an orthodox minister to stay among them." Presbyterians, groused
Anglican clergymen in these years, owed their churches to "idle fellows that
have left their lawful employment, and preach and baptize without orders";
many unchurched Marylanders, they went on, regarded the Anglican sacraments as so many "needlesse Impositions."[15]

Quakers found Anglican establishment especially repugnant, and through
their close contacts with English Friends they helped to account for the several disallowances of Maryland church acts. In the 1690s the Third Haven
Meeting in Talbot County denounced the church tax as anti-Christian and
proclaimed that no Quaker or any other person "ought to pay it Either directly or indirectly." Besides reaffirming their aversion to "fighting or takeing
away mens lives," members of the West River Meeting resolved to contribute
nothing "towards maintaining Idollatrous priests nor their houses of Worship." Some Quakers eventually served jail sentences for acting on that resolve. Before 1702, while the establishment issue technically remained open,
Friends kept careful records of the tobacco they were forced to contribute
and the property they lost in fines for refusing to pay; in 1699 they counted
forty thousand pounds of tobacco lost on the Western Shore and as much as
one hundred thousand seized on the Eastern Shore. The courts offered no
recourse. Fruitlessly petitioning the governor for relief, Maryland Friends
wrote English Quakers to complain of their "Suffering for Priests Wages"
and traveled to London to petition for disallowance. Their defeat in 1702
came with a small concession, for the law incorporated an English rule permitting affirmation in court testimony. Most Quakers still stood outside the
political process, however; in 1704 Queen Anne ordered the royal governor,
at that time John Seymour, to continue to demand the oath of allegiance from
all Maryland officeholders.[16]

Catholics swore that oath, but refused to take others that repudiated papal
authority and denied the doctrine of substantiation. If tested, they thus

could hold no public office or serve on juries after the revolution of 1689. Concentrated in the oldest Western Shore counties, Catholics numbered almost three thousand persons at the beginning of the eighteenth century; eight priests and three brothers administered to the several parishes. Protestant leaders, never doubting that Catholics abhorred Anglican establishment, believed that these few papists bore watching. Authorities noted the changing ethnicity of incoming indentured servants, though fewer in number, the latest servants to arrive in Maryland were predominantly Irish Catholic. Furthermore, the imperial struggle between England and France, which in 1702 grew into Queen Anne's War, had a religious cast that fostered Protestant mistrust of Catholics in general. Bray argued for the appointment of a suffragan bishop in Maryland partly as "Necessary to prevent [the] increase of Romanism." But for the curbs royal government imposed, wrote Anglican clergymen, "the Insolence of the Romish priests . . . would soon be Intolerable in these parts." Governor Seymour in 1704 drew on his military bearing and the prevailing hostility toward Catholics to berate priests for saying mass in churches. That "Exercise of Superstitious Vanities," he said, demonstrated their intent by such "gawdy shows and Serpentine policy to amuse the multitude and beguile the unthinking weakest part of them." The General Assembly in October placed a twenty-shilling duty on Irish servants to discourage "Importing too great a number of Irish Papists." Statutes of the same year—the first, at Seymour's request, aiming "to Prevent the Growth of Popery"—outlawed public baptisms and masses, Catholic schools, and any attempt to convert Protestants to Catholicism.[17]

Anglican establishment thus gave rise to two distinct minorities in Maryland. Quakers in the early eighteenth century worshipped freely in their meetinghouses, conducted their business, and concentrated on maintaining their separation from the rest of society. A few of them strayed; elders admonished younger Quakers who married outside the faith or entered public service despite the ban on oaths. William Edmondson, son of the delegate who left the 1692 royal assembly rather than swear, took the required oath in 1701 and served as a Talbot County magistrate. Edmondson's brother Thomas sat in the lower house of the assembly from 1719 to 1722, as did Thomas Dixon and the younger John Hudson. Most Quaker families followed the example of the Chews of Anne Arundel County, focusing attention on their businesses, caring for their own, and prospering. In like manner Catholics in the period quietly went about their lives. They heard mass and received the sacraments only in private homes and in the dwellings maintained by small communities of priests. A few Catholics never dropped from public view, even during royal rule. Henry Darnall, distantly related by marriage to the Calverts, sat on the third Lord Baltimore's land council and served as his agent and receiver general; Darnall owned more than eighteen thousand acres of land, one hundred slaves, and a store. At the same time

Charles Carroll, an Irish immigrant who had risen to influence before the revolution of 1689, acted as Baltimore's solicitor and register of the land office. He amassed property that placed him and his son among the wealthiest men in the colony.

The plight of Quakers and Catholics did not improve, as they thought it might, when in 1715 old Lord Charles died and King George I suddenly returned full proprietary privileges to Benedict Leonard Calvert, fourth Lord Baltimore and an Anglican convert. He died soon thereafter, and the guardians of his eldest son and successor, Charles (a sixteen year old), spurned the Friends' recommendation that he restore their political freedom. Governor Seymour's successor, John Hart, remained in office for five years after the Calverts' restoration and, like Seymour, believed Catholic plots pervasive in the colony. It infuriated him that Carroll retained authority under the new proprietor. Indeed, Darnall having died, Carroll had fallen heir to Baltimore's chief offices in the colony. Carroll's dispatch in collecting proprietary fees, fines, and taxes—and his refusal to take the Oath of Supremacy—pushed Hart over the edge. In 1718 the governor asked for, and the assembly readily passed, an act depriving all unsworn Catholics of the vote. The ideal of toleration lay in ruins.

⌒◦∝◦⌒

Another early ideal had been social hierarchy. Though by the beginning of the eighteenth century life in Maryland little resembled the manorial settlement at St. Mary's, a few Quakers and Catholics and a small portion of all Protestants had fulfilled Cecil Calvert's dream of a transplanted nobility. They formed a wealthy elite whose good fortune actually owed less to medieval favor than to sharp practice.

Maryland planters—so many of whom lived within musket shot of saltwater—had from the beginnings of the province found the bay and its navigable rivers an open invitation to trade. Rarely were they subsistence farmers who grew only what they needed to live. Even small producers back from the water put axles through their hogsheads and rolled them (on what became known as rolling roads) to nearby wharves; they grew tobacco for market and watched the market closely. Committed to tobacco exports, planters of Maryland and Virginia stood at the mercy of forces in the Atlantic economy which few of them could discern and which largely were beyond their reach. Overproduction and uncertified quality, they realized, dropped prices and undermined demand. Yet late-seventeenth-century attempts to control the size of the tobacco crop and regulate quality, both unsuccessful, ignored uncanny elements in the tobacco trade. Distance and sailing time made the business uncertain. Planters sold their crops or shipped them on consignment based on price information at best many months old. Whether they dealt with a consignment trader, English sea captain, independent merchant, or factor (an agent for an English or Scottish firm), tobacco growers

"The Conveyance to Market." From William Tatham, *Historical and Practical Essay on the Culture and Commerce of Tobacco* (London, 1800). *McGregor Library, University of Virginia*

had scant idea what the value of a harvested crop would prove to be on reaching Britain. The size of the spring planting represented a similar gamble. Supply affected tobacco prices and the planter's profits; so did the availability of English ships, freight and insurance rates, sales commissions, English import duties, and unpredictable decisions in foreign courts—for much of the tobacco exported to England found its market on the Continent. Clearly wartime disruption of commerce between 1702 and 1713 lowered Maryland tobacco prices. More remotely, English reexport duties dampened trade with the Dutch.

Tobacco growers understood well that credit made all the difference in this developing region. Obtaining credit, but particularly being in a position to provide it, followed astute judgment and some good luck. From the earliest years of the province a few planters, themselves owing British creditors, had not only grown tobacco but acted as middlemen for the smaller planters in their locale—accepting for shipment the tobacco they produced and selling them imported goods in exchange or on credit. The arrangement had mutual advantages. Planter-traders earned profits on both the shipping and the store. Small growers, whose few hogsheads were not enough to detain an English ship captain, could consolidate their crops with those of a larger neighbor and then purchase from his store the needles and thread, powder and shot, glass and metalware, needed for the coming year. The size of these enterprises often was small, as the estates of William Fishwick of Dorchester County and John Connor of Kent illustrated. Fishwick's debtors, 162 in number, owed him only a little more than three pounds each, while Connor's 123 debtors averaged just under five pounds. Merchandisers like Fishwick and Connor may have begun among the lesser tobacco growers or have arrived in Maryland with money to invest. Others started out as factors.

Whatever their beginnings, these planter-merchants had gained considerable economic advantage by the late seventeenth century, and the rich promised to grow richer in the eighteenth. With family or business connections in England, friendly contacts with shippers, and additional income from dealings with local planters, they reaped the richest profits when tobacco prices were high. When, in addition to war, satisfied demand and leveled-off production meant lean years for tobacco growing, they weathered the storm most comfortably. Their uncollected debts and outstanding loans gave them assets they could use in parlaying for credit with London firms; their liquidated landholdings or credit reserves enabled them to pay the high purchase price of slaves as black labor became available. During Queen Anne's War they may also have profited from outfitting the royal warships that patrolled the Atlantic for French privateers and put into the Chesapeake for provisions. On the return of peace these planter-merchants stood poised to capture the lion's share of the market, which fattened in 1723 when the Walpole ministry took mercy on the languishing tobacco trade and removed reexport fees. In the same year the French government restored the tobacco monopoly there to a company whose directors decided to import Chesapeake Orinoco from England.

During the ensuing period of comparative prosperity—tobacco exports rose from about thirty million pounds in the 1720s to one hundred million by the 1770s—the best-situated Marylanders rode the crest and raised their net worth even higher. Among them were members of the professions. A successful physician and surgeon in Annapolis, Charles Carroll, invested his fees in shipping and land; in the early eighteenth century he grew as wealthy as his Catholic cousins who bore the same name. Dr. Carroll's son, who

A Chesapeake tobacco wharf and factor. Cartouche from "A Map of the Inhabited part of Virginia containing the whole Province of Maryland," drawn by Joshua Fry and Peter Jefferson, 1751. *MHS*

reached his twenties in the 1740s, wisely chose the law. Before 1700 it had not been unusual for litigants to plead their own cases; lawyers often had been clerks who needed to supplement their salaries. Afterward lawyers became a close-knit group of educated practitioners, men only, whose income derived almost entirely from law practice. Of seven attorneys practicing before the Prince George's County Court in 1710, all but one were professionals. Eastern Shore lawyers performed before as many as four county courts, which met in succession; Western Shore attorneys, besides attending the same circuit on the other side of the bay, often argued cases before the provincial court. Benefiting, as the Talbot Court observed, from the fact that trade "Causeth many Suits Att Lawe," the busiest lawyers normally joined the ranks of the county rich.[18]

On both shores wealth grew steadily concentrated in these years. Talbot County merchant-planters, lawyers, merchants, and officeholders, all of whom in 1733 numbered thirty men or a mere 2 percent of the taxable or nondependent population, held more than 45 percent of all property in the county. In 1680 only one Talbot planter had been worth two thousand pounds; half a century later one merchant-planter alone, Richard Bennett, claimed twenty thousand pounds in property. Members of this elite enlarged the size of their slaveholdings as well as their share of all slaves. While very few small planters owned slaves (some still held white servants), large planters tended increasingly to hold slaves in large numbers. In Charles and Prince George's counties by 1733 less than 10 percent of slaveholders held 43 percent of all black bondsmen.

Together with these trends, changes in the social makeup of the colony both lent stability and tightened hierarchy. At some point in the early eighteenth century, men and women born in Maryland became a majority of the population, which climbed to about forty-three thousand in 1710 and nearly doubled in the next twenty years. Better health, an improved ratio of women to men, and younger marriages provided the basis for this growth. Native-born children were less susceptible to the diseases that had decimated newcomers. Not facing the terms of service that delayed marriage among seventeenth-century servants, they wedded earlier—men before age twenty-five, women in their late teens. The continuing, though declining, preponderance of males in the population and their eagerness in seeking mates did most to explain the younger age of marriage among women. Once established, the pattern quickly worked a revolution in the colony, which before had been so grimly dependent on settlers for population growth. Having married younger, native couples ordinarily had larger families than did immigrants—on average as many as nine births—and their grown children did also. Lower mortality rates and a longer life expectancy among native Marylanders meant that more parents lived to see their children reach maturity. In material terms this demographic change meant that fathers more likely lived long enough to acquire property that they could pass on to their children, that their children would live to inherit, and that families, over generations and through intermarriage, consolidated their wealth in each locality. On the Eastern Shore in 1700, for example, perhaps half of the landowners were linked to each other by marriage or kinship ties.

The rise of the native-born had political effect as well. Governor Seymour, who did not always have his way with the lower house of assembly, wrote the Board of Trade and Plantations with alarm and impatience that the natives "by the name of Country borne" stood aloof "from the rest of her Majestys Subjects." He meant that Marylanders had begun to think of themselves as such and to use their identity as a bond in struggles against "outside" authority. Sitting in the lower house between 1700 and 1715 were thirty-seven delegates whose fathers had served in Maryland offices. Six members could point to grandfathers who had held political posts. Two burgesses of long service—Thomas Brooke, a Catholic converted to Anglicanism, and Edward Lloyd II of Talbot County, in 1701 a councillor—belonged to the third generation of Marylanders who had been in public life. Their families had had connections with the proprietor.[19]

Most of the men assuming political prominence in the early eighteenth century, however, reflected the later success of merchant-planters and lawyers. Their names included Bordley, Dulany, Hammond, Frisby, Addison, Dashiel, Harris, Pearce, Tasker, Tripp, and Ward. With their families and friends intermarried, they formed a network of Protestant officeholders, justices, vestrymen, and militia officers. As in Virginia, they saw their sons appointed to posts of ascending responsibility. Daniel Dulany, born in Ireland, had arrived in Maryland in 1703 as an indentured servant; after working in the law office of George Plater, he became a leading professional, served as attorney general of the colony, and sent his son to England for study. Edward Lloyd, his brothers Philemon and James, and brothers-in-law Richard Tilghman and Matthew Tilghman Ward, exercised considerable power on the Eastern Shore. The Addison family of Prince George's County carried similar weight on the Western Shore. Thomas Addison assumed his dead father's place on the council at age twenty-nine. His half-sister married Thomas Brooke, also on the council. Brooke's son-in-law, related to the Lees of Virginia, joined the council in 1715. Another Addison brother-in-law, Benjamin Tasker, benefited from Addison's influence, as did a son-in-law, James Bowles, and more relations among the Dent and Smith families of Charles and Calvert counties. An act the assembly passed in 1704 illustrated the territorial sensibility that worried Seymour. Intended "for the Incouragement of Learning and Advancement of the Natives of this Province," it aimed at absentee officeholding and—excepting direct commissions from the Crown—required three years' residence in Maryland before appointment to posts of trust and profit.[20]

For the less advantaged among the white native-born, this orderly world limited opportunities. Compared to the mid-seventeenth century, it disappointed ambition. Since people lived longer and some families had accumulated power, political responsibility even in the newer counties came less often to men of mean education and experience. The more discouraging realities were economic. While tobacco prices for many years remained less than a penny a pound, land prices more than doubled between 1680 and 1700. During those years and later, war-related trade disruptions kept the cost of imported tools and other planters' necessities high. The price of servants stood beyond the reach of many freed men; that of slaves had climbed far too high for them to consider. Under these conditions freed white servants found it difficult to establish themselves in tobacco planting and indeed could foresee little profit in it. While in 1660 only about 10 percent of the householders in Maryland did not own the land they lived on, that proportion had tripled by the first of the eighteenth century. In 1705 one-third of the households in Charles, Prince George's, and St. Mary's counties had formed on rented land. On the Eastern Shore—where a new county, Queen Anne's, appeared in 1706—land eastward, away from creeks, rivers, and the bay, offered hope for some would-be planters, and the small planter's share of the wealth remained roughly the same from 1680 to 1710. Yet the poorest people, often ex-servants, tended to leave tobacco-growing counties and become permanent tenants. Many of them left Maryland altogether.[21]

At the bottom of the social scale, in the slaves' quarters, changing patterns of life helped somewhat to make their isolation endurable in the eighteenth century. Not that blacks settled easily into slave communities. Newly landed Africans, who continued to arrive in large numbers until about 1740, did not always embrace the ways of seasoned and native blacks or adapt smoothly to slavery. An African brought to Charles County in about 1730 contemptuously regarded the slaves he met there as a "vulgar race, beneath his rank, and the dignity of his former station." Among immigrant slaves, men outnumbered women about two to one, so native slaves and African newcomers competed for mates, sometimes violently. Africans did not at first adopt the seasoned slaves' subtle forms of resistance. "A new Negro, if he must be broke, either from Obstinacy, or, which I am more apt to suppose, from Greatness of Soul, will require more hard Discipline than a young Spaniel," wrote an English visitor to Worcester County in mid-century. "You would really be surpriz'd at their Perseverance; let an hundred Men shew him how to hoe or drive a Wheelbarrow, he'll still take the one by the Bottom, and the other by the wheel; and they often die before they can be conquer'd." As in Virginia, where fugitive slaves almost succeeded in establishing a colony in the mountains, a few blacks in Maryland apparently banded together across the Monocacy River in the late 1720s, "entertained and encouraged," according to the assembly, to live with an Indian tribe in the "Back-Woods." Later, in 1739–40, Prince George's County whites uncovered a plot whereby Jack Ransom, a native black, and his followers, likely African born, were to rise up and slay their white masters and families. Ransom was tried and hanged for the offense. Stephen Bordley, an Annapolis lawyer, said much of the fears Ransom struck in whites when he wrote that the slaves, after killing white men and uniting blacks on both shores, had planned to take the remaining white women as wives.[22]

Several trends suggested that the loneliness and dispersion of blacks would diminish with time. First, the number of black women born in Maryland reached a level high enough to have an impact on the Negro birth rate. African women—usually arriving in their twenties, often in poor health, placed under great stress during the passage to the Chesapeake, and relatively few in number—tended to have few children. In the 1720s, certainly after 1730, the black population began a natural increase that paralleled white growth. In a sampling of Negroes in Charles and Prince George's counties between 1711 and 1720, 120 black females between the ages of 16 and 50 had 182 children; in the nine years after 1721, 188 slave women in their fertile years had 383 children. An Anglican clergyman on the south side of the Potomac observed in 1724 that the Negroes were "a very prolifick people among themselves." He would have come closer to the truth had he said that native-born blacks were healthier than imported Africans, had children earlier, and lived longer. The change appeared in Maryland at different times in different localities, depending on the proportion of immigrants in the black population and the ratio of men to women. It affected the slave experience on both shores. Slave families in Maryland, still by no means the rule, became more common in the eighteenth century than before.[23]

Increasingly concentrated in large holdings, slaves took safety in numbers. They more often slept in quarters of their own, where they began to gather the personal and collective resources so peculiar to oppressed people. They drew on the African culture from which many slaves could recall being torn, borrowed from the English, Christian society encasing them, and learned from everyday experience. They developed a common, pidgin language peculiar to themselves and traded techniques for survival on the plantation. Besides passing along folk stories and remedies, blacks among themselves posed questions that could only call for religious answers. Finally, held on larger plantations, slaves found themselves employed at a variety of tasks in the eighteenth century. Some were trained as house servants. Others learned manual skills like blacksmithing, carpentry, and coopering. Masters entrusted a few native blacks with responsibility for the work of others. Living under their master's control but imposing black order on the quarters, raising their children to endure, slaves slowly constructed a community of their own.

⚶

In 1705 the Virginia historian Robert Beverley described Marylanders as sponging "upon the Blessings of a warm Sun, and a fruitful Soil"—as being too lazy to use art or industry to improve Nature's gifts. Twenty-five years later Ebenezer Cook published a hopeful sequel to his earlier satiric verse. In 1730 tobacco prices again were low and the colony tasted hard times. *Sotweed Redivivus: Or the Planters Looking-Glass* warned that "It's Industry, and not a nauseous Weed, / Must cloath the Naked and the Hungry feed." Cook looked forward to the day when his fellow planters would put the lie to remarks like Beverley's—would drain marshes, plant cereals, and build ships "to sound / Great-Britain's Channel, and in Cash abound."[24]

This call for a diversified Maryland economy finally received an answer. Beginning in the late seventeenth century, New England vessels bound for the Caribbean had found it profitable to stop in the Chesapeake for grain that they then traded in the West Indies—where planters concentrated on profitable sugar production—for rum, sugar, and slaves. When sailing in the other direction they took on wheat at Oxford or Annapolis for sale in Boston, Salem, and Rhode Island seaports. Many of the planters who first supplied this market lived on the inland stretches of sandy Eastern Shore soil that did not produce the best tobacco; common planters, they fell below the planter-merchants, who could allocate their slave labor to corn and wheat as well as

tobacco, and stood ahead of those farmers whose debts forced them to produce tobacco for its meager but dependable income. Interest in cereal crops
grew in the 1740s, when Philadelphia merchants, busily exporting wheat to
Europe, began looking south to broaden their supply network. Gradually
the plow necessary to wheat growing became as familiar to Baltimore, Cecil,
and especially Kent county planters as the tobacco hoe. They were likely as
well to raise sheep for the local wool markets and, given the foreign demand
for foodstuffs, to keep hogs and cattle for curing. By 1760 Kent County had
almost entirely given up tobacco—despite its continuing good prices—and
switched to wheat and livestock farming. Wheat did not exhaust the soil as
quickly as tobacco or require the sot-weed's constant care. Though like tobacco it left the planter highly dependent on market shifts, demand for the
time being kept pace with increasing production.[25]

Promoting diversified agriculture, this rise in grain markets also encouraged Maryland shipping. Using Chesapeake Bay as a highway and sporting
ground from the days of earliest settlement, Marylanders of all ranks considered themselves boatmen whom Nature had intended to be amphibious: except for the upper Potomac and lower Susquehanna, the rivers were fairly
free of strong currents, and the pines, mulberries, chestnuts, and oaks required for shipbuilding rose in abundance not far from the navigable arms
of the bay. Claiborne had a shipwright in his employ on Kent Island when
Lord Baltimore's settlers entered the Chesapeake. Later—so many planters
having their own wharves or piers—shallops, flat-bottomed barges, canoes,
skiffs, and pinnaces (like the *Dove*) became common on the bay, doing much
of the day-to-day work that wagons or carriages did in neighboring Pennsylvania. Marylanders fished and transported cargoes in small boats that
evolved from practical experience.

Chesapeake shipwrights applied similar trial and error in designing larger
vessels, which they began to fashion in earnest by the early eighteenth century. Maryland shipyards in those years produced a few large and bulky
ships, some for sale to England, displacing several hundred tons and well
suited for tobacco transport. Other craft, most between twenty and fifty tons
and gaily trimmed, appeared as Maryland merchants and skippers entered
the New England and Caribbean trades. In the West Indies, where colonists
often sailed without the protection of British convoys, circumstances placed
a premium on speed and maneuverability. Pirates, French privateers (who
nearly wiped out the Maryland merchant marine during Queen Anne's War),
and then the attractions of illicit commerce with non-British islands urged
Maryland shipbuilders to modify traditional rigging to build speed. Single-
masted sloops and particularly two-masted schooners emerged as distinctive
Chesapeake designs and became the envy of foreigners. Shipyards at Third
Haven and Island Creek in Talbot County, at Chestertown in Kent, and
at West River near Annapolis earned high reputations for their work—
especially after they began using white oak at about mid-century. Shipbuild-

"Shipyard at Gray's Inn Creek," c. 1767. Overmantel panel from Spencer Hall, Kent County, showing the wide variety of vessels common in the eighteenth-century Chesapeake, including, from left to right, log canoe, brig, sloop, tobacco ship, schooner, and shallop. *MHS*

ing attracted skilled British sailmakers and developed reliable sources of rope and duck. Seafarers of the period considered ship chandlers at Annapolis and Chestertown equal even to those of Norfolk for the quality of their equipment and repairs (sailing into northern Chesapeake ports also helped to rid hulls of the boring worms that accumulated in saltwater). Well fitted, the graceful craft of Maryland began a wider search for markets. In 1731 an assembly report to Benedict Leonard Calvert mentioned a few Maryland ships sailing across the Atlantic to the Azores and Madeira. They carried homegrown products like grain, lumber from the Pocomoke River region, naval stores, pork, beef, and tobacco in trade for fruit, wines, and salt. By the 1750s Maryland vessels had reached Lisbon, Cadiz, and other ports of southern Europe.

Grain exports also stimulated the town growth that had eluded Maryland—despite legislative encouragement—since its founding. Tobacco marketing called for seasonal activity on the part of a few factors or ships' supercargoes at villages like Oxford, Joppa Town, and Port Tobacco—each serving a locality with its own name for leaf quality. In 1747 the Maryland assembly passed a tobacco inspection act that established dozens of points in the colony, roughly fifteen miles apart, each with a warehouse and complement of inspectors. At least from early April until the end of August, when inspectors had to be on duty, these places became important; they seldom led to new towns. By contrast wheat, corn, and livestock brought year-round economic activity that fed itself. General farming called for wagons, and they for teamsters and craftsmen who created a demand for goods and services. Since wheat shipments usually left in the fall, surplus corn in the spring, tavernkeepers and small merchants established themselves permanently along the routes to Philadelphia, at headwaters and transfer points like Elkton, and at ports like Chestertown. Furthermore, wheat traveled best to the Caribbean as flour (during the tropical summer, grain could grow "hot" and spoil). Wheat exports encouraged mills and they, too, gave rise to town life.

To Marylanders with venture capital, the falls of the major Western Shore rivers soon became points of interest beyond their natural beauty. Georgetown, a Prince George's County village perched where oceangoing vessels reached the Potomac rapids, began to develop as a mercantile location that looked west for future prospects. Another reason for exploring the fall line lay in water power. The swift waters of Western Shore streams had an important application in milling. One such run, eventually known as Jones Falls, offered particular attraction because it fed into a basin of the northern branch of the Patapsco River, where a large sheltered cove might make a fine harbor. In August 1729 the assembly passed an act providing for a town—not the first to be called Baltimore—on a portion of this site owned by the Carrolls. Within a short time commissioners purchased the land and laid out plots on the west bank of the creek, opposite a hamlet called Jones Town. Boundaries grew several times, and in 1745 Baltimore Town and Jones Town merged. Seven years later, when John Moale drew a sketch of Baltimore, it included twenty-five buildings, mostly wooden homes, spaced widely over the hillsides that sloped gently toward the water. Lot owners there jealously regarded the growing community downriver at William Fell's point, where deeper water permitted larger vessels to berth. Ships visiting both communities took on grain from the countryside to the west and flour milled on the Jones Falls, the Patapsco River, and the Gunpowder River to the north. Though growing, and the site of popular spring and fall fairs, Baltimore remained a small town.

Economic vitality on the Patapsco also owed something to the home-financed iron mills of the Baltimore Company, located on the south branch of the river not far from the village. Formed in 1731, the company exploited Baltimore Town's location as a shipping point and a variety of resources. It planned to turn local hardwoods into charcoal for the furnaces, and to make use of the abundant water power at the site. Iron deposits were so rich that they littered the surface of the ground. Still, the business involved risk. An earlier iron venture in Maryland, the Principio Company, had received the backing of British investors; the Baltimore enterprise, requiring more than thirty-five hundred pounds for the land, slaves, plant, and supplies necessary to put it in operation, necessarily drew upon some of the colony's wealthiest men—Daniel Dulany the Elder, Benjamin Tasker, Sr., and several members of the Carroll family—who considered the risks worth taking. The company did not disappoint them. Between 1734 and 1737 it shipped 1,977 tons of pig iron to England, usually in and among the hogsheads aboard tobacco ships. Dulany and the others put first returns into further building. By the 1740s equipped with a forge, the Patapsco firm manufactured bar in addition to pig iron. Eventually it consisted of several furnaces, three forges, thirty thousand acres of land, and engaged the labor of one hundred and fifty slaves. Except during the mid-1740s and afterward, when King George's War caused trade disruptions, the company fared well. By 1756 there were

"Baltimore in 1752, From a sketch then made by John Moale Esq. deceased, corrected by the late Daniel Bowley Esq. 'from his certain recollection, and that of other aged persons, well acquainted with it, with whom he compared Notes.'" Aquatint engraving by William Strickland, 1817. *MHS*

six ironworks in Baltimore County. Dr. Carroll's son, Charles Carroll the Barrister, touted Baltimore Company iron as "not in the Least Inferior" to the best Swedish product.[26]

Shrewd in meeting the British need for iron, men like the senior Dulany also played a prominent part in developing the Maryland backcountry, where iron, copper, limestone, and water power lured the investor. Dulany's own interest in the Piedmont frontier had begun in 1721, when he entered into partnership with a Prince George's County planter, John Bradford, who had extensive frontier experience. Bradford located some two thousand acres of bottom land up the Potomac—"Above Ye Inhabitants," as maps of the time noted simply. He surveyed them for Dulany, who, living in Annapolis, secured warrants for the tracts and applied for patents. Benjamin Tasker joined Dulany in 1727 by acquiring a patent for 7,000 acres about twelve miles above the Potomac, on the west bank of the Monocacy, a parcel the new owner described as "Tasker's Chance."

The name fit because for many years serious obstacles lay in the path of western settlement in Maryland. To start game in the Piedmont hills, Indians for many years had set brush fires, which at times burned so fiercely that sailors forty miles off the Atlantic coast could smell the smoke. These devastated areas became notorious for their emptiness and scrub growth. Travelers through the northern and western reaches of old Baltimore County reported "Barren Hills," rocky soil, an absence of trees that pioneers needed to build homes and fences, and nothing to eat but berries. Added to these discouraging accounts were fears that Indians on the upper Potomac, led in the 1730s by a chief who called himself Captain Civility, would inflict reprisals should whites, in his words, "press too much upon us for We have given no body Land." Furthermore, much western Maryland land had been surveyed by speculators who obtained warrants for large claims that they, unlike the Dulanys and Taskers, then failed to patent—hoping to avoid paying the proprietor quitrents. Settling on warranted lands held out the likelihood of disputes to which newcomers "could not hope Easily to see an End," as Dulany himself said when speaking for an assembly committee.[27]

That land disputes could be bloody the Calverts and Penns proved by carrying their boundary differences well into the eighteenth century. The migrations of Pennsylvania-German farmers—whose superior husbandry, sobriety, and prosperity made them highly desirable citizens—exacerbated the problem. In the 1730s their rising numbers had caused some of them to move into the attractive farmland southwest of the Susquehanna, where both proprietors had claims and where both, hoping to win the Germans' allegiance, invited them to settle. Caught in the midst of a border war, the Germans often did not know to whom they owed taxes. The situation would have delighted William Claiborne. In Claiborne's absence Thomas Cresap, a fearless Marylander who had been born in George Calvert's Yorkshire County and had practiced feuding with Pennsylvanians on the Susquehanna, established a fortress home in the contested region south of Lancaster—on a 500-acre grant from Charles Calvert, fifth Lord Baltimore. In addition to several Maryland commissions, Cresap took with him friends who were glad to fight and his wife, a Prince George's County woman who carried a rifle, two pistols, a tomahawk, a scalping knife, and, in her boot, a small dagger. Cresap classified farmers whose allegiance lay with Pennsylvania as poachers, squatters, or traitors, and he raided them mercilessly. In 1736, after a fourteen-hour seige, a Pennsylvania sheriff and his small army finally arrested the cursing Cresap on many charges and took him to Philadelphia. There, by reports, he turned to someone and loudly remarked, "Damn it, Aston, this is one of the Prettyst Towns in Maryland!"[28] The next year the king ordered Cresap's release and put an end to the Penn-Calvert feud by placing a moratorium on all grants in the contested territory. By then many Germans had quit Maryland for Virginia. They passed through the Monocacy country, crossed the Catoctins to the Antietam valley, and forded the Potomac on a wagon trail that became known as the Monocacy Road.

Dulany's interest in western development coincided with a political consideration that he shared with Lord Baltimore. In 1732 Charles Calvert paid a visit to the colony and issued a proclamation placing the settlement of western Maryland on the most favorable possible terms. But during the Penn truce the locus of trouble shifted southward: the Virginia government seemed intent on making grants along the upper Potomac, and the whereabouts of the "first Fountain" of that river, which the Calvert charter established as the southwestern boundary of Maryland, remained vague. Settling the Monocacy region might avert another border conflict by strengthening Baltimore's claim to that western land. It would also make Dulany, a member of the governor's council after 1742, a fortune. In the fall of 1744, after a weather-shortened trip up the southern (he thought main) branch of the river, Dulany wrote the proprietor that the land of western Maryland equaled if it did not surpass "any in America for natural Advantages"; it had rich soil, timber, stone for building, some marble, and was "very healthy." With the aid of the now-famous Cresap, Dulany patented more and more claims in the Monocacy River and Antietam Creek valleys, including the old Tasker claim and Cresap's "Long Meadow" surveys, until his holdings approached twenty thousand acres. The threat of war with Captain Civility subsided in 1744, when Maryland adhered to tradition. Observing that the Indians of the Five Nations would settle for "nothing less than Blood or Money," the assembly purchased their rights to all land between the Potomac and Susquehanna rivers.[29]

In this climate Dulany's fruit ripened. To Germans, Swiss-Germans, and Scots-Irish marching through western Maryland, he offered farms of one hundred to three hundred acres at modest prices—at first at a loss. He foresaw that these "quiet, honest, and Industrious" farmers—"the fittest people that can be to Settle a New Country"—would grow grains, raise cattle, and soon demand a center for markets and services.[30] In 1745, according to an arrangement with Lord Baltimore which gave him subfeudal authority, Dulany laid out a town on the eastern edge of Tasker's Chance with lots that he rented rather than sold. The community, named Frederick Town for Lord Baltimore's son, flourished as an assortment of artisans, merchants, and professional men arrived and took up lots. Those German families who first availed themselves of Dulany's promotion—Lays, Millers, Brunners, Stoners, Schleys, Steiners, and Schultzes—used their own language to spread word of the landlord's terms and advertise the vibrancy of Frederick Town.

The area became the fastest growing in Maryland. Some of the newcomers had landed at Baltimore Town from the lower Rhine; others moved down from the western bank of the Susquehanna. First a Lutheran then a Reformed church appeared in Frederick. For the time being Dulany's subordinates winked at the Anglican church tax there, an oversight that appealed to the Germans because so many of them had left Europe to escape religious impositions. After the assembly created Frederick County in 1748, voters elected Dulany's son to the lower house. By 1750 the county seat—home to a thousand inhabitants—was the largest town in Maryland, with wagon roads connecting it to Annapolis and Baltimore Town. In the next year alone sixty wagons loaded with flax seed arrived on the Patapsco from Frederick County, and many more with wheat. In western Maryland no more talk was heard of barren hills or lazy citizens. In the colony as a whole the seventeenth-century economy of tobacco growing and imported goods had given way to a more complex one that included grains, milling, ironmaking, and various small crafts and cottage industries.

⁓⋙⁓

The natives of Maryland, an exuberant contributor to *London Magazine* wrote in 1746, "enjoy a Life much to be envy'd by Courts and Cities." He heaped praise on the habit of hospitality—Marylanders sought after strangers greedily, he said, and let "Mirth and Glee" reign supreme. The Englishman was used to colder people and weather alike; "my Spirits have been sometimes raised so much," he declared, "that I have almost forgotten I was of another clime, and have wish'd myself for ever amongst them." Better served than some sojourners in the colony, he found Maryland a place of "full Tables and open Doors."[31]

The homes Marylanders invited visitors into gave the best evidence of stability in the colony. Houses eventually reflected particular taste and an experimental approach to building; not surprisingly, innovative trends coincided with the increase in native-born population. Generally they led away from the steep gables and small windows of imported English style and pointed toward more comfortable, brighter, and airier houses. Early planters, facing stark needs, had built a simple "great room" and an upstairs divided into bedrooms. After about 1710, by various roof designs that included the "catslide" of the saltbox type and the hipped gambrel, Marylanders began to construct houses two rooms deep and often a full two stories high. Planters also added "telescoping" wings, either wooden or brick, onto the end walls of existing structures. Cedar Park in Anne Arundel County—first built with earthfast posts and clapboard sheathing in about 1703 and then expanded, partly with brick, in about 1736—typified the drift toward deeper, larger, more durable homes. So did Bryerwood and The Retreat in Charles County, and Boston Cliff (1729), Otwell, and Crooked Intention (1717, 1730) in Talbot. Though only one room in depth, an artful two-story brick mansion in Worcester County, Genezir (c. 1732), exemplified the tendency toward vertical reach. On the lower Western Shore a characteristic form eventually became the two-room-deep house with double chimneys at one or both ends of the house, the brickwork enclosing a door or a small nook—a chimney-pent. New styles reached western Maryland only after a time lag and then conformed to material conditions there. Families breaking ground on their first farm ordinarily made good use of available timber and built one-room homes of logs, sometimes hand-hewn so as to fit more tightly and to make flat walls. They tried to build their cabins near a spring, which, besides water, supplied a means to cool milk and other foods. The Germans

Upper left, Hard Bargain, Charles County, c. 1768. *Upper right*, Cedar Park, Anne Arundel County, c. 1703/36. *Lower left*, Genezir, Worcester County, c. 1732. *Lower right*, Bard's Fields, St. Mary's County, c. 1750. Etchings by Don Swann, originally published in *Colonial and Historic Homes of Maryland* (Baltimore, 1939). Swann, a well-known mid-Atlantic artist, strove to document early Maryland houses at a time when many of them were falling into ruin. *S. Donovan Swann, Jr.*

of Frederick County set an example by constructing solid houses of the limestone so abundant in the "barren" region.[32]

The wonderful variety of Chesapeake foods already was proverbial. In comfortable circles one found luxury items like sugar, coffee, and spices, imported wines and rum, and bread made from wheat flour. At the same time Nature distributed her bounty rather evenly. As elsewhere in colonial America, corn probably supplied half the calories of every person's diet, rich and poor, bound and free. Ground and baked, it made an unleavened, loose bread called johnny cake, hoe cake, or pone—the best of which, according to a visitor, "when cut and roasted tastes almost like warm white bread." Corn also could be ground into a coarse meal that after cooking became a porridge served with milk or cider; malted into beer, it provided a common

"View from Bushongo Tavern 5 miles from York Town on the Baltimore road." From *Columbian Magazine* (Philadelphia, 1788). *Mariners' Museum, Newport News*

drink. To supplement this staple in the eighteenth century Marylanders had, in the words of another traveler, "good Beefe [usually salted] and Bacon sometimes Mutton and abundance of Greenes as Cabbages, Parsnips, Turnips, Carrots, [sweet] Pottatoes Simnels [wheat breads] squashes and watter mellons and also abundance of other things too tedious to be here incerted." Ham, pickled and smoked, along with chickens, milk cows, and honey, enriched and sweetened this fare. Orchards, a mark of German husbandry (though from the seventeenth century technically required of all Maryland landholders), for the first time produced a marketable surplus. Besides being healthful fresh fruits, apples, pears, quinces, and peaches furnished the makings of cider and other drinks that permitted, at least during the fall, less reliance on the shallow wells of the lower country. An Anglican minister in Maryland believed the cider "where it is rightly ordered not inferior to the best white wine." Pressings left over from cider making, chestnuts, and the fruit that dropped on the ground Marylanders fed to their hogs. A visitor to Annapolis thought those animals ate better than the Hyde Park gentry of London. Upcountry Germans earned a deserved reputation for the baked dishes and preserves they made from strawberries, huckleberries, cherries, and grapes.[33]

To this domestic supply Marylanders added game and fish, developing recipes that later became distinctive to them. Venison, bear, squirrel, and wild turkey (dressed turkeys could exceed forty pounds) pleasantly varied the Chesapeake diet. Taking deer was common enough seriously to deplete their numbers by 1757, when the assembly sought to limit the killing season. Truly delectable additions to the table came from the creeks, rivers, and the bay. Crabs, oysters, and clams abounded on the bottoms so widely accessible, and "a surprising variety of excellent fish"—bass and bluefish, shad, sturgeon, sheepshead, drumfish, and catfish—flourished in the Chesapeake mixture of saltwater and freshwater. One seine at Kent Narrows in the eighteenth century yielded a catch, mostly perch, of 173 bushels. Apparently Marylanders were only late in realizing the taste of terrapin soup. Out of wild fowl they made a host of dishes that were said to "abound amongst the humble cottagers." Indeed, canvasback and geese landed in season with such profusion that they made the water off Bohemia Manor look like turf, as another admirer put it, "and when they flew up there was a rushing and vibration of the air like a great storm coming through the trees, and even like the rumbling of distant thunder."[34]

In places like Chestertown gentlemen got together to share news and comment, to "pass away their spare Hours agreeably, and to good purposes." They aimed for civility. More commonly pastimes among native Marylanders grew out of the ruggedness of life in a new society trying to imitate the old. Among some people drinking developed into a sport; planters were "so Generous one to another," an Englishman noted approvingly, that if one came by a gallon of brandy "halfe a dozen honest ffellows" would go "to pay him a vissitt and never leave hime tell all be out." Turkey shoots, besides bringing together rural people whose social occasions were few, allowed demonstrations of prowess that assumed added importance where men still outnumbered women. Cockfighting, which like bear and bull baiting had English origins, also grew popular in the tidewater. It served similar purposes—combat by proxy in the pit displaying the viciously competitive side of a society that provided advancement to only a few and no doubt occasionally allowing the poor man's rooster a sweet victory over the cock belonging to a merchant or large planter.[35]

Nothing, however, represented the values so crucial to the common planter in Maryland, as in Virginia, better than racing horses over a quarter-mile stretch. These events, accompanied by heavy wagering, often took place at country crossroads, ordinaries or taverns, and near the tobacco-loading points where planters rubbed shoulders and competed for good prices. Violent affairs with few rules, these races placed a premium on the skills and derring-do that marked real life. They also demonstrated a man's willingness to defend his reputation, his honor, through his quickness in accepting challenges, the speed of his horse, the size of his bet, and prompt payment of his gambling debts. Accompanied by exuberance utterly at odds with the Quaker faith—"Drunkeness, fighting, Hooping, hallowing, Swearing, Cursing, Wrestling," and contested finishes—horse races understandably caused the Friends anxiety (and the rowdy delight) when they coincided with yearly meetings, as they did in Anne Arundel and Talbot counties in 1715. A special act of the upper house forbade the sale of liquor within two miles of the meetinghouses.[36]

After the 1730s horseflesh figured prominently in further examples of sport as social expression—the efforts of the Chesapeake-born gentry to imitate English country gentlemen. Foxhunting with hounds and livery made its appearance in those years, large planters vying with one another in the quality of their packs and the elaborateness of their entertaining. Helping to distance themselves from the madding crowds at quarter-races, planters in southern Anne Arundel County formed an exclusive social and sporting circle they called the South River Club. There were similar clubs in nearby counties, but none, thought a contemporary, so "well-regulated and sorted like Birds of a Feather."[37] In 1746 the South River Club made a point of drinking toasts and firing a cannon to celebrate the royal victory over Scottish Jacobite rebels at Culloden Moor. Meantime Maryland men of means like Samuel Ogle, governor (with interruptions) between 1731 and 1752, his brother-in-law Benjamin Tasker, Jr., Dr. Thomas Hamilton of Prince George's County, and Samuel Galloway of West River joined a circle of Virginians in importing and breeding blooded stock. The first thoroughbred had been brought to Virginia in 1730; over the next forty years nearly one hundred English horses and mares descended from the Middle Eastern "foundation" stallions arrived in the Chesapeake. Their owners began racing according to English rules that tested the blooded horses' endurance as well as speed—usually running three heats at distances of three or four miles.

Anyone could plainly see that the thoroughbred symbolized social station. Only the wealthy could afford to invest in thoroughbreds, only blooded horses stood a chance racing against others, and their beauty was unmatched by the ordinary planter's smaller, though sturdy, mount. In 1743 Ogle and others in and around Annapolis formed an English-style jockey club and in two years began holding plate, purse, and cup races that drew entries from all over the Chesapeake region. Upper and Lower Marlborough, Joppa Town, Elkridge, and Chestertown staged similar fall and spring events. A celebrated sweepstakes race between Maryland and Virginia champions took place in December 1752 in Gloucester County, Virginia. William Byrd III, who had put up his horse Trial against all challengers, watched in surprise as Tasker's imported mare Selima defeated Trial and several other entries for a heavy purse of Spanish coin. Later, after four days of fall racing at Annapolis, the royal customs official William Eddis assured a London correspondent that "there are few meetings in England better attended, or where more capital horses are exhibited."[38]

While this love of display and outdoor sports did not rule out reflection, arts, and letters, neither did the emphasis on prowess and practical expertise much encourage things intellectual among the gentry. Maryland legislators

THE
Commendation
of Cockes, and Cock-
fighting.

Wherein is fhewed, that Cocke-
*fighting was before the com-
ming of Chrift.*

LONDON,
Printed for *Henrie Tomes*, and are
to be fold at his Shop ouer a-
gainft Graies Inne gate in Holburne,
1 6 o 7.

Left, An early-seventeenth-cen-
tury British volume touting the
gentleman's sport of cockfighting. *Folger Shakespeare Library.*
Below, "The End of the Hunt."
Artist unknown, American or
British, probably mid-eighteenth
century. *National Gallery of Art,
Washington, D.C.*

in this period did recognize the importance of schools, and occasionally made gestures toward establishing them. An act passed in 1723 erecting a school and board of visitors in each county sought to improve the "natural Abilities and Acuteness, (which seems not to be inferior to any)" of Maryland youth. A few years later the assembly ordered schoolmasters, whose income partly derived from levies on imported Irish servants and black slaves, to take under instruction all the poor children their visitors or overseers believed practicable. Schools in Queen Anne's, Kent, and Somerset counties stood on firm ground in the 1730s and 1740s, and Frederick established a school soon after its founding. The Anglican academy of the Reverend Thomas Bacon in Talbot and Samuel Finley's Presbyterian school at Nottingham, Prince George's, earned glowing reputations in the mid-eighteenth century. Yet legislated support for education never matched the need. King William's School in Annapolis, a small group of buildings enclosed by a wall on the south grounds of the state house, never prospered as Governor Nicholson had hoped—its funding, based on fur exports and duties on enumerated luxuries, never proved adequate. Its sister academy in Talbot never materialized. Most counties failed to open free schools.[39]

Among the reasons for these shortcomings, which included the jealousies of shore and denomination, the indifference of the planting gentry may have been fatal. The average planter in Virginia and Maryland alike in the eighteenth century preferred horses and cards to books. Most of them fretted about education only if they believed themselves successful enough to acquire some sign of breeding. Each family of substance saw to its own, and if adequate, the schooling of young men—women's roles, men agreed, required little learning—seldom could have been called rigorous. "The young fellows," said a visitor simply, "are not much burden'd with Study." Typically this training involved the attentions of a tutor, followed by a few years at a rural minister's academy, and then immersion in planting. Some students went on to Annapolis or Williamsburg, where the College of William and Mary benefited from tobacco taxes levied on both Maryland and Virginia exports. A small number served an apprenticeship in a law office or merchant house, and fewer still enjoyed an English education and read law at the Inns of Court in London.[40]

Not eager to tax themselves for schools, men of this intellectual experience kept books that met their immediate needs. There were noteworthy exceptions, libraries that an educated Englishman or Continental gentleman would proudly have shown visitors. The Reverend Bacon of Talbot County, the Eastern Shore factor and small planter Henry Callister, Daniel Dulany the Elder, Dr. Charles Carroll and his son, the Eastern Shore student of agriculture John Beale Bordley and his half-brother, Stephen Bordley of Annapolis, all assembled distinguished libraries. But understandably the planter's reading habits reflected his interests and condition: his library contained fewer Latin and Greek classics, folios of English literature, and multivolume histories than tracts on farming, law, politics, and practical mathematics—including navigation. For light reading a Maryland gentleman might have turned to London periodicals like Addison and Steele's *Tatler* and *Spectator*. Planters' libraries, besides the Bible, usually included such catechistic tracts as an anti-Quaker booklet entitled *The Snake in the Grass* and the Book of Common Prayer.

The fifth Lord Baltimore's brother, Benedict Leonard Calvert, who before his death in 1732 served four years as governor of Maryland, had been educated at Oxford and come to America in hopes of writing a history of the colony during his term. In letters home that were overly harsh but indicative of the intellectual gossamer he found and the mercantile focus he noticed in Chesapeake society, he described Maryland as "this unpolished part of the universe." "Our Conversation runs on planting Tobacco and such other improvements of trade," he reported ruefully, "as neither the Muses inspire, nor Classic Authors treat of."[41]

Had the polished Governor Calvert lived longer, he might have grown well pleased with life in Maryland; quite likely he would have enjoyed Annapolis. From humble beginnings it had grown "rich and opulent," wrote Cook in *Sotweed Redivivus*. He sang of Annapolis as "The famous Beau *Metropolis* / Of *Maryland*." Andrew Burnaby, an English minister given to understatement, discovered the town to be pleasant—small and neat—at mid-century, when the town fathers purchased its first fire wagon. Consisting of perhaps one hundred and fifty households, visited regularly by ships in the British trade (though not promising as a deepwater port), it had begun to earn a reputation for luxury and culture. Many leading Maryland families—the Carrolls, Bordleys, and Dulanys among them—had made their homes in Annapolis, where the "grave and ancient enjoy the blessings of respectable society," noted William Eddis, "while the young and gay have various amusements to engage their hours of relaxation."[42]

Annapolis artisans proved the town at least somewhat deserving its renown for opulence. For many years Marylanders of means had purchased New England furniture and Philadelphia silver while preferring English luxury items to all others. Now, if they wished (and not all did), they could patronize a growing number of local silver and goldsmiths, makers of cabinets and clocks, and portrait painters. In about 1730 Philip Syng, Sr., moved to Annapolis from Philadelphia to open a silver and watch shop. Possibly after an apprenticeship with Syng, John Inch in 1741 began plying his trade in the capital. There, as in Chestertown, Easton, and Baltimore Town, the work usually ran to repairing imported pieces and making commonplace items like knee buckles and simple jewelry. Inch, no different from the others, supplemented his craftly income by keeping a tavern, renting boats, trading in sugar, and dealing in indentured servants. In 1743 he received a commission to make a silver trophy for the Annapolis races, a simple but original creation that must have given him much pleasure. Within three years John Anderson, an arrival from Liverpool, began working in Annapolis, making furniture "in the neatest, cheapest, and newest mode." Later Annapolis craftsmen included William Faris, a well-known silversmith in the southern colonies, and the talented cabinetmakers Gamaliel Butler and John Shaw.[43]

Annapolis also became the center of literary and artistic life on the Tobacco Coast. After 1726, with the arrival of an English-born printer, William Parks, the town had a press, and the next year, in the *Maryland Gazette*, the first newspaper in the Chesapeake. In addition to printing the official proceedings and acts of the assembly, Parks published political broadsides, literary works like Cook's poetry, an almanac, a primer, and religious sermons. When Parks left for Williamsburg in 1737, a gifted member of an old colonial printing family, Jonas Green, took his place in this publishing work. In 1745 Green revived the *Gazette*, which had lapsed in 1734. He began writing political and critical pieces—and accepting locally written material—that gave the paper weighty voice and sparkling character. By opening a bookstore in Annapolis, Green's assistant on the *Gazette* between 1758 and 1766, William Rind, added further to the intellectual liveliness of the town.

Thus Annapolis suggested the importance of urban focus and patronage in the life of expression. Many a planter with his wife and children played musical instruments and performed for themselves and neighbors; Annapolis attracted instructors in dance and drew professional musicians who by the 1740s performed regular concerts. Some of the chamber music heard there was the work of the Reverend Bacon, an estimable amateur composer, whose parish had an active musical calendar of its own. The curtain went up on Maryland theater in June 1752, when a "Company of Comedians" began a two-month stand playing John Gay's *The Beggar's Opera* and David Garrick's *The Lying Valet*. This troupe later divided its time between Annapolis and Williamsburg, with occasional performances at Upper Marlborough, Port Tobacco, and Chestertown to please crowds attending horse races. By 1770 the appeal of these theatrical and musical events led to a subscription drive to build a new playhouse in Annapolis. When it opened in the fall of 1771 it apparently was the first brick theater in the colonies. One member of the audience that evening, George Washington, often attended plays and races in the capital.

The inner and fastest wheel in Annapolis cultural circles was the Tuesday Club, made up of a dozen or more gentlemen of Annapolis and its locale (but countless honorary members) who after 1745 gathered at members' homes to share convivial Tuesday evenings. The clubbers tended to be professional or clerical, though Witham Marshe had made his mark as a scribe during negotiations with the Iroquois in 1744. Several of them were born in Scotland; all were educated. They delighted in whimsy, wit, and science,

Title page illustration from John Playford's *The Dancing Master* (London, c. 1725). *Folger Shakespeare Library*

poked ceaseless fun at one another, conducted an annual parade through the streets of Annapolis, and supplied much of the talent that went into local music making and essay and verse writing for the *Gazette*. Secretary of the club, and with Jonas Green one of the founders, was Dr. Alexander Hamilton, an Edinburgh-trained physician whose interests extended from smallpox research to illustrating books to belles-lettres. Clergymen in the circle included Henry Addison, rector of St. John's Parish, Piscataway, Prince George's County, and a graduate of Queen's College, Oxford; and Thomas Bacon, who crossed the bay for meetings and served as official songster. Bacon's brother Anthony was a member, as was the elder Dulany's son and Hamilton's brother-in-law, Walter Dulany. Because Charles Cole was wealthy and liked to entertain, the members named him perpetual president. The Tuesday Club turned in one of its most amusing performances when in 1745 it used the *Gazette* to satirize the poetry of a worthy Anglican divine, Thomas Cradock, who belonged to a rival group known as the Baltimore Bards. A poetic "war" ensued in the pages of the Annapolis paper, much to the delight of many readers. Hamilton's mock "History" of the Tuesday Club, describing its "downfall" from simple fun and fare to "luxury and excess," typified the enjoyment its members took in deflating the pompous and laughing at themselves. Hamilton's own persona in the tale was "Loquacious Scribble, M.D.," and in it the bard might have spoken for Maryland in poking fun at Virginia dignity: Colonel William Fitzhugh, a member of the club who had moved to Maryland from Virginia, became "Col. Comico Butman"; Hamilton's stuffy opening discussion of the club's background and pedigree apparently lampooned the introduction the Virginia writer William Byrd wrote to his "History of the Dividing Line."

The Georgian home of mid-eighteenth-century Maryland epitomized the

"Second grand Anniversary Procession" of the Tuesday Club. Pen and ink drawing attributed to Dr. Alexander Hamilton, 1747. *MHS*

order, balance, and gracious living that marked life at the highest reaches of society. A style that owed much to Christopher Wren's designs for middle-class English homes during Queen Anne's reign, Georgian design came to America by way of several architectural handbooks published in England in the late 1720s. By about 1732, when work began on the central part of Read-bourne, a brick country house in Queen Anne's County, the style clearly had arrived in both Maryland and Virginia. In early colonial form the brick Georgian mansion stood two stories high, with hipped or gabled roof and sashed windows placed evenly on either side of a paneled, pedimented front door that opened into a great hallway and staircase. Interiors, calculated to be just as imposing yet comfortable, featured high ceilings, richly carved woodwork around doors and fireplaces, and a floor plan as ordered as the facade. In the third quarter of the century, builders added hyphens and wings to central blocks, creating the five-part houses that marked the apogee of colonial architecture.

Employing the imported craftsmen who put up these structures, successful Marylanders soon made the elegance and symmetry of Georgian architecture—including its towering chimneys—a statement of their own achievements. Annapolis did not grow as Nicholson had planned, but its brick Georgian town houses were stunning in their variety. The Worthington and Callahan families built brick homes on the new design. At the corner of Back or Tabernacle Street (later College Avenue) and King George Street, Dr. William Stevenson completed another such structure—the brick laid in alternating long- and short-side Flemish bond—not long before his death in 1739. In about 1731 Edmund Jenings, secretary of the colony and a member of the council, began building a noteworthy dwelling, all brick, on four acres at the foot of East Street, northeast of the city dock. The most imposing Annapolis town houses expanded on the Jenings model. William Paca built one with thirty-seven rooms and extensive gardens to the rear; the home of the third-generation Annapolis merchant James Brice had three-foot-thick walls and chimneys towering seventy or more feet above the street. Craftsmen-architects like William Buckland, drawn by the superior means and soaring ambitions of leading Annapolitans, fashioned buildings that helped make the Maryland capital, as people then said, the Athens of America.

The Georgian style produced especially impressive designs in Prince George's County, where Thomas Snowden's Montpelier (1740) and Belair (1746), Samuel Ogle's home and the site of his horse farm, testified to the continued profits to be made in tobacco. But handsome mid-century houses also commented on the increasingly varied wealth of Marylanders. One occupant of a Georgian town house in Annapolis, William Reynolds, earned his livelihood by making beaver hats, using the main floor of his home as an ordinary or tavern, marketing dry goods, weaving stockings, keeping a livery stable, and selling theater tickets. In Talbot County, Ratcliffe Manor, begun in 1757, was the property of Henry Hollyday, a local official and planter–salt merchant. Samuel Galloway's five-part Tulip Hill mansion in Anne Arundel County, begun in about 1756, lay near his profitable West River shipyard. The builder of Readbourne, James Hollyday, a Prince George's native, had married the widow of Edward Lloyd II; his diversified farming followed prevailing practice on the Eastern Shore. In Baltimore County the ironmaster Caleb Dorsey built Belmont in 1738.

"On my arrival in Maryland, I thought there was something pleasanter in the Country than in Virginia," wrote a French gentleman in 1765; he thought the land "beter Cultivated and setled." Capitalizing on the riches of earth and water, Marylanders where possible placed their homes to complement both—to take in fully "the very beautiful prospects" visitors seldom failed to note. While the boxwoods and terraces did have English prototypes, the

The MAIN FACADE of

The Brice House - Annapolis - Maryland

(as restored.)

Built in 1740 — Scale of Feet

0 10 20 30 40

Hugh A. Simpson Del.

Brice House, Annapolis, 1767–73. From *Great Georgian Houses of America*, vol. 2 (New York, 1937).

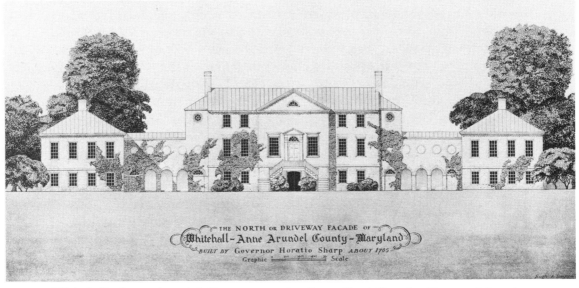

THE NORTH OR DRIVEWAY FACADE OF

Whitehall - Anne Arundel County - Maryland

BUILT BY Governor Horatio Sharp ABOUT 1765

Graphic — Scale

Whitehall, Anne Arundel County, c. 1765. From *Great Georgian Houses of America*, vol. 1 (New York, 1933).

Chesapeake setting—gardens sloping gradually from house to waterside—lent extraordinary beauty to some of these homes. In the 1760s distinguished travelers found a welcome at Horatio Sharpe's yet unfinished Whitehall, seven miles from Annapolis, an ambitious country house that borrowed classical forms. As if serving as a symbol of Maryland at the time, Whitehall struck William Eddis as being of excellent design, the living spaces "well fitted up and perfectly convenient." The grounds surrounding the house he believed "so judiciously disposed that utility and taste are everywhere happily united; and when the worthy owner has completed his extensive plan," Eddis wrote, "Whitehall will be one of the most desirable situations in this or in any of the neighboring provinces."[44]

CHAPTER 3

Revolutionary Persuasion

The Revolution was not so much a war as something that took place "in the Minds of the People," John Adams wrote Thomas Jefferson after they both had retired from public life, "and this was effected, from 1760 to 1775." In May 1773 Annapolis townspeople staged a political rally that illustrated Adams's point. The gathering was a mock-burial service—not for a defeated candidate in the recent House of Delegates election; he had escaped embarrassment by dropping out of the race. The funeral was for a document. In the coffin lay a copy of the governor's proclamation of 1770 reasserting the proprietary right to establish the fees officials charged for public services. Heading the procession to the town gallows were two flags, one inscribed "Liberty" and the other "No Proclamation," whose bearers flanked the two victorious candidates, Matthias Hammond and William Paca. Behind the pine box walked a gravedigger carrying a spade. All was silence except for muffled drumbeats and fifers playing a march for the dead. Hammond and Paca made graveside speeches, the coffin was lowered into the ground, and small cannon fired shots of little mourning.

By this elaborate ceremony and similar ones, Marylanders experienced a double revolution. Before cutting ties with Great Britain, they rejected a proprietary order that was almost a century and a half old. The crowd, "a great concourse of citizens, and gentlemen from the country," suggested the groundswell of popular participation that the business of resistance encouraged—a link between the local issue that brought Hammond and Paca victory in that last colonial election and the Continental movement for independence. This liturgy for a document also made clear the importance of political concepts in the change of mind Adams referred to. "The Proclamation / The Child of FOLLY and OPPRESSION," read an inscription on the coffin: "It is wished, that all similar attempts against the rights of a free people may meet with equal abhorrence; and that the court party, convinced by experience of the impotency of their interest, may never hereafter disturb the peace of the city by their vain and feeble exertions to bear down the free and independent citizens."

With the cat of revolt let out of the bag, gentlemen and people whom gentlemen regarded as lesser sorts maneuvered to set the direction and distance of change. No one in Maryland and certainly not John Adams in Boston knew what the outcome of revolution would be. "That is so eccentric a Colony," Adams said of Maryland in 1776, "sometimes so hot, sometimes so cold; now so high, then so low—that I know not what to say about or to expect from it." Yet "when they get agoing," Adams finished, "I expect some wild extravagant Flight or other from it. To be sure they must go beyond every body else when they begin to go."[1]

⚭

Most mid-eighteenth-century Marylanders thought of themselves as loyal subjects of the king. Born and reared in one of the oldest English colonies in America, six weeks' or more sailing time from the Mother Country, they were somewhat like children, they themselves admitted, dependent upon the wisdom and strength of the parent nation. In this view the British mercantile system had as its object the good of the whole family. Marylanders learned to live within it. Growing the Orinoco tobacco that did not command much of an English market, they might have complained of the "enumeration" policy by which their staple traveled first there or to Scotland before being reexported to the European continent. Since the Maryland iron industry began by making bulk rods and bars for export to Britain, the Iron Act of 1750—prohibiting colonial manufacture of finished iron products—had less effect in Maryland than in Pennsylvania, but it frustrated economic growth all the same. The lords of trade and plantations, expecting Maryland and Virginia to produce revenue by growing tobacco, also prohibited the importation of salt into the Chesapeake—a restriction that prevented the export of salt-cured fish. The assembly did protest against the rule between 1730 and 1760, the proprietor himself petitioning the board on behalf of the colony. Marylanders endured economic regulation for practical reasons as well as emotional ones. Sailing the Atlantic and Mediterranean, colonists benefited from the respect others paid the Royal Navy; a strong homeland provided a foil against the stratagems of the French and Indians to the west.

One home measure that greatly angered "children" in the Chesapeake concerned crime and punishment. Great Britain, changing rapidly from a country of rural villages with common pasture lands to an industrial-commercial nation, spawned a huge number of urban vagrants and law-breakers. Officials differed on how to punish these offenders until 1717, when Parliament, perfecting what had been a haphazard and small-scale enterprise, adopted a policy of transportation, banishing convicts to the American colonies (usually for seven years). Though publicly subsidized, transportation remained a private business tied to shipping patterns. As a result, almost all of the convicts left England in vessels that made summer landings in Philadelphia or the Chesapeake to take on tobacco, corn, or wheat. In the

"Representation of the Transports going from Newgate to take water at Black-friars"—a contemporary, sardonic view of convicts marching from prison to a vessel bound for America. *Newgate Calendar,* London, n.d.

half-century after Parliament enacted transportation, more than ten thousand British vagabonds, thieves, and cutthroats made their way to Maryland as laborers who during their sentences could be bought and sold as indentured servants.

Typically males of humble origins, the convicts arrived at either Annapolis or Baltimore chained in groups of ninety or more, "wretched, ragged, and lean," as one of them recalled. Buyers came aboard, looked in mouths, and haggled over prices. Low as they were, these prices made convicts, sold in lots of five or fewer, attractive investments to marginal planters. Some of these people had skills that made them invaluable as coopers, blacksmiths, carpenters, bricklayers, wheelwrights, glassblowers, and the like. A few knew or learned something of clerking in shops. Most of them had no trade they could ply within the law; if they did not go into farming, they went to users of heavy labor. The Principio and Baltimore iron firms, among others, used felons as diggers, woodcutters, and drovers. Convicts worked in lumbering and shipbuilding. The felon population grew largest in the economically diverse counties near the major ports. Indeed criminal labor became one barometer of industrial activity. By 1755 in Baltimore, Anne Arundel, Charles, and Queen Anne's counties one adult white male in ten was a British convict.[2]

Even proponents of transportation admitted that it dumped the "Scum and Dregs" of Britain on American shores. Most of the ruffians looked the part—often deformed by scars, missing ears or fingers. They could be fearsome in appearance, ruthless, and threatening to their owners. One developed a "wild look" if taxed with anything to do; another's master noted that he had an "insolent daring Aspect" when provoked. To judge from the *Maryland Gazette,* which printed an average of thirty-three runaway notices a year, convict labor did little to edify the master-servant relationship—always potentially explosive. No doubt the felon's attitude made a difference. One convicted thief, Mary Stanford, said that "living in foreign Parts was worse than a disgraceful and shameful Death at Home" and pleaded to be hanged rather than sent to the Chesapeake. James Brown declared himself "terrified and affrighted" by the labor convicts there were said to do. Another felon described the work as "intended for Horses and not for Christians." The low, grubbing conditions in which many masters lived must also have influenced their dealings with these servants, who bore "the stamp of infamy."[3]

In any event, accounts of abuse, which had not been strikingly common in cases of earlier indentures, appeared often in letters to England and in the public record. Joseph Lewin was purchased by "a very rigid, severe Master" who beat him "cruelly and unmercifully." In August 1747 the *Maryland Gazette* remarked on the "rigorous Usage and Ill-treatment of Masters to Servants." Four years later a convict working in a field went berserk while his master and mistress attended a funeral, attacking their children with an axe and kitchen knife. Another convict, who reportedly had cut off his hand rather than work another day in Maryland, died in a Philadelphia street. A few stories had happy endings. Convicts with skills did well in servitude and afterward. A transported Oxford thief became a Baltimore County physician with "bisness a nuf for 2." Sarah Wilson, who apparently had once served in the queen's household, escaped to South Carolina and passed herself off as royalty, promising the planters whose hospitality she enjoyed commissions, promotions, and favors. But most convicts lived miserable lives. Drunkenness was common among them, and in 1747 the Annapolis coroner noted the increasing incidence of felon-servant suicide.[4]

Americans could do little about convict transportation except to repeat protests against it. "I wish you would be so kind," William Byrd II wrote a friend in England, "as to hang all your felons at home." Benjamin Franklin's suggested remedy was for America to return the favor and ship rattlesnakes to England. The Maryland council complained in 1719 that transportation, threatening the peace and property of the colony, would discourage worthier immigration and prompt settlers then in Maryland to depart. Aside from the danger that convicts would cause a crime wave, Marylanders and Virginians worried that they might unite in rebellion with slaves. The provincial court in 1721 reported criminal prosecutions much increased since the "late Importation of Convicts," and the grand jury in 1723 predicted that felons would teach their "Wicked Practices" to servants and Negroes. While no harmony developed between white convicts and black slaves and the actual criminal influence of imported felons remained difficult to gauge, Maryland lawmakers struggled to discourage their sale. The lower house considered demanding a bond of every purchaser to help ensure the good conduct of his felon-servant, and opponents of transportation later proposed a head tax on each convict landed in Maryland.[5] Such legislation stood no chance of British approval. Convict transportation remained in force, many Marylanders holding that the policy punished them, not the criminals.

More than differences with British authority, quarrels with the proprietor and his friends occupied the minds of Maryland political leaders after Lord Baltimore's restoration in 1715. The soothing language of Baltimore's governor (and uncle), Charles Calvert, did not change the basic truth of conflict between the interests of the proprietor and those of ordinary Marylanders. In an address to members of the lower house in October 1722 Calvert said that Lord Baltimore stood to them "as a Bountifull Indulgent Father towards a dutiful Deserving son"; the governor in the same message announced that the proprietor expected to redress the balance between his prerogatives and their "Privileges" and that Baltimore had vetoed two acts of the previous session.[6] In the royal period gubernatorial vetoes had been rare, and in English practice no monarch had turned down parliamentary legislation since 1707. The young Lord Baltimore seemed not to have read his history.

He had read the Maryland charter, however, and he expected to exercise his rights fully. Tenant-in-chief of the colony, he, like his forebears, collected numerous minor fines, manor rents, and fees for ferries, commissions, and licenses. When one purchased land, the "caution money" went to the proprietor. The proprietor was entitled to rents on patented land, but since 1719, when the assembly had passed short-term export duties that were supposed to be "equivalent" to the quitrents (they raised more than five thousand pounds in 1731), this principal source of income had become subject to house appropriation, renewals, and bargaining. The proprietor also enjoyed revenue from the old port or tonnage duty that the assembly enacted for defense in 1661; since the royal period the duty, amounting to as much as fourteen hundred pounds a year, had gone to Lord Baltimore as private income. The restored proprietor claimed monies the assembly in 1704 had raised for the then-royal governor by taxing each exported hogshead of tobacco twelve pence.

Besides supplying Baltimore's personal income and supporting the Anglican church, Marylanders through assorted payments contributed to a governmental structure that burdened them considerably and left most of them on the "outside." Allowances for sitting legislators, judges, and their clerks represented reasonable public costs. But a complex system of fees made any official transaction in Maryland expensive and inconvenient. The provincial chancellor collected fees for 32 duties that included sealing an original writ (five pounds of tobacco) to sealing a land patent (ninety pounds). The secretary of the province earned from five to more than two hundred pounds of tobacco for 127 listed services. Sheriffs were due nine pounds of tobacco for swearing a witness in county court. The number of their paid functions exceeded 60. The commissary general or judge of probate listed 43 fees, the county court clerks 61. Various criers, inspectors, deputies, registers, and keepers collected fees or commissions, as did the surveyor general and examiner general of the land office and naval or port officers. All of them served at the pleasure of the proprietor or his chosen principals. Lord Baltimore filled the Anglican parsonages. As before the 1689–92 revolution, the governor represented him in the colony. Members of the council of state—the proprietor's appointed advisors and the upper house of assembly when it met—held many of the most lucrative offices. Without tendering posts of honor and profit, Governor Calvert's successor wrote Baltimore, he could not easily persuade a man to sit on the council. Adding a touch of mystery to the establishment was Lord Baltimore's "court" in London—his behind-the-scenes principal secretary and one or more quiet assistants who were available to plead the proprietor's causes before British officials. In Maryland supporters of the proprietary regime adhered to a faction known as the "court" party that at times filled as many as four of every ten seats in the House of Delegates.

Events in the colony pointed toward eventual confrontation between friends of Baltimore's court and its critics. The proprietor claimed the right to set fees by his charter authority to create offices; members of the lower house saw those fees as taxes that only they could levy. Since 1635 the lords Baltimore had claimed the right to decide the extent to which the common law and acts of Parliament applied in Maryland; the lower house claimed all the protections of English law.

Issues dividing the better-off and the less well-to-do easily led to bitter exchanges on these fundamental, constitutional disagreements. A glut in the tobacco market having brought another drop in prices in 1722, elections of that year returned to the lower house a majority of delegates who were eager to repeal a recent law prohibiting shipment of low-quality "trash" tobacco. Though the measure placed a burden on poor planters, the council refused to consider repeal. In response house members, with an eye on the plainness of their constituents, called the proprietor's councillors "Assistants to Prerogative and Dependent on it." Seizing the moment, Daniel Dulany and Thomas Bordley wrote resolutions requiring judges "To do equall Law and right to all the Kings Subjects rich and poor"—even when commanded otherwise by letters from the king or proprietor—and to determine cases according to the statutes and "reasonable Customs of England and of this province." Lord Baltimore and his attorneys recognized in the Dulany-

Bordley resolutions a challenge to proprietary power and quickly disallowed them. In retaliation the house refused to compensate councillors for their expenses, caustically remarked on their personal interest in the proprietary establishment, called for the election of sheriffs, and suggested the reduction of all the fees Baltimore's officers received. The council complained that house members turned "everything into banter and ridicule."[7] When in 1725 the governor called for new elections, anti-court delegates cleverly used the printing press to make their case against proprietary privilege.

Lord Baltimore sent his younger brother Benedict Leonard Calvert to replace Charles and pacify the delegates, but the 1728 session, the first in several years, produced more acrimony. Still concerned with the hardships of ordinary planters, the lower house legislated a limit on the number of tobacco plants one could put in, and as part of the same austerity measure scaled down by about 25 percent the salaries that the established clergy and all proprietary officers received. The house reenacted the measure prescribing the duties of judges and adopting English law. The proprietor once more refused his assent—leaving nothing in the statute books that provided for collection of his fees and threatening to bring government to a standstill.

Members of the lower house protested what they called a violation of "our happy constitution," and again they took their case outside the state house doors. Through the Annapolis printer William Parks, Dulany in December 1728 published a pamphlet arguing that "the *People of Maryland* are *Freemen*" entitled to all the protections of English common and statute law. If Marylanders permitted the proprietor to deny them those privileges, they would render their "Lives, Liberties, and Properties, Precarious." Among provincial complaints was the lack of paper currency that would promote economic growth and offer an alternative to tobacco payments of some fees; unless the house wrote a law making the paper system conditional on Lord Baltimore's approval, the council refused its assent. Exploring the record of earlier assemblies with his provincial history in mind, Benedict Calvert in October 1729 wrote his lordship a long letter offering perspective on all the issues that excited the lower house and the "proud, petulant and Ignorant planters" who tried to keep "the Common necessary Support of Government so much under their Thumb."[8]

Lord Baltimore took matters into his own hands. After sending Samuel Ogle to replace his brother, who died returning to England, he himself sailed to Maryland, landing in November 1732. Greeting him and Lady Baltimore at Annapolis were bonfires, cannon salutes, a poem in the *Maryland Gazette*, and the cheers of townsmen warmed by free rum punch. Not for almost a half-century, since 1684, had a Lord Proprietor sat in the province. The social swirl in the capital that winter reached new heights of elegance, but all the while Baltimore attended to business—the controversy with the Penns, settlement of western Maryland, and above all the spring meeting of the assembly. He inspected the revenue books, consulted with lawyers, saw

Left, Daniel Dulany the Elder (1687–1753). *Right*, Thomas Bordley (1682–1726). Both paintings by unidentified artists, c. 1715. *MHS*

firsthand the need for currency in the colony. He sent for Daniel Dulany, before whom he dangled three choice places in the proprietary establishment—agent and receiver general, judge of the vice-admiralty court, and attorney general.

Then, in March, Baltimore presided over a watershed session of the assembly. He consented to an act floating ninety thousand pounds in one- to twenty-shilling notes, to be backed by tobacco export revenues invested in Bank of England stock. Surprising members of the lower house, Baltimore rejected a bill continuing the equivalency-of-quitrents scheme. Instead his lordship revived the system of collecting rents and ordered Dulany, the former house leader now crossed over to the proprietor's side, to arrange for gathering them. Removing another form of leverage that the lower house had employed in recent years, Baltimore next announced that his governor in the colony would be paid by the 1704 duty rather than by periodic appropriation. Refusing to bargain over officers' fees, the proprietor in April 1733 simply published a new list setting them forth, as his brother Benedict had advised, and left for England that summer.

❧

Much as did the career of Sir Thomas Lawrence, Dulany's decision to join the proprietary forces illustrated the sway of self-interest in Maryland politics. The proprietary-antiproprietary struggle may have appeared simply to

be between "ins" and "outs." Yet despite Dulany's choice and the real rewards that went with allegiance to Baltimore's court, political ideas also were
at issue. Leaders of the lower house had assumed a role in Maryland that
closely paralleled that of late-seventeenth- and early-eighteenth-century
British Whigs, many of them landholding squires who between sessions of
Commons sat in the country and scornfully watched the ploys of clever men
in the corrupting royal court. They worried about the course of concentrated
power. From the speeches and writings of Whig or Opposition leaders like
Algernon Sidney, John Trenchard, Thomas Gordon, and James Burgh, colonials adopted principles that made sense to their own experience. Only a jealous regard for liberties (including discretionary powers that the lower house
gradually had acquired) would preserve them. One had to be suspicious of
all government power (especially when distant) and keep a tight hand on
the public purse strings. A constitution balanced among the one, the few,
and the many (king, lords, commons; proprietor, council, and House of
Delegates) provided the best security against the tyranny of any one element. Protections of law and constitution, grounded in human experience
and sacred providence, had to be defended at all costs. In the eyes of many
Maryland burgesses the proprietary system with its "placemen," privilege,
and arbitrary authority closely resembled the self-serving and cliquish court
at London's Whitehall. Delegates who imitated its opponents called themselves the "country" party.

Having lost Dulany to defection and Bordley to early death, the country-
men remained quiet for several years after Lord Baltimore's departure. Better
prices helped to account for the peace and quiet Governor Ogle hoped to
maintain. Nonetheless, in time new house leaders emerged—Dr. Charles
Carroll (a convert to Protestantism), James Tilghman of Talbot County,
Edward Tilghman and Robert Lloyd of Queen Anne's, Thomas Ringgold of
Kent—and members of the House of Delegates remained sensitive to slight.
Ogle's calm turned to storm in 1738, when the lower house ordered an apology from an Eastern Shore justice of the peace; accused of misconduct, he
had called the delegates sons of bitches and worse. Ogle sent the angry burgesses home and directed a new election. The next assembly turned out to
be even more refractory. With Carroll serving as one spokesman, it restated
the case for English law in Maryland and protested Lord Baltimore's arbitrary
setting of officers' fees. It refused to renew a law for defense taxes unless the
governor agreed to the appointment of an agent in London to represent the
concerns of the people, as distinguished from the proprietor, of Maryland.
Ogle refused and prorogued this assembly, as well. Maintaining that because
the dismissed lawmakers had passed no laws they had not constituted an
assembly, Ogle kept in force the old arms duty for another year—it was
supposed to expire, he argued, "at the end of the next Session of Assembly."[9] The governor's high-handed approach proved his downfall. The next
spring, when British authorities demanded financial support for a war with

Spain, house members tied a modest money bill to a reduction in proprietary officers' fees. Ogle, enraged and frustrated, challenged a delegate to a duel. The house ordered his arrest for breach of privilege.

During the 1747 assembly session the stalemate ended long enough for house and council to agree on a tobacco inspection act that carried both political and economic importance. Maryland Orinoco leaf never enjoyed a high reputation among London or Scottish buyers, and after the Virginia assembly in 1730 passed an act regulating the quality of exports from that colony, demand for the Maryland product dropped even lower. Calls for a similar Maryland law had been loud among larger planters. Advocates of the inspection bill wrote persuasive pieces for the *Maryland Gazette*; opponents argued that a typical small planter might harvest 1,500 pounds of tobacco, only 1,000 of which would clear inspection, and that rents would leave him only 200 pounds, or about £1 13s. for a year's purchases. The competitive disadvantage of Maryland tobacco finally won over most critics; the inspection act passed after long debate and many votes. At designated points throughout the colony, locally chosen officials were to grade superior Maryland leaf and to burn the "trash" that failed inspection. For approved hogsheads planters received certificates that sufficed for payment of fees requiring tobacco. Yet the lower house did not accept inspection without squeezing concessions from its enemies on the governor's council. The act forced proprietary officers to accept currency as well as tobacco certificates in payment; it also reduced by about one-quarter and fixed by law the fees of proprietary officers—thus setting aside Lord Charles's exercise of prerogative fourteen years before. Councillors and proprietor accepted this portion of the law in order to gain the whole, calculating that inspected tobacco, worth more, actually would sustain the level of officers' compensation.

When inspection passed, delegates and councillors drank toasts in the council chamber to one another's health. The rarity of that concord became apparent in the years following. Ogle's successor, Thomas Bladen—whose wife was Lady Baltimore's sister and whose sister had married Benjamin Tasker—found the delegates truculent and mean spirited. After obtaining an outlay of £4,000 for a governor's residence, Bladen discovered that the money went far enough only to complete the first floor of his ambitious plan. He returned to the delegates for more funding at the same time he and they differed on the powers the house could confer on emissaries to a planned meeting with the Iroquois. The house declined to make any additional appropriation for "Bladen's Folly," and the unfinished mansion, exposed to the weather and "going to ruin," testified to the political impasse. Far more serious than housing the governor was protecting the frontiers. When in October 1753 another governor, Horatio Sharpe, appealed for funds to help thwart the French intrusion into the Ohio country, he also met with rebuff. While members of the lower house stated a willingness to aid neighbors and repel invasion, they then saw no "pressing occasion" for a money bill. Fierce independence and jealousy also marked the response of the house to the Albany Plan of the next year. Though Benjamin Franklin's proposal for a loose American union won acceptance in none of the colonies or in London, members of the Maryland house not only rejected the plan, they denounced it as a scheme that would "ultimately subvert" their "happy form of government." It might "destroy the rights, liberties, and property of his Majesty's loyal subjects."[10]

Sharpe's tact and firmness and the cruel realities of frontier war suppressed political rivalries once again in the summer of 1754. Word then reached tidewater Maryland of George Washington's surrender at Fort Necessity in western Pennsylvania. The loss of Washington's small force opened the way to French invasion and brought fears of hostile Indian raids. Revealing a hope that some of the tribes would remain friendly, the assembly appropriated £6,000 "towards the defence of the colony of Virginia, attacked by the French and Indians; and for the relief and support of the wives and children of the Indian allies that put themselves under the protection of this government." Volunteer militia units readied themselves to defend settlements like Jonathan Hager's Elizabeth Town near Antietam Creek, which, in the great valley between North and South mountains, stood dangerously exposed. Frederick Town became a rendezvous for troops organized in eastern Maryland. Thomas Cresap at Oldtown, the site of an ancient Indian settlement far up the Potomac, received a commission to raise a company of rangers. These reinforcements made their way westward to Fort Cumberland, on the high ground where Will's Creek met the Potomac and where Washington had established his line of defense. Sharpe, a veteran who temporarily commanded British forces, busied himself gathering supplies for the expedition that finally fell under the command of General Edward Braddock. In the offensive of July 1755, combining British regulars with colonial forces, Braddock refused to employ lessons provincials had learned bitterly in frontier fighting. The savages might have proven formidable "to your raw American militia," he said, "but upon the king's regular and disciplined troops, sir, it is impossible they should make an impression."[11]

Braddock's heedless advance upon Fort Duquesne led to the "most scandalous and disgraceful defeat that ever was heard of," in the words of Daniel Dulany, Jr. Afterward Indians burned farms and murdered families from Fort Cumberland, which the British military abandoned, eastward a hundred miles. A few settlers, like Thomas Cresap's son Michael on Conococheague Creek, barricaded themselves in strongholds; "dressed and painted like Indians" except for their distinguishing red caps, they then ventured forth on raiding parties in the forest, where they killed with vengeance and scalped their victims. Residents as far east as Baltimore and Annapolis heard warnings of Indian attacks. Private persons offered bounties for dead Indians. Governor Sharpe braced for a possible uprising of slaves, servants, and convicts. Rumors spread of Catholic sympathy for the Indians' allies the

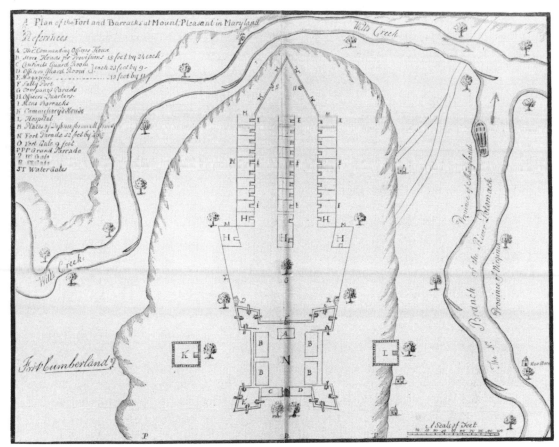

Plan of Fort Cumberland, 1755. From William H. Lowdermilk, *History of Cumberland* (Washington, D.C., 1878). *MHS*

French; "clamors against Popery," Dulany reported, "are as loud as ever." In the midst of this terror and confusion, the governor's only immediate support came from subscription money he obtained from councillors and "gentlemen of the country." Not until May 1756, after a twelve-week session of the assembly, did Sharpe have another military supply bill. By that enactment, £40,000 went primarily toward construction of a fort west of Elizabeth Town, on the Potomac near North Mountain. The fort was named after Frederick, the sixth Lord Baltimore, who had succeeded to the title when Lord Charles died in 1751.[12]

The failure of the Maryland lower house to cooperate fully in financing the war outraged royal administrators and the proprietary elite alike. As usual, an embarrassing deadlock turned on what the country party in the house viewed as a constitutional issue. In this case the question was whether the proprietor should permit taxation of his own lands or use of his own revenues, which delegates still regarded as too high, in paying for the defense of his province. The power to tax, delegates maintained, lay with them, and they guarded that right firmly. "Unhappy is the condition of that people," they wrote in a resolution that later underwent softening, "whose frame of government has such clogs thrown into the wheels of it as will not permit such motions as are absolutely necessary for their own defense and security . . . but at the expense of their rights and privileges." Faced with such "obstinacy," as Sharpe described it, the council finally agreed to the May 1756 bill on terms the lower house had insisted upon. In addition to laying duties on unmarried men according to their means and on luxuries like wines, spirits, and billiard tables, the act placed a tax of twelve pence per hundred acres of land—including Lord Frederick's own holdings. Thus the supply law violated Sharpe's instructions on the special status of proprietary property. It also levied a double tax on Roman Catholic landholders, nasty proof of Protestant fears, and thereby forced Sharpe to deviate from other orders that he respect religious nondiscrimination. The measure provided for house commissioners to work with the governor on the Indian negotiations and defense policies that the proprietor claimed to be his prerogative. Sharpe signed the bill even with its specific instructions on spending.[13]

The country party clearly had learned an old Whig lesson about exploiting circumstances. Maryland's poor showing in the imperial war effort (London newspapers carried sarcastic remarks on Baltimore's wartime sacrifices) greatly embarrassed Lord Frederick, who agreed to the supply law. The next year, when the house tied more appropriations to a 5 percent charge on his quitrents and the incomes of proprietary officers, the council refused assent and in Annapolis yet another pamphlet criticized the proprietary system. Maryland delegates continued to win notice in their defense of local rights.

⌒∞⌒

Vigilant on behalf of liberty, jealous of property rights and constitutional protections, the country party by no means welcomed anyone into its Spartan band. Love of liberty did not carry with it a friendly regard for the "leveling" radicalism of classical democracy. No less than the councillors of Lord Baltimore's "court," members of the country party in the House of Delegates expected deference from those persons beneath them. Usually they received such respect. The "Generality of a Neighbourhood," wrote the *Maryland Gazette* in 1762, by and large "think and act in most Things as some one leading Man among them (of whose Understanding they have a good Opinion) instructs them, and whom they have accustomed themselves to look upon as an Oracle, whose Speeches are infallible."[14] While small planters may have made good followers in these years, a great many other white Marylanders remained beyond the pale of political life—indeed, faced a tough battle to survive.

In several respects the political structure of the colony stood open to criticism. Representation in the assembly increasingly favored the Eastern Shore counties, where white population growth failed to keep up with that on the other side of the bay. After the creation of Frederick County in 1748, both shores contained seven counties and therefore sent an equal number of delegates, four from each county, to Annapolis. That town, succeeding to a privilege earlier allowed St. Mary's City (and a center of court party strength), elected two burgesses. By 1760 neither the Eastern Shore as a whole nor the lower Western Shore any longer registered gains in numbers. Elsewhere in the following decade population increase averaged 20 percent. After the French abandoned Fort Duquesne late in 1758 and the threat of Indian attack subsided, Frederick County—all of old Prince George's west of Rock Creek—grew rapidly, by 54 percent between 1765 and 1775. Both Eastern Shore sensibility and the caution of the proprietary regime prevented a political adjustment to reflect population trends. In 1760 Lord Frederick's principal secretary advised against creating any new counties, pointing out that every new division "by increasing the Number of Delegates increases the number of opponents to the Government."[15] Thirteen years later, when another proprietor answered the pleas of northern Baltimore County citizens by allowing the creation of Harford County, Eastern Shore legislators successfully sustained the balance between shores by obtaining Caroline.

Maryland electoral requirements in these years, besides prescribing oaths that Catholics could not take in good conscience, conformed to an act of 1715. Seeking to follow English precedents "as near as the Constitution of this province will Admitt," that statute limited house membership and voting for delegates to freemen who had patented fifty acres of land or (hereby including well-off tenants) held a "visible estate" worth £40 sterling. By British tradition, electors also had to be native to the realm, at least twenty-one years old, and have paid taxes within twelve months of the election. While requirements for Annapolitans were slightly more relaxed, Maryland law excluded a sizable body of freemen. Virginia at the same time required that white freeholders own only twenty-five acres or hold a long-term lease on that much land. In Prince George's and Talbot counties in the mid-eighteenth century 57 percent of private landholdings smaller than fifty acres were freeholds that would have earned one the right to vote in Virginia. The "visible estate" provision introduced a subjective element, but £40 sterling represented no small sum. The native-born citizenship requirement hindered voting among the Germans of western Maryland. A parliamentary naturalization act of 1740 supposedly invited non-British Protestants in the American colonies to enter the political fold, at least so far as to vote (it did not extend to officeholding), but its complexities prompted Daniel Dulany, Jr., in 1758 to seek a simplified act for Maryland. That measure, important to property titles as well as to political participation, passed the lower house but failed in the council. While Maryland law did not specifically exclude free blacks (as did Virginia) otherwise qualified from voting, custom generally did not encourage them. About one in three white adult males in Maryland could not meet property or religious stipulations.[16]

Few men able to vote found the political process simple or office accessible. County justices established the time of elections, usually no more than a few weeks hence, and the sheriff saw to publicizing the event in church and tavern. On election day the sheriff presided, opening and closing the polls, verifying qualifications, and directing the county court clerk to record each elector's choice—voiced for all to hear—between the gentlemen who "stood" before the public. Candidates presented themselves, as a rule, only after waiting their turn and securing the approval of their peers. Though these office seekers might have complained of the inconvenience of the canvass, their bid largely meant writing letters, soliciting friends, and—until the lower house in 1749 detected abuses among victorious court party candidates—setting out the wine punch and cookie "treats" or pork barbeques that rewarded a journey to the polls. Given the distances between Frederick, for example, and the Conococheague valley or the Georgetown region down the Potomac, justices in some counties established a second polling place or extended the election period over several days. Sheriffs did not enforce the compulsory voting law stiffly; usually about half the eligible voters turned out. While an occasional person of meager property may have hoodwinked the sheriff and voted, Maryland requirements successfully kept the polls and doors of office closed except to the men whose property ensured their political responsibility, their stake in society. Except in Annapolis, small property owners were spectators, and delegates, as William Eddis noticed, were "generally persons of the greatest consequence in their different counties."[17]

Those of lesser consequence in Maryland found their part of the population increasing as the eighteenth century wore on, which meant that politically more and more men were locked outdoors. Land ownership, as always the best index of one's success in the colony, lagged behind the rate of population growth, especially in the older counties. A continuing reason for the rise in tenancy lay in a lack of capital; former servants and convicts who had served their terms could not afford to buy land and labor. A newer cause arrived with Lord Charles's decision to reconstruct the quitrent system, which urged planters to meet their fees by working as much of their land as possible—with tenants if not with slaves. Land costs rose again in eastern Maryland in 1763, when Parliament under the Bute ministry closed land west of the Appalachians to colonial settlement. The pattern varied only slightly on Eastern and Western shores. In Prince George's County in 1771 a population of more than 18,000, with about 2,500 free males, yielded only 775 freeholders. Between 1756 and 1771 population in the county had grown 27 percent, property owners by less than 5 percent. Though Talbot County grew by 32 percent in that period, land ownership declined 7 percent; Queen

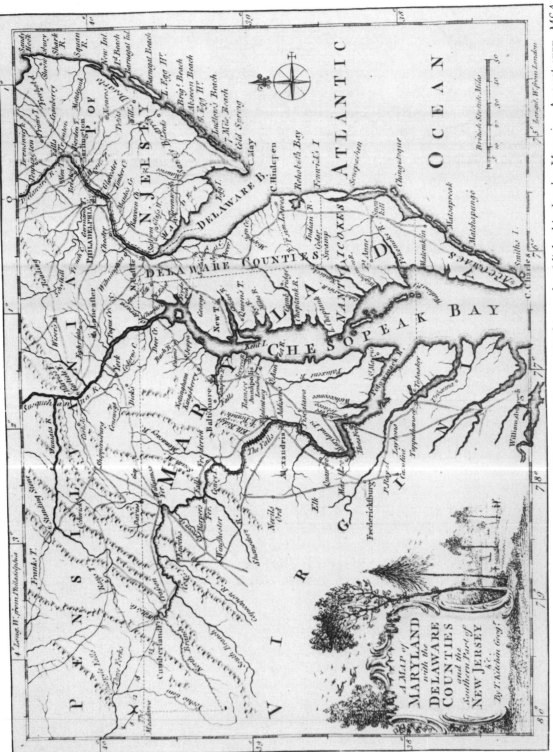

"A Map of Maryland with the Delaware Counties." Drawn by Thomas Kitchin and published in *London Magazine*, August 1757. *MSA*

Anne's grew by 20 percent overall, freeholds by only 4 percent. Baltimore, where population increased in these years by more than 55 percent, registered a gain in landholding—including town lots in Baltimore Town—of 37 percent.[18]

Such figures support contemporary observations of squalor and desperation in the lower ranks of whites. While many "honest industrious" planters with "a small portion of Property" were to be seen in Prince George's County, wrote a native, a "great Part of our People" could be found in "the no less honest, but more poor and laborious one, who rents Land." An English Jesuit priest serving in St. Mary's County in 1759 wrote home that he believed the common people around him "very poor, and not to be compared with the rest of our colonies." His later impressions of the Eastern Shore, where most land had been taken up, were even dimmer. His parishioners consisted of "poor, miserable, abandoned families." Maryland, he wrote, once was a good place for the poor, "but now it is well peopled, the lands are all secured, and the harvest for such is now over." Slaves worked the landlord's land, he reported, "and, of consequence, white servants, after their bondage is out, are strolling about the country without bread." Tenants of Lord Baltimore, before the sale of his twenty-three proprietary manors after 1767, paid lower rents and held longer leases, but their lives were as simple as their approach to farming was "gloomy and barbarous."[19]

Frequently saddled with debt, tenants greatly feared its consequences. The law came to the aid of debtors in certain ways, by encouraging the collection of small debts out of court before a single justice so as to limit court and attorneys' fees, by limiting interest charges, and by allowing debt payment in crops other than tobacco. Otherwise the judicial system kept debtors on a tight leash. They could not leave the colony without a pass, subject to jail and attachment of their property. If a creditor won a suit against a debtor whose assets failed to cover the amount owed, the debtor landed in jail. The condition of Maryland jails remained a scandal throughout this period. The original Annapolis prison, a two-story brick structure twenty-five by fifteen feet, proved so badly constructed that it virtually collapsed of its own weight. A 1731 building, a little larger, consisted of one room atop another; sanitation facilities, limited to a pipe upstairs and a pit in the ground below, offended the prisoners, "the Neighbours and all that pass thereby." Prisoners avoided freezing in winter only by cutting away ceiling joists to burn as firewood; in summer men and women—for whom there were no separate quarters—suffered upstairs from the stench rising from below. Lord Charles on his visit to Maryland thought these conditions "Unchristian." Truly, wrote a committee of the assembly in 1736, "the Gaol of Annapolis besides being a place of Restraint and Confinement has also been a place of Death and Torments to Many Unfortunate People."[20]

County jails seldom were in any better condition, and imprisonment in them left debtors to the mercies of sheriffs. Appointed by the proprietor, sheriffs carried out responsibility for collecting, on a commission basis, various proprietary revenues, which between 1756 and 1766 included quitrents at 10 percent. If a sheriff were "very active and diligent punctual & well acquainted with the People of his County & their Circumstances," according to Lord Baltimore's last governor, he could make the office pay as much as £300 sterling a year. On the cutting edge of Lord Baltimore's collection system, sheriffs also received prisoners' fees that provided little incentive for careful bookkeeping or kindness. Some appointees apparently found it tempting to keep men confined after they should have been released and to hold down costs of food and other necessities. Though presumably most sheriffs were firm yet fair, they could be peremptory, even harsh, with their prisoners. In 1730 inmates of the Prince George's County jail complained to the assembly that the sheriff had "Abused some Languishing Prisoners" and threatened others with "Cruel and Severe Usage for Petitioning the Assembly for their Liberty"—a complaint that led only to a reprimand from that body. The Charles County sheriff, Richard Lee, Jr., gained notoriety in 1769 by keeping fifteen debtors in a jail cell only that many feet square during severe winter weather, then whipping the two prisoners who wrote an appeal to the assembly. When the house petitioned the council for action against this proprietary officer, who had decided to spend the rest of the year in Virginia, it found "not sufficient Ground arising from the Behaviours of the said Sheriff to inflict a further Punishment on him by removing him from his Office." [21]

The convicted debtor whose family could not make good on his debts remained in jail unless he could persuade governor and assembly to release him. Between 1707 and 1774, 845 prisoners, 32 of them women, successfully petitioned for their freedom, and after 1765 the number of released debtors rose to an annual average of about 60 persons. Another 250 requests the assembly denied. Most of these debtors returned to society on condition that they sell all their real and personal goods—except for family clothing, bedding, and the tools of their trade, if any—and divide the proceeds among their creditors. This crude form of bankruptcy amounted to a resolve to sell oneself into servitude. A petition from one Jonathan Martino in 1769 made just that proposal, suggesting the depths to which the poor in Maryland could fall in the period. A prisoner for ten months in a "Clos Dungon," starved, cold in winter, stifled in summer, Martino wrote that he was forty, the father of four. "Your Patitioner is not able with all the small Estate to Comply with his Raspacttive Creditors which he would Be Willing to Surrander up so that he Could obtain his libarty," Martino wrote the governor, as best he could; that liberty, he continued, "he is not like to Get Except Your Excellancy will take it in Your Serious Consideration and Grant that thare may be An Act made Ether to Sall him or to Ralass him out of his Misarable and Daplorable Confindment." [22] By 1768 the assembly had begun establishing almshouses or workhouses for the poor, and in the next eight years provided seven counties with trustees by whose authority the poor would be made to work in return for public housing. Filling the houses posed no problem.

⚬⚬⚬

Planters never hesitated to buy in the spring against the late summer's crop, so that Maryland indebtedness was scarcely confined to tenants or the poor. According to time-honored patterns, small and middling planters borrowed from Maryland merchants or the large merchant-planters. After the 1730s Scottish factors, representing the Glasgow firms most aggressive in the Continental tobacco market, prospered in the Potomac and Patuxent regions by selling on credit. Large planters and merchant-planters often shipped their hogsheads on consignment to British firms, to whom they usually were indebted. Some of them dealt with Maryland merchants who handled large quantities for export.

A growing number of these merchants established themselves in Baltimore Town, where falls and harbor became especially important in marketing Western Shore and Susquehanna Valley wheat. Commercial opportunities begged for investors. Among the earliest were John Stevenson, an Irish-born physician who pioneered in flour exports, and Darby Lux, a British ship captain until the early 1740s, when he settled in Baltimore and went into dry goods. Twenty years later Lux's son William, a town commissioner, had risen to local political prominence while building the family trade in partnership with Daniel Bowly. During the 1760s Baltimore flourished as never before. The French and Indian War spurred demand in the British Empire (and elsewhere, making illegal trade attractive) for Chesapeake products and drew talented newcomers to the town—German merchants and craftsmen from Frederick County, the Scotsman Ebenezer Mackie, and Robert and Samuel Purviance, who were Irish born. Scots-Irish from Pennsylvania and Delaware—John Smith, William Buchanan, James Sterrett, Mark Alexander, and Alexander McKim—moved to Baltimore, mostly attracted by the lucrative wheat and flour market. Ships of Baltimore registry, always entering and clearing through the customshouse at Annapolis, engaged in coastal trading with Virginia, North Carolina, Boston, and Newfoundland; they carried tobacco, iron, and wheat to British ports and grains to Spain and Portugal. From England they imported dry goods, hardware, servants, or convicts. From southern Europe, if they obeyed the law, they returned either in ballast or with Madeira wine. A few ventured to Africa for slaves. Many smaller vessels sailed to the Caribbean sugar plantations with flour, bread, or biscuits, commonly returning with sugar, molasses, rum, or slaves.

Establishing partnerships that spread risk, intermarrying, and drawing younger members of their families into business, these first Baltimore merchant-investors laid a firm foundation for later moneymaking. Their credit arrangements, though vulnerable, enabled them to act as wholesalers of

British imported goods. They diversified their holdings. William Lux built a ropemaking factory—a ropewalk—on his Baltimore County estate. The Purviances and Sterretts entered shipping after setting themselves up as brewers. In 1761 John and Charles Ridgely, already exporters, built iron furnaces on wooded land at Northampton—where a typical assembly of convicts, indentured whites, slaves, and hirelings produced pig iron for England. Other ambitious merchants put money in rum distilling, shipbuilding, and town lots. While property at Fells Point and Baltimore Town varied in value, one could reasonably expect a rise. For every Lux there were hundreds of sailors, carpenters, caulkers (who made the wooden vessels watertight), stevedores, millers, teamsters, bricklayers, and clerks. Many investors obligated themselves heavily.

Indebtedness was nothing new in Maryland, but it reached a new level between 1759 and 1763, when Maryland planters and merchants acquired a long-term trade imbalance: they imported far more than they produced or could pay for, made purchases far in excess of the value of their crops or sales. Planters in Anne Arundel, Baltimore, Frederick, Prince George's, and Talbot counties selling on consignment to the London house of William Molleson, for example, each owed about £15 sterling; numerous smaller planters carried debts of £6 or £8 with Molleson's stores in Bladensburg, Georgetown, and Pigg Point in Anne Arundel County. In 1763–64 Samuel Galloway, who bought entire cargoes for his own merchandising house, owed one London merchant, Sylvanus Grove, £1,097 and another, Thomas Philpot, £734. Themselves unable to make collections, Lux and other Baltimore merchants dropped deeply into debt with London firms. At the same time, British traders dunned Maryland debtors with high interest charges, and retirement of paper bills issued in the 1750s reduced the amount in circulation by one-half. Then, in 1761, oversupply led to a fall in the Continental tobacco market, a drop in prices paid Maryland growers, and the failure of many Glasgow trading houses. Similar problems beset the West Indies grain trade. Believing the former belligerents overextended, Dutch bankers after the peace of 1763 tightened credit. London firms called in their own debts to meet demands, and soon the shock wave struck Maryland debtors. "Every honest fair trader fail'd more or less on my right hand and my left," explained Henry Callister, a factor who had gone into merchandising himself and by 1765 was ruined. "It is madness now to sue for debts. If people are not able to pay you must let them walk off or stay to defy you."[23]

Thus the Stamp Act—a principal British measure to recoup costs of the French and Indian War through taxation, and through it to confirm parliamentary jurisdiction in the colonies—landed among Marylanders like a thunderbolt. Earlier acts affecting New England imports and lands beyond the western borders of Maryland had created little stir. In the spring of 1765 Jonas Green of the *Maryland Gazette* broke word of the stamp duties, which Parliament required after 1 November for all legal papers, pamphlets, and newspapers, and began publishing articles critical of the act. Green printed a letter from London announcing that Zachariah Hood, a small Annapolis merchant who was in London on business, had accepted the post of collector for Maryland. Hood became the first target of Stamp Act opponents, whose leaders—William Lux and Annapolis lawyers like Thomas Johnson, William Paca, and Samuel Chase—tended to be younger men, often indebted and impatient. Since winning admittance to the bar in 1763, Chase, a large, heavyset fellow of strong ambition, had made a business of defending debtors. Himself overdrawn in speculative deals, he did not avoid controversy; a small Annapolis group calling itself the Forensic Club expelled him in these years "for extremely irregular and indecent behavior," a verdict he accepted gladly. In 1764 he had helped to form a coalition that placed two workingmen on the Annapolis council and then won a seat in the House of Delegates. The Stamp Act furor placed Chase in his element. Before Hood's return Chase led a crowd that hanged the collector in effigy. Immediately after Hood arrived in Annapolis another mob burned the warehouse storing the stamps.[24]

"Our Province (Maryland)," the frightened official wrote superiors in New York, "is extreamly heated." A French visitor in Maryland wrote that wherever he went that summer, including Galloway's home, Tulip Hill, talk soon turned to the Stamp Act. At a shipboard dinner party near Baltimore—the captain treated planters who had loaded tobacco on his vessel—generous drinks led to loud bragging about harvests, and the Frenchman expected the aroused growers to fall on one another until somebody spoke of the tax. "Then was they Damning their souls if they would pay and Damn them but they would fight to the last Drop of their blood before they would Consent to such Slavery."[25] In an October issue of the *Gazette* Green wrote that he would shut down the paper rather than pay the stamp tax. Before closing, however, he printed and advertised a long, unsigned essay entitled *Considerations on the Propriety of Imposing Taxes in the British Colonies, For the Purpose of Raising a Revenue.*

Everyone soon learned that the pamphlet came from the pen of Daniel Dulany, Jr., whose education at Cambridge and legal training at the Inns of Court commended his opinion on this constitutional question. Dulany's father had died in 1753; in June 1761 the younger man, gaining by his father's service, accepted proprietary office and a place on the council. There the former Frederick County delegate raised the eyebrows of his new colleagues by showing signs of sympathy for his old ones in the house. Sharpe noted in a letter to Lord Baltimore that the younger Dulany, who urged the use of his lordship's license fees for frontier defense, was "fond of being thought a Patriot Councillor and rather inclined to serve the People than the Proprietor." Perhaps more legalistic than partisan, Dulany earlier had conceded that the colonies might justly share the costs of the French and Indian War—"but

The *MARYLAND* GAZETTE.

105

[XXIst Year.] THURSDAY, *September* 5, 1765. [N°. 1061.]

From the BOSTON EVENING POST, *August* 19.

Bondage is Ign'rance, and be that sees,
Needs no directer Cure for that Disease;
Knowledge and Liberty, go Hand in Hand,
Fools only will obey, when Knaves command.
The sordid Yoke no longer can be borne,
When once he sees, he must the Odious Scorn

IT is well observed by an ingenious political Writer, That the first Article of Safety, in Princes and States, lies in avoiding all Councils, *or Designs of Innovation, in ancient and established Forms and Laws,* especially those concerning LIBERTY, PROPERTY and RELIGION; *which are the Possessions Men will ever have most at Heart,* and be most tenacious of retaining: By avoiding which *Designs of Innovation,* they will leave the Channel of *known and common Justice* clear and undisturbed.

The next Thing wherein *that Safety* consists, is, *pursuing the true and common Interests of the Nation, or People they Govern;* without espousing those of any Party or Faction; or, if *these* are so formed in a State, that they *must* incline to one or other, then to chuse or favour that which is most *popular,* or wherein the *greatest or strongest Part of the People* appear to be engaged. For as the *End of Government* appears to be *salus populi,* so the *Strength of the Government* is *the Consent of the People:* From whence arose the Maxim of *Vox populi, Vox Dei:* That is, the Governors who are but *few,* will ever be forced to follow the *Strength of the Governed,* who are *many,* let them be either People or Armies, by which they Govern.——The People are the Bulk of Mankind, for whose Sake, it is not amiss to believe, that Government was originally erected.

These very just and pertinent Observations, must naturally lead us into some Reflections on the present unhappy Situation of Affairs in the Northern Colonies. The People inhabiting the several Governments in *North-America,* are generally true and loyal Subjects to the KING, and have for a long Time enjoyed the Privileges of *British Subjects,* and tasted the Sweets of *English Liberty.* It is no Wonder then, that the most distant Approaches of *Arbitrary Power* should spread a general Consternation among them. The Notices of the STAMP-ACT in particular, have raised the *Alarm,* and transmitted it thro' the whole Continent, and it is generally considered, as an Encroachment, unprecedented and unconstitutional, pregnant of innumerable Woes and Calamities, to the oppressed People. An Act, which, when it takes place, the Evils of it will perhaps be more *sensibly felt,* than at present can easily be imagined. The best that can now be said of it is, that it must be considered as an *entering Wedge,* or Introduction to future Oppressions and Impositions.— It is generally thought (and that not without good Reason) that this *Trojan Horse, this Engine, big with exorbitant Mischiefs,* was projected and framed in one of the principal Northern Governments. And if any of the Sons of *New-England,* descended from *worthy Ancestors,* were concerned in its *Formation,* with a View to Lucrative Posts and Employments, how can they hold up their Heads, amidst the Reproaches and Execrations of a justly enraged People? Can they think to escape the *Scourge of Tongues?* Or that they will not be *burlesqu'd,* and *pasquinaded* in every *News-Paper,* and *lampoon'd* by every *Pamphleteer?* But not to dwell upon this disagreeable Subject any longer, we shall only recommend to such Gentlemen a serious Perusal of those most apposite Lines in *Addison's Cato.*——

O PORCIUS, *is there not some chosen Curse,*
Some hidden Thunder in the Stores of Heaven,
Red with uncommon Wrath, to blast the Man
Who owes his Greatness to his Country's Ruin?

At a Town-Meeting of the Town of Providence, *in the Colony of* Rhode-Island, *on the* 13th *Day of* August, 1765.

It is Voted and Resolved, *That the following Instructions be given to the Gentlemen, who represent this Corporation in General Assembly.*

AS a full and free Enjoyment of *British* Liberty, and of our particular Rights as Colonists, long since precisely known and ascertained by uninterrupted Practice and Usage from the first Settlement of this Country down to this Time, is of unspeakable Value, and strenuously to be contended for by the dutiful Subjects of the best Frame of Government in the World, any Attempts to deprive them thereof must be very alarming, and ought to be opposed, although in a decent Manner, yet with the utmost Firmness.——We conceive that some late Resolutions of the Parliament of *Great-Britain,* for taxing us without our own Consent, have a Tendency to divest us of our most valuable Privileges as *Englishmen:* and that the Measures adopted by the Ministry and the Parliament in this Behalf, if carried into Execution, will be a manifest Infraction of our inherent Rights, as Members of the *British* Government, and unspeakably injurious in the present distressed and involved State of the Colony.

The Ministry, in Justification of this Encroachment upon the incontestible Rights of his Majesty's liege Subjects in these Parts of the World, have pretended that the Colonies are represented in Parliament by the *British* Members. The contrary is so evident, that a bare Denial of the Position is sufficient to refute it.

The Refusal of the Parliament to hear the humble Petitions of the Colonies against the Stamp-Act, the Enlargement of the Admiralty Jurisdiction, and the burdening Trade, we look upon as a great Grievance, and directly against our Rights as Subjects.

With the utmost Concern and Dread we consider the Extension of the Powers of the Court of Admiralty; and must freely declare to the whole World, that we look upon our natural Rights to be diminished in the same Proportion as the Powers of that Court are extended: And in this Particular we are unhappily distinguished from our Fellow-Subjects in *Britain.*

We then think it needful, in this critical Conjuncture, to give unto you, who are our Deputies, some Instructions to be by you observed in your Representation of us in General Assembly.

In the first Place, we recommend it to you, in the most express Manner, to use your utmost Endeavours, that Commissioners be appointed by the Assembly to meet with the Commissioners from the other Colonies on the Continent, at *New-York,* on the first Day of *October* next, agreeable to the Proposal and Request of the Province of the *Massachusetts-Bay,* signified to this Colony, in order to unite in a Petition to the King, for Relief from the Stamp-Act, and other Grievances.

In the Choice of these Commissioners, we are assured, from our Knowledge of your Virtue, that you will pay more Attention to Merit, Skill in public Business, and a Zeal for the Welfare of the Colonies, than to any other Consideration.

We likewise request you to do all in your Power, consistent with our Relation to *Great-Britain,* towards postponing the Introduction of the Stamp-Act into this Colony, until the Colonies may have Opportunity to be heard in Defence of such just Rights, as they will be deprived of by an Execution of it. And to this End, that you endeavour to procure our essential Rights and Privileges to be asserted in General Assembly, by Votes or Resolves to the following Effect, *viz.*

1. That the first Adventurers, Settlers of this his Majesty's Colony and Dominion of *Rhode-Island,* and *Providence* Plantations, brought with them, and transmitted to their Posterity, and all other his Majesty's Subjects since inhabiting in this his Majesty's Colony, all the Privileges and Immunities, that have at any Time been held, enjoyed, and possessed by the People of *Great-Britain.*

2. That by a Charter, granted by King *Charles* the Second, in the fifteenth Year of his Reign, it is declared and granted unto the Governor and Company of this Colony, and their Successors, that all and every the Subjects of his said Majesty, his Heirs and Successors, which were then planted within the said Colony, or which should thereafter go to inhabit within the said Colony, and all and every of their Children which had been born there, or which should afterwards be born there, or on the Seas going thither, or returning from thence, should have and enjoy all Liberties and Immunities of free and natural Subjects within any of the Dominions of his said Majesty, his Heirs or Successors, to all Intents, Constructions, and Purposes whatsoever, as if they and every of them were born within the Realm of *England.*

3. That his Majesty's liege People of this Colony have enjoyed the Right of being governed by their own Assembly, in the Article of Taxes and internal Police; and that the same hath never been forfeited, or any other Way yielded up, but hath been constantly recognized by the King and People of *Britain.*

4. That therefore his Majesty, or his Substitutes, together with the General Assembly of this Colony, have, in their representative Capacity, the only exclusive Right to lay Taxes and Imposts upon the Inhabitants of this Colony; and that every Attempt to vest such Power in any Person or Persons whatever, other than the General Assembly aforesaid, is unconstitutional, and hath a manifest Tendency to destroy *British,* as well as *American* Liberty.

5. That his Majesty's liege People, the Inhabitants of this Colony, are not bound to yield Obedience to any Law or Ordinance, designed to impose any internal Taxation whatsoever upon them, other than the Laws and Ordinances of the General Assembly aforesaid.

And inasmuch as it hath lately been drawn into Question, how far the People of this his Majesty's Dominion of *Rhode-Island* have the Right of being tried by Juries, we earnestly recommend it to you to procure an Act to be passed, if it may be done, declaring that the Courts of Common Law only, and not any Court of Admiralty, have, and ought to have Jurisdiction in all Causes growing and arising in this Colony, on Account of levying or collecting any internal Taxes, or of any Matters relating thereto: And that such Process and Way of Trial shall hereafter be had and used in such Matters, as have been usual and accustomed Time out of Mind. And further, that no Decree of any Court of Admiralty, respecting these Matters, shall be executed in this Colony.

We think that an Address of Thanks ought to be voted by the General Assembly to those Gentlemen, who distinguished themselves at the last Session of Parliament, in Defence of Liberty and the Colonies; in particular to General *Conway,* and Colonel *Isaac Barré.*

As to other Matters, not of such general Concernment as the foregoing, we leave their Management to your Prudence and Judgment, in which we put the greatest Confidence.

A true Copy.

Witness, JAMES ANGELL, Town-Clerk.

LONDON, *June* 22.

ON the 15th at Night a dreadful Fire broke out at Wapping, which destroyed Thirty-one Dwelling-Houses, besides Ware and Out-Houses. Some Vessels took Fire, but were saved; most of the Inhabitants lost their All, several had their Arms and Legs broke, in endeavouring to save their Children from the Flames. It is suspected this Calamity was occasioned by some wicked Incendiaries.

It is assured that no less than 42 Changes will soon take Place in Departments of Consequence to the Public, among which we hear, from good Authority, the following are already fixed.

President of the Council, Duke of Newcastle.

Secretaries of State, Duke of Grafton, and Mr. Pitt.

First Lord of the Treasury, Earl Temple.

Chancellor of the Exchequer, Mr. George Grenville.

Secretary of War, Sir George Saville.

Lord Lieutenant of Ireland, Marquis of Rockingham.

Master of the Horse, Duke of Portland.

Charles Townshend, Esq; to continue Paymaster of the Forces.

A printed skull and crossbones marked the "place to affix the stamp" in an editorial protesting the Stamp Act in the *Maryland Gazette* of 5 September 1765. *MSA*

so many things are to be considered in making a regulation of this sort just and effectual," he said, "that I dread the consequence of Parliament's undertaking it."[26]

Considerations, a brief for moderate resistance, claimed that Parliament had failed. From the principle that no Englishman could be taxed without representation, Dulany proceeded to ask whether colonists enjoyed either direct or "virtual" representation in Parliament. Obviously they elected no one. Just as clearly, he maintained, no member guarded their interests while pursuing the "common good"; the "notion of a *virtual representation*," he wrote, "is a mere cob-web, spread to catch the unwary, and entangle the weak." Only the General Assembly, where Marylanders sent representatives, could impose internal taxes. While he did not challenge "the subordination and dependence of the colonies," Dulany argued that members of Commons had no right to give or grant property that did not belong to them.[27] In an appendix to his pamphlet he also wrote of the colonists' economic grievances against Britain—the duties, monopolies, and trade restrictions that stymied colonial development and skimmed off planters' profits; he warned that the Mother Country might be devouring the hen that laid golden eggs. Yet he abhorred the rebellion that Chase, Lux, and Paca had helped to foment. He urged orderly opposition to the Stamp Act. Easily the most influential American protest against that measure, Dulany's pamphlet went through additional printings as far north as New York and Boston and even in London, where its language appeared in later parliamentary debate. For a spell Marylanders followed Dulany's recommendation of lawful protest. Three leaders of the country party, Edward Tilghman, William Murdock, and Thomas Ringgold, attended the peaceful Stamp Act Congress, which met in New York in October.

Early in 1766, with government offices still closed and business at a standstill, some opponents of the law chose to ignore it and assert their own authority. The Frederick County Court began issuing writs bearing no stamps. Green defiantly resumed publication of the *Gazette*. In 1763 Baltimore skilled workers—known in that day as mechanics—had enrolled themselves in a social, fire-fighting, and quasi-military company that antistamp merchants now wanted to enlist on the side of colonial rights; tied to Baltimore ships and trade, these workers needed scant prodding. Early in 1766 Lux, Mark Alexander, and others joined with them to form a chapter of the Sons of Liberty, an association "for the maintenance of Order"—which opponents believed a gross distortion—"and Protection of American Liberty." Riding a tide of popular feeling in Annapolis, Chase and Paca led more Sons of Liberty, who again included tradesmen and fellows of a rougher sort. Chase's credentials were impeccable. In March he aligned himself with disgruntled Annapolitans who complained that the mayor and aldermen had misappropriated funds and passed ordinances too restrictive on the common man's purchase of rum and keeping of dogs. City officials, who included Daniel

Dulany's brother Walter and the rich merchant John Brice, rejected the charges in a public letter and described Chase as a "Busy restless Incendiary—a Ringleader of Mobs—a foul mouth'd and inflaming Son of Discord and Passion—a common Disturber of the public Tranquility." With such a talented upstart in the lead, the Sons of Liberty petitioned Dulany, who then served as proprietary secretary, for the reopening of courts and provincial offices. Green gleefully printed every such appeal, and Dulany complied only four days before news arrived in Annapolis that the Stamp Act had been repealed.[28]

Indebtedness provoked fury at the stamp tax; it also led to nonimportation, a commercial tactic that illustrated well the connection between economic interests and mercantile resistance in Maryland. For Baltimore merchants like Lux, refusing to order more British goods until Parliament revoked the Stamp Act answered private as well as patriotic ends. "I do not intend importing any more goods till I have squared the old score or at least half of it," he wrote an associate in September 1765. In November of that year traders in Baltimore agreed to an informal arrangement similar to those adopted in Philadelphia and New York. Two years later, under guise of imperial trade regulation rather than taxation, the Townshend Acts laid new duties on a wide range of British products entering the colonies. Thereafter patriots in the northern colonies, though seldom the merchants, demanded a stronger nonimportation policy. Gradually the mercantile community bowed to the pressure. In March 1769, after Philadelphia merchants decided on a boycott, Baltimore shippers and traders took the lead in devising a Maryland plan. In doing so they demonstrated the leverage Philadelphia creditors exercised over many of them and insured that they, not others, enumerated the boycotted items and exceptions. In June an Annapolis meeting of lawyers, merchants, and planters produced an agreement to govern policy in all waterside counties.[29]

Cynics could not help noticing that the Maryland nonimportation agreement of 1769 left open so many holes that it amounted to a list of goods merchants there wanted the British to sell at a lower price. Even patriots could be swayed by self-interest, and the market for American staples reached record-high levels after 1766. As opportunity knocked, Maryland merchants had moved quickly to gain advantages that would satisfy creditors and build profits. Net returns from tobacco in this period reached £6 to £10 a hogshead; short wheat crops in Europe lifted the value of grain so high that little went to the West Indies. Baltimore Town had risen accordingly. In 1768 it replaced Joppa as the county seat and was a town of more than 350 houses, Lux boasted, "more adding every day." Seventy or eighty ships a year loaded wheat, flour, and flaxseed at the Fells Point docks. Annapolis and Oxford port record books showed that between 1767 and 1772 ship arrivals from Britain generally increased each year.[30]

In the midst of such trading and growth, nonimportation understandably struck Baltimore and Annapolis merchants as a necessary evil at best. The two shippers accused of violating its provisions in Baltimore escaped penalty. Two of four Annapolis nonimportation leaders in the spring of 1769 later committed an egregious violation of the June accords. An ad hoc committee did refuse them permission to unload their cargo. But Philadelphia merchants complained that Marylanders shamelessly used the boycott to gain competitive advantage. When English merchants approached the ministry to repeal the Townshend duties, Lord Hillsborough, the secretary of state, told them correctly that shipments to Maryland and Virginia never had been heavier. Chase and Lux had fallen out by the late 1760s—a business arrangement between them had disappointed Chase—and therefore attempts to stir support for nonimportation among Baltimore merchants failed for reasons that mixed the personal, political, and economic. Maryland merchants dropped the pretense as soon as they heard in the fall of 1770 that the government had set aside duties on all goods except tea.

⟳↭⟲

The strands of disaffection with a "parent," country or Whiggish political thought, lower-class grievance, and mercantile self-interest—all came together in the next six years to assault proprietary favoritism and imperial restriction alike. The process—irregular and almost imperceptible until 1774—began with a final fight between the lower house and proprietary establishment over fees.

Much overlaid animosity served as a foundation for this new round in the ancient struggle, but Frederick Lord Baltimore's personal character and that of his friends made it all the more difficult for Marylanders to bend to his will. Late in 1766 Frederick had sent his old Oxford chum the Reverend Bennet Allen to fill the next comfortable church vacancy. On arriving, Allen chose the pulpit at St. Anne's Church, Annapolis, until something richer came along. At first the Dulany family greeted Allen as they usually welcomed people dear to the proprietor. Soon he, a heavy drinker, and his traveling companion, a woman Allen said was his sister, had worn out the Dulanys' welcome and become the butt of irreverent jokes. Allen tried to even the score by publishing insulting verse in the *Maryland Gazette* (he thought himself a fine poet; an English reviewer said his work was "enough to make a dog howl"). Bennet narrowly avoided a duel with Samuel Chew, head of the vestry and Daniel and Walter Dulany's stepbrother. Later, when the reverend seated himself at the truly lucrative All-Saints parish, Frederick, he so alienated his congregation that the vestrymen bolted the doors to keep him out of church. "A man of some talents, but no principles" (said another cleric), Allen took to climbing in a window before dawn so as to "preach" and claim the parish income. His flock chased him from Frederick. In Philadelphia Allen issued further attacks on the Dulanys. Visiting Annapolis in 1768, he suffered a public beating from Walter Dulany.[31]

That year other church scandals surfaced. A St. Mary's County parson had not preached for three years and stood accused of murdering a slave; another minister "was said to be not only an habitual Drunkard but also to live in adultery." Lord Baltimore might have been embarrassed by the state of the Maryland church, but in the late 1760s he himself had fled to the Continent rather than face charges that he had brutally raped a seamstress whose reputable family scorned his offer to buy them off. Before the uproar over the Townshend duties, the lower house debated whether to form a commission of laymen and clergy to regulate established churchmen—the best of whom, in the words of an Anglican minister writing the bishop of London, appeared like lights here and there "shining in a dark place."[32]

To countrymen the hope of reducing officers' fees never had diminished. In October 1770 the tobacco inspection law that also regulated clergy incomes and proprietary fees expired while the lower house considered a measure to renew it. While discussing this charged issue, the house must have grown every bit as raucous as it had appeared only a few years before to Thomas Jefferson. Used to the stately capitol in Williamsburg and self-conscious decorum of the House of Burgesses there, the young Virginian had been struck by the informality of proceedings in Annapolis. He described the Maryland delegates as a "mob (for such was their appearance)," sitting and lounging on the benches, "divided into little clubs amusing themselves in the common chit chat way," addressing the speaker "without rising from their seats, and three, four, and five at a time without being checked."[33] In the fall of 1770 voices doubtless rose when someone pointed out that despite the death of the inspection law, William Steuart, a clerk of the land office in Annapolis, still collected fees. Probably rising four and five at a time, country party members successfully urged passage of a resolution ordering the proprietary officer jailed—only the assembly had the right to tax Marylanders. House members may also have argued that this gesture of defiance would welcome Sharpe's successor as governor, Lord Frederick's brother-in-law Robert Eden, as he should be greeted.

A likable former officer in the Coldstream Guards, Eden handled matters in military fashion. He consulted his council, prorogued the house long enough to release Steuart, and adamantly refused to consider all the fee-reduction proposals the reconvened house sent him. On 26 November, after the delegates adjourned, Eden coolly issued a proclamation leaving officers' fees at their 1733 levels. Thus, while other colonies enjoyed a lull in agitation in the early 1770s, Marylanders outside the proprietary establishment seethed. Planters at Port Tobacco and Upper Marlborough, at Indian Landing in Anne Arundel County, and in Queen Anne's County formed their own inspection committees to maintain the quality and price of Maryland leaf as prosperity continued. Everyone read with interest the printed report of a house committee that made clear the exorbitant amounts officers received each year: the provincial secretary, Dulany, between £1,000 and

£1,500; the clerk of the land office £1,800 or more. One of the Carrolls be-lieved men could be found to fill clerkships for £300. In the 1771 elections, house candidates made full use of the fees issue, which preoccupied the October session. Neither the house nor Eden and council budged, and the governor at last dismissed the delegates. During the uneasy period that fol-lowed Eden's supporters warned against radical change. Letters to the *Mary-land Gazette* took the cautious view that extralegal inspection, like the volun-tary militia plan of 1755 and the later proposal that private subscribers send an agent of the people to London, amounted to a dangerous breakdown of order. Jonathan Boucher, Allen's replacement as rector at St. Anne's and a fast friend of the Dulanys, recalled that the "times were grown beyond mea-sure troublesome: men's minds were restless and dissatisfied, for ever dis-contented and grumbling at the present state of things, and for ever project-ing reformations."[34]

In the battle for men's minds Boucher and his friends did not overlook the rising importance of pamphlets and newspaper essays, but employing these weapons carried risk. Lord Frederick's death in 1771 vacated all proprietary commissions. By Frederick's will, the new proprietor turned out to be his illegitimate son, Henry Harford, and court men exerted themselves to dis-play loyalty and win appointments from Harford's guardians. Dulany's own energy may have issued from various sources—a hope to sustain his place in court and council by defending order but also a hidebound sense of legal-ity. Not long after the Stamp Act crisis Dulany had published a booklet de-fending the proprietor's right to tonnage duties. In January 1773, as elections for another House of Delegates approached, he wrote a dialogue for the *Maryland Gazette* between two Maryland freemen, the carefully crafted ar-guments of the "Second Citizen" finally convincing the other of the legality of Eden's fee proclamation. Appearing so soon after the court party's un-pretty scramble for places, the Dulany letters only sharpened popular anger at the fee system. In early February he discovered that a challenger assuming the "First Citizen" persona had risen to meet him, and the exchange dazzled readers into July. Dulany as "Antilon" relied on a narrow interpretation of the Maryland charter. "First Citizen" took a constitutional approach that drew parallels between Baltimore's fees and the fees early English kings had allowed retainers to collect; the medieval model had evolved into public fees rightly provided for by parliamentary appropriation (which, in the case of Maryland, implied that the House of Delegates exercised supreme local pow-ers). "First Citizen" won applause from "Independent Whigs" and other friends in the columns of the *Gazette*.

What made the series all the more exciting, however, was the common knowledge that young Charles Carroll, the English- and French-educated Catholic whose father had lived in Annapolis for many years, was writing the "First Citizen" pieces. Like his father legally denied a part in the political process, Carroll had returned from Europe in 1765 and settled in Annapolis (though identifying himself by the extensive family acreage called Carroll-ton, in the upper Patapsco River valley). In 1762, studying law in London, Carroll had met Dulany, Jr., and taken an instant dislike to him. Dulany seemed self-important, humorless; *"c'est un homme bizarre,"* Carroll wrote his father, whose own low opinion of Dulany grew out of their troubled partnership in the Baltimore ironworks as well as the Dulanys' connection to the all-Protestant court party. Bad blood between the families went back many years. In 1769 Lloyd Dulany had written so maliciously of Carroll of Carroll-ton's father that the younger man had felt obligated to avenge those words with "a brace of pistols"—an offer Dulany had avoided by dismissing Carroll as a "silly little puppy" and "dirty little rascal." Illustrating a change that took place in more than one elite Maryland family, Carroll's father hoped "First Citizen" would destroy Dulany but not alienate Eden, while the son saw both councillor and governor as belonging to a system that demanded fundamental reform.[35]

The "First Citizen" series helped to coalesce leadership of a new antiproprietary coalition that came to be known as the "popular party" and to bring it victory in the spring election. Reviving the Annapolis-Baltimore alliance, the new network formed around Samuel Chase and the Catholic Carrolls. Carroll of Carrollton's cousin and active supporter, the Annapolis attorney of the same name, had married a daughter of Matthew Tilghman, the Talbot County planter and house speaker. Also on friendly terms with Chase, Carroll the Barrister thus provided a link with two important legislative figures. Thomas Johnson, the anti–Stamp Act leader who served as legal advisor to the Carroll family, and William Cooke, whose sister before her untimely death Carroll of Carrollton had planned to marry, gave the circle around "First Citizen" additional weight. William Paca had read law with Stephen Bordley in Annapolis and briefly at the Inns of Court. A member of the House of Delegates, Paca maintained friendly relations with Eden in the early months of 1773 and fed the circle news of the governor's activity. In Baltimore support for "First Citizen" centered on important merchants like Lux, Samuel Purviance, and Charles Ridgely. Rapprochement between Lux and Chase helped to redraw the Annapolis-Baltimore axis, as did Carroll of Carrollton's commercial training and sympathy for Maryland traders. Further aiding supporters of "First Citizen" in early 1773, Paca and Chase became embroiled in another newspaper debate with the Reverend Boucher over clerical salaries. Boucher argued that in the absence of fees legislation, the tobacco tax for the vestries reverted to higher levels that had prevailed before the 1747 fees act. Allen's mischief and that of some other proprietary appointees to the church left Boucher scant support. In May popular party candidates won convincingly. The Dulanys, Carroll of Carrollton wrote his father afterward, stood "humbled, and what is still more galling they have great reason to fear an end of their powers, influence and future promotion."[36]

Deepening crisis in the British Empire cast doubt upon anyone's accustomed power, influence, or promotion. The participation of ordinary folk in protests against proprietary rule had begun to change the game of politics. Earlier, in 1766, deadlock between house and council over the question of who should salary the upper chamber's clerk had prevented passage of an act to pay people to whom the province owed money—many of them soldiers and small military suppliers. Thomas Cresap and a body of deerskin-clad friends with long rifles had spoken of marching on Annapolis to impose reason on the councillors. Anger over Eden's fee proclamation led to public displays attended by nonvoters, debtors, and others who enjoyed baiting the powerful. The "minds of a certain Rank of men," someone wrote in the *Maryland Gazette*, had been "poisoned to such a Degree, that far from being ashamed of resisting subordinate Authority, they even glory in their audacious Insults of Government itself." [37]

Just as during the Stamp Act crisis, a few audacious men with political influence tried to ride the horse of rising anger. Among the daring were John Hall and Matthias and Rezin Hammond, longtime members of the country party with homes in Annapolis and Anne Arundel County. After the 1773 assembly elections they split with leaders of the new popular party in formulating a tobacco inspection and fees bill. Chase, Paca, and Johnson— perhaps hoping not unduly to offend the governor, who planned consultations in London—drew up a recommended list of fees; Hall and the Hammonds attacked it as too generous. Playing on the sentiment against proprietary officers (also reflecting sharp differences between Matthias Hammond and the Carrolls over their adjoining property bounds in the county), the radical Hall-Hammond faction sent the fee schedule down to defeat. Then, in May 1774, the Boston committee of correspondence called for resistance to the British coercive acts by closing all trade with the Mother Country. Carroll's friends and the Hall-Hammond group fought for leadership of the Annapolis meeting that considered the Boston call, each side outdoing the other as stalwart spokesmen for American rights. The emotional gathering concluded with a statement demanding that no Maryland lawyer prosecute any debt owed to a British creditor as long as the Boston Port Act remained in force.

It proved difficult to keep a lid on growing unrest. The Annapolis resolves, also favoring nonimportation and nonexportation, appealed to Maryland planters because of the economic misfortune that frustrated them once again. Improved wheat harvests in the south of Europe in 1770 lowered the price of that staple, which merchants had relied upon, and then the next year tobacco and lumber prices also fell. European depression in 1772 had severe repercussions in the Chesapeake. Poor Marylanders suspected factors of foul practices. Familiar cries about debts and down markets resounded at county meetings, where smaller planters finally dominated talk of the Annapolis resolves. British firms complained to no avail of the no-collection policy. During the early summer of 1774 public meetings at Charles Hungerford's tavern in the lower district of Frederick County, at Frederick Town, and in Jonathan Hager's Elizabeth Town all took a firm stand against the coercion of Boston. In June an Annapolis meeting sent friends of the Carrolls—Chase, Johnson, and Paca from the Western Shore, Matthew Tilghman and Robert Goldsborough from the Eastern—to the Continental Congress, which first met in Philadelphia that September. At home the Hall-Hammond radicals found a suitably explosive issue in the October arrival of the brigantine *Peggy Stewart*. Belonging to a critic of debt renunciation, Anthony Stewart, the vessel entered Annapolis harbor loaded with two thousand pounds of tea on which Stewart had paid the detested duties. Hall and Hammond circulated handbills calling for a public meeting on the nineteenth of the month.

Accounts differ as to what happened next. Leaders of the crowd—Rezin Hammond, Charles Ridgely, two young Anne Arundel physicians, Charles Warfield and Ephraim Howard, and firebrands from Elk Ridge and Baltimore—entertained motions to tar and feather Stewart and burn his vessel. Hammond and Ridgely escorted Stewart to the ship while on shore Chase, home briefly from Philadelphia, and Charles Carroll the Barrister won the crowd's approval of a lesser punishment—burning of the tea only. Clamor for destruction nonetheless won out, and the *Peggy Stewart* went to the torch by its owner's hands. A few bystanders watched the fiery ritual terrified at its implications. "If this is Liberty, If this is Justice," wrote John Galloway to his father at Tulip Hill, "they certainly must have a new code of Laws on Elk Ridge." The infamous and rascally affair, he went on, "makes all men of property reflect with horror on their present Situation[;] to have their lives and propertys at the disposal & mercy of a Mob is Shocking indeed."[38]

This affair gave the popular party an air of comparative moderation, and at the Continental Congress its leaders gained the same reputation. The Maryland delegation played a prominent part in locating the middle ground between radicals and conservatives, between the urgent pleas of New England and the practical needs of the northern commercial and southern planting colonies. Marylanders voted against a plan of colonial union that Joseph Galloway of Pennsylvania proposed as a conservative device. Chase, Paca, and Johnson developed friendships with John Adams, who hoped for radical action. Adams grumbled that his Chesapeake colleagues too readily recognized Parliament's power to govern imperial commerce. Yet he praised Johnson's "extensive" knowledge of trade; he wrote of Paca's skills as a deliberator and Chase's warmth as a speaker. At the same time James Duane, an especially conservative New Yorker, believed that the commercial interests that his colony and Maryland shared made them fast allies. They also agreed on the British right to regulate trade. "The Maryland arguments in which you had so great a share on this essential point were unanswerable," Duane later wrote Chase, "—they never were attempted to be answered, yet unhappily they produced no conviction." Along with Virginia and North Carolina delegates, the Marylanders wanted to delay nonexportation long enough to ship at least one tobacco crop and begin the climb out of debt. Johnson served on the committee that proposed a compromise Congress adopted: nonimportation after 1 December 1774, nonexportation a year later.[39]

In November, the Continental Congress then adjourned, Maryland patriots faced another balancing act. The congressional agenda of enforcing nonimportation required local action. In taking it, defenders of colonial rights—except for the Hall-Hammond men—hoped to keep "the common sort" under control; since the burning of the *Peggy Stewart*, a Scottish trader wrote home, those people "seem to think they may commit any outrage they please." Popular party leaders called elections that sent delegates to a Maryland convention in Annapolis. Though by its nature a revolutionary body— it presumed to rule in place of proprietor, governor, and assembly and claimed to draw its powers from the people—the convention still tried to tread the path of resistance lightly. To broaden its support it acted on the problem of indebtedness, though moderately: it set up barriers making it difficult for merchants who violated the nonimportation policy to collect debts in court. Members elected the radical John Hall to a standing committee of correspondence. Joining Chase, Paca, Johnson, and Tilghman in that group were two more of the original "First Citizen" circle—Carroll the Barrister and Carroll of Carrollton himself. Moderation paid dividends from the proprietary elite; late in 1774 Major Daniel of St. Thomas Jenifer joined the resistance after losing favor with Eden, who rightly suspected the receiver-general of being a secret correspondent with Carroll of Carrollton's father. The convention assured compliance with the policy of nonimportation by establishing committees of observation made up of local leaders like the western Marylanders John Hanson, Henry Griffith, Baker Johnson, and Jonathan Hager, who had cast their lot for resistance. Struggling against the British plan "to enslave America," patriot leaders appealed for a union of "all ranks of men" and recommended "that all former differences about religion or politics and all private animosities and quarrels of every kind from henceforth cease and be forever buried in oblivion."[40]

Despite this wish, outside events and extralegal measures badly divided Marylanders. In late March 1775 members of the Bush River, Harford County, committee of observation issued resolves urging independence and pledging themselves, in memorable words, "to Each Other & to our Country . . . at the Risque of Our Lives & fortunes." About two weeks later, when word reached Maryland of the bloodshed at Lexington and Concord, patriot feeling of an ethnic cast stirred up the Baltimore Irish, who in gangs went looking for Englishmen. Under convention authority, militia units organized in many counties, watchful of rumored British invasion from both the west and

A gallery of revolutionary-period statesmen. *Top left*, William Paca (1740–99) by Charles Willson Peale, 1772, *MHS*. *Top right*, Samuel Chase (1741–1811) by Charles Willson Peale, c. 1773, *MHS*. *Lower left*, Charles Carroll of Carrollton (1737–1832) by Sir Joshua Reynolds, 1763, *Yale Center for British Art*. *Lower right*, Thomas Stone (1743–87) by John Beale Bordley, 1835, *Maryland Commission on Artistic Properties*.

the Chesapeake. "Every province is learning the life of arms," an Annapolis merchant wrote to London; "you may depend that we will die before we give up our liberties and have our property at the disposal of a damn lot of rascally ministers." In July 1775 the *Totness*, carrying a cargo of boycotted goods, ran aground on a sand bar in the mouth of the West River. Annapolis area radicals quickly burned the vessel, repeating the *Peggy Stewart* assault on property. Late that month the provincial convention, issuing a printed and signed proclamation as the "Association of the Freemen of Maryland," recommended a state of defense and formed a council of safety—an executive arm made up of eight patriots from each shore and headed by Jenifer. "All power is getting fast into the hands of the very lowest people," Governor Eden wrote in the fall of 1775. "Those who first encouraged the opposition to government and set these on this licentious behavior will probably be amongs't the first to repent thereof."[41]

Truly the times tried men's souls. Many people felt confused. Extralegal committees of observation duplicated the powers of justices of the peace, whom Eden tried and failed to keep on his side. "Voluntary contributions" (placing heavy pressure on slackers) supplied the early militia companies. Those units did not always bring comfort to men of property, who noted that they lacked discipline and elected their officers. With war broken out in New England and familiar law and order breaking down at home, some members of the colonial elite voiced their loyalty to the Crown. They clung to the established order; place in the proprietary structure, dependence on the British government, commitment to the Anglican church, and family ties in England—all played a part in one's choice. Though families naturally weighed the wealth that rebellion risked, at bottom anxiety about disorder decided most elite Loyalists. The Reverend Boucher feared tenant rebellion, convict uprisings, and slave conspiracies. The "laboring classes," he warned, "instead of regarding the rich as their guardians, patrons, and benefactors, now look on them as so many overgrown colossuses, whom it is no demerit in them to wrong." Boucher spoke for many other loyal subjects in Maryland in claiming that king and Parliament ruled with "parental tenderness." Before leaving Annapolis for England in 1775 he placed two loaded pistols on the pulpit cushion at St. Anne's and delivered a farewell sermon. "As long as I live," he concluded defiantly, "yea, while I have my being, will I proclaim 'God save the King!' "[42]

Not all Loyalists belonged to the rich or well-placed, however, and not all Marylanders of meaner circumstances approved the *Peggy Stewart* and *Totness* riots. Humble people could either go ahead faster than the rich and well-born popular party leaders, hoping to move them out of their usual orbits and thereby gain advantage. Or they might look upon the revolutionary movement with a debtor's dislike for a creditor. More than a few humble Marylanders resisted the resistance. Defying the Association of Freemen, they became known as "nonassociators." One of them, Robert Davis of Anne

A Maryland four-dollar note (printed in Annapolis by Frederick Green in July 1775, with woodcuts by Thomas Sparrow) circulated a crude but doubtless effective picture of Mother England and King George III as abusive parents. *MHS*

Arundel County, spoke disrespectfully of the local committee leaders and threatened to shoot the militiamen who came to arrest him as "damned rebel sons of bitches." Out fishing, a Dorchester County wheelwright told an inquirer that he would never muster for the patriot militia. "The gentlemen," he said according to a report, intended "to make us fight for their lands and negroes, and then said damn them (meaning the gentlemen)"; if some of them were killed "we should have the best of the land to tend and besides could get money enough." Poverty aside, conversion to Methodism accounted for especially conservative sentiment among the people on the lower Eastern Shore. An Anglican reform movement that John Wesley directed from Britain, Methodism stressed heartfelt involvement in the spiritual life, a piety that meant it. Circuit-riding preachers, raising their voices against the emptiness of rote liturgy, carried the Methodist good news to every remote settlement on the Shore. Emotional faith and scorn for vanity, making the Methodists natural opponents of the high-and-mighty planters, now estranged them from the cause of the Tilghmans, Goldsboroughs, and others.[43]

Eden thought one British regiment would quash resistance. His belief at least reflected the caution of Maryland convention leaders, many of whom rested content with their commanding position over Lord Baltimore. They hardly approached revolution in haste. On 12 January 1776 they instructed

Jonathan Boucher (1738–1804), who believed the colonies should remain loyal children. Engraving by P. Conde after original painting by W. J. Thomson. *MHS*

delegates in Congress to agree to nothing declaring the colonies independent "without the previous knowledge and approbation of the Convention of this province." Later in the month Tilghman, Johnson, and Jenifer, holding discussions with Eden, left him with the impression that they were "so far from desiring an independency that if the establishment of it were left to their choice, they would reject it with abhorrence." In April the convention's executive body, the council of safety, stiffly reprimanded two Baltimore patriots for moving too quickly and exceeding the bounds of good taste. Samuel Purviance, chairman of the committee of safety there, and Samuel Smith, John Smith's seagoing son and an early volunteer in the Baltimore Independent Cadets, had seen a report that Governor Eden planned to depart Annapolis. Smith led a body of men to the capital in a nearly successful effort to capture him. Administering the tongue-lashing, Jenifer may silently have thanked the radicals, whose excesses reflected well on the moderation he believed to be of future political importance. The episode illustrated what

Richard Henry Lee of Virginia called "namby pamby" hesitation among both Marylanders and Virginians. On 21 May the Annapolis convention unanimously renewed its hesitant instructions to the delegation in Congress. As that body considered declaring independence, Thomas Stone, who along with John Beale Bordley had declined to serve on the first council of safety, darkly referred to developments in Philadelphia as giving a "fatal stab" to any future colonial-British tie. "Thus alas! are we proceeding by degrees to that crisis we so much deprecate," moaned James Hollyday. In June another council of safety member, Benjamin Rumsey, wrote that he had taken care "so as not to fall into Independence," though he admitted a willingness to prepare for it as an "absolute Necessity."[44]

Prodding from Congress had much effect. On 7 June Lee submitted independence resolutions, while Jefferson, John Adams, and others grew short with New York, Pennsylvania, Delaware, and Maryland delegates. "Maryland hung heavily on our backs," Jefferson later testified. Except for Matthew Tilghman, Chase, and Paca, Adams recalled, "neither the state of Maryland nor [any] of their Delegates were very early in their conviction of the necessity of independence, nor very forward in promoting it." In the middle of June, Chase and the rest left for Annapolis, hoping to return with support for independence and a French alliance. Governor Eden sensed the tilt and departed, the convention and council of safety seeing him off in friendly fashion on 21 June and even sending Virginia a request for his safe conduct. "I presume Maryland soon will join company," Adams wrote Chase impatiently; "if not, she must be left alone."[45]

Leaders more hesitant than Chase and the Hammonds may have realized with Carroll of Carrollton, who had just returned from a diplomatic mission to Canada, that the war forced Maryland to choose between independence and total dependence. During the week following Eden's departure, the convention debated these unappealing alternatives. Outdoors the elements that daunted Loyalists clamored for action. Patriot petitions arrived from Western Shore county committees, militia units eager for a decision, and the Baltimore Sons of Liberty—whom the governor had thought the most "pronounced rebellious and mischievous" people in the province. Even at the eleventh hour many convention members may have agreed with Eden's assessment. Arguments over independence left pieces of the old leadership lying about in odd places. Former proprietary men like George Plater III of St. Mary's joined Jenifer in supporting revolution. Earlier spokesmen for colonial rights—Robert Alexander, a Baltimore merchant who also served on the council of safety, and James Tilghman of Talbot—chose loyalism, as quietly did Daniel Dulany. Colonel Richard Lloyd, firm for independence, pulled the doubtful Robert Goldsborough "by the Nose" toward a break with the Mother Country. Finally voting by members instead of county blocs, the convention on 28 June directed Maryland delegates in Congress to concur with their colleagues "in declaring the United Colonies free and independent states."[46] On 3 July the convention formally made that declaration on its own and then set elections for an August meeting that would write a state constitution. Shorn of proprietor and Britain alike, some Marylanders (and some more bravely than others) completed the shift in mind that Tom Paine spoke of in *Common Sense*. Paine asked whether it was in the interests of a man to be a boy all his life.

Revolutionary leaders in Maryland hoped next to minimize revolutionary change—to control the constitutional convention so as not to lose their standing and to manage the war so that it did little to upset the old order. Again they walked a fine line. Military necessity forced a calling out of as many of the able-bodied as possible; the requests of the powerful for sacrifice invited pleas among contributors for political change and social equality. Although the provincial convention had lifted some restrictions on voting in the late summer of 1775—allowing immigrants, Catholics, Quakers, and freeholders with less than fifty acres of land to vote for delegates to the de facto provincial government—many Marylanders of lesser station remained disqualified. In July 1776 convention members, leaving no doubt as to their conservative bent, decreed that all persons voting for delegates to the constitutional convention had to meet all the old colonial property requirements.

Common people and their friends groused disgustedly. Demonstrations against election judges occurred at polling places on both shores—in Queen Anne's and Worcester, and in the lower district of Frederick that plans called for making into a new county. Freemen gathered at the Prince George's County election point and declared that "every taxpayer bearing arms" should have the vote "at this time of public calamity." They dispersed the convention-appointed election judges and installed men who did not quibble over one's landholdings or visible wealth. In Kent County election officials managed to close the polls before a similar disturbance took place. John McClure of Baltimore County believed that only the "clever" candidates, appealing to the people, succeeded in winning seats, and where lay the difference, he asked the young merchant Mordecai Gist, "between being disqualified to vote or having a vote when these men are to represent you?" The precaution of denying the suffrage to soldiers on active service and of forbidding militia musters on election day backfired on the council of safety in Annapolis, where Maryland troops belonging to the "Flying Camp" of Continental light infantry had stopped on their way to duty in New Jersey. One of the soldiers approached the poll and was told that he did not qualify. Quickly other troops surrounded the judges, shouting that if they could fight they could surely vote, and threatening the life of Captain Thomas Watkins, who had questioned the soldier's property holdings. Persuaded to reassemble on Gallows Hill outside the town, the troops listened as some speakers argued for obedience to the law and others advised using their muskets to register a vote. Someone explained the property rule, which the men knew all too well; the whole company, shouted an enlisted man, probably wasn't worth £40 in visible estate.[47]

To private soldiers and humble folk expecting change in Maryland, the season looked promising. Leading Western Shore members of the old country party like Thomas Contee, Robert Tyler, Josias Beall, Walter Tolley, Jr., and John Moale lost in the August elections. Thomas Stone, who finally had signed the Declaration of Independence, went down to defeat. Carroll of Carrollton, Paca, and Johnson lost their seats in Anne Arundel County; only last-minute maneuvering in Annapolis and Caroline County assured their appearance at the convention, which numbered among its seventy-six members fifty men who never had served in the provincial assembly. Some of them owed prominence to their role in the emerging war effort—Samuel Beall of Elizabeth Town and Samuel Hughes were important ironmakers of western Maryland. Other newcomers were Germans like Henry Schnebely and David Shriver and Catholics—besides Carroll of Carrollton, Ignatius Fenwick and Jeremiah Jordan. More members than usual classified themselves as farmers rather than planters. Reform seemed imminent. Signifying the thinking of a vocal minority, Annapolis militia units issued a bill of recommendations that included electing county justices and sheriffs, putting an end to plural officeholding, and placing a greater share of land taxes on the wealthy. Perhaps Rezin or Matthias Hammond wrote the "Watchman" essay that caused such a stir in the *Maryland Gazette*. Without free suffrage, read the piece, the people would be "meer beasts of burden." "*Each Citizen of a state who lends his aid to the support of it, has an equal claim to all the privileges, liberties and immunities with every of his fellow countrymen.*"[48] Long conflict between upper and lower houses in Maryland and the example of revolutionary Pennsylvania also produced talk of a unicameral legislature.

Depending on one's point of view, the constitution that later emerged proved either a stunning disappointment or a victory for moderation. Despite the influx of new faces, experienced men—Carroll of Carrollton, Paca, Chase, Matthew Tilghman, Robert Goldsborough, and George Plater—dominated the meeting and formed the committee that actually wrote the new state constitution. Reported on 11 September, it left government in the hands of the propertied. To sit in the lower house, elected annually, one had to own £500 in real or personal property; to serve in the senate, on the governor's executive council (a holdover from the colonial structure), as a delegate to the Continental Congress, or as sheriff, the minimum stood at £1,000. Only men worth £5,000 qualified to act as governor. While ordinary voters elected sheriffs and members of the lower house, the assembly named the congressional delegation as well as the governor—who served a one-year term and could not succeed himself more than twice. Every five years an electoral college made up of men worth at least £500 chose senators, and the constitution provided for slightly heavier representation of the more populous Western Shore.

Rezin Hammond, Cockey Deye from Baltimore Town, Charles Ridgely and John Stevenson from Baltimore County, and other champions of the common Marylander from Harford and the new Montgomery County managed few gains in the convention. The constitution left in force the ancient requirement of a fifty-acre freehold. On the other hand, it confirmed the restoration of political rights to Catholics, and did nothing to proscribe free blacks, otherwise qualified, from voting. Most important, the convention allowed men who did not own land to vote if they held £30 worth of property in "current money"—which in effect cut the old qualification of £40 sterling in half. The 1776 constitution, which passed in October, increased the proportion of free males who could exercise the suffrage by roughly 10 percent in most counties—by a mere 5 percent in Worcester (where nonlandowners were very poor), by 13 in Montgomery and 20 percent in Washington County, the old upper district of Frederick.[49] Old beliefs about the importance of property in shaping government policy obviously remained strong. Novices in public life clearly paid men like Carroll, Chase, Paca, and Tilghman personal respect.

Conservative influences also showed in the Maryland Declaration of Rights, a listing of forty-two individual guarantees and limits on government. The convention voted down a proposal to forbid enslavement of black newcomers to the state; one clause respected the duty of "every man" to "worship God in such manner as he thinks most acceptable to him" but protected only "persons professing the christian religion." Even so, the declaration represented the full flowering of Whiggish political thought, beginning with the principle that "all government of right originates from the people, is founded in compact only, and instituted solely for the good of the whole." The following articles established as inviolable the rights to free speech and press, petition, trial by jury, and frequent elections; they promised freedom from unwarranted searches and seizures, excessive bail, and self-incrimination. Reflecting the Whigs' fear of military rule and American colonial experience with resident British forces, the declaration placed military power beneath civil authority and prohibited standing armies and the quartering of soldiers in private homes without permission. It provided for a separation of executive, legislative, and judicial powers. By forbidding plural officeholding, disestablishing the Anglican church, and condemning the poll tax that had gone toward Anglican ministers, the convention pointedly rid Maryland of the proprietary establishment and colonial rule. Though the committee that drafted the declaration had access to similar documents already adopted in Virginia and Pennsylvania, Marylanders went beyond those models in outlawing ex post facto laws and bills of attainder.[50]

The revolution in attitudes that marked revolt against proprietor and royal rule—including the idea that no man is better than another—and the bitterness of division in Maryland over the rightness of independence itself forced Maryland leaders to undergo a "revolution of mind" not entirely encompassed in John Adams's remark. Military necessity and civil disorder weighed heavily on the new state's leaders. British warships remained in control of the bay, welcomed fugitive slaves (three of whom in August 1776 killed a Dorchester County white man while trying to escape), landed supplies for their supporters in Somerset County, and conducted foraging operations as far north as the St. Mary's region. Militia units ordered there grew sickly and unruly, and citizens requested their withdrawal. In the summer of 1776 essays in the *Maryland Gazette* and in the *Journal* of Baltimore made the obvious connection between love of liberty and service, and conversely between toryism and refusal to support the new military. In Baltimore battles broke out between the militant Sons of Liberty, now called the Whig Club, and armed Loyalists. An Anne Arundel County militia unit demanded new officers' elections because one of their captains had said "that a poor man was not born to freedom but to be a drudge on earth." [51]

On the Eastern Shore, where Lord Dunmore's raids and his threat to enlist slaves in putting down rebellion in Virginia frightened Maryland white folk, large numbers of the poor continued to flout patriot or "rebel" authority. Methodist circuit riders like Francis Asbury and Freeborn Garrettson looked to Wesley in England and refused to take patriot oaths. One militia officer described their antirevolutionary preachings as "the greatest stroke the British Ministry ever struck amongst us." Dorchester County militia leaders reported their troops "very lukewarm in the opposition, difficult to be got together, and when collected, in such bad discipline they are not (in their opinion) to be relied on, paying but little regard to the instructions of their officers." Unable to organize the men who worked on the water, another officer called them "a set of Poor, Ignorant, Illitorate People. Yet," he conceded, "they are Artful and Cunning as Foxes." Worcester County troops deserted in defiance of a brutal company officer. An infamous Tory guerrilla (or simply pirate) named China Clow threatened patriot supply points at the head of the bay and also freed slaves, probably more in defiance of authority than for humanitarian reasons. Riots broke out on the Eastern Shore over shortages of salt, and bands of poor men—adding to what William Fitzhugh earlier had called "democratical confusion"—plundered the supplies of the wealthy. [52]

For the Revolution to succeed—and at this point some patriot leaders had doubts it would—support at home had to be combined with success in the field. Members of the first state legislature, meeting in February 1777, somberly faced the first of these objects and passed laws that penalized themselves and violated some of their own cherished principles. One of the measures, a tax bill, abolished the head or poll tax that in colonial times provided most of the funds required to support the provincial government, and in its place established a progressive tax on various kinds of property. By 1781 Maryland tax laws covered the value of iron mines, merchants' inventories, slaves, real estate, and improvements. Special provisions for the poor allowed tenants to deduct their assessed tax bill from their annual rent and debtors to reduce their interest payments by the amount of their tax bill (to offset these provisions, the state did not consider a creditor's receivable accounts as taxable property). Another important wartime provision floated paper currency, which, though greatly below the value of sterling money, Maryland required creditors to accept in payment of all debts. Chase and Charles Ridgely, two supporters of the bill, did indeed owe large sums themselves. But the measure, imposing considerable sacrifice on creditors, had the support of almost all the legislators, who still overwhelmingly represented wealth and station. Carroll of Carrollton referred to the bill as the "price of Revolution"; "No great revolution can happen in a state without revolutions or mutations of private property," he wrote, pointing to the practical need to win wide support for the state government and the patriot cause. His father, retaining the principle of repayment of borrowed money in full value, viciously attacked Chase for promoting the scheme, called its supporters "highwaymen and pickpockets," and nearly broke with Carroll of Carrollton over the question. Father and son traded views on the lengths to which persons of integrity might go to win popular favor in tumultuous times.[53]

Quite a distance, many of them agreed. Together with tax and currency legislation, the creation of the state government helped to build links between the new establishment and ordinary Marylanders. Tax commissioners, purchasing agents for the war effort, loan subscription committees, and the like permitted leaders in Annapolis to make patronage choices at the local level which William Eddis compared to the old proprietary system. "The persons now employed, greatly, very greatly, exceed every former establishment," he commented; "the present rulers most amply reward the laborers in their vineyard." Yet the expedient had high purpose and apparently worked. Of the 414 persons selected to fill new offices, 335 never before had been a part of government. To deal with the problem of loyalism and disorder, the early state assemblies offered both olive branch and sword. A strong bill for the suppression of Tories and traitors carried heavy penalties. The state courts, meeting on the Eastern Shore for the first time in April 1778, prudently adopted a policy of leniency toward those men—virtually all of them either landless or hardscrabble planters—found guilty of disloyalty, generally levying a fine in paper currency. By the end of the year, when British operations shifted to Georgia and the Carolinas, "disaffected" persons remaining behind lost a vital source of encouragement. China Clow remained at large, but a semblance of order returned to the Eastern Shore.[54]

Plagued with internal strife, Maryland made war contributions far heavier than one might have expected. Of course its citizens sacrificed as did patriots throughout the new states. To supply the army during the first winter of the war, local authorities commandeered half of every household's extra blankets, paid for them in paper currency, and later in the same manner sought one pair of shoes and white yarn stockings from every housekeeper. In Cecil, Harford, and Baltimore counties, as elsewhere, farmers on the army's line of march lost wagons, cattle, horses, grain, and other property to the military—receiving only paper in exchange. Early in 1780, when the Continental Congress turned to the states for supplies in kind, the Maryland quota for army foodstuffs stood at 20,000 barrels of flour, 200 tons of hay, and some 56,000 bushels of corn. On top of these calls Robert Morris, congressional finance superintendent, the following summer requested enough Maryland ships and boats to transport 7,000 men from Head of Elk to Virginia and laid another heavy demand for provisions—beef, pork, salt, and rum besides tobacco and grain. These burdens fell on county committees and after them on Maryland farmers and watermen on both shores. The 1781 episode demonstrated how grudgingly citizens accepted paper currency (especially when French forces had hard money) and illustrated the reluctance of local committees to impress private property. Still, Maryland officials succeeded in gathering nearly 4,000 barrels of flour, 2,000 of salt, herds of cattle, and large quantities of forage for Washington's troops, many of whom went down the bay in private vessels. Marylanders later filled special army orders for picks and shovels, gunpowder, cannon, and the spirits that made water potable.

Several Maryland towns bustled and profited. Frederick served as a powder depository and Hessian prisoner-of-war camp. At Annapolis, a mustering and shipping point, the state established a hospital, first on State Circle, in 1776 and then leased one of the town's two tanning yards to make military leatherware. At one point in hot weather the council of safety suspended tanning because of its "intolerable stench." Citizens avoided putting up soldiers in their homes, and with reason; troops left the Annapolis jail damaged beyond repair and in their search for firewood did not improve several vacant dwellings there. Baltimore, spared Norfolk's destruction and the occupation that hamstrung Philadelphia and New York, enjoyed another growth spurt as a supply depot between northern and southern theaters of operation, a landing and loading point that required fortification, and a center of wartime manufacturing. In the winter of 1776–77, when the British threatened Philadelphia, Congress moved to Baltimore and sat at Jacob Fite's tavern on Market (later Baltimore) Street. The assembly legislated geese and pigs off of major thoroughfares and tried to widen some of them to speed war-related traffic. In winter months scavengers ravished outlying woodlands for fuel, and food prices rose sharply. Baltimore attracted another wave of aggressive merchants—among them William Patterson and the Scottish-born Robert Gilmor—who eagerly invested in wartime shipping and industry. Baltimoreans built water-powered factories to do work colonial restrictions had left to England alone: dyeing and carding wool, making linen, manufacturing paper and hardware. Jesse Hollingsworth, who had come to Baltimore from Cecil County, William Moore, and the partners Joseph Ellicott and Hugh Burgess supplied French and Continental troops with flour. In 1780 Baltimore obtained its own customshouse, severing its official reliance on Annapolis.

Maritime grievances against Britain helped to explain the dominance of patriots at Fells Point and Baltimore, and merchants, shipbuilders, and sailors there applied themselves eagerly to the business of naval warfare. As early as October 1775 Congress ordered two cruisers, *Hornet* and *Wasp*, outfitted in Baltimore for attacks on hostile British vessels and in December commissioned a shipyard at Fells Point to produce the twenty-eight-gun *Virginia*. Unfurling the Continental colors in Baltimore for the first time the following summer, Joshua Barney, a Baltimore County native, had assembled a full crew for the *Hornet* by the end of a single day. Barney's later career reflected considerable credit on Maryland, as did the exploits of Captain James Nicholson, a Chestertown native and ranking American naval officer after January 1777. The Maryland council of safety began commissioning its own vessels in mid-1776 to rid shallow waters of the many British boats and barges that harassed shipping and carried scavenging parties. A few craft in the Maryland navy—the *Defence* with twenty-two six-pounders, brigs *Friendship* and *Amelia*, and the twenty-two-gun sloop *Hebe Johnson* among them—made captures in the bay and sailed outside its mouth. Most of the vessels, lightly armed galleys and forty-two-foot barges that drew only fifteen inches of water, patrolled the tributaries of the bay and, in 1776–77, challenged Lord Dunmore's forces off the lower counties.

The most damaging blow Marylanders dealt to the enemy at sea, however, came not from commissioned warships but from armed privateers—vessels carrying letters of marque and reprisal that authorized them to take prizes later condemned in admiralty courts and divided as booty. The forms and rules governing privateering had been one of the earliest pronouncements of the Continental Congress. Between the spring of 1776 and the end of the war, Baltimore, then with a population of some six thousand, became home port to about 250 privateers—most the now-famous bay schooners and sloops that enabled a small crew to sail with great speed and maneuverability. The rewards and adventure of privateering strongly attracted Maryland sailors, and because the practice so well combined patriotic service and individual enterprise, financial backers were no more difficult to find. Prominent merchants and millers of the city—John Sterrett (the city's leading shipper, with interests in 23 vessels), Jeremiah Yellott, Charles Ridgely, Thomas Todd, Andrew Skinner Ennals, Hollingsworth, the Smiths and Purviances—led the business. Joining in it were captains and speculators, hitherto little known, whose skill and luck started their fortunes. Non-Baltimoreans like

John Johnson of Annapolis, Levin Gale of Somerset County, and Robert Morris of Philadelphia bought interests in privateers, as did Dutch and Spanish investors. Fighting some memorable naval battles in the bay and cruising the Atlantic, Maryland privateers severely crippled British commerce, driving up insurance rates and by one estimate taking 559 sail between 1776 and 1778 alone. They also gained American forces badly needed war supplies like powder, arms, and clothing, and provided income to the state through charges made for licenses, admiralty court costs, and the public share of some prizes. The speed and daring of Maryland privateer crews enabled the state to run the British blockade of capes Henry and Charles with cargoes of corn, wheat, and flour. Sold in the French West Indies, Chesapeake products helped the legislature supply its troops in the field.

The recruitment, provisioning, and disciplining of those soldiers posed some of the most serious problems Governor Thomas Johnson and the assembly faced during the war. In addition to the unreliability of many Eastern Shore militia units, the lack of adequate arms left the defenses of the state precarious for much of the early Revolution. Only gradually did iron foundries like that of Samuel Hughes on Antietam Creek, a gunlock factory established at Frederick in 1776, and captures begin to meet the needs of Maryland naval and military services. At the outset of war, recruiting instructions explicitly required "great Regard to moral Character; Sobriety in particular." "You are to inlist no Man," read one set of orders, "who is not able bodied, healthy and a good marcher, nor such whose attachment to the liberties of America you have cause to suspect. Young hearty robust men who are tied by Birth Family Connections or property to this Country; and are well practised in the use of firearms are by much to be preferred."[55]

At first the assembly relied on such volunteers, who received a bounty and a promise of future land grants, to fill the eight regiments of Continental infantry Congress requested of the state. Later measures forced vagrants and invited free blacks as well as servants—whose masters were compensated—into military service. By 1778 the failure of these plans forced the legislature to enact a complicated draft act that allowed one to send a substitute. The foreign-born, British convicts, and British deserters were not acceptable under the recruitment laws. The 1778 act and another in 1780 nonetheless succeeded in collecting for service men who, commonly the most desperate in a given county, counted need among their motives for joining. Such men may not have approached the rigors of campaigning with the highest sense of duty.

All the same, Maryland troops in Continental service generally acquitted themselves well and at war's end belonged to the core of the American army. Among the first southern soldiers to reach Washington's forces at the siege of Boston late in the summer of 1775 were the volunteer western Marylanders of Michael Cresap and Thomas Price. All expert shots, they left Frederick "painted like Indians, armed with tomahawks and rifles, dressed in hunting-shirts and moccasins," and in a mere three weeks covered the 550 miles to Boston. Their long-range accuracy had an immediate effect on unwary British troops. During the disastrous fighting around New York the following August and September, infantrymen commanded by General William Smallwood, a Charles County native who had served in the lower house of assembly, earned first honors for Maryland at the battle of Long Island, when the left and center of the outflanked American line broke and began a flight to the rear. On the right, led at the time by Major Mordecai Gist, stood four hundred of the earliest Maryland troops to enlist in the war, wearing the red and buff uniforms first adopted by the Baltimore Independent Cadets. Using bayonets more than fire, Gist's men sacrificed themselves trying to cover the retreat. Five times they swept into a British force that held the Cortelyou House and its commanding position, losing in the attempt more than half their number killed, wounded, or captured. Tench Tilghman, a native of Talbot County and member of Washington's staff, proudly reported home that "no regular troops ever made a more gallant resistance," while another aide to Washington wrote that Smallwood's men "inspired the whole army."[56] Later, reinforced with Maryland companies of the Flying Camp, the Marylanders played a conspicuous part in other rear-guard actions at Harlem Heights and White Plains.

The Maryland Line served three years with Washington in New York, New Jersey, and Pennsylvania, and then, in the spring of 1780, spent what must have been a bittersweet few days passing through their home state— marching to Head of Elk and then sailing down the bay to face Cornwallis's threat in the Carolinas. At a succession of bloody encounters that summer and through September of the next year—Camden, Cowpens, Eutaw Springs, and Hobkirk's Hill among them—the Old Line won further renown in fighting that always cost the British heavy losses. Under two colonels on whom General Nathaniel Greene depended in the southern campaigns, Otho Holland Williams and John Eager Howard, Maryland troops made up a third of the southern army and with the Delaware Continentals often formed the center of the American position. "Nothing could exceed the gallantry of the Maryland Line," wrote Greene, commending the troops who at Hobkirk's Hill fought one of the worst hand-to-hand struggles of the war and helped to bring about the British surrender at Yorktown. "Cols. Williams and Howard, and all the officers, exhibited acts of uncommon bravery, and the free use of the bayonet, by this and some other corps, gave us the victory."[57]

The Maryland Line may have owed its success to the commonness of outdoor sports in the Chesapeake country and the ruggedness of life on the western Maryland frontier. By all reports Maryland troops received superior training from Smallwood, a rigorous disciplinarian whose earliest subordinate officers had a reputation for élan. "There were none by whom an un-

"Battle of Long Island—Retreat of the Americans under Gen. Stirling across Gowanus Creek." Engraving by Jas. Boudine after an original painting by Alonzo Chappel, c. 1866. Maryland troops placed themselves between the wreckage of Stirling's army, in the foreground of this sentimental rendering, and the advancing British. *MHS*

officerlike appearance and deportment could be less tolerated," wrote a Pennsylvanian, "than by a city-bred Marylander, who, at this time, was distinguished by the most fashionably cut coat, the most macaroni cocked hat, and the hottest blood in the union."[58] First discipline, then experience must have made a difference in handling citizen-soldiers. Along with seasoned noncommissioned officers, field leaders like Gist, Samuel Smith, Williams, and Howard shaped and tempered the Maryland Line. Fighting in both north and south, Maryland troops—along with Delaware and Virginia Continentals—could not help but take a large view of the conflict and may for that reason have fought with uncommon zeal. Perhaps even poverty and indebtedness—turned into democratic yearnings—came into play. The Maryland Line represented under arms the change in mind that preferred winning independence (and all it promised) to standing by old ways.

In any event, Maryland veterans could be irreverent. After the Yorktown

Military leaders of the Revolution. *Upper left,* William Smallwood (1732–92). *Upper right,* Otho Holland Williams (1749–94). *Lower left,* John Eager Howard (1752–1827). Paintings by Charles Willson Peale, c. 1782, for his Philadelphia museum's "Gallery of Great Men." *Independence National Historical Park Collection. Lower right,* Mordecai Gist (1743–92) by Luther Terry, after Charles Willson Peale, 1837. *MHS*

surrender Washington ordered American and French soldiers, moving at the same pace, to take ceremonial control of the British redoubt. The Marquis de Lafayette marched in front of some Maryland troops, who could see little point to mere ceremony (or diplomacy). Legend had it that a sergeant from Emmitsburg bellowed "Hurry, general, those d—d Frenchmen will get in before us yet."[59]

CHAPTER 4

Realizing the New Republic

I n the 1790s Baltimore became the fastest-growing city in the country. Outsiders complained that the cost of living was higher than in London, and land values in the bustling harbor area climbed constantly. Colorful pennants, each of them representing a different firm, announced major ship arrivals from an observatory atop the hill overlooking the basin. At Fells Point hundreds of vessels—brigantines, scows, schooners, and sloops—lay tied up along wharves that stretched into the water like fingers. In the crowded streets teamsters drove draft horses hitched two, four, or even six to a wagon—"every detail of the harnesses and carriages," someone reported, "bearing evidence of care and neatness." Three markets—one on Hanover Street, another on Harrison, and a third across the Jones Falls marsh at Fells Point—supplied housekeepers with meat and produce and were busiest on Thursdays and Saturdays. Nearly half the three thousand or more houses were brick, two and a half stories high. Holes cut in the wooden eaves gave asylum to swallows—"for it is believed," a visitor explained, "that their affection for a home brings prosperity to its inhabitants." Baltimoreans enjoyed cards and dancing and attended two theaters, though one was "little better than a heap of loose boards." A leading hotel in town, the Indian Queen at the corner of Hanover and Market streets, served food that pleased even the French. When guests retired they were given slippers to wear; slaves polished shoes or boots and before morning left them outside one's door.

A boomtown of special character, Baltimore mixed slave and free, land and water, the romantic and the rowdy. It left varied impressions. Chateaubriand recalled that entering the harbor was like sailing into a park. Walking the upper Jones Falls left another visitor fairly enraptured. "The rocky bed over which the water flows, a grist mill with its turning wheel and the intermingling of the numerous phases of rural life with those of a commercial and maritime city are extremely pleasing," he wrote, "and linger in the mind of him who returns to the city along the banks of the stream." Still, low tide revealed an inner harbor slime that gave off foul vapors, especially after summer showers. The stench convinced outsiders of what the natives denied—that the air was sickly. Holding his nose for other reasons, an Englishman wrote that once a vessel tied up at Baltimore the crew "waited not even a twilight to fly to the polluted arms of the white, the black, the yellow harlot." Gentlemen and ladies of the city were "mild, obliging, and hospitable," said a grateful foreigner—they pressed one "to make a longer stay in every house he visits." "Collected from all quarters," wrote yet another European, Baltimoreans "are bent on the pursuit of wealth; to get money honestly, if they can, but at any rate to get it."[1]

In the spring of 1783 Congress agreed to the treaty ending war with Britain and on 23 December, standing before a meeting of Congress at Annapolis, George Washington resigned his commission and returned to private life. Peace, though welcomed, neither resolved squabbles among the states in Congress nor settled differences within states. It remained uncertain what shape the newly founded republic might take. Many Americans doubted that a free society could survive the centrifugal forces of selfishness, corruption, and democracy.

One issue that nicely demonstrated interstate suspicions and the potential for selfishness in the new republic involved western lands. To encourage army enlistments, Congress in September 1776 proposed that each state grant a bounty of land to officers and soldiers—up to five hundred acres to high-ranking officers, one hundred to each enlisted man. The Maryland convention returned a message that the state had little land it could claim as its own and could ill afford to purchase western territory to meet the request or match competition from landed states. Marylanders pointed out that if larger states claiming imperial domains could use their lands to pay their soldiers and fund their public debt as they pleased, Maryland and the other states having no such claims "must be so weakened and impoverished, that they can hold their liberties only at the will of their powerful neighbours." Taking the lead among the landless states, Maryland finally refused to ratify the Articles of Confederation until its neighbor to the south and others surrendered their western claims to the Congress and accepted definite boundaries. No state should stand in the Union as a preeminent power, Marylanders declared. Back lands claimed by the British Crown, "if secured by the blood and treasure of all, ought in reason, justice, and policy, to be considered as a common stock, to be parcelled out by Congress into free, convenient, and independent Governments, as the wisdom of that body shall hereafter direct."[2]

The motives for this constructive obstinacy were mixed, and they included self-interest. A few powerful Marylanders held shares in land companies with Ohio country claims that were good only if Virginia stepped aside. Governor Thomas Johnson, whose interest in western land and ironmaking had included extensive purchases in the Indian Spring and Catoctin regions of Washington County, owned shares in the Wabash Company. So did other Maryland investors. Eventually Samuel Chase, Charles Carroll of Carrollton, and William Paca also bought into the Ohio-country scheme, and shareholders sat in the convention that issued the appeal for congressional authority in the west. Still, the view that the west should belong to all the states reflected opinion that ran deep in the Maryland convention and perhaps embodied a view of the future that even went beyond the traditional Maryland jealousy of Virginia. Besides the problems "imperial" Virginia would pose in the federation, Marylanders considered the growth of the west. In the 1770s English-speaking settlements beyond the Appalachians—at places like Vandalia in the Illinois country and Watauga in far western North Carolina—had issued calls for self-government. There was good sense in the argument that a union of states would endure only if it suppressed imbalances of size and power and allowed for western political development under the authority of the Congress, where states had equal weight. Virginia finally turned over its western lands on terms that satisfied its views of sovereignty, and Maryland thus had an indirect part in the Northwest Ordinance of 1784, the farthest-reaching decision the Confederation Congress made.

Illustrating less ambiguously the play of opportunity in Maryland public life, Samuel Chase's wartime and postwar career confirmed the worst fears that self-government led to self-indulgence. A member of Congress in the summer of 1778, Chase had used knowledge of an impending government flour purchase to buy up large quantities of Baltimore grain and make himself and his partner, John Dorsey, a tidy profit. Later, learning of confidential plans in Congress to lift an embargo on tobacco exports, Chase bought up all the tobacco he could find. By the 1780 legislative term, Chase, a leader in the House of Delegates, had acquired enough money to begin making loans; he and his friends in that session repealed the earlier legal tender act, thus making debts payable in currency of greater value than issued paper. Chase ruled the house "without control," Carroll of Carrollton believed; "the acts of that branch of the legislature respecting money matters seem calculated to answer his particular contracts and interests." At the same time, Chase began purchasing Maryland paper issues, and in a proposed tax bill introduced a clause that would have pledged the faith and credit of the state to redeem paper at two-thirds its value in hard currency. Another public issue that yielded private gain in these years involved confiscation. Learning that the British had seized Maryland's Bank of England stock (a legacy of the 1733 paper money act), the assembly in 1780 voted to seize Loyalist and British property in the state.

Chase and a group of speculators close to him were prominent among purchasers of these town and rural holdings, which were worth about £500,000 and included the extensive Principio Ironworks in Cecil County.

"A Front View of the State-House &c. at Annapolis the Capital of Maryland." Engraving from *Columbian Magazine* (Philadelphia, 1789). *MHS*

Apparently Chase and cohorts began with several plans to insure that they might buy up the choicest properties. By one scheme, attached to the 1779 version of the bill, auctions were to take place in January, when few competitors would likely leave their firesides. Indirect evidence suggests that speculators hit upon a far more sophisticated arrangement. Daniel of St. Thomas Jenifer, by the early 1780s friendlier to Chase than to the Carrolls, served as intendant of the revenues and exercised supervisory power over the sale of confiscated property. Jenifer quietly disallowed for "irregularities" the purchases Chase and his syndicate made of some important properties, with the result that they went to the same men for far less than the bid price. The confiscation law permitted these purchases to be made on credit, a provision most buyers took advantage of, and in November 1787 purchasers of Loyalist and British property owed the state more than £303,000. By that time Chase, along with other speculators in that property like Jeremiah Townley Chase of Annapolis (Samuel Chase's first cousin once removed), Charles Ridgely of Baltimore County, William Paca, and the state attorney general, Luther Martin, once again had become advocates of paper money.[3]

Because the world of Maryland leadership was so small, Chase's "desperate circumstances"—his "imprudence, incapacity, and extravagance," as one enemy put it—carried large significance. The senate severely reprimanded Chase in 1778; after recalling him from the congressional delegation, the General Assembly even passed a law prohibiting merchants from serving in Congress. Believing with reason that Carroll of Carrollton had led the movement to censure him, Chase, protesting his innocence, engaged Carroll in a savage newspaper exchange during the late summer of 1781. Neither man ever quite forgave the other for what appeared in print. With Chase leading the House of Delegates and Carroll standing as a towering figure in the senate, new actors played the old scenes of conflict between upper and lower houses. Chase curried popular favor by calling members of the senate Tories. Carroll opposed the paper money act of 1785 as irresponsible and tainted with self-service. In the eyes of Carroll and others Chase and his friends had gotten drunk on the wine of self-rule. Gaining privately from public service, they exemplified the corruption that had brought decay to earlier republics.[4]

More alarming, Chase drew on a deep well of resentment among common folk, for whom the Revolution brought expectations of lighter taxes and less aristocracy. They detested any plan that smacked of elitism. An act of 1785 fit that description by appropriating proceeds from certain state licences and fines—about £3,000 annually—toward support of two colleges, one in Annapolis, the other in Chestertown. Though one critic wondered whether these cities might turn out to be "places where vice and debauchery abound," the main objection to the measure, which wisely appealed for support from both sides of the bay, lay in its aristocratic overtones. Enemies of the college act noted that it obliged the poor to pay for educating the wealthy. "Is it not assisting and invigorating that dangerous effort in civil society to aggrandize the few, and depress the many?" asked an "Old Soldier" from Washington County; "the rulers of the state," wrote another suspicious citizen, "mean to establish ranks among us, and begin their scheme by founding a College, wherein the lordly sons of our future nobility will be trained up, uncontaminated by a mixture with boys of plebian mould."[5]

Common Marylanders expressed deepest anger over money matters, for indebtedness plagued and taxes severely burdened them. At the end of the war the state owed nearly £1,648,000, with yearly interest payments amounting to about £20,000—sums hardly imaginable a few years before. In 1782 estimated property tax receipts, £264,348, amounted to an average of £1.11.0 per white person—or about half one's yearly income. Taxes looked to climb higher. Congress relied on the states to shoulder the staggering Continental debt; Maryland legislators, like lawmakers elsewhere, first wanted to build courthouses, pay state salaries, and service the debt owed to Marylanders. Meanwhile a typical planter might have been in debt to a British creditor (who now tried to collect), a local merchant, and the tax collector; like Chase and friends though on a smaller scale, he might owe the state for an earlier purchase of confiscated land. Indeed, the seizure of Lord Baltimore's manors had enabled many tenants, on credit, to climb into the landowning bracket and obtain the vote.

Economic laws and currency policy affected everyone's livelihood. Debtors naturally preferred to pay their debts and taxes in inflated or depreciated currency (while their crops commanded more paper than hard coin, they could make required payments at the face value of the notes), while creditors avoided such payments. Trying to collect family debts in these years, John Galloway simply refused to accept depreciated Continental paper. Maryland paper money in circulation, printed late in the war, carried the promise of staggered redemption between December 1784 and May 1786. In the fall 1784 session the assembly passed a "consolidating act" that established a single fund to redeem outstanding paper. The act made the depreciated money climb back toward its face amount in value. It also hastened the return of open-handed creditors, spurred tax collectors, and pained people who were in debt.

Eventually the weight of debt had to fall on government and citizen alike. It did after November 1785, when too many imports and too much American production dropped commodity prices. Perhaps half of all Baltimoreans took direct or indirect part in commerce, and the economic falloff threw many of them out of work. Others felt the pinch as well. Early in 1786 more than three hundred Baltimore County residents signed a petition asking the governor to postpone tax collection until after they had taken in their wheat crop. "We really are in a most deplorable condition," read a similar Western Shore petition, which also noted the prevailing low prices for wheat, tobacco, and lumber. "Our property is at the mercy of sheriffs and collectors and sold, will not bring one third its real value." Most Maryland lawyers refused to take debt actions, perhaps for the same reason that a British factor in Charles County made out his will and took precautions against being assassinated. In June 1786, when the factor did try to sue debtors, about a hundred men gathered at the courthouse and rioted. They dispersed only after the justices, their sympathies clear, persuaded the factor to drop his suit. Later that year the campaigns both for the house and for senate electors enabled enemies of the "LORDS or MIZERS of the state" to vent their frustrations. "Wealthy men, in general, are proud and arrogant, and despise the inferior classes of life," declared an Anne Arundel County handbill. Rich creditors, read a letter in the Baltimore *Maryland Journal*, delight in "making men, who are in every way worthy to be their equals, either submit to their . . . extortion, or languish in gaols, whilst their wretched families linger out a miserable existence at home."[6]

Thus, to advocates of order and friends of property rights, the postwar Maryland experience illustrated well how fragile, how vulnerable to unrest, self-government could be—within the states and among them alike. On the one hand Marylanders quarreled over legislation that decided whether debtor's or creditor's ox would be gored worse; on the other, leaders divided over federal issues like the role the hard-pressed states should play in settling the congressional debt. In late 1786 and early 1787 conflict between Maryland debtors and creditors worsened. Members of the House of Delegates proposed additional paper money and debtor-relief legislation. The senate defeated it because it ignored property rights. Paper money partisans, asking whether they were "to be made slaves to a few designing rich men," threatened to instruct senators how to vote and force them to obey; making an important shift from earlier concepts of representation, they argued that senators, like delegates, must do the people's bidding. In response a Frederick horse troop organized and pledged itself to protect the senate from "all tumults, secret and traitorous conspiracies, attempts or combinations whatsoever."[7] At Philadelphia the Congress, presided over by John Hanson, had become so powerless and stricken by problems of funding that it had trouble assembling a quorum. It hardly offered a place for the discussion of pressing practical matters like those Maryland and Virginia faced in regulating commerce and navigation on the waters they shared. The new states could not agree on their Potomac River boundary, much less on standard import duties. Though shippers in both states admitted the need for a lighthouse at Cape Henry (the British had talked about building one since about 1731), Annapolis and Richmond legislators now could not come to terms on how to pay for it. A productive conference on such issues, held at Washington's home in March 1785, prompted delegates to recommend a later session at Annapolis, where, at James Madison's suggestion, deputies from all the states would be welcomed.

Absorbed in local affairs, Maryland leaders did not play the parts they might have taken in the critical business that followed. No Maryland representatives attended the Annapolis meeting of September 1786. In May of the next year, when delegates from all the states met in Philadelphia to discuss improving the Articles of Confederation, neither Chase, who that spring declared bankruptcy, nor Carroll of Carrollton attended. Each feared leaving Maryland to the devices of the other. Daniel of St. Thomas Jenifer, late revenue intendant, represented the large view of a few Marylanders that the federal Congress ought to exercise stronger powers of taxation—ought to address the states' common debt. Of the Marylanders who did attend, Luther Martin took the most active role. Martin, a College of New Jersey (Princeton) graduate whose father had been a poor farmer in Jersey, voiced reservations that blended political science with private interest. He objected that the "Virginia Plan" and its provision for heavy large-state representation eventually would oppress the smaller ones (at the time Maryland was sixth among the thirteen states in population) and accused some members of the convention of secretly being monarchists (Alexander Hamilton had in fact recommended a president for life). Martin made the most of class antagonism at home by noting that the Constitution would, "by the imposition of a variety of taxes, imposts, stamps, excises, and other duties," jeopardize gains common people had won since the Revolution. The proposed govern-

Left, Daniel of St. Thomas Jenifer (1723–90) by John Hesselius, c. 1765, pictured early in his career. *National Portrait Gallery, Smithsonian Institution. Right*, Luther Martin (1748–1826). Engraving by W. A. Wilmer after a painting by an unknown artist of c. 1815. *MHS*

ment, he said, would "squeeze from them the little money they may acquire, the hard earnings of their industry, as you would squeeze the juice from an orange . . . and then let loose upon them their private creditors."[8]

With voting qualifications set as they were in Maryland, no one could say how many citizens in 1788 truly favored the stronger Constitution proposed in Philadelphia. Spokesmen for the debt-ridden, including William Paca and the beleaguered Chase, echoed Martin's doubts about the document, which carried property protections, prohibited state money, and likely would help British creditors. Their "anti-federalist" appeal struck a responsive chord in Anne Arundel, Baltimore, and Harford counties, where debtors and holders of confiscated British estates worried about their future welfare. During the campaign for delegates to the state ratifying convention, newspaper essays signed "Betsey Cornstalk" and "Farmer" tried to expose the Constitution as "the most artful plan that ever was formed to entrap a free people." Refuse this "new-fangled" scheme, begged an ordinary Marylander, "and extricate yourselves and posterity from tyranny, oppression, aristocratical or monarchical government."[9]

Leading supporters of the Constitution, known as federalists, centered on the Maryland Senate and carried considerable prestige. They included Carroll of Carrollton, his cousin Daniel Carroll, Thomas Johnson (who in the 1775 Congress had nominated Washington to be commanding general of American forces), Edward Lloyd, George Plater, Robert Goldsborough, Thomas Sim Lee (governor between 1779 and 1782), and Judge Alexander Contee Hanson, who published a persuasive proratification pamphlet. Actually federalists relied less on their prestige or political theory than on traditional market-oriented ambitions that drove so many Marylanders—making the most of the bay as a shipping outlet and taking advantage of every resource. Empowered to regulate and protect commerce, the new Congress might end petty conflicts among American ports and thereby promote trade, standardize the currency essential to it, erect tariff barriers beneficial to domestic manufacturing, and undertake various internal improvements. By means of concerted foreign policy and an active navy, the proposed federal government likely would encourage exports of Chesapeake products as well.

Meeting in Annapolis the week of 21 April, the Maryland convention agreed to ratification by a vote of 63 to 11. Chase, Paca, and Martin argued that the Constitution ought to be amended on as many as twenty-two points, limiting congressional powers to those specified and explicitly protecting the private and civil liberties contained in the state's own Declaration of Rights. After Paca voted for ratification the convention appointed a committee under him to consider such proposals, but friends of the document finally grew tired of debate and adjourned. They noted that ratification in Maryland could only improve chances of acceptance in Virginia. Opponents flattered themselves that the Virginians might pick up the standard of a bill of rights.

Doubtless Marylanders who could vote followed their pocketbooks in deciding the issue of ratification. More than a few convention members, all of whom were the wealthy and privileged sort who had ruled in the past, held the Continental securities that the new government could repay far more readily than the Confederation Congress. Yet economic interest reached well below the level of property owners and creditors. Besides market-oriented farmers on both shores of the bay, ordinary seamen, workers in shipyards, and mechanics all joined in the hope that the new federal order would bring prosperity. In May 1788, when word reached Baltimore that the required nine states had ratified the Constitution, thousands of sailors and common workers, along with ship captains and merchants, paraded cheering through the streets of the city until they reached the lofty site (afterward called Federal Hill) of a huge picnic and fireworks display. In the middle of the procession was a miniature warship, christened *Federalist*, fifteen feet long. Built for the occasion, placed on wheels and drawn by four horses, it was "commanded" during the parade by Joshua Barney himself. Barney later put the boat into the Patapsco and sailed it first to a rousing welcome at Annapolis and then to Mount Vernon, where he presented the little vessel to a startled Washington as a gift from Baltimoreans. Seven hundred of them from all ranks already had signed a petition calling on the first federal Congress to cut the "commercial shackles" that kept America from becoming "independent in fact as well as in name."[10]

⟳⟲

Booming confidence and high expectations belonged to Baltimore as nowhere else in America. The first federal census in 1790 counted 13,500 persons there, placing it behind only Philadelphia, New York, and Boston among American cities; a decade later its 26,000 surpassed Boston and seemed to rival Philadelphia. By 1790 six Baltimore newspapers carried word of the far-off events that affected markets. Between 1790 and 1797 the total tonnage of Baltimore-owned vessels jumped from 13,500 to almost 60,000. Regular packets, established in the 1780s, sailed from Baltimore to Rhode Island, Georgetown, Alexandria, Norfolk, and Charleston. Larger vessels followed the established ocean lanes to London, Liverpool, Dublin, Le Havre, Rotterdam, Bremen, Lisbon, Cadiz, and the Canary Islands; laden with foodstuffs, they still sailed to the Caribbean and ventured into South American waters for coffee and other tropical goods. Baltimoreans built a small but steady commerce with China and the East Indies. The French and Dutch continued to be the best customers for Maryland tobacco, made direct purchases after the Revolution, and in the 1790s placed trade consuls in Baltimore. Shipping, manufacturing (which after 1784 included sugar refining), and the boldness of Baltimore merchants continued to account for this phenomenal rise. Samuel Smith, now a militia general and warden of the port, obtained a subcontract to supply the official French tobacco monopoly. American ships in the Mediterranean had lost British naval protection against North African pirates; Smith had his London agents bribe officials for the passports that gave him clear sailing and distinct advantage in those waters. His ships falsified documents to avoid French and British restrictions on West Indian trade. Robert Oliver, a young Scots-Irishman who had arrived as a commercial agent in 1783, soon entered into a partnership with another immigrant, Hugh Thompson, and began a hugely successful career by providing commercial services (consignment agents, purchasers, debt collectors) to European firms. "Men generally persue their own interests," Oliver wrote in his record book, "without regard to any other persons."[11]

In the exciting post-Revolutionary years men of affairs devised altogether new ways of doing business and tackling projects. Earlier, relying on personal contacts and trust built up over years of trade, merchants largely had handled credit functions among themselves. The needs and ambitions of Baltimore commerce prepared the ground for banks. Robert Morris of Philadelphia had established the first American bank late in the Revolution; its success, despite the view of many farmers that it manipulated prices and elevated some citizens over others, led to similar experiments in New York and Massachusetts in the 1780s. Having failed in 1782 to locate enough subscribers, Baltimoreans in 1790 succeeded and obtained a state charter for the Bank of Maryland. By 1807 they had established three more banks. Besides issuing paper money (redeemable for hard coin) and easing the flow of commercial affairs, banks attracted deposits that created a credit reservoir—they made capital available for investment as never before. There were other signs of change as well. To a joint-stock fire insurance company founded in 1787 (the first in the United States), Baltimoreans in the next twenty years added ten more mutual associations—half of them marine insurance firms. Chartered companies built bridges over the Jones Falls and the Patapsco. Another began water service in Baltimore. Freshwater springs had sufficed until the early 1790s, when these sources dried up or grew foul tasting. In 1804, after several false starts, a joint-stock company began work on a system to pipe water from the upper Jones Falls to the city, at first using wooden logs bored to four inches. No single person could have built the waterworks: Baltimore banks and companies announced the arrival of corporate, impersonal, endeavor.

Nonetheless, inventiveness wore many faces, and the excitement of phenomenal growth in Baltimore left plenty of room for individual effort. The city became the center of statewide interest in applied science—a trend the steamboat pioneer James Rumsey vividly illustrated. In the 1780s Rumsey, a Cecil County native whom Jefferson described as "the most original and the greatest mechanical genius I have ever seen," had hoped to solve a major problem of inland navigation by using steam to propel a boat upstream. By September 1784, working at Shepherdstown, Virginia, he had completed a model of his craft and impressed Washington with its "vast importance." Rumsey next constructed a full-size boat using a boiler and other parts made at Frederick and Baltimore. While his neighbors believed him mad, the inventor plodded on alone, and for the sake of secrecy made his first experimental voyages at night. The prototype vessel suffered damage in a sudden storm. Finally, in December 1787, Rumsey launched his steamboat, took on six passengers, and proceeded to chug and hiss up the Potomac near Shepherdstown. By later accounts one of the distinguished witnesses, General Horatio Gates, shouted with excitement, "My God! it moves!"—and yet despite this impressive performance, financial backing proved difficult to find. Rumsey died in London, where he had gone to seek it, and Robert Fulton's later success with a different steam engine eclipsed Rumsey's considerable achievement.[12]

Because the federal government greatly simplified the patenting process (previous protection had to be obtained from state legislatures), Maryland inventors after 1789 eagerly set about finding ways and means of getting things done more easily. Baltimore, hard at work, lent them encouragement. Millers on the Patapsco adopted the improved system of Oliver Evans, by which the same water-powered train driving the stones also turned the machinery that brought up wheat and carried off flour. The problem of mud in

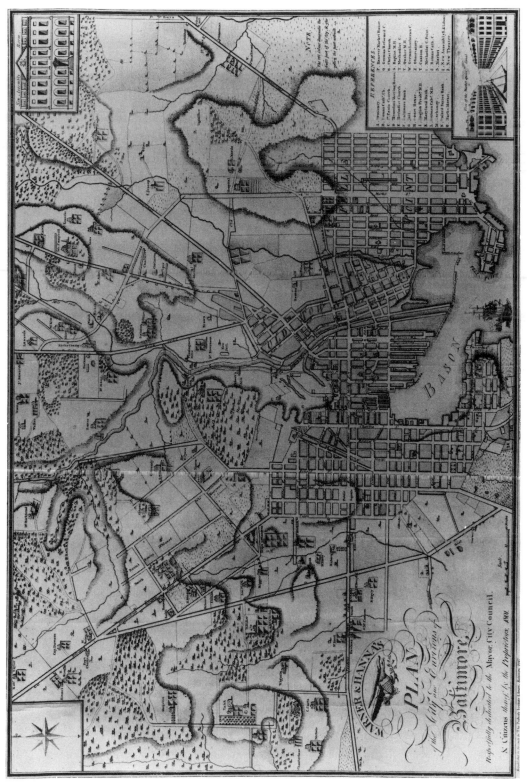

"Warner & Hanna's Plan of the City and Environs of Baltimore," 1801. *MHS*

the inner harbor led Peter Zacharie to build a dredging machine in 1791. Later he patented a device for cutting nails from rods. James Long devised a new way to nap hats. In 1803 Thomas Moore of Brookeville advertised a device he called a refrigerator. Thomas Bruff, unusually versatile, developed a new coffee mill, an improved tooth-extracting machine, and a better way to make spoons. William Faris (or Ferris) dabbled in carriages and water-raising devices.[13]

Raising water—so that it could power a wheel, usually to turn a grist mill—also became the mania of a native Virginian, Englehart Cruse, who made a name for himself in Baltimore in the early 1790s by trying to perfect a steam system that would run a mill at the end of a pier. His machine would save time and money by enabling ships laden with grain to make flour while tied up. Cruse published handbills that described glowing possibilities for the engine. He sent a sketch of it to Washington and in 1791 received a patent from Secretary of State Jefferson, who on principle preferred not to grant such "monopolies." Unfortunately the prototype engine never worked as well as Cruse wished, and in 1793 he declared himself bankrupt. Unbeknown to Cruse, who later went on to Charleston, South Carolina, the British already had built a direct-drive steam gristmill that far outdid his raised-water machine. Cruse's energy, if nothing else, illustrated the positive relationship between boom and experimentation.[14]

As in older American cities, ethnicity more than wealth but no single factor dictated one's place of residence in Baltimore. Probably more Germans made their homes west than east of the Jones Falls. On the southern edge of the city lived descendants of French Acadians; expelled by the British from Nova Scotia, they had landed in Baltimore a bit awkwardly during the French and Indian War. More French refugees—fifty-three ships with white planters and their families, together with some blacks and mulattoes—arrived in 1793, when a slave uprising in the French colony of Saint-Domingue (soon Haiti) turned into race war. Those who stayed in the city added to its cosmopolitan, biracial flavor. In 1800 nearly three thousand slaves lived in Baltimore, many of them, house servants, dwelling with well-to-do white families dispersed throughout the city. The rest worked as craftsmen, seamstresses, stevedores, teamsters, or laborers, and apparently either boarded with their masters in the city or—contracted to Baltimore companies by planters—established their own lodgings. White construction laborers congregated on Bridge (later Gay) Street. Artisans and laborers lived east of the Jones Falls in old Jones Town or Old Town. There they joined a few Jewish families who in 1801 acquired a small cemetery plot from Charles Carroll of Carrollton. Sailors boarded around the Fells Point docks, but merchants and sea captains also lived near the water. In 1799 John Hollins and James Buchanan built mansions on Calvert north of Baltimore Street. At the same time lawyers lived near the city courthouse along with persons of lesser income.[15]

The hodgepodge pattern of wealth and color did not quite signify equality. John Adams, attending Congress during the first winter of the war, had remarked that the Baltimore gentry held "all laboring people and tradesmen, in such contempt, that they think themselves a distinct order of beings." A few wealthy families sustained Adams's point; besides town houses, they owned estates on the hilltops that looked down on the city. In the mid-eighteenth century Charles Carroll the Barrister had built Mount Clare mansion, a handsome Georgian summer home southwest of the town. Originally standing on a 2,300-acre plantation, Mount Clare in time gave over most of its land to iron mining, milling on the Gwynn's Falls, and shipbuilding on the lower Patapsco. Marrying the daughter of an original town commissioner, William Lux had obtained a similar seat, Chatsworth, half a mile from the town, where Adams said Lux lived "like a Prince."[16]

In establishing similar summer or country homes, later Baltimoreans pursued this patrician ideal. They also paid respect to the danger of yellow fever, a malady that arrived with the Saint-Dominguean refugees in 1793 and for many years afterward ravaged the city in August and September. Thus Robert Gilmor's Beech Hill, William Patterson's Hampstead Hill, east of the city, and Robert Oliver's Green Mount to the northeast combined healthful escape with the aura of planting. Colonel John Eager Howard, son of a planter (and governor between 1788 and 1791), built Belvidere, a massive home with greenhouse and formal garden, on a ridge north of Charles Street. Farther north and west lay Bolton, the seat of the merchant George Grundy, whose thirty acres provided room enough for brick barns, stables, sheds, smoke- and icehouses, a gardener's house, slave quarters, orchards, and extensive hayfields. David Harris, a banker, enjoyed showing friends around Mount Deposit.

These estates reflected the taste, occasionally the talent, and of course the vanity of leading Baltimoreans. Far to the north of the city, on property known as Homewood, Carroll of Carrollton's son ordered a classic Georgian country house built in about 1801. Samuel Smith may have had a hand in laying out his oddly shaped house, Montebello, which he named after a French victory over the Austrians in 1800. Nicholas Rogers, a flour merchant who had been an aide to generals Ducoudray and De Kalb during the Revolution, worked with a local carpenter-builder in designing a home three miles northwest of the basin and then in rebuilding the house after a fire in 1796. Rogers took special pains in landscaping his villa, clumping deciduous trees and evergreens so as to enhance autumnal foliage. Druid Hill and other Baltimore country estates became favorite subjects of Francis Guy, the British-born artist who in the early nineteenth century lived in the city and boasted that his landscapes had "been taken by the best judges to be one hundred years of age." He eagerly painted Baltimore vistas and accepted fat commissions for portraying town-and-country gentlemen strolling about the gardens with family or guests.[17]

A sometime dyer, tailor, and dentist, Guy also painted busy mills on the Jones Falls, but more commonly working people appeared in the distance. Close-up, as he well knew, they presented a colorful though not always happy picture. Workingmen supplied most members of the voluntary fire companies that competed boisterously when the fire bell clanged—for insurance companies paid volunteers according to the number of blazes they put out. Joining the old Mechanical Company were later ones named Union, Friendship, and Mercantile. According to an agreement reached in March 1787, leaders of these companies requested citizens, in the event of a nearby blaze, to aid volunteers by placing candles in their windows (to light the street) and keeping two leather buckets available. Companies named certain members "lane-men." Armed with eight-foot staffs, they cleared a path from the closest water source to the fire. Others, wearing white-topped hats, acted as "property men" whose job was to protect the household goods firemen took out of a burning house.

The larger the city became the heavier the demands it placed on informal civil arrangements, and in 1796 the municipal structure, like business life, began to take more formal shape. A disastrous fire in December of that year, consuming six buildings on Light Street and threatening the famous Fountain Inn, led to a public meeting and further fire regulations. Extending the old voluntary system, civic leaders organized a patrol network and demanded enforcement of the two-bucket-per-household rule and a law requiring chimneys to be swept properly once a month. Because of the fire's suspicious origins, the near-disaster also provided a good excuse to discipline people who occupied the lowest rungs on the social ladder. Twelve resolutions, which included a call for public wells on every street, twice mentioned the need to police vagrants and disorderly persons; the committee recommended that masters and mistresses keep slaves, servants, and apprentices at home after nine at night. Members of the fire committee may have joined men of property and standing in petitioning the General Assembly for a city charter. Mechanical Company volunteers, among others, opposed the measure—less government left service responsibilities to democratic groups like their own. Rural assemblymen, themselves worried about disorder in the bustling city, bowed to advocates of incorporation. On the last day of 1796 Baltimore received a charter creating city courts, a mayor, and a bicameral municipal council.

A city of newcomers, Baltimore at times left its thousands of low- and middling-income workers anxious and afraid. With reason they worried for their health; when epidemics of yellow fever broke out, the disease took its highest toll in the increasingly crowded and poor section of the city east of Jones Falls. German immigrants after 1783 had the benefit of a Baltimore society expressly formed to "guard them from the oppression and barbarity

"View of Mr. Tagert's House and Mr. Pennington's Mill from the New Bridge" by Francis Guy, 1804. *Peabody Institute of the Johns Hopkins University*

of unfeeling men." [18] Members of fire companies jealously guarded them be-cause they served functions beyond answering bells—they helped to knit people together. They provided one way for the men, at least, to "belong," to set themselves off from vagrants and servants. Yet no institutions in the city offered the uprooted more comfort than the churches. In 1790, when only one in ten Americans belonged to a church, Baltimore rolls listed four times that figure. Over the next four decades the number of Baltimore con-gregations grew from eleven to nearly fifty, their membership as a portion of the total population remaining about double the national average. Shocked by the variety of faiths in the city, the New England geographer and Congre-gational minister Jedidiah Morse, writing in 1799, had to doubt that Balti-moreans practiced any religion at all.

Some denominations grew because new members arrived in Baltimore, crowding churches and then spilling over to form others. Roman Catholics established themselves especially well, partly through the efforts of John Carroll, whose background, besides priestly duties in southern Maryland, included diplomatic service. In 1776 Father Carroll had joined his cousin,

Vignette from Baltimore Fire Insurance Company policy, designed by Maximilien Godefroy, c. 1815. The artist offers a vivid glimpse of the terror of city fires in an age of independent fire companies and limited municipal water supplies. *MHS*

Carroll of Carrollton, and two others—Benjamin Franklin and Chase—on a brief and barren mission seeking Canadian support for the Revolution. The choice of his fellow priests to lead the American clergy, Carroll had been consecrated bishop of Baltimore in 1790. The diocese covered the entire country and in 1800 governed only fifty priests. Seven of them were in Baltimore, where Catholics increased from eight hundred in 1790 to several thousand in the first years of the nineteenth century. Two parishes proved the church's immigrant cast and comparative poverty. French emigrés had founded St. Peter's, which was enlarged in 1784; twelve years later, to meet spiritual and temporal needs among the incoming Irish, Catholics formed St. Patrick's Church at Fells Point. Not for sixty-five years did St. Patrick's, made up almost entirely of workingmen and their families, have an American-born pastor. At St. Peter's perhaps as many as two of three parishioners belonged to lower-income families.

Other churches sprang up as quickly as newcomers arrived. Since 1773 Baptists had conducted services at Front and Fayette streets in Old Town. Quakers had moved their Patapsco Meeting from the country to Aisquith and Fayette streets in 1781. The old Anglican, now Protestant Episcopal, church stood bereft of public support in Maryland but still held its old property. Baltimore Episcopalians, all originally belonging to St. Paul's Church, grew steadily and claimed members through all social ranks. The German Reformed congregation (following the Heidelberg catechism) built a new church near the Jones Falls bridge in 1785; finding the spot too risky (flood-waters destroyed it in 1786) and too noisy, its members sold the building to the Episcopalians and started another one in 1795. Presbyterians, heavily composed of wealthy merchants, informed a new minister that they expected "to be treated according to custom with dainties and luxuries, leaving the loaves and fishes, the sackcloth and ashes to the more humble minority." The Presbytery of Baltimore formed in 1786. Three years later, when the First Presbyterian congregation found its church too small, it began raising one of the city's most impressive structures: a twin-towered classic revival building at Fayette Street and Guilford Avenue. John Hargrove built his Swedenborgian Temple of the New Jerusalem in 1799 and soon began publishing *The Temple of Truth* as an antidote to an infidel booklet, *The Temple of Reason*.[19]

The branching of Protestant churches often grew out of internal divisions—personal, theological, or both. Lutherans, enlarging their church in 1785, fell into a dispute over pastors. Johann Siegfried Gerock and the younger man, Johann Daniel Kurtz, finally signed a peace compact pledging one another "sincere brotherly respect." Kurtz went on to become a Lutheran leader of national eminence. A second Presbyterian congregation organized under John Glendy, who was known for his old-fashioned attire and use of expletives. The Episcopalians built Trinity Church after 1805, when a popular assistant pastor at St. Paul's, Elijah Rattoone, stood accused of drunkenness. Significant differences arose over questions of religious orthodoxy and styles of piety—congregations could split angrily over the place of emotional expression in the liturgy. A schism in the Baltimore German Reformed church prompted Philip Otterbein to form an evangelical, Separatist Reformed congregation. Under his dynamic and long-lived leadership, the Separatists grew quickly in numbers in the city and twice built larger churches in this period. Joseph Bend, pastor of St. Paul's Episcopal, had a tiff with another assistant, George Dashiell, whom Bend accused of "inexcusable levity." Instead of organ music, Dashiell encouraged loud singing; he relied on extemporaneous rather than printed prayers. His preaching Bend described as "not unworthy of a camp meeting."[20]

The Reverend Mr. Bend looked askance at a series of awakenings that swept the city in these years (one coincided with the 1800 yellow fever outbreak) and that owed much of their impetus to surging Methodism. American Methodists, like the Catholics, made Baltimore their home. Before the Revolution, Methodists had been strong at Fells Point, where they built the Lovely Lane Church. During Christmastide 1784 Lovely Lane provided the site for a conference of sixty Methodist ministers who followed their English leader, John Wesley, in separating formally from the Church of England. In the newly organized American church, Francis Asbury, who had been preaching in Baltimore, served as superintendent, and for many years afterward Methodists held their annual meetings there. At each general conference Asbury exhorted his fellow churchmen, in the Methodist manner, to

"The Ordination of Bishop Asbury, and Organization of the Methodist Episcopal Church, Dec. 27th, 1784." Engraving by A. G. Campbell after a painting by Thomas Coke Ruckle, 1882. *MHS*

feed the fires of religious awakening; "Lord," he prayed, "look upon our city congregations, for they are a valley of dry bones." The yearly sessions brought Methodists public notice that they turned to pious purpose. During the week of the May 1800 conference, outdoor preaching yielded two hundred conversions—"many fell down," as the Methodists said, "slain with the sword of the spirit."[21]

Aggressive Methodist preaching stirred and won over many Baltimore working people. From fewer than a thousand in 1790, Methodists over the next several decades climbed to thirteen thousand and eventually became the largest communion in the city. Outside Baltimore, under tents that attracted farmers and urban workers alike, they conducted meetings that further swelled their ranks. In September 1804 a gathering fifteen miles out the Reisterstown Road drew more than one thousand persons late in the week and five thousand on Sunday. Fanny Lewis, a young Baltimorean who attended another such meeting, described it as "a day long to be remembered and a night never to be forgotten." She had found "the pearl of great price. The preachers all seemed as men filled with new wine," she testified. Some people in the crowd cried on their feet, "others prostrate on the ground, as insensible to every earthly object; while the Master of assemblies was speaking to the hearts of poor sinners, who stood trembling under a sense of the power and presence of a sin-avenging God." Shunning this emotionalism, clerics of stricter faiths accused evangelical preachers of fondling young women in paroxysms of religious joy (Methodists set regulations on worship in 1820); in any event, Episcopalians and Methodists agreed that sin continued to make great strides in Baltimore. Stephen Grellet, a traveling preacher, complained in 1809 that "the spirit of the world" had "taken deep root" in Methodist meetinghouses there. Next year Methodists decried "backsliding and declension" in the city; too many people had given themselves over to fondness of drink, "love of dress, the love of unprofitable company," and "the inordinate love of money."[22]

Though as a rule women accounted for a large share of denominational growth, revivals appealed strongly to men. Perhaps by blasting worldliness, Methodists unwittingly helped many workingmen square themselves with their economic world: the same drive for efficiency that encouraged inventiveness and incorporation led to changes in Baltimore manufacturing and they, in turn, tended to leave the worker's yearning for material gain unfulfilled. Laborers in skilled trades like tailoring, shoemaking, and shipbuilding traditionally had learned the craft as apprentices, then journeymen, working under a master, whose authority over them (apprentices frequently lived in the master's household) resembled that of a father over children. This arrangement functioned well as long as the craft met a small market, with demand limited to special orders or retail sales.

The explosive growth of Baltimore in the 1790s, and even more the abundant markets that the city tapped by land and water, prompted masters to meet demand with larger-scale production. One way was to hire more journeymen, who soon complained of their low pay and the likelihood that they would remain permanent wage earners. Organized into a society, Philadelphia journeymen in 1794 sponsored their own shops in competition and defined fair practices they hoped to force upon masters; similarly in Baltimore journeymen appealed to the public for sympathy. In June 1799 the Baltimore *American and Daily Advertiser* published complaints that master tailors, who in effect had become factory owners, built superb houses, bought extensive plantations, invested in shipping, and lived "in a state of luxury equal to men of the first rank." Less happily, the journeyman who actually made the overpriced suits spent the prime of his youth in tedious employment, "almost deprived of eye sight, his constitution impaired, and his circumstances precisely as they were years before."[23]

These trends continued because manufacturers in Baltimore had no trouble finding the cheap labor that undercut the journeyman's effort to sustain his rank and pay. Wealthy Baltimore artisans of all trades owned slaves in 1800, but brickmakers and shipbuilders relied heavily on black labor. David

Stodder, one of the richest men in Baltimore, owned seventeen slaves in 1800 and apparently employed most of the men among them as caulkers at his shipyard on Harris Creek southeast of Fells Point. Other leading ship-wrights—John Steele, James Biays, and Joseph Despeaux, a refugee from Saint-Domingue—owned their own blacks and also hired caulkers from other firms. In trades where work depended less on contract and tools were simpler, master artisans capitalized on white apprentice labor that the city orphans' court and county trustees of the poor supplied from children who were abandoned, illegitimate, or declared indigent. Their labor agreements resembled the indentures of colonial servants, and the court's caseload in-dexed the level of flotsam the rapidly changing city produced: between 1794 and 1800 the Baltimore orphan's court handled on average 109 contracts a year, a figure that rose between 1811 and 1815 to 300. Almost all these chil-dren found their way into the clothing, woodworking, and shoemaking in-dustries. Employers exploited every source of ready labor.

Thus invisible market trends and civil power alike foredoomed the jour-neymen's cause—dampening their hopes of better times under the Consti-tution. Baltimore directories listed 81 percent more apprentices in the city in 1815 than in 1796. More and more of them appeared in the tax lists as prop-ertyless, and no longer were they likely to live with the master craftsman as part of his family. In 1809 authorities punished thirty-seven members of a shoemakers' union for conspiracy after they attempted a strike.

Heavily involved in the export of flour and other agricultural commodities, Baltimore shippers owed their rise not only to advantageous market condi-tions abroad but to aggressive development of the city's hinterland—a pro-ject that brought them into competition with Potomac interests and high-lighted various differences within the state. Much of the Baltimoreans' good fortune had origins in colonial Pennsylvania politics—the reluctance of the Quaker government to build decent roads linking the interior to Philadel-phia. As a result the rich produce of the Susquehanna River basin had fol-lowed its easiest course, downriver. By 1770 most roads in south-central Pennsylvania, like the river, led south toward the loading point at Charles Town, where shallops left for Baltimore. After the Revolution, taking advan-tage of wartime profits, Baltimore merchants heated up their rivalry with Philadelphia by organizing a company to dig a canal along the treacherous lower Susquehanna. The canal never proved as much a success as a flat-bottomed boat designed in 1794 by a German miller on the Juniata River. Said to resemble an ark, his craft cleared falls, rocks, and rapids with ease when rain raised the river, and before long enterprising farmers followed his example. In the 1790s producers of wheat, cattle, lumber, iron, coal, plaster of Paris, and salt as far north as the Genesee Valley of New York looked to

Baltimore as a market. For a short time Pennsylvania retaliated by declaring it a misdemeanor to remove rocks and debris from its section of the lower Susquehanna.

Of equal importance to Baltimore were the fields and hands of western Marylanders, to whom improved roads reached out in these years to form a spider's web of economic ties. In 1787 commissioners laid out twenty-foot-wide roads to Frederick and Reisterstown as well as toward York, Pennsylvania; a few years later the assembly authorized a highway twice that width, ambitious on paper, to connect some of the busy outlying mills (including those of John Ellicott, Elisha Tyson, and the Jessop brothers, William and Charles) with Baltimore. These official gestures acknowledged the poor condition of most Maryland roads at the time. Travelers uniformly referred to them as frightful, miserable, and worst in the union. On steep side slopes passengers sometimes had to lean out windows on one side of a carriage to prevent it from overturning, the driver shouting commands—"Now gentlemen to the right"—as if he were the captain of a sailboat. While horses had to be halted to rest every three or four miles, drivers, on whom everyone depended so completely, often used the stop to slake their thirst with a drink of local whiskey. These men knew what they were up against. "We saw ourselves confronted with abominable roads," wrote a Frenchman leaving Baltimore for the west in 1791, "where one runs the risk of being upset at any moment on sharp stones or of being thrown into mudholes." [24]

In the end turnpike companies and the Ellicotts themselves actually built the new roads north and west of Baltimore. These companies, like the bridge corporations, received charters from the General Assembly granting them exclusive rights to sell stock, build, and collect tolls in exchange for their public service. The work was expensive and proceeded slowly. Employing gravel on established roadbeds where possible, building bridges out of stone, the chartered companies pushed ahead at the rate of nearly ten thousand dollars per mile. By 1807 reports made to Albert Gallatin, secretary of the treasury, revealed that the road from Baltimore to Frederick extended for thirty miles, the Reisterstown or Hookstown pike out Franklin Street for ten miles. By 1818 the turnpike through Frederick had passed west as far as the village of Boonsborough. Disputes over the course of the road and the high cost of construction in the mountains brought a temporary halt to extensions of that highway, which eventually reached Watkins' Ferry (or Williamsport) and Elizabeth Town (officially Hagerstown after 1814) in Washington County. Not until 1821—under pressure from the legislature—did private capital complete the turnpike to Cumberland, the eastern terminus of the federally financed National Road to the Ohio River. At that time turnpikes also connected Baltimore to Washington, Georgetown to Frederick along Braddock's route of 1755, Hagerstown to Westminster, Westminster to Baltimore. On the pike between Boonsborough and Hagerstown in the early

1820s, American roadbuilders first used macadam (layers of compacted crushed gravel) as a surface. A product of economic demand, these Piedmont Maryland turnpikes—then considered among the best in the country—handled heavy wagons in bad weather, made travel feasible year-round, and further hastened economic growth in the region.

In Frederick and Washington counties much of that development was the work of the German families who still made up the greatest part of the population. Frederick Town increased in population until in 1800 it numbered more than twenty-six hundred persons, of whom about three hundred were black. Some of the newcomers were former Hessian prisoners who found the people and country so attractive they remained behind. In 1785 an entire community of more than three hundred persons under a prominent Bohemian glassmaker, John Frederick Amelung, arrived in Frederick County and settled on the Monocacy at a place they called New Bremen. Though Amelung eventually failed—he chose to make more crystal than windowpane—everyone who passed through Frederick commented on the town's vitality and "brisk inland trade." A proudly published list of artisans working there at the end of the eighteenth century included tobacconists, saddlers, joiners, combmakers, shoemakers, weavers, wagon makers, hatters, gunsmiths, painters, watch- and clockmakers, potters, glovers, butchers, brewers, and silver-, copper-, and tinsmiths. To meet the needs of a growing community, the people of Frederick resorted freely to lotteries, which required legislative permission and provided another index to private and civic change. Frederick between 1801 and 1817 staged thirty-four lotteries, probably more than any other Maryland town; they helped to finance projects as different as buying fire engines, deepening wells, and repairing the town's seven churches.[25]

As before the Revolution, outsiders commented on the industry, intelligence, and cooperation of the German farmers in Frederick County. Approaching Frederick "the country very much improves in appearance," an Englishman remarked in the early nineteenth century; "the farms present a succession of fine fields, of young Indian corn, wheat, rye, oats and clover." Besides growing the fine wheat crops that were the foundation stones of local prosperity—there were eighty grist mills around Frederick in 1798—German farmers planted flax for what became a highly profitable linen and paper trade. They also found time to produce colored thread, long-yarn stockings, and leather products like harness. Farmers throughout the Frederick economic basin relied on Matthias Bartgis's English- and German-language newspapers for market reports. Bartgis recommended that people in Funkstown, Elizabeth Town, Sharpsburg, and the Virginia communities of Shepherdstown, Martinsburg, and Winchester appoint circulation committees of fifty-two men, each of whom would journey to Frederick once a year to pick up the latest issue. Perhaps some of those committees formed. Community spirit in Middletown, a village of twenty-six houses in the valley between

Frederick and Elizabeth Town, was so high in 1791 that all religious sects shared one church—a practice that led a Frenchman to write with astonishment that "nearly all the sects tolerate each other and the sectarians respect each other."[26]

As a gateway to the west, Elizabeth Town had famous inns and its full share of near-frontier entertainment. Taverns included the Globe, Scholl's Black Bear, and Ragan's Indian King. At Beltzhoover's Inn townspeople staged a memorable banquet for Washington in the fall of 1790. Stone's Tavern gained a reputation for being a nest of gamblers. Virginians crossed the Potomac to enter cockfights at Ladle Spring. Until crowds made the game too dangerous, men gathered in town to play "long bullets"—a game of tossing a four-pound ball at a point on the ground, the nearest throw winning. Horse races, with the usual betting and fighting, took place on the southern edge of town, not far from the large marsh that forced a dogleg turn in the main north-south thoroughfare, Potomac Street. In 1793 a showman offered townspeople a glimpse of his camel, "the greatest natural curiosity ever exhibited to the public on this continent." Annual musters of the local militia unit, the Washington Blues, brought two thousand men into town for patriotic gaiety.[27]

Elizabeth Town had grown large enough by 1791 to support four newspapers and generate interesting local controversies. Residents then complained to the assembly that people living on the hilly main streets had made them impassable by digging ditches to divert rainwater for their private use. In the same year commissioners set about building a new, two-story market and courthouse in the public square that Jonathan Hager had planned as the center of the town. Before long a dispute flared over what weather vane should go atop the new structure. Germans wanted to use the tin profile of a fat and satisfied burgher, "Old Heiskel," which had been used on the old market; members of the Freemasons' lodge, who must have included Scots-Irish (and who finally had their way), preferred the compass and square symbol of marketplaces everywhere. Ethnic differences inherent in such a harmless squabble showed themselves more readily in the number of churches in the small town, which in 1805 consisted of only about 250 houses, most built of logs. Besides the two German congregations common to western Maryland communities—the Lutheran and Reformed—the city at the time also had Episcopal and Catholic parishes, Presbyterian and Methodist congregations. Varied in settlement, Elizabeth Town and its countryside of Germans to the north and Irish along the Potomac became, like Frederick, a lively rural publishing center. John Gruber's *Westliche Correspondenz* issued from a press that produced a large volume of German-language religious works and Gruber's best-known publication, the town almanac, first printed in 1797.

Hustle, diversity, and growth even extended from the Antietam and Conococheague valleys to the more forbidding terrain beyond North Moun-

tain—farther west than the village of Hancocktown, where Maryland separated Pennsylvania and Virginia by only a few miles, and above Thomas
Cresap's famous outpost at Oldtown. Fort Cumberland, the small settlement
above Will's Creek, benefited from land grants the state made to troops of
the Maryland Line. Five years after the peace with Britain, nearly four hundred families had moved into the region west of the old fort, as did a fugitive
member of the French nobility and younger sons of established Maryland
families—among them Daniel Cresap, George Dent, John and David Lynn
from Frederick Town, Thomas Beall "of Samuel" and also of Frederick, and
Andrew Bruce of Frederick County.

Opportunity knocked at this far western site. Answering petitions that
complained of the distance to court in Elizabeth Town, the assembly in 1789
created Allegany County and named Cumberland its seat. The village, its
land values boosted and its leadership in line for county offices, soon bore
evidence of its new importance. A log cabin served Lutherans and Methodists alike until 1789, when the Methodists, whom a circuit rider met once
a month, built their own meetinghouse—the first in western Maryland.
Catholics had a log church after 1792, and enough downstate Episcopalians,
likely merchants and lawyers among them, had arrived in Cumberland by
1803 to establish another congregation. Cumberland had a Wednesday-
Saturday market after 1795, and a primitive academy after 1799, by which
time new county taxes had paid for a simple two-story public building—
courthouse above, jail below. Early inhabitants hopefully called the place a
"queen city." Nestled among high mountains the Cresaps had made famous
when battling Indians, facing westward toward "the Glades"—an expanse
of inviting meadowland—and toward valleys that lay along the Potomac,
Cumberland justified every reference to its natural setting.

Nature offered obstacles as well as vistas. As the town spread to the eastern bank of Will's Creek, commissioners struggled to build a bridge strong
enough to withstand its periodic flooding, and they fought a losing battle
until construction of an iron-chain bridge in the 1820s. More serious were
problems of access to markets. The town provided Maryland a portal to
the Ohio country, and forward-looking townspeople considered prospects
bright for trade with that region as well as with Pittsburgh to the north. The
road to Baltimore, long and expensive, appeared a less likely route than the
Potomac; but rocky and winding, shallow in spots, elsewhere quick and
treacherous, the river untamed did the people of Cumberland little good.
Joining them in favor of improving Potomac navigation were merchants in
other Maryland river towns like Williamsport and above all in Georgetown,
the offloading point that now lay in the District of Columbia.

Ways to open the Potomac had been talked about since colonial days. As
early as 1762 Washington had studied plans for clearing the river from the
Great Falls to Fort Cumberland. Meeting at Annapolis in 1784, commission-

Old courthouse and public square, Elizabeth Town. From Mary Vernon Mish, *Jonathan Hager, Founder* (Hagerstown, 1937). The Washington County Courthouse, built c. 1776 and replaced in the federal period, stood on stilts, allowing room below for a farmers' market. *MHS*

"View of Fort Cumberland, Maryland." From Adlard Welby, *Visit to North America* (London, 1821). *MHS*

ers from Maryland and Virginia, Washington among them, had formed the Potomac Company to finance improvements to the river. Plans were to build locks around five of the worst falls and a road from the farthest navigable point on the north branch of the river to one of several rivers that flowed into the Ohio. Both states purchased one-tenth of the company's 500 shares, and within five months the company raised £40,000—the largest portion of subscribers living in Alexandria, Georgetown, Frederick, and the Shenandoah Valley of Virginia. By 1789 barge traffic safely plied the river between Oldtown and Great Falls, a distance of 180 miles, and locks were completed as far upriver as Williamsport. The following year Washington, after passing through Elizabeth Town, floated freely the entire distance to Mount Vernon.

The Potomac Company, the turnpike companies reaching out from Baltimore, and the small manufacturers in western Maryland outlined economic progress that one could not find in every corner of Maryland. Varying soil quality remained a primary determinant of wealth, and indebtedness still plagued planters and farmers in many parts of the state. In Cecil County, still heavily wooded, visitors found idleness and poverty. Harford County, remaining rough and underdeveloped, gained nothing in per capita wealth between the Revolution and 1790 and thereafter grew slowly in population. Immediately west of Baltimore farmers struggled on middling land. "The leanness of the sheep and of the horned cattle gives evidence of the sterility of the soil," noted Ferdinand-M. Bayard in the summer of 1791; crops seemed "to be wrested from a stingy earth." More than one wayfarer complimented Maryland on its handsome new State House, which the assembly first used in 1779; a Charles Wallace–William Buckland structure with fine interior details, it had an ornate cupola styled after the Schlossturm tower in Karlsruhe, Germany. Except when the legislature met, however, Annapolis by the early nineteenth century had become little more than a county seat and local market. On the sandy soil back from the bay, northern Anne Arundel County showed travelers little cultivated land. The country looked "barren, producing only Shrubs & Pines."[28]

Elsewhere in Maryland prospects were little brighter. While along the Patuxent River one noted fields and fences and the rich loam of the valley, Prince George's County, still devoted to tobacco and corn, contained varied soil and piney woods that harbored many pockets of poverty. Farther south, planters gradually were shifting from tobacco to corn and wheat, but already much of the land lay ruined. Between Port Tobacco and Hoe's Ferry the flat and sandy country wore "a most dreary aspect." Close to the Potomac in Montgomery County, tobacco lands for the time being yielded good crops; inland one found clay, gravel, and few improvements. "The change in the face of the country after leaving Frederick is gradual, but at the end of a day's journey a striking difference is perceptible," wrote Isaac Weld after a trip through Montgomery to Washington. "Instead of well cultivated fields green with wheat . . . large pieces of land which have been worn out with the culture of tobacco are here seen lying waste, with scarcely any herb to cover them." In the 1790s the county lost population.[29]

Along with one-crop tobacco planting, slavery received its full share of the blame for the poverty and backwardness of the black counties. "Everything in Maryland and in Virginia bears the stamp of slavery," wrote Brissot de Warville, "the parched soil, the badly managed farming, the ramshackle houses, and the few scrawny cattle that look like walking skeletons." He was struck by the differences in appearance between Quaker and slaveowning farms, and the ease with which Marylanders picked up their slaves and belongings and headed for new lands in places like Kentucky and Georgia. Weld thought that southern Maryland looked "as if it had been deserted by one half its inhabitants." When the land no longer supported a planter's family and slaves, many people did indeed leave. Between 1790 and 1800, the heavily slave counties of Calvert, Charles, and St. Mary's lost white and black population alike.[30]

Across the bay from Baltimore, Eastern Shore Marylanders recovered gradually from wartime confusion and damage. Production of "genuine white wheat" on the Sassafras Loam of Talbot, Queen Anne's, and Kent counties provided a good income to farmers there. As in the late colonial period, they shipped much of their harvests overland to points on the Delaware River for export through Philadelphia. Sandy soil in the lower counties encouraged the planting of corn and sweet potatoes. Shipbuilding at St. Michaels continued important in the late eighteenth and early nineteenth centuries, as did lumbering on the Pocomoke; between 1790 and 1810 the population of Worcester County grew from 7,626 to 11,490. Together with Oxford, Chestertown—a village of elegant brick and many more wooden houses—still served as a port whose vessels carried wheat and other products to Baltimore and beyond.

Relatively poor and debt-ridden, however, the Eastern Shore also grew more isolated. It developed a flavor all its own. Outsiders believed the people there different, blaming "moist, sultry, and disagreeable" summer air for the "agues and intermittent fevers" that bothered inhabitants and accounted for their "sickly appearance." Shifting transportation patterns gradually brought in fewer non-natives to make such unflattering comment. The colonial route from the north to Annapolis often took itinerants down the Eastern Shore and then by boat to the capital. The rise of Baltimore diverted most traffic down the bay from Frenchtown on the Elk River. Meanwhile independent-minded Eastern Shoremen as early as 1776 had proposed a clause in the Declaration of Rights permitting either shore to secede from the other; more successfully they demanded balance in the state structure. The constitution provided two state treasurers and land office registrars, one per shore, and alternate general court sessions on each side of the bay. Talbot Court House, the site of the Eastern Shore offices and meetings, soon grew in size and became known as East Town or Easton. A large courthouse built there in

1794 at state expense fostered a lingering hope that occasionally the assembly might also convene at the Eastern Shore capital.[31]

This apartness must have owed something to measures taken to suppress Eastern Shore Tories during the Revolution. It clearly drew on economic differences. When in 1801 discussion centered on a canal to connect the upper Chesapeake and lower Delaware bays—a project heartily endorsed in Philadelphia and on the Eastern Shore—most resistance to it came from Baltimore. State incorporation of so many Baltimore banks also grated on Eastern Shore residents, who said they could obtain a loan only with a Baltimorean's co-signature. In 1804 the assembly finally chartered a Farmer's Bank with an Easton branch. Soon the Easton *Star* reported that Baltimore interests were trying to buy a controlling share of the institution while denying "favors" to its Eastern Shore depositors.[32] Bypassed, noting the expansion of the Western Shore with its fresh lands and abundant capital, Eastern Shoremen regarded Baltimore and the west with the jealousy the state had taken to land-rich Virginia in the Confederation period.

⌒﹏⌒

The tobacco planters' economic slump made them especially watchful of Baltimore and its commercial rise; foreign events and the policies of the new federal government also applied heat to political feelings in the 1790s. Early rivalries naturally grew out of the ratification struggle—and shore loyalties. When in 1789 the assembly balloted for the first U.S. senators, the Eastern Shore demanded and received one of its own, John Henry, Jr., a Dorchester County landholder whose legislative service dated from 1777 (the other seat went to Carroll of Carrollton). Friends of the Constitution, facing the problem of smoldering anti-federalist sentiment in Anne Arundel, Baltimore, and Harford counties, passed an election law by which voters throughout the state chose six congressmen (candidates had to be residents of their districts) according to a general ticket never before used in Maryland; "anti" strength in a few localities, they calculated, would disappear under weight of federalist feeling in the state as a whole. Members of the opposition, recognizing the ploy, could only try to thwart it by printing confusing tickets, calling federalist candidates "dangerous to public liberty," and in western Maryland attempting to drive a wedge between German and native-born voters. When anti-federalists placed on their own ticket the popular Joshua Seney, a Queen Anne's lawyer and former member of both Congress and assembly, federalists revised theirs and put him on it. These machinations were beside the point. For all the reasons Maryland had supported constitutional ratification—interest in exports and internal improvements chief among them—voters in 1789 sent strong supporters of the federal government to Congress and for the electoral college selected candidates pledged to Washington for president.[33]

Soon self-interest, regional and personal, began to erode federalist unity.

Alexander Hamilton's proposal as treasury secretary to fund the debt of the federal government, paying current holders of securities full face amount, received the support of most Marylanders, who like William Smith could not resist the temptation to spread word of the program to friends and relatives. Smith's son-in-law Otho Holland Williams, now a militia general and Baltimore federalist, busily began buying the depreciated paper that held out hope for high profits. "Send me your money," he wrote a friend, "I'll make what I can on't. There's no danger of loss." Hamilton's collateral plan, to assume the debts of the states, received a mixed response among Marylanders. Since the state had taken steps to finance a portion of its own liabilities, funding promised to be of help only in paying off a wartime obligation to Dutch bankers. Resolutions condemning assumption appeared on the floor of the House of Delegates in late 1790 and two of them passed—only to be rescinded in a doubtful procedure. The curious failed to pry loose an explanation for the turnabout, but later it became clear that Marylanders held a considerable amount in state securities—which had become the last public paper available at bargain rates. Siding with James Madison and prominent members of the Virginia delegation, Michael Jenifer Stone of Maryland resisted Hamilton's plans because they violated equity and limits on federal power; assumption, he said, might be convenient, but "for a people who have parted with their liberty the most convenient government is an arbitrary one." Stone went down to defeat in the next election.[34]

Passage of Hamilton's financial program finally depended on a compromise that proved highly divisive among Marylanders. They, like Virginians, long had advocated the permanent location of the federal capital somewhere farther south than New York or Philadelphia. Hardships of travel from the southeast and the harshness of northern winter weather counted in their thinking; so did their aversion toward distant government. Possible sites had included the lower Susquehanna, Annapolis, the upper Potomac (Washington, thinking of military defense, briefly considered the point where the Conococheague met the river), and the lower Potomac-Anacostia basin below Georgetown. Baltimoreans, General Williams at the fore, at first supported the Susquehanna because of its likely boost to Baltimore commerce, then strenuously promoted their own city as the new capital. The terms of the final compromise that Jefferson, Madison, and Hamilton worked out in the summer of 1790—Virginia's support for assumption in return for northern votes for a Potomac capital—angered some Marylanders, who felt slighted, and pleased others. Senator Carroll's cousin Daniel Carroll, who owned land in the proposed federal district, supported the relocation measure. William Smith of Baltimore did not; he peevishly observed that, even if the federal buildings went on the Maryland side of the river, they "will be so situated as to give Virginia all the Advantages" of viewing them.[35]

These two men belonged to clusters that for a brief time jostled in Maryland political life as the "Potomac" and "Chesapeake" factions. Potomac partisans, claiming to be the heartiest supporters of Washington and his secretary of the treasury, had interests that lay in Potomac River development or ground plots in the new capital; more of them belonged to the old landholding families, increasingly impoverished, along the lower river. Chesapeake adherents centered in Baltimore business and among small farmers who carried debts and harbored doubts about the new federal structure. In Baltimore vengeful motives helped to account for a doubtless fraudulent 99 percent voter turnout in the 1790 congressional elections, which the Chesapeakes won handily. Anger over the new capital's location also brought together strange companions: old supporters of creditors and the Constitution—Judge Alexander Hanson, Philip Key, and the powerful Smith brothers, Samuel and Robert—and their erstwhile enemies who had favored paper money and worked against ratification: Samuel Sterett, a badly indebted Baltimore merchant, and Samuel Chase. Earlier Hanson had looked on Chase "with horror . . . and detestation"; now the judge referred to him as a man of "good understanding" who had been "the mover of almost everything this state has to boast of." Eastern Shoremen stood to gain mainly by being courted. In the fall 1790 elections the Chesapeake faction placed William Vans Murray, a Dorchester attorney and former delegate from the Eastern Shore, on its ticket, just as the Potomac group tried to win the endorsement of the Eastern Shore lawyer and firm federalist James Tilghman.[36]

Washington's efforts to fill federal offices posed hard choices for some leading Marylanders. Like Carroll of Carrollton—after a few years he resigned his U.S. Senate seat, believing the Maryland Senate a more important body—they could not decide where prestige lay. Robert Hanson Harrison, Maryland chancellor in 1789, turned down the president's invitation to the U.S. Supreme Court. Thomas Johnson, then chief judge of the distinguished Maryland General Court, accepted the same offer but later, having stepped down, declined Washington's request that he serve as secretary of state. Howard refused the secretaryship of war in 1795. Others, drawing on the fulsome Maryland experience with political patronage, eagerly sought places in the new order. Washington rewarded Congressmen Daniel Carroll and George Gale for their support of funding and assumption by naming Carroll a commissioner of the District of Columbia and Gale a collector of internal revenue for Maryland. Otho Williams, who had held a state customs post in the 1780s, now leaped to what he called "the main chance" and busily wrote letters seeking help in obtaining the federal collectorship at the port of Baltimore. Washington appointed the former Continental officer to that post and later looked to both him and James McHenry, another veteran, for advice in filling other federal jobs. McHenry, who unsuccessfully had asked for a diplomatic post in Europe, counseled the use of lucrative offers to win over prominent anti-federalists. One of them, William Paca, soon accepted a seat on the federal district court bench. Samuel Chase, notorious foe of creditors and an unamended Constitution, lost little time in announcing his conver-

Left, Thomas Johnson (1710–91) by Charles Willson Peale, 1788. *Maryland Commission on Artistic Properties. Right*, Dr. James McHenry (1753–1816) by Charles Balthazar Julien Fevret de St. Memin, 1803. *MHS*

sion to federalism. Serving as a state judge in Baltimore, Chase as early as July 1789 wrote Washington that he had "for some time, wished to be employed by the national government." Several months later he wrote again, to congratulate the president on his inauguration and to offer himself for a seat on the Supreme Court. Washington ignored these supplications, which Chase begged him to keep within his own breast. "I do not wish," he explained, "to afford my political Enemies (for I never had any private ones) an Opportunity to Mortify and insult me."[37]

Chase's skill at making enemies played a considerable part in Maryland political life during these years. So did European developments that impinged on the trade, livelihoods, and sentiments of Marylanders. After Hamilton's financial policies no issue created more of a stir than the French Revolution and British attempts to contain it. At first declaring the same ideals of liberty that had produced the movement for American independence, the Revolution in France claimed broad early support in Maryland. Members of both factions in the state (friends of the Constitution and Potomac men now assumed the name Federalists; most Chesapeake partisans, gradually siding with the opposition in Congress, called themselves Republicans) praised the French for throwing off the yoke of monarchy. Baltimore gentlemen, if not others, succumbed to the change toward simplicity in fashion that the Revolution inspired. Men discarded powdered wigs, cut their hair close, wore trousers rather than knee breeches, and adopted the short-waisted, high-collared jackets that went with "pudding bag" cravats. A Republican Society formed in Baltimore to advocate in America some of the reforms radicals demanded in France. Its agenda included manhood suffrage and more popularly chosen officials; the society affirmed the right of the people to instruct representatives how to vote on legislation. When the Revolution turned bloodier and began to consume its leaders in the Reign of Terror, Marylanders as other Americans divided bitterly over its implications. Wearing a black cockade in one's hat signified adherence to order over "mobocracy" and affection for the British, on whom the French declared war in 1793. The red cockade marked one as a friend of liberty and equality, a foe of things British and aristocratic.

As tempers flared between wearers of the black and red cockades, Marylanders, facing the maritime dangers posed by the French-British conflict, found themselves groping for a middle course between violent reaction and sacrifice of principle. Each belligerent considered American trade with its enemy fair game. In November 1793 the British declared the French West Indies, so important to the Baltimore wheat-export trade, closed to neutral vessels. In a few months they had seized about two hundred and fifty American vessels, among them the *Sampson*, Joshua Barney captain. News of Barney's capture put the British consul in Baltimore at considerable risk, and he wisely took refuge in Philadelphia. Angry Baltimoreans debated what to do next. Both Federalists and Republicans joined the volunteer military companies that formed against possible British attack. Merchants and seamen largely supported the shipping embargo that the administration imposed in the spring of 1794 to protest violations of neutral rights. Soon afterward the Jay Treaty—Washington's gesture toward peace—revived party feeling. The conciliatory treaty struck most Maryland Republicans as accepting far too many conditions on American trade with British dominions. In July 1795 a large public meeting in Baltimore urged the president to reject Jay's work. Yet the agreement did offer some commercial gains; leading shippers argued that half a loaf was better than none. Senators John Henry and Richard Potts (a state judge from Frederick County who had succeeded Carroll of Carrollton in 1793) parted with other southerners and voted in favor of the controversial measure. During later debate on implementing the Jay Treaty, Samuel Smith, Baltimore congressman since 1793, explained that his constituents disliked it but he foresaw fewer evils from acquiescence than rejection. He called for a pause in hateful disagreements over the treaty. Public affairs, he warned, must reflect some unanimity; "a House so nearly divided against itself could never thrive."[38]

Marylanders sensed the balance between order and liberty teetering one way, then another. When in the summer of 1794 western Pennsylvania farmers rose up against Hamilton's excise tax on distilled spirits, neither Federalists in western Maryland nor Republicans in Baltimore hesitated to answer

Washington's call to arms. In a matter of days all 5,418 Maryland troops, under Samuel Smith as militia general, were in the field. Still, persons sympathetic to the Whiskey Boys planted a liberty pole in the Elizabeth Town square. In Baltimore that year, to believe Judge Chase, government nearly gave way to the mob violence so much in evidence near Pittsburgh. At the expiration of the spring embargo, Fells Point patriots had tarred and feathered a captain who signalled his pro-British feeling. Despite popular support for the rioters and a loud demonstration when they appeared in court, Chase denied every motion to dismiss charges against the ringleaders—among whom were the shipbuilder David Stodder and some minor public officials; when the mob threatened to tear down Chase's house he delivered a tirade against popular lawlessness. His stand so pleased Federalist party leaders that Washington shortly afterward named him to the Supreme Court, where by 1800 his notoriety was complete. In the aftermath of the XYZ affair and French assaults on neutral rights, Federalists in Congress passed alien and sedition laws that tested anew the equilibrium between law and freedom. Chase again proved himself a champion of order. As judge on the federal circuit that included Maryland, he snipped out newspaper passages he considered offensive to elected officials and placed them before grand juries. He once kept a jury empaneled an extra day hoping it would hand down indictments against Republicans.

Disaffection with Federalist policy and Chase's hellbent efforts to enforce the rule of law helped to strengthen Maryland Republicans. Earlier than in most other states, partisans in Maryland, besides employing the newspaper essays and barbeques of colonial days, used parades, bonfires, and even illegal voting to fatten their tallies, and such campaign competition sharpened differences between Federalists and Republicans. Hamilton's excise tax and Washington's suppression of the Whiskey rebels probably helped to soften Federalist strength in far western Maryland. By supporting the alien act, which made it more difficult for immigrants to become United States citizens, Federalists endangered their support among German farmers and confirmed the suspicions of Irish newcomers to Baltimore—who hated the Federalists for their favoritism toward Britain. Preparing for the anticipated war with France in 1798, the Adams administration succeeded in obtaining from Congress a direct tax on houses, land, and slaves—a measure that fell hard on all Maryland farmers. The sedition act, which arch-Federalist James Lloyd of Talbot County had introduced in the Senate and which Jefferson called the onset of an American reign of terror, provoked emotional reaction among many Marylanders. Newspapers in Frederick and Elizabeth Town protested its violation of "blood-bought liberties." James Ash, a Baltimore Federalist, wrote James McHenry, then serving as Adams's secretary of war, that he opposed trying "to *exterminate*" Republicans—a "delightful way to introduce a *civil war*"; "it is much better," he said, voicing Maryland moderation, "to *reform* than to *destroy*."[39]

Federalists lost congressional seats in the 1798 election, and in 1800 the Maryland popular vote went to Jefferson for the presidency. But the most important political change of the period emerged shortly afterward in the General Assembly. It did not come about as a strictly party measure. Perhaps believing that future Federalist strength lay in popular appeal, Michael Taney of Calvert County, an ardent member of that party in the house, had introduced in 1797 a constitutional amendment "to abolish all that part of the form of government which requires property as a qualification for voting or for office." So preposterous did the suggestion sound to members of the indirectly elected state senate that Joseph H. Nicholson, one of the Republicans who spoke against it, drew laughter by offering to grant the vote to women and children as well as unpropertied men. Unfortunately for Nicholson and other opponents of suffrage reform, the bill captured public attention; legislators who opposed it—both Federalists and Republicans—faced tough campaigns for reelection. Next year Nicholson and some of his friends switched their position, but as late as 1799 the senate forestalled passage by insisting on either £30 visible property or taxpaying as a qualification. Finally, in 1801, reformers succeeded in winning a majority in the senate. Victory for the suffrage proposal quickly followed, the amendment becoming part of the constitution in 1802 when the next assembly passed a confirmatory act. Free white males who had lived in Maryland for one year and were twenty-one years of age and over received the vote in state elections and thereafter voted by ballot rather than viva voce. Seven years later another Federalist, John Hanson Thomas of Frederick County, successfully proposed an end to a second tradition from colonial days: property qualifications for public office. In 1810 the assembly confirmed both that amendment and another extending the 1802 suffrage reform to cover federal elections.

These changes did not bring a revolution in voting patterns. By defining one's visible estate in terms of inflationary money, the constitution of 1776 itself had expanded the electorate. Without doubt unqualified voters had taken part in some elections—challenges filed by losers gave evidence of more than a few irregularities, like those in the Baltimore canvass of 1790. Even so, the amendments of 1802 and 1810 transformed one of the most conservative constitutions of the revolutionary years into one of the earliest examples of democracy in the country. A principal reason for the change lay in economic and social diversity that in turn produced Federalist-Republican competition. By the early nineteenth century few members of either party enjoyed such security in office as to shrug off charges of flouting the popular will. Blessed or plagued (depending on their view of society and government) with factional rivalry, Maryland leaders found electoral reform in their best interests.

To many thoughtful Americans independence opened the way for, indeed demanded, new awareness of social need and social wrong. They asked what kind of society would take shape in the new republic. Answering that question, Marylanders faced some issues and avoided others. A growing minority noted the contradiction of slavery in a land of liberty. Black bondage had grown so familiar, so much a part of everyday life in eighteenth-century Maryland, that most whites, slaveowners or not, thought nothing of it. They neither championed slavery nor challenged it; they simply accepted it. To jump the ruts of common belief one had to reflect with studied detachment or feel a peculiar urge. The religious doctrines of inner light and universal redemption supplied such powerful impulses.

Shared hostility to slavery first surfaced in Quaker conviction and evangelical Protestant piety. As early as 1760 Quakers, standing outside Maryland political life and knit closely with members of the faith beyond the tobacco-growing colonies, had admonished one another to withdraw from the slave trade. Later the struggle for independence and the example of Quaker antislavery in Britain and Pennsylvania completed the turn in moral sensibility. At a memorable meeting in the midst of war, Maryland Quakers in 1778 called on one another to free their bondsmen and abjure slaveholding. Quaker slave ownership nearly disappeared in Maryland, and in 1787 the Yearly Meeting in Baltimore shifted focus to the system itself. Slavery, declared the meeting, was wrong—wherever men held others in bondage, regardless of whether slaveholders were Friends. Equally opposed to property in humans was a fringe group that flourished in Caroline County during and after the Revolution. The Nicholites followed the path of a Delaware farmer, Joseph Nichols, and later a Marylander, James Harris. Like the Quakers, whom they eventually joined, the Nicholites wore undyed clothing (slave labor produced colorful fabrics) and in the early 1790s asked themselves whether they did "bear a faithful testimony against Slavery in its various branches, and provide in a suitable manner for those in their families that have had their freedom secured to them." [40]

Methodist moral criticism owed much to its own apartness from the world—to humility incompatible with the slave order. Garrettson and other itinerant Methodists preached that all mankind stood equal in God's eyes; the path to salvation lay open to everyone, black and white alike. At the Christmas Conference of 1784 Methodists made the wrong of human bondage a foundation stone of their faith. The Methodist service book condemned slavery for oppressing souls "capable of the image of God." Slavery violated the Golden Rule and "the unalienable rights of mankind." After the Revolution public meetings in Queen Anne's, Kent, Talbot, Caroline, Dorchester, and Worcester counties—where Methodism had grown especially strong—chided the General Assembly to act on slavery. At the same time, again joining with Quakers elsewhere, Maryland Friends adopted the strategy of hold-

ing up slavery to the public eye. They, too, petitioned the House of Delegates
to rid Maryland of black bondage.[41]

In the 1790s, as earlier, legislators set aside these petitions by comfortable
margins. Hesitant to tamper with property rights and worried about uncon-
trolled blacks, they reflected widespread caution. The ambitions of nonslaveholders also figured in these votes. Spokesmen for upper bay and western
counties (where blacks were few but hopes of slave ownership not to be
discounted) usually split on antislavery petitions, and delegates in the house
viewed with suspicion any senate proposal on so fundamental a social issue.
Except for the unworldly message of the Methodists, early antislavery expression did coincide closely with success. It was easy to conclude that the
rich aimed to right themselves at the expense of their inferiors. Quakers as a
group had continued to make substantial economic gains. Secular spokesmen against slavery—Carroll of Carrollton, Nicholas Hammond (an English-
born Dorchester County planter and slaveholder), and William Pinkney, a
rising Harford County lawyer who had studied with Samuel Chase—stood
on the side of education and accomplishment. In 1789 charitable gentlemen
in Baltimore established a Maryland Society for Promoting the Abolition of
Slavery and the Relief of Poor Negroes and Others Unlawfully Held in Bondage. Before long these reformers had a membership list of more than two
hundred persons and an office in the center of the city. The abolition and
relief campaign included taking doubtful masters into court—testing the
cases of blacks who claimed to be free.

Antislavery got mixed up with the politics of privilege. In the fall of 1789
the Baltimore gentlemen themselves called on the assembly to act against
slavery. In the house their plea received support from Pinkney, whose committee recommended slave emancipation "by silent and gradual steps, with
the consent of the owner." That same session the senate considered an abolition bill that Hammond introduced. He, along with John Hall and Carroll
of Carrollton, formed a committee to confer with the delegates on language
agreeable to both houses. Carroll's message to the house noted "the great
importance of this subject, whether considered with a view to the persons
whom it concerns, or to the advantage and happiness of the community at
large." Despite Pinkney's efforts, however, the house by a vote of 39 to 15
refused to confer. During the next session the senate again tried and failed
to prod the delegates on the slavery issue, and in 1791 their spiteful regard
of senate and station became fully visible. The house then heard complaints
that the abolition and relief group had become a menace. Its "wealthy and
influential" members, read the committee report, dragged out contested servitude cases until it no longer paid to dispute them. Delegates described
the tactics of this "powerful society" as "improper, indecent, and unjusti-
fiable."[42] It later disbanded.

Though organized antislavery failed in these years, black population
change demonstrated white ambivalence about black bondage. For some

Maryland slaveholders the misgivings were economic; failing planters, if they did not move west or south, could sell their slaves out of state. Such sales were common enough that foes of slavery in these years introduced several bills, all falling short of passage, which aimed to limit or at least regulate slave commerce—to prevent, for example, the breakup of black families. By another pattern slaveholders freed their bondsmen in Maryland, an avenue that opened wider in 1796. That year, as the assembly republished state laws, a senate amendment removed a rule in force since 1752 and permitted masters to free slaves by will or during the master's last illness. Making out "deathbed" freedom papers, Maryland masters—while avoiding personal sacrifice—eased their consciences and freed their children from the burdens of slaveholding. Further, Maryland courts after the Revolution took a comparatively liberal view of slave "freedom suits." For almost twenty years in the late seventeenth century Maryland law had enslaved any white woman giving birth to a black father's child. After 1681 the assembly adopted the prevailing rule that children followed the mother's slave or free status. In the 1780s and 1790s state judges heard "repeated Applications" from blacks who claimed white female ancestry. After 1786 the courts accepted oral recollection as evidence in such cases, greatly increasing chances of a successful petition. Ten years later antislavery leaders counted 138 decisions on the side of freedom. "Hundreds of negroes," sourly wrote Luther Martin, attorney general in 1797, "have been let loose upon the community by the hearsay testimony of an obscure illiterate individual."[43]

Maryland free blacks rose sharply in numbers between the Revolution and early nineteenth century. The change came with noteworthy suddenness on the Eastern Shore. There were antislavery societies at Choptank and Chestertown, and the Quaker-Methodist influence argued strongly for moral motives among the membership. In 1790, 421 free blacks and slightly more than 1,000 slaves lived in Caroline County; in 1820 free blacks numbered almost 1,400, while the slave population had grown only to about 1,500. Free blacks in Dorchester in the same interval grew from about 500 to nearly 2,500, the slave population declining slightly from the 1790 level of 5,337. Talbot slaves stood at about 4,700 throughout the period, while free blacks increased from 1,076 in 1790 to 2,234 in 1820. In 1790 only one in thirteen Maryland blacks was free. In 1810 the number was one in three.[44]

Better acquainted with free blacks than most other Americans, white Marylanders nonetheless viewed this growing social anomaly—blacks who were not slaves—with mixed feelings. To be sure, there were examples of black talent and white patronage. Joshua Johnson, perhaps a West Indian immigrant, became well known in Baltimore as a portrait painter whose commissions included works for Samuel Smith as well as for antislavery gentlemen and their families. Benjamin Banneker, a largely self-taught mathematician and surveyor whom Andrew Ellicott had aided, took part in laying out the federal district and published his own almanac. Banneker sent his

Benjamin Banneker's *Almanac* for 1795, Baltimore. *MHS*

1792 edition to Jefferson, whose ambiguous praise typified the attitudes free blacks had to overcome in these years. Even the Methodists disappointed them. Baltimore blacks and whites together had built the Methodist chapels at Lovely Lane and Strawberry Alley, where early seating arrangements and burial plots knew no color bar. By the late 1790s, welcoming new converts by the thousands each year, Methodists had turned their backs on militant antislavery and grown uncomfortable with mixed congregations. Black members understandably felt betrayed at these developments, which nonetheless had a beneficial effect in promoting black institutions. Jacob Fortie in 1787 took the lead in founding a Colored Methodist Society. Later the white abolition and relief group gave black Methodists use of a building on Sharpe Street. Although Bishop Asbury disapproved of black separatism, Fortie and other free blacks struggled to rent another structure on Fish (later Saratoga) Street. Both churches became formally independent in 1797–98. Not long afterward, when Daniel Coker arrived, black Methodists had their own minister. Coker as a slave boy on the Eastern Shore had gone to school with his young master and then, a runaway, received Methodist training in New York. At first without freedom papers in Baltimore, the Reverend Coker had to conceal his identity. Later he was among founders of the African M. E. church in the United States.

The rights of free blacks in Maryland declined just as quickly as their numbers increased. After 1796 they could not testify in court cases involving the question of a black's being free or slave. Later measures permitted slaves, otherwise barred from the courtroom, to testify against free blacks, against whom the legislature also passed a strict vagrancy law. In 1806 the assembly circumscribed the freed black's right of assembly and required him to obtain a permit to own a firearm or dog. According to a law of 1807 free blacks visiting Maryland could stay no longer than two weeks. As if friends of unpropertied whites had to prove that somebody truly inferior still stood outside the body politic, Maryland suffrage reform arrived at the expense of free blacks. The 1802 amendment denied them the vote.

Limiting or preventing black freedom belonged to a larger pattern of self-regulation. Independence called for self-discipline (supposedly lacking in blacks); self-government depended on an ordered society in which people of means taught responsibility to others and indeed exercised stewardship over them. Baltimore population growth, seasonal shifts in maritime work, and the usual price and export swings brought considerable disorder in the form of unemployment and hardship. Stretching beyond the reach of the county almshouse, Baltimoreans responded with noteworthy private efforts. In 1792 a group of private persons formed a corporation—never quite as active as need required—"for the Relief of the Poor and Distressed of every Sect or Religious Denomination Whatsoever." The harsh winter of 1804–5 led to a public meeting and resolutions that organized a soup kitchen for the indigent. Located behind Harrison Street, it drew on volunteer financial aid and the unsold produce of nearby Center Market vendors. In January 1806 benefactors established a fund to support St. Peter's (Episcopal) School, a home for orphans too young to be bound out in servitude. Trustees included Edward Johnson, sometime Baltimore mayor, and a gentleman-planter turned Methodist, Harry Dorsey Gough of Perry Hall. The Reverend Joseph Bend of St. Paul's joined others in founding the Baltimore General Dispensary, a place where the poor obtained at least short-term medical care, and, with Dr. James Smith of the city, in promoting smallpox vaccination among all strata of citizens. Private philanthropy, by easing the pain of growth, helped to promote growth and preserve order; organized benevolence also showed how the work of shaping free society begged for volunteers to improve everyone's lot.

Underwritten by wealthy gentlemen, these projects had an unintended effect—they gave women a part they could play in public life without shocking their husbands or friends. Women in "unwomanly" pursuits remained rare in the state and exceptions appeared mostly in the working class. Mary

Katharine Goddard, whose quarrelsome brother in 1773 had established the *Maryland Journal* in Baltimore, singlehandedly published that newspaper between 1779 and 1785 and survived the stresses of the period. According to the 1796 Baltimore directory, spinsters, many of whom had no choice but to work, accounted for between 2 and 3 percent of all heads of households. About 5 percent of the six thousand women in Baltimore and Fells Point at that time worked, many of them as laundresses, milliners, and seamstresses. Journeymen in this period complained that master tailors sedulously hunted up every woman who could "make her own Children's clothes" in order to turn out cheap apparel. Widows occasionally took over their husbands' rough businesses—one a brickyard and another a plastering company. All the same, the domestic sphere remained the place most Maryland women expected to spend their lives. Unlike neighboring states, Maryland did not require masters to teach apprentices or white servants the rudiments of learning, so poor women of that background usually were illiterate. Among the well-to-do, few families provided daughters with anything more than drawing-room skills like music and fancy stitching. Catharine Carroll, daughter of Charles and Mary of Carrollton, studied arts and sciences in English schools. By and large women stayed at home and bore children—an average of five per family in the city—and cared for others.[45]

Increasingly, so said social observers, women in the wealthiest families hired or purchased wet nurses to free themselves for other pursuits. Even if this comment voiced mere impression, the work of philanthropy pulled more and more upper-class women out of the drawing room. An unusual case involved Elizabeth Seton, a New York merchant's widow who had moved to Baltimore to raise her children in a Catholic environment. In September 1808, with the aid of a Sulpician priest, William Dubourg, Seton opened a school for girls outside the city on Paca Street. The next year, having expanded her vision to an order of teaching nuns, Seton moved the spiritual community to Emmitsburg. Most women stayed closer to home and tended earthly needs alone. At St. Paul's Episcopal Church ladies organized a Benevolent Society of the City and County of Baltimore in February 1800, planning to relieve the distress of homeless girls. About the same time others formed an interdenominational Female Humane Association that set about teaching poor girls reading and writing and basic handicrafts. In 1808, after receiving a charter renewal, this academy became the Orphaline Charity School. It operated under the management of nine "discreet female characters." In the next few years the women who answered the call to service had family names, all prominent, like Tiernan, Owen, Hollins, Schroeder, Brice, Nelms, Lucas, Bond, and Gill.[46]

Exploring all the promises of free society, Marylanders considered no issue more important than preparing young people for the duties of liberty. Yet education caused disagreement over everything except its value to free citizens. Opposition to public colleges in the 1780s had broken down an impressive plan. Its author, William Smith, was a Scots immigrant, Anglican churchman, and revolutionary-era Loyalist who served as head of the University of Pennsylvania until 1780. In Chestertown he transformed Kent Academy into Washington College and then lent his weight to the movement to make old King William's School into St. John's College. It had been his idea to unite both institutions as the University of Maryland. All the while he made prescient changes in the Washington College curriculum. Besides traditional lessons in Latin and Greek, young gentlemen studied English literature, modern languages, history, mathematics, and science. Smith tried to meet objections of elitism. He established a practical course for sons of farmers and craftsmen who wished to learn income-earning skills; he actively sought scholarship money for poorer students. Washington College flourished on this plan and St. John's grew stronger under Smith's influence until, in 1789, this pioneer withdrew from academic life in hopes of receiving an Episcopal church bishopric.

Critics of the public university favored spending tax money instead on common schools, on diffusing knowledge rather than paying for an educated aristocracy. A leading spokesman for this position emerged in Samuel Knox, a testy though liberal-minded Presbyterian minister who lived for a time in Bladensburg and between 1797 and 1803 served as principal of the Frederick Academy. When first at Frederick, Knox wrote an essay on schooling that won a prize from the American Philosophical Society; within two years he sent the legislature a copy of his paper and published it for a long list of subscribers, from local lawmakers to George Washington. Fully enjoying his celebrity, Knox deserved it at least for his originality—he stepped out of both elitist and sectarian molds by advocating nonreligious public education. A pompous college here and there might give the illusion of literary character, he warned, but without "proper subordinate nurseries of students" the state would enjoy neither general knowledge nor scientific improvement. The pyramid of learning needed a base under its apex. He recommended a system of state-supported primary schools on the parish level, academies in each county, state colleges, and finally a national university. He did not mince words. "In all ages," he wrote, "it has been the policy of those governments that existed by the slavish ignorance of the people to establish one or two sumptuously endowed schools for the sons of fortune and affluence— the expecting brood of despotical succession, leaving the canaille, the ignorant herd, to live and die, the *profanum vulgus*, the despised, enslaved, and stupid multitude."[47] Knox in 1800 proved how far ahead of his time he was by defending Jefferson's unorthodox religious beliefs during the nasty presidential contest of that year. Later Jefferson returned the compliment—relying on Knox's ideas, and Smith's too, in drawing up a plan for a pathbreaking university in Virginia. At home sharp imagery merely had a negative effect. In 1798, apparently taken by Knox's arguments, the assembly reduced the appropriation for Washington College in favor of a few Eastern

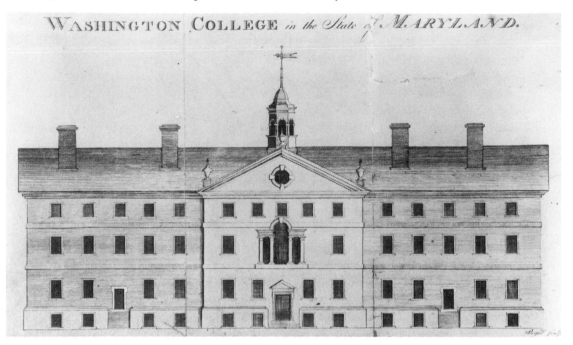

"Washington College in the State of Maryland." Engraving by Henry D. Pursell, published in William Smith's prospectus for the college, 1784. The simplicity and classical symmetry of the building illustrated early-republican hopes and values. *MHS*

Shore schoolhouses. In 1806 parsimonious legislators and enemies of privilege cut state appropriations for Washington and St. John's colleges to nothing. Though in these years the assembly authorized lotteries for academies in places like Rockville, Emmitsburg, and Middletown, it failed to act on Knox's plea for a uniform system of common schools.

At the same time religious leaders worked hard to build their own schools. Soon after the Baltimore Christmas conference, Methodists—combining Asbury's name with that of Wesley's emissary in the United States, Thomas Coke—had begun building Cokesbury College in Harford County. Coke strongly felt the release of disestablishment, rejoicing that the "anti-Christian union" between government and Anglican church (whose ministers he called "parasites and bottle companions of the rich and great") had been broken. Methodists planned the college as a training ground for preachers and accepted students, paying and poor, as young as seven years. The boys faced the sternest self-discipline, rising promptly at five in the morning—"of vast importance to both body and mind"—and spending seven hours a day at study. They learned languages and science. "But our first object," stated a circular of 1785, "shall be . . . instilling into their minds the principles of true religion—speculative, experimental, and practical—and training them in the ancient way that they may be rational, spiritual Christians." College regulations permitted students to bathe only singly and in the presence of the master or someone appointed by him. When not at their books students applied themselves to gardening, woodworking, and outdoor exercise. The college refused to call it play, for "those who play when they are young will play when they are old."[48] Besides this rigorous schedule, visitors also remarked on the lack of feather beds. Whatever the enrollment, financial problems persisted. The academy relied on annual collections at Methodist meetings, where the educated colonial clergy lived in bad memory. In 1795 fire destroyed the wooden main building and forced Cokesbury to Baltimore. There, despite fund-raising efforts, the school collapsed.

Maryland Catholics fared better under the leadership of Bishop Carroll, who resisted every attempt to place American Catholics under foreign administration or influence. A Jesuit college at Georgetown, opening in 1791, ensured that young men no longer had to travel abroad for a Catholic education. The same year at One-Mile Tavern in Baltimore, Carroll saw to the founding of a diocesan seminary, St. Mary's, for training priests. At first St. Mary's accepted only young men prepared traditionally in French or Spanish schools; in 1803 it opened to Americans, and though classes remained small, the General Assembly in 1805 chartered it as a university. Lesser schools grew up as well. Besides encouraging Elizabeth Seton, the bishop later guided Catholics in establishing academies in Baltimore and Georgetown, and in 1808 colleges for men and women—Mount St. Mary's and St. Joseph's—near Emmitsburg.

Though Carroll's intentions were sectarian, his idea of a peculiarly American Catholicism reflected a cultural mission he shared more broadly with other Marylanders in the period. Through the benevolence of the better-born and the improvement of everyone, they believed, free citizens might successfully preserve their unique way of life. As long as his clerical duties permitted, Carroll belonged to a Baltimore Society for Promoting Useful Knowledge, whose members in 1805 greatly regretted his formal resignation; he served for many years as president of the Baltimore Library Company, which in 1800 had almost ninety members and more than four thousand volumes.

Until 1807 Baltimore merchants and shipbuilders considered wartime profits worth every risk. Largely owing to Caribbean trade created by conflict between Britain and France, exports from Baltimore grew steadily, surpassing those from Philadelphia between 1798 and 1800. Though they dropped slightly during the next several years of peace, exports again reached record heights after 1804. Baltimore ships carried American goods to England and the British West Indies, as the Jay Treaty permitted. Enormous profits rewarded the reexport trade, which in the *Polly* case of 1802 British admiralty judges had held open. Except for contraband (war-making goods), Britain allowed neutral trade even between its enemies and their colonies, provided the cargoes first passed through neutral ports. Baltimore vessels thus visited places like Haiti and Martinique, sailed home to offload French products, and then reexported them as legal cargoes.

Controlling the high seas after Nelson's victory at Trafalgar in 1805, Britain quickly became what a Baltimore newspaper called "the merciless marauder of the seas."[49] The admiralty court reversed itself; the *Essex* decision of 1805 declared that if collectors rebated import duties (as Americans did when "neutralizing" cargoes), the reexport trade became illegal, violating an old rule against continuous voyages between enemy ports. When the French tried to injure Britain by placing restrictions on Continental ports, the British retaliated by declaring French ports blockaded. Taking advantage of the Jay Treaty, ships of the Royal Navy resupplied in Norfolk and then stood off the mouth of the Chesapeake to harass Maryland and Virginia shipping that might violate the narrow British view of neutral rights. While French captains considered any American ship that submitted to British search a collusive enemy and made their own captures, the British proved the worse offenders by maintaining the right to search American ships for deserted British seamen. By 1807 probably more than a thousand Maryland sailors had been caught in this net and served unwillingly on British men o' war. Then in June 1807 the British warship *Leopard* fired on the United States frigate *Chesapeake* off Norfolk, killing several seamen, wounding eighteen, and carrying away four "deserters"—three of whom proved innocent. Marylanders joined in the furious call for war.

Jefferson's chosen response, an embargo on all American exports (no one sailed legally except in the coastal trade), had the support especially of Baltimore Republicans, but for a time Federalists too approved the middle course between war and submission. "All ranks & degrees at this time are satisfied that it was a measure both proper & well-timed," wrote John Hollins in the spring of 1808, "& which saved the mercantile men from total ruin." Before long the strain became severe. By the end of the year the value of Baltimore exports, from more than $7,500,000 in 1805, had dropped to a mere $1,904,700. More than a thousand sailors were registered in Baltimore in 1806, and with the embargo most of them lost work. The temptation to defy the law grew too strong for some Maryland shippers, who never had been ones to ignore the lure of high profits. Using papers that got them out of port on coastal voyages or simply stealing away from the creeks and inlets of the bay, they returned to the old practice of smuggling. Secretary of the Treasury Albert Gallatin complained that Marylanders made a lucrative business of illegal trading and called on Samuel Smith's brother Robert—a Baltimore maritime lawyer serving as Jefferson's secretary of the navy—to crack down on the lawbreakers. John Randolph of Roanoke, himself alienated from the president, criticized Jefferson's embargo by pointing to its many evasions in Maryland; he claimed that in 1808 one hundred thousand barrels of flour left Baltimore alone.[50]

"The Union Manufactories of Maryland on Patapsco Falls Baltimore County." Drawing attributed to Maximilien Godefroy, c. 1810, showing a typically self-sufficient mill complex of the period: the large mill itself, managers' and workers' housing (with laundry set out to dry), and a brick kiln. *MHS*

Such chicanery aside, wealthy Baltimoreans softened the economic impact of the embargo by investing in factories that began making products ordinarily imported. Merchant-shippers turned to manufacturing, especially of textiles. Three hundred Marylanders subscribed a total of $1 million in establishing the Union Manufacturing Company in 1808. Another corporation appeared the year following with capital of $100,000, and Nathan Levering's Powhatan Mills began producing textiles in 1811. Patterned after a Philadelphia firm, the Athenian Society of Baltimore provided warehousing for home-made textiles that the society sold on commission. Its sales jumped from $17,608 in 1809 to almost $81,000 in 1812. The rise of textiles in Baltimore provided some out-of-work seamen and millers with jobs. It also created companies that made the most of recent technology; emerging, well-funded Baltimore textile firms quickly adopted new steam-powered equipment, which gave them a considerable advantage over smaller manufacturers. As merchant-shippers turned to textile manufacturing they also shifted their attention from foreign to domestic markets, where until this time (and except for pre-1807 imports) the small craftsmen-clothiers had operated on their own.[51]

These developments produced pressures that welled beneath the surface of Baltimore life like magma forming inside a volcano. Even after the Republicans repealed the embargo and then—by various plans that sought to punish violators of neutral rights—tried to return American ships to the seas, trade but slowly recovered and unemployment in Baltimore remained a problem. Baltimore banks reflected the division in the city between established, elite money and the craftsmen's struggle for capital: to compete with the Baltimore, Maryland, and Union institutions, groups like tanners, tailors, shoemakers, and leatherworkers formed the Mechanics' Bank in 1806 and the Franklin Bank four years later. A Federalist party resurgence in the city helped to raise tensions by polarizing opinion and feeling. Led by aggressive young lawyers like Jonathan Meredith, Virgil Maxcy, William H. Winder, and a former South Carolinian who had married Catharine Carroll, Robert Goodloe Harper, Baltimore Federalists complained of the embargo in their own newspaper, the *Federal Republican*. Its editor, Alexander Contee Hanson, Jr., a Montgomery County native and son of the Federalist judge, called Jefferson "His Gallic Majesty" and otherwise antagonized Republicans to the point that Hanson carried a pistol to defend himself.[52]

Scoring well in the 1808 elections, young Federalists in Baltimore reveled in their adversarial position. They recruited volunteers and gathered support from along the Potomac and in Anne Arundel County, where suspicion and jealousy of Baltimore remained strong. In June 1812, when President Madison called for a congressional declaration of war against Britain, the *Federal Republican* described him as a dupe of Irish immigrants. A mob no doubt made up of the immigrant laborers and unemployed whom Hanson held in contempt next destroyed his office and ran him out of town. On 26 July the editor returned with armed friends—young men with names like Pringle, Gaither, Gwinn, Kennedy, Warfield, and Schley; a young lawyer, David Hoffman; and two old revolutionary soldiers, "Light-Horse Harry" Lee of Virginia and James Lingan of Maryland. Hanson and his company barricaded themselves in a brick building on South Charles Street and waited for the latest issue of the paper to arouse Baltimore Republicans. They did not wait long. By nightfall of 27 July rioters had surrounded Hanson's fortress. The besieged Federalists fired into the crowd, killing one man. Anarchy reigned throughout the night. Twenty-four hours later, after authorities had persuaded the Federalist band to surrender and marched the men to jail, the mob broke open the jail and tried to beat to death every "monarchist" and "aristocrat" it could lay its hands on, singing a weird chant whose words went, "We'll feather and tar every d__d British tory / And this for American glory."[53] Remarkably, Lingan alone was killed in that night of terror. Survivors wore hideous scars and were missing some eyes and teeth. Critics of popular rule, holding themselves vindicated, published an account of the riot entitled *Portrait of the Evils of Democracy*. Class, ethnic, and regional differences in Baltimore and Maryland had produced one of the worst civil outbreaks in American history to that time.

Most Marylanders saw the War of 1812 as the second for American independence; Federalists, who after the Hanson riot gained heavily in the House of Delegates, considered it "unwise and impolitic"—merely an excuse for a campaign against Canada. Maryland Federalists never obstructed the war effort as did party members in New England. Maryland subscriptions to government war loans exceeded those of the northeastern states and of Virginia as well, and many Federalists dutifully contributed to the $3 million raised in Baltimore in 1813. In June of that year the British admiral Sir George Cockburn, whose ships commanded Chesapeake waters, stiffened Marylanders on the war issue by raiding and heavily damaging the helpless town of Havre de Grace. But Federalists charged that Madison's calling up the state militia for federal service was a dangerous precedent, complained that the administration spent more on defenses in Virginia than in Maryland, and made wry comment on the Republican generals who seemed to sniff a battle in every western breeze. When in late August 1814 British forces under Admiral Sir Alexander Cochrane sailed up the Patuxent, landed at Benedict, and passed through Upper Marlboro on their way to Bladensburg and Washington, Federalists used the embarrassment of the Madison administration as a campaign issue.

Circumstances came together to make Maryland sword-point of the republic. As the riot of June 1812 proved, Baltimoreans—their fellow seamen impressed, their shipping disrupted by the British—took great pleasure in twisting the Lion's tail. During the war 126 privateers sailed from the city, almost all of them built along the now-completed lines of the "Baltimore Clipper" that had been developing since the mid-eighteenth century. The sleek clipper proved a champion in this irregular naval warfare. Baltimore privateers claimed more than 550 British prizes—one-third of all ships seized during the war and fully half of those captured by American private vessels. While Baltimore seamen and merchants enjoyed their patriotic revenge, the practice paid both owners and crews exceedingly well. Baltimore's booty eventually amounted to $16 million. So attractive was the risky work— usually half the proceeds of a capture went to officers and crew—that many apprentices in the city deserted their masters to sign with privateer captains. Familiar with maritime skills, Marylanders of both parties took pride in the clipper's deadly swiftness. Everyone cheered the victories of the small American navy, whose few frigates included the thirty-eight-gun *Constellation*, launched from David Stodder's yard in September 1797. The "splendid actions of our heroic marine band" against Britain, a Federalist wrote the Annapolis paper, should "convince us that we are not inferior to that nation in naval tactics, of which she herself must be fully satisfied."[54]

Once the scene shifted from the high seas to the British landing in Maryland, the entire country watched to see whether citizen soldiers could stand up to veterans of the Napoleonic wars. First a motley force of volunteers and militia under William Winder tried to establish a defense at Bladensburg on 24 August. Winder may have had legal skills; they were not military ones, and he had little help. His uncle Levin Winder, Federalist governor of the state, had not actively prepared the state's defenses, and with President

"Admiral Cockburn Burning & Plundering Havre de Grace . . . done from a Sketch taken on the Spot at the time." Etching attributed to William Charles, 1813. *MHS*

Madison and several cabinet members visiting General Winder's camp as an experiment in executive leadership, confusion prevailed. British regulars appeared in front of the American troops and maneuvered with what the militiamen thought mechanical precision and coolness. British rockets, which the Americans had never before seen, rushed at them with a terrifying noise. The British attack on these men, some of whom had no uniforms and looked to the British like simple "country people," was devastating. "The militia ran like sheep, chased by dogs," was the angry remark of one American. A few officers tried to rally the fleeing first line; a second rank—too far to the rear—consisted almost entirely of four hundred sailors and marines under Joshua Barney. Earlier in the year the secretary of the navy had requested Barney, who predictably had busied himself as a privateersman, to command the flotilla defending the upper Chesapeake. Having filled that role as well as his barges and numbers allowed (fighting a sharp engagement at St. Leonard's Creek before scuttling his boats), he had disembarked his men and reported to Winder, who considered Barney outside his command. Barney and his men, perhaps along with the first-line stand of the old Baltimore militia regiment, the Fifth Maryland, offered most of the meager resistance the invaders met that unhappy day. Barney's men fought a desperate rearguard action until the British turned their flanks and took the wounded Barney prisoner.[55]

With public buildings in Washington burned and the government in full flight, the British had only to seize Baltimore, third-largest city in the country and notorious "nest of pirates," to make the American humiliation complete. No one could doubt that Baltimore was Admiral Cochrane's next target; a few voices recommended surrender as preferable to annihilation, banks began moving specie to safer locations, and some Philadelphians enjoyed watching a rival squirm. Yet the city had grown by meeting demand, calculating the odds, seizing opportunity, and these habits served well in an emergency. The rough-and-tumble practice of popular involvement now produced numerous committees volunteering special services. City committeemen and local militia leaders met and voted to turn over defense of Baltimore to Samuel Smith, U.S. senator since 1803 and commander of the militia division that included the city. The officer responsible for Fort McHenry, George Armistead, and senior naval officers whose ships happened to be in port—the redoubtable John Rodgers among them—agreed, putting aside service rivalries and the usual regulars' contempt for militia officers. John Eager Howard, who had four sons in the army, made the formal request and Smith quickly agreed—with the provision that Governor Winder give him emergency powers.

"A Baltimore Clipper." Watercolor by W. J. Huggins, c. 1815. The Dorchester County–built clipper *Catch Me Who Can* quickly exchanges her false British ensign for her true American colors as she engages a British warship. *MHS*

USF *Constellation*, a foundation warship of the U.S. Navy, likely the largest sailing ship ever constructed in Baltimore, and mostly the work of black labor. In his private journal in 1826, a midshipman drew one of the earliest known illustrations of the vessel. *MHS*

Samuel Smith's talent for organization, usually put to commercial use, now became a military asset even more valuable than his revolutionary experience. Smith called for the reassembly of militia units that had collapsed in "the Bladensburg Races." On 27 August he ordered citizens to gather on the exposed eastern edge of the city to begin digging earthworks, and soon a line of trenches stretched from Hampstead Hill (in the area later known as Patterson Park) to the shore of the Northwest Branch. "White and black are all at work together," wrote a young woman describing the scene. "You'll see a master and his slave digging side by side. There is no distinction whatsoever." When militia regiments from Pennsylvania and Virginia arrived the next day, Smith had them drill from sunrise to sunset. The War Department ordered cannon transferred from Fort McHenry to Washington. Observing that while the guns were federal property the carriages belonged to Baltimore, Smith answered that the department would have to carry off the tubes by hand. The army quartermaster ran out of money. Smith quickly negotiated a loan of $100,000 from Baltimore banks. Women of the city organized to roll bandages. Hundreds of private citizens contributed cash—Samuel Chase sent $100—and provided needed materials like bricks, hay, horses, shoes, tents, canteens, and knapsacks. By the end of the month Smith had assembled more than sixteen thousand defenders, who began to grow tired of soldiering in the two weeks the British took to decide whether to move against the city. On Sunday 11 September, when signal guns announced the arrival of about fifty British ships at the Patapsco's mouth, many troops were at church services. John Gruber, minister at the Light Street Methodist Church, dismissed his congregation with a blessing that concluded, "May the Lord bless King George, convert him, and take him to heaven, as we want no more of him." [56]

Rather than waiting, as Winder had at Bladensburg, Smith advanced—sending his men toward North Point, where he expected a British landing. Down the peninsula marched several Baltimore regiments under John Stricker, including William Pinkney's battalion of riflemen and the Fifth Maryland, with its companies of Independent Blues and Mechanical Volunteers. Joining them were a company of sharpshooters from Hagerstown under Thomas Quantrill, some small artillery pieces, and several companies of Pennsylvania militia. When Stricker's force finally picked a fight it lost—but not before riflemen shot and killed General Robert Ross, conqueror of Washington, and artillerymen, stuffing their guns with scrap metal, inflicted severe punishment on the invaders. Afterward British troops slowly continued their advance toward Hampstead Hill. Admiral Cochrane moved his ships under Cockburn up the Patapsco. Having heard of American atrocities during fighting in Canada, Cochrane ordered Ross's replacement to show Baltimore no mercy. One officer wrote his wife that although he did not enjoy "blood and destruction," his heart was "deeply interested in the coercion of these Baltimore heroes, who are perhaps the most inveterate against us of all the Yankees, and I hope they will be chastized even until they excite my pity, by which time they will be sufficiently humbled." [57]

All day on the thirteenth and for much of the night British ships stood off star-shaped Fort McHenry and tried to fulfill Cochrane's promise. The five bomb ships carried mortars that could loft 200-pound shells a distance of two miles. Each vessel sent forty or more shots an hour at the defenders, who may have guessed what General Armistead knew—that the magazine probably would not withstand a direct hit. Fort McHenry's guns could reach at most 2,800 yards. Though each time the British edged close enough Armistead's men fired away, they spent most of their time waiting for the shells to burst overhead or drop in their midst. A hit on one parapet killed two defenders and injured others. Another bomb, crashing into the magazine, failed to explode before a nimble defender doused the fuse with water. Into the rainy evening the cannonade continued, killing two more soldiers at McHenry. In the city, fire companies watched for incoming rockets and en-

Left, General Samuel Smith (1752–1839). *Right*, General John Stricker (1758–1825). Both by Rembrandt Peale, 1816. After the defense of Baltimore in 1814, the city commissioned portraits to honor four distinguished officers—Smith, Stricker, Armistead, and Barney. *Peale Museum, Baltimore City Life Museums*

"A View of the Bombardment of Fort McHenry." Aquatint engraving by John Bower, c. 1814–15. The artist probably had watched the British attack from the Observatory on Federal Hill. *MHS*

forced the rule against lights (during another night attack, citizens of St. Michaels had hung lanterns in trees to throw off British gunners). Action reached a climax between about one and four in the morning, when the British bungled a coordinated land-sea assault. Buildings in Baltimore shook while the fort came under its heaviest rocket, bomb, and cannon barrage. Surrender seemed to some witnesses only a matter of time.

On a truce boat eight miles downriver, Francis Scott Key, a Georgetown lawyer and brother of that staunch Federalist, Philip Barton Key, had been watching the spectacle through a spyglass. Detained by the British while seeking the release of an Upper Marlboro physician whom the British had seized, Key that night forgot all political differences with the Baltimoreans, whose troops an enemy soldier called "a parcel of tailors and shoemakers." Dawn the next day, foggy and wet, came late, and Key's anxiety for the defenders must have brought his heart to his mouth as he focused the glass on McHenry. The flag, he soon wrote, was still there: a marvelous 30-by-42-foot banner that Mary Pickersgill, a widow who made pennants for Baltimore shipowners, had produced the year before. "It is my desire," Major Armistead then had written Samuel Smith, "to have a flag so large that the British will have no difficulty seeing it from a distance."[58] Key's sentiments on seeing the flag himself after all those hours—the pride and relief he shared with other Americans watching this battle from afar—helped to stir the love of country that made the new republic a new nation. During the worst of the bombardment, troops in Fort McHenry had laughed when a rooster suddenly climbed a parapet and crowed defiantly. In the same way, cocky, rowdy, pragmatic Baltimore had given the country something to cheer about.

CHAPTER 5

Suspended between Memory and Hope

AT No. 14, FAYETTE ST., FORMERLY EAST.
MAYGER & WASHINGTON,

On the Fourth of July in 1828, Marylanders strikingly juxtaposed past and future in christening two monumental projects. Up the Potomac from Georgetown, at Little Falls, President John Quincy Adams, literally the son of a Founding Father, took up ceremonial shovel to begin work on the C&O Canal. His first thrust hit a stubborn tree root, as did his second. Adams, who strongly supported federal aid to economic and cultural projects, stripped off his coat to the crowd's cheers and kept struggling until the ground yielded. At almost the same moment, on what was left of the Mount Clare plantation southwest of Baltimore, Charles Carroll of Carrollton, the last surviving signer of the Declaration of Independence, took part in laying the first stone of the B&O Railroad. Then ninety-one, Carroll luckily had no trouble turning his own spadeful of soil. Verse written for the occasion had predicted as much: "The hand that held the pen / Never falters, but again / Is employed with the spade, to assist his fellow-men." A crowd of five thousand people—dignitaries, groups of skilled workers, merchants, common people, and children waving flags—watched as brothers of the Masonic Lodge put the stone into place.

Across the bay in Talbot County a black youth spent that summer learning his place in slavery—a labor system rooted in colonial necessity and staple-crop agriculture. The son of a white father and slave mother, Frederick earlier had left his grandmother's cabin on an outlying farm and begun work at Edward Lloyd's Wye River plantation. There he first saw a windmill "with its wide-sweeping white wings" and a boat with sails. He also saw his first whipping—punishment meted out to a young woman for seeing a man her master disapproved of. "When let down she could hardly stand," Frederick recalled. "I was terrified, hushed, stunned, and bewildered." He doubtless joined other hungry slaves in filching apples and pears from Colonel Lloyd's fine orchard (during the summer months people came from Baltimore, Easton, and Annapolis to see the lush gardens at Wye River). Lloyd finally had the fences surrounding the trees spread with pitch; any slave found with tar on his clothing got an immediate lashing from the chief gardener. Frederick played with one of the Lloyd children, ran errands for the master's family, and enjoyed the "gala days" when slaves from all the Lloyd farms gathered to collect their monthly allowances of cornmeal and pork. Later, having escaped slavery, he admitted that Maryland bondage might deserve its reputation for comparative mildness. He told, too, of overseers named Severe and Gore, whose names befit their regimes, a poor farmer named Covey who boasted of being a slave breaker and whose beatings and kickings almost killed Frederick, and the unpredictable whippings stable slaves got from gentlemen who had trouble with the spirited Lloyd horses. The slave's songs, so far from proving contentment, Frederick Douglass wrote, "represent the sorrows of his heart; and he is relieved by them, only as an aching heart is relieved by its tears."[1]

After 1815 no American state portrayed as vividly as did Maryland the contrast between slavery and steam power, past and future, convention and change—between what Ralph Waldo Emerson called the party of memory and the party of hope.

☙❦❧

Having fought with verve on privateers and gallantly defended Baltimore in 1814, Marylanders looked forward to renewed prosperity. The end of war brought mixed blessings. In Baltimore civic leaders mounted two projects that reflected the city's sense of triumph. One of them, a monument to George Washington, originally had been planned for the site of the old city courthouse. In 1815 the organizing committee held a lottery to finance the endeavor and finally decided not to put up the monument in the city itself, where homeowners feared the structure might topple on them, but to accept John Eager Howard's donation of some rural land on the northern edge of Baltimore. Howard's forested hill was near his Belvidere mansion and a spot called Howard's Park, where the public for many years had been free to roam. Like the park, which one visitor described as exhibiting "one of the finest landscapes in nature," the site of the new monument commanded a breathtaking view of the city (about a mile south), its harbor, and Fells Point.[2] Robert Mills, a native South Carolinian who had studied architecture with Jefferson and then in Philadelphia with the foremost American architect of the day, British-born Benjamin Henry Latrobe, submitted the winning design. Mills began with a massive square base on which he placed a simple, 168-foot Doric column. Atop the shaft he portrayed Washington, 16 feet high, as the general resigned his commission in Annapolis. The cornerstone of the monument, inlaid with objects like coins, Baltimore newspapers, and a copy of Washington's farewell address, was put in place 4 July 1815. A few months later, on the first anniversary of the defense of Baltimore, another ceremony marked the beginnings of a smaller though more elaborate structure commemorating the dead at North Point and Fort McHenry. Because of financial and other complications, work on the monuments continued well into the 1820s.

Before the war Baltimore had been, and for several years afterward remained, an exciting city for architects. Sudden wealth and rapid growth had meant much building. Robert Cary Long, Sr., a Baltimore native who studied architecture informally and spent an apprenticeship in carpentry, designed several structures in the early nineteenth century, including the Union Bank building and the famous Holliday Street Theater. His best-known structure, completed in 1817, may have been new St. Paul's Episcopal Church, a Greco-Roman building with bright interior marblework. Latrobe himself, busy with responsibilities in the federal city until moving to Baltimore in 1817, also had a hand in the cityscape. Part of Bishop Carroll's plans for American Catholicism had been a cathedral that would stand as a sign of the church's independence and strength. Carroll accepted Latrobe's design in 1805, and though construction began almost immediately, not until 1818, three years after Carroll's death, did the landmark near completion. Mills, who had moved to Baltimore in 1815, that year designed a series of rowhouses on Calvert Street—too far northward to sell quickly—in which he justified Latrobe's comment that he was "an excellent man of detail, and a very snug contriver of domestic conveniences."[3] Overseeing labor on the Washington Monument, Mills also drew plans in 1817 for a new Baptist church that resembled a flattened Roman Pantheon.

The designer of the Battle Monument, Maximilien Godefroy, a Frenchman who had fled Napoleonic rule, had been in Baltimore since 1805 as professor of civil and military architecture at St. Mary's College. There he had planned a Gothic revival chapel that represented the earliest such attempt in the United States. Though soon widely imitated, Godefroy's ornate building did not please him as much as the neoclassical form—simple geometric solids of the sort Latrobe and Mills also preferred—that he used more famously in his Unitarian Church, begun in 1817 at the northwest corner of Charles and Franklin streets. A cube with a large dome, Godefroy's church featured Tuscan archways over the entrance and an interior made colorful with a maple pulpit set on a base of green and white marble. Collaborating with Latrobe, with whom he began on friendly terms, Godefroy at about the same time took classical patterns to the task of designing a bank and stock exchange. Their solution, the H-shaped Merchant's Exchange Building on South Gay, became the most important structure in Baltimore. Under its central dome merchants conducted their daily affairs. Three-story wings provided office space for lawyers, clerks, traders, and eventually the federal customs office, city government, and post office as well. A fireproof cellar insured the safe storage of records. In the five years after the peace with Britain, Baltimore supplied architects one of their most exciting work sites in the country, and Greek Revival structures proliferated. Later, when Ralph Waldo Emerson

"View of the center of the Baltimore Exchange on Gay Street." Original design drawing by the architects, Maximilien Godefroy and Benjamin H. Latrobe, 1816. The Exchange housed a reading room with up-to-date news of ships' arrivals and departures; on a catwalk within the dome, shipowners could see merchants' house flags flying at the Federal Hill Observatory. *MHS*

paid his first visit to Baltimore, he thought the interior of the Unitarian church "noble" and its exterior "quite unlike any in the city." All this building and planning made citizens' spirits soar. In June 1816 a new Baltimore magazine described the city as "the Athens of America." Emerson bestowed his highest compliment: "in general & in particular," he said, Baltimore "looks like Boston."[4]

Unitarians and New Englanders in fact helped to give the city its intellectual vibrancy in the postwar years. The visits of several Unitarian preachers earlier had galvanized Baltimoreans who found the church's doctrines attractive. Many Unitarians, according to the young Harvard graduate Edward Hinckley—who joined a small but significant number of New England businessmen in Baltimore—were men "of the highest standing in wealth, manners, and influence." One of their leaders, Nathaniel Williams, declared that he "would rather be opposed to the whole city of Baltimore than to a few individuals in Boston." Early in 1819 Unitarians invited Jared Sparks, Hinckley's classmate, to assume the pulpit of the new First Independent Church. In May an elder of the heterodox theology, William Ellery Channing, came to Baltimore and gave an ordination sermon that defended Unitarians against "unwarranted use of reason in the interpretation of Scriptures," argued that the meaning of the Bible was "to be sought in the same manner, as that of other books," and protested "the irrational and unscriptural doctrine of the Trinity."[5]

Channing's sermon rocked the city in controversy and opened what became for Sparks a raucous, if rewarding, several years in Baltimore. Joseph Bend's successor as rector at St. Paul's, William E. Wyatt, engaged Sparks in a running newspaper and pamphlet exchange. A Princeton divine come to Baltimore to install a Presbyterian pastor attacked Unitarians for being "no Christians" at best, "immoral" at worst. When yellow fever briefly struck Fells Point in September 1819, a clergyman declared the sickness to be a sign of God's displeasure that a "Synagogue of Satan" had been established in the city. Sparks in January 1821 began publication of his own monthly, the *Unitarian Miscellany and Christian Monitor*, which soon reached a circulation of two thousand. At one time or another he welcomed as visiting preachers such noted Harvardians—and notorious independents—as Henry Ware, John Kirkland, John Gorham Palfrey, and Francis Parkman. "A strong spirit of inquiry is rapidly making its way among the people here," Sparks reported home soon after taking up his burden, "and prejudice is certainly sinking by degrees." Gradually, writing two sermons a week and fending off multiplying enemies, he lost spirit. "They assail me on all hands," he complained late in 1821; "as if my measure were not yet full, the Catholics are beginning to empty their quivers."[6]

Promoting the life of the mind in postwar Baltimore just as actively, though less seriously, were members of the Delphian Club. Organized in 1816 ("through a sort of Unitarian efflorescence") by Tobias Watkins and John Pierpont, the Delphians met Saturday evenings in members' homes— "there to eat bread and cheese, and settle the affairs of the universe." They were a varied lot. From 1816 to 1818 Watkins, an army surgeon, also edited the *Portico*, a literary magazine that gave writers in Baltimore and its surrounding area an outlet for their work. William Gwynn, an Irish immigrant and after 1813 editor of the *Federal Gazette*, served as president beginning in late 1824. His quaint Italianate home behind the newspaper office, designed by Robert Cary Long, Sr., and known as the Tusculum (the rabble called it "Gwynn's Folly"), provided a headquarters for the club. Other members included the master of the Bladensburg Races, William Winder, the proud Robert Goodloe Harper, and John D. Readel, a physician who for many years acted as club secretary. Rembrandt Peale, son of Charles Willson Peale, maintained informal ties to the group. In 1816–17 Henry Marie Brackenridge, son of the Pennsylvania jurist and writer, counted himself a member while practicing law in Baltimore. Francis Scott Key, whose poetic description of the battle for Fort McHenry recently had been set to music and performed at the Holliday Street Theater, attended Delphian meetings when in town, along with William Wirt, a Bladensburg native and Virginia lawyer who maintained a practice in Baltimore after joining Monroe's cabinet as attorney general in 1817. That year Wirt also published a life of Patrick Henry. Besides Pierpont, a Yale-educated merchant who had gone bankrupt in Baltimore and who later became a Unitarian minister in Boston, two other New Englanders added to the middle- or meeting-ground character of the club. John Neal, a Quaker from Portland, Maine, wrote romances and poetry while studying law. Paul Allen of Rhode Island, partly responsible for a history of the Lewis and Clark expedition in 1814, served as editor of the *Morning Chronicle* between 1818 and 1824. Meanwhile John Pendleton Kennedy, a handsome young fellow who considered law practice tedious and confining, published in the *Portico* and sought his own sanctuary in the literary life.[7]

The published work of the Delphians, thanks in part to their skilled Baltimore friends, appeared with the same brief intensity of the British rocket barrage over Fort McHenry. Printers like Thomas Murphy, William Wooddy, and J. Robinson (the last had offices in both Baltimore and Frederick) handled most of the books the group produced; publishers or booksellers/publishers—John Hopkins, Joseph Cushing, and Franklin Betts among them—aided in their appearance and promotion. With the help of the Cushing and Jewett firm on Howard Street, Brackenridge in 1817 completed a history of the late war with Britain. Allen projected, but relied on Neal and Watkins to write, a history of the American Revolution that a local shop printed. In 1821 the conservative Baltimore gentleman Thomas W. Griffith (French revolutionaries had imprisoned him for helping nobility escape the country) published two more early histories, *Annals of Baltimore* and *Sketches of the Early History of Maryland*. That year Baltimore printers also put out Allen's five-canto poem, *Noah*. Meanwhile Neal wrote with an enthusiasm that observers believed his greatest asset and liability alike; he worked, he said, with "marvellous rapidity." His *Keep Cool, a Novel Written in Hot Weather* appeared in 1817, underwritten by Joseph Cushing. Two books of his verse came out in the next two years. While outsiders published two other Neal creations, a Baltimore firm in 1823 produced *Randolph*. Masked as a novel, this book really cataloged his complaints against sundry people and almost occasioned a duel between Neal and a son of the late William Pinkney (whom even a friend had described as "vain of his vanity"). That year Robinson also published Neal's *Seventy-Six*, a popular romance of the American Revolution.[8]

Bright as did shine the Baltimore literary scene, it faded—partly because of deaths and departures and perhaps also because slave society demanded order that eventually stifled mavericks, whether religious, literary, or social. After leaving on a mission to the new South American republics, where Baltimore merchants discovered rich trading opportunities, Brackenridge rejoined the Delphians briefly before accepting in 1821 a federal appointment in Florida. Neal, after a sexual indiscretion, felt obliged to resign his Delphian membership in 1820. His next failure was an unsuccessful courtship

267

The Delphians at the Hall of the Flamen.

a drawing representing a meeting of the Club, at the Hall of Odopaus Oligostichus, Delphian Flamen &c, together with some explanatory verses, which his Ludship read.

The DELPHIAN CLUB met at Odopaus Oligostichus's Hall.

Poetical Explanation.

By A. Kennckkofritz, Duke of Pipes, Historical Painter &c.

When Time with whirring wings has flown,
And Delphians, spent their life, are gone,

"The Delphians at the Hall of the Flamen." Drawing by James H. McCulloh, Delphian Club Records, vol. 5, 10 February 1821. Beside the sketch McCulloh wrote a poem for future Delphians: "When Time with whirring wings has flown / and Delphians spent their lives are gone / How would they grieve to see no trace / Of person, lineament, or face / Of those who once in wit and fun / Composed the Club for '21!" *MHS*

of Peale's cousin Sarah, a painter in her own right. Members of polite society made clear their objections to *Randolph,* and Neal left Baltimore for Britain in December 1823. The Reverend Sparks had resigned his pastorate in April of the same year in order to find peace and begin a life of George Washington. Allen died in 1826. The promising young poet Edward Coate Pinkney followed him two years later.

Rembrandt Peale, often busy with commissions, had hoped to settle in Baltimore. Some of his earliest work had been profile drawings of John Ross Key and Matthew Tilghman and portraits of Nicholson, Hanson, and Cohen family members. In the spring of 1797 Rembrandt and his brother Raphael had tried to establish their own gallery and natural history museum in Baltimore as the elder Peale had done in Philadelphia. By 1799 they had abandoned the project. After several trips to Europe, and a Baltimore unveiling in 1811 of a large painting of Napoleon mounted for war, Peale renewed his pledge to open an institution on the Chesapeake. He wrote Jefferson that it would differ from his father's in being "more properly a Museum of Arts and Sciences"; though the museum would not neglect natural history, Peale expected to direct his "chief attention to the formation of a picture Gallery and Depository of the course and products of manufactures."[9] Support appeared ample—Henry Robinson opened his purse generously—if for no other reason than Baltimoreans always stood ready to challenge Philadelphia. Peale asked Robert Cary Long, Sr., to design what would be the country's first planned museum. Built on Holliday Street, it turned out to have a three-story, residence-like front with extralarge windows, a columned porch and loggia, and a square, two-story gallery to the rear (overrunning Long's estimate of five thousand dollars, the museum finally cost Peale fourteen thousand). Huddled with his family during the British attack of September 1814, Peale had planned to beg the British if they broke through the defenses on Hampstead Hill to spare the place as a dwelling.

Later that year—with portraits of statesmen and military and naval heroes, a few copies of Charles Willson Peale's work, and some bones borrowed from the Philadelphia institution on display—Peale's Baltimore Museum and Gallery of Fine Arts opened as "an elegant Rendezvous for taste, curiosity, and leisure." As part of the effort to draw crowds to the museum, Rembrandt in June 1816 borrowed an idea from another brother, Rubens, who had managed the Philadelphia museum—he installed lamps that burned natural gas and pledged thereby to light the museum "every evening until the public curiosity be gratified." The innovation did impress Long and a few other Baltimore investors; they obtained a charter from the assembly, formed the Gas Light Company of Baltimore, and in 1817 put gas streetlights in Old Town. Financial troubles plagued Rembrandt as in the late 1790s, however, and Rubens joined him in an attempt to make the enterprise profitable. Egyptian mummies, chanting Indians, and an armless woman who did stunts with tools held in her teeth were added to the usual attractions. Relieved of bookkeeping duties, Rembrandt produced a 24-by-13-foot, highly allegorical work depicting *The Court of Death*, which Baltimoreans viewed in 1820 before the painting left on tour. In May 1822 Rubens bought his brother's interest in the museum and Rembrandt himself left Baltimore for New York and Philadelphia. While Sarah Peale remained a portrait painter of considerable productivity in the city, the museum went into eclipse.[10]

Academics suffered a similar fate in Baltimore. In 1812 the General Assembly, hopeful of resurrecting plans for higher education in the state, had granted a university charter to Baltimore physicians who, for profit, operated a college of anatomy and medicine. The college owed its beginnings to Charles F. Wiesenthal, Prussian immigrant and state surgeon-general during the Revolution, who in the 1780s had made formal the informal apprenticeship method of training young doctors: he accepted students at his home on Gay Street and behind it built a small laboratory for their use. Since 1799 the Medical and Chirurgical Society that emerged from this experiment had authority to grant licenses to trained practitioners and prosecute the unfit. Popular outrage at grave robbing and dissection had hampered Wiesenthal, and in 1807 a mob tore down the college laboratory. The assembly acted that year to protect the institution by incorporating it. John Beale Davidge, an Annapolis native with Scottish medical schooling, and others began building a faculty, gathering students, and searching for new quarters. The doctors turned over fund raising to the worldly wise; John Eager Howard donated a plot of land at Greene and Lombard streets. A month before war broke out with Britain, Baltimoreans broke ground for a new anatomical classroom building that Long, Sr., designed as a small Roman Pantheon.

With its new University of Maryland charter, the faculty projected an enterprise (tuition going directly to professors) offering degrees in law, divinity, and even arts and sciences besides medicine. Prominent clergymen agreed to join the faculty on a part-time basis. In advertised weekly lectures the Reverend Wyatt, later known as "Dr. High-Church," aimed "to promote correct principles and pious habits among the young Gentlemen of the Institution." Other enlisted lecturers, apparently expecting rich rewards in high enrollments, included a state judge, Charles W. Hanson, in philosophy; John E. Hall (editor of a unique professional magazine, the *American Law Journal*), in what may have been the first separate history position in the country; and an Episcopal rector, George Ralph, in English and rhetoric. Principals of local academies offered more classes in mathematics, classical languages, and basic science. David Hoffman, a survivor of the 1812 Baltimore riot, planned the most ambitious curriculum of all. At the time young men prepared for the legal profession by reading lawbooks in an attorney's office; a few of them first attended college and later aspired to be statesmen. Hoffman contributed a syllabus of readings that marked a large step forward in legal schooling. *A Course of Legal Study, Respectfully Dedicated to the Students of Law in the United States*, appearing in 1817, soon won high praise from leading lights in Ameri-

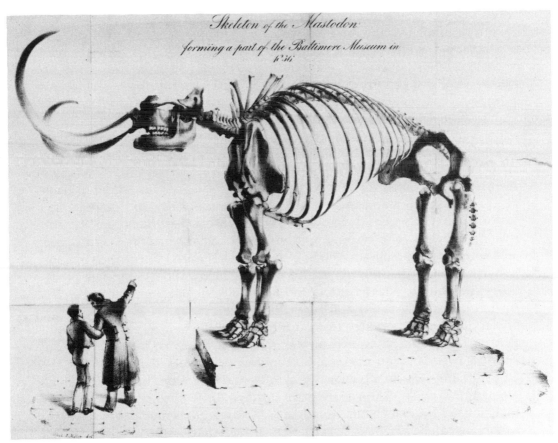

"Skeleton of the Mastodon forming a part of the Baltimore Museum in 1836." Drawn by Alfred Jacob Miller, 1836. One of three mastodon skeletons Charles Willson Peale excavated in rural New York, the fossil became a major attraction at Rembrandt Peale's Baltimore Museum. *MHS*

can law. In 1823 Hoffman began lecturing according to this plan, teaching three four-month terms that included Saturday moot courts.[11]

Trouble developed because the "university" lacked focus and direction; it suffered from an excess of individualism so typical of the age. Robert Smith, who briefly served as Madison's secretary of state, accepted the unsalaried provost's post in 1813 only to resign it in 1815. His successor, James Kemp, Episcopal bishop of Maryland, seemed content performing ceremonial duties until he retired in 1826. Arts and sciences lecturers tried gimmicks like free introductory lectures and chemistry sessions with "magical demonstrations." They taught irregularly and saw no need to coordinate their classes. In 1824 John Allen on the mathematics side led an attempt to begin anew and offer a full curriculum. Newspaper notices, damning with faint praise, declared that the university supplied an education "as good as any in Baltimore." Few students responded, and faculty members returned to their true careers. Hoffman's law institute faced equally low enrollments. In 1829, trying to stir more interest in the course, he published his lectures. But the two-volume set cost far less than tuition ($120 a term) and Baltimore living expenses, and students grew even scarcer. Hoffman later resigned and left for Europe to write fiction.[12]

Intellectual and artistic life in Baltimore competed unfavorably with pressing material problems. The state stood divided as it had been in the late eighteenth century—roughly along a northeast to southwest line through Baltimore. The northern and western counties and upper Eastern Shore looked to the future with confidence; with good markets, reasonable tariffs, and reliable currency (money consisted of minted coins, bank-circulated paper, and commercial promissory notes), those areas figured to prosper in commercial farming, trading, or manufacturing. In the oldest counties of the Western Shore, to a lesser extent in the middle Eastern Shore, slaveowners relied on tobacco growing and generally resisted change.

Marylanders had profited from European war; the return of peace brought painful readjustment. British products flooded the American market, depressing Maryland factories that had sprung up to meet demand during the embargo and war. In 1814 Washington County investors had built a small woolens mill on Antietam Creek at Funkstown. Its manager had complained that Hagerstown merchants would "purchase few homemade goods as soon as foreign can be obtained."[13] Exporters of Maryland grain and flour (wheat in the region suddenly suffered attacks from the dreaded Hessian fly) now met competition from European growers; Marylanders largely filled gaps created when foreign crops fell short. British Corn Laws of 1815 restricted American imports to periods when local wheat surpassed a set high price. Maryland tobacco exports remained far below the level of 1790. Eastern Shore lumbermen lost out to Baltic woods the Europeans could buy after the war. The stagnant West Indian economy did nothing to increase demand for either Chesapeake forest or farm products, and in any event British and French vessels had resumed their role in the Caribbean trade.

After the peace treaty with Britain, questions about the proper role of the federal government in economic development produced rancorous debates with far-reaching implications. Acting too late to save the Antietam Mills, which changed hands in 1816, Congress that year laid frankly protectionist duties on selected foreign products, established a second Bank of the United States, and spent more money on internal improvements. Maryland mirrored the country at large in dividing over these measures. Manufacturers and their employees voiced support for tariffs. The state benefited from the National Road (opened between Cumberland and Wheeling in 1818) and a strong navy. For these reasons the Federalist party, discredited at large

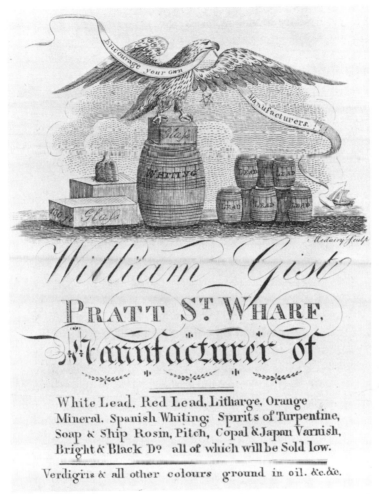

A paint manufacturer's advertisement showing strong support for protective tariffs. From *R. J. Matchett's Baltimore Directory for 1824. MHS*

for opposing the war and talking about separating New England from the Union, claimed strength in Maryland long after it ceased to be a force elsewhere.

Living in a diverse economy and society, Marylanders in general treated constitutional theory more pragmatically, with less piety, than did Virginians and other Southerners. Yet tariff walls kept the cost of clothes and hardware artificially high; slowing imports and raising duties abroad, they hurt Baltimore shipping. Maryland planters knew well that if federal power reached far enough outside constitutional bounds it might fall on slavery. Controlled by rural delegates and senators, the General Assembly in 1818 sought to restrict one federal intrusion by requiring banks opened "without authority of the state" to pay a tax on issued notes or an annual fee of $15,000. In the ensuing Supreme Court case, *McCulloch* v. *Maryland* (old and alcoholic Luther Martin argued for the state against Daniel Webster and two other Marylanders, Pinkney and Wirt), Chief Justice John Marshall struck down the Maryland law as "a tax on the operation of an instrument employed by the government of the Union to carry its powers into execution." Citizens still divided on exactly where those powers lay and the extent to which states exercised countervailing rights under the Constitution.[14]

Baltimore began losing ground to other American seaboard cities for geographic and maritime reasons that earlier had spelled success. Shippers discovered that the Baltimore Clipper carried disadvantages in peacetime, when vessels did not have to be fast and maneuverable so much as heavy and dependable—yet Chesapeake shipwrights had never specialized in making ponderous ships. Dredging of the Baltimore inner harbor had been tried with limited means and limited success. Sailing in and out of the bay for Liverpool, the leading British port, cost valuable time. While Marylanders took justifiable pride in their road improvements, it took sixteen to eighteen days for a loaded Conestoga wagon with its six-horse team, sometimes traveling day and night, to make the journey from the Ohio Valley to Baltimore. New York City by comparison enjoyed a large, deep-water harbor, easy access to the sea, and a shorter distance to Britain—making the city a logical entrepôt for goods going to and coming from that country. Clever Americans realized that, with European peace, large fortunes lay westward—in the marketing opportunities that would arise as settlers moved into the Ohio and Mississippi river valleys. In 1817 New Yorkers financed and began building a canal that they planned, incredibly, to cross the length of the state and connect the Atlantic port with Lake Erie and the west.

Another credit collapse in 1819 heightened the aura of crisis. Overproduction of cotton in the southern states, overly liberal credit to purchasers of public land there, and mismanagement of the national bank accounted for the fall, which struck hard at Baltimore firms. Many of them went under, closing shops and shipyards and throwing seamen, clerks, and laborers out of work. "The trade of this city was never more depressed," reported the British consul in Baltimore—"pecuniary embarrassments beyond anything ever before known, many failures, more expected and no one knows who to trust." Samuel Smith, since early 1816 serving a second series of congressional terms, recorded one of the saddest stories of financial failure. Smith had left his business in the hands of a partner, James Buchanan, who also acted as president of the Baltimore branch of the national bank. Buchanan joined other officials in irregular ventures that included lending themselves bank funds to make marginal stock purchases in the hope of selling at high profits. Without informing Smith, Buchanan had bought about $300,000 worth of stock in the name of their partnership. Congressional inquiries uncovered Buchanan's scheme. John Quincy Adams, like his father a moral critic of Baltimore, thought no city in the Union its rival for the "complication of profligacy." Smith and Buchanan, wrote Adams approvingly, fell "with a crash which staggered the whole city of Baltimore and will extend who knows how far." Smith had to sell Montebello; he contemplated suicide. About a hundred prominent merchants went bankrupt.[15]

The panic marked a watershed in the social history and economic growth of Baltimore. General Smith slowly recovered. He and his wife cut expenses and lived on his modest pension and meager congressional salary; their son, John Spear Smith, bought back Montebello and made it a working, paying farm. Even so, Smith's ill fortune—his literal discredit—helped to mark the decline of one commercial aristocracy, the elite that had arisen during the wars and trading opportunities of the preceding half-century. In the 1820s some of those wealthy Baltimoreans settled into the comforts of urban land-ownership, deriving income largely from rents drawn from city properties. They intermarried with the rural gentry of Frederick and Baltimore counties and made up a social register of old and still-proud Baltimore families. Another group consisting in part of Buchanans, Calhouns, Hollinses, and Leverings left trade for textile and other manufacturing. Still more leading or aspiring Baltimoreans adapted to the monetary and credit changes dictated by the shakedown of 1819. Now under capable and honest directors, among them the South Carolinian Langdon Cheves, the second Bank of the United States forced one change. Its notes circulated throughout the country, enabling buyers to make purchases in undiscounted paper; small merchants and wholesalers no longer depended on the advances, the credit patronage, of a single Baltimore merchant, and marketing practices shifted accordingly. Another change substituted institutional for personal borrowing. Before 1819 a merchant obtained credit on his word or a friend's endorsement; afterward he needed collateral and signed legal papers.

Alexander Brown typified new approaches to financiership and merchandising. Born in Northern Ireland, he first had entered the Irish linens trade in Baltimore and then widened his net. After the War of 1812 he sent his several sons to Liverpool, Philadelphia, and New York to establish branch offices and also acquired agents in southern cotton ports. So conservative was the elder Brown that he amounted to a pioneer. Rather than extend long credit to old friends, he insisted on short-term deals and payment in cash. By tradition Brown would have placed surplus capital in local real estate. Instead he reinvested in the firm. Unlike the few, high-risk efforts of Baltimore merchants bred to neutral trading during European war, his ventures tended to make small returns while representing little if any risk. After the 1819 panic, Brown bought ships and purchased bank stock at fallen prices. His strong position gained him a reputation for reliability and the respect of Cheves, who helped Brown's agents assume responsible posts at branch banks in southern cities.

Brown & Sons gained most from the lucrative export trade of the period—

the sale of southern cotton to England. Brown's Liverpool branch provided shippers with credit, insurance, and other services. The Baltimore office accepted bills of exchange for the shipped cotton, paid planters cash for two-thirds or three-fourths the cotton's total value, and then—an innovation—issued its own bills (sold for less than their value-when-due, usually due in ninety days) at a slight profit. The reliability of the company helped to make its bills especially desirable and more in demand. Brown set another precedent and added to his profits by smartly playing the market for bills—selling his own during the export season, when the exchange rate was high, buying those of other companies when demand and prices were low. By the late 1820s Brown & Sons had established itself as a powerful force in international trade and banking.[16]

Equally innovative were the Cohen brothers of Baltimore in the lottery business. In 1812 Jacob I. Cohen, Jr., had acted as one of several vendors—agents who sold a block of tickets at a small profit—in the successful lottery for the College of Medicine. Soon thereafter he and his brothers Mendes, David, and Philip established Cohen's Lottery and Exchange, a firm devoted solely to vending tickets and handling the various local bank notes people used to buy them. After the panic lotteries became big business—both because in hard times the small investor supplied the readiest source of capital and because Cohen developed into a prodigy of salesmanship. He published a weekly newspaper advertising current lotteries and offering miscellaneous commercial news, like commodity and stock prices and the discount rates (current value in Baltimore) of outside currencies. His brothers eventually opened branch offices in New York, Philadelphia, Richmond, Norfolk, and Charleston. By 1826 Cohen competed with a dozen other Baltimore lottery firms with names like Allen's Truly Lucky and Waite's Truly Fortunate. Colorful posters appeared on walls and posts everywhere. Drawings drew large, cheering crowds. Cohen advertised that he paid off numbers within ten minutes of their winning—no small feat with grand prizes sometimes as high as $100,000, others $50,000. He devised a system that paid small sums to last-digit ticket holders, whom he then enticed to buy more tickets. Cohen's paper reported stories of heaven-blessed small or share-of-ticket purchasers whose winnings fed their families or paid the mortgage. Many of them lived as far away as Massachusetts, Kentucky, and Crawford County, Georgia. In the late 1820s, with the return of moderate prosperity, the Cohen brothers left lotteries and entered banking, using their experience at changing different currencies to build one of the most successful firms in Baltimore.[17]

Lotteries enhanced a gambling spirit that made Marylanders watch transportation developments with a sharp eye. Steamboats, using energy of fearsome power, had begun to appear on the Chesapeake before the war with Britain. In design they followed the *Clermont*, built by Robert Fulton, whose New York monopoly forced them onto other waters. In 1813 two forward-

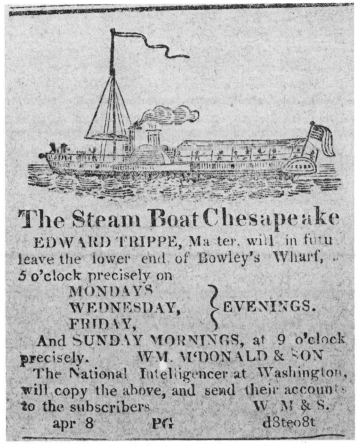

The Steam Boat Chesapeake

EDWARD TRIPPE, Master, will in futu
leave the lower end of Bowley's Wharf, at
5 o'clock precisely on
           MONDAYS
           WEDNESDAY,   } EVENINGS.
           FRIDAY,   }
    And SUNDAY MORNINGS, at 9 o'clock
precisely.   WM. M'DONALD & SON
   The National Intelligencer at Washington,
will copy the above, and send their accounts
to the subscribers   W M & S.
    apr 8   PG   d8teo8t

Advertisement for the Union Line. From the *American and Commercial Daily Advertiser*, 24 April 1816. *MHS*

looking marine financiers in Baltimore, Andrew F. Henderson and William McDonald, joined Edward Trippe in launching the steamboat *Chesapeake*. Two years later the Philadelphia-built *Eagle* sailed through the Virginia Capes and up the bay under command of a Connecticut native, Captain Moses Rogers. At first steamboats merely served as connectors for stage lines—carrying passengers between Frenchtown or Elkton and Baltimore (winds were notoriously undependable on the upper bay), or, in the case of the *Washington*, running between the federal city and stage terminals at Potomac and Aquia creeks in Virginia. Gradually they made longer voyages. In late 1815 Captain Rogers took the *Eagle*, a boat so simple it lacked a pilot-house, on a week-long trip from Baltimore to Richmond and back, proving the feasibility of service to points up and down the Chesapeake. Rogers piloted the vessel while standing on top of one of the paddle-wheel covers; he stomped on the main deck to signal the boilermen below. By 1819 a

Frenchman, fascinated by *"les bateaux à vapeur,"* counted about a dozen Chesapeake Bay steamboats, whose novelty made excursion trips from Baltimore to Yorktown and other points of interest highly fashionable. In 1828 the formation of the Maryland and Virginia Steam Boat Company marked the first attempt to coordinate land and water service between Philadelphia and Norfolk. Weekly packets made the Baltimore to Norfolk run in about twenty-four hours.

Early bay packets left some problems unsolved. Passengers put up with smoke and soot aft of the stack. They noted poor ventilation in the cabin below. A local newspaper described the Baltimore-built *Virginia*, launched at Flannigan's Wharf in 1817, as a "very large and staunch boat, elegantly fitted." Longer than the *Eagle* by twenty-six feet and four feet broader of beam, the *Virginia* carried a boiler built of copper instead of cast-iron. Her engine, producing forty-four horsepower, turned the paddles eighteen times a minute for a cruising speed of six knots. Still, the boiler used crudely evaporated sea water, slowly salting the machinery, and burned so much wood (up to 100 pine logs every hour, more in fog and storms) that the boat had only limited space for freight and passengers. The *Virginia* carried auxiliary sail and often had to use it.[18]

Meantime commercial rivalries with New York and Philadelphia encouraged Marylanders in the mid-1820s to invest in a variety of internal improvement schemes. Old ones had proved of doubtful worth. The Susquehanna Canal, its locks narrow and upkeep costs high, had fallen into disuse by 1815. The Potomac Company eased downriver traffic with chutes around the falls, but rocks still made the trip advisable only when the river was high. Maryland owned much stock in both firms, whose financial condition counseled prudence (in 1822 the Potomac Company owed more than $175,000). Nonetheless, pressure on legislators mounted from several directions, especially as the Erie Canal neared completion. For generations people had talked about a canal between the upper Chesapeake Bay and Delaware River. New Yorkers had shown that talk could lead to action. Mathew Carey, the Philadelphia publisher and promoter, fanned interest in the project, and in April 1824 work began on the Chesapeake and Delaware Canal. The Maryland legislature committed itself to $50,000 worth of company stock—twice Delaware's contribution, half of Pennsylvania's interest. In 1825 Congress appropriated another $300,000 to the C&D because of its military value.

That canal ran about thirteen miles over fairly level ground. Supporters of another ditch revived Washington's dream of a canal between the lower Potomac and upper Ohio, an estimated distance of 342 miles with a rise of about three thousand feet. At a conference held in the federal city late in 1823 a number of distinguished gentlemen subscribed to the plan. Albert Gallatin of Pennsylvania, treasury secretary under presidents Jefferson and Madison, believed it possible, as did the honorable Charles Fenton Mercer of Loudon County, Virginia, and two important District of Columbia residents,

Francis Scott Key and the Georgetown merchant John Mason. Marylanders at the meeting included Joseph Kent (then governor), Frisby Tilghman and Thomas Kennedy of Washington County, and George C. Washington. Taking a national view and hoping for federal support, the meeting urged the Potomac canal as another form of National Road, a tie between the federal capital and the growing west. President Monroe mentioned the project in his next state of the union address. In January 1824 Virginia chartered the Chesapeake and Ohio Canal Company.

Financial issues and the queries of experts postponed the project. The army corps of engineers placed the cost of a canal to Pittsburgh at more than $22 million—far more than the convention had estimated (the Erie had cost $7 million)—and argued for larger dimensions. Engineers, whose expertise grew more specialized and invaluable as improvement schemes multiplied in the country, recommended 398 locks and noted the need for a four-mile tunnel at the summit of the Allegheny Mountains. Not until the spring of 1828 did Congress subscribe $1 million to the canal, thus meeting conditions the Maryland assembly had laid down three years before. The state obligated itself to $500,000 worth of C&O stock. Word of congressional approval set off celebrations in Washington City, Georgetown, Leesburg, Martinsburg, Oldtown, and Cumberland. Western Maryland fell victim to canal fever.

Philip E. Thomas of Baltimore served as Maryland commissioner to the interstate board of directors but resigned within a year; despite talk of a canal connecting Baltimore with the C&O at Point of Rocks or Georgetown, the project clearly would benefit the Potomac region alone. Indeed, canal mania had reopened the Pandora's box of internal Maryland rivalries. Allegany, Washington, Frederick, and Montgomery county supporters of the Chesapeake and Ohio won some votes from Eastern Shoremen with promises of state appropriations for dredging rivers and draining marshes on their side of the bay. Hard-bargaining delegates from the upper Eastern Shore probably traded support for the Potomac canal for Western Shore votes in favor of the Chesapeake and Delaware enterprise. Legislators from Baltimore and the upper Western Shore largely had opposed both ventures. Earlier they had received no state help for a proposed new canal up the Susquehanna. To make the plight of Baltimore more desperate, Pennsylvanians were placing dams on the river upstream from the states' border line (surveyed by Charles Mason and Jeremiah Dixon in the 1760s). Built to siphon off water to the new canals feeding Philadelphia, these dams injured as well as insulted because they also kept farmers from floating their arks downriver to Port Deposit or Havre de Grace.

Just as the prospect of hanging concentrates a man's mind wonderfully, the specter of losing in the war for western trade forced Baltimore commercial leaders to consider innovation over imitation. They apparently first talked about taking a bold step at a dinner held at John Eager Howard's home in the fall of 1826. Philip Thomas's brother Evan, returned from Britain, had reported with enthusiasm on a new British road of double rails. The one he had seen was used to haul cars filled with coal from mine shaft to waterside. It featured a chugging steam engine that made much noise and that he thought probably not as reliable as horsepower. At first amusing, the image of rails and loaded cars quickly suggested a possible answer to a serious economic problem. Twenty-five Baltimore businessmen considered the idea worth exploring and met the following February at the house of George Brown, a son of the banker. Some of them noted that a barrel of wheat costing one dollar at Wheeling accumulated four dollars in transportation expenses before reaching Baltimore. They studied the performance of British railways—which, so limited, decided nothing. The committee argued for going ahead. In Britain "many judicious and practical men," read the published report, believed that railroads eventually would "supersede canals as effectually as canals have superseded turnpikes." [19]

Members of the assembly could find no reason to oppose the plan, and in February 1827 Maryland chartered the Baltimore and Ohio Railroad. The charter held the company to certain restrictions. The road had to be started in two years and laid to the western border of Maryland by 1837; the state reserved to itself one-third of the thirty thousand shares, which sold at $100 each, and allowed the city of Baltimore to purchase another five thousand. The charter exempted the railroad forever from all state taxes—a provision that one founder, Robert Oliver, had considered as likely to pass the legislature as the Lord's Prayer. Terms may have been generous, but the venture had no precedent; the risks seemed huge, and railroad leaders had stated their intention of going ahead with or without state aid (Philadelphians, cautiously choosing canals, had waited for legislative financing). Public support boded well for the corporation. Within eleven days citizens in Baltimore, Frederick, and Hagerstown had bought all the stock available for public purchase.

Compared to railroad mania, canal fever was perfect health. The B&O prospectus looked for settlers to reach the Rocky Mountains within thirty years, "or even to the Pacific Ocean"; it asked readers to imagine how wide and rich a western market the railroad ultimately might tap. The strait-laced *Niles' Weekly Register*, published in Baltimore since 1811, suddenly waxed eloquent over organization of the B&O. "Thus will scientific power conquer space," it read, "and even the Alleghenies sink, as it were, beneath the pressure of unconquered steam, nay, the laws of gravity give way before the march of mind!" Actually the value of steampower on a railroad had no more been demonstrated than the advantage of a railroad over a canal. The terms of the B&O charter deliberately gave the company rights to run on its rails "all machines, wagons, vehicles, or carriages of any description whatsoever." Trying an idea that one would expect to germinate in Baltimore, Evan Thomas conducted trials with a railroad car under sail, which worked well as long as the wind kept abaft. Another contraption—with a horse walking

Steam Engine & Machine Manufactory,

AT No. 14, FAYETTE ST., FORMERLY EAST,

MAYGER & WASHINGTON,

Respectfully inform the public that they are ready to receive orders for Steam Engines, locomotive or stationary, PUMPS of all kinds, PRESSES of all kinds, Rolling Mill and other SCREWS. Iron and Brass TURNING of every description. LATHES and circular SAWS fitted up according to the most approved patterns. MILLWRIGHT & PATTERN MAKING in all their varieties. Rail Road CARS, and repairing of machines in general. They have also a separate shop for WOOD and IVORY TURNING.

The first locomotive steam engine used by the Baltimore & Ohio Railroad, later nicknamed the "Tom Thumb." From *Matchett's Baltimore Director* (Baltimore, 1831). *MHS*

a treadmill that turned drive wheels—met an end when it struck a cow and overturned. By the summer of 1830 Peter Cooper, a New York merchant with Baltimore investments, had built a crude "steam carriage" (in later legend known as *Tom Thumb*) that could attain a speed of twenty miles per hour on a straightaway; it could chug and hiss up to Ellicott's Mills and back to Baltimore with a car of B&O directors, all together weighing several tons. Riders at first expected it to burst or fly apart. The engine ran so fast, said one trial passenger in August, "as to terrify the whole party."[20]

Experiments with steam coincided with many a somber speech and sermon, for in these years of comparative security and wild expansion the last of the Founding Fathers passed to their reward. Sons and daughters spoke brashly of progress; at times they were moved to reflection. On 4 July 1826, as if by summons, both Thomas Jefferson and John Adams had died—fifty years to the day after signing the Declaration of Independence. In 1832, four years after emerging from the past to bless nineteenth-century progress at the B&O groundbreaking, Carroll died. As he departed he invited comparison with Jefferson—if only because Maryland's sister state now had taken to complaining of her diminished role in public affairs and declining economic fortunes. Both Carroll and Jefferson had spent their lives as large slaveholders who quietly opposed the institution, entertained amicably the many pilgrims who came to visit them in late life, and taken great pride in their children and grandchildren. Jefferson, however, had mistrusted government, harbored mixed feelings about cities, banks, and industrial development, and placed confidence in the good judgment of an informed people. Fond of designs, he spent many years building and rebuilding Monticello. Carroll by contrast divided his time between a town house in Baltimore, where he enjoyed city life, and Doughoregan Manor, which struck a visitor as so haphazardly functional as to have "but little pretension either to beauty, variety or excellence." A planter whose wealth included stocks and foundries as well as land, he had never doubted the Hamiltonian connection between government and private enterprise. Believing himself a hard realist rather than designer, Carroll had fretted about widened suffrage and the popular election of officials. In the Jeffersonian years he went so far as to command employees to vote Federalist. Jefferson dreamed of transcontinental liberty; Carroll lived to launch a railroad that had ambitions of reaching the Ohio River.[21]

⌘

In broaching the connected problems of agricultural reform, slavery, and freed blacks, Marylanders illustrated both the hopeful spirit of the age and the obstacles any reformer faced in a slave society. Exhausted soil, gullied fields, abandoned lands—all had been the subject of commentary for many years. Along with visitors, natives like John Beale Bordley—an enlightened Eastern Shore planter of the eighteenth century—had called for a scientific approach to agriculture. After 1815 several societies formed to promote the cause. One emerged in Annapolis and Anne Arundel County late in 1817, held a contest or two, then disappeared. Another organized the following spring at a meeting at Gadsby's Tavern in Baltimore. Robert Smith and Edward Lloyd emerged as leaders of the group, which called itself the Maryland Agricultural Society. It adopted a constitution that divided officers evenly between Eastern and Western shores and provided for six "curators" from both areas whose duties included finding and distributing (at whose cost was not clear) all seeds, roots, and fertilizers that might be of value to neighboring farmers. At the November meeting of the society Lloyd, vice-president, issued a public appeal that began with an often repeated observation. "Lands generally in Maryland are nearly exhausted," he wrote; "our agriculture is sinking to its lowest stage of degradation."[22]

To publish such dire warnings and spread word of new agricultural methods, the society soon depended on John Stuart Skinner of Baltimore. A lawyer by training, Skinner had grown up on a Calvert County farm and never tired of talking about land, livestock, and horses. In 1816 James Madison appointed him Baltimore postmaster, and with the aid of a regular income Skinner, who shared the president's interest in agricultural reform, began writing about his favorite topics in a paper he entitled the *Maryland Censor*. An early article excoriated tobacco as a "loathesome weed" and challenged planters to substitute "reason and reflection in place of old fashions." Then in 1819 Skinner began publishing the *American Farmer*, a monthly magazine intended for the broadest possible audience. As the corresponding secretary of the Maryland Agricultural Society after 1820, Skinner used the *American Farmer* and later the *American Turf Register* to sound the call for new crops, improved field management, and knowledgeable animal breeding—especially of race horses.[23]

For a few years reform seemed to gain momentum. Several farms became showplaces—Skinner's at Maryland Tavern outside Baltimore (he had the aid of Robert Oliver and Isaac McKim), Lloyd's Wye River plantation, Robert Smith's dairy farm near Baltimore (he sold skimmed milk in the city for 2¢ a quart), Charles Ridgely's Hampton, and the estate of Charles Carroll's son-in-law Richard Caton. Prominent landholders like Colonel Nicholas Bosley of Hayfields, William E. Williams in Frederick County (he was son of the revolutionary war officer), Roger Brooke in Montgomery County, Tench Tilghman, Robert H. Goldsborough of Talbot, and Joseph Muse of Dorchester assumed local reform leadership. By 1825 each shore held a separate annual exhibition, usually at a gentleman's home. There, donated silver plate went to owners of the finest imported cattle and sheep, "the best cultivated farm," producers of exceptional butter, cider, and household manufactures, and the most ingenious farm implements. Plowing and reaping contests drew interested spectators. Officers of the society made speeches congratulating progressive planters. Western Shore members agreeably postponed a fall cattle show to the spring of 1825 so that Lafayette could make a brief appearance (the Eastern Shore chapter tried in vain to secure a similar visit), and at the affair dignitaries from Virginia and New Jersey joined Maryland politicians in toasting advances in husbandry. That meeting, according to the *American Farmer*, "consisted more exclusively than it had ever before done, of highly respectable landholders and gentlemen known for their practical skill & intelligence."[24]

Under the auspices of such men a number of useful experiments were made in these years. Skinner and the others demonstrated clearly the value of crop rotation, deep plowing, and the application of burnt lime and marl to worn-out fields. Devon, Alderney, Teeswater, and short-horned Durham cattle made their appearance in Maryland, along with crops like cotton, sorghum, and—in Dorchester County—rice. Attempts were made to control the Hessian fly and wheat rust by washing seed in various mixtures of lime or saltwater—although John Piper of Allegany County, a leading experimenter, still took care to plant according to moon phases. Among others, the Stablers of Sandy Spring, Montgomery County, tried silkworm culture. Increased attention to fruit growing led in 1832 to the formation of a state horticultural society. In the early 1830s the patronage of Tench Tilghman enabled Obediah Hussey to build a prototype reaper that could harvest seventy-five acres of wheat in only five days and that for a time rivaled Cyrus McCormick's machine.

Yet reformers tripped over old stumbling blocks, one of them the pride of small farmers who found the Maryland Agricultural Society little more than another gentlemen's club. Working farmers cared nothing for essays on applying manure or speeches about bone meal. Machinery contests at fairs, instead of drawing farmers, developed into promotional affairs between competing manufacturers. Apparently trying to attract common planters to the 1821 meeting of the society, Skinner advertised a fight between two buffalo. The Baltimore *American* noted that an ordinary farmer's bull, taken to that exhibit, could not compare with imported strains and predicted that next year many plain men would be afraid to enter "for fear of being excelled." At the 1826 show scarcely anything, Skinner himself admitted, had been entered by one who earned his living at farming. Skinner favored regular sales rather than exhibits. Cattle shows, he wrote in 1839, remained "in too great degree contests of pride and wealth." People who called themselves "practical farmers" continued in the 1830s to get together of a winter's evening and in some counties to stage yearly public events. "King Alcohol" might assert himself at the larger gatherings, as he did at one Charles County fair—disturbing Port Tobacco "to a considerable degree"—but most county fairs, at once peaceful and exciting, followed the example of Frederick and Queen Anne's, where dinners and songs replaced silver plate, imported bulls, and theories of improvement.[25]

Agricultural reform in Maryland carried heavy irony; the more a planter needed to invest in agricultural improvement, the less likely he had the means to do so. Farmers in western Maryland, practicing the diversified husbandry that Lloyd recommended to everyone in the state, had little worry about soil exhaustion or a reliable cash crop. Large landowners, as in the case of Nicholas Bosley, might own the lime beds needed for soil enrichment or, like the Carrolls, have enough income from other sources, including the sale of slaves, to finance experiments. In the 1830s and 1840s population figures for southern Anne Arundel, lower Prince George's, Charles, Calvert, and St. Mary's counties gave continued evidence of outmigration, poverty—and room for change. "Let us then reform our system," read the Upper Marlboro *Gazette* in 1839, "reduce our Tobacco crop—thereby enhancing the value of the article—and assume more of the character of Farmers."[26] And yet, for the small, slaveholding tobacco grower who dominated the region,

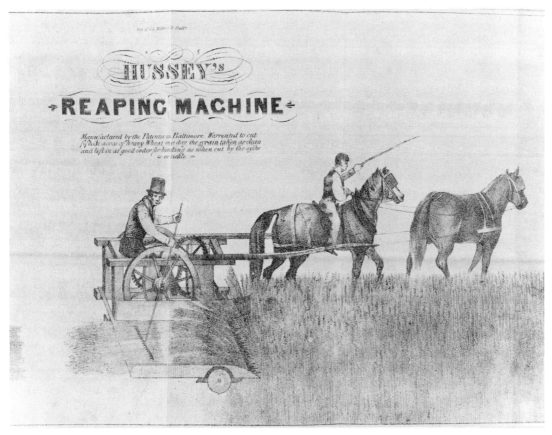

"Hussey's Reaping Machine." Lithograph by Edward Weber & Co., Baltimore, 1838. *MHS*

the well of agricultural progress came up dry. Improving one's farm required capital that he could not spare or did not have. Blooded stock, any cattle, commanded high prices and took land out of cash-producing tobacco to grow hay or make pasture. Commercial fertilizer (South American guano began arriving in Baltimore in 1843) cost dearly if one were trying hard to make ends meet.

Though the hardscrabble slaveowner might consider the comparative worth of free and slave labor, he found himself in a closed circle of dilemmas—despite his vaunted liberty. Long habit and soil composition argued in favor of staying with a familiar crop; unsteady tobacco prices and the indifference of slaves made experiments risky. New implements were of no interest—the only way to pick hornworms off tobacco plants and harvest the leaves was by hand. Slaves may have been notoriously inefficient when set against free workers, but southern Maryland as other rural areas suffered a chronic labor shortage. Seasonal work did not always keep whites and free blacks in the countryside; with good acreage scarce, people tended to move on. Slaves, if one managed to feed and clothe them, at least provided a steady labor force. Holding blacks had another benefit—it gave even the poorest planter some measure of status in his own eyes and those of other whites. He might be poor and miserable, but a small Maryland slaveholder still could ride a horse out to the fields to watch a gang of blacks working beneath him. Though wedded to comparative unproductivity, he still might put on airs for outsiders or boast at the country store.

Elsewhere, in the forward-looking western and northern counties and Baltimore City, a few men and women heaped criticism on slavery. Using issues at the federal level as an excuse to speak out, Marylanders for a time conducted debates that one seldom heard farther north or south. In 1819–20 the Missouri controversy—whether Congress should admit the new state with a proslavery constitution—produced antislavery meetings in Baltimore and, in Hagerstown, an antislavery petition to the General Assembly. The Frederick *Bartgis's Republican Gazette* expressed sorrow that Missouri so early had declared its "avaricious determination" to rely on slave labor. A Baltimore paper announced someone's plans for a pamphlet proving that slavery was constitutional and Christian; a wit calling himself "Another Slaveholder" quickly replied that his own booklet—besides making "a reasonable windfall of cash"—would prove that owning slaves was so far from wrong "that no man can be a Christian who does not hold them" and that enslaving Africans was so just that Americans should carry off "the children of any other nation, when the same can be done with impunity."[27] The Baltimore *Federal Gazette* announced that it no longer would carry the advertisements of slave dealers.

During the 1820s, when slavery in most states dropped from public view, Marylanders continued to discuss it. The Maryland legislature heard several memorials on the subject. In 1826 citizens of Baltimore County petitioned for a law that would "eventually but gradually and totally extinguish slavery in Maryland." Similar pleas in the next few years came from Baltimore City, Harford and Frederick counties. Self-interest, James Fenimore Cooper predicted in *Notions of the Americans,* surely would provide the "entering wedge" of gradual abolition in Maryland, where citizens would begin to see "that they would be richer and more powerful without their slaves than with them." In 1828, when Cooper wrote, he based this view on promising trends. Judging by numbers alone, Maryland slavery had begun a gradual decline. The state's slave population dropped between 1810 and 1820, from about 111,500 to 107,400; by 1830 it had fallen by another 5,000. "The history of emancipation in Maryland has proved that manumission begets manumission," wrote an antislavery Baltimorean in 1825—"that they increase even in a geometrical proportion."[28]

Some of the slave decrease, as earlier, resulted from masters taking their property to the south and west. Other masters freed their bondsmen by will or deed (often with conditions and restrictions), and the number of freed

"An Overseer doing his duty." Watercolor by Benjamin H. Latrobe, 1798. After spending time in Maryland, Latrobe produced one of the rare images of American slaveholding. *MHS*

blacks swelled in the state from some 30,000 in 1810 to nearly 50,000 in 1830. Many freed Negroes went to Baltimore, where they hoped to find jobs as servants, teamsters, laundresses, and shipyard workers. There they formed a class with some friends and many enemies. Increasingly they lived apart from their white employers or patrons; the number of free black households in the city climbed sharply from 103 in 1820 to 687 ten years later. Free blacks competed for jobs. They posed a threat to slavery; if they did not purchase slaves with the idea of freeing them or teach slaves to read or how to escape, they simply showed bondsmen that not all blacks were slaves. To many sympathetic whites, moreover, the free blacks' condition did not speak well of black freedom. City death records, kept after 1824, proved that the mortality rate was highest among free blacks. A Northern visitor found "no strong attachment to slavery" in Baltimore, but a nearly universal attitude among slaveholders that freeing blacks by itself did them no favor. "That the moral and physical condition of the free negroes in Baltimore is worse than that of the slave, is a fact to which all intelligent men with whom I have conversed most fully bear testimony."[29]

Marylanders struggled with the question of free blacks, whose ambiguous status—neither slave nor completely free—well portrayed the social and moral suspension of Maryland. Since the late eighteenth century state law forced free blacks to obtain work; if they did not, and refused to leave Maryland, or left and returned, they faced sale into bonded labor for varying periods. Free Negroes—many with white blood and some free because they inherited the status of their white mothers—had access to the court system, but could not testify against whites. In 1818 the assembly decided no longer to imprison free blacks convicted of serious noncapital crimes, but instead to flog them, banish them, or sell them into servitude for the length of time whites would spend in prison for the same offense. Opposition to the last feature of the law formed because some blacks sold into servitude disappeared into slavery farther south. In 1826 legislators restored prison terms, followed by banishment, for a variety of offenses.

In 1817 Francis Scott Key, Robert Goodloe Harper, and Robert H. Goldsborough had been among the founders of the American Colonization Society. Aiming to solve the problem of freed blacks by returning them to Africa, the society brought together Northern and Southern members with potentially different objectives. The society might indirectly encourage the manumission of slaves; it might strengthen the slave order by removing an irritant. The Maryland auxiliary, its members mainly citing the advantages of free over slave labor, became one of the most active in the Union. Local chapters formed in Anne Arundel, Prince George's, Montgomery, Frederick, Washington, Queen Anne's, Dorchester, and Talbot counties. In 1827 the General Assembly appropriated $1,000 to further the society's work. Four years later differences between Marylanders and the parent group, which spent money raised in Maryland on emigrants from other states, came to a head. A colonization meeting held at the Baltimore Athenaeum—its leaders John H. B. Latrobe, son of the architect, and Judge Nicholas Brice of the Baltimore City court—declared the Maryland society virtually autonomous. Then, in December 1831, the bloody Nat Turner slave uprising in Virginia gave white Marylanders, especially in heavily black counties, grounds for fright. Whites urged the assembly to take courses that ranged from abolishing slavery to reenslaving newly freed blacks.

Legislators chose no radical course. In the spring of 1832, following recommendations of a House of Delegates committee under Henry Brawner, they passed a bill further restricting the liberties of Maryland free blacks. The 1832 statute required free blacks outside Annapolis and Baltimore to find a white minister for church services. Black vendors needed a new certificate to sell farm products (whites suspected widespread thievery) and liquor. A provision discouraging the return of free blacks who left the state contained exceptions to cover sailors, teamsters, and the like. The assembly also chartered the Maryland State Colonization Society, established a state board to oversee "the Removal of Coloured People," and set aside $20,000 for 1832 and up to $200,000 over the next twenty years to repatriate all free Negroes who were willing to return to Africa.[30]

Maryland's colonizing blacks in Liberia carried interesting parallels to Lord Baltimore's settling his province exactly two centuries before. Purposes of the expedition, so redolent of white self-interest, nonetheless sounded a moral tone. Each black couple had to carry a marriage certificate. Every adult swore to abstain from liquor. Members of the American Board of Foreign Missions, among the first parties to depart, planned to conduct religious instruction of both emigrants and natives. The Maryland settlement would be separate from the original American Colonization Society site at Monrovia so as to lie on better land and to avoid the "vicious habits" and "intervals of idleness" there. Gaining lessons from the Monrovian settlers' experience, Maryland emigrants carried instructions to practice farming rather than indulge in the rum trade. They also took with them a constitution and bill of rights. Everyone agreed to abide by laws that the society would frame until the colony grew strong.[31]

In September 1833 the Maryland Society appointed James Hall, a New England physician who had practiced in Liberia, as a kind of Leonard Calvert to oversee establishment of the new colony. Two months later, with nineteen blacks from Washington and Frederick counties and Baltimore City (only seven of whom were adult males), Hall and an assistant, the Reverend John Hersey, sailed from Baltimore on the brig *Ann* for Africa. Once at Cape Palmas, about two hundred fifty miles down the coast from Monrovia, Hall refused to ply native leaders with the liquor that whites often employed in land negotiations. He traded arms and manufactured housewares for several hundred acres he believed sufficient to sustain the newcomers. Like the first Englishmen in the Chesapeake, the settlers at first suffered a seasoning period and therefore learned much from the Maryland blacks who earlier had arrived in Liberia and now joined the latest settlement. By the late summer of 1834, Maryland in Liberia, as the settlers called Cape Palmas, had grown into a village of twelve private houses, a fort, jail, community kitchen, church, school, and several buildings for the shelter of new arrivals. In 1837 the settlement had more than two hundred people and a black governor, John Brown Russwurm. Maryland's success subtracted from the cause of Monrovia, so that the older colony's attitude to the new one remained jealous if not hostile for many years. Nonetheless, other states followed the Maryland example of independent action in Liberia. New York with Pennsylvania, and Louisiana cooperating with Mississippi, eventually founded similar colonies.

While members of the Maryland Society prayed for the survival of their colony, various critics at home scoffed at it, and blacks jeered. "We consider the land in which we were born our only 'true and appropriate home,'" declared a meeting of Baltimore free blacks in 1831, "and when we desire to remove we will apprise the public of the same, in due season." Free blacks

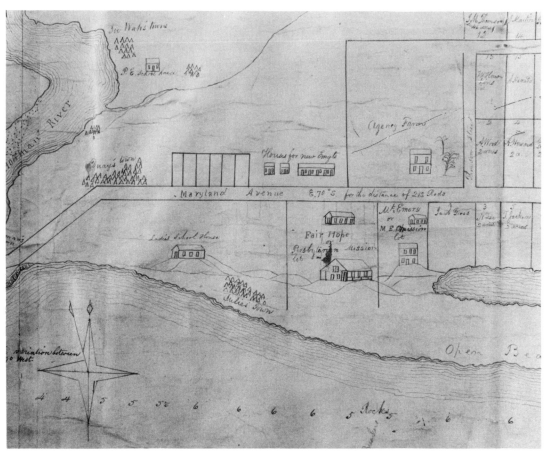

Detail, "The Town of Harper and its Vicinity at Cape Palmas, Maryland in Liberia." Lithograph by T. Campbell, Baltimore, 1834. Mission churches and schoolhouses dominated the scene in Maryland's free black settlement. *MHS*

went down to the docks to try to change the minds of rural slaves who had taken freedom at Cape Palmas over Maryland slavery. "The prejudices of the coloured people in Baltimore and other large Towns, against African Colonization, are so strong," reported a white agent, "that distributing literature among them would be to throw it away." Meantime Daniel Raymond, a Baltimore lawyer and student of political economy, observed that the Maryland black population grew by as much as forty-five thousand each year; blacks had increased by some 30 percent between 1790 and 1810 (for whites the figure had been only 13 percent). He raised serious doubts that a colonization program could settle blacks at a speed anywhere near their growth rate—and in fact no more than a few hundred Maryland blacks finally agreed to emigrate. Believing correctly that free blacks did not increase as rapidly as slaves, Raymond argued that emancipation offered whites more advantages than tightening the slave system, which he blamed for Maryland's diminished population, the "comparative unproductiveness of the earth, in consequence of imperfect cultivation," and "the idle, dissipated habits, and consequent moral degradation, which always characterizes a portion of the inhabitants of a slave state." But he went beyond condemning slavery for being uneconomical. To anyone who believed in the moral government of the Lord, this pattern readily demonstrated God's "hot displeasure against slavery." The footsteps of an angry deity, Raymond declared, "are plainly visible throughout a state where slavery abounds."[32]

A few voices in Maryland joined Raymond in speaking to the wrong of slavery itself. Elisha Tyson, a Philadelphian who came to Baltimore as a merchant, left business to become an active worker in the antislavery movement; he helped many blacks prove their freedom in lawsuits. Benjamin Lundy, a New Jersey–born Quaker whose newspaper, *The Genius of Universal Emancipation*, vigorously opposed slavery and the slave trade, moved to Baltimore from Tennessee in 1824. Lundy published a plan for the gradual abolition of slavery the next year, and while on a speechmaking tour of the North in 1828 made a larger contribution to the antislavery cause. He persuaded an outspoken young New Englander, William Lloyd Garrison, to return with him to Baltimore and serve as co-editor of the *Genius*. Though Lundy supported black emigration to Haiti, his paper—expanded and made a weekly—soon also reflected Garrison's uncompromising hostility to slavery as a sin and to colonization as "visionary." Garrison's editorials demanded "immediate and complete emancipation, the religious and secular instruction of freed blacks, and an end to the insulting policy of deportation." "Slavery is a monster," Garrison told Baltimore readers, "and he must be treated as such—hunted down bravely, despatched at a blow."[33]

Marylanders could neither suppress the slavery issue nor agree on it. In 1827 a Baltimore slave dealer brutally assaulted Lundy, who always chose his words carefully. Garrison did not, and in 1829, when he described fellow Yankees engaged in trading Maryland slaves to New Orleans as "highway robbers and murderers," a Baltimore jury took only fifteen minutes to find him guilty of libel. His counsel, Charles Mitchell, served for free, and Judge Brice, who pronounced the jail term that lifted Garrison from obscurity, may have opposed slavery (he did at least support colonization). Garrison, Lundy, and Raymond all left Maryland not long after. Lundy declared that "the spirit of tyranny" in Baltimore had become "too strong and malignant." Leaders of the Maryland State Colonization Society, trying in 1833 to clarify their position and obtain aid from friends north of the Mason-Dixon Line, avowed as their wish to hasten as best they could "the arrival of the period when slavery shall cease to exist in Maryland."[34]

Maryland newspapers carried reports of such astounding advances that one could not help but feel confident. Released energy seemed to justify every bright view of the future. Improvements in transportation became a marvel. The B&O—like the Erie Canal, proof of Yankee ingenuity—scored impressive successes. Even its bridges were remarkable, for they beautifully combined artistry and engineering. The four-span Patterson Viaduct over the upper Patapsco, completed in December 1829, soon became a landmark. Benjamin Henry Latrobe, Jr., later designed a 700-foot-long stone bridge, the Thomas Viaduct, with eight arches that supported trains more than 60 feet above the river. After giving up stone sleepers for wooden ties, the company laid track only slightly behind schedule.

Progress also appeared in the form of improved steam locomotives, which soon replaced the horse on the railroad. Cooper's device had proved the skills of native labor and the workability of steam engines, but he could not fulfill a contract the B&O signed with him, and in January 1831 the company conducted a competition for an American-built steam locomotive. Phineas Davis, a York, Pennsylvania, watchmaker, won with an upright boiler or "grasshopper" engine that could pull loads weighing as much as twenty tons up the grades west of Baltimore. His *York* locomotive hauled the first train to Frederick in December 1831 (taking along horses for the governor's barouche) and created a popular sensation. The Baltimore to Washington branch went as far as Bladensburg in the summer of 1835, when a thousand or so spectators rode down in four festive trains. Bladensburg natives lined the tracks to greet them, and livestock gave way to machinery. Cows, horses, pigs, and turkeys scurried in all directions; a bull considered, then decided against, advancing on the "terrific object."[35]

The steamboat, suddenly rivaling the clipper as the rightful queen of the bay, cast a similar spell. Travelers now wrote eagerly of the size and speed of the boats, their bright signal flags and powerful engines. When in 1834 two vessels stopped briefly at the head of the bay and came abreast to "tranship" some passengers, an Irish actor, Tyrone Power, reported that the escaping steam made "a noise that might have drowned the voice of Niagara." Once passengers had been exchanged, he continued, "the paddles began to move, the lashings were cast off, and away the boats darted from each other with startling rapidity." Many of the boats offered considerable comfort. Sleeping and washing accommodations seemed luxurious compared to those in jolting stagecoaches and the lottery of rural hotels. Steam from the boilers cooked vegetables; roasting meat turned on a spit run by gears off the engine. In early winter, when New England peddlers journeyed southward for the plantation trade, the decks of these vessels might be covered with horses and loaded carts. At most times they invited promenading (the upper deck bore that name) and the well-bred—along with everyone who wanted to be taken as well-bred—went up to be seen. The many boats, the stillness of the Chesapeake, the setting sun, an ample deck "covered with many well-dressed and *some beautiful passengers*," wrote an English naval officer, "combined to produce a most enchanting effect."[36]

Between 1831 and 1843 ten steamship firms operated out of Baltimore, and with the growth of railroads competition among carriers mounted. In 1832 the Maryland and Virginia Steam Boat Company looted its treasury to buy a rival's flagship and later boasted that its *Kentucky* could make the Baltimore to Norfolk voyage in about thirteen hours. At first great distances gave the advantage to steamboats, with railroads in a minor role. After 1831 the Chesapeake and Delaware Canal, opened in 1829, faced competition from a short railroad connecting the Delaware River at New Castle and the bay at French-town. By the late 1830s an inland or "upper" rail route between Philadelphia and the South—making use of the B&O, a new Richmond, Fredericksburg, and Potomac railroad, and a line to the Carolinas—challenged the speed and convenience of the bay steamboats. The Maryland and Virginia Company countered by hiring a railroad to whisk passengers toward North Carolina as soon as they landed in Norfolk. Eventually land and water firms had agents pass out handbills to travelers as they arrived in Baltimore. The sheets made blustery claims either for railroads or for boats and warned of horrible fates on alternative lines. Steamboat companies downplayed the danger of a boiler explosion—a notorious hazard on the Mississippi. In 1824 a mishap on the *Eagle* had left one person dead; an explosion aboard the Baltimore to Charleston packet *Pulaski* cost a hundred lives off Cape Hatteras in 1838. But by and large Baltimore steamboats shunned racing and escaped serious accidents. In 1840 the Maryland and Virginia firm declared that it had gone twenty-five years in perfect safety—so that the "croakings about 'Fogs,' 'Rough Weather,' 'Storms,' 'Risks,' 'boats urged to the top of the speed' &c." were "altogether the humbugs of a fruitful imagination, gotten up to impose upon the credulous."[37]

Steam power did excite the imagination; one way or another, it affected the lives of ordinary men and women on both sides of the bay. Industrialists found applications for the steam engine in Baltimore sugar refining, flour milling, glass cutting, plaster making, and spice grinding. Steam power appeared in Baltimore sawmills; it freed textile mills from their dependence on water. In the 1830s the Patuxent Manufacturing Company turned the village of Laurel into the largest cotton-milling center below the Mason-Dixon Line. Mainly supplying foreign markets, the company used crude steam machinery and took advantage of low land and labor prices there; it employed more than five hundred persons and relied heavily on the Washington Branch of the B&O. Steam power sped up the wagon-based economy, made possible entirely new exchanges, and created voracious demand. The railroad carried dry goods, groceries, plaster, boards, and bricks out of Baltimore. Trains returned with farm products that brought the B&O quick profits. Within three months of opening to Frederick, the B&O hauled 32,670 barrels of flour from that city. Baltimore fuel prices dropped mercifully during the cold win-

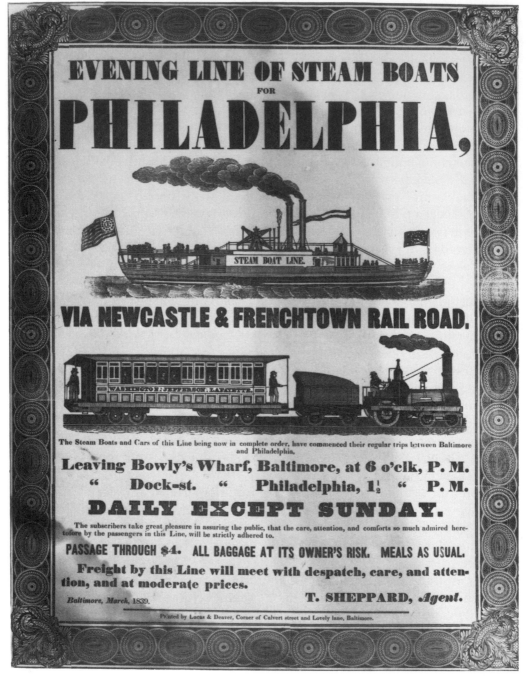

Broadside, "Evening Line of Steam Boats for Philadelphia," Baltimore, 1839. *MHS*

ter of 1831–32 because large bundles of firewood arrived by rail. Managing unusually heavy loads, the railroad also expanded markets for western Maryland lime and granite. Investors realized that eventually the railroad would tap another Allegany County resource. Steam boilers at first relied on wood, but coal had distinct advantages. Reports furnished by the state geological survey (established in 1833) confirmed the economic value of Cumberland bituminous coal. The legislature rapidly began chartering coal companies.

Early-nineteenth-century progress struck the oyster tonger like a cold front. For generations digging oysters had been an individual effort or local business. The always-abundant shellfish lived on the muddy bottoms of creeks, rivers, and the bay, down to thirty feet below the surface. During the winter harvesting season they provided a principal means of livelihood to many Maryland families along the water. Watermen went after "ayrsters," as they called them, using long-handled, scissors-action tongs that left a tonger exhausted after a few hours' work and thereby placed natural limits on the size of a catch. The railroad lengthened the distance iced oysters could travel before they spoiled; making them more profitable, it helped in the 1820s to attract New York and New England oyster boats to the Chesapeake. Employing cable-drawn, chain-bag devices—dredges—as they raked over the oyster beds, "drudgers" vastly increased the size of a day's take (indeed, they had badly depleted their Northern sources) and threatened the tonger with extinction. Watermen did not react kindly. Answering their pleas, the assembly in 1830 made it illegal for nonresidents to harvest oysters in Maryland waters and two years later outlawed dredging entirely. Northern packers sidestepped the first measure by setting up plants in Baltimore. Demand for oysters continued to grow apace with railroad expansion, while Eastern Shore leaders mounted a campaign for a railroad line of their own.

Meantime Maryland voters came to associate problems of economic development and federal authority with enormously colorful figures who quarreled over the presidency. Many of them migrants from their place of birth, they gave politics renewed intensity. Under Presidents Jefferson and Madison, secretaries of state had acted as understudies to the chief executive and later assumed his office with the approval of a caucus of congressmen. As the Federalist party waned, the caucus made its choice without fear of challenge. Then, in Monroe's second term, several men besides Secretary of State John Quincy Adams made themselves available for the highest office. The Virginia-born Georgian William H. Crawford, treasury secretary and strict constructionist, won endorsement from the caucus, which critics said was undemocratic. Secretary of War John C. Calhoun of South Carolina, at the time a firm nationalist, claimed strength north and south. Henry Clay, a Kentuckian (also born in Virginia) who at Ghent had scandalized Adams by staying up all night playing cards and spitting tobacco juice, stood behind his "American System" of high tariffs and internal improvements. He enjoyed wide popularity among manufacturers and westerners. Andrew Jackson, a Tennessean with South Carolina roots and hero of the New Orleans victory that followed the battle of Baltimore, had fought several duels and been accused of murder and bigamy. He commanded grass-roots support among people who did not always know or care where he stood on issues. When the electoral college vote of 1824 ended in a tie, the House of Representatives—Clay having thrown his support to Adams—awarded the presidency to Adams. The New Englander named Clay his secretary of state, and friends of Jackson, who had received the highest electoral vote, then charged corruption—a term humming with Revolution-era fears. Jackson's loss gave him the vengeful loyalty of a growing following of Americans who made him a symbol of the common man's struggle against favoritism and privilege.

The 1828 campaign in Maryland provided a harbinger of things to come: a local office seeker frantically tried to prove that he had not missed the battle of Baltimore, as his opponent charged; Adams men made the tactical error of calling themselves the "thinking party." Opposing the "thinkers" was an odd assortment of Maryland Jacksonians whom the promise of power and patronage rewards held together. In Anne Arundel County and Annapolis local leaders with Jeffersonian sympathies, Horatio Ridout and Gabriel Duvall's son, Grafton Duvall, had formed the earliest Jackson committee in the state. Samuel Smith had taken William Pinkney's seat in the U.S. Senate upon Pinkney's death in 1821; he and Edward Lloyd, at first Crawford men, jumped on the Jackson bandwagon just in time. Early supporters of Calhoun like Virgil Maxcy, a Massachusetts-born lawyer who owned an Anne Arundel County farm, and John Pendleton Kennedy of Baltimore joined the Jackson camp when the Carolinian agreed to run as Jackson's vice-president. Former Federalists like William Beall in Frederick and in Baltimore George H. Steuart and Benjamin Chew Howard, son of the revolutionary officer, further leavened the Jackson ranks with people who believed Old Hickory committed to internal improvements.[38]

Roger Brooke Taney, whose father had introduced the 1802 suffrage reform legislation in the General Assembly, stood with Jackson from the beginning. Born in Calvert County, educated at Dickinson College in Pennsylvania and trained in the law, Taney had married Anna Key, sister of Francis Scott Key. In 1800 he, too, had moved west—as far as Frederick, where opportunity beckoned. Later a Federalist leader, he found himself after 1821 without a party to lead. In 1824 he moved his practice again, this time to Baltimore, where with other lawyers of high reputation—Reverdy Johnson, John H. B. Latrobe, and John Van Lear McMahon, a Princeton graduate from Cumberland—he served as counsel for the B&O. In 1827 Governor Joseph Kent, another Calvert County native and former Federalist, named Taney state attorney general.

Though Jackson did not win the state in 1828 (Adams polled 25,527 to his 24,565), his Maryland friends looked forward to patronage appointments. Soon the Jacksonian glue dissolved. The old warrior Samuel Smith, assum-

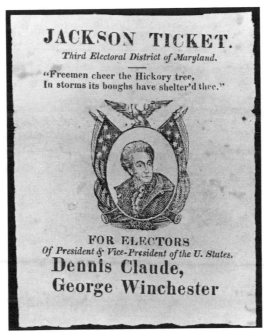

Jackson ballot, probably for Montgomery County electors, 1824. *Kensington Historical Society/MHS*

ing that he alone would direct the distribution of federal jobs, passed out more plums to erstwhile Republicans than to ex-Federalists. He tended to favor men with family connections rather than party service—to follow the old recipe. Resentment of Smith began to build. Worse, Jackson in office chose courses that severely tested the loyalty of Maryland party leaders. He proved himself merely a lukewarm ally of internal improvements at congressional expense; the Constitution, he decided, only permitted federal projects that had possible military value and crossed state lines. In the spring of 1830 the president vetoed a bill to finance a road southward from Maysville, Kentucky, greatly embarrassing his friends in Maryland. Next rejecting federal aid for a turnpike from Washington to Frederick, Jackson left considerable doubt that he would approve expenditures for the C&O Canal or the B&O Railroad. Officers of the B&O, under Taney's influence, refused to scuttle hope—as a plan of interstate scope, the railroad might still win federal aid.

Jackson's enmity for the Bank of the United States (he held it responsible for the panic of 1819) provided his opposition another catalyst. Late in 1831, when bank directors applied for an early charter renewal, Taney, whom the president that year had named federal attorney general, strongly advised against approving it. Taney doubtless regarded the bank suspiciously because of its Philadelphia location; it made Baltimore's trade rival a financial center and placed much authority in the hands of old-line Philadelphians like the sitting director, Nicholas Biddle—whose stuffiness matched his probity. Taney's more serious objections drew upon his experience as a director of a Frederick bank and the Union Bank of Baltimore. He was convinced that the federally chartered institution—directors appointed by the president of the United States—hampered economic growth and concentrated economic power. Its status as a creditor to private banks and its favored position as depository of federal funds combined for an unhealthy effect. Better, thought Taney, that the federal government leave banking private and competitive. "It is a fixed principle of our political institutions to guard against the unnecessary accumulation of power over persons and property in any hands," he wrote in an antibank report. "And no hands are less worthy to be trusted with it than those of a moneyed corporation." [39]

Once reelected in 1832, with diminished support in Maryland, the president declared war on the "monster" bank as a citadel of privilege. To carry out his plan of removing federal deposits from the bank and its branches and placing the money in various private or "pet" banks (one of them the Union Bank), Jackson in the fall of 1833 made Taney acting secretary of the treasury. Taney and the president broke open a hornet's nest of controversy. National bank shareholders joined the hue and cry against "King Andrew." John Pendleton Kennedy, though a Union director, openly condemned the bank war as foolish and destructive; given Taney's association with Union, he suspected shady dealings. The Union president, Thomas Ellicott, a sober, black-dressed Quaker who was among the first B&O directors, caught Kennedy one morning and reprimanded him for biting the hand that fed the bank. In reply Kennedy attacked Taney, denounced Ellicott for his complicity in the "flimsy affair," and wished Jackson impeached for assuming the authority of removal. Along with many other ex-Federalists, Kennedy left the Jackson fold bitterly. Most stockholders in Maryland banks applauded the president's campaign—even when Biddle, trying to build support for a new charter with a show of force, tightened credit and redeemed massive numbers of private bank notes. The resulting economic slowdown only strengthened Jacksonian resolve. Taney rallied young and rising entrepreneurs everywhere in Maryland. Rely upon it, he told a home audience, if the president restored federal funds to the national bank, it would win rechartering. "And if, after its enormities, it obtains its charter for a single year, the contest is over, and we may quietly resign ourselves to the chains with which it is prepared to bind us." [40]

In a collision between the C&O Canal and the B&O Railroad companies, Maryland offered another example of how differing approaches to economic development crossed in the age of Jackson. Both the canal and railroad planned to build west along the banks of the Potomac, where the river had cut narrow paths through the mountains. Directors of the C&O believed that their charter conveyed special status to the company, granting it a preemptive right of way along the river bank, and that the courts should protect their particular right despite any arguments that the railroad might ultimately carry wider benefits to the state than the canal. In 1828 the canal company sought an injunction in Washington County Court prohibiting the railroad from laying track along the bank of the river between Point of Rocks and Harpers Ferry. Railroad engineers and canal surveyors literally butted into one another at Point of Rocks, and the future of both projects lay in doubt as the higher courts tried to untangle the mess. An 1829 Maryland chancery ruling went in favor of the railroad—since the canal had not actually reached Point of Rocks, it could not prevent the B&O from continuing its course. In January 1832 the Court of Appeals reversed that decision and agreed with counsel for the canal company—even unused privileges belonged by contract or "prior right" to the C&O. According to John Buchanan, the chief judge who spoke for the majority of three, economic progress might be slower if government honored such unused charter rights, but the courts had to enforce contracts.[41]

The majority and minority opinions represented legal ideas that compared like the horse and steam engine on the railroad. Differing with Buchanan, Judges Stevenson Archer and Walter Dorsey argued that the law, instead of protecting status conferred by contract, should uphold action directed to the purposes of a charter, and that since the B&O had shown more energy in meeting the obligations of its charter, the railroad ought to have first building rights on the Potomac bank. Their view clearly favored the display of energy in economic development and more openness of competition. Eventually it prevailed. In the short run canal and railroad companies agreed to a compromise that William Cost Johnson of Frederick and others worked out in the House of Delegates, and the B&O reached Harpers Ferry in late 1834. Three years later the B&O and C&O controversy provided legal background to Taney's decision in the *Charles River* v. *Warren Bridge* case. By then Jackson's choice as chief justice of the United States Supreme Court, Taney in that famous opinion reflected both Jacksonian ideas of free competition and the B&O argument for economic energy. He upheld a state's right to grant charters that created competition; to vacate a Boston bridge monopoly did not impair the right of contract.

⌒⋙⋘⌒

American ferment in these years drew a tribe of Europeans who found the country a political and social workshop—fascinating for what it might tell of the future. During Jackson's first term two French noblemen, Alexis de Tocqueville and Gustave de Beaumont, arrived in America to conduct a survey that led finally to Tocqueville's *Democracy in America*. They visited Baltimore because concerned with United States prison reforms, and in the mid-1830s Maryland offered an interesting specimen. The state had built its first prison northeast of the city in 1811 and enlarged the structure in 1829, after a commission of merchants and lawyers found it wanting. Later, begrudgingly, the assembly had appropriated funds for a new building. Maryland authorities then faced problems of design reflecting rival theories of penology. Near Philadelphia, Pennsylvanians had constructed a prison based on the principle of absolute confinement (removed from evil influences, one came to a realization of moral rightness and social duty); in New York, at Auburn, prisoners worked at hard labor (moral reform of grown criminals weighed less than stiff punishment).

Maryland took a middle course. The Pennsylvania prison had a central tower for guards with radial appendages for individual cells. In designing the new Maryland penitentiary, Robert Cary Long, Jr., applied the Philadelphia layout to a shop that fit the work purposes of the Auburn plan. Maryland officials left moral improvement up to the prisoner. Each male inmate supposedly had a solitary cell for sleeping and a copy of the Bible; the prison allowed weekly services but hired no permanent chaplain as Auburn had. Most interesting about the Maryland plan was its self-supporting, profit-making character. Male inmates—who usually numbered between 350 and 400 and consisted largely of thieves—worked for contractors in textiles, shoemaking, stonecutting, and nail manufactory; female prisoners, crowded into the old building after 1837, made combs, brushes, bags, brooms, and hats. Prison labor earned enough between 1822 and 1839 to render state appropriations unnecessary. After 1828 wardens and guards even drew their salaries from prison profits. By 1842 prisoner income paid $69,000 toward prison construction costs. Tocqueville noted that prisoners pocketed sums for "overwork" and thereby created a prison underworld of bribery and corruption—an evil the state eventually corrected. Critics of the Maryland plan wondered whether "pecuniary interests" might drive officials to abuse inmates and criticized the neglect of moral improvement. But in 1841 directors of the prison stated that in many individual cases work and economy had produced an "evident deep contrition." Whatever its drawbacks, the Maryland prison exemplified the Jacksonian ideal of cheap government.[42]

Self-government and the fetish for equality, wrote Tocqueville, led Americans to answer a multitude of civic and social needs by forming associations. Dealing with drunkenness had become one glaring social need—as travelers' journals and institutional reports of the time demonstrated. Maryland almshouses sheltered a great many men whom drink had left unemployed; apparently pauper children often were victims of drunken parents. During the early years of the century pleas for temperance had come from pulpits and lecture halls—from religious leaders and the well-to-do membership of the Maryland State Temperance Society. In the spring of 1840 a tailor named William K. Mitchell and a few other Baltimore workers, after drinks at Chase's Tavern on Liberty Street (and partly as a joke), attended a visiting clergyman's temperance lecture. Afterward they agreed that temperance might be a good thing but also that antidrink ministers were "a parcel of hypocrites." "I'll tell you what," said a blacksmith, George Steers, "let's form a society and make Bill Mitchell president." The men agreed to give temperance of their own making a serious try: We hereby form a society "for our mutual benefit," read a statement that each member signed, guarding against "a pernicious practice which is injurious to our health, standing, and families," and pledging "ourselves as gentlemen that we will not drink any spiritous or malt liquors, wine or cider." The Washington Temperance Society—named for the Founding Father—met regularly at Chase's Tavern until the society began to grow and the tavern owner forced it out. The group moved to a carpenter's shop and then rented a hall and began holding public meetings. At them no speaker pronounced the path to righteousness. Instead, reformed drinkers told their own stories—a completely novel and wholly Jacksonian idea.[43]

The Washingtonians grew rapidly, a reform movement led by the reformed. "Let every man be present," went the motto, "and every man bring with him a man." At weekly meetings, someone reported, the "whole society is considered a 'grand committee of the whole.'" In a few months the movement attracted John H. W. Hawkins, a Baltimore-born hatmaker who turned his back on twenty years of excessive drinking and found his true calling as a self-help temperance spokesman. In February 1841 he and a few other Washingtonians attended the state temperance society meeting in Annapolis and even addressed the General Assembly on the evils of drink. "He is a man of plain, good common sense," a listener later wrote about Hawkins, "with a sincerity about him, and easy way of expressing himself, that every word took like a point-blank shot." Mitchell, Hawkins, and other "Reformed Drunkards" made highly publicized trips to New York and Boston in early 1841. There newspapers told of intemperate persons tearfully coming forward to sign the pledge against drink that the Baltimoreans called "the second declaration of independence." In April, after only a year, the Washingtonians claimed one thousand members in Baltimore alone—many of them "drunkards of many years standing"—and conducted a triumphant parade through the streets of the city. By May 1842 delegations from Baltimore had established societies in towns from Brattleboro, Vermont, to Richmond; deputies held meetings in Pittsburgh, Wheeling, and then went on to Cincinnati and St. Louis. Women of the movement formed Martha Washington societies. In 1843 the American Temperance Union estimated that the Washingtonians had obtained abstinence pledges from "a half million hard drinkers often drunken, and a hundred thousand sots."[44]

Tocqueville carried home especially vivid impressions of democratic politics—wherein Americans either joined the crusade against privilege and too much government or stood up for property rights and "moderation." Toward the end of Jackson's first term, nominating conventions began choosing party presidential and vice-presidential candidates, and because of Baltimore's transportation ties and Maryland's location between the poles of New England and the cotton South, the city became a favored meeting place. In the fall and early winter of 1831 two anti-Jackson groups met in Baltimore. The smaller party, the Anti-Masons (opposed to secrecy, playing on Jackson's Freemasonry), nominated William Wirt to be chief executive—the first Marylander so honored. The following spring the Jackson party, by then known as Democrats, went to Baltimore for more political hoopla. To the joy of hotel owners and tavernkeepers, the Democrats again repaired to Baltimore in 1835. By then the president's critics called themselves Whigs, after the revolutionary heroes against tyranny. In 1840 the Whigs met in Baltimore to choose a candidate to oppose Jackson's successor, Martin Van Buren. In Maryland as elsewhere, Democrats and Whigs formed state and local central committees that held their own conventions. Their ongoing rivalry (voters decided some election almost every year) encouraged mass participation and electoral frenzy.

Even more so than earlier in the century, party competition and party balance in Maryland recommended against one's being tarred with the brush of aristocracy. Candidates made it their business to get out among the people to deliver speeches, attend oyster roasts, and march in parades. At a typical rural rally south of Hagerstown, drums beat, a military band played from a wagon, and Whigs laid out enough bread, mutton, beef, pork, and miscellaneous "eats" for one or two thousand persons. Opposing candidates, speaking at these events together, never failed to arouse listeners. "We throw the gauntlet and challenge our adversaries to the Battle ground of Debate," explained the Jackson man Henry R. Warfield in 1837, using a variety of metaphors; and "altho they know we use neither the tomahawk nor the scalping knife—yet we play upon them so steadily and well directed a fire from our seventy four pounders, that most of them are blown ski high before the battle is half ended."[45] Buttons, badges, and ribbons bedecked the party faithful, who found such speechmaking and the excitement of electioneering a welcomed break from daily routine. During the 1840 campaign, when Van Buren faced "Tippecanoe and Tyler Too," Whigs in Cumberland and Hagerstown adhered to party practice by rolling a heavy balloon, eight feet in diameter, through the streets at night while a partisan crowd carried torchlights and chanted slogans about keeping the ball rolling.

Party newspapers in Baltimore and many of the counties generated heat, if not light, before each canvass. When Democrats held a rally, the Whig press ignored it; if the turnout was disappointing (a visitor called one instance a "manifest failure"), the Democratic paper inflated attendance figures. A Whig in Cecil County complained of being at a distinct disadvantage—the party there had no voice "to respond to and refute the many calumnies" of the Jacksonian *Cecil Gazette*.[46] Partisan papers also served the cause by publishing and circulating the speeches of political champions, campaign biographies, and party sheet music. A Baltimore paper advertised the sale of one hundred copies of a Henry Clay address for only a dollar. "The World Is Too Much Governed," read the masthead caption of Francis

"National Convention of Whig Young Men." Lithograph published by George Willig, Jr., Baltimore, 1840. The rally for Harrison at the Canton race track—featuring the candidate's trademark log cabin, hard cider, and a speech by Henry Clay—drew 25,000 party faithful. *Peale Museum, Baltimore City Life Museums*

Preston Blair's pro-Jackson *Washington Globe*. The *Sun* of Baltimore, first published by the New Englander Arunah S. Abell in May of 1837, cost the common man only a penny; though expressly independent, it could not hide its Jacksonian spirit and after 1840 proclaimed "Light for All" with each issue. *Niles' Weekly Register* assumed Whig leadership in the state before moving from Baltimore to Washington City in 1836. First the *American Whig* succeeded it and then the *Log Cabin Advocate*—titled to identify Whigs, too, with frontier democracy. On most election days 70 or 80 percent of eligible Maryland voters turned out, casting color-coded party "tickets" that thwarted the privacy of the ballot but permitted every voter to take a clear stand.

Winning elections meant dividing the spoils. Earlier, Jefferson had spoken of filling offices half with Federalists and half with Republicans. William Frick's appointment as Baltimore customs collector in January 1837 signaled the triumph of party professionals—men who relied on patronage for a living—over the Samuel Smiths who looked upon public office as a civic responsibility. Organizational loyalty became an end in itself—and a means to patronage. Party men made no apologies. Before a state election of the fall of his first year as collector, Frick ordered a building contractor to hire more Democrats and fire Whigs. Since campaigns cost money, finance committees dunned well-heeled party ornaments and collected "taxes" from partisans on government payrolls.

High stakes made jobbery and pointed charity commonplace; in Baltimore City outright fraud followed close behind. "Whiskey flows like water, & money abounds very much," Hezekiah Niles wrote Henry Clay on the eve of an 1830 Maryland election. Niles claimed that in the closely contested counties Jacksonians had showered needy voters with coats, hats, and boots. The needy in Baltimore multiplied. Immigrants arriving there, mostly young men (as in the seventeenth century), numbered eight thousand in 1832—four times as many as four years before—and many of them failed in the struggle for work. Paupers seeking shelter at the city almshouse rose to five hundred in these years. About one in three had been in Baltimore less than half a year; about a third were foreign born, most of them Irish. White adult males could vote after one year's residence—but election day made a native out of many a newcomer. "In this state," explained an unapproving observer of Maryland politics, there always has been a "floating vote" of "loafers, rounders, and rowdies" who "lean against lamp posts during the day and knock store-boxes around at night, and who care a fig for neither party, having no knowledge or interest in the principles which divide the more reflecting portion of the people of the country." Ebenezer L. Finley of Baltimore admitted to Tocqueville that he had "seen elections carried through the almshouse poor."[47]

Had Tocqueville spent more time in Maryland, he would have witnessed a sorry democratic spectacle—a state badly divided by local interests, loyalties, and suspicions trying to reform its constitution. The document offered a plump target in the 1830s, and clamor for readjustment mounted with publication of the 1830 census figures. They showed that about one-fourth of the population elected a majority of legislators. Two senators and two members of the House of Delegates spoke for the 80,000 residents of Baltimore, whose level of representation had not changed since the city population had stood at 26,000. Annapolis, normally a quiet town of several thousand, sent the same number to the State House. Spokesmen for the older counties tightly guarded the apportionment of delegates (four per county, regardless of population) and senators (six for the Eastern Shore, nine for the Western); they defended the practice of electing one federal senator from each shore and governors from either the Eastern Shore or the lower Western Shore. John McMahon in his *Historical View of the Government of Maryland*, published in 1831, noted that "shore jealousies" and twin government offices had given Maryland "the character of a confederacy of two shores" rather than the integrity of an ordinary state.[48]

Party feeling stoked the fires of reform. Jacksonians, powerful in Baltimore, declared the 1776 frame of government rife with elitism and inequity.

Maryland Whig strength largely coincided with former Federalist areas—the Eastern Shore and southern and western counties; except for disgruntled westerners, Whigs enjoyed disproportionate power in Annapolis and of course defended restraints like the electoral college that chose state senators. That body, argued John McMahon, placed the legislature "beyond the momentary prejudices and passions, and hasty and short-sighted views, which at times pervade every community."[49] In 1831 Whig electors chose an entirely Whig senate. The 1836 vote gave the Whigs twenty-one out of forty seats in the college, despite a Democratic edge of three thousand popular ballots. Francis Thomas, a Frederick County Democrat, hit upon a clever plan that would force either reform or constitutional crisis. Democrats kept their nineteen electors at home. Without a quorum the college could not elect a senate; without a senate there could be no assembly; without a legislature no governor could be chosen.

Thus Democrats employed minority tactics in the name of majority rule, and, oddly, they succeeded despite defeat. Illustrating the irony of their position, outnumbered reformers at a Cumberland meeting in the fall of 1836 angrily doused the lights and stamped out of the hall. Victories in both presidential and House of Delegates elections that season emboldened Whigs, who charged Jackson men with opening the door to revolution and chaos. A defiant gathering in Hagerstown, meeting to praise the boycotting "Glorious Nineteen," appeared willing to cross that threshold; it declared that it was time to "recur to first principles." "If the revolutionary spirit, now stalking amongst us is not promptly subdued," retorted *Niles' Weekly Register*, upon Maryland radicals would "rest the fearful responsibility of being the first in the country of Washington, to give liberty a mortal wound." Anticipating the blow, the Planters Guards of Prince George's County offered their services to the Whig governor, Thomas W. Veazey of Cecil. Finally enough Democratic electors caved in to give the college a quorum, it chose a Whig senate, and then, surprisingly, the new assembly—though securely in the hands of conservative forces—went on in March 1837 to pass an omnibus reform measure. With the necessary consent of the following assembly, Whigs agreed to grant Baltimore City as many delegates as the largest county, to provide for the popular election of state senators and of governors (governors' homes had to lie successively in eastern, western, and southern districts of the state), and to abolish the old governor's council.[50]

⁊⁘⁊

This Whig turnabout may have aimed to solidify the party's position—the party afterward could claim to represent both reform and order while the Democrats stood mostly for anarchy. The need for order, a word Whigs often used, had grown abundantly evident to them. Labor violence had become the rule rather than exception. In August 1831 Irish workers battled blacks in Frederick County; after police arrested the ringleaders, a Gaelic mob rescued them. Armed with stone hammers and carrying an improvised flag, laborers on the B&O at Sykes Mills quit work that year and threatened to tear up the rails they had laid unless they received the $9,000 owed them in wages. Work did not resume until a militia force from Baltimore surprised and arrested strike leaders. In early 1834 gangs of Irish on the C&O project fell upon each other, leaving five men dead before soldiers arrived from Fort McHenry to quell the disturbance. In the fall workers on the Washington Branch of the B&O turned on a supervisor and brutally killed him. Militiamen took three hundred prisoners. Elsewhere Germans fought French. Though women escaped violence, they formed several new skilled trades associations, including a Female Union Society and United Seamstresses Society, and did voice anger. Complaining that widows and women with "sickly or worthless husbands" earned only a dollar or less a week, they challenged wage reductions, called strikes, and demanded (instead of a sunrise-to-sunset work schedule) a ten-hour day during the months of longest daylight.[51]

A wave of arson shocked Baltimoreans in early 1835, and that summer, following the financial collapse of several Baltimore banks, violence again rocked the city detractors called "Mobtown." Private bank expansion—reckless issuing of paper currencies—brought on the catastrophe, which Whigs attributed to Jackson's and Taney's policies. The Bank of Maryland became a celebrated case, especially among debt-plagued working families. During 1831 about a thousand persons had been locked away in the city jail for owing a creditor $10 or less; although that year a law abolishing imprisonment for debts under $30 had gone into effect, the legislature had repealed it in 1833.[52] Now bank officers declared themselves insolvent and escaped freely while small depositors lost $2 million in savings. Common people built up steam as published audits uncovered Bank of Maryland mismanagement bordering on fraud—the bank had issued circulating notes in excess of its specie reserves by a ratio of 50 to 1. Chief culprits appeared to be Evan Poultney, former president, and Reverdy Johnson, John Glenn, and Evan T. Ellicott, directors.

On 6 August a group of men gathered in front of Johnson's home and broke his windows with stones. Suddenly the city exploded. Mayor Jesse Hunt tried to defuse anger by holding a town meeting that only assembled people for another assault on Johnson's home and those of other directors, on whose possessions the mob took glad revenge. Hunt's constables were helpless to quell the disturbance. Pillaging, shooting, and bonfires continued through the night of the eighth. In the end Samuel Smith, then eighty-three years old, called on orderly citizens to arm themselves under his command, as in 1814. Even after quiet returned, gangs of boys roamed the streets looking for trouble. Antagonism between rich and poor simmered because Johnson and other victims of the bank riot managed to win indemnities from the Whig-controlled assembly.

The failure of the Bank of Maryland supplied a forecast of bleak times, as

"Bank of Maryland Affair." Lithograph by "Jack Downing" (pseudonym of Seba Smith), 1834, lambasting the bank's directors, whose stock manipulations had brought disaster to depositors. *MHS*

the state government learned to its acute embarrassment. Maryland spending and bond issues for canals and railroads continued cheerfully in the 1830s—without the direction of a board of public works, unaccountably abolished in 1828. In 1834 the new legislature allocated half a million dollars to the B&O to finance its Washington Branch (later a moneymaker) and issued state bonds to support building of a rail line, begun in 1829, from Baltimore to the Susquehanna River at York, Pennsylvania. Labor and financial troubles had cost the C&O its federal and Virginia support in 1833, when Maryland had extended another $2 million credit; in 1836 the assembly lent $3 million more. That year the B&O received another $3 million and legislators, rolling logs with energy, supplied inducements to various local (all unsuccessful) projects like an Eastern Shore railroad and canals linking both Baltimore and Annapolis to the Potomac. By 1840 the state had invested nearly $7.2 million in the C&O, which had yet to return a dollar. Yearly interest payments on the total state internal improvements debt of about $15 million, much of it owed to foreign investors, amounted to $585,000.

Like many other states, Maryland stood vulnerable to any economic slow-down. Another one began quietly in 1836, when the Jackson administration declared gold and silver coin alone payable for public debts. The next year a drop in European cotton prices placed a strain on American banks, most of which had committed the sin of the Bank of Maryland. Foreign creditors recalled what money they could. The economy fell to an all-time low, and the state of Maryland faced the prospect of bankruptcy.

Elected public servants found life hard in the decade that followed. Legislators considered repudiating the state debt, seizing C&O assets, and various other plans of escape. Perhaps serving a single three-year term helped to guide the first popularly elected governor, William Grason, a Queen Anne's County Democrat, on an honorable course; he opposed repudiation and urged higher taxes. Twice in 1841 the Whig-controlled legislature responded, raising the real- and personal-property tax rate—first to twenty cents and then twenty-five cents on each hundred dollars of assessed value (a seven-fold increase); it also passed a constitutional amendment forbidding state assistance in public works projects. Grason's successor, former Jacksonian congressman Francis Thomas, spent much of his term embroiled in a personal dispute with the governor of Virginia, whose fifteen-year-old daughter Thomas married soon after winning the governorship and then spurned, publicly questioning her chastity. Adding to Thomas's troubles, many Maryland citizens refused to pay the late high taxes. Popular anger gave the 1844 gubernatorial election to a Prince George's Whig and former Democrat, Thomas G. Pratt. Pratt succeeded in obtaining a series of new measures distributing the tax burden among marriage licenses, acts of incorporation, inheritances, clerks' and registrars' fees—even, over Democratic objections, raising the price of public stamps. The assembly cut state salaries and abolished some jobs. Though the state never adopted repudiation, Maryland between October 1841 and January 1848 made no payments on its debts.[53]

The panic of 1837, its effects lingering into the early 1840s, spurred the violent and made many a weak man strong. Getting and keeping jobs became especially vicious business. In August 1839 Irish workers on the C&O not far from Cresap's Oldtown, fearful of losing their work, located a threat in nearby German employees of the same company. After enjoying plenty of cheap whiskey, the Irish armed themselves and fell on their rivals like "incarnate devils"—as a German priest put it—beating men and destroying property. One German died of injuries. In Baltimore political conflict continued, despite the hopes of Whigs who had backed the reform measures of 1837. Party stalwarts wanted jobs; the unemployed needed an outlet for their frustration. During the gubernatorial election of 1838 the Whig press reported that Democratic rowdies "stationed themselves at the corners of streets to waylay and attack with clubs, pistols, and stones, every prominent Whig that passed along." Democratic assaults on a Whig parade in 1840 left one man dead and another nearly so.[54]

Especially because earlier there had seemed so much reason for optimism, the disturbances and downturns of the late 1830s left many Marylanders troubled, angry, or simply stunned by the pace of change. Steam, it turned out, rewarded some people and displaced others. In the early 1830s Peter Cooper and other investors bought the O'Donnell country estate (named Canton to mark O'Donnell's successful foray in the China trade) southeast of Baltimore. There Cooper built factories that supplied the railroad with machinery; Canton's rail lines and docks made the site an important intersection between Maryland products and their markets. In other parts of the city workers made rail cars and built copper boilers. Good rail connections cheered those farmers in Prince George's, Anne Arundel, and Baltimore counties who grew food for urban tables. The Philadelphia, Wilmington, and Baltimore Railroad opened service in 1837. Within three years Maryland strawberries, finding a market in New York City, served as a lure for agricultural change, especially on the Eastern Shore. As the B&O pushed westward, farmers in Frederick and Washington counties found it profitable to ship grain directly to Baltimore. Many rural millers and distillers went out of business. Applications of steam power threatened even the traditional farmer's wife, according to Skinner's magazine. "As every good is said to bring its attendant evil," joked the *American Farmer* in 1839, the arrival of labor-saving machinery "has had the bad effect of nearly depriving the housewife of all economical employment; leaving her no resource to keep off ennui, except to read novels, whip the children, scold her husband, and kill flies!"[55]

Marylanders who favored stability found themselves uneasy. Obviously material improvement and political openness carried conflict and uncertainty. Bowing to democratic pressures in the 1837 omnibus reform bill, disturbed by the discontent that followed the panic of that year, watching investment in steam boilerworks, chemical manufacturing, and coal, men and women of old families sought distance. One response was to become a curmudgeon. A retired Eastern Shore congressman, John Leeds Kerr, mused that "politics is now become a complete trade and what is worse every fellow follows it fool or knave & aspires to the best jobs. This subject[,] once the study of patriots & statesmen, is now conveyed to such hands as to make it disgusting." "It is humiliating to confess it," wrote the Whig writer Brantz Mayer in these years, "but money making and president making are the two great occupations of all our people—public and private. . . . Possession, not enjoyment, is the great aim; so that Possession at length becomes enjoyment itself." He knew of "good men" in America, "but unfortunately they are neither rich nor in power." John Pendleton Kennedy for his part tried to revive the literary scene he had known in his youth. Earlier he had served as a patron to Edgar Allan Poe, the troubled young writer who in 1833 won a small prize for his story entitled "Ms. Found in a Bottle" (during a later stay in the city, Poe evidently fell victim to party thugs who seized the poet and used him as a multiple voter; plied with drink, he died after being pulled from a gutter). Kennedy now suggested his own misgivings about the present by writing romantic histories of the Revolution and of seventeenth-century Maryland. More directly in *Quodlibet*, which appeared in the fall of 1840, he published a farcical account of Jacksonian Baltimore. A one-term Whig congressman, Kennedy poked fun at renegade bankers and Democratic politicos—one of whom (Kennedy perhaps alluded to Taney) changed the name of his ancestral home, "Quality Hall on Poplar Flats," to "Equality Hall on Popular Flats."[56]

In January 1844, a group of twenty Baltimoreans who included Kennedy, John Spear Smith, John Van Lear McMahon, Robert Gilmor, Jr., Brantz Mayer, John H. B. Latrobe, Joshua Cohen, Charles J. W. Gwinn, and Severn Teackle Wallis founded the Maryland Historical Society. Through it, cynics would have said, they expected to tout their own families' considerable part in that history. However true, they also set about saving the artifacts, art, and records of the past that belonged to all. Kennedy already had recovered colonial records that had been collecting mold in the State House. Gilmor had asked members of old families for significant letters, which he placed in huge scrapbooks. In 1845 the society commissioned a young artist to render portraits of unsung or unpainted revolutionary heroes. The founders of the society hoped to cultivate a sense of continuity and preserve a heritage that appeared all the more fragile and valuable in the flux of the 1840s. The first exhibit, in 1848, avowedly public and thus perhaps an attempt to reach out even to the men who had rioted against Reverdy Johnson and the rest or who threw sticks and stones at well-known Whigs, tried to make respect for art and historical lore a means of restoring some of the equilibrium they believed lost in their age.

Establishing an institution that preserved for preservation's sake alone, early patrons of the Historical Society aimed for reverence in an age of irreverence. They swam against the currents of derring-do individualism, volatile politics, and forward-looking industry. Emerson, who had paid Baltimore another visit in 1843, might have saluted their effort while giving it scant hope of success. "Charles Carroll the Signer is dead, and Archbishop Carroll is dead," he lamented, "and there is no vision in the land."[57]

〜✵〜

From the outside, life in slavery did not appear harsh. In 1832 Kennedy, who as a boy had made memorable visits to relatives in Virginia, published a romance of plantation life, *Swallow Barn*. In it he wrote affectionately of country gentlemen, lawyers, and parsons, of planters' mistresses, and of slave children who darted about the bushes "like untamed monkeys" or sat around blankly like turtles on a millpond log. Kennedy's book reflected the attitudes that most white Marylanders took to blacks—to racial differences, if not to slavery itself. He described "stout negro-women," the "prolific mothers of this redundant brood." Elderly black men, including the ludi-

Edgar Allan Poe (1809–49), as seen in a daguerreotype taken in Lowell, Massachusetts, in 1848—the last known image of the poet.

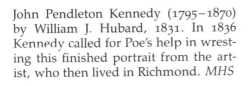

John Pendleton Kennedy (1795–1870) by William J. Hubard, 1831. In 1836 Kennedy called for Poe's help in wresting this finished portrait from the artist, who then lived in Richmond. *MHS*

crous old bachelor named "Jupiter," wore "faces shortened as if with drawing strings" and had noses that ran "all to nostril." "I should not hesitate," said Kennedy's narrator, to pronounce slaves "a comparatively comfortable and contented race of people, with much less of the care and vexation of life I have often observed in other classes of society."[58]

As a lawyer, Kennedy might have based this portrait of slavery partly on statute and case law. If the law provided a guide, Maryland slavery in the nineteenth century had grown markedly more humane than in the colonial period, when slaves had been subject to punishments as draconian as hanging for stealing and loss of a hand before hanging for arson. Striking a white man in the eighteenth century left a slave liable to ear-cropping. Such "severe and very uncouth laws," as *Niles' Weekly Register* described them in 1826, later fell from use and then from the books. Punishments for serious crimes like murder varied in this period between sentences that were no different from those given whites, and the sale of slave criminals out of state. Throughout the early nineteenth century whippings—no more than thirty-nine lashes—supplied punishment for slaves convicted of petty offenses in county or magistrates' courts. Maryland law limited the master to ten lashes, prohibited him from abusing slaves, and required him to supply blacks (just as indentured servants in the earlier period) with adequate food, clothing, shelter, and rest. There were incidents of masters being hauled into court to answer charges of slave abuse and of constables standing between owner and slave. White Marylanders spoke of the "ameliorated condition" of nineteenth-century society and of the salutary "changes that have taken place in public opinion" on proper slave treatment.[59]

Nonetheless, the law could by no means warrant the good behavior of masters, overseers, or persons hiring slave labor; William Green, who fled bondage on the Eastern Shore, remarked that a master had "all the power over the poor panting slave, and let him treat him as he will, the slave has no power to lay his grievance before any human being." Blacks themselves made valuable witnesses on this count, and runaways told many stories of severity and even cruelty. Stephen Pembroke, a Washington County slave who admitted that he also knew slavery's "moderate degree," reported that one of his three masters was "a rigid and wicked man," that he had seen blacks "tied up, whipped, shot, and starved." "I know one man who gave his slave one hundred and fifty lashes in two days," Pembroke said before a New York City audience, "and on the third day he died. He crept into the field, and his master supposing he was sleeping, went up and cowhided him, but he was cowhiding a corpse, thinking he was asleep!" Frederick Douglass wrote of whites who shot slaves at point-blank range and of a black man who was killed with a hatchet. One cold winter day a slaveowner in William Green's experience had forced an old woman who was supposed to look after the sheep but could not locate them to stay outdoors until she did. Later she was found frozen to death under a fence. John Thompson told of a southern Maryland master who would walk behind slaves as they picked tobacco worms and make them eat any they had missed. After an absence from the plantation the same man would occasionally gather slaves together and reassert his authority by whipping them "all around." It seemed to amuse him and his children, Thompson wrote afterward, to force slave husbands to whip their wives, mothers their daughters, and fathers their sons.[60]

Accounts of ill treatment had origins in all parts of Maryland, but several fugitives noted the bleakness of life in Prince George's County, where whites, outnumbered by blacks, felt a special need to make slaves stand in fear. George Ross, held in Hagerstown, had heard that Prince George's slaveholders were "a little harder than they are in the upper part of the State." Thompson called the county as different from the neighborhood in which he had grown up—apparently Calvert—"as Alabama is from Kentucky." His new masters in Prince George's considered "whipping as essential to the good of

"Perry Hall Slave Quarters, with Field Hands at Work" by Francis Guy, c. 1805. Guy portrayed Maryland slaves in Baltimore County working peacefully at a time when John Pendleton Kennedy and people like him gained fond memories of plantation life. The painting descended in the family of a freed Perry Hall slave. *MHS*

the soul as the body." In all the heavily black counties, especially following an actual or rumored slave uprising, whites patrolled the roads at night. According to a Prince George's County black, Dennis Simms, the slave caught more than a short distance from his master's home without a written pass was "unmercifully whipped," and he claimed that he knew of two absentee slaves who also suffered branding with an *R* on their cheek. Overseers in Simms's experience lost no opportunity to inflict the hated "nine and ninety-nine" (mocking the legal limit of ten strokes)—a flogging that went on until the slave lost consciousness or begged for mercy.[61]

Slave women could suffer particularly galling abuse. Life on an isolated farm and the many responsibilities of a planter's wife did not always produce women of great patience; many a black cook or house servant felt the wrath of a white woman frustrated, jealous, or simply lonely. One plantation mistress, "very rich and equally cruel," in the words of a fugitive slave, would sometimes attack her gray-headed kitchen servant "with shovel, tongs, or whatever other weapon lay within her reach," and then, exhausted, complain until her husband administered a whipping. In Baltimore County a young white girl described her neighbor as a "fiend in woman's shape" for having a black servant stripped and whipped by several men. Willingly or unwillingly, slave women on occasion became embroiled in illicit affairs with their masters, and upon discovering these encounters, mistresses could more easily direct their rage against slave than husband. Thompson perhaps exaggerated when he said that one master he served under was "the father of about one-fourth of the slaves on his plantation, by his slave women." A black man from Charles County said only that slave women there "paid the price" for being attractive. Illustrating well the hidden sexual element in the slaveholder's power over his bondswomen was the sale of a Maryland slave girl in 1830. Born of a black mother, she was the seventeen-year-old daughter of a deceased slaveowner whose estate had gone to auction. When she mounted the block her appearance created a stir among buyers. She broke into tears at the lurid questions they put to her, and her refusal to answer them, read an account in a London newspaper, "met with blood-chilling oaths." She sold for the extravagant price of $1,700.[62]

Making the most of these exhibitions, white and black abolitionists also leveled the charge of slave breeding against Southerners. Frederick Douglass reported an egregious example. The Talbot County farmer who tried to "break" him purchased a twenty-year-old black woman "for *a breeder*," hired a black man from a nearby planter, and then "fastened" them together at night. After a year the woman gave birth to twins, whom the farmer "regarded as being quite an addition to his wealth." With every incentive to encourage slave fecundity, Maryland slaveholders often did refer to a young black woman's health and stature. Whether as a rule they tried or succeeded in hastening slave reproduction, however, no one seems to have known. A Frederick County slaveowner described a black woman as being twenty-six and "in the prime of life"; she had been a house servant in childhood and when of age was "turned out for breeding," which may merely have meant allowed to find a mate. Ross knew of no instance where slaves were raised for the purpose of selling, but on his farm of thirty or forty slaves the older ones were sold as the younger blacks came of age. If slaveowners could get good bargains, he recalled, "they would sell the young just the same. I have often heard of slaves being kept for the purpose of breeding," Ross said, "but I have never seen it."[63]

Scarcely any generalization held up for Maryland slavery except perhaps that in this northernmost slave state (in Delaware slavery almost had disappeared by the 1830s), the peculiar institution had grown peculiar indeed. Most slaves still worked in the fields, gangs of men and women, as an outsider phrased it, "toiling under the harsh commands of the overseer." Some masters tried to vary the rural work pattern to their advantage; an Eastern Shore agricultural reformer, calling himself "the Great Labor Saving Man," embarked on what a slave later wrote was a plan "to make one man do the work of two" by getting his blacks up two hours before sunrise and keeping them at work after dark husking corn. One result was that he marketed 1,500 to 2,000 barrels of corn a season. Another was that his young slaves of eighteen or twenty years "looked to be thirty and thirty-five years old." Generally Maryland planters and farmers, as elsewhere in the South, followed a

"Mistress Overseeing the Plantation." Etching by Adalbert Volck, c. 1860. Volck, a German-born silversmith, dentist, and proslavery satirist who lived in Maryland in the 1850s, gave slaveholding the benefit of every doubt in this alluring view of self-possessed mistress, busy and deferential bondsmen, healthy crops, and pasture overrun with fat livestock. *MHS*

sunrise-to-sunset regimen, with work hardest during harvest season and Sundays left free. On the large plantations of the lower Western and middle Eastern Shore, labor for a few slaves grew highly specialized. Lloyd's Wye House blacks worked as coopers, cartwrights, millers, shoemakers, blacksmiths, and weavers.[64]

Since most Maryland slaveholders owned but a few blacks, odds increased that slaves worked as domestic servants, did odd jobs, or spent time hired out in the state's varied economy. Charles Ball, who grew up near Leonardtown, was told that if he behaved himself he might become a waiter or overseer—stations that appeared to him "to be the highest points of honor and greatness in the whole world." Green served as a servant, then as a jockey, until he objected to the gambling that surrounded horse racing; his master, "being quite a conscientious man in some things," next made him a waiter. Later Green accompanied a physician on house calls. Slaves served as hands on the vessels that sailed between Eastern and Western shores and as cooks and stokers on the steamers that plied the bay. A traveler on a ferry crossing the Susquehanna in the dead of winter pitied the seven blacks who took turns standing at the bow breaking river ice with long wooden clubs. Each stint left them exhausted and covered with frozen splashes. In sharp contrast, slaves labored in iron foundries between Frederick and Baltimore and in Cecil County; believing blacks to be especially tolerant of heat, whites thought them "particularly suited to such an occupation."[65]

Leased to small manufacturers, wagon masters, shipbuilders, and the like, slaves in Baltimore—about four thousand in 1830, three thousand in 1840—lived a peculiar life that brought both pleasure and pain. They found that contractors often cared less than their masters did about their well-being. "I was never abused much by my own people," testified a former Maryland slave; "I was abused by those to whom I was hired out." On the other hand, slavery in the city permitted blacks to live a life partially beyond the gaze of whites. Some masters went so far as to allow slaves to act as their own agents in finding work, so that a slave like Douglass, a caulker at Fells Point, might see his master only once a week, when he paid over a portion of his wages. City slaves, besides sometimes living in their own rented quarters and having friends among free blacks, exercised some control over their own time, attended black churches, and found release in the black grog shops that emerged in Baltimore backstreets and alleys. "A city slave is almost a freeman, compared with a slave on a plantation," Douglass later wrote. Enjoying "privileges altogether unknown" to their brothers and sisters in the country, helpful to runaways from the tobacco fields, urban slaves represented, many whites realized, a threat to the slave order itself.[66]

As much as the Maryland economy, the natural environment affected slavery in the state—and again with double-edged results. Winters could be bitter cold. Few slaves who left a record of their experience in Maryland slavery failed to comment on their frequent discomfort in that season—despite the care many masters took to provide them with extra winter clothing. Apparently a typical planter issued slave men shirts and trousers made of coarse sacking, "such as grocers keep salt in," for summer, and women a jacket and skirt of the same material; winter wear consisted of rough black-and-white woolen suits that slaves called "nits and lice." Children wore nothing more than oversized cotton or woolen smocks. Blacks normally got a pair of shoes each year, roughly measured and crudely made of ox-hide. Some blacks called them "program" shoes because they often were so large that the toes had to be stuffed with discarded playbills. Except during the winter months, slave housing generally seemed to suffice. Most rural blacks (domestic servants and slaves belonging to a small farmer might have slept in the master's house) lived in one-story log or boarded structures, which may have had windows, but never glass, and only the simplest wooden door. Floors were of dirt or planks. Slaves usually slept on straw bedding or wooden benches; William Green complained of lying down on a "bunch of straw on the cold damp earth." Fireplaces in such huts provided only a little heat and much draft during the cold months, so that survival called for ingenuity and cooperation. Slave children took empty sacks from storehouses to use as extra bedding. Mothers made quilts from scrap cloth and slept next to their

Frederick Douglass (1817–95). From *Narrative of the Life of Frederick Douglass, an American Slave* (Worthy, near Leeds, 1846). *McGregor Library, University of Virginia*

younger children. Men covered windows as best they could and, according to Green, organized watches to keep the fire burning hot through the nights.[67]

At the same time the location of most Maryland slaves near the bay or its tributaries helped measurably to supply a nutritious diet. Food seems rarely to have been a source of complaint among Maryland slaves. According to Douglass (who hastened to add that there were exceptions), Eastern Shore slaveholders followed the rule, "No matter how coarse the food, only let there be enough of it." John Thompson, describing a harsh regimen, said that slaves got a peck of corn, two dozen herrings, and about four pounds of meat per week—probably a more appetizing ration than slaves typically received on cotton or sugar plantations in the Gulf South. Another slave received a peck of corn each week throughout the year and a "tolerable supply" of pork in December, when the hogs were butchered. Apparently it was not unusual for Maryland slaves to have their own vegetable gardens—

though they could tend them only after working hours, which sometimes meant by moonlight. Slaves in Frederick and Prince George's counties, and probably elsewhere, supplemented their food supply by hunting the rabbit, possum, and raccoon that could make "a real treat" of a pot pie. Above all, slaves benefited from Maryland waters, and in many instances they did their own fishing. Charles Ball described himself as fortunate in living between the Patuxent and the bay; he enjoyed an "abundance of fish in the spring and as long as fishing season continued," and afterward a salt herring every day supplemented his allowance of corn. "Our food was very plain," recalled an old Maryland ex-slave, whose diet had included "fat hog meat, fish and vegetables raised on the farm and corn bread made up with salt and water." He stressed that his favorite meals consisted of the "fish and crabs cooked in all styles by mother."[68]

Maryland slaves did not hunt, fish, and garden like freemen, but even if rural blacks only occasionally secured their own food they demonstrated a level of self-help that slaves in the Old Southwest commonly did not enjoy. It would be difficult to imagine a slave in the Cotton South owning a hunting dog named "Ruler," as did a Charles County black who had trained the animal to jump and take off a man's hat on command. In the quarters, with many restrictions to be sure, slaves elaborated on this theme. Playing, praying, and trying to build stable domestic arrangements, they at least to a limited degree fashioned their own lives. "After work was done," a black remembered afterward, "the slaves would smoke, sing, tell ghost stories and tales," and dance to music played on home-made fiddles. The longevity of African folk customs among them made itself plain in the blacks' ability, in the frequent absence of white medical help, to "doctor themselves" with their own herbs, teas, and salves. Slave children amused themselves with mumbletypeg, rings, and marbles—although Frederick Douglass portrayed his own childhood as austere and joyless. When on holidays, especially Christmas, whites paid heed to their slaves, blacks did what they could to make a tradition of it—holding masters to their own graciousness. One black described the scene: "Christmas morning we went to the big house and got presents, and had a big time all day." Labor itself provided slaves with the means of community. Corn shuckings each fall brought blacks from several plantations together in a barn, where music, food, and drink accompanied work. After the last barrel of corn was hauled to the crib, dancing followed until late in the night. Slaves along the lower Potomac, testifying further to their success in piercing the blinds of bondage, blew a conch shell to signal nighttime social gatherings, and at times sang across the river to Virginia blacks, who would "sing back" to them.[69]

The whippings, sales, and living conditions of slavery did nothing to promote stability or authority in the black family, but evidence suggests that

Maryland slaves struggled against every obstacle. Allowed a few weeks "leisure" for childbirth, slave mothers afterward did what they could to care for their infant children. John Thompson wrote that if mothers had humane masters or overseers they might obtain permission to nurse the newborn between breaks in the work schedule; he might have noted the ways in which a skillful slave mother played on a slaveholder's view of himself as humane. According to Charles Ball slave mothers often went to bed with empty stomachs rather than refuse their hungry children. The powerlessness of slave fathers, who in addition might well live on a farm apart from their wife and children, made their place in the slave family especially ambiguous. Whites assumed that slave fathers counted little in the quarters and seldom felt enduring love for mate or children. Black testimony weighed against that jaundiced view. Ball developed a close relationship with father and grandfather alike. His father visited the family Saturday nights and always brought "apples, melons, sweet potatoes, or, if he could procure nothing else, a little parched corn, which tasted better in our cabin," Ball wrote, "because he had brought it." Later, when Ball's mother was sold away, his father became so despondent that his master decided to sell him as well, and ultimately the boy's grandfather assumed as best he could the role of parent. William Green told of slave fathers, living in barracks-like huts, who built board or blanket partitions for their families and thus became "a great man amongst them."[70]

Blacks struggled to shape their own lives within slavery; masters tried to control blacks but could not deny their humanity. This push-pull relationship became especially interesting in the shaping of black religion. Whites tried to make the gospel a means of discipline. "The ministers used to preach—'Obey your masters and mistresses and be good servants,'" complained a former Eastern Shore slave; "I never heard anything else." Slaves recognized the ploy and resisted it—either outwardly or quietly. Ball's grandfather—who had been born in Africa, claimed noble blood, and clung to African religious beliefs—warned younger blacks that these Christian teachings were the "inventions of designing men." By singing Protestant hymns in the tobacco fields, John Thompson could throw his Catholic master, who believed orthodox instruction of his blacks to be a solemn duty, into "spasms of anger." Forced to attend an Episcopal church in southern Maryland, usually seated in the rear balcony, slaves felt indifferent because the service bore so little relationship to their own experience—it aimed, as they said, "above our comprehension." Several fugitive slaves, besides telling abolitionists what they wanted to hear about Southern religion, voiced the resistance slaves mounted to "white" faith by declaring that they would rather belong to unchurched masters who drank and played cards than to pronounced Christians.[71]

Slaves found the singing, heart-centered, hope-for-deliverance strains of evangelical Christianity far more compelling than high-church white liturgy or the message of St. Paul's Epistle, and to celebrate their own kind of Christian expectation they obviously preferred their own churches. Thompson recalled a wave of conversions to Methodism among the slaves of southern Maryland, significant in part because it proved that slaves on neighboring farms could communicate with one another. The awakening "produced great consternation among the slaveholders," who apparently disagreed on how best to respond to it. In this instance they established patrols to break up black religious assemblies. Thompson's master, employing another tactic, purchased a slave fiddle player and for a time distracted his slaves with what Thompson called "worldly pleasures." Where blacks were not numerous, as in Carroll County, slaves attended an "old side" Methodist church in which a black minister preached. In southern Maryland Episcopalian and Methodist slaveholders joined in building a chapel for slaves, then cautiously installed a white minister. Even there, Thompson testified, whites occasionally allowed a "qualified and licensed" black to preach, and in Prince George's County during these years a free black known as "Parson" Rezin Williams conducted black prayer meetings with the sufferance of slaveholders. They conceded what was unavoidable, for slaves risked almost any punishment to assemble clandestinely, sing spirituals, and offer one another the support faith supplied.[72]

Thus in many subtle ways slaves succeeded in insisting on their humanity and forced, in a sense of the word, slaveholders to live up to their own professed ideals. Escaped slaves—the exceptional blacks who by acting became abolitionists—blamed the slave order for its evil effects on whites while acknowledging many examples of kindly treatment in Maryland. George Ross described the master from whom he escaped as "a very nice man, and very much a gentleman. He never laid the weight of his hand upon me to whip me." William Green pronounced Edward Hamilton "a humane man to be a slave-holder." While strict, he was "generally kind to his servants; yes, I must say very kind to them in the way of feeding and clothing them." Hamilton's children were of a piece—Green "never knew one of them to strike a servant in anger." A former slave from Frederick County said that owners there "as a whole were kind" to blacks and gave them money to spend when the crops were good. An aged ex-slave, Charles Coles, came close to portraying Kennedy's romanticized slaveholder in his recollection of Silas Dorsey. Coles's memory may have turned selective with age; nevertheless, he said that Dorsey was "loved by all who knew him, black and white, especially his slaves."[73]

Maryland slaves had been in the state for generations, frequently held by the same white families or living in the same localities. This pattern helped explain why many whites referred to their bondsmen as "their people" and were reluctant to divide or sell them south, and why blacks greatly feared that fate. It was not unusual for wills to stipulate that slaves had to remain within Maryland. Newspaper advertisements of slave sales often carried conditions to the same effect. Slaves in their later writings vividly remembered both the threats severe slaveowners made of sale southward and the assurances of a kindly master or mistress that they would never be sold out of the neighborhood. Since the promises of a well-intentioned slaveholder could not always be kept, estate sales often produced deeply affecting scenes for blacks and whites alike. Charles Ball recalled one from his childhood. His new master had clothed the black boy in one of his own children's frock shirts and was leaving the site of the sale when Ball's mother, whom the master could not afford to purchase, went to a trader from the lower South. The Marylander, Ball later wrote, "seemed to pity her, and endeavored to soothe her distress by telling her that he would be a good master to me, and that I should not want anything."[74]

Without doubt the nearness of free territory also had an effect on Maryland slaveholders and worked to keep the worst features of slavery in check. Cruelty invited action on an impulse that few whites denied to exist among slaves and that fugitives said was universal among them—the urge to freedom. In the upper counties of both shores a slave could cross the Mason-Dixon Line after a night or two spent in hard running or a few days under sail. Frederick Douglass correctly noted the average slave's ignorance of geography, yet slaves ran off with increasing frequency in the 1830s and 1840s and friends of fugitive slaves grew in numbers and efficiency. Opponents of slavery developed a secret, word-of-mouth network—the "underground railroad"—leading from Maryland into Pennsylvania and New York, each household offering refuge and occasionally transportation to those blacks who could muster the strength to leave loved ones and risk heavy punishment by running off. On the Eastern Shore, Harriet Tubman, herself an escaped Maryland slave, repeatedly returned on missions to conduct blacks across the inlets and through the forests she knew so well. Tough and resourceful, Tubman became legendary for her "military genius." Once, after a daylong wait in a swamp without food, one of her party spoke of turning about and taking his chances back on the plantation. Tubman pointed a pistol to his head and told him to "Move or die."[75]

With escape inviting (though never simple) for slaves, Maryland slaveowners faced the need actually to talk about subjects that may never have surfaced elsewhere in the slave South. Marylanders labored to convince their slaves that Canada had been oversold—that nothing grew there, that it was too cold for horses, hogs, and cows (much less for non-natives), and that half of everyone's income went to the Queen of England. Blacks, who often knew better, heard that Pennsylvania and New York were filled with ogres who recaptured fugitives and sold them south. "I don't think a great many believed those stories," Ross commented, "for we knew they were told to keep us there." Pretending to believe forbidding accounts of Canada or feigning disinterest, a slave nonetheless could know that white anxiety about runaways gave him some advantage. An Eastern Shore slave, after unloading a cargo of Canadian wheat, casually asked his master how it could have

Harriet Tubman (1820–1913). *MHS*

grown in ice. "I never saw anybody tied up and cut and slashed as they say it was in Virginia and New Orleans," said Joseph Smith after making his way to Canada; Maryland slaveholders were afraid to whip their blacks "because they knew, if they did, they would run away from them." One noticed something of the game whites and blacks played under these conditions in a master's telling his slaves that they had been treated well "and it would not be fair for them to go away," or in the almost pathetic plea William Green heard from one of his masters: "I do everything I can to make you comfortable and happy, and this is the way you go on."[76]

Finally, wanting to believe that they were indeed good masters and given their declining proportion in the state, Maryland slaveholders had to be especially concerned with their image in the public eye. In most slave states planters dominated the legislature. After the 1837 constitutional reforms, planters in counties like Talbot, Anne Arundel, and Prince George's could not ignore the truth that sheer numbers probably lay with citizens who had no vested concern with slave property; as a protection, that omnibus bill included the proviso that slavery could be abolished in Maryland only with a unanimous vote of the legislature. By the 1830s, bearing in mind the fury of distant abolitionists, planters everywhere in the South pledged themselves to view slaveholding as a form of Christian stewardship. Maryland masters lived in the midst of outspoken antislavery sentiment. In Baltimore, Douglass wrote, few people were "willing to incur the odium attaching to the reputation of being a cruel master." Charles Ball believed that his "sullen and crabbed" master was "ashamed to abuse me, lest he should suffer in the good opinion of the public."[77]

Determined at the very least to protect their property rights and themselves from uprisings like that of Nat Turner, Maryland slaveowners wavered between anxious proslavery and calculating self-doubt. In August 1835 in Annapolis a public meeting of planters appealed to the General Assembly to pass a law that would stamp out the writings of "certain deluded fanatics" who would promote "a general servile insurrection." Seven years later a similar gathering, which was planned to be much larger than it turned out, called for statutes discouraging manumission, restricting free blacks, and by various devices making escapes from slavery more difficult. For all this bluster, owners could refer to slaveholding as a "source of vexation," as did Charles Goldsborough, a former congressman and governor, in writing a Mississippi friend in 1834. In his seventieth year, Goldsborough pondered what to do with his black laborers. If he kept them at all, he had to keep them well, he explained, yet they consumed all they made and notwithstanding his kind treatment of them were prone to run off. He could simply sell them to a slave trader, but prices stood below their real worth and, besides, the transaction was "inevitably to a certain degree inhuman and offensive to one's own feelings." Searching for a middle course, Goldsborough hoped to send them en masse to work on a Mississippi cotton plantation, where they would suffer "no possible severance of connections" and would be "sure of being as well treated as they ever were." He died before acting on his plan.[78]

CHAPTER 6

A House Divided

Maryland by the mid-nineteenth century had become a sectional netherland, a mix of free and slave economy, Northern and Southern culture. The state partook of both Yankee "go-aheadism" and Cavalier leisure, gave itself completely to neither. Cambridge, Easton, Chestertown, Annapolis, and Southern Maryland nestled themselves in the ways of the past and on the surface might have been tidewater towns or tobacco lands anywhere in the South; Westminster, Frederick, Hagerstown, and Cumberland continued to grow, prosper, and boast of their advancing fortunes. Baltimore resembled Philadelphia or New York in its commercial banks and varied manufactures. At the same time the city impressed visitors as being gay and charming in a way entirely its own. The songs of black hucksters selling fruits and vegetables, dairy products and poultry, filled the morning air. For the outdoor life, the state had no peer, wrote a correspondent to the *Spirit of the Times*; "old Maryland" stood "preeminent, for hospitality, shooting, fishing, and sporting, in each and every particular." Oysters, crabs, terrapin, and canvasback truly had made Baltimore hotels like Barnum's famous as far away as London.

One also noticed the pleasantness of Maryland in polite relations between men and women. Maryland women from families of accomplishment seemed to bring out the courtly best in the gentlemen who paid them attention, and traditionally they had many admirers. Passing through Baltimore in the 1850s, an Englishwoman—though noting that they had a habit of eating everything, including oysters, with their knives, leaned both elbows on the dining table, and gloried a bit in the "braverie" of their colorful clothes— wrote that Maryland ladies were celebrated all over the Union. The most a Kentuckian could boast, she reported with slight dismay, was a sure rifle, a fine horse, and "a Maryland *gal* for his wife." A London lawyer discovered the proverbial phrase "Baltimore beauty" to be perfectly apt. Henri Herz, an Austrian-born pianist and composer who lived in Baltimore at mid-century, found women there positively distracting. "At my concerts," he confessed, "I was carried away to see so many beautiful faces all at once." He made it a practice to wave to the Maryland belles with his right hand while continuing to play with his left—a feat they applauded with delight.

Not to be outdone, young Maryland gentlemen of the day tried to win that applause by taking up chivalry. The sport of "jousting"—galloping on horseback in medieval costume and spearing rings—gained popularity in this romantic period and often included a ceremony crowning a queen at the posttournament ball. "The Knights looked well and fought gallantly," wrote a Maryland woman of an especially chaste event near Leonardtown. After ceremonies acclaiming the winner, "the Knights rode in order to the Town and the maids to their homes."[1] To sober Northerners jousting was a sure sign of Southern influence.

A better index might have been the state of education. Maryland offered an example of a slave state in which legislators, having spent large sums on internal improvements, were eager neither to support elitist colleges nor to provide for a general system of public schooling. Education thus hung somewhere between Northern interest in public schooling and Southern regard for the academies that prepared gentlemen for public leadership or ladies for social confidence. Catholics had a women's school, St. Joseph's, at Emmitsburg; well-to-do Methodists sent their daughters to academies in Annapolis and Baltimore—the Baltimore school receiving $1,500 annually from the General Assembly. Another college for women opened at Mount Washington in Baltimore County in 1856. Until retiring that year, Almira Lincoln Phelps, a New England native transplanted to Howard County, served as headmistress at the Episcopalian Patapsco Female Institute. She recognized that daughters of slaveholders posed special problems to an educator; a North Carolina congressman with daughters enrolled at the institute complained that Phelps did not pay enough attention to the development of feminine charm. Ahead of her time, she replied that she aimed to give women all the advantages young men received in college.

Men's institutions got along as best they could. Washington College in Chestertown—closed after a fire in 1827—triumphantly reopened in 1844, won limited state funding four years later, and enjoyed a period of modest prosperity. St. John's College in Annapolis, struggling financially, its trustees convinced that the 1806 withdrawal of state aid violated its charter and therefore amounted to breach of contract, finished students irregularly in the 1840s. At the 1849 commencement, William H. Tuck, an 1827 graduate who soon served as a Court of Appeals judge, seized the opportunity to speak on "the educational problems and requirements of the times." Newton University, founded in Baltimore in 1845, promised to impose "no rules, laws, or regulations of a sectarian or party character." While the college recommended its regular curriculum of languages, history, belles-lettres, and math, it also offered a three-year course in commercial, mechanical, and sci-

"A Maryland Tourney: Riding at the Quintain." Silhouette signed "T. F. H., 1841." *MHS*

entific subjects that produced "practical men and good citizens." Also in Baltimore, the University of Maryland slowly recovered from its unhappy experience in the years 1826–39, when the assembly had tried to make it a combined undergraduate college and professional school. Once more a private institution with strong medical, dental, and pharmaceutical faculties (though missing its earlier law school), it reflected growing specialization in mid-nineteenth-century professional life but also the somewhat haphazard manner that Yankees put down as Southern. Its faculty declined a donation of $10,000 virtually because spending the sum would be too much trouble. John Pendleton Kennedy, elected provost of the university in 1850, joked of his unfitness for the post and his unwillingness to let its duties draw him from more pleasurable occupations. "Think of a Provost with his coat off at billiards!" he wrote a friend.[2]

Unfamiliar with the township system of local government typified in Massachusetts and Pennsylvania, many Marylanders, like Virginians, resisted a general system of free public schools. In the 1820s Littleton Dennis Teackle of Somerset County had drawn up a program that would have divided each county into districts and distributed the two-dollar annual cost of educating a child among taxable citizens—each of whom, Teackle, figured, would have paid about sixty-two cents a year. An act of 1825 substantially adopted this plan while leaving the counties free to accept or reject it. Voters in six counties, among them Teackle's own, turned it down, postponing any statewide system of public education. As in other slave states, private academies in Maryland varied greatly in quality. Few measured up to Charlotte Hall, which for a time received monies from St. Mary's, Charles, and Prince George's counties, employed three teachers in the classics, and accepted twenty "free students." Another academically respectable academy, St. James, east of Hagerstown, had been chartered as a "college" in 1843; the Episcopal bishop of Maryland, William R. Whittingham, perhaps planned to build it into an institution to rival Mount St. Mary's, which thrived under the Reverend John McCaffey as a leading middle-states Catholic college. In Baltimore City and Frederick, Washington, and Allegany counties small free schools, some with one teacher, had become numerous by 1850, when the census placed Maryland's white illiteracy rate at about 5 percent. In this respect the state ranked between New England and New York (about 2 percent) and Virginia (8.6 percent).

The fortunate geography of Maryland continued to stimulate investments that few other Southerners found enticing. As the nineteenth century wore on, mineral wealth and ship, canal, and rail enterprises tied the state less to staple crop agriculture and ever more to manufacturing, Ohio Valley farming, and foreign exchange. In October 1850 the C&O Canal finally reached Cumberland. Long hampered by financial shortages and labor troubles, the canal company completed work on the fifty-mile stretch between Dam Number 6 at Great Cacapon and the Queen City using private money (in 1844 the legislature, itself in fiscal trouble, had released the company from earlier ties to the state). Though originally supposed to extend much farther than Cumberland, the canal became profitable enough as a conveyor of Western Maryland flour, wheat, and corn. Freight tonnage on the canal, a mere 60,000 in 1841, reached 86,000 in 1848 and two years later almost 102,000. Recognizing the close tie between farm productivity and the canal's success, company officials in 1848–49 offered special low toll rates on fertilizer headed upriver. Meantime the canal suffered from seemingly endless problems of maintenance and order. Each year banks caved in, muskrats burrowed under the towpath, floodwaters damaged both channels and locks, and boatmen broke rules against iron-tipped poles and untowed boats. Users of the "Big Ditch," as Potomac Marylanders called it, complained of delays, sunken wrecks, and drifting rafts. As always in need of funds, company directors watched developments in iron mining west of Cumberland and welcomed the bituminous coal traffic that the George's Creek Valley began to produce in quantity.

The canal literally faced an uphill contest in competing with the B&O, which eventually solved problems that would have broken the canal company. Having arrived at Cumberland (running on the Virginia side from

Harpers Ferry) eight years before the C&O opened to that city, the railroad faced both political and practical difficulties in reaching the Ohio River. Alive to the economic benefits of a cross-state railroad, Pennsylvania in the mid-1840s withdrew cooperation, forcing B&O planners to stay outside the state's boundary. In the summer of 1848 chief engineer Benjamin H. Latrobe, Jr., his predecessor, the feisty Jonathan Knight, and a New Englander, John Child, completed a survey that mapped the best route to the Ohio and estimated the cost of building west from Cumberland at more than six million dollars. The next year leadership of the company passed to a young and energetic board member, Thomas Swann. Swann cleverly used the plight of the B&O to activate the competitive juices and tap the pocketbooks of Baltimoreans, among them some younger men whose wealth had charted recent economic gains in the city—George Peabody, a New Englander with London banking ties, and Johns Hopkins, a Quaker merchant with heavy interests in development of the B&O.

Realizing the dangers of further delays (the Maryland and Virginia legislatures already had extended the deadline for completion to the Ohio), Swann focused all the resources of the road on the drive to Wheeling. Five thousand men and 1,250 horses went to work. Eleven tunnels had to be bored, two of them extraordinarily long: Broad Tree (163 miles from the Ohio) extended 2,350 feet; Kingwood (83 miles) ran to 4,100 feet, an unprecedented length. Delivering supplies to workers on the far side of each mountain required a switchback system that Mendes Cohen, a nephew of the B&O director of the same name, devised while serving under Latrobe. A company builder at the Mount Clare shops, Ross Winans, designed the slow but powerful engines that pulled twelve-ton loads up the steep switchbacks. B&O engineers constructed a 650-foot iron bridge—stone viaducts took too long to build and had grown too costly—over the Monongahela, the longest such structure in the country. Work proceeded with an enviable safety record. On Christmas Eve 1852, at a lonely spot 18 miles east of Wheeling, the tracks joined. In January, Maryland and Virginia dignitaries met at Wheeling for a rightly exuberant ceremony. After a quarter-century of trial, rails linked the Chesapeake Bay and Ohio River.

Practical developments ensured the primacy of rail over canal. Though Winans played a large part in locomotive technology during the 1830s and 1840s, the B&O had decided against relying on its own builders and gone to the open market for its engines. Philadelphia manufacturers supplied the next generation of steam locomotives, which, both powerful and fast, left no doubt that trains could run over the rugged terrain between Cumberland and Wheeling. Their boilers and driving rods, instead of vertical as in the early grasshoppers, lay parallel to the tracks. With forward "trucks" or sets of small wheels in front of the four drivers—along with "cowcatchers," gaping smokestacks, and racy cabs—the locomotive assumed its classical form. Between 1848 and 1854 revenues permitted the B&O to increase its number of engines from 57 to 207. With more of them available, none had to be in constant service, making it possible to maintain them properly and thus minimize repair costs over long service. After completion of the line to Wheeling, Cohen experimented successfully with coal-burning boilers, and before long coal replaced wood on B&O tenders. He also designed a new pressure gauge that allowed firemen to know exactly how much fuel to burn to sustain a level of steam. This simple device saved the company an estimated ninety-five thousand dollars each year.

Criss-crossing much of the state, taking many engineering and operational lessons from the B&O, other railroads made their own marks. Annapolis had a line to the B&O tracks at Elkridge, Hagerstown its own rail connection to Harrisburg. Eastern Shore lines remained incomplete for want of capital. At mid-century the Baltimore and Susquehanna line connected Jones Falls factories and the Harrisburg intersection with the new Pennsylvania Railroad. In 1850 the company also completed work on a new, gas-lighted Calvert Street Station, then the largest in the country and a model of simplicity and function. It went up on the site of an old waterworks and stood only five blocks from Barnum's Hotel. Another company, the Philadelphia, Wilmington, and Baltimore, connected those cities and in February 1850 opened its President Street Station just east of the harbor. Two years later the B&O left a haphazard Pratt Street depot and moved to the site on which the company in 1856 built Camden Station. Baltimoreans long had argued about land use, the proper pathways of railroads, and the noise of steam locomotives within the city. These new stations, along with track and wharfage construction at Canton and after 1848 at Locust Point, represented the state of the struggle between the railroads—which in 1845 won the nighttime right to use steam engines to carry heavy freight like coal and iron ore over city tracks—and the draymen, who needed hauling work but after 1847 faced higher taxes on their draft animals. Even after completion of the new, closer-in stations, passengers from Philadelphia to Washington detrained at President Street for a horsecar trip to the B&O terminus at Camden Street.

On the water, Maryland by mid-century had recovered from the financial reverses of 1837 and registered progress. In October 1852 Maryland ship pilots, angered by a recent act that permitted skippers to do their own bay and large-river piloting, formed a professional association with stiff membership requirements. During the next legislative session the association lobbied successfully for a bill making pilotage compulsory (unless shipowners paid an annual fee that a commission then divided among pilots) and establishing regular, if modest, rates. While ship captains disagreed that pilots alone knew Maryland waters well enough to navigate without mishap, the new law, partly satisfying a special interest, included general considerations of safety and insurance costs. In 1855 the state began planting offshore lighthouses (the first beacon had gone up at Bodkin Point in about 1820) according to a new, screw-pile design. Auger-like pilings, turned into the soft bay bottom, solved the problem of anchorage that until then had frustrated construction of effective warnings on the bay's sandy shoals. The first one went off the mouth of the Patapsco at Seven Foot Knoll.

With travel safer than ever and the economy healthy, steamboats thrived. The Maryland and Virginia Steam Boat firm, a victim of the depression, gave way in 1840 to the Baltimore Steam Packet Company. Later known as the Old Bay Line, it resumed the daily service between Baltimore and Norfolk and demonstrated its prosperity in the early 1850s by ordering two new vessels, the *North Carolina* and *Louisiana*. Magnificent, white-painted side-wheelers with copper-covered wooden hulls, the steamships measured well over two hundred feet in length and incorporated the latest mechanical advances and creature comforts. Passengers who had nowhere to sit except on the main deck later remarked on the pervasive smell of liquor (shipboard bars did such business that captains and crews demanded a share of the profits) and the puddles of tobacco juice. More commonly travelers praised the boats as "elegantly carpeted and furnished . . . with the most profuse gilding, mirrors, ottomans, etc."[3] By 1858, agreements with rail lines to the north and south of the Chesapeake made the Old Bay Line a chain linking sections together. The company sold through tickets from New York City to Wilmington, North Carolina.

Maryland shipbuilding, most extensive in the slave states, enjoyed a rebirth of its own in the 1850s as shipping patterns once again called for fine-lined sailing vessels. Trade between Baltimore and New Orleans—with its Mississippi shoals—required vessels of shallow draft; trips to China, which fully opened its doors to Western commerce in 1842, and after 1849 runs to the California gold fields placed a premium on speed. Expanded as far as its design would permit, the Baltimore Clipper played a last part in the glory days of sailing. The *Ann McKim*, launched in 1833, 493 tons, joined the square stern, low freeboard, and heavy after-drag of the Baltimore Clipper hull (usually of about 250 tons) with the three-masted ship rig. Striving for the capacity of the packet ships then common to oceangoing commerce, the *Ann McKim* anticipated the large, full-sail clippers later famous in the California and China trades. Baltimore shipyards produced their share—*Rattler* (1842, 539 tons), *Architect* (1847, 520 tons), *Grey Eagle*, and *Grey Hound*. In the spring of 1850 the Bell brothers of Baltimore, Edward Johnzey and Richard Henry, accepted a commission to build a speedy ship of 550 tons burden for the busy traffic around Cape Horn. Their three-masted *Seaman*—136 feet long, 28 feet of beam, and drawing only 15 feet of water—slid into the basin at the end of September. Two months later, under Captain Joseph Myrick, the *Seaman* made its first New York to San Francisco passage in 107 days, registering the second-best time any vessel had made on that journey; her return sailing time, 94 days from San Francisco to Capes Henry and Charles, set a record for sailing ships that no one ever surpassed. With such success to prompt them, the Bells in July 1851 launched a sister ship, the *Seaman's*

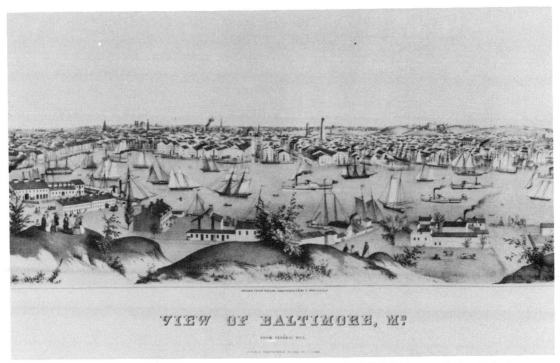

Detail, "View of Baltimore, Maryland, from Federal Hill." Lithograph by Edwin Whitefield, 1841. From atop Federal Hill a group of gentlemen and ladies marvel at the active port and city beneath them—the countryside on the north almost having receded to the horizon. *MHS*

Bride. While Baltimore did not produce as many ships as Maine, New York, or Philadelphia in these years, it hummed with activity that made shipbuilding one of the four leading sources of city employment. Yards in Talbot and Dorchester counties turned out their own working vessels for bay waters.

All these economic advances worked to change the character of the people who called Maryland home. Elsewhere in the slave South social homogeneity helped enormously to preserve a white order based on black bondage. Maryland by 1850 had attracted a high proportion of free-state immigrants. Of about 55,500 non-Maryland-born persons in the state that year (perhaps 9,000 of them having arrived since 1840), only about 12,500 outsiders had arrived from the slave region to the south and west. More important, no eastern slave state approached Maryland in number or proportion of foreignborn. Of about 418,000 Maryland whites in 1850, almost 54,000, or nearly 13 percent, had been born abroad—half of them in Germany, about 20,000 in Ireland, 4,500 in England, Scotland, and Wales, and the rest in twenty-five different countries. Baltimore, that census year a city of nearly 170,000 people and twenty wards, had doubled in size since 1820 and accounted for almost 36,000 of the foreign-born. Germans in the city were numerous

The *Seaman's Bride* under construction, 1851. An early
daguerreotype depicted the Bell brothers on the deck of
their nearly completed clipper ship. *MHS*

enough to support publication of three newspapers in their language, clubs,
musical and athletic groups, and schools. While the ratio of foreign to native-
born in Maryland resembled the average for the entire United States at this
time, a significant comparison lay with sister states below the Potomac: more
foreign-born persons lived in Maryland in 1850 than in the other old slave
states—Virginia to Georgia—combined. True, newcomers might adopt the
ways of their new home, but the German papers in Baltimore were openly
and actively abolitionist.

During the 1850s the peculiar qualities of Maryland both heated up politics
within the state and, in sectional debate, gave its spokesmen an in-between
perspective that counseled coolness and compromise. Sectional conflict followed upon United States military successes. Maryland volunteers, serving
in a regiment that included District of Columbia troops, had fought in the

Mexican War and been involved in some of the heaviest fighting around Monterrey; the rich bounty of western territory that fell to the country at war's end in 1848 proved even deadlier than enemy musketry. David Wilmot's proposal that the federal government prohibit slavery in the lands won from Mexico set off hateful exchanges between slave and free states and quickly raised other acrimonious issues: how much trouble Northerners should take in returning fugitive slaves to the South (as the Constitution required of them) and whether Congress should permit slave trading in the federal capital (where by law it governed). Doubting that slaveholders' rights would survive intact in this crisis, Southern radicals called a convention to meet in June 1850 at Nashville, where they hoped to prod their states to consider secession.

Invited to participate, Maryland leaders all declined. Throughout the year public feeling in the state overwhelmingly favored peaceful settlement and a return to business. Governor Philip F. Thomas in his yearly address to the assembly—he was a Democrat, to the dismay of his traditionally Whig Eastern Shore family, and the legislature was overwhelmingly Whig—spoke of the need for moderation. The governor made his only political mistake in suggesting Maryland make common cause with the South should the sectional quarrel come to blows. On 4 March, in bad weather, five thousand Baltimoreans staged a bipartisan rally at Monument Square under a banner that read (paraphrasing a line Andrew Jackson had addressed to John Calhoun in 1831) "The Union Must and Shall be Preserved." Another such meeting, this one called by Baltimore businessmen, was held in June. All the while Maryland congressmen and Whig senators James A. Pearce of Chestertown and Thomas G. Pratt of Annapolis lent their support to Henry Clay's omnibus compromise bill, which in late summer suffered defeat. The Baltimore *Sun* wrote that the bill's "murder" was the fault of "Northern and Southern abstractionists." Newspapers in Rockville and the Eastern Shore echoed these sentiments. Finally it was Senator Pearce, introducing Clay's measures one by one, who broke the deadlock and secured passage of the hopeful 1850 compromise. Henry Winter Davis, a Baltimore lawyer and son of a former president of St. John's College, expressed the prevailing Maryland view when he wrote that the "North is filled with the fanatics of liberty, as the South is with the Quixotes of slavery." "In the name of God," wrote another Marylander in a letter he wished every American could read, "take the Compromise of 1850 and don't let us hear any more about this matter."[4]

Politics in Maryland itself did much to direct the state's course over the next few years, at the same time that, in Washington, sectional issues became more and more difficult to manage within party bounds. Congressional debates had made it obvious that most spokesmen for Southern rights were Democrats while the old opposition party—which for many years had won regular, if narrow, victories in Maryland federal elections—had divided so bitterly between "Conscience Whigs" and "Cotton Whigs" that it lay nearly broken as a countrywide force. Most Maryland Democrats eschewed the extreme rhetoric of the Calhouns and Yanceys. Whig leaders in Maryland faced the unhappy prospect of belonging to a party with declining hopes of retaining the presidency. Then, in 1850, the matter of constitutional change in the state, subdued but not quieted after the 1837 reforms, returned to the fore. Malapportionment had remained a complaint in Baltimore and the western counties. Eastern Shoremen, though still unwilling to concede power to their traditional rivals, found the state's fiscal problems so severe (taxes recently had gone up to cover the heavy state debt) that a convention, as a means of tightening controls on spending, carried some appeal among them as well. Yet opposition in the Whiggish, slaveowning counties of Southern Maryland divided the party, and generally Whigs found themselves standing behind the Democrats in pro-reform publicity. In the western counties this image proved a severe disadvantage. During the 1850 gubernatorial canvass, coinciding with the election of delegates to the constitutional convention, the victorious Democrat Enoch Louis Lowe of Frederick, whose campaign newspaper was entitled the *Maryland Reformer*, had little trouble promoting himself as the better friend of progress.

The constitutional convention of 1851 was not a resounding success, but the encounter with reform worsened the plight of Maryland Whigs. From the start convention members placed themselves in bad odor by spending a week bickering over a choice for chairman. They went on to write a mixed bag of changes. New curbs appeared on legislative spending. The convention created new offices (state comptroller, commissioners of public works and lotteries, and county commissioners) while making formerly appointive local positions (judge of the orphans' court, county clerk, justice of the peace, and constable) elective. Henceforward state senators ran for reelection every four instead of six years. While the growing counties of the Western Shore did gain by the apportionment formula the convention finally agreed to, and Baltimore City enhanced its part of the General Assembly from one-sixteenth to one-eighth, opponents of drastic reform had enough votes to prevent election of the House of Delegates strictly on the basis of county population. Even as voters ratified the constitution, comment was critical almost everywhere: if a county did not lose representation, it did not gain enough. A Cumberland wag totaled the cost of the meeting and the length of the new constitution and argued that, at a cost of a dollar and a half per word, it was "about the hardest bargain of modern times."[5] The biggest losers, the Whigs, realized that they had won seats in the western counties only by running with Democrats as "fusion" candidates—suppressing their party identity—and that the state government, already susceptible to Democratic pleas, now consisted of even more offices that Democrats likely would win. In the 1852 contest between Winfield Scott and Franklin Pierce, the Democrats carried Maryland for the first time in a presidential election.

In these circumstances—sectional tensions still high, Whig party in decline—the cauldron of Maryland bubbled near boiling. Always combining dislocation and benefit, change in the state now brought a new round of fears. Since the 1830s private groups had been meeting to discuss the threat to old ways that accompanied the influx of immigrants, to ask what had happened to the former influence of the native-born. Secretive about their doings, members of these lodges had parried all questions by answering "I know nothing." Detractors called them "Know-Nothings," suggesting that they represented ignorance. In truth they spoke for bewilderment. Their malaise perhaps had something to do with the very speed of communication, the quickened pace of life. By 1848 the telegraph, first tested between Baltimore and Washington in 1844, made possible nearly instant news reporting from such faraway places as New Orleans. The Baltimore *Sun* soon made extensive use of the telegraph and wrote that it resulted in the "complete annihilation of space."[6]

The Know-Nothings may also have reflected a Christian native's uneasiness about the growing Jewish presence in Baltimore. Since 1826 Jews had been able to hold public office in Maryland, but change had come only after struggle and several defeats. In 1818, after receiving petitions from Jewish Baltimoreans, delegates Thomas Kennedy of Washington County had proposed and William Pinkney of Baltimore had written a constitutional amendment removing the religious test for state officeholding. The federal Constitution prohibited such restrictions, and the measure had the support of lawyers like Henry M. Brackenridge and John Van Lear McMahon as well as spokesmen for religious equality, among them John S. Tyson, William G. D. Worthington, and Ebenezer S. Thomas of Allegany. Kennedy, a Scots-born admirer of Jefferson, said he knew no Jews personally but declared that one's religion "is a question which rests, or ought to rest[,] between man and his Creator alone." "The right to put up one religion, is the right to put down another," said Tyson, who won praise from the Catholic bishop John England of South Carolina. Despite its merits, the "Jew Bill" or "Kennedy's Jew Baby" became a test of party loyalty and went down to defeat in that session and again in 1822–23; Kennedy himself lost his seat for a term when an opponent charged that Jewish equality would bring Christianity "into popular contempt." Once reelected, Kennedy introduced another measure that produced more acrimony and further pleas for religious rights. In February 1825 the bill at last passed—by one vote, with eighty legislators abstaining. Confirmed narrowly in the next assembly, the amendment opened places of public trust to anyone who believed in an afterlife—to Jews but not atheists.[7]

Of German origins, and for many years small in number, Baltimore Jewish families had formed the Hebrew Congregation (or Stadt Schule) in 1829. This Orthodox group moved from friendly rooms to available houses until Robert Cary Long, Jr., designed the first synagogue in the city. Long's Greek Revival structure retained the traditional gallery for women but introduced Ameri-

can (or Gentile) pews in the place of benches; it opened in 1845 in the heart
of the old German-Jewish community centered around Lombard Street in
Old Town. Another synagogue organized on Eden Street in Fells Point. A
third—Reformed—split from the Baltimore Hebrew Congregation in 1854
and built a temple on High Street, and then a fourth—Oheb Shalom (Lover
of Peace)—tried to steer a middle course between Orthodoxy and Reform-
ism. Despite theological differences, all these congregations clung to German-
language services.

German Jews by the mid-nineteenth century had achieved considerable
social distinction in the state. Reuben Etting earlier had served under Jefferson as federal marshal for Maryland. Both Solomon Etting, Reuben's father,
and Jacob Cohen had lobbied for Jewish rights in the 1820s. After passage of
the Kennedy amendment Etting and Cohen, well known as directors of the
B&O, won seats on the city council. In 1846 Joshua Cohen, Jacob's younger
brother and a prominent University of Maryland physician, played a part in
removing a reference to Christians in an old law that limited black court
testimony against whites; at the 1851 constitutional convention Dr. Cohen
with partial success advocated the end of all religious references in state
charter and laws. The number of Jews in Baltimore neared seven thousand
in the late 1850s, when Jewish leaders included the banking Cohens and
merchants and clothiers like the Ettings, Friedenwalds, Hutzlers, Hamburg-
ers, Levys, and Sonneborns. Leopold Blumenberg, an officer in the Fifth
Maryland, demonstrated that Jews could serve in the city's proudest militia
unit.

Most of all, however, Know-Nothings were disturbed by electoral, labor,
and miscellaneous violence and angered by "foreign ungrateful refugees."
In Baltimore gangs calling themselves Plug-Uglies, Red Necks, Blood Tubs
(who soaked the heads of erring voters in a vat of pig's blood), and Butt
Enders combined drinking with intimidating rivals at polling places. Baltimore fire companies, many of them Irish or German clubs, had become "jealous as Kilkenny cats of one another"; rumored to set fires in order to engage
in contests, wrote an astonished visitor, "they scarcely ever lose an opportunity of getting up a bloody fight." Labor groups, recovering from the long
depression after 1837, brought together at least two currents of anxiety. Better-off Marylanders worried because laborers seemed to begin with a premise of natural conflict between propertied and poor; native-born union members harbored animus toward the immigrants who served as strikebreakers.
In 1853 labor unrest reached a new peak. That spring and summer Allegany
County coal miners (in some districts nine out of ten miners were foreigners)
struck for more pay, threatening livelihoods all along the C&O Canal. Limestone workers in Baltimore County also went on strike. Laborers in the western Maryland iron fields and Harford County textile workers struck for a
ten-hour workday.[8]

Objecting to use of the Protestant Bible in Baltimore public classrooms,

"A Sketch, from The New Tragic Farce, of 'Americans Shall Rule America' as enacted by Mayor Swann of Baltimore, and his wonderful 'Star' Company." Pen and ink drawing by unknown artist, 1858. The caption accused Swann of being behind Know-Nothing violence and rendered pithy dialogue: "Hello!! Red-neck—Seen any thing worth Shooting, up this way to day?" "No—nothing of any Count worth speaking of—Some of the Fellers racked out a 'Lager Beer' just now, and winged a few Dutch,—But I'm tired o' shooting Dutch and Irish, I am! If I don't kill something else soon, I'll spile!" *MHS*

Catholics in 1852–53 sought state funds for parochial education. Thomas Kerney, a Baltimore delegate and chairman of the education committee, introduced a bill that would have allowed commissioners to allocate to parochial schools "so much of the common School Fund as in their judgment may be just and reasonable." Quickly recognizing a no-win situation, members of the assembly tabled the measure in several consecutive sessions. Running quarrels over the Kerney bill poisoned relations between Protestants and Catholics, particularly since the numbers and political weight of Catholics were increasing with immigration. Few people recalled that in 1840 the Catholic clergy, seeking a fair solution, had seriously doubted whether introducing the Bible "as an ordinary class book into schools" would prove "beneficial to religion." One's position on the Kerney bill drew on deep beliefs and cultural identity. The bill gave free rein to the imagination. Opponents saw it as a "conspiracy against the diffusion of knowledge" and the dark design of a "foreign priesthood."[9] In the fall of 1854 the *Hagerstown Herald and Torch Light* fanned anti-Catholic sentiment by publishing a story about a nun who had "escaped" from the late Mother Seton's convent in Emmitsburg and whose accounts of abuse titillated readers. A crowd in Baltimore burned a papal emissary to American bishops in effigy. Friends of a mentally unstable priest took him by rail from Annapolis to a Baltimore hospital. Onlookers said that he had been kidnapped and held prisoner.

In the spring of 1853 nativists threw off their cloak of secrecy and got involved in politics, first as the Order of the Star Spangled Banner or Know-Nothings, then as affiliates of the countrywide American party. Members came out against the Kerney bill and in favor of the Maine Law—a temperance measure proposed in the assembly. The Know-Nothings drew on rural discontent over the pace and "morbid love" of change and the ballooning power of Baltimore; the *Worcester County Shield*, a Know-Nothing voice on the Eastern Shore, called the mid-1850s "this age of wild and reckless fanaticism" and referred sarcastically to "Beautiful Baltimore"—so "petted and pampered and indulged" that its citizens had begun to think of the city "as *all* Maryland." The new party organized under the banner Americans Shall Rule America. Charles Benedict Calvert, a Prince George's County Know-Nothing with distinguished bloodlines, wrote the *Port Tobacco Times* urging a movement to "bring back the government to its original purity."[10] Nativists did not have to be Anglo-Protestants with forebears like Josias Fendall or John Coode to participate in the soul-searching—or belong to the Protestant branch of the Carroll family, as did an active Know-Nothing publicist, Anna Ella Carroll. Friedrich Anspach, a Lutheran minister in western Maryland, published a number of nativist pamphlets in these years, the best known of which, *Sons of the Sires*, made an impassioned plea to the native-born to restore the republic of the Founding Fathers. Troubled Marylanders, many of them former Whigs but ex-Democrats in Baltimore as well, heeded the call. In the fall of 1855 Know-Nothings took control of the Baltimore city government, filled all the state judgeships up for bid, elected several state commissioners, gained the balance of power in the legislature, and won four of the six Maryland congressional seats.

On the subject of slavery, the state Know-Nothings tried to maintain the moderation that appealed to most Marylanders. Henry Winter Davis, now a congressman and Know-Nothing leader, told colleagues in Washington that "the way to settle the slavery question is to be silent on it." But events made silence impossible. Opening the Kansas territory to antislavery and proslavery elements in 1854—leaving slavery in the future state constitution to settlers to decide—Congress both had repealed the Missouri Compromise (prohibiting slavery north of Missouri and above its southern border to the west) and produced an orgy of frontier violence. With Kansas bleeding, politicians in Congress found it difficult to discuss much of anything peaceably. In May 1856 Preston Brooks assaulted and nearly killed Charles Sumner on the Senate floor. The Baltimore *Sun* decried both the abolitionist's "venomous invective" and the South Carolinian's brutal reprisal.[11]

The presidential election that year forecast the fate of moderation as crisis worsened. Maryland Know-Nothings supported the American party candidate, Millard Fillmore, an ex-president and former Whig, and his running mate, the Tennessean Andrew Jackson Donelson. Like the Whigs earlier, the American party split between supporters of the ticket and "North Americans" who thought both men soft on slavery. The only state Fillmore carried was Maryland. Once again without patronage hopes at the federal level, Maryland Know-Nothings faced a bleak future. Democrats won many votes in the state by running a Pennsylvanian who refused to condemn slavery, James Buchanan. His refusal cost him much Northern support and thus bolstered the new Republican party that was fundamentally hostile to Southern interests. Standing against slavery in the territories, favoring a high protective tariff, free land for homesteaders, and federal support of internal improvements like western railroads, Republicans protested that they would not touch slavery in the states below the Mason-Dixon Line and Ohio River. Yet not even Marylanders doubted that, in Republican hands, congressional power and presidential appointments could greatly undermine slaveownership and its way of life. In slaveholding Southern Maryland, Catholic enough to back away from the Know-Nothings anyhow, voters drifted toward the Democratic camp because it offered a more likely check on "Black Republicanism."

With the old parties in disarray, extremists and novices on both sides found opportunities for advancement, and when tempers were feverishly hot, inexperience could take a heavy toll. Maryland Know-Nothings proved a partial exception to the general rule. Most of them had never before run for public office, and once in the General Assembly might have abruptly passed laws, as one nativist proposed, outlawing Catholic convents as "priests' prisons for women."[12] Instead, Know-Nothings exercised restraint, as if the anti-Catholic rhetoric that had helped them win office embarrassed them once in power. At national conventions of the American party, in fact, Maryland Know-Nothings worked to define the enemy as immigrants rather than Catholics.

On the other hand, rowdyism at Baltimore polling places—instead of abating as the scions of the sires took control—grew worse. Whether the "enemy" was an Irish newcomer or an Irish Catholic, Know-Nothing appeals at election time encouraged intense public interest, attacks and counterattacks, and immense fraud. In October 1856 the Baltimore city elections produced pitched battles between Know-Nothings and Irish Democrats near

Monument and Calvert streets and at the Lexington Market. Besides throwing brickbats and swinging clubs, opposing sides pulled pistols and drove some voters to seek cover behind the white marble town-house steps that visitors found so beautiful. Four people died in the fray and at least fifty, in the words of a laconic physician, were injured "more or less dangerously."[13] To keep some kind of order during the later Fillmore-Buchanan contest, the Democratic governor, Thomas Watkins Ligon, placed militia units on alert and offered them to Thomas Swann, now the Know-Nothing mayor. Swann calculated the effects of an increased Democratic turnout and refused help. When the riot fully unfolded somebody started firing a cannon. Ten persons were killed and more than two hundred and fifty wounded. Mayor Swann took his own measures to keep peace during the two elections in the fall of 1857, which made up in stuffed ballot-boxes what they lacked in street violence.

⌁⌁⌁

Concern for order, locally and generally, mounted. Prominent Baltimore business and professional men, along with some clerks and skilled workers, formed a City Reform Association in 1858. Led by the established lawyer and slavery opponent George William Brown, reformers promoted change in the city police and fire departments. People in other parts of the state still looked with horror upon the metropolis; an Annapolis newspaper expressed "shame and disgust" at irregularities that cast a pall on every Baltimore election return.[14] Meanwhile Americans debated Chief Justice Taney's most famous and infamous decision, handed down the year before, declaring that a slave like Dred Scott did not escape his condition by being moved into free territory. The federal Constitution, Taney declared, never had contemplated black citizenship. Excoriated by abolitionists, Taney's majority decision did not comfort moderate Marylanders either, because it dismissed the old Missouri Compromise as unconstitutional in the first place—Congress had no power to prevent slaveholders from taking their human property anywhere they chose. How could one compromise without establishing a north-south line? Must every western territory undergo the bloodbath and then electioneering fraud that had made such a mess of Kansas?

Sectional suspicions grew darker and darker, and while arguments about escaping slaves and freeing blacks tended toward theory in Massachusetts or Alabama, in Maryland they could not have been more concrete. Having played a leading part in the effort to colonize freed blacks in the 1830s, Marylanders faced anew the question of the free black's place in society. One reason for the failure of colonization lay with the blacks themselves—they steadfastly refused to leave home. By 1850, more free blacks lived in Maryland than in any other state of the Union. In ten years the gap widened; the 1860 census counted almost 84,000 "free people of color" in Maryland (Virginia that year had 58,000, Pennsylvania 56,000). They lived all over, but were concentrated on the Eastern Shore and in Baltimore City. To encourage their departure, state and city legislation kept them out of jobs like policeman and steamboat captain and from fields like the militia, politics, and law.

Whites expected them to work at menial tasks, especially in the country. Caroline County offered an example of population shifts and rural labor demand that caused friction between free blacks and whites. From the first of the nineteenth century its black population had grown more than four times as fast as that of whites, while the percentage of blacks who were slaves had dropped from about 80 to 20. Meantime Eastern Shore farmers found it hard to interest free blacks in labor contracts that rewarded them with little more than "victuals and clothes" and assigned them the common agricultural and domestic work they had done as slaves. Blacks who did labor usually worked "Christmas to Christmas," living as a tenant on a landowner's farm, or performed seasonal work like harvesting crops; if women did not join the men in the fields they washed clothes or served as house maids.

At the same time a few free blacks in the country managed to prosper as skilled workers—some of them in shops, others as itinerants. A Talbot County free black earned a wide reputation as a shoemaker who also could build boats, wagons, and wheels. On the lower Eastern Shore free blacks worked as sawyers. In Chestertown and Cambridge the most successful butchers were free blacks. Until someone discovered a copy of Harriet Beecher Stowe's *Uncle Tom's Cabin* in his back room, a Salisbury free black managed to do very well as a shopkeeper. Captain Robert Henry of Pocomoke City became a successful shipowner and trader, carrying on business between Maryland and Virginia ports. To judge from white patronage, the most successful restaurants in Chestertown, Easton, and Princess Anne were those of free blacks, and when in 1845 the federal government opened a naval school at Fort Severn, Annapolis, the first chief steward there was a local black freeman. Elsewhere on the Western Shore free blacks had a hand in the hard work of ironmaking, blacksmithing, and farming. At Ellicott's Mills they made barrels and harness of noted quality.

Most conspicuous in Baltimore, free blacks and mulattoes found their position increasingly vulnerable in the 1850s. Twenty-five thousand of them lived there, more than in any other American city, and they had done much to build a society of their own. A few had attained some status as tobacconists, confectioners, grocers, or clothiers; one, Lewis Wells, was a physician. After 1847 Baltimore free blacks supported two Masonic lodges. Besides their African Methodist Episcopal churches—now numbering about fifteen—they had established two banks (with almost twenty-one thousand dollars on deposit) and more than thirty mutual aid or insurance societies. They also banded together in their residential patterns. Free blacks (and some slaves) formed backstreet neighborhoods in Fells Point and Old Town and to the west and southwest of the harbor; they bore ironic or tell-tale names like Happy Alley, Welcome Alley, Strawberry Alley, and Whiskey Alley.

Baltimore blacks provided evidence of community strength in this period by trying to place their children's schooling on a firm foundation. For many years outsiders had commented on the church sabbath schools and their seriousness of purpose; after a visit in 1847 a black Baptist minister from Virginia said he found the colored people of Baltimore "advanced in education, quite beyond what I had conceived of." Still, the sabbath schools left many gaps to be filled. In early 1850 the Reverend Moses Clayton, Nathaniel Peck, and Captain Daniel Myers and other black leaders dared to petition the mayor and council for part of the city's school allocations. Maryland law neither prohibited black education nor encouraged it; though Clayton and the others had the support of 126 whites who questioned why blacks should be taxed to support schools for whites only, the mayor and council abided by tradition and declined the request. Over the next decade black churches, the black Catholic Oblate Sisters of Providence, and some white friends—Methodists, Quakers, Presbyterians—managed to open fifteen schools for black children in Baltimore. That of William Watkins, who was self-taught except for some training with Daniel Coker, had the highest reputation: "He was strict," a former student remembered, "from the first letter in the alphabet to the last paragraph of the highest reader."[15]

All the while free blacks discovered their jobs shrinking as white immigrants forced their way into the Baltimore labor market. This process, begun in the 1830s, accelerated as the number of unskilled whites in the city increased and as skilled whites controlled certain occupations with guilds open to themselves alone. By the 1850s free blacks for so long had dominated barbering, blacksmithing, and carriage driving that whites avoided that work as "black." Free Negroes made slight advances during the decade in oystering, though perhaps not owning their own boats, and in bricklaying as Baltimoreans put up structures less likely to burn. Other work, earlier shared between white and black, gradually went to whites. City directories for 1860 listed far fewer free blacks than earlier as laborers, sawyers, washers, draymen, and the like. This process did not always occur peacefully, particularly after the economic downturn of 1857. In May of the next year whites attacked black workers in a Fells Point brickyard, shooting one. That summer fights between black caulkers and whites trying to "bust" the longtime Negro hold on those jobs grew vicious enough to force the closing of Skinner's shipyard. In June 1859 whites belligerently offered themselves as replacements for blacks on the city horse-drawn railway system—but only at a raise from $1.00 to $1.25 per day. Soon after, a mob attacked blacks at another shipyard. Thugs whom police took into custody later went free for lack of white witnesses. The *Sun* referred to a "reign of terror" on the Baltimore docks.[16]

These tensions did not improve with news of John Brown's raid on the Harpers Ferry federal arsenal that October. Brown's unlikely, even maniacal, plan was to arm Virginia slaves and begin a war to free all Southern bondsmen. His vision carried racial conflict to its hideous conclusion, and his force included several free blacks. Maryland militia units, some from Baltimore, gladly joined in capturing Brown. In the superheated atmosphere following the raid—with military companies forming in the state to repel madmen, keep order, and protect white families from racial holocaust—free blacks stood near the top of the suspected enemies list. Baltimore constables in December 1859 answered a call that a fight had broken out at the black caulkers' annual ball. What the police found after breaking in provided plenty of ammunition for the various white Marylanders who resented free blacks in a slave state. The caulkers had drawn a likeness of Brown on the ballroom floor and labeled it "The martyr—God bless him." Also on the floor were outlines of Virginia governor Henry A. Wise (who had seen to Brown's execution), "a huge Ethiopean" who apparently struck a menacing pose, and an inscription that the *Sun* described as "unfit for publication." Forty-nine blacks were arrested. Laws pertaining to the free Negro now received the full attention of authorities. The next year three blacks in Harford County were prosecuted for "being members of a secret association," violating a law of 1842. Police in Somerset County and Annapolis conducted searches for weapons among free blacks. Rural Marylanders believed free blacks and slaves had set house fires and tried to poison whites.[17]

Evidence that Maryland free blacks incited slaves to rebel or helped them to escape did not have to be enormous; protests to the contrary aside, slaveholders so near free territory were in good position to worry. Indeed, with Northern states, Pennsylvania among them, passing "personal liberty" laws in these years—statutes making recovery of fugitives legally difficult and expensive—Maryland slaveowners suffered directly from one of the celebrated complaints Southerners made while weighing the Union. The number of blacks who escaped slavery never was entirely clear. According to census figures 279 Maryland slaves fled the state between June 1849 and June 1850—though at least another 47 were captured and imprisoned in Baltimore. In the year before the 1860 census, Maryland fugitives numbered 115 (about as many as from Virginia and Kentucky), with another 70 caught and jailed in Baltimore alone.

Only a few incidents were needed to fuel fears that free blacks aided and abetted slave resistance. In July 1845 a gang of 30 or 40 Charles County slaves had gathered together and covered considerable distance (presumably with the help of District of Columbia free blacks) before armed whites overwhelmed them near Rockville. Whites held a meeting at Port Tobacco and gave free blacks there until 1 December to leave the county. In 1847 a gang of free blacks in Hagerstown tried to free fugitive slaves detained in the jail there. Six blacks near Cambridge were arrested in 1849 on charges of aiding escaped slaves. In 1857 a Baltimore court sentenced a free black to banishment from the state for the same offense.[18]

White Marylanders could not agree on what to do about the "free Negro problem" or slavery either. Though immigrants had little love for their free black competitors, many of them, in particular the Germans who fled political oppression after collapse of the 1848 revolution, abhorred slavery. Eastern Shore farmers continually complained during harvest season that free blacks could not be "induced to work," though many of these same people, former slaveholders, had helped bring on their predicament by acting on antislavery principles. Baltimore slaveowners knew that the abundance of free blacks dropped wages and thus made hiring out slaves less profitable. Partly for that reason Baltimore slaves had declined in number between 1850 and 1860, from almost 3,000 to 2,218. In fact, slavery in the state as a whole had continued its decline during that period, from 90,368 to 87,189. Alone of the slave states, Maryland had almost as many free as enslaved blacks. The tendency of the first group to grow larger and the second smaller caused white Marylanders anxiety, yet the economic feasibility of slavery remained a doubtful question. The price of tobacco reached a low point of 5¢ a pound in 1850 (it had been 20¢ in 1810), and Marylanders continued to discuss farm reform and new crops that meant using free labor. Some slaveholders sold their bondsmen to traders who sent them southward. Stories circulated of other planters who simply turned their backs while their slaves ran off. A Bel Air man claimed that poor farm prices left him glad that his slaves had escaped. John Giddings of Prince George's County gave his blacks food and directions to the Mason-Dixon Line.[19]

When the General Assembly convened in early 1860 it briefly considered restoring a simpler order with all blacks in some kind of bondage. Militant slaveholders and planters in need of dependable labor (petitions arrived from Cecil, Somerset, Anne Arundel, and St. Mary's counties) lobbied in favor of proposals that would have ended manumission, forbidden blacks from peddling, traveling, holding their own church services, or having their own schools, and punished some offenses—among them carrying books or papers of an "inflammatory character" and any crime for which a white went to prison—with slavery. Unless free blacks found regular jobs, local commissioners would assign them masters under terms that involved renewable contracts and amounted to peonage. Since by Taney's dictum free blacks could not be citizens, the state, some legislators argued, had an obligation to "restrain their freedom and make them useful and subordinate laborers." "Free-negroism thoughout this State must be abolished," declared Curtis W. Jacobs in defense of the bill that finally emerged from his House of Delegates committee on "the Free Colored Population." He aimed to force his colleagues to decide whether Maryland would be a Southern state "or whether she shall go into the arms of the abolitionists." Significantly, the Jacobs bill passed the assembly as a referendum, to be decided in the counties of Southern Maryland and the Eastern Shore alone. Also significantly, voters there turned it down. The plan would have put the "evil example" of freed blacks in the slave quarters. It would have saddled slaveholders with slavery.[20]

∽∾∾

This curious referendum helped prepare Marylanders for the decision the country faced in the November presidential election. Democrats split. At the regular Charleston convention they nominated John Breckinridge, the choice of proslavery, positive-protection-of-slavery Southern Democrats; another faction, meeting in Baltimore at the Front Street Theater (where the main floor caved in), offered voters Stephen A. Douglas. On the Kansas-Nebraska formula, Douglas wished to leave slavery to future territorial voters. The Republican party—its slogan "Free Soil, Free Labor, and Free Land"— mustered small numbers in Frederick and Carroll counties and claimed support among pro-tariff Allegany County workers, except the Irish. Baltimore German immigrants applauded the Republican plank against slavery in the territories. Yet Lincoln had little hope of success in Maryland. The Free Soilers, Republican forebears, had won only 21 Baltimore votes in the 1852 presidential election; in 1856 the Republican candidate John Frémont had captured a mere 214. To help organize the House of Representatives in early 1860, Henry Winter Davis, who first and last despised Democrats, had cast a deciding vote for a Republican, William Pennington of New Jersey. At home that decision won him burning in effigy and obtained assembly resolutions condemning him. Miners in Pompey Smash raised what they believed was the first Lincoln campaign pole below the Mason-Dixon Line; someone cut it down, and after the Lincoln Club president put it back up, he had to stand guard over it with a shotgun. In places support of the Republicans made one an abolitionist. A Charles County Republican, believing he could deliver 15 or 20 Lincoln votes there, vowed to stand firm "although," he said, "it may cost me my life."[21]

Workingmen in Baltimore, so many of them loyal Democrats, made life miserable for Republicans. In May of the election year, Montgomery Blair, a Missouri-born, moderate Republican leader, left his Silver Spring estate to make a speech in Baltimore. He had to contend with a howling mob. When the Germans staged rallies, opponents pounded them with stones, garbage, and eggs. Thick-skinned Republicans formed a chapter of the party's Wide Awakes, whose active members marched to rallies wearing green capes and slate-colored caps with red trim. One night during the campaign the Wide Awakes staged a torchlight procession that wound up at the Holliday Street Theater. Democrats and various rowdies, having waited in the galleries, drowned every Republican speaker in a chorus of groans, bahs, coughs, wheezes, and sneezes. A Wide Awake leader who visited the gallery to call for quiet was thrown down the stairs. By the time police arrived, the meeting had become a brawl and someone had mounted the stage armed with a pistol. Another open Republican in Baltimore, the hapless abolitionist William Gunnison, suffered like an early Christian martyr; "the presence of ladies alone," wrote an unfriendly paper of an assault made upon him, "spared him the application of boots and shoes to that point of the human anatomy where kicks 'Hurt honor more than twice two thousand kicks before.' "[22]

Marylanders by and large wanted both to uphold Southern rights and to hold the Union together. Their choice narrowed to the Democrat Breckinridge and yet another ticket that formed in the state itself—at a "Constitutional Union" convention held at the First Presbyterian Church in Baltimore during May 1860. The new party, combining old Whigs and Know-Nothings in an uncertain alliance, nominated John Bell, a pro-Union Tennessean, for president and a Massachusetts conservative, Edward Everett, for vice-president. Bell and Everett sought to unite moderates throughout the country. Western Marylanders and leading Baltimoreans welcomed their appeal. The Cumberland *Civilian & Telegraph* endorsed the Constitutional Union party. Brantz Mayer, lawyer and man of letters, voiced the now-familiar cry that differences over slavery were false alarms, "political bugabooes, that are as harmless and hollow as ghosts manufactured out of sheets and pumpkins." John Pendleton Kennedy, who earlier in the decade had served well as Fillmore's secretary of the navy and then had withdrawn from politics, wrote an English friend that slavery agitation represented a political "trick," a sentiment others in the makeshift party echoed. Kennedy came out of retirement at Mount Vernon Place to speak for Bell. Constitutional Union men avoided discussing sectional issues, pointing out instead the value of steadiness, the rule of law, the protections contained for both sides in the Constitution. They warned of the radical drift of Breckinridge's platform. Frederick newspapers referred to Breckinridge men as "seceders"; the Baltimore *American* noted "the rampant and controlling spirit of disunion" as being "a distinguishing feature of his supporters."[23]

Though in the state Breckinridge's Democracy carried the taint of secessionist threats, his candidacy also defended rights that many Southern and Eastern Shore Marylanders—as possible slaveholders in the west—might wish to exercise, or that they held inviolable given their view of the compact Americans had entered into in 1789. A Montgomery County paper expressed "abhorrence" at the unwillingness of Bell to speak "upon this most vital and all-important question of slavery in the territories." For many months before the election the *Sun* refuted the charge that Southern rights stood for aggressiveness or radicalism. Lovers of the Union, wrote *Sun* editors, should ask themselves not whether the South would secede, but when the arrogant North would recede—give up its hostile designs on Southern property. "Maryland Must and Will Be True to the South," read a hopeful banner painted for a Breckinridge meeting in Monument Square.[24]

Unfortunately the November elections settled nothing. Lincoln won more

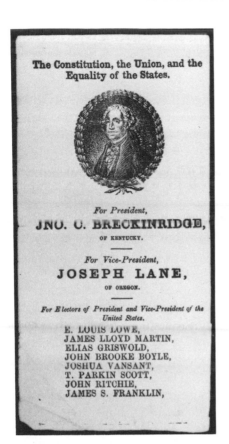

The Constitution, the Union, and the
Equality of the States.

For President,
JNO. C. BRECKINRIDGE,
OF KENTUCKY.

For Vice-President,
JOSEPH LANE,
OF OREGON.

For Electors of President and Vice-President of the
United States.

E. LOUIS LOWE,
JAMES LLOYD MARTIN,
ELIAS GRISWOLD,
JOHN BROOKE BOYLE,
JOSHUA VANSANT,
T. PARKIN SCOTT,
JOHN RITCHIE,
JAMES S. FRANKLIN,

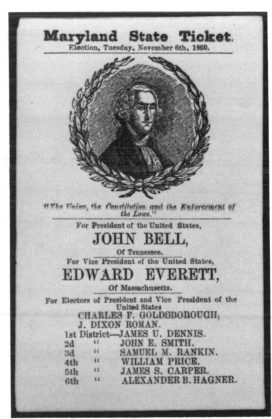

Maryland State Ticket.
Election, Tuesday, November 6th, 1860.

"The Union, the Constitution, and the Enforcement of
the Laws."

For President of the United States.
JOHN BELL,
Of Tennessee.
For Vice President of the United States,
EDWARD EVERETT,
Of Massachusetts.
For Electors of President and Vice President of the
United States
CHARLES F. GOLDSBOROUGH,
J. DIXON ROMAN.
1st District—JAMES U. DENNIS.
2d   "   JOHN E. SMITH.
3d   "   SAMUEL M. RANKIN.
4th   "   WILLIAM PRICE.
5th   "   JAMES S. CARPER.
6th   "   ALEXANDER B. HAGNER.

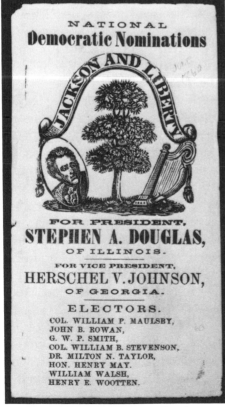

NATIONAL
Democratic Nominations

JACKSON AND LIBERTY

FOR PRESIDENT,
STEPHEN A. DOUGLAS,
OF ILLINOIS.
FOR VICE PRESIDENT,
HERSCHEL V. JOHNSON,
OF GEORGIA.
ELECTORS.
COL. WILLIAM P. MAULSBY,
JOHN B. ROWAN,
G. W. P. SMITH,
COL. WILLIAM B. STEVENSON,
DR. MILTON N. TAYLOR,
HON. HENRY MAY.
WILLIAM WALSH,
HENRY E. WOOTTEN.

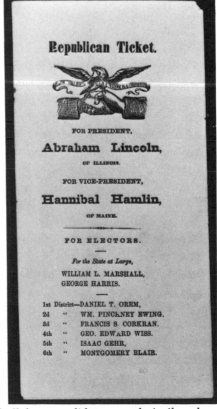

Republican Ticket.

FOR PRESIDENT,
Abraham Lincoln,
OF ILLINOIS.

FOR VICE-PRESIDENT,
Hannibal Hamlin,
OF MAINE.

FOR ELECTORS.

For the State at Large,
WILLIAM L. MARSHALL,
GEORGE HARRIS.

1st District—DANIEL T. OREM.
2d   "   WM. PINCKNEY EWING.
3d   "   FRANCIS S. CORKRAN.
4th   "   GEO. EDWARD WISS.
5th   "   ISAAC GEHR.
6th   "   MONTGOMERY BLAIR.

Election tickets, 1860. Maryland supporters of all four candidates used similar slogans and symbols in avowing loyalty to Constitution, Union, and liberty. *MHS* than five hundred votes in Allegany County, over a hundred in Cecil and Frederick, and about a thousand in Baltimore City. Douglas strength followed the same pattern, with Washington, Carroll, and Baltimore counties added. Bell and Everett carried 47 percent of the vote outside Baltimore City and all the counties except Talbot and Worcester east of the bay and St. Mary's, Charles, and Prince George's on the Western Shore. Breckinridge nonetheless ran a close second in all the counties except those with Lincoln-Douglas leanings. Democrats in Baltimore City, having successfully identified themselves with electoral and police reform, carried the day by over two thousand votes. The total Maryland popular vote thus went to Breckinridge by six-tenths of a percentage point. Badly divided in selecting a new president, Marylanders had objected overwhelmingly to "black Republicanism." Nearly half of them had supported as their first choice a kindly old statesman who seemed to hope that the political weather might someday clear. Soon that hope seemed terribly forlorn. Between December and early 1861 the states from South Carolina to Texas seceded, calling on Marylanders to make another choice, this one between staying in or leaving the Union that now had a Republican in its highest office.

The quarrel over Maryland secession began as soon as Lincoln's election became clear, and it engaged a full range of reason, emotion, and prayer. "May God in his mercy avert the dangers" that impend "so threateningly," prayed the Frederick *Herald* in mid-November. Shortly afterward Presbyterians in Baltimore held a large "Union prayer meeting." Newspapers like the *Centreville Advocate* and *Patapsco Enterprise* argued in favor of secession. In December, after the secession of South Carolina, some Baltimoreans hung the Palmetto flag out their windows. "Southern Volunteers" formed in Baltimore, while a Reisterstown company adopted the blue cockade that signified Southern rights. A Harford County militia unit wrote the governor, Thomas Holliday Hicks, begging to be mobilized against the "Black Republican hordes of the North." Newspapers overflowed with opinion: some Marylanders favored armed neutrality, others economic reprisals against the North, others a strengthened fugitive slave law as the price of keeping the state in the Union. Pro-Union feeling grew more vocal with news that more states had followed South Carolina's lead. In January Union men staged rallies in Frederick, Baltimore, and Cumberland. George William Brown, now Baltimore mayor, left no doubt that in his opinion state policy ought to be adherence to the Union. Henry Winter Davis, remaining unpopular at home as one who was willing to deal with the incoming Republicans, played a large role in congressional efforts to find a sectional compromise, at one point suggesting admission of New Mexico as a slave and Kansas as a free state.[25]

The Union or secession issue involved procedure that bogged down revolution and focused attention sharply on one man. If Maryland were to withdraw from the Union, the decision would require a convention elected for the purpose. Only the General Assembly could call such an election, and the legislature, convening every other year under the 1851 constitution, was not due to meet until 1862. Everyone watched to see whether the governor would call a special session. Nothing could properly have prepared Hicks for this crisis, but to many observers he cast an unusually small shadow. Son of a Dorchester County planter, he had risen slowly as county sheriff and member of the House of Delegates. He had gained a reputation in the state for talking seriously now and again of Eastern Shore secession. In 1857, when it was the turn of the Eastern Shore to supply the executive, he had won the governorship as a Know-Nothing. Now Hicks claimed to know of a plot to take the state out of the Union if the assembly met. Plot or not, the Democratic legislature in 1860 had resolved, "if the hour ever arrive when the Union must be dissolved," to cast Maryland's "lot with her sister states of the South and abide their fortune to the fullest extent." It was no secret that counties where Breckinridge had polled well still enjoyed heavy representation in the assembly. The Speaker of the House of Delegates, Elbridge G. Kilbourn of Anne Arundel, had openly sided with the seceded states. Kilbourn commented that the situation was too serious to allow the governor to go it alone.[26]

Hicks faced his duty ruefully and cautiously. Though sympathizing with the South as a critic of personal liberty laws, he counted himself a strong Union man and furthermore doubted the wisdom or workability of secession. In late November 1860 he had announced a wait-and-see policy; nothing, he wrote the month following, should be done before the people had time to reflect. As pressure mounted, Hicks's resolve seemed to strengthen. True to his Eastern Shore and small-state heritage, he hated above all things to be bullied. South Carolina, Alabama, and Mississippi sent letters or emissaries urging the governor and Maryland to act. Hicks reportedly said that disunion remedied no wrongs done the South "and Maryland should not seem to give countenance to it by convening her legislature at the bidding of South Carolina." When in January 1861 Mississippi departed the Union, he noted on the back of the envelope that had brought him the telegraphed news, "Mississippi has seceded and gone to the devil."[27]

The governor continued his balancing act throughout the early months of 1861 while excitement, war fever, and rumors filled the air. A gathering of citizens disgusted with the governor's inaction met in Baltimore in February and again in March, threatening to call an extralegal convention to debate secession. Meantime Hicks, on his own power, appointed a committee of Marylanders—Reverdy Johnson, Augustus W. Bradford, Benjamin Chew Howard, John T. Dent, John W. Crisfield, William T. Goldsborough, and J. Dixon Roman—to attend a conference that opened 4 February at the Willard Hotel in Washington. There border-state and Northern moderates made a desperate attempt to formulate a sectional compromise. The nationalism that gloried in the defense of Fort McHenry provided Hicks with emotional leverage in these highly charged circumstances. He told a delegation from Talbot County that secessionists in the District of Columbia had poised themselves to take over Washington City should Maryland move. Wavering Marylanders must have agreed with the governor that the prospect of an isolated and pillaged federal capital was shocking and unacceptable. Lincoln's necessary rail passage through Baltimore in late February gave rise to plenty of whispered rumors of a kidnapping or assassination, though no one ever produced the names of the supposed conspirators. A Maryland woman wrote the governor of a plan she had been told about involving three thousand men who were determined to prevent Lincoln from taking office. The Baltimore City Guards planned to take part in the military parade at Lincoln's inauguration. A reporter for the *New York Tribune*, hoping that General in Chief Winfield Scott would "assign them a proper place" if they did, described the guards' sympathies as "fully understood."[28]

Despite the conciliatory tone of the president's address on 4 March, the practical problem of handling federal garrisons within the seceded South offered scant room for compromise or delay, and in mid-April, when South Carolinians fired on Fort Sumter and Lincoln called on the states to gather seventy-five thousand troops to put down the rebellion, Marylanders faced the most difficult question yet placed before them: whether to arm themselves and force fellow Americans to remain in the Union, whether to cooperate at all in the war against Southern independence. Having expressed scruples against Union-by-coercion, Hicks found himself tottering. Military units sporting the blue cockade, fired by action in Charleston, waited menacingly for the state to secede. Enough Baltimoreans demonstrated against answering the president's call that Hicks felt compelled to visit the city and see for himself. On 17 April he traveled to Washington to confer with Lincoln and his highest aides, advising them against pressing the troop request and warning them of the tinderbox that was Baltimore—through which Lincoln's army presumably would pass. Later that day the secretary of war sent Hicks written assurances that the administration would employ Maryland soldiers only to defend federal property within state boundaries and to protect Washington. On 18 April the governor issued a plea for calm, assured citizens that any federal force passing through the state would be directed only to the defense of the capital, and promised in the pending congressional elections to listen to the voice of Maryland on the issue of Union or secession. The next day, staying with Mayor Brown in Baltimore, Hicks had begun drafting the Maryland muster order when the public voice reached him from the streets.

The riot of 19 April eventually became legendary. At about 11 A.M. the 6th regiment of Massachusetts volunteers arrived from Philadelphia at the President Street Station. The troops then proceeded by single horse-drawn cars along Pratt Street to the B&O station for the trip to Washington. Most of the

"Passage through Baltimore." Etching by Adalbert Volck, 1861. Allan Pinkerton's agents recommended that President-elect Lincoln slip through divided Baltimore in the dead of night, thus prompting Volck to pick up his poison pen.
MHS

seven hundred men had made it, hazarding shouts and stones, when some bystanders dumped a cartload of sand and threw some anchors on the tracks ahead of the last few cars, halting them and turning them back. Soon afterward Mayor Brown, demonstrating the new official attitude toward disorder in Baltimore, arrived on the scene and ordered the debris cleared. Brown next met the last companies of troops running up Pratt Street, pursued by a mob throwing cobblestones at the "invaders," screaming insults, and firing an occasional pistol shot. For a time the mayor rode at the head of the men in an effort to safeguard their passage. "The soldiers bore the pelting of the

"The Sixth Massachusetts Regiment Repelling the Attack of the Mob in Pratt Street, Baltimore, April 19, 1861." Wood engraving from *Frank Leslie's Illustrated Newspaper,* May 1861. *Peale Museum, Baltimore City Life Museums*

pitiless mob for a long time under a full trot," an eyewitness wrote, "& more than three of them were knocked & shot down, before they returned the assaults."[29]

When the troops returned fire all hell broke loose, as many bystanders as rioters falling in the melée. Marshal George Kane—head of the Baltimore constabulary that the assembly in 1860 had placed under control of a state commission—finally managed to form a police line at the rear of the troops and hold the mob at bay. The soldiers left for Washington, shooting out the windows of their cars. Four soldiers and twelve Baltimoreans lay dead, and scores were injured, the first real bloodshed of the Civil War. At an afternoon rally in Monument Square both Brown and Hicks (the governor fearing for his life) appealed for peace. Aiming to prevent troop movements and further bloodshed, the mayor and police board—either with Hicks's permission or with his acquiescence—directed Kane and militia units to burn railroad bridges north of the city. One junior officer at Fort McHenry, expecting attack, threatened to train his guns on the Washington Monument. If you do, a representative from the city replied, "there will be nothing left of you but your brass buttons to tell who you were."[30]

Lincoln agreed to defuse the situation and wait for tempers to cool; he and

Maryland leaders, among them the president of the B&O, John W. Garrett, struck a deal whereby federal troops bound for Washington would bypass volatile Baltimore, steaming from Havre de Grace to the naval school and then proceeding by branch lines to the capital. A Pennsylvania regiment turned about at Cockeysville and left for the border. But in these critical days the administration could ill afford to temporize for long. As soon as sufficient troops arrived in Washington to defend the city, General Scott promised, he would assign ten thousand men to hold Baltimore and secure the rails and bridges above the city. On 22 April General Benjamin F. Butler landed a force at Annapolis and began repairing the Annapolis and Elkridge Railroad, which its directors had begun to tear up to prevent its military use. Butler cleverly offered to help put down the local slave uprising that rumors described as imminent. While helpless to slow the growing federal presence, Hicks rejected the offer as unnecessary. Later, when Butler occupied the Relay House B&O station, just seven miles from Baltimore, he issued an ultimatum based on the belief that a Maryland farmer had poisoned one of his men. The general declared he could put an armed soldier in every household he chose.

Squeamish about forcing the South to return to the Union, perhaps realizing that events were beyond one person's power to control, Hicks on Monday, 22 April, called a special session of the General Assembly for Friday of that week. Northern commentary, until then complimentary toward the Maryland governor, wrote him off as a secessionist pawn. The Lincoln administration quietly planned every necessary measure, including "the bombardment of their cities," should legislators vote to arm against the Union.[31] In these perilous circumstances one might have expected a referendum or test of the public will. Actually voters filled only a few places according to prevailing sentiment—one seat in Washington County and nine places in Baltimore (the assembly earlier had vacated them by reason of fraud). A "States Rights and Southern Rights" gathering in Baltimore nominated candidates, including Severn Teackle Wallis and Ross Winans, who ran unopposed; the western seat went without opposition to Lewis P. Fiery, a strong Union man. With Butler in Anne Arundel County, Hicks decided to convene the assembly in the Frederick Courthouse, where—students of his motives reflected—lawmakers would not be surrounded by Union troops but would sit in the midst of Union sympathizers.

Most Marylanders probably wanted to be left alone. State government, roughly reflecting that wish, appeared paralyzed. Neither the governor nor the assembly found any decisive course appealing. A hand-carried invitation from Virginia to join the Confederacy got a cold reception. The senate published resolutions denying its authority to decide the secession question. Hicks in his address wanted neither league with the seceded South nor any active Maryland role in invading another state—and no passage through

Maryland of forces with that hostile intent. A memorial to the House of Delegates from Prince George's County called for immediate secession, but the delegates demurred, again for lack of authority. A few outright secessionists, Coleman Yellott of Baltimore among them, spoke of calling a convention to consider leaving the Union. Yellott, who had commissioned a steamboat to bring Eastern Shore legislators across the bay, introduced a bill for the "public safety" that would have created a commission to stand above the governor, prepared the militia for defense of the state, and presumably taken Maryland into the Confederacy. His bill went down to defeat—not even Wallis supported it—on grounds that it threatened "a Military Despotism." At the same time delegates turned down a request to reopen rail links to the North; repaired, legislators agreed, they would invite the invasion of "fanatical and excited multitudes, whose animosity to Baltimore and Maryland is measured by no standard known to Christian civilization." Resolutions authorized a commission to Lincoln protesting Maryland's treatment as "a conquered province."[32]

The assembly adjourned, and finally geography, economy, old patriotism, and the harsh reality of military law combined to keep Maryland officially in the Union camp. The events of 19 April both demonstrated and spent anger; the hostility of the mob may have had as much to do with transgressed neutrality—being bullied—as with support for Jeff Davis's government. Gradually, as usual, a reaction to the violence set in. On the twenty-eighth, the commander at Fort McHenry reported that a sailing ship had passed down the Patapsco freighted with men cheering his garrison and flying the Union colors stem to stern. Pro-Union Marylanders staged a convention in Baltimore on 2 May, planning to organize a party around loyalism. The destroyed railroad bridges did such harm to the local economy that there was talk of food shortages in Baltimore. They underwent repairs.

John Pendleton Kennedy, who earlier had tried to chart a course for all the border states in the crisis, next published a masterful pamphlet arguing strongly against Maryland secession on the basis of self-interest. The free-trade policy planned for the Confederacy would ruin Maryland manufactures, he wrote. Direct Confederate taxes on populous Maryland would multiply its existing tax burden as much as twelve times. Out of the Confederacy Maryland might lie vulnerable to a Southern blockade of Capes Henry and Charles, he said, but the United States could do the same to a Confederate Maryland and shut off commerce with Ohio and Pennsylvania as well. Though historically tied to Virginia, Maryland still had to decide its own course and should realize that its future truly lay not with stagnant eastern Virginia but with growing western Virginia. Kennedy also noted, as had Hicks and other Marylanders, that the state had no defensible northern frontier. Confederate Maryland would be the first region to be swept by recurrent war—and would lie on a boundary as unfriendly to slavery as Canada's. Widely circulated, this *Appeal to Maryland* doubtless had an impact on the popular will. "Maryland has no cause to desert our honored Stars and Stripes," wrote Kennedy. "Out of this Union there is nothing but ruin for her." [33]

❧

Clinching the question, Lincoln used military power to quell disorder, restore links between Washington and the North, and keep Maryland beyond the reach of would-be secessionists. On 27 April he directed Scott and his subordinates to suspend the writ of habeas corpus anywhere along a line between Washington and Philadelphia where federal officers met resistance. Without precedent, this measure enabled the military to seize and hold indefinitely anyone suspected of disloyalty. On the rainy night of 13 May General Butler quietly entered Baltimore and occupied Federal Hill, and thereafter he and his successors employed their authority to considerable effect. Much of it bore directly on the war and the eagerness of many Marylanders—whom Butler described as "malignant and traitorous"—to contribute to the Confederate cause. Butler seized twenty-seven hundred muskets, ammunition, and other stores he had reason to believe were headed southward. He closed shops he suspected of manufacturing Confederate military supplies, outlawed unsanctioned assemblies, and forbade display of the Bonnie Blue Flag. Federal officers arrested known Confederate recruiters. Shortly after Butler's arrival old Ross Winans, who in 1859 had made four thousand pikes to be used against abolitionists, landed in jail partly for building a steam-powered, four-wheeled cannon that he tried to get through Union lines to Harpers Ferry (federal troops found it unreliable). Though Winans on 16 May took the prescribed oath "not openly or covertly [to] commit any act of hostility against the Government of the United States," his reputation remained with him. Union authorities later considered hunting in a Baltimore convent for the "Winans cache" that according to rumor lay hidden there, ready for an uprising of Confederate sympathizers. [34]

Over the summer of 1861 the hand of the federal government fell firmly on the shoulders of Marylanders. Troops encamped in Patterson Park and on the railroad avenues into the city. Soldiers on Federal Hill, overlooking what a Union officer called a neighborhood "rank with disunion," dug fortifications and planted cannon that could reach three-fourths of the city. Federals began improvements on Fort McHenry, which had few defenses on its land side. Military engineers surmised that the McKim mansion and Potter's Race Course, both in east Baltimore, needed entrenchments and troops. Both places commanded the 8th ward, "one of the most disloyal in the city." Murray Hill to the north and on West Baltimore Street the home of George Hume Steuart also assumed strategic value (Steuart, a pro-Confederate with long service in the Maryland militia, had fled to Charlottesville, Virginia; in April his son had resigned from the army and embraced the Confederacy). By August more than forty-six hundred Union soldiers had taken up positions in Baltimore. Others in the military Department of Maryland occupied Annapolis, defended Relay House and the railroad to Washington, and were headquartered at Cockeysville and Havre de Grace to safeguard the railroads to York and Philadelphia. Federal troops encamped in Cumberland, Williamsport, and other points along the C&O Canal. Union commanders continually requested more men, estimating the number needed in and around Baltimore at seven thousand and describing the city as an excellent place to break in raw recruits.[35]

Union men and women were happy to have order at last, but there was no mistaking the weight or character of federal power. Mid-June congressional elections in Baltimore corresponded with the arrival of General Nathaniel P. Banks—a Massachusetts Republican, former Speaker of the House of Representatives and state governor—who had steeled himself for any challenge. He assured Mayor Brown that no Union soldiers would be permitted to leave their posts or otherwise interfere with the election, that he had confidence in the Baltimore police "to suppress ordinary election tumults." He also had his men armed with forty rounds each and prepared to march instantly; he ordered liquor stores closed and warned Brown that if the people took advantage of the situation "to organize anarchy and overthrow all forms of government," responsibility for whatever resulted would be theirs alone. Before departing in July he brought some of his troops in from the countryside so as to exercise a "moral effect upon the disaffected inhabitants of the city." Marylanders who voted returned a pro-Union delegation to Congress.[36]

Banks's replacement, John A. Dix, approached his duties with puritan pleasure. A New Hampshire native who in the 1820s had studied law with William Wirt, Dix had no doubt that since 1812 Baltimore domestic violence had been the worst in the Union. "A city so prone to burst out into flame, and thus become dangerous to its neighbors," he later wrote, "should be controlled by the strong arm of the government wherever these paroxysms of excitement occur." Dix extended the crusade against secessionist flags and paraphernalia to the latest Confederate colors, red and white—their appearance together, he said, was provocative. Amused Baltimoreans issued a mock bulletin in the name of "His Majesty (Abraham 1st)," requiring all persons having red hair and moustaches to have one side or the other dyed blue. One stanza of a song celebrating "Dix's Manifesto" went: "On Barber's pole, and mint stick / He did his veto place / He swore that in his city / He'd red and white erase."[37]

"In times of civil strife," read an earnest War Department order of the day, "errors, if any, should be on the side of the safety of the country." The Lincoln administration left considerable room for discretionary power among its friends and little for dissent, doubt, or even indifference among others. Baltimore police, by reports reaching General Scott, had discouraged citizens from greeting Union troops with food and water. Banks ordered Marshal Kane arrested on 27 June; several days later, at four in the morning, Union troops seized all four members of the city police board and put them in cells at Fort McHenry without specifying charges against them. Afterward the city lay under the authority of provost marshals. Military forces seized former governor Thomas G. Pratt early in the summer, Judge Richard Henry Alvey of Hagerstown (he opposed coercion of the South), and Baltimore Congressman Henry May, who favored peace negotiations with the Confederacy. In the fall, as the assembly prepared to reconvene, the army arrested twenty-six suspicious or pro-secession legislators—Winans (again), Wallis, and Kilbourn among them. The clerks of the house and senate went to Fort McHenry. Pinkerton secret service agents jailed the editors of two newspapers devoted to Maryland secession: Frank Key Howard (grandson of Francis Scott Key) and William Wilkins Glenn of the Baltimore *Daily Exchange* and Thomas W. Hall of the *South*. After also arresting Mayor Brown in a dispute over payment of Baltimore police during federal occupation, Dix complained in September that Fort McHenry had grown so crowded with prisoners that one cell had twenty people in it. So many disloyalists had been placed in tents on the drill field that there was "hardly room left for the guard to parade."[38]

Whatever the value of Lincoln's object, saving the Union, these means led to serious questions and earlier had produced a dramatic confrontation between the president and the Maryland native, then eighty-four, who sat as federal chief justice. The protagonist was John Merryman, a Baltimore County Democrat who in 1861 was president of the Maryland Agricultural Society and an officer in a local militia unit that under orders had helped break Baltimore's rail links after the 19 April riot. For that act federal troops arrested him in May. Merryman's friends quickly obtained a hearing with Chief Justice Taney in his capacity as judge on the federal circuit court for Maryland. Taney had issued a writ of habeas corpus, calling on the commander holding Merryman at Fort McHenry to bring him to court on 27 May and explain the reasons, if any, for his imprisonment. Though Taney feared his own arrest, he believed it important to defend the rule of law against arbitrary authority, even in perilous times. "I am an old man, a very old man," Taney had said to his friend the mayor, "but perhaps I was preserved for this occasion."[39]

At the appointed hour a blue-coated officer with red sash appeared in Baltimore federal court and handed the chief justice a paper. It announced that authorities suspected Merryman of treason and repeated that they, under presidential power, had set aside the habeas corpus protection. Taney ordered the Union general, George Cadwalader, to appear in court the next day, but there was scant hope he would obey and none of compelling him. The chief justice then wrote Lincoln an opinion that amounted to a lecture: the president assumed a power that the Constitution granted not to him but to the Congress; military officers had no right to arrest anyone not subject to army discipline except by judicial order. If the executive and the military

Baltimore from Fort Federal Hill. Photograph probably taken in September 1862, when Union troops had fortified the position Butler secured in the spring of 1861. *Peale Museum, Baltimore City Life Museums*

Roger Brooke Taney (1777–1864), the chief justice who, in his last, sad years, defied President Lincoln in the belief that no circumstances set aside constitutional safeguards. *MHS*

usurped such power, Taney declared with stirring choice of words, "the people of the United States are no longer living under a government of laws, but every citizen holds life, liberty, and property at the will and pleasure of the army officer in whose military district he may happen to be found."[40]

Dix's rule, like Lincoln's presidency, exhibited some latitude and humanity under the circumstances. Dix demanded proof of a person's alleged disloyalty and discharged some prisoners on insufficient evidence. He advised Union troops not to assume that Marylanders carrying shotguns on a "sporting excursion" were rebel soldiers. He did not use troops to search private homes and declined a request from Harford County that the army administer loyalty oaths at polling places. A few Confederate sympathizers Dix kept in perspective. One exotic war prisoner was Richard Thomas, who called himself "Zarvona" and who became known as "the French Lady" for his part (bustled and petticoated) in capturing a steamboat and sailing it into Confederate waters. After capturing "Zarvona" on another escapade, Dix eventually paroled him as a small man, "crack-brained," whose danger related directly to his stature.[41]

Still, no one could mistake the folly of open opposition to the federal government. Lincoln had made no reply to Taney's defense of civil liberties in *Ex parte Merryman*. The arrests continued. Perhaps the most abusive of them involved Richard Bennett Carmichael, a state circuit court judge for Talbot, Queen Anne's, and Kent counties. Objecting bitterly to arbitrary arrests on the Eastern Shore, Carmichael instructed grand juries to indict anyone making or abetting them. Late in 1861 Secretary of State William Seward ordered Dix to arrest Carmichael. Dix described Carmichael's courtroom statements as "inflammatory" and "insulting" to the federal government but postponed action on the advice of Eastern Shore Unionists who feared that more harm than good would come from forcibly quieting the judge. When a bill came down against Dix's deputy provost marshal for the Eastern Shore, Dix wrote Augustus Bradford, newly elected governor (and father of a Confederate officer), that Carmichael was a dishonor to the state. Finally, in late May 1862, federal troops entered Carmichael's court at Easton and literally pulled him off the bench. When Carmichael kicked back, he was pistol-whipped into submission. First taken to Fort McHenry, the judge spent six months in prison with no charges ever filed against him. Except for the staunchest supporters of the Union cause, Marylanders found Carmichael's arrest, as much the manner as the deed itself, appalling.[42]

A Maryland native in Louisiana, James Ryder Randall, wrote a poetic protest to all these attempts at military control, "My Maryland," and Baltimoreans set it to music. The song became popular among all Southern soldiers. James J. Archer, a Marylander who as a Confederate general later fell at Gettysburg, conveyed home the same sentiments. "Our Maryland is throttled," he wrote sadly. "Every day I see her across the Potomac—the armed heel of the disgusting despot trampling upon her bosom."[43]

Militarily nothing had been settled in May 1862. Since early spring elusive Confederate foot soldiers under Stonewall Jackson and Richard S. Ewell had struggled with Union forces for control of the Shenandoah Valley, one avenue into the Confederacy. The federals held onto outposts at Strasburg and Front Royal. John R. Kenly, a Baltimore native who briefly had been provost marshal in that city, commanded the Union detachment near Front Royal. His regiment, the 1st Maryland, provided the main line of defense. Beginning a thrust designed to tie down as many Union troops as possible, Jackson late in May left his encampments at New Market and Luray and headed north. His movements typically escaped the notice of federal officers, whose cavalry remained wanting, and on 23 May the head of his column of about ten thousand men approached the unwary defenders of Front Royal. To deliver his surprise (and without knowing who his adversaries were), Jackson chose another 1st Maryland, led by Bradley T. Johnson of Frederick. Rarely, even in a conflict that pitted many a brother against brother, did men from the same state face each other in combat.

The skirmish that day did not decide much, but it was sharp, and celebrated at the time. Kenly's men delayed the Confederate advance as long as possible, spreading themselves thin to cover the two roads and pair of bridges to their rear. Jackson, who did not bestow lavish praise, reported that against this "spirited resistance" the Confederate Marylanders "pushed forward in gallant style." After several hours the larger Confederate force prevailed. Union troops withdrew across the bridges in good order until Southern cavalry broke through and spread havoc among them. Severely wounded, Kenly was captured along with more than five hundred of the federal 1st Maryland and most of their stores.[44]

Fugitives who made it to Williamsport said that the Confederates had flown a black flag, shot into an ambulance, and given no quarter. Outraged at that news, Union men in Baltimore stalked the city and beat up Southern sympathizers. Not until early June, after Kenly was exchanged, did it become clear that the Confederates had treated him and his men well. Indeed, among the Marylanders who that evening found old friends and relatives in another uniform, the brief fight had purged hostility in a way that civilians could scarcely understand. "Colonel Kenly says many officers of the First Maryland Confederate Regiment visited him," read the *Sun* on 6 June, and they had been "particularly kind."[45] The fact remained that many citizens of the old state, having grown up on the middle ground between the Potomac and Mason-Dixon Line, were trying to shoot one another.

The Marylanders in gray had gone south by various routes. Many of them had joined military companies that formed in response to sectional tensions of the 1850s and that consisted of Southern rights men; they, like others, left the state and offered their services to the Confederate government when the opportunity for Maryland secession passed. After quitting federal service, young George H. Steuart—known in the army as "Maryland Stuart" to distinguish him from J.E.B. Stuart—had recruited Baltimoreans for the Confederacy. In the spring of 1861 Isaac R. Trimble, a West Point graduate who worked as an engineer for the Baltimore and Susquehanna Railroad, assumed command of a pro-secession "Volunteer Un-Uniformed Corps," many of whose members showed up in Confederate service. For good reason Governor Hicks so doubted the loyalty of the Maryland militia at the outset of war that he thought better of calling it into service. Maryland militiamen like those under William H. Dorsey and George R. Gaither (Butler called them "violent rebels") headed south, some as soon as Virginia seceded, others when the Union army entered Maryland. Most Maryland Confederates—who came from all over the state but heavily from Baltimore and the slaveholding counties—made their way individually or in small groups. Butler had noticed squads of men hastening toward Harpers Ferry and at first did not know whether he could stop them or what to do with them if he did. Soon the noose tightened, and joining the Confederate army during the war became an adventure in itself. Soldiers spoke of traveling an "underground railroad" of their own in Southern Maryland, of night crossings to Mathias Point, below Port Tobacco, or to Chantilly Bluffs, opposite St. Mary's County.[46]

The Maryland presence in Confederate service, if not large, was noticeable. Probably not more than five thousand men at any one time served under the state colors, which included a battle flag "Presented by the Ladies of Baltimore" and a headquarters pennant bearing the Crossland cross bottony. Not counting emigrés, thousands more (as many as twenty thousand Maryland men later called themselves Confederate veterans) found their way into Virginia regiments and various other units. Gaither led horsemen who made up K Company of J.E.B. Stuart's 1st cavalry; the Maryland Guards, a Baltimore militia unit, served with the 21st Virginia Infantry. Volunteering strenuously, obviously devoted to the cause, these Marylanders performed service that did them disproportionate credit. The 1st infantry, organized of companies mustered at Harpers Ferry, Point of Rocks, and Richmond, distinguished itself at First Manassas, leading the flanking charge that began the Union collapse. After Front Royal the regiment took severe losses in a fight with a noted regiment of Pennsylvania "Bucktails" at Harrisonburg, Virginia, there winning the right to attach a buck's tail to its standard. Later in 1862, at the battle of Gaines Mill below Richmond, the 1st Maryland halted a Confederate retreat by standing dressed on the colors, shot and shell raining down, while other units rallied around them. From time to time the Confederate war department tried to combine the proud Maryland infantry regiment with other units from the state—the small horse corps formed around Ridgely Brown of Montgomery County in the spring of 1862 and one of several artillery batteries the state supplied the Army of Northern Virginia. Briefly in 1862 the 1st regiments of infantry and cavalry did serve alongside

Marylanders who formed the Baltimore Light Artillery. Yet for the time being the "Maryland Line" existed mostly on paper and in the minds of Maryland Confederates.

Like the Kentuckians who called themselves an "orphan brigade," these troops spent most of the war cut off from their state—lacking military supplies, official recognition, even mail service. They worried with reason that Union authorities would harass their families and confiscate their property; they borrowed, begged, or captured what they needed. Early in the war Colonel Johnson's wife, a North Carolina native, traveled to Raleigh to plead the regiment's cause. She returned with gray uniforms and rifles that were far superior to standard Confederate arms. The Baltimore Light Artillery, like so many other Confederate batteries, fought with antiquated cannon until it won rifled guns as battle trophies. When Henry Clay Mettam succeeded in making his way from Pikesville to Richmond and located the 1st Maryland Cavalry, he had to wait while an agent for the company commander looked for horses in North Carolina (each trooper paid for his own mount). During lulls in the fighting recruiters stole home to seek replacements or money for military supplies. Often these men were captured or failed to return.

Even in the summer of 1862, when Lee's force seemed indomitable, it did not lure as many fence sitters as Maryland Confederates hoped. Lieutenant George Booth, proud of his "somewhat unruly" company of Irish-Americans, needed replacements when in early September the army crossed into his home state—a brass band leading the way and playing "Maryland, My Maryland." Booth reckoned that his bare-footed troops may have evoked the sympathy of a fellow Marylander but likely "did not inspire his confidence." He gauged correctly. The strain of the march and dusty conditions, besides the usual shortage of supplies, left Lee's men looking tired and bedraggled—not the sort a young fellow would jump to join. Dr. Lewis H. Steiner, a prominent Frederick Unionist, complained that the Confederates smelled like ammonia and referred to pro-Southern cheers for Jackson's vanguard as "feeble." A Clear Spring farmer, Otho Nesbitt, described the Confederates who camped near Hagerstown as "a hard, drab-colored set—long, lanky, and tawny"; "the dirtiest men I ever saw," wrote another onlooker, "a most ragged, lean, and hungry set of wolves." Lee had hoped to swell his ranks in Maryland. During that campaign the Army of Northern Virginia attracted perhaps two hundred Maryland recruits.[47]

Union officials, who finally recruited about 25,000 white volunteers (and about 5,000 sailors and marines), faced their own peculiar obstacles. In May 1861, once Hicks felt comfortable issuing a call for the Maryland troop quota, loyal Baltimoreans, along with contingents from Baltimore, Howard, and Frederick counties, quickly formed the 1st Maryland under Kenly. Western Marylanders that summer and fall organized companies to thwart Confederate sallies across the Potomac. As a polite gesture to loyal members of the old Fifth Maryland, the federal government swore them and their recruits

"The Charge of the First Maryland Regiment at the Death of Ashby." Lithograph by A. Hoen & Co. after a drawing by W. L. Sheppard and C. A. Muller, 1867. The war in its romantic phase, as recalled in the bittersweet times afterward. *MHS*

into service under that number. The 2d infantry regiment was also raised in Baltimore in September. A few weeks later the War Department accepted a "legion" made up of foot, horse, and artillery troops organized by William J. Purnell, a Worcester County native who was the Baltimore postmaster. During the next year Union enlistments slowed. The promise Hicks had received that Maryland troops would serve only in defense of the state and Washington did not hold for long, but many Union soldiers belonged to three regiments in the "Potomac Home Brigade"—supposedly defensive forces. Others served only on garrison duty at the military prison at Point Lookout, as pickets in Southern Maryland and on the Eastern Shore, or as occupying forces in the Shore counties of Virginia. Federal officers tried to fill quotas east of the bay by naming two infantry regiments "Eastern Shore" rather than simply Maryland units. One Shore company was disbanded when it refused to serve anywhere except at home.

A great many Marylanders, especially in the western counties, wished to see the Union preserved; there nonetheless remained much reluctance to force people to stay in it. The occupation of Baltimore did not help efforts to recruit a light-infantry regiment that General Dix himself sponsored and that never filled. Maryland failed to meet troop quotas in 1862, and in August Governor Bradford began organizing a draft under John A. J. Creswell of Cecil County. Immediately military authorities noticed a migration of young men toward Philadelphia. At about the same time the state and localities,

Company I, 5th Maryland Volunteer Infantry, c. 1862. An amply supplied Cecil County unit, recruited to fill the regiment traditionally from Baltimore, rests arms to pose for a passing photographer. *Historical Society of Cecil County*

including Baltimore City, offered bounties to volunteers, as did the Philadelphia, Wilmington, and Baltimore Railroad. Union recruiters in some areas faced personal danger trying to compile the draft lists required to raise troops. When some of them called for protection, General John E. Wool, department commander, commented acidly, "If the state of Maryland cannot enforce enrollment let it be put under martial law." In the fall of 1862 federal troops, including the cavalry of the Purnell Legion and the 4th Maryland Infantry, aided draft enforcement in Southern Maryland.[48]

Although skirmishes along the river boundary with the Confederacy were frequent, Union soldiers of Maryland did not truly feel their mettle tested until the Army of Northern Virginia entered the state in force. Much of Lee's army occupied Frederick for a week, beginning Saturday, 6 September. Lee used the time to issue a formal appeal to Maryland. Colonel Charles Marshall, a Marylander on his staff, drafted a message assuring the state of Southern friendship and offering to assist, as he put it, "in regaining the rights of which you have been despoiled." Bradley Johnson, acting as provost marshal in his home city, called on Marylanders to think of Fort McHenry's victims, "the insults to your wives and daughters, the arrests, the midnight searches of your houses. Rise at once in arms," he concluded, "and strike for liberty and right!"[49] Calculated at once to court an unseceded slave state, prey on Northern weariness, and obtain European aid for the Confederacy, Lee's daring campaign might have won the war. Instead, with Jackson's men detached to capture Harpers Ferry, the main body of Southern troops found itself driven through two gaps in South Mountain west of Middletown and almost into the Potomac at Sharpsburg, a village of about thirteen hundred people.

Maryland soldiers suffered as severely as any in the Army of the Potomac during the terrible engagement that followed on 17 September, a day that began with low clouds and a Union assault that sent the sound of cannon rumbling all the way to Hagerstown, seventeen miles north. Hurrying down the Hagerstown–Sharpsburg turnpike, a reporter for a Northern newspaper described the horrifying sound that met him as "at first like pattering drops upon a roof; then a roll, crash, roar, and rush, like a mighty ocean billow upon the shore, chafing the pebbles, wave on wave, with deep and heavy explosions of the batteries, like the crashing of thunderbolts." [50]

Probably at about the time he arrived, soldiers of George S. Greene's division of the Twelfth Corps—including the 3d Maryland (in service only since February) and infantry of the Purnell Legion—were climbing over stout farm fences and throwing themselves into the center of the smoky and confused battle. They attacked through the destroyed Mumma farm and East Woods toward the Dunker church, which charge and countercharge since dawn had left pockmarked and filled with wounded. Not long afterward the 5th Maryland, led by Leopold Blumenberg, and part of a Second Corps division commanded by a West Pointer and Baltimore native, William H. French, moved through the Roulette farm and assaulted southward. They ran into opposition at a sunken lane filled with Southern troops who (taking ghastly casualties themselves) for nearly four hours crouched and poured such fire into their attackers that the dead soon lay heaped in rows and "the broad, green leaves" of corn "were sprinkled and stained with blood." A little before noon the 2d Maryland, part of Ambrose Burnside's force on the Union far left, took heavy losses trying to cross over the narrow Antietam bridge that Georgians covered with four hundred muskets and artillery fire. "The 2d Maryland had some good soldiers in it," wrote a regimental surgeon of Northern birth. "These boys just stood up to be shot down." Later in that day that seemed to have no end ("The sun seemed almost to go backwards, and it appeared as if night would never come," one soldier remembered), Battery A, Maryland artillery, posted itself in what was left of David R. Miller's cornfield. Crumpled men lay there by the hundreds; "we could not get into position," James H. Rigby of Baltimore wrote, "without striking them with our wheels." On this dismal spot and in a second position Battery A won acclaim for withstanding heavy fire and helping to repulse Confederate counterattacks. [51]

By the end of that inconclusive day more Americans had died in battle (4,800) than on any other single day in history, and another 20,000 lay injured. "The crying of the wounded for water, the shrieks of the dying, mingled with the screeching of the shells, made up a scene so truly appalling and horrible," Rigby reported home, "that I hoped to God, that I might never witness such another."[52]

✧

Living where Marylanders did, the war was no stranger, but the battle of Antietam brought home its carnage in focused horror. On the nineteenth of September, when Nesbitt rode to the battlefield, he could tell where the Confederates had formed by a mile-long line of bodies—"the dead lying along it as they fell," he wrote in disbelief. "Nearly all lying on their backs as if they hadn't even made a struggle." Burial parties worked for days. Some families in and around Sharpsburg had left for safer quarters when the armies began choosing their ground; others had sought refuge in their cellars, as during a tornado. Though only one of them, a small girl, had been killed during the storm, it still had been a terrible ordeal, and everyone who left came home to frightful devastation. Horses of a Confederate artillery battery lay where they had been struck in the town square. Barns, homes, livestock, and crops had been destroyed. "Fences were everywhere broken down, trees shattered, the ground ploughed up in furrows" from artillery shot, wrote a New York soldier on the twentieth. Farmers discovered unexploded shells in fields and haystacks. Meanwhile physicians tried to care for the seriously wounded, whose injuries in that era carried a good chance of leading to death. Churches and public buildings in Williamsport, Keedysville, Boonsboro, Hagerstown, and Frederick served as makeshift hospitals—as did barns (preferred for their open space) for miles about. St. Paul's Episcopal Church in Sharpsburg, badly damaged by Union artillery fire, housed Confederates, the Lutheran Church Union men. No one overlooked the piles of arms and legs lying outside these places. "The minnie ball," wrote the 2d Maryland's surgeon, "does not permit much debate about amputation." On the northern edge of the battlefield Union surgeons built a tent city to shelter their patients, blue and gray. The tents remained there as late as December.[53]

The enormous scale and intensity of civil war placed new importance on organizations. Casualties on the magnitude of those at Sharpsburg called for coordinated relief, and women played a large part in a new set of benevolent organizations. Clara Barton, a New Englander who performed heroic service during and after Antietam, proved an exception in her vigorous independence. The United States Sanitary Commission, a private group that aimed broadly at the soldier's personal welfare, received heavy subscriptions in Baltimore, made purchases there, and had a large hand in supplying the army hospitals in Annapolis—one at St. John's College, the other in the vacated buildings of the naval school. Another group, the Christian Commission, applied evangelical energy to the spiritual and medical needs of Union troops. Immediately after Sharpsburg, its Baltimore committee journeyed to the battlefield and by later report was "very active in its exertions." The

Confederate dead at Antietam, 18 or 19 September 1862. Reality replaced the romantic in Alexander Gardner's classic photograph. *MHS*

Christian Commission did not, however, cater to Catholics; an Annapolis parish priest successfully petitioned the Sanitary Commission to deliver Catholic Bibles to Maryland regiments. The Union Relief Association of Baltimore—joining which gave proof of one's loyalty—held regular meetings to roll bandages, box personal articles for the comfort of Maryland troops in blue, and hear patriotic speeches. On leaving Baltimore in 1862, General Dix singled out the ladies of this association for special thanks; the records of philanthropic devotion, he wrote with a flourish, "do not contain a brighter example of self-sacrificing service than that which is to be found in their own quiet and unobtrusive labors." In the McKim military hospital, they worked hard and openly after the battle of Antietam.[54]

No organization played a more important role in the war effort than the B&O, whose rail network was as vital to the Union as its field armies and (Marylanders knew) as valuable to Baltimore as to the Union. B&O tracks connected Washington with North and West alike, and though military tonnage during the war years climbed beyond anyone's expectation in 1861, the value of the Maryland railroad also was psychological. Union forces expended vast resources to protect the B&O tracks in Virginia, where they ran

"The Baltimore Sanitary Fair at the Maryland Institute." Woodcut from *Frank Leslie's Illustrated Newspaper*, 14 May 1864. Pro-Union Baltimoreans flocked to an event that benefited army hospitals. *Peale Museum, Baltimore City Life Museums*

through country friendly in places, hostile in others. Confederate raiding parties, some of them under the command of a colorful Maryland cavalry-man, Harry Gilmor, constantly tore up track, derailed trains, tried to make off with locomotives, and burned bridges. The span over the Potomac at Harpers Ferry went down five times. John Garrett's solution became an orga-nizational model. His steady men at the Mount Clare shops piled up all de-bris for reuse. "There are millions of pounds of damaged iron," the *American Railroad Journal* reported with amazement in 1863, "but it is not lost to the company, for no matter how small the piece, it is collected, placed into melt-ing furnaces and again wrought into such parts of engines and cars as are required." Insofar as possible Garrett made short sections of the line inde-pendently functional—so parts of the system could be used even when a break occurred. Always on good terms with Secretary of War Edwin M. Stan-ton, Cameron's replacement, and with Lincoln himself, Garrett never surren-dered control of the company to the military. He cared less about his em-ployees' politics than their loyalty to the B&O.[55]

Garrett's cooperation, despite early misgivings about the war, told the tale of the Maryland home front: division no one denied, but life somehow went on. Residents of Deal Island claimed loyalty to the Union but carried on a lucrative trade with the Confederacy, usually eluding Union gunboats. Military authorities in Baltimore continued to suppress Southern supporters and, with members of the Union League, to press everyone for outward signs of Union feeling. In August 1862 the Baltimore council required a loyalty oath of all city officials, schoolteachers, and employees. Two people were arrested for waving a window curtain at passing Confederate prisoners. Provost marshals banned the sale of "evil, incendiary" secessionist sheet music in the spring of 1863, when a bank president went to prison for tipping his hat to captured rebels. General Robert C. Schenck, then military commander, went so far as to round up women who seemed to be spying on Union movements and send the ladies to Confederate lines. Frank Howard published his recollections of imprisonment for Southern sympathies, *Fourteen Months in American Bastiles*, in early 1863. When it went into a second edition, troops seized all unsold copies and threw one of the printers in jail (Howard was left unharmed). On 3 July 1863 Schenck issued an order "requesting and recommending" that every house display the American flag on the fourth. Police took down the numbers of flagless residences. After the battle of Gettysburg, during which Maryland soldiers fought each other near Culp's Hill, Baltimoreans were forbidden to receive or entertain wounded from Lee's army. Relatives of a Confederate artilleryman killed at Gettysburg met to bury him in Greenmount Cemetery. After the funeral Union troops arrested all the adult males who attended, only clergy excepted. Union officers forbade public prints to put "CSA" after the names of Marylanders killed in Southern service and shut down additional newpapers on loyalty charges.[56]

Churches, offering some sanctuary, and families, where divisions were private, vividly portrayed the conflicts that the war imposed on Marylanders. All denominations suffered some sort of wartime disruption. Earlier having tried to avoid the slavery question, Benjamin Kurtz of the *Lutheran Observer* decided when secession was the issue "to lie low and keep dark"; for the next two years he tried to hold his middle ground by arguing for gradual slave emancipation only. Methodists came under attack in Baltimore for being, too many of them, laggards in suppressing the rebellion. The mob angered by reported atrocities against Kenly's Maryland regiment in 1862 had broken up services at the Independent Methodist Church, and the following year that meeting and another received orders to display a large American flag or be judged. The minister of the Strawbridge Chapel went to jail in 1863 for pro-Southern sympathy. Priests at the Catholic cathedral in Baltimore refused to say the usual prayer at the end of mass for civil authorities because it contained a clause about saving the Union. Bishop Francis P. Kenrick then determined to say it himself, but every time he did some parishioners stood up and left and others made noises "by a great rustling of papers and silks." In Baltimore, rabbis serving the seven thousand or so Jews in the city voiced three positions toward the war. Benjamin Szold led a majority of the faith who clung to neutrality during the conflict. Bernard Illoway condemned violence against a neighbor's institutions, asking "Where was ever a greater philanthropist than Abraham, and why did he not set free his slaves?" David Einhorn, strongly pro-Union, advised Jews to "remember Egypt." Episcopal Bishop Whittingham called for a Sunday of prayer and thanksgiving after Gettysburg. The rector at Mount Calvary Church, A. A. Curtis, wrote that to him Union victories were simply "steps and stages toward eventual ruin," "matters of humiliation and not of thanksgiving."[57]

Whittingham replied by withdrawing his name from the list of pew holders at Mount Calvary—he did not wish to be "associated with a body treasonably ungrateful for Divine mercy shown in the deliverance of the State from an invasion of armed rebels and thieves." A Baltimore father wrote his son in Harford County that if he did name his baby boy Jefferson Davis Colburn, as contemplated, he must not forget to add "Beelzebub." "Between the blue forces and the gray we were ground between two millstones of terror," recalled Lizette Woodworth Reese, later an accomplished poet and then a young girl living out York Road north of Baltimore. Her grandfather was a fervent states' rights secessionist. One of his sons, a Unionist, joined the federal army. Reese's mother married a Southern sympathizer and another daughter wedded an abolitionist. One night Union soldiers came to arrest the grandfather but by mistake stumbled on the abolitionist son-in-law. "Why, boys," he sang out from a second-story bedroom window, "the old gentleman has a son in the Union Army."[58] The troops left without a prisoner.

Passing through Maryland, Confederates found such divisions of mind baffling, maddening. In Frederick in September 1862 some Marylanders had hung out buckets of water for thirsty Southerners, prepared them decent food (one South Carolina surgeon never before had tasted apple butter), and in a few cases given them the very shoes off their feet. "The ragged were clad, the shoeless shod, and the inner man rejoiced by a number and variety of delicacies," testified one of Jackson's officers. Southern-sympathizing Marylanders by their own admission held Lee, Jackson, and Stuart in awe. Baltimoreans smuggled a dress uniform to Lee. Henry Kyd Douglas, a Jackson staff officer with ties to Washington County, wrote that as soon as the tents went up outside Frederick during the campaign into Maryland, townspeople, "especially ladies," had flocked to catch a glimpse of the famous generals in gray. William W. Blackford, Stuart's scout, later wrote of a fancy ball held for the general and his officers at the Frederick Female Academy during that campaign and of the unbounded delight Marylanders a month later took in the gray cavalry as it passed through Emmitsburg on a long raid. "Though only a mile or two from the Pennsylvania state line," Blackford wrote, "the people here seemed to be intensely Southern in their sympathies and omitted no opportunity of showing us attention during the short half hour we passed among them."[59]

Lovely farms and fat livestock in the state (especially impressive after war-torn Virginia) held out promise, if Maryland would only secede, of a well-fed Confederate army able to fight indefinitely. A North Carolina soldier remarked on the "fine thickly settled country, splendid farms & houses with plenty" he saw in western Maryland—yet in Buckeystown "the houses were all shut up & nearly all the people looked as if they had lost a dear friend." "There was a surfeit of enthusiasm all about us," Douglas remarked more sharply, "—except for enlistments." Maryland's divided sympathies lived in Southern memory. On a Sunday before Antietam, when General Jackson attended a German Reformed church in Frederick, the undaunted minister prayed for Lincoln (not noticing that Jackson had fallen asleep). A Frederick farmer gave Jackson a mare to ride in battle. Stonewall mounted, but she wouldn't move; he gave her spurs and then—Douglas called the mare a "Trojan gift"—she rose up and threw the general on his back so severely that he lay there for half an hour. When the Confederate column left Frederick, natives flew Confederate and Union colors alike (Barbara Frietschie evidently waved the Stars and Stripes later, at men in blue) and drew various cries from the troops. A buxom woman wearing a small Union flag caused a riotous comment about storming breastworks; General Howell Cobb, a division commander who had served in Buchanan's cabinet, endured catcalls but found a few listeners while trying to make a secessionist speech. When the Confederates passed through Middletown, "two very pretty girls" ran down to Jackson's men wearing red, white, and blue ribbons in their hair and carrying Union flags. Laughing, they "waved their colors defiantly in the face of the General. He bowed and lifted his cap and with a quiet smile said to his staff, 'We evidently have no friends in this town.' "[60]

In June 1863 first Confederate cavalrymen and then Union infantry passed through the hamlet of Union Mills, almost entirely made up of the Shriver clan. One family, nonslaveholders who supplied five sons to the Confederate side, welcomed Stuart's famished cavaliers with a heavy breakfast—the horsemen fingered the hotcakes off the griddle before they were ready—and sang the Confederate commander's favorite tune, "If You Want to Be a Bully Boy, Jine the Cavalry." Later that day another Shriver household, pro-Union slaveowners, greeted their champions in blue with a picnic lunch and music on the family piano.[61]

By 1864 the character of the war had changed, the Southern star had sunk on the horizon, and campaigns of Union and Confederate generals alike became exercises in vengeance. Earlier Southern attacks on the C&O Canal had attempted to halt traffic on what might eventually become an asset to the Confederacy; after 1863 the raids aimed at maximum destruction—breaching the canal's banks, exploding locks, burning boats, and stealing mules. In the summer of 1864 Confederates under Jubal Early crossed the Potomac to travel in Frederick County for a third time, hoping to pull some of Grant's forces away from Lee's front. Southern troops set out to even the score, to repay the Union for its burning and pillaging in the Shenandoah Valley. Confederate horsemen under John McCausland entered Hagerstown and delivered a ransom note demanding $20,000 (they missed a digit, intending to call for $200,000) and a large assortment of clothing and supplies. The banks and merchants produced the money and most of the other articles, but another Confederate force broke into stores and took what they wanted. Confederates seized the Reverend John B. Kerfoot, headmaster at St. James Academy, and one of his faculty members, hoping to trade them for a Virginia churchman whom Union troops had captured. Middletown had to pay $5,000 and Frederick—once Union forces retreated—a full $200,000. Many farmers lost horses to the Confederates, as they usually did, as well as "money, meat, chickens, cattle, sheep, & anything that came their way." Pro-Union newspaper offices in Boonsboro and Frederick were destroyed. Baltimoreans faced an invasion scare of the same kind they had experienced in the two preceding summers. Militia and volunteer units mustered. Authorities closed shops selling spirits, curtailed travel without passes, and kept a watchful eye on suspected Southern sympathizers. Residents worked on earthworks. Prices shot up as food grew scarce.[62]

Early's campaign, designed as an armed feint, accomplished little more than to remind Marylanders how tiresome the war had grown. Among Frederick County farmers, Early's offensive and the failure of federal troops to prevent wholesale seizures dropped "Union stock" to about 25 percent of par value, wrote Jacob Englebrecht, who was so disgusted that he himself rated the cause at only 5 percent. Another example of fatigue came from the other side. Confederate Marylanders, now united in the Maryland Line, included horsemen under Johnson and Gilmor, whom Early dispatched on a separate raid.

Aside from burning Governor Bradford's home north of Baltimore (retaliating for the destruction of the Virginia governor's house in Lexington), the two Maryland Confederates conducted a thrust that almost acquired a comic or festive air. Gilmor's troopers scattered the few Union soldiers in Westminster by charging with drawn sabers, then stopped to admire a young woman who waved a kerchief out her window. Early ordered a ransom of clothing from the town fathers; they proved hard to locate, and Gilmor persuaded Early to drop the demand. Outside Baltimore, Johnson and Gilmor captured a train only to have the engineer fix the locomotive so that it could not be moved. The raiders captured another one, and this time, after gallantly giving passengers their luggage, set the train afire and backed it onto the bridge over the Gunpowder River. Guards jumped into the water, but the bridge failed to catch fire and federals repaired it in three days. A captured Union general, elderly though he was, made good his escape. At Owings Mills Johnson's men came across a railroad car loaded with ice cream. Some of the western Virginians had never seen it before and thought it was frozen mush. Gilmor's men rode off with canteens, cups, and even hats filled, slurping it at a gallop. Several of the Marylanders then enjoyed sneaking to their homes for a quick visit, right under the noses of federal troops. Johnson and Gilmor

Lieutenant Colonel Harry C. Gilmor (1838–83), looking proud and fit at the height of the conflict. *MHS*

had planned to sweep down to Point Lookout prison the night of 12 July, free the Confederates held there, and then re-arm them from captured Washington arsenals. Wisely, they abandoned the scheme. Later, after a far more destructive McCausland raid on Chambersburg, Pennsylvania, on 30 July, Johnson and Gilmor protested that the ransom demanded of Hancock— $30,000 in cash and 5,000 cooked rations—was excessive for so small a village. Hancock was spared.

❧

"In Carroll County there were so many people who were Union men that it was dangerous for whites in some places to say they were Rebels," an ex-slave remembered long after the war. "This made the colored and white people very friendly."[63] While no doubt true to one slave's experience, this impression did not hold widely; for most blacks the war imposed pressures and carried hopes that hardly made relations between themselves and whites more comfortable. Slaveholders resisted change to their labor system. Most white Marylanders remained unsettled about the numbers of free blacks. Near war's end, after outside prodding and by a circuitous route, Unionists made Maryland the first slave state to abolish slavery.

At first the Union army steered clear of any role in domestic arrangements.

Unruly slaves in Anne Arundel would have looked in vain to General Butler in April 1861. One of Dix's first duties involved the return of runaways who believed that Union troops were abolitionist friends. He ordered slaves captured by a cutter on the Severn turned over to civil magistrates at Annapolis and later directed the return of Dorchester County fugitives to their owners. "We wage war with no individuals," Dix wrote a Wisconsin officer. "Do not interfere in any manner with persons held in servitude." To avoid "misrepresentation or cavil," Dix wanted no blacks within military camps. When citizens in Washington County complained that an army officer encouraged insubordination among slaves, the local Union commander issued a reprimand and promised in the future to turn disobedient soldiers over to state authorities for trial.[64]

Holding the military on a tight leash, the Lincoln administration tried to strike a balance between its radical antislavery wing, with leaders like Horace Greeley of New York and Charles Sumner, and party moderates like Edward Bates of Missouri and Montgomery Blair, who knew well the political needs of border-state Unionists. Slowly the party center moved toward emancipation; surely Lincoln's military aims carried him along as well. Late in 1861 Republicans in Congress introduced a measure to abolish slavery in the District of Columbia, compensate slaveowners, and provide a fund for voluntary resettlement of the freedmen. On 6 March of the next year, believing that an end to slavery in the border states would deny them to the Confederacy and hasten the war's end, Lincoln sent Congress a proposed resolution urging those states to adopt gradual emancipation. He offered federal financial aid "to compensate for the inconveniences public and private, produced by such a change of system."[65]

Maryland Unionists hesitated. Soon after suggesting these resolves, Lincoln met privately with border state congressmen and senators, including John W. Crisfield, an Eastern Shore representative and Lincoln's former colleague in the House, and Cornelius L. L. Leary, an "independent Unionist" from Baltimore. Unionists had united on a conservative platform: suppressing the rebellion, preserving the Union, leaving slavery alone. Both the District bill and the compensated emancipation plan threatened unanimity among these erstwhile Know-Nothings, Democrats, Whigs, and Republicans. Crisfield and other Maryland leaders hedged, asking for more time and firm assurances of federal aid. While Congress passed the compensated-emancipation resolution easily, the entire Maryland delegation voted against it or abstained. Lincoln's proposal reached the House of Representatives just as legislators in Annapolis were about to adjourn. They took no stand on it and sidestepped another serious issue. According to the 1851 constitution, the assembly after each census had to conduct a referendum to learn whether voters favored another convention. Rural members, apprehensive that a new constitution might dismantle slavery, used parliamentary delays to defer the poll.

Congress passed the District measure that spring, and the family networks and travel patterns of free blacks quickly spread word of it. Slaves in Montgomery and Prince George's counties began departing for Washington and freedom. In April 1862 the Baltimore *Sun* reported that between one hundred and two hundred slaves were leaving for Washington weekly from the Maryland countryside. Whites watched in frustration. Reverdy Johnson, senator-elect, began preparing lawsuits to test the constitutionality of the law, which seemed to violate the terms of Maryland's land cession for the federal district. Learning that federal marshals in the District refused to honor the 1850 fugitive slave law, Governor Bradford registered futile protests with Lincoln and Attorney General Bates. Bradford's position was as helpless as Hicks's had been in the secession crisis. Losing slaves himself, he told delegations of slaveowners that calling out the militia to protect slavery would only result in disastrous clashes with federal troops; the slaveholder had to accept his losses as a cost of war, "one of the direct and anticipated fruits of this atrocious rebellion, got up under a pretense of establishing a better security for this very species of property."[66]

Editors of the *Montgomery County Sentinel* believed that the District emancipation act, besides providing a haven for runaways, promoted the likelihood of racial war—it created a hatchery for slave insurrection. Freeing the slaves might do away with that fear, but for whites in early 1862, just as in the 1820s, talk of emancipation raised the specter of living in a heavily black society. If Maryland suddenly freed its slaves, Brantz Mayer observed in an article for the Baltimore *American*, the combined black population would exceed 170,000 persons, many of them competing for jobs, others becoming a public burden. Attempting such a social revolution in the midst of political rebellion would be foolhardy, and freeing blacks who then would lose in the struggle for survival was no kindness to them. It was, he concluded, not so much emancipation as the emancipated that Marylanders need fear; the time was rapidly arriving "when the *Negro question*, rather than the *Slavery question* . . . would become of paramount importance in its bearing on labor and taxation in Maryland." A Dorchester County meeting put it more bluntly: Maryland was in danger of becoming "the free Negro state of the Union." "If in the providence of God," the resolves declared ungenerously, "this country was intended as a home for the exclusive occupation of the white man, there should be no dark spots upon it—it should be white all over."[67]

As 1862 wore on, a welter of events strengthened antislavery sentiment all the same. The Baltimore *American* cited figures showing land in nonslaveholding counties to be worth twice as much as in slaveholding areas; it declared that if all Maryland slaves ran off, the result would be a "prodigious gain." Unionists in Baltimore, angry that the assembly had failed to call a convention referendum, described slaveholders as longtime oligarchs. Meanwhile Lincoln—who protested that events controlled him, not the opposite— made shrewd patronage choices and kept to a gradualist policy. In April the

American printed a letter Postmaster General Blair wrote a Maryland friend favoring "separation of the races" after the slow dismantling of black bondage. Under consideration for a federal post, former governor Hicks, still a slaveholder, called Lincoln's compensated emancipation plan as much a stroke "against ultraists of the North as at Southern fanatics." Frederick Schley of the Frederick *Examiner*, switching his editorial stance, also endorsed Lincoln's scheme—and soon afterward became a collector of federal revenue. In a militia act of July 1862 Congress freed "rebel"-owned slaves and their families when a slave enlisted in the Union army. A sterner confiscation act (unenforceable except when slaves escaped to Union lines) freed all slaves belonging to masters supporting rebellion. Lee's retreat after Antietam permitted Lincoln to confirm that policy. White Marylanders largely greeted the Emancipation Proclamation with coolness, while Baltimore free blacks saluted the president by presenting him with an inscribed, pulpit-sized Bible. The *American* spoke for many citizens when it called slaveownership "a fleeting interest, one that all must recognize as doomed." [68]

Wartime expedients took their toll on Maryland Unionism. In May 1863, dissatisfied with "the old Bell and Everett" moderates, the leadership of the Maryland Union League met in Baltimore and formed what it called the Unconditional Union party. At the local level the league took its strength from the people who rolled bandages and sent sundries to Union troops. At the convention its spokesmen—among them Baltimore criminal court judge Hugh Lennox Bond, Henry Winter Davis, Henry Hollyday Goldsborough, and Henry Hoffman, sergeant-at-arms of the House of Representatives and a Davis man—demanded action on slavery and state constitutional reform. In part the Unionist split followed old lines. Among the Unconditionals were many former Baltimore Know-Nothings like Davis. Marylanders loyal to the established Unionist central committee, calling themselves Conservative Unionists, included Republican regulars and many former Democrats, who in places—especially the Eastern Shore and Southern Maryland—retained power at the county level. Led by Bradford, Johnson, Hicks (a U.S. senator after Pearce's death in 1862), and former Baltimore mayor Thomas Swann, conservatives aligned with Montgomery Blair, whose personal differences with Davis and policy quarrels with Republican radicals were growing more serious. Union victories at Gettysburg and Vicksburg that July helped the Unconditional Unionists gain momentum as the fall elections approached. Closely following the radical Republicans in Washington, they recommended emancipation without compensation in the border states. Conservative Unionists accused them of "toadying to the administration"; they were "prisoners on duty for the cause of abolitionism." Unconditional Unionists labeled the conservatives Copperheads, rebel sympathizers, and Democrats. [69]

Agreeing that slavery was doomed, Conservative and Unconditional Unionists located a divisive issue in the administration's recruitment of black soldiers. Baltimore free blacks had offered to help defend the city after the April 1861 riot—when Mayor Brown said he would call on them if needed. Later the army had employed them in building fortifications around Baltimore, and General Schenck had urged the administration to form them into line units. The War Department established the Bureau of Colored Troops the same month as the Union League's Baltimore convention, and in mid-July 1863 William Birney, son of the Kentucky abolitionist, set up office in Baltimore. Recruiting proceeded briskly that summer, black sergeants making the pitch for army life at nineteen recruiting stations throughout the state and a band of black musicians from Hagerstown marching in parades and performing at rallies. While free blacks joined in large numbers, they knew that Negro troops received less pay than did whites in uniform, and as the pool of willing free blacks dried, Birney's enthusiasm led to excesses. Filling the ranks of the 4th U.S. Colored Infantry in about seven weeks, Birney emptied the Baltimore City jail and ostentatiously freed slaves being held in Baltimore slave pens by District of Columbia owners trying to evade the emancipation law of 1862. His civilian agents, many of them black, had no authority to accept bondsmen. Some Maryland slaves, lacking their master's permission to volunteer, nonetheless ran away that summer and left the paperwork to the authorities—as did a Howard County man named Joe Nick. His escape to Ellicott City occasioned an embarrassingly winless contest among local bloodhound owners.[70]

In the early stages Lincoln's use of black troops pleased only Unconditional Unionists—most of whom were never so radical as to suggest that black and white soldiers stood equal to each another. Small farmers, suffering the usual labor shortage, favored slave recruitment; they grumbled that by taking free blacks into the army the federal government threw the little man on the mercy of slaveholders and their bondsmen-for-hire. Slaveowners supported recruitment of free blacks as one means to get rid of them and where possible used the state statute book to limit their property losses (in August 1863 a Union recruiter in Frederick went to jail for violating a law that punished anyone aiding slaves to escape). Black recruitment especially angered whites in heavily black areas. Talbot County citizens protested against black companies strutting about in their midst. A St. Mary's County slaveholder badgered his congressman to do something about the fugitive slaves who found sanctuary in the Leonardtown military hospital. Masters missing slaves alleged that their men had been impressed. Reports of irregularities in Maryland grew so numerous that Lincoln in September suspended black recruitment there and negotiated with Bradford and other state leaders. In early October, by General Order 329, the administration established a plan that became the model in other border states. Lincoln agreed not to enlist Maryland slaves unless free blacks failed to fill assigned draft quotas. After a thirty-day grace period, however, recruiting officers would take slaves regardless of whether they had their master's permission, the federal government paying loyal slaveholders three hundred dollars a head for their lost property. To collect, they had to produce papers freeing the recruits.

That fall, in an election many Marylanders charged was influenced by the military, Unconditional Unionists won a clear majority in the General Assembly, and friction between military and slaveholders peaked—a mark of the masters' frustration as the clock of bondage wound down. Upper Marlboro slaveowners complained bitterly that black recruiters on a steamboat were "harassing us, plundering us, and abducting our negroes." Near Camp Stanton in St. Mary's County, two whites killed a black lieutenant for enticing slaves to join the army. By early 1864—with talk of manumission on the increase, the thin fabric of Maryland slavery tearing at every corner—tension between military and civilian changed dramatically. Slaveholders seized on the army as a means of avoiding financial loss. Military officers defended themselves against another excess: they often refused, they said, to accept slaves whose owners had given up trying to force them to work and wanted them put into service. In the year following General Order 329 the federal government paid more than $14,000 for enlisted Maryland slaves. During that period nonslaveholders seemed content that ex-slaves counted toward the Maryland draft quotas. Former slaveowners complained of delays in obtaining compensation.[71]

Joined on the surface and in large issues, bickering behind the scenes, Conservatives and Unconditionals (forty-seven of whom had run as "Emancipationists") steered the ship of state to the end of the war. When the legislature met in January 1864, it quickly set about calling a constitutional convention. Members heard an unusual series of addresses—apparently by invitation—that were designed "to instruct them in the path of duty." Blair, Hicks, and Swann spoke on the need for a convention, Swann in particular demanding that the "steed of Emancipation" be whipped and spurred until "the whole state of Maryland, from its center to its circumference, shall be awakened to an edict of universal Emancipation." The assembly called for an election of convention delegates. Restricted to men loyal to the Union (perhaps as many as two-thirds of all Maryland electors did not vote or were prevented from casting a ballot), the vote affirmed the need for a convention and overwhelmingly selected emancipationists to attend it. The convention met in Annapolis in late April and sat until September—with interruptions for the national Republican convention in Baltimore, held in early June, and Early's raid in July. A minority of some thirty-five members, mostly Democrats from the Eastern Shore and Southern Maryland, lost every substantive issue and made sarcastic motions about suspending debate entirely.[72]

Though enacting reforms, the new constitution contained several notoriously pungent features. The Unionist majority pushed through an article awarding House of Delegates representation on the basis, not of total popu-

OATH
TO BE ADMINISTERED TO EVERY VOTER.

"I do swear (or affirm) that I am a citizen of the United States, that I have never given any aid, countenance or support to those in armed hostility to the United States, that I have never expressed a desire for the triumph of said Enemies over the Arms of the United States, and that I will bear true faith and allegiance to the United States, and support the Constitution and Laws thereof, as the Supreme Law of the land, any Law or Ordinance of any State to the contrary notwithstanding ; that I will in all respects demean myself as a Loyal citizen of the United States, and I make this oath (or affirmation) without any reservation or evasion, and believe it to binding on me."

QUESTIONS
For the use of Judges of Election

1. Service in the Rebel Army.

Have you ever served in the rebel army?

2. Aid to those in Armed Rebellion.

Have you ever given aid to those in rebellion?
Have you never given money to those intending to join the rebellion?
Have you never given money to their agents?
Have you never given money, clothing or provisions for the purpose of aiding the emigration of persons from this State to the South?
Have you never sent money, clothing or provisions to persons in the South since the rebellion?

3. Comfort and Encouragement to Rebellion.

NOTE.—Comfort or encouragement means advocacy, advice in favor of. We aid the rebellion by giving money, clothing and provisions ; we give it comfort and encouragement by our words. A man who has advocated the cause of rebellion, who talked in favor of Maryland going with the South, who rejoiced over the victories of the rebel armies, has given comfort and encouragement to the rebellion.

Have you ever given comfort or encouragement to the rebellion?
Have you never in conversation, attempted to justify the course of the States in rebellion?
Have you never expressed a wish for the success of the rebellion or its army?
Have you never in conversation, discouraged the cause of the Federal Government?
Did you rejoice over the downfall of Fort Sumpter?

4. Disloyalty.

NOTE.—If the Judges are satisfied that a man is disloyal to the United States ; it is their duty to refuse his vote, for such a person is not a "legal voter" of the State of Maryland.

Are you a loyal citizen of the United States?
Have you been loyal ever since the beginning of the war?
Have you ever rejoiced over the defeat of the Union army?
Have you ever rejoiced over the success of the rebel army?
When the Union army and the rebel army meet in battle, which do you wish to gain the victory.

NOTE.—After interrogating the person offering to vote, the Judges may hear other evidence to prove or disprove his statements, and must be governed by the weight of testimony.

Broadside, "Oath of Allegiance," 1864. *MHS*

lation (dear to heavily black counties), but of white population. The majority adopted a stringent loyalty oath and granted wide discretionary powers to election officials—they could judge for themselves whether one took the oath in good faith. An oath required of officeholders declared the U.S. Constitution and federal laws supreme in the land, "any law or ordinance of this or any other state, to the contrary, notwithstanding"—a clause striking at the states' rights interpretation of the federal compact. Another article disqualified from voting or holding office everyone who had served in "the so-called Confederate States of America," who had given aid or comfort to enemies of the United States, sent them "money or goods or letters or information," even those men who "by open word or deed declared adhesion" to the South. Arguably necessary as war measures, these oaths and proscriptions applied even after war's end—forever, unless one obtained an act of assembly restoring citizenship or served in the federal military. Finally, to seal acceptance of the new charter, the majority voted to impose these stringent election restrictions on the ratification vote itself—an irregularity that brought forth jeers of protest from the outvoted rural members. The convention succeeded in its single most important object by the end of June. It adopted a Declaration of Rights that included an article abolishing slavery and involuntary servitude: "all persons held to service or labor as slaves, are hereby declared free."[73]

Though the issue may have been settled at home, Marylanders like everyone else fought on until the following spring. Maryland sailors on the Union side served under Louis M. Goldsborough in the Atlantic blockading squadron; they fought on western rivers and in battles for strategic Southern coastal points. Although by the late months of the war the South virtually had no navy, Maryland natives had played conspicuous parts in the glory days of the Confederate sea service. Its ranking officer, Raphael Semmes of Charles County, skippered the celebrated sea raider *Alabama* until its sinking in June 1864, and Franklin Buchanan of Baltimore had commanded the *Virginia* (earlier *Merrimack*) when in May 1862 the ironclad challenged the *Monitor* at Hampton Roads. A brigade of Union Marylanders took part in the brutal fighting in the Spotsylvania County wilderness in late 1864. The Confederate 2d Maryland, successor to the 1st, made a name for itself in critical battles like Gettysburg but also, as the war became a matter of attrition, struggled in ugly engagements at places important only to the soldiers who lost friends there: the Weldon Railroad, Peebles Farm, Squirrel Level Road, and Hatcher's Run. Eventually forming six regiments (8,718 men), black Marylanders made bloody assaults on Fort Fisher, North Carolina, and then, during Lee's last defensive stand, charged into the fatal Petersburg Crater—a huge hole blasted by tons of gunpowder beneath the Confederate lines. Many of them, unable to climb out of the loose earth, were trapped and killed.

No less than other Marylanders who fought in that meaningful American war, they knew why they were there. In October 1863 the Baltimore *Daily Gazette* published in dialect words that someone had overheard a newly enlisted black soldier saying in prayer. "King ob Kings and God ob battles," he had asked, "Help us to be able to fight wid de union sojers de battles for de Union. Help us to fight for de country—fight for our own homes and our own free children and our children's children." [74]

CHAPTER 7

Gilded Age, Humble Lives

"M en's minds," observed the Baltimore *Sun* in August 1865, "are filled with vicious schemes of extravagant gains." On one level schemes and gains made up much of the postwar Maryland record—wherein powerful men left deep tracks. Politicians like Governor Thomas Swann handled issues by making trades, knowing whom to talk to, feeling their way through problems. They made the parliamentary process work in their favor and knew how to swing elections. Swann had his eye on the next assembly balloting for U.S. senator. Unwilling to let wartime Unionism slow his postwar career, the governor in 1866 appointed voting officials who ignored state loyalty restrictions and allowed many Democrats and ex-Confederates to return to the polls. When they did, they elected legislators who called a constitutional convention to undo as much done in 1864 as possible. Presiding over it was Judge Richard B. Carmichael—the same man Union troops had arrested on the bench. Not a single Republican attended the 1867 convention, and for years afterward Maryland Democrats went to the polls mindful of wartime wounds while Republicans clamored about corruption. In 1870, without Maryland's ratification, the Fifteenth Amendment gave the vote to blacks. Thereafter Maryland politics became a kind of greenhouse in which Marylanders voted in high percentages, Republicans always ran a close second, and Democrats won every statewide election.

Interesting foliage grew in the hothouse of one-party rule, and the urge to join in postwar prosperity—to get rail access to markets—raised the temperature. Before the war Oden Bowie and other Prince George's County leaders had obtained a charter for a Baltimore and Pope's Creek Railroad that they planned to run from Baltimore to a Potomac crossing in Charles County. Doubting that it would pay, John Garrett declined B&O involvement. So, in the summer of 1867, Bowie journeyed to Philadelphia and for two hours waited outside the office of Thomas Scott, president of the Pennsylvania Railroad. The company at the time competed fiercely with the B&O on several fronts. One of Scott's cherished desires was to break the B&O

monopoly on the Baltimore to Washington trade. Bowie conceived of a Baltimore and Pope's Creek feeder line that would make Scott's dream come true. Perhaps Scott offered Bowie all the aid he needed; in any event, eminently an artist of the possible, Bowie returned from Philadelphia and announced himself a Democratic candidate for governor. He won the party nomination in October, when one of Arthur Pue Gorman's close friends in the Howard County delegation suddenly and unaccountably switched his vote. As governor, Bowie, with his friends' support and over the violent objections of Garrett and B&O investors, in 1869 managed legislative approval of a Pennsylvania Railroad line to Washington.

These men made their mark on the state. Scott's company provided Southern Maryland new connections to market, and communities named Waldorf and La Plata sprang up around local shipping points. Maryland sent to Washington one of the most influential senators of the late nineteenth century. Still, the age that powerful and political men gilded also belonged to the ordinary, working people of Maryland, who as usual could tire of speeches. In September 1876 Montgomery County celebrated the centennial of American independence at the Rockville Fair Grounds. Allen Bowie Davis, chairman of the program, said it would feature odes and addresses. "These exercises will be interspersed with vocal and instrumental music," he announced. Then would follow the fair's final object—"an old-fashioned social feast or pic-nic."[1]

Though the constitution of 1864 left many grudges to be settled, it also did lasting good. It abolished gubernatorial election districts, reestablished the office of attorney general, and reformed the public works office. Joshua Cohen had called on Governor Bradford and the Baltimore delegation to remove every religious test for public office and thus eliminate "this last remnant of a by-gone prejudice"; the Declaration of Rights dropped the word *Jews* from references in article 37 to tests for officeholders, who still had to declare a belief in Christianity, God, or an eternal state of rewards and punishments. Article 8 of the Unionist constitution of 1864 provided for a uniform, centralized system of tax-supported public schools, and public opinion forced Democrats at the 1867 convention and in the next assembly (though they restored some authority to localities) to leave this provision intact.[2]

At last the state of Maryland taxed its citizens to support education. Property owners paid ten cents on each one hundred dollars of assessed value to a school fund that the state distributed to the counties and Baltimore according to school-age population. A Presbyterian minister and former president of St. John's College, Libertus Von Bokkelen, served as the first salaried superintendent of public instruction; largely filling an advisory role in Annapolis, he oversaw administration and curriculum. County and Baltimore City commissioners hired teachers, chose textbooks, and built schoolhouses. The school law of 1868 required counties to build one secondary school and as many elementary schools as election districts. Trustees of the old academies, which remained eligible for limited state support, chose between joining the more heavily funded public school system and standing independently. At least on the statute books, Maryland schools compared favorably with those in most parts of the Union. A state normal school for teacher training, chartered in 1865, conducted classes in a series of Baltimore buildings before moving to Towson.

The end of the war did not quite bring the jubilee that slaves had imagined freedom to be. Maryland ex-slaves fared better than blacks farther south, but they faced a hard struggle for equality. In 1866 whites raided and broke up a black Methodist meeting near Annapolis. Newspapers made light of the episode by referring to the rocks they had thrown as watermelons. For a short while after emancipation, orphans' court judges bound black children over to their former masters as apprentices. The Maryland "black code"—requiring blacks to find employment, outlawing black testimony against whites, restricting Negro travel and assembly—did not fall until Congress in 1866 passed a civil rights act and federal courts began applying it. Judge Hugh Lennox Bond argued the justice of black voting, and John R. Kenly, after the war a Baltimore lawyer, said he favored black suffrage because he believed in the brotherhood of man. Politically, however, not even Maryland Republicans would touch the Negro suffrage issue. Nor did the party advocate black public schooling in the immediate aftermath of emancipation. "The people," reported Joseph M. Cushing, a Baltimore delegate to the 1864 convention, were "not ready" for such an idea. Instead, blacks enrolled in classrooms that opened under the sponsorship of private societies to aid former slaves or, in hostile Southern Maryland, under authority of the federal Freedmen's Bureau.[3]

White friends of the freedmen in Baltimore became especially active. Predominantly Quakers, they included Cushing, Judge Bond, William J. Albert, and the Boston-born Unitarian minister John Ware. In August 1864 these men formed the Baltimore Association for the Moral and Educational Improvement of the Colored People. By the end of 1865, struggling financially, the Baltimore association had established seven black schools in the city. Caulkers' Hall housed one of them, Methodist churches three others; most of the schools handled two hundred or more pupils. In the counties the association opened eighteen smaller schools. Besides the three Rs, blacks studied geography and practiced "declamation." Young women learned sewing. Blacks flocked to these makeshift classrooms in such numbers that it became difficult to build and staff them quickly enough. Judge Bond made urgent fund-raising appeals at home and to the north. By 1867, when the association budget ran to more than seventy-six thousand dollars and its activity peaked, it had established more than a hundred schools, concen-

"Arrival of Freedmen and their Families at Baltimore, Maryland—an Every Day Scene." Wood engraving from *Frank Leslie's Illustrated Newspaper*, 30 September 1865. *MHS*

trated on the Eastern Shore and in Baltimore. Enrollment in the city reached twenty-five hundred or more, in the counties about five thousand. The association founded a normal school in Baltimore to train black teachers.

Since black education seemed to signal social revolution, rural whites largely refused to take part in the movement. In places black schooling became risky business. Whites assailed a teacher in Havre de Grace and a jury failed to convict them; a black teacher on the Eastern Shore reported that drunken white men had reeled into her classroom and frightened her students. Arson destroyed eleven schools in Baltimore, Cecil, Kent, Queen Anne's, and Somerset counties (the governor offered a reward leading to the arrest of persons responsible in Kent). All the while blacks held meetings to raise money and plan more building. Many of them worked days and attended classes at night. Typically, and proudly, a teacher at Church Creek, Dorchester, wrote that her pupils "read well in the First Reader, and are to commence Arithmetic at once."[4]

Strong free-black traditions in Baltimore helped to account for gains there. In October 1865 Frederick Douglass, then a Washington resident, spoke at

ceremonies dedicating the Douglass Institute for "the intellectual advancement of the colored portion of the community." Douglass praised Baltimore
blacks for showing that the "higher qualities attributed to the white race"
belonged to the Negro as well—and for exercising them vigorously "as the
dark cloud of slavery rolls away." That fall white caulkers in the city, not as
pleased to see the weather change, struck shipyards, protesting the high
number of blacks in the caulking trade. In response Isaac Myers, son of free
Negroes and a graduate of the Reverend Jacob Fortie's school in Baltimore,
gathered black and white capital and organized a Negro cooperative shipyard—the Chesapeake Marine Railway and Dry Dock Company. Within a
few years the firm employed several hundred black caulkers. Building on his
success, Myers in 1869 called a statewide convention of skilled blacks to find
ways of gaining economic parity in Maryland. Myers next led the struggle to
form a national black labor union. Baltimore blacks in the meantime demanded the vote, an end to legal discrimination, and the opening of the
professions and trades. In 1867, for the first time in the state, Baltimore authorities agreed to allocate black taxes toward black primary schools. Until
1871 Negroes could only ride on the outside platforms of Baltimore omnibuses, unless accompanied by a white person (in bad weather black women
and white children were known to arrange a temporary liaison). That year,
after a lawsuit and much agitation, the city did away with segregated public
transport.[5]

⌘

Those human changes were for the better. The impact of the war on Maryland business did not appear so clearly. Some firms gained; others lost. In
the first few years of conflict, with Southern suppliers and transportation
routes disrupted, processing of agricultural products in Baltimore had fallen
off. The scarcity of cotton slowed most Patapsco mills. The Kettlewell and
Ober fertilizer firm shut down during the war for lack of Southern markets.
The amount of tobacco inspected at Baltimore—a figure dependent on production in Southern Maryland particularly—decreased from 77,000 pounds
in 1860 to about 44,000 in 1865. Changes in demand, a drop in available shipping, and the attacks of Confederate privateers—an ironic turn-
around—all had an adverse effect on Baltimore's foreign trade. Coffee imports went down almost by one-half between 1861 and 1863. In similar fashion rail and canal destruction hampered commerce; coal shipments via the
B&O declined from almost 500,000 tons in 1860 to 172,000 the following year,
though gradually building back up. Baltimore dry goods companies like
those of Daniel Miller (a Shenandoah Valley native) and John W. Bruff suffered because of the large number of uncollectible debts in Virginia and other
seceded states. Hugh Sisson, a dealer in marble, had a contract to provide
stone for the new South Carolina capitol when the state left the Union.

Balancing these tales of woe were the successes of a few enterprising firms

"The Chesepeake Marine Rail Way & Dry Dock Co. of Baltimore, Md." Tinted
lithograph by E. Sachse & Co., Baltimore, 1868. *MHS*

that did war-related business. Inspected flour in Baltimore, responding to
the needs of military provisioners, climbed from 890,000 in the first year of
war to over 1 million barrels in 1863 and 1864. Bushels of corn sold also rose
slightly, reflecting the number of horses in army service. One model of enterprise, William Wilkens, made the war pay by following the army and snip-
ping the tails of dead horses; home in Baltimore, he made mattresses and
upholstery. On a larger scale, government contracts supplied the iron company belonging to Horace Abbott, a New Englander, with lucrative business.
The Abbott foundry flourished making plates for federal ironclads, including
the pioneer *Monitor*. Federal patronage of the B&O helped enormously to
fill the company coffers and service its debt; gross earnings from the main
line alone climbed from about $4 million in 1862 to more than $10 million in
1865. Another beneficiary of the war was Enoch Pratt, a Massachusetts-born
merchant and banker who, when Union troops entered Baltimore in May
1861, had shouted "Glory Hallelujah, gentlemen, we are safe!" Later he
greatly enhanced his fortune selling horseshoes and like articles to the army
and by 1865 had become one of the leading hardware dealers in the country.
Johns Hopkins—of Quaker upbringing, always an opponent of slavery, and
a strong Union man—also gained by filling government contracts.[6]

"The Result of the Fifteenth Amendment And the Rise and Progress of the African Race in America and its final Accomplishment, and Celebration on May 19th A.D. 1870." Tinted lithograph published by Metcalf & Clark, Baltimore, 1870. Local blacks, celebrating their newly won right to vote, marched through Mount Vernon Place, past the town houses of John W. Garrett and Enoch Pratt on West Monument Street. Border vignettes illustrated free black schools and churches. *MHS*

As Maryland recovered from the dislocation of the Civil War, its place in the re-united states declined by several economic measures. Among American cities Baltimore fell to sixth in population in 1890, its gross product from eighth to thirteenth, its number of wage earners from fifth to seventh. Maryland ranked twelfth in the country in 1860 in the value of its products. Thirty years later the state stood fourteenth. In 1849 Maryland manufactures accounted for 3 percent of the country's total, by 1914, 1.6 percent. Both James Higgins in his *Succinct Exposition of the Industrial Resources and Agricultural Advantages of Maryland*, published in 1867, and George Washington Howard in *The Monumental City: Its Past History and Present Resources* (1873) contributed to the puffy promotional literature of the time. Actually Baltimore and the state grew a bit slower than the pacesetters and fell slightly behind their competitors during the "industrial age."

Looking at Baltimore City itself, however, the postwar period justified practically every claim Higgins and Howard made. As if triumphantly to demonstrate their survival of civil war, Baltimoreans began work on a city hall that George Frederick designed to stand second to none—a domed building of enormous dimensions and Victorian detail. Dedicated with great ceremony in 1875, it overlooked a rapidly growing city. Between 1870 and 1900, when Baltimoreans numbered close to 900,000, population almost doubled. About 126,000 were newcomers, of whom all but 12,000 had been born Americans—about 80,000 whites and 35,000 blacks. Of the white native-born, 7 out of 10 were Marylanders. Most black immigrants also had grown up in the state—although an influx of Virginia- and North Carolina–born Negroes lowered the percentage of Maryland natives among Baltimore blacks from about 92 percent in 1870 to 79 percent in 1900. Rather alone among American cities in the late nineteenth century, Baltimore increased at the expense of its state.

Opportunity in the city depended on trade and manufactures, which in turn depended on transport. Coastal shipping resumed and grew rapidly. Steamboats—some of them war-surplus vessels carrying cargo—offered improved schedules to bay landings. The larger Baltimore to Norfolk boats became exemplars of postwar opulence, with velveted, brass-appointed, and chandeliered first-class quarters; new boats provided second-class accommodations for domestics and the increasingly numerous drummers or salesmen. Steamship companies established regular service to Havana, Liverpool, and the Continent. The North German Lloyd Line reached a cooperative agreement with the B&O, enabling the railroad to connect directly to European ports. When the line's steamer *Baltimore* arrived from Bremen in March 1868, making the first of many regular voyages (bringing immigrants over, returning with produce and tobacco), thousands of people turned out for a parade to celebrate the event. People besides stockholders in the Pennsylvania Railroad cast a jealous eye on the B&O. Garrett's system, while laying more rails at Locust Point and building coal wharves and grain elevators there, operated tax free and charged fully what the market would bear for delivered coal. Baltimore interests began raising money to complete the Western Maryland Railroad, chartered in 1853. Competition, they told subscribers, would drive down the coal costs that virtually every industry faced in the conversion to steam power.

Railroads exerted awesome influence, civic and economic. Scott of the Pennsylvania Railroad controlled the Northern Central (earlier the Baltimore and Susquehanna) and coveted an outlet to the water at Canton. Directors of his feeder line to Washington, the Baltimore and Potomac, wanted a link from the southwest to the Northern Central. Baltimore city fathers in the early 1870s bowed to railroad pressures and permitted a new corporation to dig the Union Tunnel and link the Northern Central to Canton piers. Workmen finished the tunnel in 1873. Afterward Pennsylvania oil shipments on the Northern Central doubled and the road built its own grain elevator at Canton. During the same years the Baltimore and Potomac received permission to dig a mile-and-a-half-long tunnel from Fulton Avenue to the Jones Falls Valley. The company later reneged on its agreement to build bridges across all turnpikes it crossed, explaining the *Sun* comment that the road worked "like an invading force, stealthily entrenching itself by night." In 1876 the General Assembly obligingly decided to tax tunnels at no higher rate than common track.[7]

Baltimore businesses and manufacturers provided many jobs, some more tempting than others. Dry goods firms and wholesale grocers did not take long to resume their trade in Virginia and now West Virginia, and soon hired the necessary clerking and transport help. Fertilizer companies once again supplied Southern customers with South American guano. Slaughterhouses and meatpackers met the growing needs of a crowded city and the seemingly bottomless foreign demand for refined lard, bacon, and barreled pork and beef. Wheat received in Baltimore climbed to more than 3 million bushels in 1870 and to 36 million in 1880, bushels of corn from almost 8 million in 1870 to more than 16 million a decade later. Exports of those commodities grew by the same bullish rates. Tobacco houses enlarged their area of supply into Ohio and Kentucky and produced cigars for a national market. While Baltimore gradually lost to competitors in leather tanning, sugar refining, and the making of boots and shoes, its furniture, glass, paint, lumber, spice, and rye whiskey establishments remained strong after the war, as did the manufacture of high-grade pig iron for buildings, bridges, stoves, and steam-heating equipment. After 1869 copper smelting recovered from problems of supply, changing its source of ore from Cuba and Chile to the American West. Meantime William Knabe, a piano maker, and fifteen other musical instrument firms employed among them almost seven hundred persons. Baltimore in the 1880s became a leading producer of straw hats.

In the twenty years following the Civil War the city became best known, however, for its important clothing and canning industries. The technology of canning—preserving food by boiling it in jars or cans—had developed in France in the early nineteenth century and received commercial application in the United States in about 1820, when Thomas Kensett, an Englishman familiar with the process, began canning oysters and other delicacies in New York. Kensett moved to Baltimore in 1826. Handling oysters in season and fruits and vegetables in the warmer months, he made canning a year-round industry. Canned foods had a ready market in ship provisioning, especially during the California gold rush, and grew in demand during the war, though production problems prevented the army from buying large quantities for troops. First the use of calcium chloride (raising the boiling point of the water preserving the foods) and then, in the 1870s, steam pressure cookers greatly hastened the process and enabled canners to meet large demand. For many years Baltimore stood as the leading canning center in the country. Toma-

John W. Garrett (1820–84). The B&O president as he appeared in *Baltimore Past and Present, with Biographical Sketches of its Representative Men* (Baltimore, 1871). MHS

Detail, "Baltimore and Ohio Rail Road Tide-Water Terminus, Elevators, etc., Locust Point, Baltimore." George W. Howard's *The Monumental City, Its Past History and Present Resources*, 2d ed. (Baltimore, 1876) featured Garrett's extensive rail and shipping complex just a few years after its completion. MHS

toes, corn, peaches, oysters, and cheap labor were abundant. Ships brought Welsh and other tin for the cans, which for the time being workers made by hand. By 1870 there were more than one hundred packing houses in Baltimore, the firms of Kensett and William Numsen and Sons among the leaders. Canning, in turn, stimulated the manufacture of tin sheeting and packing cases.

Making the most of the newly invented sewing machine, Baltimore clothiers—German and German Jewish—had a large part in the city's postwar rise as a clothing center. Even by 1859 they had claimed a large segment of the regional market; during the war they made heavy profits supplying army uniforms. Afterward the ready-made clothing industry demonstrated again the complementary nature of economic development, for the railroad helped enormously to make the city a national supplier of that basic need. Baltimore struggled for supremacy with New York companies as the B&O reached westward—to Chicago in 1875, with branch lines to Sandusky on Lake Erie and various trunks in Pennsylvania, West Virginia, and Ohio. Baltimore companies made men's and boys' work outfits like overalls and heavy shirts, women's finery, and summer-weight clothes. Dry goods merchants like Henry Sonneborn and Company, antebellum wholesalers of northern-made apparel, turned to manufacturing their own clothing and used their established trade connections to market their products. The ready-to-wear clothing industry, using pre-cut, interchangeable parts, demonstrated the increasing dominance of the factory system in Baltimore. The widespread advertising Baltimore clothing firms did after the war pointed the way for other industries. Sonneborn opened offices in New York and Chicago and eventually employed seven full-time salesmen throughout the country. By 1880 a quarter of the Baltimore clothing market lay in Ohio and the middle western states, some smaller fraction in New York and New England, and more than a third in Virginia and southward.

The southern focus of Baltimore trade and industry represented a double-edged attempt to recapture and expand profitable old markets and to be helpful to old friends. Daniel Miller, the dry goods merchant, helped to organize and then served as treasurer of an Agricultural Aid Association that collected $80,000 in the spring of 1865 to provide Virginia farmers with stock, tools, and seed. Goldsborough S. Griffith—owner of a wallpaper and upholstery company, leader in the Reformed church, and wartime chairman of the Christian Commission in Maryland—served as president of the Maryland Union Commission, which that same year aimed "to save by timely generosity the thousands of refugees whom the tides of war have cast upon our hands." In April of 1866 Baltimore women led by Mrs. Benjamin Chew Howard formed yet another group, the Southern Relief Association, which, after a fair at the Maryland Art Institute, sent net receipts of $164,570 to committees in every formerly Confederate state except Texas. In 1867 the Maryland General Assembly appointed commissioners to distribute an appropriation of $100,000 "for the relief of the destitute people in the States wasted by civil war." The B&O and Maryland steamships carried all relief freight without charge.[8]

Business followed charity, with both sides gaining. Baltimore firms readily sold on credit to southeastern customers after the war, and these risks paid dividends. By the 1880s a heavy proportion of tobacco, cotton, grain, and livestock that city firms handled came from southern sources—either via coasting vessels sailing from Norfolk and Savannah, or by rail. As in the clothing trade, so in groceries and manufactured commodities, the southeast along with Kentucky and Tennessee provided Baltimore with important mar-

Advertisement of Hurst, Purnell & Co., in George W. Howard's *The Monumental City, Its Past History and Present Resources,* 3d ed. (Baltimore, 1878). Showing their cast-iron storefronts in larger-than-life size, Baltimore retailers and wholesalers boasted of their growing importance in the regional economy. *MHS*

kets. Meantime Baltimore capital, with the firms of Alexander Brown & Sons, Wilson and Colston, and Middendorf and Oliver in the fore, helped considerably to rebuild the defeated region, investing in steamship lines, urban transportation, utilities, cotton mills, coal, iron, and phosphate mines, lumbering enterprises, and railroads. Richard H. Edmonds of the *Manufacturers' Record*, a paper enthusiastically supporting Baltimore investments in the South, claimed that $100 million in Maryland money had gone there by 1900. Whatever the amount, Baltimore investors financed the Atlantic Coast Line and Seaboard railroads and spent heavily on the Southern Railway System. In the late nineteenth century, declared the *Record*, what Chicago was to middle western prosperity or San Francisco to growth on the Pacific coast, "Baltimore will be to the South."[9]

⌒⚬⌒

A typical legislative turnabout in these years benefited the Eastern Shore, where lack of capital had posed a serious regional problem for generations. By a plan the General Assembly had proposed in 1856, a Queen Anne's and Kent Railroad would run tracks to Elkton, and from there supply traffic to Baltimore. In 1867 the legislature, pledging a public subscription of more than $110,000, revised the 1856 measure and freed the company to connect instead with the Delaware Railroad—a branch of Scott's Pennsylvania. The Queen Anne's and Kent company went into receivership in 1874, but branches of the Delaware Railroad, adding to the busy steamboat schedule, reached Chestertown, Centreville, Oxford, Cambridge, Crisfield, and Berlin.

So well did these links function that the outside world rediscovered the Eastern Shore, which placidly had gone about its own business since post roads began following the other side of the bay in the late eighteenth century. Writers for national magazines like *Scribner's* and *Harper's* visited the peninsula and reveled in its "arborescent bays and rivers," its forms and angles ("bridges, broken roofs, and queer rivercraft"). Eastern Shore settings made for twilights "of exquisite softness or splendor." Around Centreville the woods, where not of scrub pine, "loomed like green walls and towers against the sky." Old-fashioned stores carried placards for medicines and labor-saving devices in the windows. Centreville's brick mansions, wrote George Alfred Townsend, son of a Methodist minister and native to the peninsula, had "traditions of paint clinging to their warped eaves and porticoes." Un-pruned gardens seemed "the more beautiful for their wild luxuriance." Charming Easton was easier to enter than leave. In Oxford it was "always afternoon," commented Bayard Taylor; a half-hour's stroll was worth a night's sleep. Cambridge had a salt creek "bordered with some of the snuggest old mansions of timber and brick which could please an artist's eye." Townsend noticed old Episcopal churches covered with ivy that made them appear like "crotcheted pinnacles carved in green." Gravestones bore the crests, shields, and ciphers—the "heraldic phantoms"—of a departed soci-

Light Street near Pratt, c. 1880. Stevedores and carters on Light Street bustled to feed the many steamboat lines connecting Baltimore to the South. *MHS*

ety. Every outsider took note of the grand estates that one seldom could see from the roads, only the water, and remarked on the abundance of wild birds and fish. In Worcester County, Berlin turned out to be an agreeable surprise, a warm and cozy place. The Maryland ocean beach—its great waves "like tame elephants"—was the finest Taylor had seen for coastal bathing.[10]

The quiet people of the Shore won over all sojourners, one of whom had expected to encounter "frank discontent" over the results and losses of the war. Though whites believed that Negro farm laborers sang less than in slavery and thus could not be as happy as before, former slaveowners, while complaining of their poverty, largely accepted their fate with philosophy. Black coachmen did not appear to be "made miserable by their freedom." Old landed families eagerly discussed genealogy with New York writers and cultivated "an affectionate regard for the past." A few elderly gentlemen seemed to have been "shut up in Sleeping Beauty's castle," so antiquated were some of their ideas (one fellow advocated laws prescribing different costumes for different social classes). Ordinary Shoremen, of unmixed English stock, left the impression of being "rough and ignorant, but very good-natured," temperamentally independent and democratic. The eastern Marylander, Townsend wrote, was "the Virginian without his institutions and

Tonging for oysters in a log canoe, c. 1890. *MHS*

dogmatism." Quakerism and Methodism, he believed, had softened society and downplayed pretension. Two centuries of isolation had produced curiosities like Holland's Island, said to be governed in intellectual things by one man who wrote everybody's letters, told them the news "when it got tolerably old," and informed them "of the deep abstrusities of politics." Eastern Shore simplicity also produced wonderful modesty. A Berlin tavernkeeper apologized that all he could offer guests was "chickens and sich." He then laid out a fried-chicken dinner with fresh fish and oysters that made his visitors marvel and left them "satisfied to the very marrow."

By all reports produce farming on the Shore had created a lively and promising economy. Leaving Elkton traveling south, one immediately plunged into peach country where, in the spring, trees colored the landscape pink for fifty miles. The Sassafras River region, Townsend wrote, was to peach culture what the Marne was to wine. Blackberries grew in abundance. Cornfields around Centreville produced heavy shocks of golden corn in the fall. Flat and rich, the area was "Illinois under a warmer sky." Farmers in Somerset County grew sweet potatoes for northern markets or strawberries that bands of itinerant blacks picked in the summer. At Westover railroad junction in strawberry season one heard "a Babel of noises, ever increasing," as cart after cart rumbled up to the station "in a cloud of dust like a miniature thunder-storm." Soil on the Maryland Eastern Shore, said one observer, had an advantage over that of Virginia in that it seemed only discouraged, not exhausted, and there was plenty of muck and marl available for enrichment. Recent rail connections meant that produce delivered to Dover, Delaware, on an afternoon could reach New York City by the next morning. Shoremen seemed willing to grasp at the economic possibilities of the region. Young people were "awakened to the fact that the world had changed."

Federal rivers and harbors money in the postwar years explained some economic optimism on the Shore. With authority to contract extensive public works projects in the Chesapeake region, the army corps of engineers in the early 1870s began clearing, widening, and deepening rivers and creeks from the Elk to the Pocomoke. These operations usually cleared a channel one hundred feet wide and eight feet deep, with excavated mud often thrown behind wooden dikes that had a long-term habit of rotting and giving way. Elkton and Centreville benefited from the channel dredgers, after whose work farmers around Chestertown and Crumpton could ship their corn and wheat down the Chester and steamboat companies could carry heavier cargoes to Queenstown. There, mail packets left every other day for Baltimore and large vessels often sought refuge in storms. Expecting to ease boat traffic between the Chester River and Eastern Bay, the army deepened the channel separating Kent Island from the mainland; before that task began, the state in 1874 replaced the old Kent Narrows causeway with a drawbridge. Between 1871 and 1879 the army spent $32,500 to improve the harbor at Cambridge (its population doubled in twenty-five years) and more to clear the Choptank upriver. Steamboats in the 1880s reached as far as Denton and Greensboro. A Choptank Steamboat Company captain described the effect of channel deepening as "almost phenomenal in its benefits to commercial interests." Hampered by poorly constructed dikes, dredge crews labored up the Wicomico to Salisbury, where the Maryland Steamboat Company opened service in 1882. Afterward local produce had a convenient route to Baltimore markets.[11]

Another way the Shore changed involved fishing—especially for shad, bluefish, rockfish (the local name for striped bass), and menhaden, a small fish used for oil and meal. Taking fish in large numbers traditionally had depended on seines (or haul seines) that groups of men anchored on the bank and then hauled by boats called shad galleys in a wide semicircle of water, closing it to complete the catch. When the haul seine went out at night, it was set with lanterns and singing that gave the labor a romantic glow; to Howard Pyle of *Harper's* the men appeared "like phantoms engaged in some fantastic work." In real life seine fishermen relied on the permission of, or paid, the landholders from whose bank they worked. In about 1835 Baltimore thread makers began selling closely woven nets that caught fish by entangling their gills. Lightweight, these nets could be dragged behind a skiff by one or two men using the water freely. After the war, marking the rise of commercial fishing in the region, New Jersey scows working Chesapeake Bay began setting huge nets anchored by piles. In 1880 fishing inter-

"St. Mary's at Parker's Wharf near Solomons." Artist unknown, c. 1890. Docked, hands waiting to unload cargo, the *St. Mary's* typified smaller paddle-wheel steam-boats that served the Eastern and Western shores. *J. Dawson Reeder, Jr. MHS*

ests set several hundred pound nets at river mouths along the lower bay. The pound net increased the scale of the fishing industry; it also led to conflicts over fishing rights and jealousy among men who pursued the same catch employing different methods. All fishermen using nets found the crab a nui-sance. In the early 1870s a few Marylanders began selling crabs for their tasty meat; most watermen cursed them for fouling nets. Channel fishermen "find their work so obstructed by the crabs that they trample upon them or crush them with clubs," read an early report.[12]

More than anything else, the Eastern Shore owed its rising fortunes to the constantly climbing demand for oysters. So popular had the shellfish become that Marylanders in 1865 changed their minds about dredging. With Eastern Shore support, the assembly that year passed a measure permitting natives (them alone) to dredge in state waters fifteen feet or deeper. Since no one wished to compete with large Northern companies that surely would employ steam-powered vessels, the law limited dredgers to sailing craft. The oyster rush was on.

The boom continued for many years, and it made the most of traditional Maryland boat-building skills. For generations tongers had harvested oysters in small, two-masted sailing vessels known as log canoes because they had evolved from the dugouts of the Chesapeake Indians. These indigenous craft took several forms. Most watermen could build them at home using axe and adze to cut and shape the four or five large logs that made the heavy, durable hull. One improvement in the age-old design owed to economic choices made by some antebellum oystermen. Instead of turning their catches over to "runners" or "buy-boats," they obtained full wholesale price by taking the oysters to market themselves. Enlarging their canoes made the trips more profitable, and the brogan resulted. A centerboard canoe thirty to forty feet in length, the brogan had a fixed bowsprit, a jib with two raked masts, and a narrow, open deck. Other developments followed the amended oystering law. Many of the Maryland oystermen who stood to gain by the no-steam restriction owned or worked on one-masted sloops, two-masted schooners, and pungies—late versions of the Baltimore Clipper. About sixty feet in length and ocean-worthy, the pungy could easily handle dredging equipment.

Experience proved it cheaper and easier to enlarge the brogan for that purpose, and someone, perhaps using the Scottish word for oyster, named the new boat the bugeye. It became the Maryland dredger's workhorse. At first using fifty- or sixty-foot logs, later plank-on-frame construction, Eastern Shore builders fashioned boats that set leg-of-mutton sail on twin, raked masts like the brogan's. Bugeyes were different in having covered decks with a small cabin aft of the mainmast; they eventually carried wheels that replaced tillers. Block and tackle atop the foremast lined up with the main hatch to ease loading and unloading. Bugeyes were powerful enough to pull

Moore & Brady oyster can label, c. 1880. With a rakish pungy schooner in the background, one of Baltimore's many canneries touted its special "deep sea" (i.e., dredged) oysters. *Peale Museum, Baltimore City Life Museums*

the heavy dredge over oyster beds and large enough to stow substantial catches. Painted every bright color but the tabooed blue, they served as the mainstay of the bay oyster fleets for most of the late nineteenth century.

As the industry developed, some oyster packers moved to the source itself. Isaac Solomon of Baltimore transferred his operations to the Calvert County island that later bore his name. In the early 1870s Crisfield, a tiny community on Tangier Sound with a rail link to the Delaware line, became home port to more than six hundred oystering sailcraft. In those years tongers and dredgers marketed about 10 million bushels of oysters a year at Crisfield, and a record 15 million in 1884. In season several thousand men, women, and children worked in the dozen or more packing houses there, some filling barrels with oysters and ice, others sitting over buckets, shucking with astonishing dexterity. "She seizes an oyster," reported an onlooker of one woman, "inserts the thin knife between the shells, and with a quick turn of the wrist the shell is opened, the oyster cut loose and dropped into the pan, all with one movement." Shuckers took loaded buckets to a "skimmer" who washed the oysters, graded them, and prepared them for same-day shipping. Profits were considerable. Packers paid watermen about a quarter dollar per bushel, which usually produced a gallon shucked; at the end of each day they gave shuckers another fifteen cents or so for every shucked gallon. A processed gallon sold for a dollar. Each working day twenty or thirty boxcars loaded with oysters left Crisfield for Wilmington, 135 miles north on the railroad, and workers rolled barrels onto the steamers that waited for runs to Baltimore, Washington, and Norfolk.[13]

The men who worked on the water composed a breed unto themselves. They deserved their reputation for being clannish, suspicious of outsiders, and secretive about their work. Brought to trial, a saying went, a Shoreman was likely to face a jury made up completely of relatives. According to a report George Brown Goode made to Congress in these years, tongers could be judged comparatively docile, but "indolent and improvident." They had little ambition beyond having a house and part ownership in a boat, which in warm weather they used for fishing and hauling produce to Baltimore. "It is too often the case," read Goode's report, "that tongers, especially many of the negroes, who comprise about one-third of the total number, will work only one or two days at a time, and then remain idle until necessity forces them again to earn a few dollars."

Dredgers did work that every observer believed the worst on earth or water. Boats went out Monday morning and returned Fridays. Crews received a third of the gross income—two-thirds going to boat maintenance and the captain—and it often amounted to a pittance. Confined after hours to crowded, smoky, and vermin-infested quarters, crewmen faced even worse conditions while working. Bugeyes carried two windlasses, one on each side amidships, which four men turned to haul in the loaded dredges. Turning the windlass, recalled one old oysterman, was "like pulling in anchor while the boat was sailing." They work "poorly clad and with every garment stiff with ice," read the gruesome congressional report, "while the wind dashes the fast-freezing spray over them, hour after hour winding away at the wind-lass, pulling a heavy dredge, or else stooping, with backs nearly broken, culling oysters." Men lost fingers and toes to frostbite and suffered from "oyster hand"—an infection that could follow the smallest cut. Oystermen from the lower rural counties of Maryland provided "some few who are re-spectable and honorable men." Crews aboard Baltimore boats, on the other hand, proved that dredgers, "taken as a class, form perhaps one of the most depraved bodies of workmen to be found in the country."[14]

When dredgers hit shore it was with a vengeance. After landing at the Pratt Street wharves, oystermen took their small pay and spent it "in de-bauchery amid the lowest groggeries and dens of infamy to be found in cer-tain portions of Baltimore." Crisfield was no better, only smaller. People took excursions to see this curiosity on the lower bay, the closest thing the East had to a Dodge City or Abilene. Buildings had holes in the floorboards for emptied shells. Many structures went up on stilts standing in the marshes. Reeking of "defunct oysters" (as one sensitive visitor said), the place pro-duced other smells as well. Crisfield boasted a justice of the peace, Harvey Johnson, who owned a beer hall and presided there. "Gentlemen the court is now in session," he would say each morning, "but I call your attention to the fact that business is still going on at the bar." Burgess's Saloon featured an on-premises boxing ring. Customers with differences could settle them in pleasant, sawdusted surroundings—egged on by cheering drunks. In one bare-knuckles bout of the period Haynie Bradshaw, normally a pillar of the Methodist church but a huge man quick to anger, bloodied a series of Vir-ginia watermen, one of whom earlier in the day had asked him, "Hey, ain't you one o' them dumb Smith Islanders?" Dance halls and bars so proliferated on Goodsell's Alley that a body could scarcely sleep at night; one tormented boarder quieted down unruly oystermen by firing a shotgun out his window until they dispersed. Chorus girls at a place called Blizzard's offered notori-ous comforts to the lonely. Such all-night, broad-daylight vice offended many people on the peaceful Eastern Shore. One day in August 1873 the Methodist ladies of Salisbury arrived by train at Crisfield, pitched tents for a giant prayer meeting, and launched a crusade to save the wayward souls there. For hours the harvest was gratifying. Then suddenly, as if the Lord preferred Eastern Shore prosperity to piety, torrents of rain and deadly light-ning bolts snuffed out the revival.[15]

"Dredging in Maryland," wrote Edmonds of the *Manufacturers' Record*, "is simply a general scramble, carried on in seven hundred boats, manned by fifty-six hundred daring and unscrupulous men, who regard neither the laws of God nor man." Competition in the oyster business gave the race to the swift. Agents of rival packers got into fist-fights on the docks over whose catch belonged to whom. Watermen who felt cheated did not resort to legal action. Packers stretched profits at the expense of the buyer by adding water to the oysters' natural "likker." Like the powerful H. C. Rowe of Connecticut, pioneer in transatlantic oyster marketing, out-of-state speculators found ways to register their boats in Maryland—bribery and native stand-ins among them. To fill out crews, captains of oyster boats had agents pull bums off Baltimore streets at two dollars a head or by varied skulduggery trick immigrants (called "paddies," as if they were Irish) from as far away as New York to sign on. "We don't care where he gets them," a captain said, "whether they are drunk or sober, clothed or naked, just so they can be made to work at turning a windlass." In later years federal courts revealed cases of whole crews held captive until put ashore penniless, and of murders on the water. An immigrant who made trouble could be "paid at the boom"— disappearing when it came about and caught him blindside. State law reserved beds in water shallower than fifteen feet for tongers. Yet by 1880 special legislation enabled Talbot, Dorchester, and Somerset counties to license scrapers (smaller-scale dredgers) within their waters. Scrapers often crossed county lines at will—many of them trawling at night in black-painted boats with muddied sails. Angry tongers responded by building blinds and shooting at the intruders.[16]

In a half-hearted display at imposing order on disorder—dredgers exerted heavy influence in Annapolis—the assembly in 1868 had provided for an oyster police force. Its first commander, a Kent Islander named Hunter Davidson, struggled for years to enforce the laws, but he thought them far from adequate. Maryland statutes, he reported in 1869, did nothing for the oyster except "to open wide the door for its enemies." While Davidson coordinated efforts from a steam side-wheeler, his men fanned out on twelve sloops armed with small cannon and rifles. They patrolled the Manokin River mouth, Holland Straits, Honga River, and Swan Point off Rock Hall. Dredgers vowed to kill the police chief, who awoke one night in January 1871 to find the most famous pirate of all, Gus Rice, on board his flagship with a picked lot of assassins. Davidson managed to save himself and force the surrender of some pirates. Rice escaped as he always did. The following spring an oyster police vessel, the *Mary Compton*, armed with an old muzzle-loading cannon, sank a renegade dredge boat in the mouth of the Annemessex River. Such episodes had more effect on illegal dredging than fines, which Davidson saw captured pirates pay without flinching. Discouraged, he resigned in the early 1880s and the oyster force became a hitching rail for Democrats who had earned a spot on the state payroll. Dredgers then likened the police to green-headed flies—pesky but not dangerous.[17]

Meanwhile Maryland and Virginia nearly went to war over their exact lower Chesapeake boundary and rights to the millions of dollars worth of oysters on the bottom. By an agreement the states had made in 1785, Virginians had free access to the Potomac (all of which lay within Maryland) and Marylanders enjoyed the same rights in the Pocomoke River, whose channel

"The Pirates Attacking the Police Schooner *Julia Hamilton*." Engraving from *Harper's Weekly*, 1 March 1884. Such battles in the period's oyster wars claimed national attention. *George Peabody Library of the Johns Hopkins University*

partly marked the Maryland southern limit on the Eastern Shore. Virginians objected when Maryland dredgers worked Pocomoke Sound, where rights were ambiguous. Boundaries across the bay itself lay uncharted. Fights between oystermen from the two states led to a fruitless meeting of Maryland and Virginia representatives in 1872. Five years later commissioners agreed to draw the line from the lower Potomac to Smith's Point on the Virginia side and from there to Watkins Point on the Pocomoke.

Virginia seemed to gain more from this agreement, though Maryland retained rights to the rich banks of lower Tangier Sound. Ill feeling got no better along Pocomoke Sound. Maryland oystermen, not blameless, complained to no avail that Virginia police did little to stop Virginians from crossing over to their side of the "line of '77" when their own beds grew light. In December 1883, frustrated Marylanders shot at Virginians who ventured into Maryland waters, and then conducted retaliatory raids on Virginia beds. A Virginia police schooner, *Tangier*, chased them back to Smith Island. There twenty-five or thirty oystermen opened fire on the Virginia craft, threw up barricades, and dared the captain of the *Tangier*—who had used his own gun—to attempt a landing. He sailed back to Onancock without accepting the challenge. Responding to the affront, the Virginia assembly soon voted more money for its oyster patrols and raised the penalties for poaching to confiscation of one's boat and a prison term of one to three years. Maryland watermen clung to the belief that they should share in Pocomoke Sound oysters. In 1894, deciding a case involving a Somerset County man convicted under Virginia law, the Supreme Court upheld the exclusive right of Virginia to oysters on its side of Pocomoke Sound (and Maryland rights on the other). Settling the legal question, the justices could do nothing about the bad blood and desperate competition, or the violence that erupted time and again.

∾×∾

Marylanders on the Western Shore, increasingly aware of the emerging national economy, could not cheer its arrival with full-throated enthusiasm. The role of the state in fruit and vegetable canning did bring profits to Western Maryland growers, who increased their apple and peach acreage in these years. In 1869 Louis McMurray, a Baltimorean, established a canning plant on West All Saints Street in Frederick, and on some days during harvest season wagons loaded with "sugar corn" stretched all the way from the factory entrance to Market Square.

Still, times were not easy for the sturdy yeomen west of Baltimore, partly because of federal monetary policy. During the war the Lincoln administration had floated large issues of paper currency called "greenbacks" that eventually appeared in such large quantity as to depreciate seriously in value. In 1865–66 many Western Maryland farmers, trying to replace fencing and livestock lost during the war, borrowed these inflated dollars at high interest rates. Then, as the government in 1869 demanded public payments in gold and in 1873 ended the use of silver coinage, farmers had to make payments in money that effectively was worth twice as much as the dollars they had borrowed. Together with declining European demand for American farm goods after 1871, the "hard money" program that the Republican party made into law placed severe pressure on Maryland farmers. Many of them lost their mortgaged lands. Hagerstown in the 1870s performed melancholy service as a rendezvous point for local farmers and their families (some from Pennsylvania and West Virginia) who left the region for the West on special trains.

The rural Western Shore economy both reflected and caused social change after the war. Farm opportunities being uneven, the move of so many Marylanders to Baltimore made much sense. As this pattern of migration developed, however, many farmers felt a labor shortage that drove up the cost of wages and added to their worries. In the richer Western Shore counties a slow movement toward mechanization helped to meet the labor problem. In the 1880s Washington, Frederick, and Carroll county farmers, familiar with

Montmorency Farm, Montgomery County, 1895. *Margaret M. Coleman and Anne D. Lewis*

corn and wheat production, stood in good position to take advantage of the new agricultural implements—sowing machines, corn huskers, and wheat threshers—that Baltimore and Hagerstown companies made and advertised in periodicals like the *Southern Farmer and Planter*. Even so, such machinery required heavy investment and did not remove the fact of middle western competition in national corn and wheat markets. Maryland farmers found themselves trapped by the economy of scale. Midwestern producers, working relatively larger fields that yielded heavy crops, drove down prices and made it useless for one to farm marginal land.

Fortunate Marylanders remained as competitive as possible by putting only their better soil under the plow. Southern Maryland farmers, more than a few feeling the loss of slave-invested capital, hoped for better times. In tobacco country the labor shortage was most noticeable, and there blacks might have benefited from well-paying farm work. The record suggests that tobacco planters had ways of combining to place a ceiling on wages. In any case the freedman, like the free black of the antebellum period, often preferred moving to Baltimore to remaining in the country. Blacks who stayed in the counties tended to become sharecroppers (tenants who worked the land for a share of the profits) or, in smaller numbers, tenants who paid cash rent. By 1880, 70 percent of rural Marylanders owned their own land (almost all were white), about 23 percent were sharecroppers, and the rest tenants. Nothing in these arrangements changed for many years. Tobacco remained the leading Southern Maryland crop, labor-intensive as always and therefore immune to mechanical invention. Its market lay in France, Holland, and Germany; prices, though steady, showed no tendency to climb.[18]

During the same years important changes took place in flour milling, an agricultural industry that had changed little since the eighteenth century. Water-powered flour mills, important to the early economy of the entire state, used millstones or "burrs" set close together. One run through them, called the "first break," produced a good grade of flour and much leftover material, including bran, known as "middlings." After the Civil War millers began experimenting with two innovations. One, a purifier that sifted and resifted flour ground with the stones set farther apart, made a marketable product of the middlings that most country millers threw away. Another new device revolutionized milling by using steel or porcelain rollers, acting together in series, to crush the wheat instead of grinding it—a process that made for a whiter flour and also minimized waste. These new designs found their most avid proponents in the middle west, in Minnesota, where local wheat—a hard, red grain—required much handling to satisfy the popular preference for white flour. The national magazine for the milling industry wrote glowingly of sifted and rolled flour. Maryland millers, who in fact worked with a softer and lighter strain of wheat, took notice. Since Minneapolis ground wheat the way Baltimore canned oysters, the force of competition left them little choice.

A few Maryland mills became showcase businesses. The Gambrill Mill, at Orange Grove in Baltimore County, installed rollers in its old structure in 1879. The same firm, advertising its product as the oldest brand-name flour in the country, built a wholly new, steam-powered roller mill on the Pratt Street sites of two old Baltimore mills in 1881–82. Built of granite, seven stories high, the plant had cleaning equipment and magnets to draw stray nails from the final product, "Patapsco Superlative Patent Flour." Eastern Shore mills like J. E. Biscoe's in Queen Anne's County and J. F. T. Brown's old Wye Mills went to rollers. Most of the rural millers able and willing to make the investment in new machinery lived on the Western Shore. Shriver's Union Mills converted to rollers in the early 1880s. The Ceresville Mill, a Frederick County landmark dating from 1813, converted to rollers and in 1888 received front-page coverage in the *American Miller*. The journal described D. S. Boyer's Hagerstown mill on West Franklin Street as a model, "talked about in almost every nook and corner of the east"; in 1889 a group of 211 millers, gathered for a meeting, came down from Chambersburg to see the successful plant. Yet in the hurry to keep up with developments, other country millers in Maryland overextended themselves. In 1887 a converted Westminster miller had to sell his business, worth $60,000, to cover liabilities that totaled $100,000. Firms at Park Mills and Owings Mills followed. The number of working flour mills in Maryland of all kinds began

Advertisement of Patapsco Flouring Mills, from *The Trade, Commerce, & Manufacture of Baltimore* (Baltimore, 1886). By 1860 most Maryland factories had made the switch from water to steam power, enabling entrepreneurs to build mills wherever they wished; some water-powered mills converted on site. *MHS*

losing out in national competition and dwindling in number. In 1880 there had been more than 500. Eight years later, by one count, that figure had dropped to 221.[19]

Otherwise Western Maryland became a region of specialty manufactures that paralleled its profitable apple and peach crops. These manufacturing companies never assumed large proportions in the state—by the end of the century Baltimore accounted for 96 percent of all Maryland industry—but they supplied jobs and gave character to the larger towns west of the Patapsco. In the late 1880s and early 1890s Frederick, gaining slightly in population, added knitting mills, a brush-making plant, and brickworks to its prosperous canning industry. Hagerstown grew more rapidly, benefiting from railroad ties that became elaborate after the war. Baltimore City and Washington County capital built a branch of the B&O that opened in 1867. It ran from Weverton to Hagerstown, passing through Sandy Hook, Keedysville, and Funkstown. In 1872 the Western Maryland Railroad, with more local money and after suspiciously high expenses, completed the line between Hagerstown and Baltimore. Another railroad, the Shenandoah, connected Hagerstown to Sharpsburg, Shepherdstown across the Potomac, and Waynesboro down the Valley of Virginia. The old Cumberland Valley line, by then a part of the Pennsylvania system, provided service to Harrisburg and Philadelphia. Hagerstown businessmen referred to their home as the hub city.

Industry in Hagerstown may not have been successful in every instance, but the survivors reasonably claimed excellence. William Updegraff, member of an old business family in the town, began making gloves in 1865, at first for the few people who required odd sizes and unabrasive material, later to fill an expanding urban market for the expensive, handmade variety. In 1880 Updegraff's firm, relocated on the site of an old brewery, produced six thousand pairs a year and employed fifty persons. In 1867 a company making doors, window sashes, and shutters opened shop to supply local and perhaps Baltimore builders. That same year Updegraff helped to establish an agricultural implement company. Making clover hullers, grain planters, and hay rakes for a national market, the firm in 1881 sent eleven loaded cars of equipment to Michigan and Indiana on the B&O. Two Hagerstown companies began making wooden spokes for wagon wheels after the war, drawing wood from Virginia on the new railroad, using steam-powered saws and lathes, and operating equipment an onlooker called "as powerful as it is curious" to bend metal strips for rims. The Hagerstown Steam-Engine and Machine Works, formed in 1867 and reorganized in 1874, built threshing machines and furnished metal castings for its neighboring farm equipment company, rollers for grist mills, and machinery for paper mills—one of which John Stonebraker had built on the Antietam east of town in 1864 and rebuilt after a fire in 1873. Along with William T. Hamilton, governor from 1880 to 1884, and persons with such old local names as Wingert, Byers, Bennett, Tice, Schlotterbeck, Roessner, and McComas, Updegraff also invested in the later-famous pipe-organ works that a Dane, M. P. Möller, brought to America in 1872 and to Hagerstown in 1880. Briefly in the late nineteenth century Hagerstown had its own bicycle plant. Its farm equipment company moved to Ohio in 1888; the Hagerstown Machine Works closed later.[20]

After the Gambrill firm, one of the earliest and most successful roller mills in the state had been established at Cumberland in about 1882, producing Richard D. Johnson's "Best and American Eagle Flour." The success of this plant, and of another one on George Street called Anchor Mills, testified to the robust economic health of far western Maryland at the time. Population in Allegany County, which in 1872 lost its territory and 12,000 persons west of Big Savage and Little Savage mountains to a new county named for the B&O president, still grew from about 28,000 in 1860 to almost 40,000 in 1880. Cumberland authorities built two new bridges over Wills Creek and, for the first time, bridged the river into what now was West Virginia. A new city hall opened in time for centennial celebrations in 1876. "The largest, finest, and most costly building of the kind in Maryland, outside of the city of Baltimore," it provided first-floor space for a city market; above were rooms for fraternal orders and a multistory auditorium or Academy of Music that featured orchestra, balcony, art work on the ceiling, and a handsomely painted draw curtain depicting, boasted the town's newspaper editor, "The Decline of Carthage."[21]

The C&O took much of the credit for tying the Queen City to downstate markets. In the five or six years after 1869 the canal enjoyed its period of greatest success and highest returns. A new C&O president, James C. Clarke, set about to strengthen dams and improve the seventy-four lift locks between Cumberland and Georgetown. Canalmen had built their boats so large that pedestrian bridges in Georgetown became hazards except when the craft were fully loaded. By 1870 all the lower bridges had come down and been replaced. Besides constant maintenance headaches, Clarke wrestled with problems like enforcing the ban on Sunday pleasure boating (he decided to open the canal as a public thoroughfare) and serious operational issues. By water-lease arrangements, millers along the canal ran off C&O water to operate their mills. The poorly gauged system led to much abuse and in dry spells hampered traffic flow. Clarke tried but largely failed to impose controls on the millers. He also faced problems of volume. In 1875, when the canal handled a record 973,805 tons of freight, more than five hundred boats, averaging 112 tons burden, plied the canal. They occasionally backed up at the locks, and when the loading of vessels at Georgetown slowed—a condition Clarke could little influence—as many as eighty boats lined up single file, wasting time. Heavy loads on the C&O made the canal's various weaknesses stand out all the more prominently. Drought in 1872 aggravated differences with the millers. Heavy rains left the towpaths muddy and impassable. Mules caught sick and went lame (in the end boat-

The basin at Cumberland, c. 1890, where C&O Canal boats awaited another load of Maryland coal. *Allegany County Historical Society*

men turned them loose to die in the strip between canal and river). Floods struck in 1873 and 1874, causing damage limited only by Clarke's expensive improvements. In winter months canal usage fell off as usual.

Life on the canal at its zenith involved long hours but left some fond memories. Boats followed a common design, with a compartment for mules forward, a center section with hatches to the hold, and a rear crew's cabin, covered in summer with an awning. Aft, on the roof, one crew member managed the tiller, which called for a steady hand to keep the boat from swerving between towpath and "vern" side. Boatmen changed mules every four or six hours and guided them by special cries ("whoa" did not mean stop) that a mule handler had to deliver "in all the right accents, inflections, and quavers." As a boat captain approached a lock, as far as a quarter- or half-mile away, he tooted a tin horn for service, and in passing through the locks—where the boats fit "like a nickel in a slot"—the crew took great care. The rest could be easy. "We were tied up to no regular hours and lived in Arcadian simplicity," wrote a one-time traveler on the canal. Boatmen often worked twelve-hour days, he went on, but spent much of the time "reading, sleeping, viewing the landscape, or telling stories, in which all but the boy driving could take part." They purchased what they needed from stores and warehouses along the canal and cooked over coal-burning stoves. When they could, boatmen supplemented the usual fare of bread and ham by picking blackberries or going after the turtles that the canal (with snakes) had in abundance. They accepted more than a few stolen pigs; "there were some," wrote the same chronicler, "in fact too many, whose perception of the right of property was very dim." Yet the canal was a place for families as well. Wives of boatmen kept young children safely on harnesses and strung out wash on bow-to-stern lines. Lock tenders and their own families lived in small stone houses furnished by the company. They visited one another via passing boats.[22]

Cumberland's several rail lines made business difficult for the C&O. They forced the canal company several times to lower rates—a strategy that kept up traffic but dangerously lowered income. Incorporated in 1868, the "Pennsylvania Railroad in Maryland" finally finished a controversial line (it crossed another) that connected Cumberland to the main Pennsylvania track and New Jersey ports near New York. By 1876 the Western Maryland also took part in Cumberland's rise, sending cargo down the canal in barges and then by rail from Williamsport to Baltimore. Yet the B&O, like the National Road earlier, truly gave Cumberland its character and made it an important way station. In 1871 the B&O opened a branch line to Pittsburgh—a milestone that the Duquesne Band from that city helped to mark, along with the usual speeches, food, and heavy drink. The road long ago had built shops, sheds, and sidings in its Cumberland yards; in 1872, aiming to make the B&O as independent as possible, Garrett opened a plant in Cumberland, employing eight hundred persons, to turn out rails for the double-tracking then under way to the west.

The same year the company proudly opened the Queen City Hotel, a brick building that cost the B&O a quarter of a million dollars. Like the Cumberland city hall, it offered a good example of the highly decorative, "ginger bread" style that captured American architecture after Appomattox. Connecting four-story wings was a two-story center structure with a "tastefully finished" roof and a tall, ornately windowed cupola. Around the entire first floor designers placed a 400-foot-long porch or piazza with highly detailed wrought-iron posts and railings. Eaves and window tops displayed additional flourishes; fountains, evergreens, and shrubbery embellished the grounds—several acres bordered by town and railroad. Open to any visitor, though intended primarily for B&O passengers, the hotel, like the Queen City herself, faced the train tracks.[23]

Had a guest at the hotel been able to ride the Cumberland and Pennsylvania line or the George's Creek Railroad heading west, he soon would have entered the region that directly or indirectly affected every dollar circulating in Maryland west of North Mountain. The panhandle depended for its wealth almost entirely on minerals. Iron ore, though it did not prove as profitable to process as iron from beds in West Virginia, provided jobs in Garrett County and at mills at Lonaconing and Mount Savage west of Cumberland. Limestone deposits in the cliffs overlooking Cumberland made the Hydraulic

Cement Company one of the leading producers in the country in 1880; Hydraulic cement's transverse strength or breaking point was the highest of all domestically manufactured concrete.

Counting for more than anything else in this age of steam was coal. Some of the richest beds of bituminous coal in America lay in the George's Creek region—roughly five miles wide, between Dan's Mountain and Big Savage, and twenty-five miles long, from the Pennsylvania border to the town of Westernport where George's Creek met the Potomac's north branch. Corporations had formed to mine Maryland coal soon after the assembly chartered the B&O and C&O. The first, the Maryland Coal Company, obtained authority to purchase up to five thousand acres of land with mineral rights and powers to build railroads from its beds to Cumberland or the canal. Other firms received similar charters, many of them with capital supplied by New Yorkers like August Belmont and Erastus Corning and New Englanders who included John Murray Forbes and John F. Winslow. Highly rated as shipboard fuel, George's Creek coal also attracted Edward Cunard of the packet line. In 1864 William Aspinwall, a founder of the Pacific Mail Steamship line, and friends had combined some of their holdings and formed the Consolidation Coal Company, later the largest in the United States.

After the war Maryland coal became one of the state's chief products and exports. Although Maryland dropped from fourth in coal production among the states in 1880 to eleventh twenty years later, the importance of the product turned on its undisputed quality. "Genuine George's Creek coal," an industry journal declared in this period, "occupies a class by itself and is in a much firmer condition than any of the other Bituminous products." Money invested in Maryland coal mining increased from $605,000 in 1850 to almost $23 million in 1910. Tonnage during the same period increased from about 197,000 to 4.5 million (in 1907 the figure peaked at 5.5 million tons). About a third of it went down the canal, the rest by railroad to the "tidewater trade." George's Creek coal fueled roller mills and canning plants in Maryland, bunkered steamships in Baltimore, left that city and Washington in the coastal trade, and in 1872 reportedly went to buyers from the East Indies, Egypt, the Caribbean, Brazil, Chile, and elsewere. The U.S. Navy was a faithful customer. In 1873 the Royal Navy began buying Cumberland coal for its West Indian stations.[24]

The bituminous beds west of Cumberland lay either on the surface or in the high ground above the valley floor, making it easier and cheaper to mine and allowing the industry in Maryland to escape typical problems. At first workers had used picks and shovels in the open air, taking coal that they could see beneath their feet. By the mid-nineteenth century, surface beds gone, miners began digging tunnels or "headings" into the hills and mountains. Headings followed a pattern that lessened the danger of cave-in and aided air circulation, one of the principal problems miners faced. Two parallel shafts 30 or 100 feet apart, each 9 or 10 feet wide and usually about 8 feet high, penetrated the vein. Crossheadings connected the main shafts at various distances, leaving natural pillars as supports. Chimney-like holes ran from selected spots to the surface above; beneath these shafts a hot stove increased circulation by forcing heated air up and drawing fresh air into the tunnels. Doors at the tunnel mouths regulated the flow. To promote drainage—water was another problem—miners dug the headings at a slight upward incline until they reached the center of a mountain, then dug downward. The horizontal shafts of Cumberland mines, sparing owners expensive hoisting and pumping machinery, were far less dangerous than the vertical mines of Pennsylvania and West Virginia, particularly in an emergency. The explosive gases called "fire damp," common to mines elsewhere, hardly appeared in the Maryland coal fields.

The work was hard, however. Men labored in "rooms" off the headings and cross-headings, each chamber placed far enough from the next to leave supporting coal. All was darkness except for the small space directly in front of a miner, who wore a cap fitted with an oil-burning lamp. Working in pairs, miners used picks to make two narrow vertical cuts as far as six feet apart and three or four feet deep and next dug as deeply along the base of the block, finishing the undercutting by lying on the floor, vulnerable to slips that would crush them instantly. They then were ready to "take down" the coal, driving wedges into the top edge of the cut until the coal fell in chunks weighing as much as a ton—forcing them to jump nimbly. Two miners in this manner could take down about ten tons of coal a day, and since they were paid by the ton they spent no more time than was necessary putting up timbers and laying track for the cars that carried out loaded coal. They also paid close attention to whose turn it was to use the limited number of cars—two drivers with two cars each might serve forty or more men. Only coal carried to the company weighmaster made money. Only by overloading the two-ton cars could miners be assured that each load would count as full. Miners took pains to load pure coal. Given any sign of shale or clay in a car, the weighmaster docked a worker an arbitrary ton. The men may have escaped fire damp, but they constantly suffered from breathing carbon-filled air, known as "black damp," which, they knew, eventually corroded the lungs and killed a man. The New York writer William Cullen Bryant described miners emerging from a Maryland shaft—blackened head to foot, lamps askew—as like "sooty demons" with "flaming horns."[25]

These men and their families made up another unusual feature of Maryland mining. Even before canal and railroad brought serious commercial ventures, Maryland coal companies—British investors having their say—had imported experienced Scots and Welsh workers to the George's Creek Valley. They came to Maryland because work there resembled the labor they knew in Britain and because of the opportunities America offered. One could earn enough to purchase land, perhaps become a farmer. With such ends in view, they brought their families. As the number of Maryland miners rose from

George's Creek coal miners, c. 1890. *Allegany County Historical Society*

928 in 1860 to about 3,500 in 1886, these ethnic patterns largely held—with Cornish, Irish, and a few Germans and Eastern Europeans added. Though the first mining settlements consisted of "company" housing, Maryland firms found it more profitable to sell houses to miners than keep them, and a comparatively high proportion of Maryland miners became homeowners. Perhaps pressure from Cumberland business interests accounted for a Maryland statute of 1868 outlawing the "company store" in the Allegany fields; at any rate (though miners accused some shops of sharp practices and cozy relations with the coal firms), Maryland miners managed to steer clear of the chronic indebtedness that reduced many workers in Pennsylvania and West Virginia to peonage. Laborers in those states during this period differed also in ethnicity and marital status. Many of them arrived as bachelors from Eastern Europe, expecting to stay in this country only long enough to save some cash and return. Observers frequently noted the peculiar character of miners in the George's Creek Valley. "The population here," reported a Maryland mine inspector in 1876, "partake of the hardy character of the mountains around them and are a healthy and industrious people."[26]

⁓ϗ⁓

Few of them are "idlers," the inspector continued, and "the hive is almost entirely free from the presence of drones." Coal company managers may have shared this high regard for the George's Creek miners in 1873; they may also have likened the mines between Frostburg and Westernport to bee-hives—smoothly running, organically whole. Miners, though more moderate in Maryland than elsewhere, eventually viewed themselves differently—as stung by big coal. Over the last decades of the nineteenth century they struck the coal companies five times. Other Maryland manufacturing wage earners, who grew from 4 percent of the population in 1860 to 8 percent in 1880 and then remained at about that proportion, conducted their own strikes. Never as large a percentage as in some industrial states, workers in Maryland gradually realized that to adjust grievances and cut a larger slice of company income, they had to stand united.

In the coal fields tension between ownership and labor had as many sources as the headers had rats. Wages during the last years of the war had soared to a dollar a ton; afterward, when contraction in the coal industry led Maryland companies and others to cut pay, workers near Cumberland had resisted but finally accepted a scale of 65¢ a ton. The practice of "offtakes," or deducting costs of company services from a worker's paycheck, caused occasional friction. Legitimate charges included rent for families in company buildings, fees for medical services, and a dollar a month for each child in the "colliery schools." Coal companies also set arbitrary deductions to cover costs of sharpening and maintaining workers' tools, which often were company property, and took out home-fuel charges that did not always give miners a cut rate. Workers had little reason to place trust in weighmasters, and in the spring of 1873 issues of weights and measures brought about open conflict and work stoppages. Laborers at the Hoffman mine wanted a check of the company scales; at the Midlothian shaft miners demanded the right to place a check-weighman on duty with the weighmaster.

Airing these complaints in the *Frostburg Mining Journal* that April, an advertisement the miners placed in the paper went further: "Next, we call your attention to the UNION principle," read the piece. It called a meeting late in the month to consider forming an association "for the better protection of our interests." There were reasons to be cautious about forming a union in 1873. Pennsylvania miners had struck frequently in the period, and radicals, known as "Molly Maguires," had taken violent measures for which family men and homeowners had little taste. Organizing might mean coordinating with these laborers or striking in support of them regardless of the wishes and needs of Maryland miners. In May 1873 representatives from most George's Creek mines agreed to establish a "Miners' and Laborers' Protective and Benevolent Association of Allegany County, Maryland." Its leadership included Peter Cain and Scottish-born Thomas Brown, who had been a labor spokesman in 1853. Charging a membership fee of one dollar, the group aimed only at local services. It pledged itself to care for disabled members, to protect the lives and health of miners, spread news on all issues affecting them, "abolish as far as possible, all strikes; and to adopt, in their place,

ARBITRATION." No member was to strike without "the cognizance and approval of the General Board." The association in the beginning had no fund to support strikes.[27]

The mentality of Maryland miners stood somewhere between a worker's looking out for his concerns alone and a consciousness that viewed the interests of all laborers as one. In the fall of 1874, after leaders of the Miners' National Association made a series of appearances arguing the case for a national organization, the Allegany group affiliated with the larger union. Events soon demonstrated that Maryland miners as yet had no desire to sacrifice income for the principle of solidarity. The depression Maryland farmers faced after 1873 also brought hard times to Pennsylvania coal fields, where companies cut back wages. Workers there struck again, shifting demand to Maryland. Between 1873 and 1875 George's Creek miners escaped the worst effects of economic depression, and no appeals from the Miners' National moved them to stop work in support of other workers. Maryland miners commented that their counterparts in Ohio and Illinois seemed unhappy unless out on strike. "It's no use telling these men that they are filling the Pennsylvania contracts and ask them to stop," wrote a Frostburg observer in June 1875. "They would only laugh at you. Some of them are glad to hear of strikes in Pennsylvania." Maryland miners did raise $300 for destitute workers in Mercer County there; instead of striking in solidarity with them, however, they found the meaning of community closer to home. Lonaconing miners took a leaf from the experience of British labor unions and organized consumer cooperative stores in the town—one Scottish and the other Irish. Maryland miners petitioned the assembly for laws governing mine ventilation, scales, and worker safety. They dropped out of the national association, which soon vanished anyway, its leadership on trial for conspiracy.[28]

The hurly-burly competition of postwar America made provincialism an unaffordable luxury, especially in labor. After 1871 a mine at Clearfield, Pennsylvania (where miners received a mere 40¢ a ton), produced a grade of bituminous coal competitive with that of George's Creek. Within five years Maryland companies claimed that their part of the bituminous market had declined more than 40 percent while the Clearfield share had increased by 30 percent. Something had to give, and the operators espied high wages. In the early months of 1876 the New Central, American, and Maryland companies announced wage cuts of ten cents for the upcoming season. Meeting in angry sessions, workers voted to strike those companies; those men still employed at 65¢ agreed to pay as much as 5¢ a ton loaded for relief of the strikers. Throughout that hard year some miners worked, others did not, and everyone found it difficult to make ends meet. Quarrels among the companies postponed the workers' day of reckoning and illustrated the play of competition at the management level. The Consolidation Coal Company conducted a campaign to break local competitors by paying its employees full wages and charging the other companies high rates on the Cumberland and Pennsylvania Railroad, which it then owned. Alert to profitable side-lines, the B&O began buying a controlling interest in Consolidation Coal. Consolidation defied a new law ordering its rail rates reduced. Meanwhile miners who worked for that firm could not have believed their good fortune permanent; the Cumberland *Alleganian* cautioned that "by and by under the soft velvet glove it will show the miners the iron hand beneath."[29]

In 1877 the national economy hit its lowest point, and some Marylanders believed the Armageddon of class war had arrived. Miners in the Cumberland coal fields carried old grievances into the new year. They protested that the companies, still paying workers for two tons a carload, had installed cars built to carry more—and thus shortchanged them every time a car went to the scales. The 1876 legislature had passed an act meeting some labor appeals; state mining law now required operators to supply scales at the mouths of the mines. But workers doubted the accuracy of company weights and measures, and one inspector found at the Swanton Mine a set of scales that reduced the process to a joke—chalk marks on a beam signifying nothing and old hammer heads, spikes, and other junk piled on the counterscale. The weighmaster admitted it was all "guess-work."[30] Then, early in the year, most of the coal companies lowered wages to 50¢ a ton. The B&O applied pressure by refusing to haul coal until wages went down and then threatening to boycott any company that failed to hold the line. Badly hurt by the preceding year's hardships, workers broke ranks. Sixty or more men—apparently not experienced miners—agreed to the fifty-cent scale. Regular workers threatened them with violence; company toughs called "bulldozers" disrupted labor meetings. Bitterly, George's Creek miners went to work.

They watched that summer while other workers mounted their own struggles. Labor-management conflict on the railroads, as in the mines, pointed out the direction American economic life had taken after the war. Railroad expansion in the past decade had cost heavily. Rivalries among major eastern roads, together with the effects of depression, had brought most of them to the edge of bankruptcy by 1877. Large companies had grown large by competing well against, even devouring, other companies, yet at some point their competition became self-destructive. In April of that year the B&O, Pennsylvania, New York Central, and Erie met to negotiate an end to the "rate wars" that nearly had ruined them. Out of the meeting there also came an agreement to cut wages. While mining and railroad companies earlier might have seen themselves as patrons and benefactors, differences in interest between owners and workers had become too clear to ignore. B&O employees complained that the road gave them only two or three days of work a week. The company sent engineers and firemen out on freight trains that took them far from home and made no provision for them while they awaited, sometimes for days, a train in the other direction—the B&O refused to issue the passes that would have allowed trainmen a free return ride.

Promotion policies and work classification produced more grievances. The railroad announced wage reductions to take effect Monday, 17 July.

Depending on one's sympathies, what happened next was either a labor strike or an insurrection against lawful authority. On Sunday, 16 July, B&O firemen walked off the job at Camden Junction outside Baltimore, where the line to Washington left the main stem. Company agents fired them immediately. As tempers flared the B&O obtained the services of the Baltimore police, who, though outside city limits, arrested the malcontents for inciting to riot. The next day thirty-eight engineers left their jobs in support of firemen; the strike soon included laborers at the Mount Clare shops. Roused from their beds late Monday night, B&O officials learned that strikers at Martinsburg, West Virginia, had halted trains at that important relay station. On Tuesday morning an engine derailed near Spring Gardens in South Baltimore—as if sabotaged. That afternoon word arrived that B&O workers at two other West Virginia points had struck. Later in the week striking rail workers in Pittsburgh exploded in anger—looting, burning, and sending "Communistic madness" (said the industry detective Allan Pinkerton) through the region. At Cumberland disgruntled elements included C&O canal boatmen, on strike since mid-June, and B&O steel workers, who recently had been laid off. Assembled to protest against the moneyed interests, some workers let themselves go. They broke into B&O boxcars and helped themselves to perishable goods.[31]

At the end of that eventful week, workers knew plainly on whose side authority lay. On Tuesday John King, Jr., B&O vice-president, had sent the governor of West Virginia, Henry Mathews, an urgent telegram requesting a militia call-up to protect B&O property at Martinsburg. Rumors circulated that the troops sympathized with strikers. The stories need not have been true; West Virginia politicians knew their debts to the railroad. B&O officers soon goaded Mathews into requesting the aid of federal troops at Martinsburg, and then sent President Hayes a long telegram supporting the call, which the chief executive honored. Hearing of disturbances in Cumberland, sleepless railroad managers decided to ask Governor John Lee Carroll to dispatch the Maryland militia there. On Friday, 20 July, the order went out to James Herbert, late commander of the Confederate 2d Maryland, who agreed to ring "Big Sam"—the bell traditionally pulled in times of peril. Big Sam began ringing about six o'clock that evening, when Baltimore workers left their jobs, and as the 5th and 6th regiments mustered and moved to Camden Station, Baltimoreans turned out as they had not since the nineteenth of April, 1861.

Mobs of men and boys seized on the moment to vent anger that had built up over several years of hard times. The B&O became their scapegoat and the militiamen objects of scorn as railroad dupes. In trying to move from armory to train station, the 6th Maryland, traveling in company-size groups, fired at will into the people who stoned them. Ten of the rioters died; another

"The Great Strike—the Sixth Maryland Regiment Fighting its way through Baltimore." *Harper's Weekly,* 11 August 1877. *MHS*

twenty-five were injured. Late in the evening a crowd of about fifteen thousand amassed around Camden Station, where King, Governor Carroll, Mayor Ferdinand C. Latrobe, General Herbert, and police officials maintained their watch. With some members of the mob doing their best to destroy B&O cars and telegraph office, Governor Carroll at about 10 P.M. granted King's wish and wired President Hayes to send U.S. troops to Baltimore as well. City police began arresting the chief rioters—who turned out not to be strikers so much as practiced streetfighters. There were disturbances on Saturday, but comparative calm returned to the city on Sunday.

The B&O strike both polarized labor and management and embarrassed labor leaders who needed to avoid radical tags. Its effect on the labor movement was not immediately clear. Most Americans, natives who feared imported violence or immigrants who wanted to fit in, abhorred lawlessness and shrank from any hint of the revolutionary. The Brotherhood of Locomotive Engineers promised to punish B&O strikers. Eugene Debs, a young organizer for the Locomotive Firemen's Union, warned his men against siding with "anarchy and revolution." Out of long habit, many workers remained loyal to the B&O rather than joining the strike, and John Garrett wanted the B&O to remain a hive of faithful bees. Every man who stands "squarely against the tyrannical influences of the demagogues" and does his duty now, he wrote on 28 July, when the strike almost had been broken, "will win position and entitle himself . . . to the confidence of the Company in the future." Garrett had no concept of a legitimate labor strike; just as during the war, the good of the country depended upon the good of the railroad. "Let them see that the arm of the law is extended with instantaneous effect against them," he said of strike leaders. "We have the power. We have the public sentiment with us. We have the interests of the whole people in accord with us against a few." A Baltimore merchant took a larger-minded approach in writing the *Sun*. "The strike is not a revolution of fanatics willing to fight for an idea," he argued. "It is a revolt of workingmen against low prices of labor which have not been accompanied with correspondingly low prices of food, clothing, and house rent."[32]

In the ten years after the B&O strike, the Knights of Labor, a national society with origins in postwar Philadelphia, did as much as any organization to voice labor grievances in Maryland. The order drew strength from its fraternal character and moderate policies. Strikes it viewed only as a last resort; local assemblies were left open to skilled and unskilled alike (although city workers usually gathered by trade) and to women and blacks. In 1878 the Knights formed an assembly in Baltimore. That year locals also formed in the Allegany County coal region, where finally the K of L had eighteen assemblies. Cumberland canal boatmen, woodworkers, hod carriers, and factory men each had their own local. Workers in Elkton, Northeast, Port Deposit, Bel Air, Havre de Grace, Ellicott City, Bladensburg, Hyattsville, and Hagerstown formed "mixed" local assemblies.

The Knights did register gains in Maryland. They stressed education—both encouraging the self-improvement of members and taking their case to the public. Their leaders had noted that few trustworthy sources provided evidence of the workers' plight or the trends that might persuade legislators to act on labor's behalf. In 1884, with the strong support of the K of L, the General Assembly passed a bill creating a state Bureau of Industrial Statistics. Maryland joined twelve other states and the federal government in making regular assessments of laboring conditions. Too, the order in Maryland succeeded in avoiding the condemnation of the Catholic church, which forbade the faithful from joining secret societies and in papal pronouncements also had criticized socialist ideologies. In the early 1880s two priests in Maryland coal country, Valentine F. Schmitt of Frostburg and James O'Brien of Lonaconing, took comparatively tolerant stands on the oaths and rituals of the "Noble and Holy" Knights while seeking direction from Archbishop James Gibbons of Baltimore. Gibbons, who as a young priest had divided his time between parishes at Fells Point and Locust Point, later permitted Catholic workers to join.

Many Catholic miners enlisted in this fraternal struggle, and in the late 1870s the Knights of Labor claimed 1,750 members in the Maryland coal region. But the union again failed when it counted. Maryland miners had learned that their strength depended on the will of men who worked in other eastern coal shafts; in 1880 George's Creek families sent money and food to sustain a Clearfield strike that sought wages of 65¢ a ton. In the following year Frostburg miners felt bold enough to publish guidelines for labor policy in the local newspaper: $2.50 a day minimum wage, five tons per man a standard day's production, a ten-hour work day. Union miners were to take a fired man's place until his case underwent investigation. With the unity the K of L provided, miners successfully demanded that boys be allowed to work with their fathers and that company charges for sharpening tools not exceed half a cent per ton loaded. Then in 1882 the companies dropped wages to the per-ton rate of 50¢ that Clearfield workers had accepted. Maryland miners struck—and also lost. In 1884 their pay dropped to 40¢. Either alone or organized, they faced obstacles beyond their power, for the time, to remove: the American fear of labor militancy, the power of big industries, and the availablity of cheap labor.

❧

In Baltimore, where most cheap labor was available, the lives of ordinary people drew a telling picture of the urban experience in post–Civil War America. Beginning in the 1850s, horse-drawn public coaches or omnibuses had permitted middle-income Baltimoreans to live in neighborhoods a distance from the center of the city—around Union Square, out Broadway, and along Madison Avenue. Even these newer homes, however, had alley houses for black and Irish servants. As late as 1870 Baltimoreans of varied backgrounds and income lived somewhat scattered throughout the city.

In later years, with increasing dispatch, Baltimoreans who could afford to move from the old city did so, creating in their wake space that new immigrants crowded into. As usual with migration, some forces pushed and various attractions pulled. Expanding companies bought blocks of houses near the basin, tore them down, and put up warehouses. Old commercial buildings came down and taller ones, often made with iron facades like the one made famous by the Sun Building, took their places, emphasizing the differences between work and home life. Few people whose incomes permitted a

Row house construction, c. 1890. Workers pause in front of a row like others that filled newly expanding, middle-class sections of Baltimore. *MHS*

Union Passenger Railway, c. 1890. *MHS*

choice wished to live amidst "the din and confusion of business," as a contemporary put it, "the noise of carts and drays, the shaking and jostling of wagons and vehicles, the rattling of omnibuses."[33]

Developers for their part lured customers to new houses that went up by several thousand each year during the 1880s—reaching and extending beyond the city limits at North Avenue. As earlier in the century, these row houses followed the styles that more expensive homes had established as the norm; many of the postbellum houses imitated the Italianate patterns set at places like Mt. Vernon Place before the war. Often three stories high, they had gaslights, hot water, central heating, and conveniences like doorbells and speaking tubes. New housing responded to population growth; it also had sources in "advance credit" arrangements by which property owners, piecemeal and at reasonable rates, lent contractors the cash they needed to build. Joseph M. Cone, who liked to put up a hundred similar buildings at a time, used this method in developing the northwestern part of the city, including the Edmondson estate, which became Harlem Park.

The boom also depended on an improved transportation network. Omnibuses jolted over cobblestone streets and sank in mud. The new horsecars, running on rails, were far more reliable, and owners of suburban land were clever enough to win horsecar franchises that made their housing attractive. Citizens Railway ran lines from Druid Hill Park to the wharves and then eastward to Patterson Park. It had a part in developing land along Madison Avenue. The Frick lines extended service to Peabody Heights, out Edmondson Avenue to Harlem Park, and along Fulton Avenue. A new horse-drawn railway with double-decker cars ran between Baltimore City Hall and Towson, another out Harford Road and Homestead Avenue. With these lines in place, Baltimoreans tended as never before to settle according to means and ethnicity. Better-off Germans moved out the northeast corridor to newer homes on Harford and Belair roads and up Broadway to North Avenue. Jewish families of wealth moved to Eutaw Place, an elegant new neighborhood with a wide boulevard that styled itself after both the Parisian Champs Elysées and Unter den Linden in Berlin. Baltimore churches, which until 1850 had been located within a half-mile of Baltimore and Calvert streets, followed the migration outward. Bishop Whittingham thought the Episcopal flight worldly; a Baptist leader called it letting the poor "go to perdition."[34]

Truly the working people of Baltimore took what was left over, but not all of them were sorry for it. In 1877, a depressed year, many of them had protested economic hardship by rioting. In 1886, a good year, eleven thousand took to the streets again, this time parading through the city on Labor Day, 1 May, wearing uniforms or marching under banners according to trade and place of work. Among them were piano makers, shoemakers, hatters, shipworkers, barbers, oil workers, paperhangers, tobacco workers, stonemasons, millers, and longshoremen. The eight-hour parade made several points about the city and the people who worked with their hands. It displayed the momentary strength of the Knights of Labor, who that year chartered sixty-eight new assemblies in Baltimore, reaching a peak of more than a hundred locals. The parade also demonstrated organizational strength among blacks. Negro grain carriers made up one K of L local; at the 1886 national meeting in Richmond, Virginia, the Maryland delegation included at least one black representative. Observers of the parade commented on the apparent fraternalism among black and white brick makers, who received cheers for their part in the housing surge. The parade betrayed divisions of labor and ethnic dominance in certain kinds of work. Marching B&O workers were mostly Irish, butchers German. The butchers, instead of wearing aprons and carrying cleavers as they had in earlier parades, rode in carriages or atop black horses while black employees behind them carried the tools of the trade. Revealing for what people saw, the parade spoke volumes because of who did not appear—the thousands who claimed no trade and had no skill.

Cheap labor, complementing late-nineteenth-century technological changes, led to the mature factory system—to the skilled-crafts decline that Baltimore journeymen had feared as early as the Jefferson years. Mechanization brought revolutionary change in some industries, allowing companies to lay off unneeded workers and visiting hardship on many households. In the canneries machines replaced the men who made cans, labeled, and boxed. The Baltimore shoe industry in 1873 had employed 4,000 persons in thirty companies. By 1890 a mere eighteen firms did the same work or more with 846 hands. Among the men who actively supported B&O workers in the July 1877 riot were Baltimore box makers, sawyers, and can makers—victims of mechanization. In the 1886 parade, proudly or apprehensively, men from a furniture plant carried a mock-up of a steam-powered saw.

As firms replaced skilled with low-wage, unskilled labor, they relied heavily on women and children. Between 1870 and 1890 the Baltimore working class changed accordingly. While the number of men earning wages nearly doubled, the number of women doing so almost quadrupled. At the end of the century children below the age of sixteen made up about 5 percent of the city work force. Whole broods of children accompanied their mothers to the canning plants, where women eventually accounted for more than half the adult employees. Women also worked in tobacco plants, the boot and shoe industry; they made tinware and bottled chemicals and drugs. Women formed their own K of L assemblies and marched in the 1886 parade. In the summer months many of them took their children to labor camps on the Eastern Shore. Living in barracks-like sheds, they there picked fruits and vegetables or worked in the seasonal canneries. Unskilled labor fueled the workingman's deepest fear—a drop in the value of labor itself.

After 1880 the supply of inexpensive, willing labor increased with an influx of foreign immigrants who made a social and economic impact alike. Either docking at Locust Point, where immigration authorities checked their health, or arriving by rail from New York, the newcomers had little or no

Women's shucking department, W. H. Killian Co., c. 1890. *MHS*

property or education; their clothes and habits were as strange as their language. An early report of the state Bureau of Industrial Statistics noted that Italians had "dispossessed the colored and Irish labor on the railroads and along the waterfronts, and have filled the streets of our cities with fruit vendors"; others it described as "unfortunate outcasts" who "come to us generally in great distress and poverty."[35] To break the 1882 Maryland coal miners' strike (the B&O stood to lose money both as a carrier and as a stockholder in Consolidation Coal), Garrett had shipped some of these immigrants directly from Locust Point to guarded camps in the George's Creek Valley. In Baltimore, Polish, Lithuanian, and Latvian labor joined blacks shoveling coal into the holds of ships at the basin, taking their chances with steam-powered machinery that burned and mangled unwary tenders, doing the heaviest work at the Spring Garden oil storage facility, handling garbage for the Irish refuse haulers, working on city projects, or in hard times breaking rocks for charity organizations that offered soup for gravel.

Many of the new arrivals were Jews fleeing czarist persecution in Russia and Eastern Europe. More than 24,000 of them arrived in Baltimore between 1881 and 1890, and another 17,000 in the next decade. Not all of them stayed, nor did German Jews in the city—who numbered about 10,000 in 1880—feel prepared to encourage them to stay. The secretary of the Emigrant Aid Society that native Jews established to deal with the newcomers wrote his counterpart in New York to halt the flow toward Baltimore—there were no jobs for them. In the end German Jews nonetheless did their best to safeguard the immigrants' welfare. In August 1882 they took up a collection for 269 "Russians" (as all were called), most of whom had no work. Almost half the thirty-eight hundred dollars raised went toward resettling Russians in the West. When immigration officials began turning away Russian Jews with red eyes, supposedly because they had contracted trachoma, Baltimoreans wrote Jews in Warsaw not to wash with saltwater aboard ship—the reason for the unhealthy appearance. After 1882 federal law permitted immigration inspectors to turn away anyone likely to become a public burden. Later, when officials demanded a one-thousand-dollar bond for each of 58 Russians detained at Locust Point to guarantee their solvency, Baltimore Jews offered the buildings of their Hebrew Hospital and Orphan Asylum as security. At a meeting of Baltimore Jews on the Russian issue someone said the newcomers ought to return to Europe. William Schloss protested in an appeal that finished by quoting the Old Testament: "Hear, O Israel: the Lord is our God, the Lord is One."[36]

Those Jews who stayed in Baltimore often found their niche in the clothing industry, which before the war had been especially concentrated in a three-block square northwest of Charles and West Baltimore streets. Making ready-to-wear clothes on a large scale had brought about several work patterns. Some apparel could be made in factories, where a few tailors oversaw the work of thirty or more unskilled workers, each of whom accomplished one simple task—cutting patterns or sewing buttons—as the garment took shape. More in evidence after the Civil War, the factory system accounted for many of the women and even children who joined the Baltimore labor force in the late nineteenth century. By another practice clothiers gave simple jobs to families to do at home—a piecework hangover from earlier cottage-industry practices. State surveys revealed that even with the rise of factories many women still worked at home, sewing up to eighteen hours a day for three to five dollars a week. Manufacturers of certain garments—especially men's coats—preferred putting out jobs to contractors, who in turn hired enough men, women, and children to accomplish the work. The contractor's profit in the competitive industry depended on his undercutting others and then underpaying or "sweating" his work force to ensure a return. The contracting system divided labor so it did not have to be done in the commercial district, and by the 1880s contractors had begun using the attics and lofts of Baltimore dwellings for this work. As they did, the clothing district spread along East and West Baltimore streets, southward toward the docks, and northeastward.

Penniless, highly vulnerable to the labor market, Eastern Europeans quickly fell prey to sweatshop operators. Neighborhoods in Old Town and East Baltimore—though one could not always tell from the outside that the upstairs or rear of a building housed a sweatshop—offered studies in density, poverty, and strangeness. North Exeter Street became "a crowded place of tenement houses, saloons, filthy shops, foul odors, hideous noises"; buildings in the area commonly displayed "broken shutters and unsightly curtains." The Orthodox Jewish among the newcomers brought with them an attachment to the *mikve* or public bath, which struck the German Jews as hopelessly Old World; the industrial statistics bureau observed that in the 5th and 6th wards of Baltimore "the Anglo-Saxon dialect is seldom heard." The new immigrants were said to despise soap. "The women go unkempt," wrote a reporter visiting East Baltimore, "the men unwashed." In 1889 a young German-Jewish woman, Henrietta Szold, daughter of Rabbi Benjamin Szold and in later life a leading Zionist, opened a school for Russian immigrant children in East Baltimore, where she also chose to live. Most youngsters, she said, grew up knowing "only drudgery and grinding work. Their home life is not enticing. They became Americans," she noted sadly, "in naught but levity, shocking grammar, and the despicable smartness of the street and factory."[37]

Meantime, as neighborhood changes eroded the urban tax base, Baltimore City and County haggled over the developed belt that had wrapped itself around the city beyond its 1817 boundaries. Beginning with the 1864 constitution (at the behest of Baltimore County), the state permitted urban annexation only with the consent of the people in outlying territory. City officials hungered for the revenue the belt produced but had to make annexation attractive enough to win the referendum; Baltimore County commissioners figured that the suburbanites, only a third of the county population, yielded two-thirds of its tax income. An annexation bill that the assembly passed in 1874 suffered defeat because county officials warned of higher taxes and the city badly timed a rate increase. In the next fourteen years contractors built 10,000 new houses beyond North Avenue, and the belt population to the north and west approached 38,000 people. Lacking adequate water, police, and fire services, suburban Baltimoreans began reconsidering the issue. Mayor Latrobe put together a package that included half-rate taxes for twelve years in the annexed disticts, and in Annapolis powerful fellow Democrats guided the measure through the legislative mill. In the referendum of 1888—each district voting separately—Baltimore County residents one mile north and west of the old city line voted to join Baltimore City.

Not all built-up areas lay within the new boundaries. Along the Patapsco's Anne Arundel County shore, development proceeded swiftly after 1878, when the state had purchased the Light Street Bridge (over the Middle Branch of the Patapsco) and made it toll-free. In 1882 the B&O laid track to Curtis Bay and in the 1890s built a coal pier there. Other heavy industries joined the railroad, and factory neighborhoods grew up at Brooklyn, Fairfield, Wagner's Point (named for a cannery that hired many Poles), and Hawkins Point. Across the river, East Baltimore rejected annexation and continued to develop in its own way. Canton had grown into an industrial lot with railyards, warehouses, canning, bottling, and fertilizer plants, sawmills, forges, copper refineries, and Abbott's ironworks. Aggressively building railroad connections before and after the Civil War, borrowing against the estimated future value of its newest land acquisitions, and recruiting labor from Germany, Switzerland, Austria, and Britain, the Canton Company in the 1870s emerged as a prime example of paternal industry. It made draining and planning decisions still untried in Baltimore City. Laying out streets and avenues in Canton and, after 1870, in adjacent Highlandtown, the company graded and paved them, mapped twenty-five hundred lots 20 by 100 feet, and offered workers housing at bargain rates. Owners promised "Even he who earns only $480 a year may own a home." They gave land for churches and built recreation halls.[38]

Stable residential patterns in Canton and Highlandtown proved how attached people had grown to their work and community. Fathers and sons worked at the same factories. Locals consisted heavily of foreign-born in 1880, and they placed a high value on family and church. Illustrating both the ethnic character of the area and its cooperative spirit, just before the turn of the century, when Ukrainians began arriving there in numbers, St. Stanislaus Polish-Catholic parish offered the newcomers, Slavs of the Eastern Rite, free use of its church building. Though East Baltimoreans made a point of keeping their stoops clean, they also took pride in the town's broad-shouldered character. Highlandtown had attracted coal oil refineries, distilleries, breweries, and slaughterhouses—"nine-tenths of which," according to a resident, "were driven out of the city because municipal ordinances defined them as obnoxious." Possible industrial regulation, but also laws touching one's after-work way of life, made annexation unappealing in 1888: Baltimore City had closed saloons on Sundays. City spokesmen appeared in Highlandtown to defend annexation but left when it became clear their speeches might start a riot.[39]

Always a city of diversity, Baltimore in the 1890s became a confederation of neighborhoods. Served by the Broadway Market, Fells Point retained its nautical flavor. Around the base of Federal Hill, James F. Morgan, an active

contractor-speculator, built scaled-down Italianate row houses for the workers in that neighborhood. Mount Clare–Carroll Park (or Pigtown, apparently
so-called for once being a slaughterhouse assembly point) formed another
low-income area made up of B&O workers and employees of the Bartlett-
Hayward Company, a stove and iron work manufacturer that had bought the
Winans locomotive works. In the 1870s, still on the scene, Ross Winans used
London prototypes in building experimental tenement housing for B&O
workers on Parkin Street, just east of the Mount Clare shops; Winans's son
Thomas, who before the Civil War had played a large role in developing the
imperial Russian rail system, owned land to the south, toward Ferry Bar, on
which he built additional worker housing. Building upon Honey Alley, Baltimore blacks formed a neighborhood known as Sharp-Leadenhall—roughly
between Federal Hill and Camden Station and extending along the tracks to
the south. South Baltimore, stretching from Federal Hill to Locust Point,
became a community of two-story houses built for employees of surrounding companies. Served by the old Cross Street Market, natives lived amidst
B&O yards, streets that needed paving, saloons, shipyards, and plants turning out fertilizer, chemicals, paint, kitchenware, and canned foods. The revised city boundaries encompassed Waverly, a Victorian village of frame
houses out York Road, and old Gwynn's Falls milling towns like Dickeyville.
In the Jones Falls valley Baltimore also acquired a community of textile-mill-
ing towns—Remington, Stone Hill, Brick Hill, Druidville, Sweetaire, Clipper,
Hampden, and Woodberry—collectively known as Hampden-Woodberry.

These mill villages consisted largely of company-owned stone and brick
houses. Mill owners, who themselves lived in larger homes on the surrounding hills, often controlled the factories for generations and their own paternalism toward employees withstood all but the sternest efforts to organize
unions. In the 1880s the Knights of Labor listed but two assemblies in Hampden-Woodberry. One-quarter of the workers in these years were children.
Some of them recalled sledding on nearby hillsides during slack periods on
a winter's day; fathers also were known to punish boys who presumed to
"strike." Women made up a large part of the cotton milling work force. Some
entire families had to put in hours at the prevailing wage rates.

It nonetheless spoke of the better side of the arrangement that mill owners
in Hampden-Woodberry encouraged workers to save money for their own
homes. Savings societies, like ground rents, had become familiar in Baltimore. Housing construction in the 1880s proved that putting them together
produced more row houses. Assuring the property owner an annual income, ground rents promoted intensive development; by saving a working
family land costs, they also helped laborers become homeowners. Savings
institutions had a like effect. They usually had between fifty and two hundred subscribers, whose average deposit stood at $300 (larger banks might
have twenty-one thousand depositors with an average balance of more than
$1,000), and made low-interest loans in typical amounts of between $100 and

$1,500. They first appeared in Baltimore before the Civil War, one of the practical devices the German/Slavic-Catholic Redemptorist fathers introduced to help their struggling parishioners. Later in the century employers had a hand in forming yet others. Builders established some of the savings societies to promote sales. Most organized because ordinary people saw their advantages. They incorporated the aspirations of an ethnic group, a neighborhood, or workers in a single company. The names people gave the societies made clear how important certain values were to them—Perseverance, Harmony, Enterprise—or stated a belief that better times were inevitable: Permanent, Perpetual, Progressive. Employees of the B&O and Pennsylvania railroads had savings plans. Germans had their William Tell and Germania savings and loans. Bohemians named one for St. Wenceslaus. Polish families formed their own societies, Jews others. These associations tended to pull together people who then sought housing that later kept them neighborly.

Maryland working people played as hard as they worked. Oyster dredgers proved the point. Every Maryland city of size had an address, saloon, or block where one could repair at quitting time to pursue pleasure somewhat along the Fells Point–Crisfield model. Other activities, more usual, less scandalous, threw light on several late-nineteenth-century social themes. Increasing structure in a workingman's life may have had a part in promoting friendly societies. Ethnic differences led to enjoyments that both proclaimed ethnicity and built bridges to larger culture. The ten-hour workday had become common in the 1890s, some trades even winning nine-hour days. The rise of "off-hours" leisure, along with improvements in national communication, contributed to the development of popular sport.

On the Eastern Shore hunting long had been a favorite pastime of the waterman, whose life never quite succumbed to industrial rhythms. Spring migrations of small wading wildfowl, flickers, and hawks brought out Shoremen with a taste for bird pies or need for cash. Gunners most religiously went after the canvasback and mallards and the Canada geese that visited the Chesapeake in large numbers each autumn. Then traveling south, the birds fed on the bay's grasses and hid in its abundant marshes. Two centuries of experience had taught Maryland hunters the science of duck blinds, the nasty trick of setting nets below the water surface to entrap diving birds, and the finer arts of dog training. Dogs could be taught to perform antics on the shore to pull ducks within shotgun range. Others swam after downed birds, even breaking ice to get there; bred of Newfoundland stock, long-haired, usually dark brown or tan, the best ones formed a breed known as the Chesapeake Bay Retriever. With their favorite dogs along, many Shoremen preferred hunting wildfowl as they went after oysters—in special boats. Disguised sculls made floating blinds. The gunning skiff emerged as a shallow-draft boat with a spot on the bow for a large-caliber punt gun, whose blasts satisfied the worst human greed. In the 1890s, when the popular taste for canvasback equaled that for oysters, sport gave way to commerce—to live decoys, blinding lights, and multiple-barreled shotguns.

At the mercy of the weather (and unable to work when ice covered the bay), watermen wrestled with empty time and the pull of family that was central to their evangelical beliefs. Shoremen discussed hunting and fishing regulations, along with plenty of other topics, at the riverside or wharf stores, where men gathered off the boats to pass their time. There they had a weekday (or cold weather) tradition of passing around a bottle of local whiskey for every five tubs of oysters brought in. On warm Sundays, by contrast, watermen and their families might well enjoy a fish fry, church outing, or picnic. In a piece for the *Sun* in 1882 Frederic Emory of Queen Anne's County recalled such lazy afternoons spent rowing, fishing, and sailing, and gatherings on elm- and cedar-shaded river banks where "crabs, oysters, and fish just from the water were cooked in a pot suspended over a huge fire of logs or roasted in the coals."[40]

Miners west of Cumberland, facing their own layoffs in the winter months, when ice halted shipments on the canal, indulged themselves in what outsiders thought rude and boorish amusements. Actually they fused British and Maryland traditions. Scots miners introduced curling on icy creeks and the canal. Miners enjoyed shooting matches in which they fired at twenty-one live pigeons; in 1874 winner and runner-up hit eighteen and seventeen, and the Cumberland *Civilian and Telegraph* declared it likely "the most successful shooting ever done in the United States, by laboring men." Saloons—the miners may have preferred to call them public houses—formed one cornerstone of mining communities. Tiny towns on St. George's Creek like Barton and Pekin had six or seven pubs. Lonaconing supported twelve tippling houses and Frostburg twenty places that combined eating and drinking. One Frostburg resident believed it "disgraceful" that grog shops infested "every available space" and were "established on every corner." Men who fought five tons of coal a day thought nothing of pounding on one another, if the price were right. Prizefights, though illegal, provided furtive entertainment as "sparring exhibitions." Cock fighting, well grounded in Maryland and remembered from the British coal fields, became commonplace in Allegany County. Purses grew invitingly high. Vale Summit or Pompey Smash, a town as tough as its name, managed cock fights so that, when beaten by outsiders, townsmen seized the winning birds. Only two things could call a meeting of Maryland coal miners, a puzzled union organizer said in 1891, "prize fighting and chicken-sparring."[41]

More peaceably, Marylanders illustrated the postwar importance of the secret, fraternal society. Three such groups had hatched in the state. Maryland Red Men claimed to grow out of an Annapolis chapter of the Sons of Liberty during the Revolution. The Odd Fellows, a British association, had their American beginnings in Baltimore not long after the War of 1812. Knights of Pythias, taking as their model the legendary Greek's willingness to sacrifice himself for a friend, organized in Baltimore in 1867. These groups, and others with equally mysterious passwords and handgrasps, enjoyed considerable success in the post–Civil War years. Frederick, not a large town in 1880, had two masonic lodges, one "commandery" of the Knights Templar, a Knights of Pythias lodge, another of the Knights of Honor, an "encampment" of Odd Fellows, and a tribe of the Independent Order of Red Men. Most of the various conclaves and chapters had been chartered after the war, when Hagerstown residents organized lodges of Odd Fellows, Knights of Honor, and a council of the Royal Arcanum. At the same time new lodges of Masons, Odd Fellows, and Knights of Pythias sprang up in Cumberland.

So unlike the antebellum Know-Nothings in being apolitical and open armed, these postwar secret societies made interesting period pieces. Some of them were upright and abstemious; in the Jackson years a few teetotaling Red Men had split to organize "improved" and "independent" branches of the parent order. Catholic and Jewish associations usually had insurance, orphan care, and charitable fund raising as their primary goals; Negro groups, like the Mutual Brotherhood of Liberty the Baptist minister Harvey Johnson and others formed in Baltimore in 1885, continued the mutual-help efforts of earlier free-black organizations. But in their search for harmless fun, members also shed sidelight on the age. Probably the factory's dangers made after-hours fraternity especially attractive to workers—it provided them a chance to let off steam, as the saying went, after a trying day on the job. The lodges and conclaves also provided temporary escape from domestic duties—from the heavy responsibilities that society defined for males in the Victorian household. Finally, the secret societies gave members a few hours of welcomed equality. In a "wigwam" or the like, a clerk could learn the firm's politics and tell stories on his boss. A wage earner might scale heights his job never permitted. He might even outrank his foreman.

Baltimore immigrants kept memories of the Old Country alive, enjoyed themselves, and tried to melt in the American pot. Germans, whose numbers sharply increased in the late nineteenth century, patronized more than two dozen breweries. "The manufacture of lager beer," proclaimed a Baltimore chronicle of 1881, "is conducted by large establishments and upon the most extensive scale."[42] Leading local brands—on tap at taverns and beer gardens, some available in jugs and bottles—included Bauernschmidt, Chesapeake, Dukehart, Eagle, Gunther, Helldorfer, National, and Vonderhorst. Since 1863 the popular American Brewing Company had produced its beer on North Gay Street, in an ornate brick building with towers, spires, and stained-glass windows. A likeness of Gambrinus, patron saint of brewers, overlooked its heavily decorated main door.

The Germans also made their presence felt by a year-round sequence of

Helldorfer Brewery, Canton. From a program for the Brewers' and Maltsters' Convention held in Baltimore, 1887. *MHS*

social and cultural occasions. They conducted gymnastics events and singing contests. Musically ambitious middle-class choirs—the Liederkranz and Germania Männerchor—appealed to Baltimore Germans, who also formed more modest, folk choirs like the Arion. Origins of the Arion lay with an *arbeiter gesangverein* (workers' singing society) that the city prosecuted in 1872 for drinking at Sunday night meetings. Germans loved picnics, one of which in these years brought together fifteen hundred Knabe employees who loudly applauded recited poems honoring pianos, lager beer, and Limburger cheese. Every Christmas season brought performances of German classics and raising of a "Christmas Bush" at the German Orphans' Home. Shooting societies held annual festivals that ran for days and involved much beer drinking and merrymaking before a champion marksman emerged. Intensely German, these functions could also dull ethnicity by making it familiar to others (gradually lessening its "strangeness") and demonstrating love for America. Sponsors of a "Grand National Bottle Dance" in 1872 presented contest winners with French champagne, two German wines, and Irish whiskey. At a meeting of the American *saengerbund* in Baltimore, orators praised Wodan (German god of war) and Charlemagne, Luther and Cromwell, Franklin and Jefferson.

Recreation and transportation grew symbiotically in Baltmore, where for many years a notoriously backward transit system left little choice but local enjoyments like staying at home, attending church activities, or patronizing the neighborhood saloon. The horsecar made it much easier for everyone, especially people of limited means, to move about. As they did—thanks to an early program linking water, transportation, and parks—they helped to build an impressive city park system. In the late 1850s, when Baltimoreans had clamored for more public green space, Mayor Thomas Swann and the city council had laid a farsighted tax on public transit fares—a penny on a nickel ticket—and put the revenue toward water reservoirs that also created new parks. Before the Civil War the city purchased the old Rogers estate, Druid Hill, as part of the water-supply system. By the 1880s the attractions of Druid Hill included nine picnic groves spaced over 693 acres, two lakes, boats for hire, winter skating, sloping lawns, a refreshment stand, and a well-stocked zoo that introduced city dwellers to wild and domestic creatures alike. To mark the opening of another reservoir, Loch Raven, citizens in September 1881 held the first of several "Oriole Festivals"—three days of Mardi Gras–like revelry. Baltimore horsecars (and the railroads that brought out-of-town visitors) helped to swell the crowds one year to about 150,000 persons, who watched the floats go by, attended costume balls, or marched to the "Oriole Quickstep."

In the mid-1880s electric streetcars extended the range of city amusements. Baltimoreans rode the streetcars to visit old Patterson Park, Federal Hill (a park since 1879), and new open sites—the Carroll Mansion park in the southwest corner of the city and Clifton Park in the northeast. The new German schützen park northeast of the city, blending rifle range and picnic grounds, relied on the trolleys. Streetcar companies opened amusement parks at the end of their lines for summer recreation at a cost of only a nickel round-trip. Some of them provided outlying amusements that altered the courtship habits of young people, who earlier might have spent more time with each other's parents or at a corner soda fountain. One mecca, out Reisterstown Road near Belvedere Avenue, called itself Electric Park. The Lake Roland Railway opened Lakeside, a wooded area with a merry-go-round and picnic pavilion. Westward on North Avenue was Ridgewood Park. Riverview, below Canton on the Patapsco, proved popular as a beer garden. Streetcars swelled crowds at Pimlico or "Old Hilltop," an oval track on Belvedere Avenue where in 1870 the revived Maryland Jockey Club had begun seasonal horse racing and where, in 1877, most members of Congress suddenly had repaired en masse to see a sweepstakes run. Lines also served a spot that in the mid-1890s became all the rage. As The Vineyard, the estate of William Gilmor, Sr., the land in 1840 had been the site of one of the first chivalric tournaments in Maryland. Now near 25th Street and Greenmount Avenue, it was the Union Base Ball Park.

Changes in leisure time, law, and taste had produced the era of professional sports for mass audiences, horse racing and baseball serving as examples. In antebellum times gentlemen bred and raced thoroughbreds, making polite wagers on the results; their sons wore white uniforms and straw

"Maryland Jockey Club." Colored lithograph by A. Hoen & Co., Baltimore, c. 1875. *MHS*

hats to play ballgames that a few friends may have watched. After the war the turf gained wider interest in Maryland and small-scale betting became frenzied business, legalized in 1890. Crowds thronged to the track, drinking and fighting were common, and one had to choose companions carefully. A similar rise in spectatorship and business structure transformed baseball. The first openly salaried players in the country, the Cincinnati Red Stockings, visited Baltimore in 1869 for a game out Madison Avenue against a team of local all-stars, the Marylands, who said they were "champions of the South." Though the champions lost handily, 47 to 7, the game fired public interest in the sport. Railroad travel allowed teams in different cities to play regular schedules, and in 1871 a National Association of Professional Players formed, with standardized rules and franchise holders who established parks, sold tickets, and paid salaries. Until 1874, when it dissolved, a team in the league known as the Lord Baltimores developed a reputation for both losing and (rightly or wrongly) throwing games so as to reap gambling profits. Spectators could be riotous. Players were known to drink between innings.

Baltimore baseball recovered under the guidance of Harry Vonderhorst, co-owner of the brewery of that name and a heavy, bearded man who realized full well the appeal of the game. After 1875, the National Association having expired, a new National League embodied reform—barring liquor, punishing players caught gambling, and outlawing Sunday games. So far from joining the "white ribbon" league, Vonderhorst entered his ball club in the American Association that baseball entrepreneurs, several of whom sold liquor, organized in 1882. Quickly called the "beer and whiskey" league, it included the old Cincinnati club (which refused to ban beer), the Philadelphia Athletics, and the New York Metropolitans. One of the league slogans claimed that it put baseball "within the reach of everyone." At his own field Vonderhorst charged not the National League's "aristocratic" admission fee of half a dollar, but a mere quarter. He built a grandstand, with an upper deck, which seated about six thousand, and in an attempt to give the game more respectability sometimes hired bands to play dance music nearby, set out picnic tables, and admitted children free. Pleasant as the "ball park"– beer garden must have been, the team at first floundered. When someone asked Vonderhorst how business went, he supposedly answered, "Vell, ve don't vin many games, but ve sell lots of beer."[43] In 1883, by then at Union Park, the enterprise showed a profit of thirty thousand dollars. Also that year, in a stroke of genius that may first have come to Billy Barnie, the team manager, Vonderhorst decided to name his club after the small birds that bore Lord Baltimore's colors.

The Orioles remained a middling team for a long time. Their fans (so-called because fanatics) consoled themselves by watching the club evolve. In 1885 a left-handed Baltimore pitcher, Matt Kilroy, set a record never broken by striking out 513 batters in one season (the pitcher's mound then was closer to home plate by ten and a half feet). Kilroy dazzled crowds with his ability to pick off runners at first base. In 1887, truly tireless, he won 46 games and lost 20. In 1889 Baltimore-born Frank Foreman, who argued that his own arm never got sore either, won 25 and lost 21 games while the team finished in fifth place. Wilbert Robinson, an overweight catcher with honed skills in purple language, joined the team in 1890. Surprisingly, Robbie stole bases. He also hit; in a nine-inning game with St. Louis, he batted successfully in all seven times at bat. In 1891 Barnie and the Orioles obtained an eighteen-year-old New Yorker, John McGraw, who at five feet, six inches and about 120 pounds was Robinson's opposite in everything except creative swearing. Gamecock-tough, with piercing black eyes and a terrible temper, McGraw, a third baseman, seemed always to be starting fights with someone who towered over him. Batting, he had a rare ability to hit to all fields. In 1892 Vonderhorst signed a new manager, Ned Hanlon, who had played for many years at Detroit. Hanlon's eye for talent soon brought together an explosive combination of players in Baltimore. He traded his predecessor as player-manager for Joe Kelley, a young and struggling outfielder. Hanlon acquired an apparently anemic hitter from the Pennsylvania coal fields, Hugh Jennings, who played shortstop. Among other newcomers were Dennis "Big

"The Winning Game of 1897. Boston vs. Baltimore." The world-champion Baltimore Orioles that year tried to win (and nearly did) an unprecedented fourth straight National League pennant at Union Park. The game drew the largest ballgame crowd yet seen in the city—30,000. *James H. Bready*

Dan" Brouthers, a powerful first baseman with a thick moustache, and "Wee Willie" Keeler, who was smaller than McGraw.

After 1893, the year Oriole Bill Hawke pitched the first no-hitter in professional ball, the team came into its own. McGraw and Jennings attended a New York college in the off season, coaching in exchange for tuition charges. McGraw spent the winter of 1893–94 teaching his friend to stay in the batter's box (he placed the cage behind Jennings so he had no choice), to step into pitches, and to place his hits wherever he wanted them to go. At the Macon, Georgia, training camp Hanlon toyed with his batting order until the lineup began with several hitters who could poke the ball through any hole in the infield or foul off pitches indefinitely. McGraw, Keeler, Jennings, and Kelley became masters of the hit-and-run: the base runner broke for second and the hitter stroked the ball into either right or left field, depending on whether shortstop or second baseman covered second base. Hanlon's hitters also perfected the "Baltimore chop"—a ball hit so hard into the ground in front of homeplate that it stayed in the air while the batter reached first base. The

Orioles developed defensive tactics against double-stealing and fake throws that lured runners off base for "sucker" outs. To open the 1894 season (when electric streetcars began running to Vonderhorst's Union Park), fifteen thousand people watched the home team unveil its new game against the New York Giants. The Orioles swept the four-game series, leaving the New York manager, John Montgomery Ward, dumbfounded. "Trick stuff by a lot of kids," he said, and referred to his rule book. Playing the champion Boston Beaneaters for the first time that year, the Orioles were down 3 to 1 in the ninth inning until thirteen consecutive batters played hit-and-run. They won 15 to 3.[44]

By 4 July the other eleven teams in the latest National League (it earlier had admitted four cities from the moribund American Association) conceded Baltimore a chance of winning the pennant. Hanlon, realizing the weakness of Orioles pitching, had made midseason deals with second-division clubs for several promising young "hurlers"—George Hemming, "Kid" Gleason (small but feisty, he fit well into the Baltimore program), and "Duke" Esper— to help John "Sadie" McMahon, the only dependable starter. Baseball watchers nonetheless expected the Orioles to fade. Instead they became more intimidating—sharpening their spikes before games with ceremony the other dugout could not miss. Their base stealing, if predictable, still was effective. McGraw liked to take advantage of the game's single, behind-the-plate umpire. On first base, when something distracted the official, he could steal third by skipping second, running the more direct path behind the pitcher's box. Playing defense at third base with a man on second, he planted himself inside the bag so that the runner had to slow in making the outside turn for home—often a deadly delay at the plate. In another defensive move, McGraw got behind a runner on third and found something to grasp. Playing St. Louis that season, McGraw had a firm hand on an opponent who undid his buckle; as the run scored, McGraw stood holding an extra belt. Besides ensuring that the ground in front of the plate at Union Park was good and hard, Tom Murphy, the Orioles groundskeeper, landscaped the third-base line so that bunts, crucial to the Baltimore offense, tended to roll fair. Murphy also let the outfield grass grow lush and a bit high. In it the Orioles planted an additional ball or two for critical plays.

Playing superb baseball—less by foul means than fair—the Orioles won the pennant that year, and repeated in 1895 and 1896. They revolutionized the game. They won by hard work, but also with pluck and guile—a style their fans recognized as their own.

CHAPTER 8

Non-Pilgrim's Progress

By the turn of the century half of all Marylanders lived in Baltimore, where economic growth assaulted natural beauty. Arriving at the city by water meant plying the Patapsco. The slowly flowing river carried by-products of industries like fertilizer making and tanning, contained heavy proportions of raw sewage, and "emitted a stench as cadaverous and unearthly as that of the canals of Venice." It took a traveler past a growing concentration of industrial sites. At Sparrows Point, where until 1872 there had been a picnic ground known as Holly Grove, a Maryland subsidiary of Pennsylvania Steel in the early 1890s finished construction of four blast furnaces, a rail mill, and other assorted plants, piers, and rail yards. Their smokestacks and those of factories in Canton and on Locust Point dropped soot that coated paint, got into eyes, and made one cough. From the south travelers rode the royal blue B&O "along scores of dirty streets with shabby little one and two story dwellings, largely inhabited by Negroes," wrote a reporter for a London paper, "with plentiful supplies of pigs, chicken coops, and swarming children." From that direction, he said, one might well think Baltimore to be "a dirty, dreary, ramshackle sort of place."

If the train arrived from the north and entered Union Station, however, travelers stepped into another Baltimore. Down Charles, a "fine street, full of character," black servants washed the large windows and swept the stone steps of fashionable town houses—all of which had "a certain Southern aspect very picturesque to one coming from the more commonplace Northern towns." Here and there carriages with drivers in livery waited outside, making a strange picture next to the new electric and telephone poles. In the February 1896 issue of *Harper's*, Stephen Bonsal wrote that the stately buildings at Mount Vernon Place, together with the Washington Monument and its four green squares, presented "the most imposing site to be found in any American city." The British writer felt "thankful so quiet a city is to be found in the same country which contains New York and Chicago."

He might better have said that the rumblings were often agreeable. Progress in Baltimore, if not the pious pilgrimage John Bunyan had written of, made it one of the most exciting cities in the United States. Several elite families living near Mount Vernon Place had made philanthropic contributions that soon benefited not only Baltimore and Maryland, but the nation. Men of probity led attempts at political reform. Members of the medical profession and earnest women attacked long-festering social problems. Bonsal entitled his article "The New Baltimore." He thought its citizens carried themselves with the civic pride that "Plutarch says somewhere is characteristic of the sons of famous cities" and that "is so enviable and makes so much for happiness." "Baltimore as we know it," declared a native, "is a city of schools, libraries, lecture courses, university advantages, and all that can conspire to the cultivation of intellect."[1]

For affluent Marylanders life was pleasant indeed. Breakthroughs in railroads, steel, oil, and merchandising allowed individuals to accumulate unprecedented wealth, and there was yet no tax on income. As late-nineteenth-century architecture suggested, the age gave rise to studied display among those who could afford it (and among their imitators)—to many-turreted, heavily ornamented styles of life. Then as always, wealth sought its own. Late in the Civil War, Union General Lew Wallace had outraged proper Baltimoreans by turning the Maryland Club, founded in 1857 as a haven for men of station in Baltimore, its membership by invitation only, into a shelter for homeless ex-slaves. In the early 1890s the club moved to new quarters on Eager and North Charles streets. E. Francis Baldwin and Josiah Pennington, who designed the Romanesque structure, had it built of Baltimore County white marble; with its great hall, oaken beams, and large fireplace, pronounced *Harper's*, it compared favorably "with the best examples of London club-land." Its regional cuisine and wine cellar earned the admiration of every visitor. An offshoot that finally found quarters on Mount Vernon Place, the Baltimore Club formed in 1878 when younger members departed from the customs of tippling and wagering. Other clubs, the Merchants' and the University, brought together elites in somewhat different circles. The Germania Club, established in 1840, served as a retreat for leading Baltimore businessmen of German parentage and for the Germans sent to manage the Baltimore-Bremen tobacco trade. Jewish men of wealth dominated the Concordia Club, organized in 1847 as a German liberal society, and the Phoenix Club, which they began in 1866. High dues ensured that only the eminently successful could apply for admission. The wives of these gentlemen formed charitable and social clubs that followed the same pattern.[2]

Recreation among Maryland elites offered interesting studies in social preference and self-identification. While true that trends in athletics at the time pointed toward spectatorship and betting, genteel sport remained participatory and became more and more self-consciously exclusive. Owners of

Lurman family picinic, c. 1890. A well-to-do Maryland family relaxed by picnicking at Wye Plantation, taking along vintage wines, abundant baskets, servants, dogs, and camera. *MHS*

pleasure craft in the Choptank River organized the Chesapeake Bay Yacht Club with the stated aims of purchasing real estate, improving navigation, and pursuing "scientific and social purposes." Combining water and fitness, several rowing clubs, including L'Hirondelle Boat Club in Baltimore and others on the Severn and at the naval school (returned to Annapolis in September 1865), fostered competition among young gentlemen. Sailing and rowing placed emphasis on individual daring and strength, clearly of value if one's social beliefs drew upon Charles Darwin's theory of natural selection; these activities were beyond the means of ordinary people, who perhaps were less fit for survival. Young gentlemen in the Baltimore business district in these years established the Baltimore Athletic Club. They obtained the services of an ex-heavyweight boxer named Jake Kilrain to teach them how to fight scientifically. Another example of sport that served an identifying function was lacrosse—an Indian game that had been forgotten in the Chesapeake region until in 1878 a group of young men from wealthy Baltimore families saw it played at a Newport polo club. They were so taken by the game that they bought sticks and carried lacrosse back with them. South of New York the game became the preserve of Baltimore private school boys, college men, and then clubs of alumni that played rugged contests with northern teams.[3]

City dwellers liked to get to the country or take to the water when Maryland summers descended; obviously not all could manage the escape from noise, crowds, heat, and humidity. Baltimore storeowners and small manufacturers might send their families to live with country relatives; others commuted from rented summer houses outside the city. Along the Potomac above Washington two Philadelphians, Edwin and Edward Baltzley, bought land in 1889 for a resort they planned to call Rhineland on the Potomac. Their efforts faltered the following year when a large Germanesque hotel, a castle built of wood, burned (soon after the brothers turned the Glen Echo property into a national meeting site for the Chautauqua religious and self-help movement). Meantime families of great means journeyed to the Virginia springs, summered at northern spas like Saratoga Springs or Newport, or spent vacations at upland retreats along Maryland railroad lines. A mountaintop resort and amusement park called Pen-Mar northwest of Thurmont provided visitors cool glades not far from the Western Maryland tracks. Near Oakland in Garrett County the B&O under John Garrett built Deer Park, a splendid highland hotel (another Baldwin and Pennington design, this one in Swiss Alpine manner) with elaborate wooden cottages and springs of pure mountain water nearby. In 1886 President Grover Cleveland and his bride spent their honeymoon at Deer Park, where, said travel brochures, guests were "strictly of the highest order" and earth, air, sky, and water joined "to render summer life a positive charm."[4]

New rail links, especially on the Eastern Shore, and improved steamboat service on the bay combined to make waterside recreation into a new industry. Most of the demand originated among middle-class Baltimoreans. Donning the new, lightweight, summer fabrics, they could escape hot weather by taking one-day excursion boats from the Light Street wharves to places like Tolchester Beach in Kent County. Opened in 1877, Tolchester offered amusements under wooden shelters, boating, and a swimming beach for persons willing to brave nettles. Betterton Beach lay to the north, where the Sassafras River met the Chesapeake. Hotels there catered to families that could afford weekly stays. On the other shore, below Annapolis at the mouth of the Severn, the B&O established Bay Ridge, an enormously successful retreat for Baltimoreans and Washingtonians. One could reach it only by train from Bladen Station in Annapolis or by Baltimore steamboat—landing alongside a thousand-foot pier with a fishing and crabbing platform at its end. Bay Ridge had a large hotel, a restaurant that could seat hundreds at a time, and a boardwalk with a two-decked, gaily painted pavilion full of curios and concession stands. There were picnic grounds, a merry-go-round and ferris wheel, and a bandstand where musical and dance groups performed to appreciative crowds. They were white only; managers in 1892 refused entry to Frederick Douglass's son Charles, a Civil War major, who soon established a summer retreat for black professional families at nearby Highland Beach. Meanwhile Bay Ridge proved so popular that Pennsylvania

"Pen-Mar Park." Colored lithograph by A. Hoen & Co., Baltimore, c. 1885. *MHS*

Railroad investors planned a similar park, Chesapeake Beach, for upper Calvert County. They began building a spur line of the same name between the bay and the Bennington junction on their Baltimore to Washington line.

Railroad rivalry also accounted for the rise of Ocean City, where land speculators turned out glittering brochures (failing to mention the area's notorious mosquitoes) and talked of making the hamlet another Atlantic City, New Jersey. For many years a trickle of visitors to the ocean shore had crossed Sinepuxent Bay in small boats-for-hire. The Atlantic Hotel, first on the beach, went up in 1875. The following year the Wicomico and Pocomoke Railroad completed a bridge over the Sinepuxent. The planked trestle served carriages as well as trains and greatly eased travel to the beach. After 1891 Baltimoreans could make the trip in less than six hours—taking a steamboat from Light Street to Claiborne, then boarding the Baltimore and Eastern Shore Railroad (which had taken over the Wicomico and Pocomoke) for the final leg. Such outings were supposed to be affordable to "a large number of the nicest people from the North, South and West." By 1892 the Sinepuxent Beach Company, a group of developers from Baltimore and Washington,

Tolchester Company poster, c. 1895. *MHS*

had bought and "modernized" the Atlantic Hotel, surveyed broad avenues and intersecting streets, and begun selling individual lots for summer cottages. Sinepuxent developers praised the Ocean City beach as "firm and unchangeable."[5]

A few Marylanders preserved the traditions of the country gentry. At old manor houses, those families fortunate enough to have been born to comfort and to have retained wealth supported Bonsal's comment in *Harper's* that largely "your Baltimoreans are stay-at-home folk." The Marylander's "keen appreciation of open-air life," he said further, owed much to comparatively low tax rates on land. In lower Montgomery County, as trolleys from Washington began the suburban development so noticeable in Baltimore, horsemen formed the Dumblane Club in 1885 to hunt foxes, but finding few quarry, and apparently tiring of dragging (dogs tracking a scented sack), members soon dispersed. There were active hunting societies in the Green Spring Valley and at Elkridge. Bonsal praised the Murray Hanson hounds in Howard County and S. S. Howland's kennels outside Annapolis; with such dogs, Marylanders could "hunt as long and as often as flesh and blood, human and equine, can stand." Merging rigor and the outdoors, "country clubs" at first imitated the old fun of foxhunting, then took inspiration from less expensive British models. On the Dumblane terrain in 1892 Francis G.

Enjoying the beach in front of the new Plimhimmon Hotel, Ocean City, c. 1900. *MHS*

Newlands, Nevada senator and land speculator, formed the Chevy Chase Club (named after an eighteenth-century manor nearby), where Scottish golf and the popular English pastime of tennis replaced hunting and riding as chief amusements. At the same time a country club appeared in Catonsville. In 1896 Baltimoreans founded a similar, members-only institution on the northern fringes of the city.[6]

⌒∾⌒

Besides demonstrating the individual rewards possible in the explosive nineteenth-century economy, Maryland wealth cameoed two major themes in American folklore: the dream of success and the generosity of the winner. Most of the institutions that gave Baltimore its fame were the work of men who, like Rockefeller, Carnegie, and Mellon, rose from humble origins and then gave lavishly for the common good. George Peabody had established the pattern. After rising as a merchant-banker in Baltimore from 1814 to 1837, Peabody had moved the center of his enterprises to London, where he generously supported American and British causes alike. In the old Puritan manner, Peabody believed his success a mark of God's favor and a trust that carried responsibilities toward others. Though absent many years from Baltimore, he harbored a wish, occasionally mentioned, to share his wealth with the city. In 1857, after John Pendleton Kennedy visited London and discussed the terms of his proposed gift, Peabody returned to Maryland and prepared its final form. Construction of a large marble structure began that year on the southeast corner of Mount Vernon Place, a location Peabody preferred and paid extra money to obtain. His contributions grew until they amounted to almost $1.5 million.

After the war trustees disentangled their varied interests and set the Peabody Institute safely on its course. In 1867 Nathaniel Holmes Morison, a New Hampshire native who for twenty-five years had been a prominent schoolmaster in Baltimore, assumed all executive duties. Following Peabody's plan, the institute aimed to provide public lectures, establish a music academy and art gallery, and aid worthy students in their academic progress. Lectures at the institute, as many as thirty a year, introduced Baltimoreans to scholars of all disciplines and regions of the country. The art gallery housed a small collection that included the work of an esteemed Maryland sculptor, William H. Rinehart, and, by means of a gift from John Garrett, replicas of great European sculptures. As a musical conservatory the Peabody had to find its own path. It first offered lectures on musical subjects, with musicians playing illustrative pieces, then assembled regular faculty, accepted students, and found an orchestra director. In 1871 trustees named as head of the conservatory a Danish musician and composer, Asger Hamerik, who strengthened both instruction and symphonic performances. One of Hamerik's best musician-students was a struggling young poet from Georgia, Sidney Lanier. As a captured Confederate soldier at Point Lookout in the winter of 1864–65, Lanier had entertained troops with a flute that he concealed up his sleeve. A lover of poetry and music, he happily enrolled himself at the Peabody "among the devotees of these two sublime arts."[7]

With zest Morison proceeded to fulfill another of Peabody's objectives—assembling a library. A few respectable academic libraries already had appeared in the city; Loyola College had more than 21,000 volumes, St. Mary's Catholic seminary had 15,000. Peabody (who died in 1869) and Morison deserved credit for taking a qualitative approach to the institute collection. It became a distinguished reference library, marking changes in the very approach (with publications rapidly growing in number) one necessarily took to intellectual endeavor: students had to read selectively and learn how to find what they needed. By 1876 the Peabody library included 70,000 scholarly and rare editions of immense research value. Morison developed a classification system that made it simple to locate and reshelve the books. To house the enormous collection, E. G. Lind, who had designed the original building, drew plans for a library wing. Completed in 1878, Lind's structure featured an interior that was one of the more spectacular in the city. Six floors of stacks had open centers and balconies with ornamental railings that overlooked the reading room below. Above it Lind placed a large skylight that illuminated the working area and in metaphor emphasized its purpose.

Pathbreaking quality at the Peabody had a counterpart in the unheard-of availability of more popular volumes in Baltimore. "Public" libraries in the city and in other Maryland towns had followed the general pattern of group sponsorship and subscription membership. Several of them had enjoyed success. The Odd Fellows library contained about 25,000 books. The old Library Company of Baltimore, declining in membership during the Jacksonian years, had donated its 11,000 volumes to the Maryland Historical Society in 1856. The Mercantile Library Association, formed in 1839 when younger clerks and businessmen found the Library Company too expensive, perhaps too stuffy, had grown quickly. It circulated books and conducted lecture programs in the antebellum period, occupying, after 1848, rooms in the Athenaeum Building. In 1873, when the library consisted of more than 31,000 volumes, membership cost a modest three (for workingmen) or five dollars a year. Small-town citizens began to show the same appreciation for books and self-help. After the war Salisbury residents opened a lyceum and library. In the late 1870s an organization of Hagerstown women purchased the old St. James Academy library and placed its nearly three thousand volumes at the disposal of the community. Annual library dues were three dollars. Washington County went so far in 1904 as to put books in a wagon and take them to every crossroads community.

While these societies circulated books invitingly, the truly "free" library system in the country owed much to the example of Enoch Pratt. A product of public schooling and another New Englander with a keen sense of duty to the commonweal, Pratt in late life quietly studied schemes for public li-

Peabody Library interior, c. 1885. *Allan Hirsh, Jr.*

braries. In 1865, under careful trusteeship, he had established a free school and public library in his Massachusetts boyhood home; later he noted the success of a Workingmen's Institute, with library, in Canton. As treasurer of the Peabody trust, he knew the high objectives of the institute library. He saw a glaring need for something else. In 1881 workmen on Mulberry Street began digging a foundation for a structure that the hardware mogul at first did not identify. By the time the decorous, white marble building was finished, the city (and General Assembly according to usual form) had agreed to an arrangement by which Pratt's bequest of $833,000 went into Baltimore bonds—eventually producing $50,000 in annual interest and tying the city to library upkeep. Branches of the Pratt, each with 15,000 volumes, opened in all four corners of the city. As first director of the library system, trustees selected Lewis Henry Steiner, the Frederick physician who after the war had served as superintendent of Frederick County schools. In January 1886, when the library opened, its volumes—particularly heavy in history, religion, and English literature—numbered 28,000. That first year 26,000 Baltimoreans received library cards, and patrons made 400,000 withdrawals. Before his death in 1896, Pratt himself used the library, sometimes needling the staff with comments about procedure.

Harper's called the Walters residence on the west side of Mount Vernon Place a "modest and unpretentious dwelling"—as William T. Walters, who had risen from ordinary beginnings, evidently wanted it. While a young man he had worked in the iron country of western Pennsylvania, and then, with saved money and considerable acumen, had become a produce merchant, relocated in Baltimore, and joined efforts to build the Northern Central. Having acquired Southern sympathies planning railroads below the Potomac, he took refuge in Paris during the Civil War. Afterward, especially following the hard times of the mid-1870s, Walters played a large part in consolidating those lines, which promoted and profited from the growth of Virginia and North Carolina produce farming. Eventually comprising more than ten thousand miles of track, the network in 1893 became the Atlantic Coast Line. In the same years Walters, his neighbor Enoch Pratt on West Monument Street, and others made the Safe Deposit and Trust Company a leading source of Baltimore capital. Walters's son Henry, born in 1848, had all his father's talents plus the advantages of schooling at Loyola College in Baltimore, Georgetown in Washington (where he finished a master of arts degree in 1871), the Lawrence Scientific Institute at Harvard, and yet more studies in Paris. Combining skills in management and engineering, the younger Walters later completed the railroad empire his father had begun.[8]

The diversity of their genius occasioned comment: though so much of their time and energy went to the brutally competitive business of railroad building, father and son just as diligently pursued the aesthetic. Both men collected art. The elder Walters had become enchanted with French paintings during his time in Paris and then had bought a few objects. His early acquisitions included Joseph Turner's *The Grand Canal in Venice*, an excellent example of that master's work. Most of the collection, however, reflected an interest in artists comparatively unknown in America—Camille Corot, François Millet, the watercolorist Léon Bonvin, and Henri Rousseau—whose *Le Givre—Winter Solitude* the contemporary critic Martha J. Lamb called "weird but simple" after seeing it in Baltimore. Walters purchased rare jewelry, porcelain—chiefly Viennese and Oriental—and sculptures that included many Rinehart pieces.[9]

An art student as well as patron, Walters amassed a "connoisseur's collection." He attended exhibitions in Paris and Vienna, where he advised artists on subjects and commented on their technique. When in 1884 one of Baron Leys's pupils, Alma-Tadema, completed a difficult but admirable watercolor, *Xantha and Phaon*, the artist wrote from London that Walters "must always look at this picture as a result of your last visit to my studio." Walters became an amateur authority on the French Romantic sculptor Antoine-Louis Barye, criticism of whose work he compiled and published, with his own preface, in 1884. Before his death ten years later, he added two wings onto the Mount Vernon Place home as galleries and regularly opened them to the public. Henry, besides being a steady patron of American yachting, carried on his father's work. "There is no art collection, public or private, accessible to the people of this country," wrote Lamb, "where so many real treasures may be enjoyed, and no private art collection in any quarter of the world of such munificent proportions and genuine value."[10]

Doubtless the philanthropy of these men did arise from a moral sense of debt and responsibility; it may also have derived from personal sadness or incompleteness. Except for the elder Walters, the Baltimore givers had no children to accept their love and continue the family name. Like Peabody, Johns Hopkins, another philanthropist, never married. Unlike the rest, he was a native Marylander, born on an Anne Arundel tobacco plantation into a family of Friends with seventeenth-century roots in the county. In Baltimore, maintaining a townhouse on Saratoga Street and presiding over a magnificent country home at Clifton, on the northeastern edge of the city, Hopkins had become a peculiar figure. Though remaining a Quaker, he enjoyed wine and champagne and considered installing a billiard table in his home on Saratoga. While the railroad he financed tied together the middle of the nation, he refused as a rule to travel beyond the city. His austerity kept colleagues and his few friends at arm's length. He suffered from insomnia, dressed almost carelessly, walked whenever he could, and took frank pleasure in collecting dividends and closing a good business deal. Hopkins declined at one point to recarpet his house because, he had said, he would rather earn interest on the money it would take. During his lifetime he gave no hint that he had generous plans for his wealth.

Yet the Quaker reliance on education had been part of his upbringing. He had suffered from cholera and seen its ravages visited on Baltimore—to-

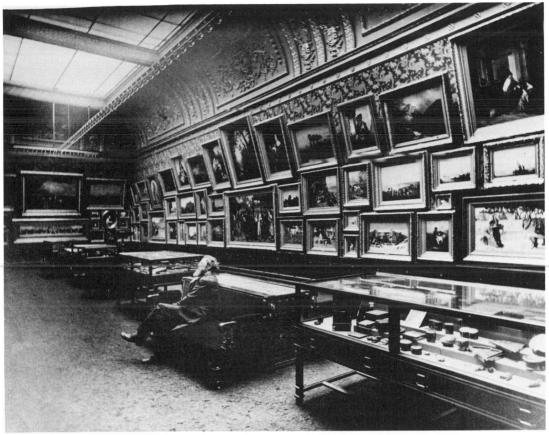

Interior of the original Walters Art Gallery, 1884. *Walters Art Gallery*

gether with outbreaks of smallpox and yellow fever. He fell under the influence of Peabody. At his death in 1873 Hopkins left seven million dollars for a university and hospital to bear his name.

❦

Rarely did means and need so nicely intersect. In medicine and higher education new ways of looking at things had ignited intellectual revolt and promised important changes. The willingness to innovate clearly surfaced in postwar America. The war had altered the minds of many men who had fought in it, Oliver Wendell Holmes, Jr. (seriously wounded at Antietam), among them: new arms and mass killing made them impatient with old theories. Darwin offered an inductive view of the development of life over millions of years and thereby questioned man's concept of himself. At the same time, industrial growth and the impact of new immigrants recommended fresh approaches to timeless human problems while introducing new ones. At Harvard, Charles W. Eliot had undertaken as president a program of curriculum reform. Encouraging postgraduate schools in law and science, Eliot also allowed students in the college to choose electives like modern over classical languages and tried to retire the old classroom practice of rote recitation. Learning ought to prepare one for life in practical terms, argued reformers, and education mirror American experience. Trustees and faculty at other colleges continued the old debate on how properly to conduct intellectual training, and to what purposes.

State colleges, many of them founded after Congress in 1862 passed the Morrill Land-Grant Act, supplied an answer to the second question by emphasizing public service. The Maryland Agricultural College in Prince George's County exemplified that peculiarly American idea. The assembly had established the school just before the war, mostly through the efforts of Charles Benedict Calvert, the Riverdale Know-Nothing elected to Congress in 1860 who bloomed as an ardent agricultural reformer. After passage of the Morrill Act in 1862, the college became the state land-grant institution. Its several buildings stood on a hill behind the old Rossborough Inn, a stagecoach tavern on the Baltimore-Washington pike, and on soil so poor as to be a teaching aid. Away from the "unhealthful atmosphere and the impure, corrupting associations of the city," thought one advocate, the college would nurse young Maryland farmers (actually, at first, they were planters' sons) into physical health, "simple-minded virtue, and pure and undefiled religion." In 1864 students and faculty had greeted Bradley Johnson's Confederates warmly, causing patriotic outcry, and afterward trustees endangered public support for the college by appointing as presidents a succession of ex-Confederates or, in the case of Samuel Register, a professor of revealed religion who neglected agricultural science. In the 1870s, with Morrill money providing a small yearly stipend of about six thousand dollars, the College Park school made halting progress. Students chose six courses of instruction from among seven: ancient or modern languages, English, mathematics, physics, chemistry, civil engineering, and agriculture. Conforming to the Morrill Act, students conducted military drill—their gray uniforms with U.S. insignia pleasing neither Union nor Confederate veterans. The university soon became a fertilizer-testing post for the state and, with federal money, a farm experiment station.[11]

At the private University of Maryland Medical School, where professors still used the hospital as part of their private practice, important changes had begun in a field that still included a wide variety of quacks and home-remedy artists. Earlier in the century the university had relied on the lecture method and theories of disease and surgery on the Scottish model. After the Civil War such bookish and general study began giving way to specialized work and the clinical approach that French physicians had developed by 1850. Five new faculty members assumed duties after clinical experience in Paris. They included several Marylanders; Christopher Johnston taught surgery, Francis Donaldson throat and chest diseases, and Samuel Claggett Chew drugs or materia medica. John Julian Chisholm and Francis T. Miles, both South Carolinians, earned wide reputations—Chisholm in ophthalmology and Miles in neurology. William Travis Howard, a North Carolinian, taught obstetrics according to the French formula—putting students in wards, teaching not with discourses but with manikins and by having students observe and assist at childbirth. This teaching trend, from classroom to hospital, received impetus from discoveries that made hospitals places where mending and healing took place. Anesthesia permitted less traumatic surgery. Medical men also then realized that fresh air and cleanliness reduced complications in wounds and hastened recovery from illness. With this finding evident, an untiring English woman, Louisa Parsons, founded a nursing school that enjoyed considerable success at the university hospital.

The Hopkins trustees—overlapping sets for university and hospital—gathered in 1874 to plan the work left to them. Certainly the size of their endowment freed their creativity. Living in a state that always had combined old and new and where pragmatism had been a necessary rule, they perhaps felt the same urge that had moved the founders of the B&O: they launched schools taking the best of the tried while trying something altogether new. A hospital building committee—Garrett of the B&O joined Quaker businessman Francis T. King and Galloway Cheston, a flour merchant; Alan P. Smith, Hopkins's own doctor; state attorney general Charles J. M. Gwinn; and Baltimore judge George W. Dobbin—began preparations for a structure on the East Baltimore land Hopkins had purchased before his death. University trustees, who again included Garrett, Gwinn, and Dobbin, asked European and American educators for their conception of the ideal university. Trustee George W. Brown, the victim of Union proscription who now sat as a city judge, had some ideas of his own; James Carey Thomas, a Quaker physician and religious leader, reported himself "engrossed and deeply interested in reading up University subjects." Reverdy Johnson, Jr., son of the wartime Maryland senator and postwar minister to Britain, had studied law at Heidelberg and knew the lay of European higher education. Exploratory letters went out to many university leaders. The most helpful of them—Eliot of Harvard, Andrew Dickson White of Cornell, and James B. Angell of the University of Michigan—agreed that the best choice for Hopkins president would be a Connecticut-born educator who then served as president of the University of California, Daniel Coit Gilman.[12]

For Gilman the new university promised to be the beacon that for many years he had wanted to light. Forty-three years old in 1874, he had studied at Yale and Harvard, then spent a year at the University of Berlin, where the standards of German scholars had made a deep impression on him. Returned to Yale, Gilman had been an instructor at the Sheffield School of Science. Both there and at California he had urged the reform of American universities. He agreed with the trustees that the Hopkins institutions should set out to be the most eminent in the nation—drawing students "first from Maryland and the states near to it, but soon also from the remotest parts of the land." The university would be primarily a graduate school, the faculty made up of specialists devoted not merely to passing along learning, but, in the earlier words of George Brown, intent on adding "something by their writings and discoveries to the world's stock of literature and science." Ample fellowships at Hopkins would support graduate students, who earlier had not received much encouragement at American colleges; students would conduct their own research, gathered around a professor in "seminaries" or seminars in the German tradition. The new president pledged himself to create a university out of men rather than buildings. Early in 1875 he made trips to American colleges and then, in the summer, to Britain and the Continent in a talent search that also brought him into touch with prominent European academics. Able to offer new faculty as much as four thousand dollars, a tidy annual salary at the time, Gilman realized that even that sum would move few established scholars. Like Jefferson founding the University of Virginia, he said, he sought "men of promise rather than fame."[13]

While gratifying, his success was not at first complete. Several Germans and Harvard men to whom Gilman offered jobs declined. When the Johns Hopkins University opened in October 1876, chairs in English, philosophy, and history remained vacant. Nonetheless, the university from the beginning offered instruction in German and such abstruse studies as Sanskrit and Semitic languages. It established itself as excellent in the fields its faculty represented. Gilman eventually assembled an impressive array of ambitious young researchers and a few older, long-frustrated scholars. Basil Gildersleeve, who walked with a limp received in Confederate war service, arrived as a professor of Greek from the University of Virginia. The move agreed with him. "I certainly did not dream," he wrote, "that so much enthusiasm was left in me." Another Hopkins professor, A. Marshall Elliott, virtually founded the study of Romance languages in America. Gilman in 1879 went to the Peabody for Sidney Lanier, who while a lecturer at Hopkins wrote major studies of English verse and the English novel. In 1881 Herbert Baxter Adams, holder of a Ph.D. from Heidelberg and one of the first graduate fellows admitted to Hopkins, received a faculty appointment in history and political economy. Emphasizing political institutions, his seminars stimulated students like Woodrow Wilson and Charles Homer Haskins, and repelled others—J. Franklin Jameson and Frederick Jackson Turner among them—who fertilized historical thought with their own interpretations. James T. Ely, a critic of laissez-faire theory (and hence of unregulated corporate growth), handled seminars in political economy. Charles Sanders Peirce, an important figure in early American philosophy, lectured on logic in the early 1880s before returning to Harvard. G. Stanley Hall, his successor, became an influential student of experimental psychology.[14]

In assembling a science faculty, Gilman and the trustees kept in view their plans for a pathbreaking medical school. One of Gilman's first selections was

Herbert Baxter Adams addressing the history seminar, Johns Hopkins University, c. 1885. This image from Charles K. Edmunds, "A Half-Century of Johns Hopkins," *Review of Reviews* (November 1926), may be the only one ever taken of Adams at work in a celebrated setting of American scholarship. *MHS*

a youthful instructor of physics at Rensselaer Polytechnic Institute, Henry A. Rowland. Rowland recently had published an article in a British journal of science; Yale editors of its American rival had turned down the piece, believing Rowland too young to be working on electricity. A zany but brilliant mathematician, James J. Sylvester, finally agreed to leave England for Baltimore after holding out for a salary of six thousand dollars. Another Englishman, Henry Newell Martin, filled the professorship Gilman wished to establish in biology—a field generally neglected in American academics to that time. When the Hopkins president met Martin in New York he thought Martin "more youthful in appearance" than he had expected, but giving signs of "learning, force & a spirit of work." In chemistry Gilman's choice was Ira Remsen, a young New Yorker with a Munich, Göttingen, and Tübingen background who immediately began building the most advanced laboratory in the country. By a custom Gilman believed important to departmental integrity, Sylvester, Rowland, Remsen, and Martin picked their own assistants. Complementing Martin, William Keith Brooks, a Harvard Ph.D. who chewed tobacco, taught courses in morphology (the structure of living things) and developed a special interest in marine biology.[15]

As the first true university in the New World, Hopkins became America's most stimulating place—a distinction it maintained easily until its graduates and similarly trained scholars carried seeds to other institutions. A writer for *Scribner's*, sent to investigate life at Hopkins, wrote with some amazement that graduate students were "permitted and directed how to grow, not molded, and hammered, and chiseled into form." Aside from its graduated

Ph.D.s, the most visible fruit of the new university was its variety of academic publications. At Hopkins scholars at last could realize the urge to make known their findings, to test their ideas in print. Beginning in 1877–78, Remsen published *Notes from the Chemical Laboratory* and Martin *Studies from the Biological Laboratory*. Sylvester, who carried his unpublished manuscripts around in a footlocker, followed with the *American Journal of Mathematics*. In the 1880s Gildersleeve founded the *American Journal of Philology*, Adams the series of one-topic books *Studies in Historical and Political Science*, and Elliott *Modern Language Notes*. A journal of archeology went to Princeton with Arthur L. Frothingham; Hall took the *American Journal of Psychology* with him to Clark University. By the early 1890s these serials, along with other academic printings and scholarly circulars, appeared under the auspices of The Johns Hopkins Press, arguably the first of its kind in the country.[16]

Relations between "The Hopkins" and the community made clear how far the new university intended to stretch intellectual bounds. While true, as *Harper's* said, that the university "added to the social life of Baltimore a great number of charming and agreeable men and women, who have been made very welcome," Gilman walked a tightrope, protecting scholarly ideals (the Hopkins motto became The Truth Shall Set You Free) while calming public fear of infidelity and elitism. In an early history course Adams chose as one reading Edward Clodd's *The Childhood of Religions*, a volume that according to Adams gave "some idea of the kinship of Indo-European religious ideas." The recently named Episcopal bishop of Maryland, William Paret, denounced the book as "unjust, unfair toward the Bible & Christian Religion." Gilman called these comments to the attention of Adams, who apparently struck the book from his list while having graduate students read it anyway. Gilman had to tread carefully about the issue of science and religion. Martin in biology had studied under Thomas Huxley, a champion of Darwinian evolution theory. In 1876 Gilman had Huxley deliver the address that formally opened the university. Gilman, a vigorous nonsectarian, courted danger by omitting prayer from the day's events, and in Huxley's text a few listeners found confirmation of Hopkins's godless purpose. "He says not a word about the science of *morals*," wrote an angry Baltimorean, "and of course he takes no account of revealed *religion*." Gilman countered such attacks by personally conducting voluntary chapel services for students and publicizing the number of courses (like Oriental languages) that related to theological studies. When biology students put a bust of Darwin in their laboratory, Gilman suggested that likenesses of some other scientific heroes might make the evolutionist less conspicuous.[17]

It delighted Gilman that he could point to immediate, practical returns on the Hopkins investment. In 1878 Brooks established a summer research station, the Chesapeake Zoological Laboratory, on a six-acre pile of rocks off Hampton Roads. Besides making preliminary surveys of the oyster beds, he did important research on oyster propagation. The European oyster sheltered its spawn within its shell. Brooks learned that the Chesapeake oyster instead released its young into the water, where swift currents and predators took their toll. The seeding of Chesapeake oyster beds—one practical way to maintain the industry—would have to depart from the French model and make use of tanks or protected, shallow waters. These and other findings, soon published in *The Oyster: A Popular Summary of a Scientific Study*, interested a wide readership. Brooks appeared frequently at Annapolis to speak on behalf of bills limiting the size of harvested oysters and regulating dredgers; he warned that the bay would go "flat broke if the oysters give out" and counseled "prompt and decisive action." [18]

Gilman countered the image of elitism with reconsidered attention to undergraduate study and by inviting everyone in the community to an early university lecture series. Though one faculty member derided the series as "starring in the provinces," its subjects, which included the law and "popular astronomy," proved of great interest. Two visitors from New England, James Russell Lowell and Francis J. Childs, "captured the town," boasted Gilman in the spring of 1877; Baltimoreans talked of "the Chaucer and Dante revival" much as they did of two leading evangelical preachers, "Moody & Sankey!" Settling undergraduates at Hopkins was more difficult. Mr. Hopkins, proclaimed the Baltimore *American* early on, wanted "education for the people and not sinecures for the learned." In 1883 John Garrett publicly doubted that Hopkins did enough for local young men. Many of them prepared not far from the original university buildings on and about Howard Street, where Baltimore City College had moved in 1875; once admitted, they felt "as welcome as redheaded stepchildren." In 1889, when Gilman appointed a new dean of college studies, undergraduate enrollment climbed to 141 and Remsen noted anxiously that "student spirit" rose "as never before." Students that year put out a yearbook, played pranks in class, and opened a fourth fraternity. But the main reason for school spirit lay with the Hopkins lacrosse team, which went undefeated for the first of many seasons. During the excitement students serenaded Gilman with a "Hopkins Yell" that shattered the heavy air of graduate study. [19]

At the time, lacrosse triumphs meant less to Gilman than ripening plans for the medical school, which had awaited completion of the hospital. Trustees in the late 1870s learned that the hospital's very design required answers to yet-unanswered questions. If disease grew out of bad earth or air, how should one lay out wards; should surgical patients be placed above or below the sick; was it better to put up permanent buildings or wooden ones that could be destroyed as they became contaminated with "hospitalism" and cheaply replaced? Hopkins committeemen toured notable hospitals and solicited new ideas from architects and medical men. Among them, John Shaw Billings, an army medical officer in Washington, soon emerged as the most interesting and ardent planner. Billings recommended a design that incorporated theories of medical schooling as well as disease. Senior students should be kept close to their patients. The nurses' training school provided for in the Hopkins bequest—presumably with the University of Maryland example in mind—ought to be housed separately. Billings included laboratories in his plan, and wrote of the need to publish medical findings. The hospital could be of permanent construction, he said, but should consist of a main building with connected pavilions (somewhat like the University of Virginia) to the north and south of a grassy mall, spaced and directed so as to maximize air and sunshine. Though the trustees had an architect in John R. Niernsee, a Vienna-born veteran of the Confederate army, they named Billings superintendent of construction. Begun in the summer of 1877, the hospital, minus its southern row of pavilions, finally opened in May 1889.

Gilman's concept of medical schooling, besides owing much to Billings, drew on his own experience at Sheffield, his supreme confidence in science, and his determination to impose strict academic standards. As the hospital neared completion he began assembling medical faculty members who would build on the scientific freshness and rigor of Remsen and Martin. Martin won notoriety by conducting experiments on the hearts of live dogs; physiology, he stated boldly and with Gilman's blessing, "is concerned with the phenomena going on in living things, and vital processes cannot be observed in dead bodies." Gilman's first appointment in medicine proper, William Henry Welch in 1884, confirmed the university president's commitment to microscopic science and belief that it belonged in medicine. Another Connecticut native, a son and grandson of physicians, Welch as a Yale student briefly had considered departing the pattern and becoming a classicist. After deciding on medicine he had attended the College of Physicians and Surgeons in New York City and later traveled to Germany to work in the famous laboratory of Julius Cohnheim, a leader in the early study of pathology, particularly inflammation, at the University of Breslau. At Bellevue Hospital in New York when offered the Hopkins position, Welch quickly accepted. To head the department of medicine Welch favored a young Canadian, William Osler, who after finishing at McGill University in Montreal also had pursued European studies and then taken a professorship at the University of Pennsylvania. In New York, Welch had known William Stewart Halsted, a New Yorker younger even than Osler, as a brilliant teacher with an interest in the biological problems of surgery. Gilman hired him in February 1889. Howard Atwood Kelly, a mere thirty-one years old, soon left the University of Pennsylvania to become professor of obstetrics and gynecology at Hopkins.[20]

Gilman's project—he became director of the hospital in 1889, when King fell ill—nearly ran onto the shoals of financial trouble in the late 1880s, but in the end crisis brought with it an advance. The magnificent Hopkins bequest relied heavily on B&O stock, which at first paid 10 percent dividends. Badly encumbered with debts following track expansion in the 1870s, mismanaged after Garrett's death at Deer Park in 1884, the company curtailed dividend payments in 1886 and then paid none in 1888–90. The railroad went into receivership in 1896, underwent reorganization at the hands of New York and Chicago investors, and reemerged as a blue-chip corporation, though no longer owned by Marylanders, in 1899. While the B&O languished, Gilman faced his own expenses. Support for academic journals, always judicious, suffered. Faculty salaries briefly came from the building fund. The admission of the first medical school class was put off. Gilman wisely began building an endowment apart from the original gift.

In these dire circumstances a group of patrons came to the rescue. Heading the list were Garrett's wealthy daughter, Mary, and M. Carey Thomas, another trustee's daughter, who had a German doctorate and in 1885 had founded the Bryn Mawr School. They with others offered to help finance the medical school with a gift of one hundred thousand dollars. In doing so they also applied pressure on the trustees to make an amendment to their ambitious academic plans—to make them more forward-looking by admitting women to the Hopkins medical classes. Until then the place of women in medicine had been set according to Victorian sexual regimen. Housed separately, nurses at Hopkins were to have superintendents whose duties included safeguarding the nurses' honor. Billings, in a remark that reflected this paternalism, wrote that Hopkins nurses must be "of unspotted morals and chastity," and that "no woman shall be subordinate to a man." Mary Garrett and M. Carey Thomas went a step further: all women enrolled need not be nurses.[21]

Opening in 1893, the Johns Hopkins School of Medicine at once earned a high reputation for admissions standards, research excellence, and professional leadership. Students arrived with undergraduate degrees, courses in physics, chemistry, and biology on the Hopkins premedical model, and a "good reading knowledge of French and German." Basic anatomy, so much involving memorization, became a premedical course. Isabel Adams Hampton, first head of the nursing school, and her successor, Mary Adelaide Nutting, placed that program on a firm academic standing; Hampton founded the *American Journal of Nursing* and published several nursing textbooks. By principle that finally led to truly full-time staff, Hopkins faculty members placed their teaching duties ahead of private practice. To ensure the smooth functioning of school and hospital, teaching department heads—Kelly in gynecology, Halsted in surgery—also headed that branch of the hospital service staff. Just as at the university, research and advanced training became the hallmarks of the Hopkins Hospital. Welch made the laboratory a third leg in medical training: besides learning medical theory in lecture hall and library and dealing with cases in the clinic, medical students spent hours investigating the bacteria and studying the tissue samples that only gave up their secrets under a microscope. Following Billings's early suggestion, Welch in 1889 began publishing his findings—first in the *Bulletin of the Johns Hopkins*

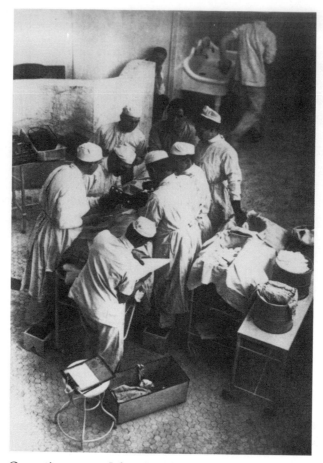

Operating room, Johns Hopkins Hospital, 1904. Perhaps the best-known photograph of early modern medicine. Dr. William Halsted operated in the Hopkins surgical amphitheater, employing antiseptic dress and the rubber surgical gloves developed there.
Johns Hopkins Medical Institutions

Hospital as well as in longer *Reports*, after 1896 in the soon prestigious *Journal of Experimental Medicine*. The textbooks of Osler, Kelly, and other Hopkins faculty remained for many years the highest authorities in each of their fields.[22]

Academic, scientific to a degree revolutionary, medical training at Hopkins later received criticism for being impersonal. Yet it excelled for human reasons. A new system of chief residents and assistant residents in each department, all supported with modest financial aid, provided immediate care to patients and steeped the talented young people who gathered at Hopkins in extensive clinical experience. Osler took students into the wards with him for discussion of medical histories and diagnoses. The Hopkins method placed a young doctor "in a position and an attitude of mind which enables him to go on a student for the rest of his life," Welch wrote, and indeed most

Hopkins physicians went on to pioneer in medical training elsewhere. Welch himself was a delightfully approachable man who loved desserts, cigars, and his bicycle; on the subject of Orioles baseball in the early 1890s he became, by his own admission, "an enthusiast, even a crank." To celebrate his fiftieth birthday, students and former students—led by William T. Councilman, a Baltimore County native who later taught at Harvard—held a dinner for him at the Maryland Club and in the German manner gave him a commemorative book of their research work. A quarter-century before, he told them gratefully, a festschrift of such research had been inconceivable in America.[23]

In 1906, when John Singer Sargent painted a group portrait of Welch, Osler, Halsted, and Kelly, he entitled it simply *The Four Doctors.*

⌒⌒⌒

Maryland politics remained far more interesting than antiseptic. At issue in Congress were critical economic questions like tariffs and currency, in Annapolis problems like railroad privileges, taxes, coal mine regulation, and policing of the oyster beds. Arthur Pue Gorman and Isaac Freeman Rasin represented the art of political brokerage and grass-roots organization as well as anyone in America. In their heyday they gave newspaper cartoonists plenty of inspiration. "Free" Rasin, short and stout, wore a trimmed beard and carried himself with bluster. Gorman, with a Roman-looking face and grave appearance—he always dressed in "ministerial blackness"—prided himself on being a quiet, behind-the-scenes conciliator who never showed emotion.[24]

Both of them had emerged from humble origins, developed an early love for politics, and as young men escaped military service in the Civil War. Rasin's family had deep roots in Kent County, where Rasin was born in 1833. After attending Washington College he moved to Baltimore and entered the millinery and straw goods trade while also getting involved in ward-level politics in East Baltimore—first as a Know-Nothing and then Democrat. In 1864 his friends elected him to the Democrats' city executive committee. Three years later, when loyalty oaths and "Unionist" rule fell by the wayside, Rasin as a party regular won election to the clerk's office of the Baltimore City court of common pleas. Gorman's political apprenticeship, quite different from Rasin's though equally instructive, took place in Washington, where he had gone in 1850, age eleven, to act as a Senate page. How his father, a Woodstock and then Laurel quarryman, managed to win the appointment (two Maryland congressmen, both Democrats, saw to it) was not clear, but the boy understandably found politics more appealing than the schooling he never completed. He literally learned at the feet of larger-than-life figures like Clay, Calhoun, Webster, and Douglas. As Senate postal clerk during the war he made occasional trips to the front as a courier and during Early's campaign—"ready to surrender on first demands"—barricaded himself in the Senate Chamber. After the war President Johnson named Gorman a federal revenue collector for Maryland, in which role he began building political fences while also taking part in early baseball organizing. In 1869, when Grant and the Republicans turned out Democratic officeholders, Gorman lost his appointment.[25]

The following year these remarkable characters met in a back room of the old Baltimore city hall, quickly recognized each other's talents, and before very long had established themselves as the foremost political powers in Maryland. Their reign offered lessons in political science and history. It certainly owed a great deal to the Democrats' hold on the state (a case largely of one-party rule), and yet it belonged to a particular time and place. Rasin and Gorman were more than products of a political environment; their own personalities and political skills helped to shape the environment, to ensure that Democrats maintained their control.

Baltimore politics resembled sport—or club membership. In rooms over a store or pool hall each ward had its Democratic club, where men could gather to play cards and talk politics. Ward leaders combined toughness and easy familiarity. One of them, John J. "Sonny" Mahon, a genial fellow in the downtown 9th ward, led a gang that "could pretty well clean up anything that came against" it. Rasin drew these ward leaders into a network of men whose services he could count on as long as he had goods to deliver. In 1870, at age nineteen, Mahon pledged fealty to Rasin's organization in exchange for a state tobacco warehouse job that paid a princely $2 a day. Rasin later made this understudy messenger for the mayor's office, then city council doorkeeper—both posts worth about $900 a year. Consulting with Rasin, ward heelers like Mahon and their closest friends nominated candidates for local office, and nomination amounted to election. Mahon eventually thought he deserved a seat on the city council. "I talked to the Old Man about it," he later explained, "and he wanted me to go there and be his representative. Of course, there wasn't any trouble about it. I could have nominated and elected anybody I wanted in that ward, and everybody knew it." On election day Rasin preferred to take nothing for granted—dissident or Independent Democrats occasionally challenged the ring—and because voters still made their choices without privacy, muscle and money counted. With "walking-around money" in their pockets and using various powers of persuasion, local Democrats got out the white vote, rewarded the faithful, and made trouble for the rest. The ring ruled—in the streets and at City Hall. After 1875 Ferdinand C. Latrobe, grandson of the architect and son of the B&O lawyer, served as mayor almost without interruption for twenty years, becoming as much a fixture in the political life of the city as Rasin himself. Yet the city charter left Latrobe nearly powerless. The mayor stood on friendly terms with Rasin while holding, or pretending to hold, himself aloof. Given universal suffrage, said Latrobe in a revealing comment, a machine like Rasin's was unavoidable and perhaps helped make democracy work.[26]

Left, Arthur Pue Gorman (1839–1906), c. 1885. *MHS. Right*, Isaac Freeman Rasin (1833–1907). *Enoch Pratt Free Library*

In the state as a whole Republicans counted enough strength to claim more than four out of ten votes in most gubernatorial and presidential elections (U. S. Grant nearly carried the state in 1872). That strength nonetheless was spotty. In Western Maryland the majority of voters earlier had pledged themselves to the cause of the Union, and in the late nineteenth century they stood by the Grand Old Party. Its leadership (Henry Winter Davis had died at the end of 1865) fell to John Creswell, who received the postmaster general's post under Grant and filled the position well, and Judge Hugh Bond of Baltimore, who remained a spokesman for black equal rights. Blacks, grateful for emancipation and the Fifteenth Amendment, voted Republican in Baltimore City; in heavily black Southern Maryland they gave the party of Lincoln dependable majorities. Republicans in northern and western counties might safely espouse Negro rights. Elsewhere fear of blacks, along with memories of strenuous wartime efforts to hold Maryland in the Union, kept the majority of white Maryland voters in the Democratic fold—or drove them into it. During close campaigns Democrats baited opponents on race. Personal followings in the party became a constant—the basis of factions that ebbed and flowed according to the rivalry of railroads, secret deals, patronage choices, broken promises, and petty rebellions.

Gorman's rise illustrated all these themes. After winning a seat in the House of Delegates in 1869, Gorman attached himself to the grandson of William Pinkney, William Pinkney Whyte of Baltimore. With B&O help Whyte defeated Oden Bowie—the friend of the Pennsylvania Railroad—for the governorship in 1871. Aiming at the next U.S. Senate vacancy, Whyte obtained Gorman's support (and threw out James C. Clarke, a Bowie man) by naming him C&O president. Still in the legislature, Gorman filled various canal positions with chosen men, criticized railroad rates and privileges (especially those of Garrett's B&O), and in all ways championed the cheap transportation of George's Creek coal. He built a political following up and down the Potomac. With his backing (Gorman in 1873–74 became House of Delegates Speaker) and Rasin's, Whyte won the assembly balloting for senator in 1873 while returning the incumbent, William T. Hamilton, to private life. Hamilton, a Washington County native who had helped make Gorman a page, dedicated himself to winning the next gubernatorial contest and gaining revenge on the Whyte "ring." This old patron ran headfirst into Gorman's plans to sponsor John Lee Carroll of Howard County for the governorship.

It soon became clear that Maryland politicians fell into two camps—"ins" and "outs"—and that it paid to be one of Gorman's friends. The 1875 state Democratic convention, held in Baltimore at the Art Institute, supplied a textbook example of personal politics. Backstairs and smoky-room bargaining sessions were frenzied. A seasoned parliamentarian, Gorman skillfully outmaneuvered Hamilton, whose frustrated supporters started fist-fights over procedural points. Gorman emerged the winner; Hamilton and friends angrily nominated their own slate and courted favor with the Republicans. State elections that year produced what someone called the "Potato Bug Campaign," partly because potato bugs ruined the summer crop, mostly because party regulars referred to Hamilton men as being yellow and nasty, like the insects. Electoral violence in Baltimore, where police arrested 209 blacks and whites for fighting, rivaled the eruptions of the 1850s. Victory went to the regular Democrats, who afterward marched to Rasin and Gorman's music. In 1880 Gorman completed the circular epic. He surprised Whyte by defeating him in the legislature and went to Washington again, this time as senator.

In the Senate Gorman became a powerful force in Democratic councils and national legislation. At home he built a "state crowd" of cronies who saved him from the mistakes of Hamilton and Whyte. He kept his political base secure. L. Victor Baughman, an ex-Confederate and former Hamilton man, edited the Frederick *Citizen* and served as state comptroller in these years. He embraced Gorman and served as his lieutenant in Western Maryland—where in 1886 Republicans defeated Baughman in a race for Congress. Murray Vandiver of Harford County served Gorman devotedly, managing campaigns so as to free the senator from worrisome detail. In 1892 legislators elected Vandiver Speaker of the House of Delegates. Barnes Compton led Gorman men in Southern Maryland, where outnumbered whites were staunchly Democratic. On the Eastern Shore Jesse K. Hines of Kent County, John Walter Smith of Worcester, and Elihu E. Jackson, a wealthy lumber businessman from Wicomico County, allied themselves with Gorman. Jackson, elected to the House of Delegates in 1882 and senate in 1884, went on to serve as president of the senate and as governor in 1887; he once wrote Gorman that three-quarters of his income went toward keeping Wicomico Democratic (between 1870 and 1895 Democrats won every election there). Smith, a Snow Hill lumber producer and banker, won election to the assembly in 1889 and then to Congress in 1898. He afterward served as governor and U.S. senator. Detractors called this clique the Old Guard.

When Gorman's friend Grover Cleveland won the presidency in 1884, the Old Guard entered the promised land. Cleveland had risen in New York by favoring civic reform. Gorman became a notoriously successful party fund raiser by dunning the New York City interests Cleveland abhorred. He advised the reform president to make good use of federal patronage and himself enjoyed a free hand with Maryland appointments. Gorman had Rasin installed in a lucrative customs job in Baltimore. Two Gorman men, former U.S. Senator James B. Groome and Edwin Warfield, joined Rasin in the customs office. Gorman secured the federal district attorney's job for Thomas G. Hayes, the postmaster's post in Baltimore for I. Parker Veazey, and the U.S. marshal's salary for George H. Cairnes, a physician and party loyalist. Robert M. McLane, then governor, and Frederick Raine went to diplomatic posts in France and Germany. Sonny Mahon got a job as treasury department special agent in Baltimore; earning $8 a day, he thought he had "all the money in the United States." Two more of Rasin's fast friends obtained Washington jobs as chief of the Treasury Department appointments division and (of all things) Interior Department inspector of Indians. The elderly Severn Teackle Wallis, speaking for Independent Democrats, went to Washington to protest Gorman's unchallenged influence. It was a futile attempt. Those were the days, said the Rasin ward heeler Jim Lewis, when "knighthood was in flower."[27]

Urban problems foiled these gallants, however; governing Baltimore made the machine squeak. Believing with Mayor Latrobe that "manufactures will not go where taxes are excessive," Baltimoreans in these years got along on painfully low city budgets and went deeply into debt floating capital improvements loans that Rasin and Latrobe believed would ultimately raise the tax base. Evasion of levied taxes kept revenues about 30 percent short of assessments. Baltimore's two-chamber city council, which lent itself to combinations and vote trading, passed budgets that income did not cover, forcing the mayor (with Rasin in the background) to pick and choose the improvements that would go ahead. In order to plead for local projects, many residents in the 1880s formed neighborhood associations whose leaders scrambled for Rasin's favor like children in a poor household fighting for crumbs. All the while businessmen and city contractors knew they had to make payments to the party in return for city jobs.[28]

School administration and building offered a glimpse of this homely system at work. "Our buildings are less costly, our teachers' salaries lower, and our general current expenses, and cost per pupil, less than in almost any other large cities in our country," the president of the Baltimore Board of School Commissioners noted proudly in 1873. The Rasin ring left that record intact. Critics rightly called the school board "a product of the ward politicians"; to it lower-branch councilmen named longtime members of the Democratic clubs. So avidly did board members curry political favor, testified one observer, "that at one time to have already served a term or two as school commissioner was regarded as the best possible training and qualification for an aspirant for a seat in the City Council." The board selected principals and their assistants, annually renewed teachers' contracts (annual turnover ran at about 10 percent), and decided whether and how to make any improvements to the city schools. Teachers, like street pavers, had no choice but to make contributions to the Democratic party. "Political influence," a Baltimorean wrote, "appears to play a much greater part in appointment than merit."[29]

Precisely because politicized, the schools always worked in someone's favor; the ring could indeed be highly sensitive to public pressure. Henry E. Shepherd, former literature and history teacher and principal at City College, served as Baltimore school superintendent in the late 1870s. Shepherd got into a running battle with the state superintendent, Alexander Newell, a Towson Normal School instructor who had become a nationwide advocate of manual or vocational high schools and wanted one built in Baltimore. Schools did not teach trades, Shepherd maintained; they transferred culture. At first Baltimore commissioners dismissed the manual training idea as too expensive. But newspapers found the Newell-Shepherd controversy lively material and aligned according to political posture. The *Sun*, then friendly to Rasin, wrote that introducing the trades into the classroom would be "foreign to the genius of our institutions." The *American*, Rasin's arch-enemy, endorsed manual schools because they would dignify labor, and condemned Shepherd, presumably Rasin's stooge, as an elitist. This appeal soon generated support for a manual school that the politically astute commissioners could not ignore, and they trimmed their sails. Shepherd resigned in 1882, protesting the decline of classical education and complaining about graft in the school system; the *American* described Shepherd's departure as a sacrifice to the political machine. The manual training school opened in 1884. Renamed Polytechnic ten years later (and known thereafter as Poly), it soon furnished Hopkins, the naval school, and Baltimore industry with eager young men trained in engineering and mathematics.[30]

Results in the school building program were far less salutary. In 1870 only about three in ten school-age Baltimore youngsters attended school, for many of them worked; in 1900 attendance stood at only four in ten. Yet the city grew so rapidly from the late 1870s to the mid-1890s that enrollment increased by more than sixteen hundred pupils a year. Shortsightedness and lack of funds exacted high costs. The commissioners tried stopgap measures like renting space in empty buildings. Schools went up without steam heat, adequate light and ventilation, or space in the yards. Schoolrooms commonly had twice as many pupils as they were designed to hold. "The heat and stifling air, and nauseating effluvia in some of the rooms," noted a visitor to one Baltimore school in 1878, "is indeed such as a human being has hardly been compelled to live in since the time of Jonah." In the winter children sitting close to coal and wood stoves were too hot, those a few seats away too cold. These stoves posed an obvious fire hazard, yet a long-delayed inspection of 1880 revealed thirty schools in which several rooms opened onto narrow halls or steep stairways. According to reports some parents were "unwilling to endanger the health of their children" by sending them to school. Ward leaders and councilmen naturally had only the interests of their backyards in mind. Neither superintendent nor building inspector had the power to coordinate the needs of the various wards and the city as a whole. In the absence of planning, new buildings did not always suffice. When in 1890 school number 20 opened, it already was obsolete—children without classrooms had to sit on the front steps.[31]

Equally serious were shortcomings in water management. Although Baltimore had made heroic attempts to improve its water-supply network during and after the war, problems persisted. In 1877 a Baltimore County newspaper described Lake Roland as a "receptacle of filth" from nearby sinks and a slaughterhouse—explaining why "Towsontowners never drink any water when they go to the city." Loch Raven Reservoir, with its marvelous tunnels to Lake Montebello and Lake Clifton, captured national attention in 1881. Next year the city sued a manufacturer whose privies and pigpens discolored the Gunpowder before it reached Loch Raven. Though the court ordered the offenses removed, Baltimore collected no damages because the city could not prove the nature of the "divers injurious ingredients and substances" pigs and privies put in the water supply.[32]

Even as Baltimore sought fresh drinking water, the city for many years put off facing the companion issues of waste and drainage, which rapid growth made critical. Many households ran water closets into tanks that "odorless excavating" services pumped out from time to time, carrying the effluence to "night soil" dumping grounds outside the city. Other houses had backyard privies that eventually contaminated the ground water—even though in places like Fells Point people still relied on neighborhood wells. New row houses or neighborhood developments often went up with sewer lines that merely ran pipe to the nearest stream. While a city ordinance prohibited

Odorless Excavating Apparatus, c. 1890. *Baltimore Sunpapers*

connecting a privy with a storm sewer, one easily obtained a permit for a basement drain by making a contribution to the local councilman or ward heeler. Basement drains introduced the danger of deadly sewer gas. To carry off sewage much of Baltimore still relied on the Jones Falls. During dry seasons its stench made an impression even on natives who stood downstream or downwind. The plea of a Southwest Association president during these years demonstrated the nagging problem of localism. "Relieve us of the stagnant rivers," he cried at a dinner for Latrobe. "When North Baltimore sends us its refuse we demand that the city pass it on to the next fellow." In 1880 a special commission recommended building separate storm and sewage pipes under Baltimore with public money; thirteen years later, nothing having been done, another group went further and called for pumping treated human waste into the bay below Baltimore. Night soil contractors condemned the plan.[33]

Ill equipped to make long-range or large-scale plans, the Rasin-Gorman machine succeeded for many years because it serviced at least some local needs and satisfied human emotions. One set of feelings related to the Civil War and the men who had fought in it. As veterans of the conflict approached old age, they, somewhat like the philanthropists, sought ways to live beyond themselves. More than forty chapters of the Grand Army of the Republic formed in Maryland, the Dushane Post in Baltimore growing especially strong. Union veterans reunited each year for speeches and reminiscing. A Confederate army-navy society formed in Maryland in 1871, and the Association of the Maryland Line organized in 1881. That year ex-Confederates in Frederick unveiled a granite and marble statue of a soldier at rest arms. Soon afterward, not to be outdone, Union veterans there erected a similar monument. Dedicating statues and staging encampments stirred memories and carried undertones. In Maryland patriotic rituals helped to exorcise the ghost of Lincoln's assassin, John Wilkes Booth, the deranged Harford County–born actor whose deed had shocked so many Marylanders shortly after Lee's surrender. They enabled Maryland Confederates, who at Manassas had called the Star-Spangled Banner that "damned old gridiron," to reaffirm their loyalty.[34] Conversely, they reminded voters that Democrats had not imprisoned fellow Marylanders.

Above all, commemorative gestures appealed to state pride and aimed at reconciliation. In 1888 the legislature passed two measures friendly to old soldiers. It turned over the former federal arsenal near Pikesville to leaders of the Maryland Line association, who planned to make it a home for elderly Confederate veterans, and voted funds for Union monuments at Gettysburg (Maryland was one of the last states to do so). William D. Burchinal, a Kent County senator and Union veteran who voted in favor of the Confederate Soldiers' Home, served as one of the Gettysburg commissioners. According to the commissioners' report, dedication ceremonies that October surpassed those even of Ohio and Pennsylvania for color and participation. Little wonder if true, for special excursion trains from Hagerstown, Westminster, and Baltimore carried military bands, national guard units, firemen, veterans from all over the state, and a host of spectators to the scene of the event. The color sergeant carried a new Maryland flag—Crossland red and white quartered with Lord Baltimore's black and gold. Orators in their own way tried to restitch the torn fabric of Maryland. "The suspicions, the bitterness, the animosities necessarily engendered by a protracted Civil War," declared Colonel James C. Mullikin of Easton, "have departed from our state never to return." Colonel Theodore F. Lang, chairman of the commissioners and GAR department commander, saluted the Confederate Marylanders who had assaulted his men on the very ground where everyone stood; the Union monuments did not mark the victory of one side over the other, he concluded. "These columns stand for union." Governor Elihu Jackson said that even mentioning the deeds done at Gettysburg reopened "wounds in the hearts of thousands of widows and orphans."[35]

Thriving on sentimentality, Gorman, Rasin, and their friends epitomized something that was disappearing just as surely as the Civil War veteran: informal, highly personal ways of settling accounts. Rasin "knew everything and everybody," according to a Baltimore newspaper reporter, staying closely in touch with workingmen and clubmen alike. His lines in the city were "numerous and marvelous." Claiming that he never put anybody unfit into office, he learned quickly of ingratitude. One did not flirt with Rasin's anger—he shouted abuse at every foe and knew secrets embarrassing to many

"Governor E. E. Jackson and Staff, At the Dedication of Maryland Monuments, Gettysburg, October 25, 1888." *Report of the State of Maryland Gettysburg Monument Commission* (Baltimore, 1891). *Alderman Library, University of Virginia*

people who could withstand abuse. Gorman only appeared to be different. Unshaken and philosophic when suffering attack, he "neither forgave nor forgot his enemies"—so many of whom were associated with the B&O. In 1878, fighting a rate war with the Pennsylvania Railroad, Garrett had sought release from an agreement by which the B&O turned over one-fifth of its Baltimore-Washington passenger revenues to the state in repayment for public support in building the line. Then C&O president and a state senator, Gorman had permitted that release only after forcing Garrett to surrender the railroad's tax-free status and agree to regulation of rates on coal and other raw materials so as to benefit the canal. Two years later friends of the B&O conducted a legislative inquiry that tried without success to show that Gorman mismanaged the C&O (key company records later disappeared). In the 1880s Gorman's patronage appointments greatly irked the railroad.[36]

It was easy to expect the worst and get along with officials who both conceded and illustrated human weaknesses. Police ignored as harmless the private lottery called Policy—some of them may have collected profits from it—and winked at the late-night matches between black fighters held at the Eureka Athletic and Social Club in Baltimore, partly because so many public figures attended them. Sailing into Baltimore, oyster and produce boats passed harbor police a few choice specimens of their cargo in exchange for occasional help. When a shopkeeper wanted to enlarge a sign above his door, he did not bother seeking a permit; he slipped his councilman a few dollars and hung it. Rasin's clerkship in the city court involved banking the fines and fees he collected. At the time—with his men distributing food baskets to the needy at Christmas—few people knew or cared that he put interest accrued on those funds to his own purposes if not into his pocket.

The plain people of Baltimore, believed a native son, had grown accustomed to this old-fashioned manner. It kept money in circulation and made for "a spacious and stimulating communal life." [37]

The Progressive impulse drew strength from several sources. On one level anybody who felt he had been cheated might listen to calls for reform. State inspection and ventilation laws of 1876 and 1878 satisfied very few Western Maryland coal miners, for example. A stronger bill, which passed both senate and House of Delegates in 1886, mysteriously disappeared on its way to the governor's desk for signature—adding weight to the view that the coal companies got their way in Annapolis. Watermen were philosophical about large trends, if not indifferent to them. Yet tongers ran behind dredgers in the oyster race, and legislators in the 1880s, under the sway of dredgers and packing companies, provided the oyster navy nothing more than an annual pittance. State power politics played a role as well; John K. Cowen, the highly respected general counsel for the B&O, fought the Gorman machine for reasons that began with tax rates and comparative corporate privilege. Mostly the Progressive movement reflected the growing influence of civic-minded and educated city dwellers. Though one might have agreed with Mayor Latrobe that politicians like Rasin were necessary evils, the costs of "boss" rule—fraud, localism, and poor urban services—made for growing dissatisfaction among prominent Baltimoreans, middle-class managers, and professionals. They relied on the findings of contemporary science, preferred organization and efficiency to waste and mismanagement, and subscribed to an ideal they called "good government."

In their attempts to reorganize charities, Baltimoreans in the 1880s foreshadowed the Progressive attack on duplication and poor coordination. After about 1862 the city council apparently ceased making grants to the old almshouse trustees and instead began making annual grants to a proliferating number of charity groups. A state Court of Appeals decision of 1875 declared the practice illegal without legislative authority but did not prevent the city from contracting with private agencies for charity work. In 1870 seven institutions received $22,000 for care of the sick and for orphan and poor relief; ten years later fifteen groups received appropriations of $100,000 for those purposes. Critics claimed that the relief groups fostered pauperism. In any event, the city had no means of inspecting these houses or hospitals, auditing their accounts, or influencing their policy; Baltimore made grants in large sums rather than for a particular purpose. With such shortcomings in mind, President Gilman of Hopkins in 1881 attended an Albany, New York, meeting of the American Social Science Association, a national group dedicated to studying such problems, and there he heard one speaker explain the advantages of a London society that oversaw all charitable work there. Gilman and a group of community leaders soon formed a similar Baltimore Charity Organization Society. It developed a system of investigating and registering charitable cases in the city, keeping watch on institutions, and publishing a directory of them. The COS met needs that had gone neglected and supervised overall relief efforts. It tried to make charities rational.

Less subtly, a public utilities revolution in the 1880s invited renewed attention to old policy issues. Alexander Graham Bell's telephone, proven feasible in 1876, arrived in Maryland soon afterward. In January 1879 two Bell affiliates in Baltimore, Augustus G. Davis and John Henry C. Watts, opened a phone exchange on the corner of Baltimore and South streets. At first there were about ninety Maryland Telephone Company subscribers, seventy-six of them businesses, connected to a crude switchboard that "hello boys" operated. "No recent invention has been so well received by the general public and so fully endorsed by the press," read the company announcement of that year, "and no wonder, for the results are *astonishing*." At the same time, Gorman had telephones installed the entire length of the C&O, forming the longest system then in service and raising the ire of cautious bondholders. In 1883 the Baltimore company and its Washington, D.C., counterpart combined to form the Chesapeake and Potomac Telephone Company. C&P growth proved the widespread value of the phone, which designers dressed up to fit on a small desk or look like a handsome box. Elkton, Cumberland, Frostburg, Frederick, Hagerstown, Annapolis, Westminster, and Chestertown had Bell telephone companies by the mid-1880s; in 1890 more than twenty-two hundred Baltimoreans had taken phone service, and the figure climbed about six times in ten years.[38]

Electricity, an invisible and mystifying form of energy, first appeared commercially in Baltimore in 1880, when W. T. Russell, a B&O telegraph operator fascinated by Thomas Edison's discoveries, installed dynamos in the basement of the Sun Building and wired them to several outdoor lamps. Soon Russell began putting up poles and stringing wires for the United States Electric Company, which took over a furniture factory on Pratt Street for its steam-powered generating plant. Investors like Summerfield Baldwin and another enterprising telegrapher, J. Frank Morrison, raised two hundred thousand dollars to establish the Brush Electric Light Company in the city; in 1882 at East Monument and Constitution streets it began building the first plant in the country designed solely for generating electrical energy. Brush electricity powered a small, experimental trolley line that ran along North Avenue beginning in 1885. Later (alternating current appeared in 1888), two more Baltimore firms built generating plants. In 1886 the Brush Company started a "day circuit" that opened the way for newly developed Baxter electric motors. They had their earliest impact in the nearby clothing industry, driving large knives that cut multiple pieces at once.

Everyone sang the praises of the telephone; it instantly summoned the family doctor or easily placed an order at the local grocer's. Baltimoreans boasted of the electric street lights the city installed in the 1880s (they drew amazing swarms of summer-night insects). Yet the new conveniences brought problems. Overhead service lines for electricity firms, telephone lines, and wires for electric streetcars soon became so plentiful as to shade Baltimore streets on the brightest day. In 1889 the city council granted the C&P permission to place its downtown phone lines underground—a process that went on for years and caused much disruption. The remaining telegraph and electric lines in the business district belonged to eight different companies and left the city, as someone said in the mid-1890s, bound down, "Gulliver-like."[39] They posed a danger as well as spread blight. Broken lines—common in ice storms and high winds—could cross onto each other and start fires or drop onto pedestrians. The new utilities came at other costs as well; users pressed for laws governing rates. Telephone tolls remained high, in the view of customers, even after 1893, when Bell's first patents expired and a competing firm, the Home Telephone and Telegraph Company, appeared in Baltimore. Increased public dependence on utilities raised questions about their regulation for the common good.

A revived and self-conscious legal profession in Maryland helped to shape the good government concept, and changes in legal training marked the lawyer's new sophistication. In 1870 a few Baltimore lawyers decided to reopen the University of Maryland School of Law, which had remained moribund since David Hoffman's departure in 1832. Robert N. Martin of the city superior court played a part in the school's reappearance (Hopkins planned, but for many years did not open, a law school), along with a former Hoffman student, Judge George Dobbin, and John Prentiss Poe, a Princeton graduate, prominent Baltimore attorney, and arch-conservative. Early classes met at night in rooms on Mulberry Street; in 1884, with students numbering thirty or more, the school moved to a new building near the medical institutions. It resurfaced because the law, like so many other features of late-nineteenth-century American life, no longer permitted haphazard training. Commercial and industrial growth, besides creating new fields of legal specialization, demanded regularity and system. Maryland was one of the first law schools in the country to adjust accordingly. To staple courses in constitutional law, procedure, evidence, and equity, the faculty added new ones in sales, surety, corporations, insurance, copyrights, commercial notes, and admiralty law. Professors took students to observe the city judiciary and presided over moot court competitions. Students included the sons of German-Jewish merchants and clothiers and increasingly were college graduates and non-Baltimoreans.

The school molded a generation of Maryland lawyers whose professional training and attention to legal process posed clear threats to the Old Guard's personal style and shady practices.

Lawyers hated to lose cases before tainted judges. Severn Teackle Wallis, speaking outside the Baltimore City criminal court, once pointed to it as a "sink of iniquity into which no honest man enters without a shudder and from which no scoundrel emerges without a triumph." All city trial judges, five of them, constituted the supreme bench, and in 1882 the terms of four judges expired. Most lawyers agreed that two of the incumbents, refusing to rotate each year among the courts, belonged to Rasin and ought to be replaced. The *Sun* followed suit, standing in favor "of *good laws interpreted by good judges*." Yet in October a convention of Democrats, bosses cracking the whip, nominated a ticket that included William A. Fisher, first president of the Baltimore Charity Organization, but also the two objectionable party servants. Thereafter a coalition of some 350 citizens published a protest, named its own slate of candidates (which overlapped Rasin's by naming Fisher), and mounted a furious "new judges" campaign. The city shook with speeches and demonstrations, and in November the alliance dealt Rasin his first political defeat. Spirits lifted, reformers next hoped in 1885 to defeat Rasin's choice for mayor. During that frenzied contest William L. Marbury, a young Prince George's County native and recent Maryland law graduate, risked a beating (and nearly got one) by telling a crowd in the 17th ward that its politics were "controlled by a dirty clique of rowdies." Rasin's machine, then being oiled in the first year of Cleveland's presidency, triumphed all the same. Roughnecks patrolled polling places; Rasin's ring counted the votes. Demanding fair elections, honest government, and the punishment of official wrongdoing, reformers next organized the Baltimore Reform League.[40]

The league voiced the offended sensibility of patrician and professional Baltimore. Longtime Rasin opponents and Independent Democrats provided its original leadership: Wallis, dean of the Baltimore bar, helped to form the league, as did Cowen of the B&O. Charles Marshall, former secretary to General Lee, also joined at the beginning; he once sat next to Rasin on the train to Washington and bluntly told him he ought to be in jail. S. Davies Warfield, onetime Baltimore postmaster and an early member of the Maryland Civil Service Reform Association that formed in 1881, played a prominent part in shaping the league. Most of its charter members, like Marbury and his Maryland law classmate William Cabell Bruce, were young lawyers or college graduates from old families; they had names like Baldwin, Howard, Semmes, Reynolds, Taylor, and Williams. Another founder, Charles J. Bonaparte, departed the mold somewhat—a Republican and a Catholic while most members of the group were Democrats and Protestants, usually Episcopalians. He nonetheless bespoke the league's blue blood and zest for crusade. Grandson of the illustrious Betsy Patterson and Napoleon's youngest brother, a Harvard graduate and overseer of the college, independently

Left, Severn Teackle Wallis (1816–94), c. 1885. As a member of the bar, conservative Democrat, and above all Baltimore patrician, Wallis challenged Gorman's rule. *MHS*
Right, Charles Joseph Bonaparte (1851–1921) and wife, Ellen Channing Day, c. 1875. A recent graduate of Harvard College and Law School, Bonaparte here revealed some of the satisfaction that riled his enemies. *MHS*

wealthy, Bonaparte had immersed himself in Baltimore charities and civil service reform; he had organized a local chapter of the Society for the Suppression of Vice, which tried to reconstruct prostitutes and keep saloons out of nice neighborhoods. Bonaparte's sense of noblesse oblige approached the European. In a pamphlet he compared free public schools to soup kitchens. Even to those of equal station he seemed awfully proud and aloof, and of course machine politicians detested him. It may have been Rasin's friend James Hodges, mayor in 1885, who called Bonaparte "the Imperial Peacock of Park Avenue."[41]

Reform strategy called for exposing Old Guard corruption, winning public support for change, and then throwing the rascals out. John C. Rose, a Maryland Law School product and league counsel, soon began a survey of electoral curiosities. Election officials in Baltimore, appointed by a state board whose members sat at the pleasure of the governor, predictably turned out to be agents of the Democratic party. Registration rolls omitted blacks and raised white voters from the dead. In the 9th ward, Sonny Mahon had 186 Democrats listed as living in three houses, and 72 others quartered over a friendly saloon. City clerks threw obstructions in Rose's path by declaring key records confidential, but the new judges held them open. League members drafted bills to reform voter registration and elections, and in 1888 and 1890 the General Assembly passed watered-down versions.

As popular interest in reform issues began to grow, ownership of the Baltimore *Evening News* in 1891 fell to a zealous young Virginian, Charles H. Grasty, who developed close ties to the Reform League. Two of its members gave Grasty financial support—Lawranson Riggs, another university law school graduate, and Julian LeRoy White, who had attended Cambridge University and studied economics under Ely at Hopkins. Two other wealthy young Baltimoreans, Douglas H. Gordon and Thomas K. Worthington, helped Grasty with money and editorials. The part the *News* played in Baltimore reform offered an example of the new role some newspapers assumed in the 1890s. During the Jacksonian period many papers had been party sheets, and in the late nineteenth century the Baltimore *American* continued in this vein to speak for the Republicans. The Baltimore *Herald*, developing another theme of the old penny press, played on human interest stories. The *World* spoke plainly to the working families of Baltimore. Various German-language papers retained ethnic identity—covering German weddings, funerals, and the like—with fewer readers as immigrants' children grew up as Americans. The *Sun*, until 1887 under the control of its founder, Arunah S. Abell, esteemed itself as a gentlemanly paper with a voice somewhat official, never vulgar.

Grasty by contrast had learned the news business as a reporter for the muckraking Kansas City *Star*, which in turn took its inspiration from the energetic Joseph Pulitzer paper in New York. The *News* sought accuracy with a nonpartisan commitment to "clean government." One of Grasty's early ambitions was to expose police collusion in the lottery business—while also pointing out how the lottery preyed on the hopeful but ignorant poor. Reporters examined the ruse from every angle, then interviewed police authorities who, unaware of the investigation, denied the existence of gambling in Baltimore. After the story appeared Grasty and his co-editors found themselves indicted for criminal libel. Defending them was Marbury, who in an earlier voting case had done service for the Reform League and now obtained an acquittal of the *News* by cleverly turning its trial into a further-embarrassing exposé of official misfeasance. Grasty's paper spoke plainly of injustice and human suffering. In the spring of 1892 the *News* began a series of articles exploring the high rates and financial irregularities of the Consolidated Gas Company, formed of three competing firms in 1880. It published accounts of shocking filth in Old Town's crowded and smelly sweatshops and quoted the health commissioner on his frustrating lack of authority. The

News described graphically the poverty, unemployment, and open sewers of southwest Baltimore. "Foul streets, foul people, in foul tenements filled with foul air; that's 'Pigtown.' "[42]

The impact of these stories defied precise measurement. *News* circulation in the city, however, eventually passed thirty-four thousand (almost as high as the *Sun's*), and signs of awakening public sentiment appeared among labor, church, and grass-roots groups. The hard times of the mid-1890s, if not the reform spirit, made Baltimore working people restless; in January 1893 unemployment among skilled workers alone stood at 38 percent. Edward Hirsch, a typesetter for the *Sun* and later a prominent labor spokesman, cooperated with anti-machine reformers, as did Jacob Schonfarber, a carpenter and old Knights of Labor leader in the city who in 1889 began publishing a weekly magazine devoted to labor reforms that presupposed honest government. Clerical converts to reform had stirring influence among wage earners, well-to-do, and middle class alike. Henry M. Wharton, a lawyer who served as minister of the Brantley Church in West Baltimore, the largest Baptist congregation in the city, asked members to see the effects of boss rule as their moral responsibility. "If the church does not thunder forth its anathema against wickedness in high places now, in the name of all that is good," he cried, "what is the reason for its existence?" The Reverend Hiram Vrooman had grown up in Kansas and spent time at Harvard and as a newspaperman before entering the seminary. In 1893 he assumed the pulpit at the venerable Church of the New Jerusalem, where he determined to fuse religion and politics "until the mighty ring of this city is purified." Vrooman, who had three equally active brothers in Baltimore, soon formed a Union for Public Good that joined religious, charity, reform, and labor organizations in the struggle for ethical government.[43]

Nonpartisan good government clubs formed in many Baltimore wards, Bonaparte acting as coordinating chairman. Women's groups, always active in Baltimore charities, came out for political reform. The most prominent among them, the Arundell Good Government Club, organized as an offshoot of the elite Arundell Club. Arundell activists divided their time between the campaign to admit women at the Hopkins Medical School and the fight to dismiss the Old Guard.

❧

If acceptance of the informal had helped to account for the Old Guard's dominance, this rising tide of organized indignation spelled trouble for it. Reformers first marshalled their forces for a full attack in the fall elections of 1895. At the Democratic convention that year reform Democrats, led by a Baltimore iron and copper manufacturer, William Keyser, found Senator Gorman's power formidable. The senator anointed John E. Hurst as his candidate for governor and simply summoned the others to his Carrollton Hotel room and advised them to withdraw. After the raucous convention about one hundred and fifty Keyser men met to absolve Maryland Democrats of their party allegiance. Young Reform League Democrats had no trouble with an independent course; Bruce, then a state senator, spoke for them as they departed. Some older party men also left in disgust. The disappointed would-be nominee for governor, Tom Hayes, split with the Old Guard, as did the longtime loyal Democrat William Whyte. The *Sun* had passed to Edwin F. Abell, the founder's son, and been critical of Gorman since the preceding summer—Gorman had parted ways with President Cleveland over tariff policy. During the 1895 campaign the paper published a barrage of editorials against "The Dual Despotism of Gorman and Rasin." Cowen and directors of the B&O had fresh quarrels with Gorman, who recently had opposed a rate-pooling bill the B&O favored.[44]

Republicans made hay in this sunshine. Lloyd G. Lowndes, a Cumberland banker, and George L. Wellington, another Allegany countian, worked to rebuild the state party, whose Baltimore leadership included important Reform League members like Rose, Robert Garrett (grandson of John W.), George R. Gaither (Maryland law graduate, cotton merchant, and son of the Confederate officer), the Jewish attorney Lewis Putzel, William F. Stone (city party chairman), and a textile industrialist, Alcaeus Hooper. In August the GOP state convention, held in Cambridge, selected Lowndes as the Republican candidate for governor. Rose himself drafted the reform platform that the Republicans adopted. Meeting separately in October, Baltimore City Republicans nominated Hooper for mayor and declared the need to divorce politics from city government.

Baltimoreans did not soon forget the 1895 campaign. Regular Democrats again tried to make race an issue. They reproduced a picture of black and white Pennsylvania schoolchildren, describing the awful scene as the result of Republican rule there (on close look the children were smiling), and encouraged the belief that a Republican victory would bring a New York–style public accommodations law fining or imprisoning any white man "who does not welcome the negro to his restaurant, his table, bed, theatre, &c." Machine Democrats passed out bogus handbills that reserved the galleries of Republican meeting places for "colored ladies and their escorts." Rasin men in the city staged a parade to prove their undiminished strength. Sonny Mahon, wearing a red shirt and white cap, led the John J. Mahon Democratic Club. Old Guard dignitaries rode in carriages and waved to the crowds. But the crowds were smaller and quieter than usual; the ward heeler's occasional food baskets and inside connections at city hall had failed to satisfy many hard-pressed Baltimoreans. Rasin's choice of a large bell at the head of the procession also backfired. A *Sun* reporter wrote that the bell and demonstration alike sounded the death-knell of the machine.[45]

A Democratic split, but also the enthusiasm of amateur reformers, made a difference that November. A group of Baltimore business and professional people established a fund to reward persons uncovering election-day irregularities. Roger W. Cull, chairman of the Reform League committee on elections, asked for volunteers to watch Baltimore polls for repeaters and arm-twisters. Fifteen hundred people answered the call, and their backgrounds proved the extent of citizen concern. Republicans and representatives of splinter parties like the prohibitionists and socialists turned out as poll watchers. So did members of women's groups, college students, retailers, and men with dealings in the harbor who had decided that machine rule was bad for business. Dr. Kelly of the Hopkins Hospital volunteered to serve in one of the roughest wards, Marsh Market; Professor W. J. A. Bliss of the Hopkins physics department stood watch in Mahon's 9th ward. An elderly Presbyterian minister who had defended the cause of Union in 1861 again volunteered, this time "under the pending danger to the Ballot Box." On election day violence flared as expected. A poll watcher took a beating after someone pointed him out as a "Reform League snipe." Alfred S. Niles, a Maryland law graduate and the president of the 12th ward Good Government Club, got a black eye; Bliss had his jaw broken. White toughs roamed some of the wards firing guns in the air to intimidate black Republicans, one of whom was shot and killed; two others suffered serious wounds.[46]

These desperate acts changed nothing. Nearly nine out of ten eligible men voted in Baltimore, and Marylanders elsewhere went to the polls in high numbers. Their votes went for reform. Lowndes carried the state by a margin of twenty thousand. In Baltimore Hooper won the mayor's race handily. He ran most strongly in the wealthy, old-family sections of the city but picked up new votes for the Republicans in virtually every ward. Mahon's 9th and a few other working-class wards went down with the Rasin machine. In races for General Assembly seats, Democrats fared well in only a few counties: Worcester, Wicomico, Queen Anne's, Caroline, Harford, Montgomery, and Calvert. Republicans won control of the legislature, Baltimore City Council, and state Board of Public Works. When in January 1896 the legislature convened, Sydney E. Mudd, a Charles County Republican, won the House of Delegates speakership and William Cabell Bruce the senate presidency.

More defeats for the Old Guard followed. In the presidential contest of 1896 Maryland veered from the Democratic column for the first time since the Civil War—though most voters apparently found the choice between William Jennings Bryan (the Democrat favored expansion of the money supply through silver coinage) and William McKinley (a high-tariff Republican) unattractive. Gorman, who had hoped for another nominee, campaigned loyally for Bryan and made vigorous speeches for him at Snow Hill, Laurel, and Hagerstown. Bryan's loss was Gorman's as well. Then, in 1897, the Republicans won a narrow victory in the General Assembly race—Rasin thought another two thousand dollars would have won it—and Gorman lost his own bid for reelection. At the turn of the century the state again went for McKinley.

Before the political pendulum swung back toward the middle, Republicans and reformers had the legislature to themselves and succeeded in making a few changes in the political structure. An 1896 election law, passed at the insistence of the Reform League and with Bruce's pivotal help in the senate, introduced an improved form of the Australian or secret ballot, which legislators first had adopted—in a manner that actually used state election machinery to strengthen the Democratic party—in 1890. The assembly in 1896 set aside the statute providing the Eastern Shore one Maryland seat in the U.S. Senate, a reform that obviously aided the GOP, whose strength lay west and south of Baltimore. In 1898 the General Assembly granted Baltimore City a charter to replace the original one of 1796. The new charter emerged from a bipartisan commission chosen by Republican mayor William T. Malster, who, not himself a fanatical reformer, made good selections in Gilman of Hopkins, Senator Whyte, Mayor Latrobe, and Gaither and Putzel. Besides strengthening the mayor's office, Baltimore's new charter established several boards designed to place critical decisions beyond the reach of ward heelers and machine councilmen. A new, citywide school board hired a superintendent with workaday independence in teacher employment, curriculum, and administration. A Board of Estimates, made up of three elected and two appointed members, set fiscal policy and granted franchises (utility franchises now carried a statutory limit of twenty-five years). An independent Board of Awards replaced the city council as grantor of contracts for city work. The 1898 charter represented compromises between reformers and old pols and between Democrats and Republicans. It moved mayoral elections from the fall to the spring, when voters could choose mayors solely on the basis of city issues (and Republicans might stand a better chance of winning).

Professional awareness had helped to bring about this new legislation, and, fittingly, Maryland attorneys at about the same time formed a state bar association. Constitutional quirks and Maryland law itself long had fostered provincialism. The *Sun* once noted that, in a two-volume set of the state code, the volume of local laws was fatter by some 250 pages than the one covering general statutes; not a lawyer in Maryland "pretends to know anything about any county save that where he practices." Trying to take a larger view, attorneys from Allegany County and Baltimore in 1896 issued a call that nearly a hundred of their colleagues answered by gathering in August at a Washington County retreat. As temporary chairman they elected Poe, who eight years before had published an ambitious new compilation of Maryland law. Without a state bar association, he now said, "we cannot do all that we should for the improvement and reform of the law." The group established permanent committees on legal education and reform of laws and courts, and in a year its membership more than doubled. Next summer at Ocean City, after debating whether appeals court judges should wear robes and wigs, members began a discussion of criminal law reform and agreed on upgrading legal education. They recommended that the university adopt a three-year law curriculum and that a state board of examiners (similar to those recently established in medicine, pharmacy, dentistry, and veterinary practice) examine all applicants to the bar. Judge James McSherry of Frederick, first association president, spoke of the need to close the guild to the unfit; its overcrowding "by utterly incompetent and unworthy persons" threatened the "ascendancy of the profession." McSherry admitted that one "cannot well fix a moral standard as you may prescribe an intellectual one."[47]

While professionals set standards that also closed ranks, Maryland politicians of both parties proved that reformers had a long way to travel. Republicans were not angels. Lowndes, who had interests in a George's Creek coal company, used his pocket veto to kill two bills raising inspection and ventilation standards in Allegany County and another, improved, measure against company stores. Democrats accused the House of Delegates Speaker of using his podium as an auction block; Mudd himself defined an honest man as "a bastard who will stay bought." A congressman in 1900, Mudd had his district census padded to allow flexibility at election time. His successor as house Speaker, Louis Schaefer, went on to be arrested as a jewel thief. Republican redistricting efforts in Baltimore City showed that the GOP could be as guilty of partisanship as the Democracy.[48]

These missteps helped Democrats to regain lost ground. They elected Tom Hayes Baltimore mayor in 1899. John Walter Smith, the Democratic work-

"The Machine in Disrepair," 1899. McKee Barclay of the Baltimore *Sun* poked fun at the Democrats' electoral malfunctions toward the end of the century. *MHS*

horse and Gorman friend from Worcester County, began a four-year term as governor in 1900. In Annapolis, Democrats applied their working majority in ordering a recount of the 1900 census. Asked if it would be bipartisan, Gorman, active in retirement, said, "Well, they took one census. Now we'll take one. That's bipartisan, isn't it?" Regular Democrats proposed yet another revised election law. The 1896 measure used party symbols—Jackson and Lincoln logos—to identify candidates, and permitted illiterate voters (including many blacks) to cast ballots with the aid of an official. Democrats said the law made influencing the ignorant all too easy. A new act, passed in 1901, replaced symbols with letters. Gorman completed his comeback in 1902 when Democrats, maintaining a slim majority in the assembly, chose him for the U.S. Senate term that began the following year. In 1904 his past willingness to compromise on the tariff question and his criticism of Republican imperialism abroad brought him enough praise outside Maryland that he considered running for his party's presidential nomination. At home that year Edwin Warfield, a Baltimore banker who long ago had been Gorman's understudy in Howard County, assumed the governor's chair.[49]

Maryland politics remained entertaining. Gorman's friends on the Eastern Shore—Smith, Elihu Jackson, and Joshua W. Miles—all made credible claims on the other U.S. Senate seat in 1905. The eventual winner, Isidor Rayner, was a German-Jewish Baltimore attorney who had served in Congress and as Maryland attorney general from 1899 to 1903. He recently had proved his talent for oratory and gained much popularity during a naval court of inquiry; he defended Rear Admiral Winfield Scott Schley, a Marylander whose rivals had tried to rob him of credit for the American victory over the Spanish at Santiago. Brazenly by Maryland standards, Rayner in 1905 took his senatorial campaign to the public. His enemies trotted out the opinion of the late Severn Teackle Wallis (who had died in 1894) that Rayner had so completely lost any moral sense that he resembled "the blank Leaf between the Old and New Testament." Calling him the "the most consummate windbag Maryland has ever produced," Gorman wanted anybody else but Rayner with him in the Senate.[50]

These players produced a pungent scene in state political theater. Greatly moved by a spirit of reconciliation, Rasin in the 1894 Baltimore congressional campaign had forced Rayner to step aside in favor of Rasin's old foe, John Cowen. Rasin later tried to make amends by helping Rayner win the attorney general's office. Once there, however, Rayner discovered Rasin's custom of pocketing interest from his clerk's fees. Recalling 1894, he demanded payment of the amount owed, with interest. In 1905 Rasin actively took part in Gorman's effort to find an anti-Rayner candidate until the showdown party caucus, when he suddenly delivered Baltimore's crucial votes to none other than Rayner. Rayner publicly embraced Rasin at the new Carvel Hotel in Annapolis. According to Gorman's journal, the new senator secretly repaid Rasin the twenty thousand dollars he earlier had collected.

Cynics and outsiders may have snickered at the state's uneven progress, but reformers could point to positive gains. Progressives won appointments that gave them new opportunities. In 1899 Lowndes named Schonfarber assistant director of the state Bureau of Industrial Statistics, a position he used to press for workingmen's reform laws. After 1900 Mayor Hayes appointed Reform League men to the Baltimore tax appeals court and Joseph Packard, league president, to the school board. Governor Warfield named Alfred Niles a judge of the city superior court. Reform leaders controlled neither party, but at times they held the balance of power. The support Hayes got from the *Sun* and the Reform League—they preferred him to the unpredictable Mayor Malster—helped to elect the Democrat and then, when he tried to form yet another city machine, to defeat him in 1903 and elect the reform-minded son of President Cleveland's minister to France, Robert McLane. In Annapolis legislators like Bruce, Putzel, and a dynamic Jewish attorney, Isaac Lobe Straus, repeatedly, if for a time unsuccessfully, introduced bills to regulate campaign finances and establish civil (enemies called it "snivel") service reform. At the 1900 session of the assembly Jacob Moses, a Hopkins and Maryland law graduate from Baltimore, won passage of a proposed constitutional amendment granting the city a fourth election district. Voters later approved the change, which still left Baltimore badly underrepresented in Annapolis. Reformers made further advances at the 1902 assembly session. Straus wrote a bill providing for direct primaries in the state, a measure that would have ended boss-controlled conventions. He and independents defeated a regular-Democrat substitute bill and at least won passage of a law applying to Baltimore City wards.

∽∾

While in politics reformers tried to eliminate the bosses and establish fair government, the Progressive ethic also recommended expert approaches to grimy problems that the bosses had either ignored or fed upon. Many of them affected Marylanders far more directly than primary elections or a nonpartisan census. At the 1902 session of the General Assembly, David J. Lewis, a miners' association lawyer and Democratic senator from Allegany County, won passage of a bill that miners in the George's Creek region had wanted for a long time. Regulating miners' working conditions, the law set stringent clean air and safety standards, ordered the printing of mine inspectors' reports, forced companies to provide the state with maps of the shafts, and established weighing and docking rules. Lewis, who himself had gone into the mines at age nine, also steered through the legislature a "cooperative insurance" or workmen's compensation bill. Employers and workers in hazardous occupations like mining, quarrying, railroading, and construction contributed to a fund that paid dividends to families of men killed on a job posing "inherent risk." The Lewis measure "introduces a new principle into American labor legislation," wrote an economics professor at Hopkins; it recognized that "the burden of trade risk should not fall primarily on the workmen." Later overturned in the courts, the act apparently passed the assembly because the coal companies feared something worse, an unfriendly employers' liability law.[51]

Legislators also showed an interest, albeit insufficient, in saving the Chesapeake Bay oyster industry. Rapacious dredging in the 1880s had proven the Hopkins biologist William Brooks all too correct. Harvests from the supposedly "illimitable" oyster beds of the 1870s had dropped from fifteen million bushels a year to under ten million by 1890. During the hard winter of 1892–93 the take was even lower. This decline forced yet another change in vessel design, for Maryland yards abandoned the bugeye and developed the graceful skipjack. Single-masted, with sweeping triangular sails, the smaller skipjack had a shallow, V-shaped bottom and was simpler and less expensive to build. Whatever the watermen sailed, they had to claw to make a living from the dwindling supply of oysters. At Rock Point, where the Wicomico joins the Potomac, dredgers fought pitched battles with one another and marine police in the 1890s. Swepson Earle, then state conservation commissioner, said that three killings a week at Rock Point "created no civic resentment, while many weeks during the oyster season marked the departure from this life of as many as five or six men." In 1900 more Chesapeake oyster-canning plants closed than opened.[52]

Learning from such hard experience, Maryland took some of Brooks's advice. Redrafted legislation in 1900 elaborated on penalties for trying to market "unmerchantable" oysters, raised the number of measurers and inspectors, forbade packing companies from accepting oysters between 8 P.M. and 6 A.M. (when pirates worked), and encouraged the dumping of shells to catch spat and the planting of seed oysters. More vessels of the fisheries force patrolled the bay and Potomac. In 1904 Maryland and Virginia declared again their resolve to punish oyster poachers on the Potomac; the states agreed to place confiscated oysters on the river bottom and not to hamper spring seeding above Cobb's Point–Colonial Beach. A Baltimore delegate, B. Howard Haman, sponsored a bill that encouraged the leasing of oyster seed beds and established a state Board of Shellfish Commissioners to grant and govern them. Passing in 1906, the law also called for a survey of the entire Chesapeake bottom in order to identify the areas most suitable for oyster farming. Chesapeake watermen, rugged individualists to the core, saw the bay as open to anyone; they resisted the attempt to reserve private seed beds. Still, the Haman law recognized the oyster as a limited resource and marked a small step toward its scientific management. Charles C. Yates, a U.S. Coast and Geodetic Survey engineer, spent six years and took almost 160,000 soundings to produce the 1912 survey that has remained in use since.

Watermen may have been right in saying seed beds would benefit corporations over individuals. Often, however, Progressives took what they believed was the side of the people against the big companies. George Stewart

Brown, a Baltimore councilman and Reform League member who had studied economics at Hopkins under Ely, championed the cause of utility regulation in the early years of the century. Brown believed that some urban services called for "public monopolies" that would end the senseless and destructive competition of utility companies yet prevent a single firm from becoming a threat to the consumer. He proposed a commission to investigate local electricity rates. Mayor Hayes appointed one, and it found that Baltimoreans paid 15 percent more than did citizens of any other large American city. Brown agreed with the commission report that Baltimore ought to erect its own municipal generating plant and the state create a public franchise commission to negotiate with the companies more nearly as an equal. These ideas struck many people, even some Reform Leaguers, as too radical. Legislators in Annapolis granted the city authority for the plant (Baltimore built only a small one, for city parks), but utility lobbyists helped to defeat the idea of a state commission. Meantime Brown attacked the high rates of street railway companies and advocated higher taxes on utility giants.

Reformers hoped to make advances everywhere in the state, but Baltimore Progressives looked no farther than their backyards for heavy work. Their cause brought together religious caring, social awareness, and scientific finding. Many leaders in social reform, clerics like Cardinal Gibbons with a keen interest in the poor and downtrodden, tried to stir consciences. After 1895 the Reverend Vrooman easily redirected his sermons from bossism to crowded tenements or sickly children. The Connecticut-born pastor of the First Congregational Church, Edward H. Lawrence, conducted classes on "the problems of the modern city" and invited reformers like Jacob Riis to speak in his church. Lawrence preached the need not merely to carry Christian charity into action, but to place oneself into poor neighborhoods. In 1893 he and a Hopkins graduate student had established a settlement house in southwest Baltimore (similar to Jane Addams's famous Hull House in Chicago), where they made plans to offer a kindergarten, classes in handicrafts and sewing, and a boys' athletic program. After Lawrence's untimely death later that year, Bernard C. Steiner, Hopkins professor and son of the first Pratt Library director, helped to organize a Lawrence Memorial Association that continued and expanded Lawrence's work. Meanwhile the YMCA carried the "social gospel" to dark corners of the city. Old St. Paul's Episcopal Church, the Unitarians, and the Presbyterians sent missions downtown. The Daughters of Israel began tending to Russian Jewish girls in East Baltimore, extending the earlier work of Henrietta Szold—who in 1893 left Baltimore for Philadelphia to become editor of the Jewish Publication Society.

A growing number of Baltimore women took a logical step by adding social to political reform. The energy of these women—some of whom had gone so far as to call for the right to vote—spoke well of their educational experience at a time when a great many people considered a woman's only proper place the home. Some had studied at Bryn Mawr in Philadelphia or

Henrietta Szold (1860–1945), just before departing Baltimore, 1893. *Jewish Historical Society of Maryland, Inc.*

Smith in Massachusetts. Others, having their ambitions raised closer to
home, benefited from schooling at the Women's College of Frederick (under
auspices of the German Reformed church, it opened in the old Frederick
Female Seminary in 1893), Woman's College of Baltimore, or Notre Dame of
Maryland.

The School Sisters of Notre Dame had founded their institution, the first
Catholic women's college in the country, in 1873. Its brick Gothic buildings
went up in woodland, then in the county, out "Charles Street Avenue."
Though adhering to traditional views of the woman's family and social role,
the sisters followed Almira Phelps by insisting that their liberal arts curriculum stand on a par with that of men's colleges. By 1893 the college offered
courses that prepared graduates for school teaching, which even tradition-
alists could view as a branch of the home, and in 1899 awarded its first bac-
calaureate degrees. Early in the new century, warmly patronized by Cardinal
Gibbons, Notre Dame boasted that it sent a woman "into the world with the
ability to see, feel and act for herself and for others, in the fullness of distinctively feminine power that is not an imitation of masculine force."[53]

Similar ideas lay behind the founding of a Methodist college for women closer to downtown Baltimore. Chartered in 1885 and opening three years later under the Reverend John F. Goucher, Woman's College prepared its students according to Goucher's belief that one's education must work to the good of others. Thaddeus Thomas, teaching sociology and economics, took a reformer's bent to his material. Lilian Welsh, who taught physiology and hygiene and played a large part in the activism of the Arundell Club, also made the message of service clear. A student said that no one could leave her classes "without a deepened sense of personal responsibility for civic sanitation and generally improved physical conditions." Most of the 510 women who attended the college between 1892 and 1910 realized this aim. Sixty percent went into teaching, and another 14 percent into social work. Thomas, echoing Goucher, thought women had "a natural capacity for dealing with the child, the immigrant, and the pauper." But graduates may well have chosen service fields over law or business because of their attractions. Welsh emphasized the formative, shaping power of public school teachers; early social workers in Baltimore like Mary Richmond and Mary Willcox Brown provided attractive models for young women in the city.[54]

Never before had Maryland women played such an active and effective public role. Richmond served as president of the Baltimore Charity Organization Society (later Federated Charities). She began arguing the case for increased government action to improve the lot of poor people. Brown spoke of the child's right to an education and of the need to keep children out of factories and off streets. Worried that many Baltimore youngsters had no place but the streets to play in, Eliza Ridgely in 1899 started a Children's Playground Association. After hearing Jane Addams speak in 1900, Mrs. Benjamin W. Corkran formed a Baltimore chapter of the National Consumers League. The Arundell Good Government Club, by far the most conspicuous women's group, endorsed child welfare legislation. Arundell leaders in these years were Elizabeth T. King (later Mrs. William M. Ellicott) and Elisabeth Gilman (daughter of the Hopkins president); its members, besides teachers and nurses, included women who had broken into the ranks of physicians. King also took part in organizing a Maryland Federation of Women's Clubs. Based in Baltimore, the federation built a network of women whose concerns ranged from the slop of oyster-packing houses to the dangers children faced in the George's Creek coal mines. In 1902, cooperating with the new school superintendent and the Baltimore delegation to Annapolis, the Arundell Club and the Charity Organization Society obtained compulsory school attendance and juvenile court legislation for the city. Supporting Schonfarber of the industrial statistics bureau, women's groups helped that year to ensure passage of an act forbidding the labor of children younger than twelve. The new law required children between the ages of twelve and sixteen to obtain permits and meet health and literacy tests.

Interior of a packing company, Baltimore, July 1909, by Lewis W. Hine. *Photographic Collections, Albin O. Kuhn Library and Gallery, University of Maryland, Baltimore County*

Women's groups had strong allies among the people who had mastered the skills and theories of contemporary medicine. Laboratory discoveries had social implications; doctors and nurses quite naturally fostered a growing belief that public leaders had some responsibility for environments. Thomas Buckler, a University of Maryland Medical School physician and early student of cholera, had pioneered in this role, publishing in the 1870s two studies that called for improved water supply and waste treatment; in 1882 Dr. W. C. Van Bibber had read a paper before the Maryland Medical and Chirurgical Faculty on "The Drinking Waters in Maryland Considered with Reference to the Health of the Inhabitants." The research of Welch and others located the source of many diseases in microbodies and the environments that harbored them. At the Hopkins Hospital, medical students in the 1890s learned that physicians could not avoid being public figures. Osler, whose indictments of contaminated food had helped to account for the first Maryland pure milk law in 1894, dedicated himself to relieving the sorrows and griefs "of the ordinary man, of the plain, toil-worn woman." Welch gave addresses on topics like "Sanitation in Relation to the Poor" and "External Sources of Infection." He sought to train "young men and women for careers of usefulness in the relief of human suffering and in the promotion of general welfare." Later, public health leaders William Sidney Thayer, a Bostonian who joined Osler at Hopkins, and Charles Phillips Emerson, who favored free medical aid to the poor, eagerly accepted this responsibility, as did Edith Holt Bloodgood, who launched the "lighthouse" movement for the blind. Kelly, who believed that a sound moral and social order depended on healthy women, included among his students Edith Houghton Hooker, an early proponent of scientific sex education, hygiene, and birth control, and Flora Pollack, who after 1903 waged war on venereal disease.[55]

The Maryland Public Health Association mobilized people sharing the belief that science could improve life. It organized in 1897, after Governor Lowndes appointed Dr. John S. Fulton of the University of Maryland to the state Board of Health. Fulton gathered medical, social, and religious leaders to discuss the board's future course. Lowndes himself attended the meeting, convened in the hall of the Maryland Medical and Chirurgical Faculty, along with Bonaparte, Gilman, and Cardinal Gibbons. Chairing sessions at the meeting, Osler and Welch urged an attack on the conditions that harbored disease; they called, in fact, for a new discipline, preventive medicine. More than three hundred Marylanders, about a quarter of them laymen and women, joined the association, which elected Welch president and Fulton executive secretary.

The association soon began publicizing the dangers of airless sweatshops, dirty people and streets, and untreated sewage. Welch's testimony in 1897 on the probable effect of dumping diluted waste water into the bay—the spread of typhoid fever—helped to defeat that proposal. The scientific authority of physicians added weight to a cleanliness movement already under way in Baltimore. A Congregational minister in Canton, Thomas M. Beadenkopf, and Eugene Levering, banker and charity patron, had made appeals for public baths since 1894. Five years later, with Baltimore budgets remaining low, Henry Walters stepped forward to provide the city with two public showers. Located on South High Street and at Columbia Avenue and Callender Alley, these baths made a start at personal hygiene, provided relief during the hot months of the year, and even enabled the poor to do laundry. Later the city used wooden, portable sprinklers for the same purposes. The Public Health Association took up Welch's earlier demand for an infectious disease hospital in Baltimore and in 1902 obtained a Baltimore City factory-inspection program that soon began closing down sweatshops.

The association also began a drive to combat the leading public health enemy in Baltimore, tuberculosis. The "white plague" or consumption afflicted perhaps ten thousand Baltimoreans and killed about one thousand each year. At least since the autumn of 1900 Osler had attacked colleagues, politicians, and fellow citizens for their failure to act against this "serious peril," which mainly afflicted the less fortunate. In early 1902 he and Welch chaired a meeting at Hopkins to arouse public concern. Turning aside the mayor's humorous opening remarks, Osler scolded the audience for doing "not one solitary thing that a civic community should do" to help consumptives in Baltimore. Widely reported, Osler's barbs finally began to stick. That spring Governor John Walter Smith appointed a state Tuberculosis Commis-

Top, "Before Enforcement of the Sweatshop Law," January 1904. *Bottom,* "After Enforcement of the Law," December 1904. *Report of the Bureau of Industrial Statistics and Information of Maryland* (Baltimore, 1904). With this study of the same workspace, the bureau argued for strict enforcement of new industrial legislation. *MHS*

sion. In January 1904, following a commission report, the Hopkins Hospital and public health authorities staged an exhibit on the dangers and causes of tuberculosis, complete with shocking photographs of crowded tenements and sweatshops. Thousands of Baltimoreans attended. Soon afterward a Maryland Association for the Prevention and Relief of Tuberculosis organized, with statewide chapters, and by the end of the 1904 legislative term it had helped to win passage of a model state law. The act moved against people who spat in public, required the registration of tubercular patients, made it the duty of physicians and local health boards "to provide for the safety of all individuals occupying the same house or apartment," and ordered disinfection of patients' homes after their death. Other states soon adopted the "Maryland Plan." In 1906 the state appropriated money for a sanitarium north of Baltimore and another near Hagerstown. In the second decade of the century the incidence of tuberculosis in Baltimore began a decline.[56]

In the Municipal Art Society, Baltimoreans had still another progressive service organization. Created in 1899, it drew heavily from people who belonged to the Reform League. Gilman served as president. William Keyser, then league president, sat on the board of directors. Another league member, Theodore Marburg, was the wealthy son of a German emigré of 1848. Marburg had studied at Hopkins, Oxford, and the Paris Free School of Political Science; his large view and interest in political economy gave the Art Society broad scope. Acting on its artistic aims, the society commissioned a mural for city hall and placed bronze statues of Howard and Wallis at Mount Vernon Place. Going further, however, the Art Society tried to harmonize aesthetic issues and the public interest—it financed repainting of some Baltimore classrooms to prove the social benefits of bright surroundings. Ultimately it aimed to introduce principles of comprehensive city planning in Baltimore. Returning from a trip to Europe, J. B. Noel Wyatt, a society director, warned that Baltimore too long had rested on its old-time reputation for such "superficial and transient" virtues as "hospitality, sociability, low rents and cheap food markets."[57]

Early in the new century the Art Society hired the firm of Frederick Law Olmsted, Jr.—son of the writer and landscape architect—to undertake a large-scale study of the city and its surroundings. Baltimoreans took pardonable pride in their existing parks, but private development of land the city annexed in 1888 (and beyond) opened the door to willy-nilly growth. Olmsted already had a Baltimore connection; his father helped plan Sudbrook Park, a community out the Western Maryland Railroad near Pikesville. Both Olmsteds' approach to landscaping—conforming to the topography, the natural beauty of the land, instead of imposing a grid upon it—had influenced plans for subdividing the area owned by the Roland Park Company. For many years the younger Olmsted worked with Edward Bouton in Baltimore in laying out the winding streets, lovely gardens, and country club of that prestigious neighborhood. For the Art Society Olmsted applied his "romantic" conception of land use to a metropolitan area. He advised Baltimoreans to build thirty-six new parks—four- or five-acre spaces that not merely beautified the city but also provided room for workers to breathe and for children to play in (Steiner's successor at the Lawrence Association, Robert Garrett, had been a runner at the 1896 olympic games and took much interest in outdoor recreation). Olmsted recommended "outlying reservations," fringing the city with grass and woods. In southwest Baltimore, where the Middle Branch drained into the Patapsco, he advised leaving land open for another park. Widened commercial highways and scenic carriage ways, uniting beauty and utility, would radiate from the center of Baltimore. While discussing Olmsted's plan, the Art Society joined the Public Health Association in agitating for the long-discussed comprehensive sewage-disposal system.

Talk of comprehensive planning was in the air when in early February 1904 a fire started in a downtown Baltimore dry goods store. In heavy winds blowing eastward, the blaze quickly spread to adjoining structures, then to whole blocks. More than a thousand firemen fought it without success. They for many years had warned that their equipment was old, their force too small for a major emergency. No regulations governed electrical wiring, construction of tall buildings, or storage of materials like hay and kerosene. Fire departments arriving from Washington and Philadelphia found that their hoses did not match Baltimore hydrants. Desperate authorities dynamited buildings in the path of the fire in a futile attempt to contain it. It burned out of control on 7 February and through the next night, when students at Notre Dame could see flames licking the sky. As far away as Washington the fire produced an eerie light on the horizon. Supposedly fireproof buildings burned like the rest; Henry L. Mencken, a young reporter for the *Evening Herald*, recalled watching a six-story office building go up "as if it had been made of matchwood and drenched with gasoline." Finally the wind shifted southward, saving East Baltimore, and drove the fire into the harbor. The city suffered periodic floods of the Jones Falls, and there had been a large fire in 1886. Nothing compared to the 1904 catastrophe. Seventy blocks, more than fifteen hundred buildings, and twenty-five hundred businesses went up in flames. The B&O lost its main offices. Twenty banks and eight hotels disappeared. Miraculously, no one died in the fire and few people went homeless. But for many days afterward the heart of the city, reduced to heaps of bricks and ashes, lay smoldering in ruin.[58]

"To suppose that the spirit of our people will not rise to the occasion is to suppose that our people are not genuine Americans," declared the *News* even before the fire died out; "We shall make the fire of 1904 a landmark not of decline but of progress." Later Baltimoreans often made that connection, believing the fire a cause of Progressive change. Actually for a time its excitement and ruin diverted interest from problems like tuberculosis, and rebuilding efforts, consuming most of the four million dollars the city recently

From atop the Shot Tower after the February 1904 fire, one could view seventy blocks of devastation—from the Jones Falls to City Hall. *MHS*

had acquired by selling its Western Maryland Railroad stock, postponed the sewer system on which Mayor McLane had planned to spend the money. Still, the fire swept some of the slate clean for urban Progressives. McLane appointed a committee of sixty-three civic and business leaders to recommend reconstruction plans. Reformers like Keyser (chairman), Marburg, and Grasty served on the committee, which consulted with Olmsted and made a number of forward-looking proposals, including widened streets and municipal ownership of the Pratt Street docks. Property owners on Baltimore Street resisted, and private interests opposed city control over wharf use and design. Reformers in December proposed a kind of town meeting on the subject of Baltimore's future. E. Clay Timanus, mayor after McLane's suicide in June, William Cabell Bruce, then city solicitor, and George Gaither, then city council second-branch president, led support for the meeting, billed as a General Public Improvements Conference.[59]

The conference was a remarkable example of civic cooperation. Baltimoreans shed party affiliation to hold it. Besides architects, lawyers, social workers, and professors, the meeting brought together shippers, financiers, and businessmen representing coal, lumber, and tobacco; laboring men and women had their delegates, as did the German-American Independent Citizens Union and neighborhood improvement associations. Under the general leadership of E. Stanley Gary, a textile manufacturer whose father had been McKinley's postmaster general, the meeting of more than two hundred persons divided into subcommittees to examine urban issues. Conferees suggested three bond issues for the 1905 spring ballot: $10 million for sewerage, $1 million for parks, and $2 million to survey and extend city services to the area annexed in 1888. Support for the referenda came from all quarters. A corporation lawyer, Francis King Carey, told an audience that "a city will be great or small in direct ratio to the greatness or smallness . . . of its people"; a Democratic ward leader in East Baltimore, Frank Furst, said "Baltimoreans generally have awakened to the need of doing things to help the city along."[60] The three proposed bond issues passed every ward. Recognizing the cohesive power of the subcommittees, Mayor Timanus occasionally recalled them for service. Over the next six years voters passed eleven of twelve bond issues, permitting improvements in schools, fire fighting, streets, and water supply. Meantime the Burnt District Commission, successor to the Keyser Committee, widened and smooth-paved many downtown streets, made harbor improvements, put in sewer connections, and placed a height restriction on office buildings.

⁓⧓⤨

A peculiar place, Maryland neither progressed as quickly as Massachusetts, Wisconsin, or Kansas in social-reform legislation in this period nor set upon blacks with the finality of states in the ex-Confederate South. To the north and west, labor unions, heavy concentrations of urban dwellers, or farmers opposed to the unfairness of corporate giants like railroads all combined to produce a political awakening. Below Maryland, whites feared the dominance of black voters, whose recent dalliance with Populism had led to a conservative backlash. Some southern states tried "grandfather" clauses and poll taxes to keep blacks out of politics; the Virginia constitution of 1902 restricted voting to persons who could understand portions of the charter when an official read it to them.

Maryland blacks, by making progress of their own, had labored to avoid such attacks. Schools remained a primary concern to black leaders in the years following passage of the Fifteenth Amendment. The Maryland Progressive State Colored Teachers Association organized in 1886 and aimed to bring about change on the local level. Under the editorship of a young Baltimore teacher and lawyer, W. Ashbie Hawkins, the association in 1891 published its own activist journal, the *Educational Era*. The Mutual Brotherhood of Liberty pleaded with some success for more black schools in the city. Between 1867 and 1900 their number rose from ten to twenty-seven, and black enrollment from about nine hundred to more than ninety-three hundred pupils. In 1901 Baltimore school officials combined the two-year Colored High School, opened in 1882, with the black manual training school that dated from 1893. About a hundred boys and girls attended. Along with schools and integrated street cars, there were other signs of social dignity. In 1892 John H. Murphy, Sr., took over a struggling black news sheet and formed it into the Baltimore *Afro-American,* first edited by the Reverend W. M. Alexander. Two years later William T. Carr, J. Marcus Cargill, and William H. Thompson, black physicians, founded Provident Hospital to meet the considerable needs of the Baltimore Negro community. Remarking on its comparative well-being in 1891, P. B. S. Pinchback, once a Louisiana lieutenant governor, exclaimed, "I am at last in a free country."[61]

Nevertheless, there was room for improvement. Conditions in black class rooms were always worse than in white ones. The Biddle Street school, near Pennsylvania Avenue, had a yard the city used for drying manure and privies so primitive that children's feet carried foul smells into the dilapidated building. The *Afro-American* carried articles exposing these scandals. Another complaint concerned the small number of black teachers in the separate "colored" school system; of 210 instructors employed, a mere 35 were black. Officials thus slighted two local sources—the Baltimore Normal School for Colored Teachers, with origins in the old Baltimore Association, and the Methodist ministerial institute, which after 1890 called itself Morgan College. One of the victorious Republican candidates for the city council in 1895, Dr. Cargill, who had prepared for medicine at Howard University, introduced and saw passed an ordinance requiring the gradual replacement of white teachers in black schools with Negroes who had passed the qualifying examination.

Outside Baltimore, black education varied from meager to disappointing. A law the assembly passed at Governor Oden Bowie's urging in 1872 obligated Maryland counties to maintain separate but supposedly equal white and black schools. Depending on revenues, the state in the late nineteenth century provided about $400,000 for white schools ($1.69 per pupil) and about a quarter of that amount ($1.46 per child) for Negroes. County commissioners spent the state money and little more on black pupils. In 1895 seven counties—Anne Arundel, Prince George's, Charles, St. Mary's, Queen Anne's, Somerset, and Worcester—made no contributions to Negro schools from county funds. Black school buildings often were the ones whites declared unfit for their own children. Teachers in black schools received lower pay than their counterparts in the white system. Black students in Frederick County attended classes until early April, whites through the end of May. No Maryland county had a black high school, and Negro higher education received scant encouragement. Trustees of the agricultural college denied blacks admission. Its companion, Princess Anne Academy on the lower Eastern Shore, was a Morgan College outpost that Somerset County whites refused to welcome in their midst. A federal land-grant school after 1890, the academy aspired to collegiate status, but state authorities cited the small proportion of blacks in Maryland (18 percent) as reason to limit its funding.

Maryland's official stinginess cost many black young people by scaling down their dreams. At the elementary school level it produced black illiteracy figures which, if lower than in states to the south, were far higher than for Maryland whites. In 1890 more than one-third of black Baltimoreans over the age of ten were illiterate. A state survey in 1900 disclosed that 47 percent (26,616) of all registered blacks could not read or write, as compared to 8 percent (18,307) of white voters.[62]

Though Maryland blacks had begun to realize their political strength, in few localities did their numbers allow them a full share of power. In Southern Maryland total black to white population stood at a ratio of 6 to 5. In Baltimore City, whose black population was 15 percent, political activity had risen in the 1890s—blacks running as independent candidates and holding street parades that impressed black visitors. Negro voters did at times cross party lines and split their ticket. Usually, however, they voted Republican, and in one or two wards they had the votes to elect their own councilmen. In 1890, before Cargill's election, Harry Sythe Cummings won election from the 11th ward. A graduate of Lincoln University in Pennsylvania, he had gained admission to the Maryland Law School before authorities closed it to Negroes. Even earlier, in 1873, Annapolis blacks had chosen one of their own, a Republican, as alderman in the third ward.

Black illiteracy, but particularly black Republicanism in the setting of two-party rivalry, decided regular Democrats in favor of eliminating or severely restricting the black vote. Not content with the 1901 revised election law, Gorman and his friends in the fall of 1903 conducted the state election campaign largely on the race issue. "The political destinies of Maryland," declared the Democratic platform, "should be shaped and controlled by the white people of the State." Democrats described the black vote as "ignorant, corrupt, the blind instrument of unscrupulous and selfish leaders"; it posed "a perpetual menace to the prosperity and peace of Maryland." After the decisive Democratic victory, Gorman asked Poe, then dean of the university law school, to draw up a constitutional amendment that would disfranchise the Negro without violating federal law and Supreme Court decrees. The resulting Poe amendment contained a "grandfather" clause that granted the vote to everyone (meaning white males) who had been qualified before the Fifteenth Amendment went into effect and to their male descendants of legal age. According to a clause borrowed from Virginia, other male applicants had to read (or have read to them) a passage from the Maryland constitution and convince the registrar that they possessed a "reasonable" understanding of its meaning. The Democratic-controlled legislature, scheduling disfranchisement before the divisive issue of oyster seed beds, passed the amendment with little debate in the spring of 1904. Because Governor Warfield opposed it and threatened not to sign it, delegates and senators submitted it directly to the people. Voters had until November 1905 to consider the Poe amendment's merits and demerits.[63]

"In the Workshop." Baltimore *American*, 9 October 1905. Keith Culver ridiculed John Prentiss Poe and Arthur Pue Gorman for trying to frighten white voters with the specter of "Negro domination." *MHS*

Meanwhile the General Assembly imposed further regulation on black voters. It passed a bill, proposed by William R. Wilson of Queen Anne's County, eliminating every reference to party on the ballot and making it illegal for parties to post any campaign literature that identified candidates except by written word. Placing illiterate citizens in the dark, the Wilson device applied only to counties of large black population or traditional Republican strength—Garrett, Frederick, Anne Arundel, Prince George's, Charles, Calvert, and St. Mary's on the Western Shore; Kent, Talbot, Somerset, and Worcester on the Eastern Shore. Democratic supporters of the Poe amendment and Wilson law argued that, by eliminating fraud and corruption at the polls, those measures answered a Progressive prayer. Without further prompting, Snow Hill, Crisfield, and Frederick at the 1904 session obtained charter amendments that restricted black voting in municipal elections. Gorman, who in the past had acknowledged his support from "intelligent men of color," denied any ill feeling toward blacks themselves. Yet the same legislature wrote the most ambitious "Jim Crow" statutes Maryland ever placed on its books at one session. Effective 1 July 1904, railroads and steamship lines in the state (except those that passed through without stopping) had to provide "Whites Only" and "Colored" seating, dining, and sleeping arrangements and see to it that the races kept separate.[64]

Marylanders responded to these measures in their customary, atypical manner. Blacks were far more articulate and better organized than elsewhere. They had lobbied against the segregation bills when they first surfaced in 1902. Returned from visiting the Deep South, the editor of the Baltimore *Afro-American Ledger* (successor to Alexander's paper) warned his readers where segregation led—to "humiliating" and "deplorable" inequities. Black churches and clubs in Baltimore threatened never again to go on steamship and railroad excursions if Jim Crow passed. When the bill became law William G. Kerbin, the Worcester County delegate who sponsored it, returned home to a personal boycott; no black would work for him. Having campaigned for more black teachers in black schools, the educated Negro community in Baltimore might have muted its criticism of segregation, but it was among the most chagrined by that new practice. Councilman Cummings found himself directed to a black gallery at a Republican party function; concerts at the Peabody Conservatory suddenly involved segregated seating. Though unable to change the Kerbin law, Maryland blacks could at least combat the Poe amendment. They organized a Negro Suffrage League, with chapters throughout the state, to arouse black ministers, businessmen, professional leaders, and members of black fraternal lodges against disfranchisement.[65]

The race control issue exposed the old fracture in Maryland between whites who lived amidst blacks and those who did not. Manners and mores in Southern Maryland and on the Eastern Shore kept the races sharply separate. As in the old days, whites there took a paternal, sometimes patronizing, view of the Negro. They treated politely, even kindly, the black who "kept his place." They could be quickly harsh with one who did not; Princess Anne natives, for example, ostracized John Wilson, a Wilmington Methodist churchman, because on his visits to the Negro academy he shook hands with blacks, ate with them, and called black men mister. Between 1889 and 1918 the 17 lynchings that took place in Maryland numbered no more than in Nebraska (there were 78 in Virginia, 368 in Georgia). But in 15 instances blacks were victims, often for an alleged assault on a white woman, and in 12 they took place on the Shore or in the counties of Southern Maryland. North and west of Baltimore, whites in the early twentieth century just as often clung to the customs of their antebellum forebears; not closely tied to black labor or surrounded by black neighborhoods, they took little enthusiasm to issues that concerned race. White Baltimoreans reflected both habits of mind. They were proud of Joe Gans, the native son who won the lightweight boxing title in 1902 and four years later fought a celebrated forty-two-round match with Battling Nelson at Goldfield, Nevada. At home the beatings he administered white opponents caused racial free-for-alls in Baltimore streets.

This social split in the state led to callous and colorful vote trading in Annapolis. In 1904 the Poe amendment and a first version of the Haman oyster-seeding bill had brought about a deal whereby Eastern Shore legislators would support the oyster measure if the Western Shore backed disfranchisement (the trade worked, except that Warfield, believing the early Haman bill amended so as to be worthless, vetoed it). Taken as a whole, Maryland approached segregation with misgivings that the Court of Appeals expressed in 1905 while overturning the conviction of a Howard University professor. On entering Cecil County, he had refused to take a segregated seat in a railroad car. Maryland judges, speaking for the first state to interpret its own accommodation law narrowly, placed limits on the Kerbin Act in accordance with federal interstate-commerce doctrine: the law could only govern journeys that began and ended in Maryland.

Maryland whites reacted to the Poe amendment with all the diversity one might expect in the state. Lawyers attacked it as vague and of doubtful constitutionality. Bonaparte, recently named Theodore Roosevelt's secretary of the navy, led Maryland Republicans in claiming rightly that their opponents expected the amendment and Wilson election law to undercut them. Regular Democrats in Southern Maryland lent weight to that case and completed the confusion of semiliterate voters by running a John E. Mudd against Sydney Mudd in the 1905 congressional election and putting candidates of a "Repudiation party" on the ballot. Reform Democrats, noting the power the Poe amendment gave registrars, denounced it as a trick to restore the old machine to power. They organized a Democratic Anti–Poe Amendment Committee. "For my part," said Leigh Bonsal, its spokesman, "I fear much more the old Democratic ring" than "the bugaboo of Negro domination." Immigrant groups in Baltimore noted that the Poe amendment's grandfather clause and "understanding" provision cut against them as well as blacks (illiteracy among naturalized citizens ran about 7 percent). To oppose disfranchisement they formed a Maryland League of Foreign-Born Citizens, which included Germans, Poles, Bohemians, Croats, Lithuanians, Italians, Hungarians, Syrians, and Armenians. A smart ward leader in East Baltimore came out against the amendment because it likely would disfranchise the Russian Jews who followed his lead. Cardinal Gibbons, along with other churchmen voicing the tolerant theme in Maryland history, reminded Marylanders that "peace and harmony can never exist where there is discrimination." Voters defeated the Poe amendment resoundingly, 104,286 to 70,227. It lost in Baltimore by a two to one margin, and lost in eighteen of the twenty-three counties.[66]

Disfranchisement did not go away peacefully. In 1908 Isaac Straus, state attorney general under Warfield's successor, Austin Lane Crothers, submitted another amendment. Straus and the lawyers who helped him draft the proposal carefully avoided any threat to foreign-born whites and established education tests (requiring an applicant to write the full names of a series of public officals) that apparently left no room for official discretion. The next year Maryland voters rejected the complicated Straus plan less decisively, but firmly, 106,069 to 89,808. Seemingly trapped by their own rhetoric, Democratic leaders refused to give disfranchisement a decent burial. Crothers said that some test for black voting would help make the Negro "frugal and industrious and eager for an education." In 1910 two Charles County Democrats, William J. Frere and Walter M. Digges, wrote yet another amendment, this time avoiding the subtleties of the Poe and Straus proposals. Digges simply would have enfranchised all white men and required other males to have owned $500 worth of property for at least two years before registering to vote. Agreeing to submit this highly vulnerable plan to voters in 1911, the assembly also enacted a measure that allowed only whites to vote in the election. Opinion all over the country, even from the Deep South, derided the election law, which Crothers vetoed. The Digges subterfuge, patently ignoring the Fifteenth Amendment, lost by about 84,000 to 46,000.[67]

It testified to the ambiguity of progress in Maryland that the Crothers administration both emitted the Digges amendment and left behind a series of important reform acts. A Cecil County native and graduate of the Maryland Law School, Crothers as a reformer profited from circumstance. He had lost his senate seat when voters defeated the Poe amendment, then through Warfield obtained an unexpired term on the state circuit court. Crothers announced he would not seek election to the post and sat out the Edwin Warfield–John Walter Smith squabbling that followed the deaths of Gorman and Rasin in 1906–7. Crothers won the gubernatorial nomination in 1907 as a compromise candidate and took office with bipartisan support and debts to no reigning bosses.

He began by trying to redeem two party-platform planks that likely could have appeared only after the passing of Gorman and Rasin—a corrupt practices act and a state primary elections law. The governor challenged legislators in his January 1908 message to eliminate electoral bribery. "Let us cut this evil practice up by the very roots and cast it out wholly and forever from our Commonwealth," he said, in a new text for Maryland governors, "so that our elections shall be unblemished and pure."[68] Straus dusted off his earlier campaign finances bill (requiring publication of expenses and sources of income, placing limits on expenditures, prohibiting corporate contributions), and it passed before the end of March. The primary elections bill ran into regular Democratic opposition led by Gorman's son, Arthur Pue Gorman, Jr. Crothers agreed for the time being to settle for a bill modeled after one a Montgomery County reform Democrat (and nephew of Montgomery Blair), Blair Lee, had written earlier for local application. Crothers appointed bipartisan commissions to report on issues like state taxes, legislative representation for Baltimore City, public health, pure food, and education. At the August 1909 party convention Crothers, Straus, Warfield, and J. Frederick C. Talbott of Baltimore held sway. Doubtless using their sympathy for disfranchisement to collect votes from reluctant Democrats, they obtained party support for an impressive list of reform legislation.

Before the assembly reconvened, Crothers stumped the state, seeking popular support for stronger election and social-interest laws. On the hustings, and then in his 1910 message to the assembly, he demonstrated a Progressive's keen eye for waste and inefficiency by outlining the need for serious reform in Annapolis. Legislators hired too many hall "cleaners" and had too many cronies on their staffs, said Crothers, following up remarks Warfield had made in his last message to the General Assembly. Members of the assembly had hired more than 120 "extra engrossing clerks;" only California rivaled Maryland's 360 legislative employees. The state needed to eliminate the system by which many Maryland officials (like their colonial predecessors) collected their salaries from fees for services and paid only the excess, if any, into the treasury. Crothers called for a central state purchasing agency to standardize, cheapen, and clean up that process.

Once more declaring himself uninterested in future office, Crothers made the 1910 session a fitting memorial to his public life. The time had arrived for public utilities control. Consolidated Gas in 1906 had taken over electrical production in Baltimore, and recent grand jury hearings in the city had aired the complaints consumers soon had about the monopoly's high rates. Attorney General Straus, following the examples of Wisconsin and New York, drew up a bill establishing a state Public Service Commission with powers to investigate company conduct, subpoena records, and set rates in Maryland for railroads, steamships, gas, electric, telephone, and telegraph companies. Utilities critic George Brown thought the measure, which said nothing of banking and insurance, too weak, but utilities clamored in opposition. When Republicans, the Reform League, and regular Democrats introduced competing bills, Crothers called in party leaders to apply the whip. After reading them the 1909 platform, he threatened to veto all local bills if Democrats divided on the utilities issue. The Straus bill became law. Crothers signed two bills that had their origins in his 1908 commissions—one law raised pure food standards and strengthened the public health board as an enforcement agency; the other, complementing the federal Mann Act, gave police new powers to suppress prostitution. Maryland in 1910 reenacted a workmen's compensation law, which this time was voluntary and applied only to miners, and also made its first appropriation to care for the insane.

Middle-class voters continued to voice their concerns for education, cleanliness, and order, and in the next few years they enjoyed considerable success. Baltimoreans, repeating the feat of 1906, gathered in March 1911 for a three-day conference to examine their city and plan for the future. Dr. J. Hall Pleasants, a native of the city who taught at the Hopkins Medical School and served as a charity official, called on delegates to wipe out "the conditions giving rise to dependency." James Harry Preston, the Democrat who that year succeeded Barry Mahool as mayor, oversaw completion of the Baltimore sewer system and of a water filtration plant at Lake Montebello. Preston won charter amendments that brought about city civil service reforms and a unicameral city council. During the summer of 1912, at a convention held at the Fifth Regiment Armory, Democrats nominated as their presidential candidate Woodrow Wilson—who had lectured at Hopkins on reforming government. While Wilson that fall won election to the White House, Marylanders elected a General Assembly that adopted party presidential primaries, made the child labor law statewide in its application, enacted a ten-hour law for women workers, and strengthened the Haman oyster law. In 1914 legislators ordered a thorough study of statewide education, created advisory boards of parole and prison administration, established a nonpartisan tax-reform commission, and passed a compulsory workmen's compensation act. The *Sun* praised the assembly for its industry. Governor Phillips Lee Goldsborough, a Cambridge Republican, bravely appointed a commission to study reforms of the sort Crothers, who had died soon after leaving office, had recommended. The panel consisted of civic leaders of the Reform League stripe; Frank J. Goodnow, then president of Hopkins, served as its chairman.[69]

"We want to put Maryland in the front rank of the march of progress," Crothers had told a crowd while trying to explain the dream of Maryland reformers. "Standpattism in both parties is dead, we hope never to be resurrected." Challenging boss rule, expressing confidence in science, and calling for efficiency, Progressivism registered a change in ideas about government's role in American society. Yet the Maryland experience showed that the balance between public and private interest could be difficult to locate. Watermen believed that leased oyster beds violated their personal liberty. Businessmen could not agree whether widening streets after the great fire infringed on their property rights. Corporate leaders fought utilities regulation. Crothers demonstrated how Maryland Progressives strained to blend modern goals and traditional ways. "We want to be baptized not with a new Democracy, but with the old Democracy of Thomas Jefferson," he said.[70]

Mixing Jefferson and Johns Hopkins, Baltimoreans in 1911 adopted an ordinance legalizing racial segregation in housing and the next year mandated the pasteurization of milk.

CHAPTER 9

Searching for the Middle in Modern America

In the spring 1922 issue of the *Nation*, as part of a series that journal contributed to the "new literature of national self-awareness," H. L. Mencken published an essay entitled "Maryland: Apex of Normalcy." Parts of it might have drawn on Father Andrew White's impressions of 1634. The state "is bathed in a singular and various beauty," Mencken declared, "from the stately estuaries of the Chesapeake to the peaks of the Blue Ridge." Providence had spared Maryland the harsh weather, decay, "appalling bugaboos," and intractable social problems of other states. Statistically it seemed "to gravitate toward a safe middle place"—in population, value of manufactures, its percentage of native-born whites, ratio of Catholics among Christians, first and last annual frosts. In all such figures the state had "a median quality." Rural Marylanders only barely outnumbered Baltimore City residents, so the country paid the city heed but never submitted slavishly to it; nationally Maryland sometimes joined southern Democrats, other times northern Republicans, the result being a "curious moderation" in politics. In a sense it represented "the ideal toward which the rest of the Republic is striving." Still, looking at large trends that did not spare his home city and state, Mencken said that something was wrong. "Men are ironed out," as he put it. "Ideas are suspect. No one appears to be happy. Life is dull."[1]

Like steam power, canned food, and electricity, the horseless carriage relentlessly transformed the lives of all Marylanders. The "automobile," as the French Academy decided to call it, emerged in late-nineteenth-century Europe when different discoveries suddenly came together. Gottlieb Daimler made an internal-combustion engine that used liquid fuel, and in 1885 Karl Benz mounted it on a bicycle-like vehicle with a chain-drive system. French engineers experimented with improved transmission and chassis designs.

An Irishman, John Dunlop, developed a successful air-filled tire (originally for bicycles) in 1888. European races, with autos averaging speeds of fifteen miles per hour, soon advertised the motorcar's promise on the sports pages of American newspapers. Tinkerers by the hundreds began building their own versions. Sinclair-Scott, a Baltimore sheet-metal firm with contracts for body parts with Peerless, began making the Maryland in 1904, using all local craftsmen. One of the first machines to employ overhead valves, the Maryland made a favorable impression on Henry Ford. The Crawford Automobile Company of Baltimore made a sporty "gentleman's roadster." Between 1907 and 1913 Carl Spoerer's machine shop on South Carey Street in Baltimore dallied in the automobile business. The Burns brothers in Havre de Grace turned out models in 1908 and 1909, when a Hyattsville company built a strange vehicle that employed two four-cylinder engines, singly or together. Motorcars in Maryland rose in numbers as sharply as elsewhere—from about ten at the turn of the century to ten thousand in 1914.

The automobile posed problems that created an entirely new world of state regulation. The first automobilists, as they called themselves, were about as welcomed as barn burners. "Every horse on the highways felt called upon to be more or less fractious at the sight of a motor," recalled a Baltimore enthusiast in 1914, "and frequently the drivers were worse than the horses." At least one Maryland farmer refused a traveler a drink of water when he learned he was a motorist. In Baltimore police tried to keep autos out of Druid Hill Park and its tempting pathways. A state registration law of 1904, charging owners a dollar for a number they had to affix somewhere on their machine, imposed speed limits of six miles an hour in towns and twelve in the country. Even on rural roads the law required motorists to slow to six miles per hour when overtaking anyone riding, driving, or leading a horse. Members of the Automobile Club of Maryland, formed with a dozen operators in 1901, lobbied for higher speeds—in the low limits they saw a furtive plan to kill the automobile's popularity. In 1906 the assembly granted an exemption to Baltimore City, where, except for cases of recklessness, police riding bicycles seldom tried to enforce the speed limit anyway. The 1906 law also pleased the auto club because it prohibited the throwing of stones or other missiles at motorcars "without authority of the person in charge thereof." The club successfully argued against a measure that would have kept motor vehicles off roads in Dorchester County on Tuesdays and Saturdays, allowing only horsemen to attend court and market.[2]

Rural hostility to the motor vehicle gradually ebbed. In about 1911 the Lord Baltimore Motor Company began turning out trucks that made far more sense to farmers than the noisy playthings well-dressed city folk enjoyed. Ford's cheap and convenient Model T invited rural people themselves to look into the value of dependable motor carriages. The auto club, like Maryland cyclists, also proved itself a firm ally in the better-roads movement. Farmers long had petitioned the General Assembly to improve "farm to market" routes. After 1899 the drive gained momentum. That year the new state Geological and Economic Survey (consisting of the governor, comptroller, and the presidents of Hopkins and the agricultural college, all unpaid), published the first scientific study of Maryland roads and bridges. The report, the work of state geologist William B. Clark and his staff, drew upon complete data, on-site inspections, and questionnaires sent to county road commissioners, farmers, highway officials of other states, and turnpike companies.

The Clark report outlined the considerable task the state faced in repairing and upgrading its road system. The Maryland portion of the sturdy old National Road, which in 1878 the state had turned over to Allegany and Garrett counties, needed extensive work. The stone bridge over the Casselman River in Garrett County, though still sound, had lost its parapets to "neglect and wanton injury." About five hundred of the two thousand miles the report classified as main roads still belonged to turnpike companies. In several locations—to the west of Hagerstown, between Rockville and the District, and north of Reisterstown—the roads of defunct firms had fallen to the counties and remained passable. Generally Maryland highway problems mirrored the state's varied topography. While the National Road had no grades steeper than 8 percent, Clark found county roads in Western Maryland as sharp as 22 percent and therefore of limited economic use. Baltimore, Frederick, Harford, and Washington counties each had more than a hundred miles of stone-based roadway; Carroll, Howard, and Montgomery had about fifty miles of highway paved with hard surface. The rest of the state, less blessed with natural road-building materials like granite and limestone, largely relied on dirt or gravel roads. In Southern Maryland many thoroughfares in the clayish soil had sunk below ground level and some ditches had washed down to five and six feet. On the Eastern Shore the usual county road suffered from either too much clay (on the west banks of rivers) or too much sand (on the eastern side). Crushed oyster shell provided the only improved surface on the Shore, and in dry weather the shells produced a dust whose "color and adhesion" made it "a great inconvenience to householders and a positive injury to storekeepers along the roads." In any event, science had shown the wisdom of using shells not on roads but in oyster seed beds.[3]

In succeeding years the assembly tried, and then gave up, an approach to highways that left counties largely free to manage their own programs. Through 1906 the Geological Survey received four hundred thousand dollars to pay half the counties' roadbuilding costs while also setting work specifications. In Baltimore County one "survey road," a two-mile extension of Park Heights Avenue from Old Court Road to the Garrison Road, consisted of limestone and crushed gravel six inches deep. Automobilists considered it "a favorite stretch for smooth running." In 1906 work began on a "boulevard" connecting Baltimore and Washington. These piecemeal improvements—two miles in Washington County, a half-mile in Frederick—failed to satisfy either automobile owners or the real estate developers who soon grasped the effect of improved roads on property values. Some county commissioners had failed to apply for the state aid, apparently believing that Annapolis would eventually shoulder the entire burden. Others resented the specifications Clark and his highway engineer, W. W. Crosby, insisted upon; local contractors could lose money meeting the new state standards. Meantime Austin Lane Crothers made it clear that his Progressivism included strong support for better roads. Heeding that call during his first year as governor, legislators in 1908 passed a good roads bill that created a state Road Commission and floated five million dollars in bonds for a seven-year program of road improvements. The compromise measure granted Baltimore City, whose citizens held about four of every seven dollars' worth of taxable property in the state, one-fifth of the bond money to improve arterial roads. The commissioners, two of whom were to be experts from the Geological Survey, received salaries as full-time public servants. They had the power to condemn private property, including turnpikes. Maryland became the first state to provide for a system of highways built and maintained on the state's authority.[4]

There was no mistaking the sudden rise of the motorcar; its numerical increase and "development for all sorts of purposes," read an early road commission report, seemed to be "inevitable and probably fortunate."[5] Baltimore dealers, repair shops, tire merchants, and gasoline jobbers grappled for space in the pages of the *Sun*, which also carried grisly reports of automobiles hitting old women as they stepped into the street. "Auto Jacks" stole vehicles for joy rides. Each January after 1906 salesmen took over the new Fifth Regiment Armory for an Automobile Show that gave consumers an idea of what was new on the market. As auto, truck, and motorcycle owners climbed in numbers, policing them became big business as well. In 1910 the assembly established a commissioner of motor vehicles whose office registered drivers, outfitted officers to patrol the roads, and issued license plates after collecting a fee. Originally paid only once, it now stood at $20 to $25 annually, depending on automobile weight. The law exempted residents of other states from the license fee, but not operators in the District of Columbia—whose government, along with that of Delaware, for many years expected Marylanders to obtain local licenses to drive there. Speed limits on open roads went up to 25 miles per hour. For the first time, operators daring enough to challenge that restriction faced possible suspension or revocation of license. In 1913 licensing fees brought the state about one hundred thousand dollars, and the value of Maryland-owned automobiles raised the same sum in personal property taxes. The legislature, besides authorizing more bond issues, applied all these sources of revenue to road improvement and maintenance.

With such funding the road commission became an important employer in Maryland and a growing presence. Its arm reached into every county. It straightened and regraded highways, built culverts, dug ditches, replaced wooden with fabricated iron bridges, and posted signs that identified roads and gave motorists directions. Abundant money and activity brought advances in highway technology. Steam-powered equipment included mixers, shovels, and rollers of ponderous size. After 1912 the standard surface on principal highways shifted from stone and asphalt to concrete. At first, to complete the thirteen-hundred-mile system planned in 1908, the commission simply paved narrow roads; in 1914 it began a program of widening highways to fourteen and a half feet. Maryland later pioneered in a cost-saving technique by which workers added firm concrete shoulders to existing highway, then filled and crowned the old roadbed with new concrete. Eight district engineers supervised this immense undertaking, a "floating gang" with heavy equipment performing major work within each district and "patrolmen" constantly doing light labor and making weekly inspections on three- to five-mile stretches of road. The commission completed the Baltimore-Washington Boulevard and in 1910 began work on a similar route between Baltimore and Annapolis. By 1915 the state had purchased all but one of the private toll roads in Maryland (the last, a turnpike from Frederick to Woodsboro, became a state road in 1921). In 1915, at nearly double the expected cost, the commission also completed the original state system. Though seldom linking up with roads from other states, it connected all the county seats with hard-surface highway. Besides criss-crossing central Maryland, it stretched south of the National Road to Oakland in Garrett County, down the peninsulas of Southern Maryland to Solomons Island, Lookout Point, and Rock Point, up and down the Eastern Shore, and eastward to Worcester County.

The speed of these changes, and the new weight of state regulation, left different impressions among different Marylanders. Unless involved in steamboating, railroading, the hotel business, or the C&O Canal, most rural Marylanders could spend weeks and months without seeing an outsider. Boats and railroads kept travelers to their course; autos now brought them easily to main streets and back roads. Little wonder that farmers resented the intrusions of spiffy Baltimoreans whose sightseeing tours frightened livestock and knocked into fences. The auto helped to sharpen the longstanding political distinction between Baltimore and the rest of the state—a difference Baltimore newspaper cartoonists played upon when representing the city as a dapper fellow in tie, jacket, and bowler and "rural Maryland" as a troublesome coot with flat hat, overalls, and goatee. But modern developments could also divide rural communities internally. Motor vehicles and hard-surface highways promoted roadside businesses in rural areas, billboard advertising along highways, and the conversion of some family dwellings to tourist homes. Some people leapt at new ways to turn a dollar. Not everyone wished to see old ways of living disturbed.

On the Eastern Shore this division surfaced in battles over liquor. Much

Road crew, Carroll County, c. 1915. From Charles T. LeViness, *A History of Road Building in Maryland* (Baltimore, 1958).

"The Guardian and His Ward." Baltimore *Sun,* 22 March 1908. "Now look here; don't you think it's about time to dissolve this trusteeship?" asked the Baltimore gentleman of the counties. "Wa'al no," came the reply. "I like bein' guardeen so much I ain't agoin' to give it up till I have to." *Baltimore Sunpapers*

more safely than the automobile, which could be a convenience, liquor came to symbolize the worldliness that threatened to change traditional values. The former fleshpots of Crisfield, the notoriety of the Baltimore waterfront, newspaper accounts of drunken brawls and stories of homes broken by sodden watermen, all witnessed the evils of drink. Methodist ministers, who preached to so many Shoremen, always had stressed the dangers of wanton pleasure. By early 1908 all but one Eastern Shore county, after receiving permission for a local referendum, had voted to prohibit the sale of alcoholic beverages.

Only Worcester remained wet. Orlando Harrison, Berlin mayor, led the anti-saloon crusade there, while "Captain" Christopher Ludlam of Ocean City—a fisherman and small hotel owner—bitterly fought local prohibition. In 1904 the first car had reached Ocean City, which remained a small community of cottages and five or six hotels. By no means the scene of reckless abandon (at the famous Plimhimmon Hotel guests could not walk the lobby in bathing attire), Ocean City had just built a fishing and recreation pier at a cost of $30,000. Baltimore pleasure seekers had offered to rent the pier at a fat fee provided Worcester stayed wet, and throughout the local-option campaign Ocean City business leaders argued that they would lose money in a dry county. In late March, when Worcester made its choice, bells tolled all day in Berlin, Snow Hill, and Pocomoke City reminding anti-saloon forces to vote. Church women put out food and lemonade near the polls. The *Sun* noted with some surprise that election day was quiet and that Democrats made no attempt to influence the outcome. They probably saw the futility of opposing Harrison's forces—Worcester went dry by a margin of 2,905 to 846. Yet this conservative victory neither dampened differences among people nor slowed the pace of automobile-inspired change; it only postponed further struggles on the Eastern Shore. The road commission soon completed a highway to Ocean City. In 1916 a private company announced plans for regular automobile-ferry service between Annapolis and Claiborne in Talbot County.

Though people at the other end of the state had gotten along well enough before the road commission, the arrival of the motorcar raised new hopes in the Maryland mountains. The Cumberland and Westernport Electric Railway met local needs famously in the first years of the century, moving shoppers in Cumberland to richly supplied downtown stores or to the park then open at Cumberland Narrows. The railway ran to Frostburg and then down the valley to Westernport, linking together the largest far western population centers with almost thirty miles of track. Cumberland citizens in these years exhibited Baltimore-like energy. In 1908 Allegany County opened a new high school in Cumberland. After fire destroyed the old city hall, Cumberland in 1911 began building an impressive new structure. Two years later, acknowledging the importance of Cumberland as a rail junction, officials of the Western Maryland built a large new station there.

Railroads continued to play an important part in Western Maryland life, but the state's new road system met two issues of concern to people in the mountains—their comparative remoteness and limits to their supply of coal. Roads gave Oakland on the B&O a much stronger freight and passenger link to the world. Garrett County towns like Redhouse and Gorman, south of the county seat, and Thayersville, McHenry, and Accident to the north of Oakland first enjoyed a reliable route to the National Road and national markets when the road commission completed its original plans for the region. Also in 1915, using inexpensive horsecars or wagons, Allegany County began transporting students in outlying areas to its high school. Soon better roads and the motor-driven school bus enabled school commissioners to take a fresh view of academic administration, for presumably schools could consolidate so as to serve more students with better teachers. Meantime, as coal production fell off in the George's Creek Valley, auto-related industry held out hope of filling the employment gap. In September 1916 the Cumberland *Evening Times* announced happily that the Kelly-Springfield Tire Company had accepted the city's offer to construct a plant employing three thousand workers in the Queen City. Though city fathers had to donate the site, agree to extend the city limits so as to provide the factory with police and fire protection, and raise a "bonus" of $750,000 for the company, the automobile age promised to be good to Cumberland—and to all of mountain Maryland. In the winter of 1920 the state Roads Commission removed its first snow from Maryland highways.

~~~

At the same time the automobile enhanced state power, developments that Marylanders could not control increased the federal government's visibility and authority in the state. One familiar agent, the army corps of engineers, continued its extensive role in river and harbor projects. It routinely maintained the ship channels dug in the 1870s and 1880s. After 1912, when Congress passed a generous internal improvements bill, dredging operations made more changes to the Maryland waterscape. Under the stern gaze of Congressman William H. Jackson of Salisbury, army contractors further improved harbors at Queenstown, Cambridge, and Crisfield; after channel work in the Elk River, Elkton in 1916 finally obtained steamboat service to Baltimore (it proved short-lived because few people used it). The army deepened the Tred Avon River from Peachblossom Creek to Easton Point and Tuckahoe Creek between Waymans Wharf and Rolphs Landing. Dredging on Smith Island in 1913–14 opened its creeks to small craft at low as well as high tide. With far less success, though at equally great expense, engineers tried to dig channels in the oozy mud of the Manokin and Pocomoke rivers. Their failures only made them mortals; some oystermen believed them worse. Instead of piling "spoil" or dredged mud behind wooden barricades, the army had taken to dumping it farther inland, or, more often, dropping it outside the channel, in shallow water. But then spoil mud buried oysters and ruined the beds. This complaint had been heard in the 1880s at Ellis Bay, downriver from the Wicomico dredging operations. After the turn of the century it arose at Rock Hall in Kent County and at Claiborne in Talbot. For all the blessings it bestowed, the corps of engineers still bore watching.

In Annapolis the naval school, assuming new dimensions after the turn of the century, loomed larger than the sleepy town itself. Though the academy around Fort Severn had established itself firmly after the Civil War, its physical and academic modesty had befitted a small navy, divided between sail and steam, fulfilling a limited peacetime mission. Until a Supreme Court ruling in 1888, students had not been officially in service. Hazing had become a brutal tradition. Summer practice cruises, conducted aboard the old frigate *Constellation*, had carried the midshipmen to many an adventure off the East Coast; one year the ship had run aground near Cape Charles Lighthouse in heavy weather.

Navy triumphs over the clumsy Spanish in 1898–99 and new American responsibilities in the Pacific awakened Congress to the value of seapower. The navy began building a new fleet of all-steam battleships; after 1899, following a parallel course, a construction program at Annapolis replaced the old school with an academy of imperial proportions. Dredging equipment deepened two basins and used the mud to extend the shoreline. The chief architect of the project, Ernest Flagg of New York, executed a French Renaissance design in granite and bronze that stated clearly the permanence and ambitions of the institution. Bancroft Hall, resembling the Hôtel des Invalides in Paris, had four floors, four and one-half miles of corridors, and covered about thirty acres; the elaborate interior of its Memorial Hall, a treasury of naval relics, stood on equal footing with the U.S. Capitol. Flanking Bancroft were two large structures named for the heroes Dahlgren and MacDonough and used for drill and gymnastics. In the same style the Alfred Thayer Mahan Library commemorated that student of seapower in history. The new chapel had enormous bronze doors, a crypt that in 1913 became the final resting place of John Paul Jones (his grave had been discovered in Paris eight years earlier), and a dome much like that of St. Paul's in London. After 1900 applications to "Annapolis" rose in number. The curriculum, no longer divided between line and engineering courses, trained students in the new technologies of naval warfare. Twenty-five midshipmen had graduated in 1899; in 1907, when the bandmaster composed "Anchors Aweigh" for football games with the military academy, that number reached 350.

Outside the Maryland Avenue Gate, residents of Georgian-brick Annapolis viewed the rebuilt academy with mixed feelings. They basked in reflected light, for the town remained poor and off the beaten paths of commerce. The corps of engineers regarded dredging the harbor as not worth the trouble. Proud of the national eminence on the northeast edge of town, Annapolis natives supplied some of its labor (black messmen lived aboard a vessel at the academy wharf). Midshipmen on liberty helped to keep small merchants afloat; academy visitors—like legislators in the early months of even years—required hotels, restaurants, and boardinghouses. Spanish officers captured at Santiago in 1898 had spent their captivity at the academy and caused a pleasant social stir in the town. Relations between officers on duty at the academy and leading citizens could be cordial. By longstanding New Year's Day custom, ladies and gentlemen visited one another's homes for powerful drinks of eggnog and brandy.

On the other hand, the naval professionals could demonstrate arrogance in a town where, by colorful overstatement, some women were said not to have bought a new hat since Appomattox. To the dismay of Annapolitans, the post-1899 building program meant destruction of Old Government House—the Governor Eden mansion that for many years had housed guests of the governor. In 1909 the Annapolis mayor and council protested with equal futility the razing of old Fort Severn, which, sitting in front of the imposing new buildings, the superintendent had dismissed as a "wart." Navy officers marched to a national beat; they viewed most "Crabtown" natives as provincials. After the turn of the century someone at the academy published an "Annapolis Alphabet," in which *B* for Busy had pictured two cows walking up Main Street toward Church Circle and *Q* for Quaintness depicted a pig, duck, and Sambo-like black youngster carrying a water bucket down a sidewalk. Quaintness was "where / We make other Cities Despair," read the accompanying limerick. "There's a good deal we ain't / But as long as we're quaint / For the rest we don't bother to care." Annapolis town leaders considered confiscating all copies of the booklet.[6]

In 1911, outside College Park, the military made another impression on the state by establishing a school where young men would learn to operate the most astounding twentieth-century invention yet, the aeroplane. The army had selected the field over the nearby Fort Myer, Virginia, parade ground in the summer of 1909 after a survey conducted by horseback and balloon. At the new field Wilbur Wright had trained two pilots, taught a naval officer, George C. Sweet, to fly, and taken some passengers aloft, including a woman who upon returning to earth said she now understood why birds sang. Afterward army aviation descended to one broken plane, a single unsoloed pilot—a gallant fellow named Foulois—and several enlisted men with nothing to do. Then, in November 1910, at a field named Halethorpe southwest of Baltimore, an "air meet" had gathered some of the most advanced flying machines of the day. It caused quite a sensation. Winning a five-thousand-dollar prize offered by the new *Evening Sun*, Hubert Latham had flown his single-engine craft (it looked like a large dragonfly) over Baltimore City for three-quarters of an hour. The lack of a safe landing strip below made the flight especially impressive. Half a million persons turned out to see it. "City lost in wonder as Latham rides the air," exclaimed the next issue of the *Sun*. "Newest marvel of man seen at its best by multitudes

"The Twentieth Century Flyer," 1909. Twentieth- and nineteenth-century technologies suddenly came face to face when a northbound train passed near the new College Park airfield—the dramatic scene recalling the story of *Tom Thumb's* race with a horse several generations earlier. *Prince George's County Historical Society*

of breathless people."[7] Latham's example, but also aeronautical advances in Europe, prompted Congress to action. The army flying school marked the official turn from indifference to energy.

Everything about the school was experimental and exciting. Its commander, Signal Corps captain Charles DeF. Chandler, apparently qualified for the job because of his experience as a balloonist—or, as foot soldiers said, ballunatic. In April 1911 a mowing machine, plow, scraper, roller, and two army mules got to work on the landing strip, which finally stretched for about 2,400 feet on an east-west path. Four low-lying wooden "hangars" 45 feet square went up, along with a headquarters shack and a hospital tent that the army expected to figure prominently in flight training. Orders went to the Wright Company for two planes (Type B, suggesting how far things had progressed) and to the Glen Curtiss Company in Texas for three more, all of them with "push" propellers. In the absence of either instructors or students, a recruiting officer began writing and cabling old friends. Two of the first men to answer the call established the aviator legend. One lieutenant, Henry H. (later "Hap") Arnold, had fought in the guerrilla war that broke out in the Philippines in 1901. The other, Thomas DeWitt "Dashing" Milling, was a cavalry officer and the army's top polo player. They trained in Dayton, Ohio, with the Wrights for a mere ten days, logging two or three hours of flight time (most hops shorter than ten minutes) before assuming their teaching assignment at the College Park field.

The Signal Corps selected College Park because of its proximity to Washington headquarters; still in the country, the field lay only a short train or automobile ride from the War Office. This closeness almost grew into a handicap. Washingtonians and nearby Marylanders, fascinated by these ungainly, soaring machines, arrived "by train, trolley, wagons, bicycles, motor cycles, and in touring cars" to crowd onto the field and applaud each flight. Newspapermen reported record-setting events—Arnold climbed higher and higher that summer—with reverent awe. Pilots complained that stories of their defying death had grown monotonous. In fact they embraced celebrity. On 10 July, Arnold and a passenger flew into Washington, circled the now-completed Washington Monument, and buzzed the Capitol, out of which Senate members, forgetting a roll-call vote then in progress, poured waving and cheering. Later in the summer two craft set off to prove the aeroplane's overland magic by flying to a National Guard encampment at Frederick. They left at about 6:30 in the morning and crossed over Kensington, where engine trouble forced one pilot down. The other plane, with Arnold and Chandler aboard, reached Frederick at 7:20 to the shrill greeting of factory whistles. The aviators found Frederick's welcome so warm that they stayed too long. Flying home late in the day, they groped for landmarks in the twilight. Finally they gave up, landed at the Bartlett farm near Gaithersburg, and caught the B&O. The next morning, when they drove a truck out to the plane, a young boy was charging the curious a nickel apiece to warm the "cockpit" seat.[8]

<hr/>

Before 1914 the doings of the army and navy in Maryland were helpful or harmless—often simply amusing. The Great War altered that innocent relationship. After August of that year, when conflict erupted, the war greatly stimulated Baltimore industry: protected yet accessible, Baltimore once again found itself in a strategic location. Bethlehem Steel purchased the plant at Sparrows Point, expanded it for wartime production, and soon began building two steamships for the British and fifty freighters for the U.S. Navy. Baltimore Drydock and Shipbuilding bought new property on south Locust Point. The Maryland Shipbuilding Company purchased a large tract on Marley Neck, below Curtis Bay. Bartlett-Hayward had munitions contracts with the French and Russians in the million-dollar range; it developed factories on Sollers Point, between Canton and Sparrows Point, and on Washington Boulevard in southwest Baltimore. The Poole Corporation, a Delaware firm, began building large guns at its plant in Woodberry—with special police stationed in Druid Hill Park to protect against sabotage. It also produced airplanes at its plant in Hagerstown. The business leadership of Baltimore, especially the old elites of Anglo-Irish blood, heavily favored American entry into the war on the Allied side.[9]

The European war caused ethnic minorities in Maryland, as elsewhere in the country, great anguish. The Baltic states and Poland, both part of the Russian Empire in 1914, fell to German troops early in the conflict. In 1915–16, Lithuanians living near the Hollins Street Market and Baltimore Poles raised money to help friends and relatives in the Old Country. East Baltimore Jews gave $9,000 for Russian relief at a spirited rally. The Baltimore German-language newspaper *Correspondent* walked a fine line. In January 1917 it marked the Kaiser's birthday with photos, poetry, and printed fanfare but the next month warned Baltimore Germans not to defend the Kaiser's war policies—"In this case one's sense of duty must triumph over one's heart." "Germany is the land of our fathers," it reminded readers soon after; "this is the land of our children and children's children." [10]

When in April the Wilson administration mobilized for the world war it had tried to avoid, the decision had immediate impact in Maryland. Governor Emerson C. Harrington put his attorney general, Albert C. Ritchie, to work writing the measures needed to place the state on a war footing. The General Assembly created a Maryland Council of Defense, with wide-ranging authority to coordinate activities like recruiting, Red Cross work, bond sales, grocery distribution, and finding housing for war workers. Within a month of Wilson's war message, 3,000 Marylanders enlisted in the navy. The work force at Bartlett-Hayward jumped from 4,000 to 22,000. Baltimore clothing manufacturers, again taking up the job that had given many of them a start, began mass producing uniforms. With the aid of electric lights, war factories kept busy round the clock, labor strength—but also arithmetic—arguing for eight-hour shifts. In late May the army registered Marylanders for the draft. Baltimoreans of military age, 55,000 of them, signed up to the ringing of church bells and the whistles of steamboats and factories. The federal government soon activated Maryland National Guard or militia regiments—the 1st, composed of Western Shoremen, and Baltimore's 4th and 5th. In July, fearing that German U-boats might enter the Chesapeake, the administration placed the Maryland "oyster navy" and its commander, Swepson Earle, under orders of the U.S. Atlantic Fleet. The U.S. Naval Academy enlarged its plebe class to 2,000 midshipmen. Army tanks and trucks soon turned many Maryland roads, particularly the new Baltimore-Washington Boulevard, into rubble.

The military buildup had an effect on the very map of Maryland, for new camps and assorted war activities ate into the land. The army took over several thousand acres of Anne Arundel County farmland and made it a center for processing recruits—named Camp Meade after the Pennsylvania general who led Union troops at Gettysburg. Meade provided a training ground for a new unit, the 313th Infantry, made up largely of Baltimore volunteers. In the fall of 1917 the government chose Harford County marshland near Aberdeen for an artillery testing ground. In June of the next year it established yet another camp southward, at Edgewood, where army chemists began experimenting with the deadly gases that Germany had employed in France.

There was a gunpowder plant at Perryville, across the Susquehanna's mouth from Havre de Grace, and a rifle range at Glen Burnie. The grounds at Fort McHenry became the site of a sprawling military hospital, and another one went up at Evergreen. An ordnance depot appeared at Curtis Bay. The army established a camp near Highlandtown called Holabird. At North Point it built new coastal defenses, named Fort Howard after the revolutionary Maryland Line officer; on the lower Potomac the army built Fort Foote and made improvements to old Fort Washington. Farther down, in Charles County, the navy appropriated a firing range at Indian Head.

Marylanders in uniform soon faced the consequences of national service in world war. Proud of their discipline and morale, the 1st, 4th, and 5th regiments and their accompanying artillery and hospital forces left in August 1917 for final training at Anniston, Alabama. At Camp McClellan the army rudely reshuffled and renumbered them, putting most of the Marylanders into the 115th Infantry and 110th Field Artillery, and forming a new division, the 29th, composed of New Jersey, Delaware, District of Columbia, Maryland, and Virginia guardsmen. Military authorities wisely abolished a troop of Maryland cavalry with origins in the Green Spring Valley Hunt Club and a policy of hauling non-issue food and drink in a covered wagon. Army doctors declared General Charles D. Gaither, commander of Maryland troops, physically unfit for service in France; Charles A. Little and other militia officers were replaced with regular army men. The "tyrants," said one Maryland officer, referring to the longstanding jealousy between regulars and citizen-soldiers, "have had their way at last." The commander of the new "Blue-Gray" division, General Charles G. Morton, enforced strict regulations that included the manner of tying bootlaces, and Maryland troops grumbled about "carrying things too far." They felt better when a Bel Air native, Colonel Milton A. Reckord, took over the 115th. Too, camp life had its lighter moments. Soldiers organized sports events and followed the 1917 World Series via telegraph. Washington Bowie, Jr., commander of the 110th, somehow managed to stage a horse show. When Negro volunteer soldiers from Baltimore joined the horse-drawn ammunition train, partly manned by an old Virginia unit, the chances of racial tension fell with jokes about "the Baltimore Blacks and Richmond Blues."[11]

At home the war consumed enormous energy, threw citizens out of their usual routines, and distracted public attention from perennial Progressive issues like women's suffrage. The economy both boomed and shuddered, for the loss of about 62,000 men (and, for the first time, women) to the army and navy meant an influx of country people who often had to make painful adjustments to urban life. The city work force—streetcleaners and the like— lost 2,000 persons to Baltimore shipyards and steel mills. Women worked as never before in offices, many now with typewriters. Others entered nursing. Elisabeth Gilman, after signing up with the Surgical Dressings Committee in Baltimore, went to Paris and worked at the YMCA enlisted men's club.

Army recruits arriving at the hastily built Camp Meade, 1917. *MHS*

Young officers "mobilize" at Mount Royal Station, 1917. *MHS*

Wages climbed slower than prices for food, coal, and shelter. Meat and eggs grew scarce, potatoes and onions disappeared from markets, and rumors flew that the producers had them hoarded on railroad cars waiting for the prices to climb still higher. The bitter-cold winter of 1917–18 left many Baltimoreans so desperate that they burned their furniture and sent children out to pick up stray pieces of coal in railroad yards, where a locomotive killed two of them. Despite new efforts to enforce cleanliness (every day trolley companies washed their tokens), crowded living conditions in Baltimore led to new outbreaks of disease. Many persons died of influenza, which became a national problem the following winter.

All the while the massive effort to defeat the Hun brought a new experience—total war against a foreign enemy. Everyone was expected to climb aboard the war bandwagon; patriotism became a heavy duty. The General Assembly, in a compulsory work law passed in the spring of 1917, made idleness in the midst of world war an infraction punishable by forced labor. Hecklers interrupted a meeting of Baltimore pacifists. The C&P demanded a loyalty pledge of its employees. The Council of Defense, after exercising its unprecedented authority to fix food prices, began a campaign to reduce consumption—everyone was to observe Sugarless Mondays, Meatless Tuesdays, Wheatless Wednesdays, Porkless Fridays, and two-meal Saturdays. Popular pressure, the council's only means of enforcement, apparently sufficed. The Women's Civic League mounted a campaign for backyard, schoolyard, and vacant-lot "liberty gardens," and in the absence of male laborers urged women all over the state to become "farmerettes." A committee of fifty leading Baltimoreans organized a fund-raising drive to help relieve war-caused distress in the city. It adopted a tactic of mass mailings and the intimidating motto Fight, Farm, or Fork Up. Red Cross financial drives asked newspaper readers, in large type, whether they were slackers with a yellow streak.

With their long exposure to German culture, Marylanders of other origins had difficulty hating the enemy with the abstraction that mass mobilization encouraged. Nonetheless the conflict worked its cruel way. After the declaration of war the *Correspondent* pressed Maryland Germans to prove their loyalty to "the land of our choice." German-Americans joined the army in representative numbers and in Baltimore raised half a million dollars for liberty bonds. At the same time, colorful enlistment posters portrayed the German soldier as a baby-spearing barbarian. Federal authorities classified unnaturalized Germans as "alien enemies" and searched their homes with impunity. In the fall of 1918, when the 29th Division took part in the Meuse-Argonne offensive and newspapers printed long casualty lists, Baltimore Germans found themselves objects of suspicion and anger. The *Sun* carried stories about Germans bombing hospitals and letters to the editor talking about exterminating the "Hun vermin" and eliminating the Germans "as a menace to the world." Later that year German singing societies stopped meeting (the old Concordia Opera House became a straw-hat factory), the German-American Alliance dissolved itself, and the *Correspondent*, losing advertisers and subscribers, ceased publication. In September 1918 the city council renamed German Street for Lieutenant George B. Redwood, the first Marylander killed in France.[12]

In Washington the expansive task of making the world safe for democracy forced enlargement of the War and Navy departments and created frantic wartime bureaus. The thousands of administrators, military people, and clerks who gathered in the nation's capital after 1917 caused a housing shortage in the city and encouraged commercial growth. Their arrival also hastened work that had begun several years before—planning and providing for water and sewage disposal in the belt around Washington. As in the case of Baltimore, this earthy issue stood between civic leaders and further land development. In 1916 the General Assembly had created a Washington Suburban Sanitary Commission to study such a coordinated system. By the formula finally agreed upon, Governor Harrington, himself a Dorchester County Democrat, named J. William Bogley of Friendship Heights to the commission. Montgomery County selected William T. S. Curtis, a Chevy Chase lawyer and landowner, who served as chairman, and Prince George's County chose a leading land developer, T. Howard Duckett of Bladensburg.

Villages like Cabin John, Bladensburg, and Oxon Hill had long histories, but most Maryland communities surrounding the District owed their origins, surely their growth, to Washington's transportation lines. Besides serving Chevy Chase, trolleys in the late nineteenth century extended through Tenley Town and Reno to Friendship Heights. From there, after about 1890, an inter-urban electric line to Rockville advanced real estate sales at places with enticing names—Woodmont, Edgemoor, Oakmont, and Alta Vista. All of them lay within the voting district that took its name from the nearby Bethesda Presbyterian Church, dating from 1820. Garrett Park, Kensington, Silver Spring (near the old Montgomery Blair estate), and Takoma Park had grown up along the B&O's metropolitan branch—Washington to Point of Rocks—after 1868. Henry Copp, a nature-loving lawyer, headed the company that bought up the five hundred acres that led to Garrett Park; his associate, John L. Freeman, wanted to lay out a town that looked like an English village. In Prince George's County the communities of Tuxedo, Landover, and Lanham lay along the Pennsylvania Railroad tracks to Washington. Besides the B&O trunk between Washington and Baltimore, an electric line—the Washington, Baltimore, and Annapolis Rail Road—contributed to the early growth of Brentwood, Hyattsville (which engulfed Bladensburg), Berwyn–Berwyn Heights, Branchville, and Beltsville. The automobile, rapidly enlarging the areas in which one could live and still work in Washington, promoted the growth of Wheaton, on the road to Brookeville, and Somerset on River Road. Southeast of the capital, where land was modestly priced, roads connected Cedar Heights, Fairmont Heights, Maryland Park,

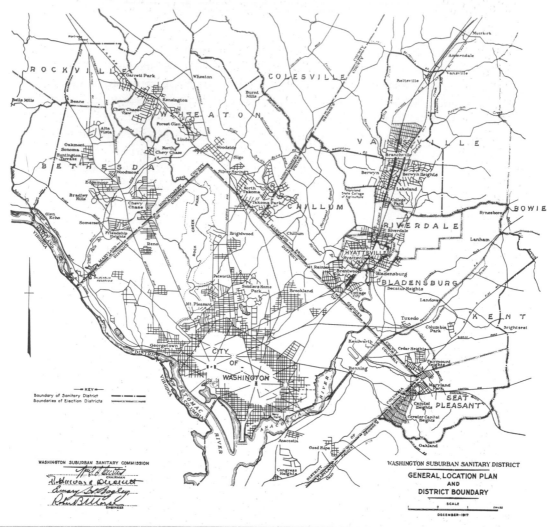

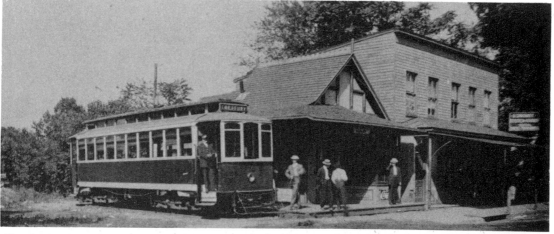

Top, Map of the Washington Suburban Sanitary District, 1917. WSSC Report, *University of Maryland, College Park. Bottom,* the Laurel trolley, c. 1900. Robert H. Sadler, Jr., photograph. *John C. Brennan and Alan Virta.* Topographical and homely views of suburban development outside Washington in those years. The Metropolitan Branch of the B&O, electric trolley lines, and then the automobile made it easier for Washington wage earners to live in Maryland.

and Capitol Heights to the Pennsylvania tracks inside the District; from the same suburbs, Benning Road ran all the way to Maryland Avenue N.E.

Divided between homeowners and real estate interests, these towns often could not decide whether they wanted to remain small or grow. Incorporation allowed them to put the local house in order—hire police or impose municipal taxes for services like water and sewerage. In the early twentieth century some of them did incorporate, others declined. Hyattsville, the largest of the suburban incorporated towns, earlier had earned notoriety for trying to grow while holding onto the simplest principles of agrarian equity—on the prompting of a town commissioner, California-born Jackson H. Ralston, it adopted Henry George's "single-tax" idea in 1892. By this scheme Hyattsville became the first community in the country to tax only the economic value of land, nothing else; supposedly fairer than any other taxing scheme, it nonetheless ran afoul of the Maryland Court of Appeals, where Judge James McSherry declared it an unconstitutional and "insufferable" burden on the landed citizenry.[13] Either because of or despite that defeat, Hyattsville grew rapidly. In 1901, when the telephone company began switchboard service at Wells's drug store, paying customers were fewer than hoped (they included the president's office at the state Agricultural College, the Melrose academy for girls, Tise's grocery store, a coal and wood dealer, and, notably, Duckett and Ford's real estate office). By 1913 phone users had multiplied so quickly that the company left the drug store and put up its own building. Montgomery County communities like Takoma Park, Silver Spring, Rockville, Kensington, and Glen Echo clung to volunteer fire companies, a reliable index of rural character. Twenty-six households in Garrett Park subscribed to service from the Potomac Electric Power Company, and yet residents took pride in their bucolic setting. In the summer months boys could go skinny dipping in the headwaters of Rock Creek. The lower creek, a major District of Columbia park after 1913, belonged to a plan of scenic areas that officials there had started to fulfill when the world war intervened. To their dismay, Rock Creek had begun to smell.

Inspections left no doubt that rural habits and rising population levels made a dangerous combination in suburban Maryland. Three out of every four houses relied on outhouses or cesspools in the backyard. Streams and ditches had grown "offensively polluted." Neighbors often shared wells, some of them driven by windmills. Most people burned refuse or fed it to pigs; only one person in twenty had regular garbage service. The same small fraction employed someone like Old Steve Bailey, a Hyattsville black man who earned a dollar a week for each backhouse he dug out. The pattern was a hodgepodge. Some incorporated communities had their own water towers; others had sewerage but no water. The incorporated town of Mt. Rainier in 1918 had just begun a municipal sewage-disposal system. Friendship Heights and Chevy Chase had private water and sewerage that cost residents dearly. Hyattsville, among other communities, could not get all the water it

Victory parade, Easton, 1919. Talbot County welcomed home native sons with music, bunting, and motorcars. *H. Robins Hollyday Collection, Historical Society of Talbot County*

needed. As summer visitors flocked to the Glen Echo amusement park, the water supply there often failed to meet demand. In that event the town simply dipped into the nearby C&O Canal. The Washington Suburban Sanitary Commission report, delivered in January 1918, pointed out that the Montgomery–Prince George's belt had grown from about twenty thousand in 1910 to thirty-two thousand people, and yet public water and sewerage served only about one person in four. More than half the private wells were probably polluted and nearly half the public sources—many "heavily impregnated with iron"—were either "unsafe for human consumption, of suspicious hygienic quality," or had "menacing" origins. If in the past the suburbs had not been completely ravaged by typhoid fever, it was "due only to good fortune."[14]

With congressional approval, the sanitary commission and District engineers forged a working agreement that permitted development in Maryland to proceed. The suburbs obtained fresh water from the District, with five pumping stations in Montgomery County and three in Prince George's providing pressure enough for home use and fire hydrants. Storm drains and waste water followed the natural logic of topography. Prince George's and Montgomery counties, generally uphill from Washington, built sewer systems that connected with the District system finished in 1907; where District terrain fed into Maryland, the Suburban Sanitary Commission took what gravity brought its way. Marylanders paid for this system, which cost about $2.2 million, at several levels. General taxation supplied the main lines. Assessments on subdivided property financed the lateral lines that served it. Each household paid the District a one-dollar-a-year usage fee.

Those households continued to rise in number, after the Armistice of November 1918 many newcomers to Washington decided to stay, and in suburban Maryland developers and builders bent to their work. Fortunately the state and federal governments cooperated in supplying vital utilities. Unfortunately, the District's modern sewage-disposal system fed untreated waste directly into the Potomac. Oystermen on the lower river complained to no avail. Before long health authorities banned bathing in the Potomac, already polluted when it reached Washington. The Anacostia continued to fill up, if not with sewage, with silt that ran off of newly exposed Prince George's pastures.

"Marylanders had stopped making history for themselves," wrote Raymond S. Tomkins about Maryland soldiers in the late war. "They had become part of the history of the United States."[15] Tomkins, a *Sun* reporter, registered a vague postwar sentiment that the state was smaller as a result of the Great War, its people entangled in world events. The conflict left marks on the reorganized troops who fought in the muddy and bloody campaigns around Verdun or served on board ships in icy waters, on Baltimore's German neighborhoods, on the men and women who had worked at war plants, on the rural people who now lived outside new military installations in Maryland or on the fringes of the growing federal capital. The Great War coincided with frightening foreign upheaval, the Bolshevik revolt against centuries of czarist power and privilege. With overseas cables buzzing and a new invention, the wireless or radio, just making its appearance, foreign events did not seem so distant. Wilson sent American troops to aid the White armies against the Red Guard. Much as Federalists in the 1790s had feared sympathizers with the French Revolution, many Americans in 1919 regarded radicals as Bolsheviks. That year President Wilson's attorney general conducted raids against suspected Bolsheviks—labor agitators and anarchists. Meanwhile the president called on Americans to face a larger role in international affairs by ratifying the League of Nations treaty. In a treaty negotiated with the Canadians in 1916 and implemented by federal statute two years later, Marylanders had a more prosaic reminder that they lived in a larger world—the treaty placed restrictions on duck and goose hunting. No longer could gunners kill wild waterfowl for sale, only for sport, now under

One weekend's kill with a big gun, c. 1900. *Harry Walsh Collection, Chesapeake Bay Maritime Museum*

strict regulation that prohibited, for example, the use of punt guns. Furthermore, two changes to the Constitution dictated reforms that ran against prevailing sentiment among many Maryland men.

⟨⟩

The modern age left Marylanders searching for a moderate middle course between government control and liberty, conscience and tolerance, tradition and more Progressive change. The state divided over the problem of drink. For prohibitionists like the Reverend Arthur H. Thompson of the Frostburg First Methodist Church and William H. Anderson, an early superintendent of the Anti-Saloon League of Maryland, the issue was moral—drink led to sin and had baneful effects on home and family. For their opponents, drinking was a matter of taste, and, as one Baltimorean put it, "the Kingdom of Heaven is not eating and drinking." [16] Not necessarily intemperate, they had grown up in families whose members enjoyed brandied eggnog in holiday season, beer at ballgames, or wine with meals.

Support for Prohibition had grown considerably since the Worcester County local-option vote of 1908. Southern Maryland had joined the dry Eastern Shore counties. Evangelical Protestant ministers in the state and local chapters of national groups like the Women's Christian Temperance Union—one of whose Kansas members, Carry Nation, became famous for chopping bars with a hatchet—lifted their voices against this evil. They lobbied at each legislative session for a new twist to voluntary, local option—a general law requiring each county to vote on the wet-or-dry question. In 1916 anti-drink forces obtained such a bill. That fall Carroll, Frederick, and Washington counties went dry; elsewhere—in Annapolis, Allegany, Baltimore, and Harford counties, the suburban belt around Washington, and above all in Baltimore City, where Prohibition lost by a margin of three to one—voters either chose the freedom to drink or refused to deny it to others. In 1918 Congress took the question out of the hands of the states and passed the Eighteenth Amendment, banning the sale and transportation of beer, wine, and liquor. With rural votes outweighing Baltimore City, the General Assembly soon ratified that measure. By January 1919 three-fourths of the states had agreed to national Prohibition, and it went into effect a year later.

While women played major roles as Maryland Progressives, the women's suffrage movement in the state faced considerable indifference and opposition. Women did not lack for leadership (though in 1894 the influential M. Carey Thomas had departed to serve as president of Bryn Mawr College). Two persuasive speakers on behalf of equal voting rights, Etta Haynie Maddox and Emilie A. Doetsch, had passed the Maryland bar examination in 1902–3 and become the first women to pratice law in the state. Lilian Welsh, the preventive medicine specialist at the Hopkins Hospital, wrote that her "greatest thrills came with the street parades" that suffragists organized in Baltimore, Annapolis, and Washington. Dr. Edith Hooker used an automo-

Alley scene, East Baltimore, 1906. John Dubas, an East Baltimore photographer, snapped some neighbors hefting samples of local brew. *Peale Museum, Baltimore City Life Museums*

Suffragists on the march in Baltimore, 1905. *MHS*

bile as a speaker's platform in Baltimore, spoke at parlor meetings on behalf of women's voting, and in 1912 began editing and publishing a newsletter, *Maryland Suffrage News*, which became influential far beyond the state's borders. Another suffragist leader and a Baltimore native, Florence E. Bamberger, studied at Columbia Teacher's College. She became the first woman on the regular Hopkins University faculty in 1916, the same year the university moved to Homewood, the old Carroll estate on North Charles Street. Only nine years before had the university accepted women in the graduate school.[17]

Women themselves differed on how to achieve the vote. In 1910 two suffragist organizations petitioned the assembly to pass two different bills. The prominent reformer Elizabeth King Ellicott had helped to form the Equal Suffrage League in Baltimore, another group with close ties to the Arundell Club. As an entering wedge, Ellicott and the league supported a measure permitting women to vote only in Baltimore elections, where presumably they would make their influence felt on topics of "women's concern"—especially schools and public health. Ellicott thought broader suffrage would follow in due course. The state Women's Suffrage Association, with Etta Maddox's sister, Emma Maddox Funck, serving for many years as president, asked for voting rights in all elections—for immediate and full equality. The more modest appeal of the Arundell group had the blessing of Baltimore

Democrats—including Mayor J. Barry Mahool and the pragmatic Sonny Mahon—and of 173,000 petitioners. The assembly nonetheless tabled both bills.

Such measures stood little chance in Maryland. They encountered the pervasive, barely spoken opposition of many men, especially Democrats, who defined chivalry so as to keep women out of the often-dirty business of politics, and who worried that women's suffrage would lead to a more than doubled black-Republican vote (indeed, the legislature still had not ratified the Fifteenth Amendment). Thus women failed even after they agreed on an agenda. In 1912 about eight hundred of them journeyed to Annapolis to lobby for a state constitutional amendment granting them the vote. This time with Republican backing, the bill again died. Four years later, as both national parties endorsed a women's vote amendment, Maryland political leaders remained cool to the notion. Edith Hooker was among the Maryland women who turned their backs on the General Assembly and petitioned Congress for the federal amendment that finally passed and went to the states in June 1919.

Fights over Prohibition and women's suffrage set the stage for Albert C. Ritchie, whose instincts inclined him to resist the growth of federal power. Ritchie, like John Pendleton Kennedy before him, combined Virginia and Baltimore and in his career wove these threads together. His mother's Cabell ancestry ran deeply into the commonwealth's history; his father, Albert Ritchie, had sat in the 1867 constitutional convention and served ably on the Baltimore Supreme Bench. Young Ritchie was a handsome blade; admirers (referring to the fashion-setting sketches of a magazine artist) described him as "almost a manifestation of the Gibson man." He graduated from Hopkins in 1896, made a tour of Europe, and studied law at the University of Maryland. After several years of private practice, Ritchie began service with the Baltimore solicitor's office in 1910 and then in 1912 joined the state Public Service Commission. As assistant general counsel to the commission, he had a hand in reducing gas and electric rates in the city, which won him popularity among consumers; one civic group leader called him "clean as a hound's tooth." In 1915, when John Walter Smith, the Democratic party chief, agreed to put Ritchie on the ticket as candidate for attorney general, Ritchie not only won but ran ahead of the ticket. After war broke out he went to Washington to work on the staff of Bernard Baruch's powerful War Industries Board. In 1919 he announced his candidacy for governor. Smith and his friends saw him as attractive and uncontroversial. Ritchie went on to defeat the Republican Harry W. Nice by 165 disputed votes. The governor-elect might have recalled that under his picture in the Hopkins yearbook classmates had predicted that one day he would win the presidency by one vote and be reelected for life.[18]

Ritchie took the governor's chair not long after another Maryland development that had political consequences, the reorganization of the Baltimore Sunpapers. The venerable morning *Sun*, the Sunday edition, and the *Evening*

Albert C. Ritchie (1876–1936) and his Virginia-born
mother, 1915. *MHS*

Sun, which first appeared in 1910, assumed their modern personality in
1919. The evening paper had been the project of Charles Grasty, who had
left Baltimore in 1908 and then returned two years later as president of the
financially restructured A. S. Abell Company. At the Sunpapers Grasty had
hired talented old hands from the *News* and *Evening Herald*, John Haslup
Adams and Henry Mencken, but also had embroiled the papers in ugly battles with political figures like the longtime Baltimore mayor, James Harry
Preston. Grasty had further difficulties as financial manager. The old crusader resigned in 1914 and five years later the presidency fell to Paul Patterson, business manager of the papers. Patterson wanted to place the Sunpapers on a new foundation. He held a series of nightly meetings with
Mencken, whose desk had been next to his when the pair had begun on the
Sun, and Harry C. Black, younger brother of the board chairman, Van Lear
Black. Harry's naval experiences in the Great War had left him cynical about
politicians and angry at the "dull and flatulent newspapers" that had to
share blame for the carnage. Patterson, Mencken, and the younger Black
agreed to a new set of rigorously nonpartisan principles that separated news
stories from editorials and governed editorial pages. The Sunpapers would

be steady, early, dependably accurate if not sensational in the Grasty manner, utterly free of special interest or rigid formula. The *Sun*, stated the memorandum later known as the White Paper, "must convince by means of sound information, unquestionable honesty and unshakable common sense."[19]

Before long it became clear that the Sunpapers—with powerful writers like Mencken, Frank Richardson Kent, John W. Owens, and Gerald W. Johnson—usually located common sense and sound judgment in Albert C. Ritchie. Ritchie began his administration appealing to old customs and a state's authority to decide its own domestic course. Recently divorced (his wife complained that in 1916 he left her and moved in with his mother), he had not marched in suffragist parades. In 1916 Ritchie had felt the need to reassure a voting-rights leader that, by opposing her cause, he did not in fact put women in a category with children, idiots, lunatics, and unpardoned criminals. He shared the sentiments of the *Sun* in early 1920, when the assembly took up the women's voting amendment. "Let Maryland be true to herself," read the paper, "to the knightly creed which recognized in true women the real inspirers of every good work and deed." Both house and senate refused assent to women's suffrage by two-to-one margins. The General Assembly went further—it passed resolutions rebuking Congress for presuming to tamper with the fundamental right of a state to define its political community.[20]

As on women's suffrage, so on Prohibition, the governor argued that the federal government had meddled in "a matter that ought to be left to the people of the states." In March, Ritchie sent a message to the House of Delegates recommending a bill that would have ignored the Volstead or federal liquor-restriction act and permitted the laboring fellow and people generally to drink light beer and wines. Along with moderates and "wets" of both parties in Maryland, Ritchie also took the position that no state law should enforce national Prohibition without a popular referendum. In the 1920 session "dry" delegates, fearing popular defeat, voted down an enforcement bill that the senate had amended to include such a plebiscite. Prohibition leaders cried out in rage at both the light-drink idea and the embarrassing referendum ploy. George W. Crabbe, then superintendent of the state Anti-Saloon League, charged the author of the original enforcement bill with "treachery." Drys classed other Maryland politicians, not all of them Democrats, as "subservient tools of the liquor interests." Crabbe described Ritchie as "a menace to the good morals of the State of Maryland."[21]

Actually Ritchie demonstrated keen political sense at a time when his party had lost popular favor. On a panoply of issues of direct concern to Marylanders he worked hard to build a popular following—and to act on his principles of efficiency and sound management. Since 1916, when the assembly acted on the Goodnow Commission report, the governor had authority to compose a budget that legislators could only reduce, not embellish (any spending the assembly wished to do had to be accompanied with a revenue-raising plan). The "executive budget" obviously added to the policy-making powers of the Maryland chief executive. Ritchie made the most of its dramatic potential by presenting his first budget to the legislature in person. Calling for increased state spending on programs dear to pre-war Progressives, he nonetheless championed strict economy. The governor recommended, and secured, immediate passage of a measure creating a Central Purchasing Bureau that would, he said, save the state enormous sums. He challenged legislators to make the internal reforms first recommended by Warfield and Crothers, and the assembly passed an appropriation for another study of the cluttered offices in Annapolis. Ritchie and members of the Ways and Means Committee agreed to make expenditures of $850,000 per year for ten years on continued road improvements. Beginning in 1916 the federal government had offered states matching grants for the purpose; as long as other states accepted federal largesse, said Ritchie, Maryland would be foolish not to take it. Even with spending on hospitals and increased salaries for public servants like highway patrolmen, Ritchie projected a reduction in the state tax rate of two cents on a hundred-dollar assessment.

The new governor made executive decisions that helped win over women and drys. In February 1920 he placed a large number of state employees—excepting direct gubernatorial appointments, teachers, and highway patrolmen—in a merit-based civil service program. Ritchie also cast a critical eye on the state school system, to which, following the survey that the assembly had ordered in 1914, legislators had made important though incomplete changes. After 1916 members of county school boards served lengthier and staggered terms, and no longer did state senators make politically inspired nominations that the governor in practice honored. The 1916 law set minimum teachers' salaries, strengthened school attendance laws, and ensured that black pupils annually spent as much time in school as did whites. Ritchie in 1920 appointed as the new state Superintendent of Schools Albert S. Cook, a student of the famous John Dewey and until then head of the Baltimore County system. Cook energetically enforced attendance laws and pressed for stiffer teacher qualification standards. Ritchie's selection as president of the State Normal School at Towson, Lida Lee Tall, proved another rewarding choice; at the end of the decade the proportion of Maryland elementary teachers who met standards then in force climbed from about 35 percent to 95 percent.[22]

Ritchie overlooked no chance for party growth. When Tennessee in August 1920 became the thirty-sixth state to ratify the Nineteenth Amendment, he and party leaders vowed to "do the decent thing and do it in a decent way"—they quickly set about registering as many women as possible.[23] The governor called a special fall session of the General Assembly, during which legislators changed Maryland laws to reflect the full citizenship of women and smoothed the registration process with an eye toward the upcoming election. Opposition remained in some quarters; the Maryland League for State Defense, made up of conservative lawyers and assemblymen, brought suit against an election official who had registered women in Baltimore. The league brief argued that Maryland had not adopted the Nineteenth Amendment and that Congress had no right to modify state voting laws without the consent of the people exercising political power.[24] Meanwhile, according to newspaper reports, almost 105,000 women registered to vote in Baltimore City, another nearly 10,000 in Baltimore County, and about 2,500 in Carroll County (the new voters for the most part split evenly between Democrats and Republicans). In the November 1920 elections women apparently accounted for the defeat of Baltimore Congressman Charles P. Coady, who had voted against passage of the suffrage amendment. Democrats, men and women, could do little for the party's presidential candidate, Governor James M. Cox of Ohio. Warren Harding's pledge to return the nation to "normalcy" appealed to Marylanders, many of whom apparently had tired of the high duties Wilson had demanded. The Republican won Maryland by a large margin.

Despite this landslide loss in the national election, Ritchie's strength in the Maryland Democratic party slowly grew. It helped somewhat that Maryland Republicans divided over Prohibition and their allegiance to the two men who then dominated the Republican party, newly elected U.S. Senator Ovington Weller and state central committee chairman Galen L. Tait. But Democrats in the state had old enmities and fights over territory to solve. Smith's control of the regular Democrats hardly compared to Gorman's in the old days. In Baltimore the situation had customary pungency. Rasin's apparent heir, Sonny Mahon, had a powerful challenger in a former understudy, Frank S. Kelly of West Baltimore, whose various exploits earned him titles like "Slot Machine" and "King of the Underworld." In 1921, in time for the fall legislative elections, Ritchie called a peace conference between Mahon and Kelly, who there hammered out an agreement on the later mayoral and councilmanic contests. Kelly agreed to support the choice of Ritchie and Mahon for mayor, Howard W. Jackson, while Kelly and his own lieutenant, William Curran, got free access to half the remaining city offices and patronage posts. Ritchie also used the government survey to his advantage. To conduct the study he had hired a Chicago consulting firm. When it recommended an executive with extensive powers, the governor in the fall of 1921 appointed a commission under Judge Charles Burke to tailor the report to what Ritchie called "those State usages and practices which experience has justified." Republicans observed that all 108 Marylanders (men and women) named to the commission were Democrats, and that they represented every county. In a candid letter to Tait, the governor admitted the commission's political as well as advisory purpose.[25]

Democrats did well in November, and in the 1922 session Ritchie reaped his reward. Under pressure from the Baltimore City delegation, the governor

that year made increased representation for Baltimore a test of party loyalty (the city in 1918 had annexed another belt, raising its size from thirty to
ninety-two square miles and its population from about 500,000 to almost
730,000). An amendment giving the city six senators and thirty-six delegates
went to voters at the next election. Ritchie also did something about the still
lamentably uneven quality of Maryland schools. His signal contribution to
the evolving system was a plan to spread Maryland's wealth evenly among
the counties for educational purposes. He successfully pressed for a general
fund into which all counties paid according to their taxable property, out of
which each county took equally for school buildings, improved teachers'
salaries, and textbooks. Though regular Democrats and those friends of
Senator Smith who filled needless jobs muttered disapproval, the General
Assembly also adopted the Burke reorganization plan. It reduced executive
and administrative agencies from eighty-five to nineteen and saved about
one hundred thousand dollars each year. The governor had the pleasant task
of inviting another reduction in the tax rate, this one of four cents. Finally,
Ritchie pushed for and won a "fewer elections" bill that saved more money;
it timed all state, city, and county elections to coincide with congressional
contests in nonpresidential years. The *Sun* endorsed the plan as "welcomed
by sane communities wearied and worn out by perpetual politics."[26]

Few people grew tired of watching Ritchie defy the federal government.
While in 1922 the governor backed a bill establishing a state Bureau of Child
Hygiene, he publicly refused federal advice on the need for another child
labor law in Maryland. In the spring of the same year, when Maryland coal
miners and others struck to protest lower postwar wages, Ritchie spurned
President Harding's recommendation that he and other governors turn out
the National Guard to protect company property. The strike had been so far
peaceful, he replied; the expense of using the militia would be high, and he
reserved the right to use his own judgment in light of his state's traditions—which, he said, truly at least for his own lifetime, included "settling
such matters as these without the aid of bayonets and rifles."[27] Ritchie did
abide by Commerce Secretary Herbert Hoover's request to form a coal commission to oversee fair distribution of that fuel in Maryland. Nonetheless, in
meetings with operators and workers, he tried to reach a homegrown solution to the crisis. In the end labor violence in Illinois undercut the miners'
position and they surrendered to the wage cut.

Ritchie literally shouted defiance to Prohibition and heavy-handed federal
attempts to enforce it. In May 1922, looking for ways to make the Volstead
Act work, President Harding acted as luncheon host to fifteen state executives, Ritchie among them, who were in Washington for the annual governors' conference. Harding made a strong pitch for a state-by-state crackdown
on the illegal flow of liquor (Ritchie's attorney general had absolved police in
the state from any obligation to do so). Afterward, according to the standard
account, the president's audience remained silent, leading him to assume

that the governors had absorbed their lesson and had nothing to say. Suddenly Ritchie broke the silence by standing up and delivering a lecture on the foolishness of federal Prohibition itself. He noted that before the Eighteenth Amendment Marylanders had met the temperance issue quite well on a local basis. Naturally they resented the Volstead law. "In the main," declared Ritchie, "they regard it as an unnecessary and drastic federal infringement on their State and personal rights." He advised federal officials to turn the matter back over to the states.[28]

Ritchie's instincts served him well on this issue. Besides a focus of local pride, the Maryland governor became a national rallying point in the struggle against dry tyranny. When in 1923 a Georgia congressman, a militant dry, toured Maryland attacking Ritchie's independence and pleading with Marylanders to rejoin the Union, Hamilton Owens of the Sunpapers drafted an editorial entitled "The Maryland Free State." In it he celebrated Maryland's independent character and suggested that perhaps, at last, it was time for Maryland to secede. Although Owens never published the piece, he soon used the "Free State" phrase and its sentiments in print, and later Mencken and others did as well. Marylanders, wets to be sure, cheered their governor on. In November 1923 Ritchie decided to make a rare bid for reelection. He won by an overwhelming majority, the first Maryland governor the people returned to a second term.[29]

⁕

Calvin Coolidge, president since Harding's sudden death in August of 1923, liked to get to bed early, keep discourse flinty, and give business a free rein. Even more attuned to normalcy than his scandal-ridden predecessor, Coolidge said simply that America's business was business. In Baltimore it had always been true. Business leaders there organized for the self-promoting or "boosting" that became so much a part of the 1920s. The Grain and Flour Exchange remodeled itself as the Chamber of Commerce and lobbied hard for federal funds to dredge the harbor; in a "spirit of working together" other groups, including the old Merchants and Manufacturers Association, formed the Baltimore Association of Commerce in the spring of 1924 and began publishing *Baltimore*, a magazine in praise of business opportunity. "There is no place in the United States," said Bethlehem Steel president Charles Schwab, "so susceptible of successful industrial development." With a ready work force, good banking, low electricity and gas costs, distribution links to the Southeast, and excellent exporting facilities, the city by many measures did well in the 1920s. The B&O, Western Maryland, and Pennsylvania railroads expanded their Baltimore grain-export terminals after the war, anticipating renewed trade with Europe. Seventh among American exporting cities in 1920, the city rose to third six years later, behind only New York and New Orleans. More than a hundred new factories located in Baltimore.[30]

"Baltimore Harbor." Etching by Sears Gallagher, 1922. *MHS*

Individual Marylanders, perhaps lying under Howard Latham's spell, kept flight on the front pages of state newspapers in these years and helped in their way to create a favorable environment for an important new industry. Marylanders played large parts in the rise of commercial aviation. John A. Hambleton, son and nephew of Baltimore bankers, had never been up in a plane in 1917 but that year left Harvard to join an army flying squadron. Returning from the war with decorations and the warm admiration of his superior, General "Billy" Mitchell, Hambleton with others founded the state's first Air National Guard unit in 1920 and a civilian flying club. He established Chesapeake Aircraft Company, flying passengers, freight, and mail into Logan Field (opened at Dundalk in 1920) from Tolchester and other local landing strips. Juan Terry Trippe's family had landed on the Eastern Shore in 1663, a few years behind the Hambletons, and the two families for generations had been in business together; Hambleton's boyhood friend, Trippe had learned to fly with the navy, missed the war, and then finished at Yale. The two men saw immense possibilities in regular flights between New York and Boston, which proved as profitable as they expected. Next, with New York financial support, Trippe and Hambleton won air mail contracts for service to the Caribbean and then Latin America. Their company eventually emerged as Pan American Airways. Meantime Van Lear Black of the Sunpapers made pioneering flights in exotic places. In June 1927, only one month after Lindbergh soloed across the Atlantic, Black hired a Dutch pilot and flew 500-mile legs from Amsterdam to Budapest, across the Middle East to India and eventually to the Dutch East Indies and back—a total of some 20,000 miles. Black regarded the trip "as having proved the practical value of the airplane for commercial travel over long distances."[31]

Reproducing the blend of personal and investment daring that earlier had created the Baltimore Clipper, several Maryland firms led in early airplane manufacturing. In Hagerstown a forward-looking shoe manufacturer, Ammon H. Kreider, and his friend Lewis E. Reisner began making small planes in 1925, at first employing assorted shops and private garages on Pennsylvania Avenue, later buying land three miles farther north. Financially taken over by a New Yorker, Sherman M. Fairchild, in 1929, the company finally produced single-engine, closed-cabin planes that became mainstays of civil aviation. Baltimore companies produced aircraft piston rings, propellers, and instruments. After the war Temple M. Joyce, a Poly graduate who as a boy had helped to refuel airplanes at the Halethorpe air show, founded the Berliner-Joyce Company and built biplanes for the army and navy. An early employee eventually bought the firm and took it to California, where it became North American Aviation.

One of the largest airplane makers in the country came to Maryland because of the state of long-range aviation at the time: since few cities anywhere had airports, many flights, especially international flights, required planes that could land in water, and the bay offered an excellent, virtually year-round site for such craft. Largely for that reason the waters off Bay Shore Park near Baltimore were an ideal location for the Schneider Cup international air races in the fall of 1925. Glenn L. Martin recognized Baltimore's advantages. A Kansas native who taught himself stunt flying, never drank, smoked, or swore, and like Ritchie lived with his mother, Martin had built airplanes for the military as early as 1913 and used the Chesapeake Bay for tests of a new bomber in 1923. Six years later (when Hambleton and Kreider both died in air accidents) Martin needed investment capital; obtaining it from the Baltimore Trust bank, he moved his plant from Ohio to a large tract

Kreider-Reisner employees tend an early monoplane, the company's model 22C-7, at a field that later became the Hagerstown airport, c. 1928. *Fairchild Industries*

on the Middle River, where he had access to the Pennsylvania Railroad, room enough to expand and build housing for his workers, and use of the bay for tests of the pontoon-equipped "flying boats" Martin specialized in making. At the time commercial aviation promised more than military contracts, and Martin's seaplanes flourished as carriers of air mail, freight, and passengers.

The oldest Maryland industry suddenly enjoyed its own prosperity. For a generation after the Civil War Southern Maryland counties had presented case studies in impoverishment—poor returns, idle fields, and population loss. Prices even for prime leaf (each crop could produce five or six different grades) stood as low as $6 or $7 a hundredweight in the early twentieth century. Maryland tobacco lacked the slow-burning heaviness required in cigars, so that Baltimore cigarmakers actually imported the leaf they used from Ohio and Connecticut. Maryland tobacco mostly furnished the French and other Continental Europeans with a strong leaf for pipes and hand-rolled cigarettes. American tastes leaned toward lighter blends; Yankees abroad choked on what the French called "pure Mar-ee-lan." Before the world war American machinery, making yet another conquest, revolutionized the tobacco industry with mass-produced and factory-packaged cigarettes. The new product located (or created) an enormous new market—but since the large companies preferred the Bright tobaccoes of southern Virginia and North Carolina and the Burleys of Kentucky, they built their factories accordingly. The smoking revolution seemed to pass Maryland by.

The Great War proved the salvation of the Maryland tobacco grower. Besides Brights and Burleys, cigarettes required a mix of quickly burning tobacco to keep them lit, a need that Arabic and Turkish sources met until war disrupted trade in 1914. Before long, with the prompting of Baltimore tobacco buyers, manufacturers discovered that Maryland tobacco burned just as quickly as imported leaf and could be had far more cheaply. Thereafter the counties of Southern Maryland supplied an essential ingredient to a rapidly growing industry. Between 1915 and 1918, prices climbed from $8.50 to $30.00 a hundredweight, and though they fluctuated in the 1920s they remained well above prewar levels. Soon observers of the tobacco economy complained that a labor shortage (the work remained as labor-intensive as in the seventeenth century) hampered expansion to meet the growing demand.

Perhaps because expectations were so high, the period nonetheless brought disappointment. Political unrest and monetary problems hampered European demand; wheat from other countries contributed to a glut on the world market. Producing basic commodities and well diversified, Baltimore escaped serious harm. Elsewhere in Maryland working people endured a period of checkered prosperity. The overproduction of flour badly pinched local roller mills, and at least two companies—Magill at Ellicott City and Rockland at Brooklandville—went under. As wheat and corn prices dropped in the postwar recession, Maryland farmers, also diversified, fell back on

Early morning in a Baltimore Jewish neighborhood, where small shopkeepers, work habits, and religious custom withstood many outside influences. East Lombard Street, c. 1927. *Jacques Kelly*

poultry, hay, vegetables, fruits, and even nuts. Ritchie in 1923 formed a governor's committee on agriculture, which reported the need for cooperatives like those already established in dairy and tobacco farming. That year farmers formed a state Farm Bureau Federation and an adjunct purchasing cooperative to pool some of their buying and selling power. The continuing development of farm machinery—gasoline-powered tractors and assorted attachments—tempted farmers, and later in the decade the new equipment was available on liberal credit. On the Eastern Shore farmers used motor vehicles to improve their position in the vegetable-growing business now called truck farming. Trucks and improved roads, complementing the labors of the army engineer corps, connected profitably to the Baltimore steamboats. The poultry industry held out high promises on the Shore, where some mills survived by converting from flour to chicken feed. Early poultrymen heaped different kinds of rolled grain on the floor and mixed it with garden rakes.

The Maryland seafood industry still lay under the plague of overharvesting. Oyster hauls disappointed skipjack crews; Marylanders took almost 5 million bushels in 1920, but afterward the figure again dropped. Watermen remained indifferent or hostile to the bed-leasing program, and before the war authorities had reclassified many beds and thus reopened them to dredging. In 1922 the new Department of Conservation—besides denying to legal hunters the few remaining Maryland deer—returned official attention to rebuilding oyster sources. An increased oyster tax soon produced $18,000 a year that went toward spreading millions of bushels of shells on depleted beds. In 1925 the oyster haul seemed to bottom out at about 2.5 million bushels. Meanwhile, as Marylanders developed a taste for spiced, steamed crab, watermen obligingly went after more of them. In 1890 the catch had been only 6 million pounds; in 1915 that figure had risen to 22 million. Seasonal variations in the blue crab population, but also heavy harvesting, accounted for the much lower take of a mere 5 million pounds in 1920. Watermen also had become involved in another form of commercial fishing—going after the bony but plentiful menhaden that provided raw material for soap, oil, and fertilizer. Before the world war menhaden processing plants on the lower Potomac and bay turned out products valued at $1.2 million. A visitor then called the boats that searched for the fish "trim and seaworthy," and noted how skippers tried to avoid the schools of bluefish that shared the menhaden's water; nets cost as much as $15,000, and the vicious blues could tear them apart in minutes.[32] The catch of menhaden, along with food fish, declined in these years.

Nor did "Coolidge prosperity" satisfy every Maryland wage earner. Business and manufacturing firms in the state successfully insisted on the open shop—their right to hire unorganized and organized employees alike. Soon after the war's end, striking Baltimore drydock workers had failed to overturn that policy; their strike, so soon after the worst of the Red Scare, played into the hands of the fearful and conforming. Unemployment in the city remained a constant in the period—though unions and boosters disagreed on the numbers. Only about 10 percent of Baltimore laboring people counted themselves as organized, most of them in building trades and textiles. But with so many workers out of jobs, the housing boom of the 1920s did not translate into stronger unions. In 1923 clothing workers failed for the same reason to win concessions at· the Mount Vernon–Woodberry Mills. The leader of the Baltimore Federation of Labor, Henry Broening, had risen from horseshoeing to obtain an education at Loyola College; cousin of William Broening, Republican mayor between 1920 and 1924, the labor spokesman emphasized moderation and self-help. His federation established a Labor College that it supported in place of vocational training in the schools and used the new medium of radio to carry the message of organized labor to a wide audience. Yet Ritchie, both parties, and probably most voters hesitated to tamper with the labor-management relationship. On the Eastern Shore canning companies and truck farmers evaded restrictions on child labor. In 1922 Western Maryland railroad workers, like coal miners, struck and won nothing more than the right to return to work at the same wages. Some of them went to jail for assaulting scabs. About 850 miners quit the coal mines for the Kelly-Springfield plant.

Though prosperity was uneven, the 1920s were good times for most Marylanders. In Baltimore enjoyable diversions included several legacies from the Progressive years, when Mayor James Harry Preston declared that citizens had as much right to "aesthetic development as they do to a sanitation department." The Baltimore Symphony Orchestra, founded in 1916 through the work of Preston and others, played under the direction of Gustav Strube. With full municipal support, it represented the first of its kind in the country. Tickets for Sunday evening concerts cost less than a dollar. The city's Park Band played to summer audiences in various neighborhoods "and by aid of stereopticon slides," boasted a resident in 1925, "the community joins in the singing of old and familiar songs." Among favorite numbers was a city anthem that a Sunpapers poet known as the Bentztown Bard, Folger McKinsey, wrote and that Emma Hemberger set to music. The Peabody Conservatory held regular recitals under Harold Randolph, longtime director. In 1929 Baltimoreans opened a city art museum on Hopkins-donated land in Wyman Park. The museum benefited greatly from Jacob Epstein's support. Epstein, a discount-clothing store pioneer, owned a fine collection of masterworks that he lent for the opening exhibit. Meantime Baltimore theater lovers patronized the Vagabonds, amateur players who had organized just before the war and now dedicated themselves to "freedom and free experiment." The Vagabonds needed only small audiences to fill their makeshift storefront-theater; its stage, remarked an early critic, "looks like the kitchenette of a modern apartment."[33]

Larger crowds attended beauty pageants at Riverview Park or enjoyed vaudeville and moving pictures at the many city theaters among them Ford's, the Lyric, the Hippodrome, the Lyceum, and the Maryland. Old-timers thought young audiences dull; only a few years before, at a showing of *Birth of a Nation*, an elderly man had given the rebel yell "and nearly started the Civil War all over again." Burlesque houses pulled away some rough customers from the theaters. Young couples had broken the male monopoly on second-floor seating, where rowdies once had ruled, and films brought with them "the habit of quietness." Besides, someone said in the late 1920s, "customers have been through a World War and have grown accustomed to scientific miracles which make the stage incidents of 'Nellie, the Beautiful Cloak Model' seem tame."[34] Most Maryland towns of any size opened moving picture theaters in these years, the automobile bringing patrons to town from the surrounding countryside.

One enterprise thrived in Maryland's peculiar setting—James Adams's floating theater. Adams, a former circus performer, had built the *Playhouse*, a huge houseboat-barge, in 1914. Each summer after the war towboats pulled it up one, then down the other, side of the bay, stopping for weekly engagements wherever agents sold enough tickets. With auditorium, box seats, and

The James Adams Show Boat at Chesapeake City, c. 1930. *Baltimore Sunpapers*

balcony, the *Playhouse* seated about seven hundred people comfortably and had space left over for eight dressing rooms and a cast dining room. The eight o'clock main show cost as little as 35¢ and featured performances of "Frisco Jennie" and "Man's Will, Woman's Way." For late-evening vaudeville acts Adams charged another 10¢. The "showboat" or "floating opera" became a regional institution. Adams's sister, for many years leading lady in most productions, earned a reputation as the Mary Pickford of the Chesapeake. In 1924 Edna Ferber toured with the company, gathering material for her later novel *Showboat*.

Horse racing and betting became big business in the twenties. Followers of the sport, thronging to places like Havre de Grace (known as "the Graw"), the Hagerstown track, the Bowie course in Prince George's County, and Pimlico in Baltimore, raised the size of winners' purses and thus lent encouragement to Maryland horsebreeders. Because Pennsylvania and Virginia had long since banned gambling at race tracks, Maryland provided a ground for testing thoroughbred blood in the Middle Atlantic region generally. But the very success of Maryland horse racing made it attractive to corrupting influences. Owners might embellish a thoroughbred's bloodline, switch horses at race time, or give the animals drugs to improve their performance. Gambling interests could pressure stewards and jockeys to throw races—to hold "boat races," for example, in which nobody challenged the predetermined winner. At the 1920 legislative session, opponents of gambling and corruption had mounted a strong attack on the "sport of kings" in Maryland. A bill to eliminate track betting passed the House of Delegates; in the senate, friends of horse racing (Ritchie himself loved the sport) helped to divert that hostility into a compromise measure. The state established a racing commission to supervise tracks and betting; the Maryland Jockey Club, which held its meetings in an elaborate Victorian clubhouse at Pimlico, continued to register thoroughbred bloodlines in the state. These reforms satisfied some if not all critics of racing, and the spring season at Pimlico continued to draw large crowds. After 1917 the Woodlawn Cup went to the winner of the prestigious Preakness Stakes, which gained national attention as the second jewel in the "triple crown" of thoroughbred racing.

Baseball probably supplied the most popular pastime of the period, and Maryland players made their mark on the game. Some of them, barred from white professional teams, played on the Baltimore Black Sox, a black league franchise that boasted a "million-dollar infield" in the 1920s. Jud Wilson, a Black Sox star in these years, joined the club in 1922 and hit .467; Satchel Paige said Wilson was so strong he could go bear hunting with a switch. In exhibition games, often staged in Baltimore, the Black Sox eventually established a record of 268 wins and 168 losses against white clubs.

Marylanders who hoped to play in the big leagues started on teams like the Salisbury Indians and Centreville Orioles, part of the class D Eastern Shore League that turned out some of the most famous players of the postwar decade. In 1923 the Easton manager, Frank "Home Run" Baker (from Talbot County, he had been American League batting leader in the prewar years), discovered the later famous Jimmy Foxx, son of a Sudlersville farmer. No doubt Baker tested Foxx's reputation for powerful hitting and throwing; according to legend, he signed the lad where he stood, in a field with his mule and cultivator. Later, at age eighteen, Foxx went to the majors as a Philadelphia Athletic. D'Arcy "Jake" Flowers, a Washington College star, played for the Cambridge Canners before signing with the St. Louis Cardinals in 1923. A Wicomico County native and a St. John's College player, Richard Twilley Porter ("Twitchey Twilley" at the plate), left his Annapolis team in 1921 for the Baltimore Orioles, then champions of the International League, a franchise owned and managed by Jack Dunn. Dunn had faced tough business decisions before the war. Owner of the old field at 29th and Greenmount, he had seen a major league competitor, the Baltimore Terrapins of the Federal League, build a rival baseball park at the northwest corner of the same intersection. Despite the remarkable success of Dunn's Orioles in the International League, Baltimoreans flocked to see the Terps. Fearing bankruptcy, Dunn in 1914 had sold his best players to major league teams.[35]

Baltimoreans in the 1920s knew all too well that among the players Dunn had been forced to sell was a left-handed pitcher, George Herman Ruth, Jr., who had been born near the B&O yards at 216 Emory Street and grown up over his father's saloon on West Camden. In that tough neighborhood Ruth had fallen in with bad company; at age seven he chewed tobacco, used language that shocked his mother, and neglected his books. Several times he landed at the St. Mary's Industrial School, a home on the western edge of the city for some eight hundred orphaned or unruly boys. Ruth turned out to be a tall, skinny, and strong fellow in his youth. He played catcher on the St. Mary's varsity team until one day he laughed too hard at his battery mate's frustration. Brother Matthias put him on the mound, where he dominated schoolboy batters and also caught Dunn's eye. With a court order making him the boy's guardian, Dunn signed Ruth to a $600 a year contract in 1914. At the minor league training camp that year Ruth pitched exhibition games against both World Series teams of the preceding season and to the amazement of onlookers struck out the most feared hitters in the major leagues—including "Home Run" Baker. Sportswriters wrote of his skills under headlines borrowed from the title of a current musical hit in New York, *Along Came Ruth*. Back in Baltimore, Ruth's pitching helped the Orioles to a commanding lead over second-place Rochester, and his confidence brimmed—he bought a red motorcycle and rode too fast on city streets. But only for a brief time. Sold to the Boston Red Sox for $6,900, Ruth played a large part in that club's later successes and in 1920 was sold for far more money to the New York Yankees. He led the American League in home runs for all but two of the next eleven years, until Jimmy Foxx overtook him. Baltimoreans could not read the papers without learning of that favorite son's spectacular career in a rival city.

The 1920s edition of Dunn's Orioles did their fans proud, but baseball lovers in Baltimore always qualified their support of a minor league team. After the war and his painful experiences in the baseball business, Dunn led a successful minor league revolt against the draft agreement that forced promising players into the majors for $7,500 or less. "I'll give Baltimore a major league team, even though it operates in the International League," he promised. "Nobody is drafting my players, and I'm not selling." Dunn largely kept his word, and his club had a heavily Maryland cast. The first baseman and frequent pitcher, Jack Bentley, had been born to a Quaker family in Sandy Spring. Max Bishop, though a Waynesboro, Pennsylvania, native, graduated from Baltimore City College. The third baseman, Fritz Maisel, was from Catonsville; later a stockholder in the club and Dunn's successor as manager, Maisel went on to serve as a Baltimore County fire chief. Dunn's son, who had played at City College and occasionally took the field, claimed credit for signing the star of the team, Bob "Lefty" Grove, who reported from Lonaconing. Grove joined the team in the middle of the 1920 pennant race with Toronto and quickly won twelve of fourteen games, striking out 88 batters in 123 innings. That season, as the year before and for the next five years, Baltimore won the International League pennant. Their margins of victory, scant in 1920 and only four games in 1925, generally were so wide that Dunn worried about keeping up fan interest. As if with that thought in mind, the Orioles only broke even in post-season "Junior World Series" play. But as Dunn slowly sold off his stars to the majors, new and younger players unfailingly met the challenge.[36]

Two Maryland baseball greats. *Left*, Babe Ruth at old Oriole Park, c. 1930. *Babe Ruth Birthplace/Baltimore Orioles Museum*. *Right*, Lefty Grove in his prime, c. 1930. *Ruth Bear Levy*

The vagaries of Maryland law and the enterprise of Elkton made the Cecil County Courthouse home to another sport, sudden marriage. With no required waiting period before nuptials and excellent rail and highway connections with New York, Philadelphia, and Wilmington, Elkton became, by its own modest admission, the Marriage Capital of the East. No-questions-asked weddings became a major source of local income in the twenties. Taxi-cab or jitney companies offered couples package deals—transportation from the rail station to the court, chapel, hotel, and back to the station—for twenty-five dollars. As competition grew fierce, sharp cabbies (they supposedly could spot love-struck couples through the windows of rail cars) included a wedding ring for the same low price. Hackers worked closely with court clerks and clergymen, who made their own share from the trade. The marriage mogul in Elkton must have been the Reverend W. R. Moon, a Baptist minister who performed ceremonies in the front room of his home. On Moon's upright piano an assistant played romantic melodies and wedding standards like "Always" and "Oh Promise Me." Preferring to be called Brother Moon, he once explained that he entered the quick-marriage business because he heard "the call of a community voice." One year, answering that call, he wedded four thousand couples.[37]

Elkton made money by catering to impulse, but the times became known for unprecedented impulse. The twenties made a mockery of moral planning. Religious leaders, among others, had hoped to brake the speed of change. Cardinal Gibbons in 1908 had forbidden Catholics at diocesan social events to dance the new steps that had revelers bending over in immodest positions. The Lord's Day Alliance clamored for and got Baltimore "blue laws" that closed all business establishments and cut out baseball on Sundays. Besides local option on liquor, opponents of moral breakdown in 1916 had obtained a state board of censors to preview the new moving pictures and excise, ban, or approve them.

Outlawing drink and banning dances simply highlighted their attractions; after the Armistice a spirit of license shocked the people who had hoped to curb it. Crime statistics in fact showed no rise, but on the level of dress, habits, and language trends broke away from experience. Young men of the fashionable set used the motorcar to attempt liberties their fathers never (or merely) dreamed about. Slang expressions among the young became deliberately startling passwords to a culture open only to the rebellious. Dance fads made the object of the cardinal's earlier concern look decorous by comparison. Moral conservatives and moderates alike took the behavior of women as a litmus test, for the well-bred Maryland woman traditionally had been a source of masculine pride. Yet young women, expanding on the freedom they or their sisters had enjoyed during the war, wore their hair bobbed, plucked their eyebrows, and, if they wished, smoked in public. Many of them no longer cared what mother, auntie, or the neighbors thought about such things. Hems of women's skirts went up above the knees. In Baltimore multiple sources of immorality came together when a young woman and some friends got drunk and drove their car into the basin.

Without state Prohibition enforcement, Maryland with reason claimed to be the wettest state in the Union. Except perhaps for rivals along the Canadian or Mexican borders, nobody had easier access to the wet world than Marylanders. A few boats offloaded liquor from the sea at Ocean City. The bay, always a smuggler's delight, soon resumed its role in illegal traffic; the Eastern Shore may have adopted local-option temperance early on, but watermen knew how to make fast money. Ships loaded with Cuban rum or German beer made nighttime deliveries on their journey up the bay. When vessels arrived, Baltimoreans could take a launch out to visit foreign friends for a party. The improved Maryland road system became an advantage to wets, who could make easy runs to sources in southern Pennsylvania, Western Maryland, or Southern Maryland. A new highway from Baltimore to Charles County (the Crain Highway, first road built on a new bed since the colonial period) became known as bootlegger's boulevard.[38]

But many consumers could avoid long travel. Baltimoreans were blessed with one of the most abundant sources of alcohol in the country—the United States Industrial Alcohol Corporation at Curtis Bay. Each year producing millions of gallons of a 185-proof fluid, it became a fountain of illegal, industrial-strength booze. A gallon of the USIA product—available in the Baltimore dealers' stronghold, a neighborhood near the Shot Tower—sold for $3.00.

Dressing up and kidding around in the 1920s. *MHS*

Cut with about a gallon of water, flavored with a few drops of glycerine, bottled and rolled on the floor to mix it, and then aged for about half an hour, it made drinkable gin. Federal agents struggled bravely to stem the flow. On one occasion they arrested six enterprising Baltimoreans who had diverted a railroad car—eight thousand gallons—from USIA for their own purpose. Agents found the car at President Street Station, carefully labeled "Olive Oil." Many people brewed beer at home, using malt and hops that stores sold openly. Basement explosions were commonplace before amateurs got the knack. Marylanders passed around recipes, and eventually the alcoholic content of these home brews reached 7 percent. Putting a raisin in the bottle before capping raised potency but also the danger of explosion. Truly serious "booties" used potato peelings, sugar, and other fermentables to make distilled alcohol. A lethal local liquor appeared under the name "Ryeola," which sold discreetly at the Cross Street Market for $1.50 a pint. Other entrepreneurs had counterfeiters manufacture brand labels or wrapped bottles of "Scotch" in old copies of British newspapers.

Baltimore stayed so wet that the saying went if a man deserved a drink, he could get one. The city never quite developed the barricaded speak-easies of other Prohibition cities. Restaurant owners flashed a red crab to signify wet-

"Farmers" violating prohibition, 1930. *A. Aubrey Bodine Collection, Peale Museum, Baltimore City Life Museums*

ness. Others, serving meals in front rooms and providing a bar in the back, winkingly advertised "Sea Food." A woman later remembered as the "beautiful blond bootlegger" ran a popular drinking retreat on Cathedral Street. Prominent citizens were known to meet at Johnny Butta's Fiorella Club in East Baltimore. A man rightly named Braumeister opened a connoisseur's beer hall on Gay Street. Even proprietors of small wet establishments might pocket as much as one thousand dollars a month, but they complained of high expenses. Landlords doubled or tripled their rent (payable in advance) as a price for silence. City police might have been idle because indifferent or because bought off. Fire inspectors had to be taken care of. Wets also claimed they made payoffs to federal agents. The "feds" did arrest the owner of a West Baltimore cafe after he aired a radio commercial boasting of "good food and everything that goes with it."

The *Evening Sun* and Baltimore wets believed themselves penalized for being city folk. Recalling the rural pattern of earlier, local-option temperance in Maryland, they noted that the Volstead Act ironically permitted farmers to make wine and cider—supposedly not exceeding .5 percent alcohol. Even city slickers knew that time turned sweet cider into hard. To publicize the unequal effect of the statute, John Philip Hill, a Baltimore lawyer who had reached the rank of colonel in the war and won election to Congress, renamed his West Franklin Street house Franklin Farms. After painting a cow on his backyard fence, he planted some apple saplings and a grape vine, hung fruit from the fence, and invited the press to keep the public posted on his attempt to make wine and cider. As he did and its alcohol level rose, Hill sent reports to the federal Prohibition commissioner. When the brew reached a rating of 6.3 percent the commissioner, lacking a sense of humor, had Hill arrested. His trial in the fall of 1924 received all the publicity he expected. A jury in U.S. District Court tasted (but apparently did not drink) his vintage, which by then had reached a 12 percent alcohol content, and found that it was "not intoxicating in fact." West Baltimore returned Hill to Washington by a landslide, and afterward any candidate in Maryland claiming to be against Prohibition had to show that he was as wet as John Philip Hill.[39]

∽✖∾

"Old West" Baltimore became the black capital of Maryland—its density owing to de facto segregation and the cohesiveness of Baltimore's Negro community. Courts had struck down city housing-segregation ordinances, but covenants produced unmistakable racial divisions. By the 1920s whites generally had fled the near-northwestern streets for all-white blocks farther north and west. As this change took place, blacks with money bought the old townhouses on Madison, McCulloh, Druid Hill, and nearby avenues. Before long virtually all Negro physicians, dentists, pharmacists, salesmen, and merchants lived in the neighborhood, and others followed, many of them newcomers attracted from the Eastern Shore or the South during the world war.[40]

Black institutions, as always, stood like piers and jetties in the fluid community. St. Peter Claver, established by Cardinal Gibbons at Fremont and Bloom in 1888, welcomed black Catholics. Other churches, some of them fleeing the heart of the city as had white congregations before them, sprung up in Old West. The Sharp Street Methodist Church, collecting small amounts for many years, finally purchased a new building at Dolphin and Etting. It had classrooms, a gallery that seated five hundred persons, electricity, and steam heat. On Druid Hill Avenue there was a Negro YMCA. Prominent black professionals belonged to the nation's second-oldest chapter of the NAACP. On side streets one found black-studies and black-rights organizations—a DuBois Circle, named for the militant black scholar, and a chapter of Marcus Garvey's Universal Negro Improvement Association. The *Afro-American* addressed a national readership from Old West. W. Llewellyn Wilson, who in the *Afro* advertised giving keyboard and musical theory classes, organized a Negro symphony orchestra. Black leaders made Primary School number 103 on Division Street a source of neighborhood pride. In 1927 Frederick Douglass High School, in more than one way a monument to black political clout, opened at Carey and Baker streets. Richmond Market lay within walking distance; the Druid Hill streetcars ran downtown. Broad streets, trees, and wide sidewalks lent Old West an air of community contentment.

That picture was not complete, however, without Pennsylvania Avenue. Middle-class blacks, like proper whites, had plenty of immorality to worry about. Together with insurance offices and real estate agencies, the avenue had hotels, clubs, burlesque houses, and theaters. Strollers in their finest traditionally took to the wide walks of the avenue on Sundays. On Saturday nights, below Dolphin Street, prostitutes walked Pennsylvania and the innocent risked violent crime. People went out anyway. Blacks from other parts of Baltimore, the state, and even Virginia and North Carolina found the sparkling nightlife of the Pennsylvania Avenue "Strip" a social mecca. They visited the Regent Theater, which won renown for its chorus lines, huge orchestra pit, and moving picture serials. Ike Dixon's Comedy Club, featuring nightly entertainment, provided Baltimore with its own Apollo (a Harlem landmark). Most famous of all was the Royal Theater, which a syndicate of blacks built in 1921–22. So eager were Old West citizens to see the theater to completion that many of them helped by paying a "dollar for a brick" as it went up. Finished, it set a standard for elegance—fancy interior and eight uniformed young women ushering patrons to their seats. The main attraction on Pennsylvania Avenue was a form of music that gave the period its name, the jazz age.

At first another example of modern depravity, jazz eventually provided an artistic middle ground between American whites and blacks. Its roots were in black music—in the blues that grew out of the Negro work experience, religious life, and culture of poverty; the piano music known as ragtime that emerged from the minstrel melodies and "cakewalk" dances of the nineteenth century; and the music of "Storyville," a section of the old French Quarter wherein New Orleans officials between 1897 and 1917 tried to restrict bawdy houses. There jazz evolved through years of nightly entertainment, bands of black musicians like Charles "Buddy" Bolden and Jellyroll Morton playing from about ten in the evening to nearly dawn, making the mournful blues and playful music of ragtime into a sound that almost forced one to dance, to cheer being alive, to enjoy the sensual. While ragtime held to fairly rigid formula, the music that observers began calling jazz (the word itself a synonym for sex) stressed freedom and above all improvisation.[41] When the police closed down Storyville, black musicians journeyed up the river and rode the railroads looking for places to play. The trick was to achieve respectability—the money suddenly was big.

James Hubert Blake, born in East Baltimore in 1883 to parents who had been slaves, illustrated one black musician's successful adaptation. Hubie or Eubie, as he came to be known, learned his father's lessons on the evils of hating and managed to survive the harsher lessons of the streets and alleys. He found music by accident. One evening while his mother shopped for groceries the young boy wandered into an organ shop. When she found the boy the storeowner had proclaimed him a genius, dared the church-loving woman to neglect a God-given talent—and sold the family a seventy-five-

Fats Waller drew a crowd at the Royal Theater, Pennsylvania Avenue, Baltimore, c. 1930. *Peale Museum, Baltimore City Life Museums*

dollar pipe organ on installments of twenty-five cents a week. Eubie learned black church and funeral music and soon took lessons that introduced him to the classics, but he later recalled that he "picked up ragtime by ear." "It just swung," he explained, "and made me feel good. It was my baby. Goodbye Beethoven." He did not know the word *ragtime* itself until he once added a quick beat and "wobble-wobble" bass to a practice number. His mother ordered him "Take that ragtime out of my house." At age fifteen he had unusually large hands and long fingers. He detested school; quite without his parents' knowledge, he got a job playing ragtime piano for tips in Aggie Shelton's bordello. He later played at Greenfeld's bar and bawdy house at the "Corner of Chestnut and Low"—he memorialized the place in song—and in the Goldfield Hotel, a handsome structure the boxer Joe Gans built with his championship winnings. Before the world war, with "Chevy Chase" and "Fizz Water," Blake became one of the first East Coast ragtimers to publish his songs.[42]

The 1920s were Blake's heyday. Several years before, playing an engagement at Riverview Park, he had met an Indiana-born singer and lyricist, Noble Sissle, whose talents with words matched Eubie's with music. In 1919 the pair joined the New York–based vaudeville circuit, singing and dancing as the Dixie Duo. Their real success came after they signed with the famous Witmark agency as songwriters. In 1921 Blake and Sissle composed a mu-

Eubie Blake (1883–1983) in a publicity photo for his second musical, *Chocolate Dandies*, 1924. *MHS/Eubie Blake Cultural Center*

sical supposedly depicting petty rivalries in a black community (also satirizing white politics), *Shuffle Along*, with new songs that delighted white audiences: "Bandana Days," "Love Will Find a Way," "I'm Just Wild about Harry," and a finale tune called "Baltimore Buzz." Cheered by critics, the show played for 504 performances on Broadway and grossed $8 million. Blake followed it with another hit musical, *The Chocolate Dandies*. Both these shows acted as cultural bridges. The music had the jump and vitality of black jazz; the characters and language labored to remain acceptable to a straight audience. Trying to break into vaudeville, Blake had received (and refused) offers to do "blackface" caricatures. Now he became a national and transatlantic celebrity. In the fall of 1925 he took a troupe to Europe and on his return to visit Baltimore granted *Sun* interviews like a statesman. He bought a lavish fur coat for his mother, assuring her that it cost a mere seventy-five dollars. Though she greeted him warmly after his tour abroad, she doubted the seemliness of jazz and show business. "He's doin' somethin' wrong," she said. "They goin' to *catch* him."[43]

Not only did the life-affirming, danceable sound of black musicians excite a growing white audience; it benefited from technological advances by which whites could listen to the partially cleansed music of "hookhouses" in their own homes. At first recordings were made by an acoustical process that only worked if musicians played loudly or shouted their songs into the recording horn. Even these primitive, mechanical recordings enlarged a musician's audience. Blake recalled an early Pennyslvania Avenue record dealer in Baltimore who pioneered in retailing them—he took a phonograph out on the sidewalk and played records that passersby stopped to hear and then came inside wanting to buy (fortunately for Blake in about 1920 he had joined the new artists' union, which won royalties for composers as their music went on piano rolls and records). After 1923 Edison's electric sound-recording system allowed musicians to make records with far greater fidelity and range of tone, and the recording industry grew rapidly in importance. Jazz artists could play as they wished, and records reproduced their music vividly. Capitalizing on these changes and playing the jazz clubs that became so popular were black musicians who had grown up in Storyville—King Oliver, Louis Armstrong, and Sidney Bechet—but also whites who loved the new medium and had a part in its popularity—Jack Teagarden and the New Orleans Rhythm Masters, the Original Dixieland Jazz Band, and the Original New Orleans Jazz Band (with Jimmy Durante and Rudy Vallee). In a few years crystal sets gave way to radios with speakers, radio stations formed networks, and jazz bands went on the air. Eubie Blake belonged to a generation of blacks who revolutionized American music.

Maybe Maryland, with its long history of urban, black-white closeness and border-state latitude, should have done more for the development of jazz. The Society for the Suppression of Vice, saving Baltimore from a full-fledged red-light district, indirectly suppressed jazz as well; the anti-prostitution act passed during the Crothers administration also had that effect. In 1919 a black bandsman, T. Henderson Kerr, had announced in the *Afro-American* that his events allowed "no jazz, no shaky music, no suggestive or vulgar dancing." Blake and Sissle took the cast of *Shuffle Along* to pre-Broadway performances at the Howard Theater in Washington and the Earl in Philadelphia—not to Baltimore. Even so, many black Baltimoreans took to the new musical form. A Grand Jazz Review, staged in the spring of 1925 at the New Albert Auditorium, headlined ten local jazz bands. Ike Dixon, Joe Rochester, Reggie Hamer, and Preston Duncan appeared often in the Pennsylvania Avenue show district. The Royal Theater, after being opened by the legendary Fats Waller, became one link in a chain of black-owned nightclubs that booked the same acts and artists. Over the years they included Chick Webb, Ella Fitzgerald, Ethel Waters, Earl "Fatha" Hines, and Pearl Bailey—who remembered rushing out to the street the first time she played the Royal to see her name on the brightly lit marquee. A Baltimorean, Joe Turner, played with Louis Armstrong's band. Cab Calloway, still a youngster in these years, remembered a "rough and raucous Baltimore Negro night life with loud music, heavy drinking and the kind of moral standards or lack of them that my parents looked down on."[44]

Equated with sex, booze, even insanity, jazz underwent constant attack from the upright press and reformers. The *Atlantic Monthly* typically observed that "almost every race and every age have known social conditions which result in an unloosing of instincts that nature wisely has taught us to hold well in check, but which, every now and then, from cryptic reasons, are allowed to break the bonds of civilization"; critics pointed out that "Buddy" Bolden, the Storyville cornet player, had fallen victim to drink and syphilis.[45] Blake hardly filled the Bolden mold, but to some onlookers he, too, pushed beyond the bounds of propriety. After the success of *Shuffle Along,* he married the daughter of a wealthy Baltimore oyster-boat owner; later he did little to disguise his taking a mistress from the cast and providing her with rooms he often visited. Jazz carried more serious implications in that it brought conspicuous wealth to many black musicians and entertainers—cause for white jealousy. A meeting place for blacks and whites, the new musical idiom defied traditional barriers between the races.

Along with motorized, rum-running lawlessness, labor tensions, and various other unsettling developments, the permissiveness of jazz gave extremists ground to stand on. In the 1920s the Ku Klux Klan, a negligible factor in post–Civil War Maryland, claimed growing membership in the state. In Baltimore the klan used mailing lists to solicit what the local King Kleagle, H. P. Moorehead, described as "picked men." In 1922 fully robed klansmen held marches in Frederick and Baltimore, and in the fall twenty-five hundred of them descended on Church Circle in Annapolis for a rally supporting "Americanism." Klan activities led to a series of *Sun* articles late in 1923, John Owens wondering if the power of the klan in Maryland might influence the election that year. No one had any firm guess as to the strength of the secret society—estimates of members on the Shore ranged from five hundred to fifteen thousand. Owens's interviews led him to conclude, persuasively, that recruits on the Shore were often farmers and oystermen and in the cities men who enjoyed controversy; most members struck him as "perfectly good, kindly people, generally without anything to occupy their minds when they quit work, looking for novelties, attracted by the idea of something mysterious." When Ritchie won reelection, the Democratic candidate for attorney general, Thomas H. Robinson, got more votes than the wet governor. Since white-sheeted drys loathed Ritchie, they might have taken credit for the difference and any embarrassment it caused the governor, but they also mistrusted Catholics. The klan (its failure to do homework truly a mystery) had supported Robinson until just before the election, when it announced that it only then had learned of his Catholicism.[46]

In the Deep South the revived klan produced a new wave of lynchings. In Maryland klansmen apparently tried to imitate the Red Men or Odd Fellows. True, they dynamited an objectionable sawmill near Smithsburg in Washington County, caught and branded a black man (who had beaten his wife), and threatened black railroad workers during a strike at Brunswick. Newspapers in the 1920s reported cross burnings all over the state. Even so, the Maryland klan avoided wholesale violence and cloaked itself in brotherly and social purposes. Moorehead in fact defended its all-white membership by comparing the klan to the Masons (who he claimed admitted no Jews) and the all-Catholic Knights of Columbus. Klansmen collected money for charity and put on robes for members' funerals. At Havre de Grace they met to lay a cornerstone for a local church whose pastor bore the status of KKK lecturer. At a Hampden klan, den clergymen performed group baptisms. Some Maryland Germans seized on the klan to demonstrate their patriotism; one loyal member had his daughter christened Katerine Karlotta Knickman.

The typically clannish qualities of the klan became apparent in the summer of 1925, when Maryland members held a series of gala rallies. In June, outside Baltimore, a reported ten thousand of them gathered to hear the Ladies Aluminum Band play star-spangled music, listen to vigorous speeches, and watch a sky-writing pilot draw "KKK" among the clouds. At Hyattsville next month and then in Baltimore for an August parade, the KKK sweated in its effort to appear powerful. Maryland leaders had none of it. State courts denied it tax-exempt status. Ritchie twice turned down its request to use the Fifth Regiment Armory, just as General Reckord, National Guard commander, kept the klan out of the armory at Westminster. Baltimore passed an ordinance requiring marchers to show their faces.

Somewhat like Maryland Democrats and jazz musicians, American writers in the 1920s searched for tenable ground in the new age. Many of them answered the wholesale destruction of the Great War, moneymaking for its sake alone, and the shabbiness of American culture by protesting. Hemingway stayed in Europe and played the hero disdainful of mortality and mere money; Sinclair Lewis wrote sarcastic novels about boosting businessmen and shallow convention. Beginning in the twenties, Samuel Dashiell Hammett, who was born in St. Mary's County, and James M. Cain, who grew up in Annapolis and Chestertown, helped to develop a new fiction that seemed not to challenge the principle of rugged individualism at all, but to make the most of it. Both of them became masters of the mystery story, writing books that at once shocked and entertained readers—and sold briskly—while raising the tough loner of American mythology to new levels in the popular imagination.

While in the early twenties Cain and Hammett had not yet met, they shared, besides their Maryland backgrounds, a youthful history of odd jobs quickly tired of, experience on newspapers, army service in the World War, and trouble with tuberculosis. Cain, who wrote first for the Baltimore *American* and then the *Sun*, considered himself a reporter who dabbled in story-telling. Hammett, whose first long-term job came as a Pinkerton operative or detective in the Baltimore office, began writing because he so enjoyed his work. His earliest story appeared in the fall of 1922 (after he had left for the West Coast), a marvel of just one paragraph: a wife and mother whose annoying child reminds her of her tormenting husband gives the boy a bath and then coolly boards a train for the west. "I know an operative," Hammett wrote next year in a series of laconic recollections, "who while looking for pickpockets at the Havre de Grace racetrack had his wallet stolen. He later became an official in an Eastern detective agency." Cain during the twenties produced magazine articles cleverly depicting stock American characters and, after reporting on labor unrest in West Virginia, ridiculing both labor leaders and management.[47]

Both men delighted in raw experience, the uncut language of the streets; they wrote of hard-boiled heroes utterly without illusion, with keen eyes and "the polite detached air of a disinterested spectator." They told of social cast-offs who included drifters, thieves, and murderers. Their most famous books eventually provided film makers with highly successful, action-filled scripts. Still, their work reached beyond the blood and prurience that became the earmarks of pulp fiction. Against the polite grain, their writing nonetheless succeeded not for its violence or sexual scenery, but for its psychological tension, chacterization, and unexpected turns. In Cain's first short story he wrote of a desperate adulterer who arranges to have his lover's husband murdered, whose treacherous accomplice by sheer chance dies himself the night of the killing, but who, always a braggart, finally winks to his pool-room cronies at the wrong moment and gives himself away. In a story published in October 1923, Hammett's Joe Shupe has a bank robber's loot thrown at his feet when police shoot the fugitive. Excitedly Shupe picks up the green bag and makes good his escape—only to find that he is too frightened and the sum too large to do anything with it. Banking it means certain capture. Leaving it in his room or even walking the streets with it carries the awful risk of losing it. The men who might be able to help him cannot be trusted with a quarter-million-dollar secret. His apparent good fortune only paralyzes and isolates him; he may have been rich and untraceable in Hammett's ironic description, but "the temptations of women and cards and the rest did not bother him now." Shupe finally discovers peace of mind and returns to his normal self when police accidentally catch and jail him.[48]

Although comparatively few readers in these years knew of Sophie Kerr, the work of this Marylander offered down-home examples of the restlessness more gifted writers took to more enduring art. Kerr grew up in Denton and studied at Hood College. In the twenties, married then divorced, she served as managing editor of *Woman's Home Companion* and wrote some fiction of her own. Her first novel, *One Thing Is Certain* (1922), told of a young woman named Louellen who lives in a place Kerr named Eden and drew along the lines of Denton. In Kerr's story Louellen, though in love with a dashing if slightly irresponsible fellow, bows to parental and community pressure and marries instead a more "acceptable" suitor—a church deacon who turns out to be unbending, boring, and cruel. In a variation of Hawthorne's *Scarlet Letter*, Louellen has an adulterous affair with the man she truly loves, and the people of hard-shell Christian "Eden" make life miserable for her. In *Mareea-Maria* (1929), a good Methodist farm lad—Kerr called him Wesley Dean—falls in love with and marries an Italian-Catholic canning worker. The gossip mill turns. Rowdies stage a mock-serenade, a shivaree, but Mareea's brickbats turn them back. One night Wesley's mother espies the couple dancing. "'Wes', her only son," she thinks, "brought up in certainty that light feet lead only to perdition. . . . And even as she looked the dance stopped and the dancers flung themselves into each other's arms, a caress spontaneous, naïve, tender, supremely forgetful. Allie Dean had never seen or known such love. It seemed to her utterly abandoned, shameless, vile. She drew away from the peep-hole, her errand forgotten." [49]

For Americans who read books or much of anything else in the twenties, F. Scott Fitzgerald above all gave the period its literary voice. *This Side of Paradise* (1920), *The Beautiful and Damned* (1922), *The Great Gatsby* (1925), and various magazine stories of young rebels with flashy cars and loose morals were all the rage. Fitzgerald became, in fact, much more than a popular author. He and Zelda, his Alabama-born wife of many quirks, came to represent license itself. They protested convention by living life to excess, so that their long visits to France and boozy, open-ended parties on the slightest pretext imitated Scott's art. The couple spent money before they had it. Fitzgerald could not stay in any one place very long without growing depressed and restless. Zelda frightened friends with death-defying joy rides on dangerous roads overlooking the Riviera. Living and telling tales of the jazz age, searching for form that fit modern experience, Fitzgerald in his writing developed a technique of undertone and main story line that bore similarities to the ragtime music he loved.

Fitzgerald took his full name, Francis Scott Key, from an illustrious Maryland background. Zelda's family, for that matter, traced its lineage to a Maryland woman who had married a Kentuckian in the antebellum period; Zelda counted Hansons, Briscoes, Coodes, and Cresaps among her forebears. Scott, from his father's stories and even his loving and supportive character itself, imbibed deeply of his Maryland heritage. Edward Fitzgerald was descended of Philip Barton Key's daughter Eliza and had grown up at Glenmary Farm near Rockville. A youthful Confederate sympathizer who aided spies and guerrillas during the Civil War, Edward afterward had tried and failed, though honorably, at several business undertakings and finally had taken the family to his wife's home among the McQuillans in St. Paul. There his ill fortune and Southern pedigree helped to leave him feeling especially alien—the self-made McQuillan men had flourished along with Minnesota flour milling in the late nineteenth century. Scott thus grew up in a home divided between the romantic past—the "reticences and obligations" of breeding that belonged to Edward Fitzgerald—and the hard-nosed business practicality of his mother's middle western family.[50]

Fitzgerald's work had more than Maryland influences, but he admitted his sense of roots. An early short story raked the ashes of Lincoln's assassination (Edward had a cousin who married a Surratt), and at the height of his fame he wrote a fond preface to Don Swann's book of etchings depicting Maryland historic homes. In his forties, then in Baltimore seeking treatment for Zelda, he took a room near Mount Vernon Place and wrote how nice it was "to look up the street and see the statue of my great uncle and to know Poe is buried here and that many ancestors of mine have walked in the old town by the bay. I belong here," he concluded, "where everything is civilized and gay and rotted and polite." Indeed, his work reflected the ambivalence that had so much to do with the history of his father's home state. Fitzgerald wrote of men and women of money, but their wealth without ethics finally brought hollow rewards, the illusion of good, sudden death.[51]

Fitzgerald had a peer in the realm of nonfiction, a writer who again illustrated the directional issues of American life in the 1920s. Governor Ritchie, drawing on old states' rights ideas, stood for limits on the growing powers of the federal government; Eubie Blake and others sought acceptance of new music that loosened old constraints. Henry Louis Mencken took on the whole modern world where it strayed from moderation, toleration, and common sense. His background was German-American West Baltimore—a grandfather had arrived with the post-1848 wave of immigrants—and, thanks to his father's cigar business, middle-class respectability. He recalled Baltimore in the 1880s as a smelly, charming city where in the summer grass overtook cobblestone streets, foods were incomparably tasty and various, and people "were complacent beyond the ordinary." The boy attended a private school whose master, Friedrich Knapp, brooked no nonsense. When not in school Mencken and his friends taunted the Irish cops in the Hollins Market–Union Square neighborhood, stole stray peaches from the corner grocer, and held long, philosophical talks with the blacks who lived in the alleys (one of them convincingly denied the existence of hell on legal grounds—"Was a chicken thief in Calvert County jailed in Baltimore?"). Mencken's favorite Christmas gift was a toy printing press, and he loved to read, though he claimed to have been born with an aversion for fairy tales and such; he read and reread *Huckleberry Finn*. As a boy he "acquired round shoulders, spindly shanks, and a despondent view of humanity." The young man graduated from Poly in 1896 and dutifully tried clerking at his father's cigar factory. He entered newspaper work the Monday after the elder Mencken died.[52]

First a reporter who looked into banalities like missing horses, then covering the police and city hall beats, Mencken took his education from earthy experience and from the books his nose led him to. He attended countless Democratic ward meetings; he specialized in pithy accounts of public hangings. After he assumed theater and music reviewing in addition to other duties, he enjoyed receiving the press agents who preceded theatrical companies with ready-to-print rave notices—men like Punch Wheeler, wearing checkered suit, loud vest, and a diamond stickpin, and the Dane with an awesome appetite, A. Toxen Worm. To relieve boredom, Mencken once took a motley collection of unemployed Italian musicians and billed them in the Baltimore *Herald* as "the Royal Palace Band and Drum Corps of Madrid," a ruse that caused a musical sensation and went undiscovered in the *Sun*.

Mencken might have continued such sport indefinitely; instead, besides writing syndicated features, he gave himself a somewhat liberal education. He read Voltaire, taught himself Darwin through Huxley and sociology by way of the pioneering student of folk habits, William Graham Sumner; he got to know the hard realism of Theodore Dreiser and the incisive character studies in Joseph Conrad's new fiction. He steeped himself in the irreverent George Bernard Shaw—whose work became the subject of a short book Mencken published in 1905. Another volume, this one on Friedrich Nietzsche's philosophy, appeared in 1908. That year Mencken's growing reputation for hard-hitting reviews won him a job as literary editor of a small, struggling New York magazine, the *Smart Set*, which called itself "a magazine of cleverness" and aimed at an avant-garde readership. After 1914 he and George Jean Nathan, another Young Turk, co-edited the magazine, Nathan supervising the New York office, Mencken working at home on Hollins Street and traveling to Manhattan once a month or so to plan future issues. Meantime Mencken wrote a regular column for the *Evening Sun*, "The Free Lance," which became the one part of the paper no Marylander wished to miss. A trip to Europe in 1912 completed Mencken's education and confirmed his attachment to Old World art, literature, and music. Utterly impatient with American provincialism, he scoffed at the prevailing view that all honor and virtue lay with the Allies. More and more he felt the outsider. When in 1917 Mencken published *A Book of Prefaces*, collecting some of his criticism, the Illinois professor Stuart P. Sherman dismissed it because Mencken's German name invited suspicion. Withdrawing from the prowar *Sun* staff, Mencken spent 1917–18 writing a monumental study of the American language.

After the war Mencken's mixed reputation reached its zenith. His book on language, demonstrating how imaginatively Americans in their own environment had met "linguistic emergencies," won deserved academic praise and yet managed to read as light-heartedly and personally as Dr. Johnson's dictionary. Discussing the American preference for the flat rather than broad *a* (as in "hurray" for "hurrah"), Mencken wrote that "To the average American, indeed, the broad *a* is a banner of affectation, and he associates it unpleasantly with spats, Harvard, male tea-drinking, wrist watches and all the other objects of his social suspicion."[53] Always efficient, Mencken assembled and redrafted "Free Lance" and *Smart Set* pieces and published them in 1919. He frankly entitled the book *Prejudices*. College students and postwar bohemians read these scathing essays with delight, as they did the *American Mercury*, a new magazine that Mencken's publisher, Alfred A. Knopf, asked him to undertake in 1924. Again an editorial writer for the *Sun*, Mencken managed also to publish a second, then third, and finally six volumes of *Prejudices* in the twenties. He wrote a book examining the topic of democracy itself in 1926 and in 1930 unabashedly produced a book about religion, *Treatise on the Gods*.

As a literary critic Mencken took a leaf from the university he never attended. In the early days of Hopkins, Gilman had established a grove where he encouraged scholars to follow truth wherever it led. Mencken placed a similar burden on the shoulders of modern writers and artists—with Darwin's bust once again on display. Before the biologist's research work, Mencken wrote in his book on Shaw, the sacredness or respectability of an idea had been enough to defend it; "since 1859 it has been necessary to prove its truth." To Mencken, Shaw's attraction lay in the irreverence, the iconoclasm, of his plays. In words that might as well have applied to himself, he said that Shaw practiced "with great zest and skill the fine art of exhibiting the obvious in unexpected and terrifying lights." Mencken praised the plays of Henrik Ibsen, the Norwegian modernist, because they helped one see the "crushing heritage of formalism and tradition, in art as well as in living." Nietzsche, whom Mencken did not fully understand, carried appeal because he seemed to agree with Mencken's own experienced view that conflict and selfishness rested at the bottom of human nature; detesting weakness and sentimentality, Mencken relied on Nietzsche for the hardened view that only self-mastery, self-discipline without illusion, offered the chance of freedom, and that those who achieved this level of awareness still faced a struggle with the inert, sheepish mass of mankind. It was fitting that Mencken savored struggle, for American cultural leaders subscribed to a different view of the artist. Professor Sherman, Mencken's vocal opponent during and after the war, summarized it when he declared that the duty of an American writer as he told a story was to "slip a spiritual goldpiece into the palm of each of his fellow countrymen."[54]

Mencken attacked the "moral uplift" consensus in American letters, the academic complacency that cheered it, and its assumptions of Anglo-Saxon superiority with all the energy Darwin had applied to his research or Shaw taken to unmasking silly social convention. Mencken accused William Dean Howells, a grandmaster of American fiction, of having caved in to "Boston notions of what is nice." Henry James, the American novelist living in London, Mencken wrote of as too English and limpid; he needed a whiff or two

Cover from the *Smart Set*, June 1922. A vignette of the jazz age: Mencken edits, Fitzgerald contributes, the new music titillates, and a friendly Satan looks approvingly on the scene, which a magazine artist colored in a lilac wash accented by devilish red. *McGregor Library, University of Virginia*

of the Chicago stockyards. When the guardians of acceptable literature—the "Genteel Tradition"—returned Mencken's fire, he ridiculed their pomposity. Meanwhile the *Smart Set*—the only "rebel" magazine that had no outside financial backing, that relied on a readership to survive—published pathbreaking American writers like Fitzgerald, Eugene O'Neill, and James Branch Cabell (along with Dashiell Hammett), and promising foreigners who included James Joyce and Somerset Maugham. Great literature, wrote Mencken in the second series of *Prejudices* in 1920, chiefly emerges from "doubting and inquiring minds in revolt against the immoveable certainties of the nation." He saw himself as a critic without debts or pretense, one of the few observers of the American scene who used plain words and refused to mince them. For a time he did fill that role and, a self-taught student, exercised pivotal influence on American writing. "My business, considering the state of society in which I find myself," he wrote in the last issue of the *Smart Set* in December 1923, "has been principally to clear the ground of mouldering rubbish, to chase away old ghosts, to help set the artist free."[55]

Particularly after launching of the *American Mercury*, Mencken turned from literature to American politics and culture generally—assaulting moral certainty wherever he located it, deriding shallowness and ignorance as its boon companions. Bitter at the treatment of Germans during the war, shocked at the quasi-legal harassment of "Reds" immediately after, he found the attorney general guilty of "a conspiracy against justice, and what is more, against common honesty and common decency." At a time when the federal courts decided against every attempt of laboring men and women to organize and granted injunctions to break strikes, Mencken in 1921 bemoaned "mill owners eager to get rid of annoying labor leaders, coal operators bent on making slaves of their miners." Our "Capitalistic masters," he concluded, not only control the government but put "maintenance of the status quo above everything else." Nowhere else in the world, he said, siding in fact more with Sinclair Lewis than the Reds, "is there such elaborate machinery for inoculating the proletariat with safe ideas." He scored the American Legion and Ku Klux Klan for their intolerance. He laughed at the automatic optimism, standard politeness, and milky platitudes of business and civic organizations.[56]

The Baltimore sage made no bones about what he saw as the root cause for so much American darkness. Never religious himself, having grown up in a home where metaphysical questions never surfaced as discussable matters, Mencken criticized a dominant strain in American life, evangelical Protestantism—especially its doctrine of interpreting scripture literally and its threats of hellfire and damnation to deviants. In the summer of 1925 the Sunpapers sent him as a special correspondent to cover one of the great dramas of the period, the Scopes trial in Dayton, Tennessee. Scopes, a teacher, had been charged with violating a state law prescribing the biblical account of creation in public schools. Mencken's reports, perhaps containing the sharpest attacks any American had made on rural religion and its values, reveled in the richness of the material—the "yahoos" and "boobs" who crowded around the courthouse; the prosecutor's imported witness, three-time presidential candidate William Jennings Bryan, a Nebraska fundamentalist; and Scopes's defense attorney, Clarence Darrow. Darrow wore wide fireman's suspenders that he gripped as he spoke. He nearly went to jail for contempt during one long argument that vaguely slighted the dignity of the presiding country judge. (The judge broke in, hoping Darrow meant no offense to the court. Darrow paused a moment, in Mencken's account, snapped his suspenders, and replied, "Your honor is at least entitled to hope.") A traveling showman and atheist landed in the Dayton jail for passing out handbills arguing that his monkey proved the similarity between man and the lower primates (he charged ten cents a look). Another innocent briefly went to jail because of a Mencken prank. The *Sun* reporter told people at a prayer meeting that a Bolshevik was arriving on the next train from Cincinnati. When it rolled into town, police arrested the only passenger to alight, a YMCA representative.[57]

Mencken rushed in where angels feared to tread—he embroiled himself in the cultural issues that caused so much public conflict in the twenties. He irreverently spoke of Prohibition as the "dry millennium" and attacked it with both comic and serious eloquence that probably no one equaled. While Ritchie told presidents that the Volstead Act infringed on local liberty, Mencken wrote that citizens above all should resist it as an affront to personal liberty—as another example of puritan fundamentalism on the march and of the unfair power of rural people over urbanites. "Such laws deserve no respect," he said, "and deserving no respect, they deserve no obedience." His appeal did not make the Menckenites, as enemies called them, anarchists so much as believers in a civil order based on social peace and tolerance. Prohibition upset peace; it "puts a premium on the lowest sort of spying," Mencken charged, "affords an easy livelihood to hordes of professional scoundrels, subjects thousands of decent men to the worst sort of blackmail, violates the theoretical sanctity of domicile, and makes for bitter and relentless enemies." He called Billy Sunday, the evangelical leader who led the dry movement, a "bumper of the boobery," a "pulpit clown" who appealed to the witch-hunting instincts of ignorant people. Mencken's reading of Nietzsche, his city-bred tastes, and intuitive psychology came together in a scathing analysis of the typical puritan. He "delights in persecution for its own sake," Mencken said, and reads with prurient glee every account of a federal agent being murdered, police searching a woman's underwear for liquor, or officials raiding a yacht. Mencken's actions spoke as loudly as his words. In 1926, when Boston authorities banned the April issue of the *Mercury* as obscene (a story entitled "Hatrack" had toasted a bony prostitute), he went there, sold copies, and stood trial. The jury acquitted him.[58]

Ignorance and intolerance always needed the pinprick of independent criticism, Mencken taught, but in modern life so did pretension and specious expertise. Though he and the *Mercury* were friendly to interesting developments in the hard sciences, Mencken registered a reaction to the scholarly-Progressive consensus that had formed in the early years of the century. Academics, so self-satisfied (and condescending toward him), he bore down upon with a vengeance. Thorstein Veblen got himself "enmeshed in his gnarled sentences like a bull trapped by barbed wire." The average professor, Mencken wrote elsewhere, "must be an obscurantist or he is nothing; he has a special and unmatchable talent for dullness" and his object is not to show the truth clearly but to prove his profundity. Pedagogues dominated publishing, he complained, penetrated government, sat on every municipal commission. During the war academics had formed a semi-official commission that supported the Wilson administration; instead of being courageous spokesmen for free ideas, they yielded, Mencken said with justification, to "the prevailing correctness of thought in all departments, north, south, east, and west." More than failed independence was at issue, however. Academic specialization had led to bogus theory and the inflation of the obvious into the esoteric. While admitting the force of Sigmund Freud's view of conflict in human nature and of unwitting processes like scapegoating, Mencken doubted the near-mystical claims that had been made for psychoanalysis. Mencken placed psychology on a plane with guesswork and hocus-pocus. Sociology, a discipline Progressives cited often, he put down as "scarcely a science at all, but rather a monkeyshine which happens to pay."[59]

Mencken regarded most Progressives as pious hypocrites. They combined genteel traditions, moral uplift, and scientific arrogance. He had no quarrel with Johns Hopkins Hospital, the battle against tuberculosis, the Baltimore sewers, or the new Maryland road system. He did, however, miss few chances to lambaste "do-gooders." He drew "Mencken's Law" from his hard lessons as a young reporter: "Whenever A annoys or injures B on the pretense of saving or improving X, A is a scoundrel." He had no trouble with granting women the vote; they had natural understanding to be envied— and impatience with "quackery." But the professional suffragist he classed as a fanatic. Still unmarried, though by no means a libertine, Mencken in the twenties found efforts to eliminate postwar license, to solve the "sex problem," foolish. "No prostitute," he wrote with typical flourish, "was ever so costly to a community as a prowling and obscene vice crusader, or as the dubious legislator or prosecuting officer who jumps as he pipes." The "forward lookers" gave neither themselves nor their neighbors rest. Once the Progressive won the direct primary, said Mencken, he demanded the short ballot. "Give him the Mann Act, and he wants laws providing for the castration of fornicators. Give him Prohibition, and he launches a new crusade against cigarettes, coffee, jazz, and custard pies."[60]

These apparently scatter-gun forays won the sage from Baltimore an international reputation as a bulldog who snapped at everything. His clipping service kept him advised of the controversies he had stirred up. A London paper said that his conceit was his undoing. A Virginian wrote that "Mencken, discussing any subject, reminds one of a dog killing a snake." "It's a wonder decent people haven't risen up and lynched him," wrote an Oklahoma clergyman. At home there were people who were tempted. Dr. Kelly, the old Hopkins Progressive, risked lampooning the lampooner by suggesting that his "mendacious friend" place "a photo-spectroheliograph on his ramshackle, tergiversating cerebrum." Mencken's attacks on evangelical religion earned him the wrath of the Eastern Shore and Maryland

Henry Louis Mencken (1880–1956). *H. L. Mencken House, Baltimore City Life Museums*

clergymen in general. A letter to the St. Michaels *Comet* asked a pointed question: "God made man and every living creature. Darwin made an error. Darrow made a mistake. But who in H___ made Mencken?" He "does not live his art," wrote Julia Johnston in the Easton *Star-Democrat*, applying one measure: "It is for him only a political weapon." An angry *Sun* reader declared with less acumen that Mencken's writings reflected "the workings of a disordered intellect." The Reverend Noland R. Best, executive secretary of the Baltimore Federation of Churches, believed that if Mencken inadvertently told the truth he would be left crestfallen. "He reminds me of three things," wrote an angry subscriber to the *Evening Sun*; "cheap perfume, a headache, and the sound of an ice-wagon going over rough stones."[61]

Not everyone understood him. Eyebrows raised, cigar firmly between his teeth, Mencken suffered fools so ungladly that strangers kept their distance. In print his sharpness and satire could leave mistaken impressions. The

Easton newspaper published comments suspecting his loyalty, and fundamentalists liked to call him a bomb-throwing radical. In truth Mencken criticized a country he loved despite its warts and lapses. He refused to join the exodus of so many writers and critics who moved to Europe in these years; writing of their choice and his, he said in the third series of *Prejudices* that while the young intellectuals set sail he remained behind, on the dock, "contentedly and even smugly basking beneath the Stars and Stripes."[62]

"That he lives in Baltimore is to Baltimore's disgrace," wrote a cleric in *Gospel Call*. Actually many Baltimoreans found him plenty of fun, and he returned the favor. In the 1926 edition of *Prejudices* Mencken explained at length why he still refused to move to New York. Manhattan was a place for making money, he wrote, Baltimore a place to enjoy it. Baltimore had a "feeling for the hearth." People owned homes and stayed in Baltimore, where, "under a slow-moving and cautious social organization, touched by the Southern sun," friendships endured and life brought agreeable charms. Mencken occupied the same Hollins Street house he had grown up in, with his mother (until her death in 1925) and brother August. He enjoyed Union Square, visiting the Peabody Bookstore on North Charles Street, playing the piano at one of his favorite small restaurants, Schellhase's, and laughing with the lifetime cronies who made up the "Saturday Night Club" at the Rennert Hotel. A hypochondriac, he took curious pleasure in visiting the hospitalized. Though he usually felt uncomfortable at large parties, Mencken dedicated himself to politeness. He so loved music that he said he would rather have written the first movement of Beethoven's *Eroica* Symphony than the Song of Solomon.[63]

Another detractor, his letter published in the *Sun*, believed one of Mencken's chief purposes "to outrage the best traditions of this State." In truth Mencken honored and upheld the peculiar Maryland spirit perhaps even better than he realized. For one thing, standing between North and South, he criticized both sections as freely as Marylanders ever had. A colonial "slaughter-house of ideas," New England, said Mencken, had confused literacy with intelligence and advanced only so far as to become a "cold-storage plant." Virginia in the twenties had grown senile; the mother of George Mason, Jefferson, and Madison had "no mind or aspiration of her own," no energy to put toward large problems. In a famous essay entitled "The Sahara of the Bozart," Mencken described the South as the epicenter of ignorance and prejudice. "Down there a poet is now almost as rare as an oboe-player, a dry-point etcher or a metaphysician," he wrote with chilling truth. "There are single acres in Europe that house more first-rate men than all the states south of the Potomac."[64]

Mencken also expressed the dread many Marylanders had of the threats modern life brought with it—government made larger by war, loyalty testing, the deadening hand of conformity, the pall of factory smoke. He sought a course that preserved historic charm while greeting the advantages of science and sound economy; he worried that his state had broken all links with the bucolic past and forgotten its character. Maryland once had a "name for gaiety," he said in the *Nation*'s "Maryland" essay, once was "a state of mind." Now the "tightening of the screws goes on unbrokenly," he warned; "the end, I suppose, as everywhere in these States, will be a complete obliteration of distinction, a wiping out of all the old traditions, a massive triumph of regimentation."[65]

Mencken searched for a civilized temperament in a new age, an aesthetic of the middle. As a critic he had the daring to write a new role in American letters—to act as intermediary between literary aspiration and a general audience. He tried to bring good books and his readership together, and, by making his reviews rollicking and readable, to widen the literate public. Mencken argued that great literature reflected life rather than moralized about it. Avoiding mere sentimentality (the mark of the Genteel Tradition), American writers would err on the other side, he said, if they created characters who were simply at the mercy of social forces (a criticism he made of Dreiser). The admonition to regard sentiment, the full range of human strengths and weaknesses, and the individual's power to choose took something from each of the classic categories of romanticism and realism and placed Mencken between the two schools of American literature that prevailed when he wrote critical pieces. His worldly-but-humane sensibility drew upon the Maryland experience, which included memories or handed-down accounts of Civil War ambiguities. The human condition, as Marylanders well knew, had much to do with anguish and imperfection. In his own age Mencken made the argument, unpopular in many quarters, that men and women were not only imperfect but not perfectible, that human problems like sin had no real solution—none that government could work—and that at bottom human experience might be mysterious. He poised himself between science, like Darwin's, that produced new insights, and what he called "the inexplicable tragedy of existence."[66]

Mencken wrote in the first issue of the *American Mercury* that the magazine aimed to supply a "middle ground of consolation for men who believe neither in the Socialist fol-de-rol nor in the principal enemies of the Socialist fol-de-rol." The world as we see it, he explained, "is down with at least a score of painful diseases, all of them chronic and incurable; nevertheless," he went on, we "cling to the notion that human existence remains predominantly charming."[67]

CHAPTER 10

Growing Up

Mencken's childhood recollections of Baltimore made up a fairy tale of lively characters and bright memories, of peace and plenty. Russell Baker remembered a different time and a different city. In the depths of the Depression he, a sister, and his widowed mother moved to Baltimore to live with relatives and look for work. His early memories described a surreal place of scant light, foul smells, and coldness. A playground bully gave him a cruel beating as the new kid in school. The family's apartment over a funeral parlor reeked of embalming fluid and boiled shrimp. To deliver his Sunday newspaper route he had to wake before dawn, scatter cockroaches in getting breakfast, and often walk past an open coffin. Once outdoors the cold air might lift his spirits, he later wrote, but the darkness, broken only by dim globes of light, frightened him—as did the pervert who stalked him early one morning—and the row houses he considered "a triumph of architectural monotony."[1] He did enjoy unwrapping the papers and reading ominous headlines that announced battles in far-off places like Ethiopia and Manchuria and the Nazi blitzkrieg against Poland. From the ceiling of his bedroom he hung model warplanes; he dreamed of being a navy ace. During the war that no one of his generation escaped, Baker quit Hopkins for flight school. He and his generation grew up in what they afterward thought of as both the best and worst of times.

"The problem of politics," Governor Ritchie said in his inaugural address of 1924, "is how to use the new. I believe it can do this by preserving what is tried and true in the old." During generally prosperous times this message carried wide appeal, and it led to a presidential campaign that had no parallel in Maryland history. Experienced, attractive, Ritchie hoped to duplicate Woodrow Wilson's rise from the New Jersey governorship to dark-horse nominee. His close advisors, weighted toward the Western Shore, believed he could do it. Among them were Howard Bruce, head of Bartlett-Hayward and a Democratic national committeeman, Kent and Mencken of the Sunpapers, the Hopkins Medical School urologist Dr. Hugh Hampton Young, and Stuart S. Janney, earlier Ritchie's law partner. Outside Baltimore Ritchie relied on help from his cousin, David C. Winebrenner III, a prominent Frederick Democrat, and William C. Walsh, a Cumberland lawyer. In Montgomery County the governor had developed close ties with the powerful Blair family. Blair Lee's son, E. Brooke Lee, a Princeton graduate and decorated veteran of the 29th Division, won election as state comptroller in 1920 and the next year became Ritchie's secretary of state.[2]

Maryland's governor would be available in 1924 as a third choice. The leading contenders that year—Wilson's son-in-law, William G. McAdoo, and the Catholic governor of New York, Alfred E. Smith—roughly split Democrats between McAdoo drys of the South and West and Smith wets of the populous East. When cautious party leaders canceled the usual January Jackson Day dinner, Ritchie held one himself in the governor's mansion. Though he denied its purpose was to launch a presidential bid, he invited more than three hundred guests. Senator Oscar Underwood of Alabama, a Democratic luminary, attended, as did Ritchie's old boss, Bernard Baruch, and the editor of the New York *World*. Ritchie seemed to display deep strength, at home and beyond. Late in March a House of Delegates resolution urged him to declare for the presidency. Ritchie addressed the Buffalo League of Women Voters, visited Democrats in New York City, and made a speech in Pittsburgh. Repeal the Eighteenth Amendment, he said repeatedly; halt the centralization of government power. He described federal aid as federal tampering. In May he appeared before a Baltimore meeting of black Democrats from eleven states. Cardinal Gibbons's successor in Baltimore, Archbishop Michael Curley, said he spoke for three hundred thousand people in declaring "no one in the country worthier or better qualified" than Ritchie "to fill the highest executive position." Ritchie won a struggle within the party over the make-up of the Maryland delegation. Assured of "favorite son" support, he—an urban, wet, states' rights Protestant—planned to lie low while MacAdoo and Smith exhausted themselves.[3]

The New York convention in July offered Ritchie a Marylander's rare chance to play center stage in national life. Howard Bruce formally nominated him, calling the Free State governor "the foremost champion of the doctrine of less paternalistic, less bureaucratic government in Washington." The floor demonstration surprised everyone; delegates from all states jumped up to join the parade that General Milton Reckord himself led through the paper-strewn aisles. Dr. Young took the state flag, mounted the speaker's platform, and then climbed atop the podium, waving the Calvert-Crossland colors. After playing many stanzas of "Maryland, My Maryland," the band took up "Dixie" to lusty huzzahs. For more than half an hour the convention cheered Ritchie, oddsmakers and pundits marveling at his spontaneous support. That weekend, not trusting chance, Ritchie men at home staged rallies in Cumberland, Hagerstown, Annapolis, Cambridge, and Salisbury; at War Memorial Plaza in Baltimore fifteen thousand people gathered to hear bipartisan, pro-Ritchie speeches that the C&P amplified with a new device, the loudspeaker. All this excitement received the planned-for coverage in the New York Sunday papers, and yet on Monday, when the delegates began voting, the Maryland governor's support never gained momentum. After more than a hundred ballots, and after Ritchie's friends in party councils pressed his case as a compromise candidate, the Democrats settled instead on John W. Davis, a West Virginia native and Wall Street lawyer whose opposition to federal spending and the Ku Klux Klan Ritchie applauded.[4]

He clung to his ambitions. Ritchie easily won a third term as governor in 1926. He continued making speaking appearances outside the state. He wrote articles on taxation, foreign relations, and politics (with titles like "Too Much Government" and "Shall We Govern Ourselves?") for national journals. Frank Kent and Hamilton Owens of the Sunpapers gave him friendly notices in similar magazines, including the *American Mercury*. A newspaperman said that Ritchie by 1928 had made "more speeches in more different parts of the United States than any other man in American life save Lindbergh and Will Rogers." Either Ritchie's aversion to a "rough and tumble" fight on the national level or his party loyalty (or both) cut short his bid in 1928. After meeting with Smith, Ritchie withdrew and pledged his support for the New Yorker. Seconding Smith's nomination, Ritchie attacked the Republican candidate, Herbert Hoover, as an engineer out of his depth. "You cannot run human government," he said in a speech that sounded like Mencken, "by dehumanized efficiency experts, who think that charts, blueprints, reports, and statistics constitute its whole sum and substance." Partisans speculated that Ritchie's withdrawal in 1928 implied Smith's backing for the Marylander in 1932.[5]

Ritchie's headlines hardly left the state a one-party preserve, but Maryland Democrats held a considerable edge. In the 1924 presidential election a large number of Baltimoreans adhered to a third party that Senator Robert M. LaFollette of Wisconsin organized. The Progressives established headquarters at the Baltimore Federation of Labor offices and selected as their leaders Elisabeth Coit Gilman and Broadus Mitchell, a Hopkins professor of economic history; the group had the support of the *Afro-American*, whose editors, along with many black leaders, had grown tired of being taken for granted as Republicans. Baltimore laboring men joined farmers in the counties in support of LaFollette, who called for government action to break up monopolies and bring down tariff walls. He won nearly thirty-three thousand votes that year, helping to defeat Davis and place Maryland in Coolidge's column. Meanwhile Republicans, a minority in the General Assembly, clung to their Western Maryland congressional seat, which then belonged to the Cumberland glassworker, labor leader, and real estate and insurance broker, Frederick N. Zihlman.

The GOP had to contend not only with a popular governor, but with distinguished Democratic leadership. In 1922 Joseph I. France, a Port Deposit physician and rugged independent Republican, lost his Senate seat to William Cabell Bruce, the Baltimore reformer who found time to write history and biography. His speeches (in 1925 Bruce told an Ocean City audience that Prohibition eventually would be "the study not so much of the political historian as of the political pathologist") reflected Ritchie's Jeffersonian approach to government and showed how the governor helped to give the Maryland Democracy coherence. In 1926 Ritchie's young friend Brooke Lee, running as a favor to the governor, won a seat in the House of Delegates and quickly became Speaker. E. Millard Tydings, a native of Havre de Grace and graduate of both the state Agricultural College and Maryland Law School, became another leading Democrat in the Ritchie years. In 1917, retaining his House of Delegates seat, Tydings had gone to France with the 29th Division; like Brooke Lee, he returned a hero. Tydings defeated Ovington Weller for the U.S. Senate in 1926 and remained there for many years after. The stature of Tydings, Lee, and the others took nothing away from Ritchie's prominence or his claim on the nation's highest office.[6]

Ritchie seemed truly destined to sit in the governor's mansion as long as he lived. Partly to his credit, the Maryland record of progressive legislation continued strong in these years. After an Annapolis conference in 1924, Maryland and Virginia agreed to legislation protecting the blue crab—both the females, which liked to lay their eggs in the salty waters inside the Virginia Capes, and the males, which usually preferred the Maryland side of the line with its comparatively fresh waters and grassy bottoms. Three years later, with Lee playing a large part, the assembly created the Maryland–National Capital Park and Planning Commission to coordinate land use in the Maryland suburbs of Washington. Public schools, especially those for whites, continued to improve; capital expenditures among the counties rose from almost $93,000 in 1920 to about $943,800 in 1930. The proportion of high school students to total enrollments rose appreciably. In 1928 the assembly required every child to finish grammar school before entering the work force. The state Roads Commission in the late 1920s began a program to eliminate railroad grade crossings—to build bridges and underpasses on major thoroughfares. Ritchie gained stature, won points for party service, and held onto his Catholic friends by standing fast against the anti-Catholic slurs that accompanied Al Smith's 1928 campaign. Methodist Bishop James Cannon, an Eastern Shore native and head of the church's board of temperance and morals, returned to Maryland to distribute leaflets declaring that a vote for Smith was a vote for the pope. "Do you suppose," Ritchie asked Maryland voters, "that the pope has been biding his time for 300 years until Smith was born?"[7]

Still, the governor had his brushes with scandal. In 1928, when shortages turned up in roads commission accounts, Ritchie had weathered the crisis by appointing an investigating committee under Edwin G. Baetjer, a leading corporate attorney and prominent Republican whose panel discovered missing funds amounting to more than $375,000 and fourteen culprits. Ritchie followed its recommendations in reorganizing the commission. During the 1926 campaign Ritchie critics said that a new Susquehanna River dam—the Conowingo, built by a Pennsylvania power interest below the Maryland line—smelled of Gorman-Rasin cronyism. In truth the construction contract worth $20 million had gone to the Arundel Corporation, a Baltimore company with many ties to Ritchie. One of its vice-presidents, former Republican governor Lloyd Lowndes, was a cousin to the Sunpapers publishers Harry and Van Lear Black; columnist Frank Kent served as an Arundel director. The colorful, up-from-poverty chairman of the corporation, Frank Furst, had been instrumental at the start of Ritchie's political career and in calling off John Walter Smith, a potential challenger, when the governor first ran for reelection. A Furst understudy, Robert B. Ennis, belonged to Ritchie's intimate circle of advisors. The governor's personal-political network in Baltimore also took in Howard Jackson, Ritchie's selection for the party mayoral nomination in 1923. While Jackson later pointed to his record of lowering taxes and improving city administration, the Baltimore *Post*—a tabloid paper that sold for a penny and delighted in attacking Ritchie—noted that Jackson had put large sums of city insurance money into his own firm and deposited city capital in the Fidelity Trust Company, where Van Lear Black and Furst exercised influence and drew profits.

Ritchie announced himself a candidate in the 1930 elections against the counsel of advisors like William Curran of East Baltimore and Howard Bruce. In 1928 both Sonny Mahon and Frank Kelly had died, leaving Democratic alignments in Baltimore badly confused, and Hoover's decisive defeat of Smith that year worsened party disorder. Eastern Shore drys panted for the governor's downfall; Independent Citizens, Inc., an anti-Catholic leftover from the Smith-Hoover campaign, claimed to have fifty thousand votes to contribute toward his defeat.

✦

Ritchie's fourth-term victory owed much to the 1929 stock market crash and its aftermath, which voters were inclined to blame on the Republicans. On one day, 29 October, investors dumped sixteen million shares on the market, and two weeks after "Black Tuesday," stocks on average had fallen to a mere 40 percent of their earlier value. President Hoover refused to consider the downturn serious; he called it not a recession but a mere "depression." Whatever the name, it baffled the experts. Its origins lay in problems far beyond the control of states: an unregulated stock market, purchases "on margin" (with only a down payment), and heedless speculation. The existing national tax structure hampered the buying power of ordinary people, yet corporate policies in the 1920s had encouraged the building of new plants and peak production that raised inventories of goods to dangerously high levels. American banks—vulnerable to sudden and massive withdrawals—made heavy investments in corporate building. Meanwhile faltering European economies could provide only a limited market for American goods. Global tariff walls frustrated such exchange in any case, and in June 1931, trying to prop up prices of manufactures and farm commodities, President Hoover signed the highest American tariff measure yet, the Hawley-Smoot Act.

The Free State escaped the earliest shock of depression. Marylanders had not fallen into dangerous industrial patterns as seriously as had citizens of other states, where automobile or refrigerator manufacturing grew too swiftly. *Baltimore* magazine to its credit had observed as early as 1927 that the country seemed to be "overbuilt." Actually the economic woes of some Marylanders cushioned the impact of the Great Crash: well before 1929 Maryland corn and wheat farmers knew that the market brought them a poor return, and even in 1928 conservative figures for unemployed persons in Baltimore ranged between fifteen and thirty thousand. For a time after the crash Maryland industrial and trading leaders remained doggedly optimistic. Baltimore businessmen in 1930—hoping to attract any investment money still available—described the city as "appreciably better off" than other Eastern ports. Maryland tobacco prices remained steady. In early 1931, when national economic indexes reported the worst news since 1914, the president of Consolidated Gas, Electric, Light and Power in Baltimore proclaimed "the basic causes of the depression have completely disappeared." "What remains," he said, "is simply fear and lack of confidence."[8]

These brave words could not hold back the rising tide of failure and unemployment. Many Maryland institutions, founded with state charters that permitted low capital reserves, stood on the brink of ruin. The Frederick Central Trust Company went into bankruptcy in 1929; Maryland Casualty Company and U.S. Fidelity and Guaranty had heavy liabilities from the sale of guaranteed mortgages. Baltimore Trust, an unstable bank with holdings of $100 million, became the state's most serious failure following the stock market crash. Alarming reports circulated that a woman of prominent family had been seen walking from Baltimore Trust to First National carrying $50,000 in cash; in September 1931 panicky depositors made a run on the bank. Two leaders of the city financial community committed suicide. In 1931 and 1932 three national banks and fifteen state banks went under. Unemployment throughout the state climbed in 1931, reaching nearly 20 percent in Baltimore. Consolidation Coal Company in the George's Creek region operated at half-strength. By the middle of 1932 just four in ten Maryland plants stood at full production and employment. A new British tariff threatened the export trade. Retailing had dropped off, and later that year the Baltimore Association of Commerce could only say that the city, though traveling a different route, had "finally arrived at about the same place" as the rest of the country.[9]

The vulnerability of longtime officeholding counted as nothing in Ritchie's career compared to the crash and its aftermath. In the summer of 1930, when Maryland farmers had enough to worry about, nature worsened their lot by inflicting a severe drought on the region. Losses stood at $38 million. President Hoover called a conference of twelve governors to discuss relief but did not invite Ritchie, who protested the snub. The Maryland Republican Galen Tait acidly commented that Ritchie had gotten what he deserved. "Practically every tenet of Governor Ritchie's theory of Maryland's relation to the nation," Tait declared, "is opposed to Maryland's true interest." When finally federal loan money became available, the governor organized a committee to oversee its division. This Maryland Drought Loan Corporation, though helpful to some farmers, required collateral, as did banks, and acted only as a lender of last resort. Its chairman, the Baltimore banker Waldo Newcomer, urged the governor to create state jobs. His words captured the urgency that gripped most of the nation. "We can't see people starve," Newcomer said, "and there seems no legal way of getting money to aid the farm laborers and some farmers who have no credit." [10]

A firm believer in voluntaryism (private action) and state self-help, Ritchie expected Marylanders to tighten their belts. Within the limits of the state budget and office structure he did what he could. The Board of Aid and Charities, which received applications for state monies, had no welfare role in the state. The General Assembly in 1931 and 1932 did vote increases for the Veterans' Relief Commission and private Maryland Children's Aid Society, and both agencies quickly spent these emergency funds. Ritchie placed the governor's prestige behind voluntary, "share the work" plans—employers pledging to avoid more layoffs and to hire new men by cutting work hours and dividing the payroll. In the spring of 1931 he set aside certain state race-track proceeds for the jobless. State authorities went ahead as soon as possible with all planned projects. "I do not know anything Maryland could do," Ritchie reported, "which has not been done in order to accelerate public building and construction work." [11]

In hard times the Maryland governor stood for old values, official economy, and he was willing to give his record a national test. Soon after his fourth-term election, he began preparing for the 1932 Democratic convention. As usual he assumed a low profile, entering no primary elections. Everybody knows you are a "'profound statesman,'" warned a Baltimore attorney in a private letter; "how can you make yourself a colorful leader?" Despite Ritchie's reserve, a poll of Democratic congressmen published that spring in *Cosmopolitan* magazine found him not far behind Franklin D. Roosevelt, the New York governor who with James A. Farley, his campaign manager, had spent two years courting party regulars. Critics of Roosevelt thought him lacking in qualifications and conviction. Amiable and philanthropic, wrote Walter Lippmann, Roosevelt was "not the dangerous enemy of anything." [12]

In contrast, the Maryland governor's message had not changed in ten years. "If you are to be inspected and suspected and never respected by your

Old-World loyalties and love of new country intersected in September 1931, when Marylanders of Hellenic descent gathered at War Memorial Plaza in Baltimore to present the governor with a Greek flag. Their spokesman compared Albert C. Ritchie to a Greek god and hoped "it will be the privilege of tens of thousands of Greeks in America to vote for him as President of the United States." *James P. Asimakes/Nicholas M. Prevas*

Government," Ritchie declared at the 1932 governors' conference, "then the army of experts and near experts who do all these things will be expert enough to see that you pay the piper, even if you cannot always call the tune." In June at Washington College commencement ceremonies (it was the bicentennial of Washington's birth) he spoke of the "strange temples" and "strange gods" that beckoned Americans. "But the altar of faith which has brought us safely through all our adventures of peace and war still stands and its fires still burn," he intoned. "I, for one, see no reason for another shrine." Many Marylanders and other Americans agreed with him. As the governor left Baltimore for the Chicago convention, more than thirty thousand people gathered to send him off. A brass band played a new favorite, "There's a President in the Heart of Maryland," and when Ritchie arrived in Chicago thousands of natives, many wearing "Win with Ritchie" armbands, lined the streets to welcome him.[13]

He had more friends and fewer votes than any other candidate there, Kent later wrote. Impressed by the size of Ritchie's Chicago crowds, Farley immediately offered the vice-president's place on the Roosevelt ticket. Ritchie declined, believing the "stop Roosevelt" forces strong enough to deny FDR the necessary two-thirds delegate vote. Besides, he told an intermediary, he would rather be governor of Maryland than vice-president. For several days the politicians played with nearly even hands. Through Brooke Lee on the platform committee, Ritchie fought successfully for an anti-Prohibition plank while Al Smith, the anti-Roosevelt leader, tried to rally delegates. On 1 June Senator Tydings delivered a dramatic nominating speech for Ritchie, setting off a forty-minute demonstration with the usual music and cheering. Just as in 1924, however, votes were more important than noise. On the first ballot Roosevelt collected 664 (still insufficient to nominate) to Ritchie's 21. At bargaining sessions next day Dr. Young, again a delegate, hoped to swing the crucial Texas delegation toward Ritchie; at Hopkins Hospital Young had operated on several of the most influential Texans and now planned, as ethically as he could, to prey on their gratitude. Somehow when the delegation met in caucus the Ritchie men were absent. John Nance Garner of Texas, then McAdoo of California (no friend of Smith) and other uncommitted delegates, soon swung to Roosevelt, who took Garner as his running mate.

Ritchie's polite exterior concealed deep disappointments. The platform fight on Prohibition, on which he placed such importance, proved a costly victory. It delayed the convention's opening, giving delegates time to forget his popular welcome in Chicago; once adopted, the plank diminished his value to the party as a wet representative. He may have felt betrayed by Smith, who never named Ritchie the logical alternative to Roosevelt (Smith found Ritchie's men amateurish), and the Maryland governor later regretted turning down second place on the FDR ticket. But Ritchie's defeat was a tribute to his integrity, his refusal to seem something he was not. His theory of discipline and economy in government expressed itself in his very demeanor, and he did not change for the sake of marketing. A New York reporter described him at the convention as "seeming to hold himself in," unable to "emerge from the campaign photograph." Restrained, a champion of small government, Ritchie lost to an ebullient pragmatist. He had fallen "out of step with too many elements in our national life," concluded the *Sun*, "to have a chance of getting the nomination."[14]

◦━◦

Ritchie returned home to find the situation growing worse. In the summer of 1932 unemployed veterans, hoping to speed passage of a measure granting them early payment of the certificates due them for world war service, gathered in Washington as the "bonus army." Like "Coxey's army" of unemployed in 1894, these petitioners received much sympathetic aid along the road in Maryland. In late May, when a contingent of three thousand arrived in Grantsville, local Red Cross volunteers provided food and found shelter for the men and their families. While Coxey's men had floated downriver on C&O barges, Potomac floodwaters in March 1924 had left the old canal little more than a relic. Aiming to shorten the veterans' stay in Maryland, Ritchie

Albert C. Ritchie leaving for Chicago, 1932. As a five-time gubernatorial candidate and twice a presidential aspirant, Ritchie may have campaigned harder than any other figure in Maryland history. *Bruce Adams*

summoned state trucks to haul the supplicants to Washington. There the "army" increased to about fifteen thousand persons and formed a ramshackle encampment on the Anacostia River mud flats. It suffered a harsh fate. Late in July President Hoover—who opposed the bonus bill for fiscal reasons—ordered regular troops to disperse the ragamuffins, handing Democrats if no one else an election-year bonus. Cheered on their return in 1918, the soldiers now fell to force that included armor, cavalry, and machine guns. It was hardly edifying, commented Ritchie as the bonus men retreated into Maryland, "to see arms and tanks and sabres and tear bombs used in this way, and men driven out at night at the point of bayonet." A Marylander friendly to the veterans offered his Anne Arundel acreage as a substitute campground. State health inspectors declared it unfit for seven thousand homeless men, however, and the governor worried about adding that number to the charity rolls. He parleyed with their leaders, and the last bonus marchers marched home.[15]

Officials breathed easier, for Maryland relief efforts had been stretched to the limit. Ritchie faced a deep crisis in public policy. In March local agricultural agents and members of the Drought Loan Corporation, naturally disposed to believe that their efforts helped, had supplied figures that showed conditions acute only in Baltimore City and Anne Arundel County. Social workers disputed this optimistic survey. Later that spring Mary F. Bogue and a staff of welfare professionals finished a more alarming report for the Maryland State Conference for Social Work. Bogue found problems of unemployment relief especially serious in eight counties and Baltimore City. The people of Cecil County, always poor, now could find scarcely any work at all. In the coal-mining counties of Allegany and Garrett, unemployment had climbed to about 7 percent. The downturn in Baltimore City had produced jobless men and women in the outlying sections of Baltimore and Anne Arundel counties. In all these areas, Bogue reported, private charity funds for 1932 already had been spent. Out-of-work Prince George's County families had made it through the previous winter because federal office employees had donated twelve thousand dollars to their relief. One could not rely on such good fortune next winter, and social workers doubted that Washington County, with its own high unemployment level, or Wicomico, where closed canneries affected the entire local economy, could make it through another winter, either. Some Eastern Shore families—too proud even to ask for aid—subsisted on watercress.

The impact of the Depression on Carroll County residents illustrated both citizen generosity and its shortfall as conditions grew grimmer in 1932. Three years earlier, after organizing a local chapter of the Children's Aid Society, women there had hired Bonnie M. Custenborder, a professional social worker, to manage day-to-day tasks. The society had deep grass-roots. Ladies of the county sewed clothing for needy children, drove children to Baltimore to visit clinics and undergo medical tests, and conducted door-to-door campaigns for one-dollar contributions. Donors included fraternal societies like the Knights of Pythias, owners of the hardware store, dime store, and beauty shop, employees of two companies—W. F. Myers' Sons and J. Stoner Geiman—and various church groups. The county commissioners added two thousand dollars in public money. At first Custenborder aided victims of fires and handled occasional cases of child neglect, poverty, and abandonment; she intended, she wrote in her first annual report, to cultivate "personalities or traits of character that will enable the individual to become self-supporting." The Depression forced a change in her constituency if not in her intentions. Much employment in Carroll County depended on its fourteen canneries, two of which closed in 1930 while the rest operated at 10 percent capacity. A cement plant at Union Bridge and the Western Maryland car shop there shut down (temporarily, said company officers) in the fall of 1931. The Congoleum plant cut back its hours. The Westminster shoe factory closed for lack of orders in early 1932, placing four hundred persons out of work.[16]

Never doubting that a child's welfare depended on that of his or her parents, Custenborder and the society went to work helping the unemployed—gathering canned food and clothes, trying to find jobs. Churches and civic groups, along with the Red Cross, relied on the society to distribute what they raised, and a county emergency relief committee of leading businessmen drew its sense of urgency from the cries of Children's Aid members. During the drought they asked residents to set aside one jar of canned vegetables to feed the hungry; during the next winter Custenborder sought clothes for the "practically naked" children she saw. In the spring of 1931 she placed members of one large family on a farm, where they planned to grow vegetables and raise a hog. For others she found only part-time work, and for others still, nothing. The burden grew heavy. Using her small apartment as an office, Custenborder tried in 1931 to answer 150 new appeals for aid; her caseload grew to almost 800 "visits" over the 565 she had had the year before. The president of the county chapter, Mrs. Frank T. Myers, appealed for volunteers. Society expenditures in 1931 climbed to about $1,200 over the 1930 level, yet contributions fell off by $777. In the early months of 1932 Myers conducted a publicity campaign to rally support for relief efforts. There were pieces in the Westminster *Democratic Advocate* and pulpit appeals in local churches. Schoolchildren took part in an essay contest—answering "Why Carroll County Should Stand Behind the Work of the Children's Aid Society." While citizens of the county did, Custenborder—who in 1932 took a voluntary paycut—felt tightly squeezed. After another year of hand-to-mouth relief work she reported "an unusual number of appeals" and predicted "the hardest winter in our history." [17]

Carroll Countians guarded vigilantly against freeloaders from Baltimore City, where the human debris of the Depression piled up quickly. Baltimore mayors faced the same choices as the governor, and early municipal responses to unemployment and suffering, however ingenious, proved inadequate. In the spring of 1930 Mayor William F. Broening had established employment guidelines for Baltimore companies, advising against firing heads of households and recommending work sharing among as many persons as possible. That December he set up a free employment service in City Hall. Deluged with more than 7,700 inquiries about jobs, the office succeeded in placing about one in five applicants for work. Broening leaned on city employees to sacrifice a fraction of their salaries to help pay for relief and to take off one day a month so as to supply others with work.

Baltimore had been at the mercy of trade fluctuations since the late eighteenth century; traditionally the city treated its downtrodden with care. After 1930 city institutions like the Community Fund, Red Cross, Family Welfare Association, Bureau of Catholic Charities, Jewish Social Service Bureau, and Salvation Army quickly spent what they had on relief efforts (Catholic and Jewish expenditures rose to about $15,000 a week late in 1930). Disbursing about $40,000 a week at the end of 1930, Community Fund leaders set the fund's goal for 1931 at $2 million, the highest target ever. Each month in the winter of 1930–31 the Family Welfare Association handled five times the hardship cases it earlier had seen in an entire year. In January, 42,000 Baltimore workers—one in eight—had no work, and "breadlines" had opened at nineteen locations in the city. About 2,750 families relied on charity. Two months later that number had risen by 1,000. The Baltimore police began accepting donations for the needy; by mid-February the department had fed 6,600 persons in station houses and supplied 7,500 families with food and fuel. That month businessmen of the Association of Commerce and other civic leaders organized a special task force, the Citizens' Emergency Relief Committee. They estimated its immediate needs at $300,000.

Baltimoreans who had a few extra dollars or cents dug even deeper. The Baltimore Federation of Labor recommended that everyone making more than $2,500 a year give 5 percent to the unemployed. In the spring of 1931 the Sunpapers and the Emergency Relief Committee organized a Lenten-season drive to conclude on "self-denial day," Good Friday, 27 March. The city provided trucks and warehouses to handle donated food and clothing. Small contributions, individual gifts, came from all parts of the city. On the day of self-denying, ballot boxes went to movie houses, markets, branches of the Pratt Library, and street corners. At noon, church bells rang and fire-house whistles blew, calling citizens to contribute. The boxes collected $90,000 during the noon hour, and the season-long drive brought in a total of $669,000. Meantime *Baltimore* magazine published stories of corporate gifts for unemployment relief—Consolidated utilities and the Savings Bank of Baltimore gave $30,000 each. Ritchie's four days of race-track receipts totaled $125,000. Yet the needs of the growing number of unemployed persons in the city outstripped charitable giving. By early September almost one in three union members had no work, while nearly another third had only part-time employment. The building trades reported 62 percent of their men out of work. On 1 October the Family Welfare Association forecast an end to its money in three weeks. "Never in the experience of the organization have we seen so much suffering and such dire conditions of want as exist now," said a spokesman. Families seeking aid rose from 3,800 in September 1931 to 14,100 in February 1932.[18]

The Depression, in the words of a Baltimorean, "presented a terror" that later generations "could never comprehend." "I've seen hundreds of people come into court," said a city judge, "admit they owed back rent and with tears in their eyes plead for a little more time in the hope their luck would change." Workers were at the mercy of distraught employers. One wage earner wrote of working sixteen hours a day for twelve dollars a week; a young boy worked in a grocery store for fifteen cents a day and carried home a loaf of bread that cost him nine cents. Husbands and fathers looked covetously at women's jobs. "All married men," according to one subscriber to the *Evening Sun*, "should start a war on the women who are keeping them and millions of other married men out of work." Women, many of them heading households, had their own angry comments. "In periods of business depression, the first thing Mr. Businessman does to reduce his overhead is to cut the salaries of his women employees," a woman who signed herself "One of Them" wrote the *Sun*. "The excuse is the old sob stuff about men having families to support." People went out in the morning in search of work, and then, having failed again, lined up outside the police station on Fayette Street and Fallsway for bread, soup, or coffee. For many years after the economy improved one could still see "a blurred, greasy mark, about elbow-high," where the jobless slowly had filed along the gray concrete wall. A widow who had been unable to make ends meet took her son and his wagon to the warehouse for the telltale packages and cans of relief groceries. On the return trip, despite the chilly air, the boy covered them with his sweater. He later referred to the food as "the edible proof of our disgrace." [19]

Ritchie and those who believed as he did found themselves caught between the principle of government economy and the fact of suffering citizens. In Baltimore, mayors and councilmen slowly caved in to monumental needs. Kicking off the special Lenten fund drive of 1931, Broening gave $50,000 from the city's contingency fund. City spending for new school construction and work on streets—so important to unemployed workers—threw the budget out of balance. In the bleak fall of 1931 Mayor Howard

A few communists and more angry unemployed paraded down a Baltimore street in March 1930. Baltimore *News American* photograph. *Jacques Kelly*

Jackson (having defeated Broening for a second time, he had announced the familiar policy of "rigid economy") swallowed his scruples and came up with $150,000—a loan to the relief organizations to be repaid the first of January, after the 1932 Community Fund drive. Yet in March 1932 (at about the time workers on the B&O agreed to donate half their paychecks over three months to relief) W. Frank Roberts of the Emergency Relief Committee reported that relief cost $50,000 each week. Just as the charities turned to the city, Jackson looked to the state. Granting Baltimore relief groups another $100,000, the mayor sought some support from Ritchie, who, in the midst of a presidential campaign, spoke against using state funds "for relief purposes in the form of donations, gifts, or doles." Doing so, he continued, would "destroy self-initiative and individual enterprise." In July Congress passed a bill permitting the new Reconstruction Finance Corporation (RFC) to lend states money for emergency relief. The mayor of Cumberland appealed to Ritchie to request that federal aid, which the states were to repay with highway tax revenues. The governor refused for the time being; "We think we will be able to take care of our own situation," he replied to another query, "without applying to the Federal Government." In August 1932 Ritchie organized a Governor's Advisory Committee on Unemployment Relief, one of the first in the country. While it conducted yet another survey of the hard times, Ritchie considered floating state bonds to cover the $3 million estimated as necessary for Baltimore relief, then in November expressed doubts about the plan—the 1867 constitution forbade the city to go into debt.[20]

Rapidly rising relief costs intersected with a downward turn in tax revenues. Marylanders wrestled with this latest crisis in the uncertain period between Hoover's November 1932 defeat (FDR's 130,000-vote victory margin in Maryland was the largest ever) and Roosevelt's March inauguration. A tax reform commission, under the old Progressive and Hopkins political economist Jacob H. Hollander, had decided that both homeowners and farmers paid an unfairly high tax rate. Just as its conclusions leaked, Mayor Jackson announced the need to charge higher property taxes to pay for 1933 outlays. A Taxpayers' War Council, claiming to represent more than twenty civic organizations, soon formed in the city. At a public meeting in early December, a crowd of four thousand assembled to boo and berate city councilmen. About the same time commissioners from seventeen counties met in Annapolis to discuss tax reduction, an object they thought feasible if the state gave up some of its gasoline tax income. In January, when the assembly convened, Ritchie suggested higher taxes on luxuries like chewing gum, soft drinks, cigars, and cigarettes. Tobacco-county delegates swarmed in opposition. After decades of low tobacco prices, growers wanted the full benefit of good times; besides, half the revenue would go to Baltimore—that portion of the state neither the Shore nor Southern Maryland wished to subsidize. Senator J. Allan Coad of St. Mary's saw fat in the state budget. Finally Ritchie and Democratic leaders backed down from the luxury tax. Adapting ideas

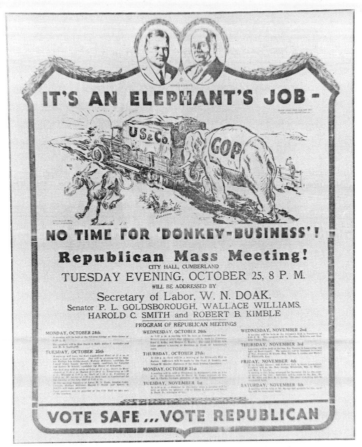

"It's an Elephant's Job." From the *Cumberland Daily News*, 22 October 1932. *Albert L. Feldstein*

In one public works project, men who may once have held office jobs cut and regraded Union and Buena Vista avenues in Baltimore, 1933. *Baltimore Sunpapers*

that emerged in debate and the earlier county commissioners' meeting, they settled on a leaner budget, a 1 percent tax on parimutuel betting, and reallocation of motor vehicle licensing revenues. The counties and Baltimore City would divide the $3 million evenly, permitting lower county taxes and financing of the Baltimore relief program.

Sheer necessity forced the issue of government involvement in relief. Baltimore City families on the relief rolls rose to almost 23,000 in the early months of 1933, a number representing about 10 percent of the entire population. The amount estimated necessary to pay for unemployment relief there climbed from $8 million at the start of the 1933 session to $12 million in early April, when the new tax-reform bill passed. In these months needy families in the counties stood at about 5 percent, but everywhere the numbers increased. Early in 1933 relief workers in Allegany County reported a 60 percent increase in destitute families over the winter months (Consolidation Coal had gone into receivership the preceding June). In Somerset, 89 families had sought charity in early 1932; a year later the number was 625. In Worcester the figure rose from 61 to 642. During the winter hundreds of families in Harford and Queen Anne's counties had broken down and sought help—the number dropping with the return of warmer weather. Dr. J. H. Janney, chairman of the Anne Arundel Relief Committee, scotched reports that all was well there; because of shortages in relief supplies, he wrote, most families receiving help got little more than starvation rations. Social workers like Custenborder in Carroll County allowed that some of these people, as she put it, "think the world owes them a living." Most of them, Ritchie's advisory committee reported in late March, would much rather work, never before had asked for aid, and might in fact perish without it. Anita Faatz, welfare director for the Board of State Aid and Charities, wrote the governor that "We need and need urgently State leadership, State planning, and financial resources if people are to be cared for next winter." Finally fiscal restraint and constitutional principle seemed less important than keeping people from starving. On 29 March Ritchie announced that he was applying for federal aid from the RFC.[21]

The Maryland governor adjusted his step to the piper, as he might have phrased it—the piper whose music held out hope of relief and recovery. In the end Marylanders had mixed reviews for FDR's performance, but in 1933 the crisis clearly called for decisive action. Ritchie's advisory committee had noted that state taxation depended on then-declining property values, while the federal government had other revenue sources—more power—than the states.

FDR quickly acted on that premise. Soon after his inauguration he called a national bank holiday and a special session of Congress. In the next hundred days the president, his "brain trusters," and the Democratic Congress tried to save the American way of life by transforming it. Congress passed banking legislation that strengthened the Federal Reserve system and took the country off the gold standard, a securities act regulating the stock market, and an Agricultural Adjustment Act (AAA) that sought to eliminate surplus crops by rewarding reductions in planting. It created the Civilian Conservation Corps (CCC), providing emergency out-of-doors work for jobless young men, and the Tennessee Valley Authority, taking federal dams and other property left over from the world war and putting them to the peaceful work of rural electrification and fertilizer making. New federal legislation extended credit to homeowners and farmers so that they could keep their homes. To raise revenues, Congress legalized and taxed beer and wine (by December a majority of states voted to repeal the Eighteenth Amendment altogether). Congress made a new National Recovery Administration (NRA) responsible for fair industrial competition and management-labor relations. The NRA recognized labor's right to collective bargaining; the Public Works Administration (PWA) within the NRA spent millions of dollars on projects to get working people off relief and money into circulation. Another act, passed in May, made outright grants to states for jobs programs. As Ritchie had suspected in late March, much federal relief money finally did not require repayment.

Hard times continued, however, and working people knew that not everyone suffered during the Depression. Soon after the 1929 crash, when Baltimore businessmen urged that the city adopt daylight savings time, working people had opposed it—in the summertime the early darkness allowed their row houses to cool down by bedtime. Rumors had spread that white-collar men wanted the extra hour for rounds of evening golf, which helped to defeat the proposal at the polls. At the same time and in a similar spirit "a Man in Overalls" had written the *Sun* that higher tariffs laid an indirect tax on "the backs of the farmers and working people, who can least afford it."[22]

As the gap between rich and poor yawned, the question of labor's rights became a flashpoint between classes. Though the famous section 7(a) of the law creating the NRA contained labor guarantees, in practice they amounted to little. Baltimore businesses, especially small firms and clothing manufacturers, resisted any attempt on the part of workers to organize, make demands, or strike. In 1932 the two largest clothing companies, J. Schoeneman Incorporated and L. Greif and Brother, had defeated a strike by firing union sympathizers, hiring nonunion workers, and calling in police to restrain pickets. Mayor Jackson proved to be a stern friend of order; he and clothing industry leaders condemned labor agitators as dangerous to public peace. Hyman Blumberg, vice-president of the Amalgamated Clothing Workers, faced the real possibility that NRA agreements might revoke gains clothing workers had made at some plants. Finally Blumberg found the NRA guidelines (wages forty cents an hour, doubling pay at some clothing establishments) fair enough, but Schoeneman and Greif ignored them. The NRA enforcement official in Baltimore, Arthur Hungerford, was a former advertising man for the *Sun*. Well intentioned, he nonetheless preferred labor peace to labor strife and declined to press the two large companies.

One might well have deserted old political ideas and grabbed for new ones. In early 1933 Maryland socialist leaders Clarence W. Whitmore and Elisabeth Coit Gilman organized a Peoples Unemployment League that soon had twenty-five hundred members and fifteen chapters in the state. That July delegates from eighty groups—besides the PUL, they included cooperative milk producers, garment workers, the Women's International League for Peace and Freedom, and the Johns Hopkins Liberal Club—met in Hagerstown for a state Congress of Farmers and Workers. Addressing the problem of adequate relief, the congress called for special laws to protect home ownership and socialize basic industries. It supported raising income tax rates in the higher brackets. The New Deal adopted some of these reforms. More radical measures Marylanders generally resisted—even in straitened circumstances. A rally the frail Communist party sponsored in Baltimore during the blackest days of the early Depression turned up only a few unhappy men; to judge from political returns and remembered kitchen-table discussions, men and women of the time scorned easy answers from left and right alike. Even so, owners sometimes lumped labor organizers, socialists, and communists together. Late in the summer of 1933 Baltimore boot and shoe manufacturers used the "lock out" to keep unionizing workers out of their shops. When employees demonstrated in protest, police arrested them. W. D. A. Anderson, NRA grievance committee chairman in the city, called the workers' tactics unnecessary and belligerent.[23]

With reason the Hagerstown congress deplored race relations in Maryland, and the Depression did little to improve them. As jobs in heavily black areas grew scarce, unemployed whites predictably tried to discourage Negro competition. In those regions it took only a black suspected of a heinous crime to put match to gasoline. One explosion occurred in December 1931 at Salisbury, where Mack Williams had been accused of murdering his white employer. A mob broke into the hospital where he lay and lynched him. Many Marylanders joined Ritchie in condemning this crime, but the local newspaper spoke of "outraged feeling" and "heroic methods"; hard up for support, townsmen also portrayed Williams as having been under the influence of communists. In November 1933 another lynching took place a few miles below Salisbury, in Princess Anne. About five thousand men thrust authorities aside and lynched a Negro who stood accused of attacking an elderly white woman. After hanging him, the mob tore apart and burned the body. In this case Attorney General William Preston Lane, Jr., an army veteran and the son of a Hagerstown newspaper publisher, learned the names of the ringleaders, who were Wicomicans, and pressed the state's attorney for action. When nothing happened Ritchie sent five hundred troops of the 5th Maryland, led by General Reckord, to Salisbury to serve warrants on the

National Guardsmen confronted whites sympathetic to accused lynching leaders, Salisbury, November 1933. Baltimore *News American* photograph. *Jacques Kelly*

suspected mob leaders. Though Reckord captured four of the nine men on Lane's list (several were "on vacation" in Virginia), a mob gathered to taunt the militiamen. Local firemen, called out to cool off the mob, turned their hoses on the troops instead. Later a Wicomico judge released the suspects before they could be taken to Baltimore for trial. The governor's enemies on the Shore expressed contempt for him, his attorney general, and the new federal presence in their lives. They joked that NRA stickers in store windows stood for Never Ritchie Again.[24]

By the summer of 1934 Ritchie had been in office so long that opposing him became sport. Challengers lined up like men at a carnival throwing baseballs to drop a clown into a tub of water. Charles Conley, a Frederick physician, ran against the disease "governitis contageosus." Howard Jackson hoped to claim the governor's chair after serving, in Ritchie's own words, as the "best mayor Baltimore ever had." He urged Ritchie to run for the U.S. Senate. Allan Coad opposed the "fifth term racket" and doubted Ritchie would run again—"No individual," he said, "could be that selfish." Tydings endorsed George L. Radcliffe for governor. A personal friend of the president and a New Dealer who with energy headed the PWA in Maryland, Radcliffe wanted to strengthen Roosevelt in Washington by replacing Republican Phillips Lee Goldsborough (the former governor had defeated Bruce in 1928) with a Democrat. Radcliffe intended to leave that Senate race open for Ritchie, who instead stated once more—he hoped for the last time—that he would rather be governor of Maryland than senator from any or all the states.[25]

Ritchie had his way with the Democrats once more. After meetings designed to avoid a messy primary, Tydings agreed to support a Ritchie-for-governor and Radcliffe-for-senator ticket. Conley taunted "Prince Albert the Fourth"—and came close to defeating the incumbent governor in the primary. Mayor Jackson feigned party loyalty but steamed unhappily. Marie Bauernschmidt, who since 1920 had served as secretary of the Baltimore Public School Association and aired her political opinions in a popular radio show, attacked the governor for appointing a notorious West Baltimore ward leader, Jack Pollack, to the Maryland Athletic Commission. Edging in for the kill, and placing value on drama, Republicans decided on Harry Nice—Ritchie's victim in 1919. On the surface the fall campaign had curiously little to do with issues. After the near-loss in the primary, Ritchie ran as a "100% New Dealer." Nice, though a good Republican, employed the slogan New Dealer, New Deck, and claimed he could obtain more federal benefits for the state. Most Maryland voters were thankful for the still-unproven New Deal and tired of their cautious (the socialists said "timid") governor. Eastern Shore whites, old drys, Baltimore blacks, and organized labor had grown especially tired. Nice narrowly won. Radcliffe defeated Joseph France. Ritchie died in February 1936.

Mostly because of Ritchie's reticence in dollar-matching programs, Marylanders received on a per capita basis less New Deal money than citizens in all but a few other states. Yet the impact of federal programs was considerable. Hoover's RFC returned Maryland Casualty and USF&G to stability (under Howard Bruce, Baltimore Trust reorganized as Maryland National Bank), and by the late summer of 1934 the Roosevelt administration announced that it had spent more than $115 million in the state—about $40 million in outright grants. Emergency Relief money already amounted to $16.5 million. The PWA spent large sums on the Chesapeake and Delaware Canal and underwrote state construction projects like the building of a new Hall of Records in Annapolis, a permanent home for the old state documents that for many years had been in Baltimore under care of the Maryland Historical Society. The Home Owners' Loan Corporation had invested $25.4 million in Maryland while saving, said Tydings, 6,000 mortgages in Baltimore alone. The AAA had put $606,000 toward reducing farm surpluses, and the Farm Credit Administration $6.7 million toward preserving farm ownership.

The CCC established thirteen camps and in 1934 had enrolled 2,600 young men in Maryland. They worked to control erosion, plant trees, build firebreaks in the woods, and conserve fish and game. They rebuilt Fort Frederick and the old Washington Monument in Washington County and made a city park in Salisbury. All the while "the clean outdoor life and healthy labor," an election-year report said, brought about a "remarkable physical and mental transformation." On the advice of Custenborder and the Children's Aid Society, the CCC took 32 lads from Carroll County; the government provided them room, board, and a small spending allowance, and gave their

Top, Civilian Conservation Corps outdoor programs especially aimed to benefit rural Marylanders like these three Garrett County young men pictured in
1936. *MSA, Robert G. Merrick Archive of Maryland Historical Photographs. Bottom*,
the beneficiary of a Farm Security Administration loan listened dubiously as
a supervisor offered advice on raising chickens, 1940. *Library of Congress*

families an additional $25 a month. Along with better times at the canneries and on the farms, Custenborder reported in the fall of 1934, the CCC, Civil Works Administration, and PWA greatly reduced the Carroll County relief rolls. In the spring of 1935 the General Assembly passed a new-deal measure of its own, creating public welfare boards in each county. Custenborder afterward returned her attention to the private care of dependent children.[26]

Friendly sources in the Roosevelt administration estimated that between 1933 and 1934 Maryland taxes paid to the federal government had climbed by almost 50 percent—demonstrating an economic turnabout and also suggesting that the New Deal would pay for itself. Doubters in Maryland, besides the wealthy whose ox Roosevelt threatened to gore, rallied around the cynical, tough old reporters, H. L. Mencken and Frank Kent. Both of them lifelong loyal Democrats, they illustrated the persistence of conservative political thought in the state. Referring to Roosevelt as "Dr. R.," Mencken used his Monday column in the *Evening Sun* to shudder at government rallies and printed propaganda on behalf of programs like the NRA. He laughed at New Deal bureaucrats, many of them so powerful as to be Washington celebrities; they were gaudy busybodies among whom "even the neophytes managed to be photographed like kidnappers or movie stars." Because Germany and Italy had fallen to spellbinding dictators, Mencken and Kent took fright at FDR's immense personal popularity and apparent disregard for constitutional restrictions. At the December 1934 Gridiron Club "roast" of FDR, Mencken began his after-dinner talk with a deep bow and the words, "Mr. President, Mr. Wright, and fellow subjects of the Reich." Kent's *Sun* column entitled "The Great Game of Politics" warned of the country's being "buoyed up by government money" and of the "great class of beneficiaries" that federal largesse created. Nationally syndicated by the end of 1934, Kent attacked New Deal "soak the rich" tax proposals as demagogic attempts "to convince the little fellow that he is going to have a free ride and that the 'Fat Cats' will pay the whole bill." The New Deal banked "on the mental poverty of the voters," Kent wrote as the 1936 campaign approached; Roosevelt depended on "the appeal of class hatred."[27]

With any threat from the Peoples Unemployment League put to rest, Kent may have based his fears on passage the year before of the Wagner Act, strengthening labor's hand in the American economy, and on recent labor violence. In August 1936 organizers representing the new and comparatively militant Congress of Industrial Organizations (CIO) had led a strike of seventeen hundred workers at Cumberland's Kelly-Springfield tire plant. The men sought union recognition, better wages and hours, and improved working conditions. Trying to keep workers satisfied with a company-sponsored "protective association," management refused to talk to CIO leaders. The company loaded a bus with nonstriking employees, secured a police escort, and headed for the picket lines—whereupon strikers stoned the bus and police threw tear gas canisters at them. Though in September the strike

National Recovery Administration troupe at the Gayety Theater, Baltimore, 1933. Officials hoped that showgirls and vaudeville acts would boost popular support for the NRA. *Peale Museum, Baltimore City Life Museums*

failed, federal officials under the Wagner Act finally ordered Kelly-Springfield to bargain with the CIO union.

Similar confrontations at other Maryland factories established labor's rights (and power) once and for all. Near Cumberland, at the Celanese Corporation textile plant in Amcelle, nine thousand workers struck in November. While the narrative of detectives, scabs, stones, and stabbings followed the old pattern, the results were new. Celanese agreed to negotiate with the CIO union, establish grievance procedures, and pay higher wages. Early the next year the United Automobile Workers (of the CIO) fought a battle to organize General Motors plants in Baltimore. Labor divided there; as many as twenty-four hundred nonstriking workers actually signed a thank-you letter for Christmas bonuses (one of their leaders turned out to be a company mole). Finally GM agreed to deal with the CIO. Across the bay at the Phillips canning plant in Cambridge, workers had to make the now-familiar decision between an aggressive national or "home" (company) union. After fighting among themselves and with the company, they affiliated with the American Federation of Labor.

Until the late 1930s Mencken and Kent played to a small but devoted anti-Roosevelt audience in Maryland. While the president lost several new counties in 1936 (Carroll, Charles, and Somerset joined Garrett and Calvert, which FDR had lost four years before), he gained about seventy-five thousand votes over his 1932 total. The president then overreached himself, in the eyes of many Marylanders. For one thing, a former professor whom FDR had made head of the Resettlement Administration, Rexford Guy Tugwell, began building a strange city in Prince George's County. Bright, famous for his idealism, Tugwell had set out to establish a wholly rational community, one that would bring together people of different incomes and backgrounds in affordable housing. He wanted to provide easy access to workplace, and to maximize pleasantry, greenery, and safety. The government bought 12,000 acres next to its Beltsville agricultural property and kept 3,600 acres of the tract for the town—217 acres for housing and the rest, in park and open land, providing a protective, green belt against the world.

Greenbelt grew up a child of reason. In 1936 relief labor, largely unskilled, began building 885 "units" on the tract, most of them "multi-family dwellings." Construction had to be kept simple. A few buildings were of brick; more were of cinder block or were wooden with a brick veneer. "Flat and pitched roofs mingle harmoniously enough," a visitor wrote, "and color has been used gaily and judiciously on the wood trim of the red or white houses." The houses went on the slopes of a crescent-shaped hill. Main roadways followed land contours while intersecting streets created five 15- to 20-acre "superblocks." Experts kept sidewalks and homes at a distance from the roads. Underpasses ensured that children could walk all over the community without crossing thoroughfares. Playgrounds abounded. Planners put the business district at a plaza in the center of town, equally accessible to all homes. Greenbelt had two new schools, with the elementary school auditorium also serving as a community center and multi-denominational church. Each of the apartment buildings had its own garden and garage; everyone had an up-to-date electric kitchen. Tugwell and his architects believed themselves "creating a stage, a theatre for the good life."[28]

Though towns emerged according to this vision near several American cities, none allowed so complete a demonstration of the ideal as Greenbelt, Maryland. Nor did "experts" and joiners of the sort Mencken derided ever enjoy more freedom. Drawing floor plans that directed traffic through the living room, designers wanted to reform the average American's habit, as someone said, of only using that space for weddings, funerals, and rubber plants. Workers for the new Works Progress Administration (WPA) designed and built "modern furniture that affords the best use of space, best decoration and best utility." Slightly undersized, the furniture made the rooms seem larger. In mid-1937 social workers conducted a laborious screening of the five thousand or so Greenbelt applicants, who filled out questionnaires and endured interviews with "senior selection specialists." The government sought lower-middle-income families who needed housing and had an interest in "group living." The pioneer settlers, white and young, typically had one or two children. Seven out of ten worked for the federal government. They loved to get involved. Besides church groups, Greenbelt soon had clubs for photography, bridge, radio, sports, widows, drama, scouting, music, journalism, and rifle shooting. At the end of Greenbelt's first year, thirty-five organizations competed for the citizen's spare time. Asked by a reporter what Greenbelters did for amusement, an early resident exclaimed, "We organize!" But that was not all they did. The birth rate in Greenbelt in 1937 and 1938 reached almost four times the national rate. Social scientists wrote articles on topics like "Eugenics at Greenbelt" and "Fertility in a Greenbelt Community."[29]

Tugwell had toured Russia in 1927 and once told an audience that Americans should "execute a concerted attack on well-stocked Tory citadels." His utopian community in Prince George's County generated more than a little controversy. Enemies viewed Tugwell's wave of the future as so much radicalism. The *American Mercury* entitled an article on Tugwell "The Sweetheart of the Regimenters," and Roy S. Braden, acting Greenbelt city manager, obligingly spoke of developing "further interest in group living as contrasted with individual philosophy." The Greenbelt school had murals depicting

Near the Greenbelt movie theater, c. 1938, patriotism and socially conscious art came together. *Larry Klein*

"Pouring Concrete," "Constructing Sewers," and "Shovel at Work." The "social realism" school also applied economic lessons, for all commercial ventures in Greenbelt were cooperatives at first financed by E. A. Filene, a philanthropist with a bent for experiment. Grocery store, filling station, beauty parlor, and the like, eventually to be community owned, paid annual dividends to townspeople. Greenbelt schoolchildren opened a gumdrop co-op.[30]

Marylanders usually welcomed more green spaces, and natives eventually grew accustomed to these interesting outsiders who published their own mimeographed newspaper. But the cost of Tugwell's scheme boggled the mind. The government spent about $15 million for the town, depending on one's accounting formula, and the cost per unit may have been as high as $10,000. Putting that figure at merely $4,423, Tugwell's men called Greenbelt a model for private builders. Critics noted that someone, if not the government, would have to pay for water, sewerage, schools, and business structures. Bound up with relief work in any case, the project understandably tilted toward the expensive. Workers took a year and spent $72,000 making a swamp into a fishpond and swimming hole. The water apparently did not invite swimming (Greenbelt critics claimed the fish died, as well), and so the government spent another $72,000 on a pool. Meanwhile residents paid the agriculture department rent that barely met operating costs and did nothing to return the taxpayers' investment. Perhaps worst of all, Prince George's County could not tax the growing federal acreage near Beltsville. The government instead paid the county an amount established by Congress "in lieu of taxes."

Tugwell had resigned by the time Roosevelt faced another hurdle with Marylanders. By so wide a margin had he won the country in 1936 that he felt strong enough next year to reorganize the federal judiciary. The Supreme Court recently had declared several New Deal programs, including the NRA, unconstitutional; by naming up to six new justices, all friendly to him, the president would gain considerable legislative leeway. Mencken and Kent jumped on the "court packing" plan as a brazen violation of separation of powers. Now they had with them the state's senior U.S. Senator, who until then had been a fairly dependable supporter of the New Deal. Tydings opposed the court reorganization measure with pointed questions on the Senate floor. The bill sought to retire justices over the age of seventy. Tydings rightly noted that sitting justices over that limit had divided on all issues, including New Deal cases, and observed that men like Holmes and Brandeis had made important contributions to the court past the age of eighty. Most effectively, Tydings asked whether supporters of the bill would seek some similar "artifice" in the future, when, perchance, the ideology of the court leaned too far in the other direction. Was the Supreme Court to become a kind of football? "We have no right" he declared, "to pack the Supreme Court of the United States to change its philosophy."[31] In August 1938 FDR set out to rid himself of wavering congressmen and senators. At a news con-

ference he singled out Tydings as a conservative wolf in New Deal wool—
"He wants to run with the Roosevelt prestige and the money of his con-
servative Republican friends both on his side." FDR called on Maryland
Democrats to support the old Western Maryland Progressive and now faith-
ful New Deal congressman, David Lewis, in the senatorial primary—to vote
Tydings out of office.[32]

Roosevelt made a big mistake. Always hostile to outside influence, whether
the subject be secession or Prohibition, Marylanders—a great many of them,
anyway—soon determined to reelect Tydings or die in the attempt. Seizing
on the sentiment he knew was there, the senator made a statewide radio
appeal within days of Roosevelt's news conference. "Let the Federal Administration and all the people of the country know that the Free State shall
remain free," he said, and "that Maryland's traditional rights will be safe-
guarded and preserved." The president kept on the offensive in early September by taking a working holiday in Maryland. He and Lewis visited
Charles County to inspect the site of a major highway bridge (later named
for Governor Nice) to be built largely with federal funds, then cruised down
the Potomac and across the bay to Crisfield. After a motorcade to Denton,
Roosevelt gave a Labor Day address that network radio carried to the nation.
He praised Lewis as a self-made man, steered clear of Tydings's name, and
pledged to try to keep the Democratic party liberal. Not even FDR's charm
worked in this case. Except for the Baltimore *Afro-American*, Maryland newspapers uniformly viewed the visit and endorsement as an intrusion into
Maryland affairs. The *Salisbury Times* reminded the president, who obviously
had not read deeply in Maryland history, that behind the Shore's hospitality
"is an independence that has existed and grown since long before the days
of the Revolution." In Lewis's hometown the Cumberland *Evening Times* likened Roosevelt's recommendation to Hitler's purge orders. On the twelfth
of September, Lewis won his congressional district while Tydings carried
Baltimore City and the rest of the counties by a total of about sixty-five
thousand votes. It was not necessary to get off the face of the earth if Mr.
Roosevelt frowned, read a triumphant *Sun* editorial. "Maryland has given
its demonstration before the eyes of all people that representative government still lives."[33]

Even with this solid evidence of independence, however, Marylanders for
the most part admired their multiterm president. Roosevelt's domestic program continued to serve them. The Rural Electrification Administration in the
thirties provided $629,000 toward the electric lines that revolutionized farm
life. By the end of the decade Maryland cooperatives, with fourteen hundred
farm families as members, had strung four hundred miles of new power lines.
Poultrymen, who needed to warm chicks in a continuing growing cycle, and
dairymen, for whom electric milking machines made life much easier, benefited especially. The state forester testified that CCC projects had advanced
conservation work on Maryland timberlands by twenty-five years. The Uni-

versity of Maryland—whose president, Harry C. "Curley" Byrd, stood at the fore of New Deal supporters in the state—received millions of dollars for academic and student buildings at College Park. In addition to the new Potomac bridge, Maryland gained by a new span over the Susquehanna above Havre de Grace. Drainage projects aided the Eastern Shore. Hard hit by the Depression, and already a beneficiary of federal aid, the B&O in 1937 applied for additional relief through the RFC. Among its bottom-of-the-barrel assets, the railroad listed title to the C&O Canal. Before long the federal government, which had been interested in the old canal since the twenties, purchased it for $2 million. Restoring the canal would be a public works project, the C&O park a retreat later Americans would consider a rich New Deal dividend. Roosevelt and other dignitaries (they included a veteran towpath mule) dedicated the lower portion of the park on Washington's birthday, 1939.

⌒∾⌒

While politicians fought over public policy and power balances in the 1930s, Marylanders survived the Depression as best they could. In late life, talking to a visitor, Joe Sutton offered a rural black perspective on this period of frightening events and unbroken pride. A Talbot County black forty-five years old in 1930, Sutton had worked his entire life on Miles Neck—mostly as a farmhand, sometimes doing a stint in a canning factory or going after oysters. He had taught himself to work on autos and once earned money as a chauffeur. He also raised Chesapeake Retrievers, selling eight-week-old pups for twenty-five dollars. His dogs developed such a reputation that orders came from as far as Boston, Minnesota, and Alaska. A man of some substance, if little money, he later recalled how rocky black-white relations grew on the middle Shore during the Depression years. One of his black acquaintances had a white neighbor who went to the bank in Easton every Saturday and offered to deposit the Negro's savings while in town. One day the black man called at the bank to learn how much was in his account. The answer was nothing. Sutton also described grimly the sport some white boys took driving backroads and trying to hit Negroes walking the shoulders— "It's been a lot of 'em killed like that," he testified, "a lot of 'em been killed a purpose on the road." The Salisbury lynching left Sutton especially sad. Some townspeople, and many blacks, believed the culprit was the victim's wayward son, who had tried to kill Williams because he had seen the murder. "Them were hard days, though," Sutton remembered. He tonged for oysters, canned them, and sold them to make a little cash. He refused welfare baskets in the second of the worst Depression years, feeling better off than others. "Course I could've got food," he explained in talking about the credit available at a country store, "but I didn't want to go into debt for it." [34]

Sutton spoke for the country Negroes who might spend their entire lives within a few miles of their birthplace. Eleanora Holiday represented the very few Maryland blacks who, like Eubie Blake a generation earlier, managed to

Billie Holiday (1915–59), Baltimore's own "Lady Day," behind the Royal Theater with friend Willie Lewis, 1947. *Gordon Anderson*

leave home for stardom. Born in Baltimore in 1915, "Billie" (for film star Billie Dove) accompanied her father, who played banjo and guitar, to New York in her early teens. There, along with Cab Calloway, she became part of a wildly popular jazz medium—the big-band music played to be danced to and called "swing." She began singing at small Harlem clubs and then in 1933 won the attention of John Hammond, a legendary talent scout, and through him of Benny Goodman, a leading bandmaster. Recording with Goodman's orchestra and then on her own, performing at places like the Apollo, Billie perfected a personal, highly expressive delivery that gave listeners to tunes like "He's Funny That Way" the sensation that she was singing it for the first time, and meant it for each of them alone. "If you find a tune and it's got something to do with you," she explained, "you don't have to evolve anything. You feel it, and when you sing it other people can feel something, too. Give me a song I can feel and it's never work." This sense of intimacy, her genius, came at a personal price; her sultry sound had emotional roots in experiences like Joe Sutton's. One of her most popular recordings, "Strange Fruit"—written especially for her—referred to the bodies of blacks dangling from trees. When she first finished singing it to an audience her listeners remained hushed, stunned. "There are a few songs that I feel so much I can't stand to sing them," Billie once admitted, "but that's something else again." Her burden proved too heavy. She began to rely on drink and drugs for support.[35]

Most Maryland blacks in the thirties had to choose between the poverty and occasional terror of the country and the slums of Baltimore. Even before the Depression many blacks on the Eastern Shore and in Southern Maryland had gone to the city. As hard times continued (two-thirds of Elkton blacks were without work in the spring of 1932), more blacks moved to Baltimore, where the Negro population rose slightly, to 17 percent. A study the Baltimore chapter of the National Urban League published in the spring of 1935 counted about fifty-five hundred black teachers, doctors, nurses, lawyers, and other professionals in Baltimore, where Negroes in 1935–1936 formed their own Monumental City bar and medical associations. Some blacks owned bakeries, gas stations, or lunch rooms. Still supporting its Colored Symphony Orchestra, Baltimore also boasted a black theater group connected with Morgan College and a 300-voice choir. There were more Negro schoolteachers in Baltimore than in any other American city. In 1935 a young Baltimore lawyer, Thurgood Marshall, won his first case as attorney for the local chapter of the National Association for the Advancement of Colored People. Sharing oral argument with NAACP attorney and Howard University dean Charles H. Houston, Marshall convinced the Maryland Court of Appeals that, in the absence of a "separate but equal" institution for blacks, the University of Maryland Law School (which five years before had denied Marshall admission) had an obligation to accept qualified Negro applicants. "What's at stake here is more than the rights of my clients," Marshall declared, "it's the moral commitment stated in our country's creed." Marshall soon turned his attention to unequal pay scales for white and black teachers, successfully taking the complaint of a Montgomery County principal as his test case. In 1938 Baltimore police accepted three blacks, one of them a woman, on the force.[36]

Though important, these ornaments and advances did little for the average Baltimore black, who worried about jobs, health, crime, and schools. Despite excellence in some classrooms (Marshall had graduated from Douglass High School), black illiteracy, at 7 percent, still stood ahead of that for whites (less than 1 percent). Negroes suffered 73 percent of all Baltimore deaths due to venereal disease and 47 percent of the tuberculosis mortality. Blacks in the city who had work largely were common laborers, domestics, or drudges in the noxious fertilizer and chemical plants. In 1933, 40 percent of the city's blacks relied on public support (13 percent of all whites did), and the figures did not improve quickly. Work open to blacks paid so little that some of them quit to "go on the relief." Black migrants comforted one another by forming small, "store-front" or front-parlor churches among themselves, trying to maintain old neighborhood ties and friendships. In such groups and extended families Baltimore blacks shared the meager food and shelter they had.[37]

Evelyn Harris, a widow trying to sustain her family of five children and hold onto her farm in Kent County, kept a one-year chronicle of her trials that shed more light on the deprivation and courage of the Depression years. "Success in life," she began with Eastern Shore simplicity, "is not spelled $ucce$$." In Chestertown at the first of the year for a required orphans' court appearance, she pleaded unsuccessfully with the county commissioners for a lower, more realistic property assessment. She paid for groceries with eggs and for a daughter's two new dresses with firewood. Many farmers paid debts with wood, and blacks—whose well-being concerned Harris beyond an employer's interest—did most of the woodcutting at her farm in exchange for food and fuel. In need of a new coat to wear to Baltimore, she paid a tailor in sweet potatoes, sausage, and apples to mend her old one, which soon tore again. The tailor bet ten dollars no one could mend it in its condition, so she patched the lining with adhesive tape. The tailor welched on the bet. Poverty on a farm she laughingly pronounced "thrilling." In February the fireplace burned "all day and most of the night with seasoned logs," she wrote, "and the lamps are so placed in the living room that the lack of electricity is a minor thing." She paid for newspapers and magazines with produce and roasting chickens—even three-cent stamps made a hole in her cash supply. She sacrificed trees for their cash value—selling locust for fenceposts and chestnut for firewood (before learning that it was premium furniture material). When the telephone company repaired downed lines, she took the surplus wire for berry vines. Rags, cleaned and dyed, made braided rugs. The sides of sheets, cut off and resewn, replaced the worn middles. Harris bought chicks with spruce saplings and called on farm women to make their own bread—"We need a permanent wave of old-fashioned cooking to lift the depression." She paid summer farm labor with lard, flour, home-killed meat, and clothing—"anything which could be used by the worker and his family." In August she sent to New York five hundred baskets of fancy number-one tomatoes. They sold for half the cost of raising them.[38]

Whether class hatred of the sort Frank Kent wrote about ever actually reared its head, Harris and other Eastern Shore natives made a sharp distinction between amateur and professional farmers. In the tight squeeze of the Depression the difference could only grow sharper. For many years people of outside wealth had been buying up old estates along the Chesapeake and its Eastern Shore rivers as country homes or hunting retreats. In the summer of 1925 the Queenstown *News* reported Centreville "aroused" at word that Wintora, an old home on Corsica Neck, had gone to the wife of a du Pont and General Motors millionaire; having paid thirty-five thousand dollars for the house and its 655 acres, she planned to make the place "a thoroughly modern country estate." Such purchases formed a pattern in the

1930s, when more than a few Eastern Shore farmers went bankrupt. A New York advertising man bought almost four miles of waterfront property and commuted to Manhattan using a seaplane. Parke Sedley, a St. Louis carburetor magnate, bought Shipping Creek Farm on Kent Island to go with his Colorado ranch. The president of Pittsburgh Steel purchased Marengo on the Miles River in Talbot County, while his counterpart at Steuben Glass became owner of Wye Plantation.[39]

For color or cheek none of the newcomers equaled Glenn and Jacqueline Stewart. Glenn, a Pittsburgh-born Ivy Leaguer whom the Foreign Service had dropped as more painful than promising, had bought large acreage across the Miles River from St. Michaels in the early 1920s. On Cape Centaur, as he called it, Stewart built a replica of the medieval Spanish Alhambra. He imported tiles, carpets, and the like, but used local labor to build much of the castle, and for the sake of authenticity required the stucco men to use their fingers as had Moorish slaves in the thirteenth century. In this incredible structure—with drawbridge, bullet-proof doors, secret compartments, and firing slits in the walls—Stewart squirreled away over a million dollars of the family fortune. He himself looked every inch the wealthy eccentric. He used a gold cigarette holder, had a moustache with pointed ends, a patch over one eye, and a face marked by a college prank (he claimed it was a dueling scar). He also had an Austrian bodyguard named Adolph, a pack of thirty Irish wolfhounds that by published accounts ate 175 pounds of beef a day, and an air-raid siren that once went off accidentally. Stewart called himself the Duke of Kent Island, which he hoped one day to own. Meantime, when not sailing the Caribbean aboard his eighty-foot black schooner, he bought more land on Miles Neck and farms on nearby Wye Island. After the Stewart divorce all Eastern Shore properties fell to Jacqueline, the distant scent of whose perfume, said a local farmer, nearly blinded his mule. She bought more of Wye Island, fenced the property, closed off a road that gave watermen access to a cove they used behind Drum Point, and evicted all native tenants.

Many of the new Eastern Shore residents added something by their presence—restoring old homes, making aesthetic points when the county commissioners decided an issue. The Centreville *Queen Anne's Record-Observer* welcomed these "delightful persons," for they loved "in advance the countryside and watersides on which they settle." Other natives noticed their No Trespassing signs and high fences. "No friendly gunning or fox-hunting or visiting," Harris wrote with clear resentment; "no friendly chats over the telephone on party lines." The children did not join the Boy Scouts or girls' clubs and went off to private schools. The parents had no reason to join the parent-teacher organizations and never joined the farmers' groups.[40]

Her principal objection to these "city men and women," however, was that they farmed merely as a hobby and undercut the efforts of the less fortunate. Visiting one of her wealthy, outsider neighbors, Harris watched in disbelief while herdsmen in starched white coveralls attended the birthing of pigs. The "porkers' palace" had hot water and an air filtering system, she wrote; imported cattle lived in quarters nicer than most houses in Kent County— "with all sorts of patented fixtures for the handling and mixing of the feeds, the latest in brushes and combs and toilet doo-dads for the 'dressing tables,' and fresh clean bedding twice a day." Echoing a complaint made in the 1830s, she noted that at county fairs the livestock native boys and their fathers raised had no hope of competing against expensive, blooded stock. During the rest of the year, on market days, estate-farm products merely took a chunk out of the ordinary farmer's receipts. Besides losing money on milk production, the amateur admitted that on the hogs he lost four cents apiece—which, he quickly added, did not include the cost of their new building. "But," Harris said to herself, "it *did* help to glut the market at that time."[41]

People forgot such complaints by taking extraordinary joy in ordinary pleasures. A group of City College students pooled their coinage and took tours in an old car one of them had. One hot day they went out to the Patapsco State Forest to go hiking and skinny dipping; discovering some ladies already there, and being without bathing suits, they discreetly went into the water one by one, sharing the single pair of boxer shorts among them. Sharing and keeping cool in hot weather became two leading Depression themes— water, so close to many Marylanders, supplied inexpensive fun and helped to keep up spirits. Harris always looked forward to the family picnics down by the shore; while during the winter her children took baths from a teakettle and wash basin, in summer they had the whole Chesapeake Bay. "Homemade rafts from shore wreckage, plus strips of home-sawed lumber," she wrote, "have given them many thrills in July and August." Unpretentious resorts like Marshall Hall below Washington and Chesapeake Beach in Calvert County drew thousands of economy-minded vacationers. Ritchie's highway program enabled a growing number of Marylanders to discover the delights of Ocean City. There in the summer of 1933 visitors found themselves caught in one of the worst storms to hit the Atlantic Coast in decades. Though waves and wind inflicted heavy property damage, the hurricane turned out to be a long-range boon to Ocean City landowners: the storm cut an inlet in the barrier sands, giving the town a harbor and making Assawoman Bay behind the town even more inviting as a fish-filled estuary. Ocean City became one of the most popular spots on the eastern seaboard for sports fishing.[42]

No doubt because so many people felt that their luck could get no worse, gambling gained in popularity in the thirties. Bingo remained a favorite pastime, successful, Harris wrote with amazement, "in every town and village where there are any concessions sold for the amusement of people." With enough kernels of corn, paper playing cards, and a few colorful prizes "displayed on a shelf and brilliantly lighted by electricity," churches and civic organizations could always depend on drawing large crowds. Victims of the Depression also flocked to the two-dollar windows at Maryland race tracks; "Any citizen with $5," said a guide to the state that writers under the WPA produced in these years, "can get on a streetcar, go to the famous Preakness, place a minimum bet on the wrong horse, invest heavily in beer and hot dogs, and return with some change." State law permitted bingo and pari-mutuel betting. It was "every man's privilege to waste his time and money" as he liked best, conceded Baltimore judge Samuel K. Dennis, "or as some express it, to go to Hades by his own route."[43]

But the "numbers game" and contraptions like the pinball machine, slot machine, and "claw machine" were not legal in May 1935, when Dennis declared the city "well nigh overrun" with unlawful gambling. He ordered police to crack down. Little wonder that their poor performance disturbed him; after an investigation begun by J. Bernard Wells, Baltimore City state's attorney, a grand jury early in 1936 indicted twenty-eight officers for their part in illegal numbers. As the story unraveled, one defendant was murdered, witnesses had second thoughts about testifying, and in July authorities had no choice but to drop all charges. The murderer went uncaught. Investigating this series of embarrassments to order, which included the worst police scandal since 1893, a committee of the city bar association later estimated that the underground numbers game grossed fifty thousand dollars a day in Baltimore.[44]

In the spring of 1937 legislators decided to make the pervasive nuisance of machine gambling into a revenue source. The General Assembly legalized devices like the pinball machine, involving "skill," so long as businessmen made payoffs not in cash but in merchandise. Owners paid thirty-five dollars a year for a license. By September of that year, after a heavy immigration of New York dealers, the number of pinball machines in Baltimore had grown to about thirty-five hundred—located in arcades, bars, clubs, tobacco shops, restaurants, billiard rooms, and pool halls. The classic downtown arcade had long rows of machines, attendants on patrol, and "a blonde cashier" who presided over a counter where customers exchanged slugs for prizes ranging from cigarettes to lamps, dolls, toasters, toiletries, silver pieces, and radios. Describing the Maryland law as being full of loopholes, owners kept their lips tightly sealed on the subject of profits. An *Evening Sun* reporter characterized the money in gambling machines as "pu-lenty." While legalizing the machines freed police from enforcing an unpopular law, the problem of defining and controlling vice did not disappear with open gambling any more than with the repeal of Prohibition. Gambling in fact generated capital for ventures like prostitution and the purchase of political influence; it offered a fertile field for the characters who had blossomed during Prohibition and explained the presence of immigrants like Coney Island Whitey, whom Mrs. Bauernschmidt in her radio programs placed on a plane with John Dillinger and Pretty Boy Floyd. Police still could be paid to wink at illegal machines like the "one-armed bandits." Perhaps with the example of open pinball machines in mind, Maryland voters in November 1938 turned down a constitutional amendment that would have permitted a state lottery.[45]

The vote betokened the durable values of most Marylanders, who like Evelyn Harris escaped worries about layoffs or poor prices by pursuing the common pleasures of the day. One could stay at home, as surely a few did, and read accounts of early Maryland; festivities surrounding the 300th anniversary of the St. Mary's landing attracted two thousand visitors to the first colonial capital on 25 March 1934 and increased popular interest in books like Swepson Earle's *Chesapeake Bay Country* (Earle still served as state conservation commissioner) and Mathew Page Andrews's *Founding of Maryland* (1933). Families listened to radio programs, which by then featured singing commercials and included popular serials, live broadcasts of dance orchestras, and game shows. Adults who could afford it went out dancing at places like the Hippodrome or Famous Ballroom in Baltimore. The Baltimore Symphony and Peabody Conservatory orchestras survived the Depression with the help of generous patrons. The Vagabond Players struggled for the scarcer theater dollar by settling into a repertoire of one-act Broadway revivals, while the Hopkins Players, with a stable academic audience, continued to produce experimental plays and classics. In 1935 Earl Larrimore and Selena Royle established a repertory company at Ford's Theater, the University Players, which included young talents like Henry Fonda, Margaret Sullavan, and Robert Montgomery. Two years later the Ford's management felt solvent enough to give the old building another remodeling. Until the late thirties, when Congress cut funding, federal music and theater projects took summer concerts and plays to rural Maryland audiences.

For forty cents the curious could get inside the East Biddle Street townhouse in Baltimore where Miss Bessie Wallis Warfield had spent several years of her childhood. Like her father named for Severn Teackle Wallis, and with proud relatives who included her uncle, "Sol" Davies Warfield, Miss Warfield had not had an ordinary young life. Her father died soon after her birth; her mother, invited to leave the house of her mother-in-law, had conducted an affair with and then married Boss Rasin's son. First married to an alcoholic navy flyer and then to Ernest Simpson, a British subject and New York broker whose business often kept him and his wife in London, Wallis in the early thirties met the Prince of Wales, who found the saucy and ambitious American woman intriguing. Mencken described the illustrious romance that followed as "the greatest story since the resurrection." In December 1936 King Edward VIII announced to the British people that he found the throne "an impossible burden" without the woman he loved. Mrs. Simpson obtained a second divorce and then became the duchess of Windsor. Many Britons believed her a moll, a tramp. Many Americans saw her as a Cinderella. If nothing else she proved again the humanity of British monarchs.

In the fall of 1937 rumors flew that the elegant couple planned an American tour, and Baltimore prepared eagerly for the visit. The curator at the Biddle Street home invited the duchess to pay a call at the museum, where, besides viewing wax figurines of royal persons, visitors sat in Wallis's bathtub (it magically made one more sensuous) and saw the kitchen from which, said a card, "came the Maryland dishes she has made famous the world over." Governor Nice and Mayor Jackson promised the couple a warm, Maryland welcome. Debutantes practiced curtsies and tried parting their hair down the middle in the duchess's manner. Rumors that the homeless Windsors might settle on an estate out Joppa Road set off a brief real estate boom in the area. A friend of a friend of the duke and duchess reportedly spent three hundred thousand dollars remodeling his home, Wye Hall, on the Eastern Shore. Sadly for all these folk, the duke and duchess canceled their travel plans.[46]

For sheer escape it was difficult to top the darkened movie hall, watching cowboy sagas in which the good guy always won or cheerful musicals with spectacular dance numbers. Theaters thrived even in the early 1930s, when the Westminster proprietor had accepted cans of food for needy families as the price of admission. According to the *Sun* in 1934, the reviewing of films had been "liberalized greatly in recent years" but in fat times or lean the Maryland Board of Censors enforced family morality on the screen; the very expression on a man's face when he kissed his leading lady came under scrutiny. Boys in Baltimore who looked eighteen (or barely so) stole away to visit the Gayety, one of the city's burlesque houses in the Baltimore Street theater district. But at least on Saturday afternoons most of the entertainment there withstood any mother's inquiry. "I'd get a quarter and it lasted all day," recalled one Baltimorean long afterward. "The No. 16 streetcar cost a nickel; a hot dog and a soda, or two hot dogs, were a nickel; and it cost ten cents to see a movie. There were a lot of theaters showing movies. Good movies."[47]

The Depression deeply affected middle- and working-class Marylanders. For young people it shaped, for older ones confirmed, the value of family ties, the stern laws of work, duty, and responsibility. By 1939 most Marylanders in their teens could scarcely remember a time when pocketbooks were not pinched, many people not out of work, relatives not needy. Hard and discouraging as those times were, "they contributed something positive," Louis Sandler wrote later, "not only to me but to most other Americans who remember them. They made us tougher, and gave us a confidence in our own abilities that we might not have learned otherwise. To this day I have a respect for material things, however small, and I appreciate them because I can remember days when we had to do without them."[48]

❧❧❧

"Whether we like it or not," Roosevelt said in his January 1940 message to Congress, "the daily lives of American citizens will, of necessity, feel the shock of events on other continents." The line drew little applause. At the

Podles Meat Market, East Baltimore, 1933. With his wife and family, Joe Podles—son of Polish immigrants, former cannery worker and lightweight boxing champion—here revealed the determination that helped so many people survive the Depression. *Baltimore Neighborhood Heritage Project, University of Baltimore*

time a majority of his countrymen were isolationists who feared involvement in yet another bloody European war, thanked God for two wide oceans, and focused their attention on decidedly serious domestic affairs. American military and naval forces had fallen to a minimum, and the army had more men than equipment. Surveying the scene, Dean Acheson—a State Department undersecretary who owned a Maryland farm and had supported Ritchie for president—hoped it true that God looked after children, drunks, and the United States of America. Segments of Maryland opinion hoped to avoid any military buildup against Germany—many Catholics thought Stalin, not Hitler, the real enemy; bankers and shippers worried about the trade disruptions a war would bring. Isolationist leaders like Charles Lindbergh lent them encouragement. "We must not be misguided by this foreign propaganda," he said, "that our frontiers lie in Europe." [49]

Newsworthy events gradually overruled or displaced the guarded sentiments of isolationism. Broadcasts of Hitler's speeches—he demanded a German Czechoslovakia—brought home the danger of war and the German dictator's maniacal personality; when Britain and France let the Germans march, Czech cries of betrayal, which radio brought into millions of American homes, appealed directly to one's sense of fairness. At least in appearance Roosevelt moved only as public opinion allowed. In May 1938 he obtained legislation for a "two-ocean" navy. Little more than a year later, after war broke in Poland, he won a revised neutrality law that permitted arms sales to friendly countries on a "cash and carry" basis. Congress later agreed to appropriate more money for warplanes. In 1940, after the fall of France and the Dunkirk retreat, the president sent the British army "surplus" arms and asked Congress for a draft law. In September he agreed to supply the Royal Navy with old destroyers. After winning an unprecedented third term in office (he denied plans to involve American boys in a foreign war) FDR received another urgent plea from Churchill. In response the president proposed the Lend-Lease Program. America, he said in his radio "fireside chat" of 29 December 1940, would become "the great arsenal of democracy." [50]

Older Marylanders knew both the economic benefits of mobilization and the human costs of war. Relying on the lessons of one world war, state officials prepared for the civic effort a second would require. In August 1940 Herbert R. O'Conor, who two years earlier had defeated Nice for the governorship, formed a state Council of Defense and Resources. A son of Irish immigrants and a product of Mahon's Baltimore ward, O'Conor had gone to the university law school and then, as Baltimore state's attorney, won national publicity for grabbing a murder suspect, wanted in Baltimore, from New York City police. Marylanders next elected him attorney general. He had a flair for prosecution. O'Conor planned to keep a sharp eye out for profiteering and unfair practices; he mentioned the need to deport subversives. Preparing further for war, about two hundred thousand young men registered for the draft in mid-October. Lined up to begin the military processing that their fathers had endured in 1917–18, they told a reporter from the Sunpapers that the draft probably was necessary, even a good thing, but most of them hoped to fight only if the country were invaded. In February 1941 men of the 29th Division reported for a year of active-duty training at Fort Meade.

If for no other reason than self-interest, Marylanders—so many connected with factories—jumped to Roosevelt's armaments call with enthusiasm. A welcomed surge in military and naval business pumped cash into the entire state economy. Edgewood and Aberdeen sprang to life with more military families and more civilian jobs. The prospect of war, causing further growth in the Washington area, brought more people into Montgomery and Prince George's counties. In 1940 Hagerstown employment improved as Fairchild Aircraft, successor to the Kreider-Reisner Company, began filling a government contract for 270 copies of its military training plane, the PT-19. Baltimore companies dealing in steel, copper, machinery, and other products faced a sudden groundswell in demand, but shipbuilding and aircraft firms there led the way. By August 1941 the total value of the past year's war-related business in Baltimore alone stood at $1.6 billion. Bethlehem-Fairfield had contracts to build 62 ships. Workers at Maryland Drydock busily repaired merchant vessels damaged by Nazi torpedoes while making the treacherous North Atlantic run to Britain. Reconverting and expanding its plant, the firm needed 12,000 new employees. Glenn L. Martin Company, then building the B26 light bomber, had $53 million in orders from the British—who were fighting an air war that everyone believed a prelude to a Nazi invasion of the island—and $687 million in orders from the army air force. Martin had 23,000 people on its payroll and expected soon to hire another 6,000. Triumph Industries in Elkton began producing mortar shells for Finland, explosives for Britain, airplane flares for France, and tank mines for Holland. More workers meant more construction work on houses, more jobs in building supply and transportation; more customers meant larger inventories and more clerks. Schools needed teachers, and while true that new workers required services from state and local government, they also enriched the revenue base—and in 1938 the General Assembly, at O'Conor's urging, had adopted a state income tax.

Marylanders rightly expected to gain from this war, but the struggle had moral content and political scale that made it truly worthy of its sacrifices. No one who could read a newspaper or listen to a radio doubted that the conflict being waged in Asia, Europe, and Africa posed militarism and totalitarianism against liberty and self-government. Italy had fallen to the rule of oppressive fascists. The German army, worse than simply an arm of another greedy nation-state, stood for uniformed cruelty, ambitions of global conquest, and racial assumptions that meant, as the Baltimore *Jewish Times* reported clearly, the persecution of Jews. Mencken, who clung to his love for German culture, at first discounted those reports. After paying Germany another visit in 1938, however, he portrayed the Nazis as a "gang of lunatics." Japanese atrocities in China and Indochina were common knowledge. Then, on the morning of 7 December 1941—early Sunday afternoon for Marylanders—the Japanese struck Pearl Harbor. Men and women never forgot the moment they heard the news on the radio. Marylanders of the 29th Division, returning from North Carolina training exercises, had halted their march in Virginia. "This is it," one of them said.[51]

Roosevelt promised that Americans of his day had a "rendezvous with destiny." Even beyond the sense of that phrase, the Second World War was a watershed, first-and-last experience. For most able-bodied males, the war meant enlisting or being drafted. Thousands of Marylanders signed up for army and navy service in the first months after Pearl Harbor (more than 89,000 eventually volunteered or went with the 29th Division; the Selective Service took another 158,000). Along with 3,700 other Marylanders during the war, Leon Uris of Baltimore joined the Marines. He later wrote a sober account of how the war made young men old, beginning with a farewell scene at Pennsylvania Station—a cavernous old structure that swallowed every echoing sound. Uris's departure captured the solemnity of a moment that so many others experienced with him. These goodbyes, final for many boys, were milestones in the lives of everyone concerned—the yet-unscathed young men themselves, but also their families, wives, sweethearts. A younger brother pleaded for a "Jap sword" when the warrior returned. The recruiting sergeant in dress blues called the roll one more time. Passing sailors shattered the silence by crowing "You'll be sorreee!" Finally the quiet youngsters climbed aboard. As the train lurched forward and picked up speed "the platform was filled with trotting and waving and shouting people. The boys in the cars pressed their faces against the windows," Uris wrote. "Faster and faster the train went until the ones outside could no longer keep pace and stopped breathlessly and waved. They grew smaller and smaller. And then the train plunged into a long black tunnel and they were gone."[52]

Army recruits went first to Meade, hurriedly enlarged, where eventually more than a million men and women from the region first encountered military haircuts, fatigues, dog tags, and close-order drill. In April 1942 military evacuation hospitals formed earlier at Johns Hopkins and the University of Maryland (Hopkins supplied the 18th and 118th, Maryland the 42d and 142d) themselves departed from Pennsylvania Station. A month later they sailed from San Francisco for points unknown. Early in 1942 troops of the 29th Division took up ad hoc defense of the Atlantic coast between North Carolina and Delaware. They next left for more rounds of training, while General Reckord, their old leader, assumed duties as commander of the Middle Atlantic Third Corps service area. In place of the 29th stood 2,700 state guards whose service the General Assembly authorized in 1941 as the main line of defense after full mobilization. To protect military objectives like bridges and water towers, the legislature approved a special military police force of 300 more men. Sightings of German periscopes and fears of Luftwaffe raids permitted the most peaceful citizen to feel the excitement of war. Governor O'Conor organized a volunteer reserve force known as minute men, 12,000 strong; mostly over-age fellows, they prepared to defend every county of the state should the Germans land. Citizens had to observe nighttime blackouts. Spotters, trained to recognize enemy airplanes by their silhouettes, served in towers along the Worcester County coast and around the bay. By late 1942, 15,000 Marylanders stood shifts in more than two hundred of these spotting stations.

Marylanders had water to protect, as well. Coast Guard auxiliaries before the outbreak of war embraced hundreds of boatowners who volunteered on both shores of the bay and up the Potomac. Flotillas organized at Baltimore, Washington, Northeast, Easton, and Ocean City; their duties included schooling less experienced boatsmen in subjects like first aid, seamanship, and maintenance. In the months after Pearl Harbor these auxiliarists, assuming police and patrol functions, freed hundreds of regular Coast Guardsmen for sea duty. Ocean City motorboats, yachts, and fishing boats served on anti-submarine patrols that early in the war took them far out into the Atlantic—without much in the way of radios or signaling devices (and at first without government life insurance coverage). In 1942 Ocean City auxiliary boats twice helped rescue seamen in distress. Other volunteers operated a special ferry across the Chesapeake and Delaware Canal (a major thoroughfare, given the submarine threat in the Atlantic), patrolled off Annapolis, and performed miscellaneous duties in the Potomac, Choptank, and Nanticoke rivers. At Baltimore an auxiliary flotilla made up largely of Maryland Yacht Club members established a constant watch off Fort Carroll. Later a Middle River patrol assisted the Martin aircraft plant there. Howard A. Kelly, Jr., commanded the nearly 2,000 Coast Guard temporary reservists in Baltimore harbor; they, with arrest powers, enforced fire and security rules, furnished armed guards, watched neutral ships for suspicious persons, captured stowaways, and kept visiting seamen in tow. Meantime the War Shipping Administration accounted for about 13,000 Marylanders who served aboard merchant marine vessels. Twice that number joined the navy.

The defense buildup proceeded so quickly, and with such sweeping effect, that the First World War seemed hardly a rehearsal by comparison. In February 1942, working for the navy, Baltimore companies began constructing an air station on 6,400 acres of condemned land at Cedar Point, St. Mary's County. Between Cecil County and Baltimore City population increased fivefold during the war. At Aberdeen Proving Ground—where in 1942 ordnance technicians improved the "bazooka" antitank weapon and found a way to waterproof tanks so that they could land on a beach—the military population grew to nearly six times its 1918 size of 5,000. Edgewood Arsenal, which soon grew to 3,400 military and more than 10,000 civilian workers, produced gas masks but also the flamethrower (Maryland natives played a large part in its development) and incendiary bombs of jellied gasoline. In May 1942 the Army Map Service moved into its new home at Brookmont, just outside the District line in Montgomery County; there an enlarged civilian staff eventually produced about 30,000 different maps for military and intelligence use. In June the navy began building an amphibious training base in lower Calvert County and military intelligence took over Camp Ritchie, the Maryland National Guard training area near the old Pen-Mar resort. Fearing a Nazi air attack on Washington, the federal government in the summer of 1942 seized property in the Camp Springs area of Prince George's

County and turned it into Andrews Field, a major air base of 4,700 acres. After dedication ceremonies in August, most Americans knew Bethesda as the site of the new Naval Medical Center—a sprawling, white marble structure with a lofty central tower.

These installations brought business—a honky-tonk strip grew up outside the gates of Fort Meade—but also carried a personal price for natives. At Solomons, government wells for navy housing dropped the water table and local families found their own wells too shallow to draw. Work on an express highway between Bolling Field in Anacostia and Andrews claimed more land in Prince George's. A hundred families had to leave their homes. "If it is essential that the government have this airport," said Robert M. Hardy, who lost a general store, "I am not going to complain. That will just be my part in the war." [53]

∽∾∾

Racial tensions did not disappear during the war. Early in 1942 police used pistols to put down blacks protesting job discrimination in Baltimore, killing ten of them. An April rally drew 2,000 Negroes, who heard Carl Murphy, editor of the *Afro-American*, urge them to take cars and chartered buses to Annapolis to lobby for their rights. Many of them did, and Governor O'Conor, a devout Catholic who publicly at least spoke of racial justice, listened as sympathetically as he thought he could in crisis conditions. He appointed a commission headed by Joseph P. Healy, district manager of Swift and Company, to report on race conditions in the state. In the short run the war defused racial tension by putting many blacks, as well as whites, back to work. Between April 1940 and November 1943 the labor force in Baltimore gained 215,000 jobs while losing 55,000 workers to military service. Migrants to the city supplied 110,000 of the needed employees, the over-aged and handicapped another 10,000, and young people entering the work force 35,000. Previously unemployed workers, a large percentage of them black, filled 40,000 wartime jobs in Baltimore, and in the state as a whole the black share of the work force climbed from 7 to 17 percent. Many of these jobs were menial, to be sure. Besides bagging fertilizer, Baltimore blacks found work manufacturing 55-gallon drums and handling heavy machinery.

"Victory," the objective, a slogan, became an ideal that produced considerable work and sacrifice. Shortages, restrictions, and service became a way of life. With national policies and local, volunteer enforcement arms, the federal government sought to control wartime consumer prices. It rationed essential goods: canned food, coffee, sugar, meat, butter and oils, shoes, tires, gasoline, fuel oil. Scarcity nonetheless raised prices, especially of food, and dictated the course of one's day. Marylanders grew familiar with the variously colored ration books and windshield stamps. Workers at arms plants received a few extra gallons of gas a week, but factory committees formed car pools and larger plants in Baltimore ran special buses or used makeshift

How Can I Best Serve My Country?

"How Can I Best Serve My Country?" From the Baltimore *Afro-American*, 17 January 1942. Editors urged young blacks, despite the discrimination they faced in the armed forces, to go when called and count on defense needs to end Jim Crowism. *Afro-American*

trailers (riders called them cattle cars) to get people to work cheaply. Trying to hold down inflation and pay for the military buildup, the government pressed workers to buy war bonds, awarding Treasury Department "Minute Man" flags to plants with high participation. In the summer of 1942 Maryland accounted for $35 million in war bonds sales. In late September, for the cost of a thousand-dollar bond, one could visit Hollywood movie stars at a Million Dollar Dinner held at the Lord Baltimore Hotel. A Schools at War program encouraged children to buy enough penny stamps to pay for a military item like a jeep or a plane; in 1943 the Maryland goal was 134 jeeps. The call went out for surplus metal, rubber, and paper. Boy Scouts collected newsprint and junk from neighbors' basements. Companies and towns made heavier contributions. Scrap iron salvaged in Western Maryland included two old railroad cars, steel rails from trolley lines in Frederick County, iron plating from the old Taneytown jail, and ornamental fencing that had graced Narrows Park in Cumberland.

Bethesda scrap metal drive, c. 1942. *Brooks Photographers/Margaret M. Coleman and Anne D. Lewis*

Voluntaryism returned to fashion. There were Red Cross chapters in Baltimore and almost every county. Volunteers manned the all-important blood donation centers, worked in the canteens accompanying them, offered help to families of those ordered overseas, put together "kit bags" and Christmas packages, and prepared for disasters natural and military. Junior Red Cross chapters enlisted the help of schoolchildren in another chief function—making life as comfortable as possible for the troops recovering from wounds. Some youngsters conducted Victory Book Campaigns, knitted afghans, and baked cookies. Others collected games, radios, and things like ping-pong and card tables. They tried to make stark hospital rooms more "homelike." Many of the sixteen thousand Montgomery County volunteers in 1942 served as "Gray Ladies" or hospital aides, tending the thousands of wounded servicemen who convalesced at the Forest Glen section of Walter Reed army hospital or Bethesda naval medical center. They helped Bethesda patients publish their own newspaper. Focusing the energies of more than a hundred local groups, the Prince George's Red Cross provided volunteer services at Andrews Field, Fort Meade, and Prince George's General Hospital. Church, fraternal, and civic groups cooperated with the Baltimore (City and County) chapter in undertaking "camp and hospital" work at military posts in the state and "adopting" Virginia and Georgia hospitals. In booking hospital entertainment the Baltimore Red Cross had enthusiastic support from workers at large plants, where apparently the boredom of assembly lines awoke every trace of musical talent. Bendix Radio, B&O, and Martin workers formed glee clubs and amateur shows that toured military bases; McCormick employees took pride in a "Hillbilly" chorus.

In the country the problem was somehow to produce more food with less of almost everything one needed to farm. Food could win the war, according to the slogan: vast military needs, an influx of war industry workers, and the demands of the Allied governments all placed a premium on agricultural produce—explaining why the government called on everyone to grow a "Victory Garden." At an early-war meeting of Maryland farmers, officials informed them of the task ahead. One farmer said he considered the production goals impossible—"but I guess," he drawled, "we'd better be getting home and starting the job." With containers scarce, Maryland farmers salvaged old crates and cans. They handled a shortage of commercial fertilizer by making more efficient use of animal and plant manures. Efforts intensified to control dairy and poultry disease, to treat crops for insects and blights. Since war production had first call on available steel, farmers largely got by without new equipment. They sold, rented, or lent their extra pieces, impro-

National Naval Medical Center, Bethesda, 1943. *National Geographic Society*

vised, and took maintenance lessons at repair centers established by the state Agricultural War Board (part of the federal system of the same name). The most serious problem involved labor. High war-industry wages drew many people off the land. The number of Maryland farmers declined from eighty thousand in 1939 to sixty-four thousand in 1944. Those who remained faced farm-labor costs of about four dollars a day—double the prewar wage. After Pearl Harbor, retired farmers went back to work, farm women drove tractors, and children pitched in harder than ever. In the 4-H Club's Feed a Fighter program, farm youngsters, after helping their parents, raised cattle and tended crops of their own.[54]

Even with such effort, however, farm families needed the aid of government and outsiders. Early in the war, by means of a special committee chaired by Philip C. Turner of Parkton, the University of Maryland Extension Service drew up guidelines to assist local draft boards in judging who should receive farm-service exemptions. These standards, the first to appear in the nation, kept seventeen thousand essential workers on the job. As a further help, Paul E. Nystrom of the extension service made plans to organize emergency farm labor—recruiting soldiers and sailors on leave, conscientious objectors, and prison inmates for seasonal work. Captured German troops, wearing dungarees marked "WP," helped to take in the 1943 tomato crop. Later, blacks from the British Caribbean arrived to work on farms and in canneries. Much of the new farm labor was homegrown. High school girls and women volunteers picked apples at a work camp near Hancock and in Anne Arundel County gathered vegetables or stripped tobacco. Many Baltimore and Washington boys, after learning how to milk a cow and drive a tractor, spent their summers hard at work.

All of it paid off richly. In the end Maryland farmers produced 40 percent more food than in prewar years with about two-thirds the earlier labor force. The Eastern Shore poultry industry, considerable in 1939, increased fivefold. Caroline Poultry Company near Federalsburg—employing about one hundred twenty-five people, half women and almost all black—reached a peak wartime volume of 200,000 pounds of chicken and turkey a week. Small in size but traditionally an important fruit- and vegetable-preserving state, Maryland led the nation in tomato canning during the war and stood fourth in all canned foods. At the height of conflict the Dulany Canning Company in Wicomico County dehydrated 40,000 pounds of potatoes or sweet potatoes (producing 8,000 pounds of dry mix) each day. Baltimore butter, made to keep at higher than normal temperatures, went to every theater of the war. The Esskay and Goetze meatpacking firms found new ways to speed up delivery on government orders.

Maryland smokestacks offered a study of modern war and an education in the close ties between defense and industry in the mid-twentieth century. The country did its part for victory with soldiers, ships, airplanes, and endless ammunition, but also with the critical banality that Maryland industry supplied—assemblies and subassemblies, bushings, toggle bolts, valves, propellers, gauges, casings, jars of insect repellent, down-filled sleeping bags, and debarkation nets. As in 1861 and 1917, Baltimore clothing firms produced uniforms on a mass scale. In Cumberland, Celanese employees made plastic that had uses ranging from blackout lenses for auto headlights to cockpit canopies. Magnus Manufacturing in Silver Spring lost money making tiny bolts for radar equipment. Cambridge workers turned out wooden pallets that were essential to rapid military shipping. A Baltimore chain-link fence maker shipped miles of it to military posts (after 1942 only the government could buy fencing). The army and navy took 350,000 tons of asphalt compound from one Baltimore firm alone. Companies in virtually every line of work converted machinery and skills to wartime needs. Brandt Cabinet Works in Hagerstown gave up replicas of eighteenth-century furniture for wooden fighter mock-ups that trained navy carrier crews. The Eveready Company in Frederick turned from household utensils to antitank mines and rifle grenades while a Westminster billboard concern built ammunition boxes. A Crisfield cutlery manufacturer won government contracts for rocket projectiles. Baltimore silversmiths converted to precision instruments. Crown Cork and Seal went from stamping bottle caps to making 9,000-pound gear rings for merchant ships and nose caps for armor-piercing ammunition.

Specialists helped to determine the outcome of this highly technological conflict. Experiments at Glenn L. Martin led to the self-sealing gas tank, enabling planes with bullet holes to fly home safely. An engineer with Consolidated Gas and Electric devised a way to heat the metal skins of airplanes as the pieces were riveted on, thus making a tighter fit and ensuring superior performance. The Charles T. Brandt Company of Baltimore, normally a sheet-metal producer, developed an airplane chute that dropped metallic flakes to confuse German radar. In 1942 several Baltimore automobile salesmen—out of work with car companies making tanks—invented a device that checked all the instruments in a four-engined bomber in three hours instead of the previous three days. Baltimore chemical firms developed a means of keeping water in lifeboats drinkable indefinitely. Several firms claimed credit for discovering plastic armor plating for merchant ships, a saving of steel. A glassblowing company researched and produced delayed-action fuses. An even more important breakthrough took place largely at the Johns Hopkins Applied Physics Laboratory in Silver Spring: development of a proximity or variable-time fuse that used a small radio to detect the nearness of a target. Other Marylanders, experienced seamen and merchant mariners, met different kinds of challenges. As boatyards around the bay turned to making small craft for the navy and Coast Guard, they excelled not only at workmanship

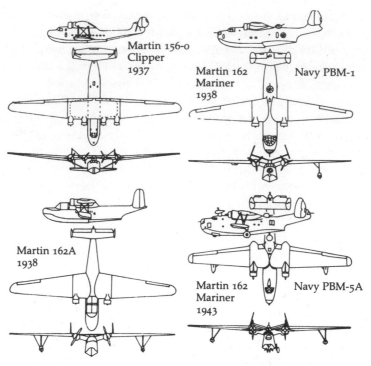

Martin's flying boats as they evolved from the China Clipper to the wartime PBM-5. *Norman G. Rubin/MHS*

but also at originality. The owner of a marina near Pasadena developed a lathe that rounded and tapered logs for masts in one-tenth the time the job had taken manually; designers at the Annapolis Yacht Yard improved the British Vospers torpedo boat's speed by 25 percent.

In military flying boats, Maryland made an especially appropriate war contribution. These craft had matured in the early 1930s, when they promised to revolutionize rescues in the open sea and communication between far-flung places. Fairchild had built a few single-engine seaplanes, most of which went to foreign buyers and suffered romantic fates like being lost in New Guinea or shot down in the Spanish Civil War. After 1932 Fokker American in Baltimore had produced a twin-engined craft for the Coast Guard called a "flying life-boat." Before the war Glenn L. Martin had won an enviable reputation for his "clippers"—graceful, four-engined craft that Pan American then used to fly passengers and airmail across the Pacific.

Martin also had become a prime supplier of navy flying boats and in the late thirties developed probably the most durable and serviceable such craft ever built, the Mariner, a twin-engined, gull-winged patrol bomber the navy designated the PBM. This plane (its hull about the size of Calvert's *Dove*) performed antisubmarine duty in the Atlantic and in the Pacific theater undertook bombing, cargo transport, and air-sea recovery missions. The tail section of the PBM, designed to twist, could frighten novice flyers by sounding as if it were about to break off. But the innovation helped remove the flying boat's greatest problems—landing and taking off in rough seas. Test pilots eventually proved that, with proper technique, the plane could operate in seas as high as ten feet. Martin built more than thirteen hundred PBMs, and, late in the war, began designing yet another flying boat, ultimately the Mars, which had a hull larger than the *Ark*'s. Martin's PBM, a product of Maryland ingenuity and love of the water, made many wartime rescues.

All merchant ships came under the control of the U.S. War Shipping Administration (WSA), which in turn employed the companies to man and maintain the vessels assigned to them. Marylanders in merchant service thus found themselves as much in the war as navy seamen, and many of them soon had stories to tell. Captain Hugh Mulzac, a black skipper from Baltimore, commanded the *Booker T. Washington* in Atlantic convoy duty; his ship, with a racially mixed crew, received high ratings. A retired naval officer in Annapolis, P. V. H. Weems, developed tables of star altitude curves, greatly reducing the time navigators in planes and ships took to fix their position. He returned to active duty as a convoy commodore, making twenty-five crossings without loss. Not everyone had such good luck. The Merchants and Miners Transportation Company of Baltimore, which the WSA eventually rated first on the Atlantic Coast in operating efficiency, supervised a total of thirty-seven merchant ships, many of them lost in action. Bull and Company lost nineteen ships and three hundred crewmen making runs to Puerto Rico. Even tugs and ferryboats went to war. In 1943 the Tolchester Line received orders to operate daytime service between Newport News and Norfolk; at night it transported troops to anchored transports and unloaded captured German and Italian soldiers. The WSA took four Bay Line packets for army transport service. *President Warfield* (named for the duchess of Windsor's uncle, company head early in the century) compiled a colorful history in England as a troop transport; *Yorktown* fell prey to German U-boats. Curtis Bay Towing tugs often steamed to the mouth of the bay to fetch damaged ships, once saving a British cruiser from sinking off Fort McHenry.

Maryland war workers wrote a memorable chapter in the state's social history. The rapid wartime buildup caused dislocation, jerry-rigged living, stretched or broken family ties, and sudden educational opportunities that really were demands. An excellent example of the war's effect on living appeared at Middle River, where Martin workers climbed from 3,500 to a peak of 53,000. This sudden development, drawing more than 100,000 people to the rural neck east of Baltimore, caused severe housing problems. The company agreed to build one house for every two the government paid for, and by September 1943 the community within a few miles of the main plant included four dormitories, about 1,200 trailers, and almost 2,000 temporary houses arranged in projects with names like Aero Acres and Victory Villa. Martin managers must have fretted about social services almost as much as they worried about B-26 or PBM production schedules. The company organized recreation and opened thirteen first-aid stations, forty cafeterias, and a cooperative nursery. It also carried on a critical training program. Practically all new employees were inexperienced (in the first three years of the war the military took 25,000 Martin workers), and educating new ones became a major industry in itself. At a cost to the company of $700 each, 40,000 Martin employees took college courses in subjects like engineering, radio, and chemistry. No time could be lost wondering what might happen to these newly trained engineers after the war.

Wartime prosperity, especially noteworthy among working people, may have changed the expectations of Marylanders. They did complain at times about pay, conditions, and bosses. After 1942 local panels (branches of the National War Labor Board) made up of public representatives like academics and clerics, company heads, and labor leaders fixed wages and arbitrated disputes, and in June 1943 Congress passed a measure to control strikes in wartime. There were work stoppages (forty-eight in 1944) and other threats of strikes at Maryland plants. Occasionally friction developed between union and nonunion workers (union leaders spoke for all workers, but no one had to join a union). More than a few plant managers noted absenteeism, especially after pay days. One employer believed its cause lay in the longtime poverty of so many of his workers—they had no experience handling money. Indeed, average per capita income in the state rose from $634 in 1939 to $1,272 at the end of the war. After adjustment for inflation this rise brought an average gain of about 50 percent, but the improvement in family income grew more marked as one moved down the economic scale. During the war the poorest one-fifth of Maryland families enjoyed a 68 percent increase in income (the richest fifth gained 20 percent).[55]

Workers went where jobs paid the most, while owners and managers tried to overcome the pervasive labor shortage. Authorities designated comparatively few industrial positions as critical and draft exempt. High school students, boys and girls, had no trouble finding after-school work. A cannery on South Eden Street in Baltimore listed 600 employees on its rolls to keep 225 active workers. At textile mills in Hampden-Woodberry, turnover was so high that War Manpower Commission officials recruited door to door. Five older employees, averaging seventy-one years of age, came out of retirement to train new workers at Hooper Mills—a company that had turned over its patents to the government royalty free, enabling war industries to produce mildew-, water-, and weather-resistant cotton duck. Managers at Mount Vernon–Woodberry Mills scoured the countryside for workers and chartered a bus to get them to work. Annual turnover was 90 percent. Finally the firm relied on weavers and spinners drawn from the military and commanded by an officer. Maryland Drydock each year trained between 3,000 and 5,000 workers in new skills and hundreds of supervisory people. Relocated from California to Baltimore, Japanese Americans worked superbly in the Sun Cab maintenance shops, but not all learned their new jobs quickly. Loane Machinery lost three key employees to the draft; replacements sent by the government employment service "required endless supervision and training." Though German prisoners relieved shortages at some plants, including the Royster Guano Company, they had scruples. One work party, under the spell of a Nazi sergeant, refused to crush oyster shells.[56]

The war changed lives in countless ways, but most noticeably by putting women in the workplace—especially in factories. By late 1943 twenty thousand women "not customarily in the labor market" filled Baltimore jobs, and the pattern repeated itself in Hagerstown, Cumberland, and elsewhere. Numerous as ever in office clerical work, women continued during the conflict to dominate the clothing industry and fill many jobs in food canning. As men left for the war, women filled places employers always had given to men. A Baltimore meatpacker reported that he had successfully hired women "in practically all operations, including those previously considered as men's jobs." Women made shoes, bottles, brushes, corrugated boxes; they worked as glaziers at a woodworks. Bethesda women's club members (one a general's wife) formed teams of two to complete nine-hour workdays at a firm experimenting with pilot-training equipment. Ruxton "war widows"— women whose husbands had gone off to fight—formed the Topflight Tool Company and began turning out specialty items like adapters for broken drills. Besides repairing Baltimore Transit buses, women for the first time drove them and acted as conductors. The Clogg Company, making things like antenna masts and X-ray machines, found women "far superior to the men available for the same jobs." At the Hagerstown Fairchild plant women served as armed guards.[57]

The real surprise came in heavy industry. Before the extreme needs of the war, no one had heard of a lady lashing down deck cargoes, feeding a blast furnace, operating a drill press, or making compressed air-hose couplings. Women worked as never before at Baltimore oil refineries and in aircraft plants. A company making inflammable and smoke-producing chemicals had one shift of black women. These jobs were hard, and they could be dangerous. Women perhaps better than men knew not to take unnecessary chances. At a Salisbury munitions plant a group calling itself WOW— Women Ordnance Workers—wore pins and sleeve insignia after pledging themselves to safety and efficiency on the job. In Baltimore 60 percent of all workers at Continental Can were women, 40 percent of them black. That company's war production included belts for machine-gun ammunition—hazardous work that caused many injuries despite safety precautions. Besides physical dangers, war work carried the seeds of fundamental social change. It violated a great many customs. Women worked night shifts with men; white women worked alongside black men. One company, 60 percent

Maryland women, among those who filled vast wartime labor demands, helped to build bombers at Glenn L. Martin in 1943. *A. Aubrey Bodine Collection, Peale Museum, Baltimore City Life Museums*

black, tried using women as crane operators. It decided that conditions were unfavorable.[58]

The war produced touching individual efforts, only a few of them recorded. An employee with initiative at Martin, for example, saved $150,000 worth of used ball and roller bearings. F. Eugene Sloan, a retired Baltimore machinist with an enviable home workshop, volunteered to make small, precisely shaped aluminum cover plates necessary in shipping airplane engines. In eleven months he made twenty-five thousand of them. A tiny firm in Towson, several of its employees in their seventies, made a part for a Martin airplane that was so complicated in design it required five days to inspect it. In Catonsville A. W. Gieske, Jr., owner of a filling station and garage, decided to avoid wartime idleness and make airplane engine valve covers on subcontract. He hired thirty neighborhood girls who worked in two shifts and several elderly black women. Of course none of them had any metalworking experience. Geiske conducted painstaking lessons at each stage of the work, and they caught on quickly. At first the shop produced one hundred covers a day. Later the girls turned out one thousand every four hours and finally one hundred thousand a month, loading them on a bus for the New Jersey contractor. Meanwhile the owner's mother, recovering from an illness, did all the firm's clerical work. In winter everyone went outdoors to find fuel for the woodstoves that supplied the shop's only heat. The black women made belts for the burring machines but also started a tradition of bringing in coffee and homemade cakes for the others.

True, workers at major plants felt pressure to produce, give blood, and buy bonds. Vying for government pennants (the Army-Navy "E" signified outstanding war service), firms awarded bonds and held rallies—sometimes with disabled veterans as speakers—to stimulate production. No doubt these devices had an effect, but blue-collar Marylanders pushed themselves, and because of them the giants and old hands of Maryland industry did more than their full share. Nine- and ten-hour shifts, "Victory Shifts" from supper to late evening, and round-the-clock operations were commonplace. B&O workers often volunteered for a second daily shift. In one war year the B&O handled nearly 3.8 million cars of freight—a record level equivalent to one car every nine seconds day and night. Workers at the Western Maryland terminal at Port Covington loaded more than 24 million bushels of grain during the war. Standard Oil employees voluntarily worked day and night to make a new grease General Eisenhower needed before the invasion of Sicily. Bethlehem, producing nearly 20 million tons of steel during the war, won an "E" and three stars. Workers at its shipyards at Sparrows Point, Fairfield, and Locust Point, working three shifts a day, seven days a week, performed superhuman tasks. At the height of the war Bethlehem-Fairfield cut the time it took to build a Liberty ship from 244 to 30 days. Charles T. Brandt, receiving many commendations, manufactured half of all the five-inch gun turrets the navy bought during the war. The Koppers Company, Bartlett-Hayward by then among its subsidiaries, received commendations for its piston rings, antiaircraft guns, and shipboard airplane catapults that were seventy feet long and weighed twenty tons. Fairchild workers turned out a new military transport, a "flying boxcar," in record time. British and American laurels showered on Bendix Radio, the main Allied supplier of aircraft communications and approach-control equipment. Workers at Chevrolet–Fisher Body made parts for two staples of the navy's Pacific air war—the Wildcat fighter and Avenger torpedo bomber. Baltimore's Consolidated Gas and Electric managed somehow to handle electrical loads that soared with Maryland war industry (Glenn Martin's needs rose from 650 kilowatts in 1939 to 16,850 in 1944, its natural gas demand from 17.6 to 185 million cubic feet). These achievements came with plenty of sweat, but also some blood. In May 1943 a "blow" at an Elkton ammunition factory claimed the lives of fifteen workers and injured nearly a hundred others.

Top, Bethlehem Steel's Fairfield shipyard. *Bottom*, some of the workers who kept it humming with activity during World War II. *A. Aubrey Bodine Collection, Peale Museum, Baltimore City Life Museums*

Marylanders under arms discovered the ancient truths of war. One felt that life was being lived faster, and needed to be—that rules had been suspended. Servicemen passing through Billie Holiday's hometown, along with war industry workers getting off late shifts and merchant seamen on liberty, helped to make the three-block Baltimore theater-burlesque district widely famous as The Block. Proper Baltimoreans thought the area seedy, and it was. Tattoo artists obliged sailors. Pinball machines relieved transients of their coinage. Entertainers like Wally Wagner and his Rainbow Room Dancers performed to roaring crowds. "Cuban reviews" preyed on the popular conception of Latin license. At the Clover and such spots beer went for fifty cents a glass and the strip shows pushed the bounds of decency—young women in scanty costumes twirled about the stage with yards of silky material trailing from their arms. A dancer calling herself Moana won a reputation for slinking to the sounds of a tom-tom; her promoters described her as "the sexy savage" and "jungle queen." Burlesque owners hired B (for bar) girls to keep patrons busy buying drinks. What the women did after hours—and what they arranged for friends—was their own business. Naturally many servicemen, away from home for the first time, fell smitten to these sirens. Late in the war, addressing "My Dear Moana," one soldier in southern France illustrated yet another wartime sensation, severe loneliness. "As I sit here on this dusty mistral-swept plateau," he wrote, "I would certainly give almost anything to be back on that dirty Baltimore Street again." [59]

For the state's hospital units the war brought the usual wartime combination of boredom, mix-up, and adventure. The Hopkins and University of Maryland forces served under General MacArthur in the southwestern Pacific. The 18th and 142d General Hospitals first set up camp on one of the Fiji Islands, where, for a while, men and women of the 142d had nothing to eat but bread, jam, and pineapple; doctors and nurses of the 118th spent much of the war near Sydney, and the 42d outside Brisbane. As the war against Japan ebbed and flowed over thousands of miles of Pacific Ocean and exotic landscape, the Marylanders generally found themselves far in the rear, treating more Fiji natives than wounded soldiers and in Australia donning dress uniforms for what they considered silly sunset parades. A twenty-five-bed section of the 42d went to New Guinea during the heavy fighting there in late 1942 and again in March 1944 traveled closer to action at Hollandia-Aitape; most doctors stayed active working on the prevention and treatment of malaria and ways to combat tropical skin infections. Back home a group of Baltimore physicians had petitioned the army to form them into another hospital unit, the 56th. They sweltered at Fort Jackson, South Carolina, until receiving orders to a northern debarkation point. The train sent to take them went to Jacksonville, Florida, by mistake. After the surgeons, physicians, nurses, and Red Cross workers finally arrived in England late in 1943, the military placed most of them in charge of a local mental hospital. They had lost their office safe filled with good bourbon and may have begun to believe the old military adage about never volunteering.

For those men who stood between all the Red Cross services, hospital units, and supply dumps and the enemy, there were additional lessons of war. Long stretches of tedium and incredible snafus gave way at times to terror, and then, with fear put aside or forgotten, men acted and reacted in suddenness, fury, resignation. Among the Marylanders who stood on the outer defenses in May 1942 was Lieutenant Milton E. Ricketts, a Baltimore-born graduate of the Naval Academy who served aboard the carrier *Yorktown* in the Coral Sea. The Japanese seemed invincible; the long-besieged American garrison on Corregidor fell to the enemy on the sixth, and Japanese ships ferried troops to the Solomon Islands not far from New Guinea. On the eighth, during the first naval battle in which the opposing ships never saw one another, Japanese planes swept down on the *Lexington* and *Yorktown*. The *Lexington* began to sink. On the *Yorktown* Lieutenant Ricketts commanded the engineering repair party, responsible for damage control deep inside the ship. A bomb passed through his battle station and exploded in the compartment below. All his men were killed, wounded, or stunned by the blast; he suffered severe injury, but until he died he managed to apply water to the fire and greatly limit the harm it did. The *Yorktown*—one of only a few aircraft carriers America had in the early war—survived to fight in the decisive battle of Midway next month.

In the first two years of the war, soldiers of the 29th Division had their fill of two leading military experiences, waiting and training. More exercises in the North Carolina mosquito swamps took up much of 1942. On 6 September they received orders to move overseas, then waited until the twenty-seventh to embark from New York. The normally grumbling infantrymen could hardly complain of the accommodations—the 29th traveled aboard the finest British liners afloat, the *Queen Mary* and *Queen Elizabeth*. The swift vessels traveled without an escort, following a zig-zag course to throw off U-boats, and arrived in Scotland in early October. By late fall the division, headquartered at Tidworth, had undertaken more training, hiking, and tedious basic instruction; in the spring of 1943, grumbling about missing the action in North Africa, the men moved to Devon and Cornwall for further exercises. That July word came that the 29th would be among the first units to make the long-planned invasion of France. Training camp moved to a beach south of Bristol, where marksmanship, swimming, and artillery-timing drills took on new meaning. The troops practiced getting down debarkation nets, moving their heavy weapons from boats to shore. An officer from Cumberland, Randolph A. Millholland, took some volunteers for a ranger unit to train with British commandos, but the high command failed to develop that good idea into a permanent specialty unit within the 29th. More practice landings—they seemed endless—took place that winter at

Slapton Sands near Dartmouth, said to resemble Normandy. At last, in mid-May, soldiers of the 29th went into confinement in camouflaged quarters along the southern coast of England. Officers began studying maps of northern France.

Men of the division had a peculiar rendezvous with destiny. Operation Overlord put them on a stretch of Normandy beach code-named Omaha at 6:30 A.M. on D-Day. Eisenhower's choice ran against two considerations. For many years the army had avoided grouping troops by locality; democratic government did not wish the bad news of modern battle, the casualty lists, to threaten morale by striking single states or towns in large batches. Though most troops headed for Normandy could call themselves citizen soldiers, only the 29th had been formed of old militia units and at its core claimed a particular place as home (nearly one in five Marylanders in the army served in the 29th; replacements included draftees from all over the country). Furthermore, among the American units scheduled to make the attack, only the 29th had seen no action in the war.

For the sake of secrecy the feelings of soldiers about to go into battle—dread, reflection, determination, fatalism—had to go unreleased in letters to loved ones. Troops of the 29th Division had much to think about: the moral stakes of the conflict, the place of northern Europe in Western culture, and the epic dimensions of a cross-Channel attack (not since William the Conqueror had an invading force successfully moved from one side of the treacherous water to the other). A reporter sent to check on the morale of the invasion force found the men of the division fairly calm. He heard no hateful references to the Germans themselves. One soldier laughed and said "now we can get started on the way home." Like any citizen-soldiers, they knew how badly military schemes could go awry. Colonel Paul R. Goode of the 175th Infantry passed around a thick book of invasion plans. "Study it and learn it," he told his men. "But unless I miss my guess, after we hit the beach, we'll have to improvise."[60]

In fact, little went according to plan. Weather delayed the invasion, which depended on closely timed parachute drops and a feint that took advantage of the Brandt radar-fooling equipment. Postponing the attack increased chances that the Germans would figure out where the Allies planned their main landings. Eisenhower gave the go-ahead order on a cloudy, windy night, gambling that the next day, 6 June, would clear. Long before light sergeants roused the men, few of whom had been able to sleep. They put on heavy packs and cartridge belts with extra loads of ammunition, waited, climbed into the landing boats, and dropped into the choppy sea. There, at "Piccadilly Circus," they waited again for all the boats to assemble—the boats circling and bobbing, spray drenching the men and leaving them shivering cold, many of them getting seasick in the water that splashed about their boots. Then, two hours from the beach, the boats of the first Allied wave (including the 116th Infantry) turned toward Normandy. When they

Omaha Beach, 6 June 1944. A now-familiar photo captured better than any other the confusion, distances, and dangers that troops of the 29th Division faced when the boat ramps went down on D-Day. *U.S. Coast Guard*

lay forty minutes offshore the Germans discovered them and began firing with heavy guns. As luck would have it, a German division had arrived in the Omaha Beach area only a few weeks before to practice repelling a cross-Channel assault. Clouds had prevented planes from knocking out beach defenses and making craters that would have given the 29th cover.

The confusion that dominates battle soon became complete. Smoke and haze obscured landmarks for the landing boat coxswains. An unexpected current running eastward carried the boats far off course. There was no time to adjust even if communications were possible, because the extensive German beach obstacles, many tipped with deadly explosives, lay but briefly exposed at low tide. The Germans had mined the three or four hundred yards of tidal flat with the exactness their industry had made famous. American tanks and landing craft took hits and disappeared. Boats carrying artillery capsized. Troops splashed into waist-deep water on sandbars and then, struggling toward shore, sank like rocks in deeper water. On the bluff overlooking the beach German machine-gun crews fired from reinforced concrete bunkers that the prelanding bombardment had failed to destroy.

At places like Tarawa or Anzio other Marylanders had jumped from boats and taken part in similar frenzy. On D-Day the 115th regiment hit Omaha

Beach only hours after the 116th, and at first like everyone else could only lie helplessly behind the bodies of the dead, the hulks of destroyed vehicles, or the remnants of a seawall while fire raked the beach. Nobody felt glorious or patriotic. The assistant division commander, Norman "Dutch" Cota—a regular army man and veteran of the North African landings—waded ashore early in the day and started shouting for the men to move forward. He saw one soldier, trying to obey, quickly shot down, another lay just beyond reach of his friends, crying "Medico, I'm hit!" several times before he died. The two regiments of the 29th left five hundred dead on the beach that morning. Units were in pieces, mixed up; the few junior officers left, noncoms, and brave men without rank could only try to rally those huddled near them. Somehow they did. Small groups—some of them artillerymen who had lost their cannon and found rifles—dashed across the open beach and struggled into the bluffs, where they could make a fight of it. Each fingerhold enabled them to destroy pillboxes and take pressure off the shoreline. The tide rose; more and more men ran the bloody race to the bluffs. At noon the Germans radioed that the Americans had been thrown back into the sea. By evening troops of the 29th Division had advanced about a mile inland.

In the weeks that followed, the 29th hardened into one of the strong units of the theater—learning the caution, the cunning, and the callousness that defines a veteran. Joined by the 175th Infantry, which landed 7 June, the division attacked west and south of Omaha Beach. It remained light until after eleven at night, and the days were hot, dusty, costly. Troops fought bitter small-unit battles for fields that the Normans since Roman times had enclosed with hedgerow fencing or *bocage*—often six or more feet of earth and tough brush. Giving the retreating Germans every advantage, the *bocage* forced troops of the 29th to improvise each day's attack; the high command had neglected to train them for hedgerow fighting. When they ran into enemy-flooded marshes on the way to Isigny, the 121st Engineers devised bridges and causeways. Fighting around St. Lô, a vital German communications center, the 29th simply beat the enemy down. Its seizure on 18 July, when a battalion of the 115th and a motorized task force entered what was left of the town, marked the climax of the Normandy offensive and set the stage for the decisive American breakout that followed. The defeated Germans were impressed with the weight of American war materiel. Equally impressive was the individual soldier's willingness to sacrifice (as a percentage of participants, Maryland combat deaths at 2 percent considerably exceeded the national rate). In the continuous fighting between D-Day and St. Lô, the 29th Division suffered about seven thousand men killed or wounded.

For men and women in service the war dragged on and on. Later in the summer of 1944 Marylanders of the division played a large part in capturing the important port city of Brest; with the 56th Hospital, they then joined the Allied drive into Germany. On the other side of the globe, the Hopkins and Maryland hospital units that had been in Fiji sailed to India, where late in

"Into the Unknown." By Richard Q. Yardley for the Balti-more *Sun*, 8 August 1945. *Baltimore Sunpapers*

1944 the military expected action. They traveled north out of Bombay on a rickety old railroad line and up the Brahmaputra River on an overloaded paddle-wheel steamer. At their "advance base" they encountered not casu-alties but foul water, giant rats, and more boredom. About the same time doctors of the 118th General Hospital landed on Leyte supporting Mac-Arthur's invasion of the Philippines. There they tended wounded troops in ankle-deep mud.

The war's end lacked nothing in drama. The Third Reich collapsed with the Allies closing in from east and west and the chancellor who had be-gun another world war killing himself in his bunker. In streets, bars, and churches Marylanders celebrated V-E Day with conditional joy. Roosevelt had died only a short time before. Pacific military and naval leaders lay awake nights thinking of the casualties still to come. Neither Marine General Julian C. Smith, a Cecil County native who had commanded the Second Marine Division at Tarawa, nor Rear Admiral Lawrence F. Reifsnider of Westminster, commander of the amphibious task force that had landed on Guam, doubted the suicidal tenacity of the Japanese. Admiral Raymond A. Spruance, born in Baltimore, had overall command of the ships and Marines who in February 1945 suffered severe losses in seizing the small, barren island of Iwo Jima. Only a handful of Americans knew about the development of a bomb that might make an invasion of the Japanese home islands unnecessary. Early in the war the president of Hynson, Westcott and Dunning, H. A. B. Dunning, and a Johns Hopkins chemist, Robert Dudley Fowler, had pioneered research in isotope separation and given the patent for the process to the government. Chase Engineering in Baltimore had sent parts for a mysterious project to Oak Ridge, Tennessee. Lieutenant Jacob Beser, an army air corpsman from Baltimore, had specialized in radar countermeasures aboard the newest American bomber, the B-29. In August 1945 Lieutenant Beser flew two missions, one to Hiroshima and the other to Nagasaki.

Before those bombs dropped, men fought wars for just and unjust reasons—killing one another by the mid-twentieth century with appalling destructive force. Afterward, not lives but life itself lay in mankind's hands: a discovered secret of physical science posed the question whether humans any longer could afford the luxury of mere tribal loyalty, of organized aggression and general war—whether in fact they had grown up.

CHAPTER 11

"Land of Pleasant Living"

After the war Marylanders like most Americans wanted to keep the country strong and have some fun. Beer and baseball fit the public mood nicely. In Garrett and Allegany counties many fans supported the Pittsburgh Pirates. On the upper Eastern Shore Marylanders were inclined to cheer the Phillies. In the counties surrounding Washington they plodded behind the luckless Senators.

Around Baltimore in the spring of 1954 baseball fever ran higher than anywhere else—in Maryland or the country. An active mayor and a circle of prominent lawyers and businessmen had concluded a deal that made the St. Louis Browns the latest Baltimore Orioles, returning major-league baseball to the city for the first time since 1902. On 15 April, the day of the Orioles' first home game, schools closed, city employees got the afternoon off, and 350,000 people turned out to watch a parade that welcomed the team to Baltimore. Milton A. Reckord, still state adjutant general, served as marshal. One float among the thirty-two carried two Miss Marylands and three Mrs. Marylands, dressed in bathing suits and furs valued at one hundred thousand dollars. Another commemorated the ten Orioles already in the baseball hall of fame. Miss Eugenia Calvert Holland and former senator George L. Radcliffe, now president of the Maryland Historical Society, acted Lord and Lady Calvert in the parade, traveling in a two-horse colonial coach. Radcliffe felt a bit silly in a bushy brown wig and a black hat with yellow plume. Riding in eleven cars, team members threw plastic baseballs to the crowd. A New Yorker described watching the parade as like seeing "the Florentine Army clanking triumphantly home after the second sack of Pisa." Put off by the baseball hysteria, Siegfried Weisberger had closed his Peabody Book Shop and departed with a Menckenesque remark—"the age of the boob is upon us." Memorial Stadium, nearly completed at a cost of $6.5 million, replaced simple stands on both sides of a football field that had been on 33rd Street since 1922. There on opening day Bob Turley and the Orioles defeated the Chicago White Sox, 3 to 1.

One of the Orioles' major sponsors, the National Brewing Company, later

"Ye Map of Maryland." By Richard Q. and Margaret B. Yardley for the Baltimore *Sunday Sun Magazine*, 13 April 1947. *Susan Yardley Wheltle*

devised an award-winning advertising campaign built around a charming view of colonial Maryland and a message whose essence, according to one of its creators, was "warmth and humor." The commercials featured a friendly sandpiper named Chester Peake, singing shellfish, dancing terrapins, and a canvasback with a striped awning. A banjo-playing, one-eyed troubadour in top hat sang a jingle that ended with the lines, "And while I'm singing I'm proud to say / It's brewed on the shores of the Chesapeake Bay." A new company slogan portrayed the region as everyman's paradise, "The Land of Pleasant Living."[1] Pleasantness implied prosperity—and more of everything.

⁓⁓

Maryland business and industrial leaders began thinking about achieving postwar prosperity as early as 1944, when a government report told them what they already knew—that Maryland was one of those "problem states" where federal war outlays had led to abnormal population growth and a heavy dependence on military production. Economic headaches followed the raucous celebrations of V-J Day just as did heavy hangovers. Maryland veterans numbered about 200,000, and in the fall of 1945, 34,000 already had come home to reclaim old jobs or look for new work. At the same time most firms filled their last wartime contracts. By October layoffs in the state numbered 45,000 persons, many of them women, almost 40,000 of them in Baltimore. Martin's work force shrank to 18,000 persons. Fisher Body and Chevrolet in Baltimore shut down for extensive retooling. After lifting of wartime price controls, Americans faced serious problems of inflation. Strikes became common as workers tried to keep wages in line with rising prices. Still, after a temporary lull, the economy proved pessimists wrong. A few Maryland firms were directly involved in one of the federal government's largest postwar needs—mothballing the World War II surface fleet. Other companies, Bendix and Westinghouse, found peaceful uses for wartime devices like two-way radios. European relief programs, further government spending, and released domestic demand kept the economy healthy for many years. In 1947 Maryland entered a period of prosperity unparalleled in its history.

Marylanders faced the large issues that preoccupied postwar America—coping with a housing shortage and managing development at the top of the list. In 1946 a Western Maryland congressman, J. Glenn Beall, introduced veterans' emergency housing legislation that permitted localities to purchase war-surplus government buildings and turn them into houses. As part of that program Baltimore and Anne Arundel county commissioners assumed control of forty-five hundred units originally sheltering war workers. Montgomery County took over about five hundred dwellings and as a five-year expedient put trailers on park land for more returning veterans. Prince George's County bought thirty-three barracks. Beginning in 1947 private in-

House Pattern, Dundalk, c. 1945. Baltimore County wartime housing, a ready model for postwar construction. *A. Aubrey Bodine Family Collection*

dustry rushed into the market. A New York construction firm built more than a thousand four-room houses, "Cape Cod" cottages, on a large tract southeast of Rockville. Workers took on the job the way others earlier had expanded Fort Meade or laid runways at Andrews Field. Bulldozers knocked over trees with dispatch and leveled acres at a time; carpenters prefabricated windows and doors in Quonset huts erected for the purpose. Homes in Veirs Mill Village—built without concern for schools, playgrounds, or access streets—sold for $8,700. Another company built a thousand small houses on land south of Baltimore at Harundale. Costing less than $7,000, they went up on concrete slabs and were made of pre-assembled pieces. Veirs Mill Village and Harundale, like many smaller housing developments that sprang up at the time, aimed at the thousands of veterans who qualified for G.I. Bill home-mortgage loans. Along with wartime growths like Aero Acres, these new developments brought swift change to suburban areas. As the boxes filled, suburban Washington and Baltimore received a heavy influx of expectant, younger, modest-income families.

Change began to place strain on Baltimore, Anne Arundel, Montgomery, and Prince George's county governments, raising weighty questions about who would decide its pace and direction. Commissioners in those places served under local potentates like "Colonel" E. Brooke Lee and his friends, who still governed in Montgomery County, and Lansdale G. Sasscer, who together with another old sponsor of the Suburban Sanitary Commission, T. Howard Duckett, ruled in Prince George's. Louis N. Phipps led Democrats in Anne Arundel; in 1938 Christian H. Kahl and Michael J. Birmingham had fallen heir to the Democratic organization in Baltimore County. Accustomed to deals, inexpensive services, and party regularity, the commissioners faced increasing criticism from suburbanites. Two earlier pieces of legislation provided interested parties with a framework for action. A state constitutional amendment of 1915 established procedures by which county voters might adopt "home rule," a county charter form of government with elected council and executive. Most citizens thereafter ignored that Progressive measure, and their leaders had no reason to remind them of it; charter government, removing local legislation from Annapolis, threatened to strike at a principal reason for the county Democrats' sway. Zoning—the power of local government to restrict land to various farm, residential, commercial, or industrial uses—had an even shorter history in Maryland. Using a standard enabling act supplied by the federal Commerce Department, the assembly in 1927 had granted that authority to Baltimore and in 1933 to smaller cities and the counties. Except for Baltimore, where there had been a zoning ordinance since 1923, few communities at the time made use of the law.

Montgomery countians had organized a charter government movement as early as 1935, when the lower county served as home to many a New Dealer. Led by members of a civic federation and the League of Women Voters, the effort owed much to a newcomer's sense of perspective, to a nonpartisan "better government" spirit that Stella Werner voiced. Campaigning strenuously for a charter, she said that the county suffered from "too much rural control" and that well before the commissioners met "matters seemed to be taken care of." Charter proponents steered the question through a preliminary test in 1942 and a charter board, Frederic P. Lee serving as chairman, wrote a home-rule document that went on the 1944 ballot. By then a committee against the charter had mobilized (the draft surrendered some powers to the Maryland–National Capital Park and Planning Commission), and the referendum narrowly lost. Procharter leaders dropped the MNCPPC provision. They kept the large issue of reform alive, and demonstrated their own property interests, by charging that Colonel Lee favored zoning action that would open the county to apartment buildings and similar low-cost housing; in July 1947, in fact, county commissioners by a vote of 3 to 2 had approved a controversial plan that permitted Harry H. Brodie to build apartments and a hotel on the Pook's Hill estate north of Bethesda. The colonel saw handwriting on the wall and tried to keep the Democratic party neutral in the charter contest. In 1948 Montgomery voters became the first in Maryland to adopt county charter local government.[2]

That year suburbanites in Baltimore and Anne Arundel counties won assurance that they would stay where they were: the General Assembly fixed the boundaries of Baltimore City as they lay. An aging matron, Baltimore suffered physical problems that promised only to get worse and that resembled the ills of any northeastern center. According to the 1940 census, no large American city had more rundown housing. Close to the harbor some twenty-six thousand dwellings, many of them a century old, still went without indoor plumbing, posed fire or safety hazards, and suffered rat infestation. Despite Baltimore's early lead in public health efforts, no city of its size in the country had a higher tuberculosis rate. Two major national highways, U.S. routes 1 and 40, ran through the heart of the city, charging through neighborhoods, creating noise, and posing special hazards to children and the elderly. Besides getting a good view of downtown drunks and dilapidation, tourists fought city traffic—wending their way around cars double- and triple-parked at places like a famous crab-cake house. "We just got to have crab cakes," natives yelled at the police who tried to move them on. "You're crazy if you think we're going anyplace else."[3]

New Rockville By-Pass, 1951. Three years after Montgomery County opted for home rule, road construction outside Rockville registered another sign of change—a new highway to divert Washington-Frederick traffic away from the center of town. *Washington Star/Washington Post Collection, D.C. Public Library*

Baltimoreans attacked the problem of "blighted areas" in their time-tested way—with as much voluntaryism and local control as possible. In April 1941 Frances Morton and other social workers had joined John H. Scarff, an architect, and Hans Froelicher, Jr., a Haverford College and Maryland Law School graduate who then was headmaster of Park School, to form a Citizens' Planning and Housing Association. The CPHA persuaded the city council shortly afterward to establish livable housing standards—to set the square footage a family of four needed, the necessary ratio of window to floor space, the amount of air required in sleeping rooms, basic plumbing needs, and the like. City ordinances of 1941 empowered fire, police, health, and public works officials to enforce the code. This strategy, using traditional means to impose enlightened regulation, became known as the Baltimore Plan. At the same time the Housing Authority of Baltimore City, tracing its origins to federal legislation of 1937, presided over low-rent and war-housing projects. These apartments, segregated by race, went up on blocks that authorities simply had razed of all old buildings. The federal government paid the difference between housing authority expenses and income from low rents.

Wartime population growth, so closely tied to war industry, gave many Baltimoreans the illusion that all was well with the city. Among others a hopeful postwar climate inspired confidence in progress—there seemed no reason here to abide the disease, homelessness, and poverty that Americans aimed to stamp out abroad. In 1945 a new city slum-clearance agency, the Baltimore Redevelopment Commission, began condemning and tearing down substandard housing, making the empty lots available to private developers and public authorities "for appropriate new uses." The housing authority built new public homes on several sites, notably at "Cherry Hill (Colored)," south of the Hanover Street Bridge. In one postwar year it received more than eight thousand new applications for low-rent housing (it had another ten thousand on file). Space permitted the commissioners, whom the mayor appointed, to place a mere 844 families. One parent of six wrote that the children had not slept in beds for fourteen months—"they have to sleep on the floor of a two-room apartment, and you know they won't get their proper rest like that and they just keep getting colds." After 1947 housing authority commissioners represented a cross-section of community interests; the board included the Reverend Don Frank Fenn, rector of St. Michael and All Angels Episcopal Church, Furman L. Templeton of the *Afro-American*, Robert G. Merrick, president of Equitable Trust, Mrs. Henry E. Corner, and a leading merchant, Walter I. Seif. The new mayor, Thomas D'Alesandro, Jr., chose them with care. First elected to the House of Delegates at age twenty-two, then a three-term Democratic congressman, D'Alesandro as mayor dedicated himself to solving Baltimore's housing problems.[4]

Deciding the best means to that end produced lively discussion among civic leaders. Froelicher, CPHA president, attacked the housing authority for

Substandard housing conditions, Baltimore, 1947, as portrayed in an official report of the postwar years. *Housing Authority of Baltimore City, Annual Report, 1947.*

being too political—generating a controversy that cost the association its Community Chest funding. He clung to the Baltimore Plan and its small government, "citizen action," self-help approach. For a time it held sway. After July 1947 a new Baltimore housing court, the first in the country, expedited cases involving housing-code violations. In its first year it heard sixteen hundred cases. A new police department sanitary squad devoted its time strictly to housing enforcement. In three years it investigated sixty-three thousand premises. Baltimore's ingenuity won wide recognition—*Reader's Digest* commended it to the nation in 1949—and enjoyed considerable support in Baltimore. The CPHA grew rapidly in size, from eight hundred members in 1946 to seventeen hundred in 1951, when it supplied all five housing authority commissioners. Reflecting a Quaker faith in his fellow man, Froelicher believed that once citizens had learned the dangers of blight they would eliminate it within their own communities. Slums in his view called for grass-roots work, and pleasant living partook not merely of material goods. "We must set a standard of living which is not of things," Froelicher wrote in the association newsletter, "but of responsibility"— "there is no 'they' to do it for 'us.' "[5]

Meanwhile, as President Truman integrated the armed forces and pressed for what he called a Fair Deal, the struggle against prejudice also began in Maryland. A principal reason lay in the leadership of Lillie Carroll Jackson, daughter of a slave, who devoted her life to rebuilding the Baltimore chapter of the National Association for the Advancement of Colored People and to making "promises of equality in the United States Constitution a reality in the lives of all people." A fundamentalist Christian, she could be spellbinding in front of an audience. She called on blacks to join in a "holy crusade to right ancient wrongs." "God opened my mouth," she once declared, "and no man can shut it." By the end of the war the Baltimore NAACP, rivaling the New York City chapter in size, counted two thousand members. Jackson urged her followers to get politically involved, and Negro voters in Baltimore roughly doubled in the dozen years after 1940; she helped to form a Maryland NAACP conference and in October 1946 took part in a Maryland Congress against Discrimination, held at the Enon Baptist Church in Baltimore. Delegates reminded Marylanders that "persecution because of race, color or creed is the carry-over of Hitlerism to our shores." Their appeal may have won converts, but at the time many Baltimore businesses posted "Gentiles Only" or "Whites Only" signs in their windows. Most theaters had "colored" seating sections. Restaurants catered to either blacks or whites. Before the Rutgers-Hopkins basketball game in early 1948, a Baltimore hotel refused a room to the visiting team's Negro member. Hopkins that year hired a black professor, but at first the faculty club refused him admission.[6]

In the early years of the century white Marylanders had debated the place of the Negro in politics. Now blacks, many of them fresh from wartime service, others having tasted employment gains in war plants, turned the tables and asked stern questions about their rights. In July 1948 white and black opponents of segregation arranged a test of Baltimore City racial policy by playing tennis at Druid Hill Park on a court reserved for whites. Police arrested them, and in November a city judge found seven protesters guilty of "conspiring to assemble unlawfully." Until then, in order not to prejudge this case involving prejudice, newspapers reported only its facts. After the decision the aging Mencken published an editorial that clearly had been brewing inside him for quite some time. As one could have expected, he chided the "so-called Progressives" who had raised the issue. He had no trouble with the judge's finding, which simply applied the law. He did take his fellow Free Staters to task for putting such a law on the books in the first place. Negroes and whites alike paid for the public grounds, wrote Mencken, and neither common sense nor common decency could keep people of different races from joining in "harmless play." "It is high time," he wrote—among his last words before suffering a crippling stroke—"that all such relics of Ku Kluxery be wiped out in Maryland."[7] Change came slowly. Three years after the Druid Hill demonstration Baltimore opened golf courses to blacks, as if many of them played golf.

While issues of housing and fairness stood on the national agenda, other postwar problems underscored the peculiar character of Maryland and lingering regional differences as mid-century approached. Western Marylanders—living a rural and small-town life—for generations had voted for moderates and gone about their business. After the war, when Fairchild in Hagerstown laid off about thirteen hundred workers and Celanese cut back in Cumberland, they worried about the future of their war-propped industries. The perennial poverty of Southern Maryland and depression in the oyster industry vexed any Maryland leader. Oyster harvests had been poor for many years and Governor O'Conor's attempt to sustain the state's conservation efforts by keeping wildlife and fish protection under a single agency failed in 1939 as watermen won another round: their friends filled the new Tidewater Fisheries office. Conservationists in the forties argued futilely that preserving the beds involved statewide issues like sewage disposal and erosion. Watermen refused, as usual, to take advantage of the oyster-culture or seed-bed laws. A commission chaired by Hopkins president Isaiah Bowman after the war estimated that watermen lost about $30 million a year by failing to cultivate oysters and also noted the dangerous shortage of the shells and seed oysters needed to "farm the Bay." Still fiercely independent, watermen preferred to search for undepleted natural beds.[8]

Many of them, Virginians included, took chances on illegal harvests. Often piloting powerful boats developed in the South Pacific war, postwar pirates motored onto the Potomac beds below the Harry Nice Bridge every moonless night; they considered outracing the undermanned and ill-equipped marine police a kind of game. In 1947 the General Assembly provided for an enlarged force of forty boats and crews. Captain Chester Cullison, a veteran Chesapeake marine policeman, took over the Potomac force and mounted a war-surplus machine gun on the *Pocomoke*. Soon he captured a boat belonging to a much-acclaimed Colonial Beach, Virginia, dredger and put it into service with the Maryland police. He ran another poacher aground, and when the oysterman sarcastically yelled for the lawman to shoot him, too, Cullison came about and filled the craft with holes. By January 1948 he had fired his entire season's supply of machine-gun ammunition. Virginia marine police decided that Cullison and his men were trigger-happy and withdrew their cooperation; Marylanders observed that Virginia pirates, tried by their own courts, got off lightly. Though Maryland officials bowed to public pressure and removed machine guns from police boats, the Virginia assembly, unplacated, adopted a law permitting powerboat dredging in parts of the Potomac. The terms of the 1785 compact required the measure to pass in Maryland before going into effect. Annapolis lawmakers shouted it down with jeers and unprintable language. The *Sun* declared itself at a loss to tell whether conflict on the Potomac "was a gang war or a neighborhood game of cops and robbers."[9]

Top, Smith Island. *Bottom,* Indian Corn in Carroll County, c. 1945–50. A. Aubrey Bodine's camera caught the pristine isolation of rural Maryland on both sides of the bay as the bridge debate raged. *A. Aubrey Bodine Family Collection*

To make things worse with her southern sister, and helping to give the state a tangier reputation than it already had, Maryland in 1949 extended a wartime allowance for Fort Meade and Anne Arundel County by legalizing slot machines in the counties of Calvert, Charles, and St. Mary's. The decision followed easily upon the pinball and claw machine measure of twelve years before. Legislators recognized the expense of suppressing the popular machines and preferred to tax what they could not stamp out. The new law had the avid support of hotel and resort owners in Southern Maryland. Wartime steamboat losses, but especially automobile competition, had hurt the packet lines and forced a cutback in the service that had made the places profitable. After the one-armed-bandit statute, taverns, filling stations, and grocery stores on state routes 2 and 4 became famous for their Las Vegas ambiance. Garish signs on U.S. 301 tried to lure truckdrivers off the road and into the gambling joints. Astonished Virginians saw casinos go up on pilings at the Potomac's southern edge, technically still in Maryland. This practice and Maryland's offensive against illegal dredging strained relations between Leah and Rachel as badly as they had been since 1877.

Marylanders quarreled with Virginians, but no worse than they quarreled among themselves. During the war, with concrete diverted to military use and fuel rationed, the state Roads Commission had postponed most of its usual work. In 1947 the General Assembly considered postwar highway plans that included a bridge across Chesapeake Bay. The bridge had been a dream at least since the 1920s, when a company had secured charter rights to build one. Doubting that enough people traveled between the shores to make it pay, Mencken, at least, had pronounced the bridge scheme "ridiculous" and "fantastic." During the Nice administration the assembly had created a Bridge Supervising Committee of seven citizens and authorized the roads commission to study the feasibility of a bridge. In 1941 the state purchased the ferryboats that filled the bill reasonably well and by then made the Annapolis to Matapeake (in place of Claiborne) run in about forty-five minutes. Travelers took the standard summertime back-ups in stride. The ferries, carrying about fifty cars a trip, allowed passengers time to relax in the fresh, salty air, visit the snack bar, throw scraps to sea gulls, and make acquaintances along the rail. Even in winter, recalled one patron, "it was pleasant to sit on a bench inside the wide windowed restaurant with a cup of hot coffee and watch the squalls whip up whitecaps on the water." Depression and war having killed earlier bridge plans, this latest proposal brought the issue to a head. Private ferryboat companies attacked the bridge, of course. So did Baltimore shipping agents, who expected any span to pose a nautical hazard; one could easily imagine freighters plowing into piers in foggy weather, perhaps bringing cars and trucks raining down to a horrible end. When civil engineers dispelled these fears, maritime spokesmen said the bridge still would spook pilots and prove to be "a mental hazard." [10]

Stiffest opposition came from the Eastern Shore, where strong sentiment ran against outsiders and disturbing changes. The same year legislators debated the bridge, the Easton *Star-Democrat* set off a flurry of zoning activity when it reported ninety new houses, eight garages, six gas stations, five warehouses, and several stores under construction in Talbot County. Later, when a Baltimore printing company arrived with the intention of building a new plant in the town, Eastonians living across the street from the site quickly objected. The town council had to weigh hard economic factors. Because silk hosiery had given way to nylons, the town had lost several small employers; high corn prices had turned local farmers away from tomato production, which meant a drop in canning employment (but also a seasonal rise in the number of visiting wild ducks and geese). The bay bridge and Easton's factory offered the Shore classic choices between development and quietude. Easton council members hesitantly forged a compromise that allowed the "smokeless and noiseless" publisher to settle there.[11] Ocean City interests pushed the bridge with all their might.

Antibridge forces made a last stand. The road from Kent Narrows to Ocean City, they said, would become a tunnel of billboards and turn the peninsula into a Coney Island. An Eastern Shore dance band, putting feelings into song, got a rise from local partygoers when it played "The Old Gray Mare" to new lyrics. The chorus ended "We don't give a damn for the whole state of Maryland / We're from the Eastern Shore." A Talbot County senator, Henry Herbert Balch, felt so strongly about the bridge that for a time he filibustered against it. Speaking for hours—singing a litany of grudges that went back to colonial times—Balch denounced Western Shore politicians, architects, engineers, the construction firm likely to build the bridge, and Arunah S. Abell (who had died in 1888) of the Baltimore *Sun*.[12] Over such protests the assembly voted a 45-million-dollar bond issue for construction of a toll bridge. In October 1949 work began on a structure that would bring Eastern and Western shores together—for better or for worse.

～∞～

Politically the state turned in the eddies formed by FDR's passage in American history. Governor O'Conor had tried to keep to the political center, loyal to Roosevelt but distanced from the New Deal. He favored legislation friendly to laboring people and teachers; he nonetheless remained a fiscally minded Democrat of the old breed who in 1942 campaigned for a second term boasting of unspent departmental appropriations and a treasury surplus of some $4.5 million. With this money he planned postwar roads projects. Higher taxes, however, helped to account for O'Conor's surplus, and the governor had lost voters on both hands. Blacks believed him a doubtful friend; enemies of the New Deal thought him too soft on Roosevelt. Theodore R. McKeldin, a Republican of growing stature and high reputation among black voters, nearly defeated O'Conor in 1942 and next year unseated Mayor Howard Jackson in Baltimore. In 1944 Maryland Democratic leaders supported Roosevelt's reelection dutifully, as soldiers. Not keen about a fourth term, they in fact had protested FDR's unprecedented third term at the 1940 convention by casting ballots for Tydings. Although the president carried Maryland in 1944, he did so barely. About one in three eligible voters went to the polls; Roosevelt Democrats, largely satisfied, stayed at home, and Republicans showed renewed strength. In the same election Tydings, still honored as an FDR critic, won another Senate term handily. At the end of the war and with Roosevelt's passing, Marylanders probably wanted the best of both worlds—the government services they had grown used to and release from government controls. In 1946 they elected as governor William Preston Lane, Jr., Ritchie's anti-lynching attorney general who ran as a Fair Dealer opposed to the Baltimore City bosses.

Lane resembled Harry Truman in demeanor and practical sense, and also in his willingness to undertake social legislation. In 1947, during one of the state's most productive assembly sessions, the governor won approval of a five-year highway improvement program that would cost $200 million. Lane also favored spending more money on Maryland schools, then at the mercy of major social developments. One involved veterans who, thanks again to the G.I. Bill, had the means their parents often had lacked for postsecondary education and now stood in large numbers on the steps of Maryland colleges and universities. At Homewood fresh youngsters in flannels and saddle shoes mixed, at first uneasily, with men in their twenties who wore division patches on their jackets, had no time for campus clowning, and scoffed at puffery. With federal assistance schools like Western Maryland in Westminster put up "vet villes" and enrolled many more new students. Reporting in 1947, a commission on Maryland higher education headed by William L. Marbury, a leading Baltimore attorney (and son of the Progressive), recommended creating "junior colleges" and expanding further at College Park. New legislation offered matching state funds to localities that built their own two-year colleges. Montgomery County already had done so; Washington County and Baltimore City soon did. For reasons of expediency and idealism—the popular demand for schooling, awareness of the egalitarianism veterans had fought for—Maryland established the principle that junior-college admissions ought to be as open as possible.

The University of Maryland handled the brunt of the load. Enrollment at College Park almost doubled between June 1946 and September of that year—from six thousand to eleven thousand students. Four women squeezed into dormitory rooms meant for two. Prince George's County turned over "tempo" buildings to the university for student housing. About seven hundred men slept on bunk beds in the armory. While the university budget grew from $4.8 million in 1945 to $9.9 million in 1948, President Byrd held the line on faculty hiring and salaries, supposedly having said "Ph.D.s are a dime a dozen." He channeled money into an extensive building program instead. A strung-out young instructor trying to handle a class of five hun-

Leading postwar Democrats, Governor William Preston Lane, Jr., on the left, and Baltimore mayor-elect Thomas D'Alesandro, Jr., enjoyed a few private words at the Preakness, May 1947. Baltimore *News American* photograph. *Jacques Kelly*

dred wrote a note that he could see "no other way out"—and left the state. At the same time the university developed a remarkable continuing education curriculum that included courses for American servicemen at foreign bases. A new American civilization program (combining literature and history) also attracted outside attention; it "inoculated" students, said an official brochure, against "various foreign isms." Beginning in 1947 a bureau of business and economic research at the university published valuable quarterly monographs, most of them on Maryland subjects. In Baltimore, nursing became a four-year program and dentistry and pharmacy trained students who scored well above the national average on state board examinations. The football team thrived under "Curley" Byrd and Coach James M. "Big Jim" Tatum; in 1949 the squad went 9 and 1 and defeated Missouri in the Gator Bowl. Making the most of all these accomplishments, Byrd cultivated political ambitions. Generous as he was proud, the president offered free tuition to students appointed by legislators (one per delegate, two per senator). On one football Saturday, using university funds, he treated a quorum of the General Assembly to lunch and game tickets.[13]

Another development forced the state to aid localities in building public schools—wartime children of newcomers reached school age soon after 1945, and Marylanders after the war had babies in sudden volume. Between 1945 and 1948 enrollments jumped by about 27,000 across the state to a total, black and white, of more than 307,000 pupils. The demand on county and Baltimore City treasuries compared to Depression relief efforts; local taxes simply could not cover the enormous public need. Lane in 1949 proposed a bond issue of $50 million for teacher salaries and construction, the money to create a loan fund available to local authorities on a three-to-one matching basis. Passage of this bill marked an important early step toward a school expansion program that continued to accelerate in the years ahead. The 1950 census revealed that in one decade the number of Maryland children below the age of ten had grown by almost 187,000, and that year public school enrollments approached 349,000. During the Lane years state funding, administered ably by Superintendent Thomas G. Pullen, led to more than two hundred new buildings or major additions; teacher salaries went up 53 percent to an annual average of $3,543. Private schools grew, as well, though not as quickly. Many Catholic taxpayers assumed a double burden—supporting public schools while paying tuition for the religious training they believed it their obligation to provide. Catholic-school enrollments in 1950 stood at 57,000, an increase of more than 20 percent over 1945 figures.[14]

Expanding the number of schools and teachers in the state raised the issue of black schooling and placed it more than ever in a practical light. Separate but equal school systems were expensive—a fact fully known to local leaders building or maintaining black classrooms. They often were a fiction, a truth all too apparent to black parents and educators and their white friends. In Baltimore after 1945 NAACP members steadily protested the condition of colored classrooms. Of fifty-eight buildings a commission in 1921 had recommended for demolition as unsafe, thirty-five still stood as black schools. Expense and the likelihood of deceit grew higher at the college level and beyond. Since Thurgood Marshall's courtroom victory in 1935, blacks had attended the university law school. That year the assembly finally purchased Princess Anne Academy and made it more nearly, if still not quite, part of the University of Maryland system. Three years later Bowie in Prince George's County became a black teachers' college and in 1939 legislators voted to take over old Morgan College, which had fallen on hard times. Meantime the state also provided scholarships for blacks who had to go elsewhere for training unavailable in local black institutions. Serving as chairman of the Southern Governors' Conference after the war, Lane helped to establish the Southern Regional Educational Board—a means of pooling the resources of segregated states and thereby enabling blacks to attend a Negro medical school, for example, even if their own state had none.

Maryland integrationists made some progress in the Lane years. Like their allies elsewhere in the country they aimed to dismantle segregation by starting at the top, where it was most vulnerable. Indeed, the poor quality of black colleges had become notorious. The Marbury Commission chided the state for unequal spending on black and white campuses; though it split on admitting blacks to graduate schools, the commission noted how difficult it was to meet the separate-but-equal test "so long as the principle of maintaining separate schools is carried through graduate and professional instruction." Carl Murphy, publisher of the *Afro-American*, wrote a minority report that argued in favor of abolishing the scholarship program and, in fields where no black schools offered postgraduate training, simply admitting students to the University of Maryland. The next year President Byrd, his critics said defending his fiefdom, renamed Princess Anne Maryland State College and recommended state funding to build it into a respectable black branch of the university. Legislators ignored the suggestion. Many of them may have preferred a stronger black college system over radical change. They nonetheless hesitated to spend the needed money as long as the federal courts applied strict measures in judging the "equality" of black institutions. Marshall and NAACP strategists drove this wedge hard. In 1950 a lawsuit opened the University of Maryland School of Nursing to Negroes. A year later—this time without legal action—a black graduate student began work at College Park.[15]

Treatment of the insane in Maryland never had been quite the same source of state pride as medical treatment, partly because of fiscal conservatism, perhaps because theories of mental disorders had lagged behind medical science or offended Marylanders. Seemingly incurable, "the insane" in the nineteenth century largely had remained with their families unless prone to violence, in which case county commissioners committed them to the local almshouse. In 1872 the Maryland Hospital (supported by state money for almost forty years) moved from Baltimore to Spring Grove near Catonsville. Later found to be without heat, Spring Grove received not the treatable, insofar as they could be identified, but "the most filthy, violent, and refractory" insane from the local almshouses. A state Lunacy Commission exercised limited control over state institutions after 1886. At Towson in 1891 trustees of the Moses Sheppard estate established the clean, kindly asylum he had wanted, and later, with Enoch Pratt funding, it grew in reputation. Overall, the struggle was uphill. Common misconceptions of Freud in the early twentieth century did not prompt public spending on mental hospitals, where presumably therapists employed his strange theory. Catholics shuddered at the analyst's attention to the sexual drive; Mencken thought America "a nest of imprisoned and fermenting sex" and yet typically dismissed one of Freud's works as "chiefly piffle."[16]

In January 1949, after prodding from the state medical society, the *Sun* in a series of articles exposed the scandalous condition of Maryland mental hospitals—children filthy, adults chained to their beds—and the Lane administration called for action. Relying on bond issues of several million dollars, legislators agreed to rebuild the six state hospitals for the mentally ill or retarded (one for blacks only, one on the Eastern Shore), raise wages for mental health employees, and establish a new department of mental hygiene. As head of the department Lane appointed Dr. Clifton T. Perkins, a psychiatrist of national renown who had been head of the Massachusetts system. Perkins came to Maryland believing that "there is no greater measure of the humanity of a state than the care it gives its mentally ill." He encouraged volunteer workers in the hospitals, permitted female nurses to tend male patients (a new practice in Maryland), and encouraged family physicians to visit the hospitals to study ways of preventing emotional disorder. Employing "industrial therapy," Perkins trained patients in skills and trades. A new division of psychiatric education and an institute at the University of Maryland helped to establish uniform state standards. Among the states, Maryland rose from nineteenth to sixth in spending for mental health. Its hospitals earned a professional reputation for excellence.[17]

Lane successfully met enormous postwar needs, but his measures cost money that bond issues did not completely cover. In 1945 Maryland spent about $37 per person on social services; in 1950 the figure had risen to $61, a little above the national average. Total state spending between 1945 and 1951 grew from about $60 million to $219 million and at a rate of 25 percent a year. Lane foundered on the rocks of higher taxes. Before he took office, an O'Conor-appointed commission chaired by Joseph Sherbow, a Baltimore City judge, had reported on tax and spending strategies. The Sherbow Commission observed that localities, dependent on property taxes alone, could not possibly pay for new public services. It recommended raising state taxes and distributing receipts among the counties and Baltimore. It suggested heavier state spending in poor counties, applying the school-equalization principle of 1922 to state services generally, and a formula, based on highway mileage, pupils, and classrooms, by which additional funds would go to quickly growing counties for new roads and schools. The assembly adopted these shared-revenue policies, including the matching-grants idea for school improvement. In raising money enough to go around, legislators figured the blame eventually would fall on the governor; in 1947 Lane persuaded them to raise income, corporation, and gasoline taxes. He also asked for and received a sales tax of 2¢ on the dollar, the first in Maryland history (though twenty-two states already had one). Taxpayers, pinched by inflation, looked at Governor Lane and saw not benefits but burdens. They scorned the sales tax (paraphrasing the popular song) as "pennies for Lane." Some of them threw pennies at the governor and his wife when they made public appearances.[18]

For a number of reasons, the sales tax only chief among them, Maryland Democrats failed to maintain their hold during the Lane years. J. Millard Tawes, the Crisfield native who had served as O'Conor's comptroller, bided his time as Lane's state bank commissioner. He had hoped to win the party nomination for governor in 1946. He later favored more ferries instead of the bay bridge and tried not to be associated with the sales tax. In Baltimore D'Alesandro had won in 1947 when McKeldin declined another term. Though in "Little Italy" his election literally caused dancing in the streets, fewer than half of all Baltimore voters had gone to the polls. The mayor busied himself making his personal position stronger. Then, in April 1947, Lane had made trouble for himself by naming Stuart S. Janney, Jr., to replace George P. Mahoney as chairman of the Maryland Racing Commission.

While "cleaning up" the sport of kings in Maryland, Mahoney had trumpeted his attacks against race fixing and the practice of doping horses. At Bel Air, in the nick of time, he claimed to have caught mobsters as they tried to substitute a ringer, Don't Delay, for All Flo; a jockey mysteriously drove off a West Virginia road before answering questions about race-track fraud, Mahoney remembered later for a series of articles written in police-gazette style. He acquired enemies. He admitted angering Pimlico managers, whom he urged to bear a heavier burden of track, stable, and grandstand improvements. Whatever Lane's reasons for dismissing Mahoney, his fitness turned out to be less important than the results of his removal. The commissioner learned of his fate at a professional gathering in Louisville, where he expected elevation to national office. Off the Maryland commission, he had to withdraw. Lane's choice of Janney embarrassed Mahoney even further, carrying symbolic injury that the governor may have not intended to inflict. Janney, a Baltimore attorney and son of Ritchie's old law partner, raised thoroughbreds with noteworthy track success. He sat easily in the saddle; for many years he rode in the point-to-point races that featured dramatic jumps over hedges and high rails. Mahoney, a paving contractor, owned expensive farms and judged show horses but did not enjoy Janney's reputation as a rider and breeder. At flat track events he may have felt kinship with the people who placed bets at the two-dollar windows. Pride injured and aspiration thwarted, he accepted his firing bitterly.[19]

Lane's discomfort finally came from his "liberal" image at a time when Marylanders had more than continued progress on their minds. While responding to twists in state party politics in the late 1940s, citizens also registered political discontent that they shared with Americans generally. Victory over the Axis Powers scarcely brought world peace; global power carried with it many frustrations—communist satellite states in occupied Eastern Europe, unrest in the old European colonies, a communist victory in China in 1949. The following June communist troops poured over the boundary between North and South Korea, dragging Americans into an undeclared war. Spies had stolen secrets necessary to make the fearful atom bomb. The Soviets invited anger, suspicion, "preparedness." Marxism, while few Americans read Marx, more than ever meant dangerous thinking. A sense of gloom and foreboding settled over the country. Many people suspected treachery. An economics instructor at St. Mary's Seminary in Baltimore, Father John Francis Cronin, wrote a long paper on "The Problem of American Communism" and in 1945 presented it to church prelates. The Maryland diocesan weekly, *Catholic Review*, warned against the rising tide of communist atheism abroad. Members of the General Assembly passed resolutions on foreign policy issues, condemning world communism as "a menace to international unity."[20]

On the national scene Marylanders unwillingly got involved in a series of sensational episodes that rocked the country and inflamed public opinion. Testifying in August 1948 before a House Committee on "Un-American Activities," Whittaker Chambers—former Baltimore resident and then a senior editor of *Time* magazine—accused Alger Hiss of having been, like himself, a member of the Communist party in the thirties. Hiss belonged to an old Baltimore family and had distinguished himself at Hopkins and Harvard Law School; he had a long record of service as a clerk to Justice Holmes and as a New Dealer in the State Department. Hiss had been secretary at the United Nations Conference of 1945. In 1948 he served as head of the Carnegie Endowment for International Peace. Vigorously denying the charges against him, Hiss appeared to stumble under the sharp questions of a young California congressman, Richard Nixon, who delighted in pursuing this privileged Easterner. The case grew personal and mysterious. When Hiss sued Chambers for libel, the former editor suddenly produced copies of State Department documents that he said Hiss had given him in 1937–38. Prosecutors could not learn with certainty what the Hiss-Chambers relationship had been before the war but pursued Hiss for perjury. One jury deadlocked; a second, based on evidence that the stolen documents had been typed on Hiss's machine and that Hiss had known Chambers later than he admitted, convicted him. Sentenced to five years' imprisonment in January 1950, Hiss never gave up protesting his innocence.

The Hiss case seemed to prove that some highly placed public officials and intellectuals had flirted with the communist enemy. Shortly after Hiss's sentencing, Joseph R. McCarthy, a Wisconsin senator, captured instant attention by claiming that he had the names of high-ranking communists in the State Department. It fell to Millard Tydings, chairman of the Foreign Relations Committee, to hear more from McCarthy, who singled out as a leading communist Professor Owen Lattimore of the Walter Hines Page School of International Studies at Hopkins. The charge stunned students and faculty at Homewood, where emigrés from Europe and scholars of all beliefs had spoken in recent years as freely as ever. George Boas, a philosopher and serviceman from both world wars, Clarence Long, a veteran who taught economics, and others formed a group in support of Lattimore's character and scholarship. When the Tydings committee met it generally found McCarthy unconvincing, finally calling the accusations against Lattimore "a fraud and a hoax." "The convenient theory that *he must have known* [that some of his associates were "communists"]," read the committee report in the summer of 1950, "has not yet become the criterion for judging a private citizen in this country." By then Lattimore already had returned to Baltimore and a noisy reception in front of Gilman Hall. Boas led the cheering—grateful, he told six hundred listeners, that the "cloud of poison gas spreading over the country has not yet smothered the faculty of The Johns Hopkins University, who remain faithful to their university motto, 'The truth will set you free.' "[21]

Besides witch hunts, the anxieties of the late forties led to retrenchment, caution, innuendo. Marylanders in 1948 passed a constitutional amendment limiting governors to two consecutive terms, just as the Twenty-second Amendment limited presidential terms. Proponents of the measures argued that for free government safety lay in numbers—in frequent turnover; there should be no more Ritchies or Roosevelts. A second constitutional change mandated annual meetings of the legislature so that the people's voice could be heard more frequently and laws passed with more dispatch (an amendment of two years later made it clear that the governor could not kill a bill with a pocket veto). In 1948, when the Baltimore Kiwanis Club got the ball rolling for an "organization of organizations" against communism, another Maryland amendment demonstrated growing fear. Approved easily in all localities, it declared ineligible for state office or employment anyone who advocated violent overthrow of the government. Better reflecting the public mood than the homecoming Lattimore received, the General Assembly next year passed a statute—commonly called for its sponsor, Frank B. Ober—outlawing "subversive" organizations and requiring public officials, from the governor down to kindergarten teachers, to take a loyalty oath.

In 1950 restless voters sought more change, and Democratic infighting helped them to find it. Mahoney sought revenge by opposing Lane, whose unpopularity plagued him, in the primary. Although the unit rule gave Lane the nomination, Mahoney got more votes. He hardly came to the incumbent's aid in the fall general election, when Lane faced Theodore McKeldin. McKeldin promised voters he would repeal the sales tax. Baltimoreans, usually Democratic, gave the former mayor a margin of forty-seven thousand votes, and McKeldin won the state with unusual ease for a Republican. Political observers found Lane's defeat unsurprising, but few people had expected Senator Tydings to lose. Tydings fell victim to dropping public confidence in government officials, to fears of wickedness in high places. His opponent, the Baltimore lawyer John Marshall Butler, shrewdly used this malaise to his advantage. Butler hired a Chicago political consultant who insinuated that Tydings and his committee had been suspiciously hard on McCarthy. No one doubted that Republicans hunted communists in government partly for partisan purposes, but O'Conor, since 1946 junior senator from Maryland, described the anti-Tydings effort as "the most deplorable resort to mud slinging and character assassination this state has witnessed in many years." On election eve, a four-page mock tabloid carried a composite picture of Tydings and the leader of the American Communist party. One "headline" read "Tydings Promised Probe, But Gave Whitewash."[22]

⌘

Theodore Roosevelt McKeldin proved the ideal governor for the times. Handsome son of a Baltimore stonecutter who later became a cop, he had been born the year the "Rough Rider" won the presidency. McKeldin's career offered convincing evidence that hard work like Teddy's paid off. To help support his family, McKeldin after finishing grammar school had taken a job as an office boy. Too ambitious to quit school, however, he enrolled in night courses at City College and next attended evening law school at the University of Maryland, graduating with honors in 1925. Meanwhile he worked at old-line Baltimore firms—Alexander Brown & Sons and the Fidelity and Deposit Company. He married the woman who taught him bookkeeping. McKeldin loved to speak and after taking a Dale Carnegie course at the YMCA was good at it; he began by handling pep talks for Fidelity and Deposit. Later, after getting involved in William Broening's 1927 campaign for mayor, McKeldin served as his honor's secretary and emissary to functions like oyster roasts and awards banquets that Broening could avoid.

The young man's drive logically led to his own campaigns for mayor and governor, and while his first efforts failed they did gain him exposure, useful connections, and admiration for his oratory. When he took office as wartime Baltimore mayor, McKeldin had applied bipartisan vigor to the task of planning for peace. Soon after the war his administration, along with Lane and federal authorities, began work on a new international airport south of the city; named for the Quaker meetinghouse that once had stood there, Friendship International could not have borne a happier or more timely title. Mayor McKeldin deserved some credit for pressing housing-code enforcement. He planned a Baltimore civic center that would attract lucrative conventions, a new wing at City Hospital for tuberculosis patients, and enlargement of the city water system by means of Liberty Reservoir on the upper Patapsco. An eminently affable fellow, McKeldin genuinely enjoyed people, both black and white, and practiced a nondenominational religion that laid emphasis on friendliness, community, and fairness. He welcomed visitors to his office with souvenirs, many of them religious, and went out of his way to mingle. As mayor he often had attended black services on Sundays, even preached at them. Politically he pursued a bipartisan course because in truth he was a party unto himself.

Self-made, self-confident, McKeldin made modernizing Maryland his business. The new governor soon appointed blacks to state commissions, created a new Commission for Interracial Problems and Relations, and opened state parks to Negroes. He championed business-like efficiency in government. His inaugural address of January 1951 pledged economy while also promising improvements to roads, hospitals, and sanitariums, the building of more schools, and a state civil defense program to help deter Soviet aggression. McKeldin appointed Simon E. Soboloff, who had been Baltimore City solicitor when McKeldin served as mayor, to head the latest commission on state administrative organization. In 1952 both assembly and voters adopted a leading Soboloff Commission suggestion, a constitutional amendment that altered the form of proposed state budgets; instead of presenting budgets in line-by-line detail, governors now would write them by "program" or state agency. Besides allowing flexibility within departments, the change bundled together appropriations by purpose and thus eased long-range forecasting. While the legislature did not follow every Soboloff recommendation, it did agree also to simplify prison and welfare administration. In 1952 McKeldin also broke ground at Jessup for a peculiar prison, the Patuxent Institution, which would house offenders noteworthy for their "persistent aggravated antisocial or criminal behavior."[23] Meanwhile the governor admitted his attack on the hated sales tax had been a mistake. The tax went up with scarcely a murmur.

Marylanders may have liked McKeldin because during his term they got around to enjoying things, and there was much to enjoy. The "casual look" became a leading theme in women's fashion; its creator, Claire McCardell, had grown up in Frederick and gone to Hood College before moving on to New York. Restoring hips and curves, to the delight of males, McCardell explained that designers had "gotten away from women's natural beauty." Music was in the air as never before. Between the end of the war and McKeldin's inauguration, Annapolis gained four new radio stations, Cumberland and Hagerstown two more each; Bethesda, Rockville, Havre de Grace, and Cambridge got their first ones. Radio aired the sentimental songs ("Oh My Papa") and nonsensical hits ("Shboom, Shboom") that were popular in the period. They also carried commercials for all the products and services that listeners wanted and many now could afford. Between 1945 and 1951 Maryland per capita income climbed 39 percent (from $1,272 to $1,769). During the fifties the rise continued, real income increasing by 70 percent, the highest gains appearing at the middle-income level.[24] Such figures meant that after postwar reconversion American manufacturers fed a seemingly inexhaustible demand for "consumer" goods—the items that made life a bit easier or more fun—like washing machines, kitchen appliances, air conditioners, vacuum cleaners, outboard motors, outdoor cooking grills.

Market analysts at Bendix and Westinghouse had been correct about radio, and about another demand too; in 1947–48 three television stations began broadcasting in Baltimore and four in Washington. Proportionately far more Marylanders owned radios than television sets, but everyone wanted a TV, especially since early television relied almost entirely on homegrown programming. In Baltimore it included the "Johns Hopkins Science Review" (Peabody Award winner in 1952 and first American program broadcast on the BBC), "Romper Room" (which eventually went on a national network), and favorites like the "Jud and Judy" variety show, "Hi Jinx," "Eddy's Prosperity Parade," and "Reward for Talent." Brent Gunts awarded prizes to contestants who identified silhouettes on a large screen; he occasionally carried live broadcasts from an ice skating rink. On Jay Grayson's "Date to Dance," local lights bounced, shuffled, and grinned at the cameras. Marvelously amateurish, TV carried unlimited commercial potential. Watching it, one could actually see all the glittering things stores and dealers carried.

Above all Marylanders wanted cars—buying them in huge numbers and then driving them to do all the things dreamed of or postponed during Depression and war. Beginning in 1949 Detroit automobile manufacturers (Maryland lost its last homemade auto, the Calvert, in 1927) began offering new models each year, and few true Americans overlooked annual changes to the streamlined, bechromed cars. In early July 1952, when Governor McKeldin in Chicago nominated his friend Dwight D. Eisenhower for president, a Baltimore dealer described the Ford as "The People's Choice." Cadillac salesmen on North Charles Street had only to say that the Cadillac owner "reserves a special place in his heart for the beautiful crest that rides high on the hood." Buick offered "lullaby smoothness." "And that Fireball 8 Engine—man," beckoned a newspaper ad, "what a docile thunderbolt you'll find it to be! What are you waiting for?" As more and more Marylanders took the bait, traffic, as one headline phrased it, busted its "highway britches." Between 1937 and 1951 the traffic count on U.S. Route 1 between Baltimore and Washington—known as billboard boulevard, "the most heavily traveled and deadliest stretch of road in the world"—rose 156 percent. On U.S. 40 to Frederick usage climbed 197 percent and on Maryland 2 between Baltimore and Annapolis 271 percent. Between Glen Burnie and the Potomac River Bridge, traffic on U.S. 301 increased 349 percent. Completion of the Delaware Memorial Bridge, connecting to the southern end of the New Jersey Turnpike, helped to account for the growing volume on U.S. 40 east of Baltimore, the Pulaski Highway. There, too, it more than trebled. These figures, said the *Evening Sun*, showed the need for more and better highways—and also that better highways led to more traffic. In that newspaper B. F. Goodrich, "First in Rubber," printed a large picture of cars clogging a two-lane road. The pre-holiday message in large type read "You'd Be Miles Ahead with Better Roads."[25]

More than a few families piled into the station wagon on a Sunday afternoon and drove across the spectacular new Chesapeake Bay Bridge, which McKeldin, Lane, Tawes, and other public figures christened on 30 July 1952. Despite a blazing sun, the ten thousand onlookers remained in what reporters called "a holiday mood." Luckily they did, for the dedication took hours—first elaborate ceremonies at Sandy Point, then a motorcade across the four-mile-long bridge for more speeches on Kent Island, where Mayor D'Alesandro and Comptroller Tawes shook hands to symbolize the meeting

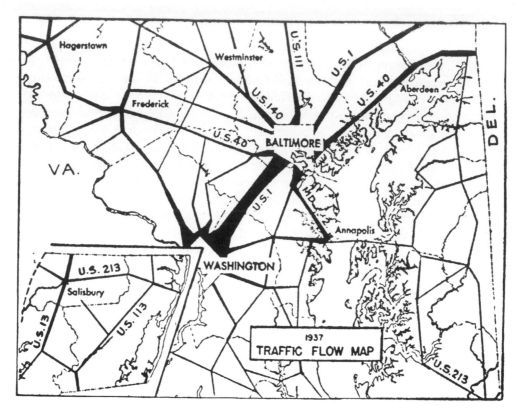

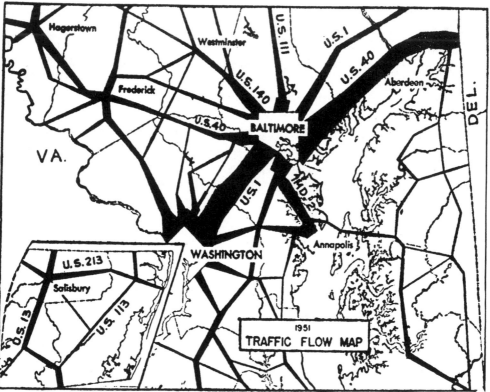

The graphic case for improved highways. Baltimore *Evening Sun*, 3 July 1952.

of the shores. During the same hours the Sandy Point–Matapeake ferries, named for governors Nice and O'Conor, sadly made their final voyages. They gave way to an impressive engineering achievement, the design of a Baltimore firm headed by J. E. Greiner. Among the longest over-water spans in the world, the bridge rested on more than four thousand steel pilings, some of them driven two hundred feet into the Chesapeake Bay floor. Battling winds and rough water, workers had installed 123 prefabricated steel pieces, each a bridge in itself, beginning at the ends and building toward the center. There a Golden Gate–like suspension span completed the structure. Photographers and artists soon made the beautiful lines of the bridge famous (a long curve on the western end allowed the center span to stand perpendicular to the ship channel). From its lofty roadway—at the center nearly two hundred feet above water—one could see sailboats fluttering in the distance and watch oceangoing freighters pass far below. Toll booth employees had to deal with motorists who "froze" at the top of the bridge and had to be driven the rest of the way across.[26]

Over a 36-hour period during the first weekend of bridge service, eighteen thousand vehicles crossed from one shore to the other—tripling the old ferry traffic and ringing up tolls much faster than anyone had expected. State officials soon regretted building only a two-lane structure. Shoremen experienced both regret and gladness—the bridge had immeasurable impact on their economy. Natives complained of the difficulty they had crossing major highways during summer weekends, the litter motorists left behind, and their big-city rudeness. A retired skipper said he had not visited the new bridge and had no desire to see it; he predicted hopefully that the first big ice on the bay would mow down the pilings like so much grass. Others capitalized on the opportunities it brought. With improved access to Baltimore-Washington markets, Eastern Shore poultry raisers, truck farmers, and seafood producers could almost completely shift their gaze from Philadelphia. Filling stations, fruit stands, and liquor stores appeared on the highways leading to ocean beaches. Church, fraternal, and veterans' groups barbequed chicken and sold it to passing vacationers. At Ocean City the thousands of added summer visitors hit like a tidal wave of money, a bit higher each season. Within a few years of the bridge's opening numbered streets, each with dozens of cottages and motels, spread north from the old center of town for miles. As either a bane or a bonanza, the Bay Bridge transformed life on the Shore.

McKeldin's triumphant drive across the bridge on dedication day—the governor seated in a shiny white convertible—deserved the attention it received, for no Maryland governor so closely identified himself with the cause of transportation and economic development. McKeldin began his administration by conducting a survey to inspect the state roads system and assess his predecessor's plans, themselves considerable, for new highways. Construction executives dream of such reports. Over the 4,700 miles of Maryland

Governor Theodore R. McKeldin led the way across the new Chesapeake
Bay Bridge on 30 July 1952. Baltimore *News American* photograph. *Jacques
Kelly*

roads, the survey discovered 6,700 dangerous curves, 12,800 spots where
depressions or low-hanging trees obstructed a driver's view, and 1,900 places
where a steep grade slowed traffic and presented more "hazards." McKeldin
appointed an advisory council to work with the state Roads Commission on
long-range planning. Together council and commission recommended rebuilding more than 3,100 miles of existing highway and laying 300 miles of
new roads.

In 1953 the legislature accepted McKeldin's highway master plan, which
projected building for twelve years. Observing that the pavement unit cost
"has far exceeded the increase of the cost of living," it estimated spending at
$568 million. In the years that followed, read a roadbuilding history of the
time, "dirt flew on highway projects in every section of the State." In 1954
McKeldin presided over completion of the Baltimore-Washington Express-

way (later Parkway); it cut through the middle of Greenbelt, which after the war the government unceremoniously sold to private interests. He oversaw construction of dual highways, many applying the "limited access" principle first embraced in 1947, between both those cities and the hubs of Annapolis and Frederick. U.S. Route 1 north of Baltimore and Route 15 above Frederick became four-lane roads. New bridges crossed the Severn and spanned the Potomac at Kitzmiller, Cumberland, and Brunswick. Placing a premium on speed and convenience, the new roads altered the time it took to go places and do things, affecting one's perspective as well as the local economy. They increasingly bypassed towns and cities, as at Westminster, where in July 1954 the governor dedicated a strip of Route 140 that went around the town and soon attracted drive-ins and similar businesses. Far more ambitious than the Westminster bypass was McKeldin's hope of building circumferential highways around Baltimore and Washington—plans that involved millions of dollars in condemned private property. New taxes on gasoline, higher license fees, and construction bonds financed the Maryland program, which, so commendably prepared, soon acted as a magnet in attracting federal "interstate" money. In 1955 McKeldin sponsored an entirely state-funded enterprise, the climax to his own public works projects. Construction began on a tunnel-expressway beneath Baltimore harbor, between Canton and Brooklyn.[27]

No Maryland governor took to highway construction more avidly than McKeldin. He rode in jeeps to survey new routes, missed scarcely a ribbon cutting, and loved to climb aboard bulldozers for ceremonial first shovels. At one such event union members protested that their rules allowed only card carriers to drive the machines. McKeldin joined the union. In Annapolis as in Washington, construction unions, road builders, car makers and dealers, oil and tire corporations, truckers, and like interests built up momentum tuned to the times. The National Highway Users Conference, also known as the "highway lobby," twice awarded McKeldin's Maryland its "Golden Milestone" for excellence.

⌒✠⌒

The reign of the roadbuilders helped to establish a context for *Brown* v. *Board of Education of Topeka*, the landmark Supreme Court case that in May 1954 struck down laws segregating schools by race. Arguing the inherent inferiority of all-black classrooms provided Thurgood Marshall one of his finest hours. Word of the decision occasioned a party—with cookies and lemonade—at Lillie Carroll Jackson's home and celebrations among NAACP members everywhere in Maryland. For a while the joy seemed justified. While in states farther south *Brown* set off a storm of protest and in Virginia led eventually to the mean-spirited tactic of "massive resistance"—official closing of public schools—much of Maryland quickly complied with the court ruling. Within a month the University of Maryland regents opened all branches to

In the years following *Brown* v. *Board*, Thurgood Marshall continued the struggle against legalized racial barriers. Here he acknowledged cheers after winning a 1958 Supreme Court contest
over school integration in Little Rock, Arkansas. *Wide World
Photos*

citizens without regard to race, and in the fall two black undergraduate students enrolled quietly at College Park—making Maryland the first state university below the Mason-Dixon Line to integrate. Baltimore benefited from
law-abiding and far-sighted leadership. Two years before the *Brown* decision,
Baltimore City School Superintendent John H. Fischer had urged the school
board to integrate Poly rather than build a new technical high school for
blacks. The board's nine members, who included Roszel C. Thomsen (later a
federal judge), Dean Roger Howell of the Maryland Law School, and Hochschild-Kohn executive Walter Sondheim, Jr., had voted in agreement. In the
summer of 1954, Sondheim having succeeded Thomsen as board president,
the commissioners ordered full desegregation in September—a full year be-

fore the court's ruling required. Under a freedom of choice scheme, 1,800 black children (out of a total of 57,000) enrolled that fall in previously all-white Baltimore schools. For a time whites picketed some integrated schools and parents kept children at home, fearful of violence. An emergency group, the Coordinating Council for Civic Unity, formed in response. Its leaders urged order, and on 4 October the police commissioner in a televised statement announced that disruptive marches broke state law by disturbing a school in session. The parades ceased.

The comparative peacefulness of Maryland integration failed to tell the whole story. Freedom of choice in rural areas hardly brought vast numbers of transfers. Two out of three Maryland blacks lived in cities, most of them in Baltimore. Between 1954 and the end of the decade, Baltimore built fifty-two new schools, thirty-seven of them in predominantly white neighborhoods. The fastest growing communities lay outside Baltimore and Washington. The *Brown* decision hardly caused suburbia's rise; people moved there in search of a better life, had begun to move before *Brown*, and many may have moved had there been no decision. Still, along with financial incentives like VA and FHA mortgage loans and federal highway funding that allowed commuters to commute and industry to disperse, fears of black-white tensions in the schools helped many white parents choose the suburbs over other places to live in the fifties. After 1954 about a thousand white pupils a year fled Baltimore City schools, which in four years were half-black. A simple pattern worked against the goal of integrated classrooms: as white, middle-class families pursued the dream of homeowning, they and their cars filled subdivisions. The subdivisions called for new schools. The new schools remained as white as the car that carried McKeldin across the Bay Bridge. Suburban Baltimore and Washington became a definable social bloc in the state, as different from Baltimore City as Western Maryland was from the Eastern Shore. The number of suburban Marylanders had doubled between 1946 and 1951 and nearly doubled again in the 1950s.

Baltimore County followed this twice-doubled pattern closely and illustrated the multiple effects of staggering suburban growth. In the 1950s row house dwellers and longtime tenants from Baltimore City moved to the county, joining families earlier drawn there by wartime work, and by the end of the decade its population approached half a million. Everybody hoped eventually to buy a house with a carport, nice back yard, and a "paramour" (or power mower—a giveaway of a local accent). Banks and builders bought up land for housing developments in huge parcels. The upward spiral produced construction millionaires and savings and loan tycoons. After 1953 the county each year issued close to ten thousand permits for new family dwellings. Enough houses went up in Baltimore County every eighteen months to shelter forty thousand people—roughly the population of Hagerstown. In 1956 Baltimore County citizens acknowledged the sweep of change and joined Montgomery countians in adopting charter rule. The

A tense moment in the desegregation of Southern High School, 1 October 1954. Baltimore *News American* photograph. *Jacques Kelly*

charter did not bring immediate release from the old organization; as first county executive Democrats elected the last president of the county Board of Commissioners, Michael Birmingham.

By 1958 the county boasted that it had registered "a century of progress in a single decade." To meet the constant demand for "home to office" and "home to market" thoroughfares, the public works department laid down 50 miles of new roads each year, resurfaced about 250 additional miles, and put up new "reflectorized" street signs. The state Roads Commission in the 1930s had installed one new traffic light in the county; in the fifties it put up twenty-six. Water lines stretched out to new developments at a rate of 50 miles a year. The county in 1958 had 725 miles of sewers—a figure that had doubled in ten years—and planned new interceptors that would connect to Baltimore City just as suburban Washington lines ran to the District. That year urban land use in Baltimore County—including residential areas, industry, roads, offices, cemeteries, and recreational sites—reached 80,000 acres. In 1950 the county had sixty-nine schools; in the twelve years .that followed—running "in high gear"—it built another sixty-five and two junior or community colleges. Baltimore County became the first in the state to use "mobile classroom units" to meet emergency needs. Its police force had a new firing range (suitably at a place called Texas), a new central records division, and "smart new uniforms." The county demolished its old office building in Towson and put up a new one that looked big enough to be a factory. A new county jail lacked visible bars; it resembled a grammar school.[28]

Montgomery and Prince George's counties rivaled Baltimore County in their growth spurt. New housing dotted the landscape in Bethesda, Rockville, Kensington, Silver Spring, and Takoma Park; newly built dwellings filled empty spaces at Langley Park, Chillum, Riverdale, Landover Hills, Cheverly, District Heights, Hillcrest Heights, Morningside Heights, and Suitland. Near Bowie the famous New York developer William Levitt in 1958 found a bargain in the old Ogle estate, Belair. Levitt built the vast subdivision according to what its middle-level managers guessed the market would bear; a kind of consumer's Greenbelt, Bowie answered the expressed needs of the average suburban family—five different model homes, though not varying much, winding, not straight, streets; plenty of interior space. By not building sidewalks (everybody had a car anyway), Levitt kept unit costs down. The Ogle mansion became a company office. As long as people could get around they seldom noticed the ravages of growth, yet every improvement invited more congestion. Widening and then making Veirs Mill Road a dual highway produced more cross-streets leading to new subdivisions. Riggs Road, leading from Adelphi to Washington, Branch Avenue southeast of Washington, and Old Georgetown and River roads in Bethesda turned from country pikes into choked thoroughfares that called for more pavement and lights. In Prince George's County the state had added thirteen traffic lights during the forties. Growth in the following decade required fifty-three, and county officials installed even more.

The shopping center—an island of commerce in a sea of housing—evolved into a monument as distinctively suburban as the pyramids were Egyptian. Roland Park in Baltimore claimed one of the earliest residential market centers in the country—a short row of English Tudor shops on Roland Avenue. Patrons drove buggies, later automobiles, into a small off-street space that serviced them. In the 1920s Sears and Roebuck had opened large stores, with parking, outside the Baltimore and Washington business districts, and in 1938 Silver Spring developers put up an unusual shopping island at the southeast corner of Georgia Avenue and Colesville Road—buildings streamlined in the modern mode. After the war the Hecht Company, with a round-cornered emporium nearby, became the first major department store in Washington to reach out to the suburban market; at Edmondson Village, out U.S. 40 in west Baltimore, Hochschild-Kohn in 1947 established a branch store, and the Meyerhoff Company filled adjoining structures with a supermarket, movie theater, and about twenty more shops. Afterward shopping centers sprang up in many places, numbers of tenants and sizes of parking lots indexing the dreams of commercial investors. Successful centers went up at Friendship Heights (Western and Wisconsin avenues) in 1949, at Langley Park and Wheaton in the mid-fifties, and at Prince George's Plaza in 1958; in 1956–58 Eastpoint and Westview opened in suburban Baltimore. These enterprises called for heavy investment (and sometimes failed). There were smaller operators also. After the war M. Cooper Walker, a builder who owned property out York Road at the Baltimore

City-County line, bulldozed an old mansion his grandfather had purchased from Frank Furst and built an apartment complex and drive-in restaurant. In the 1950s he demolished the drive-in and put up Drumcastle Center, with three stores and parking for about two dozen cars.

Architects made fat commissions designing these centers, which only occasionally did them credit. Edmondson Village copied the colonial revival style. At Friendship Heights stores followed a crescent shape on slightly sloping land. In 1955 James W. Rouse—a Talbot County native, navy veteran, and highly successful mortgage banker—broke ground for a shopping area on the old George Brown estate in northwestern Baltimore. Visiting the mansion more than a century before, according to family tradition, Henry Wadsworth Longfellow had suggested naming the place Mondawmin after the Indian spirit of the cornfields. Rouse took the old name but applied new ideas in building the 46-acre "regional retail center." He arranged stores so that people could easily walk among them. An ornamental pool and sculptured tower broke the horizontal monotony, and Rouse muted outdoor signs. At first retailers kept their distance from the unusual center; Rouse and his brother, a partner in the company, nearly failed to fill Mondawmin by the time it opened in October 1956. Two years later they had even more trouble finding tenants for Harundale—one of the first enclosed shopping "malls" in the country. Rouse was ahead of his time. Most architects in the period clung to cookie-cutter designs. Towson Plaza, more the norm than Mondawmin, opened in 1959 with "41 fine stores" and parking for 3,000 cars. The plaza had wrought-iron railings, terrazzo flower boxes, and "clean, modern lines" of precast concrete panels. According to the enthusiastic local paper, which said that piped-in music added to the holiday air, Towson Plaza enhanced "the pleasant landscape" of the neighborhood. At a nearby intersection the county installed new-fashioned signal lights that detected the flow of cars and supposedly prevented traffic jams.[29]

Rising property values and the developmental impulse made zoning fights the warp and woof of suburban politics in the fifties, and in the Washington area the battles were especially telling of county differences. The Montgomery County forces that in 1948 had won the charter struggle (by opposing cheap housing) won control of the MNCPPC in 1952. By the end of the decade the commission under chairman Herbert W. Wells, a Riverdale native, had produced its third highway master plan, another on schools and parks, and one on libraries. Its integrated view of the future appeared in a notebook entitled *Looking Ahead* (1958), which called for "orderly regional development with residential communities, shopping areas and employment centers built up in a harmonious fashion," "logical distribution of school and park facilities," a regional highway system with ample rights of way for future widening, and improved rapid transit. The MNCPPC later published a fat booklet proposing a jigsaw pattern of high population areas and open spaces reaching out from Washington through Montgomery and Prince

Interior courtyard of the futurist Mondawmin Mall, 1956. Baltimore *News American* photograph. *Jacques Kelly*

George's counties to form "wedges and corridors." Plenty of the green wedges appeared in Montgomery County; of the four corridors, three lay in Prince George's. Such plans, influential and in some parts compelling, merely advised county governments. The counties meanwhile passed zoning ordinances that had the force of law. The courts decided that rezoning could take place to rectify an original mistake or adjust to neighborhood changes.[30]

Zoning decisions, appeals, exceptions, and variances led to jostling and hustling that made clear how political the process truly was, how important market forces finally were. During the 1950s the sitting council in Montgomery limited development there to single-family homes on comparatively large lots. At the same time the upper-middle-class demand for good schools, libraries, and recreational sites called for high taxes, dissuading lower-income families from living there. The exclusive character of the county did not change; property values remained high. So valuable was land in Bethesda that an enterprising firm purchased "air rights" over a section of B&O track and put an office building above it. In 1948 the median family wealth in Montgomery County stood 4 percent higher than in Prince George's; in

The multiple effects of automobile culture and rapid development. Maryland–National Capital Park and Planning Commission, *On Wedges and Corridors* (Silver Spring, 1958).

twenty years it climbed to 34 percent higher. The MNCPPC had little choice in planning corridors to Annapolis and Baltimore through Prince George's— but they promoted industrial and commercial development, which, in turn, called for additional low-income housing. The Prince George's County commissioners, fully amenable to zoning variance requests, worked hand in hand with developers and collected campaign contributions as legal dividends. Prince George's County thus developed both more raggedly and more democratically than Montgomery. Major thoroughfares like Baltimore-Washington Boulevard in College Park, strip zoned, sprouted taverns, car dealerships, and gas stations. Garden apartments grew like crabgrass. Taxes and housing costs in Prince George's stayed relatively low, comparatively affordable.[31]

Suburban growth, the automobile, and roadbuilding—all apparently irresistible forces—had a numbing quality. The political air was stale. Endorsing Mahoney for the U.S. Senate in 1952, O'Conor had praised "his deep concern over un-American activities." Mahoney lost in the general election to J. Glenn Beall, who felt more deeply on that score. Democrats in the 1954 governor's race divided between the maverick Mahoney and the ambitious "Curley" Byrd, who vied with each another trying to sound more guarded on the subject of school integration. McKeldin, popular in the suburbs and a friend of blacks, won reelection in 1954 as easily as Eisenhower carried the state two years before and two years later. Consensus governed ideas about progress and propriety. Not many people mourned the end of passenger rail service to places like Easton, Oxford, and Sykesville. Few people noted the retirement of manned lighthouses in favor of automatic devices on the bay. In 1956 Hagerstown city fathers tore down the famous Rochester House, home of the city's first postmaster and later founder of the New York community that took his name, and put in a parking lot. In the basement plaza of Drumcastle Center the owner held fashion shows and permitted card parties sponsored by "certain carefully screened philanthropic organizations." Promoting Maryland textiles, but also indicating something of the spirit of the fifties, McKeldin declared 23–29 March 1958 "Dress Right Week." Meanwhile population growth continued, supporting every complacency. The 1960 census revealed a ten-year state growth rate of almost 33 percent—most of the increase suburban. Seven out of ten Marylanders lived between Washington and upper Baltimore County.[32]

Suburban gains spelled losses for Baltimore City. In the same period the suburbs grew by more than half a million people, Baltimore lost ten thousand. In 1950 the city on average had drawn more than seven hundred persons a month; in 1960 it lost almost a hundred each month. Those who left during the fifties greatly diminished the city's proportion of homeowning families, the educated, the affluent. In 1950 Baltimoreans had held over half the total assessed wealth in the state, the suburbs about one-fifth; in 1960 the city's share had dropped to about a third while the suburbs claimed half. Baltimore City property taxes helped to push people to the suburbs, and as the tax base declined levies climbed still higher, hastening the exodus. Baltimore's share of the black population in Maryland rose ten points, to 35 percent. Teachers' salaries fell behind those paid in the counties. In the mid-fifties downtown employment had not grown in twenty years. Businessmen noted a 12 percent drop in sales between 1952 and 1957. On some downtown blocks one in four buildings was vacant. Samuel Smith Park, largely a metered parking area, had replaced docks and shipping offices on Light Street. The problems of physical aging remained formidable. Most downtown office and commercial buildings dated from the post-1904 rebuilding effort; the newest structures, the Lord Baltimore Hotel and Baltimore Life Building, had gone up in 1927. Inadequate housing still plagued the city. The 1950 census reported seventy thousand unfit dwellings in lower Baltimore.[33]

Figures and trend lines could not quite capture the agony of the old city.

William Manchester, a *Sun* reporter who lived on the edge of the black ghetto in the early 1950s, wrote a novel about the people he met in these years—an ugly account of unredeemed lives. In places using a stream-of-consciousness technique, Manchester portrayed the monotony of misery. He described one of his characters walking home, stumbling through "thickening snow, past the 50¢ 30¢ 25¢ parking lots walled with peeling billboards hawking dead brands and forgotten candidates, past the darkened Esso Servicenters and Bargain Harry's and Money Back Mac's, up the endless U of the lightless loveless hapless alleys, into the foul crypt of the old Seventh [Ward] . . . into the land of windows without glass cheap funerals and Hadacol, land of cold water walk-ups rusting basins and rotting roofs, land of swift justice for the poor." A few years later *Esquire* magazine cast its eye on the city by way of a piece on Baltimore Street nightlife. Television drew off many theater-goers in the fifties, so that the Block had grown bawdier and seedier every year. Each club tried to be more "sexciting" than the next. In March 1956, when Tempest Storm starred at the Gayety, *Esquire* commended the area as a "neon-lighted jungle of sex."[34]

In trying to right itself, Baltimore recorded an uneven chapter in modern American urban history. Vigorous and well-intentioned, Mayor D'Alesandro in the early 1950s announced a "concerted drive ultimately to eliminate all slum and sub-standard areas" from the city. He appointed a committee of citizens, headed by Rouse, who long had been involved in the work of the Citizens' Planning and Housing Association, to advise him on housing improvement. The mayor followed its recommendation that the city use housing code enforcement to renovate whole neighborhoods instead of single dwellings—and, in the optimistic CPHA mode, to coordinate city agencies, churches, citizens' groups, and the residents themselves so as to "rehabilitate the people as well as the houses."[35]

Between 1951 and 1953 Baltimore thus conducted a Pilot Program that made fresh assaults on back-yard ruin, outdoor privies, dirt basements, dangerous wiring and the like in specified blocks of the city. Tenants did not always fare well; landlords had practiced methods of evading code requirements or passing along the costs of repairs. Poor homeowners generally benefited from the Pilot Program—they had access to a "Fight Blight" fund, raised from private businessmen, from which they could draw loans for essential improvements. Vandalism decreased in some pilot neighborhoods. Viola C. Jackson, a school principal, and Vernon F. Dobson, a probation officer and recreation supervisor, emerged as community leaders. Middle-class whites obtained useful first-hand experience with poverty. But even a young CPHA worker who wanted very much for the program to succeed admitted that it "had little success in organizing residents for the future benefit and protection of the neighborhood." Hans Froelicher led a CPHA faction that opposed the Pilot Program because it tipped the scales toward government power.[36]

An A-rab's pony lent a little warmth to an otherwise bleak winter's view of an alley near Russell Street at the end of the 1950s. *Fred G. Kraft*

In fact the war against rundown neighborhoods belonged ever more to a national campaign. In 1954 Congress passed a revised federal Housing Act (Rouse helped write it) that offered especially generous grants to cities with plans for orchestrated action. The following year D'Alesandro's planning department published a colorful and alluring booklet that marked an "in-city area" (bounded by Monroe Street, North Avenue, and Patterson Park Avenue) as a target area. Within it lived about a third of the city's population but half of Baltimore's tuberculosis patients. There one found roughly two-thirds of all Baltimore houses built before 1900, houses without indoor plumbing, and welfare cases.

The city sought to remove decay by employing different strategies, but for a time, on some fronts, the seize-and-hold of housing rehabilitation gave way to the bombing of "urban renewal." In neighborhoods like Mount Royal—one Pilot Program site—city planners hoped that code enforcement would prove sufficient. Some slums the city relegated to industrial or commercial use. It expected at all odds to separate homes from manufacturing plants

and their "personal annoyances." On Lafayette and Fremont streets and
across from the Hopkins Hospital on Broadway, the redevelopment commission planned, with federal support, to condemn and knock down houses
and then reconstruct neighborhoods with high-rise apartment buildings,
schools, and recreation and shopping centers. A transportation master plan
would send highways through rundown neighborhoods. Besides the suburban beltway, it included a Jones Falls Expressway, a harbor crossing, east
and west radial expressways leading out from the center of the city, and
main thoroughfares along northeast and northwest routes. In D'Alesandro's
booklet the city's entrance from the north, "curving gracefully through the
wooded Jones Falls valley," would be "one of the most beautiful in the Country." Elsewhere, expressways running below street level would make attractive additions to tidy, suburb-like low-income housing projects. By means
of school board, recreation and parks, public works, traffic engineers, housing authority, and redevelopment commission, the city promised to remake
blighted areas into places "where families may lead the healthy, happy, satisfying kind of life which is essential to progress."[37]

Never pessimistic, D'Alesandro laid the latest plans with new optimism.
In early January 1955, meeting at the Elkridge Club north of the city, business
and professional men formed a "private, nonprofit action group" to save
their economically stricken city. The movement belonged to local tradition—
commercial leaders seizing the reins in crisis the way Samuel Smith had organized for the British in 1814; many in the group had learned valuable
modern lessons as CPHA members. Rouse and several young men had approached Clarence W. Miles, the corporate lawyer and Orioles president,
hoping to do something about the state of the city and its pace of renewal.
If, reasoned the catalysts, Baltimore had succeeded in obtaining a major-
league baseball team, why not face the larger challenge of preserving the city
the team played for? Phone calls and personal exchanges assembled eighty-
three executive officers and presidents representing every large Baltimore
enterprise—among them the Mercantile Safe Deposit and Trust Company,
the Sunpapers and *News-Post*, the Glenn L. Martin Company, Consolidated Gas and Electric, C&P Telephone, the Canton Company, Black and
Decker, Maryland Drydock, Alexander Brown & Sons, the Western Maryland and B&O, Hutzler's, Hochschild-Kohn, the McCormick Company,
Bethlehem Steel, Equitable Trust, and the National Brewing Company.
Speeches stressed the need for resolve, and money. Robert H. Levi of the
Hecht Company noted "a civic malignancy" in Baltimore; Rouse pointed to
progress being made in Pittsburgh and St. Louis. The "Greater Baltimore
Committee" (soon known as the GBC) limited itself to one hundred mem-
bers and set dues at between two and five thousand dollars.

"It will be the task of the Greater Baltimore Committee," declared Rouse,
original chairman of its executive committee, "to get done those jobs which
desperately need to be done but which seem to hang forever in the planning

stage." The GBC gathered out of self-interest. It never claimed to be anything else but a business group. Yet it had public-private purposes that one could well call "postcapitalist"; it apparently put the lie to Marx's prediction that wealth would grow so bloated, callous, and vulnerable as to fall to proletarian outrage. Working hand in glove with the mayor and city council, GBC members intended "to help make the clock tick." On the one hand, the pace of slum clearance, about six hundred houses a year, had to improve; at that rate, noted GBC organizers, it would take 117 years to rid the city of its substandard dwellings. On the other hand, the committee had constructive plans. It established a planning council that would avoid both the "goldfish bowl" of official decision making (the GBC itself always met behind closed doors) and an outside consultant's indifference to local realities. The GBC placed its weight behind the civic center that McKeldin had proposed as mayor; it would serve as a sports arena, musical center, and convention hall. The committee demanded groundbreaking for the Jones Falls Expressway and called for improved downtown transportation. It supported new industrial districts in and around Baltimore. The GBC aimed somehow to reverse the city's self-image; William Boucher III, a Loyola College graduate, war veteran, and CPHA member who became chairman of the GBC in February 1956, believed Baltimore suffered from a "colossal inferiority complex."[38]

In an important early achievement, the GBC led the way toward reviving the maritime health of Baltimore. Several economic changes explained why the city's warehouses stood empty. Baltimore trade for many years had depended on coal and wheat exports. The St. Lawrence Seaway, begun in 1954, soon would divert midwestern grain toward that less expensive route to the Atlantic. Meantime coal production had declined in the face of cheap oil prices. Heavily tied to railroad lines—many of its wharves railroad owned—the port of Baltimore faced a serious problem in the rise of commercial trucking. In 1956 representatives of the GBC lobbied successfully for creation of a Maryland Port Authority modeled after those of New York and New Orleans. Anne Arundel County interests feared that Baltimore City would dominate the agency, but it soon proved itself a remarkably effective instrument for the good of the whole state. Granted full control over port policy and management and financed from a .5 percent duty on the profits of corporations dealing with the port, the MPA purchased the old Dundalk airfield and made it into one of the country's first modern marine terminals. Making a virtue of necessity, it pioneered in the use of containerized cargoes (truck trailer–like boxes, filled with a variety of non-bulk cargoes, which cranes could lift directly from ship to truck or railroad car). The authority eventually managed terminals at Canton, Clinton Street, Hawkins Point, and Locust Point and established promotional foreign offices. Even though the tonnage passing through the port remained about the same, the MPA, at least at first, assured that Baltimore held its own among American ports of entry.

Reviving the city itself proved far more difficult, requiring at the start

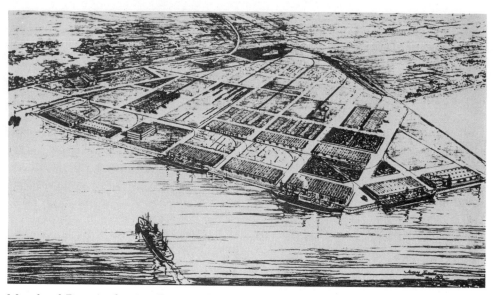

Maryland Port Authority, Proposed Dundalk Marine Terminal, Baltimore. Drawing by Turpin, Wachter, and Associates, Consulting Engineers, December 1959. *Baltimore Sunpapers*

moving and shaking that often went on behind the scenes. GBC members had strong, usually informal lines of communication to city council, State House, and various federal offices. Baltimore's delegates and senators had as their unelected but redoubtable leader Jack Pollack—long ago Mrs. Bauernschmidt's whipping boy and still boss in the heavily Jewish northwestern ward of the city. If Boucher, Rouse, and the rest kept aloof from Pollack and grass-roots politics, they dealt comfortably with D'Alesandro, who had no trouble working with ethnic Democrats. The wheels turned. An Urban Renewal Study Board declared that "piecemeal attacks on slums will not work" and recommended "a bold program that will unite public and private agencies in an all-out effort." In 1956 the city established an Urban Renewal and Housing Agency (BURHA) to seek federal funding, supposedly both to clear slums and to build low-cost housing. City legislators won clearance in the assembly for a bond issue on the civic center—which one consultant thought would fit nicely on top of an inner harbor landfill. In March 1957 work began on a state office complex on the southern edge of the Mount Royal district; costing $13.6 million and including parking for nine hundred cars, it might have been built more cheaply elsewhere, McKeldin explained, but placing it there helped to improve one of Baltimore's most blighted areas (it also increased untaxed property in the city). That November governor and mayor officially opened the Harbor Tunnel. Its approaches cut a swath through fifteen miles of city space that included housing both standard and substandard. McKeldin warned that Baltimore still needed new arteries and parking "with capacities of which we hardly have dared to dream." D'Alesandro said the tunnel proved that state and city leaders "can and do work in harmony." Taking advantage of 90 percent matching federal highway funds (called "ten-cent dollars," they flowed beneath decision making like an underground river), McKeldin and D'Alesandro did indeed start up the bulldozers in unison. Federal and state money soon broke loose for construction of the Jones Falls Expressway—an earth-moving and slum-clearance project of mammoth proportions.[39]

Drawing a downtown master plan provided a stiff test for Baltimore leaders. Having denied strenuously that it aimed to displace the Association of Commerce, the GBC faced possible rivalry from a group of merchants, some too small to join it, organized in 1954 as the Committee for Downtown. Led by J. Jefferson Miller of the Hecht Company, the committee instead joined forces with the GBC in trying to arrive at a plan that would rejuvenate an area from Federal Hill to Pennsylvania Station, from Fallsway to Paca Street. It proved an impossibly large and cumbersome project. Staff members recommended instead a single project "so bold, so dramatic, that it will shake the town by the scruff of its neck."[40]

Charles Center proved a turning point in Baltimore architecture and attitudes. It issued from the GBC planning council, mortgage banker Hunter Moss serving as chairman, and from the drawing board of David A. Wallace, a Harvard-trained urban planner who actually worked under contract for the Committee for Downtown. On paper Charles Center beguiled everyone who looked at it. The complex encompassed a 22-acre area bounded by Lombard on the south, Saratoga on the north, Charles on the east, and Liberty and Hopkins Place on the west. It included seven air-conditioned office buildings (adding 2 million square feet of new commercial space) and proved a home for the federal offices that D'Alesandro long had coveted. Architects envisioned an ultra-modern hotel of eight hundred rooms with "an adjoining executive tower." A television center with an auditorium seating three thousand would replace Ford's as the leading Baltimore theater. Completing the plan were three mass-transit terminals and as many small parks. Underground garages would park four thousand cars. On the morning of 28 March 1958, Moss, Boucher, Miller, and various GBC and Committee for Downtown leaders presented the grand scheme to D'Alesandro and a plenary assembly of city officials. The mayor listened for half an hour, in Boucher's recollection, then, with the enthusiasm he had taken to the Orioles deal, exclaimed "We're gonna do it."[41]

Private interest and elected leadership joined in a massive project for the public good. Estimated costs for Charles Center ran to more than $127 million, most of which had to come from private investors. Baltimore City, obtaining what Moss called "a tremendous bargain," would finance about $17 million, by bond issue or tax increase; limited to noncommercial uses, federal urban renewal money played no part in these figures. Moss noted that the improved tax base promised within nine years to recoup every dollar Baltimore spent (and, during construction, temporarily lost) on the project. It required an awesome use of municipal powers of eminent domain. The plan spared only the Fidelity, Lexington, and B&O buildings, Lord Baltimore Hotel, and Eglin's Garage; the axe of city condemnation would fall on 251 downtown properties. Charles Center had broad but scarcely unanimous support. The *Evening Sun* praised the GBC's "firm information gathering" and recommended that the city proceed "with caution, though without stalling." Harold Fink of the city hotel owners' association opposed the new hotel. Owners of Hamburger's store recently had spent $250,000 on renovations and pleaded to be among the properties left standing. Moss replied that "If you let one old building stay, pretty soon you have four or five, and then you have no plan. I stand for the purity of the plan." Questioned on the street, Baltimoreans generally approved of Charles Center while wondering if they would live to see its completion. "People in Baltimore are just not that modern-minded," said a bank employee. "You'll have hair on your teeth before they put that project through," declared someone equally doubtful. "In New York they'd just say 'put it up' and there it would be."[42]

The fall 1958 political campaign drew down the curtain on two incumbents and period fixtures, Governor McKeldin and Mayor D'Alesandro. Republicans nominated a World War II hero and now Second District congressman, James P. S. Devereux, to succeed McKeldin. After a Carvel Hall caucus that Birmingham of Baltimore County had arranged in January, Democrats agreed on Millard Tawes for governor. Related to the chairman of the state Fisheries Commission, Tawes had stood in line since 1939. Quietly competent, by now a master of the state financial system, he had helped to dedicate the Bay Bridge in 1952 and often appeared with a black-eyed Susan in his lapel. At the 1958 legislative session Tawes a bit belatedly had helped shape the Democratic consensus on a tax increase. With Democratic support, the outgoing McKeldin had won passage of a 1 percent increase in the sales tax (farm equipment exempted), a similar hike in the state income tax, and a rise in the cigarette tax. D'Alesandro had hoped to run for governor. He settled for a U.S. senator's spot on what Tawes and Birmingham called a Harmony Ticket. In the primaries no one rose to challenge Tawes, his choice for comptroller, Louis L. Goldstein of Calvert County, or the "harmony" candidate for attorney general, C. Ferdinand Sybert of Howard. Senatorial hopefuls, however, included Mahoney, who as usual ran against the party regulars, former ambassador James Bruce (who had supporters like Lane, Radcliffe, and Tydings), and Clarence Long of Hopkins. While D'Alesandro won the primary, the unit rule, not the popular vote, gave him the nomination. In November he fell decisively to the incumbent Beall. Tawes became the first Eastern Shoreman to occupy the governor's mansion since Harrington left it in 1920. At the polls Baltimore voters approved a Charles Center bond issue of $25 million.

Johnny Unitas throws long in the Colts' championship game of 1958. *The Indianapolis Colts*

Building Charles Center, c. 1962. Baltimore *News American* photograph. *Jacques Kelly*

During the campaign many Baltimore voters paid less attention to the politicians than to the Baltimore Colts, a team representing the city in the National Football League for only the fifth year. The Colts won game after game on Sunday afternoons. In late November they came from 20 points down at halftime to defeat San Francisco and claim the best record in their division. A month later twelve thousand of their fans, including three boisterous trainloads, traveled to New York for a game with the Giants to decide the NFL championship. *Sports Illustrated* described what happened at Yankee Stadium as "The Greatest Game Ever Played." The Colts—a collection of castoffs, as Coach Weeb Ewbank reminded them in the locker room—came from behind in the second half to tie the game and send it into overtime. After the Baltimore defense held, quarterback John Unitas, brilliantly mixing long and short passes with draw plays, moved the Colts the length of the field. Eight minutes into "sudden death" Alan "The Horse" Ameche lunged into the end zone to give Baltimore the championship. Delirious celebrations at home matched those of V-J Day. In later years natives believed the Colts' triumph helped instill the confidence needed to continue revitalization—as if the Colts' heroics ratified the Charles Center bond decision. Civic pride has many sources. Asked about a dangerous "flat" or sideline pass that set up the final touchdown, Unitas—whose Lithuanian background made him a special hero to East Baltimore—answered simply, "If you know what you're doing, there is no risk involved."[43]

⚬⚭⚬

Ribbon-cutting ceremonies, elections, and football games lent themselves to scorekeeping. Other themes of the 1950s and early 1960s escaped much daily notice. A quiet revolution took place in health care, thanks in part to the penicillin and sulfa drugs that medical researchers had discovered before World War II. Along with new antibiotics, they fought infections and permitted treatment of diseases that people earlier had accepted as a cost of living or the wages of sin. Cortisone, antihistamines, and tranquilizers relieved epidermal, allergic, and emotional distresses. New diagnostic techniques and treatments virtually eliminated the age-old threat of tuberculosis. After 1955 state health authorities administered the Salk vaccine against poliomyelitis, a scourge of the young and a fright to parents. By 1958 six out of ten Maryland water systems employed fluoride, a newly uncovered inhibitor of tooth decay.

Institutions in the state contributed heavily to medical advances. At Hopkins, where late in the war Dr. Alfred Blalock and Helen B. Taussig had made path-breaking advances in cardiac surgery, Drs. Eleanor A. Bliss and Perrin H. Long pioneered in sulfanilamide therapy; Dr. David Bodian and a polio research group helped to develop the Salk vaccine. Hopkins in the 1950s continued to pioneer in postoperative intensive care. At the same time Dr. Jonas Friedenwald, a Baltimore native, made the Wilmer Institute at Hopkins a leading center for research in eye care, especially treatment for glaucoma, and Dr. John Eager Howard, descendant of the hero of Cowpens, made advances in the prevention of kidney stones. Hopkins specialists also studied Addison's disease, pneumonia, and chemotherapy. With a vigorous new director of medical education and research, Dr. William S. Stone, the University of Maryland Hospital in the late fifties conducted important work in preventive medicine, physical therapy, and biophysics. Dr. R Adams Cowley, a Utah native and army veteran, began experimenting at University Hospital with ways to treat shock in severely injured and dying patients. The research he supervised—expensive, in many ways challenging to customary practice and disciplinary boundaries—fit uneasily into the established university program. Eventually Cowley's work led to the first shock-trauma center (specializing in the coordinated and rapid treatment of accident victims) in the nation. In Montgomery County, Bethesda developed a worldwide reputation as a center for biomedical research. The navy added wings and drew more affiliates to its medical center. A second institution, the National Institutes of Health, had begun its move to Bethesda in the mid-1930s, when Luke I. Wilson made a gift of his Tree Tops estate. In the 1950s federal spending on rare diseases and advanced clinical work led to rapid expansion at NIH. In 1961 two scientists there, Marshall W. Nirenberg and J. Heinrich Mattaei, discovered the genetic code that transfers characteristics through generations of organisms. The finding later won Nirenberg a Nobel Prize.

Beneficiaries of "wonder drugs," children who belonged to the postwar "baby boom" grew up in the fifties and early sixties healthier than any generation in history. Parents, educators, and political leaders tried to see that they received every educational and social benefit, as well. As predicted, they caused rapid expansion of Maryland schools; lines on graphs showing enrollments after 1950 resembled rocket trajectories. On average the state opened thirty new classrooms a week and hired 3,000 new teachers a year. Superintendent Pullen took rightful pride in the quality of the state system. New buildings consolidated old ones, and while more pupils than ever before rode buses to school, they presumably reaped rewards by having guidance counselors, larger libraries, and more classes with audio-visual aids. Educators experimented with new technology. Beginning in 1956 the Ford Foundation sponsored a five-year trial for educational television in Washington County, which it chose as typically American. From a central studio at the board of education building, cables on C&P telephone poles took the voices and images of the ablest teachers (handling selected subjects each day) to classrooms all over the county.[44] Generally rated successful if not widely duplicated, the system remained in place long after foundation support expired. Meantime special education for the handicapped developed into a separate field—a sign of prosperity, growing professionalism in teaching, and rising public sympathy.

Soviet launching of the first man-made satellite in October 1957 sent Maryland parents and teachers into a brief flurry of self-study. Magazine and newspaper articles asked why Johnny couldn't read, why Russian youngsters seemed to be so far ahead in technical training. Meeting in Baltimore in the spring of 1958, Maryland principals assured everyone that high school math and science enrollments had exhibited a long-term rise in the state (true at least through 1950). Maryland doubtless had more to offer than some states by way of resources. Students from public, private, and parochial schools all over the state competed each year in the Johns Hopkins Science Fair, held at Homewood. Outside Washington, especially in Montgomery County, the high proportion of students whose professional and bureaucrat parents demanded much of them helped to account for more than respectable levels of college admission. In 1958 Baltimore County boasted that its high school seniors won almost $750,000 in college scholarship money—double the 1957 amount. Nonetheless, the post-Sputnik assembly appointed a commission to examine Maryland public schools. A Columbia University professor of education spoke for some commission members who praised the system and affirmed the guiding philosophy of Pullen and his predecessor—that teachers were to excite students about learning and shape them for society. Baltimore lawyer Enos S. Stockbridge recommended a return to stricter academic standards. "If there is any error over the last decade or two," read the final report, "it has been in veering too much toward methods of developing the child's personality and in failing to place sufficient emphasis on content requirements and achievement."[45]

As the bulge of young people reached adolescence and groped for independence, adults had ample reason to consider the peculiar problems of "teenagers"—and to pay attention to their proper upbringing. A higher number if not percentage of them than before needed help finding the straight and narrow. Between 1954 and 1959 the state Welfare Department published a series on youth detention needs in various counties and Baltimore City and in 1957 produced a "blueprint" for the care and treatment of delinquent children in Maryland institutions. Baltimore County established a juvenile protective bureau in the fifties to handle cases that involved persons under eighteen years. In 1953 the same county embarked on an ambitious long-range recreational program that five years later maintained twenty-five parks, organized seasonal sports leagues, and operated seventy-five "teen centers." During the summer of 1958 more than 286,000 youngsters enrolled in Baltimore County playground programs, and youth in Montgomery and Prince George's counties joined them just as avidly. Baltimore County set the tone for these diversions when it quoted FBI Director J. Edgar Hoover. "As anti-social play contributes immeasurably to delinquency," Hoover had said, "so wholesome recreation figures prominently in the development of strong character." Taking that theme a step farther, the American Legion each summer sponsored week-long training programs at the University of Maryland campus—Boys' and Girls' State—where high school students attended classes on democratic government, marched to meals, and in the end elected their own "state officials." The teenagers examined what the legionnaires labeled Americanism.[46]

Numerous and affluent, these teenagers created a culture of their own and struggled with what social psychologist Erik Erikson called the identity crisis. By the mid-fifties young people craved their own kind of dress, frills, and music. "Rock and roll," a sound with roots in rhythm and blues, became explosively popular as the baby boomers reached adolescence. Perhaps the style could only have emerged when and how it did. Like jazz in the twenties, it voiced rebellion and adapted black music to an audience of both whites and blacks; unlike the music of the jazz age, rock and roll benefited from television dance programs and cheap, single-play disks that the young could afford. They bought them in astonishing quantities, played them until their elders craved quiet, and made folk heroes of the sensual, parentally objectionable singers who recorded them. Rock and roll drove big band music off the charts of highest-selling recordings, and marketing managers ensured that films and fads made the most of the enormous "teen" demand. This kind of youthful self-consciousness had never before appeared. It emerged not only from demography, plenty, and television, but also from Cold War fears—air-raid drills and civil defense films—and produced an uncertain mood. Concerned parents read that teenagers seemed to enjoy a movie about anger and alienation, a rebuke to educators who implicitly taught conformity, entitled *Rebel without a Cause*.

Meanwhile public support built up behind the blacks' plea for equality. Largely agreed on ends and means, white and black leaders could point to the peacefulness of desegregation in Baltimore and could be philosophical about resistance to progress. "It may well be," concluded a 1955 booklet celebrating advances in Baltimore, " . . . that the parent who on the surface is opposed to having a Negro child in the same class with his white child is, at bottom, reacting to the realization that his child may grow up with different attitudes than his own." At the same time the *Sun* published a series of front-page articles, "The City We Live In," highlighting racial injustices. Newspapers earlier had ignored blacks or patronized them; illustrating a shift in attitude common to the press in the late 1950s, the Sunpapers began to give space to black activities and social events. Sports editors backed integrated athletics (Satchel Paige of the St. Louis Browns had passed his prime when the team moved to Baltimore; the first black Oriole was a pitcher, Jehosie Heard). Despite segregationist grumbling, Baltimore and Western Shore leaders, black and white, took steps to right past wrongs. In 1956 the Baltimore City Council adopted ordinances prohibiting employment discrimination—though without penalties. Baltimore merchants decided then to permit Negro customers to try on clothes, and many city theaters and hotels dropped racial restrictions. In 1957, without fanfare, Montgomery County restaurants began to serve blacks. The state earlier had dropped separate black and white job listings and ended segregation in the National Guard. In 1959 the General Assembly considered about thirty anti-segregation bills and resolutions.[47]

To those people who looked closely, this fairly quiet progress masked what was only fairly progressive. True, Baltimore and all Western Shore counties at least paid lip service to school integration. Protests against desegregation in Westminster and a few more places had fizzled and died. Yet Maryland along with the rest of the nation fulfilled the equality pledge contained in the *Brown* decision by striking down barriers, not by seeking racial mixing. Baltimore school superintendent Fischer, opposed to legal segregation, reflected the prevailing view when he said he considered it "equally wrong to manipulate people to create an integrated situation." In 1956 about 40 percent of white pupils attended mixed grammar or high schools while about 4 percent of blacks did. In 1960 the state Department of Education and the Maryland Commission on Interracial Problems and Relations agreed that school integration in Baltimore City was "complete"—there were some black pupils in every school. Actually the number of Negro children attending predominantly black schools had risen markedly and continued to do so. Four resisting Eastern Shore counties, unintegrated in the early 1960s, testified that they were making "progress" toward freedom of choice.[48]

Another barely noticeable trend in these years concerned the quality of life—the definition of "pleasant living"—and visions of the state's future. In terms of legal and administrative structure, many of the pieces had been in place a long time. In 1933 the New Deal, through the National Planning Board, committed federal funds to states establishing planning commissions. Maryland soon had an unpaid, five-member advisory board under Abel Wolman, eminent Johns Hopkins sanitary engineer and longtime public servant. Over the years Wolman's group reviewed problems of land use, seafood conservation, public health; it combined with the University of Maryland and WPA to produce authoritative state land maps. In 1959 the commission listed more than a hundred reports, not all of them in great demand. Having had doubts about much New Deal legislation (and about Greenbelt), many Marylanders might still have associated planning with visionaries like Rexford Tugwell. In fact, postwar problems of sudden development had produced professionals whose presence had become an administrative necessity. Trained in theories of planning, constructing models of social and economic change, they wanted to advise members of the state Planning Commission and the MNCPPC the way doctors Welch and Osler at the turn of the century had counseled Baltimore mayors on the causes of tuberculosis.

Federal spending on state and local projects pushed planners to the fore. Section 701 of the 1954 Housing Act offered "planning grants" to communities, and soon federal programs carried the condition of prior planning and coordination. That incentive, if none other, forced one to take a larger view of local problems—to recognize the truth that not all problems were local. In the Washington area civic leaders in 1957 faced up to the issues they shared by forming a Metropolitan Regional Conference composed of Maryland, District, and Virginia officials. A "701" grant helped in 1963 to create the Regional Planning Council. Along with professional planners, it included representatives from Baltimore City and the counties of Baltimore, Carroll, Harford, Howard, and Anne Arundel (governed by charter since 1958). With the aid of federal money, the council aimed to qualify for still more of it. At the state level, departments of government customarily had done little in the way of planning, and yet requests for capital improvements had forced them increasingly to look ahead. They submitted proposed budgets to the planning commission, which in practice had become more heavily involved in budgetary than planning issues. Responding to all these trends, members of a General Assembly joint committee in 1957 called on state agencies to write ten-year forecasts of their needs and transmit them to the planning commission by July of 1959. That year chairman Joseph Meyerhoff asked V. O. Key, a Harvard political scientist who earlier had taught at Hopkins and worked on the Sherbow tax panel, to undertake an in-depth study of the commission and its work.

Maryland faced a mass population movement, Key wrote, that will make the great westward migration of the last century "look like a trickle," and it was by no means apparent what shape the patterns finally would take. In the year 2000, he predicted, Congress perhaps would pass "a semi-urban renewal act to undo what is being done by the subdividers with the enthusiastic cooperation of the populace." Hope lay in collaboration—among regions and layers of government—and, predictably, in sound leadership. Key challenged Maryland planners to provide some of it. Where highways ran through urban areas, the state would have to act like a city parks department. Until then the roads commission had exercised a high degree of autonomy; Key argued that the layout of highways belonged in the state planning office. City planning—involving physical structures in densely populated settings—differed from state planning, but he suggested that the state office employ urban experts to save Maryland towns the high cost of private consultants. Key recommended separation of state planning and economic development. Trying to entice business and industry to Maryland served one purpose, he said, planning quite another. He also recommended separation of governor and planning commission. Though reporting to the chief executive on proposed budgets and undertaking studies at his request, the commission ought not become "an arm of the governor," as some Marylanders had suggested in the 1958 gubernatorial campaign. Planners had to find a middle way. Key advised them neither to serve as the governor's "rubber stamp" nor to try the impossible task of working in an "insulated ivory tower." [49]

A few Marylanders stepped outside their locality and the present and tried to take a large view of mid-twentieth-century developments. In the late fifties the university business and economic research bureau at College Park issued an alarming study of the Potomac River basin. It reported that, because of poor forest management—along with the encroachment of farms, houses, and highways—wooded land on both sides of the river was only about one-third as effective as it should have been in preventing soil erosion and flooding. The resulting runoff covered downriver oyster beds with silt and required expensive dredging of the Potomac channel. Coal companies in Pennsylvania and West Virginia allowed acid to seep into streams feeding the Potomac, already deadened with various industrial waste materials. Streams like the Opequon and Conococheague picked up sewage from cities outside Maryland before emptying into the river. Fresh water demands in metropolitan Washington ran higher each year. The paper made abundantly clear the need for interstate action if the quality of the Potomac were to improve.

Thinking about the future helped to question current wisdom. In the Potomac basin study, Maryland economists criticized proposals to build an eight-lane highway along the river, and through parks, for Montgomery countians commuting to Washington. While the purity of the river depended on careful attention to natural drainage patterns—including preserved parkland—the highway debates showed that public officials regarded parks as "expendable." Herbert Wells of the MNCPPC had gone so far as to speak seriously of building a highway in Rock Creek Park; "Eventually," he remarked (with telling choice of verb), "we will have to force a road down there." The College Park criticisms rested on economic grounds—though on deeper considerations than how to turn an immediate profit. As Baltimore and Washington took over farm, forest, and "dormant" space, people assumed that current market prices ought to decide its use. Instead, according to the Potomac study, Marylanders had to ask what the land was capable of sustaining and what the public welfare cried for. The costs of preempting wilderness areas, heavy in the present, would fall even more heavily on later generations: "As urban life becomes increasingly complicated, human tensions will require accessible areas of sky, forest, and streams." "There is growing recognition," read a University of Maryland paper of 1961, "that open space in and surrounding cities is not a fortuitous amenity but a necessity for the health and survival of the cities." At the same time, scientific interest began to grow in the health, or ill health, of the Chesapeake Bay: disposal of the waste from Baltimore inner harbor dredging operations posed problems that a governor's committee addressed in 1959; two years later a coal-burning power plant on the Patuxent at Chalk Point raised questions about thermal pollution.[50]

In 1962 a longtime Silver Spring resident, Rachel Carson, contributed to this growing awareness by publishing *Silent Spring*, a study of soil, water, and air pollution in modern America. Carson, a Hopkins graduate who made full use of the NIH library in Bethesda, demonstrated that chemicals like DDT (a wartime development) and fallout from nuclear-bomb testing had disastrous consequences—on wildlife and humans alike. Since the war, chemical companies had discovered more than two hundred basic substances to kill bugs, weeds, rodents, and miscellaneous pests. Applied casually to farmland, forests, gardens, lawns, and elsewhere, they killed insects indiscriminately, poisoned wells, sickened cattle, and had the power "to still the songs of birds and the leaping of fish in the streams, to coat the leaves with a deadly film," and to linger in the soil indefinitely. "Along with the possibility of extinction of mankind by nuclear war," Carson noted, "the central problem of our age has therefore become the contamination of man's total environment with such substances of incredible potential for harm"— they could even alter the genetic code, "the very material of heredity upon which the shape of the future depends." For many weeks on best-seller lists, *Silent Spring* appeared as the large teenage population reached high school age and started college; adults as well as students read the book, but its popularity coincided with impressionability. Its opening illustration—a drawing that resembled the Middletown Valley—pictured a land worth any sacrifice to preserve. Could man in fact destroy himself through something so banal as an insect spray? Carson asked her readers. "Future historians may well be amazed by our distorted sense of proportion."[51]

As an alternative to sprawl and rapacity, another Marylander offered an experiment in proportion. In the early 1960s, having designed the Village of Cross Keys on the site of the old Baltimore Country Club golf course, Rouse revived the "new city" concept—drawing on some of Tugwell's ideas while trying to avoid the weaknesses of Greenbelt. Using secret partners and paper companies to keep prices low, he began buying twenty-two square miles of farmland west of Ellicott City. Wary residents generated stories of government plans to study tropical diseases or treat sewage on the tract; others saw the start of Washington's planned international airport (in Charles County speculators bought huge tracts for that purpose). In October 1963 Rouse went public with plans for "Columbia." Before civic groups, government committees, and chambers of commerce he for several years had criticized the growth of cities "by sheer chance—by accident, by whim of private developer and public agencies." Sprawl was reckless, inefficient, and inhumane. Rouse wanted Columbia to demonstrate urban efficiency even as it re-created small-village life. Requiring a private investment of $2 billion, Columbia would be a complete and self-sustaining city of one hundred thousand people of all income levels, virtually all of them working in firms attracted to the site. Columbia would respect the land itself—fitting "naturally into the landscape, preserving the stream valleys, protecting hills and forests," and providing parks and greenbelts.

A scoffer at government forms and bureaucratic planning, Rouse wanted his city to prove to be both more and less than Greenbelt. He planned Co-

In the fall of 1964 James W. Rouse's Community Research and Development firm unveiled this model for the new city of Columbia, planned around a 480-acre lake to be created on the Middle Patuxent River. *Columbia Archives*

lumbia to make a profit by drawing buyers to the best possible environment. "Let's examine the optimums," Rouse said to a group of advisors drawn from such widely disparate fields as economics and psychiatry. "In what size community do people feel the most comfortable? In what kind of community the most challenged? The most creative? Don't worry for the moment about feasibility. It will compromise us soon enough. Let's look at what might be and be invigorated by it."[52]

Bennett Cerf—the TV personality, publisher, and friend of the Maryland governor—once gave him a volume entitled "What I Know about Politics, by J. Millard Tawes." The book had blank pages; it drew laughs because everybody knew that Tawes's political instincts were unerring. In personal style he stood apart from his predecessor in office, the glad-handing McKeldin, and far apart from the charismatic young Massachusetts senator, John F. Kennedy, who sought Maryland support in his campaign for the presidency. Reporters covering the state capitol, believing Tawes as shy as a migratory duck, called him "J. Mallard Tawes." A London newspaper referred to him as "rather a mousy man" but went on to salute him as "a shrewd politician." His shrewdness owed everything to common sense and many years of practical experience. He obtained his modest education in Somerset County schools, at a Methodist academy in Delaware, and in a small business college. Before beginning his long stint in state finance, Tawes had worked in his father's lumbering and canning firms. Political experience showed. As governor in the spring of 1960 Tawes spoke of leading uncommitted delegates to the Democratic National Convention. Four days before the Maryland primary, licking his finger and holding it to the wind, he endorsed Kennedy instead. Humble and religious in the manner of the rural Eastern Shore, Tawes seldom acted quickly. Since he served at a time when politicians discovered the power of television, it was good for Tawes that he sought no national office.

Tawes demonstrated that charisma had little to do with effective state government. He ran for governor on a platform that included a promise to improve management of the bay and perhaps even revive the still-suffering Chesapeake oyster industry. Believing the state Planning Department "not worthy of the name," he placed planning and economic development in separate offices and put planners to work unfettered. In May 1960 Tawes called a conference of nine state governors in Annapolis to discuss shared issues. The Appalachian Regional Commission that emerged from the meeting aimed primarily at economic growth via generous federal aid. It also provided a framework for discussing Potomac basin issues like soil conservation and water quality.[53]

Tawes worked to repair Maryland's relations with Virginia, which again had scraped bottom during McKeldin's second term. One source of disaffection finally had disappeared in the spring of 1958. Henry T. Phoebus, a Republican senator from Tawes's own Somerset County, at that time sponsored a bill to remove the casinos on the Potomac's southern edge. Passage of the measure, according to the United Christian Citizens of Maryland, retrieved the state's good name and strengthened the moral fiber of its people. It surely made discussions of the Potomac oyster beds easier, and that issue had burst into open flame. Maryland in 1955 had demanded an "export tax" from Virginia watermen on the Potomac and two years later, angry over Virginia's failure to extradite a notorious poacher, acted to dissolve the 1785 compact. U.S. Supreme Court justices had urged the governors of both states to appoint members to a river commission under retired justice Stanley F. Reed. Commissioners did not act quickly enough to prevent a final gunfight on the water. Following a chase through the darkness and fog near Colonial Beach in April 1959, lawmen aboard the *McKeldin*, a converted navy PT boat, shot and killed one of their oldest quarries, Berkeley Muse. "Drudgin'," a Virginian commented sadly, "wasn't the big thing that the Maryland police made it out."[54]

Shocked at this latest violence, Tawes established new rules to govern recruitment and training of the fisheries police. He supported ratification of the cooperative agreement that the Reed Commission had drawn up and the Virginia assembly passed. At least two members of the Maryland legislature, Walter Dorsey of St. Mary's and John Sanford of Worcester, argued in favor of rejecting the new compact because, like the recent river-casino act, it surrendered powers Marylanders claimed by ancient charter. Opponents maneuvered the proposal onto the November 1962 ballot, where Dorsey and Sanford expected its defeat. To their surprise voters overwhelmingly ratified the agreement. By its provisions Congress next passed a Potomac Fisheries Commission bill, covering fishing rights, seafood inspection, and joint marine research. President Kennedy signed the bill in early December. Afterward Kennedy, Tawes, and Virginia governor Albertis S. Harrison sat down under the Capitol dome for a ceremonial luncheon that included fresh Potomac oysters.

Tawes needed little acumen to recognize two major developments of the early sixties—the continuing rise of the suburbs and the growing movement for civil rights. His first year in office coincided with reports of corruption among Maryland savings and loan associations. Lightly regulated, they advertised deceptively high interest rates, made loans on shaky second mortgages, and attracted shady managers. In the spring of 1960 Joseph D. Tydings, Millard Tydings's adopted stepson and a Harford County member of the House of Delegates, emerged as a spokesman for the suburbanites whose money was among the mismanaged deposits and who on principle recoiled from corruption and cronyism. The industry fought a Tydings bill that would have imposed stricter rules on the companies. "There must be some way," said a lobbyist, "to get rid of the rats without burning down the house." Greatly weakened, the bill passed the assembly in the last hours of the session. Tawes faced a choice between old friends and new. He sat on the measure for days and then, making what he said was one of the "most difficult decisions" of his career, vetoed it, calling the bill inadequate. He knew how closely neighborhood savings and loan associations were tied to the ordinary family's dream of homeowning—and also how generous savings and loan officers could be at fund-raising dinners.[55]

Tawes's political instincts surely guided him in dealing with reapportionment and redistricting—problems rich in social reality. Revised assembly districts would give political power to newcomers on the fringes of Baltimore and Washington and take it away from state residents whose ancestors had landed in the seventeenth century. Redrawing congressional districts either focused or diluted the power of Democrats and Republicans—of blacks, coal miners, farmers, watermen, union members, suburban professionals, the Jews who had moved into Pikesville, and the Greeks, Lithuanians, and Ukrainians who had stayed in East Baltimore. There was nothing abstract in the legal-language proposals legislators made on redistricting and reapportionment, and consensus proved nearly impossible. A constitutional amendment voters had approved in 1950—freezing the distribution of delegates until a convention met to overhaul the 1867 constitution—ironically made things worse by suspending assembly reapportionment even under the old formula.

Soon after assuming office Tawes took the safe step of appointing another blue-ribbon commission to study the apportionment issue, last examined in the Lane administration. As chairman Tawes named the longtime state attorney general, William C. Walsh of Cumberland. Walsh drafted a compromise that would respect "the political stature and importance of any area of the state." It recommended expanding the House of Delegates from 123 to 141 members and giving the new seats to growing parts. During the 1960 legislative session, bills to make those changes, opposed by the rural counties, failed as usual to pass. Soon afterward suburban leaders who included Alfred L. Scanlan, Royce Hanson, and Phillip Thorson of Montgomery County and Baltimore County Executive Christian H. Kahl met in Towson to form a Maryland Committee for Fair Representation. They issued an appeal based on the principle of equal protection of the laws. As everyone expected, the 1960 census returns (besides entitling Maryland to an eighth congressional seat) lent new weight to their grievance. While the average member of the lower house represented 25,000 persons, each Montgomery and Prince George's delegate spoke for nearly 60,000, and those from Baltimore County for 82,000. Members from Calvert, Dorchester, Garrett, Kent, Somerset, Talbot, and Worcester counties represented only about 7,000 persons.[56]

Despite loyalties to the Shore, Tawes to his credit stood behind reapportionment—a crusade that seemed unending if not lost. While legislators in these years introduced motions to name a state dog (the Chesapeake Retriever), fish (striped bass), and sport (jousting), Tawes reminded them that there was "no argument" for deferring reform. After 1962 neither did there appear to be any choice. In the spring of that year the Supreme Court in *Baker* v. *Carr* used the equal-protection principle to order legislative reapportionment in Tennessee. Almost immediately the Maryland courts, hearing a case that the Committee for Fair Representation had raised two years before, abided by that ruling and opened the door to a special session of the General Assembly. Meeting in May, legislators largely followed the Walsh Commission plan—raising the number of delegates to 142 and increasing representation for Baltimore, Montgomery, Prince George's, and Anne Arundel counties as well as for two districts in Baltimore City. Even after these changes and the naming of a third postwar commmission to study reapportionment, the fairness issue remained alive. In 1963 the Supreme Court struck down a

Georgia primary formula that used a unit rule, like Maryland's, based on legislative inequality and next year, in *Maryland Committee for Fair Representation* v. *Tawes*, declared the structure of the Free State senate unconstitutional given the "overall representation" of both houses. Maryland lawmakers quarreled further without result, and in the fall of 1965 Tawes called another special session. Better that we act, he told the assembly; it would be "far more distasteful" to have the federal courts act for us.[57] Under the new plan the number of senators ballooned from 29 to 43. In 1966 federal judges in Baltimore solved one riddle for the General Assembly. They divided the state into eight equal congressional districts.

Neither spectator to change nor an egregious example of oppression, Maryland began to experience some of the upheaval that revolutionized American race relations after 1960, when black students in Greensboro, North Carolina, conducting a lunch-counter sit-in, combined nonviolent protest and youthful idealism. Maryland blacks encountered comparatively few if any obstacles to the voting rights that Negroes in the Deep South fought to obtain. They nonetheless faced plenty of injustice and organized against it with growing enthusiasm. Old Baltimore institutions led the way at first—Lillie Carroll Jackson and the NAACP, the local chapter of the National Urban League, the *Afro-American*, and the black churches. Young people, especially college students, black and white, felt exhilarated to be on the cutting edge of "The Movement." Only a few weeks after the Greensboro protest, students mostly from Morgan State, Hopkins, and Goucher used the sit-in to desegregate lunch counters at the nearby Northwood Shopping Center. Their efforts next shifted to downtown Baltimore, where they picketed stores that held out against integration. Maryland State College students made peaceful assaults on Salisbury segregation; young people at the University of Maryland persuaded the last segregated cafe to serve blacks and then, taking a new tack, picketed College Park shops that had no Negro sales clerks. Resistance fueled the movement and provided its soldiers with red badges of courage. In 1962 white youngsters beat up blacks who wanted to swim at Riverside Park outside Baltimore.

Foreign relations helped to account for Maryland's first civil rights law. Newly independent African countries had sent emissaries to New York and Washington; much to the embarrassment of the Kennedy administration, Maryland restaurant and motel keepers refused to serve black diplomats, who soon united in protest. The State Department phoned Tawes to urge change: Maryland segregation threatened relations with friendly governments and gave the United States a regrettable image abroad. When a few restaurants agreed to serve Africans, reporters from the *Afro-American* showed up wearing togas to point out the absurdity of seating foreign, but not native, blacks. Militant black students from Baltimore and Philadelphia, some already in jail, threatened a massive "freedom ride" on the Pulaski Highway in November unless the establishments integrated.

Governor Tawes tipped his hat to the crowd during his inaugural parade, 1963. Baltimore *News American* photograph. *Jacques Kelly*

Tawes privately admitted the wrong of race discrimination as he did the unfairness of malapportionment. Hoping to avoid a civil rights fight in Maryland, he called in restaurant and motel owners and urged them to end segregation on their own. They refused without assurances that every competitor would do the same. Finally the governor, federal officials, spokesmen for the Congress on Racial Equality (CORE), and restaurant owners agreed to a compromise whereby students called off the march, most of the establishments opened to blacks, and Tawes sought a state public accommodations law. In the 1962 legislative session the bill twice went down to defeat. Next year, feeling more confident after his reelection (Kennedy's handling of the Cuban missile crisis aided Democrats all over the state), Tawes made a renewed plea for a bill opening restaurants, hotels, theaters, and recreational places to all persons, regardless of race or color. The reapportioned assembly passed it easily—though eleven counties in Southern Maryland and the Eastern Shore, along with suburban Baltimore County, won exemption from the law.

In the summer of 1963 the civil rights struggle grew particularly dramatic, and violent. On the Choptank River a major Cambridge employer, the Phillips Packing Company, had left family hands when its founders died and in 1958 gone to a national firm that later cut production. Unemployment rose, especially among blacks, and the change in ownership also weakened black community leadership—local managers no longer dispensed favors through senior black workers. Cramped in one ward, split between two factions vying to be the more indignant, blacks in the late spring and early summer listened to angry voices, one of them that of Gloria Richardson, a native of the city who had graduated from Howard University and then returned only to be frustrated in her search for work. Under Richardson's leadership—and her ties were not with Jackson's Baltimore NAACP but with more radical groups in Philadelphia and elsewhere—Cambridge blacks demonstrated defiantly for faster school desegregation, equal accommodations, and jobs. White policemen jailed two youths for participating in these marches, and on 11 June, when a juvenile court judge heard their case, blacks and whites stormed one another, causing mayhem that lasted through the night.

State police and National Guardsmen finally restored order, but tension remained high all over the state. The day after the riot, night riders in Mississippi shot and killed Medgar Evers, a black civil rights leader then on a solitary march for equality. Cambridge blacks met to pray for Evers and sing defiance at the system that kept them down. In July protests moved to the Western Shore, to the all-white Gwynn Oak amusement park in Baltimore County. There white priests, ministers, and rabbis joined blacks in the demonstration. A few months before, Archbishop Lawrence Shehan had told Catholics in a pastoral letter that they had "a special obligation" to stand at the fore of the movement to remove discrimination. One of the Gwynn Oak protesters believed that "more was needed than pious thoughts," and television carried sharp images of the arrests that followed.[58] That August about a hundred thousand civil rights marchers heard the Reverend Martin Luther King speak at the Lincoln Memorial in Washington.

Emotional events both built support for black rights and polarized white opponents. In the aftermath of the Cambridge riot Tawes displayed courage by calling for a statewide (no exceptions) public accommodations measure. President Kennedy's assassination that November, sending the nation into mourning, united public support behind the civil rights legislation he had championed at the last. Early in 1964, moved by Kennedy's death (as were congressmen who that year voted a federal civil rights law), Maryland legislators passed the bill Tawes had asked for—though it permitted segregated bars and taverns. Opponents petitioned to have it placed on the fall ballot as a referendum. They included rural whites in heavily black Southern Maryland and on the Eastern Shore. The Cambridge unrest awakened old fears of racial war among them; they voiced worries about black extremism and agitation from outside. Civil rights militants had scant support among lower-income whites in Baltimore City, many of whom lived close to public housing projects and resented what they considered black intrusion. They might be able to afford a weekend each summer at Ocean City, but on most hot days, reviewing accounts of misbehavior at newly desegregated city pools like the one at Druid Hill Park, they sweltered rather than swim.

During the spring and summer of 1964, a presidential election year, hot

Demonstrators opposed integration of Gwynn Oak Park, 1963. *A. S. Abell Television Newsfilm Archives, University of Baltimore*

feelings roiled Maryland politics. George C. Wallace, the Alabama governor who had fought black enrollment at the state university, mounted a presidential campaign that relied on whites' fear of blacks, anger at big government, and hatred of privilege. Wallace entered the Maryland primary and toured the state to noisy receptions. His mid-May visit to Cambridge, where National Guardsmen still stood duty, set off a new round of disorder and tear gas. Senator Daniel Brewster, a Baltimore County Democrat and former congressman who had won Butler's Senate seat in 1962, stumped the state representing President Lyndon B. Johnson in the primary. Brewster said that all Maryland Democrats regretted the Wallace candidacy. To Brewster's chagrin the Alabama governor carried seventeen counties and won nearly 43 percent of the total vote. That fall the open accommodations referendum demonstrated further white reaction. Though carrying by a vote of 342,000 to 301,000, the question failed on the Eastern Shore, in much of Western Maryland, and in Baltimore and Anne Arundel counties. Only Montgomery County (which, with Baltimore City, had passed its own open accommodations law in 1962) gave it a two-to-one majority. Yet in the same election Marylanders passed favorably on two leading supporters of the civil rights movement. They reelected Carlton R. Sickles the state's congressman-at-large and sent the younger Tydings, whom Kennedy had named federal district attorney, to Washington as senator. They voted overwhelmingly for President Johnson—whom Tawes and McKeldin (again mayor of Baltimore) hailed as a staunch friend of equal rights.

Marylanders who took stock might have pointed to any number of assuring signs. Tawes, a family man and moralist of the Depression era, found a way to rid the state of its evil slot machines. Ministers had written him of school-children who spent their lunch money on them. A Southern Maryland woman lost the family savings in a gambling spree and then hanged herself in her garage. Upstanding residents in lower Maryland reported rumors that mobsters controlled the slot machine supply and service businesses. In the eyes of state tax collectors, a suspicious number of apparently poor people in the southern counties drove new Cadillacs. In 1963 the governor per-suaded legislators to end the local experiment with slots, agreeing to a five-year phase-out plan that made the law somewhat less painful to its victims. Tawes used his disarmed, down-home skills in many worthwhile tasks. He negotiated an agreement with Pennsylvania and New York to begin the for-midable work of clearing the Susquehanna River of sewage, coal-mining seepage, soil runoff, and chemical fertilizers. As an Eastern Shore native, the governor could deal with watermen more easily than his predecessors. He strengthened the Department of Water Resources in 1965. Overriding water-men's objections, he established a permanent Department of Chesapeake Bay Affairs whose members, on Tawes's terms, escaped senate confirmation. A vigorous state campaign at last led to extensive reseeding of bay oyster beds.

Tawes and the General Assembly took an equally farsighted approach to state education. A 1964 measure substantially increased public school fund-ing. The following year, when Maryland ranked ninth in the country in av-erage teachers' salaries, it floated another $10 million in bonds for public education and vocational schooling. College-age students continued to climb in numbers, and the state had determined to give as many of them as pos-sible the chance for a baccalaureate degree. At College Park, where President Wilson H. Elkins had been building the university's academic reputation, enrollment surpassed thirty thousand, making Maryland the tenth-largest American university; construction there—a dozen high-rise dormitories (three, with dining hall, per "complex") and a fine arts building—proceeded at full speed. In Baltimore City a new law school building and a hospital ad-dition went up. Failing at first, Tawes finally succeeded in pushing through the legislature a bill making the five teachers' colleges four-year liberal arts and sciences institutions. Relieving the enrollment burden at College Park, the new system won support because it enabled students who could not afford college living expenses to attend classes while living at home. Com-munity colleges, multiplying in number, received enlarged state support (three hundred dollars per full-time student), as did private colleges and universities. Legislators provided for a state educational television network. In Tawes's last message to the assembly, early in 1966, he modestly cited

Powerful earth movers of the sort that made way for the Washington beltway as they appeared, almost engagingly, in a planning booklet of the period. Maryland–National Capital Park and Planning Commission, *On Wedges and Corridors* (Silver Spring, 1958).

advancement in public education as perhaps the "greatest single accomplishment" of his administration.[59]

Phenomenal growth, fulfilling Key's prophecy, seemed to sweep everything before it. Each year between 1959 and 1964, fifty thousand acres of Maryland farmland went toward suburban uses. After 1957 state tax laws came to the rescue of farmers near these growth centers and made farm use an exception to the "fair market value" standard of assessment. As a side effect, the law encouraged speculators in Montgomery, Prince George's, and Baltimore counties to buy up agricultural parcels, perfunctorily farm them, and then sell them for development at high profit. Suburban sprawl and real estate values gained momentum as the Baltimore and Washington beltways opened in 1962 and 1964. Designed to ease traffic flow, they hastened peripheral housing and commercial development. Though the rate of suburban population growth slowed somewhat (it took twenty years to double again after 1961), retail sales on the outskirts of Baltimore and Washington jumped 165 percent in the sixties (they had climbed 22 percent the decade before). Around Washington the federal government helped to shape these patterns by dispersing offices. About one in five Montgomery and Prince George's wage earners drew government salaries—the Defense Department dominating Prince George's, and Health, Education, and Welfare and agencies like the Atomic Energy Commission and National Bureau of Standards drawing professionals to Montgomery. By the mid-1960s the Montgomery County Council had swung about to favor managed growth. Next to the comparatively modest Pooks Hill apartments and not far to the north, where the Washington beltway now intersected the Rockville Pike, developers counted on building high-rise apartment structures of twenty stories or more. Zoning authorities bent to permit "cluster subdivisions" of townhouses that at first promised architectural variety, and allowed "planned neighborhoods" on self-sufficient tracts of two hundred to four hundred acres.[60]

Annapolis, for generations a "Georgian Jewel" of charming facades, narrow streets, and sleepy economy, began waking up as it grew more accessible to Washington and Baltimore. In 1960 the John Hanson Highway between Washington and the Bay Bridge neared completion and more shopping centers appeared on the Ritchie Highway. By that time speculators already had started buying up eighteenth-century houses in the hope that Annapolis would grow into the Severn River's Georgetown. Annapolitans divided roughly between businessmen who hoped to spur development and members of Historic Annapolis, Inc., a group then led by St. Clair Wright and known to critics as "Hysterical Annapolis." The two sides differed on what to do with venerable buildings that stood in the path of progress. When in 1959 the city engineer condemned the old customs house, preservationists had saved it by buying it. In 1960 both camps, each eyeing the other suspiciously, agreed to hire the Greater Baltimore Committee planning council to undertake a study that would recommend a master plan for the town. Meantime the Naval Academy wanted a new science center on a site outspoken natives preferred to let be, and merchants wanted parking lots where more old houses, mostly black residences, stood on Cornhill, Pinckney, and Fleet streets. "What do I care about quaint Old Annapolis?" declared an angry store manager. "I need some parking spaces around here and quick or I'm going out of business. To hell with quaintness."[61] In 1964 the mayor and town council issued permits for a ten-story motel across Spa Creek and a seven-story office building near the State House.

In this land of pleasant living there truly seemed to be more of everything for almost everybody. Family income, adjusted for inflation, rose more than 22 percent in the 1960s—the highest climb since a brief period during the war. Maryland taxes and spending rose as well, seemingly without ceilings. During the Tawes years, state expenditures jumped from $450.1 million to $915.8 million. In the mid-sixties about one in three Maryland high school graduates went on to college. Between 1959 and 1966 state mental hospitals, reflecting the influence of the medical profession, increased by seven, and spending for them increased from $20 million to $37 million. In 1958 there had been seventeen state parks; the Tawes administration doubled that number. Maryland unemployment in 1966 stood almost a full percentage point below the national average of 3.8 percent. In the country there were thirty-seven corporations that made net profits exceeding $100 million; twenty-two of them had major installations in Maryland. Some nine hundred federal programs benefited the state. Thanks to heavy use of commercial fertilizers, Maryland farmers set new records for per-acre yields of tobacco (1,100 pounds) and wheat (33 bushels). Apparently Maryland could afford two of whatever it wanted. In March 1965 Worcester County developers promised that, if Congress only rejected the bill to make all of Assateague Island a national park (a two-mile stretch became a state park that year), they could make the largest part of the sand bar into "a second Ocean City." Traffic so jammed the Bay Bridge on summer weekends that the General Assembly in 1966 passed a bill authorizing bonds for another one. In the fall of that year a second campus of the University of Maryland, a Baltimore County branch, opened its doors near Catonsville.[62]

One could easily misread the signs, however, as did a Baltimore native who wrote that blacks in the city, then 40 percent of the population, "don't care to riot and aren't sure what CORE means." Baltimore urban renewal had destroyed many homes, and though whites leaving the city for the suburbs created some vacancies, the black and poor still faced shortages and still fought discrimination. In November 1965 black and white demonstrators had marched through Baltimore demanding open housing laws. James Griffin of CORE predicted that "1965 will be the last year the political power structure can act without regard to the housing needs of the minority." Furman Templeton of the Urban League issued a similar warning and said he expected the drive next to attack conditions in Baltimore County. In early 1966 the Maryland State Advisory Committee to the U.S. Civil Rights Commission found "no meaningful desegregation" of schools in Anne Arundel, Calvert, Caroline, Charles, Dorchester, Kent, Queen Anne's, St. Mary's, Somerset, Talbot, and Worcester counties; under "freedom of choice," school boards used paper work and economic threats to frustrate black parents trying to move their children to previously all-white schools. Finally, following the rule that the prosperous can afford two, the Johnson administration both declared war on poverty and in 1965 went to war in South Vietnam. Most people expected victory on both fronts. High-minded federal programs like the Job Corps, summer make-work, and the Community Action Program (paying money directly to community groups for use as they saw fit) certainly raised black expectations, especially among the young. Anti-poverty made the poor angry about poverty. Maryland enjoyed unequaled prosperity; blacks were becoming increasingly aware that it was not shared equally.[63]

While Republicans in 1966 decided without dissent to nominate the Baltimore County executive, Spiro "Ted" Agnew, for governor, Democrats in the primary election scourged their foes with vengeance that showed how fortunate Tawes was to retire that year. As his successor Tawes recommended

George P. Mahoney, perennial candidate. Baltimore *News American* photograph. *Jacques Kelly*

his attorney general, the Western Marylander Thomas Finan. The Sunpapers endorsed Finan as a proven moderate and described his platform of more highways, continued educational improvement, and economic development as "intelligent, well-rounded, and constructive." Sickles, running against "politics as usual," opposed Finan as a tool of the Tawes machine. Tydings supported Sickles and declined "any sort of coalition or harmony ticket." Clarence Miles of the Orioles and GBC entered the race as an independent. Mahoney ran a campaign that reacted to talk of open housing and mimicked Wallace's visceral appeal to whites. "Your Home Is Your Castle," Mahoney declared on television, billboards, and bumper stickers—"Protect It."[64]

In October, following enlargement of Memorial Stadium, the Orioles played in their first World Series. Between 1954 and 1965, drawing average crowds of only 13,685 per game, the team had developed a reputation for inconsistency. In the series the Birds played textbook baseball. Frank Robinson, outfielder, heavy hitter, and one team leader, and Brooks Robinson, an eight-year veteran at third base, hit back-to-back home runs in the first game. Moe Drabowsky in relief and starting pitchers Dave McNally, Jim Palmer, and Wally Bunker—the last two merely twenty-one years old—performed magnificently. First baseman "Boog" Powell, bulky and powerful, and Hank Bauer, the manager whose face players said looked like a clenched fist, did their jobs equally well. The Orioles not only took the Los Angeles Dodgers in a four-game sweep, they played errorless ball and held the Dodgers scoreless for thirty-three consecutive innings.

It was easy. It was too easy.

CHAPTER 12

Renaissance:
Survival of a Sensibility

On the night of 24 July 1967, H. Rap Brown, national chairman of the Student Nonviolent Coordinating Committee and a seasoned civil rights demonstrator, stood on the hood of a parked car in the Negro section of Cambridge. Brown delivered a searing lecture on Maryland history and race relations to a crowd of about three hundred and fifty blacks. Believing them too long under sway of whites in the town and moderate or "Uncle Tom" black leadership, Brown built a bonfire out of old customs and memories. He told them to "start talking about taking your community and controlling it." No longer slaves, they must now be proud to be black; Negro?—"That's the name honky gave you," he shouted. The Cambridge police recently had hired five black patrolmen. "They give you five nigger cops"—Brown poked fun at appearances—"but they can't whip nothing but black heads. How come they can't whip no honkies?" You better get yourselves some guns, he advised his audience, which included at least one person with a tape recorder, because "the Man is out to get you." Brown scorned the treatment "the honky press" gave the black-rights movement. So far from criminal, it was political. "We're not rioting—we're rebelling," he declared, and "conditions create rebellion—not people." Before his Cambridge speech a suspicious fire had broken out at the Pine Street Elementary School, and Brown taunted local blacks for not burning it down long ago. "It's time for Cambridge to explode, baby! Black folks built America and if America don't come around," Brown cried, "we're going to burn America down!"[1] Rebirth came no easier than birth.

The explosion of Cambridge did not cause but helped to mark the beginning of an unforgettable period of violence, rebellion, and readjustment in Maryland. Not long before Brown's resonant speech, a national States' Rights party, avowedly racist, had chosen Cambridge as the site of a rally, and local blacks led by Gloria Richardson had grown understandably hostile. When

Brown finished, the blacks broke up angrily, and at about eleven o'clock that night some of them fired a shotgun at a police patrol car answering a call in the 2d ward. At 2:00 A.M. a fire broke out in the elementary school that Brown's speech had made a target. As in the 1963 riot, a white volunteer fire company declined to enter the black neighborhood without protection, and this time the flames spread quickly out of control. Besides the school, black-owned Pine Street businesses—a barber shop, cleaning service, coffee shop, record store, and "Sweetheart" Green's motel, bar, and poolroom—went up in smoke. The Democratic party headquarters burned, as if by Brown's design, as did the Zion Baptist Church on Cross Street and various houses, three of them on Dunn's Court. Oil drums and propane gas tanks exploded throughout the night. At four in the morning the flames caught high-tension wires and caused a citywide power outage. By that time a band of blacks—firemen called them "a bunch of good fellows"—had escorted men and equipment into the ghetto to fight the blaze. Five people, one a policeman, had been injured.[2]

Not for a long time did the flames die down. Governor Agnew, vacationing at his Ocean City cottage, heard of the outbreak almost as soon as it developed and left for Cambridge before dawn. At first light he toured the smoldering ruins on Pine Street, where photographers took shots of him talking to blacks. He blamed the riot on the "rabble rouser" Brown—who with warrants issued for his arrest had gone into hiding. Later in the day National Guard infantrymen from such white strongholds as Dundalk and Bel Air arrived to control the town. Their commander, Adjutant General George M. Gelston, had appeared in *Life* magazine the year before wearing a Colts jersey and explaining how the guard made room for any ballplayer in danger of being drafted. Pledging to "take care of anything that comes up," Gelston issued his men twelve rounds of ammunition each, told them to fire if fired upon, but also displayed admirable diplomatic skills—dealing as firmly with white troublemakers as with angry blacks. In the next few days and nights black leaders divided over what to do. Black and white youths alike cursed the guardsmen. Troops raided a white hangout and found it loaded with weapons. A Baltimorean representing the Union for Jobs or Income Now (U-JOIN) accused a governor's aide of "sitting on his butt" instead of delivering food and necessities to the homeless as Agnew had promised. For a second time police arrested a white civil rights worker from Baltimore, Stuart N. Wechsler, when Dorchester County sheriff Ira Johnson found his car parked illegally. "I'm running this county," shouted the sheriff to a protesting military officer. Once back on the street, Wechsler berated the governor for blaming the disturbances on one man. "If Agnew thinks that calling for the arrest of Brown will still the revolution," said Wechsler, "he's a fool."[3]

However quick to blame outsiders for trouble, Agnew handled the crisis with carefully cultivated firmness. Only son of a Greek immigrant who had owned a Baltimore lunchroom and married a widowed Virginian, he had

The morning of 25 July, Governor Spiro T. Agnew dramatically joined Adjutant General George M. Gelston on the scene of the Cambridge riot. *Baltimore Sunpapers*

come up the hard way. During the Depression the young Agnew had worked after school, attended Hopkins for a few semesters, then quit to clerk in an insurance office, where he met his wife. He served as a lieutenant throughout World War II and afterward resumed evening law school at the University of Baltimore. Failing at his own law practice, he spent several years as a personnel manager in a large grocery store. He missed the Korean War as a hardship case, and in the early fifties he and his wife bought a small home in Loch Raven, where Agnew joined the Kiwanis and handled suburban civic chores like straightening out the financial records of a swimming club. He read *Reader's Digest* pieces on increasing his "word power"—leading one fellow to comment after an Agnew flurry, "This is only the Kiwanis Club, Ted; where do you get words like this?"[4]

Agnew's political rise had been sudden and curiously linked to circumstance. In 1962 he was still struggling as a Towson zoning, labor union, and personal injury lawyer. Expecting to lose, the Republicans that year nominated him for county executive. A wealthy paint manufacturer and real estate speculator named Shuger bought the attorney a new suit of clothes, established his campaign office, and paid about half of his election expenses. Democrats obliged him—the two leading county Democrats, Birmingham and Kahl, could not cement their differences before the general election. Again in the 1966 gubernatorial race, Democrats split between Pressman of Baltimore and the Democratic primary winner, Mahoney, beside whom Agnew appeared attractively moderate. Once in office Agnew had adapted quickly, tailoring himself in the broadly appealing McKeldin style. He dressed well and befriended business. Avoiding extremes, he spoke of economic growth. In his inaugural speech as governor, Agnew expressed hope for "a new alliance" based on "people, principle, progress."[5] Ted Agnew, as unlikely a success story as any recent public figure in the state, hoped to duplicate the illustrious career of Ted McKeldin—another handsome Republican who had gone to night school and overcome hardship.

With some truth the governor claimed that he always tried to deal fairly with blacks. As personnel manager he had treated them better, said one of his bosses, than anyone else did. He had helped to get black menhaden fishermen off the Atlantic Coast organized into a union for the first time. As county executive he had taken a stand against discrimination at the Gwynn Oak amusement park (though later firing his active human relations committee chairman). He was the first Maryland governor to make a high-level black appointment, naming Dr. Gilbert Ware his advisor on health, welfare, and human relations. He appointed three blacks to state judgeships. Only a few days before the Eastern Shore outbreak, the governor had met with Roy Wilkins, national head of the NAACP, and explored ways to achieve "equal rights for all our citizens." After the Cambridge riot Agnew ordered a committee of local leaders to find a cure for what he called their "sick city" (to complete the psychiatric imagery, this group met at the Eastern Shore mental hospital), and he urged the eleven white businessmen and ten blacks to expand so as to include "responsible militants." Compared to the Dorchester County state's attorney, who denied saying that Wechsler would be shot if he returned to Cambridge, Agnew seemed reasonable and levelheaded. Still, he spared no spleen for blacks whom he defined as "irresponsible." He declared that persons inciting to riot—no matter how serious the wrong they protested—would be jailed before they finished speaking. Getting angry blacks to talk to white businessmen represented, he said, "a complete abandonment of the techniques of appeasement" that other cities had adopted when blacks turned violent.[6]

Forceful yet liberal when compared to the outright racists, Agnew had an advantage in being the first governor to work with the reapportioned legislature. He strove for bipartisanship in facing the state's tax problem. While the state taxed income and sales, localities imposed property levies that were becoming unbearable for residents of Baltimore City and counties in the Baltimore-Washington corridor. Paul D. Cooper of the state Fiscal Research Bureau and Harry R. Hughes, Caroline County Democrat and senate majority leader, had devised a reform formula that died in the House of Delegates as the assembly adjourned that election year. Agnew early in his administration held meetings with Hughes, senate president William S. James, and house Speaker Marvin Mandel to discuss a feasible tax bill. They agreed to a plan, passed in the 1967 session, by which the state income tax increased to 5 percent for the higher-income brackets, and localities had the option of laying an additional tax up to half the amount one paid the state (the state collected and then turned it back to them). Reducing pressure on property owners, the law for most Marylanders softened the blow of higher taxes.

New legislation reflected the concerns of "better-government" suburbanites and needy Baltimoreans. The assembly placed regulations on revolving credit plans and second-mortgage loan procedures. It also created the Maryland Environmental Trust, a twelve-member committee that absorbed an older "Keep Maryland Beautiful" group and aimed "to conserve, improve, stimulate and perpetuate the aesthetic, natural health, scenic and cultural qualities of the Maryland environment." One path-breaking bill governed water quality. Maryland joined Pennsylvania in requiring local governments to prepare sewage treatment plants; by means of grants and bonds the state committed itself to finance them. Maryland fell in step with the 1967 federal Clean Air Act—though meanwhile a Baltimore fertilizer company conducted and lost a court case testing the constitutionality of the act. A new commission began studying the effects of pollution, erosion, and urban encroachment on the Patuxent River valley. Ancient barriers to interracial marriage—Agnew called them a blot on the state record—went down. Maryland removed exceptions to its open accommodations law. Another bill (opponents later sent it to a referendum) outlawed discriminatory housing covenants in new developments. Agnew credited passage of such bills to Democratic and Republican members alike. He praised Mandel with collegial affection at a B'nai B'rith awards dinner. The house leader, he said, had kept a "firm hand on the tiller"—squelching discontent while puffing amiably on one of his favorite meerschaum pipes.[7]

In ordinary times Agnew might have made a fine governor, just as, in a period of comparative quiet, Marylanders might have ratified a replacement for their antiquated constitution. In the summer of 1965 Tawes had appointed a commission under the Baltimore lawyer H. Vernon Eney to study the need for a constitutional convention and to suggest changes in the structure of Maryland government (a year later, hedging his bet, Tawes named another group to examine ways to modernize the executive branch). Eney and his fellows, who included former governor Lane until his death in early 1967, recommended a convention, the assembly voted to place the issue on the 1966 primary ballot, and Marylanders, in light voting, decided to call the first such meeting in a century. There was little doubt of the need for review. The University of Maryland governmental research bureau in 1963 had published a study of the legislative process and described the number of local laws in Maryland as "unusual among the states." At the invitation of the House of Delegates, a Rutgers University professor prepared a long monograph on ways to strengthen the Maryland legislature. The Eney Commission itself produced a book-length report that accompanied its draft of a revised constitution. The draft charter, much briefer than the 1867 document,

College students outraged many Marylanders by protesting the Vietnam war—as at College Park in 1967. Baltimore *News American* photograph. *Jacques Kelly*

eliminated local laws, simplified the court system into four tiers, shortened the residency requirement for state citizenship, provided for automatic re-apportionment, and outlawed discrimination in every form. Eney served as president of the convention. Made up of delegates who reflected the new, suburban cast of the assembly, it first met at Goucher College (which had completed its move to Towson in 1952) for seminars and then convened in Annapolis on 12 September 1967.[8]

The next month, distracting Marylanders from such formal affairs as constitutional change, the anti–Vietnam war movement turned from protest to resistance—following the civil rights crusade in adopting the tactic of confrontation, physical presence, symbolic action. The anti-war campaign gained strength in step with rising American troop levels in South Vietnam. It voiced views that remained in a minority: the war was a strategic mistake, a moral wrong, or both. An umbrella group in Washington, the National Mobilization Committee, called for a burst of anti-war activity during the week of 16 October and a Washington demonstration Saturday the twenty-first. Centered in Baltimore and suburban Washington, sympathetic Mary-landers quickly enlisted in the cause. The Goucher anti-war committee held a teachers' vigil downtown. On Tuesday an "angry arts" festival, with radical poetry and irreverent humor, took place at Hopkins. Protesters later marched on the federal building in the unfinished Charles Center complex, and members of the Interfaith Peace Mission tried to disrupt the induction of draftees at Fort Holabird. Many of the Marylanders who went to the Washington rally on Saturday were college students; the anti-war movement, by no means confined to young people, counted heavily on them. Young men faced the draft and the prospect of being killed or maimed in a distant place. During the week of the protests American battle deaths rose to 171 and U.S. troops wounded in action approached 1,000.

But in deploring the expense of the war, protesters often went beyond self-preservation to ask what purpose the cost, to recoil from the arrogant use of American power, and to rebel against the traditional patriotism that simply said "My country, right or wrong." Black radicals, not alone, pointed to the high proportion of their "brothers" serving as infantrymen in the war zone; here, they said with cause, lay proof of racial bias in the draft system with its college deferments and the military service with its desk jobs for high scorers on tests. Women argued that governments led by men alone stood perpetually on a war footing. For a sizable social element, rebellion against authority became cultural—a style of life. Scoffing at convention, disdaining their parents' materialism, youth let their hair grow and adopted Asian or American-Indian clothing. Some burned incense and indulged in drugs. They listened to a new genre of folk-rock music that blasted the wrongs of society and sang of conformity as being the sound of silence.

Their rebellion confused more than a few parents and made bitter enemies. Especially in East and South Baltimore, on Eastern Shore farms, and in the small towns of Western Maryland, there were young men and women who shared their parents' sense of civic duty and like George Owens of Patterson Park High School in Baltimore did not hesitate to answer President Johnson's call; Owens joined the army at age seventeen "because," his mother said proudly after his death, "he wanted to serve his country." But Maryland parents and taxpayers had sacrificed for a great many other young people who apparently had turned against their elders, the "establishment" that had done so much for them, the values of sobriety, hard work, and "dressing right." Many adults agreed with the woman who wrote the *Evening Sun* to complain that she was "fed up with sign-carrying flower children, love-ins, campus riots and other wacky phenomena." Not since the Civil War had Marylanders divided with such emotion and conviction. When anti-war activists burned their draft cards, American Legionnaires called them traitors. When "dovish" faculty members at Maryland colleges conducted teach-ins to examine the official version of Vietnamese history and politics, "hawkish" Marylanders called for enforcement of the loyalty-test law of 1949—until, in the fall of 1967, the Supreme Court struck it down as unconstitutionally vague. On 21 October, when buses departed Baltimore for the Washington peace march, they left from War Memorial Plaza. Already ironic enough, the chosen rendezvous happened also that morning to be the site of a naval reserve awards ceremony. The scene produced a portrait of conflict on the war question. One of the boarding protesters, a student at St. Mary's Catholic Seminary, replied to the question of what made one go by saying "Something inside you—war is wrong. This is a way of expressing yourself." A veteran who was there for the navy muster looked at the antiwar people with their "HELL NO WE WON'T GO" placards and said "I'd shoot every one of the damn idiots."[9]

⁓≈⁓

In 1968, as division deepened, many a nightmare became reality. In late March–early April students at Bowie State College occupied the administration building to protest the rundown condition of classroom and dormitory space. When the college president, Samuel L. Myers, notified Agnew that the unrest made it impossible to hold classes, the governor sent state police to the Prince George's campus to clear the building. On Thursday, 4 April, a cadre of Bowie militants sat down in the State House demanding to talk with Agnew. Refusing to deal, he ordered the students arrested if they did not leave and then suddenly decided to close the college—packing the students off to home or jail, depending on their response. The superintendent of state police, Robert J. Lally, was driving to Bowie that afternoon when he heard on the radio that the Reverend Martin Luther King, Jr., had been assassinated. The civil rights leader had many faithful admirers in Maryland. Four years earlier, not long after King accepted the Nobel Peace Prize, Baltimore blacks and whites had given him a hero's welcome as he toured the state for President Johnson. He had addressed a meeting of the Southern Christian Leadership Conference at the new Civic Center in 1965, when Mayor McKeldin made him an honorary citizen of the city. In late March 1968, scheduled again to appear in Baltimore, King instead had gone to support striking black sanitation workers in Memphis. Eminently tolerant and moderate, King spoke for peaceful, constitutional change toward racial fairness. News of his murder set off rampages in the ghettos of Chicago, Detroit, Los Angeles, and elsewhere.

Black leaders in Baltimore were stunned. The Reverend Marion C. Bascom, a member of the city Board of Fire Commissioners, could only express "the shock that everybody else feels over the untimely loss of America's best friend." On Friday morning, though a reporter thought the city ominously quiet, people went to work, left for school, and did their shopping. Black leaders spoke of calling a work stoppage on Monday, the day of King's funeral. Mayor Thomas A. D'Alesandro III, son of "Big Tommy," was unusually sensitive to black demands and had been elected with black support the preceding November. "Young Tommy" ordered flags in the city lowered to half-mast "as a mark of our mourning and respect." At noon on Saturday about three hundred blacks met on Pennsylvania Avenue for a memorial service that broke up two hours later. Police saw no sign of the trouble that still rocked other cities.[10]

Nonetheless the black neighborhoods of Baltimore ignited that evening, and they burned for two days. Helmeted police first answered calls in East Baltimore, on North Gay Street, where gangs of youths, smashing into stores, met them with stones and bottles. Soon fire alarms sounded farther north on Gay, eventually spreading to North Avenue and beyond. Looters grabbed for all the furniture, clothing, and appliances that television ads placed in the typical American home. They tore steel gratings off the fronts of ghetto liquor stores and shattered the windows of food markets. Teen-agers often did the work of gaining entry. Police noted that adults followed not far behind. Except for the sirens, noise of breaking glass, and an occasional gunshot, a "carnival atmosphere" prevailed in the clerkless shops. With eleven hundred policemen battling rioters in East Baltimore, the disturbance spread to the west. At 10:00 P.M., already having declared a state of emergency, Agnew sent state police and fifty-five hundred National Guardsmen into Baltimore, banned the sale of liquor, gasoline, and firearms, and placed the city under curfew until daylight. On Palm Sunday morning "sunlight crackled" on broken glass in the streets, and by early afternoon witnesses described crowds as "larger and in uglier moods" than on Saturday night. Guardsmen, carrying ammunition but with rifles unloaded, had orders to fire only at snipers. Storeowners complained that people carried off goods with impunity. Police filled jails with the looters and curfew breakers whom they could catch and then herded more into the Civic Center. At about 6:00 P.M. Sunday, Agnew called for federal troops, who arrived from Fort Bragg less than five hours later. Regular soldiers patrolled Baltimore for the first time since the 1877 B&O strike.[11]

The Baltimore riots (similar outbreaks occurred in Washington) did not approach those of Chicago or Los Angeles in scale, but to natives they were just as disturbing. Two looters had been shot and killed in Baltimore; four other persons died in fires and a car crash and about seven hundred people suffered mostly minor injuries. Property losses stood at about $10 million—estimates were difficult to come by. The lawless orgy shocked many blacks as well as whites. Some inner-city families had fled to churches during the rioting; one Baltimorean described the looters as Barabbases who mocked King's memory and asked sadly "Who will deliver us Negroes from ourselves?" Traditional black leaders, braving abuse for being friends of "whitey," spent long hours walking the streets in an effort to restore order. Of the fifty-seven hundred persons detained, most were youthful and resentful, explained the *Evening Sun*, and evidently had started fires and thrown rocks "to repay the police for humiliating arrests and not-infrequent beatings" (since 1966 Baltimore had a special board to investigate cases of police brutality). Mayor D'Alesandro and General Gelston, both of whom had exercised considerable restraint, remained skeptical—they saw plan-

In April 1968 federal troops patrolled the streets of Baltimore for the first time since the B&O strike of 1877. *A. S. Abell Television Newsfilm Archives, University of Baltimore*

ning in the riots, for it seemed unlikely that such fury could have been spontaneous. White opinion called for punishing the ringleaders; by striking a match, black militants could "quite graphically change the face of the city."[12]

The riots and these fears brought Agnew to the forefront once more. The governor summoned a hundred Baltimore black leaders to the state office building on 11 April for what they thought would be a word of thanks for trying to quell the disturbance. The group included Commissioner Bascom, Juanita Jackson Mitchell and her husband, Clarence Mitchell, Jr. (both NAACP lawyers), their sons, state senator Clarence M. Mitchell III and Parren J. Mitchell, a Morgan State professor and director of the local Community Action Agency), educators, church pastors, and Lenny Moore and John Mackey of the Baltimore Colts. Even if Agnew did not completely plan what followed, the moment, the media, and his personality blended to produce strikingly effective political theater. Checked by a gauntlet of state policemen, the governor's guests jammed into an auditorium that seated only fifty. Though supposedly the meeting was to be private, reporters and television news cameras stood by. Dramatically delayed twenty minutes talking to Moore and Mackey (who declined to attend), Agnew marched into the hot and crowded chamber accompanied by three symbols of uniformed authority—General Gelston, Superintendent Lally, and Baltimore police chief

Donald Pomerleau. All three men seated themselves behind the governor in chairs unlabeled but originally intended for state leaders in health and welfare.

The address Agnew delivered in this setting, his own work, had alarmed several of his aides because it fanned the embers of black unrest and mistrust. "I did not ask you here to recount previous deprivations," he began, "nor to hear me enumerate prior attempts to correct them. I did not request your presence to bid for peace with the public dollar." He implied that black leaders in Baltimore were failures, moral cowards, hypocrites. When not accusatory, the statement sounded patronizing. Agnew challenged them finally to renounce black racists just as he (more safely) renounced white racists. By then two-thirds of his listeners had walked out. The confrontation made the national news networks, and Agnew's assistants soon reported that mail and telegrams ran overwhelmingly in the governor's favor.[13]

It should have come as little surprise that on 14 May Marylanders defeated the new constitution—snubbing, or worse, their reputed leaders. Tawes and McKeldin, Governor Agnew, Attorney General Francis Burch, Senators Brewster and Tydings, seven out of eight congressmen, Baltimore and Washington newspapers, leading lawyers, sitting judges, civic leaders in the metropolitan corridor, and many outspoken churchmen—all supported ratification. Reasons for the defeat, though complex, reduced to anger and fear. Convention members narrowly had voted against a provision (not necessary in the state constitution) safeguarding labor's right to organize and bargain collectively. A new plan for legislative districts of one senator and three delegates tinkered further with the identity of counties (the 1965 senatorial districts law already had) and endangered old pols with countywide networks of friends. Proposed changes in local officialdom reduced the size of the patronage pie, and mandatory county home rule spelled the end of county commissioners. A group called Save Our State argued that the new government would cost more and raise taxes. By making the executive branch stronger and placing judges beyond the reach of the electorate, the new constitution seemed to threaten popular rule.

Worse, the proposed document raised the specter of Black Power. Briefer residency rules would serve as an invitation to District of Columbia blacks, according to one rumor; heavily black Baltimore City, ran another one—completely false—might annex parts of Baltimore and Anne Arundel counties while engaged in the regional planning the constitution allowed. Precincts that had supported Wallace in 1964 and Mahoney in 1966 rejected the new charter by wide margins. Before the referendum, sound trucks roamed lower-income streets in and around Baltimore blaring "white power" slogans that only a few years earlier might have caused whites to blush. "In defeating the proposed constitution we have defeated ourselves," read a letter to the *Evening Sun*, "and again tarnished the image of our generation in the eyes of the up-and-coming idealistic generation of voters."[14]

Daily violence and civil disobedience forced every Marylander who could read a paper or watch TV to take a strong stand. During May blacks set up a tent city on the Washington Mall to protest hunger in America. Student rebels seized buildings at Columbia University in New York. Between 12 and 19 May 1968, 549 Americans died in Vietnam and 2,282 were wounded. On Friday of that week a group of nine activists broke into offices of the Catonsville draft board and carried out some 370 case files. In the parking lot they used homemade napalm to set fire to the records and then surrendered to police. One of them, Father Philip Berrigan, served as rector at St. Peter Claver Church in Old Northwest Baltimore and had been jailed earlier for throwing blood on draft files. He and others of the "Catonsville Nine"—who included his brother Daniel, a Jesuit priest—declared that their act aimed "to make it more difficult for men to kill one another." Outraged supporters of law and order demanded to know whether opposition to high taxes and welfare gave them the right to destroy government records. "Those who call Philip Berrigan a fanatic," his sympathizers replied, "need only to look at history to see that, in His own time, Jesus Christ was considered a fanatic." Over the weekend blacks in Salisbury rioted after a white policeman shot and killed a black fugitive suspected of burglary. He was a deaf-mute.[15]

In the darkness of protest, chaos, and name calling, Agnew's moon rose. When first on the national scene he felt most comfortable with fellow moderates like Republican governors William Scranton of Pennsylvania and Nelson Rockefeller of New York; he occasionally referred to himself as a Republican New Dealer. His firmness in Cambridge, affront to Bowie State, and later tongue-lashing of Baltimore blacks, however, gained him notoriety that he welcomed. Richard Nixon, who had spent several years preparing for the 1968 presidential race, noticed him, through Maryland Republicans Louise Gore and Charles S. Bresler. Agnew led the draft-Rockefeller movement until the New Yorker, failing to reach Agnew by telephone beforehand, held a press conference in late March announcing his firm withdrawal. Too late did Rockefeller relent and speak of accepting a draft; embarrassed, Agnew had switched his support to Nixon.

For a third time disarray among Democrats, and this time tragedy as well, guided Agnew's political fortunes. President Johnson had declined reelection in April and in June an assassin killed Robert F. Kennedy, probably the strongest Democrat in the race. Meeting in Chicago in July, Democrats split over the war while outside the convention hall, in full view of television audiences, police with billy clubs assaulted anti-war demonstrators. Nixon sensed ultimate victory on a platform touting order at home and "peace with honor" in Vietnam. Meanwhile he needed Maryland votes at the August convention in Miami Beach. He considered Agnew among others for his running mate. The others fell short or failed to balance the ticket. At the Republican convention Agnew nominated Nixon as McKeldin in 1952 had nominated Eisenhower. This time talk of a Maryland vice-presidential candidate proved reliable. "There is a quiet confidence about him," Nixon soon explained in an essay entitled "Why I Chose Ted Agnew." "In this atomic age the President is constantly facing the threat of nuclear war. Ted Agnew is the one in whom I would have confidence to face the threat." [16] In November, thanks to heavy Democratic votes in Baltimore City and Montgomery County, Maryland gave Hubert Humphrey a slim majority. The nation elected Nixon and Agnew.

⁓⁂⁓

The governor's elevation forced the General Assembly, in a rare vote, to choose a successor. Republicans favored an Eastern Shore congressman, Rogers C. B. Morton, a large, white-haired party regular of national prominence. Some Democrats spoke of Francis X. Gallagher, a Baltimore City Democrat who had supported the Kennedys and was a friend of Senator Tydings. On 7 January 1969, when Agnew formally resigned, the assembly voted in joint session. Morton received 26 ballots, Gallagher 15, and senate president James 13. Marvin Mandel won with 126 votes and within hours he was sworn into office, as the state manual phrased it, "in a befitting modest ceremony." [17]

The legislators went with one of their own, an experienced hand. Mandel moved into Government House knowing the ropes in Annapolis as well as any governor who ever served the state. He had been born in the Pimlico area of northwest Baltimore in 1920—then a direction of Jewish migration from the inner city—and as a Polish Jew had felt the scourge of Gentile and German-Jewish prejudice alike. Rather shy as a City College student, "Buddy" loved boxing and baseball, sold newspapers at the track, and learned the seedy side of life firsthand. While a law student at Maryland, he married his high school sweetheart, Barbara "Bootsie" Oberfeld, whose father owned a liquor store. After two years in the army Mandel in 1944 opened a law practice, which included clients on the Block, and got into politics, which out Reisterstown Road meant studying under Jack Pollack and city council member Samuel Friedel. A natural negotiator and maker of deals, the student shrank from electioneering; "Bootsie" did much of the talking among strangers. In 1951 a city justice of the peace (an appointive position that he owed to Freidel and D'Alesandro), Mandel won a seat on the party state central committee in Baltimore. Doubtless at Pollack and Friedel's urging, that group next named Mandel to fill an unexpired term in the House of Delegates. He never had to worry much about reelection campaigns and soon won the Ways and Means Committee chairmanship. Mandel was a lawmaker's lawmaker; he exercised caution, kept promises, and got results. Tawes's candidate for Speaker in 1963, he maneuvered the 1967 tax bill through the house. In 1968, chairing Maryland Democrats, Mandel raised money and tightened organization so effectively that observers gave him much of the credit for Humphrey's showing in the state.

Mandel's sudden governorship coincided roughly with a turn in public mind—away from extremism, toward political reform, economic self-help, and personal self-fulfillment. Mandel spent the first few months of his administration in a widely publicized tour of Maryland cities and county court houses, widening his circle of friends, listening and using a favorite cryptic phrase that went "Maybe we can work something out." He sensed the average Marylander's eagerness to put the house in order. Racial hostility did not disappear after the spring of 1968, but gradually whites and blacks seemed to take the riots as object lessons in radicalism of right and left. Black community leaders in Baltimore regrouped and planned political action. Whites largely stood clear of Mahoney-style rhetoric and proved willing to proceed "out of the dark ages." While no more willing than Agnew to bid openly for racial peace with the public dollar, Mandel made gestures to answer black complaints and bent his efforts to appear progressive. He restored twenty-two thousand people, many of them black, to the Medicaid rolls that Agnew had cut as an economy measure and appointed more blacks to state offices—though only about 4 percent overall. In 1969 the legislature chartered a Maryland Commission on Negro History and Culture and approved Mandel's proposal to strengthen the newly reorganized Human Relations Commission; afterward it had power to investigate complaints of discrimination in state agencies. New social services—a state-sponsored drug treatment program and a Maryland Housing and Community Development Authority to promote moderate and low-cost housing with state-underwritten mortgage loans—aimed to correct evils of concern to blacks. Government machinery, federal and state, ensured that gains made during the civil rights movement would not slip.

"Let there be no mistake in anyone's mind," Mandel declared in his first address to the assembly; "I shall govern." He seemed in fact to play the part of prime minister, his close ties to former colleagues and fellow Democrats starting a landslide of important legislation. State leaders returned to the issue of government organization. Piling committee on committee (imitating the tangled apparatus they studied) Agnew in 1968 had appointed Mandel and other legislators to examine the executive branch and its multitude of agencies and departments. Tawes's committee for that purpose, under John N. Curlett of the McCormick Company, already in 1967 had proposed restructuring the state bureaucracy according to "program" or function. In the spring of 1969, benefiting from the work of both committees, the assembly passed a measure creating four departments—natural resources, planning, budget and fiscal planning, and health and mental hygiene—each serving the governor just as executive departments in the federal cabinet served the president. The following year Mandel completed this reorganization plan with laws providing for departments of transportation (the first in the country to manage a trust fund not limited to highway spending), employment and social services, public safety and correctional services, personnel, licensing and regulation, economic and community development, and general services. With eleven secretaries to manage the discrete functions of state government beyond the treasury and attorney general's office, Maryland emerged as one of the first states to adopt the "cabinet system."[18]

Mandel's leadership and the character of the reapportioned assembly also produced a minor political miracle—resurrected constitutional reform. While the 1968 vote had not been especially narrow (56.4 percent opposed), reformers believed the electorate would have approved many parts of the revised document—the error had been in putting the whole constitution to a yea or nay vote. Feeling the pressure of pro-change elements around Washington, Mandel and his friends decided to pass on sections of the defeated constitution and then resubmit them to the citizenry as amendments. By this "side door" strategy several important provisions made their way into the charter. The residency requirement fell to six months, less for presidential elections. Voters approved machinery for congressional redistricting and legislative reapportionment every ten years and simplified the procedure for adopting home rule in the counties. Amendments established an office of lieutenant governor—he or she to be a running mate of the gubernatorial candidate—and an independent commission to fix legislators' salaries every four years. Voters approved a lengthened legislative term—from seventy to ninety days. The court system changed to the four-level plan that the Eney Commission had recommended. Above new district courts there were trial or circuit courts and a Court of Special Appeals that lightened the workload of the Court of Appeals. Eventually voters approved an amendment permitting governors and the senate the power to name and approve appellate judges for life tenure. Other sitting judges still periodically stood in uncontested elections. The Maryland court system embraced agencies like the Public Service and Workmen's Compensation commissions. It included 180 judges and staff members numbering about 1,500, and it served as a model for other state systems.

Laying plans for the reelection that some people thought he would decline in 1970, the governor appointed a commission to study the emotional issue of state aid to private, mostly Catholic, schools. He balanced racial fairness and sectarian sensitivity with hardheaded plans for economic growth. In 1969 he pushed for a Baltimore area metropolitan transit authority and the following session obtained another new authority—made up of the secretary of transportation, Harry Hughes, and six others—to promote Friendship Airport, which the state then leased from Baltimore City. In 1969 Mandel typically established a new state Council of Economic Advisors while sponsoring a consumer-protection bill. That year he proposed forty pieces of legislation. All of them became law, including an increase in the sales tax rate to four cents on the dollar. His budget for fiscal 1970, $1.3 billion, was the highest in state history.

Marylanders may have resented least the rising cost of environmental action. Legislators made significant efforts to police and preserve the soil, air, and waters of the state. In 1970—the year Congress created the Environmental Protection Agency—the General Assembly agreed to impose some of the strictest of state rules on strip mining, a method of coal extraction of particular importance in the shallow fields of Western Maryland. It could be highly destructive; maximizing profits in the absence of regulation, coal firms left the land torn up and bare, vulnerable to erosion, and a danger to water supplies. Building on a 1967 statute, Maryland obliged the companies to replant mined areas. A similar new law placed financial responsibility for cleaning up oil-polluted water on the offenders. The Department of Natural Resources in 1970 received new powers to prevent despoliation of Maryland wetlands (land below average high tide affected by the rise and fall of tides). In March 1971 the state announced that all fuel oil must meet its 1 percent limit on sulphur content. Maryland prohibited household incinerators, which were to disappear entirely by 1973, and placed limits on industrial by-product burning rates (one ton per hour) and "particulate emissions" (.03 grains per cubic foot). The state assumed responsibility for the treatment of all liquid waste water. Maryland was one of the first states to require, as opposed to encourage, sediment control at the county level.

This new agenda owed a large debt to home-grown scientific awareness; besides federal grants-in-aid, Maryland's own interesting programs attracted bright and ambitious students to environmental science. In 1968 the engineering department at College Park launched a new training course in air quality. Among the first in the country, it prepared students for work as air pollution inspectors and clean-air specialists for industry. L. Eugene Cronin directed the university's Institute of Natural Resources at Solomons Island, where in 1925 Reginald V. Truitt had opened the first state supported marine laboratory in the eastern United States. In 1969 it offered summer courses in invertebrate zoology, ichthyology (fishes), and hydrobiology. Cronin reported that jobs for trained estuarine scientists ran ahead of graduates by about one hundred a year. Hopkins professor Donald W. Pritchard served as head of the Chesapeake Bay Institute at Annapolis. Aboard a new twin-hulled research vessel named for H. Ridgely Warfield, one of William Brooks's successors in Hopkins marine research, scientists collected water samples to study "primary productivity," during which microscopic plant life or phytoplankton converted inorganic to organic material, and the base of the food chain, where microscopic zooplankton consumed phytoplankton. Work on temperature layers and circulation showed how fresh Susquehanna water flowed down the bay on the surface while, beneath, salty tidal water moved up.[19]

Attention to the Chesapeake ecosystem made the issue of nuclear power all the more salient. In the late 1960s Baltimore Gas and Electric proposed building an atomic generating plant on the white cliffs overlooking the bay in Calvert County. Marylanders quickly joined in a national debate of far-reaching importance—touching on long-term environmental safety and speaking to the industrialized world's demand for cheap and plentiful energy. Experts estimated that electrical needs in the Baltimore region would increase eight times between 1970 and the year 2000. Supporters of nuclear energy downplayed its estimated cost of $550 million; they pointed out its advantage of being a safe and reliable power source, one that did not put harmful ash into the air; critics argued that the cliffs provided a shaky foundation for the reactor, whose hot discharge water, emptied into the bay, would adversely affect (some said contaminate) fish and shellfish. Before any public hearings the utility company, with permission from federal atomic-energy authorities, began construction. Under heavy pressure, Mandel in July 1969 appointed a task force to examine the issue and decide whether "the special characteristics" of nuclear power plants posed a hazard to the "health, safety, or economy" of Maryland and thereby called for state action. William W. Eaton, a nuclear physicist and private consultant, chaired the group, which in December approved the Calvert Cliffs project but reproved the company and federal government for starting before the state could pass on its environmental impact. Traditionally reliant on studies of independent commissions, Maryland pioneered with the Eaton report—no other state thus had examined the implications of nuclear power. Soon the assembly enacted a standard-setting law requiring state approval of any future utility plant sites.[20]

Findings on issues like nuclear power, river pollution (an alarming Patuxent basin report appeared in 1968), and the biology of the bay—like the technology that successfully placed Americans on the moon in the summer of 1969—went far beyond the average person's comprehension. Scientific advances could leave one feeling dwarfed. Yet that feeling was a step toward wisdom: the astronauts' stunning photographs of the earth from space helped to place the home of life—the world that Rachel Carson's book had described as vulnerable—in wondrous perspective. Practiced in building various kinds of bridges, Marylanders wisely sought ways to make important research, the discovery that brought insight, broadly accessible. In one example, Mrs. Russell Wiltbank of Prince George's County, the first woman to serve on a Maryland county soil conservation board, began a program of talks at schools and PTA meetings. She found suburbanites perfectly willing to help on conservation projects, she said, once they were made aware "of what the problem is." As if responding to her remark that government far too zealously guarded technical knowledge, Maryland in the fall of 1968 converted an official newsletter on conservation, first published in 1923, into an attractive quarterly, *Maryland Magazine*, in which colorful photo-essays told (among other things) of scientific studies and championed the state's waters, farmland, and woodland. One typical piece spoke of the teeming and majestic Chesapeake—"Only the human animal," it noted, "threatens to disturb this successful and fecund lushness of life." Maryland Public Television, at

Constructing Calvert Cliffs, July 1969. Debates over the safety and environmental impact of nuclear power plants proved important in mobilizing citizens and shaping state policy at the end of the 1960s. *Baltimore Gas and Electric Company*

first limited to the Baltimore region but with transmitters planned for Western Maryland and the Eastern Shore, began broadcasting early in 1969; the network had immense power to inform, and one of its most successful early programs, "Hodge-Podge Lodge," undertook the environmental education of youngsters with imagination and intelligence. Meantime Cronin, mindful of the elitism ordinary people might associate with ecological awareness, welcomed public school teachers at the Solomons laboratory for courses in general marine biology.

"Public concern for the immense economic, environmental, and social values inherent in the Chesapeake Bay" prompted Mandel in 1969 to establish a Chesapeake Bay Interagency Planning Committee. Including Cronin and Pritchard, the committee soon commissioned a "comprehensive inventory of the present and anticipated problems plaguing the Bay."[21]

Pro-conservation though published by the Department of Economic and Community Development, *Maryland* reflected well the dual concerns of business and public leaders in 1970. Officials like Harry Hughes in transportation (he oversaw the Maryland Port Authority), James Bennett Coulter in natural resources, and Edmond F. Rovner in economic and community development tried to prepare for growth that blended with, rather than ravaged, state lands and waters. Nonetheless, growth was the object in view; "without a healthy economy," Coulter later remarked, "there can be no consideration of the environmental things that are held noble." Authorities in Annapolis cheered plans for an aluminum factory on rezoned land in southern Frederick County, near Buckeystown. Costing $190 million to build, it eventually would employ one thousand persons; in late 1969, before it was finished, construction workers already had boosted local bank deposits and retail sales by 16 percent. At the same time, General Electric announced plans to build a large appliance plant at Columbia. Still growing, the planned community had an outdoor amphitheater, a flourishing commercial center, and a lake that mirrored the city's relative order and harmony. One in ten houses sold for monthly payments below $120, and whites lived peacefully with the blacks who were 13 percent of the residents. Rouse had intended the attractiveness of Columbia to lure both people and industry; the GE plant, with its ten thousand or more jobs, greatly strengthened the town's economic base—which earlier had been worrisome. State officials announced that the Calvert Cliffs, Columbia, and Buckeystown projects contributed $200 million to the state economy.[22]

Continuing attention fell to the Appalachian counties of Garrett, Allegany, and Washington. Some new industry had arrived there in the 1960s. In 1961 a ladies' apparel company opened a plant in Cumberland, where six years before, Pittsburgh Plate Glass had raised employment by 1,153 workers. Mack Truck's move to Hagerstown in 1961 had boosted the economy by 3,600 jobs, and not long afterward Londontown, the Baltimore rainwear manufacturer, opened satellite factories in Hancock, Halfway, and Boonsboro. In 1968 an Appalachian Maryland Development Plan emphasized the need for more state and federal spending to plant the seeds of further economic growth in the area. By 1970 a variety of vocational and technical training programs, funded heavily with federal money, aimed to groom the labor force, stem the flow of departing young people, and draw new industry to the region. Garrett County built two vo-tech centers, one at Oakland and another at Accident. On land the Celanese Corporation donated, Allegany County in 1970 opened a school at Cresaptown. Not long afterward Washington County replaced a facility at the junior college with a new, 22-shop technical school. These centers trained high school students and adults in fields like mechanics, horticulture, electronics, printing, nursing, and secretarial skills. Meantime a strengthened state advisory council on vocational-technical education oversaw an uncommon program that supplied worker training "just about overnight" when necessary to keep or attract employers. In 1971 a New York optical firm opened a plant in Oakland after Maryland, with federal money, turned out sixty-eight new local lens grinders. Western Marylanders looked forward expectantly to completion of a long-planned

Maryland made new efforts in the early 1970s to deal with persistent poverty in western counties. *U.S. Department of Housing and Urban Development/James E. DiLisio*

interstate highway west of Hancock, a link with Ohio that might bring prosperity as had the National Road during the Monroe administration.[23]

From clammers to contractors, Marylanders on the Eastern Shore gladly put the 1967–68 unpleasantness behind them. New technology and more visitors brought new hope of rewards. Watermen benefited from two developments. In the early sixties an enterprising Shoreman, Fletcher Hanks, had invented a machine he called the "clammer whammer"—a device that hung over the side of a boat and used high-pressure water jets and a conveyor belt to make clam digging easy and highly profitable. In keeping with the new rigor in natural resources conservation, the assembly placed a limit on each power clammer of 40 bushels a day. In November 1966 Maryland had modified the age-old regulation against power dredging for oysters, setting aside Mondays and Tuesdays as "push days" when motorized "push boats" could drive the skipjacks over the beds. The law limited catches to 150 bushels a day, however, at a time when, under sail on an especially good day, a skipjack had been able to take 300 bushels (which at the dock sold for about $3 each). The value of caught Maryland seafood in 1970 reached an all-time high of $17 million—20 percent of the national total.

With the help of two agencies, economic health found its way to many places on the Shore. In the late 1960s the Wye Institute of Talbot County—a private endowment that Arthur Amory Houghton, Jr., and Clarence Miles had established to promote Eastern Shore development—advised small towns how to survive when new highways re-routed traffic and took away income: they should turn to their old waterfronts. Planners at the institute aided leaders in Pocomoke City with a study that revealed lack of housing as a prime cause for the town's sluggish economic growth. Pocomoke City adopted a city manager form of government and a master plan that included a marina to serve as a winter haven for sportsmen. The state economic development department, which in 1967 brought a brush company to Crisfield to ease its off-season unemployment rate, also helped Cambridge, where a committee of local activists overcame "a full quota of skeptics." They landed a printing factory by driving overnight to the company's headquarters in upstate New York in time for a crucial vote. "Anybody who wants us that badly," said a stunned executive, "deserves to get us." The Maryland Port Authority with federal aid dredged and widened the Cambridge channel and improved the port. By 1972 residents had sold $2.8 million in municipal bonds, built two hundred units of new public housing and a new hospital, and established two industrial parks. Such changes in leadership and attitude included making peace with racial integration and recalled the *Harper's* report, following the Civil War, that young people on the Shore had awakened to a changed world. The venturesome businessmen who spearheaded recovery in Cambridge felt confident enough to advise Federalsburg, in Caroline County, how to do it. Federalsburg established its own industrial park and hoped to obtain two hundred new jobs.[24]

At Ocean City boosters measured new jobs in the thousands, for two or three million vacationers thronged to the resort in the summer months, the number of off-season visitors climbed steadily, and twelve-month residents approached fifteen hundred. In the late sixties investors discovered an apparently bottomless market for oceanfront condominiums. Purchased rather than rented, they partially slaked the thirst for luxury among the Baltimore-Washington affluent and gave buyers a helpful income-tax deduction. The construction of "condos" proceeded full speed; "Fort Lauderdale, here we come" proclaimed one local leader. State highway authorities finished a new bridge across Assawoman Bay at 62d Street. There, in 1970, developers completed a four-million-dollar convention hall. Over the winter months its director booked big bands of the swing era to attract the "condominium crowd." At 62d Street John Whaley in 1971 built the city's first high-rise condo—a mere six-story building he named Calypso. The next year High Point, at twelve stories the tallest structure on the Shore, sold 104 apartments in only three months. Building investment in 1972 reached $60 million, 80 percent of it in condominiums.

Along the "Gold Coast" north of the new bridge, corporate interests from

Evidence of a broadly based vacation economy: mobile homes at Montego Bay, Ocean City, c. 1970. *U.S. Geological Survey*

as far away as California obtained regrettable zoning decisions. "There's no law east of the Sinepuxent," commented a Salisbury lawyer at the time. City fathers permitted developers to destroy a protective sand dune army engineers had built up after a 1962 hurricane (it blocked the view) and in places violated a state set-back rule that forbade construction too close to the beach. They ignored the rising level of Atlantic waters and the natural westward migration of the barrier island itself. Oceanographers noted that, by preventing natural shifting of the sand, unthinking Gold Coast development steepened beaches and hastened their erosion.[25]

Maryland continued to register its soundest economic gains along the Harford-to-Montgomery/Prince George's axis, where government employment, research and development firms, and new electronic technology flourished. A few Marylanders first had seen a computer in 1949, when the army installed one of the huge, humming devices at Aberdeen Proving Ground, and in the 1950s the B&O had employed newer models to handle payroll records. During the sixties federal spending on space exploration brought about swift advances in micro-electronics generally. Every breakthrough in technology promised a geometric rise in its application and provided incentive for yet faster development. The number of computers in Maryland climbed from about a hundred in 1959 to a thousand ten years later, when one of the largest served the new Social Security Administration offices in western Baltimore City. Sophisticated calculators and their data banks became primary tools in the research and development that government and business alike demanded. From the beginning Maryland claimed a share of this action. Government research centers in Maryland numbered about thirty in 1967, and the state stood third among recipients of federal research money. Professional seekers of industry in Annapolis worked hard to get more of it by attracting the private firms that secured the contracts. The state boasted of its superior universities, transportation networks, power supplies, and natural appeal. "We who live here are able to savor a little of some pleasure every day," read a Maryland brochure, "—not just on weekends." Besides being revenue producers, R&D firms had the attraction of being smokeless industries.[26]

Torn by the war and worn out by the riots, Baltimoreans paused to ask whether urban renewal brought renewed urban life. Many of them had begun to harbor doubts, even before the jolts of April 1968. Buildings of value already had fallen. The President Street Station, where Lincoln arrived in the dead of night and Massachusetts troops assembled before their dangerous trip to the B&O station, almost burned down while awaiting destruction for a proposed cross-town expressway. Inner-city highways threatened antebellum houses on Eutaw Street and the old Richmond Market on Howard. Waterloo Row, Mills's famous group of 1815 townhouses on North Calvert Street, came down for a proposed office building. Halsted of the original Hopkins medical faculty had lived in a house at Dolphin and Eutaw; it fell when the city widened Dolphin Street. "Modernization of a great city brings its rewards," the *Sunday Sun* had observed in the fall of 1965, when the Royal Theater fell, "but also leaves its losses, some of them incalculable until long afterward." Two years later Baltimoreans divided over the fate of the horse-drawn fruit and vegetable vendors, the "A-rabs" who scavenged at the wholesale market and then, singing, fanned out through the city to undersell the supermarkets. A new ordinance banned stables within three hundred feet of a residence and rebuilding soon claimed the wholesale market the hucksters depended on as a source. Phoebe H. Stanton, a Hopkins professor of art and architecture, had taken up the standard of an earlier Baltimore preservationist, Mrs. Sumner Parker. In the spring of 1968 Stanton warned that Baltimore paid too little attention to its urban heritage. "What can be done," she asked, "to retain something of the character which has grown organically as the city developed?"[27]

Just as state officials tried to weigh environmental concerns in the scales with economic growth, city leaders had to put ghetto jobs and housing ahead of urban character. Federal "affirmative action" policies helped to open up jobs for blacks—firms applying for government contracts had to demonstrate not only equal opportunity but positive efforts to hire minority workers. Businessmen also acted on their own. The Baltimore Urban Coalition, part of a national group that Rouse had helped to establish, formed a few months before the riots and met only for the second time immediately after them. Adopting the slogan "Give a Damn," it emphasized private help and community participation, aiming to unite local business, churches, civic groups, and all levels of government in the task of building black employment and financing black housing. Boucher had involved the GBC in the Baltimore chapter from its beginning. Though financed by businessmen and United Fund "Project Urban Self Help" funds, the coalition fell apart, a victim of post-riot uneasiness. Later G. Cheston Carey, Jr., Charles G. Hutzler III, Walter Sondheim, Jr., and other Baltimoreans formed a chapter of the Council for Equal Business Opportunity. Partly with federal Small Business Administration backing, the CEBO provided capital for a growing number of black businesses all over the state but primarily in Baltimore, where they ran to more than two thousand. "We've come a long way," admitted one banker in the early 1970s. "In the past two years we have become much more aware of overall needs." A "late starter," said another lender, Baltimore was "running like hell to catch up with other cities in its minority assistance programs."[28]

The work of rebuilding the downtown center went on, perhaps more deliberately after the April 1968 riots. For many years Baltimoreans had discussed what to do with Samuel Smith Park and the single pier that a Maryland Port Authority excursion boat, *Port Welcome*, still used. At pier 4 the frigate *Constellation*, brought to the city in 1955, lay needful of extensive repair, its very authenticity the subject of lively debate in the newspapers (some experts claimed that the frigate had been so completely rebuilt in the 1850s that it ought to be scrapped). In 1964 voters had turned down a bond issue of $260 million for an inner harbor complex that GBC designers had proposed. Besides a tree-lined avenue connecting City Hall to the harbor, the plan included a new municipal center, a Maryland Port Authority building, a structure for the Maryland Academy of Sciences, a marina, promenades, new shops, and an "aquarama." Despite this setback, J. Jefferson Miller of the Charles Center project agreed the following year to add development of the inner harbor to his duties. Using the Charles Center strategy, Mayor McKeldin (making, he said privately, his last pitch for lasting fame) and the city council declared the entire inner harbor an urban renewal area and condemned the properties that remained. In this case the city obtained federal funds to underwrite purchase and construction costs. Miller's Charles Center–Inner Harbor Management team achieved its first goal in September 1969, when the younger Mayor D'Alesandro, complimenting Baltimoreans on the strides they had made since the riots, installed the *Constellation* at its permanent berth at pier 1. Soon construction began on a massive inner harbor tower for U.S. Fidelity and Guaranty and, on South Charles Street, a Lutheran Medical Center.

New policies and refurbished democracy appeared in the Baltimore Urban Renewal and Housing Authority after 1968, when Robert C. Embry, Jr., took over as director. Earlier the city had seen the folly of building new high-rise dwellings for families and begun to use them only for the elderly, among whom they remained popular and serviceable. Embry, a Baltimore native and Harvard-trained lawyer, made several more changes. In the mid-sixties he had worked as a CPHA volunteer, an interlude that provided him, he said, "the best education that I received in urban and neighborhood problems." The energetic Frances Morton Froelicher (she had married Hans Froelicher) led the CPHA at the time; her example, practical experience, and maybe youthful doubts about the status quo produced Embry's approach to public housing. He established a citywide residents' advisory board, put a halt to demolition and clearance projects, and told residents that "major changes in the housing, recreation, transportation, education, and every other aspect of the community" would soon take place. This method proved immensely rewarding in human terms. "The city asked us to take part in the planning," recalled Lucille Gorham, later a leader of Citizens for Fair Housing. "Frankly, this was a new experience both for the city and for us." [29]

Embry and two assistants, Hope D. Quackenbush and Sandy Hillman, recognized that their work in housing would more likely succeed if the people they served felt fully a part of the program. They came up with the idea of a "city fair"—a means of celebrating and building pride in Baltimore's neighborhoods. At first they found little support. The mayor and other officials worried about putting blacks and whites together so soon after the riots; some people imagined glass breaking. Finally the workaday president of the city council, William Donald Schaefer, endorsed the fair, and Embry's staff obtained money from the GBC and retail merchants to hold a dinner for fifty neighborhood leaders. There Quackenbush encountered more misgivings and quibbles until at last an elderly black woman stood up and carried the motion. "This is a wonderful idea," she declared. "What we've got to do is to show our love for one another." [30]

In that spirit (and despite the springtime unrest that followed Nixon's order to invade Cambodia) Baltimoreans over the weekend of 25–27 September 1970 held their first fair. It began Friday with two thousand balloons and a "parade of neighborhoods" that led to Charles Center, where there were neighborhood exhibits, dancing, and bunting. Fells Point, Hollins Park, South Baltimore, and Govans portrayed their histories. Union Square noted its connection to Mencken. Fashionable Bolton Hill rubbed shoulders with the bootstrap South East Community Association. East Baltimore–Gay Street boasted of its recovery from the riots. Charles Village and Greater Homewood noted their distinctive charms. Blacks sold soul food; Greeks, Poles, Lithuanians, and Italians served favorite homemade dishes. A free "trolley" carried visitors to the German beer garden down at pier 1. Though organizers worried whether Baltimoreans would attend the fair, about three hundred thousand of them went and loved it. Merriment evidently did wonders for stretched nerves. On Sunday a sudden rainstorm damaged some of

Despite recent unrest, the first Baltimore City Fair in September 1970 successfully brought together many thousands of people. *Baltimore Sunpapers*

the exhibits. Early visitors and people at nearby booths pitched in to make quick repairs.

The fair proved a success because both mood and structure had changed for the better. In November Baltimore elected its first black state's attorney, Milton Allen, and the first black congressman from Maryland, the former poverty activist, Parren Mitchell. Next year Baltimoreans chose William Donald Schaefer to be their mayor.

Grainy politics in Maryland had deep roots. Proprietary government in the colonial period had made private patronage and public trust one and the same. In the late eighteenth and early nineteenth centuries, commercial opportunity had placed a premium on enterprise that Samuel Chase represented darkly and Samuel Smith more happily. After the Civil War the strength of state Democrats invited them to cut corners—making railroad, street repaving, and senatorial-election deals the way Orioles third baseman John McGraw ran the base paths.

Curious practices continued after the Gorman-Rasin-Rayner days. During the Crothers administration the Pennsylvania Railroad avoided demolition costs by literally giving away an obsolete Susquehanna River bridge to a consortium that coincidentally included the reform governor's brother and six other politicians. The new owners broke no laws and may have taken some risk, but not much. They spent $700 to cover the span so cars and trucks could use it, collected $370,000 in profits from tolls over the next thirteen years, and then sold it to the state for $585,000. Local people referred to it as the "golden bridge." Ritchie won his first gubernatorial election by a margin so thin as to arouse curiosity, directed the Conowingo Dam contract toward the Arundel Corporation, and in 1932 warned selected firms of his plans for a state bank holiday. "Let Republicans have the two-party system," the elder D'Alesandro remarked in the 1950s, "give the Democrats the jobs." Though earning modest (indeed woefully inadequate) public salaries, O'Conor and McKeldin lived their late years in exclusive Baltimore neighborhoods. Tawes, himself upright and churchgoing, had in the beer lobbyist George H. Hocker a lieutenant who made a science of the testimonial dinner. As small tokens of their esteem, contractors, insurance men, and job seekers honored the governor by buying tickets for whole tables. In 1958 Hocker, Tawes's son, and friends in Democratic circles went further in establishing the Tidewater Insurance Company—a variation on Mayor Jackson's public-private insurance arrangements in Baltimore in the 1920s. Needing performance bonds (a financial guarantee that the work will get done properly) to obtain state contracts, one found it advisable to go through Tidewater. All the while Mandel's predecessor as House of Delegates Speaker, A. Gordon Boone, developed close relationships with some savings and loan companies. In the State House legislators since the nineteenth century had used the term "bell-ringer" for a measure painful to moneyed interests, dropped at a certain price. In Baltimore City, "walk-around money" in the 1970s remained a political fact of life.[31]

State's attorneys typically looked upon these things as men of the world and as political hopefuls; in any event they lacked the resources necessary for long and complicated investigations. State attorneys general, also wrapped in political tape, had limited authority under the constitution. Thus the independent and ambitious Joseph Tydings set an important precedent in the early sixties—employing federal tools to uncover state vice. Some local leaders and constitutionalists resented this initiative; vice in Maryland, said Vernon Eney, was the business of the state alone to police. When the federal court sent Boone to jail, lusty members of the House of Delegates cheered him on his way out of the chamber (the feds who took him down were like a pack of wolves; he kept the code of silence). Pushing on, Tydings and his assistants prosecuted two congressmen, one a Marylander, Thomas F. Johnson, for mail fraud.

Tydings's successor as federal attorney, Stephen H. Sachs, kept the office active. He pursued, doggedly, the Baltimore contractor Victor Frenkil, a self-made fellow who delighted in giving away new dollar bills after he had folded them into the shapes of birds and letters of the alphabet, and who did favors for Democrats and Republicans alike. After constructing the underground garage at the Rayburn House Office Building on Capitol Hill, Frenkil's company claimed some $5 million in cost overruns. In June 1970, as a special federal grand jury in Baltimore pondered whether Frenkil and others should stand trial for improperly pressing that claim, Attorney General John Mitchell ordered the case dropped for lack of evidence. In an unusual display of independence—defying the Justice Department—the jury with Sachs's approval handed Judge Roszel C. Thomsen a sealed report on the Frenkil investigation and demanded action on it (Frenkil never was indicted on the charges). Sachs and his staff also examined a suspicious connection between Tydings's senior colleague, Senator Brewster—a member of the Postal Affairs and Civil Service Committee—and lobbyists for a Chicago mail-order house. Brewster had held great promise; a decorated Marine veteran who had inspired youngsters at Boys' State, he had disappointed his friends, lost his reelection bid in 1968, and taken to serious drink. In November 1972 a federal jury took seven hours to find him guilty of taking $14,500 in "illegal gratuities" in early 1967, when his committee voted on a proposed increase in bulk-mail rates.

Brewster's conviction came a few days after a memorable election that ultimately led to findings of far worse corruption. In the early 1970s Maryland voters divided sharply by locality on key issues like the Vietnam war and busing, the latest federal initiative to achieve racial balance in public schools. The state had two Republican senators, but they split on the war and the best means to racial equality. Charles McC. "Mac" Mathias, the Frederick lawyer and longtime congressman who had defeated Brewster, cast pro-busing votes and criticized the Nixon policy of "Vietnamization." J. Glenn Beall, Jr.—who with the help of President Nixon, the National Rifle Association, and regular Democrats had defeated Tydings in 1970—took opposite stands. Results from recently redrawn congressional districts further proved voter division in the state while also, in Mitchell's defeat of Sam Friedel in west Baltimore, demonstrating the new political power of blacks. Veteran Democrat Clarence Long, Jr., who campaigned from a house trailer, won reelection in a Baltimore County district. So did three relative newcomers: besides Mitchell, they were Paul S. Sarbanes, a Salisbury-born Rhodes Scholar and Harvard law graduate who had won a close primary for another Baltimore seat in 1970, and Frederick's Goodloe E. Byron—son of the FDR-era congressman from Williamsport, William Devereux Byron, and his successor in office, Katherine Edgar Byron. The younger Byron had chaired a commission to study Maryland zoning law in 1967–69 and in 1970 won the Western Maryland seat for the Democrats.

Republicans did well in 1972. Lawrence J. Hogan, a former FBI agent, gained reelection in a Prince George's district. William O. Mills, representing the Eastern Shore, Southern Maryland, and Harford County (Nixon had named the district's previous congressman, Rogers Morton, interior secretary in January 1971), won a full term. Gilbert Gude, educated at Cornell and George Washington universities, easily won another term in a Montgomery-Howard district. In a new district made up mostly of Anne Arundel County, Marjorie S. Holt, longtime county clerk, won after Democrats divided in the primary. These representatives underscored the range of Maryland opinion. Long strongly supported American war policies until the 1970 Cambodian invasion, then became highly critical of them. Byron, Hogan (an active busing foe), Mills, and Holt took unequivocal stands in favor of the war. Sarbanes and Gude voiced various doubts. Mitchell declared himself a pacifist. Holt's victory made the Maryland delegation, divided on important issues, half-Republican and half-Democratic.

The presidential race, having a bizarre quality, offered a less reliable index of Maryland political sentiment. During the May primary season, when Hubert Humphrey, George McGovern, and George Wallace all had vied for voters' attention, a Wisconsin man had shot Wallace as he campaigned at a Laurel shopping center. Though the Holy Cross Hospital staff in Silver Spring succeeded in saving his life, the shooting left Wallace crippled and rekindled disturbing memories of earlier assassinations. Mandel, who with Burch and Goldstein easily had won reelection in 1970, called the Wallace shooting "a horrible tragedy."[32] The near-assassination did not bring Democrats together. Delegates to their national convention, chosen according to a rigorous quota system, nominated McGovern, whose first choice for a running mate left the ticket after revelations of possible unfitness. McGovern then selected R. Sargent Shriver, a Rockville-Bethesda landowner and descendant of the Union Mills family who had married into the Kennedy clan. He had served as first director of the Peace Corps, head of the war on poverty, and ambassador to France. Marylanders finally had to choose between McGovern, whose hopes for peace represented only one side of his party and struck many Americans as too wishful, and an incumbent who still propped up a shabby if noncommunist regime in South Vietnam. After some deliberation, Nixon had decided against dropping his vice-president for someone else. Agnew had differed with Nixon on welfare reform and restoring ties to mainland China; he had committed gaffes, one of them on the Senate floor before an important vote.

He did have his own popular following, however. Indeed, after joking early on that his name was not a "household word," Agnew had gone on to become the most abrasive, polarizing vice-president in American history. He bloomed with the anti-war movement, as its unsparing enemy. In the fall of 1969, when peace marchers twice descended on Washington, he went to New Orleans to deliver a speech that he had rewritten to suit himself. Like an earlier address in Columbus, Ohio, it described as "effete" anyone who let young radicals push him around; he lit into the "effete corps of impudent snobs" who coddle college radicals and "think of themselves as intellectuals." Nixon needed someone to say bluntly what the president was thinking. Soon after the widely publicized New Orleans appearance, Nixon's speechwriters gave Agnew another text (politically he thought it suicidal) to deliver before a partisan gathering in Iowa. This speech attacked the media as insidiously "biased" against Nixon—owned and operated by a self-elected elite who did nothing more than give "instant analysis and querulous criticism." Newspapers and television people but also the American public divided over Agnew's attacks. The vice-president glowed in the publicity; a Gallup poll of early 1970 placed him behind only Nixon and the evangelist Billy Graham among the world's "most admired men." In the 1970 and 1972 elections Agnew continued throwing punches, his language copying vintage McKeldin in its studied alliteration. In 1952 McKeldin had spoken of the Truman Democrats as "plundering potentates of the Potomac" and "pusillanimous parasites." Agnew, another self-taught speechifier, won fame for calling anti-war university people "nattering nabobs of negativism."[33] Whatever the aesthetics or personal sources of his message, it resonated with the gut feelings of many unprivileged and patriotic white Americans. In Maryland Nixon-Agnew defeated the limping McGovern 829,305 to 505,781.

The federal prosecutor's office conducted itself with avowed nonpartisanship. Nonetheless George Beall, younger brother of Republican Senator Beall and Sachs's replacement in 1970, may have been pleased that so many tempting Democratic targets lay within his reach. Early in Beall's term one of his assistants, Barnet "Barncy" Skolnik, a Harvard-trained New Yorker with a special calling for cross-examination, successfully prosecuted a prominent Prince George's County Democrat and former commissioner, Jesse S. Baggett, for illegal arrangements with local contractor Ralph Rocks. Skolnik obtained the convictions with circumstantial evidence: a clear pattern of decisions made and favors received; as in the Brewster case, no written agreement or taped conversation between Baggett and Rocks provided a "smoking gun" to prove that Baggett took Rocks's bribe in exchange for a vote.

Prosecutors did not always rely on indirect evidence. Late in 1972 Skolnik (himself a Muskie Democrat) led an investigative team that included two young Maryland natives—Russell T. Baker, Jr., and Ronald S. Liebman—on a search into the politics of public works in Baltimore County. This overdue inquiry hit a seam of pure, coal-black corruption. Beginning with Towson rumors, the investigators moved ahead quickly the following spring when informants seeking immunity (later clemency) agreed to testify against big-ger subjects. Engineers, architects, and consultants came clean. Federal of-ficers hauled off subpoenaed account books by the truckload. One set of rec-ords told of "bonuses" to employees who said they then turned the money over to company executives who described having to pay cash bribes and kickbacks to get and keep county business. Paul Gaudreau said he paid kick-backs to William E. Fornoff, chief aide to the Democratic Baltimore County executive, Dale Anderson. Fingers pointed to the state's largest engineer-ing firm—a product of the booming fifties and sixties—Matz, Childs, and Associates. Informants implicated Jerome B. Wolff in the kickback scheme. Wolff later said his blood froze when Skolnik told him "I got Congressman Johnson, and I'll get you." Agnew's longtime friend, Wolff until 1970 had served as the vice-president's science and technology advisor.[34]

To this point Agnew had kept just a step ahead of embarrassing scrutiny. During his campaign for governor the Sunpapers and *New York Times* had run brief stories that touched on his connection with Al Shuger—the 1962 cam-paign financier who had helped Agnew for a reason. Shuger then needed rezoning of some land he had bought cheaply with ideas for a high-rise apartment building. In 1966 reports circulated that Agnew as the new county executive had pressed for a prompt decision in the Shuger case. No one then pursued these leads. In fact, county employees under Agnew had widened the street in front of Shuger's property, overriding planners' objections and helping Shuger's firm to profits of $378,000. Joseph Albright, a Washington reporter, explored the Agnew-Shuger friendship in a book published in time for the 1972 campaign. He also studied the benefits shared by Agnew and J. Walter Jones, Agnew's old friend from Loch Raven days. As a zoning appeals board member in 1960, Agnew decided in favor of rezoning to "industrial" a large tract that Jones recently had purchased at "residential" bargain prices. Located where the beltway later intersected the Baltimore-Harrisburg inter-state, the property in 1962 became the Greater Baltimore Industrial Park and brought Jones fifty times his original investment of $12,500. After this deci-sion Agnew became Jones's business partner. Jones sold him stock in his Chesapeake National Bank, placed him on its board of directors, came to his assistance in a Virgin Islands real estate venture, and made him an unse-cured loan of $15,000 that Agnew briefly used to speculate in Anne Arundel County—where Jones expected another industrial park to develop. When Agnew moved to Government House, Jones had a wine cellar put in for him.

As 1973 wore on, nothing sordid seemed impossible. In April John Dean's testimony before a Senate investigating committee began to unravel the Nixon presidency, and there were ripples of Watergate in Maryland. Receipts at a Republican "Salute to Ted Agnew" dinner included a padding of $50,000 from the president's reelection committee known as CREEP. Watergate hear-ings disclosed that Maryland's Congressman Mills, whom everyone believed beyond scandal, had accepted $25,000 of the same money and never reported it, as state statute required. Facing disgrace, Mills shot himself. Federal marshals surrounded the State House that spring in order to arrest James A. "Turk" Scott, a shorttime Baltimore delegate suspected of dealing in heroin. A federal grand jury indicted Clarence Mitchell III for failure to pay four years of taxes. A state senator from East Baltimore, Joseph J. Staszak, introduced a measure outlawing discount liquor sales. Staszak owned a bar where state law permitted over-the-counter purchases; asked whether he saw any conflict of interest, Staszak replied, "How does this conflict with my interests?"[35] Dale Anderson, indicted on forty-three counts touching on bribery, extortion, conspiracy, and tax evasion, at once protested innocence and announced his reelection campaign. Joseph W. Alton, Jr., Republican county executive in Anne Arundel, admitted that he was under investigation for many of the charges against Anderson; while he had done some things that were indictable, he said, he had done nothing wrong. The Maryland attorney general's office discovered that a Baltimore County state's attorney had committed "carnal bribery"—obtaining sexual favors from a woman who feared prosecution for shoplifting. Lester Matz admitted paying Vice President Agnew kickbacks for county and state business—even as Agnew sat in the Old Executive Office Building in Washington. Beclouded himself, Nixon turned his back. Agnew resigned on 10 October and in Baltimore federal court that same day accepted leniency in exchange for entering a plea of no contest (tantamount to admitting guilt) to a single count of tax evasion. As part of the agreement, the government released a statement summarizing the grand jury's massive evidence against him on a string of felony charges.

In July Marvin Mandel announced at a televised news conference that he was divorcing his wife to marry Jeanne Dorsey. People who read tabloid newspapers fully enjoyed this episode, which began in scandal, led to farce, and ended in bathos. In 1973 the affair already was several years old. Even as a successful house Speaker Mandel had grown enamored of the attractive blond who had married the son of a local political leader and often appeared in Annapolis during legislative sessions. At middle age Mandel considered his marriage stale; Jeanne, the epitome of old Maryland, Anglo-Saxon respectability, promised a fresh start and new excitement. Dorsey divorced her husband, whom the governor named assistant public defender in Howard County, and Mandel became ever more daring in arranging late-night drives and furtive rendezvous. He spent many Thursday evenings at Jeanne's waterside home in Leonardtown, where the gossip mill churned. Returning to Annapolis late one night in December 1970, the governor suffered an auto accident that cracked his skull and nearly broke open his secret. By the summer of 1973 it had become transparent to Annapolis reporters; they jokingly called the highway southward "the road to Mandel's Lay." However suspicious Barbara Mandel must have been, she learned of her husband's divorce plans by tuning in to his public statement. She first spoke of the awful strain he was under, then turned less understanding. She refused to leave Government House. How could Jeanne Dorsey be "first lady" of Maryland? she asked; she wasn't even a lady. The audience laughed as the chairman of the National Governors' Conference moved into an Annapolis motel, then to a sublet apartment.[36]

Mandel provided a rich morality tale. To win another full term in 1974 the governor had to work out something with his wife. She demanded a settlement which, including legal fees, may have cost him as much as four hundred thousand dollars. Mandel scrambled to find friends willing to help. They included Irvin Kovens, a wealthy Baltimore speculator and race-track owner also known as "the czar" or "Z," who vacationed in Florida and often employed Irving T. "Tubby" Schwartz as a business front. In 1969, after the legislature chose Mandel to be governor, the czar had sent Mandel out for some new suits and billed them to his Charlestown, West Virginia, track as "uniforms." Mandel had close ties to three newly dominant partners in Tidewater Insurance—the powerful Rodgers brothers, Harry W. III and William A., and W. Dale Hess, an old Mandel friend and client who had made real estate killings in Baltimore County where exit ramps went in for new highways.

Sadly for Mandel, federal prosecutors, again under Skolnik, notified Hess and Harry Rodgers in the spring of 1974 that they were under investigation. The governor's friends had to watch their every move. Mandel got his divorce that summer and remarried at once, but in September, just before the elections, could not lay hands on forty-two thousand dollars for his first alimony payment. Hess agreed to a complicated plan by which he and others paid that amount to a motorcycle salesman, who paid Mandel, who laundered the check through his son's bank account. Soon the Pallottine Fathers, a Catholic order in Baltimore, refinanced the Mandel loan and shielded Hess's involvement. Meanwhile the public could only judge Mandel on his considerable legislative achievements. At an early campaign dinner held at the Baltimore Civic Center the governor had raised a million dollars—more than enough to discourage opposition. In November he won by a two-to-one margin.

Thereafter Mandel's game came apart. Pursuing Hess, Skolnik and his assistants uncovered a three-year-old pattern of political pressure and secret favors. In late 1971 ownership of the dilapidated half-mile horse-racing track at Marlboro in Prince George's County had changed hands. Twelve days later, overriding the governor's earlier veto and acting on cue from Mandel's floor leaders, legislators voted to extend the number of racing days allowed the track from eighteen to thirty-six. In March Mandel requested another act (the bill failed at the eleventh hour) raising the number of racing dates to ninety-four. That fall Marlboro merged with the larger Bowie race course, where trackowners could use the Marlboro dates. Marlboro had jumped in value by $2 million. Its true owners remained a puzzle, for until 1974 Maryland race tracks could conceal their ownership as did corporations. In truth

Marvin Mandel in 1976 seated comfortably, for the time being, in the governor's office. The sign over his desk read: "May my words be gracious and tender today, for tomorrow I may have to eat them." *Washington Star/Washington Post collection, D.C. Public Library*

a series of dissemblers acted as "straw men" for Kovens, Hess, and the Rodgers brothers. Federal investigators also learned that, at the time Marlboro went to Mandel's friends, Hess gave the governor one-third interest in a Talbot County farm and closed an agreement consigning him nearly 4 percent interest in a leasing firm that paid Mandel about $520 per month. Hess later tried clumsily to backdate some papers, erase some ink, and disguise the money as legal fees. Replying to reporters' questions the spring after his reelection, Mandel insisted that in 1972 he did not know who owned Marlboro. A federal grand jury indicted him in the fall of 1975. In August 1977, after an earlier mistrial, a jury found Mandel, Hess, Kovens, the Rodgers brothers, and another defendant guilty of mail fraud and racketeering. Mandel, wrote *Washington Star* columnist Mary McGrory a bit too simply, "loved beyond his means."[37]

Maryland's embarrassment with Marvin Mandel lingered, his message having plenty of time to sink in. Hospitalized for stress in the spring of 1977, he contemplated governing through his wife, Jeanne. Blair Lee III, the for-

Governor Harry Hughes delivering his inaugural address, January 1979. *Baltimore Sunpapers*

mer Montgomery County senator and secretary of state who in 1970 had won the new post of lieutenant governor, promised to resign if Mandel allowed such nonsense. In June 1977 Mandel formally turned over the reins of government, and the lieutenant governor became acting governor. Though the patrician Lee carried on commendably, he faced a bleak political future. Burdened by his association with Mandel, he stood like a sandcastle against an incoming tide of voter outrage. Harry Hughes resigned his transportation post in May 1977, protesting Frenkil's "tainting and tampering" influence as the state began awarding contracts on the Baltimore subway system. "We've had enough of those who have betrayed the public trust," said Hughes in declaring his own candidacy for governor; he mounted a crusade "to redeem our state from the morass of corruption into which it has sunk." As running mate he selected Samuel W. Bogley III, an experienced Prince George's County councilman (the county adopted home rule in 1970) whose special concerns lay with human relations and social services. In the 1978 primary they won over Lee and Steny H. Hoyer of Prince George's, James's successor as senate president, by almost 20,000 votes and later defeated J. Glenn Beall and Aris T. Allen of Annapolis 718,000 to 293,000, the largest majority ever in a Maryland gubernatorial contest. Louis Goldstein, faithful and unimpeachable, won another term as comptroller. Former federal prosecutor Stephen Sachs won the attorney general's post.[38]

The Hughes campaign had wasted no sympathy on Mandel. Now the governor-elect made it known that he did not want Mandel (who, his conviction temporarily reversed, had reclaimed his office five days before Hughes's swearing-in) to appear at the inauguration. On 17 January 1979, the music of "Maryland, My Maryland" having reminded the crowd of the state's timelessness, Hughes spoke of newness—of his anger at the "scandal, shock, and shame" that had preceded him, of the different direction his adminstration would take. Henceforward, he promised, citizens would find their servants "beyond reproach." Immediately after taking office Hughes discovered that the Mandels had made off with furniture, crystal, flatware, and assorted historic items from Government House. Though some of the pieces were priceless, the state claimed $23,000 in stolen property.[39]

Mandel denied any wrongdoing. Agnew protested that he followed common political practice in his state. Some Maryland lawyers found fault with the federal courts' sweeping interpretation of mail fraud in the Mandel case (public officials owed their constituents, like business firms their customers, honest service, and they violated federal law whenever they abused this trust while in any way using the mails); federal judges, dividing and revoting on that issue during the Mandel appeal, made themselves and the law look foolish. Mandel's remorse, Agnew's guilt, and the possible tyranny of mail-fraud doctrine aside, the mid-1970s scandals had as important an immediate impact on Maryland politics as King's death and the riots had on open racial prejudice. In the late seventies, marking a triumph for the suburban, good-government approach to politics, the assembly passed new public ethics legislation that forced lobbyists to register, candidates and officeholders to disclose their financial holdings, companies with state dealings to admit their political contributions, and officials to open meetings to the public. Somewhat like the outbursts of April 1968, political disgrace provided an ugly groundwork for constructive change; just as the ancient Wye Oak in Talbot County withstood many a winter's storm to bud in the spring, Marylanders survived riots and scandals, even profiting from them.

The Maryland embarrassments deserved no pardon but called for perspective. For one thing, they invited comparison with a sister state that in modern times escaped such an ordeal and whose citizens scoffed at the Mandels and Agnews. At Maryland-Virginia football games in these years the Virginia student band had fun by announcing as a special guest "the governor of Maryland," whereupon a student dressed in a striped convict's suit ran onto the field. Proud of their past glory, perhaps mindful of old quarrels with Maryland on the Potomac and in the lower bay, Virginians groomed themselves at Maryland's expense. On close examination, however, Maryland's errors had been human ones where politics reflected the free play of diversity and participation. In the Virginia tradition, men of substance ruled for the "common good" with a rigorous sense of probity. In Maryland people of varied backgrounds admitted their different interests and fought tooth and nail over the direction of public policy. Recent Virginia statesmen (Marylanders might have pointed out) tended to do nothing, avoiding mistakes by trying as little as possible, wanting nothing to disturb the order of things. They sought safety in "responsible" inaction. Marylanders often had erred, but usually by acting. Indeed, on the other side of the coin bearing conflict of interest, one found the highly successful Maryland reliance on appointed state commissions to address tangled problems and, in Baltimore, the fruitful modern cooperation between public and private leadership. Studying the Maryland past made clear how and why the scandals occurred and perhaps taught citizens means to their prevention—certainly the need for vigilance. They also showed how much Marylanders had to be proud of. On the eve of Agnew's departure from Washington, Nixon held a White House meeting with Maryland senators and congressmen and joked about the state's political morality. Senator Mathias demanded an apology.

Himself a student of state history (and a senator highly respected by his peers), Mathias knew that Agnew alone did not represent the Maryland tradition. There had been war profiteers during the Revolution but also the standard of Carroll of Carrollton; chicanery in the Gilded Age but also Sol Warfield, Wallis, Marbury, Dr. Kelly, and Bonaparte. In the sixties urban-ethnic Democrats produced Mandel but also Julian Lapides, who threatened a filibuster to kill the suspicious race-track bill in March 1972; Paul Spyros Sarbanes, who after performing well in the House impeachment hearings won a U.S. Senate seat in 1976; Barbara A. Mikulski, the bright and feisty representative from East Baltimore; and the senior Mitchells—temperate radicals and moderate activists on behalf of equal rights. Republicans in the rapidly growing Maryland suburbs gave the state Agnew but also, in Gude, a gentleman-scholar who dedicated himself to the Potomac, a river that rightly belonged to Maryland and the nation alike; "This is a river," he said at a conference in November 1976, "that really cries for help."[40] Maryland's diversity had produced violence and corruption, but its openness meant everything to its character. In the late 1970s the Maryland congressional delegation contained a higher proportion of women than that of any other state, while the General Assembly had one of the highest ratios of black and female membership in the country.

⌒⋙⌒

The historical sense of Marylanders—their awareness of belonging to a place through time—began to sharpen during the period of suburban development and urban razing. Members of the Society for the Preservation of Maryland Antiquities (later Preservation Maryland) urged the state to establish a holding agency for historic buildings, and in 1961 a bill written by John Clark of Bel Air, member of the SPMA executive committee, and Senator James passed the assembly. Through the Maryland Historical Trust, Orlando Ridout IV serving as director, the state became the first in the country to make preservation a public concern. Four years later, credit going to the Montgomery County senator Louise Gore, the General Assembly established a commission to study St. Mary's City as a possible archaeological-historical work site. Both these initiatives received support in 1966, when Congress passed a national historic preservation measure requiring the states to take inventory of their venerable buildings. That year, with the aid of St. Mary's College and the Smithsonian Institution, a permanent St. Mary's City Commission set out "to preserve, develop, and maintain" the provincial capital and its environs. Historians spoke with old-time residents to put their anxiety to rest and found a sense of heritage "slumbering within them." "It needs to be awakened," said one staff member, herself a native of the town. "I think if we are skillful we can resurrect this latent sense of pride."[41]

The "awakening" became an important theme in the state—at first taking direction from steady supporters of old-line institutions like the county historical societies, the Peale Museum in Baltimore, and the Maryland Historical Society, eventually leading to new groups and extended lists of activities. Popular historical awareness mounted in city, suburbia, and country. In the late summer of 1966 Carroll County opened an agricultural museum in a building that once had been the county almshouse. Washington County commissioners in 1967 responded to the loss of Rochester House (many Hagerstownians had refused to patronize the city parking lot) by appointing an Historical Advisory Board to assist zoners and planners. An unusually active committee, it later warned of commercial encroachment on Maryland Heights opposite Harpers Ferry and at Antietam battlefield; it helped in 1970 to obtain rerouting of a highway and thereby saved a Brownsville building that dated from 1812 and contained much original woodwork. At Bowie the Ogle Mansion, which the Levitt Company finally had donated to the town, became the city hall and a public showplace, enlarged in 1968. Soon afterward the Bowie public library opened a unique horse and sporting-history collection named for Ogle's best-known champion, Selima. In 1969 the Heritage Society of Essex and Middle River in Baltimore County prevented demolition of the Ballestone Mansion, an eighteenth-century brick farmhouse on Back River. It had been threatened by a golf course. In Annapolis, a National Historic District since 1965, work proceeded on restoration of the William Paca House—the Carvel Hall hotel additions at the rear of the property, themselves of interest, having been torn down. Archaeologists in 1970 began digging to locate Paca's two-acre garden of terraces and ponds that so impressed eighteenth-century visitors. Research showed them to lie fifteen feet beneath the old hotel parking lot.

Marylanders in the 1970s rediscovered themselves, and working on historical projects, they made clear their own view that history ought to be accessible, enjoyable, and educational without being stuffy. Wilbur Hunter, director of the Peale Museum in Baltimore, refused no gifts of art or artifacts; he aimed to show the Peale's rising numbers of visitors how Baltimoreans in the past actually lived. Maryland Public Television made one of its first original productions a thirty-segment series on state history, "Stories of Maryland." The center made it easily available to schools and public groups. Lois Green Carr, St. Mary's City Commission historian, and her colleagues held seminars and published papers that drew attention from scholars studying the seventeenth century on both sides of the Atlantic. Yet the digging and reconstructing at St. Mary's also had a more commonplace object— providing the public an expense-free and instructive glance at the unvarnished colonial experience. Frederick residents purchased Rose Hill, the Thomas Johnson estate, in 1968. Four years later volunteers had made it into a museum designed so that children could actually touch exhibits. "Nothing is behind glass," explained a proud guide at Rose Hill. "They don't just see pegs full of hats in the kitchen; they try them on." Later, when the Chesapeake Bay Maritime Museum moved to new quarters (designed to blend with the eighteenth-century structures at St. Michaels), its director said the exhibits re-created "an environment, a setting which makes history live, rather than a conventional museum of shelves and glass cases."[42]

Applying the "hands-on" principle, Marylanders during the revolutionary bicentennial year of 1976 staged a variety of colorful events, all of which leavened the dough of popular history. The First Maryland Regiment, a group of military-history enthusiasts who supplied their own gear, "firelocks," and blue uniforms, appeared at Smallwood State Park in early May, then at Fort Frederick on summer weekends. Together with another outfit patterned after Cresap's riflemen, it marched, played martial music, and demonstrated the noise and smoke of revolutionary fighting. Chestertown staged its third annual re-creation of the 1774 "tea party" that month, combined with an historical Chestertown sound-and-light show. Westminster held spring and summer fairs that brought together old steam engines, Civil War troops, arts and crafts, and a fife and drum corps. Hagerstown honored its founder with a Frontier Crafts Day, Upper Marlboro touted its Famous Tobacco Barn and Antiques show, and before the weather became too cold Grantsville in the far west scheduled Pioneer Days, a fair emphasizing local history and mountain crafts. Places as different as Potomac and Princess Anne organized tours of historic homes, gardens, and churches. Several communities across the state celebrated "colonial Christmases." To be sure, not all the events Marylanders enjoyed in that bicentennial year had been organized recently, and not all of them focused on the past. But a surprising number of "things to do and see" that year did have recent origins and celebrated heritage. Fire-engine, trolley, and railroad museums testified to the nostalgia that change brought with it. At community events with historical themes natives could boast of their roots. In the suburban corridor newcomers made the discovery of local pride.

The First Maryland Regiment, one of many history-conscious groups to appear in the mid-1970s, heading for camp at Fort Frederick, c. 1974. *William L. Brown III*

Taking to the water in increasing numbers in the 1970s, Marylanders could not help but notice the skipjacks and other workboats plying the bay and its rivers. Watermen, who called the recreational boaters landlubbers, held workboat races at Cambridge, St. Michaels, and Deal Island—festivals that no weekend sailor could overlook. Interest in Maryland's nautical heritage grew rapidly. The Maryland Historical Society opened a maritime gallery in the mid-fifties, the Chesapeake Bay Maritime Museum, dating from the late sixties, offered displays on the bay's history and its ships, and in 1970 the Calvert County Historical Society founded the Calvert Marine Museum. While amateur sailors relied on mass-produced craft, most of them made of fiberglass, the three museums celebrated the high level of individual crafts-manship earlier shipbuilding had required. Old masters and students of wooden boatbuilding in the mid-seventies worked to preserve those skills, which almost had disappeared. In Allegany County local history lovers gathered around a naval reservist to build a replica of a C&O canal boat, later christened the *Cumberland*. James B. Richardson, a retired shipwright outside Cambridge known as "Mr. Jim," assembled a force of young people who in 1977 set out to construct a recreation of the *Dove*. At the same time Melbourne Smith, a seasoned builder and maritime historian from Annapolis, began work on a replica Baltimore Clipper. Receiving financial support from private sources and the Baltimore Bicentennial Commission, he set up his shipyard in the inner harbor. Early in 1977 Smith and his workers launched the *Pride of Baltimore*, a beautiful vessel, sleek, with black hull and ninety-

The *Pride of Baltimore* sailing down the Baltimore harbor channel in July 1978. *David W. Harp*

five hundred square feet of sail. Manned by a largely volunteer crew, the *Pride* set out to serve the city and state as a roving "ambassador of good will."

At the end of the decade the Maryland Historical Trust produced a booklet, *New Life for Old Towns,* to guide local leaders as they considered future policy. Rather than "scattering dozens of museum-like Williamsburgs about the Maryland countryside," the trust wanted to demonstrate how Maryland towns could "keep their historic qualities while continuing to adjust to change and maintain their economic health." The booklet reviewed the state's varied economic history, discussed the social benefits of small towns with centers, and emphasized the monetary value of a "viable Main Street." It recommended leaving downtown buildings in—or returning them to—their original form, preserving their true "personality"; it offered suggestions on landscaping, parking, managing utility wires, controlling exterior signs, and making the most of water sites. In several places community leaders acted on these ideas. "Vest-pocket" parks emerged in Cumberland. Port Tobacco began a program of restoring its many architectural treasures. The old western-road stopover of New Market in Frederick County established an historic district commission and agreed to zoning regulations that preserved the town's original charm. Still, explained the mayor, "Most everything we've passed in the way of ordinances has been through necessity." In like manner Annapolis preservationists from the beginning denied any interest in making the town a theme park; they wanted their city to remain alive, working, and spontaneous. Though the city council adopted rules governing outdoor signs and organized a committee to pass on any changes to downtown exteriors, Annapolis in the late sixties had begun holding lively sailboat shows, clam fêtes, and arts festivals at the city dock.[43]

Marylanders lived in an increasingly impersonal, interconnected world. It placed their economic future at the mercy of global trends and federal policy; it complicated economic gain with environmental considerations and tied together such unlikely partners as the spot price of Iranian crude oil and historical facades in Baltimore. In 1972–73 a Middle Eastern cartel greatly reduced the flow of oil Americans used in transportation, industry, and home heating. Yet the shortage did not bring prosperity to Western Maryland, as one might have expected, for George's Creek coal contained much sulphur. Federal restrictions kept it out of virtually all domestic furnaces (the General Assembly applied more constraints in 1975 with a law that banned strip mining on steep slopes). The state seafood business sought ways to stabilize its seasonal market; the industry struggled against high inflation that congressional spending had fueled and rising labor costs that minimum-wage regulations helped to establish. In the mid-seventies a longshoreman at the Dundalk Marine Terminal referred to the port as "Big Mama," sweating to bring home her family's bacon. Hardworking though she was, her health partly hung on rates in the federal Conrail system—which for the time being made it cheaper for ships to steam to Baltimore than to offload at Hampton–Newport News and send cargoes overland by rail.

All the while foreign competition in heavy industry slowed Sparrows Point steel mills just as it shut down factories in the Pennsylvania and Ohio "rustbelt." Demonstrating, by way of contrast, how important micro-chip technology in fields like information-processing had become to the developed world, and likely would remain, Montgomery County attracted more and more research and development firms in the seventies. Interstate 270 from Rockville to Gaithersburg, with its high-tech company headquarters and many research centers, concentrated white-collar energy much as did California's "Silicon Valley."

A Johns Hopkins University study of the period listed high wage scales and the high Maryland tax rate (about one-fourth of one's income went to taxes) among the factors that deterred new industry from settling in the state; labor unions with their accustomed demands remained strong in key sectors of the economy, and important constituencies stood prepared to resist any cutback in social services. Maryland manufacturing lost more than

In the 1970s housing developments further encroached on Maryland farmland, here in Harford County. *Baltimore Sunpapers*

sixty-three thousand jobs between the early sixties and late seventies; in 1976 there were fewer industrial wage earners in the state than there had been in 1950. Of the 3.5 million acres of Maryland's richest soil, 200,000 acres had gone to pavement or buildings by 1973. The number of Maryland farms dropped from 43,000 in 1940 to 17,500 in 1978. The typical Maryland bread-winner in 1876 had been a farmer or factory worker; a century later, one Marylander in four worked for federal, state, or local government. Tradition-ally an economic crossroads, a state of wholesalers and shippers, Maryland now lay far from the southern and southwestern regions of swiftest Ameri-can population growth.

In Annapolis and in the counties, Maryland officials in the late 1970s usu-ally found themselves reacting to such forces—and to public weariness with politicians and expensive government. State authorities responded as best they could to those factors within their grasp: Governor Hughes, like the anti-Washington president whom he resembled, stood for caution and a sense of finite possibilities. Hughes's secretary of transportation, Lowell K. Bridwell, obtained from the assembly a gasoline tax increase that resembled federal measures in both raising revenue and discouraging consumption. A larger thrust was toward tax relief of the kind signaled in 1978, when the assembly lowered the state property tax by 10 percent. The early Hughes administra-tion obtained elimination of the state sales tax on manufacturing machinery. State legislators in 1979–80 returned a short-lived state surplus to the counties and dropped the sales tax on utility bills and farm equipment. Lawmakers stayed the recent course of coping with development's natural costs, though less spectacularly than in the first Mandel years. Earlier having passed a seed-tree measure that required replanting of 5 or more acres of cut timber, the assembly in 1979 established a voluntary program that placed Maryland agricultural land in a protected-use category. While officials trimmed to the public demand for tighter state budgets, the economic and community development bureaucracy, firmly in place, turned out regular booklets on industrial opportunities in Baltimore and the counties.

In Upper Marlboro and La Plata, county government typically struggled like a ship in variable winds: federally mandated busing in the Prince George's County School System, plus the steady growth of suburban Washington, drove new residents into Charles County, where issues of land use, sewerage, and adequate schools and highways captured public attention in the late 1970s as earlier they had stirred up other counties. As the suburban belt dropped below Piscataway, blacks, along with newly arrived Asians and Latin Americans, found Prince George's housing increasingly affordable and their numbers rose. County officials and schoolteachers there struggled to meet social needs while property owners in 1978 adopted a charter amendment placing a ceiling on local property taxes.

New economic realities bred frustration but also generated constructive political controversy: the movement to preserve without embalming gained force from high prices and long lines at gas stations. People began to think about their energy consumption and expectations for the future. The Historical Trust guidebook stressed the energy-conserving advantages of small-town life. In Baltimore the preservation/conservation movement led to home-grown neighborhood revivals and produced a fight against more inner-city highways—a cause that finally met with limited success.

Federal highway officials and their allies in state business, construction, and government pressed for arteries that would complete the system the Jones Falls Expressway began and carry interstate traffic through Baltimore on north-south and east-west routes. For most of the 1960s city politicians stalled any action by debating and demanding more studies. Citizens whose homes stood in the paths of proposed routes objected to further building. They saw the Jones Falls, with its steep ramps and sharp curves, as a dangerous road and a reason to be shy of urban highways; they also pointed to problems of pollution and financial strain. Bolton Hill residents had forced abandonment of an early plan that would have buried the neighborhood under a north-south/east-west expressway intersection. Residents of Federal Hill and Fells Point resisted a scheme for an inner harbor bridge and intersection south of the business district; the plan would have obliterated the two oldest surviving communities in the city. The black neighborhood of Rosemont fought to move the route of the western highway link. By the early seventies, when federal environmental authorities raised new expressway objections on the basis of noise and air pollution, a citywide coalition of sixteen groups calling itself the Movement against Destruction (MAD) attacked "inadequate, expensive, and inconvenient transportation" everywhere in Baltimore.[44]

Controversy over "The Road" well illustrated the dynamics of urban politics in Baltimore and the friction between economic and aesthetic considerations. Mayor Schaefer strongly supported the "3-A" expressway plan D'Alesandro had decided to adopt in 1968. Completing the western entry of I-70 and the southern entrance of I-95, the plan included building a southern loop across Locust Point, a tunnel under the Patapsco near Fort McHenry, and a highway through Canton to the northeast. Another loop would connect the interstates and the Jones Falls by putting an elevated roadway through Fells Point. Schaefer in 1972 demanded the expressways (as well as mass transport) because they would encourage industrial growth and save jobs in south Baltimore. Civic associations fought to stop the I-70 highway, which would cut through Leakin and Gwynns Falls parks. Fells Point went to court to prevent destruction of its historic area, and in 1973 Locust Point residents picketed city council meetings in uniforms from the War of 1812 period. Schaefer partially relented; the latest federal highway act permitted cancellation of incomplete portions of the interstate system and the transfer of funding to mass transit. The mayor overrode opposition in the Franklin-Mulberry and Sharp-Leadenhall areas. He put through a portion of I-95 that led to the business district and, by way of a new boulevard named for Martin Luther King, Jr., into the heart of the city. A new bridge over the outer harbor completed the beltway. Fells Point escaped an elevated expressway, and the interstate in northwest Baltimore ended abruptly at Leakin Park.

As the highway debate raged, Baltimore produced an unusually successful "urban homesteading" program that might not have done well without high home-mortgage interest rates and the enthusiasm of young people. Often well employed and joiners of groups like MAD, which Locust Point residents avoided, they found city living enjoyable both for its romantic appeal and for its cash benefits. City houses cost far less than homes in suburbia. One could walk or bike to work while living in what once had been workers' housing—or even a fashionable address. In places like Union Square and Charles Village these new urban activists met to discuss replacing long-gone nineteenth-century fountains, brickwork, landscaping, and gaslights. "Preservation spreads instead of blight," one downtown dweller reported happily. "I cleaned the bricks on my house and soon other people were doing it, even some absentee landlords."[45]

As the name implied, homesteading required the pioneering spirit of frontier settlement. Architects, city planners, and others had talked for many years about the theory, by which city authorities sold derelict housing at a nominal charge on condition that the new owners restore the dwelling to its original exterior character while meeting modern building codes. In Sep-

Left, Prospective "urban homesteaders" inspect city-owned derelict housing, Baltimore, c. 1975. The more adventurous, gambling and working hard, helped to maintain the character of some venerable neighborhoods. Baltimore *News American* photograph. *Jacques Kelly. Right*, Mayor William Donald Schaefer paid a call at a Lithuanian festival in the center of Baltimore in July 1979. *Baltimore Sunpapers*

tember 1973 Schaefer and Embry announced that Baltimore would attempt homesteading. Within a few days Robert M. Windsor, director of the new home-ownership division, had more than one thousand inquiries and one hundred firm offers. The first homesteaders—whose backgrounds ranged from schoolteaching to stockbrokerage—paid a single dollar for their run-down houses in Poppleton, East Baltimore, and Harlem Park. Forty-two ramshackle row houses on Stirling Street went to homesteaders; earlier they had been scheduled for demolition, and nearby residents who wanted them gone had challenged preservationists to leave their comfortable homes and try living in them.

The city once again benefited from its own initiative. Federal loan money for homesteaders carried restrictions and might dry up. Embry recommended and voters passed a bond issue creating a fund Baltimore homesteaders could borrow from as they re-worked the old houses, many of them now available on a highest-bidder basis. Embry experimented with a row of post–Civil War houses near the Hopkins Hospital; renovating the exterior, city workmen turned the interiors of the houses into two cooperative apartment units each. The city salvaged old fixtures—doors, fireplace mantels, and the like—from demolished houses, stored them in a warehouse, and sold them cheaply to homesteaders. Not every pioneer persevered, but enough did to save areas like the Otterbein neighborhood near the inner harbor, parts of Washington Hill and Reservoir Hill, and, not far from the University of Maryland medical and dental centers, Ridgeley's Delight and Barre Circle. Second by a few days to announce its program, Baltimore in 1978 had five hundred homesteaders—about as many as all other participating cities combined. "What you have done," Schaefer told them at a Federal Hill picnic held that summer in their honor, "is to establish a mood for the city, far beyond the presence of an additional five hundred families. You have said: 'Living in Baltimore is good, and we are willing to invest ourselves in this effort.'" The old apostle of urban self-help and preservation, Hans Froelicher, Jr., had died in late 1976, but a close observer would have noticed his spirit, as well as Schaefer's celebrated enthusiasm, at the Federal Hill gathering. Each generation, Froelicher had written, has responsibility "to give new meaning to the honored phrase 'We the People.'"[46]

⁓⌇⌇⁓

The relationship between income and culture, never merely direct, still explained in some ways the resurgence of artistic vitality in these years—as perhaps did the zest for pleasure that followed the grimness and idealism of the late sixties. In the 1960s and 1970s the state's total personal income grew 64 percent faster than in the region between New York and Virginia as a whole. Most of that wealth—owing to government employment, technical industries, and research and development firms—lay in the Baltimore-Washington area. By the end of the seventies, when the Maryland population exceeded 4 million persons, eight out of ten people in the state lived in the metropolitan corridor. Concentrated numbers and wealth (and the rising proportion of two-income couples in the work force) helped the arts enormously. Marylanders in suburban Washington supported the Kennedy Center for the Performing Arts, National Theater, National Gallery Orchestra, Arena Stage, and other downtown cultural attractions; they patronized cultural programs at the University of Maryland and summer bills at Shady Grove and the Olney theater.

Baltimoreans, starting with less, eventually produced an artistic renaissance—a rebirth that at first seemed not to include the successor to Ford's famous old theater. Morris A. Mechanic, Polish-born real estate mogul, had purchased Ford's in the 1940s, demolished it for a parking garage in 1964 (when the Washington Ford's underwent renovation), and that year set out to construct the downtown stage that the GBC long had envisioned for Charles Center. The Mechanic Theater, a massive, unusual structure costing $4.3 million, opened in 1967 but soon lost money in huge sums. It twice closed in the mid-seventies. The Schaefer administration assumed its management, Embry of the housing department put in new lighting and acoustics, and the Mechanic remained open. Meanwhile Center Stage, destroyed by fire in early 1974, raised hope that Baltimore might one day make the Mechanic Theater profitable. With city help Center Stage moved into the old St. Ignatius Church/Loyola College complex at Calvert and Monument streets. By the end of 1975 it had 11,500 season ticket holders—more than twice as many as before the fire.

Giving helped all the arts. The Baltimore Opera Company, like the Chamber Music Society founded in 1950, gained new subscribers in the seventies, when rising costs posed serious problems. Under Petrus Bosman the Maryland Ballet, after near-extinction in 1978, returned the following year to a full program. Heavily endowed with public funds, the ballet relied with increasing assurance on subscribers whose number, 1,900, more than doubled between 1976 and 1979. Largely by means of generous private donations, the Walters Art Gallery (fully open to the public since 1934) completed a remarkable new wing in November 1974, almost trebling its exhibition space. The Baltimore Museum of Art owed much of its renown to the Cone sisters—Dr. Claribel (one of the earliest female students at the Johns Hopkins Medical School and one of Gertrude Stein's classmates there) and Miss Etta—both of whom, with the help of Stein and her many emigré friends, had built a famous collection centered on French impressionist and post-impressionist paintings. In 1949 Etta had donated the immense collection to the museum and then financed a wing to house it. The museum also exhibited the work of leading Maryland artists like Grace H. Turnbull, Morris Louis, Herman Maril, and Reuben Kramer. During the late seventies the BMA embarked on a massive renovation and expansion program.

The Baltimore Symphony Orchestra, with a tradition of offering special educational concerts, had begun a new chapter in 1968 when conductor Sergiu Commissiona joined the musicians. Five years later a new general manager, Joseph Leavitt, took over the delicate task of building resources and planning appearances. Friends of the BSO being generous and its reputation growing, the group performed in New York, went on foreign tours, and made recordings with major companies. In 1976 the BSO president, Joseph Meyerhoff, launched a fund-raising campaign titled "Threshold to Greatness"—an attempt to raise more than $3 million to cover salaries and operating expenses. By the end of the decade an unusual arrangement with local symphony societies in eight Maryland cities enabled the orchestra to make regular appearances on both shores. Baltimore subscribers, seven thousand in 1974–75, then numbered twelve thousand, and plans were under way to build a larger concert hall. For this worthy project Baltimore City subscribed $2.5 million, the General Assembly $7.5 million, and Meyerhoff—recalling the philanthropy of Peabody, Pratt, Walters, and Hopkins—another $5 million.

The arts revival had still other sources. Faculty members and students at the Maryland Art Institute, in the mid-sixties having taken over the renovated B&O station on Mount Royal Avenue, made themselves prominent in

In the summer of 1974, as part of the city-sponsored "Beautiful Walls for Baltimore" project, Robert Johnson painted this mural on the rear of the Baltimore *Afro-American News* building. *Baltimore Sunpapers*

the renaissance, as did musicians of the Peabody Institute—which in 1977 merged with Johns Hopkins. Morgan State had its famous Ira Aldridge Players and a renowned university choir under Nathan Carter; Notre Dame College sponsored a cultural arts program for the handicapped. At Towson, Coppin, and elsewhere the number of students in arts teaching climbed to meet the rising demand in the schools. In the early seventies Artists' Equity, a guild representing artists in public councils, obtained a Baltimore City ordinance that set aside 1 percent of every municipal building's cost for support of the arts. The funding that followed, paying for artwork inside and outside of public buildings, also enabled a city design commission to sponsor educational projects and art shows and to do away with entry fees at juried (judged) exhibitions.

Another source of funding came from Washington and Annapolis—from the National Endowment for the Arts through the Maryland Arts Council.

Established in the late sixties, the council in turn supplied Mayor Schaefer's Advisory Committee on Arts and Culture, directed by Richard Micherdzinski and then Jody Albright. This money supported a long list of local and broadly defined artwork. Grants sponsored artists' shows at community colleges and places like Homewood, Charles Center, and City Hall Courtyard; they put colorful, often abstract, impressions on neighborhood buildings and murals on construction barricades. With council funding in 1971 Norman Ross, a Baltimore black leader, established an inner-city cultural arts project that included a successful dance theater. The Maryland council staged a traveling exhibit of work done by state artists. It also helped in 1975 to establish the Baltimore International Theater Festival, the only one of its kind in the country and afterward an annual summer program of varied performances, workshops, and children's plays. Grant money also aided organizers of the Baltimore Arts Festival. In the late 1960s an exhibition of two hundred entrants at Hopkins Plaza, it later moved to the inner harbor and in 1979 featured the work of five hundred painters, sculptors, craftspeople,

Dancers entertained a youthful audience in the Cone Wing of the Baltimore Museum of Art, 1975. *Maryland State Arts Council*

dancers, and theatrical performers. That year Schaefer established CityArts, an ongoing and ambitious cultural program. The Maryland Arts Council budget, originally $50,000, rose to $1.7 million before the state austerity program forced its decline.

These developments gave youngsters a try at artistic expression and provided professionals with jobs and recognition. Yet much activity in these years owed to artists themselves; gifts and grants could create a salubrious air, but finally someone had to breathe it. Small musical groups gave one example of the self-rising character of the revival. Often unpaid and ad hoc, they sprang up so quickly that in 1974 public concerts in Baltimore had increased sixfold over their number a decade earlier and had doubled since 1969. To the Chamber Music Society, classical music lovers in 1974 added a company that later became the Pro Musica Rara. Saul Schechtman, conductor at the new Center Stage, fashioned yet another small ensemble, the Orchestra Piccola, in 1976. Two years later the Festival Chamber Players formed at Essex Community College; a "First Tuesday" concert society assembled at Goucher, which had a variety of strong arts programs. Love of art, once demonstrated, drew painters to Baltimore and gave those already there an essential sense of audience. Churches, banks, and restaurants invited artists to display their work. Like the small musical groups, local galleries generated enthusiasm between artists and public and mined the uncut diamonds of latent talent. In 1978 the Kromah Gallery, whose patron, a black businessman, wanted to take a step "towards eliminating elitism in the arts," opened with a special invitation to black artists. In the late seventies at least eight new art galleries emerged in Baltimore. Programs in dance proliferated. The Maryland Ballet relied on dancers trained elsewhere, but Bosman, who spoke of educating Marylanders to the art, hoped to develop future members of the troupe at his ballet center. In 1978 Peggy Myers, dance instructor at Towson State, formed the Movement Arts Parasol, a group specializing in Oriental dance, and Jeff Duncan moved his dance company, Impetus, from New York to Baltimore.[47]

Drama and the literary scene underwent similar, grass-roots revival. During the late seventies the Corner Theater, dating from 1967, provided a testing ground for new plays in the undercroft of the Cathedral Church of the Incarnation; the NEW PLAYERS Theater, an old group that revived in 1979, added to the dramatic opportunities the Vagabond Players, Theater Hopkins, and Baltimore Actors' Theater had supplied performers, directors, and playwrights for many years. Innovative theater companies emerged under Barry Knower at Goucher, Paul Berman at Towson State, Philip Arnoult— connected with Antioch College at Columbia—and Herbert Blau at UMBC. In 1976 Arnoult and Blau organized a groundbreaking New Theater Festival. Two years later a theater at Fells Point (the old waterfront then also had an art gallery) produced an original play, Robert Minford's *The Bird Is on the Wing*. Established societies like the Maryland State Poetry Association, the

Edgar Allan Poe Memorial Association (founded in 1907 as an offshoot of the Women's Library Club), the Lizette Woodworth Reese Association, and the Three Arts Club of Homeland sponsored lectures and offered literary prizes, as had become traditional. Still, for writers as well as musicians and dancers, the most telling developments were recent and small—poetry readings at corner cafes, small presses that printed first works, and fugitive magazines that published aspiring authors. In the mid-seventies a group calling itself the Maryland Writers Council had its own building on Franklin Street, housing small bookstore, press, and regular Friday-night readings. Daniel Mark Epstein, a poet and playwright who then found himself in Baltimore and liked it, described the place as the center of "a very intense literary community."[48]

Baltimore inspired writers without spoiling them. Marion Buchman, winner of nearly a hundred national and international poetry awards by the late 1970s, wrote in comparative obscurity. Epstein, whose verse and plays won the Prix de Rome for 1977–78, described his chosen home as "a good place to work: it's friendly, and there aren't many distractions." A black artist whom Governor Hughes named state poet laureate in 1979, Lucille Clifton, came upon a pile of her books in a Baltimore store; she found it amusing, but pleasing, that she could chat with the salesclerk without being recognized. Julia Randall, another poet and a native of the city, thanked Baltimore because, she said, it "leaves me alone, gives me space, allows me to write poems instead of 'Be a Poet.' " Josephine Jacobsen's work led to her appointment as Library of Congress poet in residence and in 1978 to a nationally acclaimed book of short stories, *A Walk with Rachid*. She called her artistic life in Baltimore "private but not isolated."[49]

Anne Tyler, who grew up all over the country, settled with her husband in Baltimore and reveled in its unique sense of time and place. A good spot for a writer, she declared, "it has a lot of depth and color." She compared living in Baltimore to being "in a time machine." In the late 1970s Tyler received increasing attention and much praise for work that explored family relationships, eccentricity, and ties to locality. Tyler's novels told of characters like Morgan Gower, who lives in a huge old Roland Park house coated with layers of paint and generations of experience. Morgan works in an ancient hardware store but cares little for money itself; he tells customers how to fix broken doors and burst pipes cheaply and reads or dozes during business hours. In *Searching for Caleb* (1976), another such figure, Justine's grandfather, takes Justine all over the country looking for a long-lost relative. Even as he travels in hopes of restoring the family's sense of wholeness, the grandfather insists that he remains a citizen of Baltimore: "All other towns were ephemeral, no account," wrote Tyler; "he shuffled through them absent-mindedly like a man passing through a string of shanties on the way to his own sturdy house."[50]

A writer's text, his or her art, rightfully stood on its own, and yet no writer could escape context. John Barth, after 1973 director of the writing seminars at Hopkins, had grown up in Cambridge during the Depression and World War II. He attended Hopkins and in 1956 published his first book, *The Floating Opera*—a novel set in Cambridge and drawing its title from Adams's Floating Theater. Four years later in *The Sot-Weed Factor*, using the form of a picaresque eighteenth-century novel, Barth retold Ebenezer Cook's epic poem describing the early tobacco coast. He eclipsed the original satire with even sharper humor and deeper explorations into rawness. A rare academic who could write powerful fiction, Barth both dealt with serious issues and maintained a comic posture. His characters dallied with suicide as the only response to an absurd world; the short stories in *Lost in the Funhouse* (1968)—following angry, pained letters to his hometown newspaper after the 1967 race riot—discussed the confusions of perception, the costs of gaining maturity. In his best-selling novel *Giles Goat Boy* he employed the legend of a boy raised by goats to write a hugely funny and yet weighty commentary on Western intellectual traditions and the passage from innocence to wisdom, from ignorance to disillusionment.

His work grew progressively theoretical, formally experimental. He intended some of his stories to be listened to, improvised dialogues between himself and a tape recorder, and deliberately used italics, dashes, and digressions about method to enliven his tales and sensitize readers. In 1973 he received the National Book Award for *Chimera*, a series of stories within stories based on the Arabian tales of a thousand and one nights. At the end of the decade Barth published a novel in the manner of the nineteenth-century epistolary romance—a book of fanciful letters between himself and his fictional characters.

Standing on a plane by itself, Barth's work set a standard for innovative American fiction in these years—it demanded close textual study—and yet the very approach Barth took to the literary craft partly revealed his roots. One could find strains of Maryland thought and experience, traces of the Maryland sensibility, in Barth's irreverence, his pragmatism, his playfulness with his readers. Barth urged American writers to rekindle creativity, to recover from what in 1967 he called the "literature of exhaustion." His writing, often criticized as overly cerebral, in fact sought a middle course—combining the emotional satisfaction of storytelling and the different rewards of imaginative technique. Characteristically, Barth compared writing to lovemaking, arguing against both "heartfelt ineptitude" and "heartless skill." He aimed to achieve what he called "passionate virtuosity."[51]

More deeply than did Mencken, though with many of the same findings, Barth in his early novels examined the conflict between traditional and modern ways, the discrepancy between the rational and nonrational in man, the ambiguity of human life itself. Todd Andrews in *Floating Opera* resists the pressures of progress, punctuality, and "success." He practices law—and is good at it—but nonetheless speaks of the limits of his own ambition, of being in no hurry. He praises "the virtues of limited consistency," daring the reader to infer "anything of a philosophical flavor" from his recited practice. Barth's characters view life in terms of relations rather than absolutes. Life is too large for moral certainty; it is like a floating opera that comes and goes on the tides—so that those who watch from the riverbank catch only glimpses of it—or like the funhouse at Ocean City, a sequence of mirrors that can make fools of us. *"Many a truth is spoke in ignorance,"* Cook's companion declares before ordering another drink in colonial Maryland; *"and many a wrong set right by chance."* Barth's sober fiction suggests that we live in a kind of "funhouse" if we choose to live at all, and in it we must find our own meaning. Each morning, preparing stoically for his possible death from a rare heart defect, Andrews pays his hotel bill; every night he writes notes for the great work he plans to call his *Inquiry.* "So," he explains to readers, "I begin each day with a gesture of cynicism, and close it with a gesture of faith"— one an act of temporality, he continues, another of eternity. "It is in the tension between these two gestures that I have lived my adult life." [52]

EPILOGUE

Placed in a world grown used to modernity, Marylanders largely preserved traditions of moderation, originality, humility, and serendipity. They preferred to live life on a human scale. Baseball again supplied useful metaphors, for while some teams tried virtually to buy championships, the Orioles over a quarter of a century won a higher percentage of games than any other major-league team—and the 1970 World Series—by playing old-fashioned ball. The club relied on fundamentals, strong pitching, sound defense, a farm system that groomed talented prospects, and player continuity. Manager Earl Weaver watched the game's statistics, played the odds, and kept opponents off balance with carefully selected pinch hitters and the old Baltimore hit-and-run. Jousting in the 1970s remained popular in Maryland, arguing for the state's ingenuity in blending past and present and, if one looked closely, its tendency toward democracy. The sport that once appealed to young gentlemen in full swoon over the Waverly romances had evolved into everyman's make-believe—colorful events that admitted anyone (a Frederick countian once rode to the rings on a mule), featured knightly "titles" that often spoofed pretension, and closed not with fancy balls but with family-style picnic suppers. Ethel Ennis, the Baltimore jazz singer whose talent seemed certain in the seventies to propel her into the spotlights of New York and Los Angeles, chose to remain at home—singing at Baltimore music festivals and an Annapolis inn. "People expect you to be a certain way if you're in show biz," she told a curious interviewer, "and that isn't who I am."

In early 1975, when officials closed the older of the two bay bridges to do repair work, someone suggested that they open the span to walkers. Though it was the kind of suggestion bureaucrats usually dismiss, Harry Hughes, then transportation secretary, agreed to it, and one day in the spring of each year pedestrians with balloons, lunches, and strollers for young children stole a march from cars and trucks and had the bridge all to themselves. Maryland preservationists wisely appealed to humane instincts. "The size and richness of much small town architecture is highly appealing," read the Historical Trust's *New Life for Old Towns*. "The buildings are of human scale; the materials and detailing reflect an earlier concern for quality and craft skills in construction." A theater student who had experienced an arts revival in San Francisco before arriving in Baltimore, Herbert Blau compared his new home favorably to that more glamorous waterside city. "The news is spreading," he said in 1977, "that Baltimore is a place . . . a city you can sort of touch; it's not too wide for the imagination."[1]

Attention to scale had no better illustration than the finished Baltimore Inner Harbor—an architectural and civic achievement that paralleled Baltimore's arts revival in the late seventies. The Convention Center opened in the fall of 1979. An unusual, three-tiered aquarium neared completion on pier 3. Baltimore and the state had begun building the 21.3-million-dollar attraction without federal money. Meantime, after considerable debate and a hard-fought referendum, Schaefer with leaders of the GBC and Charles Center–Inner Harbor Management, Inc. (then under Walter Sondheim, Jr.), directed the Rouse Company to design the focal point in the arrangement—a marketplace to lie between the Maryland Academy of Science and the new, 28-story World Trade Center. Already successful in reviving Faneuil Hall–Quincy Market in old Boston, Rouse and his architects envisioned two glass-enclosed pavilions framing the northern and western edges of the harbor and containing a variety of restaurants and shops. The opening of "Harborplace" in July 1980 marked the climax of the long effort to renew without destroying Baltimore. Maryland Public Television taped the opening festival—with balloons, music, and boats bobbing in the water—for later national airing. Mayor Schaefer, who had devised the slogan "Baltimore Is Best," triumphantly invited the entire world to the reborn city. On the evening of the first day the Baltimore Symphony performed Tchaikovsky's *1812 Overture,* a classical yet familiar piece that ended with booming fireworks. The rockets' glare may have reminded spectators of Baltimore's defense in 1814; this victory, too, turned a new page for the city.

Thirteen months later, after 18 million people had visited Harborplace and it had produced $1.1 million in tax revenues, *Time* magazine placed Rouse on its cover. In the early 1980s Marylanders could hardly have chosen a more suitable spokesman, for Rouse eloquently expressed the sensibility most of them shared. He said that somehow Americans had to achieve a balance between public and private—an old theme in Maryland life—and between profits and posterity. He made clear his belief in the driving force of individualism and the value of enlightened entrepreneurship—profit more than anything else, he said, "hauls dreams into focus." Yet Rouse insisted that dreams of economic gain encompass age-old human concerns of improving the quality of life, of making people into a community. Harborplace by itself could not sustain the shared gaiety and civic cohesion of the first city fair; free to everyone, broadly affordable, walkable, and joyous in its color and textures, it did, by Rouse's design, establish a "warm and human place, with diversity of choice, full of festival and delight." Here planning, money, and humanity intersected. Harborplace had spots for outdoor theater. It provided a stage for strolling jugglers, mimes, and colorful dancers. Its music varied from jazz to rock and to classical. Besides the multiple scents of the nearby McCormick building, the breeze carried smells of coffee, breads, crabcakes, hot pretzels, and garlic. Most important, in the food-sampling tradition of the Lexington Market, Harborplace meant shared enjoyment that

Harborplace opened with flags, tall ships, music, and enthusiastic crowds in July 1980. *Rouse Company*

broke down barriers. Blacks and whites, people of every background, *Time* reported, walked about, sat on benches, and laughed as Rouse had hoped they would. "The only valid purpose of any civilization," he said again after Harborplace opened, "is to grow better people—more creative, more productive, more inspiring, more loving people."[2]

Marylanders could claim to have fashioned an especially fertile civilization—eminently American by being democratic and diverse, yet peculiar in its version of American individualism and its vision of the good life. Far more prosaically than Rouse or the state's authors and artists, though just as clearly, some families in St. Mary's County demonstrated the persistence of the Marylander's view of the world. In 1980 they earned their livelihood much as had Calvert's settlers in the seventeenth century. Hardworking, steady though adventuresome, they loved both land and water and prized the natural rhythm of their life. They planted tobacco seedlings in early June, put out crab pots about the same time, and poked around for good clamming spots in the river. On summer mornings they sprayed and topped the to-bacco plants; nights they often spent hauling seines. In August, when dry weather permitted, adults and children went into the fields to slash, stab, and load tobacco. October brought a return to oyster tonging. Then, during the first months of the new year, the watermen-farmers scraped and repainted their boats, repaired nets, tended livestock, and did odd jobs.

They labored at the oldest life Maryland offered, and while the state as a whole pushed ahead in areas like medical research and microtechnology, these plain people kept alive the spirit that first had made Europeans and Africans into Marylanders. "It's pretty work," reflected one retired St. Mary's waterman in talking to a magazine writer; "I loved the life." Eyes bright and leathery skin wrinkled, he laughed and added, "I'd rather catch crabs than eat when I'm hungry."[3]

Middleton Evans

Notes

Bibliographical Essay

Selected Maps, Figures, and Tables

Chronology

Index

NOTES

Abbreviations

In captions to illustrations and throughout the notes and bibliography I have used the following abbreviations:

AgHist	*Agricultural History*
AHR	*American Historical Review*
AJHQ	*American Jewish Historical Quarterly*
AJLH	*American Journal of Legal History*
ArchMd	William Hand Browne, ed., *Archives of Maryland* (72 vols. to date; Baltimore: Maryland Historical Society, 1883–)
BHM	*Bulletin of the History of Medicine*
BJHH	*Bulletin of the Johns Hopkins Hospital*
CHR	*Catholic Historical Review*
CUS	Columbia University Studies in History, Economics and Public Law
CWH	*Civil War History*
HMPEC	*Historical Magazine of the Protestant Episcopal Church*
JAH	*Journal of American History*
JEH	*Journal of Economic History*
JHUS	Johns Hopkins University Studies in Historical and Political Science
JIH	*Journal of Interdisciplinary History*
JNH	*Journal of Negro History*
JSH	*Journal of Southern History*
JSocH	*Journal of Social History*
MHM	*Maryland Historical Magazine*
MHR	Maryland Hall of Records/Hall of Records Commission
MHS	Maryland Historical Society
MLR	*Maryland Law Review*
MM	*Maryland Magazine*
MSA	Maryland State Archives
MSBA	Maryland State Bar Association
MSMJ	*Maryland State Medical Journal*
NHB	*Negro History Bulletin*
PAH	*Perspectives in American History*
PMHB	*Pennsylvania Magazine of History and Biography*
RCHS	*Records of the Columbia Historical Society*
VMHB	*Virginia Magazine of History and Biography*
WMQ	*William and Mary Quarterly*

Chapter 1

1. "An Account of the Colony of the Lord Baron of Baltamore, in Maryland, near Virginia, . . . " (1633) and "A Briefe Relation of the Voyage Unto Maryland, . . . " (1634) in Clayton Colman Hall, ed., *Narratives of Early Maryland, 1633–1684*, Original Narratives of Early American History (New York: Charles Scribner's Sons, 1910), pp. 7–8, 40, 45.

2. Comte de Tillières, quoted in William Hand Browne, *George Calvert and Cecilius Calvert, Barons Baltimore of Baltimore* (New York: Dodd, Mead and Co., 1890), p. 9. See also John D. Krugler, "Sir George Calvert's Resignation as Secretary of State and the Founding of Maryland," *MHM*, 68 (1973): 239–54.

3. Cecil Calvert to Thomas Wentworth, Earl of Strafford, 10 January 1634, quoted in Browne, *George Calvert and Cecilius Calvert*, p. 42. The vessels that brought the first English settlers to Virginia were 100, 40, and 20 tons; the *Mayflower* displaced about 180 tons. See Matthew Page Andrews, *The Founding of Maryland* (New York: D. Appleton-Century Co., 1933), p. 55.

4. "Instructions 13 Novem: 1633," in Hall, ed., *Narratives of Early Maryland*, pp. 16–23. For the items Smith recommended settlers carry with them, see *A Relation of Maryland . . .* ([London:] 1635), ibid., pp. 75–77, 93–98.

5. "Instructions 13 Novem: 1633," pp. 16, 20, 23.

6. "Briefe Relation of the Voyage Unto Maryland," p. 31.

7. Ibid., p. 39.

8. Ibid., pp. 40–41; Archihu quoted in Andrews, *Founding of Maryland*, p. 61. Andrews relies on White's "Relatio Itineris in Marylandiam," a Latin version of the "Briefe Relation."

9. "Briefe Relation of the Voyage Unto Maryland," pp. 42–43.

10. For Baltimore's charter, see ibid., pp. 101–12.

11. Cecil Calvert to Leonard Calvert, 15 April 1637, quoted in John Leeds Bozman, *A Sketch of the History of Maryland . . .* (Baltimore, 1811), p. 292.

12. *A Relation of Maryland*, p. 91.

13. Ibid., pp. 91–92; Newton D. Mereness, *Maryland as a Proprietary Province* (New York: Macmillan Co., 1901), p. 51. For the 1633 terms, see Bozman, *Sketch*, pp. 283–84.

14. *A Relation of Maryland*, pp. 99–100.

15. Reverend Hugh Jones quoted in Michael G. Kammen, ed., "Maryland in 1699: A Letter from the Reverend Hugh Jones," *JSH*, 29 (1963): 369.

16. Hugh Jones, *The Present State of Virginia, from Whence Is Inferred a Short View of Maryland and North Carolina*, ed. Richard L. Morton (Chapel Hill: University of North Carolina Press, 1956), pp. 77–78, 197; Arthur Pierce Middleton, *Tobacco Coast: A Maritime History of the Chesapeake Bay in the Colonial Era* (Newport News, Va.: Mariners' Museum, 1953), pp. 97–98. Modern usage reverses the meanings of the terms stemming and stripping.

17. Russell R. Menard and Lois Green Carr, "The Lords Baltimore and the Colonization of Maryland," in David B. Quinn, ed., *Early Maryland in a Wider World* (Detroit: Wayne State University Press, 1982), pp. 193–94, 201; Aubrey C. Land, *Colonial Maryland: A History* (Millwood, N.Y.: KTO Press, 1981), p. 26; Arthur E. Karinen, "Numerical and Distributional Aspects of Maryland Population, 1631–1840," part 2, *MHM*, 60 (1965): 144–46.

18. Cecil Calvert quoted in Andrews, *Founding of Maryland*, p. 169.

19. For a full account of Ingle's capture and his relationship with Cornwallis, see Andrews, *Founding of Maryland*, pp. 113–18.

20. Burgesses to Lord Baltimore quoted in Land, *Colonial Maryland*, p. 47.

21. *ArchMd*, 1:244–47.

22. For Congregationalist complaints against "Arbitrary and Popish Government," see *Babylon's Fall in Maryland, . . .* in Hall, ed., *Narratives of Early Maryland*, especially pp. 235–36.

23. Ebenezer Cook quoted in Lorena S. Walsh and Russell R. Menard, "Death in the Chesapeake: Two Life Tables for Men in Early Colonial Maryland," *MHM*, 69 (1974): 225. This passage also draws heavily from Darrett B. Rutman and Anita H. Rutman, "Of

Agues and Fevers: Malaria in the Early Chesapeake," *WMQ* (3d ser.), 33 (1976): 31–60; Menard, "Immigrants and Their Increase: The Progress of Population Growth in Early Colonial Maryland," in Aubrey C. Land, Lois Green Carr, and Edward C. Papenfuse, eds., *Law, Society, and Politics in Early Maryland* (Baltimore: Johns Hopkins University Press, 1977), pp. 88–110; and Daniel Blake Smith, "Mortality and Family in the Colonial Chesapeake," *JIH*, 8 (1978): 403–37.

24. Hammond, with Jaspar Danckaerts and Peter Sluyter, *Journal of a Voyage to New York and a Tour in Several of the American Colonies, in 1679–80,* quoted in Gloria Main, *Tobacco Colony: Life in Early Maryland, 1650–1720* (Princeton, N.J.: Princeton University Press, 1982), p. 144n.

25. Lois Green Carr and Lorena S. Walsh, "The Planter's Wife: The Experience of White Women in Seventeenth-Century Maryland," *WMQ* (3d ser.), 34 (1977): 542–71; Menard and Carr, "Lords Baltimore and Colonization," p. 202.

26. George Alsop, *A Character of the Province of Maryland*, in Hall, ed., *Narratives of Early Maryland*, pp. 342, 357–58. This paragraph and following ones rely particularly on Russell R. Menard, "From Servant to Freeholder: Status Mobility and Property Accumulation in Seventeenth-Century Maryland," *WMQ* (3d ser.), 30 (1973): 37–64, and Lorena S. Walsh, "Servitude and Opportunity in Charles County, Maryland, 1658–1705," in Land et al., eds., *Law, Society, and Politics in Early Maryland*, pp. 111–33.

27. Reverend Joseph Mosley, S.J., quoted in Edward Ignatius Devitt, ed., *Woodstock Letters, Published by the Students of Woodstock College*, 35 (1906): 53–54.

28. Tomkinson quoted in Lorena S. Walsh, "'Till Death Us Do Part': Marriage and Family in Seventeenth-Century Maryland," in Thad W. Tate and David L. Ammerman, eds., *The Chesapeake in the Seventeenth Century: Essays in Anglo-American Society* (New York: W. W. Norton & Co., 1979), pp. 130–31.

29. Makemie quoted in Richard Webster, *A History of the Presbyterian Church in America . . .* (Philadelphia: Joseph M. Wilson, 1857), p. 89, and in L. P. Bowen, *The Days of Makemie; or, The Vine Planted,* A.D. *1680–1708* (Philadelphia: Presbyterian Board of Publication, 1885), pp. 105, 155.

30. Quakers quoted in Edward D. Neill, *Founders of Maryland as Portrayed in Manuscripts, Provincial Records and Early Documents*, Munsell's Series of Local American History, vol. 11 (Albany, N.Y.: J. Munsell, 1876), p. 131; Fox's *Journal* quoted in Land, *Colonial Maryland*, p. 64.

31. Fox quoted in David W. Jordan, "'God's Candle' within Government: Quakers and Politics in Early Maryland," *WMQ* (3d ser.), 39 (1982): 636. This paragraph and the preceding one draw heavily on Jordan's article.

32. Danckaerts and Sluyter quoted in Dieter Cunz, *The Maryland Germans: A History* (Princeton, N.J.: Princeton University Press, 1948), p. 28; Labadists on Quakers quoted in Andrews, *Founding of Maryland*, p. 304.

33. This paragraph and those following rely upon Lois Green Carr and David William Jordan, *Maryland's Revolution of Government, 1689–1692* (Ithaca, N.Y.: Cornell University Press, 1974).

34. Alsop, *Character of Maryland*, in Hall, ed., *Narratives of Early Maryland*, p. 367. See also James H. Merrell, "Cultural Continuity among the Piscataway Indians of Colonial Maryland," *WMQ* (3d ser.), 36 (1979): 560–68, and Andrews, *Founding of Maryland*, pp. 273–84.

35. Calvert and burgesses quoted in Carr and Jordan, *Maryland's Revolution of Government*, pp. 21–22.

36. Baltimore quoted in Land, *Colonial Maryland*, p. 70.

37. Reverend Yeo and Baltimore quoted ibid., pp. 65–66.

38. For quotes on Coode's appearance and politics, see David W. Jordan, "John Coode, Perennial Rebel," *MHM*, 70 (1975): 2.

39. Thomas Lord Culpeper quoted in Land, *Colonial Maryland*, p. 83.

40. Joseph quoted in Raphael Semmes, *Crime and Punishment in Early Maryland* (Baltimore: Johns Hopkins Press, 1938), p. 174.

Chapter 2

1. Rebecca Key, assembly, and Rev. Hugh Jones quoted in John W. Reps, *Tidewater Towns: City Planning in Colonial Virginia and Maryland* (Williamsburg, Va.: Colonial Williamsburg Foundation, 1972), pp. 128, 132; Cook, *The Sot-Weed Factor; Or, a Voyage to Maryland. A Satyr* (London: B. Bragg, 1708), reprinted in Bernard C. Steiner, ed., *Early Maryland Poetry: The Works of Ebenezer Cook, Gent: Laureat of Maryland, with an Appendix Containing the Mousetrap*, Fund Publication no. 36 (Baltimore: MHS, 1900), p. 29. In the late seventeenth century, Marylanders also referred to the Annapolis site as Arundelton.

2. This paragraph draws from Whittington B. Johnson, "The Origin and Nature of African Slavery in Seventeenth-Century Maryland," *MHM*, 73 (1978): 239–40.

3. *ArchMd*, 1:489, 533–34.

4. *ArchMd*, 7:204; see also Winthrop D. Jordan, *White Over Black: American Attitudes toward the Negro, 1550–1812* (Chapel Hill: University of North Carolina Press, 1968), pp. 71–82, and Jeffrey R. Brackett, *The Negro in Maryland: A Study of the Institution of Slavery*, JHUS, extra vol. 6 (1889), pp. 28–29.

5. Calvert quoted in Aubrey C. Land, *Colonial Maryland: A History* (Millwood, N.Y.: KTO Press, 1981), p. 72.

6. On the ratio of indentured servants to slaves in early Maryland, see Russell R. Menard, "From Servants to Slaves: The Transformation of the Chesapeake Labor System," *Southern Studies*, 16 (1977): 360–61, and Paul G. E. Clemons, *The Atlantic Economy and Colonial Maryland's Eastern Shore: From Tobacco to Grain* (Ithaca, N.Y.: Cornell University Press, 1980), pp. 60–61.

7. This paragraph and the preceding ones rely on Darold D. Wax, "Black Immigrants: The Slave Trade in Colonial Maryland," *MHM*, 73 (1978): 32–35; Russell R. Menard, "The Maryland Slave Population, 1658–1730: A Demographic Profile of Blacks in Four Counties," *WMQ* (3d ser.), 32 (1975): 30–35; Menard, "Servants to Slaves," p. 382; Clemons, *Atlantic Economy and Eastern Shore*, pp. 60–63; Gloria Main, *Tobacco Colony: Life in Early Maryland, 1650–1720* (Princeton, N.J.: Princeton University Press, 1982), pp. 123–37; and Allan Kulikoff, "The Origins of Afro-American Society in Tidewater Maryland and Virginia, 1700 to 1790," *WMQ* (3d ser.), 35 (1978): 232–37.

8. William and Mary and Richard Hill quoted in Lois Green Carr and David William Jordan, *Maryland's Revolution of Government, 1689–1692* (Ithaca, N.Y.: Cornell University Press, 1974), pp. 102, 113, 140.

9. Council quoted in David W. Jordan, "Sir Thomas Lawrence, Secretary of Maryland: A Royal Placeman's Fortunes in America," *MHM*, 76 (1981): 26. This section draws heavily from Jordan's article.

10. *ArchMd*, 13:421–561; quotes from pp. 467, 513.

11. *ArchMd*, 13:505–6, 546–49; 19:193; 26:261, 349–50.

12. *ArchMd*, 13:425, 450, 476. On the size of the Protestant population and its ministerial needs, see Carr and Jordan, *Maryland's Revolution of Government*, p. 204, and Nelson Waite Rightmyer, *Maryland's Established Church* (Baltimore: Church Historical Society, 1956), pp. 24–25.

13. *ArchMd*, 19:421.

14. Clergy and Bray quoted in Rightmyer, *Maryland's Established Church*, p. 46.

15. Rev. James Blair and Robert Beverley, *The History and Present State of Virginia*, quoted in Richard Webster, *A History of the Presbyterian Church in America . . .* (Philadelphia: Joseph M. Wilson, 1857), p. 89; Rev. Peregrine Cony and seven others to Archbishop of Canterbury, 14 May 1698, quoted in Kenneth L. Carroll, "Quaker Opposition to the Establishment of a State Church in Maryland," *MHM*, 65 (1970): 161.

16. Quaker resolutions quoted in Carroll, "Quaker Opposition," p. 157. This passage also relies on David W. Jordan, "'God's Candle' within Government: Quakers and Politics in Early Maryland," *WMQ* (3d ser.), 39 (1982): 628–54.

17. Anglican churchmen and Seymour quoted in Rightmyer, *Maryland's Established Church*, p. 41, and *ArchMd*, 26:289.

18. Talbot County Court quoted in Alan F. Day, "Lawyers in Colonial Maryland," *AJLH*, 17 (1973): 163.

19. Seymour quoted in Land, *Colonial Maryland*, p. 106. This paragraph and the several above rely on Paul G. E. Clemons, "Economy and Society on Maryland's Eastern Shore, 1689–1733," in Aubrey C. Land, Lois Green Carr, and Edward C. Papenfuse, eds., *Law, Society, and Politics in Early Maryland* (Baltimore: Johns Hopkins University Press, 1977), p. 164; Clemons, *Atlantic Economy and Eastern Shore*, pp. 97–108, 120–69; Menard, "Maryland Slave Population," p. 50; Russell R. Menard, "Immigrants and Their Increase: The Progress of Population Growth in Early Colonial Maryland," in Land et al., eds., *Law, Society, and Politics in Early Maryland*, pp. 98–102; and David W. Jordan, "Political Stability and the Emergence of a Native Elite in Maryland," in Thad W. Tate and David L. Ammerman, eds., *The Chesapeake in the Seventeenth Century: Essays in Anglo-American Society* (New York: W. W. Norton & Co., 1979), especially pp. 269–70.

20. Assembly quoted in Jordan, "Political Stability," p. 271.

21. This paragraph draws on Russell R. Menard, "From Servant to Freeholder: Status Mobility and Property Accumulation in Seventeenth-Century Maryland," *WMQ* (3d ser.), 30 (1973): 60; Russell R. Menard, P. M. G. Harris, and Lois Green Carr, "Opportunity and Inequality: The Distribution of Wealth on the Lower Western Shore of Maryland, 1638–1705," *MHM*, 69 (1974): 178; Clemons, *Atlantic Economy and Eastern Shore*, pp. 104–5.

22. African slave and assembly quoted in Kulikoff, "Origins of Afro-American Society," pp. 244, 238; "Eighteenth Century Maryland as Portrayed in the 'Itinerant Observations' of Edward Kimber," *MHM*, 51 (1956): 327–28.

23. Rev. Hugh Jones quoted in Allan Kulikoff, "A 'Prolifick' People: Black Population Growth in the Chesapeake Colonies, 1700–1790," *Southern Studies*, 16 (1977): 391.

24. Beverley, *History and Present State of Virginia*, Louis B. Wright, ed. (Chapel Hill: University of North Carolina Press, 1947), pt. 4, p. 83; Cook, *Sotweed Redivivus: Or the Planters Looking-Glass. In Burlesque Verse. Calculated for the Meridian of Maryland* (Annapolis: William Parks, 1730), in Steiner, *Early Maryland Poetry*, p. 36.

25. This paragraph and those below rely on Carville Earle and Ronald Hoffman, "Staple Crops and Urban Development in the Eighteenth-Century South," *PAH*, 10 (1976), especially p. 31; Main, *Tobacco Colony*, pp. 58, 77; Clemons, *Atlantic Economy and Eastern Shore*, pp. 168–205.

26. Charles Carroll, Barrister, quoted in David Curtis Skaggs, *Roots of Maryland Democracy, 1753–1776*, Contributions in American History, no. 30 (Westport, Conn.: Greenwood Press, 1973), p. 37. This passage draws from Keach Johnson, "The Baltimore Company Seeks English Markets: A Study of the Anglo-American Iron Trade, 1731–1755," *WMQ* (3d ser.), 16 (1959): 37–42.

27. References to the treeless region of northwestern Baltimore County and Captain Civility in Frank W. Porter III, "From Backcountry to County: The Delayed Settlement of Western Maryland," *MHM*, 70 (1975): 336–38; Dulany report on speculators quoted in Dieter Cunz, *The Maryland Germans: A History* (Princeton, N.J.: Princeton University Press, 1948), p. 60.

28. Cresap quoted in Aubrey C. Land, *The Dulanys of Maryland: A Biographical Study of Daniel Dulany, The Elder (1685–1753), and Daniel Dulany, The Younger (1722–1797)* (Baltimore: Johns Hopkins Press, 1968), p. 144. For another version of the remark, see Scottie Fitzgerald Smith, "The Maryland Ancestors of Zelda Sayre Fitzgerald," *MHM*, 78 (1983): 219.

29. Dulany on western Maryland quoted in Land, *Dulanys of Maryland*, p. 172; assembly on Indian title purchase quoted in Porter, "Backcountry to County," p. 340.

30. Remarks on German settlers quoted in Porter, "Backcountry to County," pp. 344–45.

31. "'Itinerant Observations' of Edward Kimber," pp. 323, 325.

32. For developments in vernacular architecture, see especially Cary Carson, "The 'Virginia House' in Maryland," *MHM*, 69 (1974): 185–96; Paula Stoner, "Early Folk Architecture of Washington County," *MHM*, 72 (1977): 512–22; and Henry Chandlee Forman, *Tidewater Maryland Architecture and Gardens* (New York: Bonanza Books, 1974).

33. Main, *Tobacco Colony*, especially pp. 195–205; "Narrative of a Voyage to Maryland," *AHR*, 12 (1907): 336; Michael Kammen, ed., "Maryland in 1699: A Letter from the Rever-

end Hugh Jones," *JSH*, 29 (1963): 370; David W Jordan, ed., "Maryland Hoggs and Hyde Park Dutchesses: A Brief Account of Maryland in 1697," *MHM*, 73 (1978): 90.

34. "Narrative of a Voyage to Maryland," pp. 329–36; William Eddis, *Letters from America*, ed. Aubrey C. Land (Cambridge, Mass.: Belknap Press of Harvard University Press, 1969), p. 32; *Maryland Gazette* and journal of Jasper Danckaerts and Peter Sluyter quoted in J. Thomas Scharf, *History of Maryland from the Earliest Period to the Present Day* (3 vols.; Baltimore: John B. Piet, 1879), 2:4 and 4n.

35. *Maryland Gazette*, 24 March 1747, quoted in Joseph Towne Wheeler, "Reading and Other Recreations of Marylanders, 1700–1776," *MHM*, 38 (1943): 43; "Narrative of a Voyage to Maryland," p. 329; Scharf, *History of Maryland*, 2:74–75.

36. Quaker complaint quoted in Matthew Page Andrews, *History of Maryland: Province and State* (Garden City, N.Y.: Doubleday, Doran & Co., 1929), p. 225n.

37. *Maryland Gazette*, 24 March 1747, quoted in Wheeler, "Readings and Other Recreations," p. 43.

38. Eddis, *Letters from America*, p. 54.

39. *ArchMd*, 34:740. The following passage draws upon Richard Beale Davis, *Intellectual Life in the Colonial South, 1585–1763* (3 vols.; Knoxville: University of Tennessee Press, 1978), pp. 282–88, 509–14, 527–38, 1292–94, 1383–96.

40. "'Itinerant Observations' of Edward Kimber," p. 335.

41. Calvert quoted in Land, *Colonial Maryland*, p. 141.

42. Cook, *Sotweed Redivivus*, in Steiner, *Early Maryland Poetry*, p. 39; Andrew Burnaby, *Travels in North America*, in John Pinkerton, *A General Collection of the Best and Most Interesting Voyages and Travels in Various Parts of America . . .* (4 vols.; London, 1819), 3:725; Eddis, *Letters from America*, p. 48.

43. Anderson advertisement, *Maryland Gazette*, 21 October 1746, quoted in Gregory R. Weidman, *Furniture in Maryland, 1740–1940: The Collection of the Maryland Historical Society* (Baltimore: MHS, 1984), p. 44.

44. "Journal of a French Traveller in the Colonies, 1765, II," *AHR*, 27 (1921): 70; Burnaby, *Travels*, in Pinkerton, *General Collection*, 3:727; Eddis, *Letters from America*, p. 14.

Chapter 3

1. Lester J. Cappon, ed., *The Adams-Jefferson Letters: The Complete Correspondence Between Thomas Jefferson and Abigail and John Adams* (2 vols.; Chapel Hill: University of North Carolina Press, 1959), 2:455; *Maryland Gazette*, 20 May 1773; John Adams to James Warren, 20 May 1776, in *Warren-Adams Letters; Being Chiefly a Correspondence among John Adams, Samuel Adams, and James Warren*, Volume 1, *1773–1777*, Massachusetts Historical Society Collections, vol. 72 (Boston: Massachusetts Historical Society, 1917), p. 251.

2. William Green, *The Sufferings of William Green . . .* (London: J. Long, [1775?]), p. 5. I am indebted to A. Roger Ekirch for allowing me to use material from the manuscript to his *Bound for America: The Transportation of British Convicts to the Colonies, 1718–1775* (Oxford: Oxford University Press, 1987).

3. Cecilius Calvert to Horatio Sharpe, 23 December 1755, *ArchMd*, 14:329; Annapolis *Maryland Gazette*, 17 December 1772 and 16 October 1751; *Accounts of the Ordinary of Newgate, His Account of the Behaviour, Confessions and Dying Words, of the Malefactors who were Executed at Tyburn* (London), 3 August 1726, p. 4, 1 June 1752, p. 80; *The Life and Actions of James Dalton . . .* (London: J. Nicholson, [1743]), p. 31; William Eddis, *Letters from America*, ed. Aubrey C. Land (Cambridge, Mass.: Belknap Press, Harvard University Press, 1969), p. 36.

4. *Accounts of the Ordinary of Newgate*, 21 October 1743, p. 9; *Maryland Gazette*, 4 August 1747, 17 April, 1 May, 16 November 1751; *Pennsylvania Gazette*, 9 and 16 May 1751, 19 May 1773; Philip Babcock Grove, "An Oxford Convict in Maryland," *MHM*, 37 (1942): 194.

5. Byrd to Charles Boyle, 5 July 1726, in Marion Tinling, ed., *The Correspondence of the Three William Byrds of Westover, Virginia, 1684–1776* (2 vols.; Charlottesville: University Press of Virginia, 1977), 1:355; Court Order, April 1721, Provincial Court Judgments, 1719–22 (p. 362) and Presentment of the Maryland Grand Jury, April 1723, Provincial

Court Judgments, 1722–24 (p. 132), MHR; *ArchMd*, 35:212–13; *Maryland Gazette*, 22 May 1755, 20 August 1767.

6. Calvert quoted in Aubrey C. Land, *Colonial Maryland: A History* (Millwood, N.Y.: KTO Press, 1981), p. 129.

7. House and council quoted ibid., pp. 131–32, 134.

8. Dulany, *The Right of the Inhabitants of Maryland, to the Benefit of the English Laws*, appendix to St. George Leakin Sioussat, *The English Statutes in Maryland*, JHUS, 21 (1903), pp. 82, 90; Calvert quoted in Land, *Colonial Maryland*, p. 145.

9. The act of May 1736 continued the tobacco duty of three pence per hogshead until 29 September 1739 unless Ogle died or was removed, in which case, the act stipulated, "at the end of the next Session of Assembly which shall happen after such Death or Removall . . . This Act shall be void . . ." (*ArchMd*, 18:470).

10. Andrew Burnaby, *Travels in North America* (London, 1775), in John Pinkerton, *A General Collection of the Best and Most Interesting Voyages and Travels in Various Parts of America . . .* (4 vols.; London, 1819), 3:725; lower house quoted in Matthew Page Andrews, *History of Maryland: Province and State* (Garden City, N.Y.: Doubleday, Doran & Co., 1929), pp. 247–48.

11. House of Delegates and Braddock quoted in Andrews, *History of Maryland*, pp. 250, 254.

12. For Dulany's remarks, see "Military and Political Affairs in the Middle Colonies in 1755," *PMHB*, 3 (1879): 21, 27; Sharpe and description of Cresap and men quoted in Andrews, *History of Maryland*, pp. 257n, 260–61. On the fears of insurrection Sharpe shared with Prince George's County residents, see *ArchMd*, 6:251, 31:246.

13. Sharpe and delegates quoted in Andrews, *History of Maryland*, pp. 255, 259.

14. *Maryland Gazette*, 8 April 1762, quoted in John C. Rainbolt, "A Note on the Maryland Declaration of Rights and Constitution of 1776," *MHM*, 66 (1971): 422.

15. Cecilius Calvert quoted in David Curtis Skaggs, *Roots of Maryland Democracy, 1753–1776*, Contributions in American History, no. 30 (Westport, Conn.: Greenwood Press, 1973), p. 31.

16. Ibid., p. 44; *ArchMd*, 30:270. See also Skaggs, *Roots of Maryland Democracy*, pp. 18–20, 65, 75.

17. Eddis, *Letters from America*, p. 64.

18. Skaggs, *Roots of Maryland Democracy*, pp. 39–42.

19. "George Meanwell" and Rev. Joseph Moseley quoted ibid., pp. 11, 42, 47; Gregory A. Stiverson, *Poverty in a Land of Plenty: Tenancy in Eighteenth Century Maryland* (Baltimore: Johns Hopkins University Press, 1977), pp. 84–85.

20. Tommy R. Thompson, "Debtors, Creditors, and the General Assembly in Colonial Maryland," *MHM*, 72 (1977): 67.

21. Donnell MacClure Owings, *His Lordship's Patronage: Offices of Profit in Colonial Maryland*, Studies in Maryland History, no. 1 (Baltimore: MHS, 1953), p. 70; Thompson, "Debtors, Creditors, and the General Assembly," pp. 70–71.

22. Martino quoted in Thompson, "Debtors, Creditors, and the General Assembly," p. 72.

23. Tommy R. Thompson, "Personal Indebtedness and the American Revolution in Maryland," *MHM*, 73 (1978): 15, 17; Ronald Hoffman, *A Spirit of Dissension: Economics, Politics, and the Revolution in Maryland* (Baltimore: Johns Hopkins University Press, 1973), p. 29.

24. Reference to Chase and Forensic Club in Elizabeth B. Anderson, *Annapolis: A Walk through History* (Centreville, Md.: Tidewater Publishers, 1984), p. 55.

25. Hood quoted in Aubrey C. Land, *The Dulanys of Maryland: A Biographical Study of Daniel Dulany, The Elder (1685–1753), and Daniel Dulany, The Younger (1722–1797)* (Baltimore: Johns Hopkins Press, 1968), p. 261; "Journal of a French Traveller in the Colonies, 1765, II," *AHR*, 27 (1921): 72.

26. Sharpe quoted in Land, *Colonial Maryland*, p. 245; "Maryland Gossip," *PMHB*, 3 (1879): 148.

27. "Daniel Dulany's *Considerations*," *MHM*, 6 (1911): 380–81, 390.

28. Francis F. Beirne, "Sam Chase, 'Disturber,'" *MHM*, 57 (1962): 78.

29. Lux quoted in Hoffman, *Spirit of Dissension*, p. 38. I am indebted to Professor Hoffman for much of the material in the following pages.

30. Ibid., p. 76. For another view of Maryland participation in the nonimportation movement of 1769–70, see Land, *Colonial Maryland*, pp. 261–63.

31. Reviewer and Rev. Jonathan Boucher quoted in James Haw, "The Patronage Follies: Bennet Allen, John Morton Jordan, and the Fall of Horatio Sharpe," *MHM*, 71 (1976): 137.

32. Report and Rev. Thomas Chandler quoted ibid., p. 148.

33. Julian Boyd et al., eds., *The Papers of Thomas Jefferson* (20 vols. to date; Princeton, N.J.: Princeton University Press, 1950–), 1:19–20.

34. Jonathan Boucher, *Reminiscences of an American Loyalist, 1738–1789* (Boston and New York: Houghton Mifflin and Co., 1925), pp. 68–69.

35. Land, *Dulanys of Maryland*, p. 241; Hoffman, *Spirit of Dissension*, pp. 103–13.

36. Carroll of Carrollton quoted in Hoffman, *Spirit of Dissension*, pp. 120–21.

37. *Maryland Gazette*, 3 October 1771, quoted in Rainbolt, "Note on Maryland Declaration of Rights and Constitution of 1776," p. 422.

38. "Account of the Destruction of the Brig 'Peggy Stewart,' at Annapolis, 1774," *PMHB*, 25 (1901): 250–51.

39. John Adams quoted in Hoffman, *Spirit of Dissension*, p. 133.

40. Bladensburg trader to brother in Glasgow, 11 November 1774, and Maryland convention, both quoted in Hoffman, *Spirit of Dissension*, pp. 136, 139.

41. The Committee of Observation, Harford County, Maryland, Record Book, 1774–77, "Bush Declaration" (Ms. 2159, MHS); Samuel Chew quoted in Hoffman, *Spirit of Dissension*, p. 139, Eden in Skaggs, *Roots of Maryland Democracy*, p. 151.

42. Rev. Boucher quoted in Edwin G. Burrows and Michael Wallace, "The American Revolution: The Ideology and Psychology of National Liberation," *PAH*, 6 (1972): 296, 298–99; "Letters of Rev. Jonathan Boucher," *MHM*, 7 (1912): 2.

43. Robert Davis and John Simmons quoted in Hoffman, *Spirit of Dissension*, pp. 147, 149.

44. Maryland convention and Eden quoted ibid., pp. 154–55; Stone, Rumsey, and Hollyday quoted in Skaggs, *Roots of Maryland Democracy*, p. 176. Lee referred to members of the Virginia convention and Maryland Council of Safety as "namby pambys" who were growing "more timid and hysterical" (Hoffman, *Spirit of Dissension*, pp. 157–58).

45. Jefferson to Adams, 12 September 1821, and Adams to Jefferson, 24 September 1821, in Cappon, ed., *Adams-Jefferson Letters*, 2:575, 577; Adams to Chase, 14 June 1776, quoted in Skaggs, *Roots of Maryland Democracy*, p. 178. James Madison thought the safe conduct message to the newly independent Commonwealth of Virginia insulting; James Madison, Jr., to James Madison, Sr., [1–15 June 1776], William T. Hutchinson et al., eds., *The Papers of James Madison* (15 vols. to date; Chicago: University of Chicago Press, and Charlottesville: University Press of Virginia, 1956–), 1:182.

46. Eden quoted in Hoffman, *Spirit of Dissension*, p. 39; Maryland convention quoted in Land, *Colonial Maryland*, p. 314. For Lloyd's reference to Goldsborough, see Herbert E. Klingelhofer, "The Cautious Revolution: Maryland and the Movement toward Independence, 1774–1776," *MHM*, 60 (1965): 302.

47. Prince George's County citizens and McClure quoted in Skaggs, *Roots of Maryland Democracy*, pp. 180–81. For the Flying Camp episode, see Hoffman, *Spirit of Dissension*, pp. 171–72.

48. "Watchman" quoted in Skaggs, *Roots of Maryland Democracy*, p. 182.

49. On gains in voter qualification after 1776, see Thornton Anderson, "Eighteenth-Century Suffrage: The Case of Maryland," *MHM*, 76 (1981): 149–51, and Rainbolt, "Note on Maryland Declaration of Rights and Constitution of 1776."

50. H. H. Walker Lewis, *The Maryland Constitution, 1776* (Baltimore: MSBA, 1976), pp. 65, 60, 35–42.

51. Anne Arundel troops quoted in Hoffman, *Spirit of Dissension*, pp. 189–90.

52. Nathaniel Potter on the Methodists, Thomas Ennals on Eastern Shore militia, and Fitzhugh quoted ibid., pp. 227, 186, 140; for the unidentified "Illitorate People" comment, see John R. Wennersten, *The Oyster Wars of Chesapeake Bay* (Centreville, Md.: Tidewater Publishers, 1981), p. 9.

53. Carrolls quoted in Hoffman, *Spirit of Dissension*, pp. 222, 211.

54. Eddis to Governor Eden, 23 July 1777, ibid., p. 223.

55. Recruiting orders quoted in Mary K. Meyer, ed., "Captain John Fulford's Company, February 13, 1776, to May 21, 1777," *MHM*, 69 (1974): 93.

56. Description of Cresap's troops from Andrews, *History of Maryland*, p. 310; Tilghman and adjutant quoted in J. Thomas Scharf, *History of Maryland from the Earliest Period to the Present Day* (3 vols.; Baltimore: John B. Piet, 1879), 2:248, 260.

57. Greene quoted in Cary Howard, "John Eager Howard: Patriot and Public Servant," *MHM*, 62 (1967): 304.

58. Alexander Graydon's *Memoirs of His Own Times* quoted in James H. Fitzgerald Brewer, *History of the 175th Infantry (Fifth Maryland)* (Baltimore: War Records Division, MHS, 1955), p. 16

59. Sergeant Curran quoted in Thomas H. Hattery, ed., *Western Maryland: A Profile* (Mt. Airy, Md.: Lomond Books, 1980), p. iv.

Chapter 4

1. For the comments of Médéric L. E. Moreau de Saint-Méry, Jacques Pierre Brissot de Warville, duc de La Rochefoucauld-Liancourt, and John Harriott, see Raphael Semmes, *Baltimore as Seen by Visitors, 1783–1860*, Studies in Maryland History, no. 2 (Baltimore: MHS, 1953), pp. 4–13. J. Davis quoted in Ronald Hoffman, *A Spirit of Dissension: Economics, Politics, and the Revolution in Maryland* (Baltimore: Johns Hopkins University Press, 1973), p. 74. See also *Chateaubriand's Travels in America*, trans. Richard Switzer (Lexington: University of Kentucky Press, 1969), p. 13, and Isaac Weld, Jr., *Travels through the States of North America . . . 1795, 1796, and 1797* (2 vols.; London: John Stockdale, 1799), 1:46.

2. Maryland convention, 9 November 1776, in Peter Force, ed., *American Archives: Fifth Series . . .* (3 vols.; Washington, D.C.: U.S. Congress, 1853), 3:178.

3. On Chase's conduct, see Hoffman, *Spirit of Dissension*, pp. 244–45, 259–60, and Forrest McDonald, *E Pluribus Unum: The Formation of the American Republic, 1776–1790* (Boston: Houghton Mifflin Co., 1965), pp. 90–99.

4. Baltimore *Maryland Gazette*, 28 September 1787, quoted in Philip A. Crowl, *Maryland during and after the Revolution: A Political and Economic Study*, JHUS, 61 (1943), p. 97.

5. Baltimore *Maryland Gazette*, 23 February, 1 April, and 17 June 1785, quoted ibid., p. 86. The following paragraphs draw heavily from Edward C. Papenfuse, "The Legislative Response to a Costly War: Fiscal Policy and Factional Politics in Maryland, 1777–1789," in Ronald Hoffman and Peter J. Albert, eds., *Sovereign States in an Age of Uncertainty* (Charlottesville: University Press of Virginia for the United States Capitol Historical Society, 1981).

6. Baltimore *Maryland Journal*, 4 and 14 July 1786, quoted in Crowl, *Maryland during and after the Revolution*, pp. 90, 101.

7. Baltimore *Maryland Gazette*, 6 March 1787, and *Maryland Journal*, 30 March 1787, quoted ibid., pp. 106–7.

8. Martin quoted in L. Marx Renzulli, Jr., *Maryland: The Federalist Years* (Rutherford, Madison, Teaneck, N.J.: Fairleigh Dickinson University Press, 1972), p. 71.

9. *Maryland Journal*, 1 April 1788, quoted in Crowl, *Maryland during and after the Revolution*, pp. 132–33.

10. Baltimore petition, 11 April 1789, quoted ibid., pp. 123–24.

11. Oliver quoted in Stuart Weems Bruchey, *Robert Oliver, Merchant of Baltimore, 1783–1819*, JHUS, 74 (1956), p. 24. On Baltimore commercial developments in these years, see Gary Lawson Browne, *Baltimore in the Nation, 1789–1861* (Chapel Hill: University of North Carolina Press, 1980), pp. 19–33.

12. Jefferson quoted in Robert D. Arbuckle, "John Nicholson and the Great Steamboat Rivalry," *MHM*, 71 (1976): 61; Washington and Gates in Matthew Page Andrews, *History of Maryland: Province and State* (Garden City, N.Y.: Doubleday, Doran & Co., 1929), pp. 381–82.

13. On local inventiveness, see G. Terry Sharrer, "Patents by Marylanders, 1790–1830," *MHM*, 71 (1976): 50–59, and James Weston Livingood, *The Philadelphia-Baltimore*

Trade Rivalry, 1780–1860 (Harrisburg: Pennsylvania Historical and Museum Commission, 1947), p. 15.

14. John W. McGrain, "Englehart Cruse and Baltimore's First Steam Mill," *MHM*, 71 (1976): 65–79.

15. This paragraph draws from Richard M. Bernard, "A Portrait of Baltimore in 1800: Economic and Occupational Patterns in an Early American City," *MHM*, 69 (1974): 341–60, and Douglas F. Stickle, "Death and Class in Baltimore: The Yellow Fever Epidemic of 1800," *MHM*, 74 (1979): 284.

16. Adams quoted in Sherry H. Olson, *Baltimore: The Building of an American City* (Baltimore: Johns Hopkins University Press, 1980), p. 15, and Annie Leakin Sioussat, *Old Baltimore* (New York: Macmillan Co., 1931), p. 91.

17. Guy quoted in J. Hall Pleasants, "Four Late Eighteenth Century Anglo-American Landscape Painters," *Proceedings of the American Antiquarian Society*, 52 (1943): 241.

18. *Maryland Journal*, 10 August 1784, quoted in Dieter Cunz, *The Maryland Germans: A History* (Princeton, N.J.: Princeton University Press, 1948), p. 179.

19. Anonymous Presbyterian quoted in Terry David Bilhartz, "Urban Religion and the Second Great Awakening: A Religious History of Baltimore, Maryland, 1790–1830" (Ph.D. dissertation, George Washington University, 1979), p. 132.

20. Lutherans quoted in Cunz, *Maryland Germans*, p. 181; Rev. Bend quoted in Bilhartz, "Urban Religion," pp. 123–24.

21. Bishop Asbury quoted in Bilhartz, "Urban Religion," p. 143.

22. Grellet and Fanny Lewis quoted ibid., pp. 143, 151.

23. *American and Daily Advertiser* quoted in Charles G. Steffen, "Changes in the Organization of Artisan Production in Baltimore, 1790–1820," *WMQ* (3d ser.), 36 (1979): 101. This paragraph also draws from Stickle, "Death and Class in Baltimore," pp. 295–96.

24. Ferdinand-M. Bayard, *Travels of a Frenchman in Maryland and Virginia . . .* , ed. and trans. Ben C. McCary (Ann Arbor, Mich.: Edwards Brothers, 1950), p. 2; Weld, *Travels*, 1:37.

25. Weld, *Travels*, 1:132–33.

26. John Palmer quoted in T. J. C. Williams and Folger McKinsey, *History of Frederick County, Maryland* (2 vols.; Baltimore: Regional Publishing Co., 1979 [Frederick, 1910]), 1:143; Bayard, *Travels*, p. 27.

27. Handbill quoted in J. Thomas Scharf, *History of Western Maryland* (2 vols.; Baltimore: Regional Publishing Co., 1971 [Philadelphia, 1882]), p. 1199.

28. Norman K. Risjord, *Chesapeake Politics, 1781–1800* (New York: Columbia University Press, 1978), pp. 8–9; Bayard, *Travels*, p. 3; Fred Shelley, ed., "Ebenezer Hazard's Travels through Maryland in 1777," *MHM*, 46 (1951): 48; "Memoranda Made by Thomas R. Joynes on a Journey to the States of Ohio and Kentucky, 1810," *WMQ* (1st ser.), 10 (1902): 231.

29. Weld, *Travels*, 1:138–39, 133.

30. J. P. Brissot de Warville, *New Travels in the United States of America, 1788*, ed. Durand Echeverria (Cambridge, Mass.: Belknap Press of Harvard University Press, 1964), p. 237; Weld, *Travels*, 1:138–39.

31. Joseph Scott, *U.S. Gazetteer* (Philadelphia: F. and R. Bailey, 1795); "Memoranda Made by Thomas R. Joynes," pp. 231–32.

32. Easton *Star* quoted in Mary Jane Dowd, "The State of the Maryland Economy, 1776–1807," *MHM*, 57 (1962): 247–48.

33. Annapolis *Maryland Gazette* quoted in Renzulli, *Federalist Years*, p. 115.

34. Williams and Stone quoted ibid., pp. 125n, 132–33n.

35. Smith cited ibid., p. 141.

36. Hanson memorandum, 25 July 1790, Ms. 1235, Chase Papers, MHS.

37. Chase quoted in Risjord, *Chesapeake Politics*, pp. 351–52.

38. *Annals of Congress*, 4th Cong., 1st sess. (1796), 1157.

39. Hagerstown *Maryland Herald*, 31 January 1799, and Ash quoted in Renzulli, *Federalist Years*, p. 202.

40. Nicholite eleventh rule quoted in Kenneth L. Carroll, "Nicholites and Slavery in Eighteenth-Century Maryland," *MHM*, 79 (1984): 128.

41. *Sunday Service of the Methodists of North America*, 1784, quoted in James M. Wright, *The Free Negro in Maryland, 1634–1860*, CUS, 97 (1921), p. 211.

42. William Pinkney and Charles Carroll quoted in Jeffrey R. Brackett, *The Negro in Maryland: A Study of the Institution of Slavery*, JHUS, extra vol. 6 (1889), pp. 53–54; *Votes and Proceedings of the House of Delegates of the State of Maryland, November Session, 1791* (Annapolis, 1792), p. 83.

43. Maryland attorney and Martin quoted in Ira Berlin, *Slaves without Masters: The Free Negro in the Antebellum South* (New York: Pantheon Books, 1974), pp. 33–34. On the number of successful freedom suits, see Anita Louise Aidt, "Ambivalent Maryland: Abolitionist Activity during the Revolutionary Period" (M.A. thesis, Georgetown University, 1980), p. 57. The figures appear in the 1796 report of the Maryland Abolitionist Society.

44. On freed blacks on the Eastern Shore in these years, see Kenneth L. Carroll, "Religious Influences on the Manumission of Slaves in Caroline, Dorchester, and Talbot Counties," *MHM*, 55 (1961): 177, and Wright, *Free Negro in Maryland*, pp. 86–89.

45. This paragraph relies on Kathryn Allamong Jacob, "The Woman's Lot in Baltimore Town, 1729–97," *MHM*, 71 (1976): 283–95. Journeymen quoted in Steffen, "Organization of Artisan Production in Baltimore," p. 112.

46. Orphaline Charity School charter quoted in J. Thomas Scharf, *History of Baltimore City and County from the Earliest Period to the Present Day* (2 vols.; Baltimore: Regional Publishing Co., 1971 [Philadelphia, 1881]), p. 594.

47. On Smith's college plans, see George H. Callcott, *A History of the University of Maryland* (Baltimore: MHS, 1966), pp. 8–15. Knox quoted in Bernard C. Steiner, *History of Education in Maryland*, no. 19 in Contributions to American Educational History, ed. Herbert Baxter Adams, United States Bureau of Education, Circular of Information no. 2 (Washington, D.C.: Government Printing Office, 1894), p. 44.

48. Coke and *Plan for Erecting a College, Intended to Advance Religion in America . . .* (1785) quoted in Steiner, *History of Education*, pp. 232–33.

49. Baltimore *American and Commercial Daily Advertiser*, 24 December 1807, quoted in John S. Pancake, "Baltimore and the Embargo, 1807–1809," *MHM*, 47 (1952): 176.

50. Hollins to Wilson Cary Nicholas, 5 April 1808, quoted ibid., p. 177; for Gallatin and Randolph's charges, see *Federal Gazette and Baltimore Daily Advertiser*, 13 September 1808, and *Annals of Congress*, 10th Cong., 2d sess. (1808), 2239.

51. On the movement toward textiles, see Browne, *Baltimore in the Nation*, pp. 55–60.

52. Baltimore *Federal Republican*, 8 and 11 July 1808, quoted in Renzulli, *Federalist Years*, p. 247.

53. War chant quoted in Frank A. Cassell, "The Great Baltimore Riot of 1812," *MHM*, 70 (1975): 256.

54. This paragraph and one above draw upon Renzulli, *Federalist Years*, pp. 294, 297–98, 301, and Jerome R. Garitee, *The Republic's Private Navy: The American Privateering Business as Practiced in Baltimore during the War of 1812* (Middletown, Conn.: Wesleyan University Press for Mystic Seaport, 1977).

55. Walter Lord, *The Dawn's Early Light* (New York: W. W. Norton & Co., 1972), pp. 119, 140. See also Frank A. Cassell, "Response to Crisis: Baltimore in 1814," *MHM*, 66 (1971): 261–87.

56. Woman observer and the Rev. Gruber quoted in Lord, *Dawn's Early Light*, pp. 235, 251–52.

57. Cochrane quoted ibid., p. 271.

58. Ibid., pp. 290, 274.

Chapter 5

1. Commemorative song quoted in Edward Hungerford, *The Story of the Baltimore & Ohio Railroad, 1827–1927* (2 vols.; New York: G. P. Putnam's Sons, 1928), 1:44; Frederick Douglass, *Life and Times of Frederick Douglass, Written by Himself* (New York: Collier Books, 1962 [Boston, 1892]), pp. 39, 49, 53; Douglass, *Narrative of the Life of Frederick Douglass An American Slave, Written by Himself*, ed. Benjamin Quarles (Cambridge, Mass.: Belknap Press of Harvard University Press, 1960 [Boston, 1845]), p. 38.

2. Jedidiah Morse, *The American Geography; or, A View of the Present Situation of the United States of America* (2d ed.; London: John Stockdale, 1792), p. 354.

3. Latrobe quoted in Richard Hubbard Howland and Eleanor Patterson Spencer et al., *The Architecture of Baltimore: A Pictorial History* (Baltimore: Johns Hopkins Press, 1953), p. 53.

4. Emerson quoted in George E. Bell, "Emerson and Baltimore: A Biographical Study," *MHM*, 65 (1970): 336.

5. Hinckley to Sparks, 19 April 1817, in Herbert Baxter Adams, ed., *Life and Writings of Jared Sparks . . .* (2 vols.; Boston and New York: Houghton Mifflin & Co., 1893), 1:127–28; Channing, *A Sermon Delivered at the Ordination of the Reverend Jared Sparks . . .* (New York: John B. Russell, 1823), pp. 4, 11.

6. Adams, ed., *Jared Sparks*, 1:180, 154; Sparks to Ann Gillam Storrow, 7 June 1819, to Charles Briggs, 22 August 1821, and to Storrow, 29 October 1821, ibid., pp. 148, 185–86.

7. John Neal, *Wandering Recollections of a Somewhat Busy Life; An Autobiography* (Boston: Roberts Brothers, 1869), p. 174.

8. Ibid., p. 173. Theophilus Parsons quoted in Robert M. Ireland, "William Pinkney: A Revision and Re-emphasis," *AJLH*, 14 (1970): 235.

9. Peale to Jefferson, 13 July 1813, in Charles Coleman Sellers, *Charles Willson Peale* (New York: Scribner's, 1969 [2 pts.; Philadelphia, 1947]), pt. 2, p. 278.

10. Opening announcement quoted ibid.; newspaper notice in David P. Erlick, "The Peales and Gas Lights in Baltimore," *MHM*, 80 (1985): 13.

11. Severn Teackle Wallis, *Baltimore Visitor*, 9 August 1834, quoted in David Hein, "The Founding of the Boys' School of St. Paul's Parish, Baltimore," *MHM*, 81 (1986): 150; Wyatt quoted in George H. Callcott, *A History of the University of Maryland* (Baltimore: MHS, 1966), p. 34.

12. Newspaper reports quoted in Callcott, *University of Maryland*, pp. 32–33.

13. Thomas Harbaugh to Henry Shafer, 23 January 1815, quoted in Betsy Bahr, "The Antietam Woolen Manufacturing Company: A Case Study in American Industrial Beginnings," *Working Papers from the Regional Economic History Research Center*, 4 (no. 4, 1981): 40.

14. Maryland statute and Marshall quoted in Paul S. Clark and R. Samuel Jett, *Luther Martin of Maryland* (Baltimore: Johns Hopkins Press, 1970), pp. 295, 302.

15. British consular report quoted in James Weston Livingood, *The Philadelphia-Baltimore Trade Rivalry, 1780–1860* (Harrisburg: Pennsylvania Historical and Museum Commission, 1947), p. 18; John Quincy Adams in Gary Lawson Browne, *Baltimore in the Nation, 1789–1861* (Chapel Hill: University of North Carolina Press, 1980), p. 76; and Frank A. Cassell, *Merchant Congressman in the Young Republic: Samuel Smith of Maryland, 1752–1839* (Madison: University of Wisconsin Press, 1971), p. 223.

16. On Brown, see Gary L. Browne, "Business Innovation and Social Change: The Career of Alexander Brown after the War of 1812," *MHM*, 69 (1974): 243–55.

17. This discussion of the Cohens relies on W. Ray Luce, "The Cohen Brothers of Baltimore: From Lotteries to Banking," *MHM*, 68 (1973): 288–308.

18. *Niles' Register*, 16 August 1817, quoted in Alexander Crosby Brown, *The Old Bay Line, 1840–1940* (Richmond, Va.: Dietz Press, 1940), p. 12; Jean Baptiste Marestier on p. 13.

19. Report quoted in Hungerford, *Baltimore & Ohio*, 1:22.

20. Ibid., pp. 25, 29; *Niles' Weekly Register* quoted in Julius Rubin, *Canal or Railroad? Imitation and Innovation in Response to the Erie Canal in Philadelphia, Baltimore, and Boston*, Transactions of the American Philosophical Society, vol. 51, pt. 7 (Philadelphia: American Philosophical Society, 1961), p. 75; Shriver family letter, 26 August 1830, quoted in Frederic Shriver Klein, "Union Mills, the Shriver Homestead," *MHM*, 52 (1957): 302–3.

21. On Doughoregan Manor, see Ralph D. Gray and Gerald E. Hartdagen, eds., "A Glimpse of Baltimore Society in 1827: Letters of Henry D. Gilpin," *MHM*, 69 (1974): 268.

22. Lloyd's remarks appeared in the Easton *Republican Star and General Advertiser*, 24 November 1818. Quoted in Vivian Doris Wiser, "The Movement for Agricultural Improvement in Maryland, 1785–1865" (Ph.D. dissertation, University of Maryland, 1963), p. 94.

23. Skinner quoted ibid., p. 97.

24. *American Farmer* 7 (1825): 89–93, ibid., p. 111.

25. *American Farmer* 8 (1826): 119, ibid., p. 112; *Baltimore American*, 23 June 1821, ibid., p. 116; *American Farmer* (3d ser.), 1 (1839): 121, ibid., p. 226; *Port Tobacco Times*, 16 November 1859, ibid., p. 320.

26. Upper Marlboro *Gazette* reprinted in *American Farmer* (3d ser.), 15 (1840): 265, 283, 305–6, quoted ibid., p. 346.

27. *Bartgis's Republican Gazette* and newspaper exchange quoted in Gerald Elton Fosbroke, "An Investigation of the Attitude of Maryland toward the Missouri Compromise" (M.A. thesis, University of Maryland, 1938), pp. 57, 69–70.

28. Baltimore County petition in Alice Dana Adams, *The Neglected Period of Anti-Slavery in America, 1808–1831*, Radcliffe College Monographs, no. 14 (Boston: Ginn and Co., 1908), p. 48; Cooper quoted in Donald J. McCauley, "The Limits of Change in the Tobacco South: An Economic and Social Analysis of Prince George's County, Maryland, 1840–1860" (M.A. thesis, University of Maryland, 1973), p. 57; *Life of Elisha Tyson, Philanthropist* (Baltimore, 1825), quoted in Ira Berlin, *Slaves without Masters: The Free Negro in the Antebellum South* (New York: Pantheon Books, 1974), pp. 30–31.

29. Ethan Allen Andrews, *Slavery and the Domestic Slave Trade in the United States . . .* (Boston: Light & Stearns, 1836), pp. 43, 53.

30. See Aaron Stopak, "The Maryland State Colonization Society: Independent State Action in the Colonization Movement," *MHM*, 63 (1968): 280.

31. Minutes, board of managers, quoted ibid., p. 284.

32. Baltimore free blacks quoted in Berlin, *Slaves without Masters*, pp. 204–5; Daniel Raymond, *Thoughts on Political Economy. In Two Parts* (Baltimore: F. Lucas, Jr., 1820), p. 436.

33. Garrison quoted in John L. Thomas, *The Liberator: William Lloyd Garrison, A Biography* (Boston: Little, Brown and Co., 1963), pp. 103, 106.

34. Ibid., pp. 107–8; Lundy quoted in David K. Sullivan, "William Lloyd Garrison in Baltimore, 1829–1830," *MHM*, 68 (1973): 75n; board of managers, Maryland State Colonization Society, 30 April 1833, in Stopak, "Maryland State Colonization Society," p. 282.

35. Bladensburg arrival described in Andrews, *Slavery and Domestic Slave Trade*, p. 84.

36. Power and Frederick Fitzgerald De Roos quoted in Brown, *Old Bay Line*, p. 37.

37. Handbill quoted ibid., p. 27.

38. This passage relies on James H. Fitzgerald Brewer, "The Democratization of Maryland, 1800–1837," in Morris L. Radoff, ed., *The Old Line State: A History of Maryland*, Publication no. 16 (Annapolis: MHR, 1971), and Mark H. Haller, "The Rise of the Jackson Party in Maryland, 1820–1829," *JSH*, 28 (1962): 307–26.

39. Taney quoted in Arthur M. Schlesinger, Jr., *The Age of Jackson* (Boston: Little, Brown & Co., 1945), p. 105.

40. Kennedy quoted in Charles H. Bohner, *John Pendleton Kennedy, Gentleman from Baltimore* (Baltimore: Johns Hopkins Press, 1961), p. 120; Taney in Schlesinger, *Age of Jackson*, p. 106.

41. Buchanan quoted in Thomas Bender, "Law, Economy, and Social Values in Jacksonian America: A Maryland Case Study," *MHM*, 71 (1976): 489.

42. *Annual Report of the Directors of the Maryland Prison, 1841* (Baltimore, 1841), quoted in Marvin E. Gettleman, "The Maryland Penitentiary in the Age of Tocqueville, 1828–1842," *MHM*, 56 (1961): 287.

43. Steers and society pledge quoted in Milton A. Maxwell, "The Washington Movement," *Quarterly Journal of Studies on Alcohol*, 11 (1950): 412–13.

44. Christian Keener on Hawkins, John Zug to John Marsh, *Boston Mercantile Journal*, New York *Daily Mail*, and 1843 report of the American Temperance Union quoted ibid., pp. 414, 417–19, 427.

45. Warfield quoted in W. Wayne Smith, "Jacksonian Democracy on the Chesapeake: The Political Institutions," *MHM*, 62 (1967): 389.

46. James S. Buckingham and Cecil Whigs quoted ibid., pp. 387–88.

47. Niles, Mason Parsons, and Finley quoted ibid., pp. 386, 391.

48. McMahon quoted in James C. Mullikin, "The Eastern Shore," in Radoff, ed., *Old Line State*, p. 161n.

49. McMahon quoted in Smith, "Political Institutions," p. 382.

50. Hagerstown meeting and *Niles' Weekly Register* quoted in A. Clarke Hagensick, "Revolution or Reform in 1836: Maryland's Preface to the Dorr Rebellion," *MHM*, 57 (1962): 352.

51. Women workers quoted in Sherry H. Olson, *Baltimore: The Building of an American City* (Baltimore: Johns Hopkins University Press, 1980), p. 99.

52. On the number of debtor inmates, see Olson, *Baltimore*, p. 93; for legislation governing imprisonment for debt in the early 1830s, see *Laws of Maryland* (1830–31), chap. 155; (1832–33), chaps. 142, 309.

53. This paragraph benefits from Alan M. Wilner, *The Maryland Board of Public Works* (Annapolis: MHR, 1984), pp. 11–23.

54. Father Guth quoted in W. David Baird, "Violence along the Chesapeake and Ohio Canal: 1839," *MHM*, 66 (1971): 122; Baltimore *Whig*, 4 October 1838, in Smith, "Political Institutions," p. 392.

55. *American Farmer* (3d ser.), 1 (1839): 177, quoted in Wiser, "Agricultural Improvement," p. 172.

56. Kerr quoted in Smith, "Political Institutions," p. 381; Mayer in Joseph W. Cox, "The Origins of the Maryland Historical Society: A Case Study in Cultural Philanthropy," *MHM*, 74 (1979): 105. On Taney and *Quodlibet*, see Bohner, *Kennedy*, p. 134.

57. Emerson quoted in Bell, "Emerson and Baltimore," p. 343.

58. John Pendleton Kennedy, *Swallow Barn, or, A Sojourn in the Old Dominion* (2 vols.; Philadelphia: Cary & Lea, 1832), 2:57, 225, 227.

59. *Niles' Register* quoted in Jeffrey R. Brackett, *The Negro in Maryland: A Study of the Institution of Slavery*, JHUS, extra vol. 6 (1889), pp. 139–40n, 142.

60. William Green, *Narrative of Events in the Life of William Green (formerly a slave), Written by Himself* (Philadelphia: Rhistoric Press, 1969 [Springfield, Mass., 1853]), pp. 7–8; John W. Blassingame, ed., *Slave Testimony: Two Centuries of Letters, Speeches, Interviews, and Autobiographies* (Baton Rouge: Louisiana State University Press, 1977), p. 169; Douglass, *Narrative*, pp. 47–49; John Thompson, *The Life of John Thompson, a Fugitive Slave . . .* (New York: Negro Universities Press, 1968 [Worcester, Mass., 1856]), pp. 18, 20, 39–40.

61. Blassingame, ed., *Slave Testimony*, p. 406; Thompson, *Life*, pp. 48–49; George P. Rawick, gen. ed., *The American Slave: A Composite Autobiography*, Contributions in Afro-American and African Studies no. 11 (17 vols.; Westport, Conn.: Greenwood Publication Co., 1972), vol. 16, Kansas, Kentucky, Maryland, Ohio, Virginia, Tennessee [each section separately paginated], "Maryland," p. 61.

62. Thompson, *Life*, pp. 31, 48–49; Georgianna Morris Diary, 1 January 1854 (privately owned); Douglass, *Narrative*, p. 49; Rawick, ed., *American Slave*, "Maryland," p. 53; Blassingame, ed., *Slave Testimony*, p. 347.

63. Douglass, *Narrative*, p. 94; Klein, "Shriver Homestead," p. 300; Blassingame, ed., *Slave Testimony*, p. 406.

64. Isaac Weld, Jr., *Travels through the States of North America . . . 1795, 1796, and 1797* (2 vols.; London: John Stockdale, 1799), 1:133; Green, *Narrative of Events*, pp. 7–8.

65. Charles Ball, *Fifty Years in Chains; or, the Life of an American Slave* (Detroit: Negro Universities Press, 1971 [New York, 1859; Lewistown, Pa., 1836]), p. 16; Green, *Narrative of Events*, p. 4; Weld, *Travels*, 1:10, 245.

66. Blassingame, ed., *Slave Testimony*, p. 438; Douglass, *Narrative*, p. 60.

67. Rawick, ed., *American Slave*, "Maryland," pp. 6–7, 45, 54, 62; Green, *Narrative of Events*, pp. 6–9; Ball, *Fifty Years*, pp. 11, 17.

68. Douglass, *Narrative*, pp. 81–82; Thompson, *Life*, p. 17; Rawick, ed., *American Slave*, "Maryland," pp. 6–7, 44, 52, 62; Ball, *Fifty Years*, p. 17.

69. Rawick, ed., *American Slave*, "Maryland," pp. 8, 18, 52.

70. Thompson, *Life*, p. 17; Ball, *Fifty Years*, p. 12; Green, *Narrative of Events*, p. 9.

71. Blassingame, ed., *Slave Testimony*, pp. 406, 411; Ball, *Fifty Years*, p. 50; Thompson, *Life*, pp. 18, 43, 56; Douglass, *Narrative*, pp. 84, 110.

72. Thompson, *Life*, pp. 19, 25–26, 43; Rawick, ed., *American Slave*, "Maryland," pp. 17, 61, 75.

73. Blassingame, ed., *Slave Testimony*, p. 405; Green, *Narrative of Events*, p. 4; Rawick, ed., *American Slave*, pp. 4–5, 45.

74. Ball, *Fifty Years*, pp. 10, 15. On the efforts of Maryland slaveholders to keep bondsmen in the state, see Brackett, *Negro in Maryland*, p. 144n, and William Calderhead, "How Extensive Was the Border State Slave Trade? A New Look," *CWH*, 18 (1972): 53–54.

75. Earl Conrad, *Harriet Tubman* (Washington, D.C.: Associated Publishers, c. 1943), p. 63.

76. Blassingame, ed., *Slave Testimony*, pp. 406–7, 410–11; Green, *Narrative of Events*, p. 13.

77. Douglass, *Narrative*, p. 60; Ball, *Fifty Years*, p. 27.

78. *Memorial of Public Meeting of the Citizens of Prince George's County, to the Legislature of Maryland, Relating to Incendiary Publications, &c.* (Annapolis [?]: n.p., 1836), p. 2; Goldsborough to Vans M. Sulivane, Grand Gulf, Mississippi, 28 August 1834, *MHM*, 39 (1944): 333.

Chapter 6

1. *Spirit of the Times*, 23 February 1850; [Mrs. M. J. Houston], *Hersperos: or, Travels in the West* (2 vols.; London, 1850), 1:219; C. R. Weld, *Vacation Tour in the United States and Canada* (London, 1855), p. 336; Henry Bertram Hill and Larry Gara, eds., "Henry Herz' Description of Baltimore," *MHM*, 52 (1957): 122; diary of Mrs. Benjamin G. Harris, 26 September 1859, Harris Papers, MHS, quoted in Jean H. Baker, *The Politics of Continuity: Maryland Political Parties from 1858 to 1870* (Baltimore: Johns Hopkins University Press, 1973), p. 11.

2. Bernard C. Steiner, *History of Education in Maryland*, no. 19 in Contributions to American Educational History, ed. Herbert Baxter Adams, United States Bureau of Education, Circular of Information no. 2 (Washington, D.C.: Government Printing Office, 1894), pp. 112, 264; Kennedy quoted in George H. Callcott, *A History of the University of Maryland* (Baltimore: MHS, 1966), p. 79.

3. J. W. Hengiston in Colburn's *New Monthly Magazine* (London, 1853) quoted in Alexander Crosby Brown, *Steam Packets on the Chesapeake: A History of the Old Bay Line Since 1840* (Cambridge, Md.: Cornell Maritime Press, 1961), p. 51.

4. Davis quoted in William J. Evitts, *A Matter of Allegiances: Maryland from 1850 to 1861* (Baltimore: Johns Hopkins University Press, 1974), p. 28; Baltimore *Sun*, 24 January, 1 and 3 August 1850, quoted ibid., pp. 75, 27.

5. Baltimore *American*, 2 June 1851, quoted ibid., p. 40.

6. Baltimore *Sun* quoted in Sherry H. Olson, *Baltimore: The Building of an American City* (Baltimore: Johns Hopkins University Press, 1980), p. 111.

7. Kennedy, Tyson, and Benjamin Calloway quoted in Isaac M. Fein, *The Making of an American Jewish Community: The History of Baltimore Jewry from 1773 to 1920* (Philadelphia: Jewish Publication Society of America, 1971), pp. 30, 32, 34.

8. Henry A. Murray, *The Land of the Slave and the Free* (London, 1857), p. 201; Anna Ella Carroll, *The Great American Battle* (New York, 1856), p. 159, quoted in Jean H. Baker, *Ambivalent Americans: The Know-Nothing Party in Maryland* (Baltimore: Johns Hopkins University Press, 1977), p. 36.

9. Kerney bill, pastoral letter of the Fourth Jesuit Provincial Council, 1840, and Baltimore *Clipper*, 12 April 1853, quoted in Mary St. Patrick McConville, *Political Nativism in the State of Maryland, 1830–1860* (Washington, D.C.: Catholic University of America, 1928), pp. 22, 25, 26.

10. *Worcester County Shield*, 13 September 1853 and 8 February 1853, and Calvert in *Port Tobacco Times*, 28 June 1855, quoted ibid., pp. 77, 110.

11. Davis quoted ibid., p. 99; Baltimore *Sun*, 24 May 1856.

12. Rev. Andrew B. Cross quoted in Evitts, *Matter of Allegiances*, p. 92. See also Baker, *Ambivalent Americans*, p. 40.

13. Baltimore physician quoted in Bernard C. Steiner, *Citizenship and Suffrage in Maryland* (Baltimore: Cushing & Co., 1896), p. 39, and Evitts, *Matter of Allegiances*, p. 98.

14. Annapolis *Maryland Republican*, 8 November 1856, quoted in Evitts, *Matter of Allegiances*, p. 110.

15. Noah Davis quoted in William George Paul, *The Shadow of Equality: The Negro in Baltimore, 1864–1911* (Ann Arbor, Mich.: University Microfilms, 1972), p. 27; unknown pupil in Bettye Gardner, "Antebellum Black Education in Baltimore," *MHM*, 71 (1976): 365.

16. Baltimore *Sun*, 29 June 1859, quoted in M. Ray Della, Jr., "The Problems of Free Negro Labor in the 1850s," *MHM*, 66 (1971): 27.

17. Baltimore *Sun*, 14 December 1859, quoted in Ira Berlin, *Slaves without Masters: The Free Negro in the Antebellum South* (New York: Pantheon Books, 1974), pp. 374–75; Harford County Criminal Docket cited in James M. Wright, *The Free Negro in Maryland, 1634–1860*, CUS, 97 (1921), p. 124; Baltimore *Sun*, 14 February 1860.

18. Baltimore *Sun*, 10, 14, and 22 July 1845; slave resistance and fugitive numbers discussed in Elwood L. Bridner, Jr., "The Fugitive Slaves of Maryland," *MHM*, 66 (1971): 33–34, 49.

19. "East Maryland" in *Easton Gazette*, 7 May 1859, quoted in Wright, *Free Negro in Maryland*, p. 153n; slaveholder lethargy mentioned in Bridner, "Fugitive Slaves," pp. 34–35.

20. Baltimore *Sun*, 2, 20, and 14 February 1860; *Sun* of 7 March quoted in Evitts, *Matter of Allegiances*, p. 137; Curtis M. Jacobs, *Speech on the Free Colored Population of Maryland, Delivered in the House of Delegates, on the 17th of February, 1860* (Annapolis: E. S. Rily, 1860), p. 7.

21. Charles County Republican partisan quoted in Evitts, *Matter of Allegiances*, p. 141.

22. Baltimore *Clipper*, 7 November 1860, quoted in Roger Bruns and William Fraley, "'Old Gunny': Abolitionist in a Slave City," *MHM*, 68 (1973): 376.

23. Mayer, Kennedy, Frederick *Herald*, 21 July 1860, and Baltimore *American*, 7 September 1860, all quoted in Evitts, *Matter of Allegiances*, pp. 146–47.

24. Rockville *Montgomery County Sentinel*, 20 June 1860, and Baltimore *Sun*, 7 September 1860, quoted ibid., p. 145; Baltimore *Sun*, 5 January 1860.

25. Frederick *Herald*, 12 and 19 November 1860 and 29 January 1861, quoted in Evitts, *Matter of Allegiances*, pp. 155, 157.

26. General Assembly quoted in George L. P. Radcliffe, *Governor Thomas H. Hicks of Maryland and the Civil War*, JHUS, 19 (1901), p. 17.

27. Ibid., p. 35n; Evitts, *Matter of Allegiances*, p. 162.

28. *Herald Tribune* correspondent quoted in Baltimore *Sun*, 6 March 1861.

29. Henry Stump (judge of the city criminal court) to Mary A. Stump, 20 April 1861, *MHM*, 53 (1958): 403.

30. George William Brown, *Baltimore and the Nineteenth of April, 1861: A Study of the War*, JHUS, extra volume 3 (1887), pp. 68–69.

31. Scott to Butler, 26 April 1861, U.S. War Department, *The War of the Rebellion: A Compilation of the Official Records of the Union and Confederate Armies . . .* (127 vols.; Washington, D.C.: Government Printing Office, 1880–1901), ser. 1, 2:602.

32. Senate debate and House of Delegates report quoted in Radcliffe, *Governor Thomas H. Hicks*, pp. 77, 79.

33. See John Pendleton Kennedy, *An Appeal to Maryland*, reprinted in Frank Moore, ed., *The Rebellion Record: A Diary of American Events . . .* (11 vols.; New York: G. P. Putnam, 1861–63; D. Van Nostrand, 1864–68), 1:368–74.

34. For Butler's proclamation from Federal Hill and the parole oath, see War Department, *War of the Rebellion*, ser. 1, 2:30, 639.

35. Dix and G. W. Cullum quoted in Charles Branch Clark, "Suppression and Control of Maryland, 1861–1865: A Study of Federal-State Relations during Civil Conflict," *MHM*, 54 (1959): 246, 250–51.

36. Banks to Brown, 13 June 1861, War Department, *War of the Rebellion*, ser. 1, 2:681.

37. Dix, "proclamation," and ditty quoted in Clark, "Suppression and Control," pp. 248–49.

38. E. D. Townsend to George Cadwalader, 16 May 1861, War Department, *War of the Rebellion*, ser. 1, 2:639; Dix to McClellan, 7 September 1861, quoted in Clark, "Suppression and Control," p. 260.

39. Taney quoted in Brown, *Baltimore and the Nineteenth of April, 1861*, p. 90.

40. See H. H. Walker Lewis and William L. Marbury, "Ex Parte Merryman," *MHM*, 56 (1961): 391.

41. Dix quoted in Clark, "Suppression and Control," pp. 260, 262.

42. Ibid., p. 255.

43. Archer to R. H. Archer, 8 January 1862, in C. A. Porter Hopkins, ed., "The James J. Archer Letters: A Marylander in the Civil War," *MHM*, 56 (1961): 125.

44. War Department, *War of the Rebellion*, ser. 1, vol. 12, pt. 1, p. 702.

45. *Sun* quoted in W. W. Goldsborough, *The Maryland Line in the Confederate Army, 1861–1865* (Baltimore: Guggenheimer, Weil & Co., 1900), p. 44.

46. Butler to Scott, 6 May 1861, War Department, *War of the Rebellion*, ser. 1, 2:624.

47. [George W. Booth], *Personal Reminiscences of a Maryland Soldier in the War Between the States, 1861–1865* (Baltimore: n.p., 1898), pp. 14, 70–71; Nesbitt quoted in Mame Warren and Marion E. Warren, *Maryland Time Exposures, 1840–1940* (Baltimore: Johns Hopkins University Press, 1984), p. 275; Leighton Parks quoted in Stephen W. Sears, *Landscape Turned Red: The Battle of Antietam* (New Haven and New York: Ticknor & Fields, 1983), p. 83.

48. Wool quoted in Charles Branch Clark, "Recruitment of Union Troops in Maryland," *MHM*, 53 (1958): 160.

49. Marshall quoted in Douglas Southall Freeman, *R. E. Lee: A Biography* (3 vols.; New York: Charles Scribner's Sons, 1934), 2:357; Johnson quoted in Harold R. Manakee, *Maryland in the Civil War* (Baltimore: MHS, 1961), p. 65.

50. Charles Carleton Coffin quoted in Robert Underwood Johnson and Clarence Clough Buel, eds., *Battles and Leaders of the Civil War* (4 vols.; New York: Thomas Yoseloff, 1956), 2:682.

51. Ibid., p. 684; Theodore Dimon quoted in James I. Robertson, Jr., ed., "A Federal Surgeon at Sharpsburg," *CWH*, 6 (1960): 150; North Carolina soldier quoted in Paul Metcalf, *Waters of Potomack* (San Francisco: North Point Press, 1982), p. 158; "Three Civil War Letters of James H. Rigby, a Maryland Federal Artillery Officer," *MHM*, 57 (1962): 158.

52. "Three Civil War Letters of James H. Rigby," p. 158.

53. Nesbitt quoted in Warren and Warren, *Maryland Time Exposures*, p. 276; Edward K. Wightman in Edward G. Longacre, ed., "On the Road to Antietam: Letters of Edward K. Wightman of 'Hawkins's Zouaves,'" *MHM*, 75 (1980): 333; Dimon in Robertson, ed., "Federal Surgeon at Sharpsburg," p. 150.

54. Edward Parmelee Smith, *Incidents among Shot and Shell . . . the United States Christian Commission during . . . the Civil War* (New York: Union Publishing Co., 1868), p. 46; Dix quoted in Clark, "Suppression and Control," p. 263.

55. *Journal* quoted in Hamilton Owens, *Baltimore on the Chesapeake* (New York: Doubleday, Doran & Co., 1941), p. 285. On Garrett's early Southern sympathies, see E. H. McDonald, "Some War History," Baltimore *Sun*, 7 December 1901, quoted in Charles Branch Clark, "Baltimore and the Attack on the Sixth Massachusetts Regiment, April 19, 1861," *MHM*, 56 (1961): 65.

56. William S. Fish, provost marshal, and Major General Robert C. Schenck, department commander, quoted in J. Thomas Scharf, *History of Baltimore City and County from the Earliest Period to the Present Day* (2 vols.; Baltimore: Regional Publishing Co., 1971 [Philadelphia, 1881]), pp. 141, 144.

57. Kurtz quoted in Douglas C. Stange, "Editor Benjamin Kurtz of the *Lutheran Observer* and the Slavery Crisis," *MHM*, 62 (1967): 298; James Cardinal Gibbons in John Tracy Ellis, *American Catholicism* (Chicago: University of Chicago Press, 1956), pp. 96–97; Illoway and Einhorn in Fein, *Making of an American Jewish Community*, pp. 96–97; Curtis in Edward N. Todd, "Bishop Whittingham, Mount Calvary Church, and the Battle of Gettysburg," *MHM*, 60 (1965): 326.

58. Whittingham quoted in Todd, "Bishop Whittingham," p. 327; Harvey Colburn to Edward A. Colburn, 16 January 1862, *MHM*, 53 (1958): 75; Lizette Woodworth Reese, *A Victorian Village: Reminiscences of Other Days* (New York: Farrar & Rinehart, 1929).

59. Jackson officer quoted in Sears, *Landscape Turned Red*, p. 87; Henry Kyd Douglas, *I Rode with Stonewall . . .* (Greenwich, Conn.: Fawcett Publications, 1961 [Chapel Hill, 1940]), p. 149; William W. Blackford, *War Years with Jeb Stuart* (New York: C. Scribner's Sons, 1945), pp. 172–73. For the Frederick side of this encounter, see Virginia O. Bardsley, ed., "Frederick Diary: September 5–14, 1862," *MHM*, 60 (1965): 132–38.

60. James Shinn quoted in Sears, *Landscape Turned Red*, p. 85; Douglas, *I Rode with Stonewall*, pp. 148, 152.

61. Frederic Shriver Klein, "Meade's Pipe Creek Line," *MHM*, 57 (1962): 140.

62. Diary of Jacob Englebrecht, 11 July 1864, Frederick County Historical Society and MHS, quoted in Richard R. Duncan, "Maryland's Reaction to Early's Raid in 1864: A Summer of Bitterness," *MHM*, 64 (1969): 256. The paragraphs below rely heavily on this article.

63. George P. Rawick, gen. ed., *The American Slave: A Composite Autobiography*, Contributions in Afro-American and African Studies no. 11 (17 vols.; Westport, Conn.: Greenwood Publication Co., 1972), vol. 16, Kansas, Kentucky, Maryland, Ohio, Virginia, Tennessee [each section separately paginated], "Maryland," p. 18.

64. Dix to H. E. Paine, 4 November 1861, War Department, *War of the Rebellion*, ser. 1, 5:641–42.

65. Lincoln resolutions quoted in Charles Lewis Wagandt, *The Mighty Revolution: Negro Emancipation in Maryland, 1862–1864* (Baltimore: Johns Hopkins Press, 1964), p. 57.

66. District of Columbia black quoted ibid., p. 64; Bradford in William Branch Clark, *Politics in Maryland during the Civil War* (Chestertown, Md.: n.p., 1952), p. 168.

67. Brantz Mayer, *The Emancipation Problem in Maryland* (Baltimore: n.p., 1862), pp. 1–3; Dorchester County resolutions quoted in Clark, *Politics in Maryland*, p. 177.

68. Baltimore *American*, 4 April 1862, quoted in Clark, *Politics in Maryland*, p. 164; Blair in the *American*, 12 April 1862, quoted in Wagandt, *Mighty Revolution*, p. 62; Hicks quoted in Baker, *Politics of Continuity*, p. 80; Baltimore *American*, 3 January 1863, quoted in Clark, *Politics in Maryland*, p. 173.

69. On Unconditional and Conservative antagonism, see Baker, *Politics of Continuity*, pp. 83, 85.

70. For the case of Joe Nick, see Rawick, ed., *American Slave*, "Maryland," pp. 58–59.

71. Upper Marlboro slaveholders quoted in Ira Berlin et al., eds., *Freedom: A Documentary History of Emancipation, 1861–1867, Selected from the Holdings of the National Archives of the United States*, Series 2, *The Black Military Experience* (Cambridge: Cambridge University Press, 1982), pp. 213–14.

72. George Earle to John A. J. Creswell, 18 January 1864, and Swann quoted in Clark, *Politics in Maryland*, pp. 190 and 191n.

73. William Starr Myers, *The Maryland Constitution of 1864*, JHUS, 19 (1901), pp. 52, 59, 67–68.

74. Baltimore *Daily Gazette*, 23 October 1863, cited in John W. Blassingame, "The Recruitment of Negro Troops in Maryland," *MHM*, 58 (1963): 29.

Chapter 7

1. Baltimore *Sun*, 16 August 1865, quoted in Sherry H. Olson, *Baltimore: The Building of an American City* (Baltimore: Johns Hopkins University Press, 1980), p. 155; Rockville *Sentinel*, 25 August 1876, summarized in Jane C. Sween, *Montgomery County: Two Centuries of Change* (Woodland Hills, Calif.: Windsor Publications, 1984). For a personal account of behind-the-scenes Maryland politics in these years, see Frank Richardson Kent, *The Story of Maryland Politics* (Baltimore: Thomas and Evans, 1911), especially pp. 5–32.

2. Cohen quoted in Isaac M. Fein, *The Making of an American Jewish Community: The History of Baltimore Jewry from 1773 to 1920* (Philadelphia: Jewish Publication Society of America, 1971), p. 24.

3. Cushing quoted in Richard Paul Fuke, "The Baltimore Association for the Moral and Educational Improvement of the Colored People, 1864–1870," *MHM*, 66 (1971): 370.

4. Mary S. Osbourne quoted ibid., p. 384.

5. Douglass quoted in Philip S. Foner, ed., "Address of Frederick Douglass at the Inauguration of Douglass Institute, Baltimore, October 1, 1865," *JNH*, 54 (1969): 177.

6. Pratt quoted in Richard H. Hart, *Enoch Pratt: The Story of a Plain Man* (Baltimore: Enoch Pratt Free Library, 1935), p. 28.

7. Baltimore *Sun*, 23 February 1872, quoted in Olson, *Baltimore*, p. 160.

8. Maryland Union Committee quoted in J. Thomas Scharf, *History of Baltimore City and County from the Earliest Period to the Present Day* (2 vols.; Baltimore: Regional Publishing Co., 1971 [Philadelphia, 1881]), pp. 155–56.

9. *Manufacturers' Record* quoted in Charles Hirschfeld, *Baltimore, 1870–1900: Studies in Social History*, JHUS, 59 (1941), p. 34.

10. The following paragraphs draw liberally from Bayard Taylor, "Down the Eastern Shore," *Harper's New Monthly Magazine*, 43 (1871): 702–8; George Alfred Townsend, "The Chesapeake Peninsula," *Scribner's Monthly*, 3 (1872): 513–24; and Howard Pyle, "A Peninsular Canaan," *Harper's New Monthly Magazine*, 59 (1879): 63–75.

11. President, Choptank Steamboat Company, quoted in Harold K. Kanarek, *The Mid Atlantic Engineers: A History of the Baltimore District, U.S. Army Corps of Engineers, 1774–1974* (Washington, D.C.: U.S. Government Printing Office, c. 1976), p. 70.

12. Pyle, "Peninsular Canaan," p. 74; William K. Brooks quoted in William H. Bayliff, "Natural Resources," in Morris L. Radoff, ed., *The Old Line State; A History of Maryland*, Publication no. 16 (Annapolis: MHR, 1971), p. 298.

13. Pyle, "Pensinsular Canaan," p. 64.

14. Samuel T. Sewell quoted in John R. Wennersten, *The Oyster Wars of the Chesapeake Bay* (Centreville, Md.: Tidewater Publishers, 1981), p. 35; Richard H. Edmonds quoted in George Brown Goode, *The Fisheries and Fishery Industries of the United States, Section V, History and Methods of the Fisheries*, 2 vols., U.S. Senate, 47th Cong., 1st sess., Misc. Document 124, part 6 (1887), 2:549–51.

15. Edmonds quoted in Goode, *Fisheries and Fishery Industries*, 2:550; Pyle quoted in John R. Wennersten, "The Almighty Oyster: A Saga of Old Somerset and the Eastern Shore, 1850–1920," *MHM*, 74 (1979): 83; Johnson and Bradshaw in Wennersten, *Oyster Wars*, pp. 20–21.

16. Edmonds and dredger captain quoted in Goode, *Fisheries and Fishery Industries*, 2:549–50.

17. Hunter Davidson, *Report upon the Oyster Resources of Maryland to the General Assembly* (Annapolis: Wm. Thompson, 1870), p. 3.

18. On the low incidence of black tenant farming, see Margaret Law Callcott, *The Negro in Maryland Politics, 1870–1912*, JHUS, 87 (1969), p. 159; for tobacco growing, see M. Whitney, "Agriculture and Live Stock," in William Hand Browne et al., *Maryland: Its Resources, Industries, and Institutions; Prepared for the Board of World's Fair Managers of Maryland* (Baltimore: Sun Job Printing Office, 1893), pp. 169–70.

19. *American Miller*, 1 October 1889, quoted in John W. McGrain, "'Good Bye Old Burr': The Roller Mill Revolution in Maryland, 1882," *MHM*, 77 (1982): 163.

20. J. Thomas Scharf, *History of Western Maryland* (2 vols.; Baltimore: Regional Publishing Co., 1971 [Philadelphia, 1882]), p. 1178.

21. Will H. Lowdermilk, *History of Cumberland (Maryland)* . . . (Baltimore: Regional Publishing Co., 1971 [Washington, D.C., 1878]), p. 427.

22. Anonymous canal journal quoted in Thomas F. Hahn, *The Chesapeake and Ohio Canal: Pathway to the Nation's Capital* (Metuchen, N.J.: Scarecrow Press, 1984), pp. 40, 45, 78–79.

23. Scharf, *History of Western Maryland*, pp. 1376, 1452.

24. *Coal Trade Journal*, 15 June 1904, quoted in Katherine A. Harvey, *The Best-Dressed Miners: Life and Labor in the Maryland Coal Region, 1835–1910* (Ithaca, N.Y.: Cornell University Press, 1969), p. 13. The following paragraphs draw heavily from Harvey's work.

25. Bryant in *New York Evening Post*, 22 October 1860, quoted ibid., p. 33.

26. Peter Cain's first annual report, MHS, quoted ibid., p. 30.

27. *Frostburg Mining Journal*, 26 April 1873, quoted ibid., pp. 169–70.

28. Letter to *Miners' National Record*, June 1875, quoted ibid., p. 181.

29. Cumberland *Alleganian*, 25 April 1876, quoted ibid., p. 191.

30. Letter from Thomas Brown to *Frostburg Mining Journal*, 19 February 1881, quoted ibid, p. 68. Publication of this letter prompted the company to order new scales.

31. Pinkerton quoted in Clifton K. Yearley, Jr., "The Baltimore and Ohio Strike of 1877," *MHM*, 51 (1956): 201.

32. Debs and letter to *Sun*, 25 July 1877, quoted ibid., pp. 210, 208–9; Garrett to [John King, Jr.], 28 July 1877, B&O Railroad Collection, ms. 2003, box 14, MHS.

33. Quoted in Michael S. Franch, "The Congregational Community in the Changing City, 1840–70," *MHM*, 71 (1976): 374.

34. Baltimore *True Union*, 8 November 1860, quoted ibid., p. 367.

35. State of Maryland, *Second Biennial Report of the Bureau of Industrial Statistics and Information of Maryland for the Years 1886 through 1887* (1888), p. 15.

36. Schloss, a leading clothier, quoted in Fein, *Making of an American Jewish Community*, p. 148.

37. Michael Aaronsohn, Philadelphia *Jewish Exponent*, 19 August 1887, and Szold quoted in Fein, *Making of an American Jewish Community*, pp. 159–60; *Second Biennial Report of the Bureau of Industrial Statistics and Information of Maryland*, p. 16.

38. Canton Company advertisement quoted in Olson, *Baltimore*, p. 154.

39. Anti-annexation remark quoted in Joseph L. Arnold, "Suburban Growth and Municipal Annexation, 1745–1918," *MHM*, 73 (1978): 114.

40. Emory quoted in Charles Branch Clark, *Eastern Shore of Maryland and Virginia* (2 vols.; New York: Lewis Historical Publishing Co., 1950), p. 854.

41. *Civilian and Telegraph*, 7 June 1866, and *Frostburg Mining Journal*, 21 March 1891, quoted in Harvey, *Best-Dressed Miners*, p. 122.

42. Scharf, *History of Baltimore City and County*, p. 423.

43. Vonderhorst (or Von der Horst) quoted without reference in Frederick G. Lieb, *The Baltimore Orioles: The History of a Colorful Baseball Team in Baltimore and St. Louis* (New York: G. P. Putnam's Sons, 1955), p. 13. Lieb apparently drew on interviews with old players and baseball writers.

44. Ward quoted ibid., p. 48.

Chapter 8

1. Henry Louis Mencken, *Newspaper Days, 1880–1892* (New York: Alfred A. Knopf, 1941), p. 53; *London Daily Chronicle* (reprinted in Baltimore *Sun*, 6 January 1894) quoted in Sherry H. Olson, *Baltimore: The Building of an American City* (Baltimore: Johns Hopkins University Press, 1980), p. 198; Stephen Bonsal, "The New Baltimore," *Harper's New Monthly Magazine*, 92 (1896): 331, 334; Jacob Frey, *Reminiscences of Baltimore* (Baltimore: Maryland Book Concern, 1893), p. 365.

2. Bonsal, "New Baltimore," p. 345.

3. Yacht club charter quoted in Richard Walsh and William Lloyd Fox, eds., *Maryland: A History, 1632–1974* (Baltimore: MHS, 1974), p. 385.

4. Alison K. Hoagland, "Deer Park Hotel," *MHM*, 73 (1978): 346–47.

5. *Ocean City, Maryland, Season of 1892: Prospectus of the Sinepuxent Beach Company* (n.p., n.d.; copy in MHS), pp. 4, 8.

6. Bonsal, "New Baltimore," pp. 343–44.

7. Lanier quoted in Edwin Mims, Jr., "Sidney Lanier," *Dictionary of American Biography*, 5:603.

8. Bonsal, "New Baltimore," p. 335.

9. Martha J. Lamb, "The Walters Collection of Art Treasures," *Magazine of American History*, 27 (1892): 246.

10. Ibid., pp. 245, 264.

11. *American Farmer*, 1 [n.s.] (1859): 144, quoted in George H. Callcott, *A History of the University of Maryland* (Baltimore: MHS, 1966), p. 143.

12. Thomas quoted in Hugh D. Hawkins, *Pioneer: A History of the Johns Hopkins University, 1874–1889* (Ithaca, N.Y.: Cornell University Press, 1960), p. 9.

13. Brown and Gilman quoted ibid., pp. 23, 6, 40.

14. Gildersleeve quoted ibid., p. 51.

15. Gilman quoted ibid., p. 49.

16. Sophie B. Herrick, "The Johns Hopkins University," *Scribner's Monthly*, 19 (1879–80): 203, quoted ibid., p. 93.

17. Bonsal, "New Baltimore," p. 344; Paret and Baltimore *American*, 15 September 1876, quoted in Hawkins, *Pioneer*, pp. 175, 70.

18. Brooks quoted in John R. Wennersten, *The Oyster Wars of the Chesapeake Bay* (Centreville, Md.: Tidewater Publishers, 1981), p. 88. See also Herrick, "Johns Hopkins," p. 207.

19. William D. Whitney, Gilman, *American* of 2 February and 6 March 1875, George Dobbin Penniman, and Remsen quoted in Hawkins, *Pioneer*, pp. 73, 23, 255, 258.

20. Martin quoted ibid., p. 143.

21. Billings quoted in Alan M. Chesney, *The Johns Hopkins Hospital and the Johns Hopkins University School of Medicine: A Chronicle* (3 vols.; Baltimore: Johns Hopkins Press, 1943–63), 1:58.

22. Ibid., pp. 312, 107.

23. Welch quoted in Simon Flexner and James Thomas Flexner, *William Henry Welch and the Heroic Age of American Medicine* (New York: Viking Press, 1941), p. 254, and Chesney, *Johns Hopkins Hospital*, pp. 106–7.

24. Frank Richardson Kent, *The Story of Maryland Politics* (Baltimore: Thomas and Evans, 1911), p. 15.

25. Gorman quoted in John R. Lambert, *Arthur Pue Gorman* (Baton Rouge: Louisiana State University Press, 1953), p. 8.

26. Mahon quoted in Margaret Law Callcott, *The Negro in Maryland Politics, 1870–1912*, JHUS, 87 (1969), p. 37. Ferdinand C. Latrobe, "Personal Memoirs of Ferdinand C. Latrobe" (two-volume typescript owned in 1968 by the mayor's daughter-in-law, Mrs. Ferdinand C. Latrobe II), mentioned in James B. Crooks, *Politics and Progress: The Rise of Urban Progressivism in Baltimore, 1895–1911* (Baton Rouge: Louisiana State University Press, 1968), p. 12.

27. Mahon and Lewis quoted in Callcott, *Negro in Maryland Politics*, p. 38.

28. Latrobe quoted in *Celebration of the 150th Anniversary of the Settlement of Baltimore* (Baltimore: King Brothers, 1881), p. 272. This paragraph draws from Joseph L. Arnold, "The Neighborhood and City Hall: The Origin of Neighborhood Associations in Baltimore, 1880–1911," *Journal of Urban History*, 6 (1979): 3–30.

29. School board president and Dr. Joseph M. Rice quoted in Charles Hirschfeld, *Baltimore, 1870–1900: Studies in Social History*, JHUS, 59 (1941), pp. 85–87, 92.

30. *Sun* quoted in Bayly Ellen Marks, "Liberal Education in the Gilded Age: Baltimore and the Creation of the Manual Training School," *MHM*, 74 (1979): 242.

31. Charles W. Chancellor, state Board of Health, quoted in Andrea R. Andrews, "The Baltimore School Building Program, 1870 to 1900: A Study of Urban Reform," *MHM*, 70 (1975): 269.

32. *Sun*, 14 April 1877 (gleaning from Towson *Union*), quoted in John W. McGrain, "Historical Aspects of Lake Roland," *MHM*, 74 (1979): 258; *Baltimore v. Warren Manufacturing Co.*, 59 *Maryland Reports* (1882) 84, quoted in John Capper, Garrett Power, and Frank R. Shivers, Jr., *Chesapeake Waters: Pollution, Public Health, and Public Opinion, 1607–1972* (Centreville, Md.: Tidewater Publishers, 1983), p. 34.

33. Southwest Association president quoted in Arnold, "Neighborhood and City Hall," p. 21.

34. [George W. Booth], *Personal Reminiscences of a Maryland Soldier in the War Between the States, 1861–1865* (Baltimore: n.p., 1898), p. 16.

35. *Report of the State of Maryland Gettysburg Monument Commission to His Excellency E. E. Jackson, Governor of Maryland, June 17th, 1891* (Baltimore: William K. Boyle & Son, 1891), pp. 73, 76, 78.

36. On the styles of Rasin and Gorman, see Kent, *Story of Maryland Politics*, pp. 16–17; on the C&O investigations, see Lambert, *Gorman*, pp. 61–74.

37. Henry Louis Mencken, *Heathen Days, 1890–1936* (New York: Alfred A. Knopf, 1943), p. 111.

38. Maryland Telephone Company quoted in Baltimore *Sun*, 21 February 1926, MHS clipping file.

39. Olson, *Baltimore*, p. 253.

40. Wallis and Marbury quoted in William L. Marbury, *The Story of an American Family*

(Baltimore: privately printed, 1966), pp. 28, 34; *Sun* quoted in Gerald W. Johnson, Frank R. Kent, H. L. Mencken, and Hamilton Owens, *The Sunpapers of Baltimore* (New York: Alfred A. Knopf, 1937), p. 153.

41. On Bonaparte, see Crooks, *Politics and Progress*, pp. 14–15, and Kent, *Story of Maryland Politics*, p. 34.

42. Baltimore *News*, 20 September 1892, quoted ibid., p. 20.

43. Wharton and Vrooman quoted ibid., p. 26.

44. *Sun* quoted in Lambert, *Gorman*, pp. 245–46.

45. Photo broadside and letter to *Sun* editor in Sun Clippings Scrapbook of 1895 Campaign, Maryland Room, Pratt Library; handbill mentioned in Lambert, *Gorman*, p. 249. See also Kent, *Story of Maryland Politics*, pp. 203–5.

46. Crooks, *Politics and Progress*, pp. 39–40; Kent, *Story of Maryland Politics*, pp. 205–6.

47. *Sun* quoted in Jean H. Baker, *The Politics of Continuity: Maryland Political Parties from 1858 to 1870* (Baltimore: Johns Hopkins University Press, 1973), p. 171; Poe in *Transactions of the First Annual Meeting of the Maryland State Bar Association* (Baltimore: MSBA, 1896), p. 3; McSherry in *Transactions of the Second Annual Meeting . . .* (Baltimore: MSBA, 1897), p. 64.

48. Mudd quoted in Lambert, *Gorman*, p. 274.

49. Gorman quoted ibid., p. 285.

50. Ibid., p. 330 and n.

51. Lewis quoted in Katherine A. Harvey, *The Best-Dressed Miners: Life and Labor in the Maryland Coal Region, 1835–1910* (Ithaca, N.Y.: Cornell University Press, 1969), p. 333; George E. Barnett, "The Maryland Workmen's Compensation Act," *Quarterly Journal of Economics*, 16 (1901–2): 591.

52. George Alfred Townsend, "The Chesapeake Peninsula," *Scribner's Monthly*, 3 (1872): 520; Earle quoted in Wennersten, *Oyster Wars*, p. 90.

53. Notre Dame College catalogue, 1912–13, quoted in Sr. Bridget Marie Engelmeyer, "A Maryland First," *MHM*, 78 (1983): 199.

54. Alumna and Thomas quoted in Cynthia Horsburgh Requardt, "Alternative Professions for Goucher College Graduates, 1892–1910," *MHM*, 74 (1979): 277–78.

55. Osler and Welch quoted in Lloyd C. Taylor, Jr., *The Medical Profession and Social Reform, 1885–1945* (New York: St. Martin's Press, 1974), pp. 5, 2.

56. Osler on tubercolosis, ibid., pp. 32, 33; *Laws of Maryland, 1904*, p. 702.

57. Wyatt quoted in Crooks, *Politics and Progress*, p. 139.

58. Henry Louis Mencken, *Newspaper Days* (New York: Alfred A. Knopf, c. 1941), p. 282.

59. *News* quoted in James B. Crooks, "The Baltimore Fire and Baltimore Reform," *MHM*, 65 (1970): 12.

60. Carey quoted ibid., p. 16, Furst in Crooks, *Politics and Progress*, p. 146.

61. Pinchback quoted in William George Paul, *The Shadow of Equality: The Negro in Baltimore, 1864–1911* (Ann Arbor, Mich.: University Microfilms, 1972), p. 254.

62. Black illiteracy in Baltimore dropped to 13 percent by 1910. Paul, *Shadow of Equality*, pp. 272, 333; Crooks, *Politics and Progress*, pp. 56–57; Callcott, *Negro in Maryland Politics*, p. 103.

63. *Sun*, 17 September 1903, quoted in Callcott, *Negro in Maryland Politics*, p. 107.

64. Gorman quoted in Crooks, *Politics and Progress*, p. 57. See also Lambert, *Gorman*, p. 245.

65. John Murphy quoted in Callcott, *Negro in Maryland Politics*, p. 135.

66. Bonsal quoted in Crooks, *Politics and Progress*, p. 61; Gibbons in *Sun*, 11 March 1904.

67. Crothers quoted in Crooks, *Politics and Progress*, p. 129.

68. Crothers quoted in Nicholas C. Burckel, "Governor Austin Lane Crothers and Progressive Reform in Maryland, 1908–1912," *MHM*, 76 (1981): 186.

69. Pleasants quoted in Crooks, *Politics and Progress*, p. 219.

70. Crothers quoted in Burckel, "Governor Crothers," p. 197.

Chapter 9

1. *Nation*, 3 (1922): 517–19.
2. See H. M. Rowe and Osborne L. Yellott, Baltimore *Sun*, 18 January 1914.
3. William Bullock Clark, *Report on the Highways of Maryland* (Baltimore: Johns Hopkins Press, 1899), pp. 207, 204.
4. *Sun*, 16 March 1908.
5. Commission report for 1908–12 quoted in Charles T. LeViness, *A History of Road Building in Maryland* (Baltimore: State Roads Commission of Maryland, 1958), p. 53.
6. Captain John M. Bowyer quoted in news clipping dated 16 June 1909 in Mame Warren and Marion E. Warren, *Everybody Works but John Paul Jones: A Portrait of the U.S. Naval Academy, 1845–1915* (Annapolis: Naval Institute Press, 1981), p. 94; William Oliver Stevens, *Annapolis: Anne Arundel's Town* (New York: Dodd, Mead and Co., 1937), p. 231.
7. *Sun*, 7 November 1910, quoted in John F. R. Scott, Jr., *Voyages into Airy Regions* (Annapolis: Ann Arundell County Historical Society and Fishergate Publishing Co., 1984), p. 82.
8. News reports quoted in William F. Lynd, "The Army Flying School at College Park," *MHM*, 48 (1953): 232.
9. This and following paragraphs rely on Sherry H. Olson, *Baltimore: The Building of an American City* (Baltimore: Johns Hopkins University Press, 1980), pp. 292–301.
10. Baltimore *Correspondent*, 4 and 6 February 1917, quoted in Dieter Cunz, *The Maryland Germans: A History* (Princeton, N.J.: Princeton University Press, 1948), pp. 398–99.
11. Raymond S. Tompkins, *Maryland Fighters in the Great War* (Baltimore: Thomas & Evans, 1919), pp. 14–15.
12. *Correspondent*, 5 April 1917, quoted in Cunz, *Maryland Germans*, p. 399; *Sun*, 24 May 1918 (a reference I could not locate), quoted in Olson, *Baltimore*, p. 301; *Sun*, 25 May 1918.
13. Judge James McSherry quoted in Philip L. Merkel, "Tax Reform 'With a Political View': The Hyattsville Single Tax Experiment in the Maryland Courts," *MHM*, 79 (1984): 156.
14. *Report on the Advisability of Creating a Sanitary District in Maryland, Contiguous to the District of Columbia and Providing It with Water and Sewerage Service, To the General Assembly of Maryland, By the Washington Suburban Sanitary Commission, 21 January 1918*, pp. 12–13 (copy available in Marylandia Department, McKeldin Library, University of Maryland, College Park).
15. Tompkins, *Maryland Fighters*, p. 12.
16. *Sun*, 1 March 1908.
17. Jeanne Hackley Stevenson, "Lilian Welsh, 1858–1938," in Winifred G. Helmes, ed., *Notable Maryland Women* (Cambridge, Md.: Tidewater Publishers, 1977), p. 394.
18. Ritchie described in Dorothy M. Brown, "Maryland Between the Wars," in Richard Walsh and William Lloyd Fox, eds., *Maryland: A History, 1632–1974* (Baltimore: MHS, 1974), p. 673, and Joseph B. Chepaitis, "Albert C. Ritchie in Power, 1920–1927," *MHM*, 68 (1973): 384.
19. On Black and the Sunpapers at this time, see Gerald W. Johnson, Frank R. Kent, H. L. Mencken, and Hamilton Owens, *The Sunpapers of Baltimore* (New York: Alfred A. Knopf, 1937), pp. 366–67, 370.
20. *Sun* quoted in Brown, "Maryland Between the Wars," p. 677. See also Ritchie to Mary Jenkins, 6 July 1916, quoted in Chepaitis, "Ritchie in Power," p. 386.
21. Crabbe quoted in William M. Bowen, Jr., "The Period of Ritchie—And After," in Morris L. Radoff, ed., *The Old Line State: A History of Maryland*, Publication no. 16 (Annapolis: MHR, 1971), pp. 128–29.
22. This passage relies on Raymond S. Sweeney, "Public Education in Maryland in the Progressive Era," *MHM*, 62 (1967): 28–46.
23. John Walter Smith in *Sun*, 19 August 1920, quoted in Brown, "Maryland Between the Wars," p. 677.
24. See *Leser et al.* v. *Garnett et al.*, 258 *U.S. Reports* 130 (1922). On newly registered

women voters, see John T. Willis, *Presidential Elections in Maryland* (Mt. Airy, Md.: Lomond Publications, 1984), p. 98 n. 45.

25. Ritchie quoted in Andrews, *History of Maryland*, p. 637.

26. *Sun* quoted in Brown, "Maryland Between the Wars," p. 681.

27. Ritchie quoted in Chepaitis, "Ritchie in Power," p. 390.

28. See Bowen, "Period of Ritchie," p. 129.

29. Johnson et al., *Sunpapers*, p. 389.

30. Schwab quoted in Brown, "Maryland Between the Wars," p. 698.

31. *Sun*, 24 July 1927.

32. Ibid., 15 March 1908.

33. Frederick Philip Stieff, "Music in Baltimore," *Art and Archaeology*, 19 (1925): 257; Linda Lee Koenig, *The Vagabonds: America's Oldest Little Theater* (Rutherford, Madison, Teaneck, N.J.: Fairleigh Dickinson University Press, 1983), pp. 16, 22.

34. *Sunday Sun*, 5 September 1929.

35. These paragraphs draw heavily on Ed Nichols, "Sports and Related Activities," in Charles Branch Clark, *Eastern Shore of Maryland and Virginia* (2 vols.; New York: Lewis Historical Publishing Co., 1950), pp. 845–48.

36. Dunn quoted in Frederick G. Lieb, *The Baltimore Orioles: The History of a Colorful Baseball Team in Baltimore and St. Louis* (New York: G. P. Putnam's Sons, 1955), pp. 147–48.

37. For the material in this paragraph I am indebted to Jacques Kelly, *A Pictorial History of Maryland* (Easton: Chesapeake Publications, 1984), p. 230.

38. These paragraphs draw on the *Sunday Sun Magazine*, 14 January 1962, and material in the clipping files, MHS.

39. On the Hill story, see Johnson et al., *Sunpapers*, p. 396.

40. This and following paragraphs rely on Roderick N. Ryon, "Old West Baltimore," *MHM*, 77 (1982): 54–69.

41. Ragtime usually followed a pattern of antecedent theme and later division by key, along with regular strong-weak rhythmic lines. See Edward A. Berlin, *Ragtime: A Musical and Cultural History* (Berkeley and Los Angeles: University of California Press, 1980), and Frank Tirro, *Jazz: A History* (New York: W. W. Norton & Co., 1977).

42. Blake quoted in Tirro, *Jazz*, p. 61. These paragraphs draw heavily from Al Rose, *Eubie Blake* (New York: Schirmer Books, 1979).

43. Blake's mother quoted in Rose, *Blake*, p. 93.

44. *Afro-American*, 4 April 1919, quoted in Susan M. Wheeler, "Jazzing with Baltimore's Blacks, 1917–1929," *MHM* (forthcoming); Calloway quoted in Ryon, "Old West Baltimore," p. 62.

45. See Tirro, *Jazz*, pp. 155–56.

46. Owens and klan leaders quoted in Brown, "Maryland Between the Wars," pp. 714–16.

47. Hammett, "From the Memoirs of a Private Detective," *Smart Set*, 70 (March 1923): 88; see also "The Parthian Shot," ibid., 69 (October 1922): 82.

48. Hammett, *The Maltese Falcon* (New York: Modern Library, 1934 [1929]), p. 90, and "The Green Bag," *Smart Set*, 72 (October 1923): 107. See also Cain, "Pastorale," *American Mercury*, 13 (1928): 291–95.

49. Sophie Kerr, *Mareea-Maria* (Garden City, N.Y.: Doubleday, Doran & Co., 1929), p. 158.

50. On the Scott-Zelda genealogy, see Scottie Fitzgerald Smith, "The Colonial Ancestors of Francis Scott Key Fitzgerald," *MHM*, 76 (1981): 363–75, and "The Maryland Ancestors of Zelda Sayre Fitzgerald," *MHM*, 78 (1983): 217–28. Fitzgerald's phrase quoted in André LeVot, *F. Scott Fitzgerald: A Biography* (New York: Doubleday & Co., 1983), p. 6.

51. Fitzgerald quoted in LeVot, *Fitzgerald*, p. 8.

52. Henry Louis Mencken, *Happy Days* (New York: Alfred A. Knopf, 1940), pp. 63, 285, 175. My discussion of Mencken draws liberally from Carl Bode, *Mencken* (Carbondale: Southern Illinois University Press, 1969).

53. Henry Louis Mencken, *The American Language: A Preliminary Inquiry into the Development of English in the United States* (New York: Alfred A. Knopf, 1919), pp. 82, 173.

54. Mencken on Darwin and Ibsen and Sherman remark quoted in W. H. A. Williams,

H. L. Mencken, Twayne's United States Authors Series, Sylvia E. Bowman, ed. (Boston: Twayne Publishers, 1977), pp. 27–28, 75; see also Henry Louis Mencken, *Prejudices, First Series* (New York: Alfred A. Knopf, 1919), p. 182.

55. For Mencken on James and Howells, see Williams, *Mencken,* p. 41.

56. Mencken quoted ibid., pp. 97–98.

57. For a synopsis of Mencken's reports on the Scopes trial, see Henry Louis Mencken, *Heathen Days, 1890–1936* (New York: Alfred A. Knopf, 1943), pp. 214–38.

58. Mencken on unjust laws quoted in Williams, *Mencken,* p. 101; Henry Louis Mencken, *Prejudices, Second Series* (New York: Alfred A. Knopf, 1920), pp. 219–20.

59. *Prejudices, First Series,* pp. 67, 70, 150–51; Henry Louis Mencken, *Prejudices, Third Series* (New York: Alfred A. Knopf, 1922), p. 278.

60. "Mencken's Law" quoted in Bode, *Mencken,* p. 251; Henry Louis Mencken, *In Defense of Women* (New York: Alfred A. Knopf, 1918), p. 140; *Prejudices, Second Series,* pp. 213–17; *Prejudices, Third Series,* p. 219. For James M. Cain's highly compatible "The Pathology of Service," dividing the modern world into busy-bodies "In Service" and those "Not in Service," see *American Mercury,* 6 (1925): 257–64. Given this grand division, Cain praised Hamilton Owens of the *Sun* for his skeptical sense of humor. "The result is that the Maryland Free State is probably the hardest State in the Union to perform Service in. Servists there have become timid and skittish. The Servist who would thrive and grow fat on ordinary abuse thinks long and hard before he braves the deadly ridicule of Mr. Owens" (ibid., p. 264).

61. For anti-Mencken remarks, see *Menckeniana: A Schimpflexikon* (New York: Alfred A. Knopf, 1928).

62. *Prejudices, Third Series,* p. 11.

63. *Menckeniana,* p. 92; Henry Louis Mencken, *Prejudices, Fifth Series* (New York: Alfred A. Knopf, 1926), pp. 241–43.

64. *Menckeniana,* p. 49; *Prejudices, Fifth Series,* p. 237; Mencken reprinted "The Sahara of the Bozart" in *Prejudices, Second Series,* pp. 136–54. See also *Prejudices, Second Series,* pp. 71, 140.

65. *Nation,* 3 (1922): 518–19. For a similar complaint about sacrificing "old charm for the sake of cotton factories, pickle factories, glue factories and what not, each with its smokestack belching forth enough smoke to befoul the nostrils of every citizen," see Francis F. Beirne, "The Late South," *Evening Sun,* 2 July 1925.

66. *Prejudices, Second Series,* p. 39. See also Williams, *Mencken,* pp. 42–47, 69–72.

67. *American Mercury,* 1 (1924): 27, 29.

Chapter 10

1. Russell Baker, *Growing Up* (New York: Congdon & Weed, 1982), p. 152.

2. Ritchie quoted in Joseph B. Chepaitis, "Albert C. Ritchie in Power, 1920–1927," *MHM,* 68 (1973): 404.

3. Curley quoted in Dorothy M. Brown, "Maryland Between the Wars," in Richard Walsh and William Lloyd Fox, eds., *Maryland: A History, 1632–1974* (Baltimore: MHS, 1974), p. 717.

4. Bruce quoted in James Levin, "Governor Albert Ritchie and the Democratic National Convention of 1924," *MHM,* 66 (1971): 112.

5. Charles Merz and Ritchie quoted in Brown, "Maryland Between the Wars," pp. 691, 692. For an example of Ritchie's Sunpapers support, see Hamilton Owens, "Ritchie of the Free State," *American Mercury,* 7 (1926): 280–87. On a possible Ritchie-Smith understanding about the 1932 nomination, see James Levin, "Governor Albert C. Ritchie and the Democratic Convention of 1932," *MHM,* 67 (1972): 282 and n. 15.

6. *Selections from the Speeches, Addresses, and Political Writings of Wm. Cabell Bruce* (Baltimore: Sun Book & Job Printing Office, 1927), p. 186.

7. Ritchie quoted in Brown, "Maryland Between the Wars," p. 693. On progress in schools, see Maryland State Board of Education, *Sixty-fourth Annual Report . . . for the Year Ending July 1930.*

8. *Baltimore* quoted in Brown, "Maryland Between the Wars," pp. 702, 730–31.

9. Ibid., p. 731.

10. Tait and Newcomer quoted ibid., pp. 735, 736.

11. Ritchie quoted ibid., p. 735.

12. Omar Hersey to Ritchie, 13 November 1931, MHS, quoted in Levin, "Ritchie and the Democratic Convention of 1932," p. 280; Lippmann quoted in Bernard Bellush, *Franklin D. Roosevelt as Governor of New York* (New York: Columbia University Press, 1955), p. xi.

13. Ritchie quoted in Brown, "Maryland Between the Wars," p. 695.

14. Baltimore *Sun*, 3 July 1932, cited ibid., p. 696.

15. Ritchie quoted ibid., p. 739.

16. Custenborder quoted in Patricia W. Levering and Ralph B. Levering, "Women in Relief: The Carroll County Children's Aid Society in the Great Depression," *MHM*, 72 (1977): 538. The following paragraphs draw heavily from the Leverings' article.

17. Ibid., pp. 539, 543.

18. Anna D. Ward, CERC, quoted in Charles M. Kimberly, "The Depression in Maryland: The Failure of Voluntaryism," *MHM*, 70 (1975): 194.

19. Judge T. Bayard Williams quoted in Brown, "Maryland Between the Wars," p. 731; Baltimore *Evening Sun* and *Sun* correspondents quoted in David Lamoreaux, with Gerson G. Eisenberg, "Baltimore Views the Great Depression, 1929–33," *MHM*, 71 (1976): 436n; Louis Sandler, "Hungry Men, Skinny-Dipping, Salamanders, and Trips," *Sunday Sun Magazine*, 16 January 1977; Baker, *Growing Up*, p. 158.

20. Jackson and Ritchie quoted in Kimberly, "Depression in Maryland," pp. 193, 195, 197.

21. Custenborder quoted in Levering and Levering, "Women in Relief," p. 540, and Faatz in Kimberly, "Depression in Maryland," p. 201.

22. Lamoreaux, "Baltimore Views the Great Depression," p. 431.

23. This paragraph relies on Jo Ann E. Argersinger, "'The Right to Strike': Labor Organization and the New Deal in Baltimore," *MHM*, 78 (1983): 299–318.

24. *Worcester Democrat and Ledger-Enterprise*, 12 December 1931, quoted in Brown, "Maryland Between the Wars," p. 719.

25. Conley and Coad quoted in Dorothy M. Brown, "The Election of 1934: The 'New Deal' in Maryland," *MHM*, 68 (1973): 410.

26. *Sun*, 28 October 1934.

27. Mencken quoted in Carl Bode, *Mencken* (Carbondale: Southern Illinois University Press, 1969), pp. 308–9, and Kent in Eugene W. Goll, "Frank R. Kent's Opposition to Franklin D. Roosevelt and the New Deal," *MHM*, 63 (1968): 164, 168–69.

28. Frances Fink, "First Resettlers," *Literary Digest*, 1 (6 November 1937): 15; Tugwell quoted in Leslie Gene Hunter, "Greenbelt, Maryland: A City on a Hill," *MHM*, 63 (1968): 116.

29. Fink, "First Resettlers," p. 15; Hunter, "Greenbelt," p. 126.

30. Tugwell quoted in Hunter, "Greenbelt," p. 116. For an example of reaction to the New Dealer, see Blair Bolles, "The Sweetheart of the Regimenters: Dr. Tugwell Makes America Over," *American Mercury*, 39 (1936): 77–86.

31. *Congressional Record*, 75th Cong., 1st sess., vol. 81, pt. 6 (1937), 6913–14.

32. Samuel I. Rosenman, ed., *The Public Papers and Addresses of Franklin D. Roosevelt . . .* (13 vols.; New York: Random House, Macmillan & Co., and Harper & Bros., 1938–50), 7:489.

33. Tydings, *Salisbury Times*, 3 September 1938, and *Sun* quoted in Philip A. Grant, Jr., "Maryland Press Reaction to the Roosevelt-Tydings Confrontation," *MHM*, 68 (1973): 422–23, 424, 433.

34. Shepard Krech III, *Praise the Bridge That Carries You Over: The Life of Joseph L. Sutton* (Cambridge, Mass.: Schenkman Publishing Co., 1981), p. 121.

35. Billie Holiday quoted in Ted Fox, *Showtime at the Apollo* (New York: Holt, Rinehart & Winston, 1983), p. 145.

36. Marshall quoted in Russell W. Bland, *Private Pressure on Public Law: The Legal Career of Justice Thurgood Marshall* (Port Washington, N.Y.: Kennikat Press, 1973), p. 8.

37. P. Stewart Macaulay, "A Study of the Negro's Problems: How They Touch All of the City," *Sunday Sun Magazine*, 31 March 1935.

38. Evelyn Harris, *The Barter Lady: A Woman Farmer Sees It Through* (Garden City, N.Y.: Doubleday, Doran & Company, 1934), pp. 31, 69, 156, 205.

39. *Sun*, 1 June 1925. The following paragraphs rely on Boyd Gibbons, *Wye Island* (Baltimore: Johns Hopkins University Press, 1977).

40. Centreville *Queen Anne's Record-Observer* quoted in Gibbons, *Wye Island*, p. 89; Harris, *Barter Lady*, p. 43.

41. Harris, *Barter Lady*, pp. 68–69, 71.

42. Ibid., p. 199.

43. Ibid., p. 232; Writers' Program of the Work Projects Administration, *Maryland: A Guide to the Old Line State* (New York: Oxford University Press, 1940), p. 204; Dennis quoted in *Evening Sun*, 20 May 1935.

44. *Evening Sun*, 20 May 1935. See also Ralph G. Murdy, director, "Report on Legalized Gambling" (paper released 13 January 1964 by Board of Directors, Baltimore Criminal Justice Commission), vertical file, Maryland Room, Pratt Library.

45. *Evening Sun*, 8 September 1937.

46. A. H. Young-O'Brien, "The Return of the Native," *Literary Digest*, 1 (6 November 1937): 19–21.

47. *Sun*, 14 October 1934; Chick Sirota quoted in Bob Litwin and Chip Silverman, "An Affectionate History of the Block: Bawdy Baltimore through the Twentieth Century," *Baltimore Magazine*, August 1979, p. 62.

48. Sandler, "Hungry Men, Skinny-Dipping, Salamanders, and Trips."

49. Rosenman, ed., *Public Papers and Addresses of Franklin D. Roosevelt*, 9:1; Lindbergh quoted in William Manchester, *The Glory and the Dream: A Narrative History of America, 1932–1972* (Boston: Little, Brown & Co., 1973), p. 200.

50. Rosenman, ed., *Public Papers and Addresses of Franklin D. Roosevelt*, 9:643.

51. Mencken quoted in Frank Turaj, "Mencken and the Nazis: A Note," *MHM*, 67 (1972): 178.

52. Leon M. Uris, *Battle Cry* (New York: G. P. Putnam's Sons, 1953), p. 10.

53. Harold Randall Manakee, comp., *Maryland in World War II* (4 vols.; Baltimore: War Records Division, MHS, 1950–58), 1:95. The rest of this chapter makes extensive use of volumes 1–3.

54. Ibid., 2:1.

55. On wartime income growth, see George H. Callcott, *Maryland and America, 1940–1980* (Baltimore: Johns Hopkins University Press, 1985), especially p. 43.

56. Manakee, comp., *Maryland in World War II*, 2:204.

57. Ibid., 2:150, 84.

58. See ibid., 2:213.

59. Litwin and Silverman, "An Affectionate History of the Block," p. 63.

60. Soldier quoted in Forrest C. Pogue, "D-Day—1944," in *D-Day: The Normandy Invasion in Retrospect*, with a foreword by Omar N. Bradley (Lawrence: Eisenhower Foundation and University of Kansas Press, 1971), p. 32; Col. Goode quoted in Manakee, comp., *Maryland in World War II*, 1:13.

Chapter 11

1. Gilbert Millstein, "'Let's Back Up Them Birds,'" *New York Times Magazine*, 9 May 1954. On the Orioles' arrival, see clippings file, MHS. Herbert D. Fried quoted in P. Susan Davis, "The Land of Pleasant Living," *MM*, 16 (Summer 1984): 6–11.

2. Werner quoted in Jane C. Sween, *Montgomery County: Two Centuries of Change* (Woodland Hills, Calif.: Windsor Publications, 1984), p. 130. On the "population swirl," see George H. Callcott, *Maryland and America, 1940–1980* (Baltimore: Johns Hopkins University Press, 1985), pp. 59–96.

3. Mark Kram wrote of his Baltimore boyhood in "A Wink at a Homely Girl," *Sports Illustrated*, 25 (10 October 1966): 99.

4. Letters of application quoted in the annual report of the Housing Authority of Baltimore, *Dear Sir—* (1948).

5. Froelicher quoted in Karen A. Stakem, "Hans Froelicher, Jr., Civic Educator," *MHM*, 77 (1982): 128.

6. Jackson quoted in "A Black Perspective: Black History in Maryland," Baltimore *Sun*, 7 February 1985, and Sherry H. Olson, *Baltimore: The Building of an American City* (Baltimore: Johns Hopkins University Press, 1980), pp. 368–69; Alexander J. Walker, Chairman, Committee to Abolish Discrimination in Maryland, "Call to the Maryland Congress against Discrimination," vertical file, Maryland Room, Pratt Library.

7. Baltimore *Evening Sun*, 9 November 1948.

8. Ibid., 13 December 1948.

9. Baltimore *Sun* quoted in John R. Wennersten, *The Oyster Wars of the Chesapeake Bay* (Centreville, Md.: Tidewater Publishers, 1981), p. 113.

10. *Evening Sun*, 13 November 1933; traveler quoted in Gilbert Sandler, "Few Remember Life Before . . . THE BRIDGE," *MM*, 15 (Summer 1983): 4; shippers quoted in Albert W. Quinn, "Contemporary Maryland," in Morris L. Radoff, ed., *The Old Line State: A History of Maryland*, Publication no. 16 (Annapolis: MHR, 1971), p. 445.

11. On developments in Easton, see Dickson J. Preston and Norman Harrington, *Talbot County: A History* (Centreville, Md.: Tidewater Publishers, 1983), pp. 311–12.

12. Sandler, "THE BRIDGE," p. 9; on Balch, see Quinn, "Contemporary Maryland," in Radoff, ed., *Old Line State*, p. 445.

13. Byrd et al. quoted in George H. Callcott, *A History of the University of Maryland* (Baltimore: MHS, 1966), pp. 339, 344, 350.

14. This paragraph relies on Callcott, *Maryland and America*, pp. 237–41.

15. *Higher Education in Maryland: A Report of a Survey by the American Council of Education with Recommendations of the Maryland Commission on Higher Education* (Washington, D.C.: American Council on Education, 1947), p. 25.

16. Report on Spring Grove quoted in Olson, *Baltimore*, p. 190; Mencken to Constance H. (Mrs. Harry C.) Black, 29 May 1919, in Carl Bode, ed., *The New Mencken Letters* (New York: Dial Press, 1977), p. 101; Henry Louis Mencken, *Prejudices, Second Series* (New York: Alfred A. Knopf, 1920), p. 32.

17. Perkins quoted in Baltimore *Sun*, 3 March 1950.

18. On state taxes and spending in the Lane years, see Callcott, *Maryland and America*, pp. 103–5.

19. For Mahoney's career as racing commission chairman, see the *Sun*, 21 April 1947, and "Horse-racing, Moral and Religious Aspects," vertical file, Maryland Room, Pratt Library.

20. Callcott, *Maryland and America*, pp. 118, 121.

21. Ibid., p. 125; Tydings Committee quoted in Earl Latham, *The Communist Controversy in Washington from the New Deal to McCarthy* (Cambridge, Mass.: Harvard University Press, 1966), p. 282; Boas in J. B. Donnelly, "The Vision of Scholarship: Johns Hopkins after the War," *MHM*, 73 (1978): 152.

22. O'Conor quoted in Franklin L. Burdette, "Modern Maryland Politics and Social Change," in Richard Walsh and William Lloyd Fox, eds., *Maryland: A History, 1632–1974* (Baltimore: MHS, 1974), p. 801.

23. G. Marie Biggs, *The Story of Jessup* (privately printed, 1977), p. 63.

24. McCardell quoted in Jo Ann Harris, "Claire McCardell, Maryland's Fashion Prophet," *MM*, 7 (Winter 1974): 4; on income levels, see Callcott, *Maryland and America*, p. 63 and passim.

25. Traffic growth articles and auto advertisements in *Evening Sun*, 3, 7, and 8 July 1952; on U.S. 1, see Charles T. LeViness, *A History of Road Building in Maryland* (Baltimore: State Roads Commission of Maryland, 1958), p. 82.

26. *Evening Sun*, 30 July 1952.

27. LeViness, *History of Road Building*, p. 169.

28. *Baltimore County Meets the Challenge: A Century of Progress in a Single Decade; County Executive's First Annual Report* (1958), pp. 7, 23, 36. See also *Baltimore County at a Glance* (1963) and University of Maryland Bureau of Business and Economic Research, *Baltimore County: Some Aspects of Change*, Studies in Business and Economy, 13 (June 1959).

29. Towson *Jeffersonian*, 8 May 1959.

30. Wells to residents of Montgomery and Prince George's counties, 19 June 1958, reprinted in Maryland–National Capital Park and Planning Commission, *Looking Ahead: A General Plan for the Maryland-Washington Regional District* (1958).

31. On Montgomery and Prince George's counties in these years, see Callcott, *Maryland and America*, pp. 64–65.

32. O'Conor quoted in Burdette, "Modern Maryland," p. 806; M. Cooper Walker in Baltimore *American*, 15 March 1959. "Dress Right Week" announced in *Evening Sun*, 5 March 1958.

33. On the plight of Baltimore in the 1950s, see Callcott, *Maryland and America*, pp. 81–85.

34. William Manchester, *The City of Anger* (New York: Ballantine Books, 1953), p. 472; Monroe Fry, "Baltimore's Mermaids," *Esquire, The Magazine for Men*, 45 (March 1956): 82.

35. D'Alesandro's earlier objective noted in Planning Commission of Baltimore City, *Urban Renewal in Baltimore* (October 1955), p. 28.

36. Martin Millspaugh and Gurney Breckenfeld, *The Human Side of Urban Renewal: A Study of the Attitude Changes Produced by Neighborhood Rehabilitation*, ed. Miles L. Colean (Baltimore: Fight-Blight, 1958), pp. 4, 35.

37. *Urban Renewal in Baltimore*, pp. 26, 16; Planning Commission of Baltimore City, *A Great New Highway in the Making!* (c. 1951), clippings file, MHS.

38. *Sun*, 6 January 1955; Boucher quoted in Weldon Wallace, "Twenty Years in Rebuilding Downtown Baltimore," *Sun*, 23 February 1975. See also *Sunday Sun*, 24 November 1968.

39. Urban Renewal Study Board, *Baltimore's Stake in Urban Renewal* (c. 1956), and *Transcript of Proceedings, Dedication Ceremonies of the Baltimore Harbor Tunnel and Approaches*, 29 November 1957, clippings file, MHS; *Sun*, 30 November 1957.

40. Downtown planning staff quoted in Wallace, "Rebuilding Downtown Baltimore."

41. D'Alesandro quoted ibid.; *Evening Sun*, 27 and 28 March 1958.

42. *Evening Sun*, 27 and 28 March 1958.

43. Unitas quoted in John F. Steadman, "'The Game': An Affectionate Memoir," *Baltimore Magazine*, 76 (December 1983): 108.

44. John R. Brugger, earlier of the University of Illinois, served as chief engineer of the project, William C. Warman of Towson as C&P liaison. The adaptable county superintendent was William M. Brish.

45. Stockbridge quoted in Callcott, *Maryland and America*, p. 250.

46. Hoover quoted in *Baltimore County Meets the Challenge*, p. 50.

47. Maryland Commission on Interracial Problems and Relations, Baltimore Commission on Human Relations, *Desegregation in the Baltimore City Schools* (July 1955), p. 32.

48. Callcott, *Maryland and America*, p. 244.

49. Key, *Report on the Maryland State Planning Commission* (November 1958), pp. 25, 32–33.

50. University of Maryland Bureau of Business and Economic Research, *Potomac River Basin, Research-Planning-Development*, Studies in Business and Economics, 11 (December 1957), pp. 13 and 15, and idem, *Retaining Open Spaces in Maryland*, ibid., 15 (June 1961), p. 1.

51. Rachel Carson, *Silent Spring* (Boston: Houghton Mifflin Co., 1962), pp. 7–8.

52. Rouse quoted in Gurney Breckenfeld, *Columbia and the New Cities* (New York: Ives Washburn, 1971), pp. 169, 174–75, 252. See also James H. Bready, "America's Top Shop Center Developer," *Sun*, 5 May 1963.

53. *Evening Sun*, 6 March 1958; Philip W. Tawes, Jr., "Millard and Avalynne: The Lives of J. Millard Tawes, the Fifty-fourth Governor of Maryland, and Helen Avalynne Tawes, His Wife" (manuscript, in possession of family, based on taped interviews), p. 106.

54. Calvin Dickinson quoted in Wennersten, *Oyster Wars*, p. 125.

55. Lobbyist quoted in *Evening Sun*, 6 March 1960, Tawes in *Evening Sun*, 8 April 1960.

56. Walsh quoted in *Final Report of the Commission for More Equal Representation in the General Assembly of Maryland* (1959), p. 14.

57. Tawes, "Millard and Avalynne," p. 112; Burdette, "Modern Maryland," p. 853.

58. Archbishop Shehan and the Rev. Eugene Carson Blake quoted in Lenora Heilig Nast, Laurence N. Krause, and R. C. Monk, eds., *Baltimore: A Living Renaissance* (Baltimore: Historic Baltimore, 1982), p. 91.

59. Tawes, "Millard and Avalynne," p. 146.

60. On retail sales, see Callcott, *Maryland and America*, p. 66.

61. J. Anthony Lukas, "What Will Happen to Annapolis?" *Sunday Sun*, 25 September 1960; Frank Henry, "Annapolis: The New Vs. Old," *Sunday Sun*, 13 May 1962; and Tony Evans, "Tempers in Annapolis Do a High Rise," *News American*, 9 August 1964.

62. Maryland Department of Economic Development, "Maryland's Economy in 1965" (January 1966), and idem, "Two Major Factors Affecting the Economy of Maryland" (1969), vertical file, Maryland Room, Pratt Library; Callcott, *Maryland and America*, pp. 63–64.

63. Kram, "Wink at a Homely Girl," p. 100; *Sunday Sun*, 7 November 1965, and *Sun*, 20 February 1966.

64. *Evening Sun*, Sickles, Tydings, and Mahoney quoted in Burdette, "Modern Maryland," p. 855.

Chapter 12

1. Brown quoted in Baltimore *Evening Sun*, 25 July 1967. I have changed the reporter's transcription of "hunky" to "honky," and capitalized Brown's reference to "the Man," that is, to whites.

2. Ibid.

3. Ibid., 25 and 26 July. On Gelston's arrangement with the Colts, see Lawrence M. Baskir and William A. Strauss, *Chance and Circumstance: The Draft, the War, and the Vietnam Generation* (New York: Alfred A. Knopf, 1978), p. 48.

4. Sam Kimmel quoted in Joseph Albright, *What Makes Spiro Run? The Life and Times of Spiro Agnew* (New York: Dodd, Mead & Co., 1972), p. 49.

5. Agnew quoted in Franklin L. Burdette, "Modern Maryland Politics and Social Change," in Richard Walsh and William Lloyd Fox, eds., *Maryland: A History, 1632–1974* (Baltimore: MHS, 1974), p. 866.

6. Ibid., p. 869; Baltimore *Sun*, 29 July 1967.

7. *Maryland Manual*, 1969–70, p. 182; Agnew quoted in Burdette, "Modern Maryland," p. 868.

8. George A. Bell and Jean E. Spencer, *The Legislative Process in Maryland: A Study of the General Assembly* (College Park: University of Maryland, College of Business and Public Administration, Bureau of Governmental Research, 1958; 2d ed. 1963), p. iii. See also Alan Rosenthal, *Strengthening the Maryland Legislature: An Eagleton Study and Report* (New Brunswick, N.J.: Rutgers University Press, 1968), pp. 32–33.

9. *Evening Sun*, 3 April, 21 May, 21 October 1967.

10. Ibid., 5 April 1968.

11. Ibid., 8 April 1968; Sherry H. Olson, *Baltimore: The Building of an American City* (Baltimore: Johns Hopkins University Press, 1980), p. 383.

12. *Evening Sun*, 12 and 8 April 1968.

13. Agnew quoted in Albright, *What Makes Spiro Run?* pp. 186–88.

14. Mrs. Sheldon Kravitz to editor, *Evening Sun*, 17 May 1968.

15. *Evening Sun*, 17 and 23 May 1968.

16. Nixon quoted in Albright, *What Makes Spiro Run?* p. 211.

17. *Maryland Manual*, 1969–70.

18. Mandel quoted in Burdette, "Modern Maryland," p. 882.

19. See John C. Schmidt, "Training Tomorrow's Estuarine Biologists, *MM*, 1 (Autumn 1968): 28–32; Earl Arnett, "Probing the Bay's Ecology," *MM*, 3 (Winter 1970): 2–5; Hal Burdett, "Mrs. Russell Wiltbank, Lady Conservationist," *MM*, 2 (Spring 1970): 31. On the air pollution program at the University of Maryland, College Park, see *MM*, 2 (Summer 1970): 32.

20. Mandel quoted in John C. Schmidt, "The Fight for a Sane Nuclear Policy," *MM*, 7 (Autumn 1974): 3.

21. Wiltbank quoted in Burdett, "Mrs. Russell Wiltbank," p. 31; Arnett, "Probing the Bay's Ecology," p. 2; Vladimir A. Wahbe to Mandel, 20 March 1972, reprinted in Maryland Department of State Planning and the Chesapeake Bay Interagency Planning Committee, *Maryland Chesapeake Bay Study* (1972). See also *MM*, 1 (Autumn 1968): 3, and William F. Hallstead, "TV's Nature Lady," *MM*, 5 (Spring 1973): 7.

22. Coulter quoted in "Walking the Ecological Tightrope," *MM*, 9 (Autumn 1976): 23; see also J. Carleton Jones, "Gearing for the Seventies," *MM*, 2 (Autumn 1969): 26–31.

23. Melvin H. Garner quoted in William F. Hallstead, "New Skills for Appalachia," *MM*, 5 (Summer 1973): 7.

24. Company executive quoted in "The Four Horsemen of Cambridge," *MM*, 5 (Autumn 1972): 15.

25. Mary Corddry, "The New Ocean City," *MM*, 13 (Spring 1981): 7. See also Mark Guidera, "Ocean City: Better Than Ever by the Sea," *MM*, 16 (Summer 1984): 28–33, and Orrin H. Pilkey, "The Twilight of Ocean City," Outlook, *Washington Post*, 26 May 1985.

26. Maryland Department of Economic Development, *Maryland . . . R & D Country* (1968).

27. "Bulldozers Doom More City Landmarks," *Sunday Sun Magazine*, 3 October 1965; Phoebe H. Stanton, "Keeping the 'There' in Baltimore," *Evening Sun*, 5 April 1968. See also "Baltimore—Horses and Wagons," vertical file, Maryland Room, Pratt Library.

28. Baltimore business leaders quoted in William F. Hallstead, "New Prospects for Black Business," *MM*, 5 (Winter 1972): 20.

29. Embry quoted in Ric Barter, "Robert C. Embry, Jr.," in Lenora Heilig Nast, Laurence N. Krause, and R. C. Monk, eds., *Baltimore: A Living Renaissance* (Baltimore: Historic Baltimore, 1982), p. 285, Gorham in Richard P. Davis, "Black East Baltimore Rebuilds," ibid., pp. 16–17.

30. Rawley M. Grau, "City Fair," in Nast, Krause, and Monk, eds., *Living Renaissance*, p. 13.

31. D'Alesandro quoted in Bradford Jacobs, *Thimbleriggers: The Law v. Governor Marvin Mandel* (Baltimore: Johns Hopkins University Press, 1984), p. 69. Jacobs also discusses Tawes, Hocker, and Tidewater Insurance. On the Susquehanna River Bridge, see Olson, *Baltimore*, pp. 290–91.

32. Mandel quoted in Burdette, "Modern Maryland," p. 897.

33. Agnew quoted in Albright, *What Makes Spiro Run?* pp. 234, 238–39; McKeldin quoted in Albert W. Quinn, "Contemporary Maryland," in Morris L. Radoff, ed., *The Old Line State: A History of Maryland*, Publication no. 16 (Annapolis: MHR, 1971), p. 451.

34. Wolff quoted in Richard M. Cohen and Jules Witcover, *A Heartbeat Away: The Investigation and Resignation of Vice President Spiro T. Agnew* (New York: Viking Press, 1974), p. 70. These paragraphs draw heavily from the Cohen and Witcover account.

35. Staszak quoted ibid., p. 40.

36. For Barbara Mandel's remark, see Jacobs, *Thimbleriggers*, p. 81. My summary account of Mandel's fall owes a great deal to Jacobs's volume.

37. McGrory quoted ibid., p. 83.

38. *Evening Sun*, 28 December 1977.

39. Hughes quoted in Jacobs, *Thimbleriggers*, p. 15.

40. Gude quoted in John T. Starr, "Maryland's Impending Water Crisis: Saving the Potomac Is Everybody's Job," *MM*, 10 (Summer 1978): 38. See also Gude, *Where the Potomac Begins: A History of the North Branch Valley* (Cabin John, Md./Washington, D.C.: Seven Locks Press, 1984).

41. Andrew Harris to editors, *Evening Sun*, 13 March 1958; 1966 bill and Mary Combs Barber quoted in James F. Waesche, "Peeling Away the Centuries," *MM*, 4 (Autumn 1971): 22–23.

42. Birch Hotz quoted in Constance Stapleton, "Yes, You May Touch: The Frederick Community Creates a Museum for Children," *MM*, 7 (Winter 1974): 8; R. J. Holt quoted in "Dateline Maryland," *MM*, 13 (Autumn 1980): 30. See also William F. Hallstead, "Maryland Tunes to Public TV," *MM*, 1 (Summer 1969): 25–28.

43. Maryland Department of Economic and Community Development, Maryland Historical Trust, *New Life for Maryland's Old Towns* (1979), p. 3; Franklin Shaw quoted in "New Market: Antique Town for Antiques," *MM*, 15 (Winter 1982): 4.

44. "Movement against Destruction" flyer, "Express Highways—Baltimore," vertical file, Maryland Room, Pratt Library.

45. Joe Anne Whitely quoted in Jacques Kelly, "New Heart for an Old City," *MM*, 8 (Spring 1976): 4.

46. Schaefer quoted in Richard P. Davis, "Urban Homesteading," in Nast, Krause, and Monk, eds., *Living Renaissance*, p. 23; Froelicher quoted in Karen A. Stakem, "Hans Froelicher, Jr., Civic Educator," *MHM*, 77 (1982): 198.

47. Kromah quoted in Lenora Heilig Nast and Jacqueline Nast Naron, "Visual Arts," in Nast, Krause, and Monk, eds., *Living Renaissance*, p. 192.

48. Epstein quoted in Clarinda Harriss Lott, "Poetry and Literature," ibid., p. 211.

49. Epstein, Randall, and Jacobsen quoted ibid., pp. 210–11.

50. Anne Tyler, *Searching for Caleb* (New York: Alfred A. Knopf, 1976), p. 7.

51. John Barth, "The Literature of Exhaustion," *Atlantic*, 220 (August 1967): 29–34; Alan Prince, "An Interview with John Barth," *Prism*, Spring 1968, p. 62.

52. John Barth, *The Floating Opera* (New York: Bantam Books, 1972 [New York, 1956]) pp. 122, 70, 50; idem, *The Sot-Weed Factor* (2d ed.; Garden City, N.Y.: Doubleday & Co., 1967), p. 398.

Epilogue

1. Ennis quoted in Sallie Kravitz, *Ethel Ennis, The Reluctant Jazz Star* (Baltimore: Gateway Press, 1984), p. 62; Maryland Department of Economic and Community Development, Maryland Historical Trust, *New Life for Maryland's Old Towns* (1979), p. 9; Blau quoted in Earl Arnett, "The Arts: Maryland's Position on the National Scene," *MM*, 10 (Spring 1978): 15.

2. Rouse quoted in *Evening Sun*, 17 November 1980, and *Time*, 24 August 1981.

3. Robert Carroll Simpson quoted in Janice Mione, "The Waterman-Farmer, A Livelihood by Choice," *MM*, 13 (Spring 1981): 2.

BIBLIOGRAPHICAL ESSAY

This listing primarily will aid the general reader and undergraduate student. Specialists and graduate students should consult the bibliographies of recent scholarly works, along with the guides that private repositories and public agencies have made available to the serious researcher. They include Edward C. Papenfuse, Gregory A. Stiverson, and Mary D. Donaldson, comps., *An Inventory of Maryland State Papers* (Annapolis: MHR, 1977–   ); Edward C. Papenfuse, Susan A. Collins, and Christopher N. Allan, comps., *Guide to the Maryland Hall of Records: Local, Judicial, and Administrative Records on Microform* (Annapolis: MHR, 1978–   ); Frank F. White, Jr., comp., *Maryland State Publications Received at the Hall of Records* (Annapolis: MHR, 1975); Morris L. Radoff, Gust Skordas and Phebe R. Jacobsen, *The County Courthouses and Records of Maryland, Part Two; The Records* (Annapolis: MHR, 1963); Michael S. Miller, comp., *The Maryland Court of Appeals: A Bibliography of Its History* (Annapolis: Maryland State Law Library, 1987); *Personal and Organizational Papers Relating to Maryland: A Guide to Holdings of the Archives and Manuscripts Department of the Special Collections Division of the University of Maryland Libraries at College Park* (College Park: University of Maryland, 1978); Eleanore O. Hofstetter and Marcella S. Eustis, comps., *Newspapers in Maryland Libraries: A Union List* (Baltimore: Division of Library Development Services, Maryland State Department of Education, 1977); Mary Gordon Malloy and Jane C. Sween, *A Selective Guide to the Historic Records of Montgomery County, Maryland* (Rockville, Md.: Montgomery County Department of Public Libraries, 1974). Richard J. Cox, *Tracing the History of the Baltimore Structure: A Guide to the Primary and Secondary Sources* (Baltimore: Baltimore City Archives and Records Management Office, 1980), and William G. LeFurgy, Susan Wertheimer David, and Richard J. Cox, *Governing Baltimore: A Guide to the Records of the Mayor and City Council at the Baltimore City Archives* (Baltimore: Baltimore City Archives and Records Management Office, 1981), offer a start at city hall, but see also paragraph below. Mary Neill Barton, "Rare Books and Other Bibliographical Resources in Baltimore Libraries," *Papers of the Bibliographical Society of America*, 55 (1961): 1–16, provides an invaluable research tool. See also John T. Guertler, ed., *The Records of Baltimore's Private Organizations: A Guide to Archival Resources* (New York: Garland Publishing, 1981).

The Maryland Historical Society—through its library, museum, and magazine—makes its own considerable contributions to the researcher. On the state's largest private manuscript collection, see Avril J. M. Pedley, ed., *The Manuscript Collections of the Maryland Historical Society* (Baltimore: MHS, 1968), and Richard J. Cox and Larry E. Sullivan, eds., *A Guide to the Research Collections of the Maryland Historical Society: General Manuscripts and Oral History Interviews* (Baltimore: MHS, 1981). Betty McKeever Key, comp., *Oral History in Maryland: A Directory*, ed. Larry E. Sullivan (Baltimore: MHS, 1981), lists files to date and participants in that growing project. See also Lynn Cox and Helena Zinkham, "Picture Research at the Maryland Historical Society: A Guide to the Sources," *MHM*, 76 (1981): 1–21, and P. William Filby, "Music in the Maryland Historical Society," MHS *Notes*, 32 (1976): 503–17. Advanced students may also make use of the extensive annual bibliographies published in the *MHM* between 1975 and 1983. Rather than trying to comment on the vast (and highly uneven) unpublished material that few readers would find accessible, I include here only a few such works and defer to Dorothy M. Brown and Richard R. Duncan, *Master's Theses and Doctoral Dissertations on Maryland History* (Baltimore: MHS, 1970; *MHM*, 63 [1968]: 412–19), and addenda: Richard J. Cox, "A Selected List of Recent Dissertations on Maryland History, 1970–1976," *MHM*, 73 (1978): 180–85; Duncan, "Master's Theses and Doctoral Dissertations on Maryland History," *MHM*, 80 (1985): 261–76. Future spring or summer issues of the magazine will bring these bibliographies up to date. While in the categories below one finds many references to Baltimore City, students will find two guides readily accessible: Richard J. Cox and Patricia M. Vanorny, "The Records of a City: Baltimore and Its Historical Sources," *MHM*, 70 (1975): 286–310, and Cox, "Understanding the Monumental City: A Bibliographical Essay on Baltimore History," *MHM*, 77 (1982): 70–111. Genealogists have useful guides in Cox, "Historical Demographers, Local Historians, and Genealogists: A Bibliographical Essay of Maryland Studies," *Maryland Genealogical Society Bulletin*, 21 (Winter 1980): 5–17, and Mary K. Meyer, *Genealogical Research in Maryland—A Guide* (3d ed.; Baltimore: MHS, 1983).

Other bibliographies of note include Richard Parsons, ed., *Guide to Specialized Subject Collections in Maryland Libraries* (2d ed.; Baltimore: Baltimore County Public Libraries, 1974); Douglas O. Michael, comp., *Western Maryland Materials in Allegany and Garrett County Libraries* (Cumberland, Md.: Allegany County Local History Program, 1977); Elizabeth Lawton and Raymond S. Sweeney, *Maryland History: A Selective Bibliography; Showing the Holdings of Some of the Major Libraries in the Baltimore-Washington Metropolitan Area* (Rockville, Md.: Montgomery County Historical Society, 1975); *The Southern Maryland Collections, Section 1, June 1979 edition: The Book Collections* (La Plata, Md.: Charles County Community College, 1979); Felix Reichman, "German Printing in Maryland: A Check List, 1768–1950," *Report of the Society for the History of Germans in Maryland*, 27 (1950): 9–70, and Frederick S. Weiser, ed., "Eighteenth Century German Church Records from Maryland: A Checklist," *The Report: A Journal of German-American History*, 38 (1982): 5–14; Gertrude Singer Nitzberg, "The Music Library at the Jewish Historical Society of Maryland, Inc.," *Generations*, 3 (December 1982): 37–38; George A. Simpson, "Bibliography of Maryland Folklore and Folklife," *Free State Folklore: The Journal of the Maryland Folklore Society*, 2 (Spring 1975): 13–20; Clay Schofield, "An Annotated Bibliography of Folklore Material in the Eastern Shore," ibid., 3 (Winter 1976–77): 19–55; P. Vivian Wiser, "Select Bibliography on History of Agriculture in Maryland," National Agricultural Library, Beltsville, Md., *Associates NAL Today*, new ser., 1 (1976): 55–85; Bruce C. Steiner, "Descriptions of Maryland," JHUS, 22 (1904); and Lawrence S. Thompson, "Foreign Travellers in Maryland, 1900–1950," *MHM*, 48 (1953): 337–43. Morgan H. Pritchett and Susan R. Woodcock, eds., *The Eastern Shore of Maryland: An Annotated Bibliography* (Centreville, Md.: Queen Anne Press of Wye Institute, 1980), lists more than twelve hundred titles, none of them from the *MHM* or other periodicals. Michael M. Reynolds, *Maryland: A Guide to Information and Reference Sources* (Adelphi, Md.: Research and Reference Publications, 1976), provides a helpful starting point on many fronts; though largely omitting journal articles and unpublished works, it lists more than two thousand entries.

A few general and reference works bear mention. Edward C. Papenfuse, Gregory A. Stiverson, Susan A. Collins, and Lois Green Carr, eds. and comps., *Maryland: A New Guide to the Old Line State* (Baltimore: Johns Hopkins University Press, 1976), revises the original Works Progress Administration guidebook, is available in paperback, and offers unexpected delights. Geographical studies of the state, which go far beyond soil classifications and mean rainfalls, include James E. DiLisio, *Maryland: A Geography*, Geographies of the United States, Ingolf Vogeler, gen. ed. (Boulder, Colo.: Westview Press, 1983), and Derek Thompson et al., *Atlas of Maryland* (College Park: Department of Geography, University of Maryland, 1977). For visual aids especially helpful to a beginning student, see Maryland Department of Economic and Community Development, Department of State Planning, *The State of Maryland Historical Atlas . . .* (Washington, D.C.: Raymond, Parish, Pine, & Plavnick, 1973). Edward C. Papenfuse and Joseph M. Coale III, eds., *The Hammond-Harwood House Atlas of Historical Maps of Maryland, 1608–1908* (Baltimore: Johns Hopkins University Press, 1982), enables one to view cartographic, economic, and a variety of other developments in a volume that itself makes up a work of art. Every two years the *Maryland Manual*, now edited by Gregory A. Stiverson, Diane Frese, and Edward C. Papenfuse, publishes a wealth of information that includes state election results. For facts and figures on presidential canvasses, see John T. Willis, *Presidential Elections in Maryland* (Mt. Airy, Md.: Lomond Publications, 1984). Frank F. White, Jr., *The Governors of Maryland*, Publication no. 15 (Annapolis: MHR, 1970), offers brief biographical sketches. Kenny Hamill, *Placenames in Maryland* (Baltimore: MHS, 1984), provides another handy reference.

Histories of Maryland, reflecting the views and purposes of their day, have done reasonably well by the state. The earliest accounts were promotional brochures and receive notice in the section for chapter 1. John Leeds Bozman, *A Sketch of the History of Maryland . . .* (Baltimore, 1811), John V. L. MacMahon, *An Historical View of the Government of Maryland from Its Colonization to the Present Day* (Baltimore: J. Lucas & E. K. Deaver, 1831), and James McSherry, *History of Maryland; from Its First Settlement in 1634 to the Year 1848* (Baltimore: J. Murphy & Co., 1849–52), relied almost entirely on legislative and court records; Bozman treated the seventeenth century while McSherry devoted most space to the colonial and revolutionary periods. J. Thomas Scharf, *History of Maryland from the Earliest Period to the Present Day* (3 vols.; Baltimore: John B. Piet, 1879), if used with caution, remains useful as a factual stockpile. Matthew Page Andrews, in his *Tercentenary History of Maryland* (4 vols., Baltimore, S. J. Clarke Publishing Co., 1925), and the abridged *History of Maryland: Province and State* (Garden City, N.Y.: Doubleday, Doran & Co., 1929), writes colorfully of politics and wars, mostly before 1865. In the 1970s two volumes helped to update the Andrews account. Morris L. Radoff, then state archivist, edited a series of essays, *The Old Line State: A History of Maryland*, Publication no. 16 (Annapolis: MHR, 1971), and Richard Walsh and William Lloyd Fox edited *Maryland: A History, 1632–1974* (Baltimore: MHS, 1974). While lacking narrative unity, both volumes contain much information. Carl Bode, *Maryland: A Bicentennial History* (New York: W. W. Norton & Co., 1978), takes a biographical approach that allows its author, an emeritus student of American literature and H. L. Mencken, to write vividly of human experience. In Donald M. Dozer, *Portrait of the Free State: A History of Maryland* (Cambridge, Md.: Tidewater Publishers, 1976), an American Studies scholar delivers an able survey. For an exemplary secondary-school survey textbook and a helpful instructors' supplement, see Suzanne Ellery Greene Chapelle, Jean H. Baker, Dean R. Esslinger, Whitman H. Ridgway, Jean B. Russo, Constance B. Schultz, and Gregory A. Stiverson, *Maryland: A History of Its People* (Baltimore: Johns Hopkins University Press, 1986), and James F. Adomanis, *Teachers' Resource Guide to Accompany "Maryland: A History of Its People"* (Baltimore: Johns Hopkins University Press, 1986).

The many recent works on Maryland counties testify to a rise in popular historical interest during and after the bicentennial celebration. Substantial and scholarly county histories of that period include Stephen Schlosnagle and the Garrett County Bicentennial Committee, *Garrett County: A History of Maryland's Tableland* (Parsons, W.Va.: McClain Printing Co., 1978); Harry I. Stegmaier, Jr., David M. Dean, Gordon E. Kershaw, and John B. Wiseman, *Allegany County: A History* (Parsons, W.Va.: McClain Printing Co., 1976); Nancy M. Warner, Ralph B. Levering, and Margaret Taylor Woltz, *Carroll County, Maryland: A History, 1837–1976* (Westminster, Md.: Carroll County Bicentennial Committee, 1976); Ray Eldon Hiebert and Richard K. MacMaster, *A Grateful Remembrance: The Story of Montgomery County, Maryland* (Rockville, Md.: Montgomery County Government and the Montgomery County Historical Society, 1976); Neal A. Brooks and Eric Rockel, *A History of Baltimore County* (Towson, Md.: Friends of the Towson Library, 1977); and Dickson J. Preston and Norman Harrington, *Talbot County: A History* (Centreville, Md.: Tidewater Publishers, 1983). James C. Bradford, ed., *Anne Arundel County, Maryland: A Bicentennial History, 1649–1977* (Annapolis: Anne Arundel County and Annapolis Bicentennial Committee, 1977), supplements Elihu S. Riley, *The Ancient City: A History of Annapolis, in Maryland, 1649–1887* (Annapolis, 1887), with much recent commentary.

A number of additional volumes, helpful in their own way, follow a topical rather than chronological format or weight coverage toward the distant past. Reuben L. Musey, *It Happened in Washington County* (Hagerstown, Md.: Washington County Bicentennial Committee, 1976), treats historic sites alphabetically. W. R. Quynn, *Bicentennial History of Frederick City and County, Maryland, 1745–1789* (Frederick, Md.: Bicentennial Committee of Frederick, 1975), and C. Milton Wright, *Our Harford Heritage: A History of Harford County, Maryland* (privately published, 1967), instruct youth while appealing to a wide audience. Louise Joyner Hienton, *Prince George's Heritage: Sidelights on the Early History of Prince George's County, Maryland, from 1696 to 1800* (Baltimore: MHS, 1972), covers a century of boundaries, Indians, churches, schools, and wars; R. Lee Van Horn, *Out of the Past: Prince Georgians and Their Land* (Riverdale, Md.: Prince George's County Historical

Society, 1976), reaches 1861. Celia M. Holland discusses family history and family seats in *Old Homes and Families of Howard County, Maryland* (privately printed, 1987). Charles Francis Stein, Jr., *Origin and History of Howard County, Maryland* (privately published in cooperation with the Howard County Historical Society, 1972), and Stein, *The History of Calvert County* (Prince Frederick, Md.: Calvert County Bicentennial Committee, 1976), combine history with coats of arms and county genealogy. Jack D. Brown, William A. Diggs, Gladys S. Jenkins, J. C. Karpiak, Elwood M. Leviner, Mary Clare Matthews, Janie MacInnis, Rona R. Schaepman, and Frederick Tilp, *Charles County, Maryland: A History* (South Hackensack, N.J.: Custombook, 1976), Regina Combs Hammett, *History of St. Mary's County, Maryland* (Ridge, Md.: privately published, 1977), and Reginald V. Truitt and Millard C. Les Callette, *Worcester County: Maryland's Arcadia* (Easton, Md.: Waverly Press, 1977), handle their subjects with loving care. Charles Branch Clark, *The Eastern Shore of Maryland and Virginia* (2 vols.; New York: Lewis Historical Publishing Co., 1950), largely thematic, provides many sidelights.

Works on Maryland communities abound, many of them appearing in the pictorial histories section below. Sherry H. Olson, *Baltimore: The Building of an American City* (Baltimore: Johns Hopkins University Press, 1980), a highly interesting urban-geographical history, replaces John Thomas Scharf's bulky *History of Baltimore City and County from the Earliest Period to the Present Day* (2 vols.; Baltimore: Regional Publishing Co., 1971 [Philadelphia, 1881]) and a civic-minded tract, Clayton Coleman Hall, ed., *Baltimore: Its History and Its People* (3 vols.; New York: Lewis Publishing Co., 1912)—both of which remain generally reliable reference works. See also Joseph L. Arnold, "Baltimore's Neighborhoods, 1800–1980," *Working Papers from the Regional Economic History Research Center*, 4 (nos. 1 and 2, 1981): 76–98, and William G. Lefurgy, "Baltimore's Wards, 1797–1978: A Guide," *MHM*, 75 (1980): 145–53. Special works on the city include Jacques Kelly, *Peabody Heights to Charles Village: The Historic Development of a Baltimore Community* (Baltimore: Equitable Trust Bank, 1976); *Reflections, Sparrows Point, Md.* (Dundalk: Dundalk-Patapsco Neck Historical Society, 1976); *Brooklyn–Curtis Bay History* (Baltimore: J. C. O'Donovan & Co., 1976); and Mark Miller, *Mount Washington, Baltimore Suburb* (Baltimore: GBS Publishers, 1981). Norman G. Rukert's volumes on historic city sites—*The Fells Point Story* (Baltimore: Bodine & Associates, 1976); *Historic Canton: Baltimore's Industrial Heartland and Its People* (Baltimore: Bodine & Associates, 1978); *Federal Hill: A Baltimore National Historic District* (Baltimore: Bodine & Associates, 1980); *The Port: Pride of Baltimore* (Baltimore: Bodine & Associates, 1982); and *Ft. McHenry, Home of the Brave* (Baltimore: Bodine & Associates, 1983)—supplement text with lavish illustrations. Gilbert Sandler, *The Neighborhood: The Story of Baltimore's Little Italy* (Baltimore: Bodine & Associates, 1974), complements text with scenes from a famous quarter of East Baltimore; see also Anna Caraveli, *Scattered in Foreign Lands: A Greek Village in Baltimore* (Baltimore: Baltimore Museum of Art, 1985).

Local histories understandably reflect love of place. On the economic fortunes of a far western community, see Robert C. Shaffer, *History of Crellin, Maryland: Story of a Double Boom Town* (privately published, 1976), and for a different story, one largely of stasis, see Lee Barron, *The History of Sharpsburg* (privately published, 1972). Though Frederick County lacks a recent textual history, there are late notes on communities; see Emilie A. and Mary B. Nakhleh, eds., *History and Society* (Emmitsburg, Md.: Chronicle Press, 1976), and Jay N. Ballentine, Jr., *Jefferson, 1774–1974, Frederick County* (Jefferson, Md.: Jefferson Bicentennial Committee, c. 1976). Anne B. Hooper, *Braddock Heights: A Glance Backward* (Baltimore: French-Bray Printing, 1975), describes life at the South Mountain resort between about 1896 and 1947. Dawn F. Thomas and Robert Barnes, *The Green Spring Valley: Its History and Heritage* (2 vols.; Baltimore: MHS, 1978), surveys the horse country northwest of Baltimore. Celia M. Holland, *Ellicott City, Maryland: Mill Town, USA* (University Park, Md.: privately published, 1970), treats that early industrial center. John W. McGrain, *Bicentennial Festival, History and Heritage: Oella—Its Thread of History* (Oella, Md.: Oella Community Improvement Association, 1976), discusses another Patapsco mill town. Ruth P. Eason, *History of the Town of Glen Burnie* (Glen Burnie, Md.: Kuethe Library, 1972), follows that Anne Arundel community from the 1880s to the suburbs; for tales of the same county, see Donald G. Shomette, *London Town: A Brief History* (Londontown,

Md.: London Town Publik House Commission, 1978), and Joseph L. Browne, *From Sot-weed to Suburbia: A History of the Crofton, Maryland, Area, 1660–1960* (Baltimore: Gateway Press, 1985). Shirley Baltz, ed., *A Chronicle of Belair* (Bowie, Md.: Bowie Heritage Committee, 1984); Evelyn Hirrel, ed., *A History of the Town of Landover Hills, Maryland* (Landover Hills, Md.: Town of Landover Hills, 1985); Darlie Norton, *A History of Suitland, Md., 1867–1976* (Suitland, Md.: privately printed, 1976); Donald Skarda, *A History of Berwyn Heights, Md.* (Berwyn Heights, Md.: privately printed, 1976); and *"I Believe in America:" Ninety Years of Community Growth and Development in the City of Hyattsville* (Hyattsville, Md.: Mayor and City Council, c. 1977), cover Prince George's communities. On Calvert, see A. Y. Dessaint, *Southern Maryland Yesterday and Today: Crab Pots and Sotweed Fields* (Prince Frederick, Md.: Calvert County Historical Society, 1984).

Elizabeth L. Kytle, *Time Was: A Cabin John Memory Book; Interviews with Eighteen Old-Timers* (Cabin John, Md.: Cabin John Citizens' Association, 1976), gathers testimony on lower Montgomery County, as does Ann Stinson, *Hoopers Island: Today and Many Yesterdays; A Brief History of Hoopers Island Compiled from the Written and Oral Accounts of the People Who Have Lived There* (Easton, Md.: Easton Publishing Co., 1975), for life along the lower Chesapeake. Cynthia Ludlow, *Historic Easton* (Easton, Md.: Historic Easton, 1979), includes illustrations and photographs; see also Norman Harrington, *Easton Album* (Easton, Md.: Historical Society of Talbot County, 1986). Dickson J. Preston, *Trappe: The Story of an Old-Fashioned Town* (Easton, Md.: Trappe Bicentennial Committee, 1976), documents the experience of that Methodist-founded community. Dickson J. Preston and Norman Harrington, *Oxford: The First Three Centuries* (Easton, Md.: Historical Society of Talbot County, 1984), examines an Eastern Shore treasure. Woodrow T. Wilson, *Crisfield, Maryland, 1676–1976* (Baltimore: Gateway Press, 1977), surveys a center of the state seafood industry. Geoffrey H. Robbins and Brian P. Henley, eds., *A Century of Seashore Hospitality: The History of Ocean City, Md., 1875–1975* (Ocean City, Md.: Ocean City Bicentennial Committee, 1975), highlights the boardwalk, means of travel, pioneer women, and churches.

Local/regional volumes of special note examine the cultural impact of economic change or the conflict between development and ecological awareness. See, for example, Kim R. Kihl, *Port Tobacco: A Transformed Community* (Baltimore: Maclay & Associates, 1982). Boyd Gibbons, *Wye Island: Outsiders, Insiders, and Resistance to Change* (Baltimore: Johns Hopkins University Press, 1977), explores recent history and social stress on the middle Eastern Shore. Randall S. Peffer, *Watermen* (Baltimore: Johns Hopkins University Press, 1979), and Lila Line, *Waterwomen* (Queenstown, Md.: Queen Anne Press, 1982), may be considered recent histories of an endangered species. Gilbert Gude, *Where the Potomac Begins: A History of the North Branch Valley* (Cabin John, Md./Washington, D.C.: Seven Locks Press, 1984), confirms the author's long interest in the health of that river. Paul Metcalf, ed., *Waters of Potowmack* (San Francisco: North Point Press, 1982), collects evocative observations of the Potomac region ranging from the seventeenth century to the 1960s. John Capper, Garrett Power, and Frank R. Shivers, Jr., *Chesapeake Waters: Pollution, Public Health, and Public Opinion, 1607–1972* (Centreville, Md.: Tidewater Publishers, 1983), treating the slow rise of responsible and far-sighted self-interest, combines history of science with political, economic, and social history.

Marylanders have not neglected the experience of discrete groups of people in the state. Dieter Cunz, *The Maryland Germans: A History* (Princeton, N.J.: Princeton University Press, 1948), remains a model of ethnic history; the Society for the History of Germans in Maryland attempts to publish recent research on the topic in an annual *Report*. Chapter bibliographies list studies in Maryland black history, which Roland C. McConnell surveys in his *Three Hundred and Fifty Years: Chronology of the Afro-American in Maryland, 1634–1984* ([Annapolis: Commission on Afro-American History and Culture,] 1985). Vera F. Rollo, *The Black Experience in Maryland* (Lanham, Md.: Maryland Historical Press, 1980), reaches out to a beginning or secondary-school audience. Harold A. Williams, *History of the Hibernian Society of Baltimore, 1803–1957* (Baltimore: Hibernian Society of Baltimore, 1957), opens one window to the Irish experience. Isaac M. Fein, *The Making of an American Jewish Community: The History of Baltimore Jewry from 1773 to 1920* (Philadelphia: Jewish Publication Society of America, 1971), narrates the story for a wide readership and carries a useful bibliography. Isidor Blum, *The Jews of Baltimore . . .* (Baltimore/Washington, D.C.: Historical Review Publishing Co., 1910), contains essays on institutions, brief biographies, and notices of business firms. Abraham D. Glushakow, *A Pictorial History of Maryland Jewry* (Baltimore: Jewish Voice Publishing Co., 1955), lacking an index, offers vignettes of leading Baltimore figures and firms. Semi-annually since 1978 the Jewish Historical Society of Maryland publishes *Generations*, a journal of local family history. Thomas Cholochwost, "Baltimore's Polish Pioneers," *Maryland Magazine of Genealogy*, 5 (1982): 3–7, begins a story that needs completion. Stephen Basarab, Paul Fenchak, Wolodymyr C. Sushko et al., *The Ukrainians of Maryland* (Baltimore: Ukrainian Education Association of Maryland, 1977), proudly documents Ukrainian contributions to life in the state. Leslie Chin, *History of Chinese-Americans in Baltimore* (Baltimore: Greater Baltimore Chinese-American Bicentennial Committee, 1976), performs the same service. Frank Porter III, *Maryland Indians Yesterday and Today* (Baltimore: MHS, 1983), discusses the seventeenth century but also the Lumbee Indians of contemporary Baltimore. In general one might see *Maryland, Our Maryland: An Ethnic and Cultural Directory* (rev. ed.; Baltimore: Baltimore Council for International Visitors, 1978); for an introduction to scholarly sources, however, consult Jean Scarpaci, *The Ethnic Experience in Maryland: A Bibliography of Resources* (Towson, Md.: Towson State University, 1978).

Winifred G. Helmes, ed., *Notable Maryland Women*, Published in Conjunction with the Maryland Bicentennial Commission (Cambridge, Md.: Tidewater Publishers, 1977), collects one hundred essays on subjects ranging from sports heroes to leading reformers. It improves upon Margie H. Luckett, ed., *Maryland Women* (3 vols.; Baltimore: privately printed, 1931), a work of Victorian quality and dimension. See also *Behind the Maryland Scene: Women of Influence, 1600–1800* (National Society of Colonial Dames of America in Maryland et al., 1977); Patricia Savella, ed., *Who's Who of Maryland Women, 1930–1976* (Maryland Division, American Association of University Women, 1976); and *Baltimore County Women, 1930–1975* (Towson, Md.: Baltimore County Chapter, American Association of University Women, 1976). Cynthia Horsburgh Requardt, "Women's Deeds in Women's Words: Manuscripts in the Maryland Historical Society," *MHM*, 73 (1978): 186–204, offers a guide to women's history sources in one repository.

Few states offer the artist or photographer lovelier material than Maryland, and because social historians now pay close attention to visual evidence, collections of prints and photographs can do far more than decorate coffee tables. Lois B. McCauley, ed., *Maryland Historical Prints, 1752 to 1889: A Selection of the Robert G. Merrick Collection, Maryland Historical Society, and Other Maryland Collections* (Baltimore: MHS, 1975), gathers a rich variety of source materials. Several masters of imagery, portraying the state as they saw it, provide us with enduring art. See Don Swann, *Colonial and Historic Homes of Maryland: One Hundred Etchings*, text by Don Swann, Jr., with a foreword by F. Scott Fitzgerald (Baltimore: Johns Hopkins University Press, 1975 [Baltimore, 1939]), and also Robert H. Burgess, *Lewis J. Feuchter, Chesapeake Bay Artist* (Newport News, Va.: Mariners Museum, 1977). Samplings of A. Aubrey Bodine's work include *My Maryland* (Baltimore: Bodine & Associates, 1952); *The Face of Maryland* and *Chesapeake Bay and Tidewater* (Baltimore: Bodine & Associates, 1967); and *Bodine's Baltimore: Forty-six Years in the Life of a City* (Baltimore: Bodine & Associates, 1973). For an evaluation, see Kathleen M. H. Ewing, with a biographical remembrance by Harold A. Williams, *A. Aubrey Bodine, Baltimore Pictorialist, 1906–1970* (Baltimore: Johns Hopkins University Press, 1985). One may also peruse Steve Uzzell, text by Carl Bode, *Maryland* (Portland, Ore.: Graphic Arts Publishing, 1983), and *Images of the Chesapeake, 1612–1984* (Catonsville, Md.: Albin O. Kuhn Library and Gallery, University of Maryland, Baltimore County, 1985).

Since the 1950s publishing technology and the techniques of photojournalism have joined with popular demand to produce a multitude of pictorial histories. Francis F. Beirne and Carleton Jones, *Baltimore: A Picture History* (3d ed., rev.; Baltimore: Bodine & Maclay, 1982 [New York, 1957]), marked an early success in that genre. A later venture, Jacques Kelly, *Bygone Baltimore: A Historical Portrait* (Norfolk/Virginia Beach, Va.: Donning Co., 1982), publishes 370 photos, many of them from Kelly's extensive personal collection, and trains the eye on a wide variety of social subjects. Suzanne Ellery Greene, *Baltimore: An Illustrated History* (Woodland Hills, Calif.: Windsor Publications, 1980), takes a business-institutional approach. Marion E. Warren and Mame Warren, *Baltimore: When She Was What She Used to Be, 1850–1930* (Baltimore: Johns Hopkins University Press, 1983), succeeds so well that we who follow cannot help but reprint some of the Warrens' selections. John Dorsey, *Mount Vernon Place: An Anecdotal Essay with Sixty-six Illustrations* (Baltimore: Maclay & Associates, 1983), more than fulfills its promise. On the port, besides the Rukert volume listed in the Baltimore section above and titles in the chapter 12 bibliography, see Robert C. Keith, *Baltimore Harbor: A Picture History* (Baltimore: Ocean World Publishers, 1982). For a commendable attempt to view the city "from the bottom up," see volume one of W. Theodore Dürr, Thomas M. Jacklin, Mary Ellen Hayward et al., *Baltimore People, Baltimore Places: A Neighborhood Album*, The Baltimore Neighborhood Heritage Series in Social History (Baltimore: University of Baltimore, 1981). Leslie Rehbein and Kate F. Peterson, eds., *Beyond the White Marble Steps: A Look at Baltimore Neighborhoods* (Baltimore: Livelier Baltimore Committee and Citizens Planning and Housing Association, 1979), and Linda G. Rich, Joan Clark Netherwood, and Elinor B. Cahn, *Neighborhood: A State of Mind* (Baltimore: Johns Hopkins University Press, 1981), may be considered contemporary social histories.

Subjects for illustrated histories extend far beyond Baltimore. James C. Johnson, *Dorchester County: A Pictorial History* (Cambridge, Md.: Western Publishing Co., 1976), nicely portrays Cambridge and environs. For fascinating glimpses of Annapolis, see Marion E. Warren and Mary Elizabeth Warren, *The Train's Done Been and Gone: An Annapolis Portrait, 1859 to 1910* (Boston: David R. Godine in association with M. E. Warren, 1976), and *Everybody Works but John Paul Jones: A Portrait of the U.S. Naval Academy, 1845–1915* (Annapolis, Md.: Naval Institute Press, 1981). Nostalgic Montgomery County albums highlight the rapidity of change there. James A. Reber, with Austin H. Kiplinger, ed., *Portrait in Time: A Photographic Profile of Montgomery County, Md.* (Rockville, Md.: Montgomery County Bicentennial Committee, 1976), concentrates on contemporary images. Jane C. Sween, *Montgomery County: Two Centuries of Change* (Woodland Hills, Calif.: Windsor Publications, 1984), with readable text, concludes with notices of leading business establishments. Margaret Marshall Coleman and Anne Dennis Lewis, *Montgomery County, Maryland: A Pictorial History* (Norfolk, Va.: Donning Co., 1984), strikingly combines the visual and textual. Ellen Marsh and Mary Anne O'Boyle, *Takoma Park: Portrait of a Victorian Suburb, 1883–1983* (Takoma Park, Md.: Historic Takoma Park, 1984), illustrates early churches, businesses, trolleys, and various landmarks in that rightly self-conscious community. Beryl Frank, *A Pictorial History of Pikesville, Maryland* (Towson, Md.: Baltimore County Public Library, 1982), does the same for the northwest Baltimore suburb. The many productions of a publishing house specializing in this genre (the Donning Co. of Virginia Beach and Norfolk, Va.)—George H. Hahn and Carl Behm III, *Towson: A Pictorial History of a Maryland Town* (1977); George and Suzanne Hurley, *Ocean City: A Pictorial History* (1979); Lee Schwartz, Albert Feldstein, and Joan H. Baldwin, *Allegany County: A Pictorial History* (1980); Nancy F. Whitman and Timothy L. Cannon, *Frederick: A Pictorial History* (1981); and Alan Virta, *Prince George's County: A Pictorial History* (1984)—complement the textual histories mentioned above.

Pictorial surveys of the entire state also demonstrate the law of supply and demand. *Maryland: A Picture History, 1632–1976*, with a commentary by Carleton Jones (Baltimore: Bodine & Associates, 1976), portrays state development up to the bicentennial. Jacques Kelly, *Maryland: A Pictorial History . . . The First 350 Years* (Norfolk, Va.: Donning Co., 1983), employing 350 photos—black-and-white and color—covers every section of the state. Mame Warren and Marion E. Warren, *Maryland Time Exposures, 1840–1940* (Baltimore: Johns Hopkins University Press, 1984), perhaps a model for the genre, publishes almost 600 of many thousands of old photographs that this father-daughter team coaxed from the attics and storage spaces of Maryland homes. Joseph L. Arnold, *Maryland: Old Line to New Prosperity* (Northridge, Calif.: Windsor Publications, 1985), skillfully traces state development, concentrating on business-economic history. For social science teachers and others equipped with a projector, a valuable pictorial survey of the state comes in the form of transparencies: Constance B. Schulz, ed., with a preface by George H. Callcott, *The History of Maryland: A Slide Collection* (Lanham, Md.: Instructional Resources, 1980).

Space permits only a short list of the many books and articles published on Maryland architecture (studies of period styles appear in chapter bibliographies below), art, and artifacts. Readings on Maryland buildings begin with their most noted student (though his followers have revised him), Henry Chandlee Forman, whose works include *Maryland Architecture: A Short History from 1634 through the Civil War* (Cambridge, Md.: Tidewater Publishers, 1968). One must see also *Three Centuries of Maryland Architecture: A Selection of Presentations Made at the Eleventh Annual Conference of the Maryland Historical Trust, Cosponsored by the Society for the Preservation of Maryland Antiquities* (Annapolis: Maryland Historical Trust, 1982), an important collection that includes Orlando Ridout V, "Agricultural Change and the Architectural Environment"; George McDaniel, "Voices from the Past: Black Builders and Their Buildings"; and Mary Ellen Hayward, "Rowhouse: A Baltimore Style of Living." Morris L. Radoff surveys public structures in *Buildings of the State of Maryland at Annapolis*, Publication no. 9 (Annapolis: MHR, 1954); *The County Courthouses and Records of Maryland. Part One: The Courthouses* (Annapolis: MHR, 1960); and *The State House at Annapolis* (Annapolis: MHR, 1972). Elizabeth B. Anderson, with Michael P. Parker and photographs by M. E. Warren, *Annapolis: A Walk through History* (Centreville, Md.: Tidewater Publishers, 1984), sketches the background of virtually every structure in the town, colonial to Victorian. Roger Brooke Farquhar, *Historic Montgomery County: Old Homes and History* (Silver Spring, Md.: privately printed, 1952), affectionately examines local landmarks. Marilyn M. Larew, *Bel Air: The Town through Its Buildings* (Annapolis: Maryland Historical Trust, 1981), treats two hundred sites and the people who created them. For an equally fascinating look at Westminster, see Christopher Weeks, *The Building of Westminster in Maryland: A Socio-Architectural Account of Westminster's First 250 Years, Including an Illustrated Inventory of over 200 Historic Structures* (Annapolis: Fishergate Publishing for the City of Westminster, 1978). On Baltimore, in addition to the chapter bibliographies below, see Richard Hubbard Howland and Eleanor Patterson Spencer et al., *The Architecture of Baltimore: A Pictorial History* (Baltimore: Johns Hopkins Press, 1953), a longtime authority; John Dorsey and James B. Dilts, *A Guide to Baltimore Architecture* (2d ed.; Cambridge, Md.: Tidewater Publishers, 1981), which posts thirteen walking tours; Natalie W. Shivers, *Those Old Placid Rows: The Aesthetics and Development of the Baltimore Rowhouse* (Baltimore: Maclay & Associates, 1981); Carleton Jones, *Lost Baltimore Landmarks: A Portfolio of Vanished Buildings* (Baltimore: Maclay & Associates, 1982); and Joanne Giza and Catherine F. Black, *Great Baltimore Houses: An Architectural and Social History* (Baltimore: Maclay & Associates, 1982).

New volumes on architecture in the state include guidebooks published with the aid of the Maryland Historical Trust: Christopher Weeks, *Inventory of Historic Sites in Caroline County* (Annapolis: Maryland Historical Trust, 1981); Weeks, *Where Land and Water Intertwine: An Architectural History of Talbot County, Maryland*; and Weeks, ed., *Between the Nanticoke and the Choptank: An Architectural History of Dorchester County, Maryland* (Baltimore: Johns Hopkins University Press, 1984).

For an introduction to collected Maryland furniture, silver, artifacts, sculpture, and paintings, see Arthur R. Blumenthal, Vicki C. Wright, Mary A. Dean, William Voss Elder III, David P. Fogle, John W. Hill, Elizabeth Johns, and Josephine Withers, *Three Hundred and Fifty Years of Art and Architecture in Maryland* (College Park: Art Gallery and Gallery of the School of Architecture, University of Maryland, 1984). J. Hall Pleasants, *Two Hundred and Fifty Years of Painting in Maryland* (Baltimore: Baltimore Museum of Art, 1945), catalogs an earlier exhibit. Also valuable is an impressive exhibition catalog, John B. Boles, ed., *Maryland Heritage: Five Baltimore Institutions Celebrate the American Bicentennial* (Baltimore: MHS, 1976), a survey of revolutionary-period objects at the Walters Art Gallery, Baltimore Museum of Art, MHS, Peale Museum, and Maryland Academy of Sciences. Special studies of note include J. Hall Pleasants and Howard Sill, *Maryland Silversmiths, 1715–1830 . . .* (Harrison, N.Y.: Robert Alan Green, 1972 [1930]); *Baltimore Furniture: The Work of Baltimore and Annapolis Cabinetmakers from 1760 to 1810* (Baltimore: Baltimore Museum of Art, 1947); *Maryland Queen Anne and Chippendale Furniture of the Eighteenth Century* (Baltimore: Baltimore Museum of Art, 1968); Jennifer Faulds Goldsborough, *Silver in Maryland* (Baltimore: MHS, 1983); Goldsborough, *Eighteenth and Nineteenth Century Maryland Silver in the Collection of the Baltimore Museum of Art*, ed. Ann Boyce Harper (Baltimore:

Baltimore Museum of Art, 1975); Gregory R. Weidman, *Furniture in Maryland, 1740–1940: The Collection of the Maryland Historical Society* (Baltimore: MHS, 1984); William Voss Elder III, *Baltimore Painted Furniture, 1800–1840* (Baltimore: Baltimore Museum of Art, 1972); William Voss Elder III and Lu Bartlett, *John Shaw, Cabinetmaker of Annapolis* (Baltimore: Baltimore Museum of Art, 1983); Gloria Seaman Allen, *Old Line Tradition: Maryland Women and Their Quilts* (Washington, D.C.: Daughters of the American Revolution Museum, 1985); and Geraldine Neva Johnson, *Weaving Rag Rugs: A Women's Craft in Western Maryland* (Knoxville: University of Tennessee Press, 1985).

Maryland transportation attracts scholars and buffs alike. See the chapter 4 bibliography for early roads, 5 and 7 for railroads and canals. The bibliography for chapter 9 introduces aviation and the automobile. Maritime Maryland, introduced in Mary Ellen Hayward, *Maryland's Maritime Heritage* (Baltimore: MHS, 1984), offers especially attractive material for illustrated histories. Marion V. Brewington, *Chesapeake Bay: A Pictorial Maritime History* (Cambridge, Md.: Cornell Maritime Press, 1953), beautifully mixes graphics and text. The authoritative work of Robert H. Burgess includes *This Was Chesapeake Bay* (Cambridge, Md.: Cornell Maritime Press, 1963), recounting experiences in shipbuilding, sailing, and fishing; *Chesapeake Circle* (Cambridge, Md.: Cornell Maritime Press, 1965), illustrating bay sail and steam craft, their work, and the people who manned them; and *Steamboats Out of Baltimore* (Cambridge, Md.: Tidewater Publishers, 1968), with H. Graham Wood, proving the romance and service of the old steamboat lines. For more on the Baltimore Steam Packet Company or Old Bay Line, see Alexander Crosby Brown, *Steam Packets on the Chesapeake: A History of the Old Bay Line Since 1840* (Cambridge, Md.: Cornell Maritime Press, 1961). John A. Hain's *Side Wheelers of the Chesapeake Bay* and *Propeller Steamers of the Chesapeake Bay* (Glen Burnie, Md.: Glendale Press, 1962 and 1964), sketch companies and vessels. Richard V. Elliott, *Last of the Steamboats: The Saga of the Wilson Line* (Cambridge, Md.: Tidewater Publishers, 1970), tells the story of a twentieth-century company that operated out of Baltimore and Washington; for a like volume on another firm, see David C. Holly, *Steamboat on the Chesapeake: Emma Giles and the Tolchester Line* (Centreville, Md.: Tidewater Publishers, 1987).

Howard I. Chapelle, *The Baltimore Clipper: Its Origin and Development* (Hatboro, Pa.: Tradition Press, 1965 [Salem, Mass., 1930]), studies the best-known Chesapeake sailing craft. On other native designs, see Marion V. Brewington, *Chesapeake Bay Log Canoes and Bugeyes* (Cambridge, Md.: Cornell Maritime Press, 1963); R. Hammond Gibson, *Eastern Shore: Chips and Shavings* (Baltimore: Chesapeake Bay Maritime Museum, 1970); Chapelle, *Chesapeake Bay Crabbing Skiffs* (St. Michaels, Md.: Chesapeake Bay Maritime Museum, 1979); Chapelle, *Notes on the Chesapeake Bay Skipjacks* (St. Michaels, Md.: Chesapeake Bay Maritime Museum, 1981); and Thomas C. Gilmer, *Chesapeake Bay Sloops* (St. Michaels, Md.: Chesapeake Bay Maritime Museum, 1982). Burgess, *Chesapeake Sailing Craft: The Fifty-Year Period, 1924–1974* (Cambridge, Md.: Tidewater Publishers, 1975), pictures and comments on commercial boats. Frederick Tilp, *The Chesapeake Bay of Yore* (Annapolis and Richmond, Va.: Chesapeake Bay Foundation, 1982), skims the literature and offers introductory notes on various small craft.

Marion V. Brewington, "Chesapeake Sailmaking," *MHM*, 65 (1970): 138–48, examines the close ties between ship building and chandling. Donald G. Shomette, *Shipwrecks on the Chesapeake: Maritime Disasters on the Chesapeake Bay and Its Tributaries, 1608–1978* (Centreville, Md.: Tidewater Publishers, 1982), logs about eighteen hundred disasters; see also Robert H. Burgess, *Sea, Sails, and Shipwreck* (Cambridge, Md.: Cornell Maritime Press, 1970). Shomette, *Pirates on the Chesapeake; Being a True History of Pirates, Picaroons, and Raiders on Chesapeake Bay, 1610–1807* (Centreville, Md.: Tidewater Publishers, 1985), exhausts that fascinating subject. Robert de Grast, *The Lighthouses of the Chesapeake* (Baltimore: Johns Hopkins University Press, 1973), traces their origins and pictures the last thirty-two of them.

Maryland intellectual, educational, and cultural themes receive attention in the chapter bibliographies that follow. George H. Callcott, *A History of the University of Maryland* (Baltimore: MHS, 1966), offers an absorbing study of a public university. Robert P. Sharkey, *Johns Hopkins: A Centennial Portrait of a University* (Baltimore: Johns Hopkins University Press, 1975), updates John C. French, *A History of the University Founded by Johns Hopkins*

(Baltimore: Johns Hopkins Press, 1946). See also George J. Fleming, "The Negro Publicly Supported Colleges in Delaware and Maryland," *JNH*, 31 (1962): 260–74; Edward N. Wilson, *The History of Morgan State College: A Century of Purpose in Action, 1867–1967* (New York: Vantage Press, 1975); Fred M. Dumschott, *Washington College: 1782 to the Present* (Chestertown, Md.: Washington College, 1980). Margaret Lynne Browne and Patricia M. Vanorny, *Piety, Chastity, and Love of Country: Education in Maryland to 1916* (Annapolis: MSA, 1984), makes a welcomed contribution; for an early, dated, general history of schooling in the state, see Bernard C. Steiner, *History of Education in Maryland*, no. 19 in Contributions to American Educational History, ed. Herbert Baxter Adams, United States Bureau of Education, Circular of Information no. 2 (Washington, D.C.: Government Printing Office, 1894). *The Public Schools of Prince George's County from the Seventeenth Century to Nineteen Hundred Fifty* (Prince George's County Retired Teachers' Association, 1976), offers a brief survey. For a short study of an important Baltimore preparatory school, see Dean R. Esslinger, *Friends for Two Hundred Years* (Baltimore: Friends School, 1983).

For a highly readable introduction to the state's writers, see Frank R. Shivers, Jr., *Maryland Wits and Baltimore Bards* (Baltimore: Maclay & Associates, 1985). See also Harold D. Jopp and R. H. Ingersoll, eds., *Shoremen: An Anthology of Eastern Shore Verse and Prose* (Cambridge, Md.: Tidewater Publishers, 1974). William F. Hallstead, "Literary Maryland," *MM*, 7 (Winter 1974): 15–20, draws thumbnail sketches of writers who were born or lived and worked in the state. For an engaging musical survey, see Lubov Keefer, *Baltimore's Music: The Haven of the American Composer* (Baltimore: J. H. Furst Co., 1962). Jane McWilliams, *The Progress of Refinement: A History of Theater in Annapolis* (Annapolis: Colonial Players of Annapolis, 1976), surveys the stage in that traditionally active theater community.

State institutional and professional histories include two valuable studies of the Sunpapers: Gerald W. Johnson, Frank R. Kent, H. L. Mencken, and Hamilton Owens, *The Sunpapers of Baltimore, 1837–1937* (New York: Alfred A. Knopf, 1937), and Harold A. Williams, *The Baltimore Sunpapers, 1837–1987* (Baltimore: Johns Hopkins University Press, 1987). Paul Winchester and Frank D. Webb, eds., *Newspapers and Newspaper Men of Maryland Past and Present* (Baltimore: Frank L. Silbey & Co. for the Journalists' Club of Baltimore, 1905), demonstrates why Johnson et al. wished to write a history of the *Sun*. Elihu S. Riley and Conway Whittle Sams, *The Bench and Bar of Maryland: A History, 1634–1901* (2 vols.; Chicago: Lewis Publishing Co., 1901), likewise fits comfortably in the "men of mark" tradition. H. H. Walker Lewis, *The United States District Court of Maryland* (Baltimore: Maryland State Bar Association, 1977), offers a lively view of the federal bench, its occupants, and its varying caseload. For a brief account of a strong collection, see James F. Schneider, *The Story of the Library Company of the Baltimore Bar* (Baltimore: Library Company of the Baltimore Bar, 1981). James D. Dilts, *The Engineers, 1905–1980* (Baltimore: Engineering Society of Baltimore, 1980), supplies a useful survey, accessible to lay readers.

Guides to the sources in state medical history include [Nancy McCall and Harold Kanarek,] *The Alan Mason Chesney Medical Archives, The Johns Hopkins Medical Institutions* (Baltimore: Archives and Manuscripts, Johns Hopkins University and Johns Hopkins Hospital, 1980); see also *BHM*, 56 (1982): 88–92, and Richard J. Cox, "Opportunities for Maryland Medical History Research at the Maryland Historical Society," *MSMJ*, 23 (1974): 56. Douglas Gordon Carroll, Jr., *Medicine in Maryland, 1643–1900* (Baltimore: Library of the Medical and Chirurgical Faculty of the State of Maryland, 1984), collects previously published articles; *The History of Medicine in Maryland, 1634–1953: An Exhibition November 16 to December 31, 1953* (Baltimore: MHS, 1953), supplies an illustrated introduction.

On advances made in nineteenth-century public health and early-modern medicine, see the bibliography for chapter 8. General studies of academic medicine in the state include major works on the Johns Hopkins University and Hospital and the University of Maryland. Thomas B. Turner, *Heritage of Excellence: The Johns Hopkins Medical Institutions, 1914–1947* (Baltimore: Johns Hopkins University Press, 1974), and A. McGehee Harvey, *Adventures in Medical Research: A Century of Discovery at Johns Hopkins* (Baltimore: Johns Hopkins University Press, 1976), supersede Alan M. Chesney's massive *The Johns Hopkins*

Hospital and the Johns Hopkins University School of Medicine: A Chronicle (3 vols.; Baltimore: Johns Hopkins Press, 1943–63). For a recent account of scientific finding aimed at preventing illness, see Elizabeth Fee, *Disease and Discovery: A History of the Johns Hopkins School of Hygiene and Public Health, 1916–1939* (Baltimore: Johns Hopkins University Press, 1987). Ethel Johns and Blanche Pfefferkorn, *The Johns Hopkins Hospital School of Nursing, 1881–1949* (Baltimore: Johns Hopkins Press, 1954), surveys that institution. Myrtle Polley Matejski, "The Influence of Selected External Forces on Medical Education at the University of Maryland School of Medicine, 1910–50" (Ph.D. dissertation, University of Maryland, 1977), sketches financial, professional, and political constraints. See also Lester H. Miles, "Med-Chi Journal History, 1839–1976," *MSMJ*, 25 (January 1976): 35–42, and Miles, "The History of Med-Chi Meetings, 1799–1977," *MSMJ*, 26 (April 1977): 37–50, 55–56; John E. Savage, "A Sketch of the History of Obstetrics and Gynecology in Maryland, 1770–1976," *MSMJ*, 28 (September 1979): 53–58; and Arthur L. Haskins, "A Short History of the Teaching of Obstetrics and Gynecology at the University of Maryland," *Bulletin of the University of Maryland School of Medicine*, 62 (May 1977): 4–12.

On other Maryland hospitals, see Toba Schwaber Kerson, "Almshouse to Municipal Hospital: The Baltimore Experience," *BHM*, 55 (1981): 203–20; Jon Michael Kingsdale, "The Growth of Hospitals: An Economic History in Baltimore" (Ph.D. dissertation, University of Michigan, 1981); and Lilian H. Hofmeister, *Union Memorial Hospital: 125 Years of Caring* (Baltimore: Community Relations Office, 1980).

Chapter bibliographies list religious histories devoted to specific periods. Gordon Pratt Baker, ed., *Those Incredible Methodists: A History of the Baltimore Conference of the United Methodist Church* (Baltimore: Commission on Archives and History, Baltimore Conference, 1972), supplies a general study of the Methodists. Bliss Forbush, *A History of Baltimore Yearly Meeting of Friends: Three Hundred Years of Quakerism in Maryland, Virginia, the District of Columbia, and Central Pennsylvania* (Sandy Spring, Md.: Baltimore Yearly Meeting of Friends, 1973), does the same for the Friends (for errata, see *MHM*, 69 [1974]: 114); see also Kenneth L. Carroll, *Three Hundred Years and More of Third Haven Quakerism* (Easton, Md.: Queen Anne Press, 1984), and Phebe R. Jacobsen, comp., *Quaker Records in Maryland* (Annapolis: MHR, 1966). Histories of single congregations include Klaus G. Wust, *Zion in Baltimore, 1755–1955* (Baltimore: Zion Church of the City of Baltimore, 1955); John H. Gardner, Jr., *The First Presbyterian Church of Baltimore: A Two Century Chronicle* (Baltimore: First Presbyterian Church, 1962); Mary Ellen Hayward and R. Kent Lancaster, *Baltimore's Westminster Cemetery and Westminster Presbyterian Church* (Baltimore: Westminster Preservation Trust, 1984); Nicholas M. Prevas, *History of the Greek Orthodox Cathedral of the Annunciation, Baltimore, Maryland* (Baltimore: John D. Lucas, 1982); *Bicentennial Histories of Old Area Churches, 1776–1976* (Cumberland, Md.: Church Women of the Greater Cumberland Area, 1976); Kingsley Smith, *Towson under God* (Towson, Md.: Trinity Episcopal Church, 1976); Constance Pelzer Ackerson, *Holy Trinity, Collington: Her People and Their Church* (Bowic, Md.: privately printed, 1978); William K. Paynter, *St. Anne's Annapolis: History and Times* (Annapolis: privately printed, 1981); and Richard O. Price, *A Brief History of the Cokesbury Memorial Church, 1784–1984* (Edgewood, Md.: Cokesbury Memorial Church, 1983).

Chronicles of state fraternal and service groups include Mary and Eben Jenkins, *The First Hundred Years: Maryland State Grange, 1874–1974* (Maryland State Grange, 1974); John P. Bauernschub, *Columbianism in Maryland, 1897–1965* (Baltimore: Maryland State Council, Knights of Columbus, 1965); and Carl N. Everstine, *History of the Grand Lodge of Ancient Free and Accepted Masons of Maryland, 1888–1950* (2 vols.; Baltimore: King Brothers, 1951).

Sports in the state have received their due. Esther J. and Ruth W. Crooks, *The Ring Tournament in the United States* (Richmond, Va.: Garrett & Massie, 1936), contains a twenty-page section on Maryland; see also Robert L. Loeffelbein, *Knight Life: Jousting in the United States* (Lexington Park, Md.: Golden Owl Publishers, 1978). On foxhunting and the traditional steeplechase, see Stuart Rose, *The Maryland Hunt Cup* (New York: Huntington Press, 1931), and J. Rieman McIntosh, *A History of the Elkridge Fox Hunting Club, the Elkridge Hounds, the Elkridge-Harford Hunt Club, 1878–1978* (Baltimore: Schneidereith & Sons, 1978). William Woodward, "The Thoroughbred Horse and Maryland," *MHM*, 17

(1922): 139–62, and David S. Gittings, *Maryland and the Thoroughbred* (Baltimore: Hoffman Brothers Co., 1932), survey the breeding of race horses; see also the bibliographies for chapters 2 and 5, and for a modern study, Robert G. Lawrence, *Maryland's Racing Industry: Its Participants, Organization, and Economic Impact*, Miscellaneous Publication no. 298 (College Park: University of Maryland Cooperative Extension Service, 1972). Joseph J. Challmes, *The Preakness: A History* (Severna Park, Md.: Anaconda Publications, 1975), offers a chronicle of that jewel in the Triple Crown. Meshach Browning, *Forty-Four Years of the Life of a Hunter*, engravings by Edward Stabler (Oakland, Md.: Appalachian Background, 1982), reprints the classic account of a legendary Maryland figure and the wilderness that developed into Garrett County. On hunting in Maryland, see also Jack Wennersten, "The Chesapeake Bay Retriever: Maryland's Own True Grit Dog," *MM*, 16 (Winter 1983): 3–7, and Barry Robert Berkey, Velma Berkey, and Richard Erie Berkey, *Pioneer Decoy Carvers: A Biography of Lemuel and Stephen Ward* (Cambridge, Md.: Tidewater Publishers, 1977). Willie J. Parker, *Game Warden: Chesapeake Assignment* (Centreville, Md.: Tidewater Publishers, 1983), recounts the experiences of a special agent in the U.S. Fish and Wildlife Service.

On team sports, see Alexander M. Weyand and Milton R. Roberts, with pen and ink drawings by Guy S. Fairlamb, *The Lacrosse Story* (Baltimore: H. & A. Herman, 1965); Bob Scott, *Lacrosse: Technique and Tradition* (Baltimore: Johns Hopkins University Press, 1976); "The Great Game," *Johns Hopkins Magazine*, 7 (April 1956): 7–9, 20–21; G. Russell Darrell, Jr., *Hotbed for Hybrids: Lacrosse and Soccer in Baltimore* (Glen Burnie, Md.: French/Bray Printing, 1978); and John Steadman, *The Baltimore Colts: A Pictorial History* (Virginia Beach, Va.: Jordan & Co., 1978). For baseball, see James H. Bready's charming and informative *The Home Team* (4th ed.; Baltimore: privately printed, 1984); Frederick G. Lieb, *The Baltimore Orioles: The History of a Colorful Baseball Team in Baltimore and St. Louis* (New York: G. P. Putnam's Sons, 1955); Ted Patterson, *Day by Day in Orioles History* (New York: Leisure Press, 1984); and the chapter 7 bibliography.

Other books on Maryland, published long ago if not histories in every instance, beg special mention as period pieces. Literate and charming—intended to bring their readers enjoyment as well as to inform them—they also convey a sense of what our parents and grandparents felt about their heritage, landscape, and water. Swepson Earle, *The Chesapeake Bay Country* (Baltimore: Thomsen-Ellis, 1923), heads this list, along with Annie Leakin Sioussat, *Old Manors in the Colony of Maryland* (Baltimore: Lord Baltimore Press, 1911) and *Old Baltimore* (New York: Macmillan Co., 1931); Paul Wilstach, *Potomac Landings* (Garden City, N.Y.: Doubleday, Page & Co., 1921) and *Tidewater Maryland* (Indianapolis: Bobbs-Merrill Co., 1931); William Oliver Stevens, *Annapolis: Anne Arundel's Town* (New York: Dodd, Mead & Co., 1937); Hamilton Owens, *Baltimore on the Chesapeake* (Garden City, N.Y.: Doubleday, Doran & Co., 1941); Hulbert Footner, *Maryland Main and the Eastern Shore* (New York: D. Appleton-Century Co., 1942) and *Rivers of the Eastern Shore: Seventeen Maryland Rivers* (Centreville, Md.: Tidewater Publishers, 1979 [New York, 1944]); Francis Sims McGrath, *Pillars of Maryland* (Richmond, Va.: Dietz Press, 1951); Francis F. Beirne, *The Amiable Baltimoreans* (Baltimore: Johns Hopkins University Press, 1984 [New York, 1951]). Gilbert Byron, *The Lord's Oysters* (Baltimore: Johns Hopkins University Press, 1977 [1957]), recounts the experience of growing up on the Eastern Shore in the 1920s.

1. From Province to Colony

One can begin study of the Calvert expedition and primitive settlement with the settlers' own writings in Clayton Colman Hall, ed., *Narratives of Early Maryland, 1633–1684*, Original Narratives of Early American History (New York: Charles Scribner's Sons, 1910). Richard J. Cox, *A Guide to the Microfilm Edition of the Calvert Papers* (Baltimore: MHS, 1973), introduces the single most important manuscript collection; Edward C. Papenfuse, Alan F. Day, David W. Jordan, and Gregory A. Stiverson, comps., *A Biographical Dictionary of the Maryland Legislature, 1635–1689* (2 vols.; Baltimore: Johns Hopkins University Press, 1978 and 1985), provides a valuable reference work for these years. Aubrey C. Land, *Colonial Maryland: A History* (Millwood, N.Y.: KTO Press, 1981), stands as the authoritative textbook, while Matthew Page Andrews, *The Founding of Maryland* (Baltimore: Williams & Wilkins Co.; New York: D. Appleton-Century Co., 1933), still worth reading, narrates the political story to 1689. Raphael Semmes, *Captains and Mariners of Early Maryland* (Baltimore: Johns Hopkins Press, 1937), delivers a colorful account of seventeenth-century swashbuckling; a companion volume, *Crime and Punishment in Early Maryland* (Baltimore: Johns Hopkins Press, 1938), extracts social history from court records. Clayton Torrence, *Old Somerset on the Eastern Shore of Maryland: A Study in Foundations and Founders* (Richmond, Va.: Whittet & Shepperson, 1935), documents that county up to royal government. On the provenance of surviving early documents, see Richard J. Cox, "Public Records in Colonial Maryland," *American Archivist*, 37 (1974): 263–75.

For a succinct account of the plans, preparations, and circumstances of settlement, see either Lois Green Carr, Russell R. Menard, and Louis Peddicord, *Maryland . . . at the Beginning* (Annapolis: MHR, 1984), or Menard and Carr, "The Lords Baltimore and the Colonization of Maryland," in David B. Quinn, ed., *Early Maryland in a Wider World* (Detroit: Wayne State University Press, 1982). James W. Foster has explored Calvert's own background in *George Calvert: The Early Years* (Baltimore: MHS, 1983), but see also John D. Krugler's series of articles: "'Our Trusty and Wellbeloved Councillor': The Parliamentary Career of Sir George Calvert," *MHM*, 72 (1977): 470–91; "Sir George Calvert's Resignation as Secretary of State and the Founding of Maryland," *MHM*, 68 (1973): 239–54; and "'The Face of a Protestant and the Heart of a Papist': A Reexamination of George Calvert's Conversion to Roman Catholicism," *Journal of Church and State*, 20 (1978): 507–31. Thomas M. Coakley, "George Calvert and Newfoundland: 'The Sad Face of Winter,'" *MHM*, 71 (1976): 1–18, treats Calvert's first colony. R. J. Lahey, "The Role of Religion in Lord Baltimore's Colonial Enterprise," *MHM*, 72 (1977): 492–511, and Krugler, "Lord Baltimore, Roman Catholics, and Toleration: Religious Policy in Maryland during the Early Catholic Years, 1634–1649," *CHR*, 65 (1979): 49–75, weigh the importance of a refuge in Calvert's motives and bring a continuing discussion up to date. Arthur Pierce Middleton, "Toleration and the Established Church in Maryland," *Historical Magazine of the Protestant Episcopal Church*, 53 (1984): 13–24, makes clear the unsympathetic context of toleration at the time. Lewis D. Asper, "The Long and Unhappy History of Loyalty Testing in Maryland," *AJLH*, 13 (1969): 97–109, begins with the harassment of Calvert and his 1633 expedition. Three essays in Quinn, ed., *Early Maryland in a Wider World*, explore the "push" factors leading to settlement: G. R. Elton, "Contentment and Discontent on the Eve of Colonization," pp. 105–18; David B. Quinn, "Why They Came," pp. 119–48; and John Bossy, "Reluctant Colonists: The English Catholics Confront the Atlantic," pp. 149–64. Erich Isaac, "Kent Island," *MHM*, 52 (1957): 93–119, 210–36, discusses the Claiborne settlement.

Harold R. Manakee, *Indians of Early Maryland* (3d. ed.; Baltimore: MHS, 1981), Christian F. Feest, "Nanticoke and Neighboring Tribes," in *Northeast*, Bruce G. Trigger, vol. ed., vol. 15 of *Handbook of North-American Indians*, William C. Sturtevant, gen. ed. (Washington, D.C.: Smithsonian Institution, 1978), pp. 240–52, and Raphael Semmes, "Aboriginal Maryland, 1608–1689," *MHM*, 24 (1929): 157–72, 195–209, introduce Chesapeake Indians, whose concept of real property W. Stitt Robinson explores in *Maryland Indian Treaties*, vol. 6 of *Early American Indian Documents: Treaties and Laws, 1607–1789*, ed. Alden T. Vaughan (Frederick, Md.: University Press of America, 1985). Recent anthropological research demonstrates the integrity of Indian culture and emphasizes the give-and-take between native and white leaders before the epidemics that virtually destroyed the tribes: Frank W. Porter III, "A Century of Accommodation: The Nanticoke Indians in Colonial Maryland," *MHM*, 74 (1979): 175–92; James H. Merrell, "Cultural Continuity among the Piscataway Indians of Colonial Maryland," *WMQ* (3d ser.), 36 (1979): 548–70; and Wayne E. Clark, "The Origins of the Piscataway and Related Indian Cultures," *MHM*, 75 (1980): 8–22. J. Frederick Fausz's essays—"Present at the 'Creation': The Chesapeake World That Greeted the Maryland Colonists," *MHM*, 79 (1984): 7–20, and "Profits, Pelts, and Power: English Culture in the Early Chesapeake, 1620–1652," *Maryland Historian*, 14 (1983): 14–23—stress the importance of the English-Indian fur trade and note the leverage it gave the natives. Francis Jennings, "Indians and Frontiers in Seventeenth-Century Maryland," in Quinn, *Early Maryland in a Wider World*, pp. 216–41, explains power relationships among the Maryland tribes and their Indian neighbors. James Axtell, "White Legend: The Jesuit Missions in Maryland," *MHM*, 81 (1986): 1–7, explores early attempts to convert the Indians. For a bibliographical guide, part of a series sponsored by the Newberry Library Center for the American Indian, see Frank W. Porter, *Indians of Maryland and Delaware* (Bloomington: Indiana University Press, 1980).

The early economy of Maryland, notable for its dependence on tobacco, receives treatment in Lewis C. Gray, *History of Agriculture in the Southern United States to 1860* (2 vols.; Washington, D.C.: Carnegie Institution, 1933), a durable general work; Arthur Pierce Middleton, *Tobacco Coast: A Maritime History of the Chesapeake Bay in the Colonial Era* (Newport News, Va.: Mariners Museum, 1953), a superb special study; and in Gloria L. Main, *Tobacco Colony: Life in Early Maryland, 1650–1720* (Princeton, N.J.: Princeton University Press, 1982), a valuable recent interpretation. See also Carr, Philip D. Morgan, and Jean B. Russo, eds., *Colonial Chesapeake Society* (Chapel Hill: University of North Carolina Press for the Institute of Early American History and Culture, 1988). Vertrees J. Wyckoff, *Tobacco Regulation in Colonial Maryland*, JHUS, extra volume, new ser., no. 22 (1936), examines the structure of incentives and attempts to establish quality standards.

The research of Russell R. Menard has contributed much to our knowledge of the tobacco economy in this period; see his "Farm Prices of Maryland Tobacco, 1659–1710," *MHM*, 68 (1973): 80–85; "A Note on Chesapeake Tobacco Prices, 1618–1660," *VMHB*, 84 (1976): 401–10; "The Tobacco Industry in the Chesapeake Colonies, 1617–1730: An Interpretation," *Research in Economic History*, 5 (1980): 109–77; and *Economy and Society in Early Colonial Maryland* (New York: Garland Publishing, 1985). See also Menard, Lois Green Carr, and Lorena S. Walsh, "A Small Planter's Profits: The Cole Estate and the Growth of the Early Chesapeake Economy," *WMQ* (3d ser.), 40 (1983): 171–96.

For an excellent summary account of the first decade or more of settlement, see Garry Wheeler Stone, "Manorial Maryland," *MHM*, 82 (1987): 3–36. See also Lois Green Carr, "'The Metropolis of Maryland': A Comment on Town Development along the Tobacco Coast," *MHM*, 69 (Summer 1974): 124–45; Henry M. Miller, *Discovering Maryland's First City: A Summary Report on the 1981–1984 Excavations in St. Mary's City, Maryland*, Archaeology Series no. 2 (St. Mary's, Md.: Historic St. Mary's City, 1986); Basil H. Brune, "The Changing Spatial Organization of Early Tobacco Marketing in the Patuxent River Basin," in Robert D. Mitchell and Edward K. Muller, eds., *Geographical Perspectives on Maryland's Past*, Occasional Papers in Geography, no. 4 (College Park: Department of Geography, University of Maryland, 1979); and Carville V. Earle, "The First English Towns of North America," *Geographical Review*, 67 (1977): 34–50. Earle, *Evolution of a Tidewater Settlement System: All Hollow's Parish, Maryland, 1650–1783*, University of Chicago Department of Geography Research Paper no. 170 (Chicago: University of Chicago Press, 1975), examines settlement, population, landholding, and economic patterns in southern Anne Arundel County. Henry J. Berkeley, "Extinct River Towns of the Chesapeake Region," *MHM*, 19 (1924): 125–34, discusses reasons for the failure of legislation establishing commercial centers; see also Kit W. Wesler, "An Architect's Perspective on the Ancient Town of Doncaster," *MHM*, 80 (1985): 383–91. For waterborne commerce, see Vertrees J. Wyckoff, "Ships and Shipping of Seventeenth-Century Maryland," *MHM*, 33 (1938): 334–42; 34 (1939): 46–63, 270–83. See the chapter 2 bibliography for the early labor system.

After extensive study of local records, historians now speak with some assurance on marriage, birth, death, and mobility in early Maryland. Lois Green Carr, Russell R. Menard, and Lorena S. Walsh—along with Gloria L. Main—have played especially important parts in researching Maryland. Menard, "Population, Economy, and Society in Seventeenth-Century Maryland," *MHM*, 79 (1984): 71–92, summarizes their findings. Walsh, "'Till Death Us Do Part': Marriage and Family in Seventeenth-Century Maryland," in Thad W. Tate and David L. Ammerman, eds., *The Chesapeake in the Seventeenth Century: Essays in Anglo-American Society* (New York: W. W. Norton & Co., 1979), pp. 130–31, makes essential reading. Several noteworthy essays explore high mortality among the first settlers: Walsh and Menard, "Death in the Chesapeake: Two Life Tables for Men in Early Colonial Maryland," *MHM*, 69 (1974): 211–27; Darrett B. Rutman and Anita H. Rutman, "Of Agues and Fevers: Malaria in the Early Chesapeake," *WMQ* (3d ser.), 33 (1976): 31–60; and Daniel Blake Smith, "Mortality and Family in the Colonial Chesapeake," *JIH*, 8 (1978): 403–37. Silas D. Hurry, "The Seventeenth-Century Tidewater: A Tentative Dietary Analysis," *Chronicles of St. Mary's*, 26 (1978): 367–73, discusses one element affecting health; on primitive attempts to treat the ill, see George B. Scriven, "Maryland Medicine in the Seventeenth Century," *MHM*, 57 (1962): 29–46.

Patterns of population growth receive critical examination in Arthur E. Karinen, "Maryland Population, 1631–1730: Numerical and Distributional Aspects," *MHM*, 54 (1959): 365–407. But compare Menard, "Immigrants and Their Increase: The Progress of Population Growth in Early Colonial Maryland," in Aubrey C. Land, Lois Green Carr, and Edward C. Papenfuse, eds., *Law, Society, and Politics in Early Maryland*, Proceedings of the First Conference on Maryland History, 14–15 June 1974 (Baltimore: Johns Hopkins University Press, 1977), pp. 88–110.

On social mobility in the period, see, besides Main, *Tobacco Colony*, William A. Reavis, "The Maryland Gentry and Social Mobility, 1637–1676," *WMQ* (3d ser.), 14 (1957): 418–28; Menard, "From Servant to Freeholder: Status Mobility and Property Accumulation in Seventeenth-Century Maryland," *WMQ* (3d ser.), 30 (1973): 37–64; Menard, P. M. G. Harris, and Carr, "Opportunity and Inequality: The Distribution of Wealth on the Lower Western Shore of Maryland, 1638–1705," *MHM*, 69 (1974): 169–84; Michael B. Sharon, "A Social Profile of the Land Owners of 1660," *Chronicles of St. Mary's*, 29 (1981): 333–44, 347–51; and Walsh, "Servitude and Opportunity in Charles County, Maryland, 1658–1705," in Land et al., eds., *Law, Society, and Politics in Early Maryland*, pp. 111–33. For a comparative view, see J. P. P. Horn, "Social and Economic Aspects of Local Society in England and the Chesapeake: A Comparative Study of the Vale of Berkely, Glos., and the Lower Western Shore of Maryland, c. 1650–1700" (D.Phil, University of Sussex, 1982). Carr and Walsh supply an important perspective in "The Planter's Wife: The Experience of White Women in Seventeenth-Century Maryland," *WMQ* (3d ser.), 34 (1977): 542–71. See the chapter 2 bibliography for architectural histories.

Provincial religious history began with tension and ended in conflict. George B. Scriven, "Religious Affiliation in Seventeenth Century Maryland," *HMPEC*, 25 (1956): 220–29, attempts to survey denominational membership. For a broad, evenhanded account of early Catholicism, see "Maryland" in John Tracy Ellis, *Catholics in Colonial America*, Benedictine Studies (Baltimore and Dublin: Helicon, 1965). Alfred P. Dennis, "Lord Baltimore's Struggle with the Jesuits," *Annual Report of the American Historical Association for the Year 1900* (Washington, D.C.: Government Printing Office, 1901), pp. 107–25, treats one feature of that experience, and links the quarrel to proprietary strategy in 1649; see also Gerald P. Fogarty, Joseph T. Durkin, and R. Emmet Curran, *The Maryland Jesuits, 1634–1833* (Baltimore: Maryland Province Society of Jesus, 1976), and Francis X. Curran, *Catholics in Colonial Law* (Chicago: Loyola University Press, 1963). Daniel R. Randall, *A Puritan Colony in Maryland*, JHUS, 4 (1884), explores the Severn settlement and its challenge to Baltimore's authority. Maryland Quakers have received the attention of Kenneth L. Carroll in *Quakerism on the Eastern Shore* (Baltimore: MHS, 1970) and in a series of articles: "Maryland Quakers in the Seventeenth Century," *MHM*, 42 (1952): 297–313; "Talbot County Quakerism in the Colonial Period," *MHM*, 53 (1958): 326–70; and "Persecution of Quakers in Early Maryland, 1658–1661," *Quaker History*, 53 (1964): 67–80. David W. Jordan discusses Quaker involvement in public life in "'God's Candle' within Government: Quakers and Politics in Early Maryland," *WMQ* (3d ser.), 39 (1982): 628–54, an invaluable work. J. William McIlvain, *Early Presbyterianism in Maryland*, Notes Supplementary to JHUS, 8 (1890), provides scholarly trim to a dated but colorful volume, L. P. Bowen, *The Days of Makemie; or, The Vine Planted, A.D. 1680–1708* (Philadelphia: Presbyterian Board of Publication, 1885). See also Bernard C. Steiner, "Presbyterian Beginnings," *MHM*, 15 (1920): 305–11. On early Anglicans, see Lawrence C. Wroth, "The First Sixty Years of the Church of England in Maryland, 1632–1692," *MHM*, 11 (1916): 1–41. The Labadists have studies in Bartlett B. James, *The Labadist Colony in Maryland*, JHUS, 17 (1899), and George A. Leakin, "The Labadists of Bohemia Manor," *MHM*, 1 (1906): 337–45.

On the experiment of toleration itself, see David W. Jordan, "'The Miracle of this Age': Maryland's Experiment in Religious Toleration, 1649–1689," *Historian*, 47 (1985): 338–59; John D. Krugler, "'With Promise of Liberty in Religion': The Catholic Lords Baltimore and Toleration in Seventeenth-Century Maryland, 1634–1692," *MHM*, 79 (1984): 21–43; Maxine N. Lurie, "Theory and Practice of Religious Toleration in the Seventeenth Century: The Proprietary Colonies as a Case Study," *MHM*, 79 (1984): 117–25; Michael J. Graham, "Lord Baltimore's Pious Enterprise: Toleration and Community in Provincial Maryland, 1634–1724" (Ph.D. dissertation, University of Michigan, 1983); and Asper, "Long and Unhappy History of Loyalty Testing," cited above. George Petrie, *Church and State in Early Maryland*, JHUS, 10 (1892), remains helpful on legislation; Jacob Hollander, "The Civil Status of Jews in Maryland, 1634–1776," *Publications of the American Jewish Historical Society*, 1 (1893): 25–39, notes the limits of toleration. Thomas O'Brien Hanley, *Their Rights and Their Liberties: The Beginnings of Religious and Political Freedom in Maryland* (Westminster, Md.: Newman Press, 1959), explores legal and Catholic roots of the two-sovereign-spheres doctrine. Carl N. Everstine, "Maryland's Toleration Act: An Appraisal," *MHM*, 79 (1984): 99–116, warns against overestimating the practical effect of that praiseworthy measure.

Studies of proprietary government begin with Newton D. Mereness, *Maryland as a Proprietary Province* (New York: Macmillan Co., 1901), still a helpful overview of offices and procedures, and Donnell MacClure Owings, *His Lordship's Patronage: Offices of Profit in Colonial Maryland*, Studies in Maryland History, no. 1 (Baltimore: MHS, 1953). See also Lewis W. Wilhelm, *Local Institutions of Maryland*, JHUS, 3 (1885). On early legal-constitutional history, see David W. Jordan, *Foundations of Representative Government in Maryland, 1632–1715* (New York: Cambridge University Press, 1987); Carl N. Everstine, "The Establishment of Legislative Power in Maryland," *Maryland Law Review*, 12 (1951): 99–121; Everstine, *The General Assembly of Maryland, 1634–1776* (Charlottesville, Va.: Michie Co., 1980); and Susan Rosenfeld Falb, *Advice and Ascent: The Development of the Maryland Assembly, 1635–1689* (New York: Garland Publishing, forthcoming). On elections, see Falb, "Proxy Voting in Early Maryland Assemblies," *MHM*, 73 (1978): 217–25. Joseph A. Smith, "The Foundations of Law in Maryland: 1634–1715," in George A. Billias, ed., *Law and Authority in Colonial America; Selected Essays* (Barre, Mass.: Barre Publications, 1965), builds on St. George Leakin Sioussat, *The English Statutes in Maryland*, JHUS, 21 (1903). For evidence of the influence of English common law in the province, see Peter G. Yackel, "Benefit of Clergy in Colonial Maryland," *MHM*, 69 (1974): 383–97. Marilyn L. Geiger, *The Administration of Justice in Colonial Maryland, 1632–1689* (New York: Garland Publishing, forthcoming), surveys the court system and the people whose lives it affected; see also Marie Hallion, "Criminal Justice in the Province of Maryland," *Maryland Historian*, 15 (1984): 3–18. Lois Green Carr, "The Development of the Maryland Orphans' Court, 1654–1715," in Land et al., *Law, Society, and Politics in Early Maryland*, pp. 41–62, combines social and legal history, as does Sophie H. Drinker, "Women Attorneys of Colonial Times," *MHM*, 56 (1961): 335–51.

Russell R. Menard, "Maryland's 'Time of Troubles': Sources of Political Disorder in Early St. Mary's," *MHM*, 76 (1981): 124–40, examines political and religious stress in the Cromwellian years; see also Lois Green Carr, "Sources of Political Stability and Upheaval in Seventeenth-Century Maryland," *MHM*, 79 (1984): 44–70. Bernard C. Steiner, *Maryland during the English Civil Wars*, JHUS, 25 (1907), and *Maryland under the Commonwealth*, JHUS, 29 (1911), provide details of that unsettled period. Lois Green Carr and David William Jordan, *Maryland's Revolution of Government, 1689–1692* (Ithaca, N.Y.: Cornell University Press, 1974), supplies a full account of the later disturbance that made Maryland a royal colony.

Private manuscripts largely lacking for early Maryland, one notes the thinness of biographies and biographical sketches. William Hand Browne, *George Calvert and Cecilius Calvert, Barons Baltimore of Baltimore* (New York: Dodd, Mead & Co., 1890), paints friendly portraits of the founders. George Boniface Stratemeier, *Thomas Cornwaleys, Commissioner and Counsellor of Maryland*, Studies in American Church History, vol. 2 (Washington, D.C.: Catholic University of America, 1922), treats a leading first settler in similar fashion. Nathaniel C. Hale, *Virginia Venturer: A Historical Biography of William Claiborne, 1600–1677* (Richmond, Va.: Dietz Press, 1951), portrays the Calverts' scourge. Earl L. W. Heck, *Augustine Herrman . . .* (Richmond, Va.: William Byrd Press, 1941), discusses the early map-maker. Edwin W. Beitzell sketches leading figures in "Thomas Gerard and His Sons-in-

Law," *MHM* 46 (1951): 189–206, and "Thomas Copley, Gentleman," *MHM*, 47 (1952): 209–23. See also McHenry Howard, "Some Early Colonial Marylanders," *MHM*, 14 (1919): 284–399; 15 (1920): 65–71, 168–80, 292–304, 312–24; 16 (1921): 19–28, 179–89. Carr and Jordan, *Maryland's Revolution of Government*, appends brief sketches of the Protestants who led the 1689 rebellion, but see also Jordan, "John Coode, Perennial Rebel," *MHM*, 70 (1975): 1–28.

2. Tobacco Coast

Obviously colonial survival and "golden age" wealth developed from the sweat of someone's brow. Manfred Jonas, "Wages in Early Colonial Maryland," *MHM*, 51 (1956): 27–38, examining a money-scarce economy, establishes one cause for the bonded labor system. Eugene I. McCormac, *White Servitude in Maryland, 1634–1820*, JHUS, 22 (1904), made an early study of the system; a more recent general account, Abbot Emerson Smith, *Colonists in Bondage: White Servitude and Convict Labor in America, 1607–1776* (Chapel Hill: University of North Carolina Press, 1947), surveys the British problems that pushed servants to the colonies and refers often to Maryland. See also David Galenson, "Immigration and the Colonial Labor System: An Analysis of the Length of Indenture," *Explorations in Economic History*, 14 (1977): 360–77. A. Roger Ekirch, *Bound for America: The Transportation of British Convicts to the Colonies, 1718–1775* (Oxford: Oxford University Press, 1988), freshly examines the experience of banished British felons.

Students exploring the origins of American slavery would do well to begin with Winthrop D. Jordan, *White Over Black: American Attitudes toward the Negro, 1550–1812* (Chapel Hill: University of North Carolina Press, 1968), an important study of racial prejudice that covers the cases of seventeenth-century Maryland and Virginia, and, for a comparative view, to consult Edmund S. Morgan, *American Slavery, American Freedom: The Ordeal of Colonial Virginia* (New York: W. W. Norton & Co., 1975). For particulars on early Maryland slave statutes, see Jeffrey R. Brackett, *The Negro in Maryland: A Study of the Institution of Slavery*, JHUS, extra volume 6 (1889). More recent and especially pertinent are Jonathan W. Alpert, "The Origins of Slavery in the United States: The Maryland Precedent," *AJLH*, 14 (1970): 189–221. For an excellent overview, see William M. Wicek, "The Statutory Law of Slavery and Race in the Thirteen Mainland Colonies of British America," *WMQ* (3d ser.), 34 (1977): 258–80. The literature on Maryland makes clear how racial stereotypes and economic imperatives conspired to establish black slavery. Russell R. Menard, "From Servants to Slaves: The Transformation of the Chesapeake Labor System," *Southern Studies*, 16 (1977): 355–90, along with Main, *Tobacco Colony*, explores the shift from white servants to black slaves. See also Whittington B. Johnson, "The Origin and Nature of African Slavery in Seventeenth-Century Maryland," *MHM*, 73 (1978): 236–45. On the rapid rise of the black population, see Menard, "The Maryland Slave Population, 1658–1730: A Demographic Profile of Blacks in Four Counties," *WMQ* (3d ser.), 32 (1975): 29–54; Darold D. Wax, "Black Immigrants: The Slave Trade in Colonial Maryland," *MHM*, 73 (1978): 30–45; and Donald M. Sweig, "The Importation of African Slaves to the Potomac River, 1732–1772," *WMQ* (3d ser.), 42 (1985): 507–24. For an important recent study in regional social and economic history, see Allan Kulikoff, *Tobacco and Slaves: The Development of Southern Cultures in the Chesapeake, 1680–1800* (Chapel Hill: University of North Carolina Press for the Institute of Early American History and Culture, 1986). Kulikoff, "A 'Prolifick' People: Black Population Growth in the Chesapeake Colonies, 1700–1790," *Southern Studies*, 16 (1977): 391–428, and "The Origins of Afro-American Society in Tidewater Maryland and Virginia, 1700 to 1790," *WMQ* (3d ser.), 35 (1978): 226–59, treat slave living conditions, acculturation, and family life—on which see as well Jean B. Lee, "The Problem of Slave Community in the Eighteenth-Century Chesapeake," *WMQ* (3d ser.), 43 (1986): 333–61.

The little that historians know of Negroes who escaped servitude depends heavily on court records, which may skew our impression of them. Ross M. Kimmel, "Free Blacks in Seventeenth-Century Maryland," *MHM*, 71 (1976): 19–25, examines the Eastern Shore; C. Ashley Ellefson, "Free Jupiter and the Rest of the World: The Problems of a Free Negro in Colonial Maryland," *MHM*, 66 (1971): 1–13, dwells on an early-eighteenth-century legal struggle in Charles County. Thomas E. Davidson, "Free Blacks in Old Somerset, 1745–1755," *MHM*, 80 (1985): 151–56, makes use of judicial, land, and tax records to examine thirty-nine subjects, most of whom, mulattoes, had been free from birth. Lathan A. Windley, comp., *Runaway Slave Advertisements: A Documentary History from the 1730s to 1790* (4 vols.; Westport, Conn.: Greenwood Press, 1983), includes a volume on Maryland fugitive descriptions. James M. Wright, *The Free Negro in Maryland, 1634–1860*, CUS, 97 (1921), remains a valuable monograph. Roland C. McConnell's contribution to Radoff, ed., *Old Line State*, ably surveys Maryland blacks, slave and free, during those years.

Political-economic studies of the royal period start with Carr and Jordan, *Maryland's Revolution of Government*, but include Jordan, *Foundations of Representative Government in Maryland*; Lois Green Carr, *County Government in Maryland, 1689–1709* (New York: Garland Publishing, 1987); Anne Leakin Sioussat, "Lionel Copley, First Royal Governor of Maryland," *MHM*, 18 (1922): 163–77; Eugenia C. Holland, "Anne Arundel Takes Over from St. Mary's," *MHM*, 44 (1949): 42–51; David W. Jordan, "Sir Thomas Lawrence, Secretary of Maryland: A Royal Placeman's Fortunes in America," *MHM*, 76 (1981): 22–44; Charles B. Clark, "The Career of John Seymour, Governor of Maryland, 1704–1709," *MHM*, 48 (1953): 134–59; and Richard Anthony Gleissner, "The Establishment of Royal Government in Maryland: A Study of Crown Policy and Provincial Politics" (Ph.D. dissertation, University of Maryland, 1968). On commerce during the royal period, see Margaret S. Morriss, *Colonial Trade of Maryland, 1689–1715*, JHUS, 32 (1914).

Bernard C. Steiner, ed., *Rev. Thomas Bray: His Life and Selected Works Relating to Maryland*, Fund Publication no. 37 (Baltimore: MHS, 1901); Samuel C. McCullough, "Dr. Thomas Bray's Commissary Work in London, 1696–1699," *WMQ* (3d ser.), 2 (1945): 333–48, and "Dr. Thomas Bray's Trip to Maryland: A Study in Militant Anglican Humanitarianism," *WMQ* (3d ser.), 2 (1945): 15–32; and Bruce T. McCully, "Governor Francis Nicholson, Patron *Par Excellence* of Religion and Learning in Colonial America," *WMQ* (3d ser.), 39 (1982): 310–33, explore the principal personalities behind Anglican establishment. For a recent assessment of its temporal and spiritual benefits, see Michael Graham, "Churching the Unchurched: The Establishment in Maryland, 1692–1724," *MHM* (1988), and the studies of Gerald E. Hartdagen: "Vestry and Clergy in the Anglican Church of Colonial Maryland," *HMPEC*, 37 (1968): 371–96; "The Anglican Vestry in Colonial Maryland: Organizational Structure and Problems," *HMPEC*, 38 (1969): 349–60; "The Anglican Vestry in Colonial Maryland: A Study in Corporate Responsibility," *HMPEC*, 40 (1971): 315–35, 461–79; and "The Vestry as a Unit of Local Government in Maryland," *MHM*, 67 (1972): 363–88. Albert Warwick Werline, *Problems of Church and State in Maryland during the Seventeenth and Eighteenth Centuries* (South Lancaster, Mass.: College Press, 1948), Spencer Ervin, "The Established Church of Colonial Maryland," *HMPEC*, 24 (1955): 232–92, and Nelson Waite Rightmyer, *Maryland's Established Church* (Baltimore: Church Historical Society, 1956), offer the standard accounts that Graham and Hartdagen reexamine with profit. Kenneth L. Carroll, "Quaker Opposition to the Establishment of a State Church in Maryland," *MHM*, 65 (1970): 149–70, demonstrates the strength of the Friends' transatlantic network. Thomas O'Brien Hanley, "The Catholic and Anglican Gentry in Maryland Politics," *HMPEC*, 38 (1969): 143–51, compares the durability of leading Maryland Catholics to that of contemporary co-religionists in England. John W. McGrain, Jr., "Priest Neale, His Mass House, and His Successors," *MHM*, 62 (1967): 254–84, discusses a Harford County priest and his furtive ministry. Vernon P. Davis and James S. Rawlings, *The Colonial Churches of Virginia, Maryland, and North Carolina: Their Interiors and Worship* (Richmond, Va.: Dietz Press, 1985), illustrates work at the point where architectural, religious, and social history meet.

Recent students of the early eighteenth century have focused on the rise of Maryland-born leaders and their world. David W. Jordan, "Political Stability and the Emergence of a Native Elite in Maryland," in Tate and Ammerman, eds., *Chesapeake in the Seventeenth Century*, explores the consequences of demographic changes. Main, *Tobacco Colony*, and Menard, Harris, and Carr, "Opportunity and Inequality," *MHM*, 69 (1974): 169–84, expose the tendency toward concentrated wealth. See also Henry M. Miller, "Transforming a 'Splendid and Delightsome Land': Colonists and Ecological Change in the Chesapeake 1670–1820," *Journal of the Washington Academy of Sciences*, 76 (no. 3, 1986): 173–87;

Robert G. Schonfeld and Spencer Wilson, "The Value of Personal Estates in Maryland, 1700–1710," *MHM*, 58 (1963): 333–43; Lorena S. Walsh, "Urban Amenities and Rural Sufficiency: Living Standards and Consumer Behavior in the Colonial Chesapeake, 1643–1777," *JEH*, 43 (1983): 109–19, and "Land, Landlord, and Leaseholder: Estate Management and Tenant Fortunes in Southern Maryland, 1642–1820," *AgHist*, 59 (1985): 373–96; and Gail S. Terry, "Wives and Widows, Sons and Daughters: Testation Patterns in Baltimore County, Maryland, 1660–1759" (M.A. thesis, University of Maryland, 1983). Nancy Baker, "Annapolis, 1695–1730," *MHM*, 81 (1986): 191–209, discusses property and taste before the golden age. Alan F. Day, "Lawyers in Colonial Maryland," *AJLH*, 17 (1973): 145–65, discovers growing income among members of a tightening profession. Planter-merchants played a central role in early capital formation; see Aubrey C. Land, "Economic Behavior in a Planting Society: The Eighteenth-Century Chesapeake," *JSH*, 33 (1967): 469–85; "Economic Base and Social Structure: The Northern Chesapeake in the Eighteenth Century," *JEH*, 25 (1965): 639–54; and "The Planters of Colonial Maryland," *MHM*, 68 (1972): 109–28.

On the market arrangements and Continental tobacco demand that profited some Marylanders, see Charles Wetherell, "'Boom and Bust' in the Colonial Chesapeake Economy," *JIH*, 15 (1984): 185–210, and Jacob M. Price's important work: "The Rise of Glasgow in the Chesapeake Tobacco Trade, 1707–1775," *WMQ* (3d ser.), 11 (1954): 179–99; "The Economic Growth of the Chesapeake and the European Market, 1697–1775," *JEH*, 24 (1964): 496–511; *France and the Chesapeake: A History of the French Tobacco Monopoly, 1674–1791* (2 vols.; Ann Arbor: University of Michigan Press, 1973); and *Capital and Credit in British Overseas Trade: The View from the Chesapeake, 1700–1776* (Cambridge, Mass.: Harvard University Press, 1980). See also Paul G. E. Clemens, "The Operation of an Eighteenth-Century Chesapeake Tobacco Plantation," *AgHist*, 49 (1975): 517–31.

Important economic shifts during the eighteenth century involved western land, wheat growing, and iron production. Paul G. E. Clemons, *The Atlantic Economy and Colonial Maryland's Eastern Shore: From Tobacco to Grain* (Ithaca, N.Y.: Cornell University Press, 1980), examines the tobacco-to-wheat revolution on that side of the bay. David C. Klingaman, "The Significance of Grain in the Development of the Tobacco Colonies," *JEH*, 29 (1969): 268–78; Allan Kulikoff, "The Economic Growth of the Chesapeake Colonies," *JEH*, 39 (1979): 275–88; and Geoffrey N. Gilbert, "Baltimore's Flour Trade to the Caribbean, 1750–1815," *JEH*, 37 (1977): 249–51, further explore diversification. On its multiple effects, see also Carville Earle and Ronald Hoffman, "Staple Crops and Urban Development in the Eighteenth-Century South," *PAH*, 10 (1976), and Peter V. Bergstrom, "Economic Diversification and Mercantile Integration in the Colonial Chesapeake, 1700–1775" (Ph.D. dissertation, University of New Hampshire, 1980). On the early iron industry, see Keach Johnson, "The Baltimore Company Seeks English Subsidies for the Colonial Iron Industry," *MHM*, 46 (1951): 27–43; "The Genesis of the Baltimore Iron Works," *JSH*, 19 (1953): 157–79; and "The Baltimore Company Seeks English Markets: A Study of the Anglo-American Iron Trade, 1731–1755," *WMQ* (3d ser.), 16 (1959): 37–60. Michael Warren Robbins, "The Principio Company: Iron-Making in Colonial Maryland, 1720–1781" (Ph.D. dissertation, George Washington University, 1972), discusses the earliest such venture. Ronald L. Lewis, "Slavery on the Chesapeake Iron Plantations before the American Revolution," *JNH*, 59 (1974): 242–54, treats the labor force often used in furnaces and forges; see also Lewis, *Coal, Iron, and Slaves: Industrial Slavery in Maryland and Virginia, 1715–1865*, Contributions in Labor History, no. 6 (Westport, Conn.: Greenwood Press, 1979). For studies of two instructive failures, see John W. McGrain, "The Development and Decline of Dorsey's Forge," *MHM*, 72 (1977): 346–52, discussing a later venture near Elkridge, and David Curtis Skaggs, "John Semple and the Development of the Potomac Valley, 1750–1773," *VMHB*, 92 (1984): 282–308, treating an overextended investor. Aubrey C. Land, "Genesis of a Colonial Fortune," *WMQ* (3d ser.), 7 (1950): 255–69, emphasizes the profits Maryland iron made.

Some of the returns went into land, although western settlement encountered early obstacles. See R. Bruce Harley, "Dr. Charles Carroll—Land Speculator, 1730–1755," *MHM*, 46 (1951): 93–107, and Aubrey C. Land, *The Dulanys of Maryland: A Biographical Study of Daniel Dulany, The Elder (1685–1753), and Daniel Dulany, The Younger (1722–1797)*

(Baltimore: Johns Hopkins Press, 1968 [Baltimore, 1955]). Edward C. Papenfuse, Jr., "Planter Behavior and Economic Opportunity in a Staple Economy," *AgHist*, 46 (1972): 297–311, argues that virgin tobacco land accessible to markets remained available in Prince George's County as late as 1776 and generally sustained a planting family for three generations. See also Hienton, *Prince George's Heritage*; John Beverley Riggs, "Certain Early Maryland Landowners in the Vicinity of Washington," *RCHS*, 48–49 (1949): 249–63; and Carol Ely, "The Northwest Hundred: Family and Society on the Maryland Frontier," *Montgomery County Story*, 22 (1979): 1–11. William B. Marye, "The Great Maryland Barrens," *MHM*, 50 (1955): 11–23, 120–42, and Frank W. Porter III, "The Maryland Frontier, 1722–1732: Prelude to Settlement in Western Maryland," in Mitchell and Muller, eds., *Geographical Perspectives on Maryland's Past*, explore physical impediments to development of the Piedmont. On another problem, see Edward B. Matthews, "History of the Boundary Dispute Between the Baltimores and the Penns Resulting in the Original Mason and Dixon Line," *Maryland Geological Survey*, 7 (1908): 105–205, which includes helpful maps; Walter A. Powell, "Fight of a Century Between the Penns and Calverts," *MHM*, 29 (1934): 83–101; and Carl N. Everstine, "The Potomac River and Maryland's Boundaries," *MHM*, 80 (1985): 355–70. On the "Maryland Monster," who, sadly, left no pictorial record of himself, see Lawrence C. Wroth, "The Story of Thomas Cresap, a Maryland Pioneer," *MHM*, 9 (1914): 1–37, and Kenneth P. Bailey, *Thomas Cresap, Maryland Frontiersman* (Boston: Christopher Publishing House, 1944). Bailey, *Christopher Gist: Colonial Frontiersman, Explorer, and Indian Agent* (Hamden, Conn.: Archon Books, 1976), treats a rugged figure whom Maryland and Virginia shared.

Frank W. Porter III, "From Backcountry to County: The Delayed Settlement of Western Maryland," *MHM*, 70 (1975): 329–49, neatly summarizes development in Frederick County, where Germans settled in large numbers; see Klaus Wust, "Direct German Immigration to Maryland in the Eighteenth Century (A Preliminary Survey)," *Report of the Society for the History of Germans in Maryland*, 37 (1978): 19–28. Porter, along with Cunz, *Maryland Germans*, makes clear the economic gains newcomers soon registered. For a durable discussion of their farming practices, see Richard Shryock, "British versus German Traditions in Colonial Agriculture," *Mississippi Valley Historical Review*, 26 (1939): 39–54. Elizabeth A. Kessel, "'A Mighty Fortress Is Our God': German Religious and Educational Organizations on the Maryland Frontier, 1734–1800," *MHM*, 77 (1982): 370–87, follows Cunz in surveying folk culture. Kessel excerpts from her valuable earlier work, "Germans on the Maryland Frontier: A Social History of Frederick County, 1730–1800" (Ph.D. dissertation, Rice University, 1981).

References to Chesapeake sporting life in the eighteenth century largely lie hidden in the writings of contemporary visitors. Horse racing has drawn more attention than gunning and other amusements. See Francis Barnum Culver, *Blooded Horses of Colonial Days: Classic Horse Matches in America before the Revolution* (Baltimore: privately printed, 1922), an account that dwells on Maryland and Virginia. Fairfax Harrison, "The Equine FFVs," *VMHB*, 35 (1927): 329–70, discusses the earliest thoroughbreds in the region. William Woodward, "The Thoroughbred Horse and Maryland," *MHM*, 17 (1922): 139–62, and Allen Eustis Begnaud, "Hoofbeats in Colonial Maryland," *MHM*, 65 (1970): 207–30, offer brief accounts. T. H. Breen, "Horses and Gentlemen: The Cultural Significance of Gambling among the Gentry of Virginia," *WMQ* (3d ser.), 34 (1977): 239–57, applies as well to Maryland.

Though one must keep the cultural achievements of eighteenth-century Maryland in perspective (see Carl Bridenbaugh, *Myths and Realities: Societies of the Colonial South* [Baton Rouge: Louisiana State University Press, 1952]), they certainly command our attention. For an exhaustive and devoted account of libraries, literature, drama, schooling, and the like, see Richard Beale Davis, *Intellectual Life in the Colonial South, 1585–1763* (3 vols.; Knoxville: University of Tennessee Press, 1978). In *Men of Letters in Colonial Maryland* (Knoxville: University of Tennessee Press, 1972), J. A. Leo Lemay offers essays on early pamphleteers, Ebenezer Cook, and members of the Tuesday Club. For a reprinting of Cook's work, see Wroth, "Maryland Muse by Ebenezer Cooke," *Proceedings of the American Antiquarian Society*, new ser., 44 (1935): 267–335, and Bernard C. Steiner, ed., *Early Maryland Poetry: The Works of Ebenezer Cook, Gent: Laureat of Maryland, with an Appendix*

Containing the Mousetrap, Fund Publication no. 36 (Baltimore: MHS, 1900). The fullest reference work on the poet is Edward H. Cohen, *Ebenezer Cooke: The Sot-Weed Canon* (Athens: University of Georgia Press, 1975); for a recent addition to the literature, see Robert D. Arner, "The Blackness of Darkness: Satire, Romance, and Ebenezer Cook's *The Sotweed Factor*," *Tennessee Studies in Literature*, 21 (1976): 1–10.

Lawrence C. Wroth, *A History of Printing in Colonial Maryland, 1686–1776* (Baltimore: Typothetae of Baltimore, 1922), surveys a fundamental element in intellectual life; Joseph Towne Wheeler, "Booksellers and Circulating Libraries in Colonial Maryland," *MHM*, 34 (1939): 111–37, and "Books Owned by Marylanders, 1700–1776," *MHM*, 35 (1940): 337–53, follows that line of inquiry. Wheeler's later articles show the attention these and other books received: "Reading Interests of the Professional Classes in Colonial Maryland, 1700–1776," *MHM*, 36 (1941): 184–201, 281–301; "Reading Interests of Maryland Planters and Merchants, 1700–1776," *MHM*, 37 (1942): 26–41, 291–310; and "Reading and Other Recreations of Marylanders, 1700–1776," *MHM*, 38 (1943): 37–55, 167–80. Wroth, "A Maryland Merchant and His Friends in 1750," *MHM*, 6 (1911): 213–24, provides a discussion of rural intellectual life. Charlotte Fletcher, "King William's School and the College of William and Mary," *MHM*, 78 (1983): 118–28, "An Endowed King William's School Plans to Become a College," *MHM*, 80 (1985): 157–66, and "King William's School Survives the Revolution," *MHM*, 81 (1986): 210–21, outline the travails of the leading colonial academy.

Carolyn J. Weekley, "Portrait Painting in Eighteenth-Century Annapolis," *Antiques*, 111 (February 1977): 345–53, examines one market that wealth in Annapolis stimulated. In "The First Professional Theater in Maryland in Its Colonial Setting," *MHM*, 70 (1975): 29–44, and "The Maryland Theatrical Season of 1760," *MHM*, 72 (1977): 335–45, Kathryn Painter Ward discusses another object of patronage. See also Robert David Ritchey, comp., *A Guide to the Baltimore Stage in the Eighteenth Century: A History and Day Book Calendar* (Westport, Conn.: Greenwood Press, 1982), and Sara Sue Shields, "A Mirror for Society: The Theater in Annapolis and Baltimore, 1752–1800" (M.A. thesis, Georgetown University, 1975). On early drama, see also Christopher J. Thaiss, "Shakespeare in Maryland, 1752–1860," in *Shakespeare in the South: Essays on Performance*, ed. Philip C. Kolin (Jackson: University Press of Mississippi, 1983).

For more on the Tuesday Club, see Robert R. Hare, "Electrico Vitrifico in Annapolis: Mr. Franklin Visits the Tuesday Club," *MHM*, 58 (1963): 62–66; J. A. Leo Lemay, "Franklin's 'Dr. Spence': The Reverend Archibald Spencer (1698?–1760), M.D.," *MHM*, 59 (1964): 199–216. Elaine G. Breslaw, "Wit, Whimsey, and Politics: The Uses of Satire by the Tuesday Club of Annapolis, 1744 to 1756," *WMQ* (3d ser.), 32 (1975): 295–306, and "The Chronicle as Satire: Dr. Hamilton's 'History of the Tuesday Club,'" *MHM*, 70 (1975): 129–39, demonstrate the power of humor in club members' writings; see also Robert Micklus, "'The History of the Tuesday Club': A Mock-Jeremiad of the Colonial South," *WMQ* (3d ser.), 40 (1983): 42–61. Breslaw, ed., *Records of the Tuesday Club of Annapolis, 1745–56* (Urbana and Chicago: University of Illinois Press, 1988), at last annotates and publishes those valuable sources. In a related project, John B. Talley plans to make available recordings of the club's musical scores; meantime, see Talley, *Secular Music in Colonial America* (Urbana and Chicago: University of Illinois Press, 1988). Breslaw, "An Early Maryland Musical Society," *MHM*, 67 (1972): 436–37, comments briefly on the Rev. Bacon's Talbot County group. David Curtis Skaggs, "Thomas Cradock and the Chesapeake Golden Age," *WMQ* (3d ser.), 30 (1973): 93–166; "The Chain of Being in Eighteenth-Century Maryland: The Paradox of Thomas Cradock," *HMPEC*, 45 (1976): 155–64; and Skaggs, ed., *The Poetic Writings of Thomas Cradock, 1718–1770* (Newark: University of Delaware Press, 1983), examine this Baltimore County pastor's secular and spiritual endeavors. David Hackett Fischer, "John Beale Bordley, Daniel Boorstin, and the American Enlightenment," *JSH*, 28 (1962): 325–42, argues that this member of the Bordley family, at least, belonged to the European Age of Reason—despite Boorstin's view of it as peculiar in the New World. For a scornful account of evangelical preaching, see Richard J. Cox, "Stephen Bordley, George Whitefield, and the Great Awakening in Maryland," *HMPEC*, 46 (1977): 297–307.

While gentlemen dominated this world, the part women played cries out for study.

Allan Kulikoff, "'Throwing the Stocking': A Gentry Marriage in Provincial Maryland," *MHM*, 71 (1976): 516–21, sheds some light on the female experience by examining ritual. James S. VanNess, "On Untieing the Knot: The Maryland Legislature and Divorce Petitions," *MHM*, 67 (1972): 171–75, unearths the few such cases the assembly heard in the eighteenth century. Katherine L. Biehl, "Economic and Social Conditions among Eighteenth Century Maryland Women" (M.A. thesis, University of Maryland, 1940), and Kathryn Allamong Jacob, "The Woman's Lot in Baltimore Town, 1729–97," *MHM*, 71 (1976): 283–95, mark beginnings and leave much to be done.

On the Nicholson plan for Annapolis, see John W. Reps, *Tidewater Towns: City Planning in Colonial Virginia and Maryland* (Williamsburg, Va.: Colonial Williamsburg Foundation, 1972). See also Baker, "Annapolis," above. For large trends in vernacular architecture, see especially Cary Carson, Norman F. Barka, William M. Kelso, Garry Wheeler Stone, and Dell Upton, "Impermanent Architecture in the Southern American Colonies," *Winterthur Portfolio*, 16 (1981): 135–96; Upton, "The Origins of Chesapeake Architecture," and Douglas C. Reed, "The Building of the Western Maryland Frontier," in *Three Centuries of Maryland Architecture*, pp. 44–57, 10–19; Henry Chandlee Forman, "The Transition in Maryland Architecture," *MHM*, 44 (1949): 275–81; Cary Carson, "The 'Virginia House' in Maryland," *MHM*, 69 (1974): 185–96; and Paula Stoner, "Early Folk Architecture of Washington County," *MHM*, 72 (1977): 512–22. Illustrated treatments of late-seventeenth- and eighteenth-century Maryland architecture include a long list of Forman's work, which modern findings occasionally alter: *Early Manor and Plantation Houses of Maryland* (2d ed., rev.; Baltimore: Bodine & Associates, 1982 [Baltimore, 1934]), introducing about six hundred pre-1800 structures; *Jamestown and St. Mary's: Buried Cities of Romance* (Baltimore: Johns Hopkins Press, 1938); *Tidewater Maryland Architecture and Gardens* (New York: Bonanza Books, 1974 [New York, 1956]); and *Old Buildings, Gardens, and Furniture in Tidewater Maryland* (Cambridge, Md.: Tidewater Publishers, 1967). Lewis A. Coffin, Jr., and Arthur C. Holden, *Brick Architecture of the Colonial Period in Maryland and Virginia* (New York: Dover Press, 1970 [New York, 1919]), assays the great Georgian buildings of the eighteenth century. Despite its title, Everett B. Wilson's *American Colonial Mansions and Other Early Houses* (New York: A. S. Barnes & Co., 1965) treats Maryland homes, exteriors and interiors. See also *Maryland Queen Anne and Chippendale Furniture of the Eighteenth Century*; Edith Rossiter Bevan, "Gardens and Gardening in Early Maryland," *MHM*, 45 (1950): 243–70; and two photographic essays—"Historic Chestertown, Md.," *Colonial Homes* 11 (January-February 1985): 60–89, and "Princess Anne Towne: A Nexus for Old Homes in Maryland's Somerset County," ibid. (July-August 1985): 54–89. On the capital itself, besides the Radoff and Anderson volumes in the general bibliography, see Deering Davis, with a foreword by Joseph Mullen, *Annapolis Houses, 1700–1775* (New York: Architectural Book Publishing Co., 1947), bountifully illustrated. On the leading builder of the golden age, see Rosamond R. Beirne and John H. Scarff, *William Buckland, 1734–1774, Architect of Virginia and Maryland* (Baltimore: MHS, 1958). Recent pieces on the Nicholson design and the grandeur of the later colonial capital include Russell J. Wright, "The Town Plan of Annapolis," *Antiques*, 111 (January 1977): 148–51, and George B. Tatum, "Great Houses from the Golden Age in Annapolis," ibid., 174–85. For an illustrated article discussing one of the most impressive Maryland country houses of the age, see Charles Scarlett, Jr., "Governor Horatio Sharpe's 'Whitehall,'" *MHM*, 46 (1951): 8–26.

3. Revolutionary Persuasion

Reprinted eighteenth-century political tracts include Daniel Dulany the Elder, *The Right of the Inhabitants of Maryland, to the Benefit of the English Laws*, in Sioussat, *English Statutes in Maryland*, appendix 2; Daniel Dulany, Jr., *Considerations on the Propriety of Imposing Taxes in the British Colonies . . .*, *MHM*, 6 (1911): 374–406, and 7 (1912): 26–59; and Peter S. Onuf, ed., *Maryland and the Empire, 1773: The Antilon–First Citizen Letters* (Baltimore: Johns Hopkins University Press, 1974). Edward C. Papenfuse and Gregory A. Stiverson, eds., *The Decisive Blow Is Struck: A Facsimile Edition of the Proceedings of the Constitutional Convention of 1776 and the First Maryland Constitution* (Annapolis: MHR, 1977), includes an introductory essay. See also Papenfuse, Stiverson, and Mary D. Donaldson, comps., *An In-*

ventory of Maryland State Papers, Volume 1, *The Era of the American Revolution, 1775–1789* (Annapolis: MHR, 1977), and, for historical perspective, Morris L. Radoff, "The Maryland Records in the Revolutionary War," *American Archivist*, 37 (1974): 277–85.

Secondary accounts continue to build on Charles A. Barker, *The Background of the Revolution in Maryland* (New Haven, Conn.: Yale University Press, 1940), a study of accumulated complaints against both imperial policy and proprietary rule. Ronald Hoffman, *A Spirit of Dissension: Economics, Politics, and the Revolution in Maryland* (Baltimore: Johns Hopkins University Press, 1973), stresses the play of self-interest among the merchants and lawyers who finally led the independence movement. Edward C. Papenfuse, *In Pursuit of Profit: The Annapolis Merchants in the Era of the American Revolution, 1763–1805* (Baltimore: Johns Hopkins University Press, 1975), focuses on commercial and political change in the capital. For background on debates over currency, see Bruce D. Smith, "Some Colonial Evidence of Two Theories of Money: Maryland and the Carolinas," *Journal of Political Economy*, 93 (1985): 1178–1211.

For comparative background on the struggle between the proprietary regime and House of Delegates, see Jack P. Greene, *The Quest for Power: The Lower Houses of Assembly in the Southern Royal Colonies, 1689–1776* (Chapel Hill: University of North Carolina Press, 1963). Robert J. Dinkin, "Elections in Proprietary Maryland," *MHM*, 73 (1978): 129–36, discusses court-country electoral rivalry in the eighteenth century. Mark J. Stegmaier, "Maryland's Fear of Insurrection at the Time of Braddock's Defeat," *MHM*, 71 (1976): 467–83, discusses apprehension of servile revolt (especially black rebellion) in those desperate weeks, when Catholics, too, came under suspicion; see also Paul H. Giddens, "The French and Indian War in Maryland," *MHM*, 30 (1935): 281–310, and Timothy W. Bosworth, "Anti-Catholicism as a Political Tool in Mid-Eighteenth Century Maryland," *CHR*, 61 (1975): 539–63.

While life in Annapolis could be opulent and imitative of European splendor, small planters and lesser folk led decidedly plain lives. Aubrey C. Land, "The Planters of Colonial Maryland," *MHM*, 67 (1972): 109–28, corrects the impression that every tobacco grower knew luxury. The plight of the white poor has received attention in Gregory A. Stiverson, *Poverty in a Land of Plenty: Tenancy in Eighteenth-Century Maryland* (Baltimore: Johns Hopkins University Press, 1977), which examines the unadvantaged on Lord Baltimore's own manors, and in Tommy R. Thompson, "Debtors, Creditors, and the General Assembly in Colonial Maryland," *MHM*, 72 (1977): 59–77. Jean B. Russo, "Free Workers in a Plantation Economy, Talbot County, Maryland, 1690–1759" (Ph.D. dissertation, Johns Hopkins University, 1983), studies the generally unsuccessful laborers out of bondage. James P. P. Horn, ed., "The Letters of William Roberts of All Hollows Parish, Anne Arundel County, Maryland, 1756–1769," *MHM*, 74 (1979): 117–32, supplies contemporary evidence that few former indentured servants escaped tenancy.

Naturally economic grievance prompted the protests of many Marylanders. Paul Kent Walker, "Business and Commerce in Baltimore on the Eve of Independence," *MHM*, 71 (1976): 296–309, surveys the deepening commercial concerns of Baltimoreans, who reacted as did other mainland colonials to the costs of imperial regulation. Paul H. Giddens, "Maryland and the Stamp Act Controversy," *MHM*, 27 (1932): 79–98, sketches reaction to a measure that injured a variety of articulate interests. Lower down the social scale, unrest among the poor in Maryland (more so than in Virginia, less so than in Pennsylvania) heated sentiment for radical change. David Curtis Skaggs, *Roots of Maryland Democracy, 1753–1776*, Contributions in American History, no. 30 (Westport, Conn.: Greenwood Press, 1973), argues that the under class demanded an ever-larger role in politics; aiming to win revolutionary debtor-relief legislation and the like, Skaggs's poor farmers and militiamen relentlessly pushed toward independence. See also Tommy R. Thompson, "Personal Indebtedness and the American Revolution in Maryland," *MHM*, 73 (1978): 13–29.

Recent studies make clear that court-country conflict within the colony—resistance to proprietary privilege—prepared more moderate minds for independence. Though exaggerated, the sins of the sinecured clergy angered many taxpayers. Josephine Fisher, "Bennet Allen, Fighting Parson," *MHM*, 38 (1943): 299–322, and 39 (1944): 49–72, discusses a case of egregious unfitness. Nelson Waite Rightmyer, "The Character of the Anglican

Clergy in Colonial Maryland," *HMPEC*, 19 (1950): 112–32, and Gerald E. Hartdagen, "The Vestries and Morals in Colonial Maryland," *MHM*, 63 (1968): 360–78, handle criticisms judiciously. David C. Skaggs, "Thomas Cradock's Sermon on the Governance of Maryland's Established Church," *WMQ* (3d ser.), 27 (1970): 630–53, introduces and reprints a contemporary attack on the blemished Anglican priesthood. For late assessments, see Skaggs and Hartdagen, "Sinners and Saints: Anglican Clerical Conduct in Colonial Maryland," *HMPEC*, 47 (1978): 177–95, and Carol Lee Van Voorst, "The Anglican Clergy in Maryland, 1692–1776" (Ph.D. dissertation, Princeton University, 1978). James Haw, "Maryland Politics on the Eve of Revolution: The Provincial Controversy, 1770–1773," *MHM*, 65 (1970): 103–29, and "The Patronage Follies: Bennet Allen, John Morton Jordan, and the Fall of Horatio Sharpe," *MHM*, 71 (1976): 134–50, demonstrate the political importance of the fees struggle. See also Neil Strawser, "Samuel Chase and the Annapolis Paper War," *MHM*, 57 (1962): 177–94; Anne Y. Zimmer, "The 'Paper War' in Maryland, 1772–73: The Paca-Chase Political Philosophy Tested," *MHM*, 71 (1976): 177–93; and Jean H. Vivian, "The Poll Tax Controversy in Maryland, 1770–76: A Case of Taxation *with* Representation," *MHM*, 71 (1976): 151–76. On the drift of the moderate-to-conservative popular party, see, besides Hoffman, *Spirit of Dissension*, Herbert E. Klingelhofer, "The Cautious Revolution: Maryland and the Movement toward Independence, 1774–1776," *MHM*, 60 (1965): 261–313.

Scholars have puzzled over the factors that led some people to support and others to shun the break from Britain. Anne Alden Allan, "Patriots and Loyalists: The Choice of Political Allegiances by the Members of Maryland's Proprietary Elite," *JSH*, 38 (1972): 283–92, examines sentiment and interest in the highest places. Without alluding to possible reasons, Dennis R. Nolan, "The Effect of the Revolution on the Bar: The Maryland Experience," *Virginia Law Review*, 62 (1976): 969–97, notes that after 1776 only two native-born Maryland lawyers (Robert Alexander and Daniel Dulany, son of Walter Dulany) openly sided with the British. On Alexander's motives, see Edward C. Papenfuse, Jr., "Economic Analysis and Loyalist Strategy during the American Revolution: Robert Alexander's Remarks on the Economy of the Peninsula or Eastern Shore of Maryland," *MHM*, 68 (1973): 173–98, and, for a popular account, Phebe R. Jacobsen, "Robert Alexander, Gentleman, Patriot . . . Loyalist," *MM*, 8 (Spring 1976): 33–37. Rodney K. Miller, "The Influence of the Socio-Economic Status of the Anglican Clergy of Revolutionary Maryland on Their Political Orientation," *HMPEC*, 47 (1978): 197–210, studies clerical beneficiaries of the established order. John R. Wennersten, "The Travail of a Tory Parson: Reverend Philip Hughes and Maryland Colonial Politics, 1767–1777," *HMPEC*, 44 (1975): 409–16, illustrates how unsettling the decision was for Hughes as for many other Marylanders. In places (especially the lower Eastern Shore) economic, status, and religious differences between the patriot squirearchy and ordinary folk led the latter by force of repulsion to tenacious Loyalism. See Hoffman, *Spirit of Dissension*, and his "The 'Disaffected' in the Revolutionary South," in Alfred Young, ed., *The American Revolution: Explorations in the History of the American Revolution* (DeKalb: Northern Illinois Press, 1976). Thomas O'Brien Hanley, *The American Revolution and Religion: Maryland, 1770–1800* (Washington, D.C.: Catholic University of America Press, 1971), includes a survey of attitudes toward independence among Presbyterians, Catholics, and Baptists (largely for) and Episcopalians, Methodists, Friends, Moravians, and Lutherans (divided), and argues that independence stimulated religious fervor. For a fruitful local study, see Jean B. Lee, "The Social Order of a Revolutionary People: Charles County, Maryland, 1733–1786" (Ph.D. dissertation, University of Virginia, 1984).

While some Marylanders simply leaned toward the British because of their military presence, Loyalism had intellectual standing. Jonathan Boucher's writings—his *A View of the Causes and Consequences of the American Revolution; in Thirteen Discourses, Preached in North America Between the Years 1763 and 1775* . . . (London, 1797) and also the more accessible autobiographical *Reminiscences of an American Loyalist, 1738–1789* (Boston and New York: Houghton Mifflin & Co., 1925)—represent some of the most complete defenses of toryism the Revolution produced. Boucher has inspired a variety of works: Robert G. Walker, "Jonathan Boucher: Champion of the Minority," *WMQ* (3d ser.), 3 (1945): 3–14;

Richard M. Gummere, "Jonathan Boucher, Toryissimus," *MHM*, 55 (1960): 138–45; Philip Evanson, "Jonathan Boucher: The Mind of an American Loyalist," *MHM*, 58 (1963): 123–36; Ralph Emmett Fall, "The Reverend Jonathan Boucher, Turbulent Tory," *HMPEC*, 36 (1967): 323–56; and Anne Young Zimmer and Alfred H. Kelly, "Jonathan Boucher, Constitutional Conservative," *JAH*, 58 (1972): 899–901. Michael D. Clark, "Jonathan Boucher and the Toleration of Roman Catholics in Maryland," *MHM*, 71 (1976): 194–203, supplies perspective on Boucher's set of mind—while Boucher fastened on the established church as a social bulwark, he allowed for Christian charity where private persons dealt with one another (and apparently hoped that Catholics would unite with Anglicans and Presbyterians in putting down "Puritan" rebels of New England and Virginia). Anne Y. Zimmer, *Jonathan Boucher, Loyalist in Exile* (Detroit: Wayne State University Press, 1978), pursues the story beyond his departure.

The political effect of the Revolution in Maryland—whether indeed the 1776 constitution brought democratic or radical changes—has not been clear until recently. David Curtis Skaggs, especially in "Maryland's Impulse toward Social Revolution, 1750–1776," *JAH*, 54 (1968): 771–86, contended that the "waters of democratic revolution swept through Maryland" in these years; John C. Rainbolt, "A Note on the Maryland Declaration of Rights and Constitution of 1776," *MHM*, 66 (1971): 420–35, argued from roll-call votes and impressionistic evidence that the new constitution represented "modest democratization" when compared to voting and officeholding restrictions in the colonial period. In "Maryland's Property Qualification for Office: A Reinterpretation of the Constitutional Convention of 1776," *MHM*, 73 (1978): 327–39, and "Eighteenth-Century Suffrage: The Case of Maryland," *MHM*, 76 (1981): 141–58, Thornton Anderson employs carefully obtained data to show uneven increases of voter eligibility in the counties after 1776. He distinguishes between gains among landowners and others and finds a continuing overall decline in landholding. His essays demonstrate that after 1776 the landed gentry remained influential—both at the polls and in office. H. H. Walker Lewis, *The Maryland Constitution, 1776* (Baltimore: Bicentennial Committee, MSBA, 1976), analyzes the document, the convention, and their context; Skaggs, "Origins of the Maryland Party System: The Constitutional Convention of 1776," *MHM*, 75 (1980): 95–117, finds enduring political differences in the clusters who supported and thwarted more daring change. John Corbin Rainbolt, "The Struggle to Define 'Religious Liberty' in Maryland, 1776–1785," *Journal of Church and State*, 17 (1975): 443–58, studies persistent limits to that concept, as does Benjamin H. Hartogensis, "Unequal Religious Rights in Maryland since 1776," *Publications of the American Jewish Historical Society*, 25 (1917): 93–107.

On the effort to finance and prosecute the war, see Ronald Hoffman, "Popularizing the Revolution: Internal Conflict and Economic Sacrifice in Maryland, 1774–1780," *MHM*, 68 (1973): 125–39, examining the concessions patriot leaders made to win wide acceptance of the war and maintain their leadership role, and Edward C. Papenfuse, "The Legislative Response to a Costly War: Fiscal Policy and Factional Politics in Maryland, 1777–1789," in Ronald Hoffman and Peter J. Albert, eds., *Sovereign States in an Age of Uncertainty* (Charlottesville: University Press of Virginia for the United States Capitol Historical Society, 1981). Philip A. Crowl, *Maryland during and after the Revolution: A Political and Economic Study*, JHUS, 61 (1943), remains worthwhile as an introductory work, but see Gregory A. Stiverson, "Maryland's Antifederalists and the Perfection of the U.S. Constitution," *MHM*, 83 (1988). Lewis D. Asper, "The Long and Unhappy History of Loyalty Testing in Maryland," *AJLH*, 13 (1969): 97–109, Thomas O'Brien Hanley, "The State and Dissenters in the Revolution," *MHM*, 58 (1963): 325–32, and Richard A. Overfield, "A Patriot Dilemma: The Treatment of Passive Loyalists and Neutrals in Revolutionary Maryland," *MHM*, 68 (1973): 140–59, examine that nettlesome issue for wartime legislators and judges. Peter G. Yackel, "Criminal Justice and Loyalists in Maryland: *Maryland v. Caspar Frietschie*, 1781," *MHM*, 73 (1978): 46–63, argues that the state prosecuted Loyalists in strict accordance with English common-law definitions of treason. Charles J. Truitt, *Breadbasket of the Revolution: Delmarva in the War for Independence* (Salisbury, Md.: Historical Books, c. 1975), makes the case for agricultural contributions on the Shore despite Loyalism there; S. Sydney Bradford, "Hunger Menaces the Revolution, December 1779–

January 1780," *MHM*, 61 (1966): 1–23, discusses one episode in the struggle to supply troops. Elizabeth Cometti, "Inflation in Revolutionary Maryland," *WMQ* (3d ser.), 8 (1951): 228–34, assays serious monetary problems that plagued the state's leadership.

Maryland military and naval contributions during the Revolution have escaped comprehensive study. Rieman Steuart, *A History of the Maryland Line in the Revolutionary War, 1775–1783* (Towson, Md.: Society of the Cincinnati, 1969), sketches officers' lives, briefly describes engagements, and lists rosters of troops. One might also consult Christopher Ward, *The War of the Revolution*, ed. John Richard Alden (2 vols.; New York: Macmillan Co., 1952), a standard military history. Richard J. Batt offers a popular summary of Long Island in "Maryland's 'Brave Fellows': A Reputation for Bravery Is Won," *MM*, 7 (Winter 1974): 29–33; see also Batt, "The Maryland Continentals, 1780–1781" (Ph.D. dissertation, Tulane University, 1974). For re-created uniforms, arms, equipment, and the like, see Ross M. Kimmel, "The Maryland Soldier, A Revolutionary War Portrait," insert *MM*, 8 (Summer 1975). Mary K. Meyer, ed., "Captain John Fulford's Company, February 13, 1776, to May 21, 1777," *MHM*, 69 (1974): 93–97, portrays earliest recruiting efforts. Arthur J. Alexander, "How Maryland Tried to Raise Her Continental Quotas," *MHM*, 42 (1947): 184–96, supplies a basic survey of recruiting legislation. On state naval forces, see Myron J. Smith, Jr., and John G. Earle, "The Maryland State Navy," in Ernest McNeill Eller, ed., *Chesapeake Bay in the American Revolution*, Maryland Bicentennial Bookshelf, (Centreville, Md.: Tidewater Publishers, 1981)—a fascinating collection of essays. William Bell Clark, *Lambert Wickes, Sea Raider and Diplomat: The Story of a Naval Captain of the Revolution* (New Haven, Conn.: Yale University Press, 1932), treats one Maryland naval hero. See also the chapter 4 bibliography and Bernard C. Steiner, "Maryland Privateers in the American Revolution," *MHM*, 3 (1908): 99–108, a listing, and Nathan Miller, "Lambert Wickes and the Continental Navy," *MM*, 8 (Autumn 1975): 31–35. Recent short studies include John M. Luykx, "Fighting for Food: British Foraging Operations at St. George's Island," *MHM*, 71 (1976): 212–19; Dean C. Allard, "The Potomac Navy of 1776," *VMHB*, 84 (1976): 411–30; and Curtis Carroll Davis, "The Tribulations of Mrs. Turner: An Episode after Guilford Court House," *MHM*, 76 (1981): 376–79—recalling the heroic efforts of a wounded soldier's mother.

Of broad significance are attempts lately under way to combine military with social and even intellectual history. Scholars would like to have enough evidence to say with assurance who carried the burden of sacrifice in the field—where soldiers came from, why they joined if they volunteered, and what happened to them after the war; one wonders how patriots squared their republican fear of standing armies with the need for the Continental Line. Edward C. Papenfuse and Gregory A. Stiverson, "General Smallwood's Recruits: The Peacetime Career of the Revolutionary War Private," *WMQ* (3d ser.), 30 (1973): 117–32, draws on 1782 enlistment records, 1783 tax assessments, and postwar pension applications to argue that troops came from the poorest class, later stayed poor, and likely joined because they needed the money. Charles Royster, *A Revolutionary People at War: The Continental Army and American Character, 1775–1783* (Chapel Hill: University of North Carolina Press for the Institute of Early American History and Culture, 1979), lays stress on motives beyond material ones—ideals of civic virtue and valor among them—and rightly scouts the notion that revolutionary soldiers who remained in service resembled European mercenaries. James Kirby Martin and Mark Edward Lender, *A Respectable Army: The Military Origins of the Republic, 1763–1789*, The American History Series, John Hope Franklin and Abraham S. Eisenstadt, eds. (Arlington Heights, Ill.: Harlan Davidson, 1982), attempts a synthesis. See also Ronald Hoffman and Peter J. Albert, eds., *Arms and Independence: The Military Character of the American Revolution* (Charlottesville: University Press of Virginia for the United States Capitol Historical Society, 1984), and E. Wayne Carp, *To Starve the Army at Pleasure: Continental Army Administration and American Political Culture, 1775–1783* (Chapel Hill: University of North Carolina Press, 1984). Barry Windsor Fowle, "The Maryland Militia during the Revolutionary War: A Revolutionary Organization" (Ph.D. dissertation, University of Maryland, 1982), examines the citizen-soldier ideal in practice.

Biographies of revolutionary-era political figures, besides Land, *Dulanys of Maryland*, include James Haw, Francis F. Beirne, Rosamond R. Beirne, and R. Samuel Jett, *Stormy*

Patriot: The Life of Samuel Chase (Baltimore, MHS, 1980); Edward S. Delaplaine, *The Life of Thomas Johnson* (New York: Grafton Press, 1927); Gregory A. Stiverson and Phebe R. Jacobsen, *William Paca: A Biography* (Baltimore: MHS, 1976); and L. G. Shore, *Tench Tilghman: The Life and Times of Washington's Aide-de-camp* (Centreville, Md.: Tidewater Publishers, 1982). Joseph H. Cromwell, *The Maryland Men Who Signed the Declaration of Independence* (Annapolis: Maryland Bicentennial Commission, 1977), introduces that group.

Understandably, Charles Carroll of Carrollton has provided the richest subject among Maryland patriots. Kate Mason Rowland, *The Life of Charles Carroll of Carrollton, 1737–1832, with His Correspondence and Public Papers* (2 vols.; New York and London: G. P. Putnam's Sons, 1898), remains important for its accuracy and reliance on family manuscripts since dropped from view. Ellen Hart Smith, *Charles Carroll of Carrollton* (Cambridge, Mass.: Harvard University Press, 1942), has stood for many years as the standard biography. In two volumes—*Charles Carroll of Carrollton: The Making of a Revolutionary Gentleman* (Washington, D.C.: Catholic University of America, 1970) and *Revolutionary Statesman: Charles Carroll and the War* (Chicago: Loyola University Press, 1983)—Thomas O'Brien Hanley emphasizes the development of Carroll's ideas; Hanley, "Young Mr. Carroll and Montesquieu," *MHM*, 62 (1967): 394–418, argues that the French philosopher's separation-of-powers doctrine influenced Carroll when he studied abroad. Ronald Hoffman, editor of the Papers of Charles Carroll of Carrollton, plans a lengthy essay on the man and his family as part of the forthcoming first volume of the project. For an interesting Carroll exhibit catalog, see Sally D. Mason, Ronald Hoffman, Edward C. Papenfuse, William Voss Elder III, Joseph T. Durkin, and Annabelle M. Melville, *"Anywhere So Long As There Be Freedom:" Charles Carroll of Carrollton, His Family, and His Maryland* (Baltimore: Baltimore Museum of Art, 1975).

Though source materials are not in every case abundant, many Marylanders of the period would make for interesting biographies. Some of them have been the subjects of sketches and exploratory works. See Joseph C. Morton, "Stephen Bordley of Colonial Annapolis" (Ph.D. dissertation, University of Maryland, 1964); W. Stull Holt, "Charles Carroll, Barrister: The Man," *MHM*, 31 (1936): 112–26; Rosamond Randall Beirne, "The Reverend Thomas Chase: Pugnacious Parson," *MHM*, 59 (1964): 1–14; Robert Drew Simpson, "The Lord's Rebel: Freeborn Garrettson: A Methodist Preacher during the American Revolution," *Wesleyan Quarterly Review*, 2 (1965): 194–211; Ralph B. Levering, "John Hanson, Public Servant," *MHM*, 71 (1976): 113–33; Cary Howard, "John Eager Howard: Patriot and Public Servant," *MHM*, 62 (1967): 300–317; Edward E. Steiner, "Nicholas Ruxton Moore: Soldier, Farmer, and Politician," *MHM*, 73 (1978): 375–93; Albert Silverman, "William Paca, Signer, Governor, Jurist," *MHM*, 37 (1942): 1–25; Jean H. Vivian, "Thomas Stone and the Reorganization of the Maryland Council of Safety, 1776," *MHM*, 69 (1974): 271–78.

On the last proprietary personalities, see Matilda Ridout, Lady Edgar, *A Colonial Governor in Maryland: Horatio Sharpe and His Times, 1753–1773* (London, New York: Longmans, Green & Co., 1912); Bernard C. Steiner, *Life and Administration of Sir Robert Eden*, JHUS, 16 (1898); Vera F. Rollo, *Henry Harford: Last Proprietor of Maryland* (Bel Air, Md.: Harford County Committee of the Maryland Bicentennial Commission, 1976); and Wallace Shugg, "The Baron and the Milliner: Lord Baltimore's Rape Trial as a Mirror of Class Tensions in Mid-Georgian London," *MHM* (forthcoming).

4. Realizing the New Republic

On early state politics and finance, see, besides Crowl, *Maryland During and After the Revolution*, Edward C. Papenfuse, "The Legislative Response to a Costly War: Fiscal Policy and Factional Politics in Maryland, 1777–1789," in Ronald Hoffman and Peter J. Albert, eds., *Sovereign States in an Age of Uncertainty* (Charlottesville: University Press of Virginia for the United States Capitol Historical Society, 1981), and Hugh S. Hanna, *A Financial History of Maryland, 1789–1848*, JHUS, 25 (1907). Jackson T. Main, "Political Parties in Revolutionary Maryland, 1780–1787," *MHM*, 62 (1967): 1–27, and Norman K. Risjord, *Chesapeake Politics, 1781–1800* (New York: Columbia University Press, 1978), trace the contours of hardship and the geographical jealousies that gave rise to factions in these years; see also Louis Maganzin, "Economic Depression in Maryland and Virginia, 1783–1787" (Ph.D. dissertation, Georgetown University, 1967). Jean H. Vivian, "Military Land Bounties during the Revolutionary and Confederation Periods," *MHM*, 61 (1966): 239; Peter Onuf, "Toward Federalism: Virginia, Congress, and the Western Lands," *WMQ* (3d ser.), 34 (1977): 353–74; and Lemuel Molovinsky, "Maryland and the American West at Independence," *MHM*, 72 (1977): 353–60, explore the part Maryland played in the states' cession of western lands. On the gathering that antedated the more famous one in Philadelphia, see Mervin B. Whealy, "'The Revolution Is Not Over': The Annapolis Convention of 1786," *MHM*, 81 (1986): 228–40, and an informative brief account, Gregory A. Stiverson, "The Annapolis Convention: A Successful Failure," *MM*, 19 (Autumn 1986): 44–47.

Recent scholarly studies of Maryland ratification—building upon Bernard C. Steiner, "Maryland's Adoption of the Federal Constitution," *AHR*, 5 (1899–1900): 22–44, 207–24—reexamine the roots of federalist strength in the state, especially in Baltimore, and explore reasons for the antifederalists' confusion in early 1788. See, in the spring 1988 issue of the *MHM*, Tina H. Sheller, "Artisans, Merchant-Manufacturers, and Manufacturing in Baltimore Town, 1776–1785"; James Haw, "Samuel Chase and Maryland Antifederalism: A Study in Disarray"; and Gregory A. Stiverson, "Maryland's Antifederalists and the Perfection of the U.S. Constitution." Edward C. Papenfuse's "Completing the Revolution in Maryland: Defining 'Vox Populi' and the Nature of Representative Government," ibid., discusses how the ratification process itself brought political change. For the thoughts of contending Maryland leaders on the subject of constitutional ratification, see Papenfuse, with Sally D. Mason, eds., "An Undelivered Defense of a Winning Cause: Charles Carroll of Carrollton's 'Remarks on the Proposed Federal Constitution,'" *MHM*, 71 (1976): 220–51, and Haw, ed., "Samuel Chase's 'Objections to the Federal Government,'" *MHM*, 76 (1981): 272–85. See also the special spring 1988 issue of *MHM* and biographies cited below.

Raphael Semmes, *Baltimore as Seen by Visitors, 1783–1860*, Studies in Maryland History, no. 2 (Baltimore: MHS, 1953), collects interesting impressions of the rapidly growing city on the Patapsco. Richard J. Cox, "Trouble on the Chain Gang: City Surveying, Maps, and the Absence of Urban Planning in Baltimore, 1730–1823, with a Checklist of Maps of the Periods," *MHM*, 80 (1985): 8–49, treats early problems of layout and includes six illustrative maps; Robert L. Alexander, "Baltimore Row Houses of the Early Nineteenth Century," [*Midcontinent*] *American Studies*, 16 (1975): 65–76, discusses the connection between economic considerations and building patterns. For the setting and reasons for Baltimore's postrevolutionary success, see Gary Lawson Browne, *Baltimore in the Nation, 1789–1861* (Chapel Hill: University of North Carolina Press, 1980); Geoffrey Gilbert, "Maritime Enterprise in the Early Republic: Investment in Baltimore Shipping, 1789–1793," *Business History Review*, 58 (1984): 14–29; Frank R. Rutter, *The South American Trade of Baltimore*, JHUS, 15 (1897), and Olson, *Baltimore*. Valuable short pieces include Rhoda M. Dorsey, "The Pattern of Baltimore Commerce during the Confederation Period," *MHM*, 62 (1967): 119–34; G. Terry Sharrer, "Flour Milling and the Growth of Baltimore, 1750–1830," *MHM*, 71 (1976): 322–33; and Sharrer, "The Merchant-Millers: Baltimore's Flour Milling Industry, 1783–1860," *AgHist*, 56 (1982): 138–50. Valuable recent studies of early republican Baltimore examine residential, morbidity, and work patterns in the city: Richard M. Bernard, "A Portrait of Baltimore in 1800: Economic and Occupational Patterns in an Early American City," *MHM*, 69 (1974): 341–60; Douglas F. Stickle, "Death and Class in Baltimore: The Yellow Fever Epidemic of 1800," *MHM*, 74 (1979): 282–99; Charles G. Steffen, "Changes in the Organization of Artisan Production in Baltimore, 1790–1820," *WMQ* (3d ser.), 36 (1979): 101–17. Gregory A. Wood, *The French Presence in Maryland, 1524–1800* (Baltimore: Gateway Press, 1978), treats the Acadians' arrival and the French influence in the later eighteenth century. Ira Rosenwaike, "The Jews of Baltimore: 1810 to 1820," *AJHQ*, 67 (1977): 101–24, and Philip Sherman, "Baltimore's Jew Alley," *Generations*, 21 (December 1981): 43–46, treat the earliest Jewish families in the city.

G. Terry Sharrer, "Patents by Marylanders, 1790–1830," *MHM*, 71 (1976): 50–59; Robert D. Arbuckle, "John Nicholson and the Great Steamboat Rivalry," *MHM*, 71 (1976):

60–64; and John W. McGrain, "Englehart Cruse and Baltimore's First Steam Mill," *MHM*, 71 (1976): 65–79, discuss technological experiments in these years. Louis F. Gorr, "Baltimore's First Public Utility," *Baltimore Engineer*, 51 (1976): 8–11, treats the waterworks.

For economic life in the hinterland, see J. Louis Kuethe, "A List of Maryland Mills, Taverns, Forges, and Furnaces of 1795," *MHM*, 31 (1936): 155–69; Mary Jane Dowd, "The State of the Maryland Economy, 1776–1807," *MHM*, 57 (1962): 90–132, 229–59; and Donald R. Adams, Jr., "One Hundred Years of Prices and Wages: Maryland, 1750–1850," *Working Papers from the Regional Economic History Research Center*, 5 (no. 5, 1982): 90–129. Bayly Ellen Marks, "The Rage for Kentucky: Emigration from St. Mary's County, 1790–1810," in Mitchell and Muller, *Geographical Perspectives on Maryland's Past*, traces the departure of poverty-stricken tobacco growers; see also Marks, "Rural Response to Urban Penetration: Baltimore and St. Mary's Counties, Maryland, 1790–1840," *Journal of Historical Geography*, 8 (1982): 113–27. Edward C. Papenfuse examines postwar farming practices in "Tobacco the Villain? A Comment on the Agricultural History of Maryland in the Decades following the American Revolution," National Agricultural Library *Associates NAL Today* (new ser.), 1 (1976): 8–10. Dwight D. Oland, "The New Bremen Glass Manufactury," *MHM*, 68 (1973): 255–72, studies the Amelung operation (and its failure) on the basis of recent archaeological excavations. Charles G. Steffen, "The Pre-Industrial Iron Worker: Northampton Iron Works, 1780–1820," *Labor History*, 20 (1979): 89–110, focuses on the Ridgely property in Baltimore County. Richard W. Griffin, "An Origin of the Industrial Revolution in Maryland: The Textile Industry, 1789–1826," *MHM*, 61 (1966): 24–36, sketches post-embargo investment in textile milling.

On the finally successful campaign to build a navigational aid at the mouth of the Chesapeake Bay, see Arthur Pierce Middleton, "The Struggle of the Cape Henry Lighthouse, 1721–1791," *American Neptune*, 8 (1948): 26–36. James Weston Livingood, *The Philadelphia-Baltimore Trade Rivalry, 1780–1860* (Harrisburg: Pennsylvania Historical and Museum Commission, 1947), examines competition that included quarrels over downriver commerce on the Susquehanna. Making Rumsey's case for being the true steamboat pioneer are Ella May Turner, *James Rumsey, Pioneer in Steam Navigation* (Scottdale, Pa.: Mennonite Publishing House, 1930); James A. Padgett, ed., "Rumsey Documents," *MHM*, 32 (1937): 10–28, 136–55, 271–85; and H. A. Gosnell, "The First American Steamboat: James Rumsey Its Inventor, Not John Fitch," *VMHB*, 40 (1932): 14–22, 124–32. See also James T. Flexner, *Steamboats Come True: American Inventors in Action* (New York: Viking Press, 1944). Charles T. LeViness, *History of Road Building in Maryland* (Baltimore: Maryland State Roads Commission, 1958), provides an invaluable introduction; see also Joseph A. Durrenberger, *Turnpikes: A Study of the Toll Road Movement in the Middle Atlantic States and Maryland* (Valdosta, Ga.: Southern Stationery & Printing Co., 1931), a durable monograph, and the recent local survey by William Hollifield, *Difficulties Made Easy: History of the Turnpikes of Baltimore City and County* (Baltimore: Baltimore County Historical Society, 1978). Accounts of the National Road seldom appear without illustrations. Archer B. Hulbert, *The Cumberland Road* (New York: AMS Press, 1971 [Cleveland, 1904]), first was published as part of Hulbert's famous Historic Highways of America series and remains useful, as does Thomas B. Searight, *The Old Pike: An Illustrated Narrative of the National Road*, ed. and illus. by Joseph E. Morse and R. Duff Green (Orange, Va.: Green Tree Press, 1971 [Uniontown, Pa., 1894]).

Maryland politics in the early national period built on internal, regional differences that external issues galvanized by the mid-1790s. Besides Risjord, *Chesapeake Politics*, see L. Marx Renzulli, Jr., *Maryland: The Federalist Years* (Rutherford, Madison, Teaneck, N.J.: Fairleigh Dickinson University Press, 1972), and a quantitative study of the lower house, L. Steven Demaree, "Maryland during the First Party System: A Roll-Call Analysis of the House of Delegates, 1789–1824" (Ph.D. dissertation, University of Missouri, 1984). Lee W. Formwalt, "A Conversation Between Two Rivers: A Debate on the Location of the U.S. Capital in Maryland," *MHM*, 71 (1976): 310–21, treats Patapsco-Potomac differences; Dorothy M. Brown, "Maryland and the Federalist: Search for Unity," *MHM*, 63 (1968): 1–21, explores divisions over issues that included the first Bank of the United States. Gary L. Browne, "Federalism in Baltimore," *MHM*, 83 (1988), pursues principal themes of the movement for ratification past 1789—when in Baltimore so many earlier friends of the

Constitution became Jeffersonian Republicans. For a valuable study of the role skilled workers played as grass-roots Jeffersonians, especially between 1794 and 1802, see Charles G. Steffen, *The Mechanics of Baltimore: Politics in the Age of Revolution, 1763–1812* (Urbana and Chicago: University of Illinois Press, 1984). William Bruce Wheeler, "The Baltimore Jeffersonians, 1788–1800: A Profile of Intra-Factional Conflict," *MHM*, 66 (1971): 153–68, explores differences over city incorporation in the mid-1790s (finding sharp lines between wealth and skilled labor, Baltimore and Fells Point) and suffrage reform. J. R. Pole, "Constitutional Reform and Election Statistics in Maryland, 1790–1812," *MHM*, 55 (1960): 275–92, cautions against overemphasizing the 1802 franchise amendment.

Malcolm C. Clark, "Federalism at High Tide: The Election of 1796 in Maryland," *MHM*, 61 (1966): 210–30, and John Kuehl, "The XYZ Affair and American Nationalism: Republican Victories in the Middle Atlantic States," *MHM*, 67 (1972): 1–20, trace the effects of presidential and foreign-policy questions on local partisans, as do Edward G. Roddy, "Maryland and the Presidential Election of 1800," *MHM*, 56 (1961): 244–68, and David Alan Bohmer, "Stability and Change in Early National Politics: The Maryland Voter and the Election of 1800," *WMQ* (3d ser.), 36 (1979): 27–50. Bohmer draws on his "Voting Behavior during the First American Party System: Maryland 1796–1816" (Ph.D. dissertation, University of Michigan, 1974). Frank A. Cassell, "General Samuel Smith and the Election of 1800," *MHM*, 63 (1968): 341–59, examines that Republican leader's efforts on Jefferson's behalf; see also John B. Boles, ed., "Politics, Intrigue, and the Presidency: James McHenry to Bishop Carroll, May 16, 1800," *MHM*, 69 (1974): 64–85. John D. Kilbourne, "The Society of the Cincinnati in Maryland: Its First One Hundred Years, 1783–1883," *MHM*, 78 (1978): 169–85, studies some ardent friends of order. Frederic Shriver Klein, "Jeffersonians in Local Politics along the Pennsylvania-Maryland Border," *Pennsylvania History*, 24 (1957): 15–28, discusses the political baptism of Andrew and Abraham Shriver as Frederick County Republicans in 1802.

Religious feeling and doctrine, always important in shaping attitudes, invite special historical attention during the postrevolutionary period, when Americans debated the course the new republic would take. Terry David Bilhartz, *Urban Religion and the Second Great Awakening: Church and Society in Early National Baltimore* (Cranbury, N.J.: Fairleigh Dickinson University Press, 1986), supplies a colorful chapter in denominational and social history. Kenneth L. Carroll has explored slavery and faith in several important pieces: besides his *Quakerism on the Eastern Shore*, see "Religious Influences on the Manumission of Slaves in Caroline, Dorchester, and Talbot Counties," *MHM*, 56 (1961): 176–97; "Nicholites and Slavery in Eighteenth-Century Maryland," *MHM*, 79 (1984): 126–33; and "An Eighteenth-Century Episcopalian Attack on Quaker and Methodist Manumission of Slaves," *MHM*, 80 (1985): 139–50. Arthur Pierce Middleton, "From Daughter Church to Sister Church: The Disestablishment of the Church of England and the Organization of the Diocese of Maryland," *MHM*, 79 (1984): 189–96, surveys reorganization of the Protestant Episcopal church, on which see also David L. Holmes, "William Holland Wilmer: A Newly Discovered Memoir," *MHM*, 81 (1986): 160–64. William H. Williams, *The Garden of American Methodism: The Delmarva Peninsula, 1769–1820* (Wilmington, Del.: Scholarly Resources, 1984), recounts the sharp rise of Methodism on the Shore following the appearance of Francis Asbury. N. C. Hughes, Jr., "The Methodist Christmas Conference: Baltimore, December 24, 1784–January 2, 1785," *MHM*, 54 (1959): 272–92, discusses formation of the separate Methodist church, including early antislavery policy. For its failure, see Donald M. Mathews, *Slavery and Methodism: A Chapter in American Morality, 1780–1844* (Princeton, N.J.: Princeton University Press, 1965). On the Catholic order begun in Baltimore, see William Jarvis, "Mother Seton's Sisters of Charity" (Ph.D. dissertation, Columbia University, 1984). Richard Shaw, *John Dubois, Founding Father: The Life and Times of Mount St. Mary's College, Emmitsburg* (Emmitsburg, Md.: Mount St. Mary's College, 1983), discusses the priest who came to Mother Seton's aid and then established a college for Catholic men. Biographies of Bishop Carroll appear below; on his rise as American prelate, see Peter Guilday, ed., "The Appointment of Father John Carroll as Prefect-Apostolic of the Church of the New Republic (1783–1785)," *CHR*, 6 (1920): 204–

48. Philip Gleason, "The Main Sheet Anchor: John Carroll and Catholic Higher Education," *Review of Politics*, 38 (1976): 576–613, discusses his part in establishing schools.

On early attempts to establish public institutions of higher education, see Callcott, *History of the University of Maryland*. Steiner, *History of Education in Maryland*, surveys primary and secondary schools. Tench Francis Tilghman, *The Early History of St. John's College in Annapolis* (Annapolis: St. John's College Press, 1984), commemorates the premier Western Shore institution. Charlotte Fletcher, "1784: The Year St. John's College Was Named," *MHM*, 74 (1979): 133–51, traces the climate of opinion, sources of college support, and Masonic influences in the period—reaching back to 1782 and the origins of Washington College as well; Anne W. Brown, "The Phoenix: A History of St. John's College Library," *MHM*, 65 (1970): 413–29, includes sidelights on the founding.

Guides to the press, private libraries, theater, and artists further index the ambitions of early republican leaders. Joseph T. Wheeler, *The Maryland Press, 1777–1790* (Baltimore: MHS, 1938), discusses Baltimore, Easton, Hagerstown, and Georgetown printers; see also Roxanne Marie Zimmer, "The Urban Daily Press, Baltimore, 1791–1816" (Ph.D. dissertation, University of Iowa, 1982). Amanda R. Minick, *A History of Printing in Maryland, 1791–1800, with a Bibliography of Works Printed in the State during the Period* (Baltimore: Enoch Pratt Free Library, 1949), remains a valuable reference work. Larry E. Sullivan, "Reading Habits of the Nineteenth-Century Baltimore Bourgeoisie: A Cross-Cultural Analysis," *Journal of Library History*, 16 (1981): 227–40, examines early libraries along with their founders, titles, and members. Jane N. Garrett, "Philadelphia and Baltimore, 1790–1840," *MHM*, 55 (1960): 1–13, explores cultural ties between the two cities, as does David Ritchey, "The Philadelphia Company Performs in Baltimore," *MHM*, 71 (1976): 80–85. See also Ritchey, *Guide to the Baltimore Stage in the Eighteenth Century*, and Christopher J. Thaiss, "Shakespeare in Maryland, 1752–1860," in *Shakespeare in the South: Essays on Performance*, ed. Philip C. Kolin (Jackson: University Press of Mississippi, 1983). On early artists, see Carolyn J. Weekley, Stiles Tuttle Colwill, Mary Ellen Hayward, and Leroy Graham, *Joshua Johnson: Freeman and Early American Portrait Painter* (Williamsburg, Va., and Baltimore: Colonial Williamsburg Foundation and MHS, 1987), a recent exhibit catalog that markedly updates J. Hall Pleasants, "Joshua Johnston [*sic*], The First American Negro Portrait Painter," *MHM*, 37 (1942): 121–49. Pleasants, "Four Late-Eighteenth-Century Anglo-American Landscape Painters," *Proceedings of the American Antiquarian Society*, 52 (1943): 187–324, treats George and Mary Beck, William Groombridge, Francis Guy, and William Winstanley. On Guy, see also Stiles Tuttle Colwill, "Town & Country: The Smaller, Greener Baltimore of Francis Guy," *American Heritage*, 32 (February/March 1981): 18–27, and an exhibition catalog, *Francis Guy, 1760–1820* (Baltimore: MHS, 1981). Robert L. Raley, "The Baltimore Country-House, 1785–1815" (M.A. thesis, University of Delaware, 1959; copy available at MHS), surveys wealthy country living in these years, self-consciously as an art form.

The rule of law and attempts to impose order in the early republic depended on strong bar and judiciary. Dennis R. Nolan, "The Effect of the Revolution on the Bar: The Maryland Experience," *Virginia Law Review*, 62 (1976): 969–97, refutes the standard view that revolutionary upheaval left American lawyers as a group weakened, discredited, and disorganized. Richard B. Lillich, "The Chase Impeachment," *AJLH*, 4 (1960): 49–72, reexamines the trial and its effect on American impeachment law. Robert M. Ireland, "William Pinkney: A Revision and Reemphasis," *AJLH*, 14 (1970): 235–46, praises Pinkney as the leading trial lawyer of the early nineteenth century; see also Ireland, *The Legal Career of William Pinkney, 1764–1822* (New York: Garland Publishing, forthcoming). For a life-and-times study of another prominent member of the Maryland bar, see Paul S. Clarkson and R. Samuel Jett, *Luther Martin of Maryland* (Baltimore: Johns Hopkins Press, 1970).

Political and social differences in Maryland produced notorious violence in these years. John S. Pancake, "Baltimore and the Embargo, 1807–1809," *MHM*, 47 (1952): 173–87, examines public response to that hopeful but ill-fated and highly coercive measure, as does Dorothy M. Brown, "Embargo Politics in Maryland," *MHM*, 58 (1963): 193–210. Victor Sapio, "Maryland's Federalist Revival, 1808–1812," *MHM*, 64 (1969): 1–17, notes the political fruits Madison's opponents harvested in the state. Several scholars have tackled the civil disturbance that gave Baltimore an unsavory reputation. Frank A. Cassell, "The Great Baltimore Riot of 1812," *MHM*, 70 (1975): 241–59, ably recounts the affair; Grace Overmyer, "The Baltimore Mobs and John Howard Payne," *MHM*, 58 (1963): 54–61, describes the violence done that actor-songwriter. Paul A. Gilje, "The Baltimore Riots of 1812 and the Breakdown of the Anglo-American Mob Tradition," *JSocH*, 13 (1980): 547–64, argues that participants exceeded the limits of contemporary out-of-doors political expression; see also Gilje, "'Le Menu Peuple' in America: Identifying the Mob in the Baltimore Riots of 1812," *MHM*, 81 (1986): 50–66.

Accounts of Maryland in the War of 1812 focus on naval contributions and the battles for Washington and Baltimore. For a good introduction see Gilbert Byron, *The War of 1812 on the Chesapeake Bay* (Baltimore: MHS, 1964). Jerome R. Garitee, *The Republic's Private Navy; The American Privateering Business as Practiced by Baltimore during the War of 1812* (Middletown, Conn.: Wesleyan University Press for Mystic Seaport, 1977), provides the authoritative work on armed merchantmen. William L. Calderhead, "Naval Innovation in Crisis: War in the Chesapeake, 1813," *American Neptune*, 36 (1976): 206–21, supplements Chapelle, *Baltimore Clipper*. Evan Randolph, "USS Constellation, 1797–1979," *American Neptune*, 39 (1979): 235–55, discusses, with illustrations, the Baltimore-built frigate that served in undeclared conflicts with France and the Barbary powers and in war with Britain; one might also see Howard I. Chapelle and Leon D. Pollard, *The Constellation Question* (Washington, D.C.: Smithsonian Press, 1970), for a discussion of the ship's later rebuilding, and the more popular work, Sanford Sternlicht and Edwin M. Jameson, *U.S.F. Constellation: "Yankee Racehorse"* (Cockeysville, Md.: Liberty Publishers, 1982). Biographies of naval leaders include Hulbert Footner, *Sailor of Fortune: The Life and Adventures of Commodore Joshua Barney, U.S.N.* (New York: Harper & Row, 1940); Fred W. Hopkins, Jr., *Tom Boyle: Master Privateer* (Cambridge, Md.: Tidewater Publishers, 1976); Irwin Anthony, *Decatur* (New York: Scribner's Sons, 1931); Charles Paullin, *Commodore John Rodgers, Captain, Commodore, and Senior Officer of the American Navy, 1773–1838* (Annapolis: Naval Institute Press, 1967 [Cleveland, 1910]). For the wartime and postwar exploits of one Baltimore captain, see Fred Hopkins, "For Flag and Profit: The Life of Commodore John Daniel Danels of Baltimore," *MHM*, 80 (1985): 392–401.

Neil Swanson, *The Perilous Fight . . .* (New York, Toronto: Farrar & Rinehart, 1945), and Walter Lord, *The Dawn's Early Light* (New York: W. W. Norton & Co., 1972), survey the military campaigns for Washington and Baltimore. For a recent synthesis, stressing the part sailors and marines took in the second, redeeming, struggle, see Scott S. Sheads, with a foreword by Walter Lord, *The Rockets' Red Glare: The Maritime Defense of Baltimore in 1814* (Centreville, Md.: Tidewater Publishers, 1987). On Barney's plan for the defense of vulnerable territory, see Donald G. Shomette, *Flotilla: Battle for the Patuxent* (Solomons, Md.: Calvert Maritime Museum, 1981), and, for related archaeological discoveries, Shomette and Fred W. Hopkins, Jr., "The Search for the Chesapeake Flotilla," *American Neptune*, 43 (1983): 5–19. Frank A. Cassell, "Baltimore in 1813: A Study of Urban Defense in the War of 1812," *Military Affairs*, 38 (1969): 349–61, discusses the preparations Baltimoreans made before and during the British offensive. See also Harry L. Coles, "1814: A Dark Hour before the Dawn," *MHM*, 66 (1971): 219–21; Paul Woehrmann, "National Response to the Sack of Washington," *MHM*, 66 (1971): 222–60; and Cassell, "Response to Crisis: Baltimore in 1814," *MHM*, 66 (1971): 261–87. A three-part series, "Fort McHenry: 1814," Richard Walsh, ed., examines the struggle for Baltimore from a military-engineering perspective: Franklin R. Mullaly, "The Battle of Baltimore," *MHM*, 54 (1959): 61–103; S. Sydney Bradford, "The Outworks in 1814," *MHM*, 54 (1959): 188–209; and Richard Walsh, "The Star Fort," *MHM*, 54 (1959): 296–309.

Biographies and sketches of Marylanders prominent in the early republic include Silvio A. Bedini, *The Life of Benjamin Banneker* (New York: Scribner's, 1972); Jane Shaffer Elsmere, *Justice Samuel Chase* (Muncie, Ind.: Janevan Publishing Co., 1980)—a supplement to the Stiverson et al. biography cited in the chapter 3 bibliography; William L. Calderhead, "A Strange Career in a Young Navy: Captain Charles Gordon, 1778–1816," *MHM*, 72 (1977): 373–86; Chester G. Dunham, "Christopher Hughes, Jr., at Ghent, 1814," *MHM*, 66 (1971): 288–99, and "A Nineteenth Century Baltimore Diplomat: Christopher Hughes Goes to Sweden," *MHM*, 72 (1977): 387–400; Bernard C. Steiner, ed., *The Life and Corre-*

spondence of James McHenry (Cleveland, Ohio: Burrows Brothers, 1907); Peter P. Hill, *William Vans Murray, Federalist Diplomat: The Shaping of Peace with France, 1797–1801* (Syracuse, N.Y.: Syracuse University Press, 1971); and Stuart Weems Bruchey, *Robert Oliver, Merchant of Baltimore, 1783–1819*, JHUS, 74 (1956). Students of Sam Smith generally rely on Frank A. Cassell, *Merchant Congressman in the New Republic: Samuel Smith of Maryland, 1752–1839* (Madison: University of Wisconsin Press, 1971); but see also John S. Pancake, *Samuel Smith and the Politics of Business, 1752–1839* (University: University of Alabama Press, 1972). On the nation's first Roman Catholic bishop, see Peter Guilday, *The Life and Times of John Carroll, Archbishop of Baltimore, 1735–1815* (Westminster, Md.: Newman Press, 1954 [New York, 1922]), and Annabelle M. Melville, *John Carroll of Baltimore: Founder of the American Catholic Hierarchy* (New York: Scribner's, 1955). For an edition selecting some, not all, of the prelate's correspondence during this critical period in church history, see Thomas O'Brien Hanley, ed., *The John Carroll Papers* (3 vols.; Notre Dame, Ind.: University of Notre Dame Press, 1976).

5. Suspended between Memory and Hope

Maryland art and architecture in the period after the War of 1812 introduce a galaxy of important American figures. On Latrobe, see Edward C. Carter II et al., eds., *The Papers of Benjamin Henry Latrobe* (Clifton, N.J.: J. T. White for the MHS, 1976), a microfiche edition of this rich collection and a guide to it; see also a growing number of important volumes, some of them distinguished examples of the printing craft: Carter, Angeline M. Polites, Darwin H. Stapleton, John C. Van Horne, Lee Formwalt et al., eds., *The Papers of Benjamin Henry Latrobe* (7 vols. to date; New Haven, Conn.: Yale University Press for the MHS, 1977–   ), with a separate series each for Latrobe's journals, engineering and architectural drawings, sketchbook and miscellaneous drawings, and correspondence and miscellaneous papers. For a true visual treat, see Carter, Van Horne, and Charles E. Brownell, eds., *Latrobe's View of America, 1795–1820: Selections from the Watercolors and Sketches* (New Haven and London: Yale University Press, 1985). On the Peales, one might begin with Charles Coleman Sellers, *Charles Willson Peale* (New York: Scribner's, 1969 [2 pts.; Philadelphia, 1947]), Charles H. Elam, ed., *The Peale Family: Three Generations of American Artists* (Detroit: Detroit Institute of Arts, 1967), and Eugenia C. Holland et al., *Four Generations of Commissions: The Peale Collection of the Maryland Historical Society* (Baltimore: MHS, 1975). Wilbur H. Hunter and John Mahey, *Miss Sarah Miriam Peale, 1800–1885: Portraits and Still Life* (Baltimore: Peale Museum, 1967), catalogs her work; see also Beverly Berghaus Chico, "Two American Firsts: Sarah Peale, Portrait Painter, and John Neale, Critic," *MHM*, 71 (1976): 349–59. David P. Erlick, "The Peales and Gas Lights in Baltimore," *MHM*, 80 (1985): 9–18, discusses that innovation. Latrobe Weston, "Art and Artists in Baltimore," *MHM*, 33 (1938): 213–27, treats artists who were drawn to the city. On Godefroy, see Robert L. Alexander, *The Architecture of Maximilian Godefroy* (Baltimore: Johns Hopkins University Press, 1975). In "Architecture and Aristocracy: The Cosmopolitan Style of Latrobe and Godefroy," *MHM*, 56 (1961): 229–43, Alexander discusses their felt duty to shape taste. Dorothy Mackay Quyan, "Maximilian and Eliza Godefroy," *MHM*, 52 (1957): 1–34, examines the architect's personal life before his departure for England in 1819. Barbara Gold, "Alfred Jacob Miller, Nineteenth Century Artist," *MM*, 5 (Spring 1973): 25–29, treats a Maryland native who painted western scenes before returning to Baltimore in the 1840s; see also William R. Johnston's two essays in Ron Tyler, ed., *Alfred Jacob Miller: Artist on the Oregon Trail* (Fort Worth, Texas: Amon Carter Museum, 1982). J. Jefferson Miller II, "Baltimore's Washington Monument" (M.A. thesis, University of Delaware, 1962; copy available at MHS), examines that architectural landmark.

On Baltimore intellectual and literary life in these years, see, besides Callcott, *University of Maryland*, John Earle Uhler, "The Delphian Club," *MHM*, 20 (1925): 305–46, and Joseph L. Yeatman, "Baltimore Literary Culture, 1815–1840" (Ph.D. dissertation, University of Maryland, 1983). Benjamin Lease, *That Wild Fellow John Neale, and the American Literary Revolution* (Chicago, 1972), sketches an irrepressible figure. George E. Bell, "Emerson and Baltimore: A Biographical Study," *MHM*, 65 (1970): 331–55, explores that mutually illuminating relationship. Robert P. Hay, "Charles Carroll and the Passing of the

Revolutionary Generation," *MHM*, 67 (1972): 54–62, discusses the climate of the late 1820s; Ralph D. Gray and Gerald E. Hartdagen, eds., "A Glimpse of Baltimore Society in 1827: Letters of Henry D. Gilpin," *MHM*, 69 (1974): 256–70, offers a Philadelphian's insights into the world of the Harper, Carroll, and Gilmor families. An important friend of the arts in Baltimore, Robert Gilmor, Jr., lacks adequate treatment, but see William R. Johnston, ed., *The Taste of Maryland: Art Collecting in Maryland 1800–1934* (Baltimore: Trustees of the Walters Art Gallery, 1984); Anna Wells Rutledge, "Robert Gilmor, Jr., Baltimore Collector," *Journal of the Walters Art Gallery*, 12 (1949): 19–39; and "The Diary of Robert Gilmor," *MHM*, 17 (1922): 231–68, 319–41, and *MHM*, 51 (1956): 1–13. Charles H. Bohner, *John Pendleton Kennedy, Gentleman from Baltimore* (Baltimore: Johns Hopkins Press, 1961), and Clarence P. Walhout, "John Pendleton Kennedy: Late Disciple of the Enlightenment," *JSH*, 32 (1966): 358–67, discuss a leading Baltimore writer and literary patron of the period.

Serious studies of Kennedy's best-known beneficiary, Edgar Allan Poe, include Arthur Hobson Quinn, *Edgar Allan Poe: A Critical Biography* (New York: D. Appleton-Century, 1941), and Edward Hutchins Davidson, *Poe: A Critical Study* (Cambridge, Mass.: Belknap Press, Harvard University Press, 1964). Dwight Thomas and David K. Jackson, comps., *The Poe Log: A Documentary Life of Edgar Allan Poe, 1809–1849* (Boston: G. K. Hall, 1987), chronicles Poe's life and work by means of chronologically arranged snippets of information. Esther F. Hyneman, *Edgar Allan Poe: An Annotated Bibliography of Books and Articles in English, 1827–1973* (Boston: G. K. Hall, 1974), supplies a key to further Poe scholarship. The circumstances surrounding the poet's untimely death continue to attract attention; see Charles Scarlett, Jr., "A Tale of Ratiocination: The Death and Burial of Edgar Allan Poe," *MHM*, 73 (1978): 360–74.

Further on lugubrious topics, see R. Kent Lancaster, "On the Drama of Dying in Early Nineteenth Century Baltimore," *MHM*, 81 (1986): 103–16, and Stephen J. Vicchio, "Baltimore's Burial Practices, Mortuary Art and Notions of Grief and Bereavement, 1780–1900," *MHM*, 81 (1986): 134–48. Lancaster, "Green Mount: The Introduction of the Rural Cemetery into Baltimore," *MHM*, 74 (1979): 62–79, treats a noteworthy shift in social values and landscape architecture in the mid-1830s.

Social and institutional studies for the period include Tina H. Sheller, "The Origins of Public Education in Baltimore, 1825–1829," *History of Education Quarterly*, 22 (1982): 23–42; Stuart C. Sherman, "The Library Company of Baltimore, 1795–1854," *MHM*, 39 (1944): 6–24; and Blanche D. Coll, "The Baltimore Society for the Prevention of Pauperism, 1820–1822," *AHR*, 61 (1955): 77–87. Coll and Douglas G. Carroll, Jr., introduce an early Thomas W. Griffith manuscript in "The Baltimore Almshouse: An Early History," *AHR*, 66 (1971): 135–52. See also Carroll, Jr., "Care of the Insane in Maryland, 1841," *MSMJ*, 28 (February 1979): 21–23. Katherine A. Harvey, "Practicing Medicine at the Baltimore Almshouse, 1828–1850," *MHM*, 74 (1979): 223–37, uses almshouse records to throw light on afflictions there and contemporary medical treatments. Marvin E. Gettleman, "The Maryland Penitentiary in the Age of Tocqueville, 1828–1842," *MHM*, 56 (1961): 269–90, examines that experiment in criminal confinement and state finance. Milton A. Maxwell, "The Washington Movement," *Quarterly Journal of Studies on Alcohol*, 11 (1950): 410–51, traces the rise and fall of a grass-roots reform effort. On the context in which the MHS appeared, see Leslie W. Dunlap, *American Historical Societies, 1790–1860* (Philadelphia: Porcupine Press, 1974 [Madison, Wisc., 1944]). Samuel K. Dennis, "A Brief Summary of the Maryland Historical Society's Hundred Years," *MHM*, 39 (1944): 1–5, and Joseph W. Cox, "The Origins of the Maryland Historical Society: A Case Study in Cultural Philanthropy," *MHM*, 74 (1979): 103–16, lay some of the groundwork for the careful study that Gary L. Browne has in preparation.

On the commercial changes and growth in manufacturing that followed the panic of 1819, see especially Browne, *Baltimore in the Nation*. Olson, *Baltimore*, further recounts those developments for the city itself; see also Edward K. Muller, "Spatial Order before Industrialization: Baltimore's Central District, 1833–1860," *Working Papers from the Regional Economic History Research Center*, 4 (nos. 1 and 2, 1981): 100–140, and Theodore Hershberg, "Nineteenth-Century Baltimore: Historical and Geographical Perspectives: A Commentary," ibid., pp. 141–55. The firm of Alexander Brown & Sons, innovative and important in the antebellum cotton trade, has been the subject of a number of studies. Frank R. Kent, with a chapter by Louis Azrael, *The Story of Alex. Brown & Sons, 1800–1975* (rev. ed.; Baltimore: Barton-Gillett Co., 1975 [Baltimore, 1925]), reprints selections from company correspondence and partially avoids the pieties of commissioned corporate histories. Edwin J. Perkins, *Financing Anglo-American Trade: The House of Brown, 1800–1880*, Harvard Studies in Business History (Cambridge, Mass.: Harvard University Press, 1975), provides the leading scholarly study. See also Perkins, "Financing Antebellum Importers: The Role of Brown Bros. & Co. in Baltimore," *BHR*, 45 (1971): 421–51, and Gary L. Browne, "Business Innovation and Social Change: The Career of Alexander Brown after the War of 1812," *MHM*, 69 (1974): 243–55. Aaron Baroway, "The Cohens of Maryland," *MHM*, 18 (1923): 357–76, introduces that family; on its rise in Baltimore banking, see W. Ray Luce, "The Cohen Brothers of Baltimore: From Lotteries to Banking," *MHM*, 68 (1973): 288–308.

On Maryland manufactures, in addition to the textile studies listed in the chapter 4 bibliography, see William A. Sisson, "From Farm to Factory: Work Values and Discipline in Two Early Textile Mills," *Working Papers from the Regional Economic History Research Center*, 4 (no. 4, 1981): 1–26; Betsy Bahr, "The Antietam Woolen Manufacturing Company: A Case Study in American Industrial Beginnings," ibid., 27–46; and Bayly Ellen Marks, "Clifton Factory, 1810–1860: An Experiment in Rural Industrialization," *MHM*, 80 (1985): 48–65. Katherine A. Harvey, "Building a Frontier Ironworks: Problems of Transport and Supply, 1837–1840," *MHM*, 70 (1975): 149–66, treats the early iron industry in Allegany County; Harvey, ed., *The Lonaconing Journals: The Founding of a Coal and Iron Community, 1837–1840*, Transactions of the American Philosophical Society, vol. 67 pt. 2 (1977), is a valuable primary source.

Location and enterprise made the nineteenth-century transportation revolution highly evident in Maryland. On the strategies different urban centers adopted in the race to reach western produce and markets, see Julius Rubin, *Canal or Railroad? Imitation and Innovation in Response to the Erie Canal in Philadelphia, Baltimore, and Boston*, Transactions of the American Philosophical Society, vol. 51, pt. 7 (1961), and Christopher T. Baer, *Canals and Railroads of the Mid-Atlantic States, 1800–1860* (Greenville, Del.: Regional Economic History Center, 1981). Alan M. Wilner, *The Maryland Board of Public Works* (Annapolis: MHR, 1984), discusses improvements legislation, financing of projects—and the consequences of overcommitment; see also Charles Fisher, "Internal Improvement Issues in Maryland, 1816–1826" (M.A. thesis, University of Maryland, 1972), and Douglas R. Littlefield, "Maryland Sectionalism and the Development of the Potomac Route to the West," *Maryland Historian*, 14 (1983): 31–52. On Maryland canals, see Littlefield, "The Potomac Company: A Misadventure in Financing an Early American Internal Improvement Project," *BHR*, 58 (1984): 562–85; Walter S. Sanderlin, *The Great National Project: A History of the Chesapeake and Ohio Canal*, JHUS, 64 (1946); Ralph D. Gray, *The National Waterway: A History of the Chesapeake and Delaware Canal, 1769–1965* (Champaign-Urbana: University of Illinois Press, 1967); and George B. Scriven, "The Susquehanna and Tidewater Canal," *MHM*, 71 (1976): 522–26. James Dilts has undertaken a comprehensive study of the B&O; meantime John F. Stover, *History of the Baltimore and Ohio Railroad* (West Lafayette, Ind.: Purdue University Press, 1987), replaces the old standard, Edward Hungerford, *The Story of the Baltimore & Ohio Railroad, 1827–1927* (2 vols.; New York: G. P. Putnam's Sons, 1928). See also Herbert H. Harwood, Jr., *Impossible Challenge: The Baltimore and Ohio Railroad in Maryland* (Baltimore: Barnard, Roberts, 1979), and Alfred R. James, "Sidelights on the Founding of the Baltimore and Ohio Railroad," *MHM*, 48 (1953): 267–309. Jack C. Potter, "The Philadelphia, Wilmington, and Baltimore Railroad, 1831–1860: A Study of Early Railroad Transportation" (M.A. thesis, University of Delaware, 1960), explores the line to the northeast. On early steamboat travel, see the general bibliography; on experimental boats, the chapter 4 bibliography. Harold Kanarek, "The U.S. Army Corps of Engineers and Early Internal Improvements in Maryland," *MHM*, 72 (1977): 99–109, treats the role of a critical federal agency and source of technical expertise—on which see also Richard J. Cox, "Professionalism and Civil Engineering in Early America: The Vicissitudes of James Shriver's Career, 1815–1826," *MHM*, 74 (1979): 23–38.

Studies of antebellum Maryland agriculture leave room for further work. Students of the topic build on or refute Avery O. Craven, *Soil Exhaustion as a Factor in the Agricultural History of Virginia and Maryland, 1606–1860* (Urbana: University of Illinois Press, 1925), a monograph that remains important despite its flaws in measurement and evidence; compare it, for example, with Papenfuse, "Tobacco the Villain?" (cited in chapter 4 bibliography). Vivian Doris Wiser, "The Movement for Agricultural Improvement in Maryland, 1785–1865" (Ph.D. dissertation, University of Maryland, 1963), relies on literary sources to survey organized reform efforts; see also her "Improving Maryland's Agriculture, 1840–1860," *MHM*, 64 (1969): 105–32. Donald J. McCauley, "The Limits of Change in the Tobacco South: An Economic and Social Analysis of Prince George's County, Maryland, 1840–1860" (M.A. thesis, University of Maryland, 1973), examines slaveholding, soil exhaustion, population shifts, and economic parameters. Harold T. Pinkett, "*The American Farmer*: A Pioneer Agricultural Journal, 1819–1834," *AgHist*, 24 (1950): 146–50, and Harold A. Bierck, Jr., "Spoils, Soils, and Skinner," *MHM*, 49 (1954): 21–40, 143–55, introduce John Stuart Skinner and his magazine; see also Jack W. Berryman, "John S. Skinner's *American Farmer*: Breeding and Racing the Maryland 'Blood Horse,' 1819–29," *MHM*, 76 (1981): 159–73, and "John Stuart Skinner and Early American Sports Journalism, 1819–1835" (Ph.D. dissertation, University of Maryland, 1976). Lucretia Ramsey Bishko, "Lafayette and the Maryland Agricultural Society: 1824–1832," *MHM*, 70 (1975): 45–67, discusses the marquis's visit and his later exchanges with Maryland friends. Laura Bornholdt, *Baltimore and Early Pan-Americanism*, Smith College Studies in History no. 34 (Northampton, Mass.: Smith College, 1949), treats Skinner's interest in South American flora.

Gerald Elton Fosbroke, "An Investigation of the Attitude of Maryland toward the Missouri Compromise" (M.A. thesis, University of Maryland, 1938), examines public response to a crisis that led Jefferson to remark that the slave states held the "wolf by the ears." On a leading Quaker antislavery spokesman, see the antiquated but still useful [John S. Tyson,] *Life of Elisha Tyson, the Philanthropist, by a Citizen of Baltimore* (Baltimore, 1825). Charles Patrick Neill, *Daniel Raymond*, JHUS, 15 (1897), and Charles J. MacGarvey, "Daniel Raymond, Esquire, Founder of American Economic Thought," *MHM*, 44 (1949): 111–22, discuss the antislavery lawyer–political economist. Two articles examine William Lloyd Garrison's Baltimore interlude: Jean Wentworth, "'Not Without Honor': William Lloyd Garrison," *MHM*, 62 (1967): 318–19, and David K. Sullivan, "William Lloyd Garrison in Baltimore, 1829–1830," *MHM*, 68 (1973): 64–79. For later state attitudes toward slavery, see Lawrence Herbert McDonald, "Prelude to Emancipation: The Failure of the Great Reaction in Maryland, 1831–1850" (Ph.D. dissertation, University of Maryland, 1974).

The attempt to colonize freed blacks in Liberia marked a typically Maryland attempt to find a "middle" solution (avoiding both racial equality and perpetual slavery) to the problems of white prejudice and black bondage. Penelope Campbell, *Maryland in Africa: The Maryland State Colonization Society, 1831–1857* (Urbana: University of Illinois Press, 1971), offers the authoritative study. Campbell, "Some Notes on Frederick County's Participation in the Maryland Colonization Scheme," *MHM*, 66 (1971): 51–59, examines rural recruitment. Aaron Stopak, "The Maryland State Colonization Society: Independent State Action in the Colonization Movement," *MHM*, 63 (1968): 275–98, summarizes the mature movement. W. Wayne Smith, ed., "A Marylander in Africa: The Letters of Henry Hannon," *MHM*, 69 (1974): 398–404, prints an emigrant's letters home to the Dorsey family. See also William D. Hoyt, Jr., "John McDonough and the Maryland Colonization of Liberia, 1834–1835," *JNH*, 24 (1939): 440–53; Samuel W. Laughton, "Administrative Problems in Maryland in Liberia, 1836–1851," *MHM*, 26 (1941): 325–64; and Charles A. Earp, "The Role of Education in the Maryland Colonization Movement," *MHM*, 26 (1941): 365–88. For abundant evidence that free blacks resisted the attempt to colonize them, see Ira Berlin, *Slaves without Masters: The Free Negro in the Antebellum South* (New York: Pantheon Books, 1974), and Roland C. McConnell's contribution to Radoff, ed., *Old Line State*; for an account of William Watkins's own struggle against the colonizationists, see Leroy Graham, *Baltimore: The Nineteenth Century Black Capital* (Lanham, Md.: University Press of America, 1982). Recent work in African history enables one to view the colony from another angle; see Harrison Ola Abingbade, "The Settler-African Conflicts: The Case of the Maryland Colonists and the Grebo, 1840–1900," *JNH*, 66 (1981): 93–109.

On the development and character of Jackson-era political parties generally, see Ronald P. Formisano, "Deferential-Participatory Politics: The Early Republic's Political Culture, 1789–1840," *American Political Science Review*, 68 (1974): 473–87. For the Maryland background of Jackson's early strength, see Mark H. Haller, "The Rise of the Jackson Party in Maryland, 1820–1829," *JSH*, 28 (1962): 307–26. Besides encouraging the active play of ordinary voters, political parties in the 1830s and 1840s developed distinctive national identities, built strong organizations that depended on divisive issues to polarize loyalists from top to bottom, from federal to local levels. W. Wayne Smith, "Jacksonian Democracy on the Chesapeake: The Political Institutions," *MHM*, 62 (1967): 381–93, describes the structures and strategies of the mature Maryland Democrats and Whigs. Smith, "Jacksonian Democracy on the Chesapeake: Class, Kinship, and Politics," *MHM*, 63 (1968): 55–67, traces some leading families, their interests, and allegiances; see also his "The Whig Party in Maryland, 1826–1861" (Ph.D. dissertation, University of Maryland, 1967). For a systematic attempt to trace changes in governing elites in Baltimore City and Frederick, St. Mary's, and Talbot counties, see Whitman H. Ridgway, *Community Leadership in Maryland, 1790–1840: A Comparative Analysis of Power in Society* (Chapel Hill: University of North Carolina Press, 1979)—a work that makes use of the sociological categories of Robert A. Dahl. In "Community Leadership: Baltimore during the First and Second Party Systems," *MHM*, 71 (1976): 334–48, Ridgway briefly sketches his findings on Baltimore. Ridgway, "McCulloch vs. the Jacksonians: Patronage and Politics in Maryland," *MHM*, 70 (1975): 350–62, leaves no doubt that the Jackson party viewed patronage as a corporate dividend. Thomas Bender, "Law, Economy, and Social Values in Jacksonian America: A Maryland Case Study," *MHM*, 71 (1976): 484–97, examines the legal implications of Jacksonian ideology in the B&O-C&O Point of Rocks dispute; John E. Semmes, *John H. B. Latrobe and His Times, 1803–1891* (Baltimore: Norman, Remington Co., 1917), sketches the career of the lawyer who helped to negotiate a settlement of that dispute. On the constitutional pressures that party struggle helped to raise in the state, see A. Clarke Hagensick, "Revolution or Reform in 1836: Maryland's Preface to the Dorr Rebellion," *MHM*, 57 (1962): 346–66.

Several valuable studies explore the unrest that unregulated competition, a large labor supply, and Irish-Catholic immigration produced. Workers did not organize without facing hostility. Richard B. Morris, "Labor Controls in Maryland in the Nineteenth Century," *JSH*, 14 (1948): 385–400, and "Andrew Jackson, Strike Breaker," *AHR*, 45 (1949): 54–68, discuss labor contracts, jail populations, and a division within the Democratic party between rising entrepreneurs and workingmen. On the class and ethnic conflict that plagued both canal and railroad projects, see W. David Baird, "Violence along the Chesapeake and Ohio Canal: 1839," *MHM*, 66 (1971): 121–34. Joseph G. Mannard, "The 1839 Baltimore Nunnery Riot: An Episode in Jacksonian Nativism and Social Violence," *Maryland Historian*, 11 (1980): 13–27, treats another example of ethnic-religious scapegoating. David Grimsted, "Rioting in Its Jacksonian Setting," *AHR*, 77 (1972): 361–97, explores class protest following the Bank of Maryland collapse, for which see also Olson, *Baltimore*.

In Roger Brooke Taney, Maryland made a signal contribution to Jacksonian America. Marvin Laurence Winitsky, "Roger B. Taney: A Historiographical Inquiry," *MHM*, 69 (1974): 1–26, surveys the literature. Carl Brent Swisher, *Roger B. Taney* (New York: Macmillan Co., 1935), though not as complete as one would wish on questions of motivation, nonetheless stands as the standard scholarly biography; Walker Lewis, *Without Fear or Favor: A Biography of Chief Justice Roger Brooke Taney* (Boston: Houghton Mifflin, 1965), differs slightly from Swisher while offering the insights of a lawyer-historian. On Taney's shift from Federalism to Jackson, see Alexandra Lee Levin, "Two Jackson Supporters: Roger Brooke Taney and William Murdock Beall of Frederick," *MHM*, 55 (1960): 221–29. Taney felt obliged to explain his involvement in the Union Bank; see Stuart Bruchey, ed., "Roger Brooke Taney's Account of His Relations with Thomas Ellicott in the Bank War," *MHM*, 53 (1958): 58–74, 131–52, and Carl Brent Swisher, ed., "Roger Brooke Taney's

'Bank War Manuscript,'" *MHM*, 53 (1958): 103–30, 215–37. Frank Otto Gatell, "Roger Brooke Taney, the Bank of Maryland Rioters, and a Whiff of Grapeshot," *MHM*, 59 (1964): 262–68, demonstrates Taney's unsympathetic attitude toward the bank-collapse victims. On an important Supreme Court case that permitted Taney to discuss which issues fell within the purview of the courts and which remained "political," see Michael A. Conron, "Law, Politics, and Chief Justice Taney: A Reconsideration of the *Luther* v. *Borden* Decision," *AJLH*, 11 (1967): 377–88. Stanley I. Kutler, *Privilege and Creative Destruction: The Charles River Bridge Case* (Philadelphia: Lippincott, 1971), treats Taney's most popular decision as chief justice. See also the chapter 6 bibliography.

Notes to this chapter cite the principal primary sources on Maryland slavery. An important recent study replaces Jeffrey R. Brackett, *The Negro in Maryland: A Case Study of the Institution of Slavery*, JHUS, extra vol. 6 (1889): Barbara Jeanne Fields, *Slavery and Freedom on the Middle Ground: Maryland during the Nineteenth Century*, Yale Historical Publications, Miscellany 123 (New Haven, Conn.: Yale University Press, 1985), argues that Maryland social and economic conditions made the black experience there especially harsh. William Calderhead, "How Extensive Was the Border State Slave Trade? A New Look," *CWH*, 18 (1972): 53–54, reexamines the question of slave sales to states in the Deep South. Elwood L. Bridner, Jr., "The Fugitive Slaves of Maryland," *MHM*, 66 (1971): 33–50, discusses slave escapes. Earl Conrad, *Harriet Tubman* (Washington, D.C.: Associated Publishers, c. 1943), sketches the life of that leader in the underground escape network. On a legendary Delaware slave catcher arrested in 1829, see M. Sammy Miller, "Patty Cannon, Murderer and Kidnapper of Free Blacks: A Review of the Evidence," *MHM*, 72 (1977): 419–23. For an introduction to the Maryland narratives, see Gerri Johnson, "Maryland Roots: An Examination of the Free State's WPA Ex-Slave Narratives," *Free State Folklore*, 4 (Winter 1977): 18–34. See also Mark Walston, "A Survey of Slave Housing in Montgomery County," *Montgomery County Story*, 27 (1984): 111–26.

John W. Blassingame et al., eds., *The Frederick Douglass Papers* (3 vols. to date; New Haven, Conn.: Yale University Press, 1979–   ), make available a rich repository of source material. *Frederick Douglass: A Register and Index of His Papers in the Library of Congress* (Washington, D.C.: Library of Congress, 1976) provides a helpful guide to the researcher. For the standard Douglass biography, see Benjamin Quarles, *Frederick Douglass*, with a new preface by James M. McPherson (New York: Atheneum, 1974 [Washington, D.C., 1948]); note also Dickson J. Preston, *Young Frederick Douglass: The Maryland Years* (Baltimore: Johns Hopkins University Press, 1980). Studies of Douglass's thought and antislavery career include Waldo E. Martin, *The Mind of Frederick Douglass* (Chapel Hill: University of North Carolina Press, 1984); William L. Van Deburg, "Frederick Douglass: Maryland Slave to Religious Liberal," *MHM*, 69 (1974): 27–43; August Meier, "Frederick Douglass's Vision for America: A Case Study in Nineteenth Century Negro Protest," in Meier and Elliott Rudwick, eds., *Along the Color Line: Explorations in the Black Experience* (Chicago: University of Illinois Press, 1976); and Leslie F. Goldstein, "Violence as an Instrument of Social Change: The Views of Frederick Douglass, 1819–1895," *JNH*, 41 (1976): 61–72. For architectural and botanical descriptions of the estate Douglass knew from a different perspective, see McHenry Howard, "Wye House, Talbot County, Maryland," *MHM*, 18 (1923): 293–99, and J. Donnell Tilghman, "Wye House," *MHM*, 48 (1953): 89–108.

6. A House Divided

Published documents of the Civil War period include Roland C. Burton, ed., "John Pendleton Kennedy and the Civil War: An Uncollected Letter," *JSH*, 29 (1963): 373–76, reprinting Kennedy's March 1850 essay for the *National Intelligencer*, "Friends of the Union to the Rescue!" Volume 1 of Frank Moore, *The Rebellion Record: A Diary of American Events . . .* (11 vols.; New York: G. P. Putnam, 1861–63; D. Van Nostrand, 1864–68), publishes Kennedy's May 1861 pamphlet, *The Great Drama: An Appeal to Maryland* (Baltimore, 1861), along with the public addresses of Governor Hicks, General Assembly resolutions, Bishop Whittingham's circular to Episcopal clergy, and assorted public papers relating to the secession crisis. Moore's later volumes deal with military rule. Frank Howard, *Fourteen Months in American Bastiles* (Baltimore: Kelly, Hedian & Piet, 1863), recounts a forced stay at Fort McHenry and elsewhere and vents wartime passions; Bayly Ellen Marks and Mark Norton Schatz, eds., *Between North and South: A Maryland Journalist Views the Civil War; The Narrative of William Wilkins Glenn, 1861–1869* (Rutherford, Madison, Teaneck, N.J.: Fairleigh Dickinson University Press, 1976), gives a view of Baltimore social and political life from a pro-Southern perspective. Military memoirs appear below. For edited primary material on engagements, one may begin with Robert Underwood Johnson and Clarence Clough Buel, eds., *Battles and Leaders of the Civil War* (4 vols.; New York: Thomas Yoseloff, 1956 [New York, 1887]). For a scholarly edition of public papers, many of them pertaining to Maryland, see Ira Berlin, Joseph P. Reidy, and Leslie S. Rowland, eds., *Freedom: A Documentary History of Emancipation, 1861–1867, Selected from the Holdings of the National Archives of the United States* (2 vols. to date; Cambridge: Cambridge University Press, 1982–)

It is well to remember that in the 1850s life went on as usual; no one at the time lived in "antebellum" America. For a comparative view of social and sporting life-as-usual, see Patricia Catherine Click, "Leisure in the Upper South in the Nineteenth Century: A Study of Trends in Baltimore, Norfolk, and Richmond" (Ph.D. dissertation, University of Virginia, 1980). G. Harrison Orians, "The Origins of the Ring Tournament in the United States," *MHM*, 36 (1941): 263–77, recounts early jousting. Anne Firor Scott, "Almira Lincoln Phelps: The Self-Made Woman in the Nineteenth Century," *MHM*, 75 (1980): 203–16, discusses the head of the Patapsco Female Institute, 1841–65; David Hein, "The Founding of the Boy's School of St. Paul's Parish, Baltimore," *MHM*, 81 (1986): 149–59, discusses the origins of another academy, founded in 1849. M. Ray Della, Jr., "An Analysis of Baltimore's Population in the 1850s," *MHM*, 68 (1973): 20–35, examines patterns of growth. Harold W. Hurst, "The Northernmost Southern Town: A Sketch of Pre-Civil War Annapolis," *MHM*, 76 (1981): 240–49, discusses the ambiance of the capital. On shipbuilding, railroad engineering, and urban architecture, see Lewis Addison Beck, Jr., "The *Seaman* and the *Seaman's Bride*, Baltimore Clipper Ships," *MHM*, 51 (1956): 302–14; Hugh R. Gibb, "Mendes Cohen: Engineer, Scholar and Railroad Executive," *MHM*, 74 (1979): 1–10; and Randolph W. Chalfant, "Calvert Station: Its Structure and Significance," *MHM*, 74 (1979): 11–22. For a charming contemporary account of a rail journey out of Baltimore, see Porte Crayon [David Hunter Strother], "Artists' Excursion on the Baltimore & Ohio Rail Road," *Harper's Monthly Magazine*, 19 (June 1859): 1–19.

James Warner Harry, *The Maryland Constitution of 1851*, JHUS, 20 (1902), surveys the revised structure of government. Several important volumes examine Maryland political life in the middle of the nineteenth century. William J. Evitts, *A Matter of Allegiances: Maryland from 1850 to 1861* (Baltimore: Johns Hopkins University Press, 1974), offers the standard treatment of state politics in the sectional crisis. Jean H. Baker, *The Politics of Continuity: Maryland Political Parties from 1858 to 1870* (Baltimore: Johns Hopkins University Press, 1973), demonstrates the durability of party ideology and leadership despite the war experience. Baker, *Ambivalent Americans: The Know-Nothing Party in Maryland* (Baltimore: Johns Hopkins University Press, 1977), focuses on the successors to the Whigs. Benjamin Tuska, "Know-Nothingism in Baltimore, 1854–1860," *CHR*, 11 (1925–26): 217–51, and an older monograph, Mary St. Patrick McConville, *Political Nativism in the State of Maryland, 1830–1860* (Washington, D.C.: Catholic University of America, 1928), explore the anti-Catholic dimensions of that movement; see also Douglas Bowers, "Ideology and Political Parties in Maryland, 1851–1856," *MHM*, 64 (1969): 197–217.

Questions about slavery in the territories agitated the country in the later 1850s, when white Marylanders also noted fearfully the rising number of free blacks in the state. In this setting Chief Justice Taney made his most controversial decision. For a discussion of the controversy, see Stanley I. Kutler, ed., *The Dred Scott Case: Law or Politics?* (Boston: Houghton Mifflin, 1967); Don E. Fehrenbacher, "Roger B. Taney and the Sectional Crisis," *JSH*, 43 (1971): 555–66; and, for the latest word in the extensive historiography, Fehrenbacher, *The Dred Scott Case: Its Significance in American Law and Politics* (New York: Oxford University Press, 1978). On free blacks, in addition to Berlin, *Slaves without Masters*, see Bettye Gardner, "Antebellum Black Education in Baltimore," *MHM*, 71 (1976): 360–66, and M. Ray Della, Jr., "The Problems of Free Negro Labor in the 1850s," *MHM*, 66 (1971): 14–32. In "'Old Gunny': Abolitionist in a Slave City," *MHM*, 68 (1973): 369–82,

Roger Bruns and William Fraley demonstrate the dangers of militant Baltimore antislavery in the 1850s. Betty Dix Greeman, "The Democratic Convention of 1860: Prelude to Secession," *MHM*, 67 (1972): 225–53, and Donald Walter Curl, "The Baltimore Convention of the Constitutional Union Party," *MHM*, 67 (1972): 254–77, treat Baltimore as a scene of partisan strife.

Studies of Maryland political leaders prominent in 1861 include Gerald S. Henig, "Henry Winter Davis and the Speakership Contest of 1859–1860," *MHM*, 68 (1973): 1–19, and Raymond W. Tyson, "Henry Winter Davis: Orator for the Union," *MHM*, 58 (1963): 1–19. Henig draws on his "Henry Winter Davis: A Biography" (Ph.D. dissertation, City University of New York, 1971). See also Milton L. Henry, "Henry Winter Davis" (Ph.D. dissertation, Louisiana State University, 1972), and Bernard C. Steiner, *Life of Henry Winter Davis* (Baltimore: John Murphy, 1916). George L. P. Radcliffe, *Governor Thomas H. Hicks of Maryland and the Civil War*, JHUS, 19 (1901), tells the story of the secession-crisis governor. Steiner, *Life of Reverdy Johnson* (Baltimore: Norman, Remington Company, 1914), narrates the life of the U.S. Senator (1845–49, 1863–68) and American minister to Great Britain (1868–69).

On the secession crisis, see, besides Evitts, *Matter of Allegiances*, Carl M. Frasure, "Union Sentiment in Maryland, 1859–1861," *MHM*, 24 (1929): 210–24, and William Bruce Catton, "The Baltimore Business Community and the Sectional Crisis, 1860–61" (M.A. thesis, University of Maryland, 1952). On the Baltimore riot, see Charles Branch Clark, "Baltimore and the Attack on the Sixth Massachusetts Regiment, April 19, 1861," *MHM*, 56 (1961): 39–71, and George William Brown, *Baltimore and the Nineteenth of April, 1861: A Study of the War*, JHUS, extra volume 3 (1887). Ralph A. Wooster, "The Membership of the Maryland Legislature of 1861," *MHM*, 56 (1961): 94–102, offers a social profile of the lawmakers whose loyalties and freedom to act—as well as those of Maryland voters—caused so much concern at the time and remain live issues (see, in the Baltimore *Sun*, the following exchange from 1984: Brice M. Clagett, "Maryland Coerced," 6 April; Jean H. Baker, "Anti-War Maryland," 7 May; Carl N. Everstine, "A Land of Unpleasant Living," 4 June; Clagett, "Maryland for Breckinridge," 21 June; Baker, "A Lost Cause," 17 July; Clagett, "Maryland, C.S.A.," 10 August; Baker, "Maryland, U.S.A.," 17 August).

Wartime politics unavoidably centered on proscription and emancipation. Charles Branch Clark, "Suppression and Control of Maryland, 1861–1865: A Study of Federal-State Relations during Civil Conflict," *MHM*, 54 (1959): 241–71, supplies a useful introduction, but see also Clark, *Politics in Maryland during the Civil War* (Chestertown, Md.: n.p., 1952), which collects several such articles and chapters from a solid dissertation. On the containment of Confederate sympathizers, see also Lewis D. Asper, "The Long and Unhappy History of Loyalty Testing in Maryland," *AJLH*, 13 (1969): 97–109; William A. Russ, "Disfranchisement in Maryland (1861–67)," *MHM*, 28 (1933): 309–28; and Sidney T. Matthews, "Control of the Baltimore Press during the Civil War," *MHM*, 36 (1941): 150–70. Robert E. Morsberger, "General Lew Wallace, Latter-Day Lord of Baltimore," *MM*, 9 (Summer 1977): 2–6, rehearses the tactics of that military authority late in the war. Until Taney died in 1864, he strenuously objected to Lincoln's arbitrary arrests, imposition of martial law, and suspension of habeas corpus in the border states. On the chief justice and his antagonist, see, besides Swisher, *Taney*, Robert M. Spector, "Lincoln and Taney: A Study in Constitutional Polarization," *AJLH*, 15 (1971): 199–214, and H. H. Walker Lewis and William L. Marbury, "Ex Parte Merryman," *MHM*, 56 (1961): 384–98. James G. Randall, *Constitutional Problems under Lincoln* (rev. ed.; Urbana: University of Illinois Press, 1964 [Urbana, 1951]), argues for the president's common sense and frequent leniency given the circumstances; Harold M. Hyman, *The Era of the Oath: Northern Loyalty Tests during the Civil War and Reconstruction* (Philadelphia: University of Pennsylvania Press, 1964) and *A More Perfect Union: The Impact of the Civil War and Reconstruction on the Constitution* (New York: Alfred A. Knopf, 1973), examine the rule of law during civil upheaval.

Charles Lewis Wagandt, *The Mighty Revolution: Negro Emancipation in Maryland, 1862–1864* (Baltimore: Johns Hopkins Press, 1964), offers the standard study of emerging black liberty in the state, but also see Berlin et al., eds., *Freedom: A Documentary History of Emancipation*. Wagandt, ed., "The Opinion of Maryland on the Emancipation Proclamation: Bernal to Russell, September 23, 1862," *MHM*, 58 (1963): 250–51, comments on the obstacles emancipationists had to overcome. John W. Blassingame, "The Recruitment of Negro Troops in Maryland," *MHM*, 58 (1963): 20–29, examines the raising of black units. Wagandt, "The Army versus Maryland Slavery, 1862–1864," *CWH*, 10 (1964): 141–48, and Dale Roger Steiner, "The Army and Maryland Emancipation" (M.A. thesis, University of Virginia, 1969), leave no doubt that military exigencies hastened dismantling of the slave system. William Starr Myers, *The Maryland Constitution of 1864*, JHUS, 19 (1901), provides a detailed study of wartime constitutional change.

Several important essays survey the part Marylanders, especially Henry Winter Davis, played in forming Reconstruction policy. See Richard Paul Fuke, "A Reform Mentality: Federal Policy toward Black Marylanders, 1864–1868," *CWH*, 22 (1976): 214–35, and "Hugh Lennox Bond and Radical Republican Ideology," *JSH*, 45 (1979): 569–86. Richard H. Luthin, "A Discordant Chapter in Lincoln's Administration: The Davis-Blair Controversy," *MHM*, 39 (1944): 25–48, treats the moderate's fall late in the war; see also Madison Davis, "The Public Career of Montgomery Blair, Particularly with Reference to His Services as Postmaster-General of the United States," *RCHS*, 13 (1910): 126–59, and William E. Smith, *The Francis Preston Blair Family in Politics* (2 vols.; New York: Macmillan Co., 1933). Herman Belz, "Henry Winter Davis and the Origins of Congressional Reconstruction," *MHM*, 67 (1972): 129–43, discusses roots of the Wade-Davis bill in plans to destroy slavery via reform of state constitutions.

Harold R. Manakee, *Maryland in the Civil War* (Baltimore: MHS, 1961), provides a synopsis of the Maryland military record and a brief bibliography. Memoirs of campaigning vary greatly in quality and reliability. One of the most highly readable and reliable firsthand accounts, Henry Kyd Douglas, *I Rode with Stonewall; Being Chiefly the War Experiences of the Youngest Member of Jackson's Staff from the John Brown Raid to the Hanging of Mrs. Surratt*, with an introduction by Philip Van Doren Stern (Greenwich, Conn.: Fawcett Publications, 1961 [Chapel Hill, 1940]), first appeared through the offices of Douglas's nephew, longtime superintendent at Antietam National Battlefield Park. W. W. Goldsborough, *The Maryland Line in the Confederate Army, 1861–1865* (Gaithersburg: Butternut Press, 1983 [Baltimore, 1900]), devotedly recounts Confederate service. Richard Snowden Andrews, *A Memoir*, ed. Tunstall Smith (Baltimore: Sun Job Printing Office, 1920); [George W. Booth], *Personal Reminiscences of a Maryland Soldier in the War Between the States, 1861–1865* (Baltimore, 1898); Harry Gilmor, *Four Years in the Saddle* (New York: Harper & Brothers, 1866); Bradley T. Johnson, "The First Maryland Campaign," *Southern Historical Society Papers*, 12 (1884): 500–537, and "My Ride Around Baltimore in Eighteen Sixty Four," ibid., 30 (1902): 215–25; McHenry Howard, *Recollections of a Maryland Confederate Soldier and Staff Officer Under Johnston, Jackson, and Lee*, with an introduction by James I. Robertson, Jr. (Dayton, Ohio: Morningside Book Shop, 1975 [Baltimore, 1914]); and "Autobiography of Commodore George Nicholas Hollins, C.S.A.," *MHM*, 34 (1939): 228–43, offer samples of Confederate reminiscences. Besides the pieces listed in Manakee, one might also see Basil William Spalding, "The Confederate Raid on Cumberland in 1865," *MHM*, 36 (1941): 33–38; "Gettysburg Described: Two Letters from a Maryland Confederate," *MHM*, 54 (1959): 210–12; C. A. Porter Hopkins, ed., "The James J. Archer Letters: A Marylander in the Civil War," *MHM*, 56 (1961): 125; and Samuel H. Miller, ed., "Civil War Memoirs of the First Maryland Cavalry, C.S.A.," *MHM*, 58 (1963): 137–69.

Secondary treatments of Maryland Confederates include David Winfred Gaddy, "William Norris and the Confederate Signal and Secret Service," *MHM*, 70 (1975): 167–88, and William Murray Rommel, "A History of the First Maryland Confederate Infantry Regiment" (M.A. thesis, University of Maryland, 1979). For a note on and illustration of the device intended for Southern service, see Timothy Nauman, "Winans' Steam Gun," *MM*, 17 (Winter 1984): 39. Charles A. Earp, "The Amazing Colonel Zarvona," *MHM*, 34 (1939): 334–43, discusses that curious figure. For an update on a Confederate spy who graduated from Mount Washington Female College in Baltimore, see Curtis Carroll Davis, "'The Pet of the Confederacy' Still? Fresh Findings about Belle Boyd," *MHM*, 78 (1982): 35–53.

Perhaps Union veterans thought their record spoke for itself; they published comparatively few reminiscences. Frederick W. Wild, *Memoirs and History of Captain F. W. Alexan-*

der's Baltimore Battery of Light Artillery, U.S.V. (Baltimore, 1912), recounts service with a Baltimore unit that once dueled gray-clad fellow townsmen. See also C. Armour Newcomer, *Coles's Cavalry; or, Three Years in the Saddle in the Shenandoah Valley* (Freeport, N.Y.: Books for Libraries Press, 1970 [Baltimore, 1895]); "Three Civil War Letters of James H. Rigby, a Maryland Federal Artillery Officer," *MHM*, 57 (1962): 155–60, covering Antietam; and William H. James, "A Baltimore Volunteer of 1864," *MHM*, 36 (1941): 22–33, including an account of Monocacy. On raising Union troops in Maryland, see, besides the section above on blacks, Charles Branch Clark, "Recruitment of Union Troops in Maryland," *MHM*, 53 (1958): 153–76, and Millard Les Callette, "A Study of the Recruitment of the Union Army in Maryland" (M.A. thesis, Johns Hopkins University, 1954).

County histories—especially Stegmaier, Dean, Kershaw, and Wiseman, *Allegany County*, Hiebert and MacMaster, *Grateful Remembrance*, and Brooks and Rockel, *History of Baltimore County*—give accounts of the many skirmishes along the Potomac and the engagements that took place during forays like Early's raid on Washington. On major Maryland engagements, see, besides Johnson and Buel, eds., *Battles and Leaders*, Warren W. Hassler, Jr., "The Battle of South Mountain," *MHM*, 52 (1957): 39–64; Stephen W. Sears, *Landscape Turned Red: The Battle of Antietam* (New Haven and New York: Ticknor & Fields, 1983); William A. Frassanito, *Antietam: The Photographic Legacy of America's Bloodiest Day* (New York: Charles Scribner's Sons, 1978); James V. Murfin, *The Gleam of Bayonets: The Battle of Antietam and the Maryland Campaign of 1862* (New York: Thomas Yoseloff, 1965); and Frank Vandiver, *Jubal's Raid* (New York: McGraw-Hill, 1960). Sears supplies a lengthy bibliography. Brad Coker, *The Battle of Monocacy* (Baltimore: University of Baltimore, 1982), surveys the most serious engagement of Early's 1864 campaign.

On prisoners of war held in Maryland, see Edwin W. Beitzell, *Point Lookout Prison Camp for Confederates* (Abell, Md.: privately published, 1972), and Harold Colson, "Point Lookout Prison: An Annotated Bibliography of Personal Narratives," ibid., 29 (1981): 365–70. William B. Hesseltine, *Civil War Prisons: A Study in War Psychology* (Columbus: Ohio State University Press, 1930), provides an overview.

Life on the Maryland home front during the war would make a book in itself. On religious divisions, see Nelson Waite Rightmyer, "The Church in a Border State: Maryland," *HMPEC*, 17 (1948): 411–21; Edward N. Todd, "Bishop Whittingham, Mount Calvary Church, and the Battle of Gettysburg," *MHM*, 60 (1965): 325–28; Richard R. Duncan, "Bishop Whittingham, the Maryland Diocese, and the Civil War," *MHM*, 61 (1966): 329–53; Duncan, "Maryland Methodists and the Civil War," *MHM*, 59 (1964): 350–68; Douglas C. Stange, "Editor Benjamin Kurtz of the *Lutheran Observer* and the Slavery Crisis," *MHM*, 62 (1967): 285–99; and Isaac M. Fein, "Baltimore Jews during the Civil War," *AJHQ*, 51 (1961): 67–96. Virginia Walcott Beauchamp, "The Sisters and the Soldiers," *MHM*, 81 (1986): 117–33, describes the work of the Sisters of Charity at Gettysburg and suggests that their service helped to dampen anti-Catholic feeling.

In "Marylanders and the Invasion of 1862," *CWH*, 11 (1965): 370–83, and "Maryland's Reaction to Early's Raid in 1864: A Summer of Bitterness," *MHM*, 64 (1969): 248–79, Richard R. Duncan gathers impressions of those unsettling experiences. Frederic Shriver Klein, "Meade's Pipe Creek Line," *MHM*, 57 (1962): 133–49, and Klein, ed., *Just South of Gettysburg* (Westminster, Md.: Newman Press, 1963), outline differences among the Shrivers. See also "A Family Letter with Views on Lincoln," *MHM*, 53 (1958): 75–78. Dieter Cunz, "The Maryland Germans in the Civil War," *MHM*, 36 (1941): 394–419, discusses a largely pro-Union group. On Montgomery County, see Virginia Campbell Moore, "Remembrances of Life along the Rockville Pike during the Civil War," *Montgomery County Story*, 27 (1984): 127–42. Alexander Armstrong, "Reminiscences of Judge Richard Henry Alvey, of Hagerstown, 1826–1906," *MHM*, 52 (1957): 124–41, includes an account of Alvey's imprisonment for Confederate sympathies. Raphael Semmes, "Civil War Song Sheets," *MHM*, 38 (1943): 205–29, proves that political conflict found its way into music. On the affection some Marylanders had for generals in gray, see Virginia O. Bardsley, ed., "Frederick Diary: September 5–14, 1862," *MHM*, 60 (1965): 132–38, and the Steuart Maryland Collection, Virginia Historical Society; as an antidote, see Lewis H. Steiner, *Report of Lewis H. Steiner, M.D., . . . Containing a Diary Kept during the Rebel Occupation of Frederick, Md.*, in Richard B. Harwell, ed., *The Union Reader* (New York: Longmans, Green, 1958). Dorothy Mackay Quynn and William Rogers Quynn, "Barbara Friet-schie," *MHM*, 38 (1942): 227–54, 400–413, closely examines the legend and its basis. Though sentiment west of Frederick may have been overwhelmingly pro-Union, see evidence of one exception in *The McKaig Journal, a Confederate Family of Cumberland* (Cumberland: Allegany County Historical Society, 1984).

Chapter 7 surveys the war's impact on education and the Maryland economy, but see Richard R. Duncan, "The College of St. James and the Civil War: A Casualty of War," *HMPEC*, 39 (1970): 265–86; Duncan, "The Social and Economic Impact of the Civil War on Maryland" (Ph.D. dissertation, Ohio State University, 1963); Walter S. Sanderlin, "A House Divided: The Conflict of Loyalties on the Chesapeake and Ohio Canal," *MHM*, 42 (1947): 206–13; Sanderlin, "The Vicissitudes of the Chesapeake and Ohio Canal during the Civil War," *JSH*, 11 (1945). 51–67; Katherine A. Harvey, "The Civil War and the Maryland Coal Trade," *MHM*, 62 (1967): 361–80; Festus P. Summers, "The Baltimore and Ohio: First in War," *CWH*, 7 (1961): 239–54; and William J. Kelley, "Baltimore Steamboats in the Civil War," *MHM*, 37 (1942): 42–52. James I. Robertson, Jr., ed., "A Federal Surgeon at Sharpsburg," *CWH*, 6 (1960): 134–51, details the human cost of Antietam; on the tribulations endured by physicians in gray, see Daniel D. Hartzler, *Maryland Doctors in the C.S.A.* (New Windsor, Md.: privately printed, 1979). For the medical advances wartime surgery and disease brought with them, see Douglas G. Carroll, Jr., "Medical Reforms in Maryland (1848–76)," *MSMJ*, 28 (November 1979): 28–30, and "Medicine in Maryland during the Civil War," *MSMJ*, 28 (July 1979): 25–32. On a news reporter who may have been an undercover Southern agent, see Daniel E. Sutherland, "'Altamont' of the *Tribune*: John Williamson Palmer in the Civil War," *MHM*, 78 (1983): 54–66.

On the Lincoln assassination, one would well begin with two recent efforts to discuss the context and various theories of murder, accusation, and execution: Thomas Reed Turner, *Beware the People Weeping: Public Opinion and the Assassination of Abraham Lincoln* (Baton Rouge: Louisiana State University Press, 1982), and William Hanchett, *The Lincoln Murder Conspiracies . . .* (Urbana: University of Illinois Press, 1983). David M. DeWitt, *The Assassination of Abraham Lincoln and Its Expiation* (New York: Macmillan Co., 1909), stands as a painstaking account. Carl Van Doren Stern, *The Man Who Killed Lincoln* (New York: Random House, 1939), and Stanley Kimmel, *The Mad Booths of Maryland* (Indianapolis, Ind.: Bobbs-Merrill, 1940), offer views of Booth's life and family. Samuel Carter III, *The Riddle of Dr. Mudd* (New York: G. P. Putnam's Sons, 1974), and Blaine Taylor, "Was the Maryland Physician a Victim or Part of the Lincoln Assassination Conspiracy?" *MSMJ*, 25 (April 1976): 35–48, mull over the Charles County doctor who treated Booth's broken leg and paid heavily for it. Alexandra Lee Levin, "Who Hid John H. Surratt, the Lincoln Conspiracy Case Figure?" *MHM*, 60 (1965): 175–84, discusses one member of the enigmatic Surratt family; see also Joseph George, Jr., ed., "'A True Childe of Sorrow.' Two Love Letters of Mary E. Surratt," *MHM*, 80 (1985): 402–5.

7. Gilded Age, Humble Lives

Published primary sources on post–Civil War Maryland include Berlin, Reidy, and Rowland, eds., *Freedom: A Documentary History of Emancipation, 1861–1867*, cited in the chapter 6 bibliography; Philip S. Foner, ed., "Address of Frederick Douglass at the Inauguration of Douglass Institute, Baltimore, October 1, 1865," *JNH*, 54 (1969): 174–83; and, a contemporary assessment, Jeffrey R. Brackett, *Notes on the Progress of the Colored People of Maryland Since the War*, JHUS, 8 (1890). George W. Howard, *Baltimore: The Monumental City* (Baltimore: J. D. Ehlers, 1873); *Industries of Maryland: A Descriptive Review of the Manufacturing and Mercantile Industries of the City of Baltimore* (New York, Philadelphia, and Baltimore: Historical Publishing Co., 1882); and William Hand Browne et al., *Maryland: Its Resources, Industries, and Institutions; Prepared for the Board of World's Fair Managers of Maryland* (Baltimore: Sun Job Printing Office, 1893), contain a wealth of contemporary information. Postbellum magazine pieces descriptive of the Eastern Shore, cited in the chapter notes, are collected and republished in Skip Witson, comp., *Old Maryland* (Albuquerque, N.M.: Sun Books, 1976).

On postwar politics, one might start with William Starr Myers, *The Self-Reconstruction of Maryland, 1864–1867*, JHUS, 27 (1909), and Baker, *Politics of Continuity*. Charles L. Wagandt, "Redemption or Reaction? Maryland in the Post–Civil War Years," in Richard O. Curry, ed., *Radicalism, Racism, and Party Realignment: The Border States during Reconstruction* (Baltimore: Johns Hopkins Press, 1969), recounts the story in a valuable comparative volume. Margaret Law Callcott, *The Negro in Maryland Politics, 1870–1912*, JHUS, 87 (1969), ably handles black enfranchisement and its aftermath. Marc V. Levine, "Standing Political Decisions and Critical Realignment: The Patterns of Maryland Politics, 1872–1948," *Journal of Politics*, 38 (1976): 292–325, examines regional party allegiance for the late nineteenth century. Robert V. Friedenberg, "John A. J. Creswell of Maryland: Reformer in the Post Office," *MHM*, 64 (1969): 133–43, sketches the career of a postwar Republican leader. In *The Story of Maryland Politics* (Baltimore: Thomas and Evans, 1911), the *Sun* political reporter Frank Richardson Kent reminisces and muckrakes; his accounts call for cross-checking. Also see the bibliography for chapter 8.

Fields, *Slavery and Freedom on the Middle Ground*, offers a compelling introduction to the problems blacks faced after gaining their freedom; for other comprehensive studies, see William George Paul, *The Shadow of Equality: The Negro in Baltimore, 1864–1911* (Ann Arbor, Mich.: University Microfilms, 1972), and Richard Paul Fuke, "Black Marylanders, 1864–1868" (Ph.D. dissertation, University of Chicago, 1973). On attempts to control the freedmen and the work of the federal agency established to aid them, see Fuke, "A School for Freed Labor: The Maryland Government Farms, 1864–1866," *Maryland Historian*, 16 (1985): 11–23, and W. A. Low, "The Freedmen's Bureau and Civil Rights in Maryland," *JNH*, 37 (1952): 221–47, and "The Freedmen's Bureau and Education in Maryland," *MHM*, 47 (1952): 29–39. Graham, *Baltimore*, covers George Alexander Hackett and Isaac Myers. Bettye C. Thomas, "A Nineteenth Century Black Operated Shipyard, 1866–1884: Reflections upon Its Inception and Ownership," *JNH*, 59 (1974): 1–12, discusses Myers's remarkable example of black enterprise.

Martha S. Putney, "The Baltimore Normal School for the Education of Colored Teachers: Its Founders and Its Founding," *MHM*, 72 (1977): 238–52, discusses the institution that in 1908 became Bowie State. On the capital, see Sallie M. Ives, "The Formation of a Black Community in Annapolis, 1870–1885," in Robert D. Mitchell and Edward K. Muller, eds., *Geographical Perspectives on Maryland's Past*, Occasional Papers in Geography, no. 4 (College Park: Department of Geography, University of Maryland, 1979). John R. Wennersten, "A Cycle of Race Relations on Maryland's Eastern Shore: Somerset County, 1850–1917," *MHM*, 80 (1985): 377–82, supplies a study one would like to have for every county; on Montgomery, see Nina H. Clark and Lilian B. Brown, *History of the Black Public Schools of Montgomery County, Maryland, 1872–1961* (New York: Vantage Press, 1978), and, for Calvert, A. Y. Dessaint, "Black Culture in Early Twentieth-Century Calvert County," *Calvert County Historical Society News and Notes*, 2 (October 1983): 10–19. George W. McDaniel, *Hearth and Home: Preserving a People's Culture* (Philadelphia: Temple University Press, 1982), makes use of methods usually divided among historians, architectural historians, and anthropologists.

Monographs and special studies of late-nineteenth-century Baltimore include Charles Hirschfeld, *Baltimore, 1870–1900: Studies in Social History*, JHUS, 59 (1941); Eleanor S. Bruchey, "The Development of Baltimore Business, 1880–1914," *MHM*, 64 (1969): 18–42, 144–60; Frank R. Rutter, *The South American Trade of Baltimore*, JHUS, 15 (1897); and Harold K. Kanarek, *A Monument to an Engineer's Skill: William P. Craighill and the Baltimore Harbor* (Baltimore: Baltimore District, U.S. Army Corps of Engineers, c. 1976). Edward F. Keuchel, "Master of the Art of Canning: Baltimore, 1860–1900," *MHM*, 67 (1972): 351–62, treats technology and labor. Helen B. Sollins and Moses Aberbach, "The Baltimore Spice Company," *Generations*, 3 (June 1982): 10–22, mentions the Brunn family enterprise; Milford H. Whitehill and Robert L. Weinberg, "Greif: One of Baltimore's Great Names in the Clothing Industry," ibid., pp. 47–51, sketches that family business.

Baltimore neighborhoods and industrial districts have been the subject of interesting recent studies. Joseph Garonzik, "The Racial and Ethnic Make-up of Baltimore Neighborhoods, 1850–70," *MHM*, 71 (1976): 392–402, surveys mid-nineteenth-century patterns. Michael S. Franch, "The Congregational Community in the Changing City, 1840–70," *MHM*, 71 (1976): 367–80, discusses church response to the exodus to new areas. Joseph

Hirschman, "Housing Patterns of Baltimore Jews," *Generations*, 2 (December 1981): 30–43, informally traces movement within the Jewish community; but see also Fein, *Making of an American Jewish Community*. On the Polish community in the 1870s, see Tomasz L. Cholochwost, "The Emergence of Baltimore's Polonia," *Polish Heritage*, 35 (1984): 12. Kelly, *Peabody Heights to Charles Village*, uses text and photos to chart growth in that fashionable neighborhood after 1870. Joseph L. Arnold, "Suburban Growth and Municipal Annexation, 1745–1918," *MHM*, 73 (1978): 109–28, treats the campaign that led to the 1888 city enlargement. On the imitative style and essential economy of working-class housing, see Mary Ellen Hayward, "Urban Vernacular Architecture in Nineteenth-Century Baltimore," *Winterthur Portfolio*, 16 (1981): 33–63.

Since 1970 sociologists and urban geographers have made considerable gains in the study of Baltimore. Besides Olson, *Baltimore*, see Olson, "Baltimore Imitates 'Spider,' " *Association of American Geographers Annals*, 69 (1979): 557–74. Edward K. Muller and Paul A. Groves, University of Maryland geographers, have made pathbreaking contributions; see their "The Changing Location of the Clothing Industry: A Link to the Social Geography of Baltimore in the Nineteenth Century," *MHM*, 71 (1976): 403–20, exploring the close relationship between immigrant concentrations and work on ready-made garments; "The Emergence of Industrial Districts in Mid-Nineteenth Century Baltimore," *Geographical Review*, 69 (1979): 159–78; and, a comparison of Baltimore and Washington, D.C., "The Evolution of Black Residential Areas in Late Nineteenth Century Cities," *Journal of Historical Geography*, 1 (1975): 169–91. In neighborhood-specific studies D. Randall Beirne has made clear the persistence of working-class populations in these years (and later); see his "Residential Stability among Urban Workers: Industrial Linkage in Hampden-Woodberry, Baltimore, 1880–1930," in Mitchell and Muller, eds., *Geographical Perspectives on Maryland's Past*, pp. 168–87; "Residential Growth Stability in the Baltimore Industrial Community of Canton during the Late Nineteenth Century," *MHM*, 74 (1979): 39–51; and "Late Nineteenth Century Industrial Communities in Baltimore," *Maryland Historian*, 11 (1980): 39–49. All these works draw on his "Steadfast Americans: Residential Stability among Workers in Baltimore, 1880–1930" (Ph.D. dissertation, University of Maryland, 1976). W. Theodore Dürr, "People of the Peninsula," *MHM*, 77 (1982): 27–53, examines South Baltimore and Locust Point. Martha J. Vill, "Immigrants and Ownership: Home Mortgage Financing in Baltimore, 1865–1914," in Mitchell and Muller, eds., *Geographical Perspectives on Maryland's Past*, examines savings banks; see also Vill, "Residential Development on a Landed Estate: The Case of Baltimore's 'Harlem,' " *MHM*, 77 (1982): 266–78. For an introduction to all this work, see Arnold, "Baltimore's Neighborhoods, 1800–1980," *Working Papers from the Regional Economic History Research Center*, 4 (nos. 1 and 2, 1981), 75–98.

On late-nineteenth-century oyster craft and steamboats, see the general bibliography. John H. Murphy, "Plain and Fancy Travel on the Bay Steamers," *MM*, 12 (Autumn 1979): 25–26, supplies an illustrated short piece. John R. Wennersten's "The Almighty Oyster: A Saga of Old Somerset and the Eastern Shore, 1850–1920," *MHM*, 74 (1979): 80–93, and *Oyster Wars of the Chesapeake Bay* (Centreville, Md.: Tidewater Publishers, 1981), handle disputes over oyster beds and offer useful bibliographies. R. Lee Burton, *Canneries of the Eastern Shore* (Centreville, Md.: Tidewater Press, 1986), treats a leading peninsula industry of the period. Paula J. Johnson, ed., *Working the Water: The Commercial Fisheries of Maryland's Patuxent River* (Charlottesville: University Press of Virginia, 1987), contains essays on the history of the Patuxent fisheries, the watermen's romantic image, and the experience of packing house workers. Carl N. Everstine, "The Potomac River and Maryland's Boundaries," *MHM*, 80 (1985): 355–69, recounts events leading up to and surrounding the 1877 survey.

Postwar economic history on the Western Shore partook of agricultural change, railroad expansion, the rise of extractive industry, and labor tension. Donald McCauley, "The Urban Impact on Agricultural Land Use: Farm Patterns in Prince George's County, Maryland, 1860–1880," in Land, Carr, and Papenfuse, eds., *Law, Society, and Politics in Early Maryland*, notes the high availability of credit there (a low incidence of sharecropping and high rate of mortgaged farms), the proximity of Baltimore and Washington markets, and the consequent shift from tobacco to diversified crops. John W. McGrain,

"'Good Bye Old Burr': The Roller Mill Revolution in Maryland, 1882," *MHM*, 77 (1982): 154–71, treats a major change in milling and the competition it brought small Maryland firms. On the completion of rail networks, besides local and corporate histories, see William B. Catton, "John W. Garrett of the Baltimore and Ohio: A Study in Seaport and Railroad Competition, 1820–1874" (Ph.D. dissertation, Northwestern University, 1959); Joseph S. Clark, Jr., "The Railroad Struggle for Pittsburgh. Forty-three Years of Philadelphia-Baltimore Rivalry, 1838–1871," *PMHB*, 48 (1924): 1–37; J. Randolph Kean, "The Development of the 'Valley Line' of the Baltimore and Ohio Railroad," *VMHB*, 60 (1952): 537–50; John C. Hayman, *Rails along the Chesapeake: A History of Railroading on the Delmarva Peninsula, 1827–1978* (n.p.: Marvadel Publishers, 1979); and Benjamin F. G. Kline, Jr., *Tall Pines and Winding Rivers: The Logging Railroads of Maryland* (Lancaster, Pa.: privately published, 1976). Thomas F. Hahn, *The C&O Canal Boatmen, 1892–1924* (Shepherdstown, W.Va.: American Canal and Transportation Center, 1980), collects life and times material; see also his *The C&O Canal: An Illustrated History* (Shepherdstown, W.Va.: American Canal and Transportation Center, 1982) and *The Chesapeake and Ohio Canal: Pathway to the Nation's Capital* (Metuchen, N.J.: Scarecrow Press, 1984). John Ralph Miele, "The Chesapeake and Ohio Canal: A Physical History" (M.A. thesis, University of Delaware, 1969), treats the losing maintenance battle. Elizabeth Kytle, *Home on the Canal* (Cabin John, Md.: Seven Locks Press, 1983), combines history and interviews with eleven people who worked on the canal.

Katherine A. Harvey, *The Best-Dressed Miners: Life and Labor in the Maryland Coal Region, 1835–1910* (Ithaca, N.Y.: Cornell University Press, 1969), represents high achievement in social and labor history. Ann Cowie, "Cardiff, Where Slate Was King," *MM*, 15 (Autumn 1982): 33–35, profiles a heavily Welsh, Harford County slate quarry of the period. Clifton K. Yearley, Jr., "The Baltimore and Ohio Strike of 1877," *MHM*, 51 (1956): 188–211; Malcolm H. Lauchheimer, *The Labor Law of Maryland*, JHUS, 37 (1919); R. T. Crane, "The Knights of Labor Movement in Baltimore," *Johns Hopkins University Circulars*, 22 (1902–3); and Jonathan Garlock, comp., *Guide to the Local Associations of the Knights of Labor* (Westport, Conn.: Greenwood Press, 1982), provide some material for the unwritten history of Maryland labor. Roderick N. Ryon, "Baltimore Workers and Industrial Decision-Making, 1890–1917," *JSH*, 51 (1985): 565–80, and Carolyn Daniel McCreesh, "On the Picket Line: Militant Women Campaign to Organize Garment Workers, 1880–1917" (Ph.D. dissertation, University of Maryland, 1975), study the help workers supplied themselves in these years. John Tracy Ellis, *The Life of James Cardinal Gibbons* (2 vols.; Milwaukee: Bruce Publishing Co., 1952), treats the Catholic prelate who was the working people's friend.

Local and older histories discuss recreation of the period, but gunning and the rise of baseball have drawn particular interest. See Harry M. Walsh, *The Outlaw Gunner* (Cambridge: Tidewater Publishers, 1971), and, on the Orioles, Bready, *Home Team*, Lieb, *Baltimore Orioles*, and John H. Lancaster, "Baltimore: A Pioneer in Organized Baseball," *MHM*, 35 (1940): 32–55.

8. Non-Pilgrim's Progress

Among contemporary and edited works that shed light on this chapter's issues, Bernard C. Steiner, *Citizenship and Suffrage in Maryland* (Baltimore: Cushing & Co., 1896), and Clayton Colman Hall, ed., *Baltimore: Its History and Its People* (3 vols.; New York and Chicago: Lewis Historical Publishing Co., 1912), prove useful.

Katherine B. Dehler, "Mt. Vernon Place at the Turn of the Century: A Vignette of the Garrett Family," *MHM*, 69 (1974): 279–92, looks into the living styles of one wealthy Baltimore family; see also Jean Jepson Page, "Notes on the Contributions of Francis Blackwell Mayer and His Family to the Cultural History of Maryland," *MHM*, 76 (1981): 217–39. Community and sporting histories in the general bibliography illuminate large themes in elite recreation. Warren and Warren, *Time Exposures*, pictures and discusses places like Bay Ridge and Chesapeake Beach. On Douglass's Highland Beach, see Carroll Greene, Jr., "The Rebuff That Inspired a Town," *MM*, 7 (Summer 1974): 49–52. Andrea Price Stevens, "Suburban Summer Resorts in Montgomery County, Maryland, 1870–1910" (M.A. thesis, George Washington University, 1980), explores Rhineland on the Potomac and its competitors; on early Chevy Chase, see Roderick S. French, "Chevy Chase Village in the Context of the National Suburban Movement," *RCHS*, 49 (1973–74): 300–329. Caleb Winslow, "Garrett Vacations in the Victorian Era," *MM*, 1 (Summer 1969): 2–7, treats hunting expeditions in far western Maryland. Allison K. Hoagland, "Deer Park Hotel," *MHM*, 73 (1978): 340–51, examines the B&O lodge in Garrett County. Patricia Catherine Click, "Leisure in the Upper South in the Nineteenth Century: A Study of Trends in Baltimore, Norfolk, and Richmond" (Ph.D. dissertation, University of Virginia, 1980), surveys developments by class and sex. Eleanor Stephens Bruchey, *The Business Elite in Baltimore, 1880–1914*, in the series Companies and Men, Business Enterprise in America, ed. Stuart Bruchey and Vincent P. Carosso (New York: Arno Press, 1976), provides a collective biography of 168 commercial leaders—examining their recruitment, business experience, memberships, and participation in civic life.

Accounts of the major philanthropists, all of them treated in Allen Johnson and Dumas Malone, eds., *Dictionary of American Biography* (22 vols.; New York: Charles Scribner's Sons, 1928–44), include William R. Johnston, "William and Henry Walters: Collectors and Philanthropists," *Walters Art Gallery Bulletin*, 27, no. 3 (1974); Franklin Parker, *George Peabody: A Biography* (Nashville, Tenn.: Vanderbilt University Press, 1971); Richard H. Hart, *Enoch Pratt: The Story of a Plain Man* (Baltimore: Enoch Pratt Free Library, 1935); and Helen Hopkins Thom, *Johns Hopkins: A Silhouette* (Baltimore: Johns Hopkins Press, 1929). The time has come for fresh studies of these figures, their motives, and their world. Roy E. Robinson, "The Peabody Institute of Baltimore: Ideas Implicit in Its Founding," *Essex Institute Historical Collections*, 106 (1970): 54–61, explores Peabody's plan as an example of instrumentalism in action. Samuel Eliot Morison, *Nathaniel Holmes Morison, 1815–1890, Provost of the Peabody Institute of Baltimore, 1867–1890* (Baltimore: Peabody Institute, 1957), surveys the contributions of an early fixture at the Institute. Luther H. Evans, "The First Sixty Years; The Enoch Pratt Free Library: An Appreciation," *Library Journal*, 71 (1946): 227–35, collects evidence of the Pratt's early importance; see also Stanley Rubinstein, "The Role of the Trustees and the Librarians in the Development of the Enoch Pratt Free Library and the Free Library of Philadelphia" (Ph.D. dissertation, George Washington University, 1978).

The Johns Hopkins University and medical institutions have received their due in scholarly attention. Franklin Parker, "Influences on the Founder of the Johns Hopkins University and the Johns Hopkins Hospital," *BHM*, 34 (1960): 148–53, explores the parts John W. Garrett and George Peabody played in shaping Hopkins's plans; see also Hugh D. Hawkins, "George William Brown and His Influence on the Johns Hopkins University," *MHM*, 52 (1957): 173–86. Hawkins, *Pioneer: A History of the Johns Hopkins University, 1874–1889* (Ithaca, N.Y.: Cornell University Press, 1960), places the university in its intellectual and social setting and provides a helpful bibliography covering early faculty members. Abraham Flexner, *Daniel Coit Gilman, Creator of the American Type of University* (New York: Harcourt, Brace & Company, 1946), covers the first president; Kathryn A. Jacob, "The Hopkins Four," *Johns Hopkins Magazine*, 25 (1974): 17–26, discusses Gildersleeve, Sylvester, Rowland, and Remsen; Hugh Kenner, "Looking for the Golden Age," ibid., 27 (1976): 53–58, treats Henry Rowland in an issue that includes other centennial pieces. See also Stewart H. Hulse and Bert F. Green, eds., *One Hundred Years of Psychological Research in America: G. Stanley Hall and the Johns Hopkins Tradition* (Baltimore: Johns Hopkins University Press, 1986). The history seminar has had its own students; see John Higham, "Herbert Baxter Adams and the Study of Local History," *AHR*, 89 (1984): 1225–39; Raymond J. Cunningham, "The German Historical World of Herbert Baxter Adams: 1874–1876," *JAH*, 68 (1981): 261–75; and Wendell H. Stevenson, "Herbert Baxter Adams and Southern Historical Scholarship at the Johns Hopkins University," *MHM*, 42 (1947): 1–20. Adams's colleagues produced *Herbert B. Adams, Tributes of Friends, with a Bibliography of the Department of History, Politics, and Economics of the Johns Hopkins University, 1876–1901*, JHUS, extra volume 23 (1902).

The general bibliography includes broad surveys in medical history. On Hopkins's early leadership, see Simon Flexner and James Thomas Flexner, *William Henry Welch and the Heroic Age of American Medicine* (New York: Viking Press, 1941); Donald H. Fleming, *William H. Welch and the Rise of Modern Medicine*, Library of American Biography (Boston:

Little, Brown & Co., 1954); Harvey W. Cushing, *The Life of William Osler* (2 vols.; Oxford: Clarendon Press, 1925); and Richard H. Shryock, *The Unique Influence of the Johns Hopkins University on American Medicine* (Copenhagen: Ejnar Munksgaard, 1953). See also Richard H. Shryock, "Dr. Welch and Medical History," *BJHH*, supplement, 87 (August 1950): 19–27; Alan Gregg, "Dr. Welch's Influence on Medical Education," *BJHH*, supplement, 87 (August 1950): 28–36; Gert H. Brieger, "The California Origins of the Johns Hopkins Medical School," *BHM*, 51 (1977): 339–52; and Frederick B. Bang, "History of Tissue Culture at Johns Hopkins," *BHM*, 51 (1977): 516–37.

Callcott, *History of the University of Maryland*, supplies background and context for "Medical Annals of Maryland, 1899–1925," a series of articles edited and compiled by Lester H. Miles and published in the *MSMJ*: John Ruhrah, "History of the Medical and Chirurgical Faculty, 1899–1925," 24 (May 1975): 62–66, (July 1975): 55–61, (September 1975): 49–53; Randolph Winslow, "Recollections of Fifty Years of the Medical and Chirurgical Faculty," 24 (November 1975): 65–70; James H. Rowland, "Summary of Obstetrical Service in Baltimore from the Late 1880s to 1926," 24 (October 1975): 46–49; I. William Nachles, "History of Orthopedics in Maryland through 1925," 25 (April 1976): 64–69; Isaac R. Pels, "A Brief History of Dermatology in Maryland through 1932," 25 (July 1976): 57–62; Jesse W. Downey, Jr., "Otology in Maryland and Baltimore through 1925," 25 (November 1976): 59–63; Jonas S. Friedenwald, "Opthalmology in Maryland through 1925," 26 (September 1977): 63–68; Charles A. Waters, "Development of Roentgenology in Maryland, 1895–1926," 26 (November 1977): 55–60; Alexius McGlannan, "Pre-1932 Surgery," 28 (January 1979): 63–66; John C. Krantz, Jr., "Pharmacology in Maryland through 1925," 28 (March 1979): 61–67; and Samuel Morrison, "Nutrition in Maryland, 1899–1928," 28 (September 1979): 105–11. See also Theodore E. Woodward, "Charles Frick: Professor of Materia Medica, 1823–1860," *MSMJ*, 35 (1986): 577–82. On dentistry, see Harry Bryan McCarthy, "History of Dental Education in Maryland" (M.A. thesis, University of Maryland, 1948).

The leading monograph of Baltimore reform, James B. Crooks, *Politics and Progress: The Rise of Urban Progressivism in Baltimore, 1895 to 1911* (Baton Rouge: Louisiana State University Press, 1968), dwells less on the political roots of the movement than on social reform; but see also his "Politics and Reform: The Dimensions of Baltimore Progressivism," *MHM*, 71 (1976): 421–27. In "From Party Tickets to Secret Ballots: The Evolution of the Electoral Process in Maryland during the Gilded Age," *MHM*, 82 (1987): 214–39, Peter H. Argersinger contributes greatly to our understanding of how state politicsm"worked" on election day and offers both a supplement to Crooks and an improvement upon Kent, *Story of Maryland Politics*. Raymond Stanley Sweeney, *Progressivism in Maryland, 1900–1917* (Ann Arbor, Mich.: University Microfilms, 1972), includes a statistical breakdown of "progressives" and "conservatives" and chapters on reform support in the counties and among labor organizations.

The targets of political reform remain a bit obscure. Rasin, who left little source material, lacks a published biography; one may begin with Mary Anne Dunn, O.S.F., "The Life of Isaac Freeman Rasin, Democratic Leader of Baltimore from 1870–1907" (M.S. thesis, Catholic University of America, 1949). M. Rosewin Sweeney, "'Sonny' Mahon and Baltimore's Irish Machine: Ethnic Politics in a Semi-Southern Setting" (M.A. thesis, Johns Hopkins University, 1979), treats Rasin's lieutenant. On Gorman, see John R. Lambert, *Arthur Pue Gorman*, Southern Biography Series, ed. Fred C. Cole and Wendell H. Stevenson (Baton Rouge: Louisiana State University Press, 1953), and Walter S. Sanderlin, "Arthur P. Gorman and the Chesapeake and Ohio Canal: An Episode in the Rise of a Political Boss," *JSH*, 13 (1947): 323–37. For personal testimony and contemporary evidence, see John Joseph Mahon, "Autobiography of a Baltimore Boss," Baltimore *Sun*, 1, 8, 15, and 22 October 1922; Ferdinand C. Latrobe, "Personal Memoirs of Ferdinand C. Latrobe" (two-volume typescript owned in 1968 by the mayor's daughter-in-law, Mrs. Ferdinand C. Latrobe II); Ferdinand C. Latrobe II, ed., "Running the City a Generation Ago," *Sun*, 1 March 1931 (clippings file, MHS); John R. Lambert, Jr., "The Autobiographical Writings of Senator Arthur Pue Gorman," *MHM*, 58 (1963): 93–122, 233–46; and "The Crescent Club of Baltimore," *Frank Leslie's Illustrated Weekly*, 63 (11 December 1886): 261–63. Bayly Ellen Marks, "Liberal Education in the Gilded Age: Baltimore and the Creation of the

Manual Training School," *MHM*, 74 (1979): 238–52, portrays the public school system before the new city charter. See also Gerald M. McDonald, "Politics and Public Works: Baltimore before Progressivism" (Ph.D. dissertation, Johns Hopkins University, 1986).

One finds colorful personalities among the Progressives as well as the bosses. Allen Walker Rumble, "Rectitude and Reform: Charles J. Bonaparte and the Politics of Gentility, 1851–1921" (Ph.D. dissertation, University of Maryland, 1971), studies one Progressive whom a few Baltimoreans believed overrated. Alexandra Lee Levin, *Dare to Be Different: A Biography of Louis H. Levin of Baltimore* (New York: Bloch Publishing Co., 1972), treats an early leader of the Federated Jewish Charities and editor of the Baltimore *Jewish Comment*. William L. Marbury, *The Story of an American Family* (Baltimore: privately printed, 1966), notices political-judicial reform leaders; H. H. Walker Lewis, *The Lawyers' Round Table of Baltimore and Its Charter Members* (Baltimore: MHS, 1978), surveys, with occasional humor, a circle formed in 1911 and made up of some attorneys and judges who took part in the earlier "good judges" struggle. Nicholas C. Burckel, "Governor Austin Lane Crothers and Progressive Reform in Maryland, 1908–1912," *MHM*, 76 (1981): 184–201, traces a career that led indirectly to Progressivism.

Marking the rise of professions like teaching and health, Progressives registered positive social changes. See Andrea R. Andrews, "The Baltimore School Building Program, 1870 to 1900: A Study of Urban Reform," *MHM*, 70 (1975): 260–74, and Raymond S. Sweeney, "Public Education in Maryland in the Progressive Era," *MHM*, 62 (1967): 28–46. Marilyn Thornton Williams, "Philanthropy in the Progressive Era: The Public Baths of Baltimore," *MHM*, 72 (1977): 118–31, discusses that Walters-financed effort.

Lloyd C. Taylor, Jr., *The Medical Profession and Social Reform, 1885–1945* (New York: St. Martin's Press, 1974), places the health concerns of Progressive Maryland physicians in a national setting. Besides the biographies above and Fee, *Disease and Discovery*, see Allen W. Freeman, "The Influence of Dr. William H. Welch on Public Health," *BJHH*, supplement, 87 (August 1950): 12–18, and Capper, Power, and Shivers, *Chesapeake Waters*. William B. Mathews, "The Beginnings of the Tuberculosis Sanatorium Movement in Maryland," *MSMJ*, 25 (August 1976): 28–31, and George H. Preston, "History of State Institutions and Private Sanitoriums for the Insane Prior to 1930," *MSMJ*, 26 (February 1977): 42–46, treat the slow rise of organized care. William Travis Howard, Jr., *Public Health Administration and the Natural History of Disease in Baltimore, Maryland, 1797–1920* (Washington, D.C.: Carnegie Institution, 1924), examined the movement for urban reform as a response, finally based on microscopic science, to repeated epidemics.

As the many essays on women activists in Helmes, ed., *Notable Maryland Women*, demonstrate, women played an important part in the Progressive movement. Alexandra Lee Levin, *Henrietta Szold: Baltimorean* (Baltimore: Jewish Historical Society of Maryland, 1976), provides a biography of a leading Progressive and later Zionist. For important records gathered in preparation for a world's fair exhibit, see Cynthia Horsburgh Requardt, ed., "The Origins of Jewish Women's Social Service Work in Baltimore," *Generations*, 5 (June 1984): 28–64. Requardt, "Alternative Professions for Goucher College Graduates, 1892–1910," *MHM*, 74 (1979): 274–81, and Sister Bridget Marie Engelmeyer, "A Maryland First," *MHM*, 78 (1983): 186–204, observe that educational experience helped stir the impulse to take on demanding social responsibilities. On whether, and if so why, more middle-class women attended college in the late nineteenth century, and other questions, see Patricia Anne McDonald, "Baltimore Women, 1870–1900" (Ph.D. dissertation, University of Maryland, 1976). Marjorie Housepian Dobkin, ed., with a foreword by Millicent Carey McIntosh, *The Making of a Feminist Lady: Early Journals of M. Carey Thomas* (Kent, Ohio: Kent State University Press, 1979), and Lucy Fisher West, comp., *The Papers of M. Carey Thomas in the Bryn Mawr College Archives: Reel Guide and Index to the Microfilm Collection* (Woodbridge, Conn.: Research Publications, 1982), make available important manuscript collections.

On Maryland's pathbreaking labor-injury legislation, proving that workers in the state had the political power to bring about reforms of their own, see Evelyn Ellen Singleton, *Workmen's Compensation in Maryland*, JHUS, 53 (1935), and Thomas D. Masterson, "David J. Lewis of Maryland: Formative and Progressive Years" (Ph.D. dissertation, Georgetown University, 1976). Joyce E. Wessel, "Learning to Cooperate: The Origins of the Maryland

State Dairymen's Association" (M.A. thesis, University of Virginia, 1980), examines the rise of organized self-interest among farmers—especially as milk-inspection laws led to increased urban demand. Joseph L. Arnold, "The Neighborhood and City Hall: The Origin of Neighborhood Associations in Baltimore, 1880–1911," *Journal of Urban History*, 6 (1979): 3–30, locates the sources of these local pressure groups in the city political culture and rising middle-class expectations. Of course Progressives often cultivated their interests as well as public health and human welfare. On the self-serving aims of Progressive zoning restrictions, see Garrett Power, "High Society: The Building Height Limitations on Baltimore's Mt. Vernon Place," *MHM*, 79 (1984): 197–219, and "Pyrrhic Victory: Daniel Goldman's Defeat of Zoning in the Maryland Court of Appeals," *MHM*, 82 (1987): 275–87. In "Mini-Revisionism in City Planning History: The Planners of Roland Park," *Journal of the Society of Architectural Historians*, 29 (1970): 347–49, and "Planning Roland Park," *MHM*, 67 (1972): 419–28, Harry G. Schalck examines the early history of that speculative development; on a nearby enterprise, see J. Gilman D'Arcy Paul, "A Baltimore Estate: Guilford and Its Three Owners," *MHM*, 51 (1956): 14–26. For a methodologically unusual study—attempting a model of public services, land values, and elite interests—see Alan D. Anderson, *The Origin and Resolution of an Urban Crisis: Baltimore, 1890–1930*, Johns Hopkins Studies in Urban Affairs (Baltimore: Johns Hopkins University Press, 1977); for a comment, see Arnold's review, *MHM*, 74 (1979): 94–96.

James B. Crooks, "The Baltimore Fire and Baltimore Reform," *MHM*, 65 (1970): 1–17, examines attempts thereafter to resolve conflicts between public and private interests. See also Christine Rosen, *The Limits of Power: Great Fires and the Process of City Growth in America* (New Rochelle, N.Y.: Cambridge University Press, 1986).

Studies in the black experience during these years lay stress on education and struggles over the franchise. See Bettye C. Thomas, "Public Education and Black Protest in Baltimore, 1865–1900," *MHM*, 71 (1976): 301–91; John R. Wennersten and Ruth Ellen Wennersten, "Separate and Unequal: The Evolution of a Black Land Grant College in Maryland, 1890–1930," *MHM*, 72 (1977): 110–17; Martha S. Putney, "The Formative Years of Maryland's First Black Postsecondary School," *MHM*, 73 (1978): 168–79; and Putney, "The Black Colleges in the Maryland State College System: Quest for Equal Opportunity, 1908–1975," *MHM*, 75 (1980): 335–43. Callcott, *Negro in Maryland Politics*, explains the appearance and defeat of anti-black voting legislation; see also Jane L. Phelps, "Charles J. Bonaparte and Negro Suffrage in Maryland," *MHM*, 54 (1959): 331–52. Suzanne Ellery Greene, "Black Republicans on the Baltimore City Council, 1890–1931," *MHM*, 74 (1979): 203–22, examines the careers of six black members of the Republican party who won city elections.

9. Searching for the Middle in Modern America

The early twentieth century brought changes that recommend a social historian's approach to the period. In a brief general history, Charles T. LeViness, *A History of Road Building in Maryland* (Baltimore: State Roads Commission of Maryland, 1958), recounts highway improvements that the automobile forced on state authorities. Rector R. Seal, *Maryland Automobile History, 1900 to 1942* (Chicago: Adams Press, 1985), supplies an interesting, illustrated survey of the industry. On the Naval Academy, see, besides Warren and Warren, *Everybody Works but John Paul Jones*, Charles Todorich, *The Spirited Years: A History of the Antebellum Naval Academy* (Annapolis: Naval Institute Press, 1984), and Peter Karsten, *The Naval Aristocracy: The Golden Age of Annapolis and the Emergence of Modern American Navalism* (New York: Free Press, 1972). For a generally reliable introduction to aviation in Maryland, see John F. R. Scott, Jr., *Voyages into Airy Regions* (Annapolis: Ann Arundell County Historical Society and Fishergate Publishing Co., 1984). William F. Lynd, "The Army Flying School at College Park," *MHM*, 48 (1953): 227–41, and Ken Beatty, *The Cradle of American Aviation: The National Aviation Field, College Park, Md.* (Hagerstown, Md.: Hagerstown Bookbinding and Printing Co., 1976), discuss that pioneer landing field. On another early installation, see James R. Dorsey, "Men at War, Edgewood Arsenal, Md., 1918," *Harford Historical Bulletin* (Winter 1986): 19–32. Contemporary accounts of Maryland military contributions during World War I include Raymond S. Tompkins, *Maryland Fighters in the Great War* (Baltimore: Thomas & Evans, 1919), and John A. Cutchins, *History of the Twenty-Ninth Division "Blue and Gray" 1917–1919* . . . (Philadelphia: MacCalla & Co., 1921). On loyalties the war divided, see Cunz, *Maryland Germans*.

Olson, *Baltimore*, and Hiebert and MacMaster, *Grateful Remembrance*, discuss the war's economic and demographic impact, as do studies of suburban Washington communities cited in the general bibliography. See also W. Edward Orser, "The Making of a Baltimore Rowhouse Community: The Edmondson Avenue Area, 1915–1945," *MHM*, 80 (1985): 203–27; Steven Lubar, "Trolley Lines, Land Speculation, and Community Building: The Early History of Woodside Park, Silver Spring, Maryland," *MHM*, 81 (1986): 316–29; Louis N. Markwood, *The Forest Glen Trolley and the Early Development of Silver Spring* (Arlington, Va.: National Capital Historical Museum of Transportation, c. 1975); William J. Ellenberger, "History of the Street Car Lines of Montgomery County," *Montgomery County Story*, 17 (1974): 1–10; Robert McQuail Bachman, "The Evolution of a Railroad Suburb: Takoma Park, Maryland, 1883–1942" (M.A. thesis, George Washington University, 1975); and John Armentrout, "The History of Land Development in Montgomery County Adjacent to the National Capital" (Tau Beta Pi thesis, University of Maryland, 1936).

On Ritchie's first gubernatorial term, its issues, and its setting, see Dorothy M. Brown, "Maryland Between the Wars," in Walsh and Fox, eds., *Maryland*; Joseph B. Chepaitis, "Albert C. Ritchie in Power, 1920–1927," *MHM*, 68 (1973): 383–404; and Joseph L. Arnold, "The Last of the Bad Old Days: Politics in Baltimore, 1920–1950," *MHM*, 71 (1976): 443–48. Edwin Rothman, "Factional Machine Politics: William Curran and the Baltimore City Democratic Organization, 1929–1946" (Ph.D. dissertation, Johns Hopkins University, 1949), examines Ritchie's urban cohorts. Emma Maddox Funck, "Maryland," in volume 6 of Ida Husted Harper, ed., *History of Woman Suffrage* (6 vols.; New York: Arno Press, 1969 [New York, 1922]), treats the movement that Ritchie resisted and finally bowed to; see also Mal Hee Son, "The Women's Suffrage Movement in Maryland from 1870 to 1920" (M.A. thesis, University of Maryland, 1962), and various contributions in Helmes, ed., *Notable Maryland Women*.

On Maryland diversions in these years, see appropriate vertical files in the Maryland Room, Pratt Library, and recollections like Michael L. Berger, "Farmers, Flivvers, and Family Life, 1900–1929," *Chronicles of St. Mary's*, 32 (July 1984): 165–75, and Lou Rose, "Social Attitudes toward Prohibition: A Calvert County Example," *Calvert County Historical Society News*, 2 (January 1983): 1–2. Marylanders who traveled by air likely made use of Harbor Field, which William G. LeFurgy discusses in "Baltimore's Municipal Airport," *Aviation Quarterly*, 7 (1983): 172–88. Ruth has two biographers: Karl Wagenheim, *Babe Ruth: His Life and Legend* (New York: Praeger Publishers, 1974), and the witty, insightful Marshall Smelser, *The Life That Ruth Built: A Biography* (New York: Quadrangle, New York Times Book Co., 1975). Robert Victor Leffler, "The History of Black Baseball in Baltimore from 1913 to 1951" (M.A. thesis, Morgan State University, 1974), and Matthew Whitehorn, "The Baltimore Elite Giants and the Decline of Negro Baseball" (M.A. thesis, Johns Hopkins University, 1981), discuss the teams that the color barrier created. Roderick N. Ryon, "Old West Baltimore," *MHM*, 77 (1982): 54–69, treats Baltimore black society in the 1920s; see also Ralph L. Pearson, "The National Urban League Comes to Baltimore," *MHM*, 72 (1977): 523–33. Al Rose, *Eubie Blake* (New York: Schirmer Books, 1979), offers a lively and amply illustrated life of Blake, with appendixes listing his music and recordings. Richard Alan Disharoon, "A History of Municipal Music in Baltimore, 1914–1947" (Ph.D. dissertation, University of Maryland, 1980), examines a pathbreaking civic program; Blanche Klasmer Cohen, "Benjamin Klasmer's Contribution to Baltimore's Musical History," *MHM*, 72 (1977): 272–76, discusses an Hungarian-born violinist who played in the first Baltimore Symphony and later conducted a Jewish Educational Alliance Orchestra. Robert Kirk Headley, Jr., *Exit: A History of Movies in Baltimore* (University Park, Md.: privately printed, 1974), offers sidelights on early films and theaters. In a similar vein, see Gilbert Sandler, "Radio as Radio Used to Be," *Baltimore*, 60 (1967): 25, 82, 87. Sheryl R. Cucchiella, photos by John Kardys and others, *Baltimore Deco* (Baltimore: Maclay & Associates, 1985), examines surviving examples of the style that surfaced in the prosperous 1920s.

One must consult Shivers, *Maryland Wits and Baltimore Bards*, on Maryland writers in this period. Among them, Hammett and Cain have won recent scholarly notice. See, for example, Sinda Gregory, *Private Investigations: The Novels of Dashiell Hammett* (Carbondale: Southern Illinois University Press, 1985); William F. Nolan, *Hammett: A Life at the Edge* (New York: Congdon & Ward, 1983); Peter Wolfe, *Beams Falling: The Art of Dashiell Hammett* (Bowling Green, Ohio: Bowling Green University Press, 1980); and Roy Hoopes, *Cain* (New York: Holt, Rinehart & Winston, 1982). Both hard-boiled authors have a volume in the Twayne series: William Marling, *Dashiell Hammett* (New York: Twayne Publishers, 1983), and David Madden, *James M. Cain* (New York: Twayne Publishers, 1970).

A short list of Menckeniana (the Enoch Pratt Free Library publishes a journal by that name) might begin with Carl Bode, *Mencken* (Carbondale: Southern Illinois University Press, 1969), the leading biography; Douglas C. Stenerson, *H.L. Mencken: Iconoclast from Baltimore* (Chicago: University of Chicago Press, 1971); William Manchester, *H. L. Mencken: Disturber of the Peace* (New York: Harper & Bros., 1950), a vivid life by a writer then working for the *Sun*; Alistair Cooke, ed., *The Vintage Mencken* (New York: Vintage Books, 1955), a sampling of his writings with a brief introduction; Malcolm Moos, ed., *H. L. Mencken on Politics* (New York: Vintage Books, 1960 [Baltimore, 1956]); William H. Nolte, *H. L. Mencken, Literary Critic* (Middletown, Conn.: Wesleyan University Press, 1966), an authoritative study; and Charles A. Fecher, *Mencken: A Study of His Thought* (New York: Alfred A. Knopf, 1978), a recent scholarly appraisal with a foreword from the publisher, Mencken's old friend. See also George H. Douglas, *H. L. Mencken: Critic of American Life* (Hamden, Conn.: Archon Books, 1978), and Edward A. Martin, *H. L. Mencken and the Debunkers* (Athens: University of Georgia Press, 1984). Fred C. Hobson, Jr., *Serpent in Eden: H. L. Mencken and the South* (Chapel Hill: University of North Carolina Press, 1974), examines Mencken's criticism of the South but mostly the flowering of Southern literature in these years; for evidence of Mencken's broadly gauged regard for genuine talent, see also Charles Scruggs, *The Sage in Harlem: H. L. Mencken and the Black Writers of the 1920s* (Baltimore: Johns Hopkins University Press, 1984).

Recent special studies include George H. Hahn II, "Twilight Reflections: The Hold of Baltimore on Lizette Woodworth Reese and H. L. Mencken," *Southern Quarterly*, 22 (1984): 5–21; David S. Thaler, "H. L. Mencken and the Baltimore Polytechnic Institute," *Menckeniana*, 65 (Fall 1983): 10–13; Gilbert Byron, "H. L. Mencken versus the Eastern Shore," *Menckeniana*, 65 (Summer 1983): 13–16; and Merritt W. Mosley, Jr., "H. L. Mencken and the First World War," *Menckeniana*, 58 (1976): 8–15. Several unpublished works will interest students of Mencken: Barbara Ione Kaufman Brown, "The Political Thought of H. L. Mencken" (Ph.D. dissertation, Johns Hopkins University, 1971); W. H. A. Williams, "H. L. Mencken: A Critical Study, 1880–1929" (Ph.D. dissertation, Johns Hopkins University, 1971); and Robert Francis Nardini, "H. L. Mencken and the Cult of Smartness" (M.A. thesis, University of Virginia, 1981). See also Fecher's bibliographical note and Betty Adler, with the assistance of Jane Wilhelm, *H.L.M: The Mencken Bibliography* (Baltimore: Johns Hopkins Press, 1961), and Adler, *A Ten-Year Supplement, 1962–1971* (Baltimore: Enoch Pratt Free Library, 1971).

10. Growing Up

James Levin, "Governor Albert Ritchie and the Democratic National Convention of 1924," *MHM*, 66 (1971): 101–20, and Levin, "Governor Albert C. Ritchie and the Democratic Convention of 1932," *MHM*, 67 (1972): 278–93, cover the Marylander's flirtation with the presidency. Dorothy M. Brown, "The Election of 1934: The 'New Deal' in Maryland," *MHM*, 68 (1973): 405–21, explores reasons for Ritchie's defeat despite FDR's widespread popularity; see also Brown, "Maryland Between the Wars," in Walsh and Fox, eds., *Maryland*. Philip A. Grant, Jr., "Maryland Press Reaction to the Roosevelt-Tydings Confrontation," *MHM*, 68 (1973): 422–37, offers a summary of news stories; Eugene W. Goll, "Frank R. Kent's Opposition to Franklin D. Roosevelt and the New Deal," *MHM*, 63 (1968): 158–71, discusses a leading critic of FDR and the changes he symbolized for many conservatives. Harry W. Kirwan, *The Inevitable Success: Herbert R. O'Conor* (Westminster, Md.: Newman Press, 1962), portrays the wartime governor as a shallow figure, competent politician. For a helpful reference, see Evelyn L. Wentworth, comp., *Election*

Statistics in Maryland, 1934–1958 (College Park: Bureau of Governmental Research, University of Maryland, 1959).

On the Eastern Shore between the world wars, see Frank Goodwin, *A Study of Personal and Social Organization: An Explorative Survey of the Eastern Shore of Maryland* (Philadelphia: University of Pennsylvania Press, 1944), a dissertation that examines population and occupation patterns, family life, leadership recruitment, and county weekly newspapers. Stanley B. Sutton, *Beyond the Roadgate: Kent County, 1900–1980* (privately printed, 1983), includes material on the University of Maryland Extension Service during the Depression; Philip J. Wingate, *Before the Bridge* (Centreville, Md.: Tidewater Publishers, 1985), contains reminiscences of Cambridge, Chestertown, and elsewhere in the 1920s and 1930s; Asbury Smith, *More Than a Whisper* (Baltimore: privately printed, 1985), recalls Smith's days as an Eastern Shore Methodist minister. Evelyn Harris, *The Farmer and His Wife; Howells Point Farm, Betterton, Md.* (privately printed, 1924), and *The Barter Lady: A Woman Farmer Sees It Through* (Garden City, N.Y.: Doubleday, Doran & Co., 1934) offer chatty but informative glimpses of Kent County truck farming in these years and of the occasional strain between natives and newly arrived wealth—on which see also Calvin Rutherford Thomas, "The Impact of Amenity Landownership on Agriculture in Talbot County, Md." (Ph.D. dissertation, University of Tennessee, 1983). Shepard Krech III, *Praise the Bridge That Carries You Over: The Life of Joseph L. Sutton* (Cambridge, Mass.: Schenkman Publishing Co., 1981), recounts black life on the Eastern Shore; in fictional form, so does Waters Edward Turpin, *These Low Grounds* (College Park, Md.: McGrath Publishing Co., 1969 [New York, 1937]).

Charles M. Kimberly, "The Depression in Maryland: The Failure of Voluntaryism," *MHM*, 70 (1975): 189–202, sketches the background for New Deal relief efforts and draws on his "The Depression and New Deal in Maryland" (Ph.D. dissertation, American University, 1974). Jo Ann E. Argersinger, *Toward a New Deal in Baltimore: People and Government in the Great Depression* (Chapel Hill: University of North Carolina Press, 1988), nicely combines political, labor, and social history; see also her "Assisting the 'Loafers': Transient Relief in Baltimore, 1933–37," *Labor History*, 23 (1982): 226–45; "'The Right to Strike': Labor Organization and the New Deal in Baltimore," *MHM*, 78 (1983): 299–318; and "Toward a Roosevelt Coalition: The Democratic Party and the New Deal in Baltimore," *MHM*, 82 (1987): 288–305. Gerard Edward McCarron, "Governor Albert C. Ritchie and Unemployment Relief in Maryland, 1929–1933" (M.A. thesis, University of Maryland, 1969), discusses a reluctant New Dealer. David Lamoreaux, with Gerson G. Eisenberg, "Baltimore Views the Great Depression, 1929–33," *MHM*, 71 (1976): 428–42, uses newspaper content analysis to survey a wrenching social experience. Patricia W. Levering and Ralph B. Levering, "Women in Relief: The Carroll County Children's Aid Society in the Great Depression," *MHM*, 72 (1977): 534–46, treats the impact of the Depression on small-town and farm families. For a retrospective view, see Constance B. Schultz, "Maryland Fifty Years Ago: Remembering the CWA and WPA," *Maryland Heritage News*, 2 (Fall 1984): 8–9.

Joseph L. Arnold, *The New Deal in the Suburbs: A History of the Greenbelt Town Program, 1935–1954* (Columbus, Ohio: Ohio State University Press, 1971); George A. Warner, *Greenbelt, The Cooperative Community: An Experience in Democratic Living* (New York: Exposition Press, 1954); and Leslie Gene Hunter, "Greenbelt, Maryland: A City on a Hill," *MHM*, 63 (1968): 105–36, introduce the Tugwell utopia. For a contemporary view, highly positive, see Francis Fink, "First Resettlers," *Literary Digest*, 1 (6 November 1937): 13–15.

Roderick N. Ryon, "An Ambiguous Legacy: Baltimore Blacks and the CIO, 1936–1941," *JNH*, 65 (1980): 18–33, discusses Negro gains after federal protections for unions and Lend-Lease industrial growth. On blacks and education in these years, see Maria Theresa Regina, "The Impact of the Depression on Black Education in Baltimore" (M.A. thesis, George Washington University, 1972); J. R. Wennersten, "Black School Teachers in Maryland, 1930s," *NHB*, 38 (1975): 370–73; and Edward J. Kuebler, "The Desegregation of the University of Maryland," *MHM*, 71 (1976): 37–49. For a study of a civil rights leader's development and practice, see Russell W. Bland, *Private Pressure on Public Law: The Legal Career of Justice Thurgood Marshall* (Port Washington, N.Y.: Kennikat Press, 1973). Hayward Farrar, "See What the *Afro* Says: The Baltimore *Afro-American*, 1892–1950" (Ph.D. dissertation, University of Chicago, 1983), studies one of the pillars of the Baltimore black community. John Chilton, *Billie's Blues: A Survey of Billie Holliday's Career, 1939–1959* (London: Quartet Books, 1975), tells that sad story with compassion. Ira DeA. Reid, *The Negro Community of Baltimore: A Summary Report of a Social Study Conducted for the Baltimore Urban League* (Baltimore: National Urban League, Department of Research and Community Projects, 1935), supplies an important contemporary assessment; see also P. Stewart Macaulay, "A Study of the Negro's Problems: How They Touch All in the City," *Sunday Sun*, 31 March 1935.

Frank Turaj, "Mencken and the Nazis: A Note," *MHM*, 67 (1972): 176–78, and Dean Banks, "H. L. Mencken and 'Hitlerism,' 1935–1941," *MHM*, 71 (1976): 498–515, recount the sage's (tardy) arrival at a negative view of German developments. On one of Mencken's contemporaries on the Sunpapers, see Fred Hobson, "Gerald W. Johnson: The Southerner as Realist," *Virginia Quarterly Review*, 58 (1982): 1–25.

George H. Callcott, *Maryland and America, 1940–1980* (Baltimore: Johns Hopkins University Press, 1985), examines the war experience with sharp analysis of the economic and demographic changes it brought to the state. Harold Randall Manakee, comp., *Maryland in World War II* (4 vols.; Baltimore: War Records Division, MHS, 1950–58), issued from a state-MHS joint effort; the first three volumes cover military participation, industry and agriculture, and the home front exhaustively, based on hundreds of questionnaires and other reports; a fourth volume publishes a Gold Star Honor Roll. See also the standard unit histories: Joseph H. Ewing, *29 Let's Go! A History of the 29th Infantry Division in World War II* (Washington, D.C.: Infantry Journal Press, 1948); Joseph Binkoski and Arthur Plaut, *The 115th Infantry Regiment in World War II* (Washington, D.C.: Infantry Journal Press, 1948); James H. Fitzgerald Brewer, *History of the 175th Infantry (Fifth Maryland)* (Baltimore: War Records Division, MHS, 1955); and John P. Cooper, Jr., *The History of the 110th Field Artillery with Sketches of Related Units* (Baltimore: War Records Division, MHS, 1953). Norman N. Rubin, "From the Sea with Wings: Maryland and the Flying Boat," *MHM*, 72 (1977): 277–87, includes much on wartime developments. Charles R. Fisher, "The Maryland State Guard in World War II," *Military Affairs*, 47 (1983): 11–14, treats the last line of defense. Karen Anderson, *Wartime Women: Sex Roles, Family Relations, and the Status of Women during World War II* (Westport, Conn.: Greenwood Press, 1981), examines these themes in Baltimore along with Detroit and Seattle. W. Edward Orser, "Involuntary Community: Conscientious Objectors at Patapsco State Park during World War II," *MHM*, 72 (1977): 132–46, discusses a sidelight on the war effort. Harry Kennard Wright, "Sun Shipyard Number Four: The Story of a Major Negro Home Front Defense Effort during the Second World War" (M.A. thesis, Morgan State University, 1972), proudly recounts a chapter in black history. On a service institution the war spawned, see *The First Forty Years: A Pictorial Account of the Johns Hopkins Applied Physics Laboratory Since Its Founding in 1942* (Baltimore: Johns Hopkins University Press, 1983).

11. "Land of Pleasant Living"

For the primary materials available on the post–World War II period, see notes to this chapter, local and county histories, and Callcott, *Maryland and America*—which will stand for many years as the authoritative study of the postwar period. Specifically on housing problems in Baltimore City, see William T. Dürr, "The Conscience of a City: A History of the Citizens' Planning and Housing Association and Efforts to Improve Housing for the Poor in Baltimore, 1937–1954" (Ph.D. dissertation, Johns Hopkins University, 1972); Karen A. Stakem, "Hans Froelicher, Jr., Civic Educator," *MHM*, 77 (1982): 193–201; and a survey of postwar blight-removal attempts that contains much on Baltimore, Martin Millspaugh and Gurney Breckenfeld, edited by Miles L. Colean, *The Human Side of Urban Renewal: A Study of the Attitude Changes Produced by Neighborhood Rehabilitation* (Baltimore: Fight-Blight, 1958). Morton Hoffman, "The Role of Government in Influencing Changes in Housing in Baltimore, 1940–1950," *Land Economics: A Quarterly Journal of Planning, Housing, and Public Utilities*, 30 (1954): 125–40, documents the diverse (and unsurprising) effects of federal spending and loans. Callcott, *History of the University of Maryland*, and J. B. Donnelly, "The Vision of Scholarship: Johns Hopkins after the War," *MHM*, 73

(1978): 137–62, discuss the arrival of veterans on college campuses. LeViness, *History of Road Building*, carries that story through the late 1950s; see also W. S. Hamill, "The Story of the Bay Bridge," *Baltimore*, 43 (July 1952): 18–19, 45–64.

The Alger Hiss case belongs to national history, but it involved Marylanders to a striking degree. The best summaries may be Allen Weinstein, *Perjury: The Alger Hiss Case* (New York: Alfred A. Knopf, 1978), and John Chabot Smith, *Alger Hiss: The True Story* (New York: Holt, Rinehart & Winston, 1976). Meyer A. Zeligs, *Friendship and Fratricide: An Analysis of Whittaker Chambers and Alger Hiss* (New York: Viking Press, 1967), explores the relationship the two men shared as a psychological problem. Athan G. Theoharis, ed., *Beyond the Hiss Case: The FBI, Congress, and the Cold War* (Philadelphia: Temple University Press, 1982), broadens the inquiry. William B. Prendergrast, "Maryland: The Ober Anti-Communism Law," in *The States and Subversion, Cornell University Studies in Civil Liberties*, ed. Walter Gellhorn (Ithaca, N.Y.: Cornell University Press, 1952), treats the notorious Maryland loyalty law; see also Lewis D. Asper, "The Long and Unhappy History of Loyalty Testing in Maryland," *AJLH*, 13 (1969): 97–109.

The end of legal segregation, a leading theme of the period, has been the subject of several valuable studies. Besides Callcott, *Maryland and America*, and Bland, *Private Pressure on Public Law*, see Martha S. Putney, "Dwight O. W. Holmes and the Maryland State Board of Education," *NHB*, 41 (1978): 920–22; Kenneth Gregory, "The Education of Blacks in Maryland: An Historical Survey" (Ph.D. dissertation, Columbia University, 1976); Samuel Lee Banks, "Descriptive Study of the Baltimore City Board of School Commissioners as an Agent in School Desegregation" (Ph.D. dissertation, George Washington University, 1976); Robert Stuart Posilkin, "An Historical Study of Desegregation of the Montgomery County, Maryland, Public Schools, 1954–1977" (Ed.D. dissertation, George Washington University, 1979); and Maureen Walsh, "An Economic Analysis of School Desegregation in Prince George's County, Maryland" (M.A. thesis, University of Maryland, 1980). Roszel C. Thomsen, "The Integration of Baltimore's Polytechnic Institute: A Reminiscence," *MHM*, 79 (1984): 235–38, recalls that first step. Lawrence Cardinal Shehan, *A Blessing of Years: The Memoirs of Lawrence Cardinal Shehan* (Notre Dame, Ind.: University of Notre Dame Press, 1982), and Sanford Jay Rosen, "Judge Soboloff's Public School Race Decisions," *MLR*, 34 (1974): 498–531, provide material on two more whites who led the struggle for integration.

Rapid suburban development, rising land values, and questions of land use and community planning also will interest future students of postwar Maryland. They will build on Robert J. Sickels, "The Illusion of Judicial Consensus: Zoning Decision in the Maryland Court of Appeals," *American Political Science Review*, 59 (1965): 100–104, and William C. Brooks, ed., *Zoning Notes: Cases of the Court of Appeals of Maryland* (Charlottesville, Va.: Michie Co., 1957). James E. Skok, "Participation in Decision-Making: The Bureaucracy and the Community," *Western Political Quarterly*, 27 (1974): 60–79, offers a turgid study of Montgomery–Prince George's county government in the mid- to late 1960s, concluding that citizens of affluent Montgomery tended to be more inclined to civic involvement and their decisions less "centralized." Mark L. Walston, "The Commercial Rise and Fall of Silver Spring: A Study of the Twentieth-Century Development of the Suburban Shopping Center in Montgomery County," *MHM*, 81 (1986): 330–39, shows how growth patterns eventually undermined the early centers just as they, at first, siphoned off trade from downtown retailers. On the conception of Columbia as an alternative community, see Gurney Breckenfeld, *Columbia and the New Cities* (New York: Ives Washburn, 1971), and Richard O. Brooks, *New Towns and Communal Values: A Case Study of Columbia, Maryland* (New York: Praeger, 1974).

Refer to chapter notes and Callcott, *Maryland and America*, for the birth of the Greater Baltimore Committee and advent of Charles Center. Especially interesting on the downtown renewal are Jane Jacobs, "New Heart for Baltimore," *Architectural Forum*, 108 (June 1958): 88–92, and Martin Millspaugh, ed., *Baltimore's Charles Center: A Case Study of Downtown Renewal*, Technical bulletin 51 (Washington, D.C.: Urban Land Institute, 1964)—containing essays by Hunter Moss, J. Jefferson Miller, David Wallace, Harry B. Cooper, George E. Kostritsky, Walter Sondheim, Jr., and others. Jacques Kelly, ed., *Eight Busy Decades: The Life of Clarence W. Miles* (Queenstown, Md: White Banks, 1986), recalls the civic concern that led to the GBC; but see also Katherine Lyall, "A Bicycle Built for Two: Public-Private Partnership in Baltimore," *National Civic Review*, 72 (1983): 531–71.

On some of the political issues that resurfaced during the Tawes administration, see John H. Michener, "History of Legislative Reapportionment in Maryland," *MLR*, 25 (Winter-Spring, 1965): 1–21, and John W. Sause, Jr., "Chronicle of the Building and Loan Industry in Maryland from 1852 to 1961," *MLR*, 22 (Winter-Spring, 1962): 1–30, 91–129. Susan Hickey Shaffer, "Slot Machines in Charles County, Maryland, 1910–1968" (M.A. thesis, University of Maryland, 1983), and Eugene L. Meyer, "Replaying the One-Armed Bandit," *Chesapeake Country Life*, 4 (April 1983): 9–11, 23, 37, discuss a colorful interlude.

Major economic, medical, and educational developments of the 1960s thus far have received limited or official coverage. *Port of Baltimore, 1955–84* (Baltimore: Maryland Port Authority, c. 1984) partly casts a backward glance on the effort to retain the state's share of import-export traffic; see also W. Gregory Halpin, "Containerization: New Life or Slow Death to the Port?" *Baltimore*, 60 (August 1967): 20–23, 45–48. Jon Franklin and Alan Dolep, *Shocktrauma* (New York: St. Martin's Press, 1980), and Thomas Bourne Turner, *Part of Medicine, Part of Me: Musings of a Johns Hopkins Dean* (Baltimore: Johns Hopkins Medical School, 1981), shed light on Maryland's medical community and its national leadership. Wilson H. Elkins, *Forty Years as a College President: Memoirs of Wilson H. Elkins*, ed. George H. Callcott (College Park: University of Maryland, 1981), collects reflections from the university's most extensive building years, the late 1950s and 1960s. William Lloyd Fox, *Montgomery College: Maryland's First Community College* (Rockville, Md.: Montgomery College, 1970), examines an experiment among the local colleges so important in a technocratic society.

12. Renaissance: Survival of a Sensibility

Primary sources for this chapter as well as chapter 11 receive full coverage in the bibliographical note in Callcott, *Maryland and America*; see also Capper, Power, and Shivers, *Chesapeake Waters*, and the various monographic reports available through the Johns Hopkins University Center for Metropolitan Planning and Research.

For a lively and thorough discussion of state politics in these years, see Callcott, *Maryland and America*. Gregory A. Stiverson, comp., *Index to the Debates of the Constitutional Convention of 1967–1968* (Annapolis: MHR, 1982), provides a helpful research tool; John P. Wheeler, Jr., and Melissa Kinsey, *Magnificent Failure: The Maryland Constitutional Convention of 1967–1968* (New York: National Municipal League, 1970), and Marianne Ellis Alexander, "The Issues and Politics of the Maryland Constitutional Convention, 1967–1968" (Ph.D. dissertation, University of Maryland, 1972), study the making of the document voters rejected. See Carl T. Richards, "Maryland's Administrative Reorganization" (Ph.D. dissertation, University of Maryland, 1972); George Stockton Wills II, "The Reorganization of the Maryland General Assembly, 1966–1968: A Study of the Politics of Reform" (Ph.D. dissertation, Johns Hopkins University, 1969); and Harry Bard's revised *Maryland, State and Government: Its New Dynamics* (Cambridge, Md.: Tidewater Publishers, 1974), for the changes made nonetheless. Laslo V. Boyd, *Maryland Government and Politics* (Centreville, Md.: Tidewater Publishers, 1987), provides another recent constitutional textbook.

Agnew prompted more than a few investigative works; they include Theo Lippman, Jr., *Spiro Agnew's America: The Vice President and the Politics of Suburbia* (New York: W. W. Norton & Co., 1972); Jules Witcover, *White Knight: The Rise of Spiro Agnew* (New York: Random House, 1972); and Joseph Albright, *What Makes Spiro Run? The Life and Times of Spiro Agnew* (New York: Dodd, Mead & Co., 1972). John R. Coyne, *The Impudent Snobs: Agnew and the Intellectual Establishment* (New Rochelle, N.Y.: Arlington House, 1972), discusses one of the controversies that made Agnew's name a household word. Richard M. Cohen and Jules Witcover, *A Heartbeat Away: The Investigation and Resignation of Vice President Spiro T. Agnew* (New York: Viking Press, 1974), relates his fall. Mandel lacks a biographer but has a critical student in Bradford Jacobs, *Thimbleriggers: The Law v. Governor Marvin Mandel* (Baltimore: Johns Hopkins University Press, 1984). Jacobs, like Frank Kent, wrote well for the Sunpapers before retiring; that Baltimore establishment fails close scrutiny in Paul Wilkes, "Baltimore's Sunpapers: Where Has Greatness Gone?" *Columbia Journalism Review*, 10 (July-August 1971): 39–46.

Black history in the 1970s, if not completely a success story, does move from violent frustration to an emphasis on educational advancement and activity within the political system. Wayne E. Page, "H. Rap Brown and the Cambridge Incident" (M.A. thesis, University of Maryland, 1970), examines that noteworthy outbreak. Paul Fairfax Evans, *City Life . . . A Perspective from Baltimore, 1968–1978* (Columbia, Md.: C. H. Fairfax Co., 1981), relates news events (including the April 1968 Baltimore riots) and a young black journalist's view of them. "Baltimore: What Went Wrong?" *Black Enterprise Magazine*, 2 (November 1971): 40–48, performs a post-mortem on the failure of the Urban Coalition. Richard Bragg, "The Maryland Black Caucus as a Racial Group in the Maryland General Assembly, Legislative Communities and Caucus Influence on Public Policy, 1975–1978" (Ph.D. dissertation, Howard University, 1979), traces behavior that combines racial concern and institutional socialization.

Negro housing and economic gain have been of interest to social scientists just as to newly elected black lawmakers. In *Power and Poverty: Theory and Practice* (New York: Oxford University Press, 1970), Peter Bachrach and Morton S. Baratz examine the Baltimore war on poverty and its ambiguous results. See also Louis S. Rosenberg, "The Low-Income Housing Effort in the City of Baltimore" (Ph.D. dissertation, Brandeis University, 1973); Sharon Perlman Krefetz, "Urban Politics and Public Welfare: Baltimore and San Francisco" (Ph.D. dissertation, Brandeis University, 1976); and Joel Ferber and Michael Braverman, "Block Grants and Baltimore: Contradictions in Community Development," Johns Hopkins University *Letters and Papers in the Social Sciences: An Undergraduate Review*, 7 (1981): 13–29. Michael A. Stegman, *Housing Investment in the Inner City: The Dynamics of Decline; A Study of Baltimore, Maryland, 1968–1979* (Cambridge, Mass.: MIT Press, 1972), offers a sobering view of slum economics. Robert B. Zehner and F. Stuart Chapin, Jr., *Across the City Line: A White Community in Transition* (Lexington, Mass.: Lexington Books, 1974), surveys response to black migration to the Prince George's County suburbs of Brentwood, Mt. Rainier, Cottage City, and Colmar Manor in 1970–71; see also Maryland–National Capital Park and Planning Commission, *The Social and Economic Status of the Black Population in Prince George's County, 1970–1980* (1985); John K. Gardner and A. Stewart Holmes, *A Profile of Poverty in Maryland* (College Park, Md.: University of Maryland Agricultural Experiment Station, 1973), and Bradley R. Schiller, *The Economics of Poverty in Maryland* (Englewood Cliffs, N.J.: Prentice-Hall, 1973), discuss the enduring poor in Baltimore, the lower counties of both shores, and Western Maryland. For an assessment of Columbia's bi-racial success (rating it a heterogeneous community coming closer each day to being a "working plural community"), see Lynne C. Burkhart, *Old Values in a New Town: The Politics of Race and Class in Columbia, Maryland* (New York: Praeger, 1981).

On state economic developments in these years, *Maryland Magazine* supplies interesting, though predictably upbeat, interviews with public officials. See "Economic Forecast for Maryland" [Joseph G. Anastasi], *MM*, 8 (Winter 1975): 45–47; "Walking the Ecological Tightrope" [James Bennett Coulter], *MM*, 9 (Autumn 1976): 18–25; Louis F. Peddicord, "Portage for People and Products, Now and Tomorrow: An Interview with Harry R. Hughes, State Secretary of Transportation," *MM*, 9 (Spring 1977): 44–48; Peddicord, "Are Marylanders Heading Back to the Farm? An Interview with Young Hance, Maryland's First Secretary of Agriculture," *MM*, 10 (Spring 1978): 17–21.

Contemporary assessments of environmental topics and historic preservation include Earl Arnett, "Probing the Bay's Ecology," *MM*, 3 (Winter 1970): 2–5; James F. Waesche, "Peeling Away the Centuries," *MM*, 4 (Autumn 1971): 20–24; J. Carleton Jones, "A Comeback in Charles County," *MM*, 5 (Autumn 1972): 2–7; and John C. Schmidt, "The Fight for a Sane Nuclear Policy," *MM*, 7 (Autumn 1974): 2–5. Charles Camp, "Perspectives in Applied Folklore: American Folk Festivals and the Recent Maryland Experience," *Free State Folklore*, 3 (1976–77): 4–15 (McKeldin Library), discusses a thriving mid-1970s program. Barbara Cole, "Maryland Forest Service, 1906–1976," *Maryland Conservationist*, 52 (1976–77): 8–11, and Eugene R. Slatick, "Maryland's Rivers—Something Special," ibid., pp. 14–19, assess progress in state environmental action. Mark R. Edwards, "The Computer as a Preservation Planning Tool: Maryland's Approach to Improving Resource Management," *Technology and Conservation*, 4 (1979): 18–25, places the state in the forefront of that movement. Thomas C. Gillmer, "The Clipper Ship: *Pride of Baltimore*," *Baltimore Engineer*, 52 (1977): 4–6, proudly documents that achievement in maritime re-creation. On the state capital, see St. Clair Wright, "Historic Preservation in Annapolis," *Antiques*, 111 (January 1977): 152–57, and Pringle Hart Symonds, "Creation of a Historic District in Annapolis," ibid., pp. 146–47. For retrospective views of two additional preservation projects, see Pamela Jayne Wolf, "Ellicott City, Maryland: A Perspective on Small Town Preservation" (M.A. thesis, George Washington University, 1981), and Dorothy Reid Jacobson, "Cultural Planning: A Perspective for Small Towns and a Case Study of Frederick, Maryland" (M.A. thesis, George Washington University, 1980).

Baltimore provides a rich study in urban conflict, reconciliation, and more conflict. Sherry H. Olson, *Baltimore* (Cambridge, Mass.: Ballinger Publishing Co., 1976), part of a comparative series on American cities, employs highly interesting maps and graphs in dissecting the city in the early 1970s. John C. Schmidt, "A New Baltimore Idea for Better Freeway Design, " *Baltimore*, 60 (January 1967): 19–21; James Bailey, "How S.O.M. [the San Francisco consulting firm of Skidmore, Owings & Merrill] Took On the Baltimore Road Gang," *Architectural Forum*, 130 (March 1969): 40–45; and Douglas H. Haeuber, *The Baltimore Expressway Controversy: A Study of the Decision-making Process* (Baltimore: Johns Hopkins University Center for Metropolitan Planning and Research, 1974), explore innovative design of, and quarrels over, city highways in the late 1960s and 1970s. Roberto Brambilla and Gianni Longo, *Learning from Baltimore: What Makes Cities Liveable?* (New York: Institute for Environmental Action, 1979), paying Baltimore compliments, contributes to a series on that question.

For a collection of interesting essays that help to answer the question while addressing the Baltimore sociocultural revival of the 1970s, see Lenora Heilig Nast, Laurence N. Krause, and R. C. Monk, eds., *Baltimore: A Living Renaissance* (Baltimore: Historic Baltimore, 1982). See also Earl Arnett, "The Arts: Maryland's Position on the National Scene," *MM*, 10 (Spring 1978): 15–16. Benjamin Franklin Carney, "The Baltimore Theater Project, 1971–1983: Toward a People's Theater" (Ph.D. dissertation, University of Missouri, 1985), studies an element in the arts revival. On the urban-homestead movement, see Richard P. Davis, "Urban Homesteading," in Nast, Krause, and Monk, eds., *Living Renaissance*; Jacques Kelly, "New Heart for an Old City," *MM*, 8 (Spring 1976): 2–7; and Tom Lake and John Bayne, "History Behind You, Costs Ahead," *Baltimore*, 70 (August 1977): 44–51. Nancy Torrieri, "Residential Dispersal and the Survival of the Italian Community in Metropolitan Baltimore, 1920–1980" (Ph.D. dissertation, University of Maryland, 1982), discusses cultural persistence in one ethnic group. For a recent guidebook, see Allen C. Goodman and Ralph B. Taylor, *The Baltimore Neighborhood Fact Book: 1970–1980* (Baltimore: Johns Hopkins University Center for Metropolitan Planning and Research, 1983).

For a hard look at the rebirth of Baltimore, see Michael C. McDonald, *American Cities: A Report on the Myths of Urban Renaissance* (New York: Simon & Schuster, 1984), especially pp. 286–95, and Donald Baker, "Is Baltimore Truly Back?" *Washington Post*, 24 November 1984. For a sour fictional view of the city, recalling William Manchester's *City of Anger* and speaking for blue-collar people who worry more about jobs than gentrification, see Robert Ward, *Red Baker* (New York: Dial Press, 1985).

Marianne Alexander, "Advancing the Status of Women," in Nast, Krause, and Monk, eds., *Living Renaissance*, discusses one group that won important, though not all, social and legal battles in the 1970s. See also League of Women Voters of Maryland, *The Maryland Experience: ERA* (1974), and Anne G. Ingram, "An Oral History Study of the Women's Equity Movement, University of Maryland, College Park, 1968–1978," *Maryland Historian*, 9 (1978): 1–25.

Memoirs and testimonial essays that throw light on recent Marylanders of note include Sallie Kravitz, *Ethel Ennis, The Reluctant Jazz Star* (Baltimore: Gateway Press, 1984); August Meier, "Benjamin Quarles and the Historiography of Black America," *CWH*, 26 (1980): 101–16, paying tribute to the Morgan State University scholar; Arnold M. Weiner, "Judge Sobeloff's Influences upon Criminal Reform," *MLR*, 34 (1974): 532–40; Frank R. L. Somerville, "'A Stature of His Own': Bishop [James Edward] Walsh, a Hero of Fifty-two Years in China, Turns Ninety," *MM*, 13 (Summer 1981): 28–29; and John H. Murphy, "Paul

Nitze, Statesman," *MM*, 15 (Autumn 1982): 12–13. Walter Hollander, Jr., ed., *Abel Wolman: His Life and Philosophy, An Oral History* (2 vols.; Chapel Hill, N.C.: Universal Printing and Publishing Co., 1981), supplies source material on an internationally respected sanitary engineer.

Eugene L. Meyer, *Maryland Lost and Found: People and Places from Chesapeake to Appalachia* (Baltimore: Johns Hopkins University Press, 1986), provides a record of late-twentieth-century life that future historians will value.

SELECTED MAPS, FIGURES, AND TABLES

The following graphics supplement text and illustrations by charting population growth, social structure, economic change, voting patterns, and the like. Drawing the hard lines of broad themes, they suggest the range of visual aids available to students of Maryland history and demonstrate the contours of modern research.

General Aids

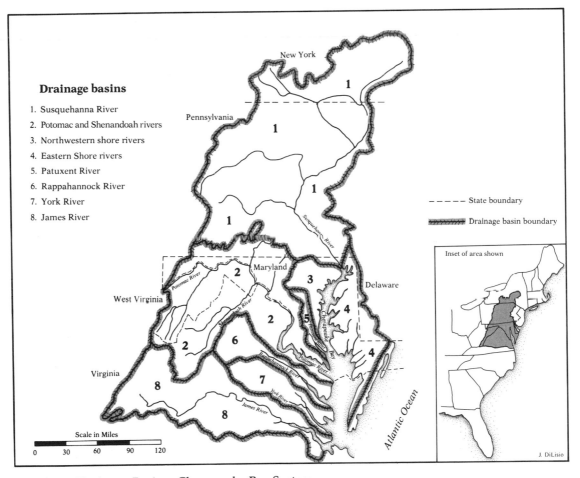

Drainage basins

1. Susquehanna River
2. Potomac and Shenandoah rivers
3. Northwestern shore rivers
4. Eastern Shore rivers
5. Patuxent River
6. Rappahannock River
7. York River
8. James River

1. Drainage Basins, Chesapeake Bay System

The extensive water network that first promoted settlement later complicated environmental protection. From Suzanne Ellery Greene Chapelle et al., *Maryland: A History of Its People* (Baltimore: Johns Hopkins University Press, 1986).

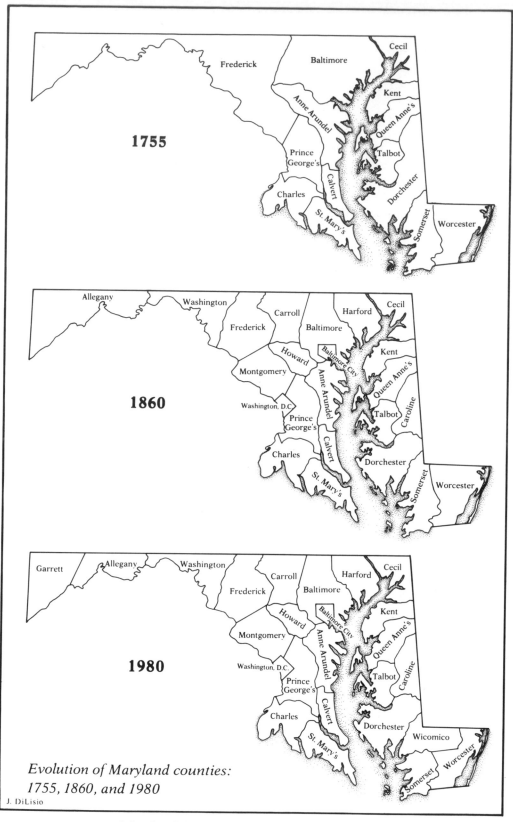

1755

Frederick
Baltimore
Cecil
Anne Arundel
Kent
Queen Anne's
Prince George's
Talbot
Calvert
Dorchester
Charles
Somerset
St. Mary's
Worcester

1860

Allegany
Washington
Carroll
Harford
Cecil
Frederick
Baltimore
Howard
Baltimore City
Kent
Montgomery
Anne Arundel
Queen Anne's
Washington, D.C.
Prince George's
Talbot
Caroline
Calvert
Charles
Dorchester
St. Mary's
Somerset
Worcester

1980

Garrett
Allegany
Washington
Carroll
Harford
Cecil
Frederick
Baltimore
Howard
Baltimore City
Kent
Montgomery
Anne Arundel
Queen Anne's
Washington, D.C.
Talbot
Caroline
Prince George's
Calvert
Charles
Dorchester
St. Mary's
Wicomico
Somerset
Worcester

Evolution of Maryland counties:
1755, 1860, and 1980

J. DiLisio

2. Maryland County Boundaries, 1755, 1860, 1980
From Chapelle et al., *Maryland*.

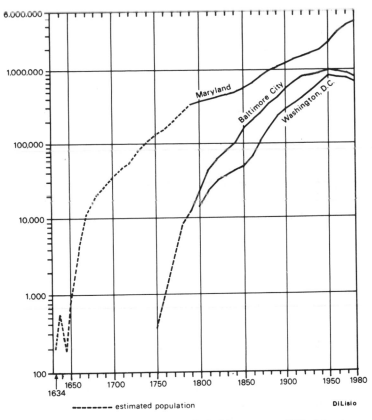

3. Population Growth, Maryland, Baltimore, and Washington, D.C., 1634–1980

Adapted from Derek Thompson et al., *Atlas of Maryland* (College Park: Department of Geography, University of Maryland, 1977).

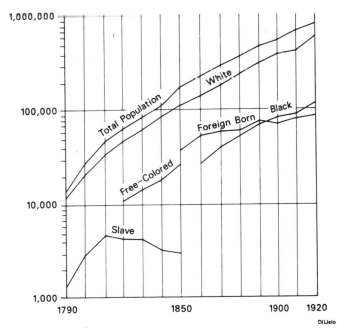

4. Population Composition, Baltimore City, 1790–1920

From Thompson et al., *Atlas of Maryland*.

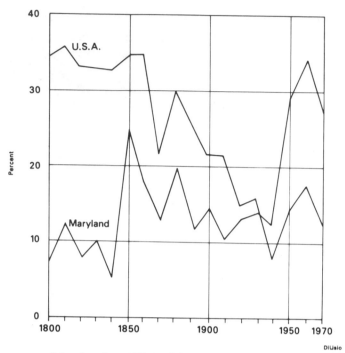

5. Maryland and United States Population Growth
Rates, 1800–1970
From Thompson et al., *Atlas of Maryland.*

Chronological References

1. Indian Tribes within the Calvert Grant, and Their Neighbors

The names of tribes and villages, c. 1620–1700, appear in their approximate locations. Arabic numerals mark the sites of reservations: (1) Broad Creek, 1711–1768; (2) Chicacoan, 1684–1768; (3) Choptank, 1669–1799; (4) Gingaskin, 1641–1813; (5) Indian River, 1711–1744; (6) Piscataway, 1668–1700. Cross-hatching represents early population centers. Adapted from Christian F. Feest, "Nanticoke and Neighboring Tribes," *Handbook of North American Indians,* William C. Sturtevant, gen. ed., vol. 15, *Northeast,* Bruce G. Trigger, vol. ed. (Washington, D.C.: Smithsonian Institution, 1978) / James E. DeLisio.

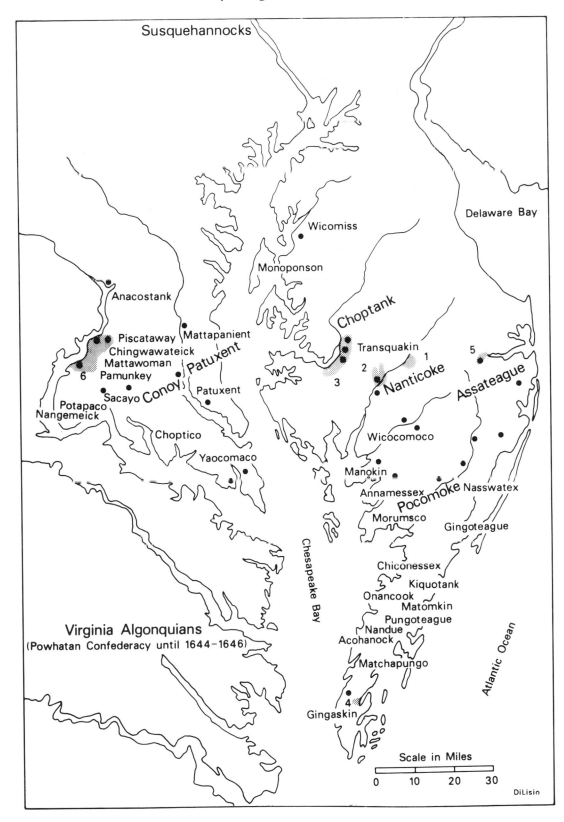

Susquehannocks

Delaware Bay

Wicomiss

Monoponson

Anacostank

Choptank

Piscataway　Mattapanient
Chingwawateick
Mattawoman　　　Patuxent
Pamunkey
6
Sacayo　Conoy
Potapaco
Nangemeick
Choptico
Yaocomaco

Transquakin　　1
2　　　5
3　　Nanticoke

Assateague

Wicocomoco

Manokin
Annamessex　Nasswatex
Pocomoke
Morumsco
Gingoteague

Chesapeake Bay

Chiconessex
Kiquotank
Onancook
Matomkin
Pungoteague
Nandue
Acohanock

Virginia Algonquians
(Powhatan Confederacy until 1644–1646)

Matchapungo

Atlantic Ocean

4
Gingaskin

Scale in Miles

0　　10　　20　　30

DiLisio

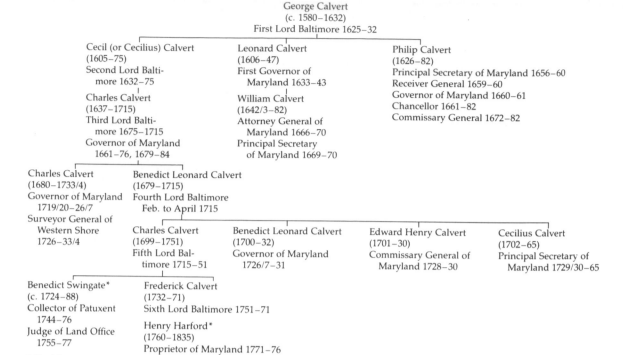

George Calvert
(c. 1580–1632)
First Lord Baltimore 1625–32

Cecil (or Cecilius) Calvert
(1605–75)
Second Lord Balti-
more 1632–75

Charles Calvert
(1637–1715)
Third Lord Balti-
more 1675–1715
Governor of Maryland
1661–76, 1679–84

Leonard Calvert
(1606–47)
First Governor of
Maryland 1633–43

William Calvert
(1642/3–82)
Attorney General of
Maryland 1666–70
Principal Secretary
of Maryland 1669–70

Philip Calvert
(1626–82)
Principal Secretary of Maryland 1656–60
Receiver General 1659–60
Governor of Maryland 1660–61
Chancellor 1661–82
Commissary General 1672–82

Charles Calvert
(1680–1733/4)
Governor of Maryland
1719/20–26/7
Surveyor General of
Western Shore
1726–33/4

Benedict Leonard Calvert
(1679–1715)
Fourth Lord Baltimore
Feb. to April 1715

Charles Calvert
(1699–1751)
Fifth Lord Bal-
timore 1715–51

Benedict Leonard Calvert
(1700–32)
Governor of Maryland
1726/7–31

Edward Henry Calvert
(1701–30)
Commissary General of
Maryland 1728–30

Cecilius Calvert
(1702–65)
Principal Secretary of
Maryland 1729/30–65

Benedict Swingate*
(c. 1724–88)
Collector of Patuxent
1744–76
Judge of Land Office
1755–77

Frederick Calvert
(1732–71)
Sixth Lord Baltimore 1751–71

Henry Harford*
(1760–1835)
Proprietor of Maryland 1771–76

* Illegitimate sons

2. Prominent Members of the Calvert Family in the Colonial Period

Adapted from Richard J. Cox, *A Guide to the Microfilm Edition of the Calvert Papers* (Baltimore: MHS, 1973).

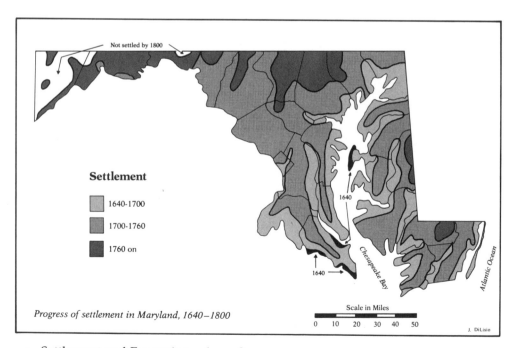

Settlement

- 1640–1700
- 1700–1760
- 1760 on

Progress of settlement in Maryland, 1640–1800

Scale in Miles
0 10 20 30 40 50

J. DiLisio

3. Settlement and Expansion, 1640–1800

Adapted from Robert D. Mitchell and Edward K. Muller, eds., *Geographical Perspectives on Maryland's Past*, Occasional Papers in Geography, no. 4 (College Park: Department of Geography, University of Maryland, 1979).

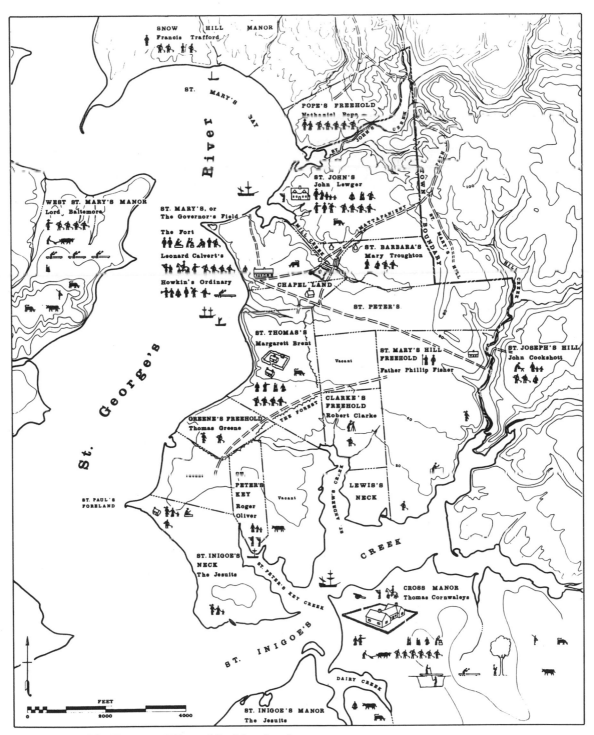

4. The Town and Port of St. Mary's, 1642
One symbol equals one person. From Garry Wheeler Stone, "Manorial Maryland," *MHM*, 82 (1987).

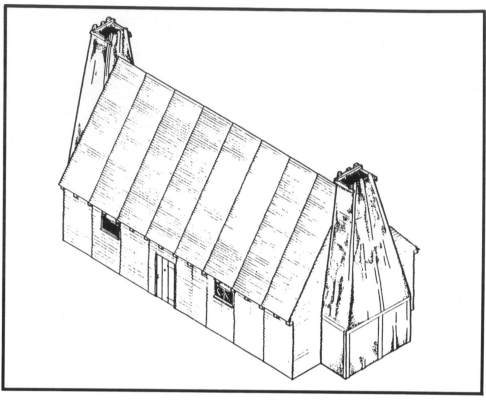

5. Conjectural Drawing of Cordea's
Hope, c. 1680
A typical planter's dwelling of the period.
Courtesy of the St. Mary's City Commission.

6. St. John's, *left*, c. 1640, and *right*,
c. 1680
John Lewger's home and public meeting place
as it may have appeared on the basis of archaeological and historical evidence. Courtesy
of the St. Mary's City Commission.

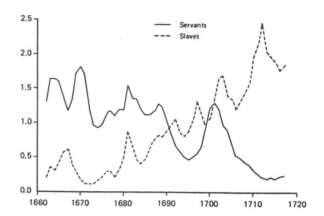

7. Servants and Slaves in Six Maryland Counties, 1662–1717

A dramatic view of the shift from white indentured servants to black slaves, based on a five-year, weighted-moving average of data gleaned from estate inventories. From Gloria L. Main, *Tobacco Colony: Life in Early Maryland, 1650–1720.* Copyright © 1982 by Princeton University Press. Reprinted with permission of publisher.

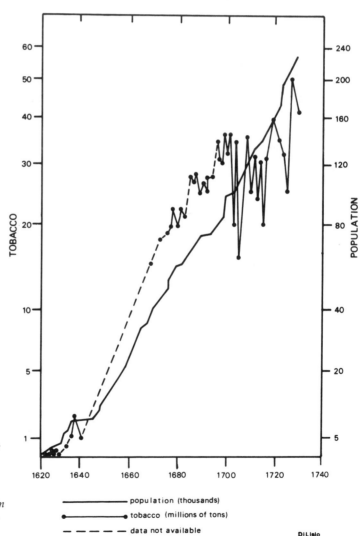

8. Population of Maryland and Virginia and British Imports of Chesapeake Tobacco, 1620–1730

Among the variables affecting migration to the Chesapeake colonies, high tobacco profits counted heavily. Adapted from Russell R. Menard, "The Tobacco Industry in the Chesapeake Colonies, 1617–1700: An Interpretation," *Research in Economic History,* 5 (1980) / James E. DiLisio.

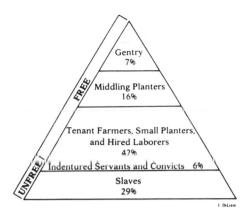

9. Structure of Maryland Society, 1755
From Chapelle et al., *Maryland*.

	White			Free Black			Slave		
	1790	1850	Percent Change	1790	1850	Percent Change	1790	1850	Percent Change
Caroline	7,028	6,096	−13.5	421	2,788	562	2,057	808	−60.7
Dorchester	10,010	10,747	7.4	528	3,848	629	5,337	4,282	−19.8
Kent	6,748	5,616	−16.8	655	3,143	380	5,433	2,627	−51.6
Queen Anne's	8,171	6,936	−15.1	618	3,278	430	6,674	4,270	−36.0
Somerset	8,272	13,385	61.8	268	3,483	1200	7,070	5,588	−21.0
Talbot	7,231	7,084	−2.0	1,076	2,593	141	4,777	4,134	−13.5
Worcester	7,626	12,401	62.6	178	3,014	1593	3,836	3,444	−10.2
Eastern Shore	55,086	62,265	13.0	3,744	22,147	492	35,184	25,153	−28.5
Anne Arundel	11,664	16,542	41.8	804	4,602	472	10,130	11,249	11.0
Calvert	4,211	3,630	−13.8	136	1,530	1025	4,305	4,486	4.2
Charles	10,124	5,665	−44.0	404	913	126	10,085	9,584	−5.0
Prince George's	10,004	8,901	−11.0	164	1,138	594	11,176	11,510	3.0
Montgomery	11,679	9,435	−19.2	294	1,311	346	6,030	5,114	−15.2
St. Mary's	8,216	6,223	−24.3	343	1,633	376	6,985	5,842	−16.4
Southern Md.	55,898	50,396	−9.8	2,145	11,127	419	48,711	47,785	−1.9
Allegany	4,539	21,633	377.0	12	412	3333	258	724	180.6
Baltimore	30,878	174,853	466.0	927	29,075	3036	7,132	6,718	−5.8
Carroll (1837)		18,667			974			975	
Cecil	10,055	15,472	53.9	163	2,623	1509	3,407	844	−75.2
Frederick	26,937	33,314	23.7	213	3,760	1665	3,641	3,913	7.5
Harford	10,784	14,413	33.7	775	2,777	258	3,417	2,166	−36.6
Washington	14,472	26,930	86.1	64	1,828	2756	1,286	2,090	62.5
Western and Northern Md.	97,665	305,282	212.6	2,154	41,449	1824	19,141	17,430	8.9

10. White, Free Black, and Slave Population by Counties, 1790–1850
Numerical evidence of the transition that by the mid-nineteenth century had made Maryland home to more free blacks than any other state in the Union. Adapted from Barbara Jeanne Fields, *Slavery and Freedom on the Middle Ground: Maryland during the Nineteenth Century*, Yale Historical Publications, Miscellany 123 (New Haven, Conn: Yale University Press, 1985).

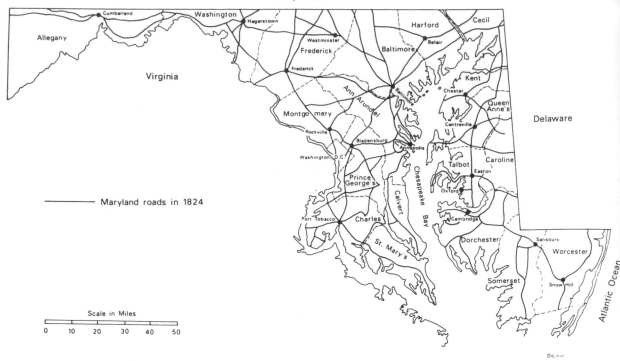

11. Maryland Roads, 1824
Adapted from Thompson et al., *Atlas of Maryland* / James E. DiLisio.

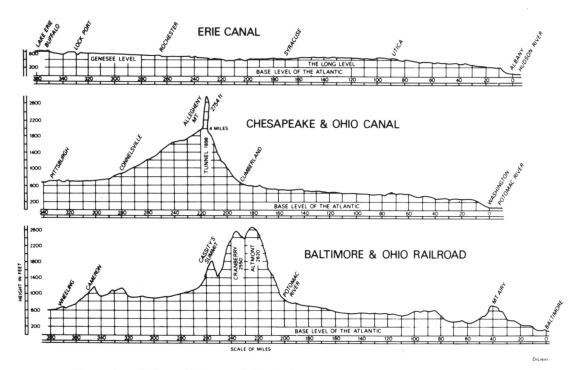

12. Trans-Appalachian Projects of the Early Nineteenth Century
The enormity of Maryland's task, compared to the topography of central New York. Adapted from Julius Rubin, *Canal or Railroad? Imitation and Innovation in Response to the Erie Canal in Philadelphia, Baltimore, and Boston, Transactions of the American Philosophical Society*, vol. 51, pt. 7 (Philadelphia: American Philosophical Society, 1961).

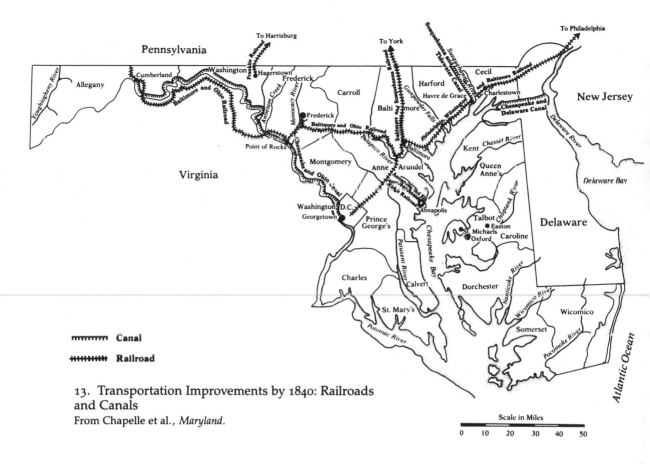

Canal

Railroad

13. Transportation Improvements by 1840: Railroads
and Canals

From Chapelle et al., *Maryland.*

Scale in Miles

0   10   20   30   40   50

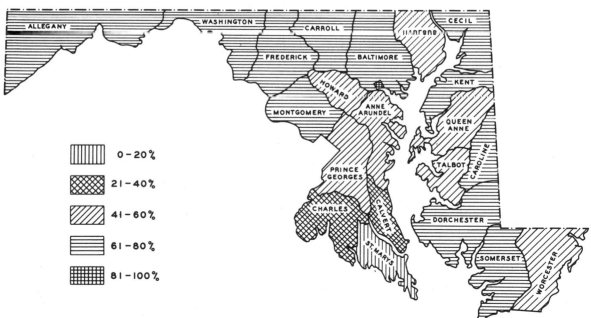

0 – 20 %

21 – 40 %

41 – 60 %

61 – 80 %

81 – 100 %

14. Geographic Distribution of Unionist Vote for Governor, November 1861

Support for Augustus W. Bradford reflected pro-Union sentiment in Maryland after the outbreak of
hostilities. From Jean H. Baker, *The Politics of Continuity: Maryland Political Parties from 1858 to 1870*
(Baltimore: Johns Hopkins University Press, 1973).

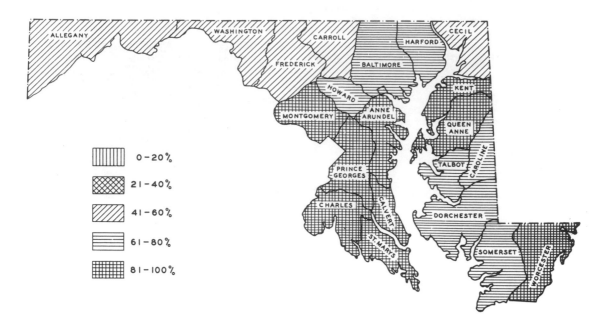

15. Geographic Distribution of Democratic Vote for President, 1868

The persistence of voting patterns following the 1867 constitutional convention. From Baker, *Politics of Continuity*.

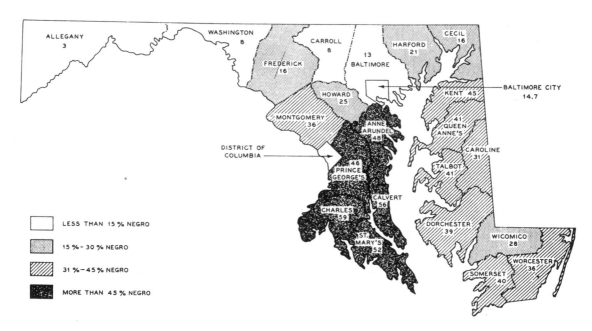

16. Negro Population, Maryland Counties and Baltimore City, 1870

After passage of the Fifteenth Amendment, Republican strength lay in Western Maryland, where there were few blacks, and in Southern Maryland, where there were many. From Margaret Law Callcott, *The Negro in Maryland Politics, 1870–1912*, JHUS 87 (1969).

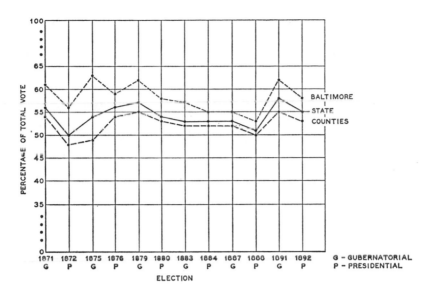

17. Democratic Party's Share of the Two-Party Vote in Baltimore City, the State, and the Counties, 1871–1892

The party claimed little more than half the vote, a thin margin of supremacy, in the late nineteenth century. From Callcott, *Negro in Maryland Politics*.

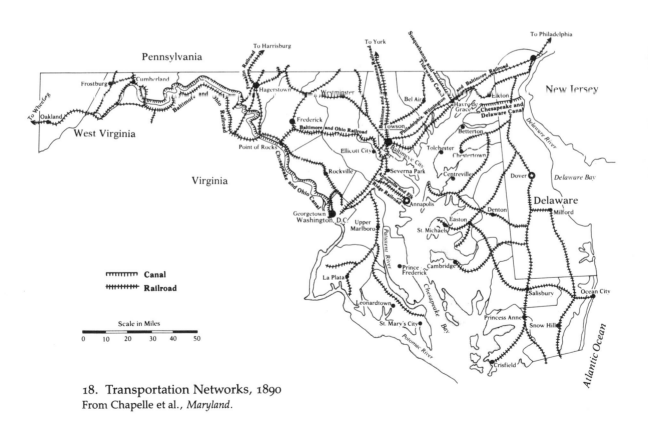

18. Transportation Networks, 1890

From Chapelle et al., *Maryland*.

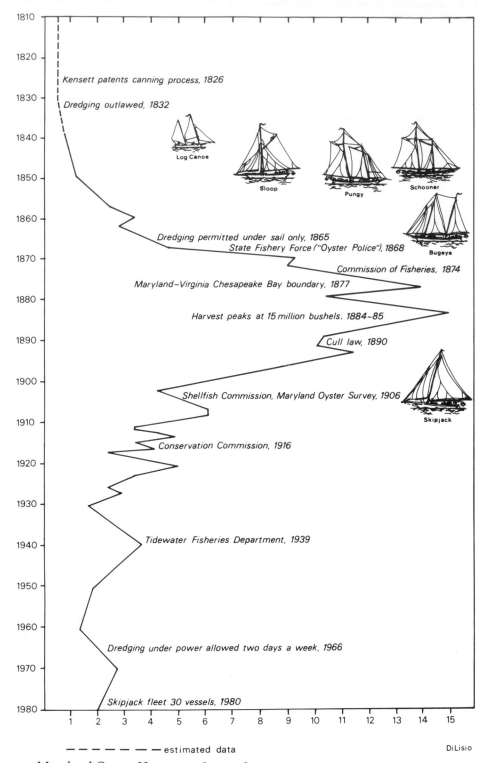

1810
1820
Kensett patents canning process, 1826
1830
Dredging outlawed, 1832
1840

Log Canoe

Sloop

Pungy

Schooner

1850

Bugeye

1860
Dredging permitted under sail only, 1865
State Fishery Force ("Oyster Police"), 1868
1870
Commission of Fisheries, 1874
Maryland–Virginia Chesapeake Bay boundary, 1877
1880
Harvest peaks at 15 million bushels, 1884–85
1890
Cull law, 1890

Skipjack

1900
Shellfish Commission, Maryland Oyster Survey, 1906
1910
Conservation Commission, 1916
1920
1930
Tidewater Fisheries Department, 1939
1940
1950
1960
Dredging under power allowed two days a week, 1966
1970
Skipjack fleet 30 vessels, 1980
1980

1 2 3 4 5 6 7 8 9 10 11 12 13 14 15

— — — — — — estimated data

DiLisio

19. Maryland Oyster Harvests, 1840–1980

Going after shellfish, nineteenth-century tongers typically used log canoes, while dredgers after the Civil War employed larger craft—sloops, pungies, schooners, bugeyes, and finally skipjacks. Adapted from chart in vertical file, Maryland Room, Pratt Library; Chapelle et al., *Maryland*; and *Sailing Craft of the Chesapeake Bay* (Maritime Museum, MHS) / James E. DiLisio.

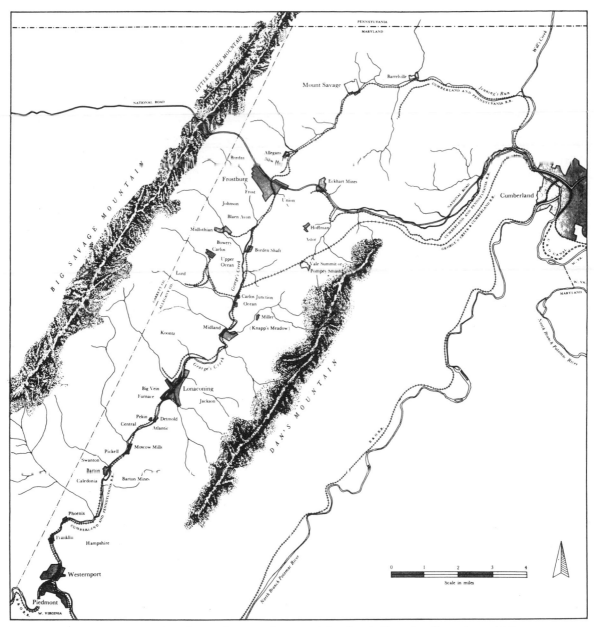

20. George's Creek Valley, Allegany County, Maryland, Showing Location of Mines

From Katherine A. Harvey, *The Best-Dressed Miners: Life and Labor in the Maryland Coal Region, 1835–1910.* Copyright © by Cornell University Press, 1969. Reprinted with permission of the publisher.

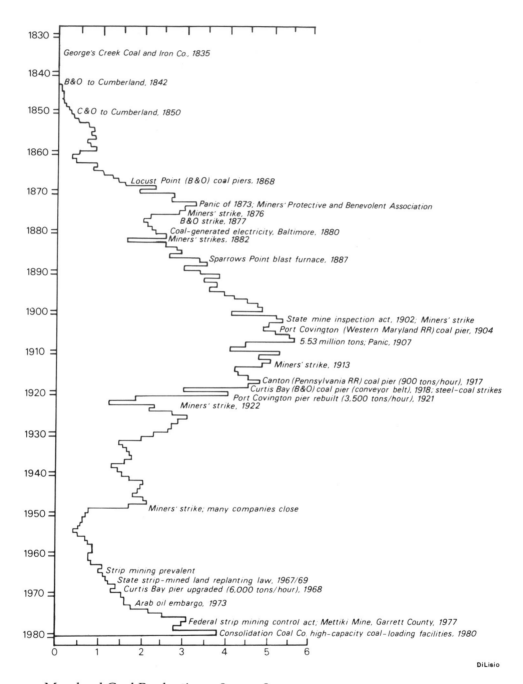

DiLisio

21. Maryland Coal Production, 1840–1980

Adapted from James E. DeLisio, *Maryland: A Geography,* Geographies of the United States, Ingolf Vogeler, gen. ed. (Boulder, Colo.: Westview Press, 1983).

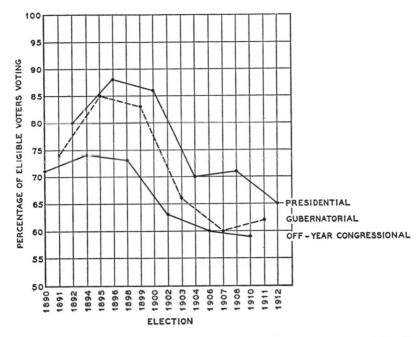

22. Effect of 1901 and 1904 Ballot–Law Changes on Voter Turnout in Maryland
A visual argument that Progressive legislation aimed to keep government clean partly by limiting the franchise. From Callcott, *Negro in Maryland Politics.*

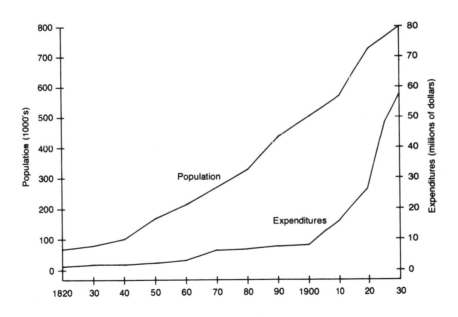

23. Baltimore Population and City Expenditures, 1820–1930
For years municipal spending lagged far behind population growth. From Alan D. Anderson, *The Origin and Resolution of an Urban Crisis: Baltimore, 1890–1930*, Johns Hopkins Studies in Urban Affairs (Baltimore: Johns Hopkins University Press, 1977).

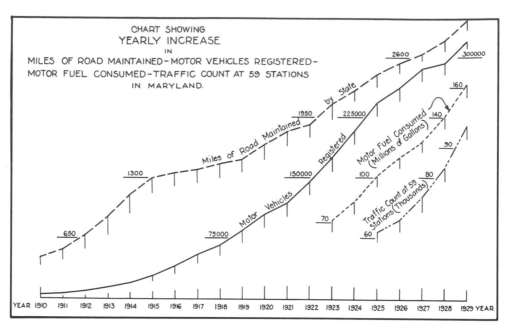

24. Miles of Road Maintained, Motor Vehicles Registered, Motor Fuel Consumed, and Traffic Count at Fifty-nine Locations in Maryland, 1910–1929
From State Roads Commission, *Annual Report*, 1930.

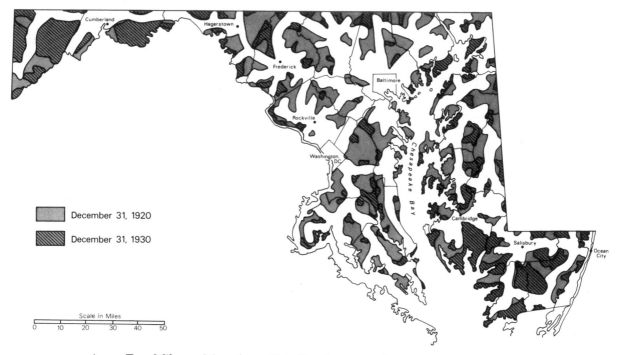

25. Areas Two Miles or More from State Road, 1920 and 1930
Adapted from State Roads Commission, *Annual Report*, 1930 / James E. DeLisio.

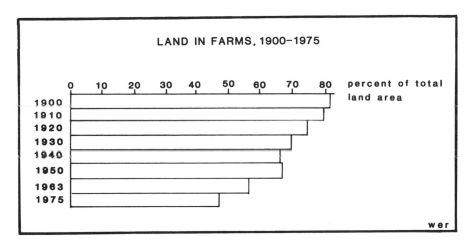

26. Land in Farms, 1900–1975
A decline interrupted only by World War II. From DeLisio, *Maryland*.

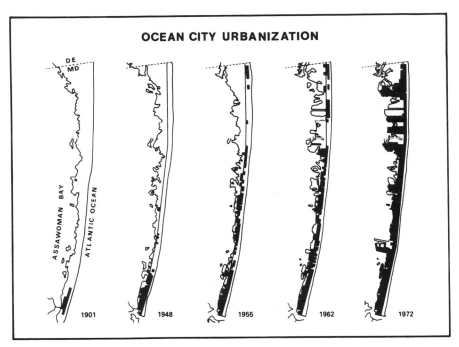

27. Ocean City Urbanization, 1901–1972
From DeLisio, *Maryland*.

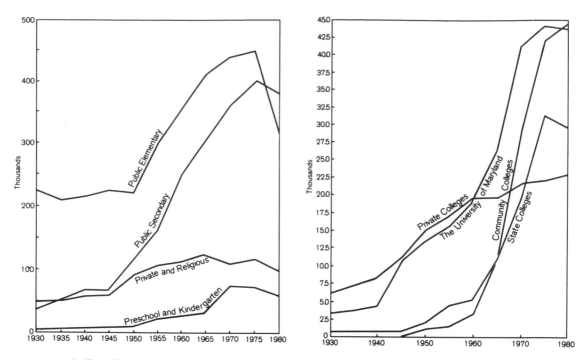

28. Enrollments in Schools and Higher Education, 1930–1980

The impact of the postwar "baby boom." From George H. Callcott, *Maryland and America, 1940–1980* (Baltimore: Johns Hopkins University Press, 1985).

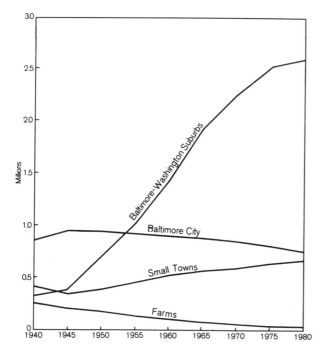

29. Population Trends, Maryland Cities, Suburbs, Towns, and Farms, 1940–1980
From Callcott, *Maryland and America.*

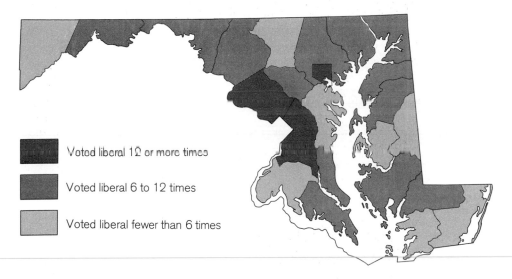

30. Support for Welfare State Liberalism, 1938–1980
Voting in nineteen gubernatorial, Senate, and presidential elections (and for congressman-at-large in 1962), Marylanders divided rather evenly on a central issue of the period—how much government could and should use its power to right social inequities and lower unemployment. From Callcott, *Maryland and America*.

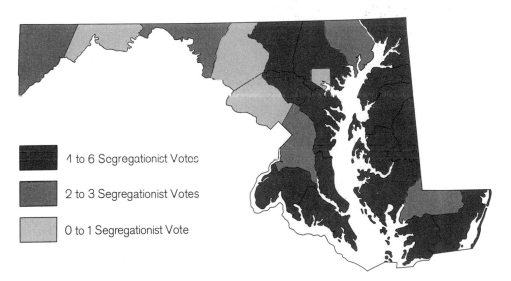

31. Votes on Segregation, 1954–1972
Dark shading reflects support for Harry C. "Curley" Byrd (for governor, 1954), George Wallace (in the 1964 and 1972 Democratic presidential primaries), and George Mahoney (for governor in 1966 and U.S. Senate in 1970) and hostility to the public accommodations bill that went to referendum in 1964. Factors at work in the lighter-shaded counties included the historic absence of a large Negro population, black population gains (as in Baltimore City and Prince George's County), suburban Washington government and professional employment, and migration from out of state. From Callcott, *Maryland and America*.

1955-1960   **1965 - 1970**

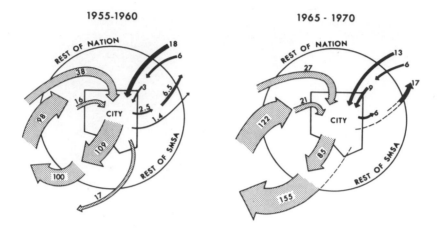

32. Migration Streams by Race

Thousands of moves made by residents of Baltimore City and the counties then in the Baltimore Standard Metropolitan Statistical Area (Anne Arundel, Baltimore, Carroll, and Howard) during two intervals. White movement (shaded) from city to suburbs was noteworthy in the five years after 1955, thereafter slowing somewhat; otherwise, white migration in the second interval intensified. Blacks (darker lines) were underrepresented in all moves, especially to the suburbs. From Sherry H. Olson, *Baltimore* (Cambridge, Mass.: Ballinger Publishing Co., 1976).

33. Black Population, Maryland and the District of Columbia, 1920–1970

Inexpensive housing in Prince George's County helped to account for the increase outside Washington, where it continued in the 1970s. From Thompson et al., *Atlas of Maryland.*

Northern Maryland: Allegany, Carroll, Frederick, Garrett, and Washington

Baltimore Area: Anne Arundel, Baltimore, Harford, and Howard

Suburban Washington: Montgomery and Prince George's

Southern Maryland: Charles, Calvert, and St. Mary's

Upper Eastern Shore: Caroline, Cecil, Kent, Queen Anne's, and Talbot

Lower Eastern Shore: Dorchester, Somerset, Wicomico, and Worcester

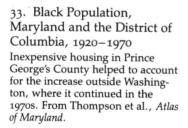

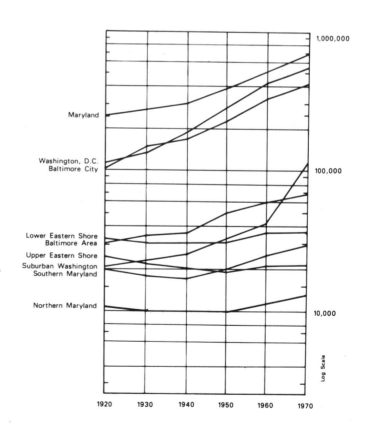

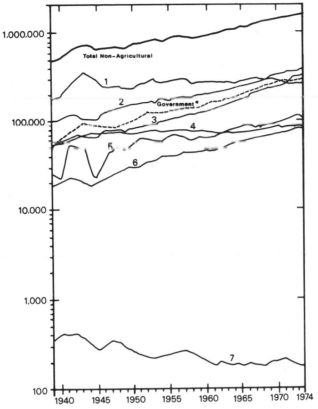

34. Civilian Employment Trends, 1939–1974

Manufacturing jobs, many involving men, dropped markedly, while employment in areas like government and service industries, often employing women, rose sharply. From Thompson et al., *Atlas of Maryland*.

1. Manufacturing
2. Trade
3. Services
4. Transportation
5. Construction
6. Finance, Insurance, and Real Estate
7. Mining
*Excludes federal civilian employment in Montgomery and Prince George's counties, about another 60,000 persons in 1974

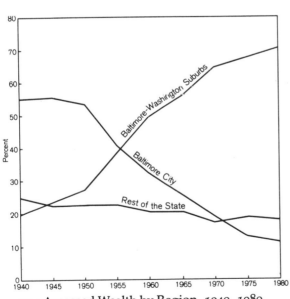

35. Assessed Wealth by Region, 1940–1980, as a Percentage of Total State Wealth

The state's largest city and the Maryland suburbs suddenly exchanged places in about 1955. From Callcott, *Maryland and America*.

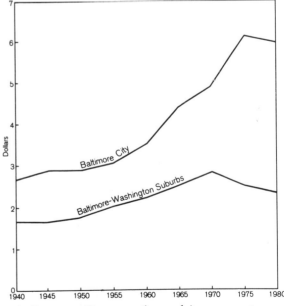

36. Property Taxes per $100 of Assessment, City and Suburban, 1940–1980

From Callcott, *Maryland and America*.

Year	Water Pollution Control Expenditures ($)	Per Capita Expenditure Rank among States	Air Pollution Control Expenditures ($)	Per Capita Expenditure Rank among States
1951	57,000	—		—
1961	160,000	8	38,000	6
1969	2,855,000	4	242,000	6
1971	13,137,000	3	973,000	4
1980	35,678,000	7	2,529,000	16

S O U R C E : U.S. Bureau of the Census, *State and Local Government Special Studies, Environmental Quality Control, 1971, 1980* (1972, 1982).

37. Pollution Control, 1951–1980
From Callcott, *Maryland and America.*

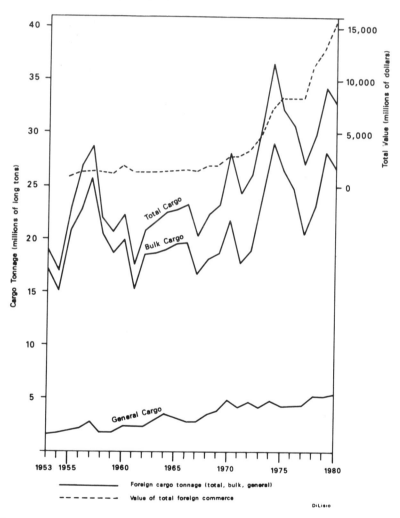

38. Foreign Oceanborne Commerce through Baltimore, 1953–1980
Bulk products include oil, coal, and grain; the category of general freight covers virtually everything that requires the handling of individual items. While total tonnage varied in these years, valuation held steady and then shot up after about 1970, due in large measure to containerized freight and foreign auto and truck imports. Source: Maryland Port Authority and *Maryland Statistical Abstract* / James E. DeLisio.

DiLisio

39. Baltimore's Foreign Oceanborne Commerce as a Share of Total U.S. and Eastern Seaboard Traffic, 1956–1980, and the Maryland Unemployment Rate, 1968–1980
The jobless rate among working-age civilians depended on many factors, but port activity, with its ripple effects throughout the state, remained an important one. Source: Maryland Port Authority and *Statistical Abstract of the United States, 1970–1982* / James E. DeLisio.

Year	Total Votes Cast in U.S.	Percent U.S. Voter Turnout	Total Votes Cast in Md.	Percent Md. Voter Turnout
1812	—unavailable—		29,577	55.7
1816	—unavailable—		10,817	19.6
1820	—unavailable—		5,379	9.4
1824	365,833	26.9	33,300	53.7
1828	1,148,018	57.6	46,873	70.3
1832	1,293,973	55.4	37,926	55.7
1836	1,503,534	57.8	49,121	67.6
1840	2,411,808	80.2	62,292	84.5
1844	2,703,659	78.9	68,660	81.4
1848	2,879,184	72.7	72,363	76.0
1852	3,161,830	69.6	75,064	72.8
1856	4,054,647	78.9	86,862	80.0
1860	4,685,561	81.2	92,649	81.1
1864	4,031,887	73.8	72,908	57.7
1868	5,722,440	78.1	92,807	72.6
1872	6,467,679	71.3	134,447	75.0
1876	8,413,101	81.8	163,756	82.7
1880	9,210,420	79.4	172,221	79.8
1884	10,049,754	77.5	185,833	79.9
1888	11,383,320	79.3	210,921	84.8
1892	12,056,097	74.7	213,275	79.9
1896	13,935,738	79.3	250,877	87.3
1900	13,970,470	73.2	264,433	85.9
1904	13,518,964	65.2	224,224	69.6
1908	14,882,734	65.4	238,531	70.9
1912	15,040,963	58.8	231,981	64.8
1916	18,535,022	61.6	262,039	68.1
1920	26,753,786	49.2	428,442	52.3
1924	29,075,959	48.9	358,630	41.0
1928	36,790,364	56.9	528,348	56.8
1932	39,749,382	56.9	511,054	51.2
1936	45,642,303	61.0	624,896	58.1
1940	49,840,443	62.5	660,135	57.2
1944	47,974,819	55.9	608,439	46.7
1948	48,692,442	53.0	599,029	41.7
1952	61,551,118	63.3	902,074	57.5
1956	62,025,372	60.6	932,827	54.6
1960	68,828,960	64.0	1,055,349	58.3
1964	70,641,104	61.7	1,116,457	54.7
1968	73,203,370	60.6	1,235,039	55.2
1972	77,727,590	55.2	1,353,812	49.8
1976	81,555,889	53.5	1,438,229	49.3
1980	86,513,296	52.6	1,540,496	50.0

40. Participation in Presidential Elections as a Percentage of Eligible Voting-Age Population, U.S. and Maryland, 1812–1980

Ratification of the Fifteenth (1870), Nineteenth (1920), and Twenty-sixth (1971) Amendments enabled new groups to vote and thus changed the basis for the "turnout" calculation. Elections following the eligibility of women and of youth aged eighteen to twenty-one years did not, however, lead to sudden surges of voter interest. By the late twentieth century, apathy among roughly half of all voting-age citizens had become commonplace. From John T. Willis, *Presidential Elections in Maryland* (Mt. Airy, Md.: Lomond Publications, 1984).

CHRONOLOGY

1629	George Calvert, Lord Baltimore, sails from Newfoundland to Virginia.
1631	William Claiborne, member of the Virginia council, establishes trading post and farming settlement on Kent Island.
1632	Charles I grants Maryland Charter to Cecil Calvert, second Lord Baltimore.
1633	English settlers on *Ark* and *Dove* depart Cowes for America (22 November).
1634–44	Leonard Calvert, governor.
1634	Calvert party, having landed at St. Clement's Island in Potomac River, celebrates Feast of Annunciation (March 25), later purchases Indian land and builds "Fort at St. Mary's City."
1635	Freemen meet in St. Mary's as a lawmaking assembly; proprietary vessels clash with those of Claiborne; Jerome Hawley and John Lewger publish *A Relation of Maryland* (London).
1636	Leonard Calvert House (later known as Country's House), East St. Mary's, serves as governor's residence and state house.
1637	Provincial records first refer to St. Mary's County.
1638	Assembly claims protections of English law; John Lewger's St. John's serves as meeting place for assembly and courts.
1639	Governor Calvert orders elections (first in province) on Kent Island and in hundreds of Mattapanient, St. Michael's, St. Mary's, and St. George's for delegates to assembly.
1642	Governor's appointment of commissioners makes earliest reference to Kent County.
1643–44	Giles Brent, acting provincial governor.
1645	Richard Ingle leads rebellion against proprietary government.
1646–47	Leonard Calvert again governor.
1647–49	Thomas Greene, governor.
1649–52	William Stone, governor.
1649	Stone invites Virginia Puritans to settle in Maryland; assembly passes An Act Concerning Religion, later known as Toleration Act (20 April).
1650	Assembly creates Anne Arundel County, divides itself into upper and lower chambers.
1652	Parliamentary commissioners displace proprietary regime.
1654	Order in council forms Patuxent, later Calvert, County.
1655	Puritans defeat Stone at Battle of the Severn.
1656	John Hammond publishes *Leah and Rachel* (London).
1657	Lord Baltimore reestablishes proprietary authority.
1657–60	Josias Fendall, governor.
1658	Order in council creates Charles County; lower house votes to constitute itself of four delegates per county, elected by freemen.
1660–61	Philip Calvert, governor.
1660	Lord Proprietary's writ proves earlier creation of Baltimore County; Augustine Herrman, first naturalized citizen of Maryland (1663), establishes Bohemia Manor.

1661–76   Charles Calvert, governor.

1662   Sheriff's writ establishes earlier creation of Talbot County.

1664   Provincial statute refers to lifetime black bondage; probable date for building of frame Secretary's Office or Council Chamber (later van Swearingen Ordinary), St. Mary's.

1666   Order in council establishes Somerset County; assembly agrees to one-year "stint" on tobacco growing, but Lord Baltimore vetoes; George Alsop publishes *A Character of the Province of Maryland* (London).

1669   Proprietary writ establishes existence of Dorchester County.

1670   Governor restricts vote to planters with 50-acre freehold or property worth £40 and officeholding to owners of 1,000 acres; Herrman completes authoritative map of Maryland (engraved, London, 1673).

1672   George Fox preaches in Anne Arundel County; Friends form Maryland Yearly Meeting.

1674   Governor forms Cecil County out of Baltimore and Kent.

1676–79   Thomas Notley, governor.

1676   Brick state house completed, St. Mary's City (incorporated, 1667); proprietor limits delegates to two per county.

1679–84   Charles Calvert, third Lord Baltimore, governor.

1679   Philip Calvert begins construction of St. Peter's, largest brick structure in province; governor grants county courts jurisdiction over civil suits.

1681   Provincial court finds Fendall guilty of conspiracy, fines and banishes him.

1682   Quakers begin building Third Haven Meeting House, Talbot County (completed 1684).

1683   Proprietor replaces headright system of land grants with "caution money" or outright purchase; assembly passes Act for Advancement of Trade or town act; Labadist community settles at Bohemia Manor.

1684–89   Council of deputy governors rules Maryland in the name of the child Benedict Leonard Calvert.

1684   Commissioners lay out Cambridge on Choptank River; Presbyterians under Francis Makemie build church at Snow Hill, first in colonies.

1685   William Nuthead establishes printing press, St. Mary's City.

1689   Protestant Associators overthrow proprietary officers.

1692   William and Mary declare Maryland a royal colony and appoint Sir Lionel Copley governor; assembly makes first attempt to establish the Church of England (successful in 1702).

1693–94   Sir Thomas Lawrence, Sir Edmund Andros, and Nicholas Greenberry briefly serve as governors.

1694–99   Sir Francis Nicholson, governor.

1694   Anne Arundell Town replaces St. Mary's City as capital; Nicholson lays out plan for city.

1695   Assembly creates Prince George's County from Charles and Calvert.

1696   Construction begins on new state house (completed 1704) and probably on St. Anne's Church (completed 1704); Nicholson and others found King William's School.

1698   Parliament abolishes Royal African Company monopoly and black slave imports increase markedly; Kent County Court House moves to New Town (later Chestertown) from New Yarmouth.

1699–1704 Nathaniel Blackiston or his appointee, acting governor.

1704–9   John Seymour, governor.

1704   State house burns (October).

1706	Assembly forms Queen Anne's County.
1708	Justus Engelhardt Kühn, portrait painter, arrives in Maryland; Ebenezer Cook publishes *The Sot-Weed Factor* (London).
1709–14	Edward Lloyd, president of the council, acts as governor.
1710	Talbot Court House (later East Town or Easton).
1714–20	John Hart, governor.
1715	Crown restores proprietary rights to Benedict Leonard Calvert, fourth Lord Baltimore (February); Charles Calvert succeeds as fifth Lord Baltimore (April); English capital finances Principio Iron Works, Cecil County.
1718	Assembly disfranchises Roman Catholics.
1720–27	Charles Calvert, governor.
1723	Assembly mandates school and board of visitors in each county.
1727–31	Benedict Leonard Calvert, governor.
1727	William Parks, Annapolis, publishes first newspaper in the Chesapeake, the *Maryland Gazette* (until 1734).
1729	Baltimore Town receives charter.
1730	Cook publishes *Sotweed Redivivus* (Annapolis).
1731–32	Samuel Ogle, governor.
1731	Baltimore Company begins ironmaking on the Patapsco River.
1732–33	Charles Calvert, governor.
1732	Boundary settlement concedes Delaware counties to Pennsylvania; commissioners lay out Salisbury Town.
1733–42	Samuel Ogle, governor.
1741	Thomas Cresap founds Oldtown on upper Potomac.
1742–47	Thomas Bladen, governor.
1742	Assembly creates Worcester County; Baptists establish first church in Maryland at Chestnut Ridge, Baltimore County.
1743	Monocacy River Lutherans under David Candler build first church in Maryland.
1744	Assembly purchases last Indian land claims in Maryland.
1745	Tuesday Club forms in Annapolis; Maryland Jockey Club organizes first races; Jonas Green revives *Maryland Gazette*; Daniel Dulany the Elder lays out Frederick Town and invites German settlement; assembly combines Jones Town and Baltimore Town.
1747–52	Samuel Ogle, governor.
1747	Tobacco inspection law establishes multiple inspection points to ensure export of only quality leaf and sets clerical and proprietary officers' fees; Michael Schlatter organizes Reformed Lutheran congregation in Frederick (May).
1748	Assembly forms Frederick County from Baltimore and Prince George's.
1750	Ohio Company establishes trading post at Will's Creek on Potomac River; about this time John Stevenson ships cargo of flour to Ireland, first in an export trade that spurs development of Baltimore.
1752–53	Benjamin Tasker, president of the council, acts as governor.
1752	John Moale sketches Baltimore Town.
1753–69	Horatio Sharpe, governor.
1754	Militiamen construct Fort Cumberland.
1755	French and Indians defeat General Edward Braddock's forces near Fort Duquesne; Indians attack western settlers; French-speaking Catholics arrive in Baltimore from Nova Scotia.

1756   Assembly supplies funds for Fort Frederick, near North Mountain.

1762   Jonathan Hager lays out Elizabeth Town (later Hagerstown).

1763   Charles Mason and Jeremiah Dixon begin surveying Maryland-Pennsylvania boundary (completed 1767); first volunteer fire company, later Mechanical Company, forms in Baltimore.

1765   Popular meetings and Daniel Dulany, Jr.'s *Considerations on the Propriety of Imposing Taxes in the British Colonies* (Annapolis) denounce Stamp Act.

1766   Sons of Liberty organize in Baltimore County.

1767   Annapolis merchants send Charles Willson Peale to London to study painting with Benjamin West.

1768   Baltimore County seat moves from Joppa to Baltimore Town.

1769–76   Robert Eden, governor.

1769   Maryland merchants adopt nonimportation of British goods; Henry Stevenson establishes first smallpox hospital in colonies, Baltimore.

1771   First brick theater in America opens in Annapolis.

1772   Work begins on new State House, Annapolis; Ellicott brothers build largest flour mill in Maryland on Patapsco River; Methodists under Robert Strawbridge build first house of worship in colonies, John Evans House, Frederick (later Carroll) County.

1773   Assembly creates Caroline County of Dorchester and Queen Anne's, forms Harford County from Baltimore, and unites Fells Point and Baltimore Town; *Maryland Gazette* carries "Antilon"/"First Citizen" debate on officers' fees; William Goddard begins printing *Maryland Journal and Baltimore Advertiser*.

1774   Provincial Convention, an extralegal body, meets in Annapolis (22 June) and sends delegates to First Continental Congress; Baltimoreans ship cargo of corn, rye, and bread to people of Boston (August); Annapolis mob burns *Peggy Stewart* (19 October); Mordecai Gist forms Baltimore Independent Cadets (December); Catoctin Furnace, Frederick County.

1775   Bush River, Harford County, patriots call for independence (22 March); rifle companies under Michael Cresap and Thomas Price depart Frederick Town to join Washington's army at Boston (18 July); Maryland Convention adopts Articles of Association of Freemen (26 July), begins recruiting troops (December).

1776   Colonel William Smallwood organizes First Battalion of Maryland (forerunner of Maryland Line), Captain James Nicholson commands Maryland sloop *Defence*; Whig Club forms in Baltimore (March); Eden departs Annapolis (26 June); Maryland Convention adopts independence resolution (3 July); Charles Carroll of Carrollton, Samuel Chase, Thomas Stone, and William Paca sign Declaration of Independence at Philadelphia (4 July); Maryland troops under Gist fight crucial delaying action at Gowanus Creek, Long Island (27 August); Maryland Convention passes Declaration of Rights and disestablishes Church of England (3 November), adopts state constitution (8 November), and creates Montgomery and Washington counties out of Frederick. Congress meets in Baltimore (20 December–4 March 1777).

1777–79   Thomas Johnson, governor.

1778   Count Casimir Pulaski raises independent troops, Baltimore.

1779–82   Thomas Sim Lee, governor.

1779   Maryland Anglicans refer to themselves as Protestant Episcopal church.

1780   Baltimore becomes port of entry.

1781   Maryland Line under John Eager Howard plays decisive part in Battle of

Cowpens (January); assembly ratifies Articles of Confederation (1 March); John Hanson elected president of Congress (5 November).

1782–85   William Paca, governor.

1782   Washington College, Chestertown, emerges from Kent Academy.

1783   Freemasons, meeting at Talbot Court House, form Maryland Grand Lodge; Congress convenes in Annapolis (26 November–3 June 1784); Washington resigns as Continental Army commander in Annapolis (23 December).

1784   John Frederick Amelung and party establish New Bremen, Frederick County, glassworks; Maryland and Virginia charter Potomac Company; Edward Warren, Baltimore, makes first balloon ascension in United States aboard balloon designed by Peter Carnes, Bladensburg (June); Methodist Christmas Conference, Baltimore, establishes Methodist Episcopal church in America; assembly charters Western Shore college, St. John's, and designates it, with Washington College, as the University of Maryland (30 December).

1785–88   William Smallwood, governor.

1785   John O'Donnell arrives in Baltimore with cargo from Canton, China; assembly agrees to compact with Virginia governing Potomac–Chesapeake Bay fishing and navigation (December); German Evangelical Reformed congregation under Philip William Otterbein builds United Brethren Church, Baltimore.

1786   Delegates from several states (Maryland not among them) meet at Mann's Tavern, Annapolis, to discuss revisions to the Articles of Confederation (11–14 September); Matthias Bartgis begins newspaper publishing in Frederick.

1787   Assembly authorizes toll roads connecting Baltimore with Frederick, Westminster, Hanover, and York; Friends' Yearly Meeting, Baltimore, condemns slavery; Methodists open Cokesbury College, Abingdon (December); James Rumsey launches steamboat on Potomac River near Shepherdstown, Virginia (December).

1788–91   John Eager Howard, governor.

1788   Maryland convention ratifies federal Constitution (26 April), adjourns without recommending amendments; parade and festival give name to Federal Hill (1 May).

1789   Assembly creates Allegany County from Washington, charters Georgetown College; Maryland Society for Promoting the Abolition of Slavery and the Relief of Poor Negroes and Others Unlawfully Held in Bondage forms, Baltimore; general meeting of Roman Catholic clergy recommends John Carroll to be pastor of American church.

1790   By papal direction Bishop Charles Walmsley consecrates Carroll bishop of Baltimore, Ludworth Castle, England (August); assembly incorporates East Town or Easton; James Cowan publishes Easton *Maryland Herald*; Stewart Herbert begins printing Elizabeth Town *Washington Spy*, first newspaper west of Blue Ridge Mountains.

1791–92   George Plater, governor.

1791   Maryland cedes territory for federal District of Columbia; Benjamin Banneker publishes almanac.

1792–94   Thomas Sim Lee (Federalist), governor.

1792   Blacks form Sharp Street Church, Baltimore.

1793   Refugees from Haitian slave uprising arrive in Baltimore.

1794–97   John H. Stone (Federalist), governor.

1794   Baltimore Equitable Society forms, first fire insurance company in Maryland;

first of many yellow fever epidemics strikes Baltimore; courthouse opens at Queen Anne's County seat (1792), Centreville.

1795   Bank of Baltimore; federal government establishes post office at Cumberland.

1796   Baltimore leaders obtain city incorporation; Maryland law forbids import of slaves for sale, permits voluntary slave emancipation.

1797–98 John Henry (Federalist), governor.

1797   David Stodder's shipyard, Harris Creek, launches United States Frigate *Constellation* (September).

1798–1801 Benjamin Ogle (Federalist), governor.

1799   Construction begins on Fort McHenry; Alexander Martin establishes Baltimore *American and Daily Advertiser*.

1801–3 John Francis Mercer (Democratic-Republican), governor.

1802   Assembly confirms constitutional amendment removing property qualifications for voting in local and state elections (granting the suffrage to adult white males) and replacing voice voting with ballots; Daniel Coker ministers to black Methodists, Baltimore.

1803–6 Robert Bowie (Democratic-Republican), governor.

1804   Baltimore Water Company forms (chartered 1792); Levi Hollingsworth establishes mining operation, Gunpowder Copper Works.

1806–9 Robert Wright (Democratic-Republican), governor.

1806   Benjamin Henry Latrobe begins America's first Roman Catholic cathedral, Baltimore (main part completed 1818); Maximilien Godefroy designs first Gothic Revival structure in United States, St. Mary's Seminary Chapel, Baltimore (completed 1808).

1807   College of Medicine of Maryland, Baltimore.

1808   Elizabeth Seton opens female academy, Baltimore; John Dubois establishes Mount St. Mary's College, Emmitsburg.

1809–11 Edward Lloyd V (Democratic-Republican), governor.

1809   Washington Cotton Manufacturing Company, Mount Washington, first in state, receives charter; Seton adopts modified rule of Sisters of Charity, establishes order in Emmitsburg; St. Joseph's College, Emmitsburg.

1810   Assembly confirms constitutional amendment extending adult white male suffrage to federal elections and amendment abolishing property qualifications for state officeholding.

1811–12 Robert Bowie (Democratic-Republican), governor.

1811   Hezekiah Niles, Baltimore, begins publishing *Niles' Register*; work begins on National Road; Alexander Brown & Sons opens as investment banking firm.

1812–16 Levin Winder (Federalist), governor.

1812   Mob attacks Alexander Contee Hanson, editor Baltimore *Federal Republican*, and party (July); College of Medicine receives charter as University of Maryland; Thomas Kemp, Fells Point, launches Baltimore Clipper *Chasseur*, later famous under command of Thomas Boyle.

1813   Assembly incorporates Hagerstown; first steamboat, *Chesapeake*, appears on bay; British conduct raids on Chesapeake targets, including Havre de Grace.

1814   Rembrandt Peale opens the Baltimore Museum and Gallery of Fine Arts, designed by Robert Cary Long, Sr. (August); sailors and marines under Joshua Barney fight rear-guard action at Battle of Bladensburg (24 August); local militia meets British at North Point (12 September) and Baltimore (13–14 September); Francis Scott Key writes "Star Spangled Banner."

1815	Baltimoreans lay cornerstones for Robert Mills's Washington Monument (July; completed 1829) and Godefroy's Battle Monument (September; completed 1825); Charles Reeder establishes steam-engine manufactory and foundry, Federal Hill.
1816–19	Charles Ridgely (Federalist), governor.
1816	Rembrandt Peale demonstrates gas lighting at his museum; Delphian Club organizes, Baltimore; Daniel Coker and other black church leaders form independent African Methodist Episcopal church.
1817	Gas Light Company incorporates to provide streetlights in Baltimore, first such firm in country (February); Godefroy begins Unitarian Temple, Baltimore; Maryland auxiliary of American Colonization Society forms, Baltimore.
1818	Savings Bank of Baltimore, first of its kind in state; Maryland Agricultural Society organizes, Baltimore; National Road opens between Cumberland and Wheeling, Virginia.
1819	Charles Goldsborough (Federalist), governor; John Stuart Skinner publishes the *American Farmer*, Baltimore; Independent Order of Odd Fellows organizes in Baltimore.
1819–22	Samuel Sprigg (Republican), governor.
1822–26	Samuel Stevens, Jr. (Republican), governor.
1822	Isaac McKim mills flour with steam power, Baltimore, first such operation in country.
1824	Work begins on Chesapeake and Delaware Canal (completed 1829); Benjamin Lundy publishes the *Genius of Universal Emancipation*, Baltimore.
1825	Marquis de Lafayette revisits Baltimore; Maryland Institute holds first exhibition.
1826–29	Joseph Kent (Republican), governor.
1826	After several defeats, "Jew Bill" passes legislature, enabling Jews to hold public office; Thomas Kensett begins canning oysters in Baltimore.
1827	Boonsboro citizens erect monument to Washington, South Mountain (July).
1828	Baltimore Shot Tower begun (June); first earth turned (4 July) for construction of Baltimore and Ohio Railroad (chartered February 1827) and Chesapeake and Ohio Canal; Maryland and Virginia Steam Boat Company offers regular Baltimore to Norfolk service; Maryland penitentiary directors appoint committee to recommend plans for expansion.
1829–30	Daniel Martin (anti-Jackson), governor.
1829	Work begins on Baltimore and Susquehanna Railroad (completed to Pennsylvania line 1832); Oblate Sisters of Providence open school for black children, Baltimore; B&O's Carrollton Viaduct, first masonry railroad bridge in country, crosses Gwynn's Falls; John M. Dyer and twelve others organize state's first Jewish congregation, Nidhei Israel, Baltimore; Chesapeake and Delaware Canal opens.
1830–31	Thomas King Carroll (Democrat), governor.
1830	Peter Cooper and other investors start earliest planned industrial area in country at Canton; B&O station at Mount Clare first in United States.
1831	Howard heirs donate land for parks to extend north, south, east, and west of Washington Monument; Maryland Colonization Society forms in Baltimore (February); B&O station, Ellicott's Mills.
1831–33	George Howard (anti-Jackson), governor.
1832	John Pendleton Kennedy publishes *Swallow Barn*; assembly passes new legislation restricting free blacks in aftermath of Nat Turner rebellion, prohibits oyster dredging; first omnibus lines appear in Baltimore.

1833–36 James Thomas (anti-Jackson), governor.

1833 Baltimore *Saturday Morning Visitor* publishes Edgar Allan Poe's "Ms. Found in a Bottle," winner of fifty-dollar prize (October); first settlers sail for Cape Palmas, Liberia (November).

1834 B&O reaches Harpers Ferry.

1835 Red Men organize Great Council of Maryland, Baltimore; Baltimore mobs demonstrate against Bank of Maryland and its directors (6–8 August); Baltimore and Washington Railroad opens (25 August); George's Creek Coal and Iron Company forms; B&O's Thomas Viaduct, first multispan masonry railroad bridge in country, crosses Patapsco River at Relay.

1836–39 Thomas W. Veazey (Whig), governor.

1837 Chief Justice Roger Brooke Taney writes majority opinion in *Charles River* v. *Warren Bridge* case; Whig-controlled assembly passes reform bill providing for popular election of governors and state senators and rotating geographical districts of successive governors; Arunah S. Abell begins publishing the *Sun*, Baltimore (17 May); voters approve constitutional amendment forming Carroll County out of Baltimore and Frederick.

1838 Frederick Douglass escapes Baltimore slavery; Philadelphia, Wilmington, and Baltimore Railroad Company forms.

1839–42 William Grason (Democrat), governor.

1839 Mercantile Library Association; Baltimore City Council establishes Central High School (later City College); David Carroll and Horatio Gambrill open textile mills, Hamden-Woodberry.

1840 Washington Temperance Society; Baltimore Steam Packet Company (Old Bay Line); Baltimore College of Dental Surgery.

1841 Maryland College of Pharmacy.

1842–45 Francis Thomas (Democrat), governor.

1842 Slaveholders' convention meets at Annapolis; B&O reaches Cumberland.

1844 Maryland Historical Society (January); Samuel F. B. Morse sends first telegraph message from Washington to Baltimore (24 May).

1845–48 Thomas G. Pratt (Whig), governor.

1845 Lloyd Street Synagogue, Baltimore, first in Maryland and a Robert Cary Long, Jr., design; Frederick Douglass publishes *Narrative* of his life in slavery; Department of the Navy establishes officers' training school at Fort Severn, Annapolis; Baltimore and Cuba Smelting and Mining Company, Baltimore.

1846 James Corner opens first transatlantic packet line, Baltimore to Liverpool.

1848–51 Philip Francis Thomas (Democrat), governor.

1848 State Agricultural Chemist, first such in country; John Nepomucene Neumann, Redemptorist priest, builds Saints Peter and Paul Catholic Church, Baltimore.

1849 Harriet Tubman escapes slavery in Dorchester County; Josiah Henson, former Charles County slave, publishes his *Life*.

1850 President Street (Philadelphia, Wilmington, and Baltimore Railroad) and Calvert Street (Baltimore and Susquehanna) stations, Baltimore; C&O reaches Cumberland (October); Sun Iron Building, Baltimore's first all-iron structure.

1851–54 Enoch Louis Lowe (Democrat), governor.

1851 Constitutional Convention adjourns (May); voters adopt new constitution (June), which recognizes Howard District as Howard County; *Seaman*, Baltimore, establishes San Francisco to Cape Henry speed record for sail (94 days).

1852	Statewide convention of free blacks, Baltimore (July); Boston Steamship Company (later Merchants and Miners Transportation) begins coastal shipping service, Baltimore; evangelical groups form Young Men's Christian Association, Baltimore (November); B&O lines reach Wheeling, Virginia (December); Thomas Kerney introduces bill to aid parochial schools; Loyola College, Baltimore; Association of Maryland Pilots.
1853	Henry Sonneborn, Baltimore, begins manufacturing clothing; Baltimore, Carroll, and Frederick Railroad (later Western Maryland).
1854–58	Thomas Watkins Ligon (Democrat), governor.
1854	Baltimore County seat moves to Towson Town.
1855	*Mary Whitridge*, Baltimore built clipper ship, sets transatlantic sailing record (12½ days) never broken; Know-Nothings win fall elections.
1856	Camden Street (B&O) Station; Hebrew Benevolent Society, Baltimore; election violence, Baltimore (October–November).
1857	Baltimore gentlemen form Maryland Club; Chief Justice Taney writes majority opinion in case of *Dred Scott* v. *Sanford*.
1858–62	Thomas Holliday Hicks (Know-Nothing), governor.
1859	Maryland Agricultural College, Prince George's County (6 October); John Brown uses Washington County farm to launch attack on federal arsenal at Harpers Ferry (16 October); first horsecar line, Baltimore.
1860	Druid Hill Park opens, Baltimore; assembly passes Jacobs bill to enslave free blacks but measure fails referendum; Constitutional Union party forms in Baltimore (May); Maryland voters give John C. Breckinridge (Southern rights Democrat) 42,482 votes, John Bell (Constitutional Union) 41,760, Stephen A. Douglas (popular sovereignty Democrat) 5,966, and Abraham Lincoln (Republican) 2,294 in presidential election; Irish-born population of Baltimore City peaks (15,536 of 212,418).
1861	Baltimore mob attacks Massachusetts volunteers (19 April); federal troops occupy Annapolis (22 April); assembly convenes in Frederick (26 April); President Lincoln suspends writ of habeas corpus between Washington and Philadelphia (27 April); Union troops occupy Baltimore (13 May); sitting on circuit, Chief Justice Taney calls in vain for the release of John Merryman (27–28 May); congressional elections return Unionist delegation, military arrests Baltimore police board members (June); Secretary of War Cameron orders arrest of secessionist members of the assembly (11 September); voters defeat states' rights candidate for governor, Benjamin Chew Howard (November); Peabody Institute (later west wing) opens in Baltimore.
1862–66	Augustus W. Bradford (Unionist), governor.
1862	James Ryder Randall writes "My Maryland"; Marylanders oppose one another at Battle of Front Royal (23 May); Confederate cavalry enters Cumberland (16 June); Union troops force Crampton's and Turner's gaps, South Mountain (14 September); Battle of Antietam or Sharpsburg leaves more than 4,800 men dead and 18,000 wounded (17 September); Stuart's cavalry rides through Washington, Frederick, and Montgomery counties during raid into Pennsylvania (10–12 October).
1863	Lee's army passes through Washington County during invasion of Pennsylvania, retreats from Gettysburg (late June-early July).
1864	Unionist convention meets in Annapolis to rewrite constitution (27 April–6 September); Confederate forces under Jubal Early demand ransoms of Hagerstown and Frederick residents (6, 9 July), defeat Lew Wallace at Battle of Monocacy (9 July), and send cavalry raiders north of Baltimore and then through Prince George's County; soldiers' vote assures adoption (29

October) of 1864 constitution, which abolishes slavery (effective 1 November) and requires strict loyalty oath of voters.

1865   John Wilkes Booth assassinates President Lincoln and escapes through Prince George's and Charles counties (April); Frederick Douglass dedicates institute bearing his name, Baltimore (October); Isaac Myers establishes Chesapeake Marine Railway and Dry Dock Company, first black-owned business in state; assembly permits oyster dredging, but only under sail.

1866–69   Thomas Swann (Unionist Democrat), governor.

1866   Library (first) of Peabody Institute opens.

1867   Assembly charters Centenary Biblical Institute; Democrats rewrite constitution (8 May–17 August), which voters adopt (18 September); constitution carves Wicomico County out of Somerset and Worcester; Isaac Freeman Rasin wins election to clerkship, Baltimore City Court of Common Pleas; Knights of Pythias form in Baltimore.

1868   State Oyster Police; Methodists receive charter for Western Maryland College (1866); B&O and North German Lloyd inaugurate regular steamship service between Baltimore and Bremen.

1869–72   Oden Bowie (Democrat), governor.

1869   Arthur Pue Gorman wins seat in House of Delegates; Myers and black caulkers in Baltimore form union (July); Wendell Bollman builds iron truss bridge for B&O, Savage.

1870   Baltimore blacks parade to celebrate passage of Fifteenth Amendment (May); University of Maryland School of Law reopens; Maryland Jockey Club sponsors racing at Pimlico track.

1872–74   William Pinkney Whyte (Democrat), governor.

1872   Assembly creates Garrett County out of Allegany, mandates separate but equal white and black schools; Western Maryland Railroad completes line, Hagerstown to Baltimore.

1873   Allegany County coal miners establish Protective and Benevolent Association (May); School Sisters of Notre Dame establish College of Notre Dame of Maryland, Baltimore, first Catholic women's college in United States; B&O opens Deer Park Hotel, Garrett County (July).

1874–76   James Black Groome (Democrat), governor.

1874   Commission of Fisheries.

1875   Ceremonies dedicate Baltimore City Hall, a George Frederick design; work begins on east or library wing, Peabody Institute (completed 1878); Atlantic Hotel, first in Ocean City.

1876–80   John Lee Carroll (Democrat), governor.

1876   Railroad/carriage trestle crosses Sinepuxent Bay at Ocean City; The Johns Hopkins University opens, Baltimore (October).

1877   Jenkins-Black Award establishes Maryland-Virginia boundary in lower Chesapeake Bay (January); B&O workers strike along line, demonstrate in Cumberland, riot in Baltimore (20–22 July).

1878   William Brooks establishes Chesapeake Zoological Laboratory, Hampton Roads; young men return from Newport, Rhode Island, with lacrosse sticks; Knights of Labor, Baltimore.

1879   Telephone exchange opens in Baltimore, first in state.

1880–84   William T. Hamilton (Democrat), governor.

1880   Consolidated Gas Company, Baltimore; electrical energy debuts in Maryland at Sun Building, Baltimore.

1881   Oriole Festival celebrates opening of Loch Raven Reservoir (September).

1882   Baltimore reformers win "good judges" election; Harry Vonderhorst sponsors Baltimore team in American Association of baseball clubs; Colored High School opens, Baltimore.

1883   Chesapeake and Potomac Telephone Company forms; B&O opens polygonal Passenger Car Shop, largest such structure in world, Baltimore.

1884–85   Robert M. McLane (Democrat), governor.

1884   Assembly under Knights of Labor pressure creates state Bureau of Industrial Statistics.

1885–88   Henry Lloyd (Democrat), governor.

1885   Baltimore civic leaders establish Reform League, black leaders the Mutual Brotherhood of Liberty; Methodists receive charter for Woman's College of Baltimore (Goucher); M. Carey Thomas founds Bryn Mawr School; Baltimore-Union Passenger Railway Company, first commercial electric street railway in country.

1886   Enoch Pratt Free Library opens in Baltimore (January); Ottmar Mergenthaler perfects Linotype machine, Baltimore; Maryland Progressive State Colored Teachers Association.

1887   Pennsylvania Steel (Maryland Steel, 1891) builds blast furnace at Sparrows Point; Frederick Law Olmsted, Sr., designs summer retreat, Sudbrook Park, near Pikesville.

1888–92   Elihu E. Jackson (Democrat), governor.

1888   Voters north and west of Baltimore City agree to annexation; Maryland flag of Calvert and Crossland colors flies at monument dedication ceremonies, Gettysburg (October).

1889   Johns Hopkins Hospital opens, Baltimore (May); floodwaters inundate Cumberland (May); Baltimore Federation of Labor; Henrietta Szold opens school for Jewish immigrant children.

1890   Morgan College forms of Centenary Biblical Institute; Columbian Iron Works, Baltimore, produces *Maverick*, first steel tanker ship in United States; German-born population of Baltimore City peaks (41,930 of 365,863); Harry S. Cummings wins seat on Baltimore City Council, first black in state to hold major elective office.

1891   Charles H. Grasty assumes control of Baltimore *Evening News*.

1892–96   Frank Brown (Democrat), governor.

1892   State Weather Service; John H. Murphy, Sr., founds Baltimore *Afro-American*; Francis G. Newlands develops Chevy Chase.

1893   Johns Hopkins School of Medicine opens, accepting women; Women's College of Frederick (later Hood).

1894   Baltimore women form Arundell Club; assembly restricts child labor, passes first pure milk law; William T. Carr and William H. Thompson found Provident Hospital, Baltimore; "Coxey's army" passes through state; Baltimore Orioles win their first professional baseball championship.

1895   Maryland Bar Association holds first convention; reformers carry Baltimore City and state elections; Charles County seat moves from Port Tobacco to La Plata.

1896–1900   Lloyd Lowndes (Republican), governor.

1896   Maryland adopts improved "secret" ballot; assembly ends practice of electing one U.S. senator from Eastern Shore, passes law restraining courts from compelling reporters to divulge their sources; state establishes office of Game Warden; Columbian Iron Works builds *Argonaut*, path-breaking submarine.

1897   Maryland Public Health Association forms, Baltimore; Frederick Law Olmsted, Jr., plans west side of Roland Park (company organized 1891).

1898	Baltimore obtains reformed city charter.
1899	William B. Clark issues report on state roads; Maryland Federation of Women's Clubs organizes (November); Baltimore Municipal Art Society forms; building program begins at Naval Academy, Ernest Flagg architect.
1900–1904	John Walter Smith (Democrat), governor.
1901	Automobile Club of Maryland; election law replaces symbols on ballots with words.
1902	Assembly agrees to compulsory school attendance in Baltimore City, adopts new regulations for miners' work conditions, forbids child labor under age twelve, and passes the country's first workmen's compensation plan (overturned in courts).
1904–8	Edwin Warfield (Democrat), governor.
1904	Fire destroys much of downtown Baltimore (7–8 February); Emma J. Maddox Funck heads Maryland Woman Suffrage Association; assembly passes Kerbin "Jim Crow" public accommodations law; Maryland Association for the Prevention and Relief of Tuberculosis forms, Baltimore; Sinclair-Scott begins making Maryland motorcar; William Hand Browne edits first volume of *Maryland Historical Magazine*.
1905	Voters defeat black-disfranchising Poe amendment (November).
1906	Haman Act encourages oyster-bed leasing, establishes Shell Fish Commission, and provides for survey of Chesapeake Bay bottom; state Board of Forestry; Elizabeth King Ellicott organizes Equal Suffrage League, Baltimore.
1907	Washington County experiments successfully with horse-drawn bookmobile; Naval Academy bandmaster composes "Anchors Aweigh"; Johns Hopkins University accepts women graduate students.
1908–12	Austin Lane Crothers (Democrat), governor.
1908	Assembly passes campaign-reform and primary-elections (for some localities) bills, creates state Roads Commission and Board of Agriculture; H. L. Mencken becomes literary editor of the *Smart Set*.
1909	Voters defeat Straus anti-black voting amendment; Greek Orthodox parish, first in state, forms, Baltimore.
1910	Assembly enacts redrafted workmen's compensation bill, passes pure food/drug and anti-prostitution measures, establishes state Commissioner of Motor Vehicles and Public Service Commission; Hubert Latham flies over Baltimore during Halethorpe air meet (November); Russian-born population of Baltimore City (including Eastern European) peaks (24,798 of 558,485).
1911	Baltimore completes sewerage system; army establishes flying school at College Park; navy uses Greenbury Point, Annapolis, as air station; Digges voting amendment goes down to defeat; Isaac E. Emerson builds Emerson or "Bromo-Seltzer" Tower, Baltimore.
1912–16	Phillips Lee Goldsborough (Republican), governor.
1912	Assembly passes ten-hour work law for women, strengthens child-labor legislation and Haman oyster law, adopts party presidential primaries; Edith Hooker begins publishing *Maryland Suffrage News*; Ukrainian Greek Catholics purchase land for St. Michael's Church, South Wolfe Street, Baltimore.
1913	Baltimore Chapter, NAACP, second oldest in country.
1914	Babe Ruth pitches for International League Orioles.
1915	Abraham Flexner and John Bachman present report on state public education; assembly passes education reform measures; voters adopt referendum and county home-rule amendments to the constitution.
1916–20	Emerson C. Harrington (Democrat), governor.

1916 Baltimore Symphony Orchestra organizes under Gustav Strube (February); assembly creates board of film censors; state Conservation Commission forms out of Fishery Force, Shell Fish Commission, and Game Warden; constitutional amendments require balanced state budgets and adopt the executive budget-forming procedure; Johns Hopkins University moves to Homewood; Vagabond Players, Baltimore, stage first performance (November).

1917 Assembly passes compulsory work law; Harrington names state Council of Defense; federal government establishes Camp Meade and Aberdeen Proving Ground; army places Maryland militia units in new 29th Division.

1918 Edgewood Arsenal; Maryland troops fight in Meuse-Argonne; Washington Suburban Sanitary Commission (created 1916) issues first report; Baltimore expands city limits; Rockefeller Foundation funds Johns Hopkins School of Hygiene and Public Health.

1919 Mencken publishes first book of *Prejudices*; Orioles win first of six International League pennants.

1920–35 Albert C. Ritchie (Democrat), governor.

1920 Central purchasing bureau reforms state expenditures; merit system replaces many politically filled positions in state government; assembly creates state athletic and racing commissions; University of Maryland unites agricultural college and Baltimore professional schools; Logan Field (earlier Dundalk Flying Field) dedicated, Baltimore; state's first Air National Guard unit.

1921 Associated Jewish Charities forms, Baltimore (January); Eubie Blake stages "Shuffle Along," New York City.

1922 Assembly adopts fewer elections and equalization of school spending among counties; KKK rallies in Frederick and Baltimore; commercial radio stations air in Baltimore.

1924 Ritchie campaigns for Democratic presidential nomination; Edna Ferber gathers material for *Showboat* aboard James Adams's barge *Playhouse*; Mencken begins editing *American Mercury*; floods destroy much of C&O Canal.

1925 Chesapeake Biological Laboratory, Solomons Island; Maryland and Virginia pass legislation protecting the blue crab, Ammon H. Kreider and Lewis E. Reisner begin building single-engine airplanes, Hagerstown.

1926 Baltimore City equalizes pay for black and white teachers.

1927 Assembly creates Maryland–National Capital Park and Planning Commission and state Commission on Interracial Problems.

1928 Assembly mandates grammar-school education.

1929 Glenn L. Martin moves aircraft plant from Ohio to Middle River; new Baltimore Trust Building, tallest structure in Baltimore; Baltimore Museum of Art opens (incorporated 1914, first exhibition at Garrett mansion, 1923), Wyman Park, Baltimore.

1930 Italian-born population of Baltimore City peaks (9,022 of 804,874); Johns Hopkins University opens Walter Hines Page School of International Relations.

1931 Citizens' Emergency Relief Committee organizes, Baltimore (February); Baltimore Trust Company, largest Maryland bank, reorganizes (forms Maryland National Bank, May 1933); mob lynches Negro in Salisbury (December).

1932 Ritchie loses second bid for presidency (June); "bonus army" travels through Maryland; Ritchie organizes Governor's Advisory Committee on Unemployment Relief, one of first in country (August).

1933 Peoples Unemployment League organizes; state Congress of Farmers and Workers convenes in Hagerstown (July); storm cuts inlet at Ocean City;

Princess Anne mob lynches black prisoner (November); Billie Holliday auditions with Benny Goodman orchestra; Abel Wolman chairs new state Planning Commission; Pratt Library, Baltimore, moves to new building.

1934   Walters Art Gallery opens (built 1909, Henry Walters bequeathed to city, 1931), Baltimore.

1935–39   Harry W. Nice (Republican), governor.

1935   Assembly creates county welfare boards; Hall of Records opens, Annapolis; Baltimore chapter, National Association for the Advancement of Colored People, revives under Lillie Carroll Jackson; Pan American flies Martin M-130 flying boat, the China Clipper, on first scheduled air-mail flight to Orient (November); Baltimore Transit Company forms of United Railways; University of Maryland School of Law opens to blacks after NAACP lawyer Thurgood Marshall brings suit.

1936   CIO strike leads to riot, Cumberland; New Deal builds Greenbelt in Prince George's County; Princess Anne Academy becomes part of University of Maryland system.

1937   Assembly votes income tax; Montgomery County equalizes pay for black and white teachers; Pan American Airways inaugurates Baltimore to Bermuda service; St. John's College adopts "great books" curriculum.

1938   FDR announces plans to purge Maryland Senator Millard Tydings (August); Maryland courts order equal pay to black and white teachers in all counties; federal government begins moving National Institutes of Health to site near Bethesda; Martin Company develops Mariner, most serviceable flying boat ever built; Silver Spring Shopping Center.

1939–47   Herbert R. O'Conor (Democrat), governor.

1939   C&O Canal opens as national park (February); Fairchild Company wins competition for army trainer with PT-19; Ritchie Highway connects Baltimore and Annapolis; Morgan College becomes part of state system.

1940   State Council of Defense and Resources (August); Martin Marauder bomber undergoes first tests (November).

1941   Maryland State Guard; O'Conor creates Board of Natural Resources, Tidewater Fisheries Department remaining separate; Citizens' Planning and Housing Association forms in Baltimore (April); Bethlehem-Fairfield Shipyard produces first Liberty Ship, *Patrick Henry* (April–September).

1942   Patuxent Air Station, St. Mary's County (February); Andrews Field, Prince George's County; Baltimore blacks protest police brutality and demand school board representation (April); O'Conor establishes Commission to Study the Problems Affecting the Colored Population; Naval Medical Center, Bethesda (August); 29th Division embarks for Britain (September).

1943   Assembly passes "work or fight" law; explosion at Elkton ammunition factory kills fifteen workers.

1944   Troops of 29th Division land on Omaha Beach (June); mayor's commission recommends new Baltimore municipal airport in Anne Arundel County.

1945   Redevelopment Commission begins slum clearance in Baltimore.

1946   Montgomery County Junior College opens, first in state; Maryland Congress against Discrimination meets in Baltimore (October).

1947–51   William Preston Lane, Jr. (Democrat), governor.

1947   Assembly votes new roads program to include bay bridge, passes sales tax (first in state history) and higher income tax; "Baltimore Plan" housing court, first in country, enforces building codes; commercial TV stations broadcast from Baltimore and Washington; Edmondson Village Shopping Center.

1948	Baltimore activists test segregated tennis court policy, Druid Hill Park; Montgomery County first in state to adopt home rule; constitutional amendments limit governor to two terms, mandate annual meetings of legislature.
1949	Assembly establishes Department of Mental Hygiene, spends heavily on public schools, passes Ober loyalty law, permits slot machines in Southern Maryland.
1950	Alger Hiss sentenced for perjury (January); Friendship International Airport begins service (June); law suit opens University of Maryland School of Nursing to blacks.
1951–59	Theodore R. McKeldin (Republican), governor.
1951	McKeldin names state Commission on Interracial Problems and Relations; University of Maryland graduate school integrates; Baltimore inaugurates pilot program to upgrade blighted housing, opens golf courses to blacks.
1952	Chesapeake Bay Bridge opens (July); Historic Annapolis, Inc., forms; Polytechnic High School in Baltimore integrates.
1953	Assembly adopts McKeldin highway master plan; state parks open to blacks.
1954	St. Louis Browns move to Baltimore, become American League Orioles; Thurgood Marshall and NAACP win *Brown* v. *Board* decision (May); Baltimore City and Western Shore counties desegregate schools using freedom of choice (September); University of Maryland integrates, first state university below Mason-Dixon Line to do so; public housing in Baltimore integrates; first black elected to House of Delegates, from Baltimore; Baltimore-Washington Expressway opens.
1955	Business leaders organize Greater Baltimore Committee or GBC (January); Maryland National Guard units integrate.
1956	Assembly creates Maryland Port Authority (MPA); Baltimore establishes Urban Renewal and Housing Agency (BURHA) and passes equal employment ordinance; voting machines first used throughout state; I-70(N) connects Frederick and Baltimore; Washington County educational television project begins; John Barth publishes *The Floating Opera*; James W. Rouse opens Mondawmin Mall, Baltimore.
1957	Maryland dissolves 1785 compact with Virginia; I-70(S) connects Frederick and Washington; Baltimore Harbor Tunnel opens (November); Cone Wing opens, Baltimore Museum of Art.
1958	GBC unveils plans for Charles Center (March); Rouse builds Harundale Mall, Anne Arundel County, first enclosed shopping center in state; MPA purchases Harbor Field with plans for Dundalk Marine Terminal (November); Baltimore Colts, NFL champions (December).
1959–67	J. Millard Tawes (Democrat), governor.
1959	I-83 links Baltimore and Harrisburg; Colts repeat as champions.
1960	Appalachian Regional Development Commission forms at Annapolis governors' meeting; Tawes creates state departments of Chesapeake Bay Affairs and Economic Development.
1961	Assembly ends political appointment of Baltimore City magistrates, charters Maryland Historical Trust.
1962	Assembly reapportions House of Delegates; Baltimore beltway and Jones Falls Expressway open; Baltimore City and Montgomery County adopt open accommodations; voters approve Reed Commission fisheries agreement with Virginia; Rachel Carson publishes *Silent Spring*.
1963	Assembly votes to phase out slot machines, passes open accommodations

measure limited to Baltimore City and twelve counties; blacks riot in Cambridge (June); black and white clergymen force integration of Gwynn Oak amusement park (July); Rouse announces plan to build Columbia in Howard County (October); Commission on Higher Education governs three-tiered college system; I-95 connects Wilmington and Baltimore; Regional Planning Council.

1964   Assembly passes public accommodations bill; Maryland Committee for Fair Representation wins court test regarding Maryland senate representation; Tawes appoints Commission on the Status of Women; Eastern Shore leaders establish Wye Institute, Queen Anne's County; Washington beltway opens; Dundalk Marine Terminal begins handling containerized cargoes.

1965   State Department of Water Resources; Assateague Island becomes state park.

1966   Assembly approves second bay bridge, passes fair employment law, creates St. Mary's City Commission, permits oyster dredging under power two days a week; University of Maryland campus at Baltimore County opens; Baltimore Orioles win World Series.

1967–69   Spiro T. Agnew (Republican), governor.

1967   Black unrest in Cambridge (July); constitutional convention meets in Annapolis (12 September–10 January 1968); voters largely reject open housing referendum; Morris A. Mechanic Theater, Baltimore, and Merriweather Post Pavilion, Columbia, open; Richard A. Henson inaugurates air service between Hagerstown and Baltimore (November).

1968   Riots in Baltimore and Washington follow assassination of Dr. Martin Luther King (April); voters reject revised constitution (May); BURHA under Robert C. Embry, Jr., establishes residents' advisory board; *Maryland Magazine* publishes first issue; Marshall W. Nirenberg, National Institutes of Health scientist, wins Nobel Prize.

1969–77   Marvin Mandel (Democrat), governor.

1969   Assembly elects Mandel to succeed Vice President–elect Agnew (January), adopts cabinet system of state government, charters state Commission on Negro History and Culture; Mandel names Chesapeake Bay Interagency Planning Committee; Maryland Public Broadcasting airs; *Constellation* moors permanently at Pier 1, Baltimore; Baltimore Gas and Electric begins construction of Calvert Cliffs Nuclear Power Plant, Solomons.

1970   Assembly passes new environmental legislation; University of Maryland Board of Regents creates Center for Environmental and Estuarine Studies; voters approve independent General Assembly salary board; Baltimore stages first city fair (September); I-70 opens from Frederick to Hancock; Orioles win World Series.

1971   Colts win Super Bowl; state adopts open housing legislation; first high-rise condominium, Ocean City; I-95 opens between Baltimore and Washington.

1972   Assembly passes state equal rights amendment, approves women's equal rights amendment to U.S. Constitution.

1973   State adopts lottery; Friendship Airport reopens as Baltimore-Washington International; Mayor William Donald Schaefer announces "homesteading" program in Baltimore (September); Agnew resigns vice-presidency, pleads no contest to felony charge (October); Johns Hopkins physicians and scientists develop first heart pacemaker; Barth wins National Book Award for *Chimera*.

1974   New wing of Walters Art Gallery opens, Baltimore.

1975   Center Stage reopens in converted St. Ignatius Church/Loyola College complex, Baltimore; Pope Paul VI canonizes Mother Elizabeth Seton.

1976   Maryland Science Center opens in Baltimore; state civic and history groups mark national bicentennial.

1977–79 Blair Lee III (Democrat), acting governor.

1977   Melbourne Smith (builder) and city of Baltimore launch replica clipper *Pride of Baltimore*, Inner Harbor, Baltimore (February); World Trade Center opens; Pope Paul VI canonizes Bishop John Nepomucene Neumann; Mandel found guilty on mail fraud charges (August), appeals decision, succeeded by Lieutenant Governor Lee.

1978   Jim Richardson (builder) launches replica pinnace *Maryland Dove*, LeCompte Creek.

1979–1987 Harry Hughes (Democrat), governor.

1979   Daniel Nathans and Hamilton Smith, Johns Hopkins Hospital, win Nobel Prizes for medicine; Baltimore Convention Center.

1980   Harborplace opens, Baltimore (July).

INDEX

References to illustrations and appended maps, figures, and tables appear in italics. Official state agencies are listed without a "Maryland" prefix (e.g., State Roads Commission). Evolving institutions generally have been entered under their titles as of 1980—e.g., Maryland State College under University of Maryland and oyster police under Natural Resources Police Force—with earlier names following in parentheses.